NEW  ES

COMPUTER CONCEPTS

JUNE JAMRICH PARSONS • DAN OJA

EDITION

11

COMPREHENSIVE

Includes access to an integrated Web site and an interactive BookOnCD. The Web site offers audio clips, labs, games, relevant links, practice tests, and more. The BookOnCD contains the entire contents of the textbook with figures that come to life as videos, software tours, and animations. See the Preface for more information!

COURSE TECHNOLOGY
CENGAGE Learning™

Australia • Brazil • Japan • Korea • Mexico • Singapore • Spain • United Kingdom • United States

COURSE TECHNOLOGY
CENGAGE Learning

New Perspectives on Computer Concepts, 11th Edition, Comprehensive

June Jamrich Parsons, Dan Oja

Executive Editor: Marie Lee

Senior Product Manager: Kathy Finnegan

Product Manager: Erik Herman

Associate Product Manager: Brandi Henson

Developmental Editor: Deb Kaufmann

Editorial Assistant: Leigh Robbins

Technology Project Manager: Jim Ruggiero

Director of Marketing: Cheryl Costantini

Marketing Manager: Ryan DeGrote

Marketing Specialist: Jennifer Hankin

Senior Content Project Manager:
   Jennifer Goguen McGrail

Photo Researcher: Abby Reip

Art Director: Marissa Falco

Cover Designer: Joel Sadagursky

BookOnCD Technician: Keefe Crowley

BookOnCD Development:
   MediaTechnics Corp.

Prepress Production: GEX Publishing Services

ISBN-13: 978-1-4239-2518-7
ISBN-10: 1-4239-2518-1

Course Technology
25 Thomson Place
Boston, MA 02210
USA

Cengage Learning is a leading provider of customized learning solutions with office locations around the globe, including Singapore, the United Kingdom, Australia, Mexico, Brazil and Japan. Locate your local office at:
international.cengage.com/region

Cengage Learning products are represented in Canada by Nelson Education, Ltd.

For your lifelong learning solutions, visit **course.cengage.com**

Purchase any of our products at your local college store or at our preferred online store **www.ichapters.com**

Printed in the United States of America
1 2 3 4 5 6 7 8 9 12 11 10 09 08

CONTENTS AT A GLANCE

TABLE OF CONTENTS

ORIENTATION

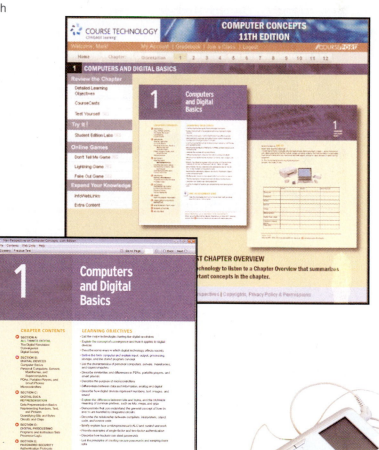

CHAPTER 1

COMPUTERS AND DIGITAL BASICS

CHAPTER 2

COMPUTER HARDWARE

CHAPTER 5

LANS AND WLANS

CHAPTER 8

DIGITAL MEDIA

CHAPTER 11

DATABASES

CHAPTER 12

COMPUTER PROGRAMMING

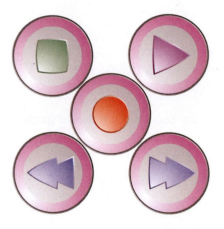

NEW PERSPECTIVES LABS

STUDENT EDITION LABS

Study Smarter: The NP11 Experience

You have purchased more than just a book...

New Perspectives on Computer Concepts, 11th Edition includes a printed book, an integrated Web site, and an interactive BookOnCD designed to provide a cutting-edge learning experience.

Want to study smarter? The NP11 Web site offers tools to help you understand the material from all angles and to thoroughly prepare for exams. Want to see the chapter concepts in action? The BookOnCD and other BookOn products bring concepts to life through figures that become videos, animations, and software tours.

The NP Computer Concepts pedagogy is like no other. Chapters are divided into three essential learning components: preparatory activities, chapter activities, and review activities. This model helps focus your learning, so that you can study more efficiently and retain information better. Web-based, book-based, and CD-based activities work together for an interactive, hands-on, and engaging learning experience.

New for this edition...

The 11th Edition packs plenty of new material. You'll find coverage of new hardware, such as the **IPHONE** and **MULTI-CORE PROCESSORS**, in addition to beefed up coverage of Macs and popular **VIRTUAL MACHINE TECHNOLOGY**.

In the context of software you'll see increased emphasis on **OPEN SOURCE SOFTWARE** and popular operating systems such as **UBUNTU LINUX**. You'll find lots of practical tips for using **WINDOWS VISTA**, and learn about the latest version of Microsoft Office with its **RIBBON INTERFACE**, and updated DOCX and XLSX file formats. This edition introduces you to **CD MASTERING** and packet writing. It showcases Web Apps such as **GOOGLE DOCS**, and offers an extended discussion of using restore points, recovery disks, and virtual machines for backups. In addition, you'll learn about **WEB 2.0**, human-powered search sites, and **REALBASIC**.

Topping off the revisions for this edition, the NP labs have been newly revised, the SE labs are now offered in version 4.0, and the BookOnCD contains lots of new and reworked screentours.

CREATE YOUR OWN LEARNING PLAN

Use the book, the NP11 Web site, the BookOnCD, BookOnFlashDrive, or other BookOn technology in **ANY WAY THAT'S RIGHT FOR YOU**. The Orientation helps you get acquainted with the wide array of NP11 technology that's at your command.

Your BookOn Plan—Seven Easy Steps

1. Use the BookOnCD, BookOnFlashDrive, or other BookOn product to take the **PRE-ASSESSMENT** and gauge what you already know.

2. Work on the Chapter opener **TRY IT ACTIVITY** for a hands-on introduction to the chapter topics.

3. Read a chapter, completing the **QUICKCHECKS** at the end of each section.

4. Work with **NEW PERSPECTIVES LABS** to apply your knowledge.

5. Complete **REVIEW ACTIVITIES** using your BookOnCD, BookOnFlashDrive, or other BookOn product.

6. Take a **PRACTICE TEST** to see if you're ready for the exam.

7. Transmit your results to your instructor on **WEBTRACK**.

Your Web Plan—Eight Steps Online

1. Listen to a **COURSECAST OVERVIEW** of chapter highlights.

2. Read a chapter, completing **QUICKCHECKS** at the end of each section.

3. Work with the **STUDENT EDITION LABS** to apply your knowledge.

4. Have some fun reviewing with **ONLINE GAMES**.

5. Use **COURSECAST FLASHCARDS** to review key terms from the chapter.

6. Check the **DETAILED LEARNING OBJECTIVES** to make sure you've mastered the material.

7. **TEST YOURSELF** to see if you are ready for the exam.

8. Store your results in the online **UNIVERSAL GRADEBOOK**.

Your Own Plan

MIX AND MATCH any of your favorite activities from the book, electronic textbook, or Web site.

THE BOOK

New Perspectives on Computer Concepts gives you the straight story on today's technology. Now in its 11th edition, the style has been carefully honed to be clear, concise, and visual.

Easy to read

A chapter is divided into five **SECTIONS**, each offering a chunk of information that's easy to assimilate in one session. **FAQS** answer commonly asked questions about technology topics and help you follow the flow of the presentation.

Keeps you on track

QUICKCHECKS at the end of each section help you find out if you understood the most important concepts. Extensive review activities at the end of each chapter include **INTERACTIVE CHAPTER SUMMARIES**, **KEY TERMS**, **INTERACTIVE SITUATION QUESTIONS**, and **CONCEPT MAPS**.

Helps you explore

ISSUE sections in each chapter highlight controversial aspects of technology. In the **COMPUTERS IN CONTEXT** section, you'll discover how technology plays a role in careers such as film-making, architecture, banking, and fashion. **INFOWEBLINKS** lead you to Web-based information on chapter topics. Work with **NP11 PROJECTS** to apply the concepts you learned, explore technology, consider globalization, build your resume, work with a team, and experiment with multimedia.

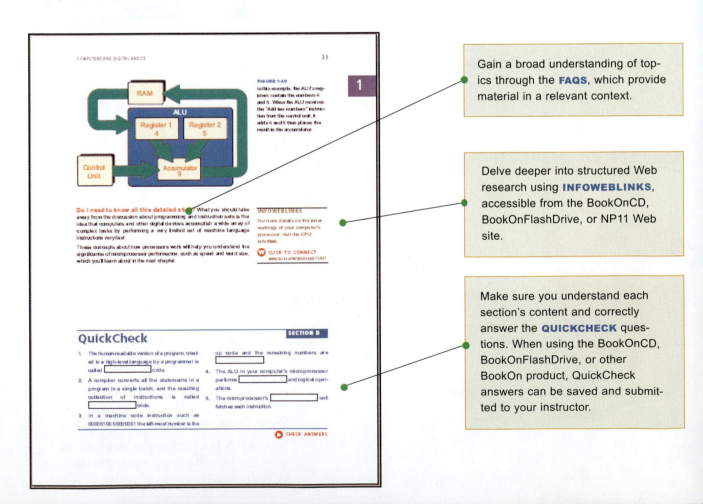

Gain a broad understanding of topics through the **FAQS**, which provide material in a relevant context.

Delve deeper into structured Web research using **INFOWEBLINKS**, accessible from the BookOnCD, BookOnFlashDrive, or NP11 Web site.

Make sure you understand each section's content and correctly answer the **QUICKCHECK** questions. When using the BookOnCD, BookOnFlashDrive, or other BookOn product, QuickCheck answers can be saved and submitted to your instructor.

THE TECHNOLOGY

The **BOOKONCD**, **BOOKONFLASHDRIVE**, and other BookOn products offer an electronic version of your textbook with multimedia and interactive activities designed to enhance your learning experience.

Works alone or with the book

Every page of the electronic textbook **MIRRORS THE PRINTED TEXTBOOK**, so use the tool that's most convenient and that best suits your learning style.

Brings concepts to life

In the electronic textbook, many photos turn into **VIDEOS**. Illustrations become **ANIMATED DIAGRAMS**. Screen shots activate guided **SOFTWARE TOURS**, so you can see how applications and operating systems like **WINDOWS VISTA** work even if they aren't installed on your computer.

Makes learning interactive

Before you read a chapter, take the **PRE-ASSESSMENT** to find out how to best focus your study time. You can master hundreds of computer concepts using the **NEW PERSPECTIVES LABS**. When you complete a chapter, try your hand at interactive, **COMPUTER-SCORED ACTIVITIES**. Take some **PRACTICE TESTS** to gauge how well you'll perform on exams. Easily transmit your scores to your instructor on **WEBTRACK**.

NP11 is available as a portable application on a flash drive. No installation is required, so you can plug your textbook into any computer, read chapters, watch multimedia figures, work on labs, and review. After you complete computer-scored review activities, you can save your scores right on the flash drive!

The electronic textbook is easy to use, packed with **MULTIMEDIA** and offers plenty of **COMPUTER-SCORED ACTIVITIES**.

Interactive **NEW PERSPECTIVES LABS** give you hands-on experience with concepts and software.

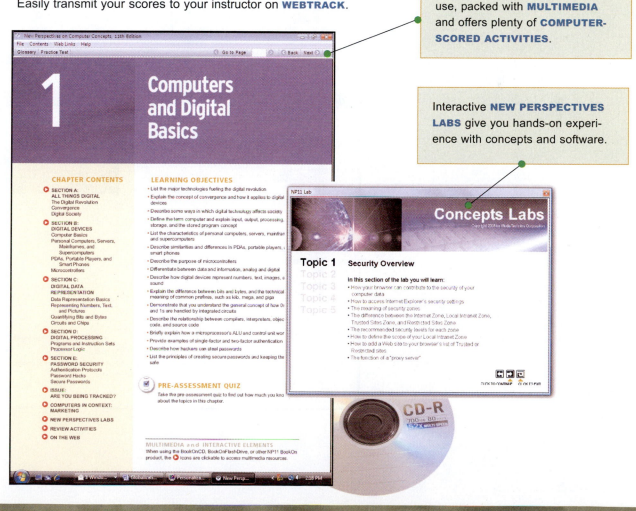

THE NP11 WEB SITE

The NP11 Web site is packed full of information and activities to accompany each chapter. Follow the directions on the inside front cover of this book to create your CoursePort account for access to the NP11 Web site.

Gives you options

Want to have fun while you review? Try an **ONLINE GAME** that packages chapter concepts into an entertaining quiz show or action game. When you're ready for some serious exam preparation, work with the **TEST YOURSELF** activity to see how well you can answer questions similar to those on your upcoming test. Need some last minute review? Load up your portable music player with a **CHAPTER OVERVIEW COURSECAST** and a **KEY TERM FLASHCARD COURSECAST**.

Reinforces your understanding

STUDENT EDITION LABS give you hands-on experience with key concepts and skills. **DETAILED LEARNING OBJECTIVES** help you determine if you've mastered all the requirements for completing a chapter.

Keeps track of your progress

CoursePort allows you to save your results from Web site activities and share them with your instructor through the **UNIVERSAL GRADEBOOK**.

Now you can listen to CourseCasts on your computer or download them to your portable music player. Audio chapter overviews and flashcards help you study while you're out and about.

Listen to chapter highlights or practice key terms with handy chapter overview and flashcard **COURSECASTS**.

Activities marked with the **CP** logo work with the Universal GradeBook to store results.

Labs, practice tests, games, and more provide many ways to explore and review.

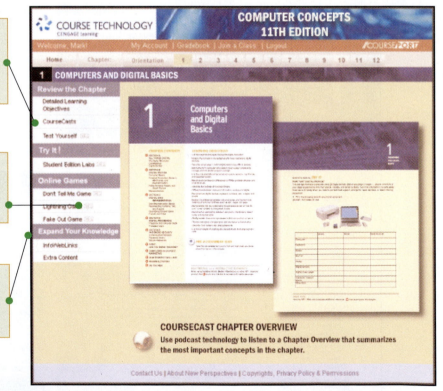

COURSECAST CHAPTER OVERVIEW
Use podcast technology to listen to a Chapter Overview that summarizes the most important concepts in the chapter.

INSTRUCTOR RESOURCES

New Perspectives instructional resources and technology provide instructors with a wide range of tools that enhance teaching and learning. These tools can be accessed from the Instructor Resources CD or at *www.course.com*.

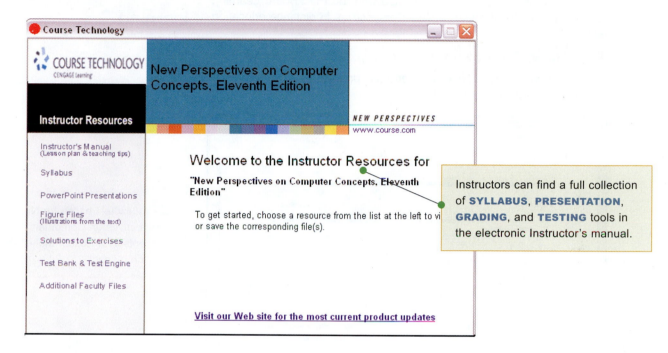

Instructors can find a full collection of **SYLLABUS**, **PRESENTATION**, **GRADING**, and **TESTING** tools in the electronic Instructor's manual.

Instructor's Manual: Help is Only a Few Keystrokes Away

The special Instructor's Manual offers bullet point lecture notes for each chapter, plus classroom activities and teaching tips, including how to effectively use and integrate the Web site content, BookOnCD content, and labs.

Course Presenter

Instructors can deliver engaging and visually impressive lectures for each chapter with the professionally-designed Course Presenter. Course Presenter is a PowerPoint presentation enhanced with screentours, animations, and videos.

WebTrack

Monitoring student progress is easy by tracking scores from BookOnCD, BookOnFlashDrive, or other BookOn products. Using the WebTrack store-and-forward system, a student can transmit scores to an instructor, who can download them at any time. Newly downloaded scores are consolidated with previous scores and can be displayed, printed, or exported in a variety of report formats.

ANNOTATIONS! Instructors can create their own text, graphical, or video annotations that students will see as they read the BookOnCD or BookOnFlashDrive. Find out more about this innovative feature in the Instructor Manual.

WebTrackIII Instructor's Page

NEW! WebTrackIII is available as a portable app that instructors can carry on a USB flash drive and use on their classroom, office, or home computer.

Universal Gradebook

For courses that take advantage of the activities at the NP11 Web site, the Universal Gradebook allows students to send results to instructors.

BlackBoard Learning System™ Content

We offer a full range of content for use with the BlackBoard Learning System to simplify the use of New Perspectives in distance education settings.

ExamView: Our Powerful Testing Software Package

With ExamView, instructors can generate printed tests, create LAN-based tests, or test over the Internet.

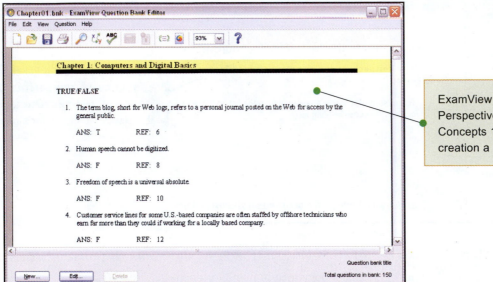

ExamView test banks for New Perspectives on Computer Concepts 11th Edition make test creation a snap.

SAM

SAM Software helps instructors teach, test, and train. It can be used to reinforce the lessons presented in this textbook and to create realistic hands-on exams. For a total teaching solution to introductory computer courses, SAM for Computer Concepts is available with SAM for Office 2007. This integrated offering provides seamless training, testing, and reporting for concepts and software skills covered in introductory computer courses. For more information about SAM Computer Concepts Training and Assessment, please visit *www.course.com/sam*.

FROM THE AUTHORS

Many of today's students have substantially more practical experience with computers than their counterparts of 10 years ago, and yet other students enter college with inadequate technology preparation. The goal of *New Perspectives on Computer Concepts* is to bring every student up to speed with computer basics, and then go beyond basic computer literacy to provide students with technical information that a college-educated person would be expected to know.

In producing the 11th edition of this very popular textbook, we incorporated significant technology trends that affect computing and everyday life. Concerns for data security and personal privacy, controversy over digital rights management, interest in open source software and portable applications, the release of Windows Vista, and the emerging Intel Mac platform are just some of the trends that have expanded coverage in this edition of the book.

Whether you are an instructor or a student, we hope that you enjoy the learning experience provided by our text-based and technology-based materials.

ACKNOWLEDGEMENTS

The book would not exist—and certainly wouldn't arrive on schedule—were it not for the efforts of our media, editorial, and production teams. We thank Deb Kaufmann for her tireless work on every detail of the project; Erik Herman for handling all the administrative tasks; Marie L. Lee for her leadership with the New Perspectives series; Kristina Matthews for her executive leadership; Jennifer Goguen McGrail for managing production; artist Joel Sadagursky for a stunning book design; Abigail Reip for photo research; and Brandi Henson for managing the supplements.

The MediaTechnics team worked tirelessly and we can't offer enough thanks to Tensi Parsons for her extraordinary devotion to desktop publishing; Keefe Crowley for his versatile skills in producing the BookOnCD, creating videos, taking photos, and maintaining the InfoWebLinks site; Donna Mulder for revising the NP Labs; Debora Elam and Fatima Lockhart for their efficient work on screentours; Marilou Potter for her invaluable contributions to research and testbank creation; Chris Robbert for his clear narrations; and Sue Oja, Debora Elam, Jaclyn Kangas, Joseph Smit, Christopher Schuch, and Kevin Lappi for checking and double-checking the alpha and beta CDs. We want to thank you all!

We also want to give special thanks to Officer David Zittlow of the City of Fond du Lac Police Department for providing photos of computer technology used in law enforcement; Bob Metcalf for giving us permission to use his original sketch of Ethernet; The University of Illinois for supplying photos of PLATO; Rob Flickenger for providing the photo of his Pringles can antenna; Jonathan Atwell for permission to use the photo of his computer mod; and Joe Bush for his distinctive photo work.

June Parsons and Dan Oja

NEW PERSPECTIVES ON COMPUTER CONCEPTS ADVISORY COMMITTEE

Spring Davidson
University of Delaware

Tom Gorecki
College of Southern
Maryland

Dennis Jirkowsky
Longview Community
College

Melissa Napper
Blue River Community
College

Matt Zullo
Wake Technical
Community College

ACADEMIC, TECHNICAL, AND STUDENT REVIEWERS

We would also like to thank past reviewers and members of previous Advisory Committees who helped provide valuable feedback that is still an influence on the 11th Edition:

Dr. Nazih Abdallah, University of Central Florida; Beverly Amer, Northern Arizona University; Ken Baldauf, Florida State University; Dottie Baumeister, Harford Community College; Paula Bell, Lock Haven University of Pennsylvania; Barbara Burns, St. Johns River Community College; Mary Caldwell, Rollins College; Chuck Calvin, Computer Learning Centers; Wendy Chisholm, Barstow College; Linda Cooper, Macon State College; Dave Courtaway, Devry University, Ponoma; Becky Curtin, William Rainey Harper College; Eric Daley, University of New Brunswick; Sallie Dodson, Radford University; Robert Erickson, University of Vermont; Mark Feiler, Merritt College; Pat Frederick, Del Mar College; Phil Funk, Southern New Hampshire University; Michael Gaffney, Century College; John Gammell, St. Cloud State University; Ernest Gines, Tarrant Count College SE; Ione Good, Southeastern Community College; Tom Gorecki, College of Southern Maryland; Steve Gramlich, Pasco-Hernando Community College; Michael Hanna, Colorado State University; Dorothy Harman, Tarrant County College Northeast; Bobbye Haupt, Cecil Community College; Heith Hennel, Valencia Community College; Gerald Hensel, Valencia Community College; Patti Impink, Macon State College; Bob Irvine, American River College; Stan Leja, Del Mar College; Martha Lindberg, Minnesota State University; Richard Linge, Arizona Western College; Terry Long, Valencia Community College; Karl Smart Lyman, Central Michigan University; Dr. W. Benjamin Martz, University of Colorado, Colorado Springs; Deann McMullen, Western Kentucky Community and Technical College; Dori McPherson, Schoolcraft College; Saeed Molki, South Texas College; Robert Moore, Laredo Community College; Ed Mott, Central Texas College; Dr. Rodney Pearson, Mississippi State University; Catherine Perlich, St. Thomas; David Primeaux, Virginia Commonwealth University; Ann Rowlette, Liberty University; Lana Shyrock, Monroe County Community College; Betty Sinowitz, Rockland Community College; Martin Skolnik, Florida Atlantic University; Jerome Spencer, Rowan University; Ella Strong, Hazard Community and Technical College; Gregory Stefanelli, Carroll Community College; Martha J. Tilmann, College of San Mateo; Michael Wiemann, Blue River Community College; Kathy Winters, University of Tennessee, Chattanooga; Mary Zayac, University of the Virgin Islands; Student Reviewers Kitty Edwards and Heather House; Technical Reviewers Jeff Harrow, Barbra D. Letts, John Lucas, Ramachandran Bharath, and Karl Mulder.

NEW PERSPECTIVES

COMPUTER CONCEPTS

JUNE JAMRICH PARSONS • DAN OJA

EDITION
11

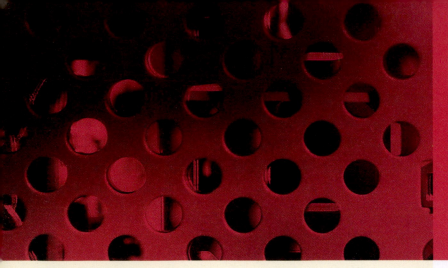

Orientation

LEARNING OBJECTIVES

- Identify the basic components of your computer system
- Identify the major components of the Windows desktop
- Use the mouse and keyboard
- Start and exit a software program
- Use the menu bar, toolbar, and sizing buttons
- Create, save, and print documents using Microsoft Word
- Use a browser
- Use a search engine to find specific information on the Web
- Create, read, and reply to e-mail messages
- Secure your computer for working online
- Take steps to protect your online privacy
- Start the BookOnCD, explore its features, and create a Tracking file
- Work with a New Perspectives Lab
- Use the Internet to connect to the New Perspectives NP11 Web site
- Explore the NP11 Web site
- Work with a Student Edition Lab

MULTIMEDIA and INTERACTIVE ELEMENTS

⌨ Keyboard icons indicate hands-on activities. When using the BookOnCD, or other BookOn product, the ▶ icons are clickable to access multimedia resources.

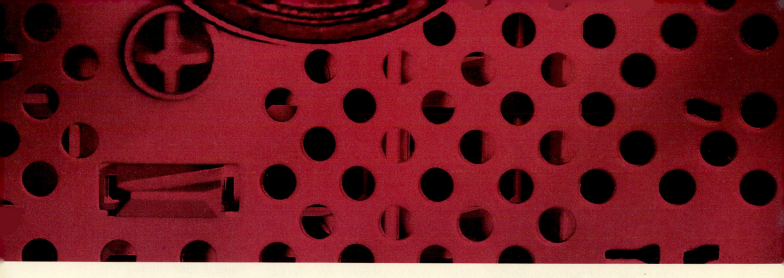

BEFORE YOU READ ON, **TRY IT**

WHAT DO I NEED TO GET STARTED?

To complete the activities in the Orientation, you'll need access to a computer, the BookOnCD packaged with your textbook (or other electronic versions of the textbook), Internet access, an e-mail address for yourself, and your instructor's e-mail address.

To make sure you have what you need, use the following checklist. Check off the boxes for each item that you have.

☐ Access to a computer. If you're using your own computer, you might need a user ID and password to log into Windows. Don't write your password down, but make sure you know what it is.

☐ Access to a school computer network. You might need a user ID and password if you'll be using a lab computer or accessing your school's network. Check with your instructor or lab manager to learn how your school handles network access.

☐ BookOnCD or other BookOn product. The BookOnCD should be packaged with your textbook and requires a computer CD or DVD drive to run. If your computer does not have this type of drive, check with your instructor. The BookOnFlashDrive requires a USB port. Your school network might provide access to the BookOnCD or BookOnFlashDrive from lab computers.

☐ E-mail address. Your instructor should explain how you can obtain an e-mail address if you don't already have one. Write your e-mail address here:

_____

☐ Instructor e-mail address. To mail in assignments, you'll need your instructor's e-mail address. Write it here:

_____

☐ Instructor WebTrack address. If your instructor will be collecting your scores with WebTrack, make sure you have your instructor's WebTrack address. Write it here:

_____

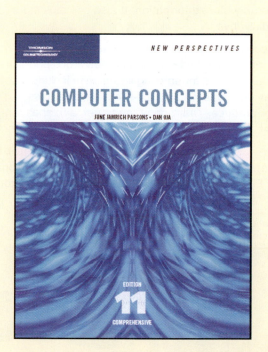

WEB SITE

Visit the NP11 Web site to access additional resources 🅦 that accompany this chapter.

SECTION A

Getting Started

WHEN YOU USE the *New Perspectives on Computer Concepts* text-book, you not only learn about computers, you also use computers as learning tools. Therefore, it is a good idea to have a basic understanding of how to use your computer. Section A is designed to get computer novices quickly up to speed with computing basics, such as turning on computer equipment, working with Windows, using a mouse and computer keyboard, and accessing Help. Work through this section next to a computer so that you can do the TRY IT! activities.

COMPUTER EQUIPMENT

What do I need to know about my computer? Your computer—the one you own, the one you use in a school lab, or the one provided to you at work—is technically classified as a microcomputer and sometimes referred to as a personal computer. A computer runs software (also called programs) that help you accomplish a variety of tasks. A typical computer system consists of several devices—you must be able to identify these devices to use them.

What are the important components of my computer system? The system unit contains your computer's circuitry, such as the microprocessor that is the "brain" of your computer and memory chips that temporarily store information. It also contains storage devices, such as a hard disk drive.

Your computer system includes basic hardware devices that allow you to enter information and commands, view work, and store information for later retrieval. Devices for entering information include a keyboard and mouse. A display device, such as a TV-like monitor, allows you to view your work, a printer produces "hard copy" on paper, and speakers produce beeps and chimes that help you pay attention to what happens on the screen.

Where are the important components of a desktop computer system? A desktop computer is designed for stationary use on a desk or table. Figure 1 shows the key components of a desktop computer system.

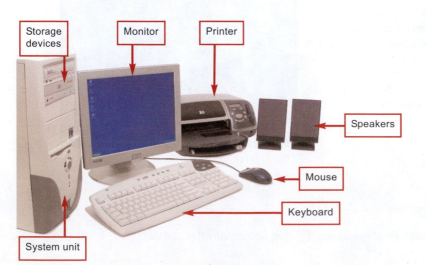

FIGURE 1

A desktop computer system includes several components, usually connected by cables.

Where are the important components of a notebook computer system?

Notebook computers (sometimes called laptops) are small, light-weight computers designed to be carried from place to place. The components of a notebook computer system, except the printer, are housed in a single unit, as shown in Figure 2.

LCD screen

Speakers

Keyboard

Touchpad

Storage devices

FIGURE 2

A notebook computer includes a flat-panel LCD screen, keyboard, speakers, and touchpad in the same unit that contains the microprocessor, memory, and storage devices. An external mouse is sometimes used instead of the touchpad.

How do I identify my computer's storage devices?

Your computer contains a hard disk, housed inside the system unit. It is also likely to have some type of drive that works with CDs. Figure 3 can help you identify your computer's storage devices and their uses.

FIGURE 3

You should use the hard disk to store most of your data, but to transport or back up data, you can use floppy disks, CDs, DVDs, or USB flash drives.

Floppy disk drive

Low-capacity storage, but an inexpensive way to transport small files from one computer to another.

CD drive

CD drives can play CD-ROMs, but can't change the data they contain. CD drives can store data on CD-Rs, CD+Rs, or CD-RWs.

DVD drive

DVD drives read CD-ROMs and DVD-ROMs, but can't change the data on them. Most of today's DVD drives can write data on CD-Rs, CD-RWs, DVD-Rs, and DVD-RWs.

USB flash drive

A USB flash drive is about the size of a high-lighter and plugs directly into the computer system unit. Capacities range from 32 million to 12 billion characters.

HOW TO TURN YOUR COMPUTER ON AND OFF

How do I turn it on? A notebook computer typically has one switch that turns on the entire system. Look for the switch along the sides of the computer or above the keyboard. When using a desktop computer, turn on the monitor, printer, and speakers before you turn on the system unit.

Most computers take a minute or two to power up, and you might be required to log in by entering a user ID and password. Your computer is ready to use when the Windows desktop (Figure 4 on the next page) appears on the computer screen and you can move the arrow-shaped pointer with your mouse.

How do I turn it off? Your computer is designed to turn itself off after you initiate a shutdown sequence by clicking the onscreen Start button, selecting Shut Down or Turn Off Computer, and following the instructions on the screen. After the computer shuts itself off, you can turn off the monitor, speakers, and printer. When using computers in a school lab, ask about the shutdown procedure. Your lab manager might ask that you log out but do not turn the computer off.

⌨**TRY IT!**

Turn your computer on

1. Locate the power switch for any devices connected to your computer and turn them on.

2. Locate the power switch for your computer and turn it on.

3. If a message asks for your user ID and/or password, type them in, and then press the **Enter** key on your computer's keyboard.

4. Wait for the Windows desktop to appear.

WINDOWS BASICS

What is Windows? Microsoft Windows is an example of a type of software called an operating system. The operating system controls all the basic tasks your computer performs, such as running application software, manipulating files on storage devices, and transferring data to and from printers, digital cameras, and other devices. The operating system also controls the user interface—the way software appears on the screen and the way you control what it does.

What is the Windows desktop? The Windows desktop is your base of operations for using your computer. It displays small pictures called *icons* that help you access software, documents, and the components of your computer system. The design of the Windows desktop depends on the version of Windows you're using. Figure 4 shows the important elements of the two most recent versions: Windows XP and Windows Vista.

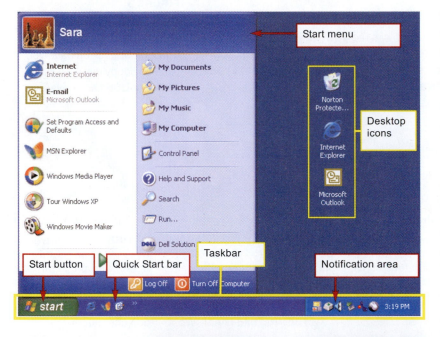

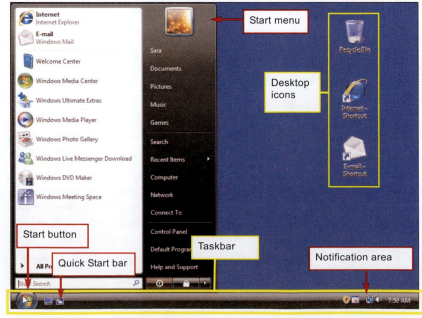

FIGURE 4

Windows desktop components as they appear in Windows XP (top) and Windows Vista (bottom).

Desktop icons can represent programs, documents, folders, or other electronic tools.

The **taskbar** contains the Start button, Quick Start bar, and Notification area. In this book, screens with a blue taskbar are Windows XP and those with a black taskbar are Windows Vista.

The **Start button** is used to display the Start menu, which lists all the programs installed on your computer.

The **Start menu** lists application and utility programs installed on your computer.

The **Quick Start bar** is always visible, making it a good place for icons that represent the programs you frequently use.

The **Notification area** displays the current time and the status of programs, devices, and Internet connections.

MOUSE BASICS

What is a mouse? A mouse is a device used to manipulate items on the screen, such as the buttons and icons displayed on the Windows desktop. The mouse controls an on-screen pointer. The pointer is usually shaped like an arrow ⌖, but it can change to a different shape, depending on the task you're doing. For example, when the computer is busy, the arrow shape turns into an hourglass ⧗ or circle ◯, signifying that you should wait for the computer to finish its current task before attempting to start a new task.

PC-compatible mice have at least two buttons, typically located on top of the mouse. Some mice also include a scroll wheel mounted between the left and right mouse buttons. Other mice include additional buttons on the top or sides (Figure 5).

How do I use a mouse? Hold the mouse in your right hand as shown in Figure 6. When you drag the mouse from left to right over your mousepad or desk, the arrow-shaped pointer on the screen moves from left to right. If you run out of room to move the mouse, simply pick it up and reposition it. The pointer does not move when the mouse is not in contact with a flat surface.

FIGURE 5

For basic mousing, you need use only the left and right mouse buttons.

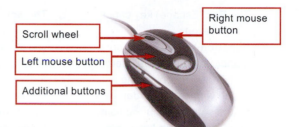

There are several ways you can manipulate on-screen objects. Although you might not be able to manipulate every object in all possible ways, you'll soon learn which mouse actions are allowed for each type of control. The following list describes your repertoire of mouse actions.

FIGURE 6

Rest the palm of your right hand on the mouse. Position your index finger over the left mouse button and your middle finger over the right mouse button.

⌨ TRY IT!

Use your mouse

1. With your computer on and the Windows desktop showing on the screen, move your mouse around on the desk and notice how the mouse movements correspond to the movement of the arrow-shaped pointer.

2. Move the mouse to position the pointer on the Start button.

3. Click the left mouse button to open the Start menu.

4. Click the **Start** button again to close the Start menu.

Action	How to	Result
Click	Press the left mouse button once, and then immediately release it.	Select an object
Double-click	Press the left mouse button twice in rapid succession without moving the body of the mouse.	Activate an object
Right-click	Press the right mouse button once, and then immediately release it.	Display a shortcut menu
Drag	Hold the left mouse button down while you move the mouse.	Move an object

Orientation

KEYBOARD BASICS

What are the important features of a computer keyboard?
You use the computer keyboard to input commands, respond to prompts, and type the text of documents. An insertion point that looks like a flashing vertical bar indicates where the characters you type will appear. You can change the location of the insertion point by using the mouse or the arrow keys. Study Figure 7 for an overview of important computer keys and their functions.

FIGURE 7

Computer Keyboard

A The **Esc** (Escape) key cancels an operation.

B **Function keys** activate commands, such as Save, Help, and Print. The command associated with each key depends on the software you are using.

C The **Print Screen** key prints the contents of the screen or stores a copy of the screen in memory that you can print or manipulate with graphics software.

D The **Scroll Lock** key's function depends on the software you're using. This key is rarely used with today's software.

E **Indicator lights** show you the status of three toggle keys: Num Lock, Caps Lock, and Scroll Lock. The Power light indicates whether the computer is on or off.

F The **Backspace** key deletes one character to the left of the insertion point.

G The **Insert** key switches between insert mode and type-over mode.

H The **Home** key takes you to the beginning of a line or the beginning of a document, depending on the software you are using.

I The **Tab** key can move your current typing location to the next tab stop or the next text-entry box.

J The **Caps Lock** key capitalizes all the letters you type when it is engaged, but does not produce the top symbol on keys that contain two symbols. This key is a toggle key, which means that each time you press it, you switch between uppercase and lowercase modes.

K The **Shift** key capitalizes letters and produces the top symbol on keys that contain two symbols.

L You hold down the **Ctrl** key while pressing another key. The result of Ctrl or Alt key combinations depends on the software you are using.

M You hold down the **Alt** key while you press another key.

N The **Enter** key is used to indicate that you have completed a command or want to move your typing position down to the next line.

O The **Delete** key deletes the character to the right of the insertion point.

P The **End** key takes you to the end of a line or the end of a document, depending on the software you are using.

Q The **Page Up** key displays the previous screen of information. The **Page Down** key displays the next screen of information.

R The up, down, right, and left **arrow keys** move the insertion point.

S The **numeric keypad** produces numbers or moves the insertion point, depending on the status of the Num Lock key shown by the status lights.

What do Alt and Ctrl mean? The Alt and Ctrl keys work with the letter keys. If you see <Ctrl X>, Ctrl+X, [Ctrl X], Ctrl-X, or Ctrl X on the screen or in an instruction manual, it means to hold down the Ctrl key while you press X. For example, Ctrl+X is a keyboard shortcut for clicking the Edit menu, and then clicking the Cut option. A keyboard shortcut allows you to use the keyboard rather than the mouse to select menu commands.

What if I make a mistake? Everyone makes mistakes. The first rule is don't panic! Most mistakes are reversible. The hints and tips in Figure 8 should help you recover from mistakes.

FIGURE 8

Most mistakes are easy to fix.

What Happened	What To Do
Typed the wrong thing	Use the Backspace key to delete the last characters you typed.
Selected the wrong menu	Press the Esc key to close the menu.
Opened a window you didn't mean to	Click the X button in the upper-right corner of the window.
Computer has "hung up" and no longer responds to mouse clicks or typed commands	Hold down the Ctrl, Alt, and Delete keys, and then follow instructions to close the program.
Pressed the Enter Key in the middle of a sentence	Press the Backspace key to paste the sentence back together.

HOW TO START SOFTWARE

How do I start programs? You can use the Start button to launch just about any software that's installed on your computer. The Start menu includes a list of recently accessed programs. Clicking the All Programs option displays a list of every program installed on your computer. You can run a program from this list simply by clicking it. Follow the instructions in the TRY IT! box to start Microsoft Paint (assuming it is installed on your computer).

⌨ TRY IT!

Start Microsoft Paint

1. Make sure your computer is on and it is displaying the Windows desktop.

2. Click the **Start** button to display the Start menu.

3. Click **All Programs** to display a list of all software installed on your computer.

4. Click **Accessories**, and then click **Paint**.

5. Wait a few seconds for your computer to display the main screen for Microsoft Paint, shown below. Leave Paint open for use with the next TRY IT!

WINDOWS CONTROLS

How do I tell the software what I want to do? Word processing, photo editing, and other software designed for use on computers running the Windows operating system is referred to as *Windows software*. Most Windows software works in a fairly uniform way and uses a similar set of controls.

Each software application appears within a rectangular area called a *window*, which can include a title bar, a menu bar, a ribbon, a workspace, and various controls shown in Figure 9.

FIGURE 9

The **title bar** displays the title of the software, the name of the current data file, and the window sizing buttons.

The **Minimize button** shrinks the window to a button at the bottom of the screen.

The **Maximize button** stretches the window to fill the screen.

The **Close button** closes the window and exits the program.

A **menu bar** displays the titles of menus you can click to select commands.

A **toolbar** displays a series of tools for accomplishing various tasks.

A **ribbon** combines the options of a menu and toolbars into a single set of controls (see Figure 11).

A **scroll bar** can be clicked or dragged to see any material that does not fit in the displayed window.

The **workspace** is the area in which your document is displayed.

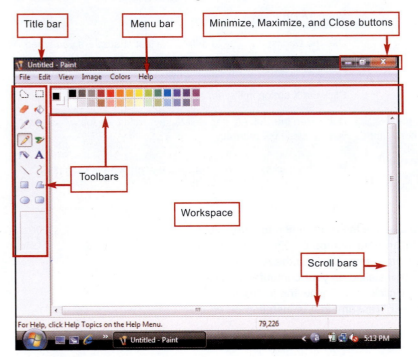

If you're unfamiliar with Windows controls, take a few minutes to complete the steps in the TRY IT! box below.

⌨ TRY IT!

Use the toolbar

1. As shown below, click the **Brush** button on the Paint toolbar.

2. Move the pointer to the workspace, hold down the left mouse button and drag the mouse to paint a shape.

3. Release the mouse button when the shape is complete.

Use the menu bar

1. Click **Image** on the menu bar.

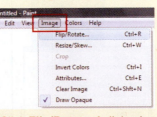

2. Click **Flip/Rotate**. A dialog box appears.

3. Click the circle next to **Flip Vertical**.

4. Click the **OK** button. Your shape is now upside down.

Use the sizing buttons

1. Click the ⬜ **Minimize** button.

2. The Paint window shrinks down to a button on the taskbar at the bottom of the screen.

3. Click the taskbar button to make the Paint window reappear.

4. Click the ❌ **Close** button to close the Paint program and remove its window from the screen. If you see a message asking if you want to save changes, click the Don't Save button.

HELP

How can I get help using software? If you've had problems using software, you're not alone! Everyone has questions at one time or another. Most software offers several sources of help, such as the following:

- **Message boxes.** When using software, it is important to pay attention to any message boxes displayed on the screen. Make sure you carefully read the options they present. If the box doesn't seem to apply to what you want to do, click its Cancel button to close it. Otherwise, set the options the way you want them, and then click the OK button to continue.

- **User manual.** Whether you're a beginner or a power user, the manual that comes with software can be an excellent resource. User manuals can contain quick-start guides, tutorials, detailed descriptions of menu options, and tips for using features effectively. Many manuals are offered online along with tools you can use to browse through them or look for the answer to a specific question.

- **Help menu.** The Help menu provides access to on-screen documentation, which can contain detailed instructions, tips, and FAQs. Answers to specific questions can be found by entering search terms, consulting the index, or browsing through a table of contents (Figure 10).

FIGURE 10

Clicking the [icon] Help button or the Help menu produces a list of help options, where you can enter search terms or browse through topics.

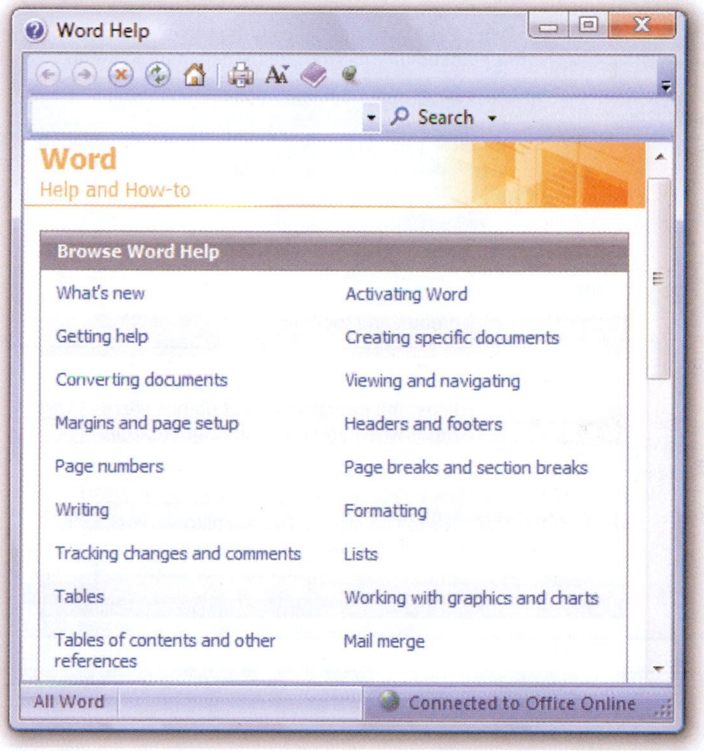

QuickCheck

1. When turning on the components of a desktop computer system, the computer's system _____ should be switched on last.

2. Instead of using the on/off switch to turn off your computer, you should use the _____ button to initiate a shutdown.

3. Ctrl+X means to hold down the Ctrl key, then press +, then press X. True or false? _____

4. The _____ key can be used to delete the last character you typed.

5. Most Windows software displays a(n) _____ bar that includes options, such as File and Help.

⏵ CHECK ANSWERS

Documents, Browsers, and E-mail

TO COMPLETE ASSIGNMENTS for your course, you should be able to work with documents, browsers, and e-mail. Section B walks you through the basics.

CREATING DOCUMENTS

How do I create and save a document? To create a document, simply type text in the workspace provided by word processing software such as Microsoft Word or OpenOffice Writer. The flashing vertical insertion point (Figure 11) indicates your place in the document. Figure 12 explains how to save a document.

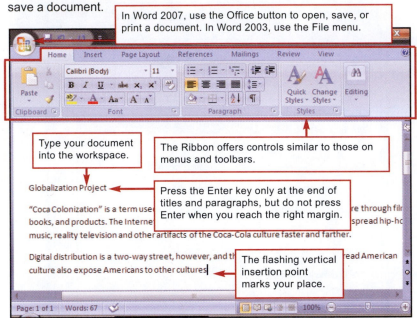

In Word 2007, use the Office button to open, save, or print a document. In Word 2003, use the File menu.

Type your document into the workspace.

The Ribbon offers controls similar to those on menus and toolbars.

Globalization Project

Press the Enter key only at the end of titles and paragraphs, but do not press Enter when you reach the right margin.

"Coca Colonization" is a term used... re through film, books, and products. The Interne... spread hip-hop music, reality television and other artifacts of the Coca-Cola culture faster and farther.

Digital distribution is a two-way street, however, and th... read American culture also expose Americans to other cultures

The flashing vertical insertion point marks your place.

Page: 1 of 1   Words: 67   100%

FIGURE 11

When typing text, you can use the following keys to move within a document and make revisions:

- **Backspace**: Delete the character to the left of the insertion point.

- **Delete:** Delete the character to the right of the insertion point.

- **Enter:** End a paragraph and begin a new line.

- **Arrow keys:** Move the insertion point up, down, right, or left.

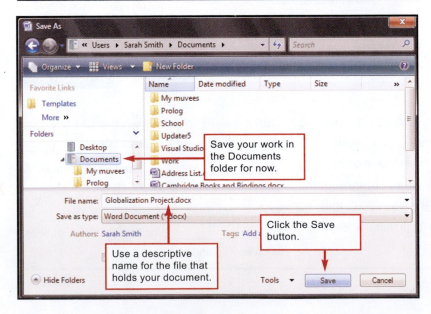

Save As

Users ▶ Sarah Smith ▶ Documents ▶

Organize ▾   Views ▾   New Folder

Favorite Links

Templates
More »

Folders

Desktop
Documents
My muvees
Prolog

Name   Date modified   Type   Size

My muvees
Prolog
School
Updater5
Visual Studio
Work
Address List.
Cambridge Books and Bindings.docx

Save your work in the Documents folder for now.

File name: Globalization Project.docx
Save as type: Word Document (*.docx)
Authors: Sarah Smith   Tags: Add

Click the Save button.

Use a descriptive name for the file that holds your document.

Hide Folders   Tools ▾   Save   Cancel

FIGURE 12

It is a good idea to save your document every few minutes, even if it is not finished. When you save a document, use the Save option on the File menu or Office button.

Your computer is probably configured to save documents on the hard disk in a folder called Documents. No need to change that until you gain more experience. File names can be several words long; just do not use the * / \ " ' : symbols in the file name.

How do I print a document? To print a document, simply click the Office button or File menu, and then select Print. Your computer displays a window containing a series of print options. If you want to print a single copy of your document, these settings should be correct, so you can click the OK button at the bottom of the window to send your document to the printer.

Can I send a document to my instructor? You can e-mail a document by using the Send option accessed from the Office button or File menu (Figure 13). To do so, you must know your instructor's e-mail address. You'll learn more about e-mail later in the Orientation, but keep this option in mind because it is a handy way to submit assignments, such as projects and term papers.

How do I find my documents again in the future? If you want to revise a document sometime in the future, simply start your word processing software, click the Office button or File menu, and then click Open. Your computer should display a list of documents stored in the Documents folder. Locate the one you want to revise and double-click it.

What should I do when I'm done? When you're ready to quit, you can close the document by clicking the Close option from the Office button or File menu. When you want to close your word processing software, you can click the [X] Close button in the upper-right corner of the screen.

FIGURE 13

Most word processing programs offer an option for sending a document as an e-mail attachment.

- In Word 2007, click the Office button, point to Send, and then select E-mail (shown below).

- In Word 2003, click File, select Send To, and then select Mail Recipient.

- In OpenOffice Writer, click File, select Send, and then select Document as E-mail.

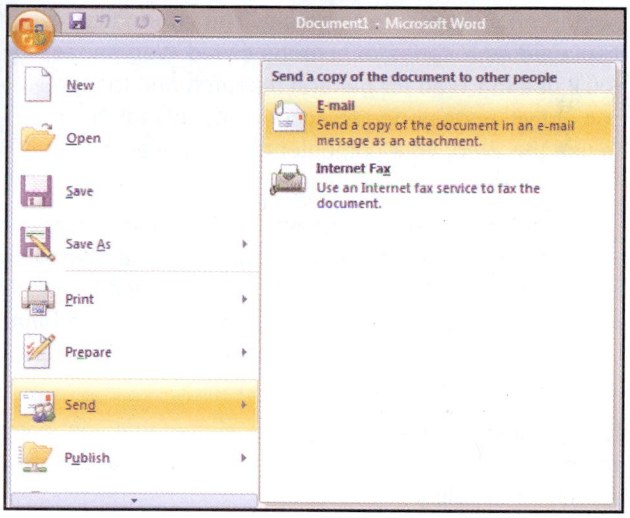

TRY IT!

Create a document

1. Click the **Start** button. Look for Microsoft Word or OpenOffice Writer in the Start menu or the All Programs menu. Click the name of your word processing software to open it.

2. Click the workspace to position the insertion point in the upper-left corner.

3. Type a paragraph. Refer to Figure 11 for keys to use while typing and revising your work.

4. When the first paragraph is complete, press the **Enter** key to begin a new paragraph.

5. Type a second paragraph of text.

Save a document

1. Click the [disk icon] **Save** icon located near the top of the window.

2. Make sure the Documents folder is selected. If not, click the ▶ button next to your user name at the top of the window and then click the Documents folder from the list. (Or use the ▾ button next to the Save In box to display a list of folders.)

3. In the *File name* box, type a name for your document.

4. Click the **Save** button.

5. When the Save As dialog box closes, your document is saved.

Print a document, close it, and exit Word

1. Click the [Office icon] **Office** button or **File** menu, and then click **Print**.

2. Make sure the page range is set to **All**.

3. Make sure number of copies is set to **1**.

4. Click the **OK** button and wait a few seconds for the printer to produce your document.

5. Close the document by clicking the **Office** button or **File** menu, then clicking **Close**. The workspace should become blank.

6. Exit your word processing software by clicking the [X] **Close** button.

INTERNET AND WEB BASICS

What is the Internet? The Internet is the largest computer network in the world, carrying information from one continent to another in the blink of an eye (Figure 14). The computers connected to this network offer many types of resources, such as e-mail, instant messaging, popular music downloads, and online shopping.

What is the Web? Although some people use the terms *Internet* and *Web* interchangeably, the two are not the same. The Internet refers to a communications network that connects computers all around the globe. The Web—short for World Wide Web—is just one of the many resources available over this communications network.

The World Wide Web is a collection of linked and cross-referenced information available for public access. This information is accessible from Web sites located on millions of computers. The information is displayed as a series of screens called Web pages. You'll use the Web for general research and for specific activities designed to accompany this textbook. To use the Web, your computer must have access to the Internet.

How do I access the Internet? Most computers can be configured to connect to the Internet over telephone or cable television systems. Internet access can be obtained from school computer labs, local service providers, such as your cable television company, and national Internet service providers, such as AOL (America Online), AT&T Worldnet, and MSN (Microsoft Network).

To expedite your orientation, it is assumed that your computer has Internet access. If it does not, consult your instructor, or ask an experienced computer user to help you get set up.

How do I know if my computer has Internet access? The easiest way to find out if your computer can access the Internet is to try it. You can quickly find out if you have Internet access by starting software called a browser that's designed to display Web pages.

Browser software called Internet Explorer is supplied with Microsoft Windows. Other browsers, such as Netscape Navigator, Firefox, and Opera, are also available. Follow the steps in the TRY IT! box to start Internet Explorer.

HOW TO USE A WEB BROWSER AND SEARCH ENGINE

How do I use a browser? A browser lets you enter a unique Web page address called a URL and jump from one Web page to another by using links. Links are usually underlined, and when you position the arrow-shaped mouse pointer over a link, it changes to a hand shape.

FIGURE 14

The Internet communications network stretches around the globe.

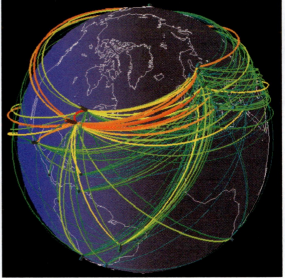

⌨ **TRY IT!**

Start your browser

1. Click the 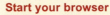 icon located near the Start button.

2. Your computer should soon display a window containing "Internet Explorer" in the title bar. (Refer to the next page.)

If your computer displays a *Connect to* box, click the **Dial** button to establish a dial-up connection over your telephone line.

You'll need to cancel the browser command and consult an experienced computer user if:

- Your computer displays a "working off line" message.
- Your computer displays an Internet Connection Wizard box.

Although browsers offer many features, you can get along quite well using the basic controls shown in Figure 15.

Go back to the last page viewed.

Close the browser window.

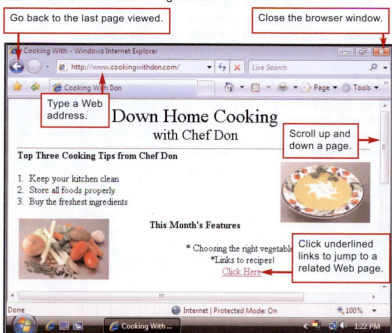

Type a Web address.

Scroll up and down a page.

Click underlined links to jump to a related Web page.

FIGURE 15

Using a Browser

A full Web address might look like this:

http://www.cookingwithdon.com

It is not necessary to type the http://, so to access the Down Home Cooking page shown here, you would type:

www.cookingwithdon.com

When typing a Web address, do not use any spaces and copy upper- and lowercase letters exactly.

How do I find specific information on the Web? If you're looking for information and don't know the Web site where it might be located, you can use a search engine to find it. Follow the steps in the TRY IT! box to "Google it" by using the Google search engine.

⌨TRY IT!

Use a search engine

1. Make sure the browser window is open.

2. Click the Address box and type:

3. Press the **Enter** key. Your browser displays the Web page for the Google search engine.

4. Click the blank search box and then type **national parks**.

5. Press the **Enter** key. Google displays a list of Web pages that relate to national parks.

6. Click the underlined **National Park Service** link. Your browser displays the Park Service's home page.

7. To close the browser, click the **Close** button.

WORKING WITH E-MAIL

What is e-mail? E-mail is a form of communication that relies on computer networks, such as the Internet, to transmit messages from one computer to another. Like regular mail, e-mail messages are sent to a mailbox where they are kept until the recipient retrieves the message. Messages might arrive at their destination within seconds, or might not arrive for a few hours. Once sent, e-mail messages cannot be retrieved.

What do I need to use e-mail? To send and receive e-mail, you need an Internet connection, an e-mail account, and software that enables you to compose, read, and delete e-mail messages. An e-mail account consists of an e-mail address (Figure 16), a password, and a mailbox. You can usually obtain an e-mail account from your Internet service provider, your school, or a Web-based e-mail provider, such as Hotmail, Yahoo! Mail, or Gmail.

How do I create and send an e-mail message? Many e-mail systems are available, and each uses slightly different software, making it impossible to cover all options in this short orientation. You might want to enlist the aid of an experienced computer user to help you get started. The steps in the TRY IT! box are designed for students who use e-mail software supplied with Windows XP or Vista.

FIGURE 16

E-mail Addresses

An e-mail address consists of a user ID followed by an @ symbol and the name of a computer that handles e-mail accounts. Ask your instructor for his or her e-mail address. It is likely similar to the following:

instructor@school.edu

When typing an e-mail address, use all lowercase letters and do not use any spaces.

🖮 TRY IT!

Create and send e-mail

1. Click the **Start** button and look for an e-mail program, such as Outlook, Outlook Express, Microsoft Mail, or Windows Mail. Click the program name to get it started.

2. Click the **Create** button to display a form like the one below.

3. Follow steps 4-6 as shown below.

7. When your message is complete, click the **Send** button. With most computers, this button places the e-mail in your Outbox.

8. Click the **Send/Receive** button on the toolbar to ship the message over the network to your instructor.

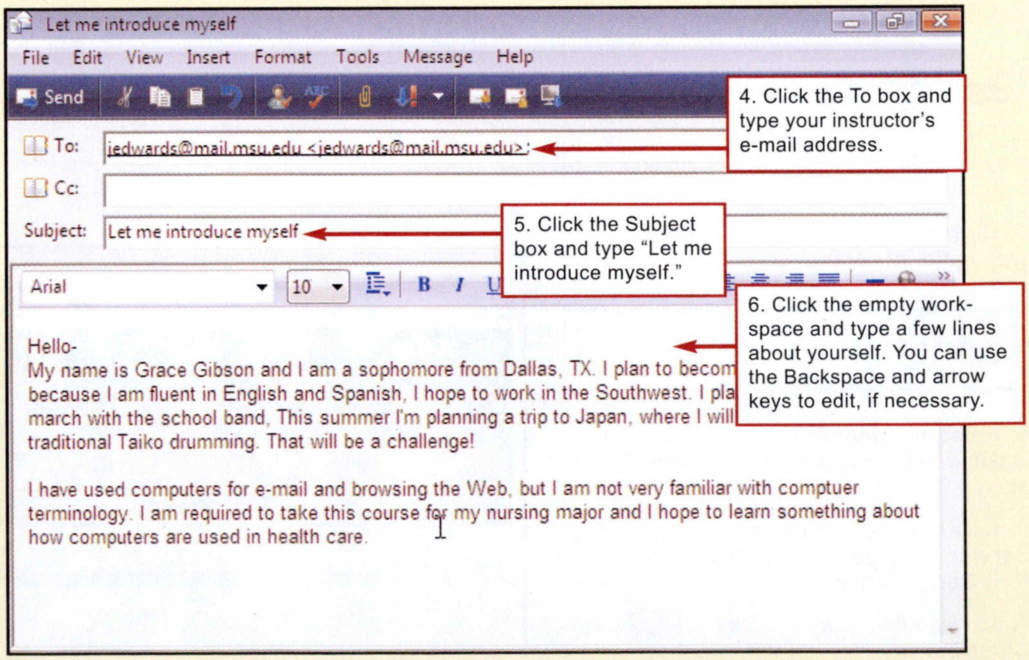

Let me introduce myself

| File | Edit | View | Insert | Format | Tools | Message | Help |

Send

To: jedwards@mail.msu.edu <jedwards@mail.msu.edu>;

Cc:

Subject: Let me introduce myself

Arial   10   B I U

Hello-
My name is Grace Gibson and I am a sophomore from Dallas, TX. I plan to becom
because I am fluent in English and Spanish, I hope to work in the Southwest. I pla
march with the school band, This summer I'm planning a trip to Japan, where I will
traditional Taiko drumming. That will be a challenge!

I have used computers for e-mail and browsing the Web, but I am not very familiar with comptuer terminology. I am required to take this course for my nursing major and I hope to learn something about how computers are used in health care.

4. Click the To box and type your instructor's e-mail address.

5. Click the Subject box and type "Let me introduce myself."

6. Click the empty workspace and type a few lines about yourself. You can use the Backspace and arrow keys to edit, if necessary.

How do I get my e-mail? As with sending mail, the way you get mail depends on your e-mail system. In general, clicking the Send/Receive button collects your mail from the network and stores it in your Inbox. Your e-mail software displays a list of your messages. The new ones are usually shown highlighted or in bold type. You can click any message to open it, read it, and reply to it, as shown in Figure 17.

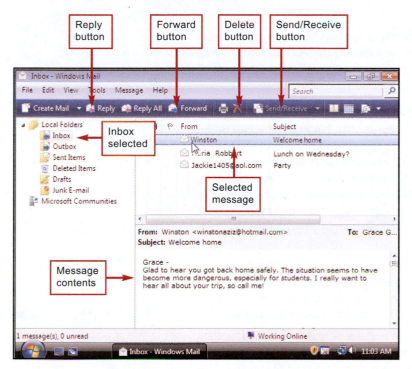

FIGURE 17

Most e-mail software displays a list of your messages. You can:

- Open a message and read it.

- Reply to a message.

- Delete unwanted messages (a good idea to minimize the size of your mailbox).

- Forward a message to some-one else.

QuickCheck

1. It is a good idea to [_____] your work every few minutes, even if you are not finished with it.

2. Software called a(n) [_____] helps you access Web pages.

3. If you don't know where to find information, you can use a(n) [_____] engine to pro-duce a list of links to Web pages that might contain the information you seek.

4. The special symbol used in e-mail addresses is [_____] .

5. An e-mail [_____] consists of an e-mail address, a password, and a mailbox.

▶ CHECK ANSWERS

Security and Privacy

AS WITH MOST OTHER facets of modern life, computing has its share of troublemakers, scam artists, and identity thieves. Section C offers some tips on navigating through the sometimes rough neighborhoods of cyberspace, while keeping your data safe and your identity private.

SECURING YOUR COMPUTER AND DATA

What's at risk if my computer is stolen? A computer can be an attractive target for thieves, but the value of a stolen computer is not so much in the hardware as in the data it contains. With stolen data such as your bank account numbers and PINs, a thief can wipe out your checking and savings accounts. With your credit card numbers, a thief can go on a spending spree. Even worse, a criminal can use stolen data to assume your identity, run up debts, get into legal difficulties, ruin your credit rating, and cause you no end of trouble.

How can I protect my computer data from theft? When you carry a notebook computer, never leave it unattended. To thwart a thief who breaks into your home or dorm room, anchor your computer to your desk with a specially designed lock you can buy at most electronics stores.

If a thief steals your computer, you can make it difficult to access your data by setting up a password. Until the password is entered, your data is off limits. A thief might be able to boot up the Windows desktop, but should not be able to easily look at the data in your folders.

Many new computers are shipped with a standard administrator password that everyone knows. If you are the only person using your computer, you can use the administrator account for your day-to-day computing, but create a secure password (Figure 18) for this account as soon as you can.

Your computer might also include a preset guest account with a nonsecure password such as "guest." You should disable this guest account or assign it a secure password.

FIGURE 18

To create a secure password:

- Use at least five characters, mixing numbers with letters, as in 2by4s.

- Do not use your name, the name of a family member, or pet's name.

- Do not use a word that can be found in the dictionary.

- Do not forget your password!

⌨ **TRY IT!**

Check the accounts on your computer

1. Click the **Start** button, then select **Control Panel**.

2. For Windows Vista, select **User Accounts** and then select **Manage another account**. (You might be required to enter an administrator password.) For Windows XP, select **User Accounts**.

3. Check the password protection on all accounts. If you are working on a school lab computer, close the User Accounts window without making any changes. If you are using your own computer, click the Administrator account and make sure it has a secure password.

For security, all active accounts should be password protected.

AVOIDING VIRUSES

What's so bad about computer viruses? The term *virus* has a technical meaning, but many people use the term loosely when referring to malicious programs that circulate on disks, in e-mail attachments, and on the Internet. This malware, as it is sometimes called, can steal your data, destroy files, or create network traffic jams. It might display an irritating message to announce its presence, or it might work quietly behind the scenes to spread itself to various files on your computer or mail itself out to everyone in your e-mail address book.

After a virus takes up residence in your computer, it is often difficult to disinfect all your files. Rather than wait for a virus attack, you should take steps to keep your computer virus free.

How can I keep viruses out of my computer? Back when viruses were less sophisticated, computer users were commonly warned not to download pirated software or open e-mail attachments from unknown senders. These two common sources of viruses still exist, but virus creators have found ways to make pirated software look legitimate and to affix your friends' names to e-mails that carry infected attachments.

Although it is a good idea to avoid pirated software and stay alert when opening e-mail attachments, the best defense against viruses is to install antivirus software such as the packages listed in Figure 19, and configure it to run continuously whenever your computer is on. You should make sure your antivirus software is set up to scan for viruses in incoming files and e-mail messages. At least once a week your antivirus software should run a full system check to make sure every file on your computer is virus free.

As new viruses emerge, your antivirus software needs to update its virus definition file. It gets this update as a Web download. If you've selected the auto update option, your computer should automatically receive updates as they become available.

FIGURE 19

Popular Antivirus Software

Norton AntiVirus
McAfee VirusScan
Kaspersky Anti-Virus
F-Prot
Softwin BitDefender
Panda Antivirus
Trend Micro PC-cillin
AVG Anti-virus
Alwil Avast!

TRY IT!

Get familiar with your antivirus software

1. Click the **Start** button, and then select **All Programs**. Look for antivirus software (refer to Figure 19 for a list). Open your antivirus software by clicking it.

Can't find any? If you are using your own computer and it doesn't seem to have antivirus software, you can connect to an antivirus Web site and download it.

2. Each antivirus program has unique features. The figure on the right shows the main screen for Norton AntiVirus software. Explore your antivirus software to make sure it is configured to do the following:

- Scan incoming e-mail
- Run continuously in the background—a feature sometimes called Auto Protect
- Block malicious scripts

3. Check the date of your last full system scan. If it was more than one week ago, you should check the settings that schedule antivirus scans.

4. Check the date when your computer last received virus definitions. If it was more than two weeks ago, you should make sure your antivirus software is configured to receive automatic live updates.

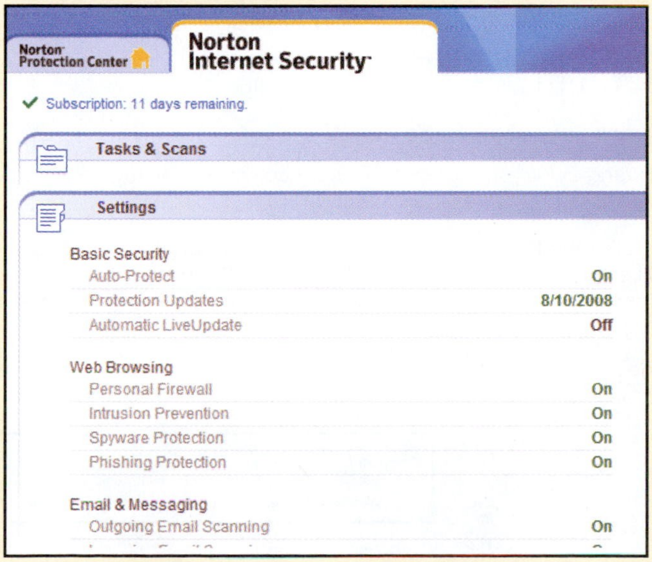

Norton Protection Center	**Norton Internet Security**	
✔ Subscription: 11 days remaining.		
Tasks & Scans		
Settings		
Basic Security		
Auto-Protect		On
Protection Updates		8/10/2008
Automatic LiveUpdate		Off
Web Browsing		
Personal Firewall		On
Intrusion Prevention		On
Spyware Protection		On
Phishing Protection		On
Email & Messaging		
Outgoing Email Scanning		On

PREVENTING INTRUSIONS

Is it risky to go online? The Internet offers lots of cool stuff—music downloads, movie reviews and trailers, online shopping and banking, consumer information, chat groups, news, sports, weather, and much more. Most Internet offerings are legitimate, but some downloads contain viruses, and shady characters called hackers control programs that lurk about waiting to snatch your personal data or infiltrate your computer. The longer your computer remains connected to the Internet, the more vulnerable it is to a hacker's infiltration attempts.

If a hacker gains access to your computer, he or she can look through your files, use your computer as a launching platform for viruses and network-jamming attacks, or turn your computer into a server for pornography and other unsavory material. Hackers have even found ways to turn thousands of infiltrated computers into "zombies," link them together, and carry out coordinated attacks to disrupt online access to Microsoft, Bank of America, and other Internet businesses.

How do hackers gain access to my computer? Intruders gain access by exploiting security flaws in your computer's operating system, browser, and e-mail software. Software publishers are constantly creating patches to fix these flaws. As part of your overall security plan, you should download and install security patches as they become available.

How can I block hackers from infiltrating my computer? Firewall software, such as the packages listed in Figure 20, provides a protective barrier between a computer and the Internet. If your computer is directly connected to the Internet, it should have active firewall software. If your computer connects to a local area network for Internet access, the network should have a device called a router to block infiltration attempts.

When a firewall is active, it watches for potentially disruptive incoming data called *probes*. When a probe is discovered, your firewall displays a warning and asks what to do. If the source looks legitimate, you can let it through; if not, you should block it (Figure 21).

Where do I get a firewall? Windows XP and Vista include built-in firewalls. If your computer uses an earlier version of Windows, you can download a third-party firewall.

FIGURE 20

Popular Firewall Software

Tiny Personal Firewall

McAfee Personal Firewall

ZoneAlarm Pro

Sygate Firewall Pro

Norton Personal Firewall

BlackICE Defender

Mac OS Firewall

Outpost Firewall

Windows Firewall

FIGURE 21

When your firewall software encounters new or unusual activity, it asks you what to do.

⌨ **TRY IT!**

Check your computer's firewall

Finding out if your computer has an active firewall requires a little detective work. Try the steps below to see if a firewall is protecting your computer from intrusions.

1. Click the **Start** button, then click **Control Panel**. Click the **Security** link or double-click the **Security Center** icon to see if the Windows Firewall is active.

2. If the Windows firewall is not active, you should check to see if a third-party firewall is protecting your computer.

3. Click the **Start** button, click **All Programs**, and then look through the program list for firewalls such as those in Figure 20. If you find a firewall listed, start it and explore to see if it has been activated.

4. If your computer does not appear to have an active firewall, you might want to download one and install it.

BLOCKING SPYWARE AND POP-UP ADS

Are some Web sites dangerous? When you access Web sites, data is transferred to your computer and displayed by your browser. Most of this data is harmless, but malicious HTML scripts, rogue ActiveX components, and spyware have the potential to search your computer for passwords and credit card numbers, monitor your Web-browsing habits for marketing purposes, block your access to legitimate Web sites, or surreptitiously use your computer as a staging area for illicit activities.

Spyware is the most insidious threat. It often piggybacks on pop-up ads and activates if you click the ad window. Some spyware can begin its dirty work when you try to click the Close button to get rid of an ad.

How can I block spyware? The first line of defense is to never click pop-up ads—especially those with dire warnings about your computer being infected by a virus or spyware! (See Figure 22.) To close an ad, right-click its button on the taskbar at the bottom of your screen, and then select the Close option from the menu that appears. Some browsers can be configured to block spyware and pop-up ads. Your antivirus software might offer similar options. You can also install software specially designed to block spyware and pop-up ads. Figure 23 lists some popular titles.

What other steps can I take to browse the Web safely? Most browsers include security features. You should take some time to become familiar with them. For example, Internet Explorer allows you to specify how you want it to deal with ActiveX components. You can also specify how to deal with HTML scripts, cookies, security certificates, and other Web-based data. If you don't want to be bothered by these details, however, Internet Explorer offers several predefined configurations for Low, Medium, and High security. Most Internet Explorer users set security and privacy options to Medium.

FIGURE 22

Some pop-up ads contain fake warnings about viruses, spyware, and intrusion attempts.

FIGURE 23

Popular Antispyware and Ad-Blocking Software

Webroot Spy Sweeper

Lavasoft Ad-Aware

Safer Networking Spybot S&D

InfoWorks SpyRemover

CA Pest Patrol

TrustSoft Antispyware

Pop-up Defender

TRY IT!

Check Internet Explorer security and privacy options

1. Start Internet Explorer. Click **Tools**, then select **Internet Options**.

2. Click the **Security** tab. Typically, your security setting should be Medium.

3. Click the **Privacy** tab. Typically, your privacy setting should be Medium.

4. Check the bottom of the window for a Pop-up Blocker option. If your version of Internet Explorer offers this feature, make sure its box contains a check mark so that it is activated.

5. If your version of Internet Explorer does not offer a pop-up blocker, check your antivirus software to see if it can provide protection. Otherwise, you can use the Start button to see if any of the software listed in Figure 23 has been installed. If your computer seems to have no antispyware or ad-blocking software, you might want to download some and install it.

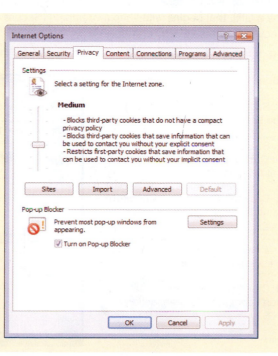

PROTECTING E-COMMERCE TRANSACTIONS

Is online shopping safe? Online shopping is generally safe. From time to time, shoppers encounter fake storefronts designed to look like legitimate merchants but that are actually set up to steal credit card information. You can avoid these fakes by making sure you enter correctly spelled URLs when connecting to your favorite shopping sites.

How safe is my credit card information when I'm shopping online? Online shopping is not much more dangerous than using your credit card for a telephone order or giving it to a server when you've finished eating in a restaurant. Anyone who handles your card can copy the card number, jot down the expiration date, and try to make unauthorized charges.

That's not to say that credit cards are risk free. Credit cards are surprisingly vulnerable both online and off. Thieves can break into merchant computers that store order information. Thieves might even pick up your credit card information from discarded order forms. Despite these risks, we continue to use credit cards.

Many people are concerned about their credit card data getting intercepted as it travels over the Internet. As you wrap up an online purchase and submit your credit card information, it is transmitted from your computer to the merchant's computer. Software called a packet sniffer, designed for legitimately monitoring network traffic, is occasionally used by unscrupulous hackers to intercept credit card numbers and other data traveling over the Internet.

How can I keep my credit card number confidential? When you submit credit card information, make sure the merchant provides a secure connection for transporting data. Typically, a secure connection is activated when you're in the final phases of checking out—as you enter your shipping and credit card information into a form and click a Submit button to send it. A secure connection encrypts your data. Even if your credit card number is intercepted, it cannot be deciphered and used. To make sure you have a secure connection, look for the lock icon. The Address box should also display a URL that begins with shttp:// or https:// (Secure HTTP), or contains ssl (Secure Sockets Layer).

⌨ TRY IT!

Identify a secure connection

1. Start your browser and connect to the site: **www.walmart.com**.

2. Select any item and use the **Add to Cart** option to place it in your online shopping cart.

3. Click the **Proceed to Checkout** button.

4. At the checkout screen, do you see any evidence that you're using a secure connection?

5. Close your browser so that you don't complete the transaction.

Secure HTTPS in URL

Lock icon in address bar at top of window or taskbar at bottom of window.

AVOIDING E-MAIL SCAMS

What are e-mail scams? From time to time, you hear about con artists who have bilked innocent consumers out of their life savings. The Internet has its share of con artists, too, who run e-mail scams designed to collect money and confidential information from unsuspecting victims. E-mail scams are usually distributed in mass mailings called spam.

What do I need to know about spam? The Internet makes it easy and cheap to send out millions of e-mail solicitations. In the United States, the CAN-SPAM Act requires mass-mail messages to be labeled with a valid subject line. Recipients are supposed to be provided with a way to opt out of receiving future messages. Legitimate merchants and organizations comply with the law when sending product announcements, newsletters, and other messages. Unscrupulous spammers ignore the law and try to disguise their solicitations as messages from your friends, chat room participants, or co-workers (Figure 24).

!	0	⚑	From	Subject
			Winston	Welcome home
			Maria Robbert	Lunch on Wednesday?
			Jackie1405@aol.com	Party
			Datamation IT Update	[SPAM] Conference Focuses on IT
			FlyCharterAir.com	[SPAM] Charter Specials
			Sonja Crowder	Receive your V1agr&a
			Dwayne Thrman	It's new and successful

FIGURE 24

Some e-mail systems use spam filters to flag suspected spam by adding [SPAM] to the subject line. Spam filters are not perfect, however. Some spam is not flagged and occasionally legitimate mail is mistaken for spam.

Is spam dangerous? Many spam messages contain legitimate information, including daily or weekly newsletters to which you've subscribed. Some spam messages, however, advertise illegal products. Others are outright scams to get you to download a virus, divulge your bank account numbers, or send in money for products you'll never receive.

Beware of spam containing offers that seem just too good to be true. For example, you might receive a message from an African businessman who is seeking your help to transfer a large sum of money from his country to yours (Figure 25). These messages are frauds.

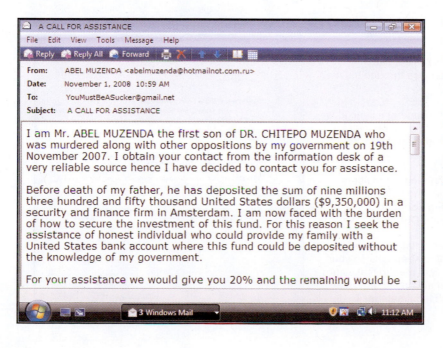

FIGURE 25

Many variations of this African money-transfer fraud—complete with deliberate grammatical errors—have circulated on the Internet for years. Victims who respond to these preposterous e-mails have found their bank accounts raided, their credit ratings destroyed, and their reputations ruined. According to the FBI, some victims have even been kidnapped!

What's phishing? Phishing (pronounced "fishing") is a scam that arrives in your e-mailbox looking like official correspondence from a major company, such as Microsoft, PayPal, eBay, MSN, Yahoo!, or America Online. The e-mail message is actually from an illegitimate source and is designed to trick you into divulging confidential information or downloading a virus. Links in the e-mail message often lead to a Web site that looks official, where you are asked to enter confidential information such as your credit card number, Social Security number, or bank account number.

The following are examples of phishing scams you should be aware of:

● A message from Microsoft with an attachment that supposedly contains a security update for Microsoft Windows. Downloading the attachment infects your computer with a virus.

● A message from America Online, complete with official-looking logos, that alerts you to a problem with your account. When you click the AOL Billing Center link and enter your account information, it is transmitted to a hacker's computer.

● A message that's obviously spam, but contains a convenient opt-out link. If you click the link believing that it will prevent future spam from this source, you'll actually be downloading a program that hackers can use to remotely control your computer for illegal activities.

How do I avoid e-mail scams? If your e-mail software provides spam filters, you can use them to block some unsolicited mail from your e-mailbox. Spam filters are far from perfect, however, so don't assume everything that gets through is legitimate. Use your judgment before opening any e-mail message or attachment.

Never reply to a message that you suspect to be fraudulent. If you have a question about its legitimacy, check whether it's on a list of known scams. Never click a link provided in an e-mail message to manage your account information. Instead, use your browser to go directly to the company's Web site and access your account as usual. Microsoft never sends updates as attachments. To obtain Microsoft updates, go to *www.microsoft.com* and click Security & Updates.

🖮 TRY IT!

Arm yourself against e-mail scams

1. Start your browser and connect to the site **www.millersmiles.co.uk** and browse through the list of recent phishing attacks.

2. Open your e-mail software and find out if it incudes spam filters. You can usually find this information by clicking Help on the menu bar and then typing "spam filter" in the search box.

3. Explore your options for configuring spam filters. If you use Windows Mail for e-mail (shown at right), you can find these settings by clicking **Tools** on the menu bar, and then clicking **Junk E-mail Options**.

Spam filters sometimes catch legitimate mail and group it with junk mail. You might want to keep tabs on your spam filters when they are first activated to make sure they are set to a level that eliminates most unwanted spam without catching too much legitimate mail.

PROTECTING YOUR PRIVACY

How much information has been collected about me? No matter what steps you take to protect your privacy, information about you is stored in many places and has the potential to be consolidated by government agencies, private businesses, and criminals.

Some databases are legitimate—those maintained by credit bureaus and medical insurance companies, for example. By law, you have the right to ask for a copy of these records and correct any errors you find. Many other databases, such as those maintained at e-commerce sites and those illegally acquired by hackers, are not accessible, and you have no way of checking the data they contain.

Can I control who collects information about me? To some extent, you can limit your exposure to future data collection by supplying personal data only when absolutely necessary. When filling out online forms, consider whether you want to or need to provide your real name and address.

You should also be careful about revealing personal information in chat rooms and other online forums. Many chat room participants are not who they appear to be. Some people are just having fun with fantasy identities, but others are trying to con people by telling hard luck stories and faking illnesses. In a chat room, never reveal personal information, such as your full name, address, or phone number. Resist the temptation to meet face to face with chat room participants. Taking simple steps to protect your privacy is an important part of your overall security plan (Figure 26).

TRY IT!

Check your privacy

1. Start your browser and go Googling by connecting to **www.google.com**. Enter your name in the Search box. What turns up?

2. Connect to **www.peopledata.com**. Enter your name and state of residence. Click the **Search** button. Notice all the information that's offered.

3. Connect to **www.ciadata.com** and scroll down the page to view the kind of information anyone can obtain about you for less than $100.

4. Connect to the Federal Trade Commission site:

   http://www.ftc.gov/bcp/conline/pubs/credit/crdright.htm

At this site, you can read about your rights to view credit reports.

FIGURE 26

Computer Security Checklist

- Use a password to protect your data in case your computer is stolen.

- Don't leave your computer unattended in public places.

- Run antivirus software and keep it updated.

- Install software service packs and security patches as they become available, but make sure they are legitimate.

- Install and activate firewall software, especially if your computer is directly connected to the Internet by an ISDN, DSL, satellite, or cable connection.

- Do not publish or post personal information, such as your physical address, passwords, Social Security number, or account numbers, on your Web site, your online resume, or other online documents.

- Be wary of contacts you make in public chat rooms.

- Don't click pop-up ads.

- Install and activate antispyware and ad-blocking software.

- Do not reply to spam.

- Ignore e-mail offers that seem too good to be true.

QuickCheck

SECTION C

1. The best defense against viruses is to use a phishing filter before opening e-mail attachments. True or false? [ ]

2. Intruders can access your computer by exploiting [ ] flaws in a computer's operating system, browser, or e-mail software.

3. [ ] is an online threat that compromises your privacy by piggybacking on pop-up ads and collecting personal information.

4. E-mail scams are usually distributed in mass mailings called [ ].

▶ CHECK ANSWERS

BookOnCD

ELECTRONIC VERSIONS of your textbook are designed to be portable, interactive learning environments. This section offers an interactive overview of the popular BookOnCD and other BookOn products have similar features.

BOOKONCD BASICS

What is the BookOnCD? The BookOnCD is a multimedia version of your textbook with photos that come to life as videos, diagrams that become animations, screenshots that open to guided software tours, and computer-scored activities that will help improve your test scores.

What's the most effective way to use the BookOnCD? If you're used to reading documents and Web pages on your computer screen, you can use the BookOnCD for most of your reading and studying. As you work through a chapter, you'll be able to view the multimedia elements in context and take QuickChecks at the end of each section. If you prefer to read from your printed textbook, you can start the BookOnCD whenever you want to view a multimedia element or work with a computer-scored activity.

How do I start the BookOnCD? To start the BookOnCD and take advantage of its interactive features, follow the instructions in the TRY IT! box below.

FLASH PLAYER

The BookOnCD requires the Adobe Flash player for displaying labs. The Flash player is installed on most computers. If the BookOnCD cannot find your Flash player when it starts, you'll be directed to go online to download and install it.

TRY IT!

Start the BookOnCD

1. Locate the button on your computer's CD or DVD drive and push it to open the tray.

2. Insert the BookOnCD into the tray, label side up and close the drive tray.

3. Wait a few seconds until the BookOnCD has loaded.

● If the main Computer Concepts screen appears, proceed to step 4.
● If an Autoplay box appears, select Run BookOnCD.exe.
● If the CD does not start automatically, click the Start button, click Computer, and then double-click the CD or DVD drive icon.

The BookOnCD allows you to save your scores for QuickChecks, practice tests, and other activities, but for this session you do not need to track this data.

4. To disable tracking, make sure the box *Save Tracking data* is empty. If the box contains a check mark, click the box to empty it.

5. Click the **OK** button. The Tracking Options dialog box closes and the BookOnCD is ready for use.

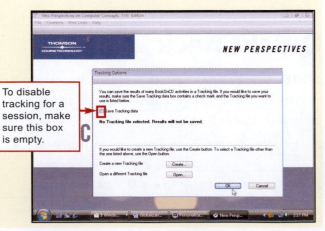

To disable tracking for a session, make sure this box is empty.

How do I navigate through the book?
The BookOnCD menu and toolbar, near the top of the screen, contain tools you can use for navigation. The Next and Back buttons turn one page at a time. To get to the first page of any chapter, you can select it from the Contents menu.

The BookOnCD pages mirror the pages in the printed book, so if you want to take the QuickCheck that's on page 21 of your printed textbook for example, you can use the Go to Page option on the toolbar to jump right to it.

What are the other menu and navigation options?
The menu bar includes a Web Links menu with options that open your browser and connect to InfoWebLinks, the NP11 Web site, and the Course Technology Web site. The menu bar also includes a Help menu where you can access instructions and troubleshooting FAQs. The Glossary button provides access to definitions for key terms. An Annotation button appears when your instructor has posted comments or lecture notes. If your instructor has not posted annotations, the button will not appear.

How do I exit the BookOnCD?
When you have completed a session and want to close the BookOnCD, you can click the [×] button in the upper-right corner of the title bar, or you can click the File menu and select Exit. Figure 27 helps you locate the Close button and BookOnCD navigation tools.

FIGURE 27

Key features of the BookOnCD menu bar and toolbar.

The Contents menu takes you to the first page of any chapter you select.

The Back button displays the previous page.

The Next button displays the next page.

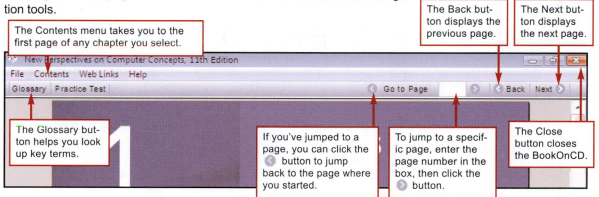

The Glossary button helps you look up key terms.

If you've jumped to a page, you can click the ◀ button to jump back to the page where you started.

To jump to a specific page, enter the page number in the box, then click the ◉ button.

The Close button closes the BookOnCD.

📇 TRY IT!

Open a chapter and navigate the BookOnCD

1. Click **Contents** on the menu bar. The contents menu appears.

2. Click **Chapter 2**.

3. When Chapter 2 appears, click the **Next** button twice until you see page 56.

4. Click the **Back** button twice to go back to the first page of Chapter 2.

5. Click the white box on the right side of Go to Page. Type **89**, then click the **Go to Page** ◉ button.

6. Click the ◀ **Go to Page** button. Now you should be back at the first page of Chapter 2.

7. Scroll down the page until you can see the Chapter Contents listing. As shown at right, you can use this list to quickly jump to Sections A, B, C, D, or E, Issues, Computers in Context, Labs, and End-of-Chapter activities.

8. Click ◉ **Section D** to jump to Section D.

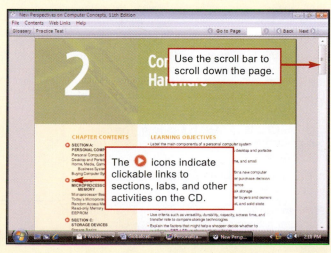

Use the scroll bar to scroll down the page.

The ◉ icons indicate clickable links to sections, labs, and other activities on the CD.

MULTIMEDIA AND COMPUTER-SCORED ACTIVITIES

What kinds of multimedia are included in the BookOnCD?
Figures in your book marked with the ⊙ icon morph into multimedia screentours, animations, and videos. A screentour takes you on a guided software tour—even if you don't have the software installed on your computer! Animations and videos visually expand on the concepts presented in the text.

How do I access screentours and other multimedia?
To access multimedia elements, simply click the ⊙CLICK TO START icon while using the BookOnCD.

Which activities are computer scored?
Figure 28 lists the BookOnCD activities that are computer scored. You can use these activities to gauge how well you remember and understand the material you read in the textbook.

Suppose you're reading Chapter 2. Work with the TRY IT! below to see how multimedia and computer-scored activities work.

FIGURE 28

BookOnCD Computer-Scored Activities

Interactive Summary

Interactive Situation Questions

Practice Tests

Concept Map

QuickChecks

Lab QuickChecks

⌨ TRY IT!

Explore multimedia and computer-scored activities

1. Use the **Go to Page** control to jump to page 79.

2. On page 79, Figure 2-23 contains a ⊙CLICK TO START icon. Click it to launch the video.

3. When you want to stop the video, click any blank area of the BookOnCD page. To restart the video, click the ⊙CLICK TO START icon again.

4. Now, try a computer-scored QuickCheck. Use the **Go to Page** control to get to page 75 and scroll down the page until you can see the entire set of QuickCheck questions.

5. Click the answer box for question 1, and then type your answer. Most answers are a single word. Upper and lower-case have no effect on the correctness of your answer.

6. Press the **Tab** key to jump to question 2, and then type your answer. Don't worry if you don't know the answer, you haven't actually read Chapter 2 yet. Just make a guess for now.

7. When you have answered all the questions, click the ⊙CHECK ANSWERS icon. The computer indicates whether your answer is correct or incorrect.

8. Continue to click **OK** to check the rest of your answers.

9. When you've reviewed all your answers, the computer presents a score summary. Click **OK** to close the dialog box.

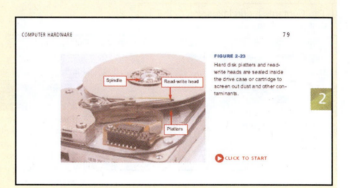

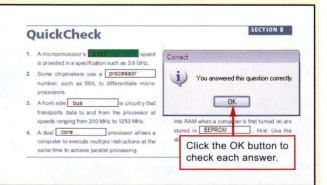

NEW PERSPECTIVES LABS

What about labs? Your textbook gives you access to two kinds of labs. New Perspectives Labs are part of the BookOnCD. Student Edition Labs are located at the NP11 Web site. You'll learn how to access Student Edition Labs in Section E.

New Perspectives Labs give you hands-on experience applying concepts and using software discussed in each chapter. Labs on the BookOnCD are divided into topics, and each topic ends with a QuickCheck so that you can make sure you understand key concepts.

In addition to lab QuickChecks, each New Perspectives Lab also includes a set of assignments located in the Lab section of each chapter. Your instructor might require you to complete these assignments. You can submit them on paper, on disk, or as an e-mail message, according to your instructor's directions.

How do I launch a lab? First, navigate to the lab page using the New Perspectives Labs option from the Chapter Contents list or type in the corresponding page number from the printed book. Click the lab's ● icon to start it.

TRY IT!

Open a New Perspectives Lab

1. Click **Contents** on the BookOnCD menu bar and select **Chapter 1**.

2. Scroll down to the Chapter Contents list and click ● **New Perspectives Labs**.

3. When the New Perspectives Labs page appears, click ● **Operating a Personal Computer**.

4. The lab window opens. Click the ➡ button to view objectives for Topic 1.

5. Click the ➡ button again to view page 1 of the lab. Read the information on the page, and then continue through the lab, making sure to follow any numbered instructions.

6. After page 8, you will encounter the first QuickCheck question. Click the correct answer, and then click the **Check Answer** button. After you find out if your answer was correct, click the ➡ button to continue to the next question. Complete all the QuickCheck questions for Topic 1.

7. For this TRY IT! you don't have to complete the entire lab. When you are ready to quit, click the ⬛ button.

8. Click the ⬛ button again. Your Lab QuickCheck results are displayed.

9. Click the **OK** button to return to the BookOnCD.

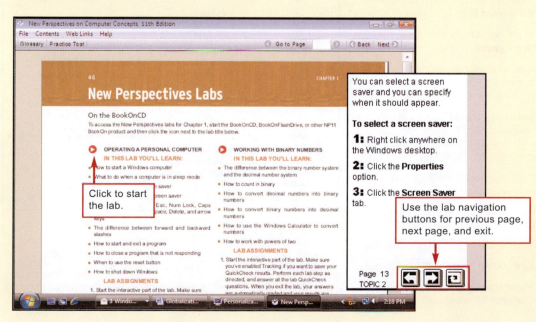

TRACKING YOUR SCORES

Can I save scores from QuickChecks, labs, and other activities?

To save your scores, you have to create a Tracking file. The file can be located on a floppy disk, your computer's hard disk, a USB flash drive, or a network drive where you have permission to store files.

⌨ TRY IT!

Create a Tracking file

1. Make sure your BookOnCD is open.

2. Click **File** on the BookOnCD menu bar, then click **Change Tracking Options**.

3. When the Tracking Options dialog box appears, click the **Create** button.

4. When the Create Tracking File dialog box appears, enter the requested data (see illustration above right), then click **Continue**. The Save As dialog box appears.

5. Use the Save As dialog box to specify the location and name for your Tracking file. (See the illustration below right.)

6. After selecting a name and location for your Tracking file, click the **Save** button.

7. Back at the Tracking Options dialog box, make sure there is a check mark in the box labeled *Save Tracking data*, then click the **OK** button. Now your Tracking file is ready to receive your scores.

Complete a Practice Test

To start tracking your scores, you can complete a Practice Test.

1. Click the **Practice Test** button located on the BookOnCD toolbar.

2. The first question of a 10-question Practice Test appears. Answer the question, then click the **Next** button.

3. Answer the remaining questions, then click the **Check Answers** button.

4. When you see your score summary, click the **OK** button. You can then step through each of your answers or view a study guide.

5. Click the **Study Guide** button. A browser window opens to display each Practice Test question, your answers, and corresponding page numbers in your textbook.

6. Click the ❌ button on your browser window to close the Study Guide.

7. Click the **Close** button on the Practice Test window to close it and save your scores.

View the contents of your Tracking file

1. Click **File** on the BookOnCD menu bar.

2. Click **View Tracking Report**. Your computer opens your browser and displays a

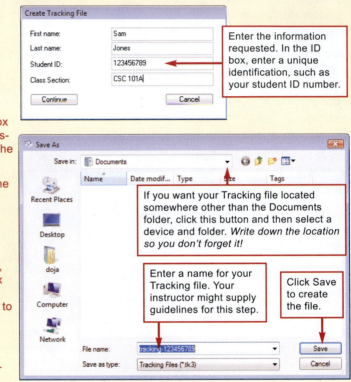

summary score for the Practice Test you completed. The list of summary scores grows as you save additional Practice Tests, QuickChecks, Interactive Summaries, Interactive Situation Questions, and Lab QuickChecks.

3. To close the Tracking Report, close the browser window by clicking its ❌ button.

How do I submit scores from my Tracking file? You can use the Submit Tracking Data option on the File menu to send your scores to your instructor. The files are sent over an Internet service called WebTrack. Before you begin, make sure you have the following:

- An Internet connection
- Your instructor's WebTrack address
- Tracking file (If you've stored your data on a USB flash drive, make sure it is connected; if your data is on a floppy disk, make sure it is inserted in the drive.)

Are the scores erased from my Tracking file when they are sent? No. Your scores remain in your file—a copy is sent to your instructor. If your instructor's computer malfunctions and loses your data, you can resubmit your Tracking file. It is a good idea to back up your Tracking file using the Back Up Tracking File option on the File menu. If your file is damaged or lost, you'll have a copy.

TRY IT!

Send your Tracking data

1. Click **File** on the BookOnCD menu bar, then click **Submit Tracking Data**.

2. Make sure your instructor's Web Track address is correctly displayed in the Tracking Data Destination dialog box, then click **Continue**.

3. Your computer opens a browser window, makes an Internet connection, and contacts the WebTrack server.

4. When the WebTrack screen appears, make sure the information displayed is correct, then click the **Submit** button.

5. When you see a message that confirms your data has been submitted, you can close the browser window by clicking the [X] button.

6. Close your BookOnCD before you continue to the next section in the Orientation.

Submit Tracking Data - Windows Internet Explorer

C:\Users\Temp\study.htm · Live Search

Submit Tracking Data · Page · Tools ·

WEBTRACK Powered by MediaTechnic's BookOnCD and BookOnWeb Technology

Tracking file:	C:\Users\doja\Documents\tracking-123456789.tk3
Name:	Sam Jones
Student ID:	123456789
Class Section:	CSC 101A
Submit to:	insturctor@school.edu

Transmit Tracking data now: [Submit]

To cancel, close the browser window.

Done · Computer | Protected Mode: Off · 100%

New Perspectives o... · Submit Tracking Da... · 2:11 PM

QuickCheck

1. When you use the NP11 BookOnCD a(n) [   ] button appears if your instructor has posted comments or lecture notes.

2. Figures in the book marked with an @ sign morph into multimedia screentours, animations, and videos. True or false? [   ]

3. New Perspectives [   ] are divided into topics and each topic ends with a QuickCheck.

4. To save your scores on computer-scored activities you have to create a [   ] file.

 CHECK ANSWERS

SECTION E

NP11 Web Site

THE INTERNET offers access to information that's useful to just about everyone, and New Perspectives students are no exception. Your textbook includes the information you need to access the New Perspectives NP11 Web site, where you can continue the learning experience you began with your printed textbook and BookOnCD.

WEB SITE RESOURCES

What kinds of Web resources accompany my textbook? The New Perspectives NP11 Web site—NP11 Web site, for short—includes activities and information to help you extend your knowledge and prepare for tests. Figure 29 highlights the features you'll find on the NP11 Web site.

FIGURE 29

NP11 Web Site Features

Detailed Learning Objectives
An expanded version of the Learning Objectives included at the beginning of each chapter.

Chapter Overview CourseCasts
Listen to a 5-minute audio presentation of chapter highlights on your computer or download to your MP3 player to study on the go.

Chapter FlashCard CourseCasts
Interact with downloadable audio flash cards to review key terms from the chapter.

Test Yourself
Each test contains 10 randomly selected questions from the chapter.

Student Edition Labs
Get hands-on practice with some of the concepts presented in a chapter.

InfoWebLinks
Follow Web links to find the most current information on equipment, concepts, and software you read about in a chapter.

Online Games
Have some fun while refreshing your memory about key concepts that might appear on the exam.

WEB SITE ACCESS

How do I access the NP11 Web site? You can get to the NP11 Web site in several ways:

- Open your browser and type *www.course.com/np/concepts11*. Your browser will display the main page of the NP11 Web site. From there, you can click links to each chapter's activities and information.

- Open your BookOnCD or other BookOn product and click any 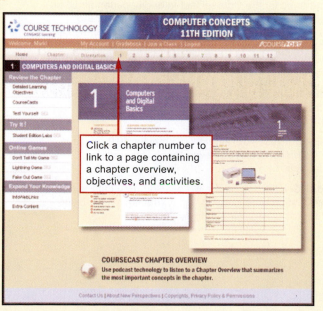 link. These links take you directly to the information or activity specified along with the link.

Do I need a password? Yes. The first time you connect to the NP11 Web site, you must register for a CoursePort account. When you have completed the short registration process, you can access the NP11 Web site. Use the New User Registration link to create your CoursePort account.

🖮TRY IT!

Access the NP11 Web site

1. Start your browser.

2. Click the address box and type:

> MSN.com - Windows Internet Explorer
>
> www.course.com/np/concepts11

Make sure to use all lowercase letters, insert no spaces, and use the / slash, not the \ slash.

3. Press the **Enter** key. The CoursePort Login screen is displayed.

4. If you are accessing the NP11 Web site for the first time, click the **New User Registration** link and follow the instructions to create your account.

5. Once you've created a CoursePort account, you can log in by entering your Username and Password, then clicking the **Enter** button.

6. The Welcome screen contains links to activities for each chapter of the textbook. Click the button for Chapter 1 at the top of the screen. Your browser displays links to activities for the first chapter in your textbook.

7. You can always return to the Welcome screen by clicking the Home button on the Chapter toolbar. Click the **Home** button now.

8. Use your browser's ☒ **Close** button to exit the NP11 Web site. If you are using a dial-up connection, you might have to manually disconnect from the Internet by double-clicking the 🖥 icon in the lower-right corner of your screen, and then clicking **Disconnect**.

Login · //COURSE**PORT**

New Students · Sign Up Now! · Returning Students and Instructors

New Students:
Sign up to enjoy this Thomson Course Technology site. This one-time process will save you time in the future. To begin, click the link below.

New User Registration

First time users can click this link to set up a CoursePort account.

Student Members: Sign in with your CoursePort Username and Password to continue.

Instructors: Use your Course.com Username and Password to log in to CoursePort.

Username
Password

Enter

Forgot your username or password?   Login Help

Once you have a CoursePort account, you can enter your username and password to access the site.

COURSE TECHNOLOGY · COMPUTER CONCEPTS 11TH EDITION

Click a chapter number to link to a page containing a chapter overview, objectives, and activities.

COURSECAST CHAPTER OVERVIEW
Use podcast technology to listen to a Chapter Overview that summarizes the most important concepts in the chapter.

WEB SITE TOUR

How do I use the resources at the NP11 Web site? The NP11 Web site is designed to help you review chapter material, prepare for tests, and extend your understanding of various topics.

When you have completed a chapter, you can work with InfoWebLinks to explore chapter topics in more depth or gather material for class projects.

If you like a challenge, use the online games as a review activity; you'll get high scores if you understand the chapter material.

Test Yourself is a great way to prepare for tests because you'll be answering questions similar to those in your instructor's test bank.

For last minute review, load up your iPod with the Chapter Overview and Key Term FlashCard CourseCasts. You can listen to them for a quick refresher on your way to the test!

Can I submit scores from Web site activities to my instructor? You can track your results from the Test Yourself, Student Edition Labs, and Online Games through CoursePort's Universal Gradebook. Follow the steps in the box below to explore the NP11 Web site and find out how to submit scores to your instructor.

📻 TRY IT!

Explore the NP11 Web site

1. Connect to the NP11 Web site and then click the link for **Chapter 1**.

2. Click the **InfoWeb** link. When you see a list of InfoWebLinks for Chapter 1, click the **Supercomputer** link. Read the short overview, and then click the first blue underlined link. Use the **Back** button on your browser window to get back to the Chapter 1 main page of the NP11 Web site.

3. To listen to a CourseCast on your computer, click the **Chapter Overview** link. You might have to wait a minute or so for the CourseCast to begin, depending on the speed of your Internet connection. If you want to store a CourseCast on your computer or portable music player, right-click the link, click **Save Target As**, and then select a location for the CourseCast file. When you are ready to continue the tour, close the audio window.

4. Click the link to the **Lightning** game. Try your hand at a few questions, and then go back to the main Chapter 1 Web page.

5. Click the **Test Yourself** link. Complete a 10-question quiz. Your scores will be saved to the Universal Gradebook.

6. Click **Gradebook** on the CoursePort menu at the top of the Chapter main page to find instructions for printing your scores or e-mailing them to your instructor.

InfoWebLinks provide lots of information to supplement what you've read in the textbook.

Online games, such as Lightning, Don't Tell Me, and Fake Out provide a fun way to review chapter material.

STUDENT EDITION LABS

How do I access the Student Edition Labs? Student Edition Labs help you review the material presented in the textbook and extend your knowledge through dynamic observation and step-by-step practice.

TRY IT!

Work with Student Edition Labs

1. Make sure you're connected to the NP11 Web site and then click the link for **Chapter 1**.

2. Click the link for **Student Edition Labs**.

3. To listen to a CourseCast on your computer, click the **Chapter Overview** link. You might have to wait a minute or so for the CourseCast to begin, depending on the speed of your Internet connection. If you want to store a CourseCast on your computer or portable music player, right-click the link, click **Save Target As**, and then select a location for the CourseCast file. When you are ready to continue the tour, close the audio window.

4. Take a few minutes to walk through the section **Guide to Student Edition Labs**.

5. Click **Select a Lab** and then click **Understanding the Motherboard** to start the lab.

6. Complete the first section of the lab, including the Intro, Observe, Practice, and Review activities.

7. When you've completed the review activity, a report containing your results is displayed. Use the Print button to print your report, or return to the NP11 Web site. If your instructor has activated your class, your score will be recorded to the Gradebook.

8. Exit the lab by clicking the [X] button.

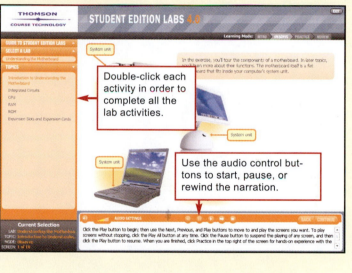

The first time you work with the Student Edition Labs, you can find out how to use them effectively by stepping through the introduction, Guide to Student Edition Labs.

Double-click each activity in order to complete all the lab activities.

Use the audio control buttons to start, pause, or rewind the narration.

QuickCheck

1. To access the NP11 Web site, you need a username and password. True or false? [ ]

2. When you're at the NP11 Web site, you can use the [ ] button to display the Welcome screen.

3. The Chapter [ ] is a 5-minute audio presentation of chapter highlights.

4. The Student Edition [ ] help you review through dynamic observation and step-by-step practice.

▶ CHECK ANSWERS

NEW PERSPECTIVES

COMPUTER CONCEPTS

JUNE JAMRICH PARSONS • DAN OJA

EDITION
11

1

Computers and Digital Basics

LEARNING OBJECTIVES

- List the major technologies fueling the digital revolution
- Explain the concept of convergence and how it applies to digital devices
- Describe some ways in which digital technology affects society
- Define the term computer and explain input, output, processing, storage, and the stored program concept
- List the characteristics of personal computers, servers, mainframes, and supercomputers
- Describe similarities and differences in PDAs, portable players, and smart phones
- Describe the purpose of microcontrollers
- Differentiate between data and information, analog and digital
- Describe how digital devices represent numbers, text, images, and sound
- Explain the difference between bits and bytes, and the technical meaning of common prefixes, such as kilo, mega, and giga
- Demonstrate that you understand the general concept of how 0s and 1s are handled by integrated circuits
- Describe the relationship between compilers, interpreters, object code, and source code
- Briefly explain how a microprocessor's ALU and control unit work
- Provide examples of single-factor and two-factor authentication
- Describe how hackers can steal passwords
- List the principles of creating secure passwords and keeping them safe

PRE-ASSESSMENT QUIZ

Take the pre-assessment quiz to find out how much you know about the topics in this chapter. ▶

MULTIMEDIA and INTERACTIVE ELEMENTS
When using the BookOnCD, BookOnFlashDrive, or other NP11 BookOn product, the ▶ icons are clickable to access multimedia resources.

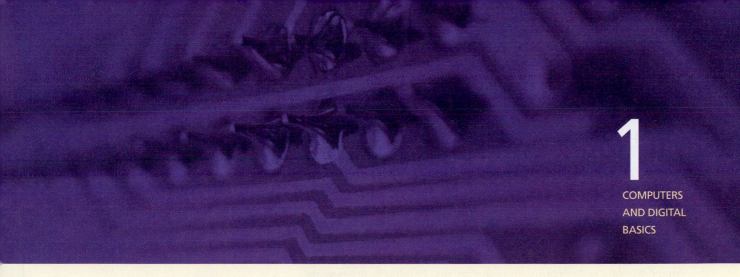

BEFORE YOU READ ON, **TRY IT**

WHAT'S MY DIGITAL PROFILE?

The average American consumer owns 26 digital devices. Before you begin Chapter 1, take an inventory of your digital equipment to find their brands, models, and serial numbers. Tuck this information in a safe place. It can come in handy when you need to call technical support, arrange for repair services, or report missing equipment.

1. Fill in the following table for any digital equipment
you own, rent, lease, or use.

	Brand	Model	Serial Number
Computer			
Keyboard			
Mouse			
Monitor			
Printer			
Digital camera			
Digital music player			
Internet or network device			
Other (list)			

WEB SITE

Visit the NP11 Web site to access additional resources Ⓦ that accompany this chapter.

All Things Digital

IN A SIMPLER TIME of poodle skirts, saddle shoes, and pony tails, consumers used a telephone to communicate, switched on a radio for music, watched the television for news, went to a movie theater for entertainment, trudged to the library for research, and headed to the nearest pizza joint for a game of pinball. Today, technology offers a dizzying number of choices for entertainment, information, and communication. It has changed the fabric of life in significant ways. We're using innovative new products, adjusting to industries in transformation, watching new markets emerge, and grappling with complex issues that have the potential to influence culture, politics, and economics on a global scale. Section A offers an overview of digital technology within the context of social and economic change.

THE DIGITAL REVOLUTION

What is the digital revolution? The **digital revolution** is an ongoing process of social, political, and economic change brought about by digital technology, such as computers and the Internet. The digital revolution became a significant factor in the 1980s, as computers and other digital devices became popular and as the Internet opened global communications.

The term digital revolution was probably coined as a parallel to the term industrial revolution, and in that sense it promises to bring about a similar level of social and economic change. The digital revolution is creating an Information Society, in which owning, generating, distributing, and manipulating information becomes a significant economic and cultural activity.

The digital revolution is ongoing. Every day new digital innovations challenge the status quo and require societies to make adjustments to traditions, lifestyles, and legislation.

What technologies are fueling the digital revolution? A constellation of technologies, including digital electronics, computers, communications networks, the Web, and digitization, are fueling the digital revolution. Before you learn about these technologies in greater detail later in the book, the following overview explains the big picture.

What's the significance of digital electronics? Digital electronics use electronic circuits to represent data. In the 1940s and 1950s engineers began to develop digital electronic devices and refine the electronic components used to build them. Transistors and then integrated circuits, which we call computer chips, were key factors in making electronic devices increasingly smaller and less expensive (Figure 1-1).

Consumers first became acquainted with digital electronics through digital watches that appeared in 1972 and then with handheld electronic calculators popularized by Texas Instruments in 1973. Today, digital electronic devices include computers, portable media players such as iPods, digital cameras and camcorders, cell phones, radios and televisions, GPSs (global positioning systems), DVD and CD players, e-book readers, digital voice recorders, and arcade games. Even cars and appliances, such as microwave ovens, refrigerators, and washing machines, include digital electronics for control, monitoring, and fault diagnosis.

> **TERMINOLOGY NOTE**
>
> The word *digital* comes from the root *digit*. In Latin, the word *digitus* means finger or toe. The modern use of the term *digital* is probably derived from the idea of counting on your fingers.

FIGURE 1-1

Digital devices, such as this wireless mouse, are built from solid state circuit boards and computer chips, making them small, light, fast, inexpensive, and durable.

Without digital electronics, you'd still be listening to bulky vacuum-tube radios instead of toting sleek iPods; computers would be huge machines, priced far beyond the reach of individuals; and your favorite form of entertainment would probably be foosball.

When did computers step into the picture? Engineers built the first digital computers during World War II for breaking codes and calculating ballistic missile trajectories. By the 1950s, a few computers were being used for business data processing applications, such as payroll and inventory management. Businesses adopted computers with increasing fervor as benefits for cutting costs and managing mountains of data became apparent.

During the antiestablishment era of the 1960s, the digital revolution was beginning to transform organizations, but had little effect on ordinary people. As with many technologies, computers were initially viewed with some measure of suspicion by consumers, who worried that impersonal data processing machines were reducing people to numbers.

When the first personal computers became available in 1976, sales got off to a slow start. Without compelling software applications, personal computers, such as the Apple II, seemed to offer little for their $2,400 price. As the variety of software increased, however, consumer interest grew. In 1982, *Time* magazine's annual Man of the Year award went to the computer, an indication that computers had finally gained a measure of acceptance by the person in the street (Figure 1-2).

As generations of computer users since that time have discovered, computers are handy devices. They displaced typewriters for creating documents, obsoleted mechanical calculators for number crunching, and took games to an entirely new dimension. Ambitious parents snapped up computers and educational software for their children and school systems set about equipping schools with computer labs.

In 1982, computers might have gained recognition in *Time* magazine, but fewer than 10% of U.S. households had a computer. Working on a standalone computer wasn't for everyone. People without interest in typing up corporate reports or school papers, crunching numbers for accounting, or playing computer games weren't tempted to become active soldiers in the digital revolution. Social scientists even worried that people would become increasingly isolated as they focused on computer activities rather than social ones. Computer ownership increased at a gradual pace until the mid-1990s, and then it suddenly accelerated as shown in the graph in Figure 1-3.

FIGURE 1-2

The computer was *Time* magazine's Machine of the Year in 1982.

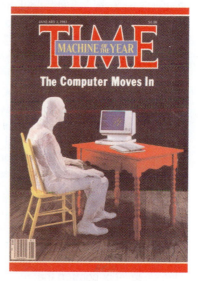

FIGURE 1-3

Household ownership of personal computers in the United States

Source: U.S. Census Bureau

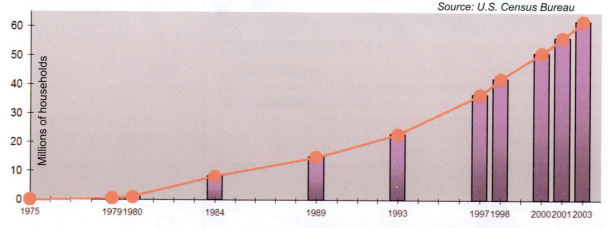

What caused the sudden upswing in computer ownership?

The second phase of the digital revolution materialized when the Internet was opened to public use. The **Internet** is a global computer network originally developed as a military project, then handed over to the National Science Foundation for research and academic use. When commercial Internet use was first allowed in 1995, companies such as AOL and Compuserve began to offer Internet access and e-mail to a quickly growing list of subscribers. **E-mail**, a form of electronic communication, was an application for the masses and finally a reason to buy a computer and join the digital revolution.

In addition to e-mail, the Internet offers many ways for people to communicate and interact. The Internet has turned the old idea of social isolation on its head; instead of computers reducing human interaction, computer networks seem to encourage new types of interpersonal communications and relationships.

Bulletin boards, which allow members to post comments and questions that can be read and responded to by others, were one of the first online social scenes. Although postings and responses were sometimes days apart, some boards attracted thousands of participants. Hostile postings led to so-called flame wars that subsided only when moderators stepped in.

Chat groups where people exchange typed messages in real time offered a more compelling environment than bulletin boards, and remain popular today. **Blogs**, short for Web logs, are personal journals posted online for general public access. A typical blog includes commentary, photos, and videos as well as links to additional information. Bloggers even enjoy the same protections under the law as journalists.

Online social networks, such as MySpace (Figure 1-4) and Facebook, have become wildly popular. To become a member of an online social network, you fill out a questionnaire to create your virtual identity and identify a list of friends. You can then choose to interact with your friends or with friends of those friends. This networking technique called *circle of friends* offers a level of comfort that members are interacting with friends of friends, rather than with strangers who might be encountered in chat rooms.

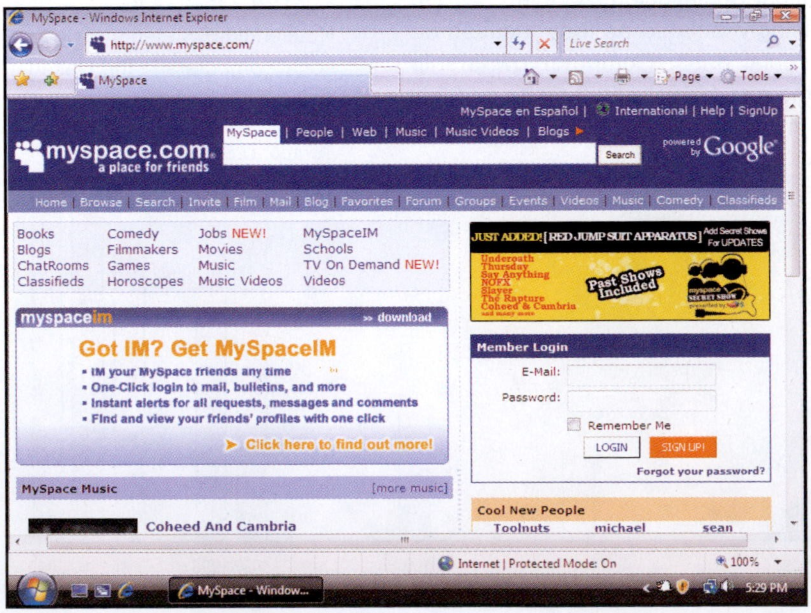

FIGURE 1-4

Online social networks offer netizens a place to look up old friends and meet friends of friends.

CLICK TO START

The Internet allows people to share resources as well as interact. Individuals' computers can be linked together in grid networks with powerful processing capabilities. One of the most ambitious grid computing efforts, SETI@home uses the Internet to connect the personal computers of more than 3 million volunteers from all over the world to analyze deep space radio signals in the search for extraterrestrial life.

A **computer network** is a group of computers linked by wired or wireless technology to share data and resources. Network technology existed before the Internet became popular, but the first computer networks were mainly deployed in schools and businesses. They were complicated to set up, unreliable, and offered only local connectivity. Network technology eventually became consumer-friendly, allowing homeowners to connect multiple computers for sharing printers, files, and an Internet connection.

Wireless networks offered even more advantages. Soon Wi-Fi hotspots sprung up in airports, coffee shops, and hotels. Whereas the Internet enhanced communications, wireless network technology offered convenience and made digital information as accessible as radio stations.

What about the Web? When historians look back on the digital revolution, they are certain to identify the Web as a major transformative influence. The **Web** (short for World Wide Web) is a collection of linked documents, graphics, and sounds that can be accessed over the Internet. The Web has changed centuries-old business models, revolutionized the flow of information, and created a new virtual world.

Online stores pioneered by Amazon.com transformed the face of retailing. Rummage sales have gone global with Web sites such as eBay. Consumers now have more direct access to products and services, such as music downloads and airline reservations.

The publisher of telephone's ubiquitous Yellow Pages used to advertise "Let your fingers do the walking." That catch-phrase has never been more true as Web surfers' fingers jog miles over their keyboards each day to find answers, read the news, get sports scores, and check the weather forecast. In 2007 there were over 100 million Web sites, each with hundreds or thousands of pages containing information.

Fallout from the massive pool of Web-based information includes the proliferation of misinformation and disinformation. Anyone can post virtually anything on the Web, so researchers and ordinary netizens who use the Web have had to develop strategies to sift for the truth.

A key aspect of the Web is that it adds content and substance to the Internet. Without the Web, the Internet would be like a library without any books or a railroad without any trains. From storefronts to online magazines to multiplayer games, the Web has made Internet access a compelling digital technology for just about everyone.

Cyberspace is a term that refers to entities that exist largely within computer networks (Figure 1-5). The virtual world isn't reality in the sense of bricks and mortar, flesh and blood. You might envision online stores as similar to the shops in your local mall, but in reality they are simply a collection of data and images stored at a Web site. The Web defines much of the landscape of cyberspace, and its graphics and sounds make things seem real.

How does digitization factor into the digital revolution?
Digitization is the process of converting text, numbers, sound, photos, and video into data that can be processed by digital devices. Some of the most obvious effects of the digital revolution can be attributed to digitization.

FIGURE 1-5

The term *cyberspace* was coined by science fiction writer William Gibson in his novelette *Burning Chrome*.

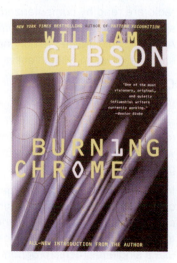

Digital images have changed the photographic industry. More than 80% of all cameras sold are digital, and the market for camera film is dwindling rapidly. One-hour photo processing labs, so popular in the 1990s, are disappearing from the strip-market landscape now that consumers can easily print their snapshots at home or from a Wal-Mart photo kiosk.

Digital imaging, such as computed tomography used in CAT scans, has had profound effects in medicine. The advantage of digital images is that they can be easily stored and transmitted. For example, rather than sending an x-ray to a consulting physician by overnight mail, a digital x-ray can be quickly transmitted over the Internet. Digital images can also be easily modified, encouraging all sorts of creative uses, but rendering photographic evidence somewhat less authoritative than it was in the pre-digital past.

Digital video is responsible for special effects in movies, new trends in 3-D animation, portable video, and surging consumer interest in home video. The film industry has become much more technology oriented and job openings reflect the need for specialists in graphics and motion video. Feature-length 3-D animated films are responsible for stunning technology breakthroughs, such as the ability to realistically depict the movement of clothing on a moving character and animate individual strands of hair or fur (Figure 1-6).

At the consumer level, computer gaming is probably the most significant force driving research into faster computers and more sophisticated graphics processing.

Digital music first became popular when Internet-based file sharing networks like Napster offered free music downloads. The term **download** refers to the practice of copying a file from a remote computer to a local computer, such as when you copy a song from the Internet to your computer's hard disk. By disregarding copyrights and enabling users to pirate copyrighted music, file-sharing networks ran afoul of the law and many were forced to shut down. Apple and other astute companies saw a business opportunity in digital music, and online music stores, such as iTunes, quickly became popular.

Online music stores are transforming the industry by changing the way music is marketed, bought, and played. The ability to purchase a single song, rather than an entire album is making recording artists reconsider some of the shovelware they've been producing to bulk up albums.

Human speech can also be digitized. Weather reports on weatherband radio are read by computerized voice synthesizers. Automated telephone systems understand caller comments by using voice recognition. United Airlines' sophisticated telephone-based reservation system can handle an entire reservation without asking customers to use their phone keypads.

CONVERGENCE

What is convergence? Your cell phone has a camera. Your clock has a radio. Your thermometer also reports the humidity. Your PDA plays digital music. All these are examples of technological **convergence**, a process by which several technologies with distinct functionalities evolve to form a single product.

In the pre-digital days, convergence often meant combining two technologically different devices in a single box. Old clock-radios, for example, combined a transistor radio and wind-up clock into a single case. Digital technology makes convergence much easier. Modern digital clock radios use a single microchip programmed for clock and radio functionality.

FIGURE 1-6

Animators at Pixar Studios created software called Fizt to individually simulate each of the 3 million hairs that flow and flutter as the furry main character moves.

1

Convergence is currently doing its magic on cell phones, PDAs, computers, portable music players, digital cameras, GPSs, and e-book readers. These devices are gradually acquiring overlapping features and seem to be headed toward becoming a single device.

Another technology in convergence is voice communication. The current mix of land lines, cell phones, and Voice over IP burdens consumers with multiple handsets, numbers, and rate plans. Most people would like to have a single telephone number that can be used while at home, at work, or traveling. The phone must have a full set of features, such as emergency 911, caller ID, and voice mail. One vision for voice communication convergence is a Voice over IP phone that operates over home-, school-, or work-based broadband Internet connections, and switches automatically to a mobile network for use in other locations.

How does convergence affect typical consumers? Convergence tends to offer enhanced functionality and convenience. An average consumer owns more than 26 digital devices. Rather than juggle a cell phone, portable media player, camera, PDA, and computer, combining their features puts your data in a single device with a single charger.

The potential downside of convergence is quality. Especially in the initial stages of development, multipurpose devices rarely offer the same quality as the standalone devices they replace. For example, digital cameras tacked onto cell phones offer lower resolution and fewer photo settings than high-end standalone digital cameras. The marketplace is usually a good testing ground where consumer spending weeds out products that don't offer an acceptable mix of quality and convenience.

Why does convergence seem to take so long? Technology sometimes outstrips society's ability to deal with it. Many aspects of the digital revolution challenge the adaptability of societies and individuals. Laws and customs tend to change more slowly than technology, therefore technologies might be ready for deployment, but people and institutions just aren't ready for them.

Apple's foray into handheld computers illustrates the barriers that can hinder convergence. In 1993 Apple introduced a handheld device called the Newton that featured a small screen, personal organizer software, e-mail, and network connectivity. You'll recognize these features as being similar to today's PDAs. Unfortunately, the Newton was too large to fit in a shirt pocket and its handwriting recognition failed to recognize all but the most painstakingly printed characters. But the real problem was that people just didn't have much use for the product and it was discontinued.

In 2004 Apple risked another foray into the handheld market, this time with a portable media player called the iPod. In contrast to the Newton, the iPod became an immediate hit because a huge population of young music lovers immediately recognized its value. By 2006 iPod fans had posted images depicting their ultimate iPod, and guess what? It merges a portable media player with a qwerty keyboard, camera, organizer software, and network connectivity. Apple listened to its customers and produced a mobile device called the iPhone. Figure 1-7 compares an early idea for the iPhone with the product that Apple eventually developed.

TERMINOLOGY NOTE

Voice over IP (VoIP) refers to voice conversations that are routed over the Internet, rather than landlines or cellular phones. It is also called IP telephony or Internet telephony.

FIGURE 1-7

iPod fans created a mockup image of their dream machine—an iPod cell phone with PDA and digital media functionality. The real iPhone with its multi-touch interface turned out to be even more innovative than the mockup.

DIGITAL SOCIETY

How does digital technology affect freedom and democracy?

Freedom of speech is the cornerstone of democracy. It can be defined as being able to speak freely without censorship or fear of reprisal. The concept is not limited to speaking, but includes all forms of expression, including writing, art, and symbolic actions. The more inclusive term *freedom of expression* is sometimes used instead of freedom of speech.

Freedom of speech is not an absolute. Most societies prohibit or repress some types of expression, such as hate speech, libel, pornography, and flag burning. Although freedom of expression is guaranteed under the U.S. Constitution, the European Convention on Human Rights, and the Universal Declaration of Human Rights, these documents recognize the necessity for some restrictions, which might vary from one society to the next. Incidents ranging from the controversy over teaching evolution in schools to the Arab world's fury over cartoons of Mohammed illustrate that societies draw the freedom of speech line in different places. The types of expression that are allowed or prohibited in a particular country are, in many respects, a reflection of its culture (Figure 1-8).

FIGURE 1-8

The 1960 movie *Inherit the Wind* was based on the trial of John Scopes who was accused of violating a state law that prohibited teaching evolution in state-funded schools.

Digital technologies and communications networks make it easy to cross cultural and geographic boundaries. News, television shows, music, and art from all over the globe are accessible on the Internet. The Internet has the potential to expand freedom of speech by offering every person on the globe a forum for personal expression using personal Web sites, blogs, chat groups, and collaborative Wikis. Anonymous Internet sites such as Freenet, and **anonymizer tools** that cloak a person's identity even make it possible to exercise freedom of speech in situations where reprisals might repress it.

Internet information that seems innocuous in some cultures is not acceptable in others. Governments, parents, and organizations sometimes find it necessary to censor the Internet by limiting access and filtering content. China has some of the most draconian Internet censorship in the world. It blocks access to Web sites such as the BBC, The New York Times, Amnesty International, and Human Rights Watch. U.S. firms allegedly supplied the Chinese government with software necessary to erect its sophisticated filtering system. Search engines Google and Yahoo! have been accused of censoring search results for China-based Web surfers.

Chinese Internet censorship seems excessive, but it is by no means the only instance of free speech suppression. eBay has banned listings for any merchandise that could "promote or glorify hatred, violence or racial intolerance, or items that promote organizations with such views (e.g., KKK, Nazis, neo-Nazis, Skinhead Aryan Nation)." Parents frequently use filtering software such as Net Nanny and CYBER sitter. The U.S. Digital Millennium Copyright Act censored technical information by making it a crime to publish information about cracking DVD and CD copy protection.

Despite attempts to censor and filter speech on the Internet, it seems clear that digital technology opens the door to freedom of expression in unprecedented ways. Limitations on Internet speech are likely to change, too, as technology evolves and as societies come to grips with the balance between freedom and responsibility.

TERMINOLOGY NOTE

A Wiki is one or more collaborative documents posted on the Web that can be viewed and changed by users. For example, Wikipedia is a collection of documents that form an encyclopedia. Visitors to the Wikipedia Web site can view definitions and information on a huge variety of topics and make changes to entries that are not correct or complete.

Has digital technology changed the way we view privacy?

Citizens of free societies have an expectation of privacy, which in the words of Supreme Court Justices Warren and Brandeis is "the right to be let alone." Digital technology use has exerted substantial pressure to diminish privacy by making it possible to easily collect and distribute data about individuals without their knowledge or consent.

In the United States, the expectation of privacy is derived from Fourth Amendment protections against unreasonable searches and seizures. The Fourth Amendment was formulated long before digital technologies such as e-mail and GPS devices. Legislation and court decisions pertaining to new technologies do not always strike the right balance between privacy and competing principles, such as free speech or free trade.

Privacy also encompasses confidentiality—the expectation that personal information will not be collected or divulged without permission. Internet marketers have a whole bag of tricks for getting personal information, and hackers are adept at breaking into sensitive databases to obtain confidential information.

Surveillance is viewed by many people as an invasion of privacy. Digital technology, such as GPS devices embedded in cell phones and cars, could allow everyone to be followed all of the time.

Some individuals dismiss the erosion of privacy saying "I have nothing to hide, so I don't care." But even they typically don't want stores, hackers, and curious onlookers to have access to data about what they buy, read, and watch, who they call, where they travel, and what they say.

Digital technology has not so much changed the way we view privacy— most citizens still have a reasonable expectation that their private lives will remain so. Instead, technology may help us develop a better appreciation for privacy and an understanding of the nuances that differentiate private and public spaces.

How does digital technology affect intellectual property?

Intellectual property refers to the ownership of certain types of information, ideas, or representations. It includes patents, trademarks, and copyrighted material, such as music, photos, software, books, and films. In the past, such works were difficult and expensive to copy.

Digital technology has made it easy to produce copies with no loss in quality from the original. Pirating—illegal copying and distribution of copyrighted material—is simple and inexpensive. It has caused significant revenue loss for software publishers, recording studios, and film producers. The fight against piracy takes many forms, from passing strict anti-piracy laws, to scrambling, encryption, and digital rights management schemes that physically prevent copying (Figure 1-9).

Digital technology adds complexity to intellectual property issues. For example, artists used to think nothing of cutting out various photos from magazines and pasting them together to form a

FIGURE 1-9

Most movie-goers have seen the rock-video style "Stealing" trailer. Consumer education is one front in the war against piracy.

▶ CLICK TO START

collage. It is even easier to download digital images from the Web and paste them into reports, onto Web pages, and incorporate them into works of art. Without permission, however, such digital cut and paste is not allowed.

Some films contain scenes that parents would rather their children not see. Even some scenes from family-oriented Harry Potter films might be too intense for young viewers. So, why not simply edit them out digitally to make a new DVD that the little tykes can watch? Such modifications are not allowed under current U.S. law, even for private viewing.

The law allows you to make a backup copy of software CDs or DVDs you legally own. However, if a CD, for example, is copy protected to prevent you from making a copy, it is against the law to break the copy protection. So, legally you have a right to a backup, but you don't have a way to legally create one!

Bucking protectionist trends are **open source** projects that promote copying, free distribution, peer review, and user modification. Linux is an open-source computer operating system that can be modified and freely distributed. Open source application software includes the popular OpenOffice.org suite, Firefox Web browser, Thunderbird e-mail, and Avast! antivirus.

Digital technology makes it possible to copy and modify films, music, software, and other data, but a tricky balancing act is required to allow consumers flexibility to use data while protecting the income stream to artists, performers, and publishers.

What effect does digital technology have on the economy?

Digital technology is an important factor in global and national economies, in addition to affecting the economic status of individuals. **Globalization** can be defined as the worldwide economic interdependence of countries that occurs as cross-border commerce increases and as money flows more freely among countries. Consumers gain access to a wide variety of products, including technology products manufactured in locations scattered all over the globe. Countries that benefit from significant technology output include the United States, China, India, South Korea, and Finland (Figure 1-10).

Global communications technology offers opportunities for teleworkers in distant countries. Customer service lines for U.S. based companies, such as IBM, Dell, and Hewlett-Packard, are often staffed by offshore technicians who earn far more than they could if working for a locally-based company.

Globalization, fueled by digital technology, has controversial aspects, however. Worker advocates object to the use of cheap offshore labor that displaces onshore employees.

Individuals are affected by the **digital divide**, a term that refers to the gap between people who have access to technology and those who do not. Typically, digital have-nots face economic barriers.

INFOWEBLINKS

You'll find links to more information on the social, economic, and political aspects of computers at the **Digital Revolution InfoWeb**.

W CLICK TO CONNECT
www.course.com/np/concepts11/ch01

FIGURE 1-10

Finland is a world leader in wireless technology. Its flagship technology company, Nokia, is responsible for about 25% of the country's exports.

They cannot afford computers, cell phones, and Internet access, or they are located in an economically depressed region where electricity is not available to run digital devices, power satellite dishes, and pick up Internet signals. But technology offers opportunity even to digital have-nots. For example, the Village Phone Project provides a small loan to entrepreneurs known as "village phone ladies" who sell minutes on their cell phones to neighbors who cannot afford their own land lines or cell phones (Figure 1-11).

Globalization is an ongoing process that will have far reaching effects on people in countries with developed technologies and those with emerging economies. Digital technology will be called upon to open additional economic opportunities without disrupting the lifestyles of currently prosperous nations.

So what's the point? Learning about digital technology is not just about circuits and electronics, nor is it only about digital gadgets, such as computers and portable music players. Digital technology permeates the very core of modern life. Understanding how this technology works and thinking about its potential can help you comprehend many issues related to privacy, security, freedom of speech, and intellectual property. It will help you become a better consumer and give you insights into local and world events.

You might even come to realize that some people who are responsible for making decisions about technology have only a vague idea of how it works. Without a solid grasp of technology problems, there can be little hope of finding effective solutions. As you continue to read this textbook, don't lose sight of the big picture. On one level, in this course you might be simply learning about how to use a computer and software. On a more profound level, however, you are accumulating knowledge about digital technology that applies to broader cultural and legal issues that are certain to affect your life far into the future.

FIGURE 1-11

In less technically developed countries such as Uganda and Bangladesh women make a living by selling cell phone time to their neighbors.

QuickCheck

1. Computer ownership increased at a gradual pace from the late 1970s until the mid-1990s, and then it suddenly accelerated after the [＿＿＿＿＿＿＿＿] opened for commercial use.

2. Online social [＿＿＿＿＿＿＿＿], such as MySpace and Facebook, added a virtual dimension to the way people interact.

3. [＿＿＿＿＿＿＿＿] is a term that refers to objects and entities that exist largely within computer networks.

4. [＿＿＿＿＿＿＿＿] is the process of converting text, numbers, sound, animation, photos, and video into data that can be processed by digital devices.

5. [＿＿＿＿＿＿＿＿] is a process by which several technologies with distinct functionalities evolve to form a single product.

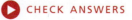 CHECK ANSWERS

Digital Devices

WHETHER YOU REALIZE IT or not, you already know a lot about the devices that fuel the digital revolution. You've picked up information from commercials and news articles, from books and movies, from conversations and correspondence—perhaps even from using a variety of digital devices and trying to figure out why they don't always work! The quintessential digital device is the computer. Section B provides an overview that's designed to help you start organizing what you know about digital devices, starting with computers.

COMPUTER BASICS

What is a computer? The word *computer* has been part of the English language since 1646, but if you look in a dictionary printed before 1940, you might be surprised to find a computer defined as a person who performs calculations! Prior to 1940, machines designed to perform calculations were referred to as calculators and tabulators, not computers. The modern definition and use of the term computer emerged in the 1940s, when the first electronic computing devices were developed.

Most people can formulate a mental picture of a computer, but computers do so many things and come in such a variety of shapes and sizes that it might seem difficult to distill their common characteristics into an all-purpose definition. At its core, a **computer** is a multipurpose device that accepts input, processes data, stores data, and produces output, all according to a series of stored instructions (Figure 1-12).

FIGURE 1-12

A computer can be defined by its ability to accept input, process data, store data, and produce output, all according to a set of instructions from a computer program.

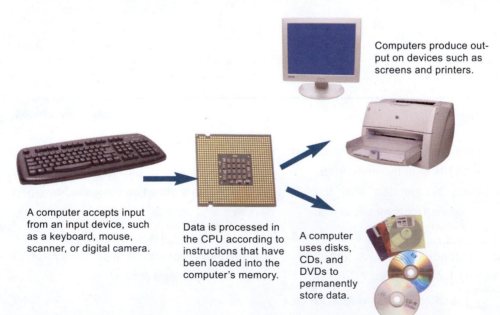

Computers produce output on devices such as screens and printers.

A computer accepts input from an input device, such as a keyboard, mouse, scanner, or digital camera.

Data is processed in the CPU according to instructions that have been loaded into the computer's memory.

A computer uses disks, CDs, and DVDs to permanently store data.

▶ CLICK TO START

What is input? Computer **input** is whatever is typed, submitted, or transmitted to a computer system. Input can be supplied by a person, by the environment, or by another computer. Examples of the kinds of input that computers can accept include words and symbols in a document, numbers for a calculation, pictures, temperatures from a thermostat, audio signals from a microphone, and instructions from a computer program. An input device, such as a keyboard or mouse, gathers data and transforms it into a series of electronic signals for the computer to store and manipulate.

What is output? **Output** is the result produced by a computer. Some examples of computer output include reports, documents, music, graphs, and pictures. Output devices display, print, or transmit the results of processing.

What does *process data* mean? Technically speaking, **data** refers to the symbols that represent facts, objects, and ideas. Computers manipulate data in many ways, and this manipulation is called **processing**. Some of the ways that a computer can process data include performing calculations, modifying documents and pictures, keeping track of your score in a fast-action game, drawing graphs, and sorting lists of words or numbers (Figure 1-13).

In a computer, most processing takes place in a component called the **central processing unit** or **CPU**. The CPU of most modern computers is a **microprocessor**, which is an electronic component that can be programmed to perform tasks based on data it receives. You'll learn more about microprocessors later in the chapter. For now, visualize a microprocessor as the little black box that's the brain of a digital device.

How do computers store data? A computer stores data so that it will be available for processing. Most computers have more than one place to put data, depending on how the data is being used. **Memory** is an area of a computer that temporarily holds data waiting to be processed, stored, or output. **Storage** is the area where data can be left on a permanent basis when it is not immediately needed for processing. Data is typically stored in files. A computer file, usually referred to simply as a **file**, is a named collection of data that exists on a storage medium, such as a hard disk, floppy disk, CD, DVD, or flash drive. A file can contain data for a term paper, Web page, e-mail message, or music video. Some files also contain instructions that tell the computer how to perform various tasks.

What's so significant about a computer's ability to store instructions? The series of instructions that tells a computer how to carry out processing tasks is referred to as a **computer program**, or simply a program. These programs form the **software** that sets up a computer to do a specific task. When a computer *runs* software, it performs the instructions to carry out a task.

Take a moment to think about the way you use a simple handheld calculator to balance your checkbook each month. You're forced to do the calculations in stages. Although you can store data from one stage and use it in the next stage, you cannot store the sequence of formulas—the program—required to balance your checkbook. Every month, therefore, you have to perform a similar set of calculations. The process would be much simpler if your calculator remembered the sequence of calculations and just asked you for this month's checkbook entries.

FIGURE 1-13

An unsorted list is input to the computer, which processes it and produces a sorted list as output.

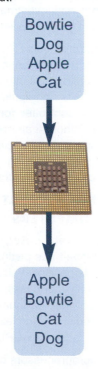

The idea of a **stored program** means that a series of instructions for a computing task can be loaded into a computer's memory. These instructions can easily be replaced by a different set of instructions when it is time for the computer to perform another task. This ability makes computers multipurpose machines.

The stored program concept allows you to use your computer for one task, such as word processing, and then easily switch to a different type of computing task, such as editing a photo or sending an e-mail message. It is the single most important characteristic that distinguishes a computer from other simpler and less versatile digital devices, such as watches, calculators, and pocket-sized electronic dictionaries.

What kinds of software do computers run? Computers run two main types of software: application software and system software. A computer can be *applied* to many tasks, such as writing, number crunching, video editing, and online shopping. **Application software** is a set of computer programs that helps a person carry out a task. Word processing software, for example, helps people create, edit, and print documents. Personal finance software helps people keep track of their money and investments. Video editing software helps people create and edit home movies—and even some professional films.

Whereas application software is designed to help a person carry out a task, the primary purpose of **system software** is to help the computer system monitor itself in order to function efficiently. An example of system software is a computer **operating system** (OS), which is essentially the master controller for all the activities that take place within a computer. Although an operating system does not directly help people perform application-specific tasks, such as word processing, people do interact with the operating system for certain operational and storage tasks, such as starting programs and locating data files.

PERSONAL COMPUTERS, SERVERS, MAINFRAMES, AND SUPERCOMPUTERS

Are computers categorized in any way? At one time it was possible to define three distinct categories of computers. Mainframes were housed in large, closet-sized metal frames. Minicomputers were smaller, less expensive, and less powerful computers that were able, nevertheless, to provide adequate computing power for small businesses. Microcomputers were clearly differentiated from computers in other categories because their CPUs consisted of a single microprocessor chip.

Today, microprocessors are no longer a distinction between computer categories because just about every computer uses one or more microprocessors as its CPU. The term *minicomputer* has fallen into disuse and the terms microcomputer and mainframe are used with less and less frequency.

Computers are versatile machines that can perform a truly amazing assortment of tasks, but some computers are better suited than others for certain tasks. Categorizing computers is a way of grouping them according to criteria such as usage, cost, size, and capability. Experts don't necessarily agree on the categories or the devices placed in each category, but commonly used computer categories include personal computers, servers, mainframes, and supercomputers.

TERMINOLOGY NOTE

The term *personal computer* is sometimes abbreviated as *PC*. However, PC can also refer to a specific type of personal computer that descended from the original IBM PC and runs Windows software.

In this book, PC refers to IBM PC descendants. It is not used as an abbreviation for personal computer.

What is a personal computer? A **personal computer** is a microprocessor-based computing device designed to meet the computing needs of an individual. It typically provides access to a wide variety of computing applications, such as word processing, photo editing, and e-mail.

Personal computers are available as desktop or portable models, and in a variety of *form factors*, a term that refers to the dimensions of the unit that holds the computer circuitry. You'll learn more about the wide variety of personal computer form factors in the Hardware chapter. For now, simply remember that computers like those pictured in Figure 1-14 are classified as personal computers.

FIGURE 1-14

Personal computer designs run the gamut from drab gray boxes to colorful curvy cases.

What is a workstation? The term **workstation** has two meanings. It can simply refer to an ordinary personal computer that is connected to a network. A second meaning refers to powerful desktop computers used for high-performance tasks, such as medical imaging and computer-aided design, that require a lot of processing speed. Some workstations contain more than one microprocessor, and most have circuitry specially designed for creating and displaying three-dimensional and animated graphics. Workstations, such as the one pictured in Figure 1-15, typically cost a bit more than an average personal computer.

FIGURE 1-15

A workstation resembles a desktop computer, but typically features more processing power and storage capacity.

Is an Xbox a personal computer? A **videogame console**, such as Nintendo's Wii, Sony's PlayStation, or Microsoft's Xbox, are not generally referred to as personal computers because of their history as dedicated game devices. They originated as simple digital devices that connected to a TV set and provided only a pair of joysticks for input.

Today's videogame consoles contain microprocessors that are equivalent to any found in a fast personal computer, and they are equipped to produce graphics that rival those on sophisticated workstations. Add-ons such as keyboards, DVD players, and Internet access make it possible to use a videogame console to watch DVD movies, send and receive e-mail, and participate in online activities such as multiplayer games. Despite these features, videogame consoles like the one in Figure 1-16 fill a specialized niche and are not considered a replacement for a personal computer.

FIGURE 1-16

A videogame console includes circuitry similar to a personal computer's, but its input and output devices are optimized for gaming.

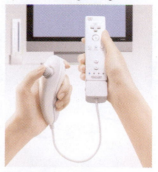

What makes a computer a server? In the computer industry, the term *server* has several meanings. It can refer to computer hardware, to a specific type of software, or to a combination of hardware and software. In any case, the purpose of a **server** is to *serve* computers on a network (such as the Internet or a home network) by supplying them with data.

Any software or digital device, such as a computer, that requests data from a server is referred to as a **client**. For example, on a network, a server might respond to a client's request for a Web page. Another server might handle the steady stream of e-mail that travels among clients from all over the Internet. A server might also allow clients within a network to share files or access a centralized printer.

Remarkably, just about any personal computer, workstation, mainframe, or supercomputer can be configured to perform the work of a server. That fact should emphasize the concept that a server does not require a specific type of hardware. Nonetheless, computer manufacturers categorize some of their computers as servers because they are especially suited for storing and distributing data on a network. Server prices vary, depending on configuration, but tend to be more similar to workstation prices than personal computer prices. Despite impressive performance on server-related tasks, these machines often do not include features such as sound cards, DVD players, and other fun accessories that consumers expect on their desktop computers. Most consumers would not want to buy a server to replace a desktop computer.

What's so special about a mainframe computer? A **mainframe computer** (or simply a mainframe) is a large and expensive computer capable of simultaneously processing data for hundreds or thousands of users. Mainframes are generally used by businesses or governments to provide centralized storage, processing, and management for large amounts of data. Mainframes remain the computer of choice in situations where reliability, data security, and centralized control are necessary.

The price of a mainframe computer typically starts at several hundred thousand dollars and can easily exceed $1 million. Its main processing circuitry is housed in a closet-sized cabinet (Figure 1-17), but after large components are added for storage and output, a mainframe computer system can fill a good-sized room.

How powerful is a supercomputer? A computer falls into the **supercomputer** category if it is, at the time of construction, one of the fastest computers in the world (Figure 1-18).

FIGURE 1-17

This IBM z9 109 mainframe computer weighs 2,672 pounds and is about 6.5 feet tall.

FIGURE 1-18

The BlueGene/P supercomputer topped the list as the world's fastest computer when it was introduced in 2007.

Because of their speed, supercomputers can tackle complex tasks and compute-intensive problems that just would not be practical for other computers. A **compute-intensive** problem is one that requires massive amounts of data to be processed using complex mathematical calculations. Molecular calculations, atmospheric models, and cosmological research are all examples of projects that require massive numbers of data points to be manipulated, processed, and analyzed.

Common uses for supercomputers include breaking codes, modeling worldwide weather systems, and simulating nuclear explosions. One impressive simulation designed to run on a supercomputer tracked the movement of thousands of dust particles as they were tossed about by a tornado.

At one time, supercomputer designers focused on building specialized, very fast, and very large CPUs. Today, most supercomputer CPUs are constructed from thousands of microprocessors. Of the 500 fastest supercomputers in the world, the majority use microprocessor technology.

PDAS, PORTABLE PLAYERS, AND SMART PHONES

Are handheld devices computers? Handheld digital devices include familiar gadgets such as iPhones, Blackberries, and Zunes. These devices incorporate many computer characteristics. They accept input, produce output, process data, and include storage capabilities. Handheld devices vary in their programmability and their versatility, however. Technically, these devices could be classified as computers, but only some are customarily referred to as computers.

What is a handheld computer? The gadgets sometimes touted as handheld computers are descended from PDAs. A **PDA** (personal digital assistant) is a pocket-sized digital appointment book with a small qwerty keyboard or a touch-sensitive screen, designed to run on batteries and be used while holding it. Originally, PDAs were not equipped for voice communications, which distinguished them from the emerging cell phone market. PDAs synchronized appointment data and contact lists with desktop computers by exchanging data over a dedicated wired or wireless connection.

A **handheld computer** is essentially a PDA enhanced with features such as removable storage, e-mail, Web access, voice communications, built-in camera, and GPS. Handheld computers also offer a variety of application software, but they do not typically run the same full-featured software versions as personal computers. Instead, they run special scaled-down versions of word processing, spreadsheet, and other application software. Examples of handheld computers include the iPhone, Palm Treo, RIM Blackberry, and Hewlett-Packard iPAQ (Figure 1-19).

INFOWEBLINKS

What's the latest news about supercomputers? Visit the **Supercomputer InfoWeb** to learn more about these amazing machines.

 CLICK TO CONNECT
www.course.com/np/concepts11/ch01

INFOWEBLINKS

Learn more about the latest PDAs, players, and smart phones by visiting the **Handheld InfoWeb**.

 CLICK TO CONNECT
www.course.com/np/concepts11/ch01

FIGURE 1-19

Many handheld computers feature a small keyboard, others accept handwriting input, and some work with touch screen icons.

How do smart phones fit into the picture? Smart phones are descended from basic cell phones that were originally designed exclusively for voice communications. Their simple design offered a numeric keypad, a small screen, and just enough memory for a few names and phone numbers. Keypad data entry required the now-familiar thumbing such as pressing the 7 key four times to produce the letter *s*.

From the cell phone's humble origins emerged a digital device called a **smart phone**, which in addition to voice communication, includes features such as full qwerty keypad, text messaging, e-mail, Web access, removable storage, camera, FM radio, digital music player, and software options for games, financial management, personal organizer, GPS, and maps.

Smart phones, like the one in Figure 1-20, contain a microprocessor and have many characteristics of computers. They are not, however, usually referred to as computers because of their origins as a special-purpose device with keypad input and limited programmability.

How are iPods classified? iPods are an enhancement on MP3 players designed to play music stored in a type of file called MP3 (which stands for MPEG-1 Audio Layer-3). The basic idea behind these players was to convert music from CDs or download it from the Web to your computer, then transfer it to the player. Sharing MP3 files on the Web became hugely popular despite its questionable legality. After many music sharing sites were shut down, Apple created a legal Web-based music store called iTunes where music is stored in a proprietary, copy-protected file format and sold by the song or by the album. The iPod (Figure 1-21) was designed as a portable music player and enhanced versions of the device now store and play video and photos as well.

iPods and similar devices are classified as **portable media players** because their main strength is playing music, showing videos, and storing photos. Like other handheld digital devices, these players have many computer characteristics. An iPod, for example, contains a microprocessor, accepts input, has significant storage capacity on its built-in hard disk, and outputs stored music, video, and images. Most portable media players, however, have very limited programmability. They are not designed for users to add software and their lack of a keyboard or touch screen puts severe limits on data entry.

Why is it hard to see much difference in handheld devices? Whether they fall into the handheld computer, smart phone, or portable media player categories, today's handheld digital devices have many features in common. The lines that separate these devices are blurry because the market is in a state of convergence. Currently, size and battery life seem to be the factors preventing a single device from integrating all the features possible for a handheld device. Technology, however, is likely to solve those problems soon.

MICROCONTROLLERS

What is a microcontroller? Have you ever wondered how a guided missile reaches its target or how your refrigerator knows when to initiate a defrost cycle? What controls your microwave oven, your television remote, TiVos, digital thermometers, watches, and clocks? Many common appliances and machines are controlled by embedded microcontrollers. A **microcontroller** is a special-purpose microprocessor that is built into the machine it controls. A microcontroller is sometimes called a computer-on-a-chip because it includes many of the elements common to computers.

FIGURE 1-20

Smart phones include qwerty keyboards, cameras, and digital music players.

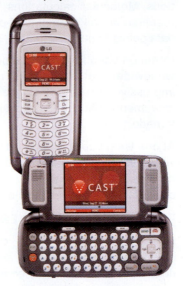

FIGURE 1-21

The iPod and other portable media players work with music, videos, and photos.

How does a microcontroller work? Consider the microcontroller in a Subzero refrigerator. It accepts user input for desired temperatures in the refrigerator and freezer compartments. It stores these desired temperatures in memory. Temperature sensors collect additional input of the actual temperatures. The microcontroller processes the input data by comparing the actual temperature to the desired temperature. As output, the microcontroller sends signals to activate the cooling motor as necessary. It also generates a digital readout of the refrigerator and freezer temperatures.

Is a microcontroller really a computer? Recall that a computer is defined as a multipurpose device that accepts input, produces output, stores data, and processes it according to a stored program. A microcontroller seems to fit the input, processing, output, and storage criteria that define computers. Some microcontrollers can even be reprogrammed to perform different tasks.

Technically, a microcontroller could be classified as a computer, just as smart phones, and portable media players can be. Despite this technicality, however, microcontrollers tend to be referred to as processors rather than as computers because in practice they are used for dedicated applications, not as multipurpose devices.

Why are microcontrollers significant? Microcontrollers, such as the one in Figure 1-22, can be embedded in all sorts of everyday devices, enabling machines to perform sophisticated tasks that require awareness and feedback from the environment. When combined with wireless networks, devices with embedded processors can relay information to Web sites, cell phones, and a variety of data collection devices. Machines and appliances with embedded processors tend to be smarter about their use of resources, such as electricity and water, so they can be environmentally friendly.

Perhaps the most significant effect of microcontrollers is that they are an almost invisible technology, one that doesn't require much adaptation or learning on the part of the people who interact with microcontrolled devices. However, because microcontrollers remain mostly out-of-sight-and-out-of-mind, it is easy for their use to creep into areas that could be detrimental to quality of life, privacy, and freedom. That innocuous GPS chip in your cell phone, for example, can be useful if you're lost and need 911 assistance, but it could potentially become a tool for surreptitious surveillance.

FIGURE 1-22

A microcontroller is usually mounted on a circuit board and then installed in a machine or appliance using wires to carry input and output signals.

QuickCheck

1. A computer accepts input, processes data, stores data, and produces [_____] according to a series of instructions.

2. The term *microprocessor* is a synonym for the term *microcomputer*. True or false? [_____]

3. The [_____] program concept enables computers to be multipurpose devices.

4. A(n) [_____] specializes in compute-intensive problems.

5. A(n) [_____] is a special-purpose microprocessor that is built into the machine it controls.

 CHECK ANSWERS

SECTION **C**

Digital Data Representation

COMPUTERS AND OTHER DIGITAL DEVICES work with all sorts of "stuff," including text, numbers, music, images, speech, and video. The amazing aspect of digital technology is that all these different elements are distilled down to simple pulses of electricity and stored as 0s and 1s. Understanding the data representation concepts presented in Section C will help you grasp the essence of the digital world and get a handle on all the jargon pertaining to bits, bytes, megahertz, and gigabytes.

DATA REPRESENTATION BASICS

What is data? As you learned earlier in the chapter, data refers to the symbols that represent people, events, things, and ideas. Data can be a name, a number, the colors in a photograph, or the notes in a musical composition.

Is there a difference between data and information? In everyday conversation, people use the terms *data* and *information* interchangeably. Nevertheless, some technology professionals make a distinction between the two terms. They define data as the symbols that represent people, events, things, and ideas. Data becomes information when it is presented in a format that people can understand and use. As a general rule, remember that (technically speaking) data is used by machines, such as computers; information is used by humans.

What is data representation? **Data representation** refers to the form in which data is stored, processed, and transmitted. For example, devices such as PDAs, iPods, and computers store numbers, text, music, photos, and videos in formats that can be handled by electronic circuitry. Those formats are data representations. Data can be represented using digital or analog methods.

What's the difference between analog and digital? For a simple illustration of the difference between analog and digital, consider the way you can control the lights in a room using a traditional light switch or a dimmer switch (Figure 1-23). A traditional light switch has two discrete states—on and off. There are no in-between states, so this type of light switch is digital. A dimmer switch, on the other hand, has a rotating dial that controls a continuous range of brightness. It is, therefore, analog.

Digital data is text, numbers, graphics, sound, and video that has been converted into discrete digits such as 0s and 1s. In contrast, **analog data** is represented using an infinite scale of values.

How does digital data work? Imagine that you want to send a message by flashing a light. Your light switch offers two states: on and off. You could use sequences of ons and offs to represent various letters of the alphabet. To write down the representation for each letter, you can use 0s and 1s. The 0s represent the off state of your light switch; the 1s indicate the on state. For example, the sequence on on off off would be written 1100, and you might decide that sequence represents the letter A.

FIGURE 1-23

A computer is a digital device, more like a standard light switch than a dimmer switch.

Digital devices are electronic and so you can envision data flowing within these devices as pulses of light. In reality, digital signals are represented by two different voltages, such as +5 volts and 0 volts. They can also be represented by two different tones as they flow over a phone line. Digital data can also take the form of light and dark spots etched onto the surface of a CD or the positive and negative orientation of magnetic particles on the surface of a hard disk. Regardless of the technology, however, digital data is always represented by two states denoted as 0 and 1.

The 0s and 1s used to represent digital data are referred to as binary digits. It is from this term that we get the word *bit—binary digit*. A **bit** is a 0 or 1 used in the digital representation of data.

REPRESENTING NUMBERS, TEXT, AND PICTURES

How do digital devices represent numbers? Numeric data consists of numbers that might be used in arithmetic operations. For example, your annual income is numeric data, as is your age. The price of a bicycle is numeric data. So is the average gas mileage for a vehicle, such as a car or SUV. Digital devices can represent numeric data using the binary number system, also called base 2.

The **binary number system** has only two digits: 0 and 1. No numeral like 2 exists in this system, so the number two is represented in binary as 10 (pronounced *one zero*). You'll understand why if you think about what happens when you're counting from 1 to 10 in the familiar decimal system. After you reach 9, you run out of digits. For ten, you have to use the digits 10—zero is a placeholder and the 1 indicates one group of tens.

In binary, you just run out of digits sooner—right after you count to 1. To get to the next number, you have to use the zero as a placeholder and the 1 indicates one group of 2s. In binary then, you count 0 (zero), 1 (one), 10 (one zero), instead of counting 0, 1, 2 in decimal. If you need to brush up on binary numbers, refer to Figure 1-24 and to the lab at the end of the chapter.

The important point to understand is that the binary number system allows digital devices to represent virtually any number simply by using 0s and 1s.

Decimal (Base 10)	Binary (Base 2)
0	0
1	1
2	10
3	11
4	100
5	101
6	110
7	111
8	1000
9	1001
10	1010
11	1011
1000	1111101000

FIGURE 1-24

The decimal system uses ten symbols to represent numbers: 0, 1, 2, 3, 4, 5, 6, 7, 8, and 9. The binary number system uses only two symbols: 0 and 1.

How do digital devices represent words and letters?

Character data is composed of letters, symbols, and numerals that are not used in arithmetic operations. Examples of character data include your name, address, and hair color. Just as Morse code uses dashes and dots to represent the letters of the alphabet, a digital computer uses a series of bits to represent letters, characters, and numerals. Figure 1-25 illustrates how a computer can use 0s and 1s to represent the letters and symbols in the text *HI!*

Digital devices employ several types of codes to represent character data, including ASCII, EBCDIC, and Unicode. **ASCII** (American Standard Code for Information Interchange, pronounced *ASK ee*) requires only seven bits for each character. For example, the ASCII code for an uppercase *A* is 1000001. ASCII provides codes for 128 characters, including uppercase letters, lowercase letters, punctuation symbols, and numerals.

A superset of ASCII, called **Extended ASCII**, uses eight bits to represent each character. For example, Extended ASCII represents the uppercase letter *A* as 01000001. Using eight bits instead of seven bits allows Extended ASCII to provide codes for 256 characters. The additional Extended ASCII characters include boxes, circles, and other graphical symbols. Figure 1-26 lists the Extended ASCII character set.

FIGURE 1-25

A computer treats the letters and symbols in the word *HI!* as character data, which can be represented by a string of 0s and 1s.

01001000   01001001   00100001

FIGURE 1-26

The Extended ASCII code uses eight 1s and 0s to represent letters, symbols, and numerals. The first 32 ASCII characters are not shown in the table because they represent special control sequences that cannot be printed. The two blank entries are space characters.

Char	Code	Char	Code	Char	Code	Char	Code	Char	Code	Char	Code	Char	Code	Char	Code
(space)	00100000	>	00111110	\	01011100	z	01111010	ÿ	10011000	╢	10110110	╘	11010100	≥	11110010
!	00100001	?	00111111	]	01011101	{	01111011	Ö	10011001	╖	10110111	╒	11010101	≤	11110011
"	00100010	@	01000000	^	01011110	|	01111100	Ü	10011010	╕	10111000	╓	11010110	⌠	11110100
#	00100011	A	01000001	_	01011111	}	01111101	¢	10011011	╣	10111001	╫	11010111	J	11110101
$	00100100	B	01000010	`	01100000	~	01111110	£	10011100	║	10111010	╪	11011000	÷	11110110
%	00100101	C	01000011	a	01100001		01111111	¥	10011101	╗	10111011	┘	11011001	≈	11110111
&	00100110	D	01000100	b	01100010	Ç	10000000	₧	10011110	╝	10111100	┌	11011010	°	11111000
'	00100111	E	01000101	c	01100011	ü	10000001	ƒ	10011111	╜	10111101	█	11011011	∙	11111001
(	00101000	F	01000110	d	01100100	é	10000010	á	10100000	╛	10111110	▄	11011100	·	11111010
)	00101001	G	01000111	e	01100101	â	10000011	í	10100001	┐	10111111	▌	11011101	√	11111011
*	00101010	H	01001000	f	01100110	ä	10000100	ó	10100010	└	11000000	▐	11011110	ⁿ	11111100
+	00101011	I	01001001	g	01100111	à	10000101	ú	10100011	┴	11000001	▀	11011111	²	11111101
,	00101100	J	01001010	h	01101000	å	10000110	ñ	10100100	┬	11000010	α	11100000	■	11111110
-	00101101	K	01001011	i	01101001	ç	10000111	Ñ	10100101	├	11000011	β	11100001		11111111
.	00101110	L	01001100	j	01101010	ê	10001000	ª	10100110	─	11000100	Γ	11100010		
/	00101111	M	01001101	k	01101011	ë	10001001	º	10100111	┼	11000101	π	11100011		
0	00110000	N	01001110	l	01101100	è	10001010	¿	10101000	╞	11000110	Σ	11100100		
1	00110001	O	01001111	m	01101101	ï	10001011	⌐	10101001	╟	11000111	σ	11100101		
2	00110010	P	01010000	n	01101110	î	10001100	¬	10101010	╚	11001000	µ	11100110		
3	00110011	Q	01010001	o	01101111	ì	10001101	½	10101011	╔	11001001	τ	11100111		
4	00110100	R	01010010	p	01110000	Ä	10001110	¼	10101100	╩	11001010	Φ	11101000		
5	00110101	S	01010011	q	01110001	Å	10001111	¡	10101101	╦	11001011	Θ	11101001		
6	00110110	T	01010100	r	01110010	É	10010000	«	10101110	╠	11001100	Ω	11101010		
7	00110111	U	01010101	s	01110011	æ	10010001	»	10101111	═	11001101	δ	11101011		
8	00111000	V	01010110	t	01110100	Æ	10010010	░	10110000	╬	11001110	∞	11101100		
9	00111001	W	01010111	u	01110101	ô	10010011	▒	10110001	╧	11001111	ø	11101101		
:	00111010	X	01011000	v	01110110	ö	10010100	▓	10110010	╨	11010000	€	11101110		
;	00111011	Y	01011001	w	01110111	ò	10010101	│	10110011	╤	11010001	∩	11101111		
<	00111100	Z	01011010	x	01111000	û	10010110	┤	10110100	╥	11010010	≡	11110000		
=	00111101	[	01011011	y	01111001	ù	10010111	╡	10110101	╙	11010011	±	11110001		

An alternative to the 8-bit Extended ASCII code, called **EBCDIC** (Extended Binary-Coded Decimal Interchange Code, pronounced *EB seh dick*), is usually used only by older, IBM mainframe computers.

Unicode (pronounced *YOU ni code*) uses sixteen bits and provides codes for 65,000 characters—a real bonus for representing the alphabets of multiple languages. For example, Unicode represents an uppercase *A* in the Russian Cyrillic alphabet as 0000010000010000.

Why do ASCII and Extended ASCII provide codes for 0, 1, 2, 3, 4, 5, 6, 7, 8, and 9? While glancing at the table of ASCII codes in Figure 1-26 you might have wondered why the table contains codes for 0, 1, 2, 3, and so on. Aren't these numbers represented by the binary number system? A computer uses Extended ASCII character codes for 0, 1, 2, 3 to represent numerals that are not used for calculations. For example, you don't typically use your Social Security number in calculations, so it is considered character data and represented using Extended ASCII. Likewise, the numbers in your street address can be represented by character codes rather than binary numbers.

How can bits be used to store images? Images, such as photos, pictures, line art, and graphs, are not small, discrete objects like numbers or the letters of the alphabet. To work with images, they must be digitized.

Images can be digitized by treating them as a series of colored dots. Each dot is assigned a binary number according to its color. For example, a green dot might be represented by 0010 and a red dot by 1100, as shown in Figure 1-27. A digital image is simply a list of color numbers for all the dots it contains.

How can bits be used to store sound? Sound, such as music and speech, is characterized by the properties of a sound wave. You can create a comparable wave by etching it onto a vinyl platter—essentially how records were made in the days of jukeboxes and record players. You can also represent that sound wave digitally by sampling it at various points, and then converting those points into digital numbers. The more samples you take, the closer your points come to approximating the full wave pattern. This process of sampling, illustrated in Figure 1-28, is how digital recordings are made.

FIGURE 1-27

An image can be digitized by assigning a binary number to each dot.

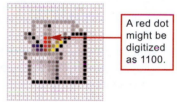

A red dot might be digitized as 1100.

FIGURE 1-28

A sound wave can be sampled at fraction-of-a-second time intervals. Each sample is recorded as a binary number and stored.

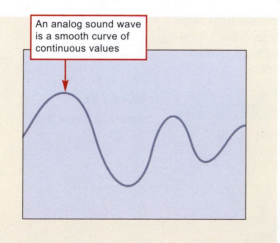

An analog sound wave is a smooth curve of continuous values

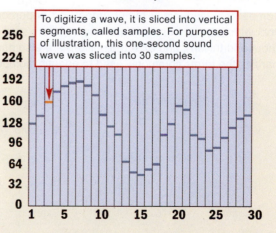

To digitize a wave, it is sliced into vertical segments, called samples. For purposes of illustration, this one-second sound wave was sliced into 30 samples.

QUANTIFYING BITS AND BYTES

How can I tell the difference between bits and bytes? The ads for digital devices typically include lots of abbreviations relating to bits and bytes. A few key concepts can help you understand what these abbreviations mean. Even though the word *bit* is an abbreviation for binary digit, it can be further abbreviated, usually as a lowercase *b*.

On older digital devices, bits were handled in groups, and terminology from that era is still used. A group of 8 bits is called a **byte** and is usually abbreviated as an uppercase *B*.

Transmission speeds are typically expressed in bits, whereas storage space is typically expressed in bytes. For example, a cable Internet connection might transfer data from the Internet to your computer at 3 mega*bits* per second. In an iPod ad, you might notice that it can store up to 60 giga*bytes* of music and video.

What do the prefixes kilo-, mega-, and giga- mean? When reading about digital devices, you'll frequently encounter references such as 50 kilobits per second, 1.44 megabytes, 2.8 gigahertz, and 2 terabytes. Kilo, mega, giga, tera, and similar terms are used to quantify digital data.

In common usage, *kilo*, abbreviated as K, means a thousand. For example, $50 K means $50,000. In the context of computers, however, 50K means 51,200. Why the difference? In the decimal number system we use on a daily basis, the number 1,000 is 10 to the 3rd power, or 10^3. For digital devices where base 2 is the norm, a kilo is precisely 1,024, or 2^{10}. A **kilobit** (abbreviated Kb or Kbit) is 1,024 bits. A **kilobyte** (abbreviated KB or Kbyte) is 1,024 bytes. Kilobytes are often used when referring to the size of small computer files.

The prefix *mega* means a million, or in the context of bits and bytes, precisely 1,048,576 (the equivalent of 2^{20}). A **megabit** (Mb or Mbit) is 1,048,576 bits. A **megabyte** (MB or MByte) is 1,048,576 bytes. Megabytes are often used when referring to the size of medium to large computer files or to floppy disk capacity.

In technology lingo, the prefix *giga* refers to a billion, or precisely 1,073,741,824. As you might expect, a **gigabit** (Gb or Gbit) is approximately one billion bits. A **gigabyte** (GB or GByte) is one billion bytes. Gigabytes are typically used to refer to storage capacity.

Computers—especially mainframes and supercomputers—sometimes work with huge amounts of data, and so terms such as tera- (trillion), peta- (thousand trillion), and exa- (quintillion) are also handy. Figure 1-29 summarizes the terms commonly used to quantify computer data.

> **TERMINOLOGY NOTE**
>
> What's a kibibyte? Some computer scientists have proposed alternative terminology to dispel the ambiguity in terms such as *mega* that can mean 1,000 or 1,024. They suggest the following prefixes:
>
> Kibi = 1,024
>
> Mebi = 1,048,576
>
> Gibi = 1,073,741,824

Bit	One binary digit	Gigabit	2^{30} bits
Byte	8 bits	Gigabyte	2^{30} bytes
Kilobit	1,024 or 2^{10} bits	Terabyte	2^{40} bytes
Kilobyte	1,024 or 2^{10} bytes	Petabyte	2^{50} bytes
Megabit	1,048,576 or 2^{20} bits	Exabyte	2^{60} bytes
Megabyte	1,048,576 or 2^{20} bytes		

FIGURE 1-29

Quantifying Digital Data

CIRCUITS AND CHIPS

How do digital devices store and transport all those bits?

Because most digital devices are electronic, bits take the form of electrical pulses that can travel over circuits in much the same way that electricity flows over a wire when you turn on a light switch. All the circuits, chips, and mechanical components that form a digital device are designed to work with bits.

At the simplest level, you can envision bits as two states of an electric circuit; the state used for a 1 bit would be *on* and the state for a 0 bit would be *off*. In practice, the 1 bit might be represented by an elevated voltage, such as +5 volts, whereas a 0 bit is represented by a low voltage, such as 0.

What's inside?

If it weren't for the miniaturization made possible by digital electronic technology, computers, cell phones, and portable music players would be huge, and contain a complex jumble of wires and other electronic gizmos. Instead, today's digital devices contain relatively few parts—just a few wires, some microchips, and one or more circuit boards.

What's a computer chip?

The terms *computer chip*, *microchip*, and *chip* originated as technical jargon for *integrated circuit*. An **integrated circuit** (IC), such as the one pictured in Figure 1-30, is a super-thin slice of semiconducting material packed with microscopic circuit elements, such as wires, transistors, capacitors, logic gates, and resistors.

Semiconducting materials (or semiconductors), such as silicon and germanium, are substances with properties between those of a conductor (like copper) and an insulator (like wood). To fabricate a chip, the conductive properties of selective parts of the semiconducting material can be enhanced to essentially create miniature electronic pathways and components, such as transistors.

Integrated circuits are packaged in protective carriers that vary in shape and size. Figure 1-31 illustrates some chip carriers, including small rectangular DIPs (dual in-line packages) with caterpillar-like legs protruding from a black, rectangular body; and pincushion-like PGAs (pin-grid arrays).

INFOWEBLINKS

Learn more about Digital electronics at the **Integrated Circuits InfoWeb**.

 CLICK TO CONNECT
www.course.com/np/concepts11/ch01

FIGURE 1-30

A computer chip is classified by the number of miniaturized components it contains—from small-scale integration (SSI) of fewer than 100 components per chip to ultra large-scale integration (ULSI) of more than 1 million components per chip.

FIGURE 1-31

Integrated circuits can be used for microprocessors, memory, and support circuitry. They are housed within a ceramic carrier. These carriers exist in several configurations, or chip packages, such as DIPs and PGAs.

A DIP has two rows of pins that connect the IC circuitry to a circuit board.

A PGA is a square chip package with pins arranged in concentric squares, typically used for microprocessors.

How do chips fit together? The electronic components of most digital devices are mounted on a circuit board called a system board, mother-board, or main board. The **system board** houses all essential chips and provides connecting circuitry between them. In Figure 1-32, you can see what's inside a typical desktop computer, a Palm Pilot, and a cell phone.

FIGURE 1-32

The electronic components of computers, PDAs, and cell phones have many similar elements, including microchips and circuit boards.

QuickCheck

1. Most computers are electronic, [_____] devices that work with discrete numbers, such as 1s and 0s.

2. The [_____] number system represents numeric data as a series of 0s and 1s.

3. A computer uses [_____] codes to represent the numerals in your Social Security number and street address, whereas it uses [_____] numbers for numeric data such as your age.

4. A(n) [_____] is approximately one billion bytes.

5. A(n) [_____] circuit contains micro-scopic elements, such as wires, transistors, and capacitors, that are packed onto a very small square of semiconducting material.

 CHECK ANSWERS

Digital Processing

COMPUTERS AND OTHER DIGITAL DEVICES process data, but how do they know what to do with it? The instructions you issue aren't 0s and 1s that a digital device can work with. So what goes on inside the box? Section D explains the programs that make digital devices tick. You'll discover that although digital devices appear to perform very complex tasks, under the hood they are really performing some very simple operations, but doing them at lightning speed.

PROGRAMS AND INSTRUCTION SETS

How do digital devices process data? Computers, portable media players, handheld computers, and smart phones all work with digital data. That data is manipulated under the control of a computer program, or software. But how do digital circuits know what those program instructions mean? Let's take a closer look at programs to see how they are created and how digital devices work with them.

Who creates programs? Computer programmers create programs that control digital devices. These programs are usually written in a high-level **programming language**, such as C, Basic, COBOL, or Java.

Programming languages use a limited set of command words such as Print, If, Write, Display, and Get to form sentence-like statements designed as step-by-step directives for the processor chip. An important characteristic of most programming languages is that they can be written with simple tools, such as a word processor, and they can be understood by programmers. A simple program to select a song on your iPod might contain the statements shown in Figure 1-33.

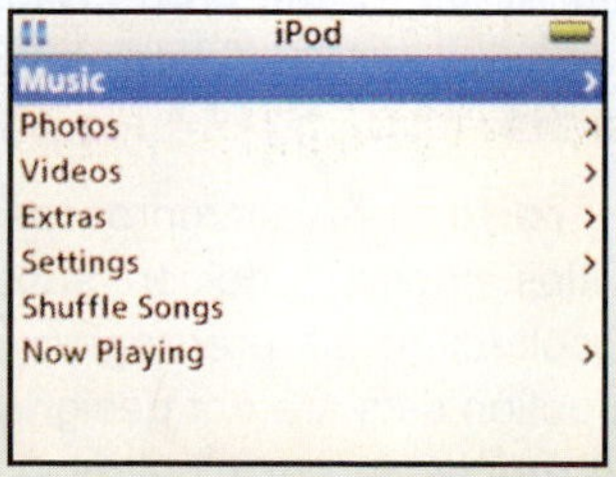

FIGURE 1-33

The program for an iPod displays a list of songs that the user can choose to play. A program works behind the scenes to display the list, get your selection, process it, and play the song.

```
Display Playlist

Get Song

Play Song
```

❚❚	iPod	▭
Music		>
Photos		>
Videos		>
Extras		>
Settings		>
Shuffle Songs		
Now Playing		>

The human-readable version of a program, like the one above, created in a high-level language by a programmer is called **source code**. Source code is an important first step in programming application software, batch files, and scripts that you'll learn about in later chapters. However, just as a digital device can't work directly with text, sounds, or images until they have been digitized, source code has to be converted into a digital format before the processor can use it.

How does source code get converted? The procedure for translating source code into 0s and 1s can be accomplished by a compiler or an interpreter. A **compiler** converts all the statements in a program in a single batch, and the resulting collection of instructions, called **object code**, is placed in a new file (Figure 1-34). Most of the program files distributed as software contain object code that is ready for the processor to execute.

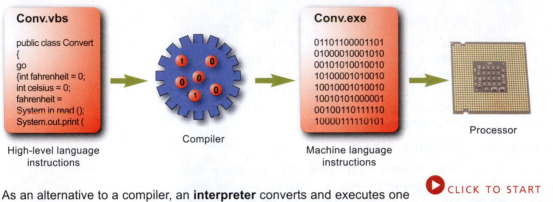

High-level language instructions   Compiler   Machine language instructions   Processor

> CLICK TO START

As an alternative to a compiler, an **interpreter** converts and executes one statement at a time while the program is running. After the statement is executed, the interpreter converts and executes the next statement, and so on (Figure 1-35).

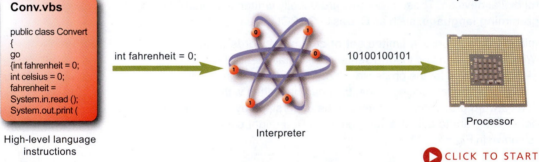

High-level language instructions   Interpreter   Processor

> CLICK TO START

Compilers and interpreters don't simply convert the characters from source code into 0s and 1s. For example, in the first line of the iPod program, Display Playlist, a compiler would not simply convert the *D* into its ASCII equivalent. No, computers are a little trickier than that.

What does the conversion process produce? A microprocessor is hard wired to perform a limited set of activities, such as addition, subtraction, counting, and comparisons. This collection of preprogrammed activities is called an **instruction set**. Instruction sets are not designed to carry out any specific task, such as word processing or playing music. Instead, an instruction set is designed to be general purpose so that programmers can use it in creative ways for the wide variety of tasks performed by all kinds of digital devices.

Each instruction has a corresponding sequence of 0s and 1s. For example, 00000100 might correspond to Add. The list of codes for a microprocessor's instruction set, called **machine language**, can be directly executed by the processor's circuitry. A set of machine language instructions for a program is called **machine code**.

A machine code instruction has two parts: the op code and the operands. An **op code**, which is short for operation code, is a command word for an operation such as add, compare, or jump. The **operand** for an instruction specifies the data, or the address of the data, for the operation. In the following instruction, the op code means add and the operand is 1, so the instruction means Add 1.

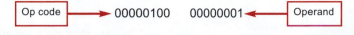

Op code → 00000100   00000001 ← Operand

A single high-level instruction very often converts into multiple machine language instructions. Figure 1-36 illustrates the number of machine-language instructions that correspond to a simple high-level program.

```
#include <stdio.h>
int main (int argc, char *argv[])
{
    int I;
    int sum = 0;

    for (I=0; I<=100; I++) sum += I * I;
    printf ("The sum 0..100=%d\n",sum);
}
```

00100111101111011111111111100000
10101111101111110000000000010100
10101111101001000000000000100000
10101111101001010000000000100100
10101111101000000000000000011000
10101111101000000000000000011100
10001111101011100000000000011100
10001111101110000000000000011000
00000001110011100000000000011001
00100101110010000000000000000001
00101001000000010000000001100101
10101111101010000000000000011100
00000000000000000111100000010010
00000011000011111110010000100001
00010100001000001111111111110111
10101111101110010000000000011000
00111100000000100000100000000000
10001111101001010000000000011000
00001100000010000000000001101100
00100100100001000000000100000110000

To summarize what you should now know about programs and instruction sets, a programmer creates human-readable source code using a programming language. A compiler or interpreter converts source code into machine code. Machine code instructions are a series of 0s and 1s that correspond to a processor's instruction set.

PROCESSOR LOGIC

What happens inside a computer chip? A microprocessor contains miles of microscopic circuitry and millions of miniature components divided into different kinds of operational units, such as the ALU and the control unit.

The **ALU** (arithmetic logic unit) is the part of the microprocessor that performs arithmetic operations, such as addition and subtraction. It also performs logical operations, such as comparing two numbers to see if they are the same. The ALU uses **registers** to hold data that is being processed, just as you use a mixing bowl to hold the ingredients for a batch of cookies.

The microprocessor's **control unit** fetches each instruction, just as you get each ingredient out of a cupboard or the refrigerator. Data is loaded into the ALU's registers, just as you add all the ingredients to the mixing bowl. Finally, the control unit gives the ALU the green light to begin processing, just as you flip the switch on your electric mixer to begin blending the cookie ingredients. Figure 1-37 illustrates a microprocessor control unit and ALU preparing to add 2 + 3.

FIGURE 1-36

Many machine language instructions might be needed to equal a simple high-level program that counts to 100.

FIGURE 1-37

The control unit fetches the ADD instruction, then loads data into the ALU's registers where it is processed.

Control Unit
ADD

ALU

Register   2

Register   3

What happens when a computer executes an instruction? The term **instruction cycle** refers to the process in which a computer executes a single instruction. Some parts of the instruction cycle are performed by the microprocessor's control unit; other parts of the cycle are performed by the ALU. The steps in this cycle are summarized in Figure 1-38.

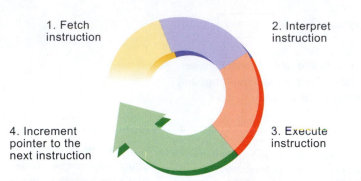

1. Fetch instruction

2. Interpret instruction

4. Increment pointer to the next instruction

3. Execute instruction

FIGURE 1-38

The instruction cycle includes four activities.

What role does the control unit play? The instructions that a computer is supposed to process for a particular program, are held in memory. When the program begins, the memory address of the first instruction is placed in a part of the microprocessor's control unit called an instruction pointer. The control unit can then fetch the instruction by copying data from that address into its instruction register. From there, the control unit can interpret the instruction, gather the specified data, or tell the ALU to begin processing. Figure 1-39 helps you visualize the control unit's role in processing an instruction.

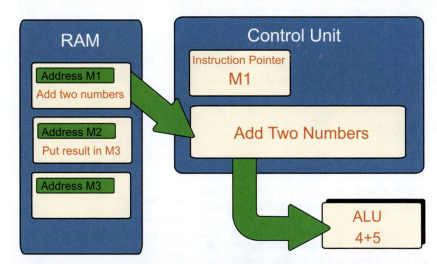

RAM

Control Unit

Instruction Pointer
M1

Address M1
Add two numbers

Add Two Numbers

Address M2
Put result in M3

Address M3

ALU
4+5

FIGURE 1-39

The control unit's instruction pointer indicates M1, a location in memory. The control unit fetches the "Add two numbers" instruction from M1. This instuction is then sent to the ALU.

When does the ALU swing into action? The ALU is responsible for performing arithmetic and logical operations. It uses registers to hold data ready to be processed. When it gets the go-ahead signal from the control unit, the ALU processes the data and places the result in an accumulator. From the accumulator, the data can be sent to memory or used for further processing. Figure 1-40 on the next page helps you visualize what happens in the ALU as the computer processes data.

What happens after an instruction is executed? When the computer completes an instruction, the control unit increments the instruction pointer to the memory address of the next instruction, and the instruction cycle begins again.

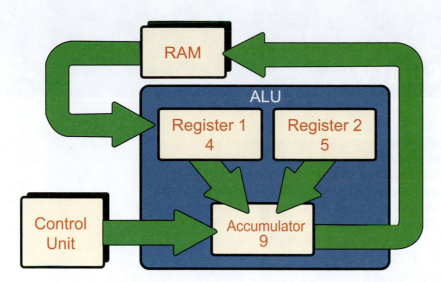

FIGURE 1-40

In this example, the ALU's registers contain the numbers 4
and 5. When the ALU receives
the "Add two numbers" instruction from the control unit, it
adds 4 and 5 then places the
result in the accumulator.

Do I need to know all this detailed stuff? What you should take
away from the discussion about programming and instruction sets is the
idea that computers and other digital devices accomplish a wide array of
complex tasks by performing a very limited set of machine language
instructions very fast.

These concepts about how processors work will help you understand the
significance of microprocessor performance, such as speed and word size,
which you'll learn about in the next chapter.

INFOWEBLINKS

For more details on the inner
workings of your computer's
processor, visit the **CPU
InfoWeb**.

 CLICK TO CONNECT
www.course.com/np/concepts11/ch01

QuickCheck

1. The human-readable version of a program, created in a high-level language by a programmer is
called [_____] code.

2. A compiler converts all the statements in a
program in a single batch, and the resulting
collection of instructions is called
[_____] code.

3. In a machine code instruction such as
00000100 00000001 the left-most number is the

op code and the remaining numbers are
[_____].

4. The ALU in your computer's microprocessor
performs [_____] and logical operations.

5. The microprocessor's [_____] unit
fetches each instruction.

▶ CHECK ANSWERS

Password Security

USER IDS, passwords, and personal identification numbers (PINs) are a fact of everyday life in the information age. They are required for activities such as using ATMs and debit cards, logging into Windows, accessing wireless networks, making an iTunes purchase, instant messaging, reading e-mail, and file sharing. Many Web sites encourage you to sign up for membership by choosing a user ID and password. Section E provides information about selecting secure passwords and managing the mountain of passwords you collect and tend to forget.

AUTHENTICATION PROTOCOLS

What is an authentication protocol? Security experts use the term **authentication protocol** to refer to any method that confirms a person's identity using something the person knows, something the person possesses, or something the person is. For example, a person might know a password or PIN. A person might possess an ATM card or a credit card. A person can also be identified by **biometrics**, such as a fingerprint, facial features (photo), or retinal pattern (Figure 1-41).

Authentication protocols that use more than one means of identification are more secure than others. Two-factor authentication, which verifies identity using two independent elements of confirmation such as an ATM card and PIN, is more secure than single-factor authentication, such as a password. Computer-related security is primarily based on passwords associated with user IDs. The level of protection offered by single-factor authentication depends on good password selection and management on the part of users.

What is a user ID? A **user ID** is a series of characters—letters and possibly numbers or special symbols—that becomes a person's unique identifier, similar to a Social Security number. It is also referred to as a username, login, screenname, online nickname, or handle. User IDs are typically public. Because they are not secret, they do not offer any level of security.

User IDs are significant because they are the name on an account, such as e-mail or iTunes, that requires a password. When you first apply for or set up an account, you might be supplied with a user ID or you might be asked to create one. Often a user ID is a variation of your name. Brunhilde Jefferson's user ID might be bjeffe, bjefferson, brunhilde_jefferson, or bjeff0918445. It is also becoming common to use your e-mail address as a user ID.

The rules for creating a user ID are not consistent throughout all applications, so it is important to read instructions carefully before finalizing your user ID. For example, spaces might not be allowed in a user ID. Hence, the underline in brunhilde_jefferson is used instead of a space. There might be a length limitation, so Ms. Jefferson might have to choose a short user ID, such as bjeffe.

FIGURE 1-41

Biometric authentication protocols include retinal scans that identify unique patterns of blood vessels in the eye.

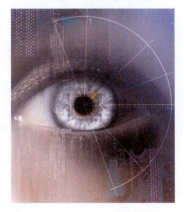

Some computers that host password-protected resources don't differenti-ate between uppercase and lowercase letters, and would consider the user IDs B_Jefferson and b_jefferson to be the same. Other computers are **case sensitive** and differentiate between uppercase and lowercase. On such computers, if Ms. Jefferson selected Brun_Jeff as her user ID, she would not be able to gain access by typing brun_jeff. To avoid such prob-lems, most people stick to lowercase letters for their user IDs.

What is a password? A **password** is a series of characters that verifies a user ID and guarantees that you are the person you claim to be. Although you might be assigned a password, typically you are asked to provide your own. In some situations you might be given a temporary password, and then asked to change it as soon as you successfully log in for the first time. Passwords and user IDs are typically created on a registration or enroll-ment screen similar to the one in Figure 1-42.

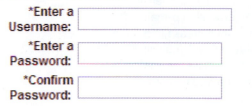

User Name & Password

*Enter a Username:	(Must be at least 8 characters)
*Enter a Password:	(Must be at least 8 characters and include one number)
*Confirm Password:	

View our privacy policy to learn how we protect your information.

ENROLL NOW!»

FIGURE 1-42

When you create an account, you are typically asked to enter a user ID and password.

What if I forget my password? Login screens for many applications provide a "forgot my password" link. Clicking this link checks your identity using your answer to a personal question. If your identity checks out, your password is e-mailed to you. A personal question provides an alternative authentication protocol to ensure that you are not a hacker pretending to have lost a password.

Personal questions and answers are usually set up at the same time you create an account. After selecting a password, you are required to choose a question that you must answer before your forgotten password is e-mailed to you. This question might be something like: What is your mother's maid-en name? What is your favorite color? or Where were you born? You should be careful about the question you choose because public informa-tion like your mother's maiden name or the town of your birth can be researched by any hacker.

What is the difference between a password and a PIN? Both passwords and PINs are classified as *something the user knows* authenti-cation methods. In practice, PINs tend to be a sort sequence of numbers that can be entered using a numeric keypad, whereas passwords tend to be longer sequences of letters, numbers, and special characters that require a full qwerty keyboard for entry. PINs are typically used with two-factor authentication protocols, whereas passwords are used in conjunction with single-factor authentication protocols.

For example, ATMs require a bank card (something you possess) and a PIN (something you know). In contrast, passwords are associated with single-factor authentication used for networks, Web sites, and other situations in which the hardware for dealing with ID cards is not available.

PASSWORD HACKS

How serious is password theft? To a hacker, obtaining the password for a specific user ID can be even more rewarding than a burglar figuring out the combination to a house safe. Once hackers get into a user account, a wealth of personal information can be at their fingertips. This information could be anything from juicy e-mail gossip to Social Security numbers, credit card numbers, bank account numbers, health data, and other private details. When someone gains unauthorized access to your personal data and uses it illegally, it is called **identity theft**. Victims of this increasingly common crime often don't realize what is happening until it's too late.

Armed with your password and other personal data, a cybercriminal can rack up bills using your credit card, apply for a mortgage using your financial data, create fake accounts in your name, send embarrassing e-mail messages, or wreak havoc on your bank account. Once a thief breaks into an online account, he or she can also change your password and you will no longer be able to log in. Password theft is serious and pervasive, so it is important to understand how hackers get passwords and how you can protect yours.

How can hackers get my password? Hackers can employ a whole range of ways to steal passwords. Some primitive means include shoulder surfing, which is looking over your shoulder as you type in your password, and dumpster diving, which is going through your trash.

Password thieves can easily find your password if you write it down on a yellow sticky note hidden under your keyboard or in plain sight on top of your monitor. If a hacker doesn't have physical access to your work area but your computer is connected to a network, your password can be discovered by a hacker using a remote computer and software tools that systematically guess your password, intercept it, or trick you into revealing it.

A **dictionary attack** helps hackers guess your password by stepping through a dictionary containing thousands of the most commonly used passwords. Password dictionaries can be found on black hat sites and packaged with password cracking software, such as John the Ripper. Unfortunately, dictionary attacks are often enough to break a password because many users choose passwords that are easy to remember and likely to be in the most commonly used list (Figure 1-43).

> **TERMINOLOGY NOTE**
>
> *Hacker* can refer to a skilled programmer or to a person who manipulates computers with malicious intent. The terms *black hat* and *cracker* are also used to refer to a malicious or criminal hacker.

FIGURE 1-43

Some of the most commonly used passwords are included in the dictionaries packaged with password cracking software. You should avoid using these passwords.

12345	internet	jordan	alex	newyork	jonathan
abc123	service	michael	apple	soccer	love
password	canada	michelle	avalon	thomas	marina
computer	hello	mindy	brandy	wizard	master
123456	ranger	patrick	chelsea	Monday	missy
tigger	shadow	123abc	coffee	asdfgh	monday
1234	baseball	andrew	dave	bandit	monkey
a1b2c3	donald	bear	falcon	batman	natasha
qwerty	harley	calvin	freedom	boris	ncc1701
123	hockey	changeme	gandalf	dorothy	newpass
xxx	letmein	diamond	golf	eeyore	pamela
money	maggie	matthew	green	fishing	pepper
test	mike	miller	helpme	football	piglet
carmen	mustang	ou812	linda	george	poohbear
mickey	snoopy	tiger	magic	happy	pookie
secret	buster	trustno1	merlin	iloveyou	rabbit
summer	dragon	12345678	molson	jennifer	rachel

The **brute force attack** also uses password-cracking software, but its range is much more extensive than the dictionary attack. Because it exhausts all possible keys to decrypt a password, a brute force attack can run for days or even as long as a week to crack some passwords.

If hackers can't guess a password, they can use another technique called **sniffing**, which intercepts information sent out over computer networks. Sniffing software is used legitimately by network administrators to record network traffic for monitoring and maintenance purposes. The same software can also be used for illicit activities. If your user ID and password travel over a network as unencrypted text they can easily fall into the hands of a password thief.

An even more sophisticated approach to password theft is **phishing**, in which a hacker poses as a legitimate representative of an official organization such as your ISP, your bank, or an online payment service in order to persuade you to disclose highly confidential information. Mostly through e-mail or instant messaging, a fake customer representative or administrator asks you to visit a Web page to confirm billing information or verify your account by providing your password, credit card number, or Social Security number. If you examine phishing messages more closely, you might realize that the Web sites referred to are fake. However, seasoned hackers try to make the URLs look as close as possible to the official Web sites they claim to represent (Figure 1-44).

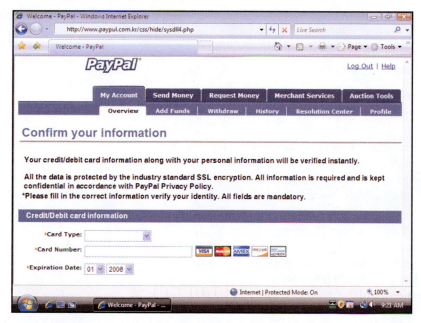

FIGURE 1-44

A fake Web site can look very similar to the real thing, but this fraudulent site originates in Korea. You should avoid clicking links in e-mail messages that attempt to get you to confirm or renew account data.

As users became better at identifying phishing messages, password thieves resorted to the use of keyloggers. Short for *keystroke logging*, a keylogger is software that secretly records a user's keystrokes and sends the information to a hacker. A keylogger is a form of malicious code called a Trojan horse, or Trojan. Trojans are computer programs that seem to perform one function while actually doing something else. They can be embedded in e-mail attachments, software downloads, and even files. Trojans are discussed in more detail in the security section of the Software chapter.

SECURE PASSWORDS

How do I create a secure password? With password theft becoming more and more widespread, security experts recommend using a strong, secure password for financial transactions such as those that involve PayPal or bank accounts. A strong, secure password is one that is easy to remember but difficult to crack. Figure 1-45 offers guidelines for selecting secure passwords and avoiding ones that are easily crackable.

FIGURE 1-45

Tips for creating secure passwords

- Use passwords that are at least 8 characters in length. The longer the password, the tougher it is to crack.

- Use a combination of letters, numbers, and special characters such as $, #, if permitted.

- Use uppercase and lowercase letters if the hosting computer is case sensitive.

- Use a pass phrase, that is, one that is based on the first letters of a verse from a favorite poem or song. For example, the words from the nursery rhyme "Jack and Jill went up the hill" can be converted to jjwuth. You can then insert special characters and numbers, and add some uppercase letters to create a password that still makes sense to you personally, such as J&J w^th! This type of password appears random to anyone else but you.

- Do not use a password based on public information such as your phone number, Social Security number, driver's license number, or birthday. Hackers can easily find this information, and other personal facts such as names of your spouse, children, or pets.

- Avoid passwords that contain your entire user ID or part of it. A user ID of bjeffe coupled with a password of bjeffe123 is an easy target for password thieves.

- Steer clear of words that can be found in the dictionary, including foreign words. Dictionary attacks can utilize foreign language dictionaries. Even common words spelled backwards, such as *drowssap* instead of *password*, are not tricky enough to fool password-cracking software.

How do I protect my password? Once you have selected a strong password, you must take steps to keep it safe. Do not share your password with anyone. Avoid writing down a password. If possible, memorize it. If you must write down a password, do not leave it in an obvious place such as under your keyboard or mouse pad. Recording passwords in an unencrypted file stored on your computer is risky, too, especially if you have more than one password. A hacker who gains access to that file can use the password to access all your accounts.

If you think one of your passwords has been compromised, change it immediately. Even if you have no evidence of password tampering, security experts recommend that you change your password periodically, say every six months. When you change your passwords, do not just make a slight variation to your current one. For example, do not change just4Me1 to just4Me2. You should not reuse your old passwords either, so it's best to keep a password history list.

Aside from good password maintenance habits, computer maintenance is also essential. Make sure that your entire computer is protected by security software, which is explained in the Software chapter.

How do I deal with all my passwords and user IDs? You can accumulate many passwords and user IDs—from online banking, your ISP, online shopping sites, online music stores, and maybe even from your favorite news and information Web sites. The more passwords and user IDs you have, the more difficult they become to remember.

How many times have you had to click on the "I forgot my password" link when you logged in to an online account? Your passwords provide the most protection if they are unique, but accessing even 25 different Web sites that require 25 different user IDs and 25 corresponding passwords requires quite a memory. To add to the confusion, you must also regularly change passwords to your critical accounts!

Instead of using 25 different user IDs and passwords, you need some way to reduce the number of things you have to memorize. First, strive to select a unique user ID that you can use for more than one site. Remember that people with your name who selected user IDs before you might have already taken the obvious user IDs. For example, when John Smith selects a user ID, you can bet that other people have already used johnsmith, jsmith, and john_smith. To keep his user ID unique, John might instead select jsl2wm (the first letters in John Smith loves 2 watch movies).

Next, you can maintain two or three tiers of passwords—the top level for high security, the second level for medium security, and the third level for low security. If you do not have too many accounts, you can opt for just two tiers—for high and low security. You can then select two passwords. Use the high-security password for accessing critical data, such as online banking, for managing an online stock portfolio, or for your account at an online bookstore that stores a copy of your billing and credit card information.

Use your low-security password in situations where you don't really care if your security is compromised. Some places on the Internet want you to establish an account with a user ID and password just so that they can put you on a mailing list. At other sites, your user ID and password provide access to information, but none of your own data (a credit card number, for example) is stored there. It is not necessary to change your low-security password very often. Figure 1-46 provides more information about tiered passwords.

Tier 1: High security
Password: BBx98$$NN26
Uses:
Online banking
PayPal
iTunes
Amazon.com

Tier 2: Low security
Password: Rover
Uses:
New York Times archive
Google
Wikipedia
PhotoSIG

FIGURE 1-46

Tiered passwords have the advantage of being easy to remember, however, the disadvantage is that a hacker who discovers one of your passwords will be able to use it to access many of your accounts.

What is a password manager? A **password manager** is utility soft-ware that generates secure passwords and stores them along with user IDs and their corresponding sites. When you want to log into an online account, your password manager recognizes the sites and automatically retrieves and transmits the appropriate user ID and password. The data stored by a password manager is encrypted to protect it from hackers. You need only one master password to access all the password manager data.

The big advantage of a password manager is that you can use unique and secure passwords for every one of your online accounts. You don't have to worry if the passwords are difficult to remember because the software keeps track of them (Figure 1-47).

FIGURE 1-47

Password managers help you keep track of all your passwords.

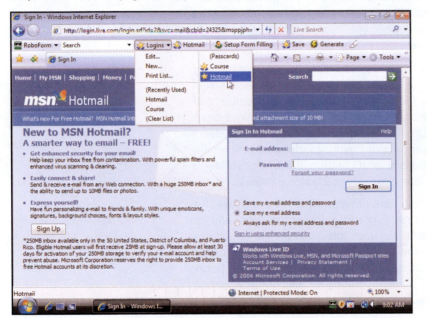

CLICK TO START

In addition to generating and tracking your passwords, most password managers provide other features, such as password strength meters and form fillers. A password strength meter indicates whether your passwords are secure enough—a feature that is useful if you've created your own passwords, rather than using your password manager to generate them. Form fillers automatically enter data into online Web forms such as those that request billing data when you order at an online shopping site. Many form fillers also match a Web form's URL against a set of valid URLs that you have provided in order to avoid sending data to a fake Web site that you have been lured to visit by a phishing message. When entering pass-words, form fillers are not collecting your password from the keyboard; therefore, a hacker's keylogger cannot secretly record keystrokes.

There are several free, shareware, or open source password managers, such as KeyWallet, Whisper 32, PasswordMaker, and Password Safe. Some password managers offer portable versions. A portable password manager does not have to be installed on a computer before it is used. Instead, you can carry it around on a USB flash drive so that your passwords are available wherever you go, such as your school lab, the library, or your work. When you remove the flash drive, your portable password manager leaves no traces of passwords behind (Figure 1-48).

For extra protection against intruders who might search your computer for passwords, a flash drive that contains a password manager can be unplugged when you are not accessing password protected sites. You can also remove the flash drive from your computer when you're out so that your nosy roommate can't snoop through your computer files.

New password management techniques are being developed, but some offer their own set of potential security problems. For example, Web-based password managers could make attractive targets for password thieves. Breaking into a single site, a password thief could harvest thousands of passwords. As new password management technologies appear, make sure you evaluate them carefully before trusting them with your valuable data.

FIGURE 1-48

Some password managers are portable so that you can carry them with you on a USB flash drive.

QuickCheck

1. A(n) [_____] protocol is any method that confirms a person's identity using something the person knows, something the person possesses, or something the person is.

2. [_____] such as retinal scans help identify people based on physical characteristics.

3. A(n) [_____] is software that secretly records a user's keystrokes and sends the information to a hacker.

4. Tiered passwords have the advantage of reducing the number of passwords you have to remember, however, their disadvantage is that a hacker who discovers one of your passwords will be able to use it to access many of your accounts. True or false? [_____]

5. A(n) [_____] manager is utility software that generates secure passwords and stores them along with user IDs and their corresponding sites.

 CHECK ANSWERS

ISSUE

Are You Being Tracked?

IN THE BOOK *Harry Potter and the Prisoner of Azkaban*, Harry acquires a magical item called the Marauder's Map, which shows the location of every teacher and student at the Hogwarts School of Witchcraft and Wizardry. A group of students at the Massachusetts Institute of Technology became fascinated by the idea of a tracking map and constructed one of their own. It is rather amazing that a fictional magic device could so easily become reality.

In the context of Harry Potter, tracking technology seems fun, but in real life this apparently innocent tracking technology could be used by governments, corporations, and possibly criminals to monitor the daily activities of ordinary people. Location privacy can be defined as the ability to prevent other parties from learning one's current or past location. Tracking technology could have a significant effect on our ability to keep our daily lives private.

A location-enabled device (sometimes referred to as a location-aware device) is one that can determine its geographic location. Most are handheld mobile devices, but tracking chips can also be embedded in items as varied as cars, shipping cartons, product labels, clothing, and passports. Three technologies are used to equip devices with location awareness: GPS, cellular networks, and RFID.

A global positioning system, or GPS, uses a receiver inside a mobile device to triangulate a location based on signals from three or more earth-orbiting satellites. GPS technology is used for handheld GPS locator devices and automobile tracking services such as OnStar. GPS is a one-way technology; data travels to the GPS device, but the device does not transmit its position back to a satellite. However, coordinates from a GPS system can be transmitted over a different network, such as the cellular phone system or wireless network. For example, a tourist might rent a virtual tour guide device that narrates points of interest on a walking tour. The device collects information from a GPS satellite and when the tourist reaches an attraction, begins narrating.

Unbeknownst to the tourist, however, the device can transmit its location to the tour operator's office. Not only does the tour operator know the tourist's location, but that information could be passed to a third party marketer or to immigration officials.

Wireless networks, such as a cellular phone system, can determine location based on the antenna to which it broadcasts. An antenna's coverage area ranges from a few miles up to 20 miles. The location of a mobile device and the person using it can be roughly determined to be within the range of the antenna it is currently transmitting to. A more precise location can be triangulated using multiple antennas. With current technology, triangulation from cellular phone antennas is less accurate than with GPS; current technology pinpoints a location to within 50-150 meters. Locations can be tracked only within range of cell towers. In contrast, GPS tracking is essentially worldwide.

Wireless transmissions are bi-directional; unlike one-way GPS, most mobile devices can transmit a location back to a base station. Cellular phone companies originally used this capability to determine when customers were roaming out of their home coverage area.

Currently, location data from cellular phones is also available for use by emergency responders to locate people in need of assistance. More controversially, bi-directional tracking devices have been embedded in rental cars to determine whether the car is exceeding the speed limit or is being used for unauthorized travel across state lines.

New child-tracking services offered by cellular phone carriers allow parents to track their cell-phone equipped children on a Web-based map. Parents can even set up boundaries and if their child crosses out of the approved area, an alarm sounds on the parent's computer or cell phone.

Law enforcement agencies have tried to gain access to location information to track suspected criminals and in some states, motor vehicle officials are considering plans to implant tracking devices in license plates.

RFID (radio frequency identification) technology is based on a special-purpose computer chip equipped with a microscopic antenna that receives and responds to radio-frequency queries from a transceiver. Whenever the chip is within range of a transceiver, its signal can be picked up. RFID chips are so small that they are almost unnoticeable. They can be implanted in animals or people, incorporated into a credit card or passport, and tucked away in clothing labels or commercial products.

RFID product labels were originally designed to streamline warehouse and retail store operations, so that products could be scanned without removing them from shipping crates or shopping carts. They became controversial because consumers were not necessarily able to locate or remove the RFID device. Further, RFID-enabled items could be linked to a specific individual if an RFID labeled item was purchased with a credit card. It also seemed possible that unauthorized people could hijack RFID signals and track a person by, for example, picking up the signals emitted by her Benneton sweater.

Tracking technology has many uses. Employers can use location data to make sure employees are not spending too much time in the smoking area or break room. Cell phone carriers can collaborate with aggressive marketers to turn your cell phone into a handheld carnival barker who tries to coax you into nearby stores or restaurants. Data from a location-enabled device could be correlated with health clinics, bars, or adult bookstores allowing trackers to make inferences about a person's lifestyle.

The use of tracking technology is spreading and it seems clear that laws and regulations are necessary to prevent abusive practices. The Communications Act of 1934 requires that carriers only use a customer's confidential information for providing services specifically requested by that customer. The so called E911 Act that required wireless service providers to equip phones with GPS capability added location data to the list of information that is supposed to be kept confidential, and it prohibited certain marketing uses of customers' location data. Unfortunately, a bill that was proposed in 2001 requiring location-based services to obtain permission from customers before disclosing location information was not passed into law.

Privacy advocates are demanding strict protocols for collecting, using, storing, and distributing location information. They face opposition, however, from law enforcement officials who would like to explore ways location technology can be used to track criminals, and prevent terrorism. Commercial interest in this technology for marketing and advertising is also high and consumers might be willing to give up some measure of privacy for economic incentives, such as free OnStar service in exchange for listening to location-based advertising while driving.

The outcome of conflicting interests will determine if location-tracking technology can be implemented in such a way that the rights and privacy of individuals are protected.

INFOWEBLINKS

You'll find lots more information about tracking devices at the **Digital Surveillance InfoWeb**.

W CLICK TO CONNECT
www.course.com/np/concepts11/ch01

What Do You Think?

ISSUE

1. Should users of location-enabled devices be informed when location tracking is in use?

  ○ Yes   ○ No   ○ Not sure

2. Do you think most people are aware of the privacy issues associated with location-enabled devices?

  ○ Yes   ○ No   ○ Not sure

3. Should users of location-aware devices be permitted to enable and disable tracking features on their devices?

  ○ Yes   ○ No   ○ Not sure

● SAVE RESPONSES

Marketing

WALKING OUT THE GATE of ancient Pompeii, you might have come across an eye-catching sign extolling the virtues of a popular tavern in the next town. The sign was a clever bit of marketing designed to target thirsty travelers and drum up business. Throughout the centuries, handbills, newspaper ads, television commercials, radio spots, and mass mail campaigns were all important tools of the marketing industry. Now, computers have opened new vistas for communicating with consumers.

The American Marketing Association defines marketing as an organizational function and a set of processes for creating, communicating, and delivering value to customers and for managing customer relationships in ways that benefit the organization and its stakeholders. A person-in-the-street definition might simply be that marketing is an attempt to sell products.

Computers first played a role in marketing as a research tool for quickly crunching numbers from consumer surveys and sales figures. Statistics derived from that data helped companies focus development efforts on the most promising products and market them effectively. Marketing research data made one fact very clear: even the most effective advertising could not convince everyone to buy a particular product. A costly prime-time television ad, for example, might be seen by millions of viewers, but many of them had no interest at all in the advertised product. To better target potential buyers, marketers turned to direct marketing.

Direct marketing attempts to establish a one-to-one relationship with prospective customers rather than waiting for them to learn about a product from general, impersonal forms of advertising, such as billboards, radio spots, television commercials, and newspaper ads. The first direct marketing techniques included personalized letters, catalogs, and telemarketing. Customer names, addresses, and telephone numbers were mined from extensive computer databases maintained by mailing list brokers. Lists could be tailored in rudimentary ways to fit target markets. Selling snow tires? Get a list of consumers in northern states. Hawking a new brand of disposable razors? Get a list of men.

"Dear Carmen Smith, you might already have won…" Just about everyone in America has received a personalized sweepstakes mailing. Initially, personalized names were crudely inserted using dot matrix printers, but today high-speed laser printers dash off thousands of personalized letters per hour and use graphics capabilities to affix signatures that appear to have been hand-signed in ink.

Telemarketing is a technique for telephone solicitation. Computerized autodialers make it possible for telemarketers to work efficiently. An autodialer is a device that can dial telephone numbers stored in a list. It can also generate and dial telephone numbers using a random or sequential number generator.

A *smart* autodialer, called a predictive dialer, increases a telemarketer's efficiency even more by automatically calling several numbers at the same time and only passing a call to the marketer when a person answers. If you've picked up the telephone only to hear silence or a disconnect, it was likely an autodialer that connected to more than one person at the same time and dropped your call. Preemptive dialers eliminate telemarketing time that would be otherwise wasted with busy signals, answering machines, and so on.

The Internet opened up dramatic new horizons in direct marketing by providing an inexpensive conduit for collecting information about potential customers and distributing targeted direct marketing. According to author Jim Sterne, "The Internet and the World Wide Web have become the most important new communication media since television, and ones that are fundamentally reshaping contemporary understanding of sales and marketing." Today, a vast amount of information flows over the Internet and marketers are trying to harness that information to most efficiently communicate their messages to prospective customers.

Market analysts are interested in consumer opinions about companies and products. Analysts for companies like Ford, Microsoft, and Sony track opinions on the Internet by monitoring message boards, discussion sites, and blogs. Software tools, such as Intelliseek and Cymfony, are similar to Google's Web search technology, but are refined to sift through blogs for conjunctions of words such as *Ford Ranger*, *love*, and *dependable* to guess that a blogger is happy with a particular vehicle.

E-commerce Web sites offer a global distribution channel for small entrepreneurs as well as multinational corporations. Consumers can locate e-commerce sites using a search engine. Some search engines allow paid advertising to appear on their sites. Clever marketers use search engine optimization techniques to get their Web sites to the top of search engine lists.

Another way to drive traffic to an e-commerce site is banner advertising that clutters up Web pages with inviting tag lines for free products. Clicking the ad connects consumers to the site. The cost of placing a banner ad depends on the click-through rate—the number of consumers who click an ad. Sophisticated banner ad software displays the banner ad across an entire network and monitors click-through rates. Not only does this software keep track of click throughs for billing purposes, it can automatically adjust the sites that carry each ad to maximize click-through rates.

The word *marketing* combined with *Internet* is often associated with the tidal wave of spam that's currently crashing into everyone's Inbox. These mass spam e-mails, however bothersome, are a very crude form of direct marketing. Typically, spammers use unscrubbed mailing lists containing many expired,

blocked, and invalid e-mail addresses. This hit-or-miss strategy is cheap. Ten million e-mail addresses can be rented for as low as $100 and server bandwidth provided by e-mail brokers costs about $300 per million messages sent.

Marketing professionals regard massive e-mail spamming with some degree of scorn because most lists don't narrow the focus to the most promising customers. Worse yet, consumers react by installing spam filters. Some spammers try to evade spam filters. More than one Web site offers marketers a free service that analyzes mass e-mail solicitations using a Spam filter simulator. If the solicitation can't get through the filter, the service offers suggestions on what to change so the message slips through.

In contrast to gratuitous spammers, marketing professionals have learned that opt-in mailing lists have much higher success rates. Consumers who have asked for information more often appreciate receiving it and act on it. Opt-in consumers are also more willing to divulge information that develops an accurate profile of their lifestyle so marketers can offer them the most appropriate products.

Most consumers would agree that the marketing industry needs professionals who are socially responsible. In describing the qualifications for marketing professionals, the Bureau of Labor and Statistics states the obvious when it says, "Computer skills are vital because marketing, product promotion, and advertising on the Internet are increasingly common." In preparing for a marketing career, a knowledge of computers, the Web, and the Internet are important. Equally important is preparation in statistical analysis, psychology, and ethics, along with coursework that covers legal and regulatory aspects of the technology-driven marketing industry.

INFOWEBLINKS

You'll find additional information about this Computers in Context topic by visiting the **Computers and Marketing InfoWeb**.

Ⓦ CLICK TO CONNECT
www.course.com/np/concepts11/ch01

New Perspectives Labs

On the BookOnCD

To access the New Perspectives labs for Chapter 1, start the BookOnCD, BookOnFlashDrive, or other NP11 BookOn product and then click the icon next to the lab title below.

▶ OPERATING A PERSONAL COMPUTER

IN THIS LAB YOU'LL LEARN:

- How to start a Windows computer
- What to do when a computer is in sleep mode
- How to deactivate a screen saver
- How to select a different screen saver
- How to use the Alt, Ctrl, Esc, Num Lock, Caps Lock, Windows, Fn, Backspace, Delete, and arrow keys
- The difference between forward and backward slashes
- How to start and exit a program
- How to close a program that is not responding
- When to use the reset button
- How to shut down Windows

LAB ASSIGNMENTS

1. Start the interactive part of the lab. Make sure you've enabled Tracking if you want to save your QuickCheck results. Perform each lab step as directed, and answer all the lab QuickCheck questions. When you exit the lab, your answers are automatically graded and your results are displayed.

2. Make a note of the brand and location of the computer you're using to complete these lab assignments.

3. Use the Start button to access your computer's Control Panel folder. Describe the status of your computer's power saver settings.

4. Preview the available screen savers on the computer you use most frequently. Select the screen saver you like the best and describe it in a few sentences.

5. What is the purpose of an Fn key? Does your computer keyboard include an Fn key? Explain why or why not.

6. In your own words, describe what happens when you (a) click the Close button, (b) hold down the Ctrl, Alt, and Del keys, (c) press the reset button, and (d) select the Shut Down option.

▶ WORKING WITH BINARY NUMBERS

IN THIS LAB YOU'LL LEARN:

- The difference between the binary number system and the decimal number system
- How to count in binary
- How to convert decimal numbers into binary numbers
- How to convert binary numbers into decimal numbers
- How to use the Windows Calculator to convert numbers
- How to work with powers of two

LAB ASSIGNMENTS

1. Start the interactive part of the lab. Make sure you've enabled Tracking if you want to save your QuickCheck results. Perform each lab step as directed, and answer all the lab QuickCheck questions. When you exit the lab, your answers are automatically graded and your results are displayed.

2. Using paper and pencil, manually convert the following decimal numbers into binary numbers. Your instructor might ask you to show the process that you used for each conversion.

   a. 100   b. 1,000   c. 256
   d. 27   e. 48   f. 112
   g. 96   h. 1,024

3. Using paper and pencil, manually convert the following binary numbers into decimal numbers. Your instructor might ask you to show the process that you used for each conversion.

   a. 100   b. 101   c. 1100
   d. 10101   e. 1111   f. 10000
   g. 1111000 h. 110110

4. Describe what is wrong with the following sequence:

   10 100 110 1000 1001 1100 1110 10000

5. What is the decimal equivalent of 2^0? 2^1? 2^8?

Key Terms

Make sure you understand all the boldfaced key terms presented in this chapter. If you're using the NP11 BookOnCD, BookOnFlashDrive, or other NP11 BookOn product, you can use this list of terms as an interactive study activity. First, try to define a term in your own words, and then click the term to compare your definition with the definition presented in the chapter.

ALU, 31
Analog data, 22
Anonymizer tools, 10
Application software, 16
ASCII, 24
Authentication protocol, 34
Binary number system, 23
Biometrics, 34
Bit, 23
Blogs, 6
Brute force attack, 37
Bulletin boards, 6
Byte, 26
Case sensitive, 35
Central processing unit, 15
Character data, 24
Chat groups, 6
Client, 18
Compiler, 30
Compute-intensive, 19
Computer, 14
Computer network, 7
Computer program, 15
Control unit, 31
Convergence, 8
CPU, 15
Cyberspace, 7
Data, 15
Data representation, 22
Dictionary attack, 36
Digital data, 22
Digital divide, 12
Digital revolution, 4

Digitization, 7
Download, 8
EBCDIC, 25
E-mail, 6
Extended ASCII, 24
File, 15
Gigabit, 26
Gigabyte, 26
Globalization, 12
Handheld computer, 19
Identity theft, 36
Input, 15
Instruction cycle, 32
Instruction set, 30
Integrated circuit, 27
Intellectual property, 11
Internet, 6
Interpreter, 30
Kilobit, 26
Kilobyte, 26
Machine code, 30
Machine language, 30
Mainframe computer, 18
Megabit, 26
Megabyte, 26
Memory, 15
Microcontroller, 20
Microprocessor, 15
Numeric data, 23
Object code, 30
Online social networks, 6
Op code, 31
Open source, 12

Operand, 31
Operating system, 16
Output, 15
Password, 35
Password manager, 40
PDA, 19
Personal computer, 17
Phishing, 37
Portable media player, 20
Processing, 15
Programming language, 29
Registers, 31
Semiconducting materials, 27
Server, 18
Smart phone, 20
Sniffing, 37
Software, 15
Source code, 29
Storage, 15
Stored program, 16
Supercomputer, 18
System board, 28
System software, 16
Unicode, 25
User ID, 34
Videogame console, 17
Web, 7
Workstation, 17

Interactive Summary

To review important concepts from this chapter, fill in the blanks to best complete each sentence. When using the NP11 BookOnCD or other BookOn product, click the Check Answers buttons to automatically score your answers.

SECTION A: The [_____] revolution is an ongoing process of social, political, and economic change brought about by technologies such as computers and the Internet. The [_____] Is a global computer network originally developed as a military project, adapted for research and academic use, and then for commercial use. [_____], a form of electronic communication, was an application for the masses and finally a reason to buy a computer and join the digital revolution. Another aspect of the digital revolution is [_____], a process by which several technologies with distinct functionalities evolve to form a single product. Technology has the potential to spread ideas, such as freedom and democracy, but it might have a chilling effect on [_____], or "the right to be left alone." It might also affect intellectual [_____] because digital technology has made it easy to produce copies with no loss in quality from the original. And although technology-driven [_____] has an effect on the economy, activists worry about the digital [_____] that separates people who have access to technology and those who do not.

▶ CHECK ANSWERS

SECTION B: A [_____] is a multipurpose device that accepts input, processes data, stores data, and produces output according to a series of stored instructions. The data a computer is getting ready to process is temporarily held in [_____]. This data is then processed in the central processing [_____]. The series of instructions that tells a computer how to carry out processing tasks is referred to as a computer [_____], which forms the [_____] that sets up a computer to do a specific task. Data is typically stored in a [_____], which is a named collection of data that exists on a storage medium, such as a hard disk, floppy disk, CD, DVD, or USB flash drive. The idea of a [_____] program means that a series of instructions for a computing task can be loaded into a computer's memory. [_____] software is a set of computer programs that helps a person carry out a task. [_____] software helps the computer system monitor itself in order to function efficiently. For example, a computer [_____] system (OS) is essentially the master controller for all the activities that take place within a computer. Computers are grouped into categories. A [_____] computer is a type of microcomputer designed to meet the needs of an individual. The term [_____] can refer to an ordinary personal computer that is connected to a network or to a powerful desktop computer used for high-performance tasks. A [_____] is, at the time of its construction, one of the fastest computers in the world. A [_____] computer is large, expensive, and capable of simultaneously processing data for hundreds or thousands of users. A [_____] computer is essentially a PDA enhanced with features such as removable storage, e-mail, and Web access. A [_____] is a special-purpose microprocessor that can control a device, such as a refrigerator or microwave oven.

▶ CHECK ANSWERS

SECTION C:

[_____] data is processed, stored, and transmitted as a series of 1s and 0s. Each 1 or 0 is called a [_____] . A series of eight 0s and 1s, called a [_____] , represents one character—a letter, number, or punctuation mark. Data becomes [_____] when it is presented in a format that people can understand and use. [_____] data consists of numbers that might be used in arithmetic operations. It can be represented digitally using the [_____] number system. [_____] data is composed of letters, symbols, and numerals that are not used in arithmetic

operations. This data is represented using [_____] , EBCDIC, or Unicode. Data is quantified using terms such as [_____] or kibibyte (1024 bytes), and prefixes, such as [_____] or mebi (1,048,576), and giga or [_____] (1,073,741,824). The bits that represent data travel as electronic pulses through [_____] circuits, sometimes called computer chips. These chips are made from [_____] materials and are housed in chip carriers that can be plugged into the [_____] board of a digital device.

▶ CHECK ANSWERS

SECTION D:

Software is usually written in high-level [_____] languages, such as C, Basic, COBOL, and Java. The human-readable version of a program, created in a high-level language by a programmer is called [_____] code. A [_____] or interpreter converts this high-level code into [_____] code. A microprocessor is hard wired to perform a limited set of activities, such as addition, subtraction, counting, and comparisons. This collection of preprogrammed activities is called an [_____] set.

Each instruction begins with an [_____] code, which is a command word for an operation such as add, compare, or jump. Most instructions also include an [_____] that specifies the data, or the address of the data, for the operation. The processor's ALU uses [_____] to hold data that is being processed. The processor's [_____] unit fetches each instruction, sends data to the registers, and signals the ALU to begin processing.

▶ CHECK ANSWERS

SECTION E:

Passwords and user IDs are the most common authentication [_____] . Password theft has become a serious security problem, that has led to many cases of [_____] theft, when unauthorized individuals gain access to personal data. Hackers guess, discover, and steal passwords using a variety of techniques. A [_____] attack tries passwords from a list of commonly used passwords. A [_____] force attack tries every possible combination of letters and numbers. [_____] intercepts information sent out over

computer networks. [_____] uses fraudulent Web sites or e-mail messages to fool unsuspecting readers into entering passwords and other personal information. A [_____] is software that secretly records a user's keystrokes and sends them to a hacker. To keep passwords safe, you should consider using tiered passwords or password [_____] software that generates secure passwords and keeps track of which password corresponds to each site you access.

▶ CHECK ANSWERS

Interactive Situation Questions

Apply what you've learned to some typical computing situations. When using the NP11 BookOnCD, BookOnFlashDrive, or any other NP11 BookOn product, you can type your answers, and then use the Check Answers button to automatically score your responses.

1. Suppose that you walk into an office and see the devices pictured to the right. You would probably assume that they are the screen, keyboard, and mouse for a [_____] computer, workstation, or server.

2. You receive an e-mail message asking you to join a circle of friends. You assume that the message was generated in conjunction with an online [_____] network, such as MySpace, and if you become a member, you will be able to socialize online.

3. You go to the iTunes music store and purchase an album. When you see the [_____] message at the top of the screen, you know that the songs are being transferred from the remote iTunes server to your local computer.

4. You're visiting an antique shop and notice a collection of old fashioned radios. They actually feature a dial for tuning in different radio stations. You immediately recognize this as a(n) [_____] device because it deals with an infinite scale of values, rather than discrete values.

5. While attending a meeting at work you hear one of the executives wondering if "unit code" would be helpful. After a moment of puzzlement, you realize that the executive really meant [_____] , and that it would allow your company software to be translated into the Cyrillic alphabet used by the Russian language.

6. You have a new storage device that offers 2 GB of storage space. It is currently empty. Your friend wants to give you a large digital photo that's 16 MB. Will it fit on your storage device. Yes or no? [__]

7. Your bank is giving customers the choice of using a 4-digit PIN or a password that can contain up to 10 letters and numbers. The [_____] is more secure, so that's what you decide to use.

8. You need to select a password for your online PayPal account. Which of the following passwords would be the LEAST secure: jeff683, hddtmrutc, gargantuan, fanhotshot, bb#ii22jeffry, or high348? [_____]

● CHECK ANSWERS

Interactive Practice Tests

Practice tests that consist of 10 multiple-choice, true/false, and fill-in-the-blank questions are available on both the NP11 BookOn products and the NP11 Web site. The questions are selected at random from a large test bank, so each time you take a test, you'll receive a different set of questions. Your tests are scored immediately, and you can print study guides that help you find the correct answers for any questions that you missed.

● CLICK TO START

Study Tips

1

Study Tips help you to organize and consolidate the information in a unit by making lists, outlines, charts, and sketches. You can use paper and pencil or word processing software to complete most of the Study Tip activities.

1. Make sure you can use your own words to correctly answer each of the red focus questions that appear throughout the chapter.

2. List the technologies that are fueling the digital revolution.

3. Give at least 5 examples of convergence.

4. Describe at least two social, political, and economic effects of the digital revolution.

5. Use a diagram to explain how a computer makes use of input, processing, storage, memory, output, and the stored program concept.

6. List, briefly describe, and rank (in terms of computing capacity) the characteristics of each computer category described in Section B of this chapter.

7. Describe the difference between system software, an operating system, application software, and a computer program.

8. Explain the difference between digital and analog.

9. List various ways to digitally represent character and numeric data.

10. Without looking back at the chapter, list as many terms as you can that relate to quantifying bits and bytes.

11. Use the terms integrated circuits, microprocessor, and system board in a meaningful sentence.

12. Describe how compilers and interpreters work with high level programming languages, source code, and object code.

13. Make a storyboard showing how a microprocessor's ALU would add the numbers 2 and 8.

14. Create five secure passwords and five passwords that might be easy to crack.

15. Fill in the blanks on the concept map shown below to show the relationships between programming and processing concepts described in this chapter.

Concept Map

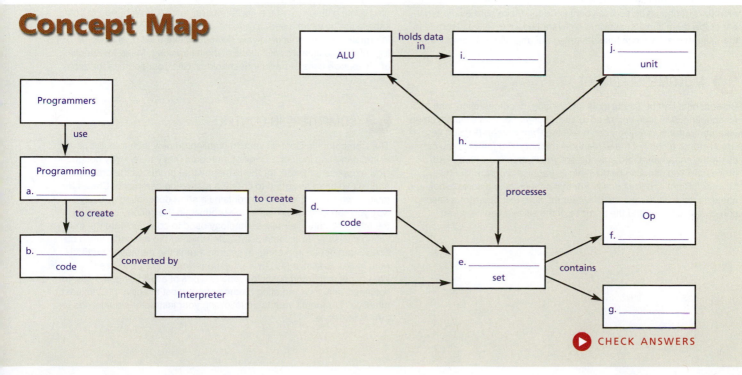

CHECK ANSWERS

Projects

CRITICAL THINKING

Whether you're taking this course to fulfill a graduation requirement, to improve your career options, or just for fun, take a few minutes to evaluate what you expect to gain from this course. Look through the table of contents of this textbook and select the five sections that you think will be most interesting, and the five sections that seem to be the least relevant to you. Incorporate your thoughts in two or three paragraphs that you e-mail to your instructor.

GROUP PROJECT

Form a group with four or five other students. Each student in the group should ask at least five friends if they have 1) a computer, 2) a cell phone, 3) a portable music player, 4) dial-up Internet access, 5) high speed Internet access. Consolidate the data from all members of your group into an Excel spreadsheet, and then graph it. How do your statistics coincide with nationwide statistics for digital ownership? Graph or write a summary and make sure you site your sources for national statistics.

CYBERCLASSROOM

Your instructor should provide each student with the e-mail addresses of four or five other students who will form a team, and designate a team leader. The team leader should find a news story about a technology issue from a source such as *www.news.google.com* and send it to one of the other students on the team. That student should add his or her opinion and comments, then send the message to another student in the group. Each student should use a different font color and initial their comments. When the message has circulated to all team members, it should be sent to your instructor. Make sure every member of the team is using antivirus software because, as you learned in the chapter, hackers can take advantage of unprotected computers.

MULTIMEDIA PROJECT

Screenshots can be useful tools for learning, documentation, and troubleshooting. Any time you need to show someone what's displayed on your computer screen, you can press the Print Screen (PrtScr) key, which stores a copy of the screen into memory. From there, you can paste the screenshot into a document you're creating with a word processor. You can also paste it into a graphics program, such as Microsoft Paint and then edit it. For this project, take a screenshot, and paste it into a Word document. Under the screenshot, enter a description of the software and the purpose of the screen you captured.

RESUME BUILDER

Several Web sites offer career aptitude assessments that claim to help you select a career that's suited to your personality and background. Use a search engine to locate three free Web-based career aptitude tests. Take the tests. If you are asked to sign up, make sure you exercise caution in the amount of personal information you divulge. After completing the tests, compare the results. Do they all point you in a similar career direction? What is your reaction to the results? Which test do you think was the most valid and why? Provide your instructor with your analysis, along with the URLs for the Web sites that provided the tests.

GLOBALIZATION

Although the Internet provides a global communications network, communication between people still depends on finding a common language. For this project, explore the Web and experiment with ways in which technology is being used to close the language gap. You might start at Google or Wikipedia and look at the selection of languages they offer. Chronicle your exploration, making sure to document the Web sites you visited. What are your conclusions about Internet use by non-English speakers?

ISSUE

The Issue section of this chapter focused on the increasing use of digital devices that can track a person's location. Tracking technology has advantages and disadvantages. It has been used to track down terrorists and to find missing children, but it can also be abused by government and private companies. For this project, begin by scanning some of the links at the Digital Surveillance InfoWeb. Add to your knowledge by using a search engine, such as Google, to scan recent information about location aware devices. Make a list of at least 10 legitimate and useful applications of digital tracking. Make another list of 10 abusive uses of tracking technology. Cite your sources for each item you list.

COMPUTERS IN CONTEXT

The Computers in Context section highlighted new technologies used in the marketing industry. Think of a product that you recently bought. Now, suppose you work for the company that produces the product and you've been assigned to create a marketing campaign. Create a table in which the first column contains a short description of every way you can think of to market the product. In the second column of the table, indicate the main technology used to communicate the marketing message. In column 3, indicate which of the methods would be considered direct marketing. In column 4 rank the marketing methods from most expensive (10) to least expensive (1). (You can use the Web to get estimated costs for various types of advertising.) Finally, in column 5 rank the marketing methods from most effective (10) to least effective (1). Submit your table following your instructor's guidelines for format and style.

On the Web

STUDENT EDITION LABS

W **CLICK TO ACCESS THE NP11 WEB SITE**
or open your browser and connect to www.course.com/np/concepts11/ch01.
Lab results can be stored in the Universal Gradebook.

Work hands-on in structured simulations practicing important skills and concepts

BINARY NUMBERS

In the Binary Numbers Student Edition Lab, you will learn about the following topics:

- Comparing binary numbers to decimal numbers
- Adding binary numbers manually
- Converting binary numbers to decimal equivalents

UNDERSTANDING THE MOTHERBOARD

In the Understanding the Motherboard Student Edition Lab, you will learn about the following topics:

- Identifying components of the motherboard, such as integrated circuits, the CPU, RAM, ROM, and expansion slots and cards
- Modifying the way Windows handles virtual memory on a system
- Installing expansion cards into a PC

CHAPTER COURSECAST

Use your computer or iPod to hear a five-minute audio presentation of chapter highlights.

FLASHCARD COURSECAST

Interact with audio flashcards to review key terms from the chapter.

DETAILED OBJECTIVES

Make sure that you've achieved all the objectives for a chapter before it's time for your test!

TEST YOURSELF

Review chapter material by taking these ten-question tests, then send your results to the Universal Gradebook.

ONLINE GAMES

Have some fun while refreshing your memory about key concepts that might appear on the next test. You can even send your results to the Universal Gradebook!

AND MORE!

At the NP11 Web site you'll also find Extra Content and InfoWebLinks.

2

Computer Hardware

LEARNING OBJECTIVES

- Label the main components of a personal computer system
- List the advantages and disadvantages of various desktop and portable computer form factors
- Describe the target markets for home, media, game, and small business computers
- List important factors to consider when shopping for a new computer
- Explain how upgrades and mods fit into a computer purchase decision
- List the factors that affect microprocessor performance
- Explain how RAM works and how it differs from disk storage
- List facts about RAM that are important to computer buyers and owners
- Describe the differences between magnetic, optical, and solid state storage
- Use criteria such as versatility, durability, capacity, access time, and transfer rate to compare storage technologies
- Explain the factors that might help a shopper decide whether to purchase a CRT, LCD, or plasma display device
- Compare and contrast the technologies and applications for ink jet, laser, and dot matrix printers
- Describe the components of a computer's expansion bus, including various types of expansion slots and cables
- Explain the hardware compatibility considerations, device drivers, and procedures involved in installing a peripheral device
- List ways you can protect your computer system hardware from theft and damage

✅ PRE-ASSESSMENT QUIZ

Take the pre-assessment quiz to find out how much you know about the topics in this chapter. ▶

MULTIMEDIA and INTERACTIVE ELEMENTS
When using the BookOnCD, BookOnFlashDrive, or other NP11 BookOn product, the ▶ icons are clickable to access multimedia resources.

BEFORE YOU READ ON, **TRY IT**

HOW POWERFUL IS MY COMPUTER?

As you read Chapter 2, you'll learn that some computers are more powerful than others because they can store more data and process data faster. To find out how your home, work, or lab computer stacks up, you'll need to know a few of its specifications. Before you begin to read this chapter, check your computer's specifications by doing the following:

1. Start your computer.

2. Click the Start button, then click Control Panel.

3. Double-click the System icon or link to open the System Properties dialog box. (If you're in Category View, click System and Maintenance first.)

4. If you see a window with tabs, make sure the General tab is displayed.

5. Record information about your computer similar to the information provided for the sample computer in the table.

6. Then, just to get an idea of the other equipment you've got attached to your computer, click the link or icon for Device Manager. (You might have to click the Hardware tab first).

7. Browse through the list. When you're done, close all the dialog boxes by clicking the ⊠ buttons.

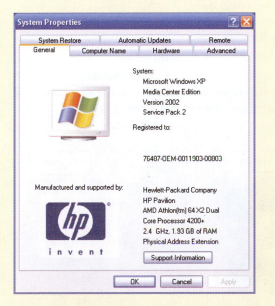

	Sample Computer	Your Computer
Computer Manufacturer	Hewlett-Packard	
Computer Model	HP Pavilion	
Processor Manufacturer	AMD	
Processor Type	Athlon 64 X2	
Processor speed	2.4 GHz	
Number of processors	1 (Dual core)	
RAM capacity	1.93 GB	

WEB SITE

Visit the NP11 Web site to access additional resources Ⓦ that accompany this chapter.

SECTION A

Personal Computer Basics

WHETHER YOU ARE SHOPPING for a new computer, using your trusty laptop, or troubleshooting a system glitch, it is useful to have some background about computer system components and how they work. Section A begins with a framework for understanding the vast number of options available for putting together a personal computer system, and then wraps up with some tips on interpreting the jargon in computer ads and negotiating the digital marketplace.

PERSONAL COMPUTER SYSTEMS

What's a personal computer system? The term *personal computer system* has at least two meanings. It can broadly refer to any computer system that uses personal computers for core processing operations. Such systems would include school labs and small business networks. In a more limited context, the term personal computer system refers to a personal computer, software, and peripheral devices that can be connected together for use by a single individual. This chapter focuses on computers in the latter context to make sure you're familiar with the hardware tools that make a computer system tick.

What are the components of a typical personal computer system? The centerpiece of a personal computer system is, of course, a personal computer. In addition, most systems include peripheral devices. The term **peripheral device** designates input, output, and storage equipment that might be added to a computer system to enhance its functionality. Popular peripheral devices include printers, digital cameras, scanners, joysticks, and speakers.

A personal computer system usually includes the components shown in Figure 2-1. These components are described briefly on the next page. They are defined and discussed in more detail later in the chapter.

FIGURE 2-1

A typical personal computer system includes the system unit and a variety of storage, input, and output devices.

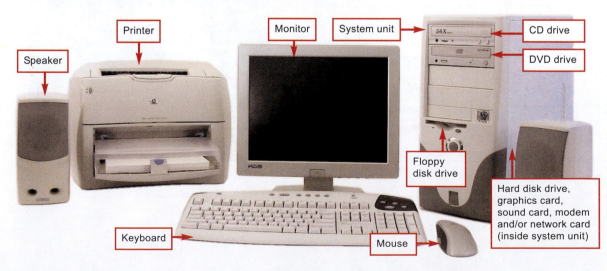

- Speaker
- Printer
- Monitor
- System unit
- CD drive
- DVD drive
- Floppy disk drive
- Hard disk drive, graphics card, sound card, modem and/or network card (inside system unit)
- Keyboard
- Mouse

 **CLICK TO START**

- **System unit.** The **system unit** is the case that holds the computer's main circuit boards, microprocessor, memory, power supply, and storage devices. Depending on the computer design, the system unit might also include other built-in devices, such as a keyboard and speakers.

- **Keyboard.** Most personal computer systems are equipped with a keyboard as the primary input device.

- **Mouse.** A mouse is an input device designed to manipulate on-screen graphical objects and controls.

- **Hard disk drive.** A hard disk drive is the main storage device on a personal computer system. It is usually mounted inside the computer's system unit and can store billions of characters of data. A small external light indicates when the drive is reading or writing data.

- **CD and DVD drives.** A CD drive is a storage device that uses laser technology to work with data on computer or audio CDs. A DVD drive can work with data on computer CDs, audio CDs, computer DVDs, or DVD movie disks. Some CD and DVD drives are classified as *read only* devices that cannot be used to write data onto disks. They are typically used to access data from commercial software, music, and movie CDs or DVDs. *Writable* CD and DVD drives, however, can be used to store and access data.

- **Other storage.** Personal computers sometimes include a floppy disk drive, which is a low-capacity storage device once found on virtually all computers. Floppy disks are disappearing as USB flash storage devices become more popular.

- **Sound system.** The sound system for a personal computer can output digital music, digitally recorded speech, and a variety of sound effects called system sounds designed to draw your attention to various messages and events. To produce sounds, a computer uses a circuit board called a sound card, which is typically housed in the system unit. A computer's sound card sends signals to speakers, which can be external devices or built into the system unit.

- **Display system.** A personal computer display system consists of two parts. Circuitry, called a graphics card, converts raw digital data into images that can be shown on a display device. Display devices, often called computer screens or monitors, present visual output, such as documents, photos, and videos. Personal computer systems can use several types of display technologies, including CRTs and LCDs. Display devices are usually built into the system unit of portable computers, but exist as stand-alone devices for computers that spend most of their time on a desk.

- **Network and Internet access.** Many personal computer systems include built-in circuitry for wired or wireless connections to a computer network. Networking features are useful for constructing a home network or connecting to public networks in coffee shops and airports. Internet connections require a modem. Modems that establish an Internet connection using a standard telephone line are often built into the system unit. Modems for cable, satellite, and other types of Internet access are usually separate components.

- **Printer.** A computer printer is an output device that produces computer-generated text or graphical images on paper.

TERMINOLOGY NOTE

The word *peripheral* is a relatively old part of computer jargon that dates back to the days of mainframes when the CPU was housed in a giant box and all input, output, and storage devices were housed separately. Technically, a peripheral is any device that is not part of the CPU.

In the world of personal computers, however, the use of the term *peripheral* varies and is often used to refer to any components that are not housed inside the system unit. Many personal computer owners do not think of a hard disk drive as a peripheral device, but technically it is one.

2

DESKTOP AND PORTABLE COMPUTERS

What is the significance of different computer designs? The industrial design principle that "form follows function" applies to computers. If you need a computer that's functional for mobile applications, you would not consider hauling around a large, heavy unit designed to remain on a desk. Instead, you would look for a computer "form" that suits your mobile "function."

In the computer industry, the term **form factor** refers to the size and dimensions of a component, such as a system board or system unit. Personal computers are available in all sorts of form factors; some are small and some are large; some are designed to remain on a desk, whereas others are designed to be portable.

What are the characteristics of desktop computers? A **desktop computer** fits on a desk and runs on power from an electrical wall outlet. The main component of a typical desktop computer is a system unit that houses the processor, memory, storage devices, display circuitry, and sound circuitry. A desktop computer's keyboard, mouse, and display screen are typically separate components that are connected to the main unit by cables or wireless technology.

The first personal computers were desktop models, and this style remains popular for offices, schools, and homes. Because their components can be manufactured economically, desktop computers typically provide the most computing power for your dollar. The price of an entry-level desktop computer starts at $300 or a bit less, but most consumers select more powerful models that cost between $800 and $1,100.

A desktop computer's system unit can be housed in a vertical case or a horizontal case. Most horizontal units are placed under the display device to save desk space. Horizontal system units were once the most common desktop computer form factor, however, they are much less popular now that manufacturers offer a wider variety of options.

One of those options is a vertical system unit, which can be placed on the desk, on the floor, or in a cubbyhole beneath the desk. The case for a vertical system unit is often referred to as a *tower*. Tower cases provide plenty of space for gamers and "modders" who want to soup up their machines by adding storage devices, lighted power cables, or accelerated graphics cards. Tower units are also the form factor of choice for computer owners who might want to upgrade components in the future because it is easy to get inside the case and swap out parts.

Another desktop computer option is a cube-shaped mini case, which is smaller than a tower unit and sometimes sports a handle. Mini cases are popular with gamers because they can be easily carried to LAN parties where they are networked together for multiplayer games.

Some manufacturers eliminate the separate system unit by incorporating computer circuitry in the back of a flat-panel screen or into a keyboard. Figure 2-2 illustrates some popular desktop form factors.

FIGURE 2-2

A desktop computer fits on a desk and is tethered to a wall outlet.

A tower unit can be placed on the desk or on the floor.

A small form factor desktop is easy to carry, but is not classified as a portable computer because it requires power from a wall outlet and does not run on batteries.

The circuitry for this desktop model is integrated into the case that holds the screen.

How do portable computers differ from desktops?

A **portable computer** (also referred to as a mobile computer) is a small, lightweight personal computer with screen, keyboard, storage, and processing components integrated into a single unit that runs on power supplied by an electrical outlet or a battery. Portable computers are ideal for mobile uses because they are easy to carry and can be used outdoors, in airports, and in classrooms without the need for a nearby electrical outlet. Portable computers are classified as notebooks, tablets, and ultra-mobiles (Figure 2-3).

What is a notebook computer?

A **notebook computer** (also referred to as a laptop), is a small, lightweight portable computer that opens like a clamshell to reveal a screen and keyboard. Notebook computers cost a bit more than desktop computers with similar computing power and storage capacity.

Notebook computers are coveted by students because they don't take up too much space in crowded dorm rooms and they are fairly easy to carry around campus. On average, a notebook computer weighs about 5 pounds, but some ultra-light notebooks weigh in at about 2 pounds. The price of an entry-level notebook computer starts around $500. Consumers often spend between $800 and $1,200, however, to get the features and performance they want. A fully-loaded notebook computer with widescreen display can cost more than $4,000.

What is a tablet computer?

A **tablet computer** is a portable computing device featuring a touch-sensitive screen that can be used as a writing or drawing pad. A *slate* tablet configuration resembles a high-tech clipboard and lacks a built-in keyboard (although one can be attached). A *convertible* tablet computer is constructed like a notebook computer, but the screen folds face up over the keyboard to provide a horizontal writing surface.

Tablet computers shine for applications that involve handwritten input. Most tablet computers are also configured to accept voice input. These capabilities are particularly useful for insurance adjusters who do most of their work at the scene of accidents and natural disasters, real estate agents who need access to data while out with clients, and healthcare workers who are moving quickly from one patient to the next.

When tablet computers were first introduced in 2002, they were priced significantly higher than notebook computers with similar processors and memory capacity. Currently, however, tablet computers are priced only slightly higher than equivalent notebook computers.

What is an ultra-mobile computer?

An **ultra-mobile PC** (UMPC) is a small form factor tablet computer designed to run most of the software available for larger portable computers. About the size of a paperback book and weighing in at 2 pounds or less, a typical UMPC does not have a physical keyboard, but one can be displayed on its small, touch-sensitive screen. UMPCs are equipped for wireless Internet access to the Web and e-mail. Many UMPCs are equipped with a camera and GPS and can be used to listen to music, watch videos, and play games. A typical UMPC costs from $500-$900.

FIGURE 2-3

Portable computers include a screen and keyboard in one unit and can run on batteries.

A notebook computer is small and lightweight, giving it the advantage of portability. It can be plugged into an electrical outlet, or it can run on battery power.

A slate is a type of tablet computer that's similar in size to a notebook computer, but features a touch-sensitive screen that can be used for input instead of a keyboard.

An ultra-mobile PC is a smaller, lighter version of the slate-style tablet computer.

HOME, MEDIA, GAME, AND SMALL BUSINESS SYSTEMS

What's the significance of designations, such as home, media, small business, or game systems? When studying computer ads and browsing vendor Web sites, you're likely to see some computer systems designated as home systems, whereas others are designated as game systems, small business systems, or media systems. These designations are created by computer vendors to help consumers sort through the sometimes mind-boggling variety of configuration options.

What differentiates a home computer from other types? The idea of a home computer system probably developed because Microsoft offered Home and Professional versions of the Windows operating system. Windows Home version targeted less sophisticated users and originally was not meant to be used extensively for networking.

Today, a **home computer system** offers a hardware platform with adequate, but not super-charged support for most computer applications, including Web browsing, e-mail, working with photos, downloading music, and working with general productivity applications, such as word processing. Software applications run at an acceptable speed, but graphics and games might be a bit slow.

The target market for home computer systems is families with young children and adults who are occasional users. A home system is often synonymous with a budget system, with prices starting at $300 including a display device.

What is a Media Center PC? Media Center PCs originated with a version of Windows that turned PCs into home entertainment devices. Today, the terms **Media Center PC**, entertainment PC, and media PC are used for any computers that include components for integrating computers, televisions, home theaters, and audio systems.

Key components of these media center computers include a remote control device and wireless keyboard that allow you to control your computer from your couch; a graphics system with TV tuner circuitry to display television programs on a computer screen; and software for displaying digital photos as a slide show on a computer screen, television, projection TV, computer projection device, or home theater (Figure 2-4). Media PCs also include a variety of connectors for speakers, VCRs, and cassette players.

FIGURE 2-4

Technologies such as Intel's Viiv and AMD's LIVE! are designed for entertainment and media PC systems that produce vivid graphics, smooth video, and vibrant surround sound.

What's so great about a gaming PC? Some of the most cutting-edge computers are designed for gaming. Not only do these machines feature the fastest processors, they are also stuffed with memory, include state-of-the-art sound capabilities, and feature dual graphics processors (Figure 2-5).

Although some manufacturers produce gaming notebook computers, most serious gamers tend to select desktop models because they are easier to customize and offer a little more power per dollar. Some overlap exists between media PCs and gaming PCs. Both may use the Windows Media Center Edition operating system for flexibility in handling video and music. Gamers like to have it all, so when they're taking a break from intense online multiplayer competition, they can relax and unwind watching their favorite Sci-Fi shows on their widescreen LCD screens.

The technophile features of a gaming computer come with a steep price premium. Computers start at $2000 and quickly climb past the $4000 price point.

What are the characteristics of small business computers? Computers marketed for small business applications tend to be middle-of-the-line models pared down to essentials. A medium-speed processor, moderate amount of RAM, and sensible disk capacity are adequate for basic business applications, such as word processing, spreadsheet analysis, accounting, and e-mail. Easy networking options allow small business computers to connect with other computers in an office environment.

With price tags under $1000, small business computers like those advertised in Figure 2-6 remain cost-effective because they are not loaded with memory, fancy graphics cards, or audio systems typical on home or media computers. Small business computers might not include a CD or DVD drive and often do not include speakers. The computers used in small businesses tend to be desktop models, rather than notebooks, because they are less expensive, easier to repair, and are less likely to be lost or stolen.

FIGURE 2-5

Game computers feature state-of-the-art components for processing, graphics, and audio.

2

NVIDIA® GeForce® 8800 GPUs and NVIDIA nForce® 600 Series MCPs
Redefine reality with the definitive gaming platform from NVIDIA. The new NVIDIA® GeForce® 8800 graphics processing units (GPUs) and NVIDIA nForce® 600 Series media communications processors (MCPs) are architected for maximum gaming performance. With up to 2X the performance of previous generations, GeForce 8800 GPUs provide unparalleled levels of graphics realism and image quality, while nForce 600 Series MCPs deliver incomparable system performance for both Intel and AMD processors.

GeForce 8800 GPUs   nForce 600 Series MCPs   BUY NOW

FIGURE 2-6

Small business owners want a cost effective solution without bells and whistles.

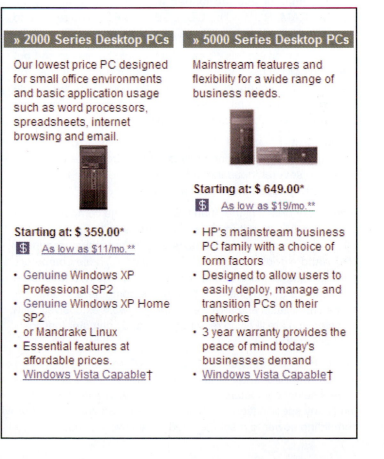

» 2000 Series Desktop PCs

Our lowest price PC designed for small office environments and basic application usage such as word processors, spreadsheets, internet browsing and email.

Starting at: $ 359.00*
$ As low as $11/mo.**

• Genuine Windows XP Professional SP2
• Genuine Windows XP Home SP2
• or Mandrake Linux
• Essential features at affordable prices.
• Windows Vista Capable†

» 5000 Series Desktop PCs

Mainstream features and flexibility for a wide range of business needs.

Starting at: $ 649.00*
$ As low as $19/mo.**

• HP's mainstream business PC family with a choice of form factors
• Designed to allow users to easily deploy, manage and transition PCs on their networks
• 3 year warranty provides the peace of mind today's businesses demand
• Windows Vista Capable†

BUYING COMPUTER SYSTEM COMPONENTS

How do I get started? The process of buying your own computer system is not cut and dried. Some experts advocate assessing your computing needs first, whereas other experts suggest researching features and prices. The trick is to do your homework for the entire system before jumping into a purchase of any one component. Remember that you will be purchasing peripherals, software, and accessories in addition to a computer. To prepare for a computer purchase you should complete the following activities:

- Browse through computer magazines and online computer stores to get a general idea of features and prices.

- Decide on a budget and stick to it.

- Make a list of the ways you plan to use your computer.

- Select a platform.

- Decide on a form factor.

- Select peripherals, software, and accessories.

Where can I find product information? You can start by looking at ads in current computer magazines, such as *PC Computing*, *PC Magazine*, *CPU*, and *MacWorld*. You might visit computer stores online or in a nearby mall to get a general idea of prices and features.

How can I make sense of all the jargon in computer ads? Computer ads are loaded with jargon and acronyms, such as RAM, ROM MHz, GB, USB, and PCI. You're sure to spot lots of this computer lingo in ads like the one in Figure 2-7.

When you complete this chapter, you should be able to sort out the terminology used in a typical computer ad. For terms you encounter that are not covered in this textbook, you can google the term or refer to online dictionaries and encyclopedias, such as Webopedia, Whatis.com, or Wikipedia.

What can I expect to pay for a new computer? Computers are sold at price points ranging from a few hundred dollars to several thousand dollars. Computer price points can be roughly grouped into three categories.

A computer priced higher than US$2,000 is the computer equivalent of a luxury automobile. Computers in this price range contain one or more fast processors, a generous amount of RAM, and a copious amount of disk space. These computers contain state-of-the-art components and should not have to be replaced as quickly as less expensive computers. Computer game enthusiasts and anyone planning to work extensively with video editing are likely to require a high-end computer that costs over US$2,000.

Computers that retail for between US$800 and $2,000 might be considered the four-door sedans of the computer marketplace because a majority of buyers select computers in this price range. These popular computers lack the flashy specifications of their state-of-the-art cousins, but provide ample computing power to meet the needs of an average user.

FIGURE 2-7

A typical computer ad provides specifications couched in lots of computer jargon.

- Intel Core 2 Duo 6700 processor 2.66 GHz with Virtualization Technology 1066 MHz FSB
- 4 MB L2 cache
- 2 GB 533 MHz SDRAM (max. 4 GB)
- 250 GB SATA HD (7200 rpm)
- 48X CD-RW + 16X DVD+RW/+R with double layer write capable
- 19" LCD TV/monitor
- 512 MB NVidia PCI graphics card
- Sound Blaster PCI sound card
- Altec Lansing speakers
- Mouse and keyboard
- External drive bays: 2 5.25" bays for disk, tape, or CD drives; 1 3.5" bay for a floppy drive
- Internal drive bays: 1 HDD bay
- 8 USB ports: 2 front, 6 back
- 2 serial, 1 parallel, and 1 video port
- 1 network port (RJ45 connector)
- 4 PCI slots and 1 AGP slot
- Windows Vista operating system
- Home/small business software bundle
- 3-year limited warranty

In the computer industry, the equivalent of a compact car is a sub-$800 computer. The technology in these computers is usually a year or two old and you can expect reduced processor speed, memory capacity, and drive capacity. Nevertheless, budget computers feature many of the same components that owners coveted in their state-of-the-art computers a few years back. You might have to replace a budget computer sooner than a more expensive computer, but it should be serviceable for typical applications.

Why is it important to figure out how I'm going to use my new computer? Computers can help you perform such a wide variety of tasks that it can be impossible to predict all the ways you might use your new machine in the future. You can, however, make a list of the ways you plan to immediately use your computer and that list can help you think about the features you'll need. Some computer-based activities require more processing or storage capacity than others. Therefore, if you have some ideas about your computer usage, you're more likely to buy the right computer and not have to purchase expensive upgrades for it later. Figure 2-8 offers some guidelines to help you evaluate how your plan for using a computer might affect your purchase decision.

FIGURE 2-8

Situations such as those listed in the left column help to narrow down the mind-boggling number of choices offered to computer shoppers.

Usage Plan	Purchase Recommendation
You plan to use your computer for popular tasks such as e-mail, browsing the Web, playing a few games, managing your checkbook, downloading digital music, and writing school papers.	A mid-priced computer with standard features might meet your needs.
You're on a budget.	A budget-priced computer will handle the same applications as a mid-priced computer, but some tasks might run more slowly.
You plan to work on accounting and budgeting for a small business.	Consider one of the business systems offered by your computer vendor.
You spend lots of time playing computer games.	Buy a computer with the fastest processor and graphics card you can afford.
You plan to work extensively with video editing or desktop publishing.	Select a computer system with a fast processor, lots of hard disk capacity, and a graphics card loaded with memory.
Someone who will use the computer has special needs.	Consider purchasing appropriate adaptive equipment, such as a voice synthesizer or one-handed keyboard.
You plan to use specialized peripheral devices.	Make sure the computer you purchase can accommodate the devices you plan to use.
Your work at home overlaps your work at school or on the job.	Shop for a computer that's compatible with the ones you use at school or work.
You want to work with specific software, such as a game or graphics tool.	Make sure you select a computer that meets the specifications listed on the software box or Web site.
You're buying a new computer to replace an old one.	If you have a big investment in software, you should select a new computer that's compatible with the old one.

How important is compatibility? Suppose that you want to do some assignments at home using the same software provided by your school lab. Maybe you want to transport data back and forth between your job and home. Or, perhaps your child wants to use a computer at home like the one at school. Computers that operate in essentially the same way are said to be *compatible*. To assess whether two computers are compatible, you have to consider if they run the same software and use the same peripheral devices.

Today, there are three personal computer platforms: PC, Mac, and Linux. The **PC platform** is based on the design for one of the first personal computer superstars—the IBM PC. The great grandchildren of the IBM PC are on computer store shelves today—a huge selection of personal computer brands and models manufactured by companies such as Lenovo, Hewlett-Packard, Dell, and Gateway. The Windows operating system was designed specifically for these personal computers and, therefore, the PC platform is sometimes called the Windows platform. Most of the examples in this book pertain to PCs because they are so popular.

The **Mac platform** is based on a proprietary design for a personal computer called the Macintosh (or Mac), manufactured almost exclusively by Apple Inc. The Mac lineup includes the iMac, MacBook, Mac mini, and Mac Pro computers, all running the Mac OS operating system.

At one time, the PC and Mac platforms were not compatible because of hardware and operating system differences. Application software designed for Macs did not typically work with PCs and vice versa.

The compatibility situation has changed because many Mac computers now use the same microprocessors as PCs. If you have a Mac computer with an Intel processor (sometimes called an Intel Mac), you can install Windows on it and run Windows software.

The ability to run Windows offers Mac owners access to software from the PC and Mac platforms, and makes it possible to use the Mac OS to run one application, then switch to Windows to run another application. This capability can come in handy, for example, if a parent who uses Windows software is sharing a computer with an elementary-school student who is working with Macs at school.

The **Linux platform** is essentially a standard PC with the Linux operating system installed. As with Intel Macs, Linux computers can be configured to boot into either Linux or Windows operating systems. Linux is typically the platform selected for technical applications.

What about software? Most computers are sold with a pre-installed operating system, which typically includes a Web browser and e-mail software. Some computers are bundled with application software that you can use to create documents, crunch numbers, and produce presentations. Check the software situation carefully. The trend today is for manufacturers to install trial software that you can use free for a few months. To continue using the software beyond the trial period, however, you have to pay for it. Such software is "included" but not "free." Buyer beware.

If you're purchasing a computer to do a task that requires specialized software, you should factor its cost into the cost of your computer system. Check the specifications listed on the software box to make sure your new computer has enough memory and processing speed to run it.

TERMINOLOGY NOTE

Computers that are compatible with the PC platform are usually referred to simply as PCs. Computers in the Mac platform are referred to as Macs.

Can I upgrade a computer to make it more powerful?
When shopping for a computer system, your budget might not stretch to cover the cost of all the equipment you want. Or, you might wonder if you can extend the life of your current computer by upgrading key components. Some components are easy to add or change, whereas others are not. Figure 2-9 summarizes the most popular computer equipment upgrades, indicates their average time for completion, cost, difficulty level, and accessibility.

FIGURE 2-9

Popular upgrades at a glance; in the Accessibility column, internal upgrades require you to open the system unit.

2

Upgrade	Time	Cost (US$)	Difficulty	Accessibility
Replace processor	1-5 hours	$200-600	Difficult and not recommended	Internal
Add memory	30-60 minutes	$50-300	Moderate	Internal
Add external hard drive	10-15 minutes	$100-300	Easy	External
Replace internal hard disk drive	1-2 hours	$50-500	Somewhat difficult	Internal
Replace graphics card	1 hour	$150-500	Moderate	Internal
Switch to wireless keyboard and mouse	15 minutes	$50-100	Easy	External
Add USB port or digital camera memory card reader	15 minutes	$20-200	Easy	External
Add second display screen	5-10 minutes	$250-500	Easy	External
Add or replace speakers	5-10 minutes	$50-500	Easy	External
Replace CD or DVD drive	1-2 hours	$50-150	Moderate	Internal

What is a mod?
Upgrades and add-ons, such as those listed in Figure 2-9, are usually sanctioned and approved by computer manufacturers and vendors. However, some creative computer owners, called modders, work with unsanctioned modifications. In the context of computing a **mod** is a custom, hand-built modification to a computer system component.

Mods are analogous to hotrods in many ways. Just as hot rod construction begins with a standard car chassis, a computer mod begins with standard, off-the-shelf components. Hot rods can be chopped and jacked, fenders removed, windows added, engines chromed, and chassis painted in day-glo colors. Computer mods often include custom paint jobs, glowing lights, and clear plexiglass side panels that offer a view of the system board.

Where do modders find components?
Modders have built computers using discarded microwave ovens, vintage televisions, gumball machines, Legos, suitcases, and toys—all items that can be picked up in thrift stores or rummage sales.

Electronic components, such as cold cathode lights and neon string lights, can be scavenged from a variety of sources. Radio Shack offers a collection of products for modders, but a much more extensive selection of modding components can be found at Web sites that specialize in modding. Figure 2-10 illustrates a creative mod that uses see-through and lighting effects.

FIGURE 2-10

Mods are customized computers that sport radical modifications, such as see-through cases and lighted cables.

Where is the best place to buy a computer? Consumers have many choices for computer vendors. Manufacturers such as Dell and Apple sell computers online at company Web sites, where you can easily configure a computer system with various features and get a price quote. The Web hosts a wide array of computer vendors. Make sure you are dealing with a reputable vendor before finalizing your purchase and providing your credit card number.

Computers and peripherals are also sold at office stores, such as OfficeMax, and electronics stores, such as Best Buy or Circuit City. You might have the option of working with a locally-owned computer boutique. Most consumer advocates suggest shopping around, comparing prices, service, and warranties.

Before you make a final decision on computer equipment or software, ask the following questions: Does your new equipment or software come with technical support? How long does the support last? How can you contact technical support? Is it free? Is the support staff knowledgeable? What is the duration of the equipment warranty? Does it cover the cost of parts and labor? Where do repairs take place? Who pays shipping costs for equipment that is sent to the manufacturer for repair? How long do repairs typically take? With the answers to these questions in hand along with your decisions about budget, form factor, and platform, you can be confident that you're making a savvy computer purchase.

QuickCheck

1. Popular [   ] devices include printers, digital cameras, scanners, joysticks, and speakers.

2. The first popular personal computers were [   ] models, and this style remains popular for offices, schools, and homes.

3. Portable computers are classified as notebooks, [   ], and ultra-mobiles.

4. Key components of a(n) [   ] Center PC include a remote control device, TV tuner, and Viiv or similar technology.

5. To assess whether two computers are [   ], you have to consider if they run the same software and use the same peripheral devices.

 CHECK ANSWERS

SECTION B

Microprocessors and Memory

A TYPICAL COMPUTER AD contains a long list of specifications that describe a computer's components and capabilities. Savvy shoppers understand how these specifications affect computer performance and price. Most computer specifications begin with the microprocessor type and speed. Computer manufacturers want consumers to think that faster is better, but is there a point at which you can pay for speed you won't need? Computer ads also contain information about a computer's memory capacity. Lots of memory can add hundreds of dollars to the cost of a computer. Consumers are right to ask "How much RAM is enough?" Section B explains how microprocessors and memory affect computer performance and price.

MICROPROCESSOR BASICS

What exactly is a microprocessor? As you learned in Chapter 1, a microprocessor (sometimes simply referred to as a processor) is an integrated circuit designed to process instructions. It is the most important, and usually the most expensive, component of a computer. Although a microprocessor is sometimes mistakenly referred to as a computer on a chip, it can be more accurately described as a CPU on a chip because it contains—on a single chip—circuitry that performs essentially the same tasks as the central processing unit (CPU) of a classic mainframe computer.

What does it look like? Looking inside a computer, you can usually identify the microprocessor because it is the largest chip on the system board, although it might be hidden under a cooling fan. Most of today's microprocessors are housed in a PGA (pin grid array) chip package, as shown in Figure 2-11.

What makes one microprocessor perform better than another? Computer ads typically include microprocessor specifications related to performance. For example, an ad might describe a microprocessor as "Intel® Core 2 Duo 2.66 GHz, 1066 MHz FSB, 4 MB Cache." A microprocessor's performance is affected by several factors, including clock speed, bus speed, word size, cache size, instruction set, and processing techniques.

What do MHz and GHz have to do with computer performance? A specification, such as 2.66 GHz, that you see in a computer ad indicates the speed of the **microprocessor clock**—a timing device that sets the pace for executing instructions. Most computer ads specify the speed of a microprocessor in megahertz or gigahertz. **Megahertz** (MHz) means a million cycles per second. **Gigahertz** (GHz) means a billion cycles per second.

A cycle is the smallest unit of time in a microprocessor's universe. Every action a processor performs is measured by these cycles. It is important, however, to understand that the clock speed is not equal to the number

FIGURE 2-11

Today's microprocessors are typically housed in a PGA chip package.

of instructions a processor can execute in one second. In many computers, some instructions occur within one cycle, but other instructions might require multiple cycles. Some processors can even execute several instructions in a single clock cycle.

A specification such as 2.66 GHz means that the microprocessor's clock operates at a speed of 2.66 billion cycles per second. All other things being equal, a computer with a 2.66 GHz processor is faster than a computer with a 1.5 GHz processor or a 933 MHz processor (Figure 2-12).

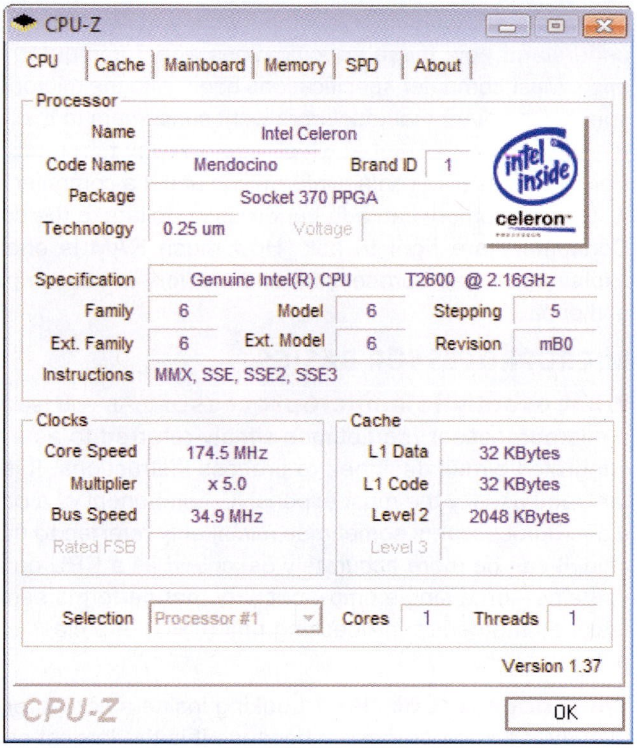

Some chipmakers differentiate chips by clock speed whereas other chipmakers use model numbers, called processor numbers (PN). Processor numbers do not correspond to a particular clock speed but they can indicate speed relative to other processors within the same family. For example, the Core 2 Duo 6700 processor has a higher processor number and is faster than the Core 2 Duo 4500. Processor numbers cannot be compared across product families, however. An Intel M 755 processor is not faster than the Pentium 4 560. Even though 755 is a larger number than 560, the M processor and Pentium 4 are in different processor families. Their processor numbers cannot be compared to each other.

What is FSB? FSB stands for **front side bus**, a term that refers to the circuitry that transports data to and from the microprocessor. A fast front side bus moves data quickly and allows the processor to work at full capacity. In today's computers, FSB speed (technically its frequency) is measured in megahertz (MHz) and ranges from 200 MHz to 1250 MHz. Higher numbers indicate faster FSB speeds. Some processor manufacturers use a technology called **HyperTransport** to increase the speed of data moving to the processor.

What impact does word size have on performance? **Word size** refers to the number of bits that a microprocessor can manipulate at one time. Word size is based on the size of registers in the ALU and the capacity of circuits that lead to those registers. A processor with a 32-bit word size, for example, has 32-bit registers, processes 32 bits at a time, and is referred to as a 32-bit processor. Processors with a larger word size can process more data during each processor cycle—a factor that leads to increased computer performance. Today's personal computers typically contain 32-bit or 64-bit processors.

How does the cache size affect performance? **Cache** (pronounced "cash") is special high-speed memory that allows a microprocessor to access data more rapidly than from memory located elsewhere on the system board. A large cache can increase computer performance. Some computer ads specify cache type and capacity. A **Level 1 cache** (L1) is built into the processor chip, whereas a **Level 2 cache** (L2) is located on a separate chip and takes a little more time to get data to the processor. Cache capacity is usually measured in kilobytes.

FIGURE 2-12

Computer ads provide processor specifications, but how about the processor in your current computer? You can discover your processor's specs using the Windows Control Panel or third-party software, such as CPU-Z.

TERMINOLOGY NOTE

Other terms for front side bus include system bus and memory bus.

Cache is sometimes called RAM cache, cache memory, CPU cache, or internal cache.

How does an instruction set affect performance? As chip designers developed various instruction sets for microprocessors, they added increasingly complex instructions, each requiring several clock cycles for execution. A microprocessor with such an instruction set uses **CISC** (complex instruction set computer) technology. A microprocessor with a limited set of simple instructions uses **RISC** (reduced instruction set computer) technology. A RISC processor performs most instructions faster than a CISC processor. It might, however, require more of these simple instructions to complete a task than a CISC processor requires for the same task. Most processors in today's personal computers use CISC technology.

A processor's ability to handle graphics can be enhanced by adding specialized graphics and multimedia instructions to a processor's instruction set. 3DNow!, MMX, and SSE-3 are examples of instruction set enhancements sometimes mentioned in computer ads. Although instruction set enhancements have the potential to speed up games, graphics software, and video editing, they offer speed enhancements only with software designed to utilize these specialized instructions.

Can a microprocessor execute more than one instruction at a time? Some processors execute instructions "serially"—that is, one instruction at a time. With **serial processing**, the processor must complete all steps in the instruction cycle before it begins to execute the next instruction. However, using a technology called **pipelining**, a processor can begin executing an instruction before it completes the previous instruction. Many of today's microprocessors also perform **parallel processing**, in which multiple instructions are executed at the same time. Pipelining and parallel processing, illustrated in Figure 2-13, enhance processor performance.

To get a clearer picture of serial, pipelining, and parallel processing technology, consider an analogy in which computer instructions are pizzas. Serial processing executes only one instruction at a time, just like a pizzeria with one oven that holds only one pizza. Pipelining is similar to a pizza conveyor belt. A pizza (instruction) starts moving along the conveyor belt into the oven, but before it reaches the end, another pizza starts moving along the belt. Parallel processing is similar to a pizzeria with many ovens. Just as these ovens can bake more than one pizza at a time, a parallel processor can execute more than one instruction at a time.

What's a multi-core processor? A single microprocessor that contains circuitry for more than one processing unit is called a **multi-core processor**. Today's dual-core and quad-core processors are faster than those with a single core. To gain maximum speed, however, your computer's operating system and software should be optimized for multi-core processing. Windows supports it, as do some games and graphics software.

What is HT? The abbreviation HT (or HTT), which appears in many computer ads, stands for **Hyper-Threading Technology** and refers to circuitry that enables a single processor to simulate two processors. Hyper-Threading speeds up some applications, but does not offer the performance boost of dual core technology.

With so many factors to consider, how can I compare microprocessor performance? Various testing laboratories run a series of tests to gauge the overall speed of a microprocessor. The results of these tests—called **benchmarks**—can then be compared to the results for other microprocessors. The results of benchmark tests are usually available on the Web and published in computer magazine articles.

FIGURE 2-13

Microprocessor designers have developed techniques for serial processing, pipelining, and parallel processing.

In serial processing, one instruction is processed at a time.

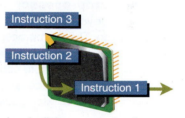

In pipelining, an instruction can begin to be processed before the previous instruction's processing is complete.

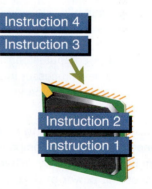

In parallel processing, multiple instructions can be processed at the same time.

TODAY'S MICROPROCESSORS

Which companies produce most of today's popular micro-processors? Intel is the world's largest chipmaker and supplies a sizeable percentage of the microprocessors that power PCs. In 1971, Intel introduced the world's first microprocessor—the 4004. Intel's 8088 processor powered the original IBM PC. Since the debut of the IBM PC in 1985, Intel has introduced numerous microprocessors that have been used by most major computer manufacturers.

AMD (Advanced Micro Devices) is Intel's chief rival in the PC chip market. AMD's Athlon and Opteron processors are direct competitors to Intel's Core, Pentium, and Itanium lines (Figure 2-14). AMD processors are less expensive than comparable Intel models and have a slight performance advantage according to some benchmarks.

Historically, Motorola and IBM were the main chip suppliers for Apple computers, but Apple began a transition to Intel chips in 2005. IBM produces RISC-based POWER processors for servers and other high-performance computers. Transmeta Corporation specializes in chips for mobile computing devices, such as tablet computers.

Which microprocessor is best for my PC? The microprocessor that's best for you depends on your budget and the type of work and play you plan to do. The microprocessors marketed with the current crop of computers can handle most business, educational, and entertainment applications. You'll want to consider the fastest processor offerings if you typically engage in processing-hungry activities, such as 3-D animated computer games, desktop publishing, multitrack sound recording, or video editing.

Can I replace my computer's microprocessor with a faster one? It is technically possible to upgrade your computer's microprocessor, but computer owners rarely do so. The price of the latest, greatest microprocessor can often get you more than halfway to buying an entirely new computer system. Technical factors also discourage microprocessor upgrades. A microprocessor operates at full efficiency only if all components in the computer can handle the faster speeds. In many cases, installing a new processor in an old computer can be like attaching a huge outboard engine to a canoe. In both cases, too much power can lead to disaster.

What is overclocking? Overclocking is a technique for increasing the speed of a computer component, such as a processor, graphics card, system board, or memory. When successful, overclocking can increase the processing power of a slow component to match that of a faster, more expensive component. Overclocking is popular with gamers who want to squeeze every bit of processing speed out of their computers.

Why doesn't everyone overclock? Overclocking is very risky. Additional electrical power pumped into a component increases heat output. Overclocked components can overheat and even catch fire. To maintain safe operating temperatures, modders install supplemental cooling systems, sometimes using heavy-duty heatsinks, big fans, liquid oxygen, dry ice, or other refrigerants.

FIGURE 2-14

Today's popular server, desktop, and mobile microprocessors.

Processor	Application
Core	Desktops, portables
Xeon	Servers
Itanium	Servers
Pentium D	Servers, desktops
Pentium 4	Servers, desktops
Pentium Extreme Edition	Desktops
Celeron Celeron M	Desktops Portables
Pentium M	Notebooks, PDAs
Mobile Pentium 4	Notebooks, PDAs

AMD

Opteron	Servers
Athlon 64	Desktops, portables
Athlon X2 Dual-Core	Desktops, portables
Turion 64	Notebooks, PDAs
Sempron	Desktops
Mobile Sempron	Notebooks, PDAs

INFOWEBLINKS

For updates on popular microprocessors, you can connect to the **Microprocessor Update InfoWeb**.

CLICK TO CONNECT
www.course.com/np/concepts11/ch02

RANDOM ACCESS MEMORY

What is RAM? RAM (random access memory) is a temporary holding area for data, application program instructions, and the operating system. In a personal computer, RAM is usually several chips or small circuit boards that plug into the system board within the computer's system unit. A computer's RAM capacity is invariably included in the list of specifications in a computer ad (Figure 2-15).

The amount of RAM in a computer can affect the overall price of a computer system. To understand how much RAM your computer needs and to understand computer ad terminology, it is handy to have a little background on how RAM works and what it does.

Why is RAM so important? RAM is the "waiting room" for the computer's processor. It holds raw data waiting to be processed as well as the program instructions for processing that data. In addition, RAM holds the results of processing until they can be stored more permanently on disk or tape (Figure 2-16).

FIGURE 2-15

A computer ad typically specifies the amount and type of RAM.

- Intel Core 2 Duo 6700 processor 2.66 GHz 1066 MHz FSB
- 2 MB L2 cache
- 2 GB 533 MHz SDRAM (max. 4 GB)
- 160 GB SATA HD (7200 rpm)
- 48X CD-RW + 16X DVD+RW/+R with double layer write capable

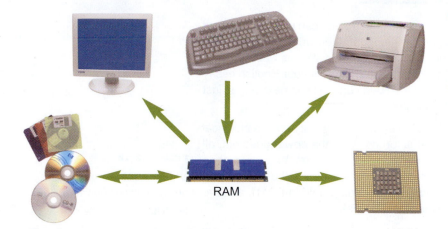

RAM

FIGURE 2-16

RAM is the computer equivalent of the waiting room at an airport or a train station. It holds data waiting to be processed, stored, displayed, or printed.

Let's look at an example. When you use personal finance software to balance your checkbook, you enter raw data for check amounts, which is held in RAM. The personal finance software sends to RAM the instructions for processing this data. The processor uses these instructions to calculate your checkbook balance and sends the results back to RAM. From RAM, your checkbook balance can be stored on disk, displayed, or printed.

In addition to data and application software instructions, RAM also holds operating system instructions that control the basic functions of a computer system. These instructions are loaded into RAM every time you start your computer, and they remain there until you turn off your computer.

How does RAM differ from hard-disk storage? People who are new to computers sometimes tend to confuse RAM and hard-disk storage, maybe because both components hold data, because they typically are "hidden" inside the system unit, or because they can both be measured in gigabytes. To differentiate between RAM and hard-disk storage, remember that RAM holds data in circuitry that's directly connected to the system board, whereas hard-disk storage places data on magnetic media. RAM is temporary storage; hard-disk storage is more permanent. In addition, RAM usually has less storage capacity than hard-disk storage.

How does RAM work? In RAM, microscopic electronic parts called **capacitors** hold the bits that represent data. You can visualize the capacitors as microscopic lights that can be turned on or off. A charged capacitor is "turned on" and represents a "1" bit. A discharged capacitor is "turned off" and represents a "0" bit. Each bank of capacitors holds eight bits—one byte of data. A RAM address on each bank helps the computer locate data, as needed, for processing (Figure 2-17).

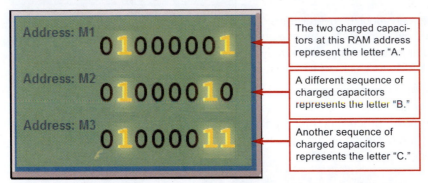

Address: M1 — 01000001 — The two charged capacitors at this RAM address represent the letter "A."

Address: M2 — 01000010 — A different sequence of charged capacitors represents the letter "B."

Address: M3 — 01000011 — Another sequence of charged capacitors represents the letter "C."

FIGURE 2-17

Each RAM location has an address and uses eight capacitors to hold the eight bits that represent a byte.

▶ CLICK TO START

In some respects, RAM is similar to a chalkboard. You can use a chalkboard to write mathematical formulas, erase them, and then write an outline for a report. In a similar way, RAM can hold numbers and formulas when you balance your checkbook, and then can hold the outline of your English essay when you use word processing software. RAM contents can be changed just by changing the charge of the capacitors.

Unlike disk storage, most RAM is **volatile**, which means it requires electrical power to hold data. If the computer is turned off or the power goes out, all data stored in RAM instantly and permanently disappears. When someone exclaims, "Rats! I just lost my document," it often means the person was entering the text of a document (which was being held in RAM), and the power went out before the data was saved on disk.

How much RAM does my computer need? RAM capacity is expressed in megabytes or gigabytes. Today's personal computers typically feature between 512 MB and 2 GB of RAM. The amount of RAM your computer needs depends on the software you use. RAM requirements are routinely specified on the outside of a software package (Figure 2-18). If you need more RAM, you can purchase and install additional memory up to the limit the computer manufacturer sets. For good basic performance, a computer running Windows Vista should have at least 1 GB of RAM. Games, desktop publishing, graphics, and video applications tend to run more smoothly with at least 2 GB of RAM.

Can my computer run out of memory? Suppose that you want to work with several programs and large graphics at the same time. Will your computer eventually run out of memory? The answer is "probably not." Today's personal computer operating systems are quite adept at allocating RAM space to multiple programs. If a program exceeds its allocated space, the operating system uses an area of the hard disk, called **virtual memory**, to store parts of programs or data files until they are needed. By selectively exchanging the data in RAM with the data in virtual memory, your computer effectively gains almost unlimited memory capacity.

Too much dependence on virtual memory can slow down your computer's performance, however, because getting data from a mechanical device, such as a hard disk drive, is much slower than getting data from an elec-

FIGURE 2-18

Minimum RAM requirements are typically displayed on the package of a software product.

Minimum System Requirements:

- Windows XP or Vista
- 1 GB of RAM
- 450 MB hard drive space
- CD drive for installation
- Mouse
- Internet connection (optional)
- Printer (optional)
- Scanner or digital camera with 32-bit twain interface (optional)

tronic device, such as RAM. To minimize virtual memory use, load up your computer with as much RAM as possible.

Do all computers use the same type of RAM? No. RAM components vary in speed, technology, and configuration. Many computer ads provide information on all three aspects of RAM, but consumers who want lots of fast RAM for 3-D gaming and desktop publishing have to wade through a thicket of acronyms and technical jargon. To unlock the meaning of RAM specifications, such as "1 GB 675 MHz Dual-Channel DDR2 SDRAM," you need an understanding of a few more acronyms and abbreviations.

RAM speed is often expressed in nanoseconds or megahertz. One **nanosecond** (ns) is 1 billionth of a second. In the context of RAM speed, lower nanosecond ratings are better because it means the RAM circuitry can react faster to update the data it holds. For example, 8 ns RAM is faster than 10 ns RAM.

RAM speed can also be expressed in MHz (millions of cycles per second). Just the opposite of nanoseconds, higher MHz ratings mean faster speeds. For example, 675 MHz RAM is faster than 400 MHz RAM.

Most of today's personal computers use SDRAM or RDRAM. SDRAM (synchronous dynamic RAM) is fast and relatively inexpensive. Innovations, such as dual-channel technology and double data rate (DDR or DDR2) have increased SDRAM speed. RDRAM (rambus dynamic RAM) was first developed for the popular Nintendo 64 game system and then adapted for use in personal computers. RDRAM is more expensive than SDRAM and is usually found in high-performance workstations. RAM is configured as a series of DIP chips soldered onto a small circuit board, as shown in Figure 2-19.

FIGURE 2-19

SDRAM is the most popular type of RAM in today's computers. It is typically available on a small circuit board called a DIMM (dual inline memory module). When adding memory to a computer, check with the computer manufacturer to make sure you purchase the correct RAM type and speed.

READ-ONLY MEMORY

How is ROM different from RAM? **ROM** (read-only memory) is a type of memory circuitry that holds the computer's startup routine. ROM is housed in a single integrated circuit—usually a fairly large, caterpillar-like DIP package—which is plugged into the system board.

Whereas RAM is temporary and volatile, ROM is permanent and non-volatile. ROM holds "hard-wired" instructions that are a permanent part of the circuitry and remain in place even when the computer power is turned off. This is a familiar concept to anyone who has used a hand calculator that includes various hard-wired routines for calculating square roots, cosines, and other functions. The instructions in ROM are permanent, and the only way to change them is to replace the ROM chip.

If a computer has RAM, why does it need ROM too? When you turn on your computer, the microprocessor receives electrical power and is ready to begin executing instructions. As a result of the power being off, however, RAM is empty and doesn't contain any instructions for the microprocessor to execute. Now ROM plays its part. ROM contains a small set of instructions called the **ROM BIOS** (basic input/output system). These instructions tell the computer how to access the hard disk, find the operating system, and load it into RAM. After the operating system is loaded, the computer can understand your input, display output, run software, and access your data.

EEPROM

Where does a computer store its basic hardware settings? To operate correctly, a computer must have some basic information about storage, memory, and display configurations. For example, your computer needs to know how much memory is available so that it can allocate space for all the programs you want to run.

RAM goes blank when the computer power is turned off, so configuration information cannot be stored there. ROM would not be a good place for this information, either, because it holds data on a permanent basis. If, for example, your computer stored the memory size in ROM, you could never add more memory—well, you might be able to add it, but you couldn't change the size specification in ROM. To store some basic system information, your computer needs a type of memory that's more permanent than RAM, but less permanent than ROM. EEPROM is just the ticket.

EEPROM (electrically erasable programmable read-only memory) is a non-volatile chip that requires no power to hold data. EEPROMs replace CMOS technology that required power from a small battery integrated into the system board.

When you change the configuration of your computer system—by adding RAM, for example—the data in EEPROM must be updated. Some operating systems recognize such changes and automatically perform the update. You can manually change EEPROM settings by running your computer's setup program, as described in Figure 2-20.

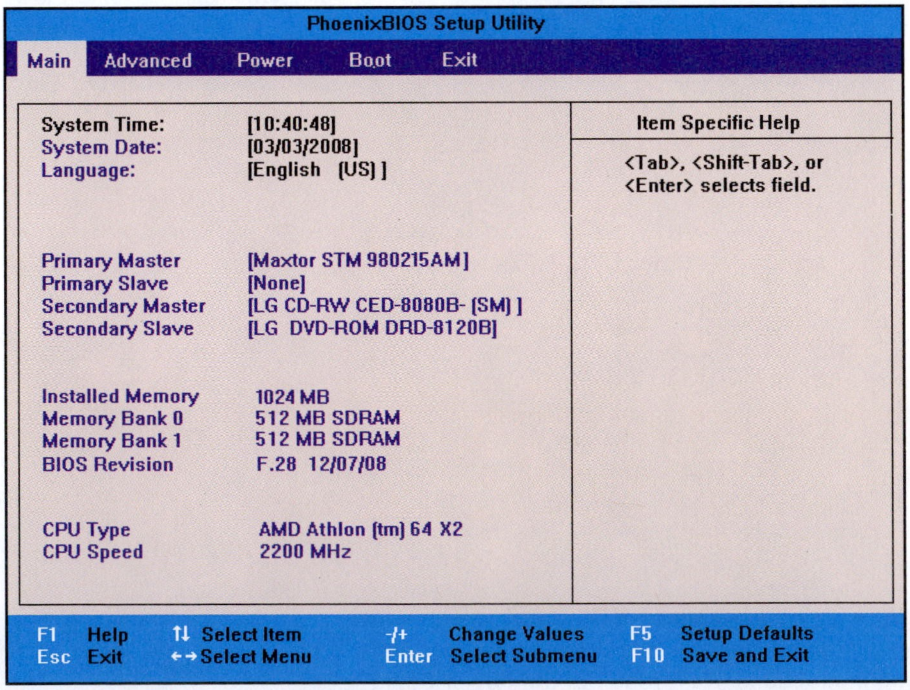

FIGURE 2-20

EEPROM holds computer configuration settings, such as the date and time, hard disk capacity, number of floppy disk drives, and RAM capacity. To access the EEPROM setup program, hold down the F1 key as your computer boots. But be careful! If you make a mistake with these settings, your computer might not be able to start.

If you mistakenly enter the Setup program, follow the on-screen instructions to exit and proceed with the boot process. In Figure 2-20, the Esc (Escape) key allows you to exit the Setup program without making any changes to the EEPROM settings.

What information about memory performance is most important? Even though ROM and EEPROM have important roles in the operation of a computer, RAM capacity really makes a difference you can notice. The more data and programs that can fit into RAM, the less time your computer will spend moving data to and from virtual memory. With lots of RAM, you'll find that documents scroll faster, games respond more quickly, and many graphics operations take less time than with a computer that has a skimpy RAM capacity.

Most ads specify RAM capacity, speed, and type. Now when you see the specification "1 GB 675 MHz Dual-Channel DDR2 SDRAM (max. 2 GB)" in a computer ad, you'll know that the computer's RAM capacity is 1 gigabyte (enough to run Windows Vista), that it operates at 675 megahertz (fairly fast), and that it uses dual-channel, double data rate SDRAM. You'll also have important information about the maximum amount of RAM that can be installed in the computer—2 GB, which is more than enough for the typical computer owner who does a bit of word processing, surfs the Web, and plays computer games.

QuickCheck

SECTION B

1. A microprocessor's [   ] speed is provided in a specification such as 3.6 GHz.

2. Some chipmakers use a [   ] number, such as 560, to differentiate microprocessors.

3. A front side [   ] is circuitry that transports data to and from the processor at speeds ranging from 200 MHz to 1250 MHz.

4. A dual [   ] processor allows a computer to execute multiple instructions at the same time to achieve parallel processing.

5. RAM is [   ], which means that it cannot hold data when the computer power is off.

6. A computer does not usually run out of RAM because it can use an area of the hard disk called [   ] memory.

7. The instructions for loading the operating system into RAM when a computer is first turned on are stored in [   ]. Hint: Use the abbreviation.

 CHECK ANSWERS

Storage Devices

COMPUTER MANUFACTURERS typically try to entice consumers by configuring computers with a variety of storage devices, such as a hard disk drive, solid-state card readers, and some sort of CD or DVD drive. What's the point of having so many storage devices? As it turns out, none of today's storage technologies is perfect. One technology might provide fast access to data, but it might also be susceptible to problems that could potentially wipe out all your data. A different technology might be more dependable, but it might have the disadvantage of relatively slow access to data.

Smart shoppers make sure their new computers are equipped with a variety of storage devices. Informed computer owners understand the strengths and weaknesses of each storage technology so that they can use these devices with maximum effectiveness. In this section, you'll find guidelines that can make you a smart storage technology buyer and owner. The storage technologies you'll learn about are now used in a variety of devices—from digital cameras to player pianos—so an understanding of storage technology can be useful even outside the boundaries of personal computing.

STORAGE BASICS

What are the basic components of a data storage system? A data storage system has two main components: a storage medium and a storage device. A **storage medium** (storage media is the plural) is the disk, tape, CD, DVD, paper, or other substance that contains data. A **storage device** is the mechanical apparatus that records and retrieves data from a storage medium. Storage devices include hard disk drives, floppy disk drives, tape drives, CD drives, DVD drives, and flash drives. The term *storage technology* refers to a storage device and the media it uses.

How does a storage system interact with other computer components? You can think of your computer's storage devices as having a direct pipeline to RAM. Data gets copied from a storage device into RAM, where it waits to be processed. After data is processed, it is held temporarily in RAM, but it is usually copied to a storage medium for more permanent safekeeping.

As you know, a computer's processor works with data that has been coded into bits that can be represented by 1s and 0s. When data is stored, these 1s and 0s must be converted into some kind of signal or mark that's fairly permanent, but can be changed when necessary.

Obviously, the data is not literally written as "1" or "0." Instead, the 1s and 0s must be transformed into changes in the surface of a storage medium. Exactly how this transformation happens depends on the storage technology. For example, hard disks store data in a different way than CDs. Three types of storage technologies are commonly used for personal computers: magnetic, optical, and solid state.

> **TERMINOLOGY NOTE**
>
> The process of storing data is often referred to as writing data or saving a file because the storage device writes the data on the storage medium to save it for later use.
>
> The process of retrieving data is often referred to as reading data, loading data, or opening a file.

Which storage technology is best? Each storage technology has its advantages and disadvantages. If one storage system was perfect, we wouldn't need so many storage devices connected to our computers! To compare storage devices, it is useful to apply the criteria of versatility, durability, speed, and capacity.

How can one storage technology be more versatile than another? Some storage devices can access data from only one type of medium. More versatile devices can access data from several different media. A floppy disk drive, for example, can access only floppy disks, whereas a DVD drive can access computer DVDs, DVD movies, audio CDs, computer CDs, and CD-Rs.

What makes a storage technology durable? Most storage technologies are susceptible to damage from mishandling or environmental factors, such as heat and moisture. Some technologies are more susceptible than others to damage that could cause data loss. CDs and DVDs tend to be more durable than hard disks, for example.

What factors affect storage speed? Quick access to data is important, so fast storage devices are preferred over slower devices. **Access time** is the average time it takes a computer to locate data on the storage medium and read it. Access time for a personal computer storage device, such as a disk drive, is measured in milliseconds (thousandths of a second). One millisecond (ms) is one-thousandth of a second. Lower numbers indicate faster access times. For example, a drive with a 6 ms access time is faster than a drive with an access time of 11 ms.

Access time is best for random-access devices. **Random access** (also called direct access) is the ability of a device to "jump" directly to the requested data. Floppy disk, hard disk, CD, DVD, and solid state drives are random-access devices, as are the memory cards used in digital cameras. A tape drive, on the other hand, must use slower **sequential access** by reading through the data from the beginning of the tape. The advantage of random access becomes clear when you consider how much faster and easier it is to locate a song on a CD (random access) than on a cassette tape (sequential access).

Data transfer rate is the amount of data a storage device can move per second from the storage medium to the computer. Higher numbers indicate faster transfer rates. For example, a CD-ROM drive with a 600 KBps (kilobytes per second) data transfer rate is faster than one with a 300 KBps transfer rate.

What's important about storage capacity? In today's computing environment, higher capacity is almost always preferred. Storage capacity is the maximum amount of data that can be stored on a storage medium, and it is measured in kilobytes (KB), megabytes (MB), gigabytes (GB), or terabytes (TB).

Storage capacity is directly related to **storage density**, the amount of data that can be stored in a given area of a storage medium, such as the surface of a disk. The higher the storage density, the more data is stored. Storage density can be increased by making the particles representing bits smaller, by layering them, packing them closer together, or standing them vertically (Figure 2-21).

FIGURE 2-21

Vertical storage produces higher storage capacities than horizontal storage.

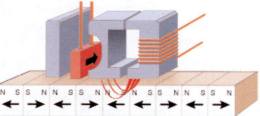

With horizontal storage, particles are arranged end to end, and use of the disk surface is not optimized.

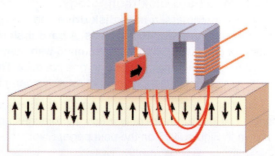

With vertical storage, particles stand on end so that many more can be packed on the disk surface.

MAGNETIC DISK AND TAPE TECHNOLOGY

What is magnetic disk and tape technology? Hard disk, floppy disk, and tape storage technologies can be classified as **magnetic storage**, which stores data by magnetizing microscopic particles on a disk or tape surface. The particles retain their magnetic orientation until that orientation is changed, thereby making disks and tapes fairly permanent but modifiable storage media. A **read-write head** mechanism in the disk drive can magnetize particles to write data, and sense the particles' polarities to read data. Figure 2-22 shows how a computer stores data on magnetic media.

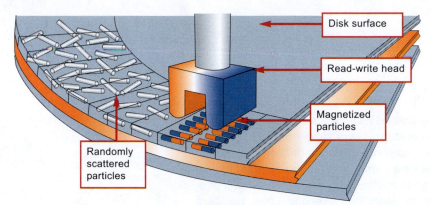

Disk surface

Read-write head

Magnetized particles

Randomly scattered particles

FIGURE 2-22

Before data is stored, particles on the surface of the disk are scattered in random patterns. The disk drive's read-write head magnetizes the particles, and orients them in a positive (north) or negative (south) direction to represent 0 and 1 bits.

Data stored magnetically can be easily changed or deleted simply by changing the magnetic orientation of the appropriate particles on the disk surface. This feature of magnetic storage provides lots of flexibility for editing data and reusing areas of a storage medium containing unneeded data.

Data stored on magnetic media can be unintentionally altered by magnetic fields, dust, mold, smoke particles, heat, and mechanical problems with a storage device. Placing a magnet on a floppy disk, for example, is a sure way of losing data.

Magnetic media gradually lose their magnetic charge, resulting in lost data. Some experts estimate that the reliable life span of data stored on magnetic media is about three years. They recommend that you refresh your data every two years by recopying it.

Why are hard disk drives so popular? Hard disk technology is the preferred type of main storage for most computer systems for three reasons. First, it provides lots of storage capacity. Second, it provides fast access to files. Third, a hard disk is economical. The cost of storing 40 megabytes of data is about a penny. You'll find hard disk drives in all kinds of digital devices, including personal computers, iPods, and TiVos.

How does hard disk technology work? As the main storage device on most computers, a **hard disk drive** contains one or more platters and their associated read-write heads. A **hard disk platter** is a flat, rigid disk made of aluminum or glass and coated with magnetic iron oxide particles. More platters mean more data storage capacity. The platters rotate as a unit on a spindle, making thousands of rotations per minute.

Each platter has a read-write head that hovers over the surface to read data. The head hovers only a few microinches above the disk surface, as shown in Figure 2-23 on the next page.

shown in Figure 2-23 on the next page.

TERMINOLOGY NOTE

You often see the terms *hard disk* and *hard disk drive* used interchangeably. You might also hear the term *fixed disk* used to refer to hard disks.

FIGURE 2-23

Hard disk platters and read-write heads are sealed inside the drive case or cartridge to screen out dust and other contaminants.

▶ CLICK TO START

Personal computer hard disk platters are typically 3.5" in diameter, with storage capacities ranging from 40 GB to 1 TB. Miniature hard drives (sometimes called microdrives), such as the 1.8" drive featured on Apple's iPod digital music player, store 30 to 80 GB.

Hard disk access times of 6 to 11 ms are not uncommon, whereas a floppy or CD takes about half a second to spin up to speed and find data. Hard disk drive speed is sometimes measured in revolutions per minute (rpm). The faster a drive spins, the more rapidly it can position the read-write head over specific data. For example, a 7,200 rpm drive is able to access data faster than a 5,400 rpm drive.

Computer ads typically specify the capacity, access time, and speed of a hard disk drive. So "160 GB 8 ms 7200 RPM HD" means a hard disk drive with 160 gigabyte capacity, access time of 8 milliseconds, and speed of 7,200 revolutions per minute. Ads rarely specify the amount of data that a hard drive can transfer, but the average data transfer rate is about 50 megabytes per second.

What's all this business about Ultra ATA, EIDE, SCSI, and DMA? Computer ads use these acronyms to describe hard disk drive technology. A hard drive mechanism includes a circuit board called a **hard disk controller** that positions the disk, locates data, and interfaces with components on the system board. Disk drives are classified according to their controllers. Popular types of drive controllers include SATA, Ultra ATA, EIDE, and SCSI. Although computer ads often specify the hard drive controller type, consumers don't really have much choice. If you want a 160 GB drive, for example, your hardware vendor is likely to offer only one brand of drive with one type of controller. Figure 2-24 shows a typical controller mounted on a hard disk drive.

The storage technology used on many PCs transfers data from a disk, through the controller, to the processor, and finally to RAM before it is actually processed. Computer ads sometimes specify this technology. DMA (direct memory access) technology allows a computer to transfer data directly from a drive into RAM, without intervention from the processor. This architecture relieves the processor of data-transfer duties and frees up processing cycles for other tasks. UDMA (ultra DMA) is a faster version of DMA technology.

FIGURE 2-24

A hard disk controller circuit board is typically mounted in the hard disk drive case.

What's the downside of hard disk storage? Hard disks are not as durable as many other storage technologies. The read-write heads in a hard disk hover a microscopic distance above the disk surface. If a read-write head runs into a dust particle or some other contaminant on the disk, it might cause a **head crash**, which damages some of the data on the disk. To help prevent contaminants from contacting the platters and causing head crashes, a hard disk is sealed in its case. A head crash can also be triggered by jarring the hard disk while it is in use. Although hard disks have become considerably more rugged in recent years, you should still handle and transport them with care. You should also make sure that you make a backup copy of the data stored on your hard disk in case of a head crash.

Can I use a second hard disk drive to increase storage space? You can increase the storage capacity of your computer by adding a second hard disk drive, which can also provide backup for your primary drive. Hard disk drives are available as internal or external units. Internal drives are inexpensive and can be easily installed in a desktop computer's system unit. External drives are slightly more expensive and connect to a desktop or notebook computer using a cable.

What is floppy disk technology? One of the oldest storage technologies, floppy disks are classified as magnetic storage because data is stored by magnetizing microscopic particles on the disk surface. A **floppy disk** is a round piece of flexible mylar plastic covered with a thin layer of magnetic oxide and sealed inside a protective casing (Figure 2-25). If you break open the disk casing (something you should never do unless you want to ruin the disk), you would see that the mylar disk inside is thin and literally floppy.

At one time, just about every personal computer included a floppy disk drive designed for high-density (HD) double-sided (DS) disks. Floppy disks are also referred to as floppies or diskettes. It is not correct to call them hard disks even though they seem to have a "hard" or rigid plastic case. The term hard disk refers to an entirely different storage technology.

A floppy disk's 1.44 MB capacity is not really sufficient for today's media-intensive applications. Many MP3 music files and photos are too large to fit on a floppy. In the past, floppy disks were extensively used to distribute software. CDs and DVDs offer more capacity for distributing the huge files for today's software applications. Web downloads offer more convenience.

What's the purpose of a tape drive? As you have learned, a head crash can easily destroy hard disk data. Protecting the vast amount of data on the hard disk is of particular concern because it would be difficult and time-consuming to reconstruct. A backup copy of the data on a hard disk can be made with a variety of storage devices, including tape drives. A **tape drive** is a device that reads data from and writes data to a long stream of recordable media similar to the tapes used in audio cassettes.

Tape drives are primarily used on business computers. Unlike CDs and DVDs, a tape backup device is not suitable for everyday storage tasks. To find out why, you need to understand how a tape drive works.

How does a tape drive work? A tape is a sequential, rather than a random-access, storage medium. Essentially, data is arranged as a long sequence of bits that begins at one end of the tape and stretches to the other end. The beginning and end of each file are marked with special header labels. To locate a file, the tape drive must start at one end of the tape and read through all the data until it finds the right header label. A tape

FIGURE 2-25

A standard floppy disk drive reads and writes data on a 3.5" HD DS floppy disk.

can contain hundreds or—in the case of a mainframe—thousands of feet of tape. Access time is measured in seconds, not in milliseconds as for a hard disk drive. Tape is simply too slow to be practical as a computer's main storage device.

CD AND DVD TECHNOLOGY

Is there a difference between CD and DVD technology? Today, most computers come equipped with some type of **CD drive** or **DVD drive**, designed to work with a variety of CDs and DVDs. CD and DVD technologies are similar, but storage capacities differ.

CD (compact disc) technology was originally designed to hold 74 minutes of recorded music. The original CD standard was adapted for computer storage with capacity for 650 MB of data. Later improvements in CD standards increased the capacity to 80 minutes of music or 700 MB of data.

DVD (digital video disc or digital versatile disk) is a variation of CD technology that was originally designed as an alternative to VCRs, but was quickly adopted by the computer industry to store data. The initial DVD standard offered 4.7 GB (4,700 MB) of data storage; that's about seven times as much capacity as a CD. Subsequent improvements in DVD technology offer even more storage capacity. A **double layer DVD** has two recordable layers on the same side and can store 8.5 GB of data. An **HD-DVD** can store 15 GB per layer on a single side; a **Blu-ray DVD** (BD) has 25 GB capacity per layer.

How do CD and DVD drives work? CD and DVD storage technologies are classified as **optical storage**, which stores data as microscopic light and dark spots on the disk surface. The dark spots, shown in Figure 2-26, are called **pits**. The lighter, non-pitted surface areas of the disk are called **lands**.

CD and DVD drives contain a spindle that rotates the disk over a laser lens. The laser directs a beam of light toward the underside of the disk. The dark pits and light lands on the disk surface reflect the light differently. As the lens reads the disk, these differences are translated into the 0s and 1s that represent data (Figure 2-27).

FIGURE 2-26

As seen through an electron microscope, the pits on an optical storage disk look like small craters. Each pit is less than 1 micron (one millionth of a meter) in diameter—1,500 pits lined up side by side are about as wide as the head of a pin.

FIGURE 2-27

CD and DVD drives use a laser to read data from the underside of a disk.

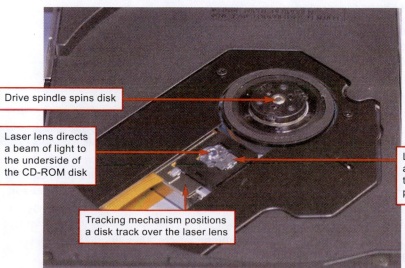

Drive spindle spins disk

Laser lens directs a beam of light to the underside of the CD-ROM disk

Tracking mechanism positions a disk track over the laser lens

Laser pickup assembly senses the reflectivity of pits and lands

The surface of an optical disk is coated with clear plastic, making the disk quite durable and less susceptible to environmental damage than data recorded on magnetic media. An optical disk, such as a CD, is not susceptible to humidity, fingerprints, dust, magnets, or spilled soft drinks. Scratches on the disk surface can interfere with data transfer, but a good buffing with toothpaste can erase the scratch without damaging the underlying data. An optical disk's useful life is estimated to be more than 30 years. Figure 2-28 illustrates the layers of an optical disk.

FIGURE 2-28

CDs and DVDs are constructed with one or more layers of recording surface sandwiched between protective plastic.

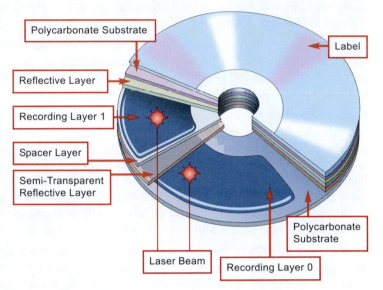

How fast are CDs and DVDs? The original CD drives could access 150 KB of data per second. The next generation of drives doubled the data transfer rate and were consequently dubbed "2X" drives. Transfer rates seem to be continually increasing. A 52X CD drive, for example, transfers data at 80 Mbps, which is still relatively slow compared to a hard disk drive's transfer rate of 5,000 Mbps.

The speed of a DVD drive is measured on a different scale than a CD drive. A 1X DVD drive is about the same speed as a 9X CD drive. Today's DVD drives typically have 16X speeds for a data transfer rate of 177.28 Mbps.

What's the significance of ROM, R, and RW? Optical technologies are grouped into three categories: read-only, recordable, and rewritable.

Read-only technology (ROM), stores data permanently on a disk, which cannot be subsequently added to or changed. Read-only disks, such as CD-ROMs, CD-DAs, DVD-Video, and DVD-ROMs are typically pre-pressed during mass production and used to distribute software, music, and movies.

Recordable technology (R) uses a laser to change the color in a dye layer sandwiched beneath the clear plastic disk surface. The laser creates dark spots in the dye that are read as pits. The change in the dye is permanent, so data cannot be changed once it has been recorded.

Rewritable technology (RW) uses phase change technology to alter a crystal structure on the disk surface. Altering the crystal structure creates patterns of light and dark spots similar to the pits and lands on a CD. The crystal structure can be changed from light to dark and back again many times, making it possible to record and modify data much like on a hard disk.

What are my choices for CD and DVD media? Several CD and DVD formats are currently popular for use in personal computers:

- **CD-DA** (compact disc digital audio), more commonly known as audio CD, is the format for commercial music CDs. Music is typically recorded on audio CDs by the manufacturer, but can't be changed by the consumer.

- **DVD-Video** (digital versatile disc video) is the format for commercial DVDs that contain feature-length films.

TERMINOLOGY NOTE

The "D" in acronyms for optical media such as CDs and DVDs formally means *disc*. In common usage, however, you will often see it spelled *disk*.

- **CD-ROM** (compact disc read-only memory, pronounced "cee dee rom") was the original optical format for computer data. Data is stamped on the disk at the time it is manufactured. Data cannot be added, changed, or deleted from these disks.

- **DVD-ROM** (digital versatile disc read-only memory) contains data stamped onto the disk surface at the time of manufacture. Like CD-ROMs, the data on these DVD-ROMs is permanent, so you cannot add or change data.

- **CD-R** (compact disc recordable) disks store data using recordable technology. The data on a CD-R cannot be erased or modified once you record it. However, most CD-R drives allow you to record your data in multiple sessions. For example, you can store two files on a CD-R disk today, and add data for a few more files to the disk at a later time.

- **DVD+R** or **DVD-R** (digital versatile disc recordable) disks store data using recordable technology similar to a CD-R, but with DVD storage capacity.

- **CD-RW** (compact disc rewritable) disks store data using rewritable technology. Stored data can be recorded and erased multiple times, making it a very flexible storage option.

- **DVD+RW** or **DVD-RW** (digital versatile disc rewritable) disks store data using rewritable technology similar to CD-RW, but with DVD storage capacity.

Are rewritable CD or DVD drives an acceptable replacement for a hard disk?
A rewritable CD or DVD drive is a fine addition to a computer system, but is not a good replacement for a hard disk drive. Unfortunately, the process of accessing, saving, and modifying data on a rewritable disk is relatively slow compared to the speed of hard disk access.

Can I use a single drive to work with any CD or DVD media?
Most CD drives can read CD-ROM, CD-R, and CD-RW disks, but cannot read DVDs. Most DVD drives can read CD and DVD formats. Storing computer data and creating music CDs requires a recordable or rewritable device. As you can see from the table in Figure 2-29, the most versatile optical storage device is a DVD R/RW/CD-RW combo.

> **TERMINOLOGY NOTE**
>
> Even though CD-ROM and ROM-BIOS both contain the word *ROM*, they refer to quite different technologies. ROM BIOS refers to a chip on the system board that contains permanent instructions for the computer's boot sequence. A CD-ROM drive is an optical storage device that's usually installed in one of the system unit's drive bays.

FIGURE 2-29

CD and DVD Capabilities

	Play Audio CDs	Play DVD Movies	Read CD Data	Read DVD Data	Create Music CDs	Store Data on CDs	Store Data on DVDs
CD-ROM Drive	✔		✔				
CD-R Drive	✔		✔		✔	✔	
CD-RW Drive	✔		✔		✔	✔	
DVD/CD-RW Drive	✔	✔	✔	✔	✔	✔	
DVD R/RW/CD-RW Drive	✔	✔	✔	✔	✔	✔	✔

SOLID STATE STORAGE

What is solid state storage? **Solid state storage** (sometimes called flash memory) is a technology that stores data in erasable, rewritable circuitry, rather than on spinning disks or streaming tape. It is widely used in portable consumer devices, such as digital cameras, MP3 music players, notebook computers, PDAs, and cell phones.

Solid state storage is portable and provides fairly fast access to data. It is an ideal solution for storing data on mobile devices and transporting data from one device to another.

How does solid state storage work? Solid state storage contains a gridwork of circuitry. Each cell in the grid contains two transistors that act as gates. When the gates are open, current can flow and the cell has a value that represents a "1" bit. When the gates are closed by a process called Fowler-Nordheim tunneling, the cell has a value that represents a "0" bit.

Very little power is required to open or close the gates, which makes solid state storage ideal for battery-operated devices, such as digital cameras and PDAs. Once the data is stored, it is **non-volatile**—the chip retains the data without the need for an external power source.

Solid state storage provides fast access to data because it includes no moving parts. Solid state storage is very durable—it is virtually impervious to vibration, magnetic fields, or extreme temperature fluctuations. On the downside, the capacity of solid state storage does not currently match that of hard disks. The cost per megabyte of solid state storage is about a penny, which is significantly higher than for magnetic or optical storage.

What are my options for solid state storage? Several types of solid state storage are available to today's consumers. The formats for these small, flat cards include CompactFlash, MultiMedia, SecureDigital (SD), and SmartMedia. A **card reader** is a device that reads and writes data on solid state storage. Sometimes referred to as 5-in-1, 7-in-1, or all-in-one card readers, these combination devices work with multiple types of solid state storage formats (Figure 2-30).

Because digital photography is so popular, many notebook and desktop computers have a built-in card reader to make it simple to transfer photos from your camera to your computer. Moving data in the other direction, a computer can download MP3 music files and store them on a solid state memory card. That card can be removed from the computer and inserted into a portable MP3 player, so you can listen to your favorite tunes while you're on the go.

For even more versatility, solid state USB flash drives and U3 drives can be used to store computer data files and programs.

FIGURE 2-30

A 5-in-1 card reader can be installed in a drive bay if one is not supplied as standard equipment.

Card reader

Memory card

What is a USB flash drive? A **USB flash drive**, such as Sony's MicroVault, the SanDisk Cruzer, or the Kingston Traveler, is a portable storage device that plugs directly into a computer's USB port using a built-in connector (Figure 2-31).

Also called thumb drives, pen drives, jumpdrives, keychain drives, or UFDs, USB flash drives are about the size of a highlighter pen and so durable that you can literally carry them on your key ring. USB flash drives have capacities ranging from 16 MB to 32 GB. They have maximum data transfer speeds of about 100 Mbps, but most commonly operate in the range of 18-28 megabytes per second. When you want to remove a USB flash drive from a computer, you should use the appropriate onscreen eject control. For example, on PCs, you would use the Safely Remove Hardware icon, located on the right side of the Windows task bar.

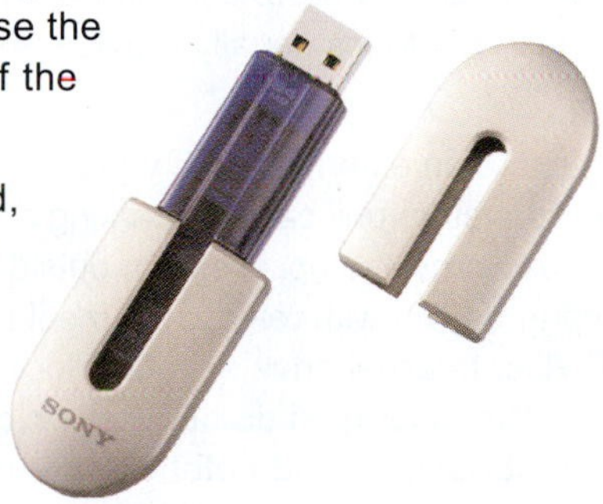

Files stored on a USB flash drive can be opened, edited, deleted, and run just as though those files were stored on magnetic or optical media. You might say that USB flash drives are the new floppy disks because not only can you access files as if they were stored on disks, but you can run software from them, too (Figure 2-32).

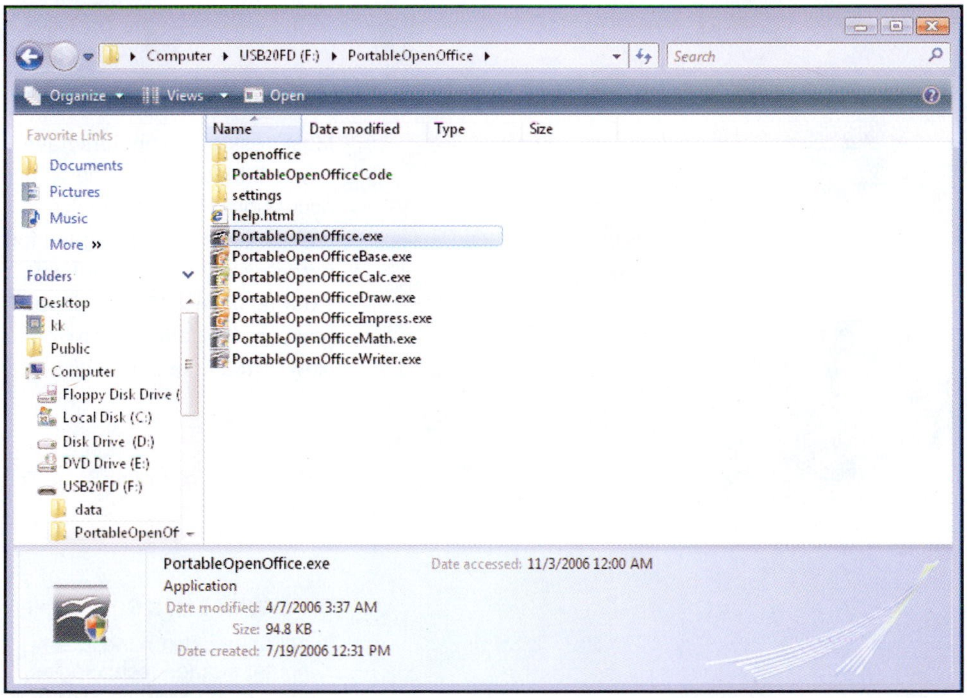

TERMINOLOGY NOTE

UFD stands for USB Flash Drive.

2

FIGURE 2-31

A USB flash drive plugs directly into a computer's USB port.

FIGURE 2-32

To run software from a USB Flash drive, you can double-click the program name in Windows Explorer.

What is a U3 drive? A **U3 drive** (sometimes called a U3 smart drive) is a special type of USB flash drive that is preconfigured to autoplay when it is inserted into a computer. It runs an application called Launchpad, which is similar to the Windows Start menu, and lists programs that can be accessed from the U3 drive. Software applications for U3 drives are available at the U3 Web site.

STORAGE WRAPUP

Can I add storage to my computer? You can increase storage capacity by adding hard drives and you can add storage flexibility by installing additional types of storage devices.

External storage devices, such as external hard disk drives, CD drives, DVD drives, and USB flash drives, simply plug into connectors built into your computer's system unit. They can be easily detached when you want to move your computer or if your external drive contains a backup that you want to store away from your computer. Before you disconnect any storage device, make sure you understand the manufacturer's instructions for doing so. On PCs, you usually have to use the Safely Remove Hardware icon on the Windows taskbar. Macs usually provide an eject icon next to the drive listing.

As an alternative to an external drive, you can install storage devices inside your computer's system unit case in "parking spaces" called **drive bays**. An external drive bay provides access from outside the system unit—a necessity for a storage device with removable media, such as floppy disks, CDs, tapes, and DVDs. Internal drive bays are located deep inside the system unit and are designed for hard disk drives, which don't use removable storage media. Most desktop and notebook computers include at least one internal drive bay and one or more external bays (Figure 2-33).

FIGURE 2-33

Most notebook computers provide bays for one hard disk drive and one CD or DVD drive.

An empty drive bay located on the side of a notebook computer

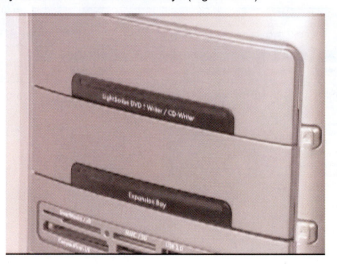

Most desktop computers have several drive bays, some accessible from outside the case, and others—designed for hard disk drives—without any external access. Empty drive bays are typically hidden from view with a face plate.

 **CLICK TO START**

INFOWEBLINKS

To get an update on the latest computer storage technologies, connect to the **Storage Frontiers InfoWeb**.

 **CLICK TO CONNECT**
www.course.com/np/concepts11/ch02

What are the relative advantages and disadvantages of each type of computer storage device? Earlier in the chapter you read that no storage technology is perfect. While hard disk drives offer fast and inexpensive access, they are not the most durable technology. CD and DVD technology is durable, but slow, and flash drives are expensive when compared to other storage media. The table in Figure 2-34 summarizes the relative advantages and disadvantages of each storage technology covered in this section.

FIGURE 2-34

Storage Technology Comparison

2

Storage device	Cost of device (Average)	Capacity	Cost of media (disk/tape)	Cost per MB (Average)	Data Transfer rate	Technology	Portable
Floppy disk	$15-30	1.44 MB	$0.24 in bulk	$0.17	62.5 KBps	Magnetic	Yes
CD-RW	$30-60	700 MB	$0.64 in bulk	$0.081	150 KBps-7.8 MBps (for 1-52x)	Optical	Yes
DVD+RW	$40-129	4.7 GB	$0.45 in bulk	$0.009	1.35-32.4 MBps (for 1-24x)	Optical	Yes
Flash drive	$14-$200	512 MB–16 GB		$0.025	10-30 MBps	Solid State	Yes
Hard drive (Internal)	$50-$400	80 GB–1 TB		$0.0005	150-300 MBps	Magnetic	No
Hard drive (External)	$70-$750	80 GB-1 TB		$0.0008	12-480 MBps	Magnetic	Yes
Tape	$500-$1000	2 GB–800 GB compressed	$2–$90 in bulk	$0.0001	2-160 MBps	Magnetic (sequential)	No

QuickCheck

1. _____ time is the average time it takes a computer to locate data on a storage medium and read it.

2. A disk drive is a(n) _____ access device; a tape drive is a(n) _____ access device.

3. Higher disk _____ provides increased storage capacity.

4. A magnetic storage device uses a read-write _____ to magnetize particles that represent data.

5. Hard disks are very susceptible to head _____ , so it is important to make backup copies.

6. Data on an optical storage medium, such as a DVD, is stored as pits and _____ .

7. CD-RW technology allows you to write data on a disk, and then change that data. True or false? _____

8. A USB flash drive uses solid _____ technology to store data and programs.

 CHECK ANSWERS

Input and Output Devices

THIS SECTION provides an overview of the most popular input and output devices for personal computers. It begins with input devices, including keyboards, mice, trackpads, joysticks, and touch screens. Next, a survey of computer display devices helps you sort out the differences among CRT, LCD, and plasma displays. A guide to printers describes today's most popular printer technologies and provides a handy comparison chart. You'll learn about other peripheral devices in later chapters. You'll also take a look at the computer's expansion bus—the components that carry data to peripheral devices. With an understanding of how the expansion bus works, you'll be able to select, install, and use all kinds of peripherals.

BASIC INPUT DEVICES

What devices can I use to get data into a computer? Most computer systems include a keyboard and pointing device, such as a mouse, for basic data input. Touch-sensitive screens offer an additional input option. Other input devices, such as scanners, digital cameras, and graphics tablets, are handy for working with graphical input. Microphones and electronic instruments provide input capabilities for sound and music.

What's special about a computer keyboard's design? The design of most computer keyboards is based on the typewriter's QWERTY layout, which was engineered to keep the typewriter's mechanical keys from jamming. In addition to a basic typing keypad, desktop and notebook computer keyboards include a collection of keys such as Alt, Ctrl, and Print Screen, designed for computer-specific tasks. Most desktop computer keyboards also include a calculator-style numeric keypad, plus an editing keypad with keys such as End, Home, and Page Up, to efficiently move the screen-based insertion point. You can even find tiny keyboards on hand-held devices—entering text and numbers is an important part of most computing tasks.

What does a pointing device do? A **pointing device** allows you to manipulate an on-screen pointer and other screen-based graphical controls. The most popular pointing devices for personal computers include mice, trackballs, pointing sticks, trackpads, and joysticks.

How does a mouse work? A standard desktop computer includes a **mouse** as its primary pointing device. Many computer owners also add a mouse to their notebook computers. A mouse includes one or more buttons that can be clicked to input command selections, such as "Start" and "Shut down." To track its position, a computer mouse uses either mechanical or optical technology (Figure 2-35).

Most computer owners prefer the performance of an optical mouse because it provides more precise tracking, greater durability, less maintenance, and more flexibility to use the mouse on a wide variety of surfaces without a mouse pad.

FIGURE 2-35

A mechanical mouse (top) reads its position based on the movement of a ball that rolls over a mouse pad placed on a desk.

An optical mouse (bottom) uses an onboard chip to track a light beam as it bounces off a surface, such as a desk, clipboard, or mouse pad.

When would I use other pointing devices?

Alternative pointing devices, such as those pictured in Figure 2-36 can be used when a mouse is not available or does not provide adequate control.

FIGURE 2-36

Alternative Pointing Devices

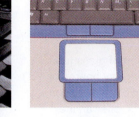

Pointing stick

Trackpad

Trackball

Joystick

A **pointing stick**, or TrackPoint, looks like the tip of an eraser embedded in the keyboard of a notebook computer. It is a space-saving device that you can push up, down, or sideways to move the on-screen pointer. A **trackpad** is a touch-sensitive surface on which you can slide your fingers to move the on-screen pointer. Pointing sticks and trackpads are typically supplied with notebook computers so that it is not necessary to carry a mouse as an extra component.

A **trackball** looks like a mechanical mouse turned upside down. You use your fingers or palm to roll the ball and move the pointer. Controlling a trackball uses a different set of muscles than controlling a mouse, so some computer owners periodically switch to a trackball to prevent stress injuries.

A **joystick** looks like a small version of a car's stick shift. Moving the stick provides input to on-screen objects, such as a pointer or an action figure in a computer game. Joysticks can include several sticks and buttons for arcade-like control when playing computer games. Some joysticks are designed for people who have physical disabilities that prevent them from using a standard mouse.

How does a touch screen work?

Tablet computers, many PDAs, UMPCs, retail store self checkouts, and information kiosks collect input from a **touch screen**, which overlays a display screen. The most commonly used touch screen technology is a transparent panel coated with a thin layer of electrically conductive material that senses a change in the electrical current when touched. This "resistive" technology is fairly durable. It is not susceptible to dust or water, but it can be damaged by sharp objects.

FIGURE 2-37

Most touch screens use resistive technology that registers a change in electrical current when touched.

The coordinates for a touch event are processed in essentially the same way as a mouse click. For example, if you touch your PDA screen at the location of a button labeled "Calendar" the area you touch generates coordinates and sends them to the processor. The processor compares the coordinates to the image displayed on the screen to find out what is at the coordinates, and then responds, in this case by opening your appointment calendar.

The resistive technology used in today's touch screens can be operated with bare fingers or a stylus (Figure 2-37). Processing technology can interpret a single touch or more complex input such as handwriting.

DISPLAY DEVICES

What are my options for display devices? A computer display screen is usually classified as an output device because it typically shows the results of a processing task. Touch-sensitive screens, however, can be classified as both input and output devices because they accept input. Three technologies are used for computer display devices: CRT, LCD, and plasma (Figure 2-38).

A **CRT** (cathode ray tube) display device uses the same sort of glass tube as a standard television. Gun-like mechanisms in the tube spray beams of electrons toward the screen and activate individual dots of color that form an image. CRT display devices, often simply called monitors, offer an inexpensive and dependable computer display. They are bulky, however, and consume a fair amount of power.

An **LCD** (liquid crystal display) produces an image by manipulating light within a layer of liquid crystal cells. Modern LCD technology is compact in size, lightweight, and provides an easy-to-read display. LCDs are standard equipment on notebook computers. Standalone LCDs, referred to as LCD monitors or flat panel displays, are popular for desktop computers. The advantages of LCD monitors include display clarity, low radiation emission, portability, and compactness. LCD technology has become price competitive with CRTs and most new computers now ship with LCD displays.

Plasma screen technology creates an on-screen image by illuminating miniature colored fluorescent lights arrayed in a panel-like screen. Plasma screens are compact, lightweight, and more expensive than LCD and CRT monitors.

CRT, LCD, and plasma screens can be equipped with NTSC (standard American television) or HDTV (high-definition television) circuitry so they accept television signals from an antenna or cable. This technology lets you simultaneously view computer data and television on the same display device using split-screen or picture-in-picture format.

Which display technology produces the best image? Image quality is a factor of screen size, dot pitch, width of viewing angle, refresh rate, resolution, and color depth. Screen size is the measurement in inches from one corner of the screen diagonally across to the opposite corner. Typical monitor screen sizes range from 13" to 21". On some displays, the viewable image does not stretch to the edge of the screen. Instead, a black border makes the image smaller than the size specified. Many computer ads now include a measurement of the **viewable image size** (vis).

Dot pitch (dp) is a measure of image clarity. A smaller dot pitch means a crisper image. Technically, dot pitch is the distance in millimeters between like-colored **pixels**—the small dots of light that form an image. A dot pitch between .26 and .23 is typical for today's display devices.

A display device's **viewing angle width** indicates how far to the side you can still clearly see the screen image. A wide viewing angle indicates that you can view the screen from various positions without compromising image quality. CRT and plasma screens offer the widest viewing angles. Graphics artists tend to prefer CRT screens, which display uniform color from any angle.

A CRT's **refresh rate** (also referred to as vertical scan rate) is the speed at which the screen is repainted. The faster the refresh rate, the less the screen flickers. Refresh rate is measured in cycles per second, or Hertz (Hz), and is

FIGURE 2-38

Display Device Technology

CRT

LCD

Plasma

INFOWEBLINKS

For up-to-the-minute information on the latest and greatest graphics cards, monitors, and LCD displays, check out the **Display Devices InfoWeb**.

Ⓦ CLICK TO CONNECT

www.course.com/np/concepts11/ch02

adjustable using Control Panel settings in Windows. A refresh rate of at least 75 Hz produces a fairly flicker-free display.

The number of colors a monitor can display is referred to as **color depth** or bit depth. Most PC display devices have the capability to display millions of colors. When set at 24-bit color depth (sometimes called True Color), your PC can display more than 16 million colors—and produce what are considered photographic-quality images. Windows allows you to select resolution and color depth. The most popular setting is 24-bit color at 1024 x 768 resolution.

The number of horizontal and vertical pixels that a device displays on a screen is referred to as its **resolution**. The resolution for many early PC displays was referred to as **VGA** (Video Graphics Array). Higher resolutions were later provided by **SVGA** (Super VGA), **XGA** (eXtended Graphics Array), **SXGA** (Super XGA), and **UXGA** (Ultra XGA). Widescreen resolutions, such as **WUXGA**, offer the same aspect ratio as high definition television. Figure 2-39 summarizes the most common PC resolutions.

At higher resolutions, text and other objects appear smaller, but the computer can display a larger work area, such as an entire page of a document. The two screens in Figure 2-40 help you compare a display set at 800 x 600 resolution with a display set at 1280 x 800 resolution.

FIGURE 2-39

Common PC Resolutions

VGA	640 x 480
SVGA	800 x 600
XGA	1024 x 768
SXGA	1280 x 1024
UXGA	1600 x 1200
WUXGA	1920 x 1200

FIGURE 2-40

The screen on the left shows 1280 x 800 resolution. Notice the size of text and other screen-based objects. The screen on the right shows 800 x 600 resolution. Text and other objects appear larger on the low-resolution screen, but you see a smaller portion of the screen desktop.

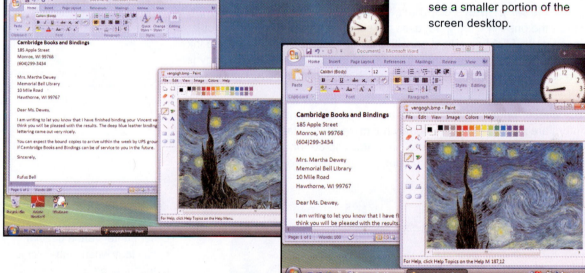

What are the components of a typical computer display system?

In addition to a display device, such as a monitor, a computer display system also requires graphics circuitry that generates the signals for displaying an image on the screen. One type of graphics circuitry, referred to as integrated graphics, is built into a computer's system board. Graphics circuitry can also be supplied by a small circuit board called a **graphics card** (graphics board or video card), like the one in Figure 2-41.

A graphics card typically contains a **graphics processing unit** (GPU) and special video memory, which stores screen images as they are processed but before they are displayed. Lots of video memory is the key to lightning-fast screen updating for fast action games, 3-D modeling, and graphics-intensive desktop publishing. In addition to video memory, most graphics cards contain special graphics accelerator technology to further boost performance.

FIGURE 2-41

A graphics card is a small circuit board that plugs into the system board.

PRINTERS

What printer technologies are available for personal computers?

Printers are one of the most popular output devices available for personal computers. Today's best-selling printers typically use ink jet or laser technology. An old printer technology called dot matrix is also used in some applications.

How does an ink jet printer work?

An **ink jet printer** has a nozzle-like print head that sprays ink onto paper to form characters and graphics. The print head in a color ink jet printer consists of a series of nozzles, each with its own ink cartridge. Most ink jet printers use CMYK color, which requires only cyan (blue), magenta (pink), yellow, and black inks to create a printout that appears to have thousands of colors. Alternatively, some printers use six or eight ink colors to print midtone shades that create slightly more realistic photographic images.

Ink jet printers, such as the one in Figure 2-42, outsell all other types of printers because they are inexpensive and produce both color and black-and-white printouts. They work well for most home and small business applications. Small, portable ink jet printers meet the needs of many mobile computer owners. Ink jet technology also powers many photo printers, which are optimized to print high-quality images produced by digital cameras and scanners.

How do laser printers compare to ink jet printers?

A **laser printer**, such as the one in Figure 2-43, uses the same technology as a photocopier to paint dots of light on a light-sensitive drum. Electrostatically charged ink is applied to the drum and then transferred to paper. Laser technology is more complex than ink jet technology, which accounts for the higher price of laser printers.

A basic laser printer produces only black-and-white printouts. Color laser printers are available, but are somewhat more costly than basic black-and-white models. Laser printers are often the choice for business printers, particularly for applications that produce a high volume of printed material.

FIGURE 2-42

Most ink jet printers are small, lightweight, and inexpensive, yet produce very good-quality color output.

FIGURE 2-43

Laser printers are a popular technology when high-volume output or good-quality printouts are required.

▶ CLICK TO START

What is a dot matrix printer?

When PCs first appeared in the late 1970s, dot matrix printers were the technology of choice, and they are still available today. A **dot matrix printer** produces characters and graphics by using a grid of fine wires. As the print head noisily clatters across the paper, the wires strike a ribbon and paper in a pattern prescribed by your PC. Dot matrix printers can print text and graphics—some even print in color using a multicolored ribbon.

Today, dot matrix printers, like the one in Figure 2-44, are used primarily for "back-office" applications that demand low operating cost and dependability, but not high print quality.

FIGURE 2-44

Unlike laser and ink jet technologies, a dot matrix printer actually strikes the paper and, therefore, can print multipart carbon forms.

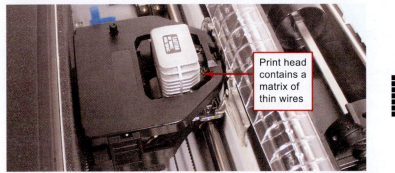

Print head contains a matrix of thin wires

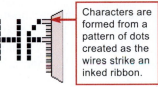

Characters are formed from a pattern of dots created as the wires strike an inked ribbon.

What features should I look for in a printer? Printers differ in resolution, speed, duty cycle, operating costs, duplex capability, and memory.

• **Resolution.** The quality or sharpness of printed images and text depends on the printer's resolution—the density of the gridwork of dots that create an image. Printer resolution is measured by the number of dots printed per linear inch, abbreviated as dpi. At normal reading distance, a resolution of about 900 dpi appears solid to the human eye, but a close examination reveals a dot pattern. If you want magazine-quality printouts, 900 dpi is sufficient resolution. If you are aiming for resolution similar to expensive coffee-table books, look for printer resolution of 2,400 dpi or higher.

• **Print speed.** Printer speeds are measured either by pages per minute (ppm) or characters per second (cps). Color printouts typically take longer than black-and-white printouts. Pages that contain mostly text tend to print more rapidly than pages that contain graphics. Typical speeds for personal computer printers range between 6 and 30 pages of text per minute. A full-page 8.5 x 11 photo can take up to 6 minutes to print.

• **Duty cycle.** In addition to printer speed, a printer's **duty cycle** determines how many pages a printer is able to churn out. Printer duty cycle is usually measured in pages per month. For example, a personal laser printer has a duty cycle of about 3,000 pages per month (ppm)—that means roughly 100 pages per day. You wouldn't want to use it to produce 5,000 campaign brochures for next Monday, but you would find it quite suitable for printing 10 copies of a five-page outline for a meeting tomorrow.

• **Operating costs.** The initial cost of a printer is only one of the expenses associated with printed output. Ink jet printers require frequent replacements of relatively expensive ink cartridges. Laser printers require toner cartridge refills or replacements. Dot matrix printers require replacement ribbons. When shopping for a printer, you can check online resources to determine how often you'll need to replace printer supplies and how much they are likely to cost. Printer comparisons often specify printing costs per page. Color printouts average 5 cents or more per page.

• **Duplex capability.** A **duplex printer** can print on both sides of the paper. This environment-friendly option saves paper but can slow down the print process, especially on ink-jet printers that pause to let the ink dry before printing the second side.

● **Memory.** A computer sends data for a printout to the printer along with a set of instructions on how to print that data. **Printer Control Language** (PCL) is the most widely used language for communication between computers and printers, but **PostScript** is an alternative printer language that many publishing professionals prefer. The data that arrives at a printer along with its printer language instructions require memory. A large memory capacity is required to print color images and graphics-intensive documents. Some printers let you add memory to improve printing of such pages.

● **Networkability.** If your personal computer system is not networked to other computers in your house, apartment, or dorm, you can attach a printer directly to your computer. If your computer is part of a network, you can share your printer with other network users, who essentially send their print jobs to your computer's printer for output. Another way to configure network printing for multiple users is to purchase a network-enabled printer that connects directly to the network, rather than to one of the computers on a network. The network connection can be wired or wireless. The advantage of a network-ready printer is that it can be placed in a location convenient for all the network users.

Figure 2-45 provides comparative information for ink jet, laser, and dot matrix printers. For specific information on a particular brand and model of printer, check the manufacturer's Web site.

INFOWEBLINKS

Before you shop for a printer, take a look at the buying tips in the **Printer Buyer's Guide InfoWeb**.

 **CLICK TO CONNECT**

www.course.com/np/concepts11/ch02

FIGURE 2-45

Printer Comparison

Printer Type	Max. Resolution	Speed	Duty Cycle	Operating Cost	Memory
Ink Jet (B&W) (color graphics)	4800 x 1200	2–7 ppm 1–2 ppm	3,000 ppm	1–7¢/page 6–18¢/page	256 KB–2 MB
Laser (B&W) (color graphics)	2400 dpi	10–20 ppm 2–4 ppm	150,000 ppm	2–4¢/page 2–4¢/page	8–120 MB
Dot Matrix (B&W)	72–360 dpi	5–6 ppm	6,000–60,000 ppm	1.5–2¢/page	2–128 KB

INSTALLING PERIPHERAL DEVICES

Is it difficult to install a new peripheral device? At one time, installing computer peripherals required a screwdriver and extensive knowledge of ports, slots, boards, and device drivers. Today, many peripheral devices connect to an external **USB** (universal serial bus) port and Windows automatically loads their device drivers, making installation as simple as plugging in a table lamp. USB is currently the most popular technology for connecting peripherals (Figure 2-46).

On most new computer models, USB ports are conveniently located on the front or sides of the system unit for easy access. Many kinds of peripheral devices—including mice, scanners, and joysticks—are available with USB connections. Several types of storage devices, such as USB flash drives, also use USB connections.

There are still occasions, however, when a simple USB connection is not available. Installing high-end graphics and sound cards for a multimedia or serious gaming computer typically requires you to open the system unit.

Whether you are working with a simple USB connection or more complex equipment, a little information about the computer's data bus will arm you with the information you need to negotiate the steps for installing most peripheral devices.

FIGURE 2-46

Plugging a cable into a USB port is the simplest way to connect peripheral devices to a computer.

How does a computer move data to and from peripheral devices? When you install a peripheral device, you are basically creating a connection for data to flow between the device and the computer. Within a computer, data travels from one component to another over circuits called a **data bus**. One part of the data bus runs between RAM and the microprocessor. The segment of the data bus to which peripheral devices connect is called the **expansion bus** (or the I/O bus). As data moves along the expansion bus, it can travel through expansion slots, expansion cards, ports, and cables (Figure 2-47).

FIGURE 2-47

The expansion bus connects the computer system board to peripheral devices.

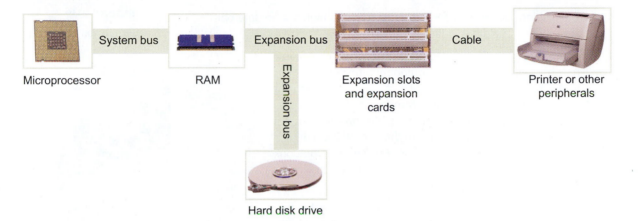

Microprocessor	System bus · RAM · Expansion bus	Expansion slots and expansion cards	Printer or other peripherals

Expansion bus

Hard disk drive

What's an expansion slot? An **expansion slot** is a long, narrow socket on the system board into which you can plug an expansion card. An **expansion card** is a small circuit board that gives a computer the capability to control a storage device, an input device, or an output device. Expansion cards are also called expansion boards, controller cards, or adapters.

Expansion cards are built for only one type of slot. If you plan to add or upgrade a card in your computer, you must make sure the right type of slot is available on the system board. Most desktop computers provide four to eight expansion slots, some containing factory-installed expansion cards, such as modems, graphics cards, sound cards, and network cards. Figure 2-48 shows how to plug an expansion card into an expansion slot.

FIGURE 2-48

An expansion card simply slides into an expansion slot and is secured with a small screw. Before you open the case, make sure you unplug the computer and ground yourself—that's technical jargon for releasing static electricity by using a special grounding wristband or by touching both hands to a metal object.

 CLICK TO START

Expansion slots are classified as ISA, PCI, or AGP:

- **ISA** (Industry Standard Architecture) slots are an old technology, used today only for some modems and other relatively slow devices. Many new computers have few or no ISA slots.

- **PCI** (Peripheral Component Interconnect) slots offer fast transfer speeds and a 32-bit or 64-bit data bus. These slots typically house a graphics card, sound card, video capture card, modem, or network interface card. PCI Express is a high speed version used by today's fastest graphics cards.

- **AGP** (Accelerated Graphics Port) slots provide a high-speed data pathway primarily used for graphics cards.

Do notebook computers contain expansion slots?

Most notebook computers are equipped with several USB ports and a special type of external slot called a **PC slot** or PCMCIA slot (Personal Computer Memory Card International Association). Typically, a notebook computer has only one of these slots, but the slot can hold more than one **PC card** (also called PCMCIA expansion cards or Card Bus cards). Notebook owners are advised to use the USB ports and PC slot, rather than opening the notebook's system unit.

What is an expansion port?

An **expansion port** is any connector that passes data in and out of a computer or peripheral device. It is similar to an electrical outlet because you can plug things in to make a connection.

An expansion port is often housed on an expansion card so that it is accessible through an opening in the back of the computer's system unit. A port might also be built into the system unit case of a desktop or notebook computer. The built-in ports supplied with a computer usually include a mouse port, keyboard port, serial port, and USB ports. Some computers also include a FireWire (IEEE 1394) port used to connect digital cameras. Figure 2-49 illustrates the major types of expansion ports on a typical desktop computer.

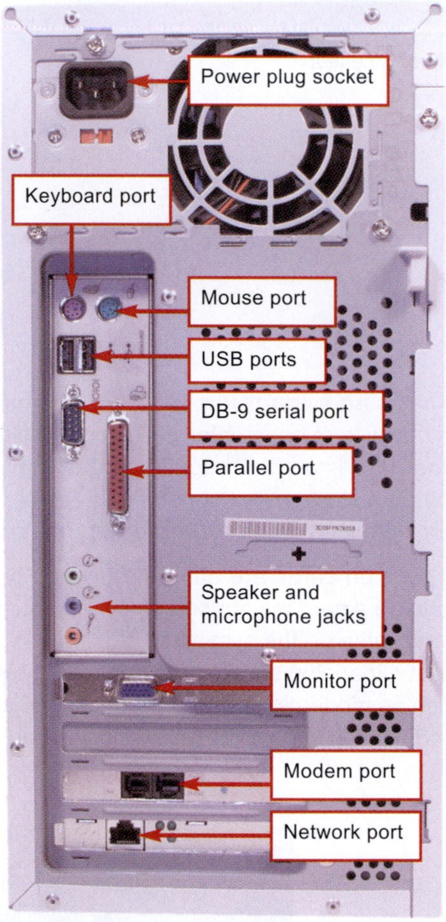

How do I know which cable to use?

With so many types of ports, you can expect a corresponding variety of cables. If a cable is supplied with a peripheral device, you can usually figure out where to plug it in by matching the shape of the cable connector to the port. Some manufacturers also color code ports and plugs to make them easy to match. Figure 2-50 on the next page provides information about the computer cables you're most likely to encounter.

Why do some peripheral devices include a disk or CD?

Some devices require software to establish communication with your computer. The directions supplied with your peripheral device include instructions on how to install the software. Typically, you use the software disk or CD one time to get everything set up, and then you can put the disk away in a safe place. You'll learn more about this software, called a device driver, in the next chapter.

Long-time computer techies probably remember the days when installing a peripheral device meant messing around with little electronic components called dip switches and a host of complex software settings called IRQs.

FIGURE 2-49

Expansion Ports

- Power plug socket
- Keyboard port
- Mouse port
- USB ports
- DB-9 serial port
- Parallel port
- Speaker and microphone jacks
- Monitor port
- Modem port
- Network port

Fortunately, today's PCs include a feature called **Plug and Play** (PnP) that automatically takes care of these technical details. Although it took several years to refine Plug and Play technology, it works quite well for just about every popular peripheral device. If PnP doesn't work, your computer simply won't recognize the device and won't be able to exchange data with it. If you've got a stubborn peripheral device, check the manufacturer's Web site for a device driver update, or call the manufacturer's technical support department.

What's the most important thing to remember about installing peripherals? Installing a peripheral device is not difficult when you remember that it's all about using the expansion bus to make a connection between the system board and a peripheral device. The cable you use must match the peripheral device and a port on the computer. If the right type of port is not available, you might have to add an expansion card. Once the connection is made, PnP should recognize the new device. If not, you'll probably have to install driver software and perhaps seek technical assistance.

FIGURE 2-50

Common Personal Computer Cables and Connectors

	CONNECTOR	DESCRIPTION	DEVICES
	USB	Connects to USB port, which sends data over a single data line and can support up to 127 devices. USB-1 carries data at speeds up to 12,000 Kbps; USB-2, at 480,000 Kbps.	Modem, keyboard, joystick, scanner, mouse, external hard disk drive, MP3 player, digital camera
	IEEE 1394	Connects to the FireWire port, which sends data at 400,000 Kbps.	Video camera, DVD player
	VGA HDB-15	Connects to the video port.	Display device

QuickCheck

1. Computer _____ devices include mice, trackpads, trackballs, and joysticks.

2. In the context of computer display technology, _____ rate refers to the speed at which the screen image is repainted.

3. The number of dots that form images and text on a monitor or printer is referred to as _____ .

4. A printer with _____ printing capability can print on both sides of the paper.

5. AGP, PCI, and ISA are types of expansion _____ .

6. A(n) _____ port provides one of the fastest, simplest ways to connect peripherals.

▶ CHECK ANSWERS

Hardware Security

THE INFORMATION that computers contain and process has become practically priceless to every PC owner. Just about everyone depends on a computer for information and communication. A stolen computer, even if it's low-priced, can be a huge loss if it holds valuable financial data or months of research. A broken PC can easily cost hundreds of dollars to repair, especially if the data is damaged and needs to be recovered. For trouble-free computer use, is important to secure and regularly maintain your computer equipment, just as you would with your home and car.

ANTI-THEFT DEVICES

What can I do to prevent my computer from being stolen?

Computers have rapidly become prime targets for thieves. Many security breaches have been traced to stolen computers. The portability of notebook computers makes them particularly easy for a thief to grab, just as a wallet or a handbag would be. Figure 2-51 contains important tips for protecting your notebook computer from theft.

FIGURE 2-51

Tips for Preventing Computer Theft

- Never leave your notebook computer unattended, especially when you are in a coffee shop, the library, or at the airport.

- If you have to leave your notebook computer in your car, never leave it in plain view. Lock it up in the trunk or cover it up.

- Carry your notebook computer in an inconspicuous carrying case.

- Record your notebook computer's make, model, and serial number and store them away from the computer. Many recovered computers cannot be returned to their owners because this tracking information is not supplied to police.

- Consider securing your notebook computer with an anti-theft device.

How do computer anti-theft devices work?

Several computer anti-theft devices are available. Most can be used for both desktops and notebook computers.

The Kensington Security Slot is a security mechanism that's factory-installed on many personal computers. It docks with a special lock that can be attached to a cable. The cable can be fastened to a desk to prevent theft as shown in Figure 2-52.

FIGURE 2-52

The Kensington Security Slot is an industry standard way to secure a computer to a desk.

Notebook computers can also be fastened with tie-down brackets or stored in a specially designed locker that can be installed under a desk or in a closet. Another option for securing notebook computers is a security plate that's affixed to the underside of the computer or to a desk (Figure 2-53).

Computer motion sensor alarms, similar to those for automobiles, can be installed on desktop or notebook computers and armed so that any movement triggers audible alarm sounds or recorded verbal warnings.

In addition to locks designed to secure a computer's system unit, there are also several types of storage device locks designed to prevent unauthorized access to your computer's floppy, CD, and DVD drives. For example, you can equip your computer with a fingerprint reader that requires your fingerprint match to access data on the hard disk.

If my computer is stolen can authorities recover it? Your chances of recovering a stolen computer improve if you have taken some steps in advance, such as recording the computer's serial number, affixing a tracking label, or installing tracking software.

STOP (Security Tracking of Office Property) plates leave an indelible tattoo on your computer equipment. It takes 800 pounds of force to remove a plate, which contains a unique ID number, a warning message, and an 800 number to report a stolen computer. Each plate ID number is registered in the international STOP database, thereby making it virtually impossible for a thief to resell a computer that has a STOP label.

Tracking and recovery software, such as Lojack for Laptops, LaptopLocate, and CyberAngel, secretly sends a message as soon as a thief uses a stolen computer to log onto the Internet. This message contains the computer's exact location and is directed to a tracking or monitoring center. Some tracking software products can be configured to delete the data on the stolen computer.

SURGE PROTECTION AND BATTERY BACKUP

What is a power surge? To ensure that your computer stays in good running condition, it is essential that you protect it from the unavoidable power surges or spikes that endanger many electrical appliances and equipment. A **power surge** is a sudden increase or spike in electrical energy, affecting the current that flows to electrical outlets. Computers and peripheral devices require a stable current and are particularly sensitive to these sudden bursts of electrical energy. The overload can slowly damage your computer's circuit boards and other electrical components. Over time, even small, repeated power surges can shorten your PC's life.

Power surges can originate from a number of sources: downed power lines, power grid switching by the electric company, faulty wiring, and large appliances like refrigerators and air conditioners powering on and off. Lightning causes extremely large power surges and consequently poses a real threat to your computer equipment.

FIGURE 2-53

Security plates are designed to lock a computer to a desk.

2

How can I protect my computer from power surges?
You can protect your computer equipment from power surges by plugging it into a surge strip instead of directly into a wall outlet. For added protection during thunderstorms, shut down your computer, turn off all your peripheral devices, and unplug the surge strip and all computer-related cables from wall outlets, including the telephone line for your modem.

What is a surge strip and how does one work?
A **surge strip** (also called a surge suppressor or surge protector) is a device that contains electrical outlets protected by circuitry that blocks surges and spikes. Some surge strips also have sockets for modem connections that prevent surges from traveling down telephone or cable lines and into your computer (Figure 2-54).

A surge strip monitors the electrical current that passes from the outlet to all the devices plugged into the strip. When it detects a surge or spike, it redirects the extra current to a grounded circuit. A big power surge can burn out a surge strip while it tries to protect your equipment. Some surge strips have an indicator light that warns you if the surge strip is no longer functioning properly. Check the manufacturer's documentation to determine if you should discard the depleted strip, reset it, or install a new fuse.

What is a UPS?
A **UPS** (uninterruptible power supply) is a device that not only provides surge protection, but also furnishes your computer with battery backup power during a power outage. If your computer is connected to a UPS when a power outage occurs, you can save what you're doing and shut down your PC properly. Depending on your system's configuration, a UPS with a high-performance battery might give you enough backup power to keep your computer up and running for several hours, allowing you to continue to work during the entire blackout or brownout.

Most UPSs have two types of sockets: one type offers battery backup plus surge protection, and the other offers only surge protection. The surge-only sockets are for printers, which use so much power that they can quickly drain the battery. Manufacturers advise against the use of battery backup for printers because it's not economical. Some UPS units also provide fax and cable modem protection. At the Web site for American Power Conversion, you'll find tips for choosing a UPS based on your system's configuration and the amount of run time you want during a power failure. Figure 2-55 illustrates the major components of a UPS.

FIGURE 2-54

A surge strip offers outlets for power plugs and might also provide protection for modem cables.

FIGURE 2-55

An uninterruptible power supply (UPS) not only protects electronic equipment from power surges, it also provides battery power during power outages.

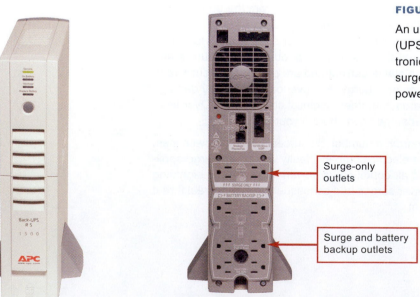

Surge-only outlets

Surge and battery backup outlets

BASIC MAINTENANCE

Can I prevent hardware problems?
Computer component failures can be caused by manufacturing defects and other circumstances beyond your control. You can, however, undertake some preventive maintenance that can add years to the life of your computer equipment, just as regular tune-ups lengthen the life of your car. Preventive maintenance can save you more than the cost of repairs; you also save the time you would've lost while tracking down problems and arranging for repairs. Regular cleaning of your PC's components and peripheral devices helps to keep your system in good condition.

How do I clean the keyboard?
Always shut down your PC before you clean your keyboard so that you don't inadvertently type in commands that you don't want your system to do. Also, disconnect your keyboard and remember where the connection is located. Flip the keyboard over and shake it gently to get rid of any small pieces of dirt between the keys. A can of compressed air is effective for blowing off the dust and dislodging larger debris. A vacuum cleaner can pop off and suck away the keys on your keyboard, so be very careful if you use one to clean your keyboard.

You can use cotton swabs just slightly moistened with a mild cleaning fluid to clean the sides of keys. Wipe the tops of the keys with a soft cloth, again slightly dampened with a mild cleaning solution. Allow your keyboard to dry before you reconnect it to your PC. Avoid spills into your keyboard by not setting your drinks too close to it. A flexible clear plastic keyboard cover can also prevent damage from spills and sticky fingers. Figure 2-56 provides more information on cleaning your computer keyboard.

FIGURE 2-56

Carefully use a Q-tip and a can of compressed air or a vacuum cleaner to remove dust and debris from your keyboard. Sticky liquids are difficult to remove. That can of pop? Better to keep it away from your keyboard.

▶ CLICK TO START

How do I get dust and fingerprints off my computer screen?
Dust and fingerprint smudges can easily accumulate on your computer screen and make it quite difficult to read. You should clean your screen on a regular basis, at least weekly. It's always best to turn off your display device before you clean because a blank screen will reveal all the smudges, dust, and dirt.

You can safely clean CRT screens with a household glass cleaner because they are made of glass. Spray the cleaner on a lint-free, soft cloth, but never directly on the screen. The dripping liquid can seep through your display device and damage the inside circuits.

Because LCD screens are not made of glass, they are more delicate than CRTs. It is safest to use commercial LCD cleaners. Again, do not spray directly on the panel. Dampen your lint-free, soft cloth with the cleaner. If you choose to purchase lint-free wipes, make sure they are non-abrasive. Some computer equipment manufacturers recommend microfiber cloths used for wiping eyeglasses.

Should I be concerned about my computer's operating temperature? High-performance processors, hard drives, graphics cards, and several other computer components generate a lot of heat. Overheating can shorten the lifespan of internal components and chips.

Most desktop computers have a fan mounted on the power supply that runs continuously to maintain the proper temperature inside of the system unit. Additional cooling fans might also be used to cool the microprocessor or graphics card. Notebook computers also have cooling fans, but the fans come on only after the processor reaches a certain temperature (Figure 2-57).

FIGURE 2-57

Fans that cool your computer vent outside the case. Keep the area around your computer clear for good air circulation.

It is important to be aware of the ventilation around your computer system and ensure that the fans are able to draw air from the room and blow it across the inside components. If your computer is in an enclosed space, such as a cabinet, you might need to cut out a hole at the back to give your PC some room to "breathe." You should also be aware of the temperature in the room in which your computer resides. Several vendors sell temperature monitors and extra cooling fans if you think your equipment is overheating.

Dust particles, dirt, and even your pet's hair can collect on and around the cooling fans and impede their performance. You should regularly use a can of compressed air or a vacuum cleaner hose to clean out debris from the vents and fans. You should, however, exercise extreme caution when you clean out your computer's system case. First, make sure that you've turned off your PC, display device, and all other related devices. Stay a couple of inches away from all components as you dust, especially if you're using a vacuum cleaner hose. Do not touch the system board, and make sure not to knock any cables loose.

Computer monitors also heat up quickly. They have top and rear vents for releasing heat, and you should keep them clear of dust, dirt, and other obstacles. Do not put papers, books, or other items on top of a monitor.

Are there any other components that need TLC? To avoid read or write errors, you also want your CD, DVD, and floppy drives to function properly. Retailers provide cleaning kits for many types of storage devices and media. Also examine your CDs and DVDs for scratches and fingerprints. Clean them with a soft cloth slightly dampened with water. If the smudges don't come off, a little isopropyl alcohol might help.

If you work with a mechanical mouse, you should clean it periodically. Unplug the mouse, remove the bottom cover and the ball inside it, and then use a cotton swab to clean out the dirt that has accumulated around the rollers. If you own a wireless mouse, you'll have to change the battery at least every six months.

What is a good computer maintenance routine? Aside from cleaning your computer equipment on a regular basis, you should do the preventive maintenance tasks listed in Figure 2-58. You'll learn how to do these tasks in later chapters.

FIGURE 2-58

Tips for Regular Computer Maintenance

- Back up your files regularly, particularly those that are most important to you. You might want to perform daily incremental backups of critical data and monthly backups of all your files. You should also test your backup procedures periodically.

- Run utilities that ensure peak performance for your hard disk drive. In Windows, these utilities include Disk Cleanup and Disk Defragmenter. It's best to do this maintenance on a weekly basis.

- Delete your browser's history and cache files on a monthly basis in order to free up space for your temporary files. The free space results in faster downloads from the Internet.

- Apply the latest operating system, driver, and security updates.

- Scan your computer for viruses and spyware once a week.

- Keep antivirus and spyware definitions updated.

TROUBLESHOOTING AND REPAIR

How can I tell if something is wrong with my computer? There are several telltale signs that your computer is in trouble. The most obvious one is your PC's failure to power up. A loud beep at start-up time can also indicate a problem. If your computer's screen remains blank or error messages appear, you might have a hardware problem.

Hardware problems can also show up as unexpected restarts at random intervals, or as a peripheral device that stops working. Some problems are intermittent and might seem to be resolved only to come back when they are least convenient to deal with.

Many seasoned Windows users have encountered the **blue screen of death** (also called BSoD), that suddenly replaces the usual graphical screen display with an enigmatic error message written in white text against a bright blue background. The blue screen of death indicates that the operating system has encountered an error from which it cannot recover, and the computer no longer accepts any commands.

Hardware problems can quickly escalate and some can eventually make your computer non-functional or make your data impossible to access. Any computer problem that prevents you from working as usual should be taken seriously. A little time spent troubleshooting can save you lots of annoyance down the road.

How do I troubleshoot a hardware problem? You might be able to solve many hardware problems by simply following the basic guidelines for troubleshooting listed in Figure 2-59.

FIGURE 2-59

Troubleshooting Tips

- Stay calm and don't jump to any conclusions until you've thought everything through.

- Write down all error messages and any other information that goes with them.

- Make sure all components are plugged in and that there are no loose cables. For example, if your display device's cable is loose, the indicator light will be off and your screen will be blank.

- If you can, try to duplicate the problem by going through the same steps that led you to it.

- Look for troubleshooting and repair tips in your user's manual, your vendor's Web site, or even through a search engine. If you search the Internet by typing in the error message number or keywords in the error message, you might discover that at least one person has already found a solution to your problem.

- Run your spyware and antivirus software. Lurking viruses, worms, Trojan Horses, and spyware (discussed in the next chapter), can cause strange and unexplainable occurrences in your computer system. For example, spyware can cause your computer to keep displaying a pop-up ad no matter how you try to close it.

- A simple reboot of your computer might clear up the problem. Windows always requires a reboot when it displays the blue screen of death on your screen. However, a more serious problem underlying a BSoD will not be resolved with a reboot. To reboot a PC, hold down the Ctrl, Alt, and Del keys at the same time. When the Task Manager window appears, hold down the Ctrl, Alt, and Del keys once again.

Troubleshooting and diagnostic tools can help you find the source of a problem and fix it. For example, Windows offers interactive troubleshooting tools formatted as a series of simple questions, answers, and recommendations. You might have to borrow a computer to run these tools if your computer is totally out of commission. Figure 2-60 illustrates a simple troubleshooting session.

FIGURE 2-60

To access a Windows troubleshooter, use the Start menu to select Help and Support, then look for the link to Troubleshooting or Fixing a Problem.

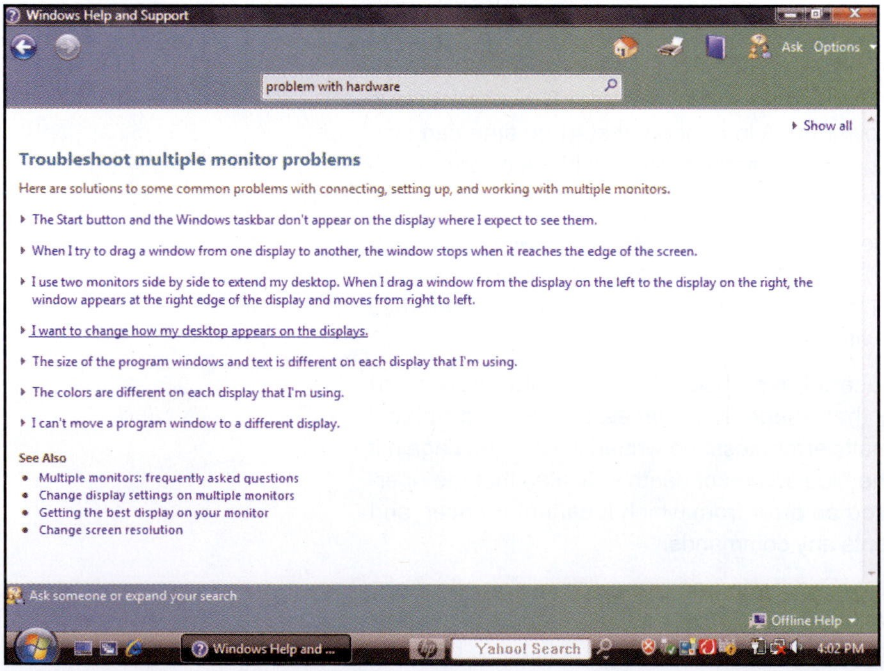

What Is Safe Mode? If Windows encounters a critical problem that is keeping it from operating normally, it starts up in Safe Mode the next time you reboot your computer. **Safe Mode** is a limited version of Windows that allows you to use your mouse, screen, and keyboard, but no other peripheral devices (Figure 2-61). While in Safe Mode you can use Control Panel's Add/Remove Programs to uninstall recently added programs or hardware that might be interfering with the operation of other components.

FIGURE 2-61

To enter Safe Mode, you can press the F8 function key as your PC boots.

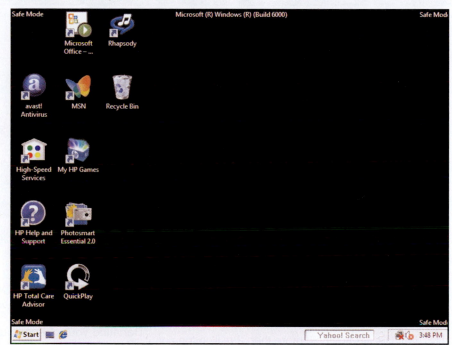

What if I can't solve the problem myself?

If you are unable to fix a hardware problem after following the basic guidelines for troubleshooting, get ready to call the technical support center for the device or component that is malfunctioning. You can also consider asking for help from a knowledgeable person or from computer repair professionals like the Geek Squad. Make sure you have all the data they might need, such as warranty information, purchase date, serial number, brand, model, and operating system. You will also have to provide the error message and all information that came with it. You might also have to describe the steps that led you to the problem.

However you resolve the problem, write down the solution. You never know when you might need it again!

QuickCheck

SECTION E

1. The Kensington Security _____ is an industry standard security mechanism that's factory-installed on many personal computers.

2. A power _____ is a sudden increase or spike in electrical energy, affecting the current that flows to electrical outlets.

3. Most UPSs have two types of sockets: one type offers _____ backup plus surge protection, and the other offers only surge protection.

4. Many seasoned users have encountered the blue screen of _____ that suddenly replaces the usual graphical screen display with an enigmatic error message written in white text against a bright blue background.

5. _____ Mode is a stripped down version of Windows, designed for troubleshooting.

▶ CHECK ANSWERS

Where Does All the e-Garbage Go?

MANUFACTURING an average desktop computer with a CRT monitor requires 48 pounds of chemicals and 529 pounds of fossil fuels, according to a United Nations University study. That makes producing a computer more materials-intensive than manufacturing an automobile. Extending the lifespan of your computer might be environmentally friendly, but keeping up with technology probably means replacing your computer every few years.

When it is time to replace your computer, is there a way to do it in an environmentally safe way? The National Recycling Coalition estimates that 500 million computers had become obsolete by 2007. In the United States alone, almost eight printer cartridges are discarded every second. A recycling company called GreenDisk estimates that about 1 billion floppy disks, CDs, and DVDs end up in landfills every year.

U.S. landfills already hold more than 2 million tons of computer and electronic parts, which contain toxic substances such as lead, cadmium, and mercury. A CRT monitor, for example, can contain up to eight pounds of lead. An Environmental Protection Agency (EPA) report sums up the situation: "In this world of rapidly changing technology, disposal of computers and other electronic equipment has created a new and growing waste stream."

Many computers end up in landfills because their owners are unaware of potential environmental hazards and simply toss them in the garbage. In addition, PC owners typically are not given information on options for disposing of their old machines. Instead of throwing away your old computer, you might be able to sell it; donate it to a local school, church, or community program; have it hauled away by a professional recycling firm; or send it back to the manufacturer. Some artists even accept old computers and use parts in jewelry and craft projects.

With the growing popularity of Internet auctions and dedicated computer reclamation sites, you might be able to get some cash for your old computer. At Web sites such as the Computer Recycle Center at *www.recycles.com*, you can post an ad for your old stuff. Off the Web, you can find businesses that refurbish and sell old computers. Goodwill stores in many communities accept old computer equipment and arrange for it to be reused or recycled.

Recycled Computer Creations by Gregory Steele, Marquette, MI

Donating your old computer to a local organization doesn't actually eliminate the disposal problem, but it does delay it. Unfortunately, finding a new home for an old computer is not always easy. Most schools and community organizations have few resources for repairing broken equipment, so if your old computer is not in good working order, it could be more of a burden than a gift. In addition, your computer might be too old to be compatible with the other computers in an organization. It helps if you can donate software along with your old computer. To ensure a legal transfer, include the software distribution disks, manuals, and license agreement. And remember, once you donate the software, you cannot legally use it on your new computer unless it is freeware or shareware.

If you cannot find an organization to accept your computer donation, look in your local Yellow Pages or on the Internet for an electronics recycling firm, which will haul away your computer and recycle any usable materials.

Despite private sector options for selling, donating, or recycling old computers, many governments are worried that these voluntary efforts will not be enough to prevent massive dumping of an ever-growing population of obsolete computers.

Many states have taken legislative action to curtail the rampant disposal of obsolete computer equipment. For example, Massachusetts has banned televisions and computer monitors from its landfills.

In Maine it is illegal to dispose of computers or monitors—they have to be recycled in an environmentally sound way. But recycling can be costly—equipment needs to be collected, sorted, disassembled, and shipped to processing or disposal plants.

Basic to the issue of reducing electronic waste is the question of "Who pays?" Should it be the taxpayer, the individual consumer, the retailer, or the computer manufacturer?

When Californians were faced with the prospect of tax hikes to deal with alarming increases in electronic waste, activists questioned if tax increases were fair to individual taxpayers who generate very little electronic waste. Now, consumers buying computers in California have to pay a recycling fee at the time of purchase.

Other lawmakers propose to make manufacturers responsible for recycling costs and logistics. "Extended producer responsibility" refers to the idea of holding manufacturers responsible for the environmental effects of their products through the entire product life cycle, which includes taking them back, recycling them, or disposing of them. Maryland requires computer manufacturers to ante up an annual fee for electronic waste disposal.

The economics of a mandatory take-back program are likely to increase product costs because manufacturers would typically pass on recycling costs to consumers.

Some manufacturers currently participate in voluntary producer responsibility programs. Consumers who buy Hewlett-Packard toner cartridges are provided with a postage-paid shipping box so they can return the cartridges for recycling. Using IBM's PC

Recycling Service, consumers can ship any make of computer, including system units, monitors, printers, and optional attachments, to a recycling center for $29.99. Greenpeace's Green Ranking rates digital equipment manufacturers on their recycling efforts and use of toxic materials.

The EPA (Environmental Protection Agency) advocates a national plan in which consumers, retailers, and manufacturers can cooperate to reduce electronic waste. Its Plug-in to eCycling Web site makes the point that "No national infrastructure exists for collecting, reusing, and recycling electronics." With laws that differ from state to state, consumers are often confused about how to dispose of their unwanted computers, monitors, CDs, and ink cartridges.

U.S. Legislators are trying to hammer out the details of an e-waste bill that provides tax incentives for companies that recycle and requires consumers to recycle computers, monitors, and other electronic devices. The United States is not alone in its efforts. Lawmakers in the European Union, Great Britain, Australia, China, and Japan are also addressing ways to manage the electronic waste stream and keep our planet green.

INFOWEBLINKS

You'll find much more information about how you can recycle an old computer by connecting to the **Computer Recycling InfoWeb.**

Ⓦ CLICK TO CONNECT
www.course.com/np/concepts11/ch02

What Do You Think?

ISSUE

1. Have you ever thrown away an old computer or other electronic device?   ○ Yes   ○ No   ○ Not sure

2. Are you aware of any options for recycling electronic equipment in your local area?   ○ Yes   ○ No   ○ Not sure

3. Would it be fair for consumers to pay a recycling tax on any electronic equipment that they purchase?   ○ Yes   ○ No   ○ Not sure

▶ SAVE RESPONSES

IN ENGINES OF THE MIND, Joel Shurkin writes, "If necessity is the mother of invention, then war can be said to be its grandmother." The military, an early pioneer in computer and communication technologies, continues to be the driving force behind technologies that have revolutionized everyday life. During World War II, the U.S. military initiated a classified research program, called Project PX, to develop an electronic device to calculate artillery firing tables; by hand, each table required weeks of grueling calculations. Project PX produced ENIAC (Electrical Numerical Integrator And Calculator), one of the first general-purpose electronic computers. When ENIAC was completed in 1946, the war was over, but ENIAC's versatile architecture could be used for other calculations, such as designing hydrogen bombs, predicting weather, and engineering wind tunnels. ENIAC's technology evolved into the computers used today.

After Project PX, the military continued to support computer research. Like most large corporations, the military used mainframe computers to maintain personnel, inventory, supply, and facilities records. This data was distributed to terminals at other locations through rudimentary networks. Because all data communication flowed through the mainframe, a single point of failure for the entire system was a possible risk. A malfunction or an enemy "hit" could disrupt command and control, sending the military into chaos. Therefore, the armed forces created the Advanced Research Projects Agency (ARPA) to design a distributed communications system that could continue operating without a centralized computer. The result was ARPANET, which paved the way for the data communications system we know today as the Internet. ARPANET was activated in 1967, but the .mil domain that designates U.S. military Web sites was not implemented until 1984.

The U.S. Department of Defense (DoD) currently maintains several data communications networks, including SIPRNet, a classified (secret-level) network, and NIPRNet, which provides unclassified services. The DoD's public Web site, called DefenseLINK, provides official information about defense policies, organizations, budgets, and operations.

Computers and communications technology have also become an integral part of high-tech military operations. U.S. Apache helicopters, for example, are equipped with computer-based Target Acquisition Designation Sights, laser range finder/designators, and Pilot Night Vision Sensors. These arcade-style controls are also used by tank drivers in the U.S. Army's 4th Infantry Division. Each vehicle in this "Digitized Division" is equipped with a Force XXI Battle Command Brigade and Below system, which works like a battlefield Internet to transmit data on the location of friendly and enemy forces from one vehicle to another using wireless communication.

Much like a video game, the Force XXI touch screen shows friendly troops in blue, and a global positioning satellite (GPS) system updates their positions automatically. Enemy troops spotted by helicopters are shown as red icons. To get information on any friendly or enemy vehicle, a soldier can simply touch one of these blue or red icons. To send text messages—much like cell phone and computer instant messaging—a soldier touches the Message button. The built-in GPS system provides location and route information, much like sophisticated mapping programs in luxury cars.

Force XXI computers are installed in shock-resistant cases and equipped with a cooling system that eliminates the need for a fan, which might pull in dust, dirt, or water. The computers run Sun Microsystem's Solaris operating system because it is less vulnerable to viruses and intrusion attacks than Microsoft Windows. To prevent enemy capture and use, Force

2

XXI computers have a self-destruct mechanism that can be triggered remotely.

In 2007 the U.S. Army began implementing its Future Combat Systems (FCS) network. According to the Army Website, FCS "enables soldiers to perceive, comprehend, shape, and dominate the future battle-field at unprecedented levels." The system uses off-the-shelf hardware, a proprietary operating system, secure data transport protocols, and a variety of specially designed applications called Battle Command software. The software helps soldiers plan missions using simulations, detailed maps, and decison aids. FCS allows soldiers to communicate voice and data over secure radio and network connections. Soldiers can also control unmanned robots and drones using a small, hand carried device. FCS research encompasses soldier-wearable computers, such as helmet-mounted displays and communications devices. "The new technology we have is going to save a lot of lives," explains one of the soldiers who tested the system. "That's the thing we're impressed about."

The military has also conducted research in computer simulations that are similar to civilian computer games. "Live" military training is dangerous—weapons are deadly and equipment costs millions of dollars. With computer simulations, however, troops can train in a true-to-life environment without physical harm or equipment damage. Flying an F-16 fighter, for example, costs about $5,000 an hour, but flying an F-16 simulator costs only $500 per hour. The military uses simulators to teach Air Force pilots to fly fighter jets, Navy submarine officers to navigate in harbors, and Marine infantry squads to handle urban combat. Military trainers agree that widespread use of computer games helps prepare troops to adapt quickly to simulations.

A 24-year-old preflight student at Pensacola Naval Air Station modified the Microsoft Flight Simulator game to re-create a T-34C Turbo Mentor plane's controls. After logging 50 hours on the simulator, the student performed so well on a real plane that the Navy used his simulation to train other pilots. Today, a growing cadre of computer and communications specialists are needed to create and maintain increasingly complex military systems.

Armies once depended on their infantry divisions, but today's high-tech armies also depend on database designers, computer programmers, and network specialists. Even previously low-tech military jobs, such as mechanics and dietitians, require some computer expertise. Happily, new recruits are finding military computer systems easy to learn, based on their knowledge of civilian technologies, such as the Internet and computer games.

Although most citizens agree that an adequate national defense is necessary, the cost of defense-related equipment, personnel, and research remains controversial. In 1961, President Dwight Eisenhower warned "We must guard against the acquisition of unwarranted influence, whether sought or unsought, by the military-industrial complex." Many socially motivated citizens and pacifists protested diverting tax dollars from social and economic programs to the military-industrial complex Eisenhower cautioned against. In retrospect, however, military funding contributed to many technologies we depend on today. For example, detractors tried to convince the government that Project PX was doomed to failure, but without ENIAC research, computers might not exist today. Skeptics saw no future for the fruits of ARPANET research, but it led to the Internet, which has changed our lives significantly.

INFOWEBLINKS

You'll find lots more information related to this Computers in Context topic at the **Computers and the Military InfoWeb.**

Ⓦ CLICK TO CONNECT
www.course.com/np/concepts11/ch02

New Perspectives Labs

On the BookOnCD

To access the New Perspectives labs for Chapter 2, start the BookOnCD, BookOnFlashDrive, or other NP11 BookOn product and then click the icon next to the lab title below.

▶ **BENCHMARKING**

IN THIS LAB YOU'LL LEARN:

- Which computer performance factors can be measured by benchmark tests

- How to run a test that identifies a computer's processor type, RAM capacity, and graphics card type

- How to run benchmarking software that analyzes a computer's processor speed and graphics processing speed

- How to interpret the results of a benchmark test

- How to compare the results from benchmark tests that were performed on different system configurations

- When benchmark tests might not provide accurate information on computer performance

LAB ASSIGNMENTS

1. Start the interactive part of the lab. Make sure you've enabled Tracking if you want to save your QuickCheck results. Perform each lab step as directed, and answer all the lab QuickCheck questions. When you exit the lab, your answers are automatically graded and your results are displayed.

2. Use the System Information utility to analyze the computer you typically use. Provide the results of the analysis along with a brief description of the computer you tested and its location (at home, at work, in a computer lab, and so on).

PROCESSOR BENCHMARKS		
Processor	Quake III Arena	PCMark
"Supernova EE"	548	5198
"Pulsar FX"	551	5020

3. From the Processor Benchmarks table above, which fictional processor appears to be faster at graphics processing? Which processor appears to be better at overall processing tasks?

4. Explain why you might perform a benchmark test on your own computer, but get different results from those stated in a computer magazine, which tested the same computer with the same benchmark test.

5. Use a search engine on the Web to find benchmark ratings for one of Intel's Core Duo processors and one of AMD's Athlon 64 Dual-Core processors. Are the benchmarks different? What would account for the benchmark results?

Key Terms

Make sure you understand all the boldfaced key terms presented in this chapter. If you're using the NP11 BookOnCD, BookOnFlashDrive, or other NP11 BookOn product, you can use this list of terms as an interactive study activity. First, try to define a term in your own words, and then click the term to compare your definition with the definition presented in the chapter.

2

Access time, 77
AGP, 96
Benchmarks, 69
Blue screen of death, 103
Blu-ray DVD, 81
Cache, 68
Capacitors, 72
Card reader, 84
CD drive, 81
CD, 81
CD-DA, 82
CD-R, 83
CD-ROM, 83
CD-RW, 83
CISC, 69
Color depth, 91
CRT, 90
Data bus, 95
Data transfer rate, 77
Desktop computer, 58
Dot matrix printer, 92
Dot pitch, 90
Double layer DVD, 81
Drive bays, 86
Duplex printer, 93
Duty cycle, 93
DVD, 81
DVD drive, 81
DVD+R, 83
DVD+RW, 83
DVD-R, 83
DVD-ROM, 83
DVD-RW, 83
DVD-Video, 82
EEPROM, 74
Expansion bus, 95
Expansion card, 95
Expansion port, 96
Expansion slot, 95
Floppy disk, 80
Form factor, 58
Front side bus, 68
Gigahertz, 67
Graphics card, 91
Graphics processing unit, 91

Hard disk controller, 79
Hard disk drive, 78
Hard disk platter, 78
HD-DVD, 81
Head crash, 80
Home computer system, 60
Hyper-Threading Technology, 69
HyperTransport, 68
Ink jet printer, 92
ISA, 96
Joystick, 89
Lands, 81
Laser printer, 92
LCD, 90
Level 1 cache, 68
Level 2 cache, 68
Linux platform, 64
Mac platform, 64
Magnetic storage, 78
Media Center PC, 60
Megahertz, 67
Microprocessor clock, 67
Mod, 65
Mouse, 88
multi-core processor, 69
Nanosecond, 73
Non-volatile, 84
Notebook computer, 59
Optical storage, 81
Overclocking, 70
Parallel processing, 69
PC card, 96
PC platform, 64
PC slot, 96
PCI, 96
Peripheral device, 56
Pipelining, 69
Pits, 81
Pixels, 90
Plasma screen, 90
Plug and Play, 97
Pointing device, 88
Pointing stick, 89
Portable computer, 59
PostScript, 94

Power surge, 99
Printer Control Language, 94
RAM, 71
Random access, 77
Read-only technology, 82
Read-write head, 78
Recordable technology, 82
Refresh rate, 90
Resolution, 91
Rewritable technology, 82
RISC, 69
ROM BIOS, 74
ROM, 73
Safe Mode, 105
Sequential access, 77
Serial processing, 69
Solid state storage, 84
Storage density, 77
Storage device, 76
Storage medium, 76
Surge strip, 100
SVGA, 91
SXGA, 91
System unit, 57
Tablet computer, 59
Tape drive, 80
Touch screen, 89
Trackball, 89
Trackpad, 89
U3 drive, 85
Ultra-mobile PC, 59
UPS, 100
USB, 94
USB flash drive, 85
UXGA, 91
VGA, 91
Viewable image size, 90
Viewing angle width, 90
Virtual memory, 72
Volatile, 72
Word size, 68
WUXGA, 91
XGA, 91

Interactive Summary

To review important concepts from this chapter, fill in the blanks to best complete each sentence. When using the NP11 BookOnCD or other BookOn product, click the Check Answers buttons to automatically score your answers.

SECTION A: The core of a personal computer system includes the computer system [＿＿＿＿＿＿＿＿] , display device, keyboard, and mouse. Personal computers come in several varieties of [＿＿＿＿＿＿＿＿] factors. A [＿＿＿＿＿＿＿＿] computer fits on a desk, runs on power from an electrical wall outlet, and can be housed in a horizontal case or vertical [＿＿＿＿＿＿＿＿] case. A [＿＿＿＿＿＿＿＿] computer (also referred to as a mobile computer) is a small, lightweight personal computer with screen, keyboard, storage, and processing components integrated into a single unit that runs on power supplied by an electrical outlet or a battery. Three categories of these computers include notebook computers, [＿＿＿＿＿＿＿＿] computers, and ultra-mobile PCs. Personal computers are sometimes designated as home, media, small business, or game systems to help consumers select the computer that's right for their needs. Although the Mac platform was not previously [＿＿＿＿＿＿＿＿] with the PC platform, the situation is changing now that Intel Macs use the same [＿＿＿＿＿＿＿＿] as PCs. Consumers can sometimes save money by installing upgrades after purchase, however replacing a [＿＿＿＿＿＿＿＿] is difficult and not recommended. Some computer owners make unauthorized modifications to their computer systems called [＿＿＿＿＿＿＿＿] . For information on the latest computers, mods, and prices, consumers can check computer magazines and Web sites.

 **CHECK ANSWERS**

SECTION B: The microprocessor and memory are two of the most important components in a computer. The microprocessor is an [＿＿＿＿＿＿＿＿] circuit, which is designed to process data based on a set of instructions. Microprocessor performance can be measured by the speed of the microprocessor [＿＿＿＿＿＿＿＿] . A specification such as 3.2 GHz means that the microprocessor operates at a speed of 3.2 [＿＿＿＿＿＿＿＿] cycles per second. Other factors affecting overall processing speed include word size, cache size, instruction set complexity, parallel processing, and pipelining. Most personal computers only contain one main microprocessor, but today's dual [＿＿＿＿＿＿＿＿] processors contain the circuitry for two microprocessors.

Computers contain various kinds of memory. Random [＿＿＿＿＿＿＿＿] memory is a special holding area for data, program instructions, and the [＿＿＿＿＿＿＿＿] system. It stores data on a temporary basis until the processor makes a data request. The speed of RAM circuitry is measured in [＿＿＿＿＿＿＿＿] or in megahertz (MHz). RAM is different from disk storage because it is [＿＿＿＿＿＿＿＿] , which means that it can hold data only when the computer power is turned on. Computers also contain Read [＿＿＿＿＿＿＿＿] memory, which is a type of memory that provides a set of "hard-wired" instructions that a computer uses to boot up. A third type of memory, called by its acronym [＿＿＿＿＿＿＿＿] , is a non-volatile chip that contains configuration settings, such as hard disk size and RAM capacity.

 **CHECK ANSWERS**

SECTION C: Today's personal computers use a variety of storage technologies. [_____] storage technologies, such as hard disks, floppy disks, and tapes, store data as magnetized particles. A hard disk drive provides multiple [_____] for data storage that are sealed inside the drive case to prevent airborne contaminants from interfering with the read-write heads. Hard disks are less durable than floppy disks, so it is important to make a copy of the data they contain. [_____] storage technologies store data as a series of [_____] and lands on the surface of CDs or DVDs. Storage technologies, such as CD-[_____], are often used for distributing software, but you cannot alter the disk's contents. [_____] technology allows you to write data on a CD or DVD, but you cannot delete or change that data. [_____] technology allows you to write and rewrite data on a CD or DVD. [_____] state storage technologies, such as USB flash drives, store data by activating electrons in a microscopic grid of circuitry.

▶ CHECK ANSWERS

SECTION D: Most computer systems include a keyboard and some type of [_____] device for basic data [_____]. For output, most computers include a display device. A [_____] produces an image by spraying electrons toward the screen. [_____] technology produces an image by manipulating light within a layer of liquid crystal cells. [_____] screen technology creates an on-screen image by illuminating miniature fluorescent lights arrayed in a panel-like screen. Image quality for a display device is a factor of resolution, screen size, dot [_____], viewing angle width, refresh [_____], and color [_____]. A typical computer display system consists of the display device and a [_____] card. For printed output, most personal computer owners select [_____] jet printers, although [_____] printers are a popular option when low operating costs and high duty cycle are important. A [_____] matrix printer is sometimes used for back-office applications and printing multipart forms. Installing a peripheral device is not difficult when you remember that it uses the [_____] bus to make a connection between the computer and peripheral device. Many of today's peripherals connect to a [_____] port. If the right type of port is not built-in to your computer, you might have to add an [_____] card.

▶ CHECK ANSWERS

SECTION E: For trouble-free computer use, it is important to secure and regularly [_____] your computer equipment. Anti-theft devices include computer locks and tie-down brackets. Computers can be protected from power surges and [_____] by connecting to a surge strip. An [_____] power supply can also protect against surges, plus it can supply backup power in case of a power outage. Keeping your computer's [_____] vents free of dust can help to keep its temperature within operational levels. You can also clean dust off the screen and shake dirt out of the keyboard. Problems such as the blue screen of [_____] require troubleshooting. Windows offers interactive troubleshooting tools formatted as a series of simple questions, answers, and recommendations. Booting into [_____] Mode can also be a helpful step in the troubleshooting process.

▶ CHECK ANSWERS

Interactive Situation Questions

Apply what you've learned to some typical computing situations. When using the NP11 BookOnCD, BookOnFlashDrive, or any other NP11 BookOn product, you can type your answers, and then use the Check Answers button to automatically score your responses.

1. Suppose you're reading a computer magazine and you come across the ad pictured to the right. By looking at the specs, you can tell that the microprocessor was manufactured by which company? [   ]

2. The capacity of the hard disk drive in the ad is [   ] GB and the memory capacity is [   ] GB.

3. The computer in the ad appears to have a(n) [   ] controller card for the hard disk drive.

4. You are thinking about upgrading the microprocessor in your three-year-old computer, which has a 2.6 MHz Pentium microprocessor and 512 MB of RAM. Would it be worthwhile to spend $500 to install an Intel Core Duo m processor? Yes or no? [   ]

5. You're in the process of booting up your computer and suddenly the screen contains an assortment of settings for date and time, hard disk drive, and memory capacity. From what you've learned in this chapter, you surmise that these settings are stored in [   ] , and that they are best left unmodified.

6. You're looking for a portable storage device that you can use to transport a few files between your home computer and your school computer lab. The school lab computers have no floppy disk drives, but do have USB ports. You should be able to transport your files using a USB [   ] drive.

7. You want to add a storage device to your computer that reads CD-ROMs, DVD-ROMs, DVD-Videos, and CD-Rs. A DVD/CD-RW will do the job. True or false? [   ]

SUP-R GAME DESKTOP MODEL EE2007

- Athlon™ 64 X2 Dual Core
- 1 GB 400 MHz SDRAM
- 160 GB UltraATA HD (7200 rpm)
- 16x DVD / 52x36x52x CD-RW Drive
- 3.5" 1.44 MB FDD
- 21" 24 dp monitor
- Dual NVIDIA® GeForce™ 6800 Ultra PCI Express 512MB
- Creative Sound Blaster® Audigy®
- Altec Lansing speakers
- Gigbit Ethernet port
- 3-year limited warranty*
- Windows Vista

$ 1299

---

8. You are a professional graphics designer. A(n) [   ] is likely to give you the best colors from all viewing angles, whereas a(n) [   ] may not show true colors when viewed from some angles.

9. Suppose that you volunteer to produce a large quantity of black-and-white leaflets for a charity organization. It is fortunate that you have access to a(n) [   ] printer with a high duty cycle and low operating costs.

CHECK ANSWERS

Interactive Practice Tests

Practice tests that consist of 10 multiple-choice, true/false, and fill-in-the-blank questions are available on both the NP11 BookOn products and the NP11 Web site. The questions are selected at random from a large test bank, so each time you take a test, you'll receive a different set of questions. Your tests are scored immediately, and you can print study guides that help you find the correct answers for any questions that you missed.

CLICK TO START

Study Tips

Study Tips help you to organize and consolidate the information in a unit by making lists, outlines, charts, and sketches. You can use paper and pencil or word processing software to complete most of the Study Tip activities.

2

1. Make sure you can use your own words to correctly answer each of the red focus questions that appear throughout the chapter.

2. Draw a set of quick sketches that show each of the following form factors: desktop tower, desktop horizontal, small form factor desktop, notebook, slate tablet, convertible tablet, UMPC.

3. Create a short consumer brochure that lists 5 characteristics that would help consumers choose among a home, media, game, or small business computer system.

4. Describe the three price-points for personal computers and indicate which price point best fits your computing needs.

5. Explain how Intel Macs are changing the old idea that PCs and Macs are not compatible.

6. Make sure you can list at least three computer upgrades that are easy and explain the upgrade that is most difficult to make.

7. List and describe the factors that affect microprocessor performance.

8. Name two companies that produce microprocessors, and list some of the models that each company produces.

9. List four types of memory and briefly describe how each one works.

10. Describe the advantages and disadvantages of magnetic storage, optical storage, and solid state storage.

11. Create your own diagram to illustrate how the data bus connects RAM, the microprocessor, and peripheral devices.

12. Summarize what you know about how a graphics card can affect a display device's resolution.

13. Make a table with three columns, labeled Input, Output, and Storage/Memory. Page through the chapter and for each device you encounter, place it in one or more of the columns as appropriate.

14. List three ways you can protect your computer from theft.

15. Make a list of ways to keep your computer clean, prevent it from overheating, and protect it from power anomalies.

16. Think about the last time you had a problem with computer hardware or software. Would any of the steps in Figure 2-59 have helped you solve the problem faster? If not, what guidelines would you add to the list in the figure?

17. Fill in the blanks on the concept map below to show the hierarchy of system unit components.

Concept Map

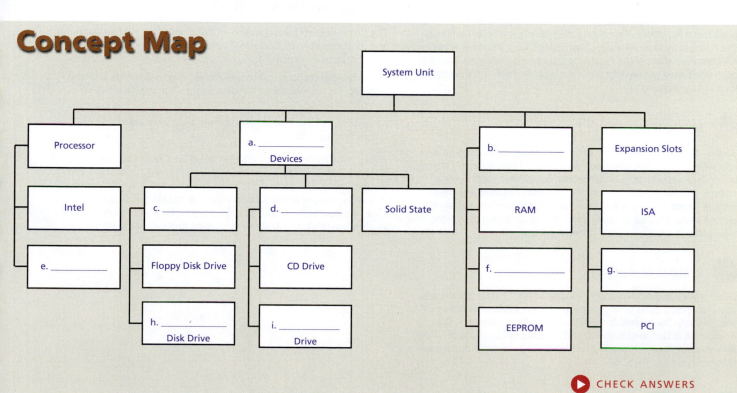

CHECK ANSWERS

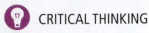

Projects

CRITICAL THINKING

Steve Jobs, co-founder of Apple Inc, coined the idea that computers should be consumer appliances like toasters that could be setup easily, used by anyone, and "democratically priced" so they were affordable to everyone. An opposing philosophy, championed by many PC owners, is that computers should be flexible modular systems that can be easily customized, upgraded, and modified by anyone with a moderate degree of technical savvy. Which philosophy do you personally prefer? What do you think is the preference of the majority of computer shoppers? If you were a computer designer, how would you provide your customers with flexibility while making it approachable for non-techies? Incorporate your ideas in a one-page e-mail message or attachment and submit it to your instructor.

GROUP PROJECT

For this project, work in groups of three or four. The group should select a digital device, such as a printer, scanner, digital camera, Web camera, digital video camera, digital music player, video capture card, digitizing tablet, or accelerated 3-D graphics card. If a member of your group owns the device, that's a plus. Create promotional materials for a tradeshow booth featuring your "product." You might include a product photo, list of specifications, and a short instruction manual. If time permits, your instructor might ask your group to present your sales pitch or a demonstration to the rest of the class.

CYBERCLASSROOM

E-mail the other members of your team a technical support question based on a hypothetical problem you're having with your computer. They should try to solve the problem using their current expertise and relevant Web sites. At the end of the project, evaluate your team's success rate based on the difficulty of the problems and the efficiency of their troubleshooting.

MULTIMEDIA PROJECT

Search the Web for "modding" and collect ideas for souping up your computer system unit, keyboard, and mouse. Make sure you check out options for clear lexan and metallic cases, along with lighting options. Download photos from the Web and print them out, keeping track of sources. Using ideas from your collection of photos, sketch out plans for your ultimate modded computer. Submit your plan along with a list of the sources you used to get ideas and images.

RESUME BUILDER

Use the Web and other resources to learn about the computers and other technologies used in your career field or profession of interest to you. Develop the information you find into a format similar to the Computers in Context section of each chapter in this textbook. Make sure you select two photos to accompany your narrative and include a list of relevant InfoWebLinks.

GLOBALIZATION

Computer ownership is growing worldwide and providing access to productivity tools and a global communications infrastructure. For this project, look for statistics and graphs showing the increase in computer ownership over time. How does it compare to telephone, television, and radio ownership? Are any aspects of this data unexpected or surprising? Gather your graphs and analysis into a two- to three-page executive summary.

ISSUE

The Issue section of this chapter focused on the potential for discarded computers and other electronic devices to become a significant environmental problem. For this project, write a two- to five-page paper about recycling computers, based on information you gather from the Internet. To begin this project, consult the Computer Recycling InfoWeb (see page 107) and link to the recommended Web pages to get an in-depth overview of the issue. Next, determine the specific aspect of the issue you will present in your paper. You might, for example, decide to focus on toxic materials that end up in landfills or barriers that discourage shipping old computers across national borders. Whatever aspect of the issue you present, make sure you can back up your discussion with facts and references to authoritative articles and Web pages. Follow your professor's instructions for formatting citations and for submitting your paper by e-mail or as a printed document.

COMPUTERS IN CONTEXT

The Computers in Context section of this chapter focused on computer and communication technologies pioneered by the military and then adopted into civilian use. For this project, research one of two topics:

- The use of notebook computers in combat environments and how design innovations for military use might affect the design of your next computer

- Developments in wearable computers and how soldiers and civilians might use them

To begin the project, survey the material in the Computers and the Military InfoWeb (page 109). Use a Web search engine to locate additional material relevant to the topic you've selected. Then write a two- to four-page paper about your findings and include graphics to illustrate your points. Make sure you cite sources for your material. Follow your professor's instructions for formatting and submitting your paper.

On the Web

STUDENT EDITION LABS

W **CLICK TO ACCESS THE NP11 WEB SITE**
or open your browser and connect to www.course.com/np/concepts11/ch02.
Lab results can be stored in the Universal Gradebook.

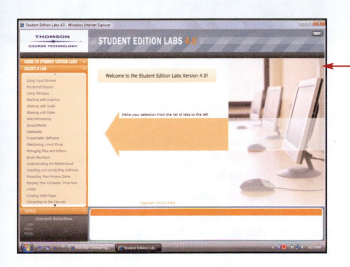

Work hands-on in structured simulations practicing important skills and concepts

PERIPHERAL DEVICES

In the Peripheral Devices Student Edition Lab, you will learn about the following topics:

- Identifying commonly used peripheral devices, such as display devices, printers, scanners, digital cameras, and storage devices

- Adjusting display properties on a monitor and printer settings on a printer

- Identifying storage devices and their appropriate uses

CHAPTER COURSECAST

Use your computer or iPod to hear a five-minute audio presentation of chapter highlights.

FLASHCARD COURSECAST

Interact with audio flashcards to review key terms from the chapter.

DETAILED OBJECTIVES

Make sure that you've achieved all the objectives for a chapter before it's time for your test!

USING INPUT DEVICES

In the Using Input Devices Student Edition Lab, you will learn about the following topics:

- Using a keyboard, including using the function keys and the numeric keypad

- Using a mouse, including double-clicking, right-clicking, and dragging objects

- Identifying other input devices, such as touchpads, stylus, microphones, and digital video cameras

TEST YOURSELF

Review chapter material by taking these ten-question tests, then send your results to the Universal Gradebook.

ONLINE GAMES

Have some fun while refreshing your memory about key concepts that might appear on the next test. You can even send your results to the Universal Gradebook!

AND MORE!

At the NP11 Web site you'll also find Extra Content and InfoWebLinks.

3

Computer Software

LEARNING OBJECTIVES

- Describe the way software is categorized and identify the purpose for each major software category
- Explain the key features and uses for word processing, desktop publishing, and Web authoring software
- Describe the major features of spreadsheet software
- Describe the key features of database software
- List the types of software available for graphics, video, music, education and reference, entertainment, and business
- List guidelines that are important for software shoppers
- Describe the rights granted by copyright law, commercial software licenses, shareware licenses, freeware licenses, open source licenses, and public domain software
- Explain how to install and uninstall software, whether it is supplied on CDs or as a Web download
- Differentiate between local, portable, and Web applications
- Describe the purpose of software updates, patches, and service packs
- List and describe the various types of malware mentioned in this chapter
- Explain how antivirus software works

PRE-ASSESSMENT QUIZ

Take the pre-assessment quiz to find out how much you know about the topics in this chapter. ▶

MULTIMEDIA and INTERACTIVE ELEMENTS

When using the BookOnCD, BookOnFlashDrive, or other NP11 BookOn product, the ▶ icons are clickable to access multimedia resources.

IS MY SOFTWARE UP TO DATE?

Chapter 3 introduces you to basic concepts about computer software. Before you begin reading, take a glance at the software installed on your home, work, or school computer. Want to know if your software is up to date? You can use the "About" feature of any software package to find its version number and discover if a service pack (SP) has been installed.

1.   Start your computer.

2.   Click the Start button.

3.   Click the All Programs option to display a list of installed software.

4.   Point to items in the list that have a ▸ symbol to see a sublist of software programs.

5.   As you read through the list of installed software, jot down the names of any that you're not familiar with. When you read the chapter, you might find out what they do.

6.   Look for Internet Explorer in the list of programs.

7.   Click Internet Explorer to open the program.

8.   Click the Help menu, then click About Internet Explorer. A dialog box appears. It contains a version number like 6.0 or 7.0, and it might also contain a service pack number like SP2. You'll learn the significance of version numbers and service packs when you read the chapter.

9.   Click the OK button to close the About Internet Explorer window, then click the  button to close the Internet Explorer program.

10. Explore the About dialog box for other software on your computer. Does it provide more or less information than the Internet Explorer Dialog box?

WEB SITE

Visit the NP11 Web site to access additional resources 🅦 that accompany this chapter.

Software Basics

COMPUTER SOFTWARE determines the types of tasks a computer can help you accomplish. Some software helps you create documents, while other software helps you block viruses or fine tune your computer's performance. Section A delves into the characteristics of application software, utilities, and device drivers.

SOFTWARE CATEGORIES

What is software? As you learned in Chapter 1, the instructions that tell a computer how to carry out a task are referred to as a computer program. These programs form the software that prepares a computer to do a specific task, such as document production, photo editing, virus protection, file management, or Web browsing.

How is software categorized? The two main categories are system software and application software. System software is designed for computer-centric tasks, whereas application software is designed to help people accomplish real-world tasks. For example, you would use system software to diagnose a problem with your hard disk drive or Internet connection, but you would use application software to edit a photo or write a term paper.

Application software can be divided into subcategories according to its use. System software includes operating systems (discussed in detail in Chapter 4), utilities, and device drivers. System software and application software subcategories are shown in Figure 3-1.

> **TERMINOLOGY NOTE**
>
> The term *software* was once used for all non-hardware components of a computer. In this context, software referred to computer programs and to the data the programs used. It could also refer to any data that existed in digital format, such as documents or photos. Using today's terminology, however, the documents and photos you create are usually classified as *data* rather than as software.

FIGURE 3-1

Software can be classified into categories.

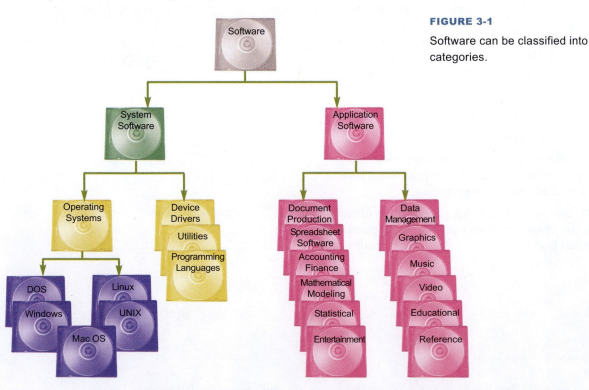

APPLICATION SOFTWARE

Why is it called application software? When you hear the word *application*, your first reaction might be to envision a financial aid application or a form you fill out to apply for a job, a club membership, or a driver's license. The word application has other meanings, however. One of them is a synonym for the word *use*. A computer certainly has many uses, such as creating documents, crunching numbers, drawing designs, and editing photographs. Each use is considered an application, and the software that provides the computer with instructions for each use is called application software, an application, or simply an *app*.

There are thousands of useful software applications designed for personal use or business use. You'll get a detailed look at some of the most popular application software later in the chapter.

What is productivity software? Some types of application software are referred to as productivity software. Many different definitions exist for this popular term. In general, however, **productivity software** can be defined as any type of application software that has the potential to help people do their work more efficiently.

The term might have originated in reference to software tools used by businesses to increase secretarial efficiency at routine office tasks, such as typing, filing, and basic bookkeeping. The applications that are most commonly associated with productivity software include word processing, spreadsheets, schedulers, and database management systems. Graphics software, presentation software, and desktop publishing software are also sometimes classified as productivity applications.

What is groupware? Another type of application software, called **groupware**, is designed to help several people collaborate on a single project using local networks or Internet connections. Groupware usually provides the capability to maintain schedules for group members, automatically select meeting times for the group, facilitate communication by e-mail or other channels, distribute documents according to a prearranged schedule or sequence, and allow multiple people to contribute to a single document.

How do I run application software? Techniques for running applications depend on your computer's operating system, but on most personal computers, you can double-click a desktop icon or select the application from a menu, as shown in Figure 3-2.

FIGURE 3-2

When using a PC, you can usually start application software using the Start menu or a desktop icon.

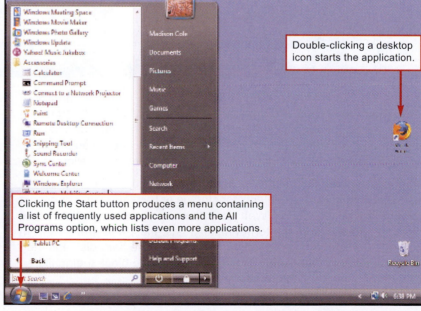

Double-clicking a desktop icon starts the application.

Clicking the Start button produces a menu containing a list of frequently used applications and the All Programs option, which lists even more applications.

 CLICK TO START

UTILITY SOFTWARE

What is utility software? A type of system software called **utility software** is designed to help you monitor and configure settings for your computer system equipment, the operating system, or application software. Examples of utility software include diagnostic and maintenance tools, setup wizards, communications programs, and security software.

Typically, utility software targets a specific task, and includes a much more limited set of features than application software. LIke all system software, utilities focus on computer-centric tasks such as blocking viruses or diagnosing hard disk errors, rather than real-world tasks such as document production or accounting. On a PC, you can access some utility software from desktop icons or the Start menu, just like application software. Other utilities can be accessed from Windows Control Panel (Figure 3-3).

FIGURE 3-3

Windows Control Panel provides access to many utilities. You can open the Control Panel using the Windows Start menu.

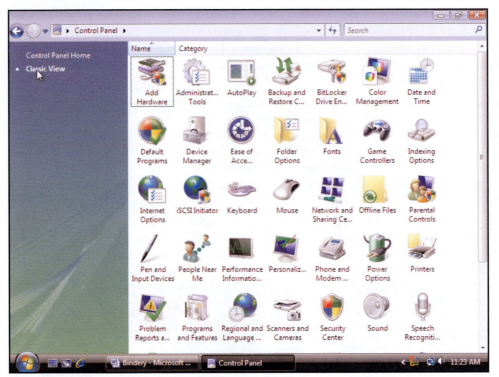

What are the most popular utilities? In recent years, antivirus software, such as Norton AntiVirus and McAfee VirusScan, has been a popular category of utility software. With the recent influx of nuisance ads, intrusion attempts, and spam, utilities such as pop-up ad blockers, personal firewalls, and spam filters have also become best-sellers.

Other security-related utilities include file-encryption software, such as PGP, that scrambles file contents for storage or transmission. For people nervous about the trail of Web sites they leave behind, utilities like 12Ghosts Wash remove Internet history lists, files, and graphics from locations that can be scattered in many parts of the hard disk. Filtering software, such as Net Nanny, is used by parents to block their children from viewing objectionable Web sites.

Acrobat Reader is a long-time favorite utility that transforms all kinds of files into a format that can be created and read by any computer on which it is installed. Acrobat is especially handy for distributing documents created using expensive desktop publishing software that's not likely to be installed on many people's computers.

Computer owners like to customize their screen-based desktops with screensavers that display clever graphics when the machine is idle. *Skins* that customize the look and feel of media players and DVD burners are also popular (Figure 3-4).

Another popular category of utility software is system utilities, such as Norton SystemWorks, and System Mechanic. These utilities can track down and fix disk errors, repair corrupted files, and give your PC a performance-enhancing tune-up.

A final group of utilities worth mentioning is designed for backing up files, cleaning up hard disks, and shredding files so they can't be recovered. Utilities such as Recover My Files, VirtualLab, and R-Undelete can help you recover files deleted by mistake.

What are desktop widgets? A **desktop widget** (sometimes called a gadget, dashboard widget, or control) is a specialized utility program that appears on a computer's screen-based desktop, looks like a control, and might display a snippet of information. Some examples of desktop widgets include clocks, calendars, calculators, news aggregators, sticky notes, and weather stations. Widgets are usually configured to autostart when a computer boots up, and remain on the desktop until the computer is shut down. Widgets can also be corralled in a sidebar or dashboard.

Widgets are sometimes designed to be transparent so that they don't obscure other objects. Figure 3-5 illustrates some popular desktop widgets.

Skins that change the appearance of Windows Media Player are an example of popular utilities.

3

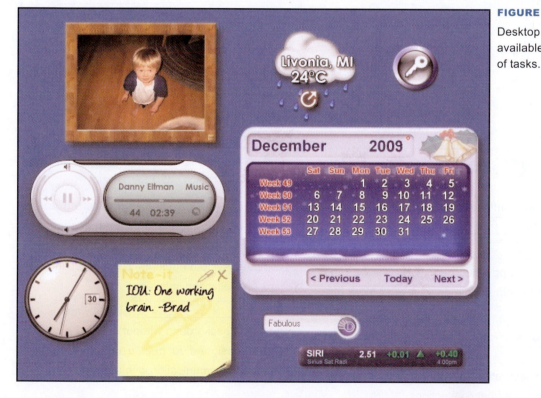

Desktop widgets are available for all kinds of tasks.

CLICK TO START

DEVICE DRIVERS

What is a device driver? A **device driver** is software that helps a peripheral device establish communication with a computer. This type of system software is used by printers, monitors, graphics cards, sound cards, network cards, modems, storage devices, mice, and scanners. Once installed, a device driver automatically starts when it is needed. Device drivers usually run in the background, without opening a window on the screen.

Suppose you connect a new printer to your computer. When you install it, you also install a printer driver. Whenever you initiate a print job, the device driver runs in the background to send data to the printer. The printer driver signals you only if it runs into a problem, such as if the printer is not connected or it runs out of paper.

On a PC, if you need to change the settings for a device driver or update it, you can usually access the driver by using the Start menu's Programs or All Programs option. Otherwise, open the Control Panel and then open the System icon. On the Hardware tab, click the Device Manager button to view a list of all your computer system hardware and corresponding device drivers, as shown in Figure 3-6.

FIGURE 3-6

The Windows Device Manager offers access to device drivers. You can typically check if they are working and change settings. You can also check the device driver's version number to compare it with the most recent version posted online.

Microsoft PS/2 Mouse Properties	? ✕

General | Driver | Details | Resources

Microsoft PS/2 Mouse

Driver Provider: Microsoft
Driver Date: 6/21/2006
Driver Version: 6.0.5600.16384
Digital Signer: microsoft windows publisher

Driver Details	To view details about the driver files.
Update Driver...	To update the driver software for this device.
Roll Back Driver	If the device fails after updating the driver, roll back to the previously installed driver.
Disable	Disables the selected device.
Uninstall	To uninstall the driver (Advanced).

OK   Cancel

QuickCheck

1. The two main software categories are application software and _____ software.

2. _____ software can be defined as any type of application software that has the potential to help people do their work more efficiently.

3. A type of application software that is called _____ is designed to help several people collaborate on a single project using local networks or Internet connections.

4. A type of system software referred to as _____ software is designed to help you monitor and configure settings for your computer system equipment, the operating system, or application software.

5. A device _____ is software usually run in the background without opening a window and is designed to help a peripheral device establish communication with a computer.

 CHECK ANSWERS

Popular Applications

MOST COMPUTERS INCLUDE some basic word processing, e-mail, and Internet access software, but computer owners invariably want additional software to increase their computers' productivity, business, learning, or entertainment capabilities. Section B provides an overview of the vast array of application software that's available for personal computers.

DOCUMENT PRODUCTION SOFTWARE

How can my computer help me with my writing? Whether you are writing a 10-page paper, generating software documentation, designing a brochure for your new startup company, or laying out the school newspaper, you will probably use some form of **document production software**. This software assists you with composing, editing, designing, printing, and electronically publishing documents. The three most popular types of document production software are word processing, desktop publishing, and Web authoring (Figure 3-7).

Word processing software has replaced typewriters for producing many types of documents, including reports, letters, memos, papers, and manuscripts. Word processing packages such as Microsoft Word and OpenOffice Write, give you the ability to create, spell-check, edit, and format a document on the screen before you commit it to paper.

Desktop publishing software (abbreviated DTP) takes word processing software one step further by helping you use graphic design techniques to enhance the format and appearance of a document. Although today's word processing software offers many page layout and design features, DTP software products, such as QuarkXPress and Adobe InDesign, have sophisticated features to help you produce professional-quality output for newspapers, newsletters, brochures, magazines, and books.

Web authoring software helps you design and develop customized Web pages that you can publish electronically on the Internet. Only a few years ago, creating Web pages was a fairly technical task that required authors to insert HTML tags, such as <a href="contents.htm">. Now Web authoring software products, such as Microsoft FrontPage and Macromedia Dreamweaver, help nontechnical Web authors by providing easy-to-use tools for composing the text for a Web page, assembling graphical elements, and automatically generating HTML tags.

How does document production software help me turn my ideas into sentences and paragraphs? Document production software makes it easy to let your ideas flow because it automatically handles many tasks that might otherwise distract you. For example, you don't need to worry about fitting words within the margins. A feature called *word wrap* determines how your text will flow from line to line by automatically moving words down to the next line as you reach the right margin. Imagine that the sentences in your document are ribbons of text; word wrap bends the ribbons. Changing the margin size just means bending the ribbon in different

FIGURE 3-7

Popular document production software includes Microsoft Word, QuarkXPress, and Adobe Dreamweaver.

places. Even after you type an entire document, adjusting the size of your right, left, top, and bottom margins is simple (Figure 3-8).

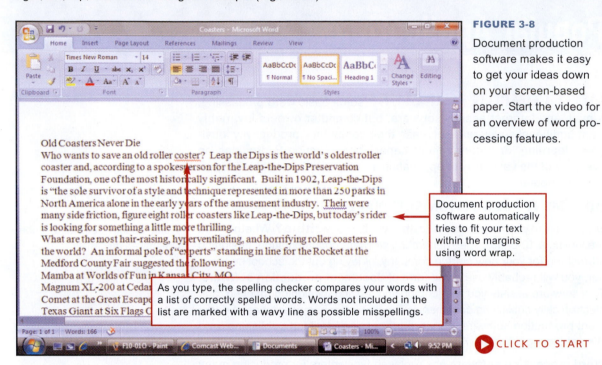

FIGURE 3-8

Document production software makes it easy to get your ideas down on your screen-based paper. Start the video for an overview of word processing features.

Document production software automatically tries to fit your text within the margins using word wrap.

As you type, the spelling checker compares your words with a list of correctly spelled words. Words not included in the list are marked with a wavy line as possible misspellings.

▶ CLICK TO START

What if I'm a bad speller? Most document production software includes a **spelling checker** that marks misspelled words in a document. You can easily correct a misspelled word as you type, or you can run the spelling checker when you finish entering all the text. Some software even has autocorrecting capability that automatically changes a typo, such as *teh*, to the correct spelling (*the*).

Although your software's spelling checker helps you correct misspellings, it cannot guarantee an error-free document. A spelling checker works by comparing each word from your document to a list of correctly spelled words that is stored in a data file called a **spelling dictionary**. If the word from your document is in the dictionary, the spelling checker considers the word correctly spelled. If the word is not in the dictionary, the word is counted as misspelled. Sounds okay, right? But suppose your document contains a reference to the city of Negaunee. This word is not in the dictionary, so the spelling checker considers it misspelled, even though it is spelled correctly. Proper nouns and scientific, medical, and technical words are likely to be flagged as misspelled, even if you spell them correctly, because they are not included in the spelling checker's dictionary.

Now suppose that your document contains the phrase *a pear of shoes*. Although you meant to use *pair* rather than *pear*, the spelling checker will not catch your mistake because *pear* is a valid word in the dictionary. Your spelling checker won't help if you have trouble deciding whether to use *there* or *their*, *its* or *it's*, or *too* or *to*. Remember, then, that a spelling checker cannot substitute for a thorough proofread.

Can document production software improve my writing? Because word processing software tends to focus on the writing process, it offers several features that can improve the quality of your writing. These features may not be available in desktop publishing software or Web authoring software, which focus on the format of a document.

Your word processing software is likely to include a **thesaurus**, which can help you find a synonym for a word so that you can make your writing more varied and interesting. A **grammar checker** reads through your document and points out potential grammatical trouble spots, such as incomplete sentences, run-on sentences, and verbs that don't agree with nouns.

Your word processing software might also be able to analyze the reading level of your document using a standard **readability formula**, such as the Flesch-Kincaid reading level. You can use this analysis to find out if your writing matches your target audience, based on sentence length and vocabulary.

Can document production software help me break bad writing habits? Most word processing, DTP, and Web authoring software includes a **Search and Replace** feature. You can use this feature to hunt down mistakes that you typically make in your writing. For example, you might know from experience that you tend to overuse the word *typically*. You can use Search and Replace to find each occurrence of *typically*, and then you can decide whether you should substitute a different word, such as *usually* or *ordinarily*.

How do I get my documents to look good? The **format** for a document refers to the way that all the elements of a document—text, pictures, titles, and page numbers—are arranged on the page. The final format of your document depends on how and where you intend to use it. A school paper, for example, simply needs to be printed in standard paragraph format—perhaps double spaced and with numbered pages. Your word processing software has all the features you need for this formatting task. A brochure, newsletter, or corporate report, on the other hand, might require more ambitious formatting, such as columns that continue on noncontiguous pages and text labels that overlay graphics. You might consider transferring your document from your word processing software to your desktop publishing software for access to more sophisticated formatting tools. For documents that you plan to publish on the Web, Web authoring software usually provides the most useful set of formatting tools.

The look of your final document depends on several formatting factors, such as font style, paragraph style, and page layout. A **font** is a set of letters that share a unified design. Font size is measured as **point size**, abbreviated pt. (One point is about 1/72 of an inch.) Figure 3-9 illustrates several popular fonts included with document production software.

INFOWEBLINKS

You can add to your font collection by downloading font files from the **Font InfoWeb**.

 CLICK TO CONNECT
www.course.com/np/concepts11/ch03

Times New Roman Font	8 pt.
Times New Roman Font	10 pt.
Times New Roman Font	12 pt.
Times New Roman Font	16 pt.
Times New Roman Font	**16 pt. Bold**
Times New Roman Font	16 pt. Green
Arial Font	16 pt.
Comic Sans MS	16 pt.
Georgia Font	**16 pt. Bold Gold**
Dotto	24 pt. Orange

FIGURE 3-9

You can vary the font style by selecting character formatting attributes, such as bold, italics, underline, superscript, and subscript. You can also select a color and size for a font. The font size for the text in a typical paragraph is set at 8, 10, or 12 pt. Titles can be as large as 72 pt.

Paragraph style includes the alignment of text within the margins and the space between each line of text. **Paragraph alignment** refers to the horizontal position of text—whether it is aligned at the left margin, aligned at the right margin, or **fully justified** so that the text is aligned evenly on both the right and left margins. Your document will look more formal if it is fully justified, like the text in this paragraph, than if it has an uneven or ragged right margin. **Line spacing** (also called **leading**, pronounced "LED ing") refers to the vertical spacing between lines. Documents are typically single spaced or double spaced, but word processing and DTP software allow you to adjust line spacing in 1 pt. increments.

Instead of individually selecting font and paragraph style elements, document production software typically allows you to define a **style** that lets you apply several font and paragraph characteristics with a single click. For example, instead of applying bold to a title, changing its font to Times New Roman, centering the text, and then adjusting the font size to 18 pt., you can define a Document Title style as 18 pt., Times New Roman, centered, bold. You can then apply all four style characteristics at once simply by selecting the Document Title style (Figure 3-10).

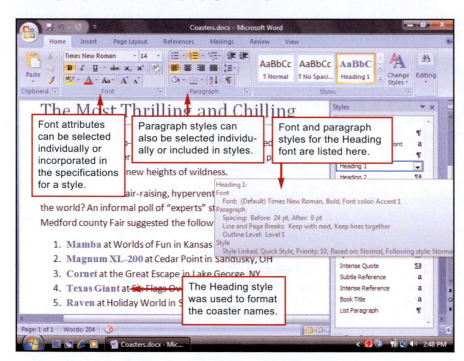

FIGURE 3-10

In this document, coaster names were formatted by selecting the Heading style with a single click instead of individually selecting a font color, font size, and font style. Now if the Heading style is changed to green, for example, all the coaster names will automatically change from blue to green.

● CLICK TO START

Page layout refers to the physical position of each element on a page. In addition to paragraphs of text, these elements might include:

● **Headers and footers.** A **header** is text that you specify to automatically appear in the top margin of every page. A **footer** is text that you specify to automatically appear in the bottom margin of every page. You might put your name and the document title in the header or footer of a document so that its printed pages won't get mixed up with those of another printed document.

● **Page numbers.** Word processing and DTP software automatically number the pages of a document according to your specifications, usually placing the page number within a header or footer. A Web page, no matter what its length, is all a single page, so Web authoring software typically doesn't provide page numbering.

- **Graphical elements.** Photos, diagrams, graphs, and charts can be incorporated in your documents. **Clip art**—a collection of drawings and photos designed to be inserted in documents—is a popular source of graphical elements.

- **Tables.** A **table** is a grid-like structure that can hold text or pictures. For printed documents, tables are a popular way to produce easy-to-read columns and rows of data and to position graphics. It may sound surprising, but for Web pages, tables provide one of the few ways to precisely position text and pictures. As a result, Web page designers make extensive and very creative use of tables.

Most word processing software is page-oriented, meaning that it treats each page as a rectangle that can be filled with text and graphics. Text automatically flows from one page to the next. In contrast, most DTP software is frame-oriented, allowing you to divide each page into several rectangular-shaped **frames** that you can fill with text or graphics. Text flows from one frame to the next, rather than from page to page (Figure 3-11).

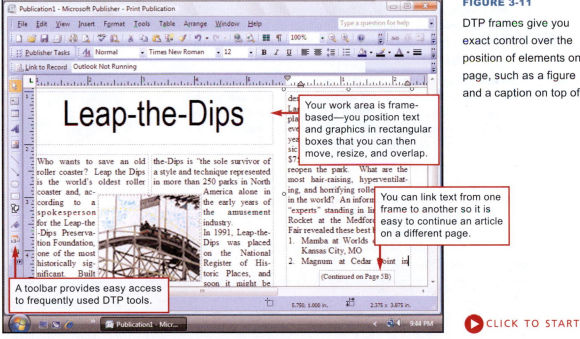

FIGURE 3-11

DTP frames give you exact control over the position of elements on a page, such as a figure and a caption on top of it.

▶ CLICK TO START

Does document production software increase productivity?

Word processing software, in particular, provides several features that automate tasks and allow you to work more productively. For example, suppose that you want to send prospective employers a letter and your resume. Instead of composing and addressing each letter individually, your software can perform a **mail merge** that automatically creates personalized letters by combining the information in a mailing list with a form letter. Some additional capabilities of word processing software include:

- Automatically generating a table of contents and an index for a document

- Automatically numbering footnotes and positioning each footnote on the page where it is referenced

- Providing document templates and document wizards that show you the correct content and format for a variety of documents, such as business letters, fax cover sheets, and memos

- Exporting a document into HTML format for use on the Web

SPREADSHEET SOFTWARE

What is a spreadsheet? A **spreadsheet** uses rows and columns of numbers to create a model or representation of a real situation. For example, your checkbook register is a type of spreadsheet because it is a numerical representation of the cash flowing in and out of your bank account. Today, **spreadsheet software**, such as Microsoft Excel or OpenOffice Calc, provides tools to create electronic spreadsheets. It is similar to a smart piece of paper that automatically adds up the columns of numbers you write on it. You can use it to make other calculations, too, based on simple equations that you write or more complex, built-in formulas. As an added bonus, spreadsheet software helps you turn your data into a variety of colorful graphs. It also includes special data-handling features that allow you to sort data, search for data that meets specific criteria, and print reports.

Spreadsheet software was initially popular with accountants and financial managers who dealt with paper-based spreadsheets, but found the electronic version far easier to use and less prone to errors than manual calculations. Other people soon discovered the benefits of spreadsheets for projects that require repetitive calculations—budgeting, maintaining a grade book, balancing a checkbook, tracking investments, calculating loan payments, and estimating project costs.

Because it is so easy to experiment with different numbers, spreadsheet software is particularly useful for **what-if analysis**. You can use what-if analyses to answer questions such as "What if I get an A on my next two economics exams? But what if I get only Bs?" "What if I invest $100 a month in my retirement plan? But what if I invest $200 a month?"

What does a computerized spreadsheet look like? You use spreadsheet software to create an on-screen **worksheet**. A worksheet is based on a grid of columns and rows. Each **cell** in the grid can contain a value, label, or formula. A **value** is a number that you want to use in a calculation. A **label** is any text used to describe data. For example, suppose that your worksheet contains the value $486,000. You could use a label to identify this number as Income (Figure 3-12).

INFOWEBLINKS

For links to today's best-selling spreadsheet software, connect to the **Spreadsheet InfoWeb**.

W CLICK TO CONNECT
www.course.com/np/concepts11/ch03

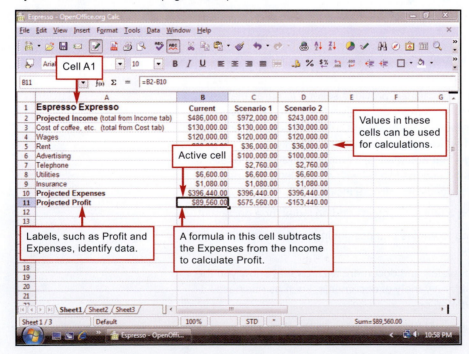

FIGURE 3-12

In a worksheet, each column is lettered and each row is numbered. The intersection of a column and row is called a cell. Each cell has a unique cell reference, or *address*, derived from its column and row location. For example, A1 is the cell reference for the upper-left cell in a worksheet because it is in column A and row 1. You can select any cell and make it the active cell by clicking it. Once a cell is active, you can enter data into it.

▶ CLICK TO START

You can format the labels and values on a worksheet in much the same way as you would format text in a word processing document. You can change fonts and font size, select a font color, and select font styles, such as bold, italic, and underline.

How does spreadsheet software work? The values contained in a cell can be manipulated by formulas placed in other cells. A **formula** works behind the scenes to tell the computer how to use the contents of cells in calculations. You can enter a simple formula in a cell to add, subtract, multiply, or divide numbers. More complex formulas can be designed to perform just about any calculation you can imagine. Figure 3-13 illustrates how a formula might be used in a simple spreadsheet to calculate savings.

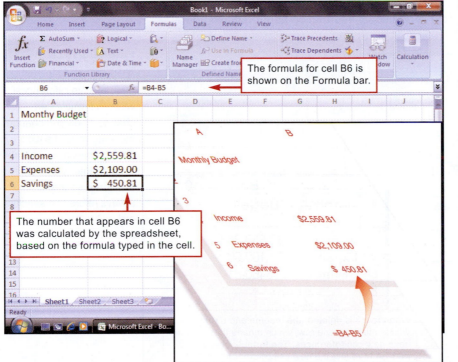

FIGURE 3-13

When a cell contains a formula, it displays the result of the formula rather than the formula itself. To view and edit the formula, you use the Formula bar.

You can think of the formula as working behind the scenes to perform calculations and then display the result.

▶ CLICK TO START

FIGURE 3-14

Functions are special formulas provided by spreadsheet software.

A formula, such as =D4-D5+((D8/B2)*110), can contain **cell references** (like D4 and D5), numbers (like 110), and **mathematical operators**, such as the multiplication symbol (*), the division symbol (/), the addition symbol, and the subtraction symbol. Parts of a formula can be enclosed in parentheses to indicate the order in which the mathematical operations should be performed. The operation in the innermost set of parentheses—in this case, (D8/B2)— should be performed first.

You can enter a formula from scratch by typing it into a cell, or you can use a built-in preset formula called a **function**, provided by the spreadsheet software. To use a function, you simply select one from a list, as shown in Figure 3-14, and then indicate the cell references of any values you want to include in the calculation.

What happens when I modify a worksheet? When you change the contents of any cell in a worksheet, all the formulas are recalculated. This **automatic recalculation** feature ensures that the results in every cell are accurate for the information currently entered in the worksheet.

Your worksheet is also automatically updated to reflect any rows or columns that you add, delete, or copy within the worksheet. Unless you specify otherwise, a cell reference is a **relative reference**—that is, a reference that can change from B4 to B3, for example, if row 3 is deleted and all the data moves up one row.

If you don't want a cell reference to change, you can use an absolute reference. An **absolute reference** never changes when you insert rows or copy or move formulas. Understanding when to use absolute references is one of the key aspects of developing spreadsheet design expertise. Figure 3-15 and its associated tour provide additional information about relative and absolute references.

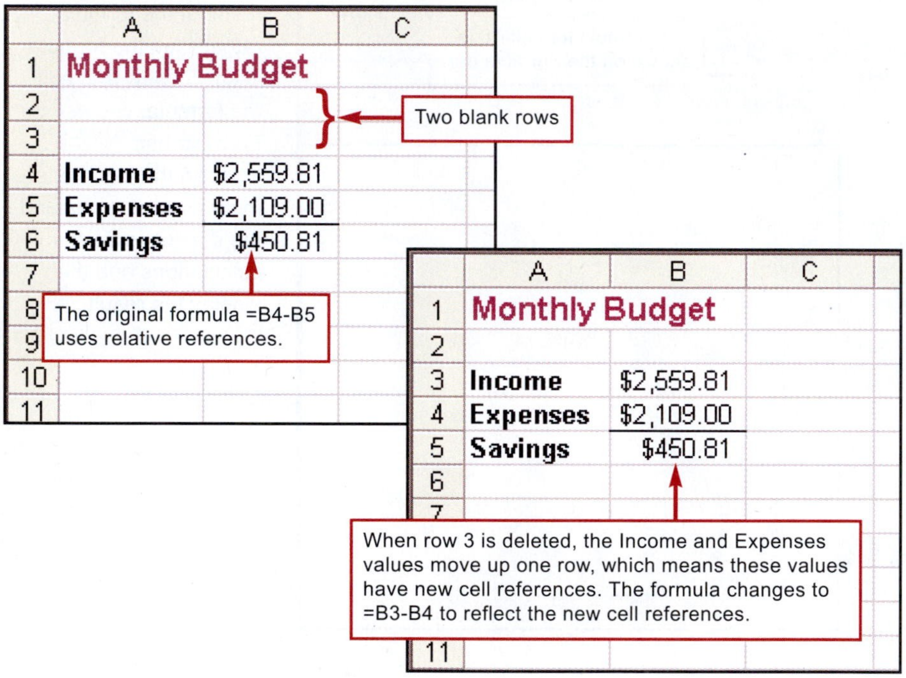

FIGURE 3-15

As shown in the examples, relative references within a formula can change when you change the sequence of a worksheet's rows and columns. An absolute reference is anchored so that it always refers to a specific cell.

▶ CLICK TO START

How will I know which formulas and functions to use when I create a worksheet? To create an effective and accurate worksheet, you typically must understand the calculations and formulas that are involved. If, for example, you want to create a worksheet that helps you calculate your final grade in a course, you need to know the grading scale and understand how your instructor plans to weight each assignment and test.

Most spreadsheet software includes a few templates or wizards for predesigned worksheets, such as invoices, income-expense reports, balance sheets, and loan payment schedules. Additional templates are available on the Web. These templates are typically designed by professionals and contain all the necessary labels and formulas. To use a template, you simply plug in the values for your calculation.

"NUMBER CRUNCHING" SOFTWARE

Aside from spreadsheets, what other "number crunching" software is available? Spreadsheet software provides a sort of blank canvas on which you can create numeric models by simply painting values, labels, and formulas. The advantage of spreadsheet software is the flexibility it provides—flexibility to create customized calculations according to your exact specifications. The disadvantage of spreadsheet software is that—aside from a few predesigned templates—you are responsible for entering formulas and selecting functions for calculations. If you don't know the formulas or don't understand the functions, you're out of luck.

In contrast to the blank canvas approach provided by spreadsheet software, other number crunching software works more like paint by numbers. It provides a structured environment dedicated to a particular number crunching task, such as statistical analysis, mathematical modeling, or money management.

Statistical software helps you analyze large sets of data to discover relationships and patterns. Products such as SPSS and Statsoft STATISTICA are helpful tools for summarizing survey results, test scores, experiment results, or population data. Most statistical software includes graphing capability so that you can display and explore your data visually.

Mathematical modeling software provides tools for solving a wide range of math, science, and engineering problems. Students, teachers, mathematicians, and engineers, in particular, appreciate how products such as Mathcad and Mathematica help them recognize patterns that can be difficult to identify in columns of numbers (Figure 3-16).

INFOWEBLINKS

For more information about popular "number crunching" software, take a look at the **Numeric Software InfoWeb**.

W **CLICK TO CONNECT**
www.course.com/np/concepts11/ch03

3

FIGURE 3-16

Mathematical modeling software helps you visualize the product of complex formulas. Here the points from a sphere are graphed onto a plane, to demonstrate the principles behind the Astronomical Clock of Prague.

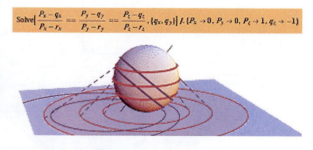

Money management software offers a variety of tools for tracking monetary transactions and investments. In this software category, **personal finance software**, such as Microsoft Money and Intuit Quicken, is designed to keep records of income, expenses, assets, and liabilities using a simple checkbook-like user interface. This software also automates routine financial tasks, such as budgeting, investing, check writing, and bill paying. Many personal financial software products provide direct links to online banking services, so you can use them to check account balances, transfer funds, and pay bills.

Personal financial software produces reports and graphs that show you where your money goes. For example, you can analyze various aspects of your cash flow, such as how much you spent on entertainment last month and how that compares to the previous month.

Tax preparation software is a specialized type of personal finance software designed to help you gather your annual income and expense data, identify deductions, and calculate tax payments. Popular products, such as Intuit TurboTax, even accept data directly from personal finance software to eliminate hours of tedious data entry.

DATABASE SOFTWARE

What is a database? The term *database* has evolved from a specialized technical term into a part of our everyday vocabulary. In the context of modern usage, a **database** is simply a collection of data that is stored on one or more computers. A database can contain any sort of data, such as a university's student records, a library's card catalog, a store's inventory, an individual's address book, or a utility company's customers. Databases can be stored on personal computers, LAN servers, Web servers, mainframes, and even handheld computers.

What is database software? **Database software** helps you enter, find, organize, update, and report information stored in a database. Microsoft Access, FileMaker Pro, and askSam are three of the most popular examples of database software for personal computers. Oracle and MySQL are popular server database software packages. For PDAs, popular choices include Visual CE, Mobile DB, dbNow, and FileMaker Mobile.

How does a database store data? Database software stores data as a series of records, which are composed of fields that hold data. A **record** holds data for a single entity—a person, place, thing, or event. A **field** holds one item of data relevant to a record. You can envision a record as a Rolodex or index card. A series of records is often presented as a table (Figure 3-17).

TERMINOLOGY NOTE

Database software is also referred to as database management software (DBMS).

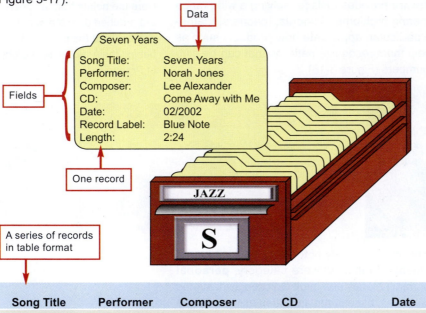

FIGURE 3-17

A single database record is similar to a Rolodex card or an index card. A series of records is usually depicted in table format.

Song Title	Performer	Composer	CD	Date	Label	Length
Seven Years	Norah Jones	Lee Alexander	Come Away with Me	02/01/2002	Blue Note	2:24
Shoot the Moon	Norah Jones	Jesse Harris	Come Away with Me	02/02/2002	Blue Note	3:57
Summertime	Janis Joplin	George Gershwin	Greatest Hits	08/31/1999	Sony	3:28
Summertime	Sarah Vaughan	George Gershwin	Compact Jazz	06/22/1987	Polygram	4:34

Some database software provides tools to work with more than one collection of records, as long as the records are somehow related to each other. For example, MTV might maintain a database pertaining to jazz music. One series of database records might contain data about jazz songs. It could contain fields such as those shown in Figure 3-17. Another series of records might contain biographical data about jazz performers, including name, birth date, and home town. It might even include a field for the performer's photo.

These two sets of records can be related by the name of the performing artist, as shown in Figure 3-18.

JAZZ PERFORMERS

Performer	Birth Date	Home Town
Ella Fitzgerald	14/25/1918	Newport News, VA
Norah Jones	03/30/1979	New York, NY
Billie Holiday	04/07/1915	Baltimore, MD
Lena Horn	06/17/1917	Brooklyn, NY

JAZZ SONGS

Song Title	Performer	Composer	CD	Date	Label	Length
Seven Years	Norah Jones	Lee Alexander	Come Away with Me	02/01/2002	Blue Note	2:24
Shoot the Moon	Norah Jones	Jesse Harris	Come Away with Me	02/02/2002	Blue Note	3:57
Summertime	Janis Joplin	George Gershwin	Greatest Hits	08/31/1999	Sony	3:28
Summertime	Sarah Vaughan	George Gershwin	Compact Jazz	06/22/1987	Polygram	4:34

FIGURE 3-18

The two sets of records are related by the Performer field. The relationship allows you to select Norah Jones from the Jazz Performers records and jump to any records in the Jazz Songs records that Norah Jones performed.

3

How do I create records? Database software provides the tools you need to define fields for a series of records. Figure 3-19 shows a simple form you might use to specify the fields for a database.

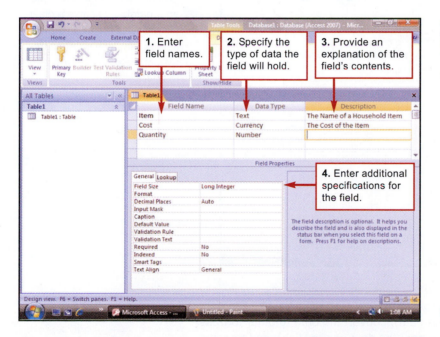

FIGURE 3-19

Database software provides tools for specifying fields for a series of records.

 CLICK TO START

When can I enter data? After you've defined fields for a series of records, you can enter the data for each record. Your database software provides a simple-to-use data entry form that allows you to easily fill in the data for each field. Instead of typing data into a database, you can also import data from a commercial database, such as a customer mailing list. You can even download databases from the Web, and then import the data into fields you have defined with your database software.

How do I locate specific data? Many databases contain hundreds or thousands of records. If you want to find a particular record or a group of records, scrolling through every record is much too cumbersome. Instead, you can enter a **query** to perform a search, and the computer will quickly locate the records you seek.

Most database software provides one or more methods for making queries. A **query language**, such as SQL (Structured Query Language), provides a set of commands for locating and manipulating data. To locate all performances of *Summertime* before 1990 from a Jazz Songs database, you might enter a query such as:

Select * from JazzSongs where SongTitle = 'Summertime' and Date < '1990'

In addition to a formal query language, some database software provides **natural language query** capabilities. To make such queries, you don't have to learn an esoteric query language. Instead, you can simply enter questions, such as:

Who performed Summertime before 1990?

As an alternative to a query language or a natural language query, your database software might allow you to **query by example** (QBE), simply by filling out a form with the type of data you want to locate. Figure 3-20 illustrates a query by example for *Summertime* performances before 1990.

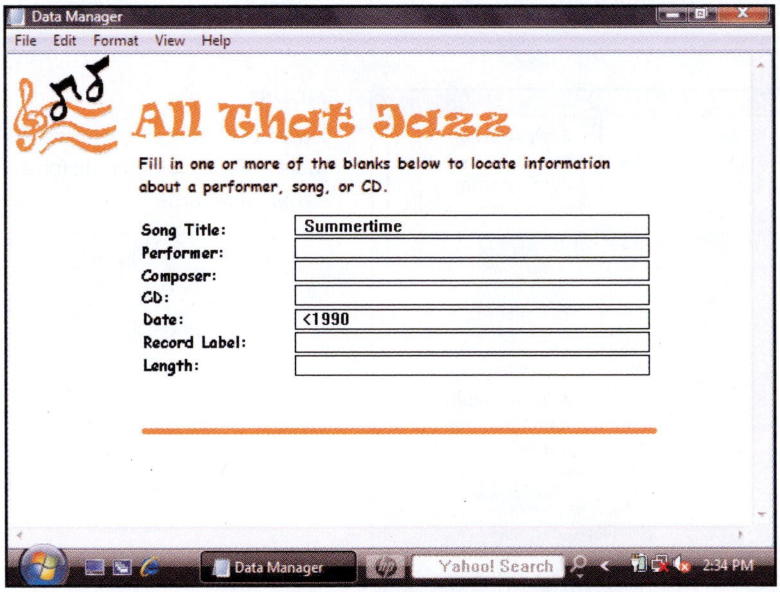

> **TERMINOLOGY NOTE**
>
> A query is a set of keywords and operators that describe information you want to find.

FIGURE 3-20

When you query by example, your database software displays a blank form on the screen, and you enter examples of the data that you want to find.

How can I use search results? Your database software can typically help you print reports, export data to other programs (such as to a spreadsheet where you can graph the data), convert the data to other formats (such as HTML so that you can post the data on the Web), and transmit data to other computers.

Whether you print, import, copy, save, or transmit the data you find in databases, it is your responsibility to use it appropriately. Never introduce inaccurate information into a database. Respect copyrights, giving credit to the person or organization that compiled the data. You should also respect the privacy of the people who are the subject of the data. Unless you have permission to do so, do not divulge names, Social Security numbers, or other identifying information that might compromise someone's privacy.

GRAPHICS SOFTWARE

What kind of software do I need to work with drawings, photos, and other pictures? In computer lingo, the term **graphics** refers to any picture, drawing, sketch, photograph, image, or icon that appears on your computer screen. **Graphics software** is designed to help you create, manipulate, and print graphics. Some graphics software products specialize in a particular type of graphic, while others allow you to work with multiple graphics formats. If you are really interested in working with graphics, you will undoubtedly end up using more than one graphics software product.

Paint software (sometimes called image editing software) provides a set of electronic pens, brushes, and paints for painting images on the screen. A simple program called Microsoft Paint is included with Windows. More sophisticated paint software products include Corel Paint Shop Pro and Procreate Painter. Many graphic artists, Web page designers, and illustrators use paint software as their primary computer-based graphics tool.

Photo editing software, such as Adobe Photoshop, includes features specially designed to fix poor-quality photos by modifying contrast and brightness, cropping out unwanted objects, and removing red eye. Photos can also be edited using paint software, but photo editing software typically offers tools and wizards that simplify common photo editing tasks.

Drawing software provides a set of lines, shapes, and colors that can be assembled into diagrams, corporate logos, and schematics. The drawings created with tools such as Adobe Illustrator and Macromedia Freehand tend to have a flat cartoon-like quality, but they are very easy to modify, and look good at just about any size. Figure 3-21 illustrates a typical set of tools provided by drawing software.

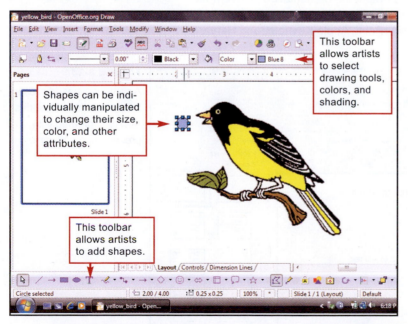

FIGURE 3-21

Drawing software provides tools for creating and manipulating graphics.

3-D graphics software provides a set of tools for creating wireframes that represent three-dimensional objects. A wireframe acts much like the framework for a pop-up tent. Just as you would construct the framework for the tent and then cover it with a nylon tent cover, 3-D graphics software can cover a wireframe object with surface texture and color to create a graphic of a 3-D object (Figure 3-22 on the next page).

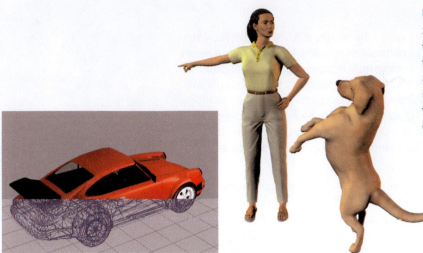

FIGURE 3-22

3-D graphics software provides tools for creating a wireframe that represents a 3-D object. Some 3-D software specializes in engineering-style graphics, while other 3-D software specializes in figures.

CAD software (computer-aided design software) is a special type of 3-D graphics software designed for architects and engineers who use computers to create blueprints and product specifications. AutoCAD is one of the best-selling professional CAD products. TurboCAD is a low-cost favorite. Scaled-down versions of professional CAD software provide simplified tools for homeowners who want to redesign their kitchens, examine new landscaping options, or experiment with floor plans.

Presentation software supplies the tools you need for combining text, photos, clip art, graphs, animations, and sound into a series of electronic slides, like those in Figure 3-23. You can display electronic slides on a color monitor for a one-on-one presentation or use a computer projection device for group presentations. You can also output the presentation as overhead transparencies, paper copies, or 35 mm slides. Popular presentation software products include Microsoft PowerPoint, Apple Keynote, and Harvard Graphics.

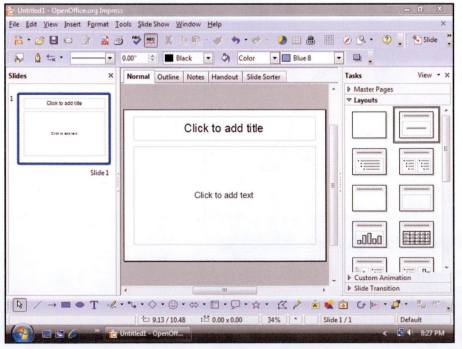

FIGURE 3-23

A computer-based presentation consists of a series of slides, created with presentation software.

CLICK TO START

MUSIC SOFTWARE

Why would I need music software? You don't have to be a musician or composer to have a use for music software. Many types of music software are available. You might be surprised to find how many of them come in handy.

It is possible—and easy—to make your own digital voice and music recordings, which you store on your computer's hard disk. Your operating system might supply **audio editing software**, such as Sound Recorder or you can download open source software, such as Audacity (Figure 3-24).

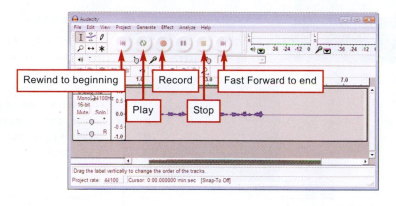

Rewind to beginning   Record   Fast Forward to end

Play   Stop

FIGURE 3-24

Audio editing software provides controls much like those on a tape recorder. Menus offer additional digital editing features, such as speed control, volume adjustments, clipping, and mixing.

Audio editing software typically includes playback as well as recording capabilities. A specialized version of this software called karaoke software integrates music files and on-screen lyrics—everything you need to sing along with your favorite tunes.

Music can be stored in a variety of digital formats on a computer or on a portable audio player, such as Apple's iPod. Digital music formats, such as MP3 and AAC, are not the same formats used to store music on commercial audio CDs. These file formats take up much less storage space than on the original CD.

A variety of software allows you to convert music from commercial CDs for use on computers and portable audio players. **CD ripper software** pulls a track off an audio CD and stores it in raw digital format on your computer's hard disk. **Audio encoding software** (sometimes called an *audio format converter*) converts the raw audio file into a format such as MP3 or AAC. After the file is converted, you can listen to it on your computer, or you can transfer it to a portable MP3 player.

Ear training software targets musicians and music students who want to learn to play by ear, develop tuning skills, recognize notes and keys, and develop other musical skills. **Notation software** is the musician's equivalent of a word processor. It helps musicians compose, edit, and print the notes for their compositions. For non-musicians, **computer-aided music software** is designed to generate unique musical compositions simply by selecting the musical style, instruments, key, and tempo. **MIDI sequencing software** and software synthesizers are an important part of the studio musician's toolbox. They're great for sound effects and for controlling keyboards and other digital instruments.

TERMINOLOGY NOTE

Some CD ripper software also includes audio encoding software so that ripping and encoding seem to happen within a single operation.

INFOWEBLINKS

At the **Music Software InfoWeb**, you'll find detailed information on popular software in this category.

W CLICK TO CONNECT
www.course.com/np/concepts11/ch03

VIDEO EDITING AND DVD AUTHORING SOFTWARE

What can video editing software do? The popularity of computer-based video editing can be attributed to video editing software, such as Windows Movie Maker and Apple iMovie, now included with Windows computers and Macs. **Video editing software** provides a set of tools for transferring video footage from a camcorder to a computer, clipping out unwanted footage, assembling video segments in any sequence, adding special visual effects, and adding a sound track. Despite an impressive array of features, video editing software is relatively easy to use, as explained in Figure 3-25.

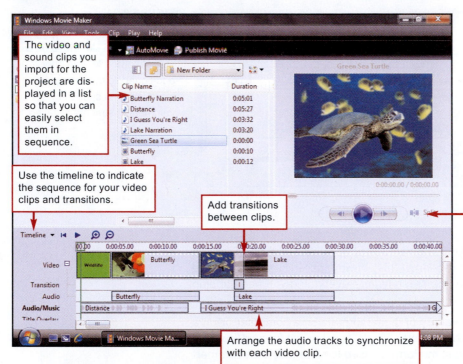

FIGURE 3-25

Video editing software helps you import a series of video clips from a camera or VCR, arrange the clips in the order of your choice, add transitions between clips, and add an audio track.

Desktop video authors now want to transfer their productions to DVDs and watch them on standard DVD players connected to television sets or projectors. **DVD authoring software** offers tools for creating DVDs with Hollywood-style menus. Just like commercial movies, desktop videos can now include menu selections such as Play Movie, Scene Selection, and Special Features. You can use the remote control for your DVD player to scroll through and select menu options. Examples of DVD authoring software include Sonic DVDit, ULead DVD MovieFactory, Apple iDVD, and Adobe Encore DVD.

EDUCATIONAL AND REFERENCE SOFTWARE

How can I use my computer for learning new things? **Educational software** helps you learn and practice new skills. For the youngest students, educational software, such as MindTwister Math and 3D Froggy Phonics, teaches basic arithmetic and reading skills. Instruction is presented in game format, and the levels of play are adapted to the player's age and ability.

For older students and adults, software is available for such diverse educational endeavors as learning languages, training yourself to use new software, learning how to play the piano or guitar, improving keyboarding skills, and even learning managerial skills for a diverse workplace. Exam

preparation software is available for standardized tests such as the SAT, GMAT, and LSAT. Web-based distance education software tools, such as Blackboard and Moodle, help instructors keep track of student progress and provide students with interactive study and testing activities.

What's reference software? **Reference software** provides a collection of information and a way to access that information. This type of software includes massive amounts of data—unlike database software, which is shipped without any data. The reference software category spans a wide range of applications—from encyclopedias to medical references, from map software to trip planners, and from cookbooks to telephone books. The options are as broad as the full range of human interests.

Because of the quantity of data it includes, reference software is generally shipped on a CD or DVD, or can be accessed on the Web. Encyclopedias are the most popular software packages in this category. Bestsellers include Microsoft Encarta and Britannica's CD. An encyclopedia on CD-ROM or the Web has several advantages over its printed counterpart. Finding information is easier, for example. Also, electronic formats take up less space on your bookshelf and include interesting video and audio clips. A single CD is cheaper to produce than a shelf full of hard-bound printed books. These lower production costs translate to more affordable products and allow an average person to own a comprehensive encyclopedia.

ENTERTAINMENT SOFTWARE

What's the best-selling entertainment software? Computer games are the most popular type of entertainment software. Over $7 billion of computer and video games are sold each year in the United States alone. Computer games are generally classified into subcategories, such as role-playing, action, adventure, puzzles, simulations, sports, and strategy/war games, as described in Figure 3-26.

FIGURE 3-26

Game Categories

Type of Game	Description	Examples
Role-playing	Based on a detailed story line—often one that takes place in a medieval world populated with dastardly villains and evil monsters—the goal is to build a character into a powerful entity that can conquer the bad guys and accumulate treasure.	Diablo, EverQuest, Icewind Dale, Planescape
Action	Like arcade games, action games require fast reflexes as you maneuver a character through a maze or dungeon.	Quake, Doom, Unreal Tournament, Enter the Matrix, Tomb Raider
Adventure	Similar to role-playing games except that the focus is on solving problems rather than building a character into a powerful wizard or fighter.	Myst, The Longest Journey, Return to Monkey Island
Puzzle	Include computerized versions of traditional board games, card games, and Rubik's cube-like challenges.	Tetris, Lemmings
Simulation	Provide a realistic setting, such as the cockpit of an airplane. Players must learn to manipulate controls using the keyboard, joystick, or special-purpose input device. A great way to get your adrenaline pumping without expenses or risks.	Flight Simulator, NASCAR Racing, Mech Warrior
Sports	Place participants in the midst of action-packed sports events, such as a football game, baseball game, hockey final, soccer match, or golf tournament. Most sports games offer arcade-like action and require quick reflexes.	NBA Live, MVP Baseball, SimGolf
Strategy	Players (one player might be the computer) take turns moving characters, armies, and other resources in a quest to capture territory.	Age of Empires, Sim City, Warcraft

How do multiplayer games work? Multiplayer games provide an environment in which two or more players can participate in the same game. Even some of the earliest computer games, like Pong, supplied joysticks for two players. Today's multiplayer games are a far cry from those simplistic games. Now numerous players can use Internet technology to band together or battle one another in sophisticated virtual environments.

Large-scale multiplayer games, such as Battlefield 1942 and EverQuest, operate on multiple Internet servers, each one with the capacity to handle thousands of players at peak times. A new twist in online multiplayer games is persistent metaworlds, in which objects remain even when play ends. If one player drops an object, for example, it will be there when other players pass by.

INFOWEBLINKS

The **Entertainment Software InfoWeb** is your link to the best game sites on the Internet.

W CLICK TO CONNECT
www.course.com/np/concepts11/ch03

BUSINESS SOFTWARE

Do businesses use specialized software? *Business software* is a broad term that describes vertical and horizontal market software, which helps businesses and organizations accomplish routine or specialized tasks.

What is vertical market software? **Vertical market software** is designed to automate specialized tasks in a specific market or business. Examples include patient management and billing software that is specially designed for hospitals, job estimating software for construction businesses, and student record management software for schools. Today, almost every business has access to some type of specialized vertical market software designed to automate, streamline, or computerize key business activities.

What is horizontal market software? **Horizontal market software** is generic software that just about any kind of business can use. **Payroll software** is a good example of horizontal market software. Almost every business has employees and must maintain payroll records. No matter what type of business uses it, payroll software must collect similar data and make similar calculations to produce payroll checks and W-2 forms. Accounting software and project management software are additional examples of horizontal market software. **Accounting software** helps a business keep track of the money flowing in and out of various accounts. **Project management software** is an important tool for planning large projects, scheduling project tasks, and tracking project costs.

QuickCheck   **SECTION B**

1. Various kinds of [   ] production software provide tools for creating and formatting printed and Web-based materials.

2. A spelling checker will find an error in "The sailor tied a complex not." True or false? [   ]

3. [   ] software provides a sort of blank canvas on which you can create numeric models by simply painting values, labels, and formulas.

4. [   ] software stores data as a series of records and allows you to establish relationships between different types of records.

5. CD [   ] software transfers files from an audio CD to your computer's hard disk.

6. [   ] authoring software allows you to add Hollywood-style menus to digital videos.

 CHECK ANSWERS

SECTION C

Buying Software

SAVVY SOFTWARE SHOPPERS have a good sense of what to buy and where to find it. Section C offers some shopping tips for expanding your computer's software repertoire. The section ends with a discussion of software copyrights—important information that will help you understand the difference between legal and illegal software copying.

CONSUMER BASICS

What are the most essential applications and utilities to have? In addition to an operating system, your computer should have browser software, an e-mail client, word processing software, a security suite, graphics viewer, and software that lets you burn files onto CDs and DVDs. You will probably also want compression software that lets you shrink big graphics files before e-mailing them, graphics software for editing photos, and some type of diagnostic software for troubleshooting hardware and software problems. For entertainment, you might want sound recording and playback software, as well as a few computer games.

Should I use the apps and utilities that come with the operating system? Most operating systems include a handful of small applications and a good variety of useful utility software. You'll want to thoroughly explore what your operating system has to offer before you spend money on third-party software. Figure 3-27 contains a list of the most frequently used apps and utilities offered by the Microsoft Windows operating system.

Software	Function
Internet Explorer	Browse the Web
Windows Explorer	Keep track of files and folders
WordPad	Perform basic word processing
Notepad	Edit text
Calculator	Add, subtract, and calculate basic functions
Paint	Edit bitmap images, such as photos
Sound Recorder	Digitize music and voice input from a microphone
Windows Media Player	Play music and videos
Backup	Make backups of hard disk files
Disk defragmenter	Arrange data on hard disk for optimal efficiency
Security Center	Set security levels for Internet and network access
Windows Firewall	Block intrusion attempts
Windows Movie Maker	Edit videos
Windows Photo Gallery	View digital photos

FIGURE 3-27

The Windows operating system includes many useful applications and utilities. You can evaluate these offerings before considering whether to supplement them with third-party versions.

If you want utilities other than those included with your computer's operating system, you can explore software offered by third-party vendors. As it turns out, third-party vendors also offer utilities designed for the same tasks as those packaged with operating systems and you might want to consider those as well.

There are two reasons why some computer owners prefer utilities produced by third-party vendors over those packaged with an operating system. Operating system utilities are sometimes not as dependable as third-party utilities designed by companies that specialize in media, system maintenance, or security.

For example, Symantec's Norton SystemWorks has a long track record of producing dependable diagnostic utilities, and McAfee's Security Suite was successfully protecting computers from viruses and intrusions long before Microsoft developed its own set of Security Center utilities.

Additionally, some operating system utilities are not as full featured as third-party versions. For example, although Windows supplies a file compression utility that reduces file size for quick transmission or efficient storage, many computer owners prefer to use third-party utilities, such as WinZip, WinAce, IZArc, QuickZip, or PKZIP, that offer a variety of compression options.

What is the advantage of a software suite? A **software suite** is a collection of software applications sold as a single package. Office suites, such as Microsoft Office, StarOffice, OpenOffice.org, and WordPerfect Office, include applications to boost basic productivity: word processing, spreadsheet, and e-mail software. Graphics suites, such as Adobe Creative Suite, Macromedia Studio MX, and CorelDRAW Graphics Suite, typically include paint, draw, and Web graphics tools. Media suites such as InterVideo MediaOne provide tools for creating music CDs and video DVDs. Security suites include tools to scan your computer for viruses and prevent online intrusions.

Purchasing a software suite is usually much less expensive than purchasing the applications separately. Another advantage is usability. Because all the applications in a suite are produced by the same software publisher, they tend to use similar user interfaces and provide an easy way to transport data from one application to another. The disadvantage of a software suite is that you might pay for applications you don't need. Figure 3-28 lists the components of several popular software suites.

FIGURE 3-28

Software suites are available in many application categories, such as productivity, antivirus, graphics, and media.

Microsoft Office 2007 Professional	**Norton SystemWorks**	**Adobe Creative Suite**	**InterVideo MediaOne**
Word	Norton AntiVirus	Adobe Illustrator	WinDVD
Excel	Norton Save and	Adobe Photoshop	Disc Master
Outlook	Restore	Adobe InDesign	Smart Backup
PowerPoint	Norton Utilities	Adobe Acrobat	Photo Album
Publisher	Norton GoBack	Professional	DVD Copy
Access	One Button		Direct
Accounting	Checkup		CD/DVD
Express	System		Disc Label
	Optimizer		

How do I know if a software program will work on my computer?

Tucked away at the software publisher's Web site or printed on the software package (Figure 3-29) you'll find **system requirements**, which specify the operating system and minimum hardware capacities necessary for a software product to work correctly.

System Requirements

Operating Systems: Windows 95/98/2000/Me/XP/Vista
Processor: Pentium class computer
Memory: 16 MB or more
Hard Disk Space: 10 MB free
Network Protocol: TCP/IP
Network Connection: 10/100 Ethernet LAN/WAN,
cable modem, DSL router, ISDN router, or dial-up modem

eCourse Internet Works
2008 eCourseWare Corp. All rights reserved. eCourse is a registered trademark of eCourseWare Corp.

Where can I find out about the latest, greatest software?

New software appears so quickly that it can seem impossible to keep up with it. However, a collection of publications and Web sites can help you keep abreast of software developments that might improve your computing experience.

Computer and technology magazines, such as *Wired*, *Macworld*, and *PC Computing*, usually include software reviews in every issue. Some magazines focus on games, while others specialize in business or power apps, but if you find a computer magazine that you enjoy reading, it is likely to include information about software that interests you.

Most computer magazines have companion Web sites and some of those significantly extend the material offered in the magazine's printed pages. ZDnet and Cnet (*reviews.cnet.com*), for example, offer in-depth comparison reviews written by experts and tested under laboratory conditions.

Consumer-oriented Web sites also offer reviews. For example, a site at *www.toptenreviews.com* contains easy-to-understand, in-depth checklists that make it easy to compare the features of popular software packages.

User reviews and ratings can be found at download sites, such as *www.download.com* and comparison shopping sites, such as *www.bizrate.com*, *Amazon.com*, and *newegg.com*. You might also find a blog or news feed that focuses on the type of software you typically use.

Where can I get software?

Software is sold in some surprising places. You might find graphics software at your local art supply store. Your favorite beauty salon might carry *Cosmopolitan*'s makeup and hairstyle makeover software. You might even find homeopathic medicine software on sale at a health food store. Of course, software is also available from traditional sources, including office stores, computer superstores, electronics superstores, and discount stores as well as local computer stores. You can buy software from mail-order catalogs, the software publisher's Web site, and software download sites.

What's included in a typical software package? The key ingredients necessary to install new software are the files that contain the programs and data. These files might be supplied on **distribution media**—one or more CDs or DVDs that are packaged in a box, along with an instruction manual. The files might also be supplied as an Internet download that contains program modules and the text of the instruction manual.

Is it better to buy software in a box or download it? Boxed software can be purchased in a store or shipped to you by mail. The box usually includes distribution CDs and an installation manual. It might also include a more extensive user manual, but many software publishers have cut costs by supplying user manuals online or as an extra cost item. The advantage of distribution CDs is their availability in case your hard disk fails and you have to reinstall your software. Boxed software can give you a physical record of your registration code, serial number, and certificate of authenticity, which might be necessary for reinstallation.

You can download software from a Web site instead of buying it in a box. Downloading can be convenient. It saves you a trip to the store and you don't have to wait for a mail order package to arrive. Depending on the speed of your Internet connection, however, downloads can tie up your computer for a few hours. Even with a fast connection a download can be interrupted and you might have to call customer service to restart it without paying for the product again.

Downloading can be risky. Some download sites display an irritating number of ads and are sometimes exploited by hackers. Software downloaded from less reputable sites might contain viruses. When possible you should download directly from the software publisher's Web site or from a download site operated by a reputable business, such as a computer magazine or retailer. In any case, it is good practice to scan downloaded files for viruses before installing them.

Prices for boxed software and Web downloads can vary, so if you have the time to shop around, you are likely to save some money.

SOFTWARE COPYRIGHTS AND LICENSES

What is a software copyright? After you purchase a software package, you might assume that you can install it and use it in any way you like. In fact, your purchase entitles you to use the software only in certain prescribed ways. In most countries, computer software, like a book or movie, is protected by a copyright.

A **copyright** is a form of legal protection that grants the author of an original work an exclusive right to copy, distribute, sell, and modify that work, except under special circumstances described by copyright laws. These exceptions include:

- The purchaser has the right to copy software from distribution media or a Web site to a computer's hard disk in order to install it.

- The purchaser can make an extra, or backup, copy of the software in case the original copy becomes erased or damaged, unless the process of making the backup requires the purchaser to defeat a copy protection mechanism designed to prohibit copying.

- The purchaser is allowed to copy and distribute sections of a software program for use in critical reviews and teaching.

INFOWEBLINKS

To read the actual text of software copyright laws, connect to the **Software Copyright InfoWeb**.

 **CLICK TO CONNECT**
www.course.com/np/concepts11/ch03

Most software displays a **copyright notice**, such as © *2008 eCourse*, on one of its screens. This notice is not required by law, however, so programs without a copyright notice are still protected by copyright law. People who circumvent copyright law and illegally copy, distribute, or modify software are sometimes called software pirates, and their illegal copies are referred to as pirated software.

Can I tell if software is pirated? Software pirates are getting more and more aggressive and pirated software is not always easy to identify. Some unsuspecting consumers have inadvertently obtained pirated software, even when paying full price from a reputable source. According to the Software & Information Industry Association (SIIA), the attributes in Figure 3-30 could indicate that a software product is pirated.

Widespread pirating of Microsoft products has led to preventive measures such as Certificates of Authenticity and expensive-to-duplicate holographic images on CD labels.

If you suspect that software is pirated, it is best not to buy it or install it. If you have questions about a product's authenticity, you can contact the SIIA or the legitimate software publisher.

What is a software license? In addition to copyright protection, computer software is often protected by the terms of a software license. A **software license**, or *license agreement*, is a legal contract that defines the ways in which you may use a computer program. Software licenses can impose additional restrictions on software use, or they can offer additional rights to consumers. For example, most software is distributed under a **single-user license** that limits use to one person at a time. However, some software publishers offer licenses for multiple users to schools, organizations, and businesses.

A **site license** is generally priced at a flat rate and allows software to be used on all computers at a specific location. A **multiple-user license** is priced per user and allows the allocated number of people to use the software at any time. A **concurrent-use license** is priced per copy and allows a specific number of copies to be used at the same time.

Where is the license? For personal computer software, you can find the license on the outside of the package, on a separate card inside the package, on the CD packaging, or in one of the program files. Most legal contracts require signatures before the terms of the contract take effect. This requirement becomes unwieldy with software—imagine having to sign a license agreement and return it before you can use a new software package. To circumvent the signature requirement, software publishers typically use two techniques to validate a software license: shrink-wrap licenses and EULAs.

What is a shrink wrap license? When you purchase computer software, the distribution media are usually sealed in an envelope, plastic box, or shrink wrapping. A **shrink-wrap license** goes into effect as soon as you open the packaging. Figure 3-31 explains more about the mechanics of a shrink-wrap license.

FIGURE 3-30

According to the Software & Information Industry Association, pirated software can sometimes be identified by these characteristics:

- Software sold in a clear CD-ROM jewel case with no accompanying documentation, license, registration card or Certificate of Authenticity
- Software that is marked as "Academic" product
- Software marked as "OEM" or "For Distribution Only With New PC Hardware"
- Software CD-ROMs with handwritten labels
- Backup disks that you receive from a computer retailer containing handwritten labels
- Poor graphics and coloring of accompanying materials (label on the inside of the jewel case)
- Multiple programs from many different publishers on a single CD-ROM (commonly referred to as Compilation CDs)
- If a computer retailer loads software on your PC, and you request the original manual and the dealer responds by saying purchase a third-party book (e.g., "WordPerfect 2000 for Dummies"), this often indicates that the software installed by the retailer is illegal
- Photocopied manuals

FIGURE 3-31

When software has a shrink-wrap license, you agree to the terms of the software license by opening the package. If you do not agree with the terms, you should return the software in its unopened package.

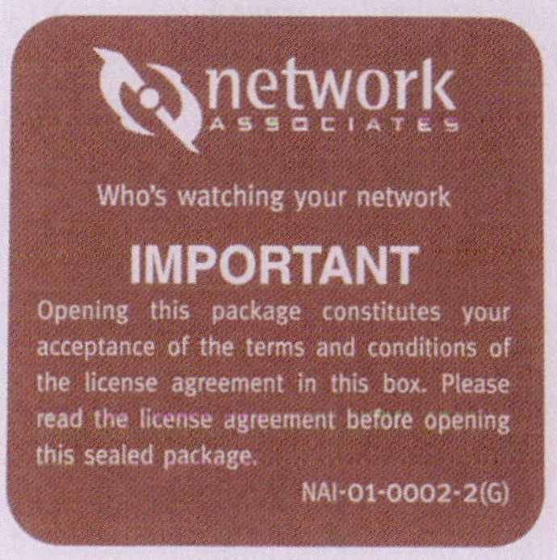

network
ASSOCIATES

Who's watching your network

IMPORTANT

Opening this package constitutes your acceptance of the terms and conditions of the license agreement in this box. Please read the license agreement before opening this sealed package.

NAI-01-0002-2(G)

What is a EULA? A **EULA** (end-user license agreement) is displayed on-screen when you first install software. After reading the software license on the screen, you can indicate that you accept the terms of the license by clicking a designated button—usually labeled OK, I agree, or I accept. If you do not accept the terms, the software does not load and you will not be able to use it.

When I accept a software license, what am I agreeing to do? Software licenses are often lengthy and written in legalese, but your legal right to use the software continues only as long as you abide by the terms of the software license. Therefore, you should understand the software license for any software you use. To become familiar with a typical license agreement, you can read through the one in Figure 3-32.

FIGURE 3-32

When you read a software license agreement, look for answers to the following questions:

Am I buying the software or licensing it?

When does the license go into effect?

Under what circumstances can I make copies?

Can I rent the software?

Can I sell the software?

What if the software includes a distribution CD and a set of distribution floppy disks?

Does the software publisher provide a warranty?

Can I loan the software to a friend?

Software License Agreement

Important - READ CAREFULLY: This License Agreement ("Agreement") is a legal agreement between you and eCourse Corporation for the software product, eCourse GraphWare ("The SOFTWARE"). By installing, copying, or otherwise using the SOFTWARE, you agree to be bound by the terms of this Agreement. The SOFTWARE is protected by copyright laws and international copyright treaties. The SOFTWARE is licensed, not sold.

GRANT OF LICENSE. This Agreement gives you the right to install and use one copy of the SOFTWARE on a single computer. The primary user of the computer on which the SOFTWARE is installed may make a second copy for his or her exclusive use on a portable computer.

OTHER RIGHTS AND LIMITATIONS. You may not reverse engineer, decompile, or disassemble the SOFTWARE except and only to the extent that such activity is expressly permitted by applicable law.

The SOFTWARE is licensed as a single product; its components may not be separated for use on more than one computer. You may not rent, lease, or lend the SOFTWARE.

You may permanently transfer all of your rights under this Agreement, provided you retain no copies, you transfer all of the SOFTWARE, and the recipient agrees to the terms of this Agreement. If the software product is an upgrade, any transfer must include all prior versions of the SOFTWARE.

You may receive the SOFTWARE in more than one medium. Regardless of the type of medium you receive, you may use only one medium that is appropriate for your single computer. You may not use or install the other medium on another computer.

WARRANTY. eCourse warrants that the SOFTWARE will perform substantially in accordance with the accompanying written documentation for a period of ninety (90) days from the date of receipt. TO THE MAXIMUM EXTENT PERMITTED BY APPLICABLE LAW, eCourse AND ITS SUPPLIERS DISCLAIM ALL OTHER WARRANTIES AND CONDITIONS EITHER EXPRESS OR IMPLIED, INCLUDING, BUT NOT LIMITED TO, IMPLIED WARRANTIES OF MERCHANTABILITY, FITNESS FOR A PARTICULAR PURPOSE, TITLE, AND NON-INFRINGEMENT, WITH REGARD TO THE SOFTWARE PRODUCT.

Are all software licenses similar? From a legal perspective, there are two categories of software: public domain and proprietary. **Public domain software** is not protected by copyright because the copyright has expired, or the author has placed the program in the public domain, making it available without restriction. Public domain software may be freely copied, distributed, and even resold. The primary restriction on public domain software is that you are not allowed to apply for a copyright on it.

Proprietary software has restrictions on its use that are delineated by copyright, patents, or license agreements. Some proprietary software is distributed commercially, whereas some of it is free. Based on licensing rights, proprietary software is distributed as commercial software, demoware, shareware, freeware, and open source software.

What is commercial software? **Commercial software** is typically sold in computer stores or at Web sites. Although you buy this software, you actually purchase only the right to use it under the terms of the software license. A license for commercial software typically adheres closely to the limitations provided by copyright law, although it might give you permission to install the software on a computer at work and on a computer at home, provided that you use only one of them at a time.

What is demoware? Some commercial software is available as a trial version, sometimes called demoware. **Demoware** is distributed for free and often comes pre-installed on new computers, but it is limited in some way until you pay for it. Demoware publishers can use a variety of techniques to limit the software. It might remain functional for a set number of days before expiring and requiring payment. It might run for a limited amount of time—for example 60 minutes—each time you launch it. Demoware could be configured so that you can run it for only a limited number of times. Or, key features, such as printing, might be disabled. Disabled features account for demoware's less-than-flattering nickname of crippleware.

Demoware publishers usually take steps to prevent users from uninstalling and reinstalling the demo to circumvent time limitations. Users who want to unlock the full version of a demo can typically do so by following links to the software publisher's Web site and using a credit card to purchase a registration code. The software can then be restarted and used without further interruption after the registration code is entered.

Is shareware the same as demoware? The characteristics of shareware sound very similar to those of demoware. **Shareware** is copyrighted software marketed under a try-before-you-buy policy. It typically includes a license that permits you to use the software for a trial period. To use it beyond the trial period, you must pay a registration fee. The original idea behind shareware was that payment would be on the honor system. Unlike crippled or time-limited demoware, shareware was supposed to be fully-functioning software.

Shareware was conceived as a low-cost marketing and distribution channel for independent programmers. Thousands of shareware programs are available, encompassing just about as many applications as commercial software. A shareware license usually encourages you to make copies of the software and distribute them to others. Copying, considered a bad thing by commercial software publishers, can work to the advantage of shareware authors, but only if users pay for the product. Unfortunately many shareware authors collect only a fraction of the money they deserve for their programming efforts.

3

Today, many shareware authors use demoware techniques to limit their programs until payment is received. The term shareware is used today to refer to programs distributed by independent programmers, whereas demoware tends to be used when referring to trial versions of software from big software firms, such as Microsoft, Adobe Systems, and Oracle.

What about freeware? **Freeware** is copyrighted software that—as you might expect—is available for free. It is fully functional and requires no payment for its use. Because the software is protected by copyright, you cannot do anything with it that is not expressly allowed by copyright law or by the author. Typically, the license for freeware permits you to use the software, copy it, and give it away, but does not permit you to alter it or sell it. Many utility programs, device drivers, and some games are available as freeware.

What is open source software? **Open source software** makes uncompiled program instructions—the source code—available to programmers who want to modify and improve the software. Open source software may be sold or distributed free of charge in compiled form, but it must, in every case, also include the source code. Linux is an example of open source software, as is FreeBSD—a version of UNIX designed for personal computers. OpenOffice.org—a full-featured productivity suite—is another popular example of open source software. You can search for open source applications at the *sourceforge.net* Web site.

Despite the lack of restrictions on distribution and use, open source software is copyrighted and is not public domain. Many open source characteristics also apply to free software (not to be confused with freeware, which you are not supposed to modify or resell). Both open source and free software can be copied an unlimited number of times, distributed for free, sold, and modified.

The philosophies behind open source and free software are slightly different, but their licenses are really quite similar. Two of the most common open source and free software licenses are BSD and GPL. The **BSD license** originated as the Berkeley Software Distribution license for a UNIX-like operating system. The license is simple and short (Figure 3-33).

FIGURE 3-33

Open source and free software applications are plentiful. Many have a very simple BSD license that ensures the source code is distributed along with the compiled software.

Software	Function
OpenOffice.org	Productivity
Thunderbird	E-mail
Firefox	Browser
Galm	Instant messenger
GIMP	Graphics editing
Gallery	Photo viewer
Blender	3D modeling and game design
Audacity	Sound editing and effects
MediaPortal	PC/TV Media Center
AVG free	Antivirus
Avast	Antivirus

open source ™

▶ CLICK TO START

The **GPL** (General Public License) was developed for a free operating system called GNU. GPL is slightly more restrictive than BSD because it requires derivative works to be licensed under a GPL. That means if you get a really cool computer game that's licensed under GPL and you modify the game to create a new level, you have to distribute your modification under the GPL license. You cannot legally market your modification under a commercial software license. There are currently three versions of the GPL license. Their differences are of interest primarily to software developers.

Should a software license affect my purchase decision?

Savvy software buyers typically consider software licenses before they make a purchase. Understanding a software license helps you stay on the right side of the law and can save you money.

Before purchasing software, make sure the license allows you to use the software the way you want to. If you plan to install the software on more than one computer or introduce modifications, make sure the license allows you to do so.

Some commercial software, such as security software, requires annual renewal. If you don't want to pay the fee every year, you might consider open source security software instead. Informed consumers tend to make better buying decisions. Just remember that many software programs exist and you can usually find alternatives with similar features offered under various licensing terms.

3

INFOWEBLINKS

To learn more about open source software and for a list of the most popular open source download sites, connect to the **Open Source Software InfoWeb**.

 **CLICK TO CONNECT**
www.course.com/np/concepts11/ch03

QuickCheck

SECTION C

1. One advantage of a software [_____] is that each application tends to have a similar user interface and it is usually easy to transport data from one application to another.

2. System [_____] specify the operating system and minimum hardware capacities required for software to work correctly.

3. If the opening screen of a software application contains no copyright notice, it is not protected by copyright law. True or false? [_____]

4. [_____] domain software is not copyrighted, making it available for use without restriction, except that you cannot apply for a copyright on it.

5. A [_____]-use license is priced per copy and allows a specific number of copies to be used at the same time.

6. [_____] source software is distributed with its source code so that it can be legally modified and redistributed.

▶ CHECK ANSWERS

Installing Software and Upgrades

IT'S SURPRISING HOW QUICKLY your collection of software can grow as you discover new ways to use your computer for school, work, and play. Before you can use software, you have to install it on your computer. As you read Section D, you'll find out how to install software from CDs or from downloads, how to upgrade your software, and how to eliminate some of the software you no longer need.

INSTALLATION BASICS

What's included in a typical software package? Whether it's on a CD or downloaded from the Web, today's software is typically composed of many files. For example, the eVideo-In Pro software includes numerous files as shown in Figure 3-34.

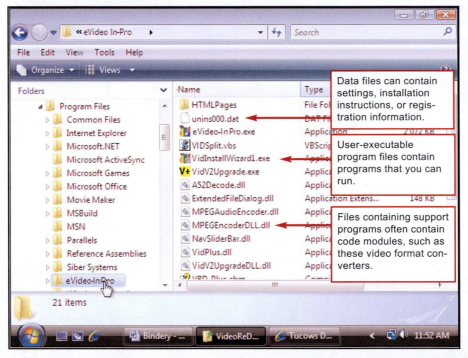

FIGURE 3-34

The files required by the eVideo-In Pro software contain user-executable programs, support programs, and data.

Data files can contain settings, installation instructions, or registration information.

User-executable program files contain programs that you can run.

Files containing support programs often contain code modules, such as these video format converters.

At least one of the files included in a software package is an **executable file** designed to be started by users or automatically launched by the operating system. These programs are sometimes referred to as EXE files (pronounced E-X-E) because of the .exe file extension appended on the program name.

Other files supplied with a software package contain support programs for the computer to use in conjunction with the main executable file. A support program can be called, or activated, by the main program as needed. In the context of Windows software, support programs often have file extensions such as .dll and .ocx.

In addition to program files, many software packages also include data files. As you might expect, these files contain any data that is necessary for a task, but not supplied by the user, such as Help documentation, a word list for an online spell checker, synonyms for a thesaurus, or graphics for the software's toolbar icons. The data files supplied with a software package sport file extensions such as .txt, .bmp, and .hlp. Figure 3-35 can help you visualize how multiple files work together as one software application.

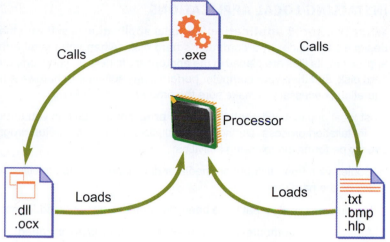

Calls

Calls

Loads

Loads

FIGURE 3-35

The main executable file provides the primary set of instructions for the computer to execute and calls various support programs and data files as needed.

With some operating systems, including Windows, one software program might share some common files with other software. These shared files are often supplied by the operating system and perform routine tasks, such as displaying the Print dialog box, which allows you to select a printer and specify how many copies you want to print. Shared files are not typically distributed with software because they should already exist on your computer. The installation routine attempts to locate these files. It then notifies you if any files are missing, and provides instructions for installing them.

Why does software require so many files? The use of a main executable file plus several support programs and data files offers a great deal of flexibility and efficiency for software developers. Support programs and data files from existing programs can usually be modified by developers for other programs without changing the main executable file. This modular approach can significantly reduce the time required to create and test the main executable file, which usually contains a long and fairly complex program. The modular approach also allows software developers to reuse their support programs in multiple software products and adapt preprogrammed support modules for use in their own software.

Modular programming techniques are of interest mainly to people who create computer programs; however, these techniques affect the process of installing and uninstalling software. It is important, therefore, to remember that computer software typically consists of many files that contain user-executable programs, support programs, and data.

Is it necessary to install software? Software installation (sometimes referred to as setup) is a process that places a program into a computer so that it can be run or executed. Installation can simply be a matter of copying files to a computer or plugging in a USB flash drive, or it can be a more formal process that requires a series of steps and configurations. Installation procedures depend on your computer's operating system and whether the software is a local, Web, or portable application.

For purposes of this discussion, we'll look at software installation under the Windows operating system. The procedure features some quirks and complexities that don't exist with the Mac and Linux platforms, and because Windows use is so pervasive, understanding how to install software on a PC is useful and practical.

INSTALLING LOCAL APPLICATIONS

What is a local application? A **local application** is software that is designed to reside on a computer's hard disk. When you install a local application, its files are placed in the appropriate folders on your computer's hard disk, and then your computer performs any software or hardware configurations necessary to make sure the program is ready to run.

Most local applications contain a **setup program** that guides you through the installation process. During the installation process, the setup program usually performs the following activities:

- Copies files from distribution media or downloads files to specified folders on the hard disk

- Uncompresses files that have been distributed in compressed format

- Analyzes the computer's resources, such as processor speed, RAM capacity, and hard disk capacity, to verify that they meet or exceed the minimum system requirements

- Analyzes hardware components and peripheral devices to select appropriate device drivers

- Looks for any system files and players, such as Internet Explorer or Windows Media Player, that are required to run the program but are not supplied on the distribution media or download

- Updates necessary system files, such as the Windows Registry and the Windows Start menu, with information about the new software

What is the Windows Registry? The **Windows Registry** is a database that keeps track of your computer's peripheral devices, software, preferences, and settings. You'll learn more about the Registry in the operating system chapter, but the important concept to understand is that when you install software on the hard disk, information about the software is recorded in the Registry.

Are all the software files installed in the same folder? Most executable files and data files for new software are placed in the folder you specify. Some support programs for the software, however, might be stored in other folders, such as Windows\System. The location for these files is determined by the software installation routine. Figure 3-36 maps out the location of files for a typical Windows software installation.

> **TERMINOLOGY NOTE**
>
> Although the term *local application* seems to imply application software as opposed to system software, it is also used in a broader sense to refer to any system or application software that is installed locally on the hard disk.

FIGURE 3-36

When you install software, its files might end up in different folders. Files for the eVideo-In Pro software are installed in two folders.

Distribution CDs

Windows\System

File name	Size	Type
eVidmdbg.dll	20 KB	Support Program
eVidodec32.dll	92 KB	Support Program
eVidwave.dll	37 KB	Support Program
Version.dll	24 KB	Support Program
eVidpodbc.dll	955 KB	Support Program
eVidgain.dll	116 KB	Support Program
eVgateway.ocx	42 KB	Support Program

Program Files\ eVideo-In Pro

File name	Size	Type
eVidpro.exe	5,500 KB	Main Executable Program
eVidpro.hlp	275 KB	Help File
eVidcore.hlp	99 KB	Help File
eVidcore.dll	1,425 KB	Support Program
eVidpro.dll	1,517 KB	Support Program
Readme.doc	65 KB	Data File
eVdplugin.dll	813 KB	Support Program
eVdtrans.dll	921 KB	Support Program

How do I install local applications from CDs and DVDs?

How do I install local applications from CDs and DVDs? The process of installing a local application from distribution CDs or DVDs is quite straightforward. You insert the CD or DVD and close the tray. A setup program should autostart and then guide you through the process of selecting the hard disk location for the program files and acknowledging the EULA. Figure 3-37 shows what to expect when you use a setup program to install local apps from CDs or DVDs.

FIGURE 3-37

Installing from Distribution Media

3

1 Insert the first distribution CD or DVD. The setup program should start automatically. If it does not, look for a file called Setup.exe and then run it.

2 Read the license agreement, if one is presented on the screen. By agreeing to the terms of the license, you can proceed with the installation.

> ● **Full Installation**
> ○ **Custom Installation**

3 Select the installation option that best meets your needs. If you select a full installation, the setup program copies all files and data from the distribution medium to the hard disk of your computer system. A full installation gives you access to all features of the software.

If you select a custom installation, the setup program displays a list of software features for your selection. After you select the features you want, the setup program copies only the selected program and data files to your hard disk. A custom installation can save space on your hard disk.

4 Follow the prompts provided by the setup program to specify a folder to hold the new software program. You can use the default folder specified by the setup program or a folder of your own choosing, You can also create a new folder during the setup process.

5 If the software includes multiple distribution CDs, insert each one in the specified drive when the setup program prompts you.

6 When the setup is complete, start the program you just installed to make sure it works.

How do I install downloaded software? The installation process is slightly different for Windows software that you download. Usually all the files needed for the new software are **zipped** to consolidate them into one large file, which is compressed to decrease its size and reduce the download time. As part of the installation process, this downloaded file must be reconstituted, or **unzipped**, into the original collection of files.

It is a good idea to store original unzipped files for downloaded software on a CD or in a hard disk folder that you back up periodically. If your computer's hard drive malfunctions, you can use these files to reconstitute your software without having to download all of it again. Figure 3-38 maps out the process of downloading and installing local apps.

FIGURE 3-38

Installing Downloaded Software

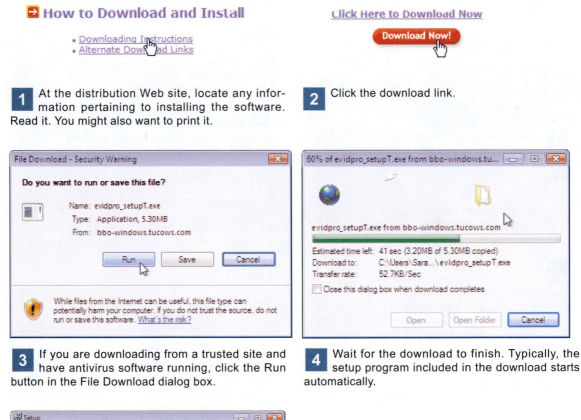

1 At the distribution Web site, locate any information pertaining to installing the software. Read it. You might also want to print it.

2 Click the download link.

3 If you are downloading from a trusted site and have antivirus software running, click the Run button in the File Download dialog box.

4 Wait for the download to finish. Typically, the setup program included in the download starts automatically.

5 Use the setup program to specify a folder to hold the new software program. You can use the default folder specified by the setup program or a folder of your own choosing. You can also create a new folder during the setup process.

6 Wait for the setup program to uncompress the downloaded file and install the software in the selected directory. During this process, respond to license agreement and other prompts. When the installation is complete, test the software to make sure it works.

Downloadable software can be provided in several different formats. Some automatically install themselves, but others require manual procedures. A downloadable file typically is set up as a **self-installing executable file**, **self-executing zip file**, or **non-executing zip file** (Figure 3-39).

FIGURE 3-39

Downloadable File Formats

Self-installing Executable Files

Under the most automated installation system, the process of downloading new software automatically initiates the entire installation process.

The software download is packaged as one large file with an .exe extension. This file automatically unzips itself and starts the setup program. You simply follow the setup program prompts to acknowledge the license agreement, indicate the folder for the software files, and complete the installation.

Self-executing Zip Files

Downloaded files with .exe extensions do not always install themselves. Some are simply self-executing zip files, which automatically unzip the software's files, but do not automatically start the setup program.

To install software from a self-executing zip file, you start the executable file to unzip the files for the new software. One of these files will be the Setup.exe program. Next, you manually start the setup program and follow its prompts to complete the installation.

Non-executing Zip Files

If you download software and it arrives as one huge file with a .zip extension, you must locate this file on your hard disk and then use Windows XP or a program such as WinZip to unzip it.

After unzipping the file, you must run the setup program to acknowledge the license agreement, indicate the folder for the software files, and complete the installation.

3

What if my software requires activation? **Product activation** is a means of protecting software from illegal copying by requiring users to enter a product key or activation code before the software can be used. Activation is usually part of the software installation process, but it can also occur when demoware times out. Failure to enter a valid code prohibits the program from launching.

Product activation is not the same as registration, which is designed to collect demographic information from consumers, although a few software publishers tie activation and registration together.

Software can be activated over the phone or more commonly on the Internet. Usually a message appears onscreen instructing you to enter a serial number or validation code supplied on the distribution medium, packaging material, or download site. The information you enter is either checked against a database or used to create a hash value.

Checking an activation code against a database, makes sure that the code you've entered has not been used before. If the code is a duplicate, the license for that copy of the software is being used by someone else and you will have to call customer service to straighten out the problem.

A **hash value** is a unique number derived from encoding one or more data sets, such as names, serial numbers, and validation codes. Product validation can create a hash value based on your validation code and your computer's internal serial number, effectively tying the software to use on one specific computer.

Validation codes are very important. You should keep a list of them in a safe place, along with other configuration information for your computer system.

INSTALLING PORTABLE SOFTWARE AND WEB APPS

What is portable software? **Portable software** is designed to run from removable storage, such as a CD or USB flash drive. Program files do not exist on the hard disk, no configuration data is stored on the hard disk, and no entries need to be made in the Windows Registry. When the media containing the portable software is removed from the computer, no trace of it is left there.

Your BookOnCD is an example of portable software. To use it, you simply insert the CD containing the program files. Other examples of portable applications include OpenOffice.org, Thunderbird (e-mail), Firefox (browser), and FileZilla (upload and download), designed to run from USB flash drives.

How do I install portable software? Portable software is so simple to install that it is sometimes referred to as install-free software. Installation is simply a matter of getting program files to the media on which they are supposed to run. For example, suppose that you want to run Portable OpenOffice.org from a USB flash drive. You can download the Portable OpenOffice.org zip file and then simply unzip it so that the files end up on the USB flash drive (Figure 3-40).

FIGURE 3-40

Portable OpenOffice.org offers word processing, spreadsheet, database, graphics, and presentation modules that can be run from a USB flash drive and transported from one computer to another.

▶ CLICK TO START

What are Web apps? A **Web application** (or Web app) is software that is accessed with a Web browser. Instead of running locally, much of the program code for the software runs on a remote computer connected to the Internet or other computer network. Web apps are available for many of the same applications that run locally, such as e-mail, calendars, databases, photo sharing, project management, maps, games, and even word processing. Google offers popular spreadsheet and word processing Web apps that allow group collaboration on projects from participants in multiple locations (Figure 3-41 on the next page).

How do I install Web apps? Some Web apps, such as Gmail and Yahoo! Mail, require no installation at all on your local computer. These applications use browser software as the e-mail client software, making it possible to access your e-mail from any computer that has a browser and an Internet connection.

Some Web applications, such as Google Earth, require a client-side program to be installed on your local computer. The Internet sites that host Web apps typically include instructions if installation is necessary. You can print the instructions if they look somewhat tricky.

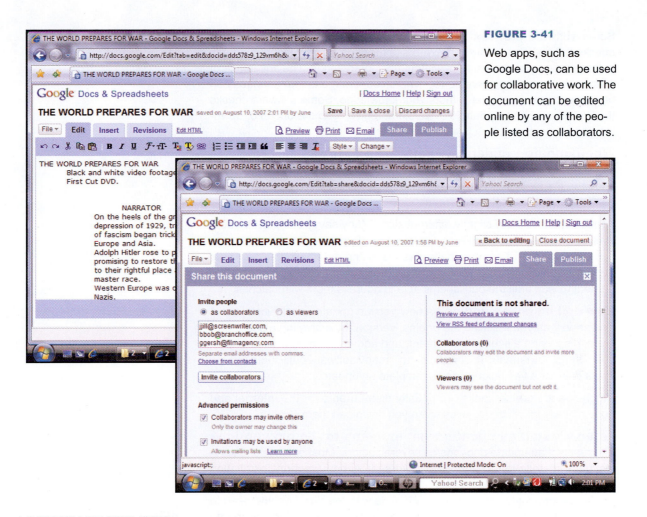

FIGURE 3-41

Web apps, such as Google Docs, can be used for collaborative work. The document can be edited online by any of the people listed as collaborators.

3

SOFTWARE UPDATES

What are updates, patches, and service packs? Software publishers regularly update their software to add new features, fix bugs, and update its security. Types of software updates (also called upgrades), include new versions, patches, and service packs.

Periodically software publishers produce new versions of their software designed to replace older versions. To keep these updates straight, each one carries a version or revision number. For example, version 1.0 might be replaced by a newer version 1.1 or version 2.0. Updating to a new version usually involves a fee, but it is typically less costly than purchasing the new version off the shelf.

A **software patch** is a small section of program code that replaces part of the software you currently have installed. The term **service pack**, which usually applies to operating system updates, is a set of patches that correct problems and address security vulnerabilities. Software patches and service packs are usually free.

How do I get updates? Software publishers have various ways of notifying customers about updates. Many allow you to set your preferences for how you would like to receive notifications and updates. If you have registered your software—usually by connecting to the publisher's Web site during or after an installation—you might receive an e-mail notice when an update is available. Alternatively, you can check the publisher's Web site from time to time.

Some software provides an Automatic Update option that periodically checks the software publisher's Web site for updates, downloads updates automatically, and installs them without user intervention. The advantage of Automatic Update is convenience. The disadvantage is that changes can be made to your computer without your knowledge. Some software checks the Web to see if an update is available and gives you the option of downloading and installing it.

When should I update my software? It is always a good idea to install patches and service packs when they become available. The revised code they contain often addresses security vulnerabilities and the sooner you patch up those holes, the better.

Version updates are a slightly different story. Many savvy computer owners wait to update for a few weeks or months after new software versions become available. The reason they wait is to find out how other users like the new version. If Internet chatter indicates some major flaws, it can be prudent to wait until the publisher is able to address them with patches.

How do I install an update? A new version update usually installs in a similar way as you installed the original version, by activating a setup program, displaying a license agreement, and adding updated entries to your computer's Start menu. To combat piracy, many software publishers require users to enter a validation code to complete an update.

Patches and service packs are usually distributed over the Internet and automatically install themselves when you download them.

When I install an update, what happens to the old version? The result of an update depends on several factors. Most patches and service pack installations cannot be reversed. A new version installation typically overwrites the old version, but you might have the option to keep the old version just in case you have trouble with the new one and need to revert back to the previous version. The documentation for the update should explain your options for retaining or overwriting old versions.

UNINSTALLING SOFTWARE

How do I know what software is installed on my computer? When working with a PC, there are several places you can look to see what software is installed. The All Programs menu lists most, if not all, of your installed applications. A few applications might not appear on this list if they were installed in a nonstandard way.

You can find information about drivers by using Control Panel's System option. Click the Device Manager option on the Hardware tab to view a list of your computer's hardware. Clicking a device from the list links to information about the device driver, including its publisher, date, and version.

How do I get rid of software? With some operating systems, such as DOS, you can remove software simply by deleting its files. Other operating systems, such as Windows and Mac OS, include an **uninstall routine**, (Figure 3-42) which deletes the software's files from various folders on your computer's hard disk. The uninstall routine also removes

FIGURE 3-42

The menu option that you use to launch a program might also include an uninstall option.

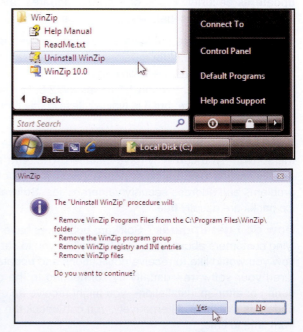

references to the program from the desktop and from operating system files, such as the file system and, in the case of Windows, the Windows Registry.

If an uninstall routine is not provided by the software, you can use the uninstall procedure supplied by your computer's operating system (Figure 3-43).

3

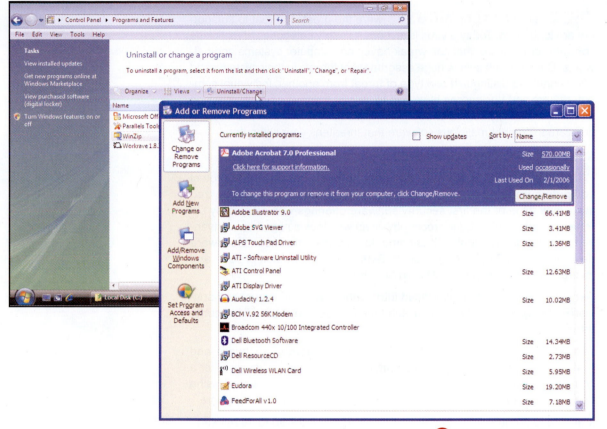

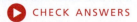 CLICK TO START

QuickCheck

1. At least one of the files included in a software package is an _____ file designed to be started by users.

2. A _____ application is software that is designed to reside on a computer's hard disk.

3. Usually all the files for downloaded software are zipped to consolidate them into one large file. True or false? _____

4. _____ software is designed to run from removable storage, such as a CD or USB flash drive.

5. A software _____ is a small section of program code that replaces part of the software you currently have installed.

● CHECK ANSWERS

Security Software

THE DAYS WHEN VIRUSES were the greatest threat to computers are long gone. Today a virus is just one of many categories of malicious software, or malware, that can wreak havoc on computer systems and networks. Deluged with such a huge assortment of threats to their systems and often unable to distinguish one type of threat from another, individual computer users and businesses have had to defend themselves by purchasing all kinds of security software. Section E explains how you can use security software to combat malicious software that threatens your computer.

SECURITY SOFTWARE BASICS

What is security software? **Security software** is designed to protect computers from various forms of destructive software and unauthorized intrusions. One of the first security software offerings was created by Dr. Peter Tippett, an emergency room physician who took a page from conventional medicine and applied it to computer viruses. The security software developed by Dr. Tippett was sold to Symantec Corporation in 1992 and incorporated into the popular Norton AntiVirus software.

Security software can be classified into various types: antivirus, anti-spyware, anti-spam, and firewalls. Each type focuses on a specific security threat.

What are malware threats? The terms **malicious software** and **malware** refer to any computer program designed to surreptitiously enter a computer, gain unauthorized access to data, or disrupt normal processing operations. Malware includes viruses, worms, Trojans, bots, and spyware.

Malware is created and unleashed by individuals referred to as hackers, crackers, black hats, or cybercriminals. The motivation behind malware is varied. Some malware is intended to be a relatively harmless prank or mildly annoying vandalism. Other malware is created to distribute political messages or to disrupt operations at specific companies. In an increasing number of cases, the motivation is monetary gain. Malware designed for identity theft or extortion has become a very real threat to individuals and corporations. Organized crime bosses, drug traffickers, and terrorists are joining forces with cybercriminals to increase the sophistication of their activities (Figure 3-44).

Emerging security threats often combine and refine old exploits, blurring the lines between viruses, worms, and other kinds of malware. For example, a Trojan horse might carry a bot that turns a victim's computer into a distribution point for a mass-mailing worm. Security experts use the term **blended threat** to describe malware that combines more than one type of malicious program. Although the nuances of blended threats are beyond the scope of this chapter, it is important to understand the threats posed by viruses, worms, Trojans, bots, and spyware if you hope to avoid identity theft and other inconvenient computing incidents.

FIGURE 3-44

Security breaches were once little more than pranks, but today's threats from organized crime and terrorists are serious concerns, not only for individuals, but for corporations and governments.

What is a virus? A **computer virus** is a set of program instructions that attaches itself to a file, reproduces itself, and spreads to other files. A common misconception is that viruses spread themselves from one computer to another. They don't. Viruses can replicate themselves only on the host computer. A key characteristic of viruses is their ability to lurk in a computer for days or months, quietly replicating themselves. While this replication takes place, you might not even know that your computer has contracted a virus; therefore, it is easy to inadvertently spread infected files to other people's computers.

In addition to replicating itself, a virus might deliver a payload, which could be as harmless as displaying an annoying message or as devastating as corrupting the data on your computer's hard disk. It can corrupt files, destroy data, display an irritating message, or otherwise disrupt computer operations. A trigger event, such as a specific date, can unleash some viruses. For example, the Michelangelo virus triggers on March 6, the birthday of artist Michelangelo. Viruses that deliver their payloads on a specific date are sometimes referred to as time bombs. Viruses that deliver their payloads in response to some other system event are referred to as logic bombs.

Viruses spread when people distribute infected files by exchanging disks and CDs, sending e-mail attachments, exchanging music on file-sharing networks, and downloading software from the Web.

What is a worm? A **computer worm** is a self-replicating program designed to carry out some unauthorized activity on a victim's computer. Worms can spread themselves from one computer to another without any assistance from victims. They can enter a computer through security holes in browsers and operating systems, as e-mail attachments, and by victims clicking on infected pop-up ads or links contained in e-mails.

Mass-mailing worms such as Klez, Netsky, MyDoom, Sasser, and Bagle (also called Beagle) have made headlines and caused havoc on personal computers, LANs, and Internet servers. A **mass-mailing worm** spreads by sending itself to every address in the address book of an infected computer. To make these worms difficult to track, the *From* line of the infected message sometimes contains a spoofed address of a randomly selected person from the e-mail address book.

Although e-mail is currently the primary vehicle used to spread worms, hackers have also devised ways to spread worms over file-sharing networks, such as Kazaa. Some worms are designed to spread over instant messaging links. Worms such as Cabir and Symbos_skulls can even infect mobile phones.

What is a Trojan Horse? A **Trojan horse** (sometimes simply called a *Trojan*) is a computer program that seems to perform one function while actually doing something else. Unlike a worm, a Trojan is not designed to spread itself to other computers. Also differing from viruses and worms, Trojans are not typically designed to replicate themselves. Trojans are standalone programs that masquerade as useful utilities or applications, which victims download and install unaware of their destructive nature.

Trojan horses are notorious for stealing passwords using a **keylogger**—a type of program that records keystrokes. Another type of Trojan called a **Remote Access Trojan** (RAT) has backdoor capabilities that allow remote hackers to transmit files to victims' computers, search for data, run programs, and use a victim's computer as a relay station for breaking into other computers.

INFOWEBLINKS

The old saying "know thy enemy" applies to malicious software. To learn more details about current threats, visit the **Virus Descriptions InfoWeb**.

W CLICK TO CONNECT
www.course.com/np/concepts11/ch03

3

TERMINOLOGY NOTE

A *spoofed address* is one that is misleading or incorrect. In the case of e-mail, it is not the actual address of the person or computer that sent the e-mail message. Spoofed addresses make it difficult or impossible to trace mail back to the sender.

What is a bot? Any software that can automate a task or autonomously execute a task when commanded to do so is called an intelligent agent. Because an intelligent agent behaves somewhat like a robot, it is often called a **bot**.

Good bots perform a variety of helpful tasks such as scanning the Web to assemble data for search engines like Google. Some bots offer online help, while others monitor chat groups for prohibited behavior and language. Bad bots, on the other hand, are controlled by hackers and designed for unauthorized or destructive tasks. They can be spread by worms or Trojans. Most bad bots are able to initiate communications with a central server on the Internet to receive instructions. A computer under the control of a bad bot is sometimes referred to as a **zombie** because it carries out instructions from a malicious leader.

Like a spider in its web, the person who controls many bot-infested computers can link them together into a network called a **botnet**. Experts have discovered botnets encompassing more than one million computers. Botmasters who control botnets use the combined computing power of their zombie legions for many types of nefarious tasks such as breaking into encrypted data, carrying out Denial of Service attacks against other computers, and sending out massive amounts of spam.

What is spyware? **Spyware** is a type of program that secretly gathers personal information without the victim's knowledge, usually for advertising and other commercial purposes. Once it is installed, spyware starts monitoring Web-surfing and purchasing behavior, and sends a summary back to one or more third parties. Just like Trojans, spyware can monitor keystrokes and relay passwords and credit card information to cybercriminals.

Spyware can get into a computer using exploits similar to those of Trojans. It can piggyback on seemingly legitimate freeware or shareware downloads. You can also inadvertently allow spyware into your computer by clicking innocuous but infected pop-up ads or surfing through seemingly valid and secure but compromised Web sites.

What does malware do? Once viruses, worms, bots, Trojans, and spyware enter your computer, they can carry out a variety of unauthorized activities, such as those listed in Figure 3-45.

> **TERMINOLOGY NOTE**
>
> A *Denial of Service attack* is designed to generate a lot of activity on a network by flooding its servers with useless traffic—enough traffic to overwhelm the server's processing capability and essentially bring all communications and services to a halt.

FIGURE 3-45

Malware Activities

- Display irritating messages and pop-up ads.
- Delete or modify your data.
- Encrypt your data and demand ransom for the encryption key.
- Upload or download unwanted files.
- Log your keystrokes to steal your passwords and credit card numbers.
- Propagate malware and spam to everyone on your e-mail address book or your instant messaging buddy list.
- Disable your antivirus and firewall software.
- Block access to specific Web sites and redirect your browser to infected Web sites.
- Cause response time on your system to deteriorate.
- Allow hackers to remotely access data on your computer.
- Allow hackers to take remote control of your machine and turn it into a zombie.
- Link your computer to others in a botnet that can send millions of spam e-mails or wage Denial of Service attacks against Web sites.
- Cause network traffic jams.

How do I know if my computer is infected? Watch out for the symptoms of an infected computer listed in Figure 3-46.

FIGURE 3-46

Symptoms of Infection

3

- Irritating messages or sounds
- Frequent pop-up ads, at times with pornographic content
- The sudden appearance of a new Internet toolbar on your browser's home page
- An addition to your Internet favorites list that you didn't put there
- Prolonged system start-up
- Slower than usual response to mouse clicks and keyboard strokes
- Browser or application crashes
- Missing files
- Your computer's security software becomes disabled and it cannot be restarted
- Periodic network activity when you are not actively browsing or sending e-mail
- Your computer reboots itself frequently

Some malware does a good job of cloaking itself, so victims are unaware of its presence. Cloaking techniques are great defense mechanisms because when victims aren't aware of malware, they won't take steps to eradicate it. Many victims whose computers were part of massive botnets never knew their computers were compromised.

Some hackers cloak their work using rootkits. The term **rootkit** refers to software tools used to conceal malware and backdoors that have been installed on a victim's computer. Rootkits can hide bots, keyloggers, spyware, worms, and viruses. With a rootkit in place, hackers can continue to exploit a victim's computer with little risk of discovery. Rootkits are usually distributed by Trojans.

How do I avoid security threats? The Orientation section at the beginning of this book listed some techniques for safe computing. That list is worth repeating (Figure 3-47).

FIGURE 3-47

Avoiding Security Threats

- Install and activate security software on every computing device you own.
- Keep software patches and operating system service packs up to date.
- Do not open suspicious e-mail attachments.
- Obtain software only from reliable sources, and before running it use security software to scan for malware.
- Do not click pop-up ads—to make the ad go away, right-click the ad's taskbar button and select the Close option.
- Avoid unsavory Web sites.
- Disable the option *Hide extensions for known file types in Windows* so you can avoid opening files with more than one extension, such as a file called game.exe.zip.

What's a virus hoax? Some virus threats are very real, but you're also likely to get e-mail messages about so-called viruses that don't really exist. A **virus hoax** usually arrives as an e-mail message containing dire warnings about a supposedly new virus on the loose. When you receive an e-mail message about a virus or any other type of malware, don't panic. It could be a hoax.

You can check one of the many antivirus software Web sites to determine whether you've received a hoax or a real threat. The Web sites also provide security or virus alerts, which list all the most recent legitimate malware threats. If the virus is a real threat, the Web site can provide information to determine whether your computer has been infected. You can also find instructions for eradicating the virus. If the virus threat is a hoax, by no means should you forward the e-mail message to others.

What if my computer gets infected? If you suspect that your computer might be infected by a virus or other malware, you should immediately use security software to scan your computer and report any suspicious program code.

SECURITY SUITES

What is a security suite? A **security suite** integrates several security modules to protect against the most common types of malware, unauthorized access, and spam. Security suites might include additional features such as WiFi detection that warns of possible intrusions into your wireless network and parental controls for monitoring and controlling children's Internet usage. A security suite, like the one in Figure 3-48, typically includes antivirus, firewall, and antispyware modules.

INFOWEBLINKS

Some Web sites specialize in tracking hoaxes. For links to these sites, visit the **Hoax InfoWeb**.

 CLICK TO CONNECT
www.course.com/np/concepts11/ch03

FIGURE 3-48

The Norton security suite includes modules for scanning viruses, detecting spyware, and activating a firewall against unauthorized intrusions.

> Norton 360
>
> **Norton 360**   PC Security
>
> Help   Support
>
> ✓ PC Security Pending
>
> | Items | Status |
> |---|---|
> | ✓ **Auto-Protect**
Your PC is protected from viruses, spyware, and other risks. | On |
> | ✓ **Firewall**
Your PC is protected from intrusions and hacker attacks. | On |
> | ✓ **LiveUpdate**
Your PC is protected from the latest known viruses, spyware, and other risks. | Last run 11/30/2007 |
> | ✓ **Virus and Spyware Scan**
Your PC is protected from viruses, spyware, and other risks. | Last run 11/28/2007
More Info.. |
> | ✓ **Email Scanning**
Your incoming email attachments are protected from | On |
>
> **Things You Can Do**
> Run Scans   Check for Updates
>
> Close

CLICK TO START

What are the advantages and disadvantages of a security suite? A security suite costs less than purchasing standalone security modules. In addition, a single interface for accessing all of the security suite's features is much less complex than having to learn how to configure and run several different products.

When installing a security suite you are typically required to uninstall or disable all other antivirus, anti-spyware, and firewall software on your computer. Most security suites cannot run concurrently with standalone security products, and overlapping security coverage from two similar products can cause glitches. Therefore, one disadvantage of security suites is that you become dependent on your security package's vendor, who becomes the sole protector of your computer from malicious code. In addition, suites may not have the best individual security components, but you cannot pick and choose. However, competition between security suite vendors tends to increase the quality of security offerings.

INFOWEBLINKS

If you don't have security software for your computer you should get it. Use the **Antivirus Software InfoWeb** to link to Web sites where you can purchase and download various types of security software.

 CLICK TO CONNECT
www.course.com/np/concepts11/ch03

Where can I purchase a security suite? The most popular security suites include Symantec Norton Internet Security, McAfee Internet Security Suite, Alwil Avast!, Trend Micro PC-cillin Internet Security, and Panda Platinum Internet Security. They can be purchased in most office, electronics, and computer stores, or downloaded from the Web.

It is also worth looking into your ISP's free security offerings. For example, Comcast provides its customers with McAfee security products, all accessible through Comcast's special toolbar. AOL gives its customers a security package that combines McAfee's main security products with its own home-grown security features, such as parental control and spam filters.

A security suite is often pre-installed on a new computer. However, usually it is demoware, so you have the option of purchasing it after the trial period, normally 60 days. Typically, there is also an annual subscription fee for continued use and regular updates. When you renew your subscription, you might have an option to upgrade to a newer version for an extra $10-20. There are also open source versions of antivirus software, which do not require annual subscription fees.

Is open source security software as dependable as commercial security suites? Open source security software, like all open source software, is distributed with its source code. Because the source code is open for examination, black hats can view the code and look for security holes. They can potentially plot strategies to disable security protection or sneak past its defenses. Proponents of open source software, however, claim that because the code is open, security holes are likely to be discovered and fixed by white hats before they can be exploited by hackers. Vulnerabilities have been discovered in both open source and commercial security products.

Whether open source products, such as ClamWin (Figure 3-49) or commercial security software, each security suite has unique strengths and weaknesses, which can change as the suites are updated. Before you purchase a security suite, read current reviews and check user ratings at consumer Web sites.

ANTIVIRUS MODULES

What is antivirus software? **Antivirus software** is a type of utility software that looks for and eradicates viruses, Trojan horses, worms, and bots. Most antivirus software also scans for spyware, although some security software publishers offer spyware detection as a separate module. Antivirus software is included in security suites or can be purchased as a standalone module. Antivirus software is available for all types of computer and data storage, including handhelds, personal computers, USB flash drives, and servers.

How does antivirus software work? Modern antivirus software attempts to identify malware by searching your computer's files and memory for virus signatures. A **virus signature** is a section of program code, such as a unique series of instructions, that can be used to identify a known malicious program, much as a fingerprint is used to identify an individual.

Antivirus software scans for virus signatures in programs, data files, incoming and outgoing e-mail and attachments, and inbound instant message attachments. Antivirus software can also watch for unusual activity such as a considerably large number of e-mail messages being sent out from your computer.

FIGURE 3-49

Open source antivirus software ClamWin comes in a portable version to protect USB flash drives.

Most antivirus programs can also scan for virus signatures in zip files, which is important when downloading zipped software and receiving zipped e-mail attachments.

How do I activate and deactivate my antivirus software?

Installation and activation procedures vary for each virus protection product. However, once you have installed your antivirus software, the best and safest practice is to keep it running full time in the background so that it checks every e-mail message as it arrives and scans all files the moment you access them. The scanning process requires only a short amount of time, which creates a slight delay in downloading e-mail and opening files.

When installing some application or utility software you might be instructed to deactivate your antivirus software. You can usually right-click the icon on your computer's taskbar that corresponds to your antivirus software and then select the exit or disable option. Do not forget to reactivate your antivirus software as soon as the installation is completed.

How should I configure my antivirus software?
For the most extensive protection from malware, you should look for and enable the features of your antivirus software listed in Figure 3-50.

FIGURE 3-50

Configuration Settings for Antivirus Software

- Start scanning when the computer boots.
- Scan all programs when they are launched and document files when they are opened.
- Scan other types of files, such as graphics, if you engage in some risky computing behaviors and are not concerned with the extra time required to open files as they are scanned.
- Scan incoming mail and attachments.
- Scan incoming instant message attachments.
- Scan outgoing e-mail for worm activity such as mass-mailing worms.
- Scan zip (compressed) files.
- Scan for spyware, sometimes called pups (potentially unwanted programs).
- Scan all files on the computer's hard disk at least once a week.

How do I keep my antivirus software up-to-date?
Two aspects of your antivirus software periodically need to be updated. First, the antivirus program itself might need a patch or update to fix bugs or improve features. Second, the list of virus signatures has to be updated to keep up with the latest malware developments. Virus signatures and other information that antivirus software uses to identify and eradicate malware is stored in one or more files usually referred to as **virus definitions**. Antivirus program updates and revised virus definitions are packaged into a file that can be manually or automatically downloaded. If your antivirus software is part of a security suite, the update might also include patches for other security software modules, such as the anti-spam module or firewall.

Most antivirus products are preconfigured to regularly check for updates, download them, and install them without user intervention. If you would rather control the download and installation process yourself, you can configure your antivirus software to alert you when updates are ready. In any case, you should manually check for updates periodically just in case the auto-update function has become disabled.

How often should I do a system scan? Most experts recommend that you configure your antivirus software to periodically scan all the files on your computer. With the proliferation of malware attacks, it's best to schedule a weekly system scan. Because a full system scan can significantly slow down your computer, schedule the scan for a time when you are not usually using your computer, but it is turned on.

You can also run a manual scan of your entire computer or of specific files. For example, suppose you download a program and you want to make sure it is virus free before you install and run it. You can use Windows Explorer to locate and right-click the downloaded file, then select the *Scan* option from the pop-up menu (Figure 3-51).

What does quarantine mean? If, during the scanning process, your virus protection software identifies a virus, worm, Trojan horse, or bot in a file or attachment, it can try to remove the infection, put the file into quarantine, or simply delete the file. A **quarantined file** typically contains suspicious code, such as a virus signature. For your protection, most antivirus software encrypts the file contents and isolates it in a quarantine folder, so it can't be inadvertently opened or accessed by a hacker. If the infected file ends up on a quarantine list, your antivirus software might give you the option of trying to disinfect the file or deleting it.

How dependable is antivirus software? Today's antivirus software is quite dependable, but not infallible. A fast-spreading worm can reach your computer before a virus definition update arrives, some spyware can slip through the net, and cloaking software can hide some viral exploits. Despite occasional misses, however, antivirus software and other security software modules are constantly weeding out malware that would otherwise infect your computer. It is essential to use security software, but also important to take additional precautions, such as making regular backups of your data.

FIGURE 3-51

Before installing and running a downloaded file, you can scan it by right-clicking the file name and selecting the Scan option.

3

QuickCheck

1. The term [_____] threat describes malware that combines more than one type of malicious program.

2. A key characteristic of [_____] is their ability to lurk in a computer for days or months, quietly replicating themselves.

3. Unlike a [_____], a Trojan is not designed to spread itself to other computers.

4. The term [_____] refers to software tools used to conceal malware and backdoors that have been installed on a victim's computer.

5. When antivirus software finds a virus signature, it typically [_____] the file by encrypting it and moving it to an isolated folder.

▶ CHECK ANSWERS

ISSUE

How Serious Is Software Piracy?

SOFTWARE IS EASY TO STEAL. You don't have to walk out of a Best Buy store with a $495 DVD Workshop software box under your shirt. You can simply borrow your friend's DVD Workshop distribution CDs and install a copy of the program on your computer's hard disk. It seems so simple that it couldn't be illegal. But it is.

Piracy takes many forms. End-user piracy includes friends loaning distribution disks to each other and installing software on more computers than the license allows. Although it is perfectly legal to lend a physical object, such as a sweater, to a friend, it is not legal to lend digital copies of software and music because, unlike a sweater that can be worn by only one person at a time, copies of digital things can be simultaneously used by many people.

Counterfeiting is the large-scale illegal duplication of software distribution media, and sometimes, even its packaging. According to Microsoft, many software counterfeiting groups are linked to organized crime and money-laundering schemes that fund a diverse collection of illegal activities, such as smuggling, gambling, extortion, and prostitution. Counterfeit software is sold in retail stores and through online auctions—often the packaging looks so authentic that buyers have no idea they have purchased illegal goods.

Internet piracy uses the Web as a way to illegally distribute unauthorized software. In Net jargon, the terms *appz* and *warez* (pronounced as "wares" or "war EZ") refer to pirated software. Some warez has even been modified to eliminate serial numbers, registration requirements, expiration dates, or other forms of copy protection. The Business Software Alliance (BSA) estimates that more than 800,000 Web sites illegally sell or distribute software.

In many countries, including the United States, software pirates are subject to civil lawsuits for monetary damages and criminal prosecution, which can result in jail time and stiff fines. Nonetheless, software piracy continues to have enormous impact. According to a BSA and IDC 2007 Piracy Study, $65 billion of software was legitimately purchased worldwide, but software worth a whopping $40 billion was pirated.

A small, but vocal, minority of software users, such as members of GNU (which stands for "Gnu's Not

UNIX"), believes that data and software should be freely distributed. Richard Stallman writes in the GNU Manifesto, "I consider that the golden rule requires that if I like a program I must share it with other people who like it. Software sellers want to divide users and conquer them, making each user agree not to share with others. I refuse to break solidarity with other users in this way. I cannot in good conscience sign a nondisclosure agreement or a software license agreement."

Is software piracy really damaging? Who cares if you use a program without paying for it? Software piracy is damaging because it has a negative effect on the economy. Software production makes a major contribution to the United States economy, employing more than 2 million people and accounting for billions of dollars in corporate revenue. It fuels economic development in countries such as India, China, and Malaysia. A BSA economic impact study concluded that lowering global piracy from an average of 36% to only 26% would add more that 1 million jobs and $400 billion in worldwide economic growth.

Decreases in software revenues can have a direct effect on consumers, too. When software publishers are forced to cut corners, they tend to reduce customer service and technical support. As a result, you, the consumer, get put on hold when you call for technical support, find fewer free technical support sites, and encounter customer support personnel who are only moderately knowledgeable about their products. The bottom line—software piracy negatively affects customer service.

As an alternative to cutting support costs, some software publishers might build the cost of software piracy into the price of the software. The unfortunate result is that those who legitimately license and purchase software pay an inflated price. The BSA and

IDC reported about 35% of the software currently in use is pirated. Armenia, Moldova, Azerbaijan, and Zimbabwe have the world's highest piracy rates. More than 90% of the software used in those countries is believed to be pirated. In China the piracy rate is 82%, down from 92% in 2003. In the United States, an estimated 21% of software is pirated. In Japan, the rate is 25%.

Piracy Rates by Region (as percent of total in use)

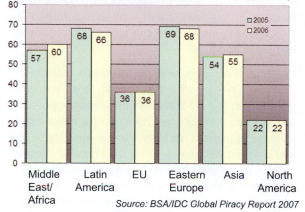

Source: BSA/IDC Global Piracy Report 2007

Although the rate of business software piracy might be declining, total piracy appears to be growing by one or two percentage points each year. Analysts fear that the Internet is a major factor in piracy growth. As Internet access becomes available to subscribers in countries such as China, piracy could skyrocket. To make matters worse, increased access to high-speed Internet connections makes it much easier to quickly download large software files.

As a justification of high piracy rates, some observers point out that people in many countries simply might not be able to afford software priced for the U.S. market. This argument could apply to China, where the average annual income is equivalent to about US$3,500, and in North Korea, where the average income is only US$900. A Korean who legitimately purchases Microsoft Office for US$250 would be spending more than one-quarter of his or her annual income.

Many countries with a high incidence of software piracy, however, have strong economies and respectable per capita incomes. To further discredit the theory that piracy stems from poverty, India—which has a fairly large computer-user community, but a per capita income of only US$1,600—is not among the top 20 countries with high rates of software piracy.

If economic factors do not account for the pervasiveness of software piracy, what does? The incidence of piracy seems to be higher among small business and individual users than corporations and government agencies. Two-thirds of college and university students see nothing unethical about swapping or downloading digital copyrighted software, music, and movie files without paying for them and more than half of the respondents believe it is acceptable to do so in the workplace.

Some analysts suggest that people need more education about software copyrights and the economic implications of piracy. Other analysts believe that copyright enforcement must be increased by implementing more vigorous efforts to identify and prosecute pirates.

INFOWEBLINKS

You can read the GNU Manifesto and other thought-provoking articles about software piracy by going to the **Copyright and Piracy InfoWeb**.

Ⓦ CLICK TO CONNECT

www.course.com/np/concepts11/ch03

What Do You Think?

ISSUE

1. Do you believe that software piracy is a serious issue?

⭕Yes ⭕ No ⭕ Not sure

2. Do you know of any instances of software piracy?

⭕Yes ⭕ No ⭕ Not sure

3. Do you think that most software pirates understand that they are doing something illegal?

⭕Yes ⭕ No ⭕ Not sure

4. Should software publishers try to adjust software pricing for local markets?

⭕Yes ⭕ No ⭕ Not sure

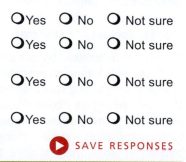

▶ SAVE RESPONSES

COMPUTERS IN CONTEXT

Journalism

IN THE ANCIENT WORLD, news spread by word of mouth, relayed by bards and merchants who traveled from town to town—in essence, the first reporters to broadcast the news. The news business is all about gathering and disseminating information as quickly as possible. Technology has played a major role in news reporting's evolution from its bardic roots to modern 24-hour live news networks.

Johann Gutenberg's printing press (ca. 1450), the first technological breakthrough in the news business, made it feasible to publish news as printed notices tacked to walls in the town square. As paper became more economical, resourceful entrepreneurs sold broadsheets to people eager for news, and the concept of a newspaper was born. The first regularly published newspapers appeared in Germany and Holland in 1609, and the first English newspaper, the Weekly News, was published in 1622.

But the news spread slowly. In the early 1800s, it took four weeks for newspapers in New York to receive reports from London. With the advent of the telegraph in 1844, however, reporters from far-flung regions could wire stories to their newspapers for publication the next day. The first radio reporters in the 1920s offered live broadcasts of sports events, church services, and variety shows. Before the 1950s, black-and-white newsreels shown in movie theaters provided the only visual imagery of news events, but television gave viewers news images on a nightly basis.

Technology has benefited print journalism, too. For decades, typesetters transferred reporters' handwritten stories into neatly set columns of type. Today, reporters use computers and word processing software to tap out their stories and run a preliminary check of spelling and grammar.

Stories are submitted by computer network to editors, who also use word processing software to edit stories to fit time and space constraints. The typesetting process has been replaced by desktop publishing software and computer to plate (CTP) technology. Digital pages produced with desktop publishing software are sent to a raster image processor (RIP), which converts the pages into dots that form words and images. After a page has been

RIPed, a platesetter uses lasers to etch the dots onto a physical plate, which is then mounted on the printing press to produce printed pages. CTP is much faster and more flexible than typesetting, so publishers can make last-minute changes to accommodate late-breaking stories.

Personal computers have also added a new dimension to the news-gathering process. Reporters were once limited to personal interviews, observation, and fact gathering at libraries, but can now make extensive use of Internet resources and e-mail. Web sites and online databases provide background information on all sorts of topics. Other resources include newsgroups and chat rooms, where reporters can monitor public opinion on current events and identify potential sources.

Most major networks maintain interactive Web sites that offer online polls and bulletin boards designed to collect viewers' opinions. Although online poll respondents are not a representative sample of the population, they can help news organizations gauge viewer opinions and determine whether news coverage is comprehensive and effective.

News organizations also accept news, images, and videos from amateur "citizen journalists" who happen upon news events armed with a cell phone or digital camera. And even CNN now reports on news stories that originate on blogs such as *slashdot.org*.

E-mail has changed the way reporters communicate with colleagues and sources. It's often the only practical method for contacting people in remote locations or distant time zones, and it's useful with reluctant sources, who feel more comfortable providing information under the cloak of anonymous Hotmail or Yahoo! accounts. Vetting e-mail sources—verifying credentials such as name, location, and occupation—can be difficult, however, so reporters tend not to rely on these sources without substantial corroboration.

For broadcast journalism, digital communications play a major role in today's live-on-the-scene television reporting. Most news organizations maintain remote production vans, sometimes called satellite news gathering (SNG) trucks, that travel to the site of breaking news, raise their antennas, and begin to broadcast. These complete mobile production facilities include camera control units, audio and video recording equipment, and satellite or microwave transmitters.

On-the-scene reporting no longer requires a truck full of equipment, however. Audiovisual editing units and video cameras have gone digital, making them easier to use and sized to fit in a suitcase. A new breed of backpack journalists carry mini-DV cameras, notebook computers, and satellite phones. Jane Ellen Stevens, a pioneer backpack journalist specializing in science and technology, has reported since 1997 from remote locations, such as a space camp in Russia.

Backpack journalists can connect their minicams to notebook computers with a FireWire cable, transfer their video footage to the hard disk, and then edit the footage using consumer-level video editing software. The resulting video files, compressed for transmission over a satellite phone, are sent to newsroom technicians, who decompress and then broadcast them—all in a matter of seconds.

One drawback of backpack journalists' use of minicams and compression is that the video quality usually isn't as crisp as images filmed with studio cameras. News organizations with high standards were once hesitant to use this lower quality video, but have found that viewers would rather see a low-quality image now than a high-quality image later. To many viewers, a few rough edges just make the footage seem more compelling, more "you are there."

A memorable tour de force in SNG was the brainchild of David Bloom, an NBC reporter embedded with the U.S. Army 3rd Infantry Division during Operation Iraqi Freedom. He helped modify an M-88 tank recovery vehicle into a high-tech, armored SNG vehicle. The $500,000 Bloommobile featured a gyrostabilized camera that could produce jiggle-free video as the tank blasted over sand dunes at 50 mph. Tragically, Bloom died while covering the conflict, but many viewers vividly remember his exhilarating reports as the Bloommobile raced down desert roads, trundled along with army supply convoys, and narrowly escaped enemy fire.

Computers, the Internet, and communications technology make it possible to instantly broadcast live reports across the globe, but live reporting is not without controversy. A reporter who arrives at the scene of a disaster with microphone in hand has little time for reflection, vetting, and cross-checking, so grievous errors, libelous images, or distasteful video footage sometimes find their way into news reports.

Jeff Gralnick, former executive producer for ABC News, remarks, "In the old days, we had time to think before we spoke. We had time to write, time to research and time to say, 'Hey, wait a minute.' Now we don't even have the time to say, 'Hey, wait a nanosecond.' Just because we can say it or do it, should we?" Technology has given journalists a powerful arsenal of tools for gathering and reporting the news, but has also increased their accountability for accurate, socially responsible reporting.

INFOWEBLINKS

You'll find lots more information related to this topic at the **Computers and Journalism InfoWeb**.

W CLICK TO CONNECT
www.course.com/np/concepts11/ch03

3

New Perspectives Labs

On the BookOnCD

To access the New Perspectives labs for Chapter 3, start the BookOnCD, BookOnFlashDrive, or other NP11 BookOn product and then click the icon next to the lab title below.

 INSTALLING AND UNINSTALLING SOFTWARE

IN THIS LAB YOU'LL LEARN:

- How to use a setup program to install Windows application software from a distribution CD

- The difference between typical, compact, and custom installation options

- How to specify a folder for a new software installation

- How to install downloaded software

- How to install an upgrade

- How to uninstall a Windows application

- What happens, in addition to deleting files, when you uninstall a software application

- How to locate the program that will uninstall a software application

- Why you might not want to delete all of the files associated with an application

LAB ASSIGNMENTS

1. Start the interactive part of the lab. Make sure you've enabled Tracking if you want to save your QuickCheck results. Perform each lab step as directed, and answer all the lab QuickCheck questions. When you exit the lab, your answers are automatically graded and your results are displayed.

2. Browse the Web and locate a software application that you might like to download. Use information supplied by the Web site to answer the following questions:

   a. What is the name of the program and the URL of the download site?

   b. What is the size of the download file?

   c. According to the instructions, does the download file appear to require manual installation, is it a self-executing zip file, or is it a self-installing executable file?

3. On the computer you typically use, look through the list of programs (click Start, then select All Programs to see a list of them). List the names of any programs that include their own uninstall routines.

4. On the computer you typically use, open the Control Panel and then select the Uninstall a Program option. List the first 10 programs shown.

Key Terms

Make sure you understand all the boldfaced key terms presented in this chapter. If you're using the NP11 BookOnCD, BookOnFlashDrive, or other NP11 BookOn product, you can use this list of terms as an interactive study activity. First, try to define a term in your own words, and then click the term to compare your definition with the definition presented in the chapter.

3

Interactive Summary

To review important concepts from this chapter, fill in the blanks to best complete each sentence. When using the NP11 BookOnCD or other BookOn product, click the Check Answers buttons to automatically score your answers.

SECTION A: Computer software can be grouped into two main categories. _____ software is designed for computer-centric tasks, whereas _____ software is designed to help people accomplish real-world tasks. These two main categories can be further divided into subcategories. _____ software is designed to help you monitor and configure settings for your computer system equipment, the operating system, or application software. Many software packages in this category appear as desktop _____ that display controls and snippets of information for clocks, calendars, calculators, news aggregators, sticky notes, and weather stations. Device _____ are a type of system software that helps a computer establish communication with peripheral devices. _____ software can be defined as any type of application software that has the potential to help people do their work more efficiently. _____ is designed to help several people collaborate on a single project using local networks or Internet connections.

 CHECK ANSWERS

SECTION B: Document _____ software assists you with composing, editing, designing, printing, and electronically publishing documents. The three most popular types of document production software include word processing, desktop publishing, and Web authoring. _____ software is similar to a smart piece of paper that automatically adds up the columns of numbers you write on it. You can use it to make other calculations, too, based on simple equations that you write or more complex, built-in formulas. Because it is so easy to experiment with different numbers, this type of software is particularly useful for _____ analyses. _____ software helps you store, find, organize, update, and report information stored in one or more tables. When two sets of records are _____, database software allows you to access data from both tables at the same time. _____ software, including paint, photo editing, drawing, 3-D, and presentation software, is designed to help you create, manipulate, and print images. Music and video editing software, educational and reference software, and entertainment software round out the most popular categories of personal computer software.

For businesses, _____ market software is designed to automate specialized tasks in a specific market or business. _____ market software is generic software that can be used by just about any kind of business.

CHECK ANSWERS

SECTION C:

Most new computers include an operating system, essential utilities, and some basic application software. If you want utilities other than those included with your computer's operating system, you can explore software offered by [_____] party vendors. When shopping for application software, consider software [_____], which are a collection of software applications sold as a single package. All the bundled applications usually have similar controls, and data can be easily transferred from one application to another. Software can be purchased in a box containing [_____] media, such as CDs or DVDs, or as a download. [_____] software, such as commercial software, is protected by copyright that grants an exclusive right to copy, distribute, sell, and modify that work to its author. Public [_____] software is not protected by copyright. A software [_____] can extend or limit the rights granted by copyright. Demoware and [_____] are distributed free of charge, but require payment for continued use. Freeware is copyrighted software that can be used for free, but cannot be altered or resold. [_____] source software is distributed with its source code, and can be modified, sold, and redistributed.

 CHECK ANSWERS

SECTION D:

The process of [_____] software places a program into a computer so that it can be executed or run. The main program is stored in an [_____] file that might call additional programs as necessary. Most programs are [_____] applications, designed to be installed or "loaded" on a hard disk. A [_____] program, included with the software, guides you through the installation process. For downloaded software, the first step in the installation process is usually to [_____] the distribution file that was compressed to conserve space and reduce download time. In contrast to local applications, [_____] software is designed to run from removable storage, such as a CD or USB flash drive. On PCs these apps require no entries in the Windows Registry. [_____] applications are designed to be accessed with a browser. Some require no installation on your local computer, whereas others require a small client-side program. Software publishers regularly update their software to add new features, fix bugs, and update its security. A software [_____] is a small section of program code that replaces part of the software you currently have installed. The term service [_____], which usually applies to operating system updates, is a set of patches that correct problems and address security vulnerabilities. To remove software from a PC, it is important to use an [_____] routine, rather than simply deleting program files.

 CHECK ANSWERS

SECTION E:

Security software can be classified into various types: antivirus, anti-spyware, anti-spam, and firewalls. Each type focuses on a specific security threat. A computer [_____] is a set of program instructions that attaches itself to a file, reproduces itself, and spreads to other files. A computer [_____] is a self-replicating program designed to carry out some unauthorized activity on a victim's computer. In the context of computing, a Trojan [_____] is a computer program that seems to perform one function while actually doing something else. For example, it might steal passwords using a type of program called a [_____] that records keystrokes. A Remote Access Trojan sets up [_____] capabilities that allow remote hackers to access files on victims' computers. [_____] programs can turn computers into zombies and link them together into [_____]. [_____] is a type of program that secretly gathers personal information without the victim's knowledge, usually for advertising and other commercial purposes. To combat malware, it is important to use [_____] software that looks for virus signatures. Most computer owners obtain this software as one module in a security [_____].

 CHECK ANSWERS

Software Key Terms

Interactive Situation Questions

Apply what you've learned to some typical computing situations. When using the NP11 BookOnCD, BookOnFlashDrive, or any other NP11 BookOn product, you can type your answers, and then use the Check Answers button to automatically score your responses.

1. You've volunteered to create some graphics for a nonprofit organization, but you'll need a variety of graphics software tools for the organization's computer. Your first choice is to consider a graphics [_____] that bundles together paint, draw, and Web graphics software.

2. Suppose that you've been hired to organize a professional skateboard competition. When you consider how you'll need to use computers, you realize that you must collect information on each competitor and keep track of every competitive event. With at least two types of related records, you'll probably need to use [_____] software.

3. Imagine that you just purchased a new software package. You insert the distribution CD, but nothing happens. No problem—you can manually run the [_____] program, which will start the install routine.

4. You are preparing to download a new software program from the Web. The download consists of one huge file with an .exe extension. You recognize this file as a self-[_____] executable file that will automatically unzip itself and start the installation routine.

5. You download an open source software program from the Web. You assume that the download includes the uncompiled [_____] code for the program as well as the [_____] version.

6. You're in the process of receiving some e-mail messages when your antivirus software pops up an alert. You assume that it has discovered a virus [_____] in an attachment for one of the e-mail messages and has [_____] the file.

 CHECK ANSWERS

Interactive Practice Tests

Practice tests that consist of 10 multiple-choice, true/false, and fill-in-the-blank questions are available on both the NP11 BookOn products and the NP11 Web site. The questions are selected at random from a large test bank, so each time you take a test, you'll receive a different set of questions. Your tests are scored immediately, and you can print study guides that help you find the correct answers for any questions that you missed.

 CLICK TO START

Study Tips

Study Tips help you to organize and consolidate the information in a unit by making lists, outlines, charts, and sketches. You can use paper and pencil or word processing software to complete most of the Study Tip activities.

1. Make sure you can use your own words to correctly answer each of the red focus questions that appear throughout the chapter.

2. List at least three examples of system software and five examples of utility software.

3. List three types of productivity software, and at least five categories of application software.

4. Compare the strengths of word processing, DTP, and Web authoring software.

5. Explain how a spelling checker works and why it is not a substitute for proofreading.

6. Draw a sketch of a simple worksheet and label the following: columns, rows, cell, active cell, values, labels, formulas, and Formula bar.

7. Explain the difference between an absolute reference and a relative reference, giving an example of each.

8. List five types of "number crunching" software that you can use in addition to spreadsheet software.

9. Describe how you would use each of the six types of graphics software described in this chapter.

10. Read the license agreement in Figure 3-32 and answer each of the questions in the corresponding figure caption.

11. Explain the differences in installing local software, portable software, and Web apps.

12. Describe the process of installing software from a distribution CD, and contrast it with the process of installing downloaded software.

13. Explain the differences between proprietary software, commercial software, shareware, open source software, freeware, and public domain software.

14. Explain the differences between self-installing executable files, self-executing zip files, and non-executing zip files.

15. Explain the purpose of a software patch and describe how it differs from a service pack.

16. Create a table that summarizes the differences between various types of malware based on their method of distribution and exploits.

17. Draw a story board to illustrate how antivirus software works.

18. Fill in the blanks on the concept map below to show the hierarchy of software described in this chapter.

Concept Map

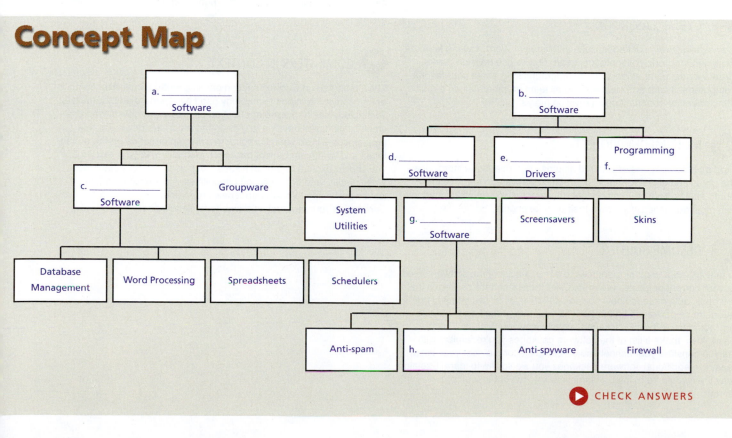

CHECK ANSWERS

Projects

 CRITICAL THINKING

Have you heard about the "24-hour rule" for software that says you can legally use any software for free for 24 hours without paying for it? How about your right to use so-called abandoned software that's no longer supported or that was created by a company now out of business? Both the 24-hour rule and the concept of abandoned software are urban legends and have no basis in copyright law. Does it seem to you that most people don't have the facts about copyrights? How strong a factor is that in the proliferation of software piracy? What are your thoughts about the connection between knowing the copyright rules and following them? Put your thoughts in order, write them up, and send them to your instructor.

GROUP PROJECT

Form a group with at least two of your classmates. Now imagine that your college (or business) has decided to negotiate with software publishers to offer students (or employees) a bundled software package at a greatly discounted price. Your group's job is to select the 15 software products for the bundle. Your group must make sure the software effectively meets the major needs of the students at your school (or employees in your workplace). Use Internet resources to look at the range of software available and make your selections. Make sure you take advantage of group members' expertise and experience with software products. Arrange your final list into categories like those in Figure 3-1.

CYBERCLASSROOM

Some productivity packages, such as Microsoft Word, include features designed for group collaboration. Learn how to use revision marks. Create a document at least three paragraphs long about your favorite computer software and circulate it to all team members as an e-mail attachment for comment using revision marks.

MULTIMEDIA PROJECT

Find a photo from one of your old albums or at an antique store. Scan the photo into digital format. Use graphics software to improve the photo quality. Your instructor might run a contest to see which students can most dramatically improve their original photos.

 RESUME BUILDER

Use the Web and other resources to compile a list of the software used in your current or future career field. Are there standard packages that job applicants need to know how to use? If so, what can you find out about those packages on the Web? If your career field does not use any standard software packages, explain why you think that is the case. Also, make a list of the software packages you're familiar with. As you consider your school and career goals for the next year, list at least five additional software packages you would like to learn. Explain why they would be helpful. Submit your lists to your instructor by e-mail.

 GLOBALIZATION

Computer games are big business. They are exported worldwide and accessed by communities of online players around the globe. For this project gather information about the most internationally popular computer games. Try some of them yourself to see what they're all about. What effect, if any, would you expect these games to have on individual players living in the cultures of 1) industrialized countries, 2) Middle-eastern countries, and 3) developing countries? Summarize your ideas in one or two pages.

 ISSUE

The Issue section of this chapter focused on copyrights and software piracy. For this project, you will write a two- to five-page paper about this issue based on information you gather from the Internet. To begin this project, consult the Copyright and Piracy InfoWeb, and link to the recommended Web pages to get an in-depth overview of the issue. Armed with this background, select one of the following viewpoints and statements and argue for or against it:

• Free software advocates: As an enabling technology, software should be freely distributed, along with its modifiable source code.

• Librarians: Copyright laws, especially the Digital Millennium Copyright Act, minimize the needs of the public and go too far in their efforts to protect the rights of software authors.

• Software Publishers Association: Strong copyright laws and enforcement are essential for companies to publish and support high-quality software.

COMPUTERS IN CONTEXT

The Computers in Context section of this chapter focused on computer and communications technology used by reporters and journalists. Technology has had a major effect on backpack journalists who use small-scale digital devices to gather and report the news. For this project, use a Web search engine to collect information on the advantages and disadvantages of backpack journalism. In your research, you should explore technical issues, such as the cost of equipment, video quality, and transmission capabilities. Also explore ethical issues pertaining to on-the-spot news reporting.
Summarize your research in a two- to four-page paper.

On the Web

3

STUDENT EDITION LABS

W CLICK TO ACCESS THE NP11 WEB SITE
or open your browser and connect to www.course.com/np/concepts11/ch03.
Lab results can be stored in the Universal Gradebook.

WORD PROCESSING

In the Word Processing Student Edition Lab, you will learn about the following topics:

- Opening, saving, and printing a document
- Moving the insertion point and entering and editing text
- Moving and deleting blocks of text
- Inserting graphics and formatting your document
- Checking your document for spelling errors

SPREADSHEETS

In the Spreadsheets Student Edition Lab, you will learn about the following topics:

- Entering labels, values, and formulas
- Selecting and naming ranges
- Inserting functions
- Formatting a worksheet
- Creating a chart

INSTALLING AND UNINSTALLING SOFTWARE

In the Installing and Uninstalling Software Student Edition Lab, you will learn about the following topics:

- Installing software from a distribution CD
- Installing downloaded software
- Understanding the differences between upgrades, updates, and patches
- Uninstalling software applications

DATABASES

In the Databases Student Edition Lab, you will learn about the following topics:

- Entering and editing data
- Understanding the relationships between tables
- Sorting data
- Creating an index
- Creating queries
- Applying filters
- Creating and modifying reports

PRESENTATION SOFTWARE

In the Presentation Software Student Edition Lab, you will learn about the following topics:

- Adding text, graphics, animations, and sound to slides
- Using slide layouts and design templates
- Understanding the slide master
- Previewing, viewing, and printing a presentation

KEEPING YOUR COMPUTER VIRUS FREE

In the Keeping Your Computer Virus Free Student Edition Lab, you will learn about the following topics:

- Using antivirus software
- Virus detection and prevention

CHAPTER COURSECAST

Use your computer or iPod to hear a five-minute audio presentation of chapter highlights.

FLASHCARD COURSECAST

Interact with audio flashcards to review key terms from the chapter.

DETAILED OBJECTIVES

Make sure that you've achieved all the objectives for a chapter before it's time for your test!

TEST YOURSELF

Review chapter material by taking these ten-question tests, then send your results to the Universal Gradebook.

ONLINE GAMES

Have some fun while refreshing your memory about key concepts that might appear on the next test. You can even send your results to the Universal Gradebook!

AND MORE!

At the NP11 Web site you'll also find Extra Content and InfoWebLinks.

4

Operating Systems and File Management

LEARNING OBJECTIVES

- Describe the way operating systems handle each computer resource

- Identify operating systems used on today's personal computers, PDAs, and servers; describe their strengths and weaknesses

- Explain the significance of multitasking, multithreading, and multi-processing

- List six steps that occur during the PC boot process

- Explain the relationship between an operating system and a user interface

- Give examples of tasks that might benefit from dual booting or virtual machine capability

- Describe the significance of file formats; list at least 10 commonly used formats and their extensions

- Create valid names for files and folders, plus demonstrate that you can construct and trace file paths

- Demonstrate how to use file management features of application software and operating system utilities

- Describe how a computer physically stores data on disks, but represents this storage system with a logical model

- Demonstrate that you can implement a viable backup and restore plan

- Compare the advantages and disadvantages of using tapes, USB flash drives, a second hard disk, CDs, DVDs, networks, and Web sites for backups

- Explain the importance of a recovery disk

- Describe the importance of restore points when using Windows

☑ PRE-ASSESSMENT QUIZ

Take the pre-assessment quiz to find out how much you know about the topics in this chapter. ▶

MULTIMEDIA and INTERACTIVE ELEMENTS
When using the BookOnCD, BookOnFlashDrive, or other NP11 BookOn product, the ▶ icons are clickable to access multimedia resources.

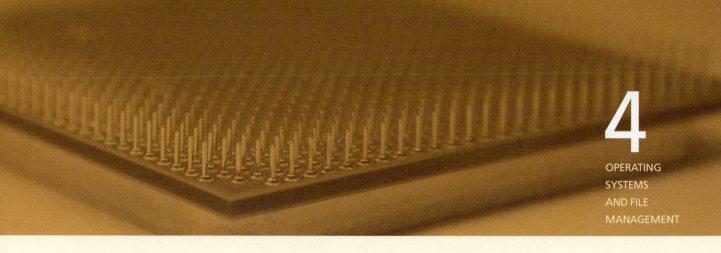

BEFORE YOU READ ON, **TRY IT**

IS MY COMPUTER'S HARD DISK GETTING FULL?

Parts of Chapter 4 focus on files—how to create them, where to store them, and how to keep them safe. Your computer's hard disk stores a high percentage of the programs you use and the data files you create. You might wonder if your hard disk is getting full. To find out, follow the steps below.

1. Start your computer and make sure you can see the Windows desktop.

2. If you are using Windows Vista, click the Start button, and then select Computer.

If you are using an earlier version of Windows, double-click the My Computer icon. If that icon is not on your desktop, click the Start button and click My Computer from the menu that appears.

3. Right-click Local disk (C:) to display the pop-up menu.

4. Click Properties.

5. A Local Disk Properties dialog box should appear containing statistics about your computer's hard disk.

6. Using the blanks on the figure below, jot down the statistics for used space, free space, and capacity, and then sketch in the slices of the pie chart for your computer.

7. Also jot down the file system used by your computer in the blank provided. You'll learn the significance of the file system when you read the chapter.

WEB SITE

Visit the NP11 Web site to access additional resources Ⓦ that accompany this chapter.

SECTION A

Operating System Basics

AN OPERATING SYSTEM is an integral part of virtually every computer system. It fundamentally affects how you can use your computer. Can you run two programs at the same time? Can you connect your computer to a network? Does your computer run dependably? Does all your software have a similar look and feel, or do you have to learn a different set of controls and commands for each new program you acquire? To answer questions like these, it is helpful to have a clear idea about what an operating system is and what it does. Section A provides an overview of operating system basics to help you understand this essential part of computer systems.

OPERATING SYSTEM ACTIVITIES

What is an operating system?

An **operating system** (abbreviated OS) is a type of system software that acts as the master controller for all activities that take place within a computer system. It is one of the factors that determines your computer's compatibility and platform. Most personal computers are sold with a preinstalled operating system, such as Microsoft Windows or Mac OS (Figure 4-1). A third operating system called Linux is typically used for high-end workstations and servers. A variety of other operating systems, such as DOS, UNIX, Solaris, and BeOS, are also available.

FIGURE 4-1

Windows (left) is typically pre-installed on IBM-compatible computers manufactured by companies such as Dell and Hewlett-Packard. Mac OS (middle) is preinstalled on Apple Macintosh computers. Linux (right) is an open source operating system that's available as a free download.

Is the Windows operating system the same as Windows software?

No. Although it is true that an operating system is software, terms such as Windows software, Mac software, or Linux software are used to refer to application software. Windows software, for example refers to applications designed to run on computers that have Microsoft Windows installed as the operating system. A program called Microsoft Word for Windows is an example of Windows software; it is a word processing program designed to run under the Windows operating system. Mac software is designed to run under Mac OS and Linux software is designed to run under the Linux operating system.

What does an operating system do? The most obvious responsibility of your computer's operating system is to provide an environment for running software. Your computer's operating system, application software, and device drivers are organized similar to the chain of command in an army. You issue a command using application software. Application software tells the operating system what to do. The operating system tells the device drivers, device drivers tell the hardware, and the hardware actually does the work. Figure 4-2 illustrates this chain of command for printing a document or photo.

FIGURE 4-2

A command to print a document is relayed through various levels of software, including the operating system, until it reaches the printer.

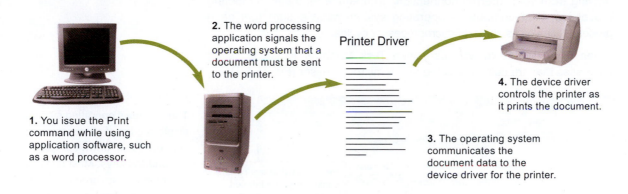

2. The word processing application signals the operating system that a document must be sent to the printer.

Printer Driver

1. You issue the Print command while using application software, such as a word processor.

4. The device driver controls the printer as it prints the document.

3. The operating system communicates the document data to the device driver for the printer.

4

The operating system interacts with application software, device drivers, and hardware to manage a computer's resources. In the context of a computer system, the term **resource** refers to any component that is required to perform work. For example, the processor is a resource. RAM, storage space, and peripherals are also resources. While you interact with application software, your computer's operating system is busy behind the scenes with resource management tasks such as those listed in Figure 4-3.

FIGURE 4-3

Operating System Tasks

	Manage memory
	Manage processor resources
	Keep track of storage resources
	Ensure that input and output proceed in an orderly manner
	Establish basic elements of the user interface

How do operating systems manage processor resources? In an earlier chapter, you learned how the control unit directs activities within the microprocessor. Operating systems also control the microprocessor—just at a slightly higher level. Every cycle of a computer's microprocessor is a resource for accomplishing tasks.

Many activities—called *processes*—compete for the attention of your computer's microprocessor. Commands are arriving from programs you're using, while input is arriving from the keyboard and mouse. At the same time, data must be sent to the display device or printer, and Web pages are arriving from your Internet connection. To manage all these competing processes, your computer's operating system must ensure that each process receives its share of microprocessor cycles.

When using Windows, you can open Task Manager to see a list of processes that are being executed by the microprocessor (Figure 4-4).

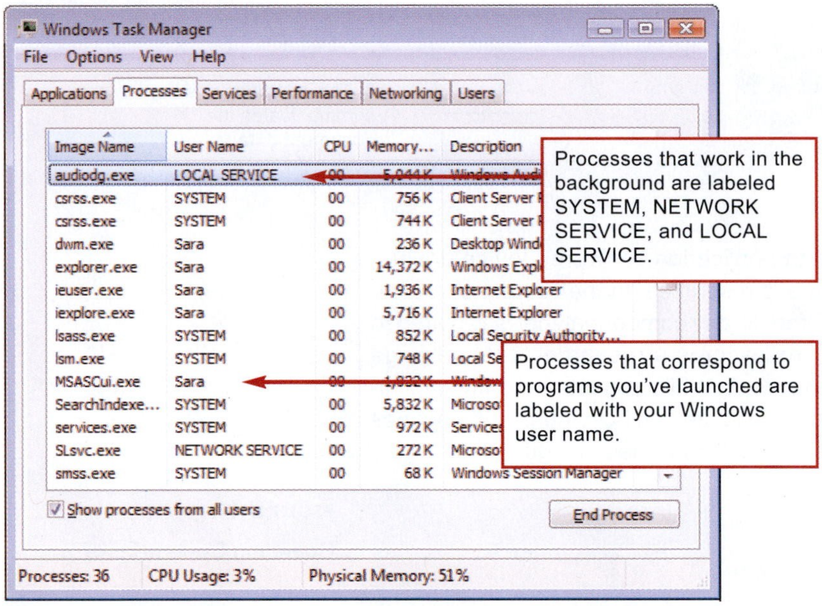

FIGURE 4-4

The Windows operating system displays a list of processes when you hold down the Ctrl, Alt, and Del keys. Most processes are legitimate programs that run in the background to carry out tasks for the operating system, device drivers, and applications. Occasionally a bot or worm will launch rogue processes. If you want to know if a process is legitimate, you can google its name using any search engine.

How do operating systems handle so many processes? During a typical computing session, your computer might run an average of 50 processes. Ideally, the operating system should be able to help the microprocessor switch seamlessly from one process to another. Depending on the capabilities of the operating system and computer hardware, processes can be managed by multitasking, multithreading, and multiprocessing.

Multitasking provides process and memory management services that allow two or more tasks, jobs, or programs to run simultaneously. Most of today's operating systems, including the OS on your personal computer, offer multitasking services.

Within a single program, **multithreading** allows multiple parts, or threads, to run simultaneously. For example, one thread for a spreadsheet program might be waiting for input from the user while other threads perform a long calculation in the background. Multithreading can speed up performance on single or multiple processor computers.

Many new computers include multi-core processors or multiple processors. An operating system's **multiprocessing** capability supports a division of labor among all the processing units.

How does an operating system manage memory?

A microprocessor works with data and executes instructions stored in RAM—one of your computer's most important resources. When you want to run more than one program at a time, the operating system has to allocate specific areas of memory for each program, as shown in Figure 4-5.

When multiple programs are running, the OS should prevent a **memory leak**—a situation in which instructions and data from one area of memory overflow into memory allocated to another program. If an OS falls down on the job and fails to protect each program's memory area, data can get corrupted, programs can crash, and your computer displays error messages, such as "General Protection Fault" or "Program Not Responding." Your PC can sometimes recover from a memory leak if you use the Ctrl+Alt+Del key sequence to close the corrupted program.

How does the OS keep track of storage resources?

Behind the scenes, an operating system acts as a filing clerk that stores and retrieves files from your disks and CDs. It remembers the names and locations of all your files and keeps track of empty spaces where new files can be stored. Later in the chapter, you'll explore file storage in more depth and learn how the operating system affects the way you create, name, save, and retrieve files.

Why does the operating system get involved with peripheral devices?

Every device connected to a computer is regarded as an input or output resource. Your computer's operating system communicates with device driver software so that data can travel smoothly between the computer and peripheral resources. If a peripheral device or driver is not performing correctly, the operating system makes a decision about what to do—usually it displays an on-screen message to warn you of the problem.

Your computer's operating system ensures that input and output proceed in an orderly manner, using buffers to collect and hold data while the computer is busy with other tasks. By using a keyboard buffer, for example, your computer never misses one of your keystrokes, regardless of how fast you type or what else is happening in your computer at the same time.

Are different operating systems needed for different computing tasks?

One operating system might be better suited to some computing tasks than others. To provide clues to their strengths and weaknesses, operating systems are informally categorized and characterized using one or more of the following terms:

A **single-user operating system** expects to deal with one set of input devices—those that can be controlled by one user at a time. Operating systems for handheld computers and some personal computers fit into the single-user category. DOS is an example of a single-user operating system.

A **multiuser operating system** allows a single, centralized computer to deal with simultaneous input, output, and processing requests from many users. One of its most difficult responsibilities is to schedule all the processing requests that a centralized computer must perform. IBM's z/OS is one of the most popular multiuser operating systems.

A **server operating system** provides tools for managing distributed networks, e-mail servers, and Web hosting sites. Mac OS X Server and Windows Server 2008 are examples of server operating systems. Technically, multiuser operating systems schedule requests for processing on a centralized computer, whereas a server operating system simply routes data and programs to each user's local computer where the actual

FIGURE 4-5

The operating system allocates a specific area of RAM for each program that is open and running. The operating system is itself a program, so it requires RAM space, too.

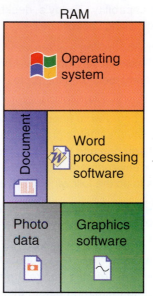

TERMINOLOGY NOTE

The term *buffer* is technical jargon for a region of memory that holds data waiting to be transferred from one device to another.

4

processing takes place. In practice, however, today's server OSs can be configured for centralized or distributed processing.

A **desktop operating system** is designed for a personal computer—a desktop, notebook, or tablet computer. The computer you use at home, at school, or at work is most likely configured with a desktop operating system, such as Microsoft Windows or Mac OS. Typically, these operating systems are designed to accommodate a single user, but can also provide networking capability. Today's desktop operating systems invariably provide multitasking capabilities.

Some operating system vendors characterize their products as home or professional versions. The home version usually has fewer network management tools than the professional version.

Do I ever interact directly with the OS? Although its main purpose is to control what happens behind the scenes of a computer system, many operating systems provide helpful tools, called operating system utilities, that you can use to control and customize your computer equipment and work environment. For example, Microsoft Windows offers its users controls to do the following activities.

• **Launch programs.** When you start your computer, Windows displays graphical objects, such as icons, the Start button, and the Programs menu, which you can use to start programs.

• **Manage files.** A useful utility, called Windows Explorer, allows you to view a list of files, move them to different storage devices, copy them, rename them, and delete them.

• **Get help.** Windows offers a Help system you can use to find out how various commands work.

• **Customize the user interface.** The Windows Control Panel, accessible from the Start menu, provides utilities that help you customize your screen display and work environment.

• **Configure equipment.** The Control Panel also provides access to utilities that help you set up and configure your computer's hardware and peripheral devices (Figure 4-6).

FIGURE 4-6

Many Windows utilities can be accessed from the Control Panel. You'll find it by clicking the Start button. The Classic View displays Control Panel utilities as icons; Category View shown here organizes the utilities into groups.

▶ CLICK TO START

USER INTERFACES

What is a user interface? A **user interface** can be defined as the combination of hardware and software that helps people and computers communicate with each other. Your computer's user interface includes a display device, mouse, and keyboard that allow you to view and manipulate your computing environment. It also includes software elements, such as icons, menus, and toolbar buttons.

How does the operating system affect the user interface? The operating system's user interface defines the so-called look and feel of compatible software. For example, application software that runs under Windows uses a standard set of menus, buttons, and toolbars based on the operating system's user interface. Originally, computers had a **command-line interface** that required users to type memorized commands to run programs and accomplish tasks.

Command-line user interfaces can be accessed from most operating systems. Experienced users and system administrators sometimes prefer to use a command-line interface for troubleshooting and system maintenance. Figure 4-7 illustrates the use of a command-line interface.

```
C:\MYDATA>PAINT
Bad command or file name

C:\MYDATA>CD\

C:\_
```

FIGURE 4-7

A command-line user interface requires users to type commands. Here the prompt C:\MYDATA> means the computer is looking at the MYDATA folder of drive C. The user has tried to start a program called Paint, but that program does not exist in the current folder, so the computer has produced an error message "Bad command or file name."

Most computers today feature a graphical user interface, abbreviated as GUI and pronounced as "gooey" or "gee you eye". A **graphical user interface** provides a way to point and click a mouse to select menu options and manipulate graphical objects displayed on the screen.

GUIs were originally conceived at the prestigious Xerox PARC research facility. In 1984, developers at Apple Computer, Inc. turned the idea into a commercial success with the launch of its popular Macintosh computer, which featured a GUI operating system and applications. Graphical user interfaces didn't really catch on in the PC market until the 1992 release of Windows 3.1.

What are the basic elements of a GUI? GUIs are based on graphical objects that can be manipulated using a mouse or other input device. Each graphical object represents a computer task, command, or real-world object. Icons and windows can be displayed on a screen-based **desktop** as explained in Figure 4-8 on the next page. An **icon** is a small picture that represents a program, file, or hardware device. A **window** is a rectangular work area that can hold a program, data, or controls.

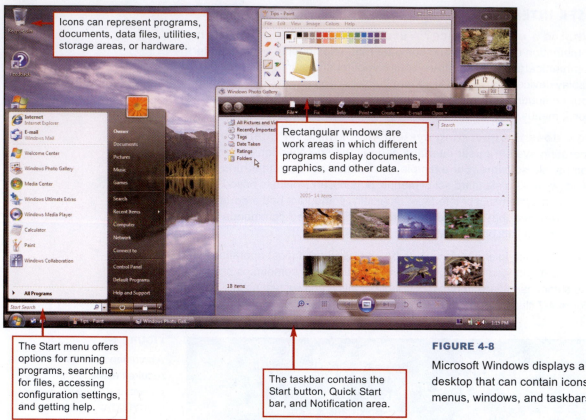

Icons can represent programs, documents, data files, utilities, storage areas, or hardware.

Rectangular windows are work areas in which different programs display documents, graphics, and other data.

The Start menu offers options for running programs, searching for files, accessing configuration settings, and getting help.

The taskbar contains the Start button, Quick Start bar, and Notification area.

FIGURE 4-8

Microsoft Windows displays a desktop that can contain icons, menus, windows, and taskbars.

A **button** is a graphic—usually rectangular in shape—that can be clicked to make a selection. Buttons can be arranged in a **menu bar**, **toolbar**, **taskbar**, or **ribbon** (Figure 4-9).

FIGURE 4-9

Buttons and command options can be arranged on menu bars, toolbars, taskbars, or ribbons (shown top to bottom).

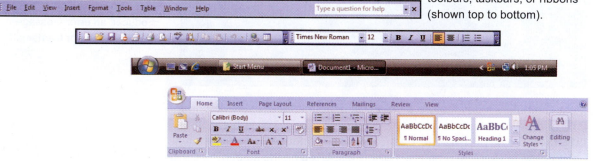

What's the point of menus and dialog boxes?

Menus were developed as a response to the difficulties many people experienced trying to remember command words and syntax for command-line user interfaces. A **menu** displays a list of commands or options. Each line of the menu is referred to as a menu option or a menu item. Menus are popular because you simply choose the command you want from a list. Also, because all the commands on the list are valid, it is not possible to invoke invalid commands that generate errors.

You might wonder how a menu can present all the commands you might want to use. Obviously, there are many possibilities for combining command words so there could be hundreds of menu options. Two methods are generally used to present a reasonably sized list of options: submenus and dialog boxes.

A **submenu** is an additional set of commands that the computer displays after you make a selection from the main menu. Sometimes a submenu displays another submenu providing even more command choices (Figure 4-10).

FIGURE 4-10

Menu options with a ▶ symbol lead to submenus.

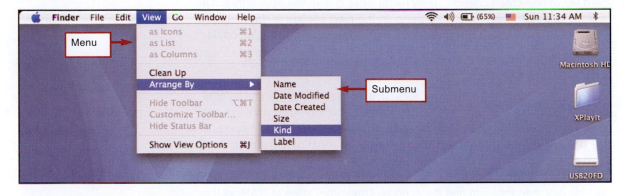

Instead of leading to a submenu, some menu options lead to a dialog box. A **dialog box** displays the options associated with a command. You fill in the dialog box to indicate specifically how you want the command carried out, as shown in Figure 4-11.

FIGURE 4-11

Dialog boxes can contain a variety of controls.

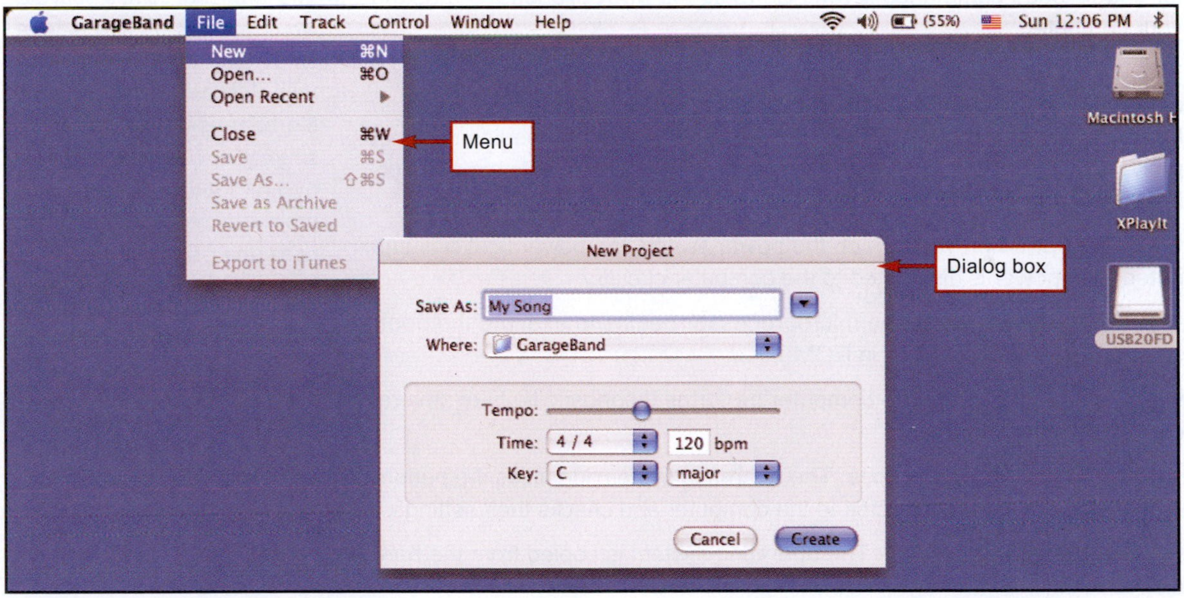

Dialog boxes display controls that you manipulate with a mouse to specify settings and other command parameters. Figure 4-12 explains how to use some of the dialog box controls that you are likely to encounter in Windows, Mac, or Linux environments.

FIGURE 4-12

Dialog box controls offer a variety of ways to enter specifications for tasks you'd like the software to carry out.

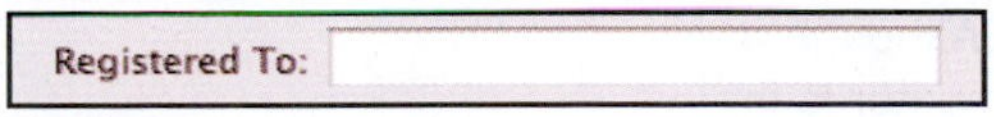

Registered To:

Text box

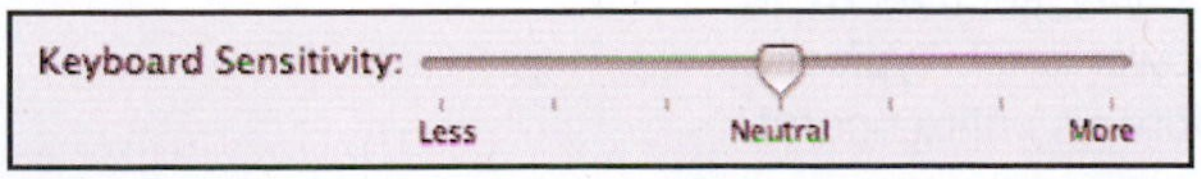

Keyboard Sensitivity: ————————⟨⟩————————
          Less   Neutral   More

Slider bar

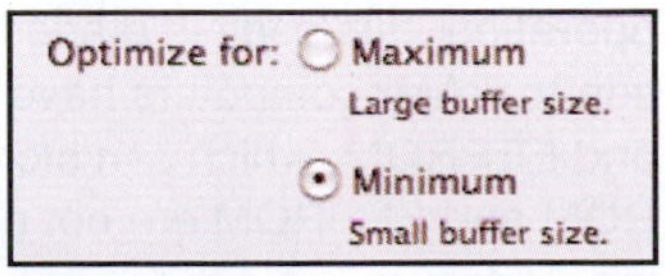

Optimize for: ◯ Maximum
                    Large buffer size.

               ◉ Minimum
                    Small buffer size.

Radio buttons

4

How similar are the user interfaces for Windows, Mac OS, and Linux? All of the popular desktop operating systems use graphical user interfaces that are more similar than they are different. Regardless of whether you use Windows, Mac OS, or Linux, you'll encounter a fairly standard set of on-screen controls. They might differ in their visual design, but it is easy to determine how to use them. In the next section of the chapter, you'll learn more about the similarities and differences in today's popular operating systems.

THE BOOT PROCESS

Where is the operating system stored? In some digital devices—typically handhelds and videogame consoles—the entire operating system is small enough to be stored in ROM. For most other computers, the operating system program is quite large, so most of it is stored on a hard disk. During the boot process, the operating system kernel is loaded into RAM. The **kernel** provides essential operating system services, such as memory management and file access. The kernel stays in RAM all the time your computer is on. Other parts of the operating system, such as customization utilities, are loaded into RAM as they are needed.

What is the boot process? The sequence of events that occurs between the time that you turn on a computer and the time that it is ready for you to issue commands is referred to as the **boot process**, or booting your computer.

Your computer's small **bootstrap program** is built into special ROM (read-only memory) circuitry housed in the computer's system unit. When you turn on a computer, the ROM circuitry receives power and begins the boot process by executing the bootstrap program. Six major events happen during the boot process:

- **Power up.** When you turn on the power switch, the power light is illuminated, and power is distributed to the computer circuitry.

- **Start boot program.** The microprocessor begins to execute the bootstrap program that is stored in ROM.

- **Power-on self-test.** The computer performs diagnostic tests of several crucial system components.

- **Identify peripheral devices.** The operating system identifies the peripheral devices that are connected to the computer and checks their settings.

- **Load operating system.** The operating system is copied from the hard disk to RAM.

- **Check configuration and customization.** The microprocessor reads configuration data and executes any customized startup routines specified by the user.

Why doesn't a computer simply leave the operating system in memory? Most of a computer's memory is volatile random access memory (RAM), which cannot hold any data when the power is off. Although a copy of the operating system is housed in RAM while the computer is in operation, this copy is erased as soon as the power is turned off. In addition to RAM, computers have non-volatile memory circuitry, such as ROM and EEPROM, which can store data even when the power is off. Typically, ROM and EEPROM are not nearly large enough to store an entire operating system.

TERMINOLOGY NOTE

The term *boot* comes from the word *bootstrap*, which is a small loop on the back of a boot. Just as you can pull on a big boot using a small bootstrap, your computer boots up by first loading a small program into memory, and then it uses that small program to load a large operating system.

Given the volatility of RAM and the insufficient size of ROM and EEPROM, computer designers decided to store the operating system on a computer's hard disk. During the boot process, a copy of the operating system is transferred into RAM where it can be accessed quickly whenever the computer needs to carry out an input, output, or storage operation (Figure 4-13).

How do I know when the operating system is loaded? The operating system is loaded and the boot process is complete when the computer is ready to accept your commands. Usually, the computer displays an operating system prompt or a main screen. The Windows operating system, for example, displays the Windows desktop when the boot process is complete.

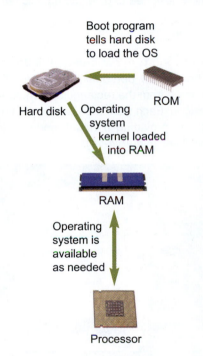

Boot program tells hard disk to load the OS

ROM

Hard disk   Operating system kernel loaded into RAM

RAM

Operating system is available as needed

Processor

FIGURE 4-13

The bootstrap program copies the operating system into RAM, where it can be directly accessed by the processor to carry out input, output, or storage operations.

4

QuickCheck

1. An operating system manages a computer's [   ] , such as RAM, storage, and peripherals.

2. To run more than one program at a time, the operating system must allocate a specific area of [   ] for each program.

3. The core part of an operating system is called its [   ] .

4. A(n) [   ] program stored in ROM tells the hard disk to load the operating system into RAM.

5. A user [   ] encompasses the hardware and software that helps people and computers communicate with each other.

▶ CHECK ANSWERS

Today's Operating Systems

CONSUMERS CAN SELECT from several operating systems for their personal computers and handheld devices. What makes these operating systems different? What are their strengths and weaknesses? Section B offers an operating system overview designed to give you a basic familiarity with their features.

MICROSOFT WINDOWS

What's the best-selling operating system? **Microsoft Windows** is installed on more than 80% of the world's personal computers. The Windows operating system gets its name from the rectangular work areas that appear on the screen-based desktop. Each work area window can display a different document or program, providing a visual model of the operating system's multitasking capabilities (Figure 4-14).

FIGURE 4-14

Microsoft Windows XP (top) and Windows Vista (bottom) use similar GUI controls, although the appearance of icons and other graphical elements is slightly different. See if you can match the elements on the Windows XP screen to those pointed out on the Windows Vista screen.

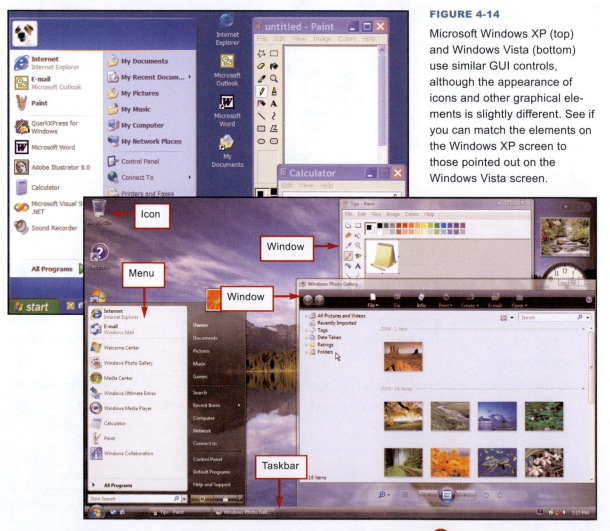

CLICK TO START

What do I need to know about the evolution of Windows? The first versions of Windows, including Windows 3.1, were sometimes referred to as *operating environments* rather than operating systems because they required DOS to supply the operating system kernel. Windows operating environments primarily supplied a point-and-click user interface, complete with graphical screen displays and mouse input. Windows operating environments evolved into today's comprehensive operating systems, which do not require the DOS kernel.

From its inception, the Windows operating system was designed to run on Intel or Intel-compatible microprocessors. As those chips evolved from 16-bit to 32-bit, and then to 64-bit architectures, Windows evolved to keep pace. In addition, Windows developers added and upgraded features, such as networking and the file system. They also refined the user interface by attempting to make it more visually attractive and easier to use. Since its introduction in 1985, Windows has evolved through several versions, listed in Figure 4-15.

What are the strengths of Windows? The number and variety of programs that run on Windows are unmatched by any other operating system, a fact that contributes to Windows being the most widely used desktop operating system. For the best selection of software, especially for games and vertical market business software, Windows is the operating system of choice.

The variety of hardware platforms that run Windows is also a significant strength. You can use a desktop computer, notebook, PDA, ultra-mobile, PC, or tablet computer and see a familiar set of Windows icons and menus. Features such as handwriting recognition contribute to the versatility of Windows, allowing it to control PDAs and tablet computers with touch screens.

The Windows user community is also a strength. A vast amount of documentation, including tutorials and troubleshooting guides, can be found online and on the shelves of most bookstores. Microsoft's official site, *www.microsoft.com*, includes thousands of pages of easily searchable information. Third-party sites, such as Paul Thurrott's Super Site for Windows, also offer tips, tools, and troubleshooting guides.

When it comes to hardware and peripheral devices, Windows offers excellent support in the form of built-in drivers and Plug and Play functionality. With the largest user base of any platform, Windows computer owners are the target market for the majority of hardware manufacturers. Many of the fastest graphics cards and the coolest joysticks are offered exclusively for the Windows platform.

What are Window's weaknesses? Windows has been criticized for two major weaknesses: reliability and security. The reliability of an operating system is usually gauged by the length of time it operates without glitches. Unfortunately, Windows tends to become unstable with more frequency than other operating systems. Slow system response, programs that stop working, and error messages can be symptoms of a Windows malfunction. Rebooting usually clears the error condition and

FIGURE 4-15

Windows Timeline

2007 Windows Vista
Featured 64-bit support, enhanced security, and more flexible file management. Also more powerful search capabilities and live icons that show document thumbnails.

2001 Windows XP
Featured an updated user interface, used the Windows 2000 32-bit kernel, and supported FAT32 and NTFS file systems.

2000 Windows Me
The last Windows version to use the original Windows kernel that accesses DOS.

2000 Windows 2000
Billed as a "multipurpose network OS for businesses of all sizes" and featured enhanced Web services.

1998 Windows 98
Increased stability was a big feature of this Windows version, which also included the Internet Explorer browser.

1995 Windows 95
Featured a revised user interface. Supported 32-bit processors, TCP/IP, dial-up networking, and long file names.

1993 Windows NT
Provided management and security tools for network servers and the NTFS file system.

1992 Windows for Workgroups
Provided peer-to-peer networking, e-mail, group scheduling, and file and printer sharing.

1992 Windows 3.1
Introduced program icons and the file folder metaphor.

1990 Windows 3.0
Introduced graphical controls.

1987 Windows 2.0
Introduced overlapping windows and expanded memory access.

1985 Windows 1.0
Divided the screen into rectangular windows that allowed users to work with several programs at the same time.

4

returns a computer to normal functionality, but the time wasted shutting down and waiting for a reboot adds unnecessary frustration to the computing experience.

Of the major desktop operating systems, Windows has the reputation for being the most vulnerable to viruses, worms, and other attacks. Some portion of Windows' vulnerability is because its huge user base makes it the biggest target. In addition, anti-establishment sentiments make Microsoft a hip adversary for rebellious hackers. Even so, Windows has many security holes which are found and exploited. Although Microsoft is diligent in its efforts to patch security holes, its programmers are always one step behind the hackers, and while users wait for patches their computers are vulnerable.

What's the difference between desktop, server, and embedded versions of Microsoft Windows? Microsoft typically offers several versions, called "editions," of the Windows operating system for various markets. Desktop editions, such as Home, Business, and Enterprise, are designed for personal computers. Server editions are designed for LAN, Internet, and Web servers. Embedded editions are designed for handheld devices, such as PDAs and mobile phones. Figure 4-16 categorizes some of the most popular past and present Windows offerings.

FIGURE 4-16

Microsoft offers several versions of Windows, designed for different computing tasks and equipment.

Personal Computers

Windows Vista Starter
Windows Vista Home Basic
Windows Vista Home
   Premium
Windows Vista Business
Windows Vista Enterprise
Windows Vista Ultimate

LAN, Internet, and Web Servers

Windows Server 2008
Windows Server 2003
Windows 2000 Server

PDAs, Mobile Phones, and Non-personal Computer Devices

Windows Mobile OS
Windows Embedded CE
Windows XP Embedded

MAC OS

Is Mac OS similar to Windows? **Mac OS** stands for Macintosh Operating System and it is the OS designed for Apple Computer's Macintosh line of computer systems. Although Mac OS was developed several years before Windows, both operating systems base their user interfaces on the graphical model pioneered at Xerox PARC. Both interfaces feature multiple rectangular work areas to reflect multitasking capabilities. Both operating systems provide basic networking services. A quick comparison of Figures 4-14 and 4-17 shows that both Mac and Windows interfaces use a mouse for pointing to and clicking various icons and menus.

FIGURE 4-17

You can tell when you're using Mac OS by the Apple logo that appears on the menu bar. The Mac OS X interface includes all the standard elements of a GUI, including icons, menus, windows, and taskbars.

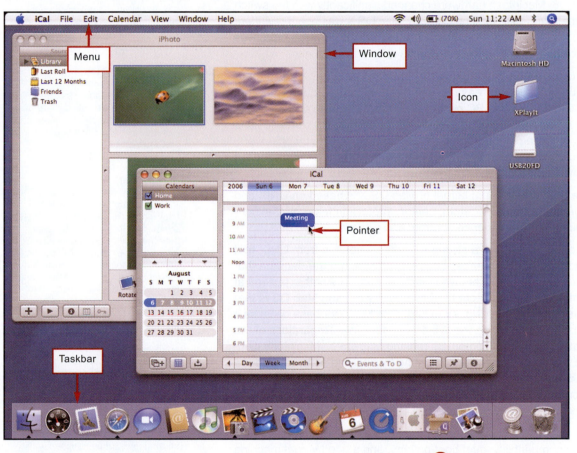

▶ CLICK TO START

What do I need to know about the evolution of Mac OS? Like Windows, Mac OS has been through a number of revisions (Figure 4-18). The original Classic Mac OS was designed for a line of Macintosh computers based on the Motorola 68000 microprocessor.

In 2001, Classic Mac OS was rewritten to run on Macintosh computers containing PowerPC microprocessors produced by IBM. The new Mac OS was called Mac OS X (the X can either be pronounced as "ten" or the letter X). Mac OS X was much more sophisticated than its predecessor, with better memory management and multitasking capabilities.

In 2006, Macintosh hardware changed significantly with the switch from PowerPC to Intel processors. Mac OS X was again rewritten. The first version of Mac OS X to support the Intel architecture was Mac OS X version 10.4, sometimes referred to as Tiger.

What are the strengths of Mac OS? Mac OS X has a reputation for being an easy to use, reliable, and secure operating system. Back when PC owners were struggling with an inscrutable command-line operating system, Macintosh owners were breezing along with a point and click GUI. According to industry observers, Macintosh developers have always been in the lead when it comes to intuitive user interface design.

The operating system kernel of Mac OS X is based on UNIX and includes industrial strength memory protection features that contribute to a low incidence of errors and glitches.

Mac OS X inherited a strong security foundation from UNIX that tends to limit the number of security holes and the damage that can be done by hackers who manage to slip in. Another factor that contributes to the security of computers running Mac OS is that fewer viruses are designed to target the Mac user base because it is much smaller than the Windows user base. Regardless of the relative security of computers running Mac OS X, Macintosh owners should practice safe computing by applying software and OS patches as they become available, activating wireless network encryption, not opening suspicious e-mail attachments, and not clicking links embedded in e-mail messages.

In addition to reliability and security, Mac OS X offers strong backward compatibility, dual boot options, and a good virtual machine platform.

What is backward compatibility? **Backward compatibility** refers to the ability to work with products designed for prior-generation hardware or software. For example, suppose you have a computer and lots of great software, but you purchase a faster machine with an upgraded operating system. If that operating system is backward compatible with the operating system on your old computer, you can use all of your old applications.

Macintosh computer developers, like their counterparts at Microsoft, have been careful to provide capabilities to run prior-generation software on new OS versions. For PowerPC Mac owners who wanted to run application software designed for the earlier generation of Mac hardware, OS X provided an emulation

FIGURE 4-18

Mac OS Timeline

2007 Mac OS X (Desktop edition for Intel processor)
Kernel ported to Intel codebase, support for old PowerPC software offered using Rosetta emulation, version Leopard.

2001 Mac OS X (Desktop edition for PowerPC)
New kernel based on Unix-like, open source code called XNU, proprietary GUI called Aqua featuring softer edges and translucent colors, multi-user, multitasking, versions Cheetah, Puma, Jaguar, Panther, and Tiger.

1999 Mac OS 9
Visually controversial metallic-look user interface, support for multiple users, Sherlock search utility searches the Internet as well as local storage devices, CD burning software, designed to run on IBM Power PC chips, Classic emulation for running software designed for Motorola chips.

1997 Mac OS 8
Full-color GUI, designed to run on Motorola 68000 and IBM Power PC processors, supported large file sizes and file names up to 255 characters.

1991 System 7/ Mac OS
User interface icons colorized, virtual memory and personal file sharing introduced, shipped with the popular QuickTime video software, balloon help identified the function of icons, 32-bit compatible.

1988 System 6
Introduced multitasking, no built-in support for virtual memory.

1984 Classic Mac OS
Grayscale graphical user interface featuring icons and menus that could be manipulated by a mouse. Singletasking, limited memory management, file system creates data forks and resource forks.

mode. An emulation program called Rosetta allows software applications designed for PowerPC Macs to run on Intel Macs. Software developers also have the option of shipping software in Universal Binary format, which includes a PowerPC and Intel version of the application. The correct version is automatically run when the application runs.

The ability to run prior-generation applications is important because software developers typically require several months to produce applications for new hardware or operating systems. While waiting for new applications, consumers can use emulators to run software they might have purchased for an older computer and have access to a much larger library of programs than would initially be available for a new hardware platform.

What is dual boot? Mac OS X on an Intel Mac offers the ability to run Windows and Windows application software in addition to software designed for the Macintosh. Software called Boot Camp is a **dual boot** utility that can switch between Mac OS X and Windows. When booting, you can select either Mac OS X or Windows (Figure 4-19). To change operating systems, you have to reboot.

FIGURE 4-19

On a Macintosh computer with Boot Camp, you can boot into Mac OS X or into Windows.

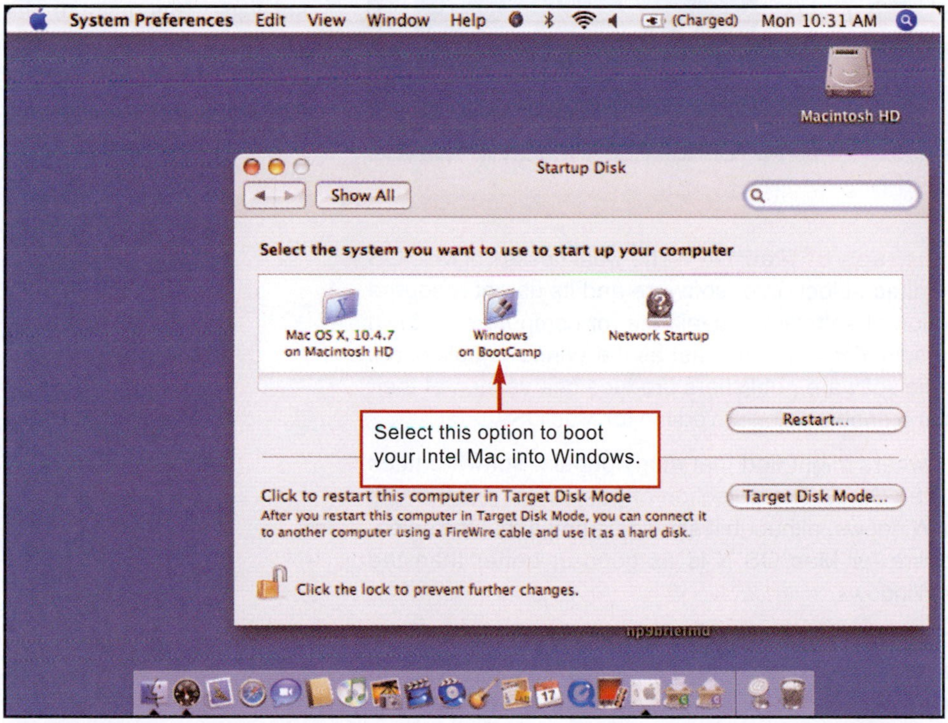

4

CLICK TO START

What is a virtual machine? Mac OS X is also a good platform for **virtual machine** (VM) technologies that allow you to use one computer to simulate the hardware and software of another. Each virtual machine has its own simulated processor (or core processor), RAM, video card, input and output ports, and operating system. Each machine can also run most software that's compatible with the virtual hardware and operating system.

Popular virtual machine software such as VMware and Parallels Desktop can run on most computers with Intel microprocessors, including Intel Macs, PCs, and generic Linux computers. The computer boots into its native OS such as Mac OS, but users can create a virtual machine running guest operating systems, such as Windows XP or Vista. The virtual machine's desktop appears in a window on the host desktop.

INFOWEBLINKS

Virtual machines are catching on fast. You can even download VM "appliances" preconfigured for uses such as Web servers or safe browsers. Find out more at the **Virtual Machines InfoWeb**.

W CLICK TO CONNECT

www.course.com/np/concepts11/ch04

Theoretically, with virtual machine software your Mac desktop could display a virtual Windows computer, a virtual Linux computer, and a native Mac OS X computer (Figure 4-20).

FIGURE 4-20

On a Mac with virtual Windows and Linux, switching from one operating system to another is as simple as selecting a window. When switched to the Windows work area, you can run games, business software, and other applications designed for the Windows OS. Clicking the Linux work area, you could run Linux applications from its vast collection of open source software. Returning to the Mac OS X desktop, you could run your collection of high-end graphics and multimedia iLife software designed exclusively for the Macintosh.

What are the weaknesses of Mac OS? The weaknesses of Mac OS include a somewhat limited selection of software and its use of resource forks. A decent collection of software is available for computers that run Mac OS, although the selection is not as vast as the Windows collection. Many of the most prolific software publishers produce one version of their software for Windows and another, similar version for Mac OS.

Macintosh computer owners might find that many popular software titles are not available for Mac OS X. The selection of games, for example, is much sparser than for Windows, although it should be noted that the selection of graphics software for Mac OS X is as good or better than the selection available for Windows.

What is a resource fork? In most operating systems a file is a single unit that contains data or program code. Files maintained by the Macintosh operating system, however, can have two parts, called forks. The **data fork** is similar to files in other operating systems. It contains data, such as the text for a document, the graphics for a photo, or the commands for a program. The **resource fork** is a companion file that stores information about the data in the data fork, such as the file type and the application that created it.

Although resource forks have advantages on their native Macintosh platform, they pose difficulties for transferring files to other platforms. In today's networked world in which everyone wants to share data, the resource fork presents a potential bottleneck to the free flow of data. To transfer Mac files to a PC, for example, requires a conversion process that bundles the resource fork information with the data fork.

UNIX AND LINUX

Are UNIX and Linux the same? The **UNIX** operating system was developed in 1969 at AT&T's Bell Labs. It gained a good reputation for its dependability in multiuser environments, and many versions of it became available for mainframes and microcomputers.

In 1991, a young Finnish student named Linus Torvalds developed the **Linux** (pronounced LIH nucks) operating system. Linux was inspired by and loosely based on a UNIX derivative called MINIX, created by Andrew Tanenbaum. Linux continues to gain popularity as an operating system for personal computers, though it is not as popular for desktop applications as Windows or Mac OS.

What are the strengths of Linux? Linux is rather unique because it is distributed along with its source code under the terms of a General Public License (GPL), which allows everyone to make copies for their own use, to give to others, or to sell. This licensing policy has encouraged programmers to develop Linux utilities, software, and enhancements. Linux is primarily distributed over the Web.

Although Linux is designed for microcomputers, rather than mainframes, it shares several technical features with UNIX, such as multitasking, virtual memory, TCP/IP drivers, and multiuser capabilities. These features make Linux a popular operating system for e-mail and Web servers as well as for local area network servers.

What are the weaknesses of Linux? Linux typically requires a bit more tinkering than the Windows and Mac desktop operating systems. The comparatively limited number of programs that run under Linux also discourages many nontechnical users from selecting it as the OS for their desktop and notebook computers. A constantly growing collection of high-quality open source software is becoming available for the Linux platform, but many of these applications are targeted toward business and technical users.

Several Web sites offer a **Linux distribution**, which is a package that contains the Linux kernel, system utilities, applications, and an installation routine. Beginner-friendly Linux distributions include Fedora, Ubuntu, and SUSE. Most of these distributions include a GUI module that provides a user interface similar to the one pictured in Figure 4-21.

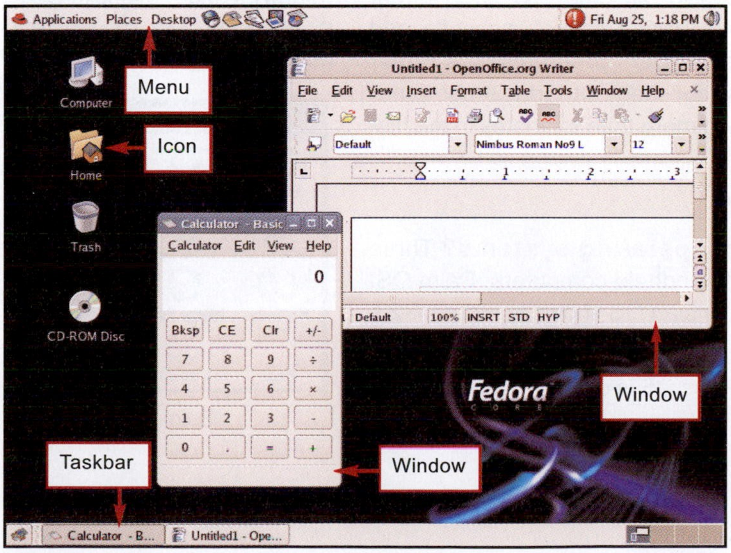

FIGURE 4-21

Linux users can choose from several graphical interfaces. Pictured here is the popular KDE graphical desktop.

CLICK TO START

DOS

Why do I keep hearing about DOS?
Old-timers in the computer industry sometimes reminisce about DOS. It was the first operating system that many of them used, and its cryptic command-line user interface left an indelible impression. **DOS** (which rhymes with toss) stands for Disk Operating System. It was developed by Microsoft—the same company that later produced Windows—and introduced on the original IBM PC in 1982. Although IBM called this operating system PC-DOS, Microsoft marketed it to other companies under the name MS-DOS.

DOS software, such as Visicalc, used command-line interfaces and rustic menus that users controlled with the keyboard's arrow keys (Figure 4-22).

FIGURE 4-22

When using Visicalc, you could press the slash key (/) to call up the main menu, which simply listed the first letter of each command. For example, F was the Format command, so if you wanted to format a cell, you pressed F to see a list of letters, such as C, L, and R—the commands for centering, left alignment, and right alignment.

```
A6                                                              C
Command:  BCDEFGIMPRSTUVW-                                     43

        A           B           C        D        E        F        G
 1Sales           42818
 2Expenses        37801
 3                ======
 4Profit           5017
 5
 6
 7
 8
 9
10
11
12
13
14
15
16
17
18
19
20
21
```

After more than 20 years, remnants of DOS still linger in the world of personal computers because it provided part of the operating system kernel for Windows versions 3.1, 95, 98, and Me.

During the peak of its popularity, thousands of software programs were produced for computers running DOS. You can occasionally find some of these programs on the Internet, and run them using the Command Prompt option accessed from the Start menu of Windows XP or Vista. DOS also offers handy troubleshooting utilities, such as Ping, Tracert, Copy *, msconfig, and netstat used by tech-savvy computer users. DOS programs look rather unsophisticated by today's standards, so for many of today's computer owners, DOS and DOS software are nothing more than footnotes in the history of the computer industry.

HANDHELD OPERATING SYSTEMS

What are the options for handheld operating systems?
Three operating systems dominate the realm of handheld computers: Palm OS, Windows Mobile OS, iPhone OS X, and Symbian OS shown in Figure 4-23.

Palm OS is produced by ACCESS, which produces a generic operating system for mobile devices called Garnet. Palm OS is currently used for popular Palm brand PDAs and smart phones.

FIGURE 4-23

Mobile devices use operating systems such as Palm OS (Below), Windows Mobile OS, Symbian OS, and iPhone OS X (next page).

Palm OS

Windows Mobile OS is an operating system built on the Microsoft Windows CE technology. As a cousin to Windows XP and Vista, Windows Mobile OS sports some features similar to those found on the Windows desktop. Windows Mobile OS is the operating system for a variety of PDAs, Pocket PCs, phone-enabled PDAs, and smartphones.

Symbian OS is a multitasking, multithreaded operating system popular on Ericsson and Nokia smartphones. Symbian can be easily programmed with languages such as C++, Visual Basic, or Personal Java, and so some interesting third-party freeware and shareware is available.

iPhone OS X

iPhone OS X is a version of Mac OS X written for the iPhone's ARM processor and optimized for touchscreen communications applications. It includes routines that manage gesture inputs, such as using your fingers to "squeeze" an onscreen graphic into a smaller size. It also includes widgets for stock quotes and weather reports.

Windows Mobile OS

Symbian OS

Are operating systems for handheld devices similar to desktop operating systems? Operating systems for handheld and desktop devices provide many similar services, such as scheduling processor resources, managing memory, loading programs, managing input and output, and establishing the user interface. But because handheld devices tend to be used for less sophisticated tasks, their operating systems are somewhat simpler and significantly smaller.

By keeping the operating system small, it can be stored in ROM. Without the need to load the OS from disk into RAM, a handheld device's operating system is ready almost instantly when the unit is turned on. Operating systems for handheld devices provide built-in support for touch screens, handwriting input, wireless networking, and cellular communications.

QuickCheck

1. The Windows operating system was designed to run on Motorola and IBM processors. True or false? [   ]

2. A(n) [   ] -compatible operating system should run application software designed for the operating system's prior generations.

3. A(n) [   ] boot computer could boot into Windows, and then reboot into Mac OS.

4. A computer configured with the correct set of [   ] machines could run Windows in a window on the Mac desktop.

5. A resource [   ] is a companion file created by Mac OS to store information about the file and its data.

6. [   ] is an open source operating system that can run on the desktop, but tends to be used for server applications instead.

7. Palm and Symbian are examples of operating systems used for handheld devices. True or false? [   ]

CHECK ANSWERS

File Basics

THE TERM FILE WAS USED for filing cabinets and collections of papers long before it became part of the personal computer lexicon. Today, computer files in digital format offer a compact and convenient way to store documents, photos, videos, and music. Computer files have several characteristics, such as a name, format, location, size, and date. To make effective use of computer files, you'll need a good understanding of these file basics, and that is the focus of Section C.

FILE NAMES AND EXTENSIONS

What is a computer file? As you learned in Chapter 1, a computer file—or simply a file— is defined as a named collection of data that exists on a storage medium, such as a disk, CD, DVD, USB flash drive, or tape. A file can contain a group of records, a document, a photo, music, a video, an e-mail message, or a computer program.

When you use word processing software, the text you enter for a document is stored as a file. You can give the file a name, such as *A History of Film Noir*. A music file, such as *Bach Brandenberg Concertos* that you download over the Internet, is stored as a file, too.

What are the rules for naming files? Every file has a name and might also have a file extension. When you save a file, you must provide a valid file name that adheres to specific rules, referred to as **file-naming conventions**. Each operating system has a unique set of file-naming conventions. Figure 4-24 lists file-naming conventions for the current versions of Windows.

Is there a maximum length for file names? DOS and Windows 3.1 limited file names to eight characters. With that limitation, it was often difficult to create descriptive file names. A file name such as HseBud08 might be used for a file containing a household budget for 2008. With such cryptic file names, it was not always easy to figure out what a file contained. As a result, files were sometimes difficult to locate and identify. Today, most operating systems allow you to use longer file names.

Current versions of Windows support file names up to 255 characters long. That limitation includes the entire file path—drive letter, folders, file name, and extension. A file name limitation of 255 characters gives you the flexibility to use descriptive file names, such as Household Budget 2008, so that you can easily identify what a file contains.

What is a file extension? A **file extension** (sometimes referred to as a file name extension) is an optional file identifier that is separated from the main file name by a period, as in Paint.exe. As you become familiar with file extensions, they will provide a clue to the file's contents. Files with .exe extensions are executable files that your computer can run. Paint.exe, for example, is a graphics utility packaged with the Windows operating system. Files with .dat extensions are typically data files. Files with .doc extensions contain word processing documents.

FIGURE 4-24

Windows File-naming Conventions

Case sensitive	No
Maximum length of file name	File name and extension cannot exceed 255 characters
Spaces allowed	Yes
Numbers allowed	Yes
Characters not allowed	* \ : < > | " / ?
File names not allowed	Aux, Com1, Com2, Com3, Com4, Con, Lpt1, Lpt2, Lpt3, Prn, Nul

Why are certain characters not allowed in a file name? If an operating system attaches special significance to a symbol, you might not be able to use it in a file name. For example, Windows uses the colon (:) character to separate the device letter from a file name or folder, as in *C:Music*. A file name that contains a colon, such as *Report:2008,* is not valid because the operating system would become confused about how to interpret the colon. When you use Windows applications, avoid using the symbols : * \ < > | " / and ? in file names.

What are reserved words? Some operating systems also contain a list of **reserved words** that are used as commands or special identifiers. You cannot use these words alone as a file name. You can, however, use these words as part of a longer file name. For example, under Windows, the file name *Nul* would not be valid, but you could name a file something like *Nul Committee Notes.doc* or *Null Set.exe.*

In addition to *Nul,* Windows users should avoid using the following reserved words as file names: *Aux, Com1, Com2, Com3, Com4, Con, Lpt1, Lpt2, Lpt3,* and *Prn.*

What else should I know about creating file names? Some operating systems are case sensitive, but not those you typically work with on personal computers. Feel free to use uppercase and lowercase letters in file names that you create on PCs and Macs.

You can also use spaces in file names. That's a different rule than for e-mail addresses where spaces are not allowed. You've probably noticed that people often use underscores or periods instead of spaces in e-mail addresses such as Madi_Jones@msu.edu. That convention is not necessary in file names, so a file name such as Letter to Madi Jones is valid.

FILE DIRECTORIES AND FOLDERS

How do I designate a file's location? To designate a file's location, you must first specify the device where the file is stored. As shown in Figure 4-25, each of a PC's storage devices is identified by a device letter—a convention that is specific to DOS and Windows. The main hard disk drive is usually referred to as drive C. A device letter is usually followed by a colon, so the hard disk drive could be designated as C:.

Although the floppy disk drive is traditionally designated as drive A and the hard disk drive is designated as drive C, device letters for CD, DVD, and USB flash drives are not standardized. For example, the CD-writer on your computer might be assigned device letter E, whereas the CD-writer on another computer might be assigned device letter R.

What is a disk partition? A **disk partition** is a section of a hard disk drive that is treated as a separate storage unit. Most computers are configured with a single hard disk partition that contains the operating system, programs, and data. However, it is possible to create more than one hard disk partition. For example, a PC owner might set up one partition for operating system files and another partition for programs and data. This arrangement sometimes can speed up the process of disinfecting a computer that has been attacked by malicious software.

Partitions can be assigned drive letters. In the example above, the operation system files would be stored in partition C. The program and data file partition would probably be designated as drive D. Partitions are not the same thing as folders. Partitions are more permanent, and a special utility is required to create, modify, or delete them.

4

FIGURE 4-25

The Windows operating system labels storage devices with letters, such as A: and C:.

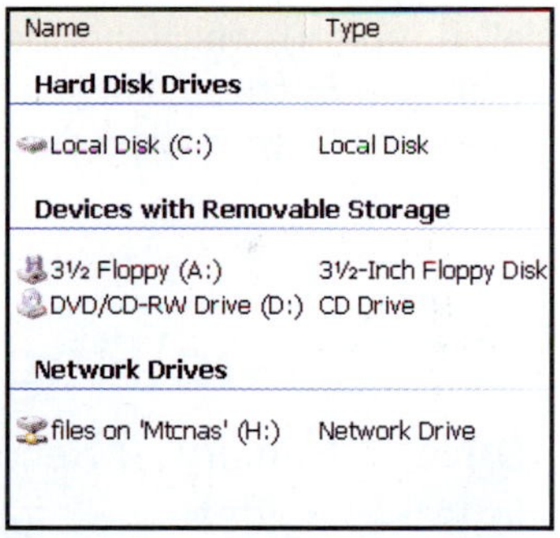

Name	Type
Hard Disk Drives	
Local Disk (C:)	Local Disk
Devices with Removable Storage	
3½ Floppy (A:)	3½-Inch Floppy Disk
DVD/CD-RW Drive (D:)	CD Drive
Network Drives	
files on 'Mtcnas' (H:)	Network Drive

TERMINOLOGY NOTE

Drive letter assignments are based on conventions that date back to the first PCs. The original IBM PCs shipped with a single floppy disk drive and it was designated drive A. An enhanced PC later shipped with two floppy disk drives, designated A and B. When hard disks were eventually added to PC systems, they were designated drive C.

Do I have to remember where I put each file? Your computer's operating system maintains a list of files called a **directory** for each storage disk, tape, CD, DVD, or USB flash drive. The main directory is referred to as the **root directory**. On a PC, the root directory is identified by the device letter followed by a backslash. For example, the root directory of the hard disk would be C:\. A root directory can be subdivided into smaller lists. Each list is called a **subdirectory**.

What is a folder? When you use Windows, Mac OS, or a Linux graphical file manager, each subdirectory is depicted as a **folder**. Folders help you envision your files as if they were stored in a filing cabinet. Each folder can hold related items, for example, a set of documents, sound clips, financial data, or photos for a school project. Windows provides a folder called *Documents* that you might use to hold reports, letters, and so on. You can also create and name folders to meet your needs, such as a folder called *QuickBooks* to hold your personal finance data.

Folders can be created within other folders. You might, for example, create a *Jazz* folder within the *Music* folder to hold your jazz collection and another folder named *Reggae to* hold your reggae collection.

A folder name is separated from a drive letter and other folder names by a special symbol. In Microsoft Windows, this symbol is the backslash (\ ). For example, the folder for your reggae music (within the *Music* folder on drive C) would be written as *C:\Music\Reggae*. Other operating systems use a forward slash (/) to separate folders.

A computer file's location is defined by a **file specification** (sometimes called a **path**), which includes the drive letter, folder(s), file name, and extension. Suppose that you have stored an MP3 file called *Marley One Love* in the *Reggae* folder on your hard disk. Its file specification is shown in Figure 4-26.

FIGURE 4-26

A file specification provides the name and location of a file.

C:\Music\Reggae\Marley One Love.mp3

Drive letter	Primary folder	Secondary folder	File name	File extension

What's the significance of a file's size? A file contains data, stored as a group of bits. The more bits, the larger the file. **File size** is usually measured in bytes, kilobytes, or megabytes. Knowing the size of a file can be important. Compared to small files, large files fill up storage space more quickly, require longer transmission times, and are more likely to be stripped off e-mail attachments by a mail server. Your computer's operating system keeps track of file sizes and supplies that information when you request a listing of files.

Is the file date important? Your computer keeps track of the date that a file was created or last modified. The **file date** is useful if you have created several versions of a file and want to make sure you know which version is the most recent. It can also come in handy if you have downloaded several updates of a software package, such as an MP3 player, and you want to make sure you install the latest version.

FILE FORMATS

Why should I know about file formats? Some operating systems do a fairly good job of shielding users from the intricacies of file formats. For example, Windows uses a file association list to link a file extension to its corresponding application software. This handy feature allows you to open a data file without first opening an application, simply by double-clicking the file from a desktop icon or selecting it from the Documents list that's accessible from the Start menu.

Of course, your application software also shields you from the messy task of searching through directories to find the files it will open. When you use the Open dialog box, most applications automatically comb through the files on a specified device and in a specified folder to display only those that have the correct file extensions.

With all this help from the operating system and your application software, it might seem that knowing about file formats is unimportant. You might, however, find it useful to understand file formats so that you can easily accomplish tasks such as those listed in Figure 4-27.

What determines a file's format? Although a file extension is a good indicator of a file's format, it does not really define the format. You could use the Rename command to change a QuickTime movie called Balloons.mov to Balloons.doc. Despite the .doc extension, the file is still in QuickTime format because the data elements in the file are arranged in a specific configuration unique to QuickTime.

The format of a file might include a header, data, and possibly an end-of-file marker. A **file header** is a section of data at the beginning of a file that contains information about a file—typically the date it was created, the date it was last updated, its size, and its file type.

A file header should not be confused with the headers appearing at the top of each page in a document created with a word processor. Instead, envision a file header as a hidden Post-It note that's attached to the beginning of a file. Although it is hidden to users, computers can read the information in a file header to determine the file's format.

The remaining contents of a file depend on whether it contains text, graphics, audio, or multimedia data. A text file, for example, might contain sentences and paragraphs interspersed with codes for centering, boldfacing, and margin settings. A graphics file might contain color data for each pixel, followed by a description of the color palette. The **file format** dictates the arrangement of this data. Figure 4-28 illustrates the layout for a Windows bitmap file and contrasts it with the layout of a GIF file.

FIGURE 4-27

Understanding file formats helps you perform the following tasks:

- Figure out the correct format for e-mail attachments that you send to friends or colleagues.
- Find the right player software for music and media files that you download from the Web.
- Discover how to work with a file that doesn't seem to open.
- Convert files from one format to another.

4

INFOWEBLINKS

The **File Formats InfoWeb** provides a list of file extensions and their corresponding software.

Ⓦ **CLICK TO CONNECT**
www.course.com/np/concepts11/ch04

Bitmap File Format	GIF File Format
File header	File header
Bitmap header	Logical screen descriptor
Color palette	Global color table
Bitmap data	Local image descriptor
	Local color table
	Image data
	End-of-file character

FIGURE 4-28

Although bitmap and GIF file formats contain graphics, the file layouts differ.

Which file formats am I most likely to encounter? A software program typically consists of at least one executable file with an .exe file extension. It might also include a number of support programs with extensions such as .dll, .vbx, and .ocx. Configuration and startup files usually have .bat, .sys, .ini, and .bin extensions. In addition, you'll find files with .hlp and .tmp extensions. Files with .hlp extensions hold the information for a program's Help utility. Files with .tmp extensions are temporary files. When you open a data file with software applications, such as word processors, spreadsheets, and graphics tools, your operating system makes a copy of the original file and stores this copy on disk as a temporary file. It is this temporary file that you work with as you view and revise a file.

To the uninitiated, the file extensions associated with programs and the operating system might seem odd. Nevertheless, executable and support files—even so-called temporary files—are crucial for the correct operation of your computer system. You should not manually delete them. The table in Figure 4-29 lists the file extensions typically associated with the Windows operating system and executable files.

FIGURE 4-29

OS and Executable Extensions

Type of File	Description	Extension
Batch file	A sequence of operating system commands executed automatically when the computer boots	.bat
Configuration file	Information about programs the computer uses to allocate the resources necessary to run them	.cfg .sys .mif .bin .ini
Help	The information displayed by on-screen Help	.hlp
Temporary file	A sort of scratch pad that contains data while a file is open, but is discarded when you close the file	.tmp
Support program	Program instructions executed along with the main .exe file for a program	.ocx .vbx .vbs .dll
Program	The main executable files for a computer program	.exe .com

The list of data file formats is long, but becoming familiar with the most popular formats and the type of data they contain is useful. Figure 4-30 provides this information in a convenient table. Where noted, a file format is associated with a particular software program.

FIGURE 4-30

Data File Extensions

Type of File	Extension
Text	.txt .dat .rtf .doc (Microsoft Word 2003) .docx (Word 2007) .wpd (WordPerfect)
Sound	.wav .mid .mp3 .au .ra (RealAudio)
Graphics	.bmp .pcx .tif .wmf .gif .jpg .png .eps .ai (Adobe Illustrator)
Animation/video	.flc .fli .avi .mpg .mov (QuickTime) .rm (RealMedia) .wmv (Windows Media Player)
Web pages	.htm .html .asp .vrml
Spreadsheets	.xls (Microsoft Excel 2003) .xlsx (Excel 2007) .wks (Lotus 1-2-3) .dif
Database	.mdb (Microsoft Access)
Miscellaneous	.pdf (Adobe Acrobat) .ppt (Microsoft PowerPoint) .zip (WinZip) .pub (Microsoft Publisher) .qxp (QuarkXpress)

How do I know which files a program will open? A software application can open files that exist in its **native file format**, plus several additional file formats. For example, Microsoft Word opens files in its native DOC (.doc or .docx) format, plus files in formats such as HTML (.htm or .html), Text (.txt), and Rich Text Format (.rtf). Within the Windows environment, you can discover which formats a particular software program can open by looking at the list of file types in the Open dialog box, as shown in Figure 4-31.

FIGURE 4-31

An application's Open dialog box usually displays a list of file formats the program can open. You can also look for an Import option on the File menu.

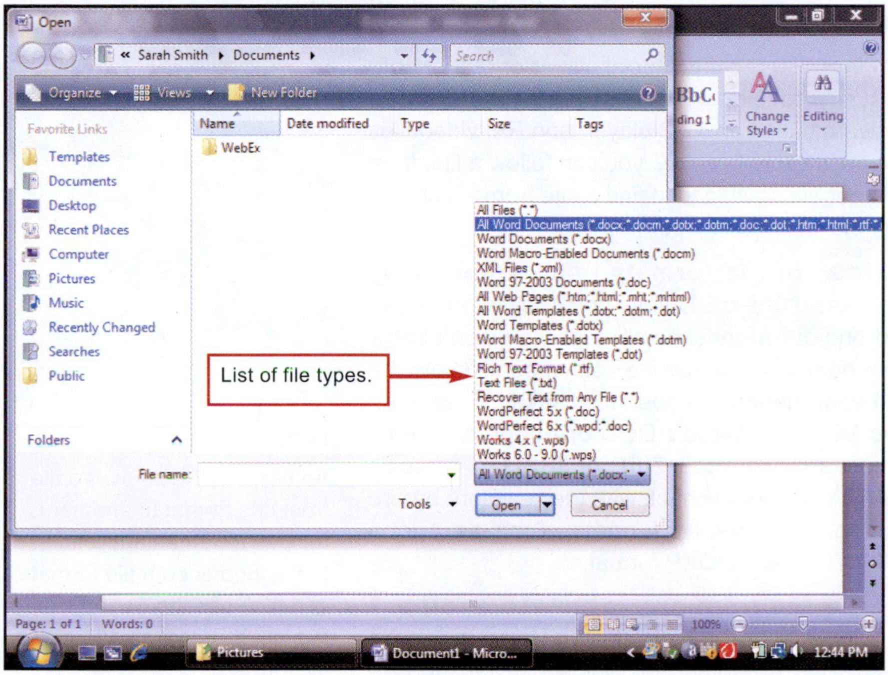

List of file types.

Why can't I open some files? Suppose you receive an e-mail attachment called Cool.tif. "Aha!" you say to yourself, "My Photoshop software ought to open that file." You try—several times—but all you get is an error message. When a file doesn't open, one of three things probably went wrong:

● The file might have been damaged—a techie would call it corrupted—by a transmission or disk error. Although you might be able to use file recovery software to repair the damage, it is usually easier to obtain an undamaged copy of the file from its original source.

● Someone might have inadvertently changed the file extension. While renaming the Cool file, perhaps the original .bmp extension was changed to .tif. If you have a little time, you can change the file extension and try to open the file. If a file contains a graphic, chances are that it should have the extension for one of the popular graphics formats, such as .bmp, .gif, .jpg, .tif, or .png. Otherwise, you should contact the source of the file to get accurate information about its real format.

● Some file formats exist in several variations, and your software might not have the capability to open a particular variation of the format. You might be able to open the file if you use different application software. For example, Photoshop might not be able to open a particular file with a .tif file extension, but Corel Paint Shop Pro might open it.

What if all my software fails to open a particular file format? Although a computer might be able to discover a file's format, it might not necessarily know how to work with it. Just as you might be able to identify a helicopter, you can't necessarily fly it without some instructions. Your computer also requires a set of instructions to use most file formats. These instructions are provided by software. To use a particular file format, you must make sure your computer has the corresponding software.

Suppose you download a file with an .rm extension and none of your current software works with this file format. Several Web sites provide lists of file extensions and their corresponding software. By looking up a file extension in one of these lists, you can find out what application software you'll need to find, buy, download, and install.

Many files downloaded from the Web require special player or reader software. For example, PDF text files require software called Acrobat Reader, MP3 music files require software called an MP3 player, and RM video files require the RealMedia Player software. Typically, you can follow a link from the Web page that supplied your file download to find a site from which you can download the necessary player or reader software.

How do I know what kinds of file formats I can send to my friends, colleagues, and instructor?
Unless you know what application software is installed on your friends' computers, you won't know for certain whether they can open a particular file you've sent. There's a good chance, however, that your friends can open files saved in common document formats such as Microsoft Word's DOC or Adobe Acrobat's PDF format; graphics formats such as PNG, TIFF, or JPEG; and music formats such as MP3 and AIF. You should check with the recipient before sending files in less common, proprietary formats, such as Adobe Illustrator's AI format and QuarkXpress's QXP format.

Is it possible to convert a file from one format to another?
Perhaps you created a Word document on your PC, but you need to convert it into a format that's usable by your colleague who owns a Mac. Or suppose you want to convert a Word document into HTML format so that you can post it on the Web. You might also want to convert a Windows bitmap (.bmp) graphic into GIF format so that you can include it on a Web page. The easiest way to convert a file from one format to another is to find an application program that works with both file formats. Open the file using that software, and then use the Export option, or the Save As dialog box, to select a new file format, assign the file a new name, and save it (Figure 4-32).

FIGURE 4-32

An easy way to convert a file from one format to another is to open it with an application that supports both file formats, and then use the Save As dialog box to select an alternative file format.

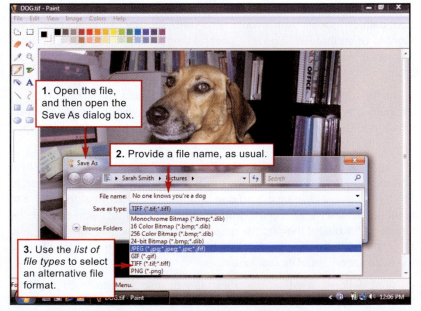

1. Open the file, and then open the Save As dialog box.

2. Provide a file name, as usual.

3. Use the *list of file types* to select an alternative file format.

CLICK TO START

Will a converted document be identical to the original? Many file formats convert easily to another format, and the resulting file is virtually indistinguishable from the original. Some conversions, however, do not retain all the characteristics of the original file. When you convert a DOC file into HTML format, for example, the HTML page does not contain any of the headers, footers, superscripts, page numbers, special characters, or page breaks that existed in the original DOC file.

When you need a conversion routine for an obscure file format, or if you need to convert between many different file formats, consider specialized conversion software, available through commercial or shareware outlets.

INFOWEBLINKS

Conversion software runs the gamut from simple shareware to industrial-strength commercial packages. The **Conversion Software InfoWeb** will help you compare what's available.

W CLICK TO CONNECT
www.course.com/np/concepts11/ch04

QuickCheck

SECTION C

1. Windows file-naming [_____] are different than for Linux.

2. When using Windows, you cannot use a reserved word, such as Aux, as a file name. True or false? [_____]

3. On a computer running Windows, the hard disk drive letter is usually designated as [_____].

4. The root directory of a disk can be divided into smaller lists called [_____], that are depicted as folders.

5. A file's location is defined by a file path, which includes the drive letter, one or more [_____], file name, and extension.

6. A file's [_____] can be important information when you are planning to transmit it to another computer over a network.

7. A file [_____] is a section of data at the beginning of a file that contains information about the file type.

8. The [_____] file format for Microsoft Word 2007 is DOCX.

 ▶ CHECK ANSWERS

SECTION D

File Management

FILE MANAGEMENT ENCOMPASSES any procedure that helps you organize your computer-based files so that you can find and use them more efficiently. Depending on your computer's operating system, you can organize and manipulate your files from within an application program or by using a special file management utility the operating system provides. Section D offers an overview of application-based and operating system-based file management.

APPLICATION-BASED FILE MANAGEMENT

How does a software application help me manage files?

Applications, such as word processing software or graphics software, typically provide a way to open files and save them in a specific folder on a designated storage device. An application might also have additional file management capabilities, such as deleting, copying, and renaming files. Take a look at an example of the file management capabilities in a typical Windows application—Microsoft Word.

Suppose you want to write a letter to your local newspaper about the rising tide of graffiti in your neighborhood. You open your word processing software and start typing. As you type, the document is held in RAM. When you are ready to save the document, click the Office button and then select the Save As option. The Save As dialog box opens and allows you to specify a name for the file and its location on one of your computer's storage devices.

Some applications also allow you to add tags for a file. A **file tag** in the context of Windows is a piece of information that describes a file. Tags are particularly handy for files that contain photos because you can describe the location, note camera settings, and name people pictured in the shot. Figure 4-33 illustrates the process of saving a Word document and adding tags.

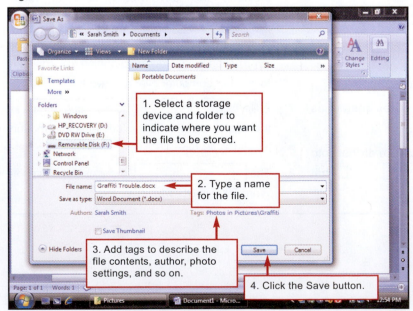

FIGURE 4-33

The Save As dialog box is used to name a file and specify its storage location. Here a file called Graffiti Trouble is being saved on a USB flash drive.

▶ CLICK TO START

What's the difference between the Save option and the Save As option?

Most Windows applications provide a curious set of options on the File menu. In addition to the Save As option, the menu contains a Save option. The difference between the two options is subtle, but useful. The Save As option allows you to select a name and storage device for a file, whereas the Save option simply saves the latest version of a file under its current name and at its current location.

A potentially confusing aspect of these options occurs when you try to use the Save option for a file that doesn't yet have a name. Because you can't save a file without a name, your application displays the Save As dialog box, even though you selected the Save option. The flowchart in Figure 4-34 can help you decide whether to use the Save or Save As command.

What other options are available in the Save As dialog box?

When you use application software, activities such as opening files and saving files require the software to interact with the operating system's file management system. When you create a file, the operating system needs to know its name. When you look for a file, the application software has to check with the operating system to get a list of available files.

Today's application software typically uses utility modules provided by the operating system to display files in the Open and the Save dialog boxes, so they look and function just like the operating system file management utility that you use to rename a file, delete a file, or create a folder. Compare the Save As window in Figure 4-35 to the Windows Explorer windows in Figure 4-36 to see the similarity.

FIGURE 4-34

Should I use the Save or Save As command?

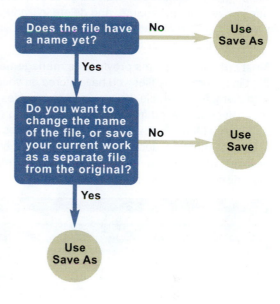

4

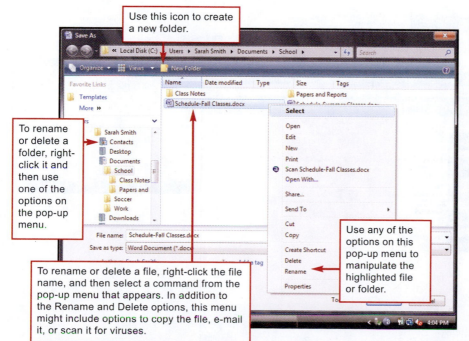

FIGURE 4-35

The Save As dialog box of most Windows applications uses the operating system's file management utility, so you can carry out a wide variety of file and folder tasks such as creating, renaming, and deleting files.

FILE MANAGEMENT UTILITIES

How does the operating system help me manage files?

Although most application software gives you access to commands you can use to save, open, rename, and delete individual files, you might want to work with groups of files or perform other file operations that are inconvenient within the Open or Save dialog boxes.

Most operating systems provide **file management utilities** that give you the big picture of the files you have stored on your disks and help you work with them. For example, Windows Vista provides a file management utility that can be accessed from the Explore option on the Start menu. On computers with Mac OS, the file management utilities are called the Finder and Spotlight. These utilities, shown in Figure 4-36, help you view a list of files, find files, move files from one place to another, make copies of files, delete files, discover file properties, and rename files.

TERMINOLOGY NOTE

Utilities called desktop search tools help you also find and access information stored in e-mails, Web pages, and contact lists in addition to data and program files. Desktop search tools are offered by third-party vendors such as Google and Yahoo! They are also being added to operating system utilities.

FIGURE 4-36

The Windows file management utility can be tailored to show files as lists (top), icons (middle), or tiles (bottom).

CLICK TO START

FILE MANAGEMENT METAPHORS

How can a file management utility help me visualize my computer's file storage? File management utilities often use some sort of storage metaphor to help you visualize and mentally organize the files on your disks and other storage devices. These metaphors are also called **logical storage models** because they are supposed to help you form a mental (logical) picture of the way in which your files are stored.

What storage metaphors are typically used for personal computers? After hearing so much about files and folders, you might have guessed that the filing cabinet is a popular metaphor for computer storage. In this metaphor, each storage device of a computer corresponds to one of the drawers in a filing cabinet. The drawers hold folders and the folders hold files.

Another storage metaphor is based on a hierarchical diagram that is sometimes referred to as a tree structure. In this metaphor, a tree represents a storage device. The trunk of the tree corresponds to the root directory. The branches of the tree represent folders. These branches can split into small branches representing folders within folders. The leaves at the end of a branch represent the files in a particular folder. Figure 4-37 illustrates the tree lying on its side so that you can see the relationship to the metaphor shown in the next figure, Figure 4-38.

The tree structure metaphor offers a useful mental image of the way in which files and folders are organized. It is not, however, particularly practical as a user interface. Imagine the complexity of the tree diagram from Figure 4-37 if it were expanded to depict branches for hundreds of folders and leaves for thousands of files.

For practicality, storage metaphors are translated into more mundane screen displays. Figure 4-38 shows how Microsoft programmers combined the filing cabinet metaphor with the tree structure metaphor in the Windows Explorer file management utility.

FIGURE 4-37

You can visualize the directory of a disk as a tree on its side. The trunk corresponds to the root directory, the branches to folders, and the leaves to files.

FIGURE 4-38

Windows Explorer borrows folders from the filing cabinet metaphor and places them in a hierarchical structure similar to a tree on its side.

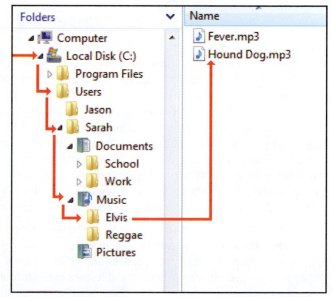

4

WINDOWS EXPLORER

How do I use a file management utility? As an example of a file management utility, take a closer look at **Windows Explorer**, a utility program bundled with the Windows operating system and designed to help you organize and manipulate the files stored on your computer.

The Windows Explorer window is divided into several window panes. The pane on the left side of the window lists each of the storage devices connected to your computer, plus several important system objects, such as My Computer, My Network Places, and the Desktop.

An icon for a storage device or other system object can be expanded by clicking its corresponding ▷ icon. Expanding an icon displays the next level of the storage hierarchy—usually a collection of folders.

A device icon or folder can be opened by clicking directly on the icon rather than on the ▷ icon. Once an icon is opened, its contents appear in the pane on the right side of the Windows Explorer window. Figure 4-39 illustrates how to manipulate the directory display.

FIGURE 4-39

Windows Explorer makes it easy to drill down through the levels of the directory hierarchy to locate a folder or file.

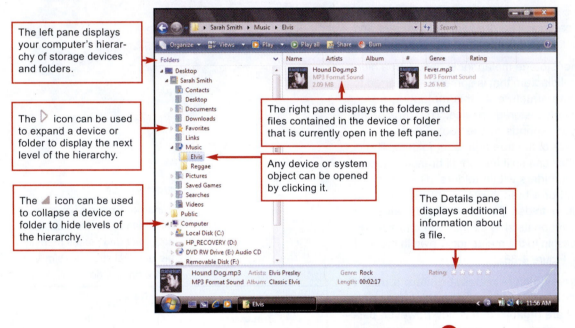

The left pane displays your computer's hierarchy of storage devices and folders.

The ▷ icon can be used to expand a device or folder to display the next level of the hierarchy.

The ◢ icon can be used to collapse a device or folder to hide levels of the hierarchy.

The right pane displays the folders and files contained in the device or folder that is currently open in the left pane.

Any device or system object can be opened by clicking it.

The Details pane displays additional information about a file.

● CLICK TO START

Can I work with more than one file or folder at a time? To work with a group of files or folders, you must first select them. You can accomplish this task in several ways. You can hold down the Ctrl key as you click each item. This method works well if you are selecting files or folders that are not listed consecutively. As an alternative, you can hold down the Shift key while you click the first item and the last item you want to select. By using the Shift key method, you select the two items that you clicked and all the items in between. Windows Explorer displays all the items you selected by highlighting them. After a group of items is highlighted, you can use the same copy, move, or delete procedure that you would use for a single item.

What can I do with the folders and files that are listed in Windows Explorer? In addition to locating files and folders, Windows Explorer provides a set of procedures (shown in Figure 4-40 on the next page) that help you manipulate files and folders in the following ways:

● **Rename.** You might want to change the name of a file or folder to better describe its contents.

● **Copy.** You can copy a file from one device to another—for example, from a floppy disk in drive A to the hard disk in drive C. You can also make a copy of a document so that you can revise the copy and leave the original intact.

● **Move.** You can move a file from one folder to another or from one storage device to another. When you move a file, it is erased from its original location, so make sure you remember the new location of the file. You can also move entire folders and their contents from one storage device to another storage device, or move them to a different folder.

● **Delete.** You can delete a file when you no longer need it. You can also delete a folder. Be careful when you delete a folder because most file management utilities also delete all the files within a folder.

FIGURE 4-40

Windows Explorer helps you delete, copy, move, and rename files.

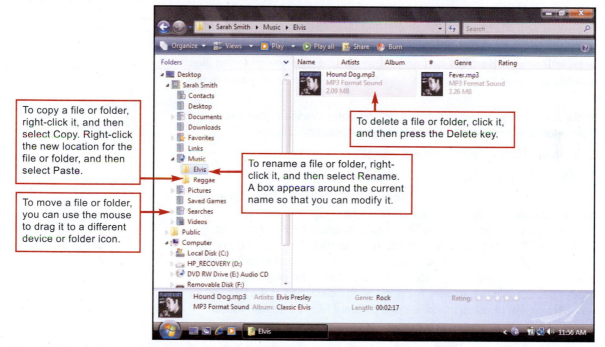

To copy a file or folder, right-click it, and then select Copy. Right-click the new location for the file or folder, and then select Paste.

To move a file or folder, you can use the mouse to drag it to a different device or folder icon.

To delete a file or folder, click it, and then press the Delete key.

To rename a file or folder, right-click it, and then select Rename. A box appears around the current name so that you can modify it.

CLICK TO START

FILE MANAGEMENT TIPS

A file management utility provides tools and procedures to help you keep track of your program and data files, but these tools are most useful when you have a logical plan for organizing your files and when you follow some basic file management guidelines. The following tips pertain to managing files on your own computer. When working with files on lab computers, follow the guidelines from your instructor or lab manager.

● **Use descriptive names.** Give your files and folders descriptive names, and avoid using cryptic abbreviations.

● **Maintain file extensions.** When renaming a file, keep the original file extension so that you can easily open it with the correct application software.

● **Group similar files.** Separate files into folders based on subject matter. For example, store your creative writing assignments in one folder and your MP3 music files in another folder.

● **Organize your folders from the top down.** When devising a hierarchy of folders, consider how you want to access files and back them up. For example, it is easy to specify one folder and its subfolders for a backup. If your important data is scattered in a variety of folders, however, making backups is more time consuming.

- **Consider using default folders.** Windows offers a set of preconfigured default folders, such as *Documents*, *Pictures*, and *Music* for storing data files (Figure 4-41). You might want to use these as your main data folders, and add subfolders as necessary to organize your files.

- **Do not mix data files and program files.** Do not store data files in the folders that hold your software—on Windows systems, most software is stored in subfolders of the *Program Files* folder.

- **Don't store files in the root directory.** Although it is acceptable to create folders in the root directory, it is not a good practice to store programs or data files in the root directory of your computer's hard disk.

- **Access files from the hard disk.** For best performance, copy files from floppy disks or CDs to your computer's hard disk before accessing them.

- **Follow copyright rules.** When copying files, make sure you adhere to copyright and license restrictions.

- **Delete or archive files you no longer need.** Deleting unneeded files and folders helps keep your list of files from growing to an unmanageable size.

- **Be aware of storage locations.** When you save files, make sure the drive letter and folder name specify the correct storage location.

- **Back up!** Back up your folders regularly.

PHYSICAL FILE STORAGE

Is data stored in specific places on a disk? So far, you've seen how an operating system such as Windows can help you visualize computer storage as files and folders. This logical storage model, however, has little to do with what actually happens on your disk. The structure of files and folders you see in Windows Explorer is called a logical model because it is supposed to help you create a mental picture. The **physical storage model** describes what actually happens on the disks and in the circuits. As you will see, the physical model is quite different from the logical model.

Before a computer can store a file on a disk, CD, or DVD, the storage medium must be formatted. The **formatting** process creates the equivalent of electronic storage bins by dividing a disk into **tracks** and then further dividing each track into **sectors**. Tracks and sectors are numbered to provide addresses for each data storage bin. The numbering scheme depends on the storage device and the operating system. On floppy and hard disks, tracks are arranged as concentric circles; on CDs and DVDs, one or more tracks spiral out from the center of the disk (Figure 4-42).

FIGURE 4-41

Windows supplies a series of default folders, including *Documents*, *Pictures*, and *Music*, that many users find convenient for storing their data.

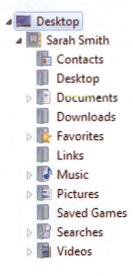

FIGURE 4-42

A process called formatting prepares the surface of a disk to hold data.

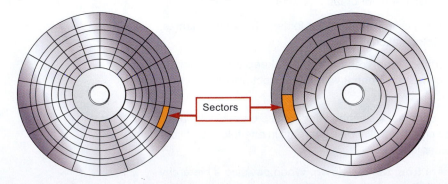

Disks are divided into tracks and wedge-shaped sectors—each side of a floppy disk typically has 80 tracks divided into 18 sectors. Each sector holds 512 bytes of data.

On a typical CD, a single track is about three miles long and is divided into 336,000 sectors. Each sector holds 2,048 bytes of data.

How does a disk get formatted? Today, most floppy and hard disks are preformatted at the factory. CDs and DVDs are formatted by the utilities that you use when you copy data files to them. Before you write data to a CD or DVD, you usually have the option of formatting the disk for mastering or for packet writing.

Disk mastering is the process of creating a CD or DVD by selecting all the files and then copying them in a single session. The process can take some time—especially when burning a full DVD. Mastered CDs and DVDs are compatible with most computers, CD players, and standalone DVD players. Mastering also works well if you want to run off several copies of a CD or DVD.

Packet writing is a recording technology that lets you record in multiple sessions. For example, you can copy a few files to a CD during one session, and then at a later date record additional files to the same CD. In Windows terminology, CDs and DVDs formatted for packet writing are referred to as Live File System discs. Packet writing is faster and more flexible than mastering, but CDs and DVDs created with packet writing might not work on all computers. A process called "closing" helps make the disks more compatible, but once a disk is closed, no more data can be added to it (Figure 4-43).

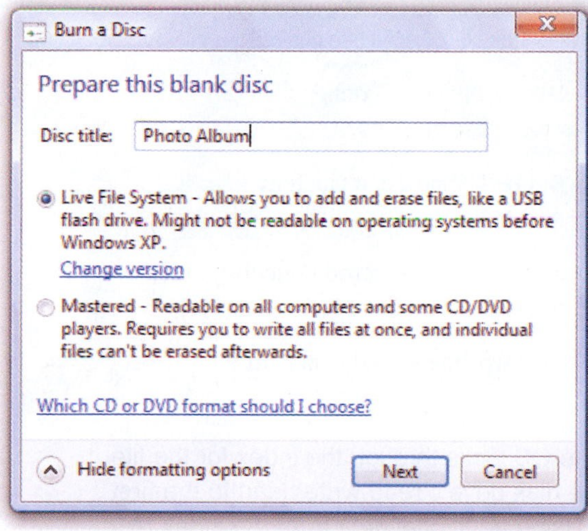

4

FIGURE 4-43

CDs and DVDs can be created using mastering or packet-writing techniques. Mastering creates disks that can be used more reliably on a wide variety of computers and standalone players. Packet writing is more flexible for disks that you plan to use only on your own computer.

How does the operating system keep track of a file's location? The operating system uses a **file system** to keep track of the names and locations of files that reside on a storage medium, such as a hard disk. Different operating systems use different file systems. Most versions of Mac OS use the Macintosh Hierarchical File System (HFS). Ext3fs (extended 3 file system) is the native file system for Linux. Windows NT, 2000, XP, and Vista use a file system called **NTFS** (New Technology File System). Windows 95, 98, and Me use a file system called **FAT32**.

To speed up the process of storing and retrieving data, a disk drive usually works with a group of sectors called a **cluster** or a "block." The number of sectors that form a cluster varies, depending on the capacity of the disk and the way the operating system works with files. A file system's primary task is to maintain a list of clusters and keep track of which are empty and which hold data. This information is stored in a special index file. If your computer uses the FAT32 file system, for example, this index file is called the **File Allocation Table** (FAT). If your computer uses NTFS, it is called the **Master File Table** (MFT).

Each of your disks contains its own index file so that information about its contents is always available when the disk is in use. Unfortunately, storing this crucial file on disk also presents a risk because if the index file is damaged by a hard disk head crash or corrupted by a virus, you'll generally lose access to all the data stored on the disk. Index files become damaged all too frequently, so it is important to back up your data.

When you save a file, your PC's operating system looks at the index file to see which clusters are empty. It selects one of these empty clusters, records the file data there, and then revises the index file to include the new file name and its location.

A file that does not fit into a single cluster spills over into the next contiguous (meaning adjacent) cluster, unless that cluster already contains data. When contiguous clusters are not available, the operating system stores parts of a file in noncontiguous (nonadjacent) clusters. Figure 4-44 helps you visualize how an index file, such as the MFT, keeps track of file names and locations.

Master File Table

File	Cluster	Comment
MFT	1	Reserved for MFT files
DISK USE	2	Part of MFT that contains list of empty sectors
Bio.txt	3, 4	Bio.txt file stored in clusters 3 and 4
Jordan.wks	7, 8, 10	Jordan.wks file stored noncontiguously in clusters 7, 8, and 10
Pick.wps	9	Pick.wps file stored in cluster 9

FIGURE 4-44

Each colored cluster on the disk contains part of a file. Bio.txt is stored in contiguous clusters. Jordan.wks is stored in noncontiguous clusters. A computer locates and displays the Jordan.wks file by looking for its name in the Master File Table.

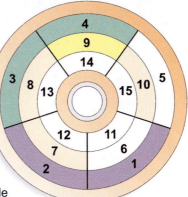

When you want to retrieve a file, the OS looks through the index for the file name and its location. It moves the disk drive's read-write head to the first cluster that contains the file data. Using additional data from the index file, the operating system can move the read-write heads to each of the clusters containing the remaining parts of the file.

What happens when a file is deleted? When you click a file's icon and then select the Delete option, you might have visions of the read-write head somehow scrubbing out the clusters that contain data. That doesn't happen. Instead, the operating system simply changes the status of the file's clusters to "empty" and removes the file name from the index file. The file name no longer appears in a directory listing, but the file's data remains in the clusters until a new file is stored there. You might think that this data is as good as erased, but it is possible to purchase utilities that recover a lot of this supposedly deleted data—law enforcement agents, for example, use these utilities to gather evidence from deleted files on the computer disks of suspected criminals.

To delete data from a disk in such a way that no one can ever read it, you can use special **file shredder software** that overwrites supposedly empty sectors with random 1s and 0s. You might find this software handy if you plan to donate your computer to a charitable organization, and you want to make sure your personal data no longer remains on the hard disk.

Can deleted files be undeleted? The Windows Recycle Bin and similar utilities in other operating systems are designed to protect you from accidentally deleting hard disk files you actually need. Instead of marking a file's clusters as available, the operating system moves the file to the Recycle Bin folder. The deleted file still takes up space on the disk, but does not appear in the usual directory listing.

Files in the Recycle Bin folder can be undeleted so that they again appear in the regular directory. The Recycle Bin can be emptied to permanently delete any files it contains.

How does a disk become fragmented? As a computer writes files on a disk, parts of files tend to become scattered all over the disk. These **fragmented files** are stored in noncontiguous clusters. Drive performance generally declines as the read-write heads move back and forth to locate the clusters containing the parts of a file. To regain peak performance, you can use a **defragmentation utility**, such as Windows Disk Defragmenter, to rearrange the files on a disk so that they are stored in contiguous clusters (Figure 4-45).

FIGURE 4-45

Defragmenting a disk helps your computer operate more efficiently. Consider using a defragmentation utility at least once a month to keep your computer running in top form.

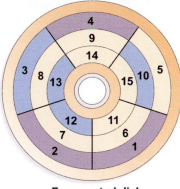

Fragmented disk

On the fragmented disk (left), the purple, orange, and blue files are stored in noncontiguous clusters.

When the disk is defragmented (right), the sectors of data for each file are moved to contiguous clusters.

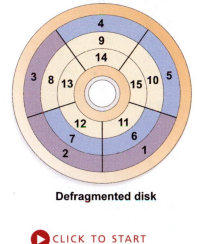

Defragmented disk

▶ CLICK TO START

QuickCheck

SECTION D

1. The [   ] option on an application's File menu allows you to save the latest version of a file under its current name and at its current location.

2. A storage [   ], such as a filing cabinet or tree, helps you visualize and mentally organize your computer files.

3. Windows [   ] is utility software provided by the operating system and designed to help you organize and manipulate files.

4. A hard disk stores data in concentric circles called [   ], which are divided into wedge-shaped [   ].

5. File [   ] software overwrites deleted files with random 1s and 0s.

▶ CHECK ANSWERS

Backup Security

COMPUTER EXPERTS UNIVERSALLY RECOMMEND
that you make backups of your data. It sounds pretty basic, right? Unfortunately, this advice tells you what to do, not how to do it. It fails to address some key questions, such as: Do I need special backup equipment and software? How often should I make a backup? How many of my files should I back up? What should I do with the backups? In this section you'll find the answers to your questions about backing up data that's stored on a personal computer. You'll begin by looking at backup basics, and then review your equipment and software options. Along the way, you should pick up lots of practical tips to keep your data safe.

BACKUP BASICS

Why do I need to make backups? Have you ever mistakenly copied an old version of a document over a new version? Has your computer's hard disk drive gone on the fritz? Did a virus wipe out your files? Has lightning fried your computer system? These kinds of data disasters are not rare; they can happen to everyone. You can't always prevent them, so you need a **backup** that stores the files needed to recover data that's been wiped out by operator error, viruses, or hardware failures.

What's the best backup plan? A good backup plan allows you to restore your computing environment to its pre-disaster state with a minimum of fuss. Unfortunately, no single backup plan fits everyone's computing style or budget. You must devise your own backup plan that's tailored to your particular computing needs.

The list in Figure 4-46 outlines factors you should consider as you formulate your own backup plan.

FIGURE 4-46

Guidelines for Formulating a Backup Plan

- Decide how much of your data you want, need, and can afford to back up.
- Create a realistic schedule for making backups.
- Make sure you have a way to avoid backing up files that contain viruses.
- Find out what kind of boot disks you might need to get your computer up and running after a hard disk failure or boot sector virus attack.
- Make sure you test your restore procedure so that you can successfully retrieve the data you've backed up.
- Find a safe place to keep your backups.
- Decide what kind of storage device you'll use to make backups.
- Select software to handle backup needs.

How often should I back up my data? Your backup schedule depends on how much data you can afford to lose. If you're working on an important project, you might want to back up the project files several times a day. Under normal use, however, most people schedule a once-a-week backup. If you work with a To Do list, use it to remind yourself when it is time to make a backup.

How do I avoid backing up files that contain viruses? Viruses can damage files to the point that your computer can't access any data on its hard disk. It is really frustrating when you restore data from a backup only to discover that the restored files contain the same virus that wiped out your data. If your antivirus software is not set to constantly scan for viruses on your computer system, you should run an up-to-date virus check as the first step in your backup routine.

How do I choose a backup device? The backup device you select depends on the value of your data, your current equipment, and your budget. Most computer owners use what they have—a writable CD, DVD, or USB flash drive. For added convenience and security, some consumers purchase an external hard disk drive (Figure 4-47). Businesses sometimes use tape drives for backups. If you have several backup options available, use the table in Figure 4-48 to evaluate the strengths and weaknesses of each one.

FIGURE 4-47

An external hard disk drive typically connects to your computer's USB port. Handy for copying data files or a full system backup, these drives can easily be disconnected when not in use and stored in a safe place.

FIGURE 4-48

Storage Capacities and Costs of Backup Media

	Device Cost	Media Cost	Capacity	Comments
Floppy disk	$30 (average)	25¢	1.44 MB	Low capacity is not practical for today's large files
Removable hard disk	$130 (average)	$50	35 GB (average)	Fast, limited capacity, but disks can be removed and locked in a secure location
External hard disk	$100 (average)	N/A	250 GB (average)	Fast and convenient, but if it is damaged, all the backups it holds are lost
Network server	Assume a business or school supplies free access	N/A	Depends on space allocated to user	Fast and convenient, but make sure that the server is regularly backed up
CD-R	$40 (average)	15¢	680 MB	Limited capacity, can't be reused, long shelf life
CD-RW	$50 (average)	25¢	680 MB	Limited capacity, reusable, very slow
Writable DVD	$100 (average)	25¢	4.7 GB	Moderate capacity, reasonable media cost, higher capacity coming soon
Tape	$2,000 (average)	$80	200 GB (average)	Expensive for capacity equal to today's hard drives
USB Flash drive	$15–$500	N/A	32 MB–8 GB	Convenient and durable, but high-capacity models are expensive
Web site	N/A	$50 per year	Depends on provider	Transfer rate depends on your Internet connection; security and privacy of your data might be a concern

Where should I keep my backups? If your backups are on an external hard disk or removable media, keep your backups in a safe place. Don't keep them at your computer desk because a fire or flood that damages your computer could also wipe out your backups. In addition, a thief who steals your computer might also scoop up nearby equipment and media. Storing your backups at a different location is the best idea. If offsite storage isn't practical, at least move them to a room apart from your computer.

How can I be sure that my backup works? If your computer's hard disk crashes, you do not want to discover that your backups are blank! To prevent such a disastrous situation, it is important to enable the read after write or compare option backup software provides. These options force the software to check the data in each sector as it is written to make sure it is copied without error. You should also test your backup by trying to restore one file. Restore the test file to a different drive or folder to avoid overwriting the original file.

DATA FILE BACKUP

What's the easiest way to back up my important data? The most important files on your computer contain the documents, images, and other data that you've created. These files are unique and might be difficult to reproduce. An easy way to back up your important data is simply by copying selected files to a writable CD or DVD. Your operating system or the utility software supplied with your CD or DVD writer includes a formatting routine that prepares a disk to hold data and allows you to select the files you want to copy, or "burn," as a backup (Figure 4-49).

INFOWEBLINKS

Interested in using a Web site for your backup? You can evaluate several of these sites by following the links at the **Web-based Backup InfoWeb**.

W CLICK TO CONNECT
www.course.com/np/concepts11/ch04

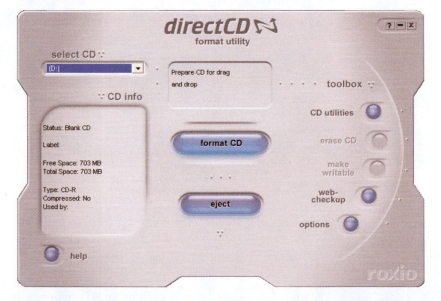

FIGURE 4-49

Use the software supplied with your CD or DVD drive to format disks and copy files.

How do I find the files I need to backup? If your strategy is to back up your important data files, the procedure can be simplified if you've stored all these files in one folder and its subfolders. For example, Windows users might store their data files in the preconfigured folders for their user accounts. Folders such as Documents, Music, and Pictures are all stored as subfolders of your user folder. With your data files organized under the umbrella of a single folder, you are less likely to omit an important file when you make backups.

INFOWEBLINKS

For more detailed information on backup techniques, such as backing up the Registry, take a look at the **Backup Techniques InfoWeb**.

W CLICK TO CONNECT
www.course.com/np/concepts11/ch04

Some applications, such as financial software, create files and update them without your direct intervention. If you have the option during setup, make sure these files are stored under your personal folder. Otherwise, you must discover the location of the files and make sure they are backed up with the rest of your data.

In addition to data files you create, a few other types of data files might be important to you. Consider making backups of the files listed in Figure 4-50.

- **Internet connection information.** Your ISP's phone number and IP address, your user ID, and your password are often stored in an encrypted file somewhere in the *Windows\System* folder. Your ISP can usually help you find this file.

- **E-mail folders.** If you're using POP e-mail software, your e-mail folder contains all the e-mail messages you've sent and received, but not deleted. Check the Help menu on your e-mail program to discover the location of these files.

- **E-mail address book.** Your e-mail address book might be stored separately from your e-mail messages. To find the file on a Windows computer, use the Search or Find option on the Start menu to search for "Address Book."

- **Favorite URLs.** If you're attached to the URLs you've collected in your Favorites or Bookmarks list, you might want to back up the file that contains this list. To find the file, search your hard disk for "Favorites" or "Bookmarks."

- **Downloads.** If you paid to download software, you might want to back it up so that you don't have to pay for it again. Downloaded software usually arrives in the form of a compressed .exe file that expands into several separate files as you install it. For backup purposes, the compressed .exe file should be all you need.

- **Validation codes and other configuration information.** If you keep a running list of validation or activation codes that correspond to your software, then it is important to copy this information in case your hard disk crashes and you have to reinstall your software. Additional configuration or procedural notes can also come in handy when it comes time to reload a hard disk after a crash.

FIGURE 4-50

Back up these files in addition to your documents, graphics, and music files.

4

How do I restore files from my data file backups? Restoring from a data file backup is easy. You simply copy files from your backup to your hard disk. If, for example, you inadvertently delete an important file and discover that you have done so only after you've cleaned out your computer's Recycle Bin, then you can retrieve the file from your backup.

If your hard drive crashes and you have to install a new one, the process of retrieving your files is a bit more complex. First, you have to reload the operating system on your hard disk. That task is explained a little later in this section. Then you have to reinstall all of your software and device drivers. As the final step, you can copy your data files back to the hard disk. To avoid a lengthy manual rebuild of your hard disk, you might consider system backups and recovery disks.

SYSTEM BACKUP

What does backup software do? To make a backup, you can use **backup software**—a set of utility programs designed to back up and restore files. Backup software usually includes options that make it easy to schedule periodic backups, define a set of files that you want to regularly back up, and automate the restoration process.

Backup software differs from most copy routines because it typically compresses all the files for a backup and places them in one large file. Under the direction of backup software, this file can spread across multiple disks if necessary. The file is indexed so that individual files can be located, uncompressed, and restored.

Where can I get backup software? Backup software is supplied with most tape drives and other backup devices. Some versions of Windows include Microsoft Backup software (Figure 4-51), which you can usually find by clicking the Start button, and then selecting Accessories and System Tools. You can also purchase and download backup software from companies that specialize in data protection software.

INFOWEBLINKS

For current links to backup software information, reviews, and manufacturers, visit the **Backup Software InfoWeb**.

W CLICK TO CONNECT
www.course.com/np/concepts11/ch04

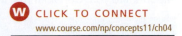

FIGURE 4-51

Microsoft Windows includes backup software with Windows XP (left) and Windows Vista (right).

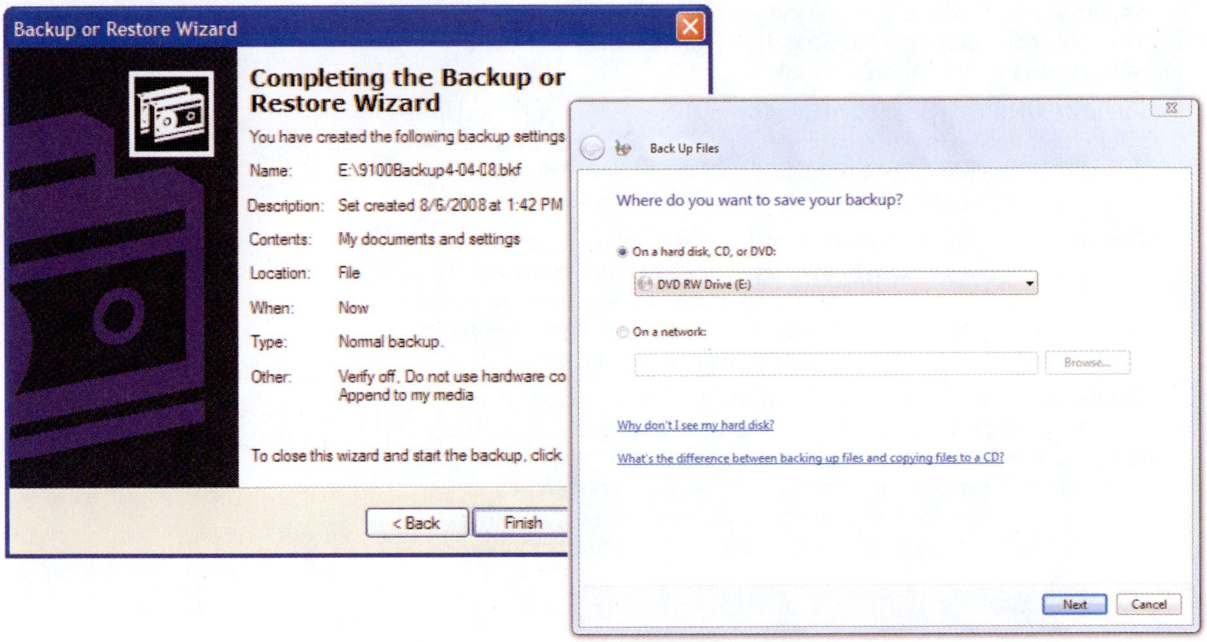

CLICK TO START

Whatever backup software you use, remember that it needs to be accessible when it comes time to restore your data. If the only copy of your backup software exists on your backup media, you will be in a Catch-22 situation. You won't be able to access your backup software until you restore the files from your backup, but you won't be able to restore your files until your backup software is running! Make sure you keep the original distribution CD for your backup software or a disk-based copy of any backup software you downloaded from the Web.

How do I use backup software? Backup software provides tools for scheduling backup dates and selecting the files you want to back up. The scheduling feature allows you to automate the backup process and reduces the chance that you'll forget to make regular backups. Backup software can also save time and storage space by offering options for full, differential, or incremental backups.

What is a full backup? A **full backup** makes a fresh copy of every file in the folders you've specified for the backup. In contrast to a full-system backup, a full backup does not necessarily contain every file on your computer. A full backup might contain only your data files, for example, if those are the files you want to regularly back up.

What is a differential backup? A **differential backup** makes a backup of only those files that were added or changed since your last full backup session. After making a full backup of your important files, you can make differential backups at regular intervals. If you need to restore all your files after a hard disk crash, first restore the files from your full backup, and then restore the files from your latest differential backup.

What is an incremental backup? An **incremental backup** makes a backup of the files that were added or changed since the last backup—not necessarily the files that changed from the last full backup, but the files that changed since any full or incremental backup. After making a full backup of your important files, you can make your first incremental backup containing the files that changed since the full backup. When you make your second incremental backup, it will contain only the files that changed since the first incremental backup. To restore files from an incremental backup, files from a full backup are restored first, followed by files from each incremental backup, starting with the oldest and ending with the most recent. Figure 4-52 describes the difference between differential and incremental backups.

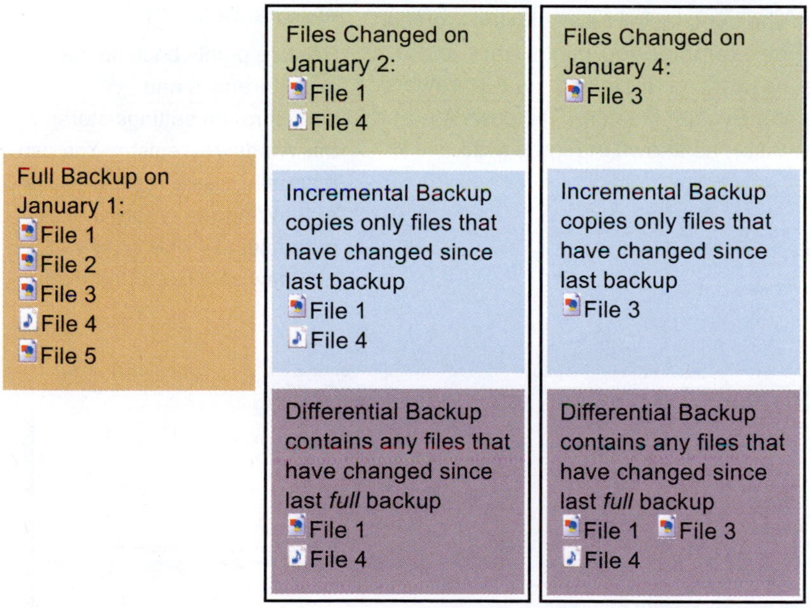

FIGURE 4-52

Suppose you have five files that you originally back up on January 1. You change two of these files on January 2. Incremental and differential backups both back up the changed files. If one additional file is changed on January 4, the incremental backup needs only back up that one file—it is the only one that has changed since the backup on January 2. A differential backup, however, will back up *three* files—those that changed since the full backup.

Full Backup on January 1:
- File 1
- File 2
- File 3
- File 4
- File 5

Files Changed on January 2:
- File 1
- File 4

Incremental Backup copies only files that have changed since last backup
- File 1
- File 4

Differential Backup contains any files that have changed since last *full* backup
- File 1
- File 4

Files Changed on January 4:
- File 3

Incremental Backup copies only files that have changed since last backup
- File 3

Differential Backup contains any files that have changed since last *full* backup
- File 1 File 3
- File 4

How many backups do I need? Most experts recommend that you keep more than one set of backups. If you use recordable CDs or DVDs for your backups, then you simply burn a new disk each time you back up. If you are using rewritable media, such as removable hard disks, tapes, or CD-RWs, then you can reuse your backups—typically by rotating three backup disks or tapes.

To maintain a rotating backup, use one disk or tape for the first backup, and then use a different disk or tape for the next backup. Use another disk or tape for the third backup. For the fourth backup, you can overwrite the data on the first backup; for the fifth backup, overwrite the data on the second backup, and so on. So that you know which backup is the most recent, write the date of the backup on the disk or tape label.

What about backing up the Windows Registry? Windows users often hear a variety of rumors about backing up the Windows Registry. The Registry, as it is usually called, is an important group of files the Windows operating system uses to store configuration information about all the devices and software installed on a computer system. If the Registry becomes damaged, your computer might not be able to boot up, launch programs, or communicate with peripheral devices. It is a good idea to have an extra copy of the Registry in case the original file is damaged.

As simple as it sounds, backing up the Registry can present a bit of a problem because the Registry is always open while your computer is on. Some software that you might use for backups cannot copy open files. If you use such software, it might never back up the Registry.

Windows users whose backup plans encompass all files on the hard disk must make sure their backup software provides an option for including the Windows Registry. Even if a full-system backup is not planned, many experts recommend that you at least copy the Registry to a separate folder on the hard disk or to a CD. If you do so, you should update this copy whenever you install new software or hardware.

What is a restore point? A **restore point** is a snapshot of your computer settings. Restore points are essentially backups of the Windows Registry. If a hard disk problem causes system instability, you might be able to roll back to a restore point when your computer was operational.

Restore points are set automatically when you install new software. You can manually set restore points, too. For example, you might want to set a restore point before setting up a network or installing new hardware. Restore points can be set by accessing System Restore (Windows Me and XP) or System Protection (Windows Vista) as shown in Figure 4-53.

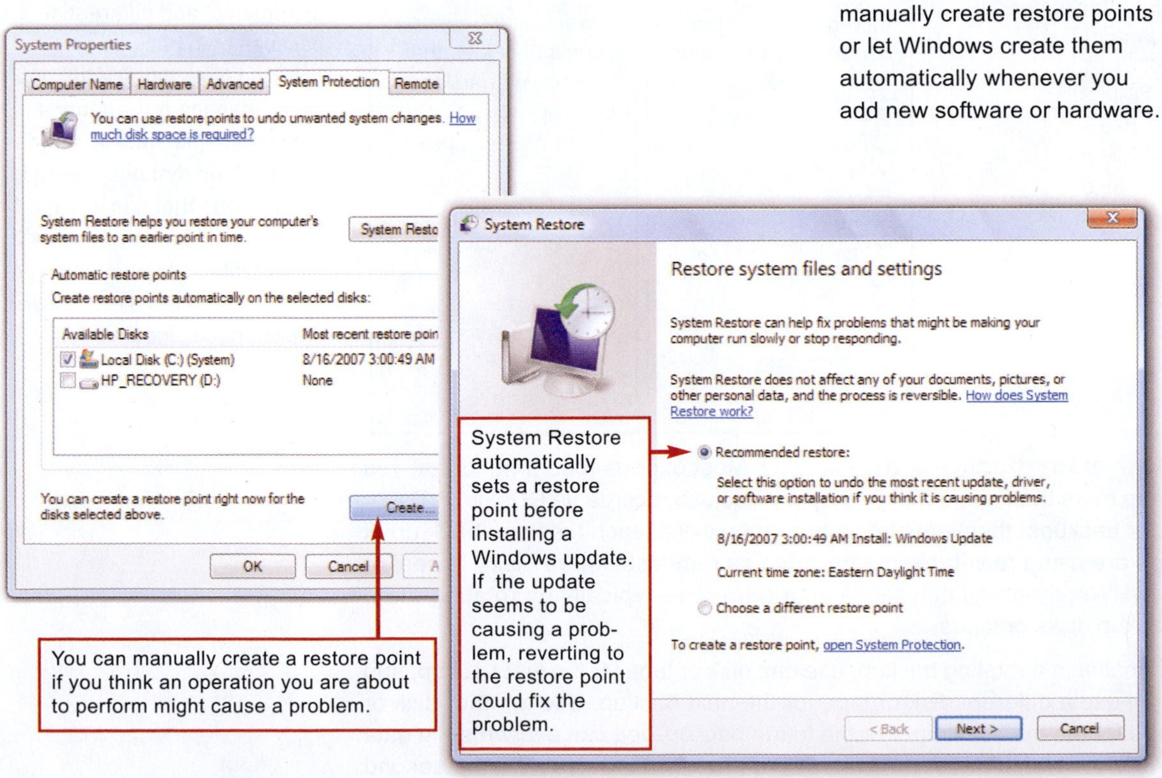

FIGURE 4-53

Restore points back up personal preferences and configuration settings stored in the Windows Registry. You can manually create restore points or let Windows create them automatically whenever you add new software or hardware.

You can manually create a restore point if you think an operation you are about to perform might cause a problem.

System Restore automatically sets a restore point before installing a Windows update. If the update seems to be causing a problem, reverting to the restore point could fix the problem.

CLICK TO START

BOOT AND RECOVERY DISKS

What is a boot disk? If your computer's hard disk is out of commission, you might wonder how it can access the operating system files needed to carry out the boot process. If your hard disk fails or a virus wipes out the boot sector files on your hard disk, you won't be able to use your normal boot procedure. For such emergencies, it is essential to have on hand a removable storage medium that you can use to boot your computer, locate the problem, and then fix it.

A **boot disk** is a removable storage medium containing the operating system files needed to boot your computer without accessing the hard disk. CDs, DVDs, and even USB flash drives can be used as boot disks. With current versions of Windows, the Windows installation CD is configured as a boot disk and can be used if your computer does not boot normally. When you insert the installation CD, you'll have the option of repairing Windows or reinstalling it. Try the repair option first (Figure 4-54).

FIGURE 4-54

The Windows installation CD allows you to repair or reinstall the Windows operating system.

4

What is a recovery disk? A **recovery disk** (sometimes referred to as a recovery CD) is a bootable CD, DVD, or other media that contains a complete copy of your computer's hard disk as it existed when shipped from the manufacturer. It contains the operating system, device drivers, utilities, and even software that was bundled with your computer. You can use a recovery disk to return your computer to its factory default state. However, a recovery disk will not restore your data files, any software that you installed, or any configuration settings you've made since you unwrapped your computer from its shipping box.

Where can I get a recovery disk? Recovery disks are sometimes included with new computers as a CD or DVD. If you don't receive one, you should check the manufacturer's Web site for a downloadable version. The operating system might also supply a method for creating recovery disks.

Several manufacturers no longer provide recovery disks. Instead, they store an exact image of the hard disk with all factory-installed device drivers and software in a hidden partition (sometimes called a recovery partition) on the hard drive.

Recovery partitions are convenient for restoring a corrupted device driver or software module because you can simply copy or reinstall the file from the recovery partition to the main partition. The files in the recovery partition are not accessible, however, if your computer's hard disk fails. Therefore, don't be misled into thinking that a recovery partition can help you restore your computer after a hard disk failure.

If your hard drive fails, you'll need a copy of the recovery partition on a series of CDs or DVDs. Consumers are supplied with a special utility to copy the entire image or selected files and drivers from the recovery partition (Figure 4-55).

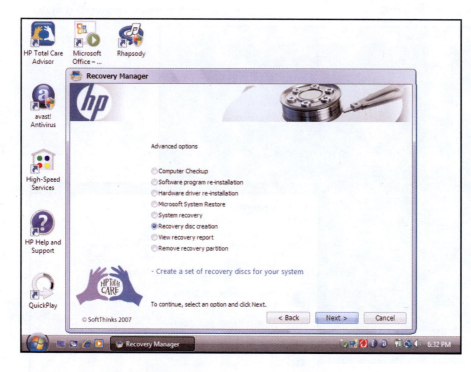

FIGURE 4-55

Hewlett-Packard's Recovery Manager helps you create recovery disks from the files stored in a recovery partition. The same utility also helps you access the recovery files to reinstall programs, copy individual drivers, or return the computer to its factory settings.

Is there any way to make a recovery disk that contains my computer's settings? You can create a **custom recovery CD** that contains your computer's current settings and device drivers. To do so, you must create a bootable image of the essential files using disk imaging software, such as Norton Ghost. Your custom recovery disk can only restore your system to its state on the date you made the image. It's important to create a new recovery disk every time you make significant changes to your hardware, software, or user settings.

Norton Ghost is a product of Symantec, which also provides a more specialized recovery disk called the Symantec Recovery Disk. In case of an emergency, you can use this disk to boot Windows, reinstall your device drivers, and establish a recovery environment where you can run tasks such as scanning your computer for viruses, restoring files and folders from a backup image, and checking disks for errors. The Symantec Recovery Disk is included with Norton Ghost and Norton Save and Restore.

Some PC manufacturers have pre-installed Norton Ghost and the recovery environment on their computers. These machines might not require the Symantec Recovery Disk. Keyboard keys are set up to start the recovery environment. Check your manufacturer's specific instructions for recovery from system failure.

The contents and capabilities of recovery disks vary. Some are designed to restore your computer to its like-new state and wipe out all your data. Others attempt to restore user settings, programs, and data. Before you depend on a recovery disk, make sure you know what it contains and how to use it in case of a system failure.

Any other backup options? Today's trend toward the use of virtual machines offers another option for backups. Reinstalling an operating system on a blank hard disk can be a bit tricky but you can avoid that problem if you run your operating system as a virtual machine.

For example, if you run Windows as a virtual machine on a Mac, you can simply back up the entire Windows machine as one folder or file. If a virus or corrupted file begins to disrupt the operation of Windows, instead of reformatting your hard disk and reinstalling Windows, you can simply copy the entire Windows machine from your backup.

So what's the bottom line? To keep your Windows data securely backed up, you can take the following steps:

- File backups. Make backups of your data files. Keep these files current so that you can restore them to your computer when necessary.

- Restore points. Make sure your computer is set to automatically create restore points. If your computer begins to behave erratically, your first activity would be to revert back to a previous restore point.

- Recovery disks. Make sure you have a set of recovery disks either supplied by your computer manufacturer or that you created from a recovery partition. If devices malfunction, try restoring drivers from these disks. If your computer's hard disk fails, you can restore the computer to its factory settings.

- System backup. If you can afford an external hard disk drive, periodically back up your entire system on it. Don't leave the drive connected to your computer, but store it in a safe place to prevent it from being damaged or stolen.

QuickCheck

1. A restore point is essentially a copy of the Windows [_____] and the settings for your computer at a particular point in time.

2. The backup process is simplified if you store all your important data files in a single [_____] or its subfolders.

3. One of the best devices for home backup is a(n) [_____] hard disk drive.

4. A(n) [_____] backup copies only those files that have changed since your last backup session.

5. A(n) [_____] CD helps restore a computer system by loading hardware drivers and user settings as well as the operating system.

▶ CHECK ANSWERS

Cyberterrorists or Pranksters?

IT DOESN'T TAKE any special digital expertise to mastermind some computer crimes. Setting fire to a computer doesn't require the same finesse as writing a stealthy virus, but both can have the same disastrous effect on data. Old-fashioned crimes, such as arson, that take a high-tech twist because they involve a computer can be prosecuted under traditional laws.

Traditional laws do not, however, cover the range of possibilities for computer crimes. Suppose a person unlawfully enters a computer facility and steals back-up tapes. That person might be prosecuted for breaking and entering. But would common breaking and entering laws apply to a person who uses an off-site terminal to enter a computer system without authorization? And what if a person copies a data file without authorization? Has that file really been stolen if the original remains on the computer?

Many countries have computer crime laws that specifically define computer data and software as personal property. These laws also define as crimes the unauthorized access, use, modification, or disabling of a computer system or data. But laws don't necessarily stop criminals. If they did, we wouldn't have to deal with malicious code and intrusions.

Computer Crime Gambits

Data diddling: Unauthorized alterations to data stored on a computer system, such as a student changing grades stored in a school's computer.

Identity theft: Unauthorized copying of personal information, such as credit card numbers, passwords, Social Security numbers, and bank account PINs.

Salami shaving: Redirecting small, unnoticeable amounts of money from large amounts.

Denial of Service: An attempt to disrupt the operations of a network or computer system, usually by flooding it with data traffic.

Information theft: Unauthorized access to a computer system, such as military or government computers, to gain restricted information.

Virus distribution: Launching viruses, worms, and Trojan horses.

Vandalism: Intentional defacement of Web sites.

Computer crimes—costly to organizations and individuals—include a variety of gambits, such as virus distribution, data diddling, identity theft, and salami shaving.

One of the first computer crime cases involved a worm unleashed on the ARPANET in 1988 that quickly spread through government and university computer systems. The worm's author, Robert Morris, was convicted and sentenced to three years' probation, 400 hours of community service, and a $10,000 fine. This relatively lenient sentence was imposed because Morris claimed he had not intended to cripple the entire network.

A 1995 high-profile case involved a computer hacker named Kevin Mitnick, who was accused of breaking into dozens of corporate, university, government, and personal computers. Although vilified in the media, Mitnick had the support of many hackers and other people who believed that the prosecution grossly exaggerated the extent of his crimes. Nonetheless, Mitnick was sentenced to 46 months in prison and ordered to pay restitution in the amount of $4,125 during his three-year period of supervised release. The prosecution was horrified by such a paltry sum—an amount that was much less than its request for $1.5 million in restitution.

Forbes reporter Adam L. Penenberg took issue with the 46-month sentence imposed by Judge Marianne Pfaelzer and wrote, "This in a country where the average prison term for manslaughter is three years. Mitnick's crimes were curiously innocuous. He broke into corporate computers, but no evidence indicates that he destroyed data. Or sold anything he copied. Yes, he pilfered software—but in doing so left it behind. This world of bits is a strange one, in which you can take something and still leave it for its rightful owner. The theft laws designed for payroll sacks and motor vehicles just don't apply to a hacker."

In 2005 a German teenager confessed to creating the Sasser computer worm that was blamed for shutting down British Airways and Delta Airlines flight check-ins, hospitals and government offices in Hong Kong, part of Australia's rail network, Finnish banks, British Coast Guard stations, and millions of other computers worldwide. The teen was given a suspended sentence of 21 months and was required to perform 30 hours of community service. Microsoft paid a $250,000 reward to the two people who tipped off German police to the virus author's identity. The teen now holds a job at a computer company that creates antivirus software.

Officials also made two arrests in connection with the Blaster worm. A 24-year-old Romanian citizen and an American teenager apparently downloaded copies of the worm source code, altered it slightly, and sent their versions back out again. The Romanian was allegedly angered by his treatment by one of his professors. The American teenager was just trying to see what he could get away with.

Under Romanian law, distributing a virus can mean a 15-year prison sentence. The U.S. Patriot Act and the Cyber-Security Enhancement Act carry even stiffer penalties—anywhere from 10 years to life in prison.

A CNET reporter questions the harshness of such penalties: "What bothers me most is that here in the United States, rapists serve, on average, 10 years in prison. Yet if, instead of assaulting another human being, that same person had released a virus on the Net, the criminal would get the same or an even harsher sentence."

Law makers hope that stiff penalties will deter cyber criminals. U.S. Attorney John McKay is quoted as saying, "Let there be no mistake about it, cyber-hacking is a crime. It harms persons, it harms individuals, it harms businesses. We will investigate, track down, and prosecute cyber-hackers."

These cases illustrate our culture's ambivalent attitude toward computer hackers. On the one hand, they are viewed as evil cyberterrorists who are set on destroying the glue that binds together the Information Age. From this perspective, hackers are criminals who must be hunted down, forced to make restitution for damages, and prevented from creating further havoc.

From another perspective, hackers are viewed more as Casper the Friendly Ghost in our complex cyber-machines—as moderately bothersome entities whose pranks are tolerated by the computer community, along with software bugs and hardware glitches. Seen from this perspective, a hacker's pranks are part of the normal course of study that leads to the highest echelons of computer expertise. "Everyone has done it," claims one hacking devotee, "even Bill Gates (founder of Microsoft) and Steve Jobs (founder of Apple Computer)."

Which perspective is right? Are hackers dangerous cyberterrorists or harmless pranksters? Before you make up your mind about computer hacking and cracking, you might want to further investigate several landmark cases by following links at the Computer Crime InfoWeb.

INFOWEBLINKS

Who's in the cybercrime news? How are cybercriminals caught? **The Computer Crime InfoWeb** provides answers to these questions and more.

W **CLICK TO CONNECT**
www.course.com/np/concepts11/ch04

What Do You Think?

1. Should a computer virus distribution sentence carry the same penalty as manslaughter?

○ Yes ○ No ○ Not sure

2. Should it be a crime to steal a copy of computer data while leaving the original data in place and unaltered?

○ Yes ○ No ○ Not sure

3. Should hackers be sent to jail if they cannot pay restitution to companies and individuals who lost money as the result of a prank?

○ Yes ○ No ○ Not sure

4. Do you think that a hacker would make a good consultant on computer security?

○ Yes ○ No ○ Not sure

▶ SAVE RESPONSES

COMPUTERS IN CONTEXT

Law Enforcement

SIRENS WAIL. Blue lights strobe the night. A speeding car slows and pulls off to the side of the road. It looks like a routine traffic stop, but the patrol car is outfitted with a mobile data computer. The police officers on this high-tech force have already checked the speeding car's license plate number and description against a database of stolen cars and cars allegedly used in kidnapping and other crimes.

Mounted in the dashboard of marked and unmarked police cars, a mobile data computer resembles a notebook computer with its flat-panel screen and compact keyboard. Unlike a consumer-grade notebook, however, the computers in police cruisers use hardened technology designed to withstand extreme conditions, such as high temperatures in parked vehicles. The dashboard-mounted computer communicates with an office-based server using a wireless link, such as short-range radio, CDPD (cellular digital packet data) technology, or Wi-Fi. With this wireless link, police officers can access data from local, state, and national databases.

One national database, the National Crime Information Center (NCIC), is maintained by the FBI and can be accessed by authorized personnel in local, state, and federal law enforcement agencies. The system can process more than 2.4 million queries per day related to stolen vehicles, wanted criminals, missing persons, violent gang members, stolen guns, and members of terrorist organizations. The officers who pulled over the speeding car received information from the NCIC that the car was stolen, so they arrested the car's occupant and took him to the police station for booking.

At the police station, digital cameras flash and the suspect's mug shot is automatically entered into an automated warrants and booking system. The system stores the suspect's complete biographical and arrest information, such as name, aliases, addresses, Social Security number, charges, and arrest date. The system also checks for outstanding warrants against the suspect, such as warrants for other thefts. Booking agents can enter those charges into the system, assign the new inmate to a cell, log his personal items, and print a photo ID or wrist band.

Automated warrants and booking systems have been proved to increase police productivity. New York City's system handles more than 300,000 bookings per year, with gains in productivity that have put nearly 300 officers back into action investigating crimes and patrolling neighborhoods.

As part of the booking process, the suspect is fingerprinted. A standard fingerprint card, sometimes called a ten-print card, contains inked prints of the fingers on each hand, plus name, date of birth, and other arrest information. Now, however, instead of using ink, a biometric scanning device can electronically capture fingerprints. Text information is entered using a keyboard and stored with digital fingerprint images.

The fingerprint information can be transmitted in digital format from local law enforcement agencies to the FBI's Automated Fingerprint Identification System (AFIS). This biometric identification methodology uses digital imaging technology to analyze fingerprint data. Using sophisticated algorithms, AFIS can classify arriving prints for storage or search the collection of 600 million fingerprint cards for matching prints.

Conventional crimes, such as car theft, are often solved by using standard investigative techniques with information from computer databases. To solve cybercrimes, however, often the special skills of computer forensic investigators are required.

Ready for left hand fingers...

Left Hand

Computer forensics is the scientific examination and analysis of data located on computer storage media, conducted to offer evidence of computer crimes in court. Computer crimes can be separated into two categories. The first includes crimes that use computers, such as transmitting trade secrets to competitors, reproducing copyrighted material, and distributing child pornography. The second includes crimes targeted at computers, such as Denial of Service attacks on servers, Web site vandalism, data theft, and destructive viruses. Computer forensics can be applied to both categories.

Whether investigators suspect that a computer is the origin of a cyber attack or contains evidence, the first step in the forensic process is to use disk imaging software to make an exact replica of the information stored on the hard disk. The disk image is collected on a write-once medium that cannot be altered with planted evidence, and the forensic scientist begins analyzing the disk image data with simple search software that looks through files for keywords related to the crime. In the case of the Gap-Toothed Bandit who was convicted for robbing nine banks, analysis of the disk image revealed word processing files containing notes he handed to tellers demanding money.

Criminals typically attempt to delete files with incriminating evidence, but a good forensic scientist can retrieve data from deleted files with undelete software or data recovery software. Temporary Internet or cache files can also yield evidence, pointing law enforcement officers to Web sites the suspect visited that might be fronts for illegal activity.

When a computer is a target of a cyber attack, forensic investigators use three techniques to track the source. The first option is to make an immediate image of the server's hard disk and look through its log files for evidence of activity coming from unauthorized IP addresses. A second technique is to monitor the intruder by watching login attempts, changes to log files, and file access requests. Sophisticated intruders might be able to detect such monitoring, however, and cover their tracks. A third technique is to create a honeypot—an irresistible computer system or Web site containing fake information that allows investigators to monitor hackers until identification is possible.

Despite the many techniques and tools available to forensic investigators, they have three main constraints. First, they must adhere to privacy regulations and obtain warrants to set up wiretaps or gather information from ISPs about their customers. Second, they must scrupulously document their procedures so that the evidence they produce cannot be discredited in court as planted or fabricated. Third, forensic investigators must examine a wide range of alternatives pertaining to the crime, such as the chance that an IP or e-mail address used to commit a cybercrime doesn't belong to an innocent bystander being spoofed by the real hacker.

Privacy, documentation, and evidentiary constraints cost forensic investigators time, and failure to adhere to strict standards can sometimes allow criminals to avoid conviction and penalties. But even within these constraints, careful forensic investigation is an important aspect of catching and convicting high-tech criminals.

INFOWEBLINKS

For more information about police and FBI technology, connect to the **Computers in Law Enforcement InfoWeb**.

Ⓦ CLICK TO CONNECT
www.course.com/np/concepts11/ch04

4

New Perspectives Labs

On the BookOnCD

To access the New Perspectives labs for Chapter 4, start the BookOnCD, BookOnFlashDrive, or other NP11 BookOn product and then click the icon next to the lab title below.

 WORKING WITH WINDOWS EXPLORER

IN THIS LAB YOU'LL LEARN:

- How to access Windows Explorer
- How to expand and collapse the directory structure
- How to rename or delete a file or folder
- The basic principles for creating an efficient directory structure for your files
- How to create a folder
- How to select a single file or a group of files
- How to move files from one folder to another

LAB ASSIGNMENTS

1. Start the interactive part of the lab. Make sure you've enabled Tracking if you want to save your QuickCheck results. Perform each lab step, and answer all the lab QuickCheck questions.

2. Use Windows Explorer to look at the directory of the disk or USB flash drive that currently contains most of your files. Draw a diagram showing the hierarchy of folders. Write a paragraph explaining how you could improve this hierarchy, and draw a diagram to illustrate your plan.

3. On a blank floppy disk or USB Flash drive, create three folders: Music, Web Graphics, and Articles. Within the Music folder, create four additional folders: Jazz, Reggae, Rock, and Classical. Within the Classical folder, create two more folders: Classical MIDI and Classical MP3. If you have Internet access, go on to #4.

4. Use your browser software to connect to the Internet, and then go to a Web site, such as *www.zdnet.com* or *www.cnet.com*. Look for a small graphic (remember, the capacity of a floppy disk is only 1.44 MB!) and download it to your Web Graphics folder. Next, use a search engine to search for "classical MIDI music." Download one of the compositions to the Music\Classical\Classical MIDI folder. Open Windows Explorer and expand all the directories for drive A. Open the Music\Classical\Classical MIDI folder and make sure your music download appears. Capture a screenshot. Follow your instructor's directions to submit this screenshot as a printout or an e-mail attachment.

BACKING UP YOUR COMPUTER

IN THIS LAB YOU'LL LEARN:

- How to start the Windows Backup and Restore Center utility
- How to create a backup job
- Which files to select for a backup job
- The implications of compressing your backup data
- How to restore data from an entire backup job
- How to restore a single file from a backup

LAB ASSIGNMENTS

1. Start the interactive part of the lab. Make sure you've enabled Tracking if you want to save your QuickCheck results. Perform each lab step as directed, and answer all the lab QuickCheck questions. When you exit the lab, your answers are automatically graded and your results are displayed.

2. Describe where most of your data files are stored, and estimate how many megabytes of data (not programs) you have in all these files. Next, take a close look at these files and estimate how much data (in megabytes) you cannot afford to lose. Finally, explain what you think would be the best hardware device for backing up this amount of data.

3. List three different types of backup media. Describe strengths and weaknesses for each. Consider the actual capacity of the media itself, the amount of backup space that it can hold, and its reliability and durability.

4. Assume that you will use Microsoft Backup and Restore Center to make a backup of your data files. Describe the backup job you would create—specify the types of files you must include. It is not necessary to list individual files.

Key Terms

Make sure you understand all the boldfaced key terms presented in this chapter. If you're using the NP11 BookOnCD, BookOnFlashDrive, or other NP11 BookOn product, you can use this list of terms as an interactive study activity. First, try to define a term in your own words, and then click the term to compare your definition with the definition presented in the chapter.

4

Interactive Summary

To review important concepts from this chapter, fill in the blanks to best complete each sentence. When using the NP11 BookOnCD or other BookOn product, click the Check Answers buttons to automatically score your answers.

SECTION A: An operating system interacts with application software, device drivers, and hardware to manage a computer's _____ , such as the processor, memory, and input/output devices. To allow two or more programs to run simultaneously, an OS can offer _____ services. Within a single program, _____ allows multiple parts, or threads, to run simultaneously. An operating system's _____ capability supports a division of labor among all the processing units. When multiple programs are running, the OS should prevent a memory _____ , that is a situation in which instructions and data from one area of memory overflow into memory allocated to another program. Operating systems are informally categorized and characterized using one or more of the following terms: A _____ -user operating system expects to deal with one set of input devices—those that can be controlled by one person at a time. A

_____ -user operating system is designed to deal with input, output, and processing requests from many users. A _____ operating system provides management tools for distributed networks, e-mail servers, and Web site hosting. A _____ operating system is one that's designed for a personal computer—either a desktop or notebook computer.

In addition to behind-the-scenes activities, operating systems also provide tools, called operating system _____ that you can use to control and customize your computer equipment and work environment. In addition, many operating systems also influence the "look and feel" of your software, or what's known as the user _____ . The core part of an operating system is called the _____ , which is loaded into RAM during the _____ process.

▶ CHECK ANSWERS

SECTION B: Popular _____ operating systems include Microsoft Windows, Mac OS, and Linux. The first versions of Windows were sometimes referred to as operating _____ rather than operating systems because they required DOS to supply the operating system kernel. Windows has evolved to keep pace with 16-bit to 32-bit, and _____ -bit architectures. Its strengths include a huge library of Windows _____ , support for a variety of peripheral devices, and plenty of documentation. Two of the weakest features of Microsoft Windows are reliability and _____ .

Mac OS evolved from the original Classic Mac OS designed for _____ computers based on the Motorola 68000 microprocessor. In 2001, Mac OS X was released for Apple's new line of computers using IBM's PowerPC processor. OS X was again revised for a line of computers using _____

processors. Mac OS X offers _____ compatibility for prior-generation applications. Intel Macs can be set up to dual _____ Mac OS and Windows. Intel Macs also offer a good platform for _____ machine technologies that allow you to use one computer to simulate the hardware and software of another. One of the potential problems with Mac OS is its use of _____ forks, which make cross-platform file sharing clumsy. Linux is an _____ source operating system that is used extensively for servers. One of the reasons it has not become a popular desktop OS is that it requires a bit more technical savvy than Windows or Mac OS. Developed by Microsoft and supplied on the original IBM PCs, _____ was one of the first operating systems for personal computers. Operating systems for PDAs are typically smaller than PC operating systems and the OS files are small enough to fit in _____ .

▶ CHECK ANSWERS

SECTION C: A computer [_____] is a named collection of data that exists on a storage medium, such as a hard disk, floppy disk, CD, DVD, or tape. Every file has a name and might also have a file extension. The rules that specify valid file names are called file-naming [_____]. These rules typically do not allow you to use certain characters or [_____] words in a file name. A file [_____] is usually related to a file format—the arrangement of data in a file and the coding scheme used to represent the data. A software program's [_____] file format is the default format for storing files created with that program. A file's location is defined by a file [_____] (sometimes called a path), which includes the storage device, folder(s), file name, and extension. In Windows, storage devices are identified by a drive letter, followed by a [_____]. An operating system maintains a list of files called a directory for each storage disk, USB flash drive, tape, CD, or DVD. The main directory of a disk is referred to as the [_____] directory, which can be subdivided into several smaller lists called subdirectories that are depicted as [_____].

▶ CHECK ANSWERS

4

SECTION D: File [_____] encompasses any procedure that helps you organize your computer-based files so that you can find them more effectively. [_____]-based file management uses tools provided with a software program to open and save files. Additional tools might also allow you to create new folders, rename files, and delete files. The Save and Save As dialog boxes are examples of these file management tools. Most operating systems provide file management [_____] that give you the "big picture" of the files you have stored on your disks. The structure of folders that you envision on your disk is a [_____] model, which is often represented by a storage [_____], such as a tree structure or filing cabinet. Windows [_____] is an example of a file management utility provided by an operating system. Windows Explorer allows you to find, rename, copy, move, and delete files and folders. In addition, it allows you to perform these file management activities with more than one file at a time. The way that data is actually stored is referred to as the [_____] storage model. Before a computer stores data on a disk, CD, or DVD, it creates the equivalent of electronic storage bins by dividing the disk into [_____], and then further dividing the disk into [_____]. This dividing process is referred to as [_____]. Each sector of a disk is numbered, providing a storage address that the operating system can track. Many computers work with a group of sectors, called a [_____], to increase the efficiency of file storage operations. An operating system uses a file [_____] to track the physical location of files.

▶ CHECK ANSWERS

SECTION E: A backup is a copy of one or more files that has been made in case the original files become damaged. A good backup plan allows you to [_____] your computing environment to its pre-disaster state with a minimum of fuss. Your personal backup plan depends on the files you need to back up, the hardware you have available to make backups, and your backup software. In any case, it is a good idea to back up the Windows  and make sure your files are free of [_____]. Backups should be stored in a safe place, away from the computer. Personal computer backups are typically recorded on writable CDs and DVDs, USB flash drives, networks, Web sites, or a second hard disk. Many computer owners depend on writable CDs for backups, and use My Computer or Windows [_____] to simply select files and copy files to the backup. [_____] drives and backup software are typically used in business situations when a full-system backup is desirable. Backup software differs from most copy routines because it [_____] all the files for a backup into one large file. In addition to file backups, you should have a [_____] disk containing the operating system files and settings needed to start your computer without accessing the hard disk.

 ▶ CHECK ANSWERS

Interactive Situation Questions

Apply what you've learned to some typical computing situations. When using the NP11 BookOnCD, BookOnFlashDrive, or any other NP11 BookOn product, you can type your answers, and then use the Check Answers button to automatically score your responses.

1. While using several programs at the same time, your computer displays an error message that refers to a program that is not responding. You recognize this message as one that might result from a [ ] leak and decide to close the non-responding program using Ctrl+Alt+Del.

2. Your friend wants to open a window on his Mac computer in which he can run Microsoft Windows and play some games designed for the Windows platform. You tell your friend to create a [ ] machine using software such as Parallels Desktop.

3. Suppose you are using Microsoft Word and you want to open a file. When your software lists the documents you can open, you can expect them to be in Word's [ ] file format, which is DOC.

4. Can you use a Windows application, create a document, and store it using the file name I L*ve NY ? Yes or no? [ ]

5. When you want to work with several files—to move them to different folders, for example—it would be most efficient to use a file management utility, such as Windows [ ].

6. When specifying a location for a data file on your hard disk, you should avoid saving it in the [ ] directory.

7. Your computer seems to be taking longer to store and retrieve files. You use a(n) [ ] utility to rearrange the files in contiguous clusters.

8. You have an old computer that you will donate to a school, but you want to make sure its hard disk contains no trace of your data. To do so, you use file [ ] software that overwrites empty sectors with random 1s and 0s.

9. You just finished making a backup on a set of DVDs. Before you depend on this backup, you should test it to make sure you can successfully [ ] the data in the event of a hard disk crash.

10. Your hard disk crashed for some unknown reason. Now when you switch on the computer power, all you get is an "Error reading drive C:" message. You use a(n) [ ] CD that contains the operating system files and device drivers needed to start your computer without accessing the hard disk.

 CHECK ANSWERS

Interactive Practice Tests

Practice tests that consist of 10 multiple-choice, true/false, and fill-in-the-blank questions are available on both the NP11 BookOn products and the NP11 Web site. The questions are selected at random from a large test bank, so each time you take a test, you'll receive a different set of questions. Your tests are scored immediately, and you can print study guides that help you find the correct answers for any questions that you missed.

CLICK TO START

Study Tips

Study Tips help you to organize and consolidate the information in a unit by making lists, outlines, charts, and sketches. You can use paper and pencil or word processing software to complete most of the Study Tip activities.

1. Make sure you can use your own words to correctly answer each of the red focus questions that appear throughout the chapter.

2. Make sure you can list and describe the four main resources that an operating system manages.

3. Explain the term *memory leak*, and describe what you can do if one occurs on your PC.

4. Describe the difference between a graphical user interface and a command-line user interface.

5. Watch your computer while it boots and revise the list on page 192 so that it reflects what happens when your computer boots.

6. Describe five tasks for which you must interact directly with the operating system.

7. Study the figures of Windows, Mac OS, and Linux in Section B. If you were to start an unfamiliar computer, describe how you would identify its operating system.

8. Discuss the pros and cons of using Linux as a desktop operating system.

9. Make a list of five file names that are valid under the file-naming conventions for your operating system. Also create a list of five file names that are not valid, and explain the problem with each one.

10. Pick any five files on the computer that you typically use, and write out the full path for each one.

11. Make a list of at least 20 file extensions you find on the computer you use most often. Group these extensions into the following categories: system files, graphics files, sound files, text files, other.

12. Describe the difference between the Save and the Save As options provided by an application.

13. Explain the kinds of file management tasks that might best be accomplished using a file management utility such as Windows Explorer, instead of the Save As or Open dialog box provided by a software application.

14. Make sure that you can describe what happens in the MFT or FAT when a file is stored or deleted.

15. Describe the various types of disks that might help you recover from a hard disk crash.

16. Discuss the backup pros and cons of CDs, DVDs, USB flash drives, external hard disks, floppy disks, tapes, and Web sites.

17. Make a list of backup tips that you think would help people devise a solid backup plan.

18. Fill in the blanks in the concept map below that illustrates the hierarchy of OS resource management activities.

4

Concept Map

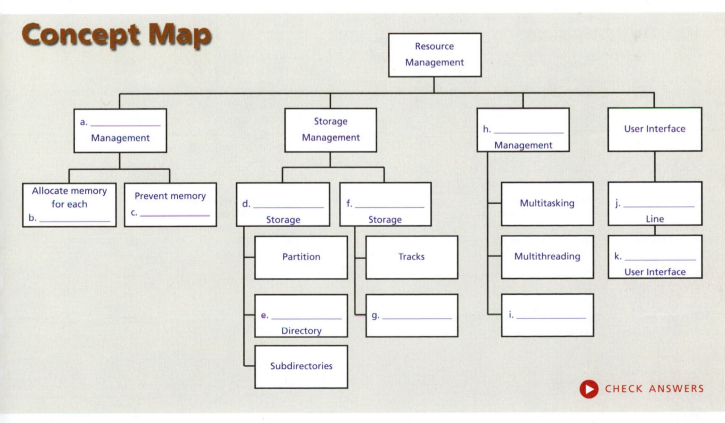

Projects

 **CRITICAL THINKING**

Think about the ways you typically interact with a computer and how the operating system factors into that interaction. What aspects of the operating system do you like? Which aspects could be improved? Organize your thoughts into an annotated list and e-mail it to your instructor.

GROUP PROJECT

Keeping files and folders organized is a skill worth developing. Work with one or two other people to streamline the organization of folders and files on a computer storage device, such as a hard disk or flash drive. The storage device should contain at least 100 files. You can have the computer generate a listing of the files by connecting to *www.support.microsoft.com*, searching for article 196158, and following the instructions you find there for "How to Create a Text File List of the Contents of a Folder." Once you have a document containing the list, you can edit it to indicate how you would rearrange the files into a better structure of folders. Use a series of indents or Microsoft Word's outlining function to show the hierarchy of files and folders. Annotate your list by indicating the kinds of files you expect to be stored in each folder.

 **CYBERCLASSROOM**

Create an e-mail message that describes your backup equipment and plan along with the date of your last backup. In the subject line, include your name and the title "Original Backup Plan." Send the message to other members of your team and solicit comments and questions.

Based on the feedback you receive, use a word processor to revise your backup plan so it gives you improved protection against losing files. Using copy and paste, add the text of your Original Backup Plan and all the comments you received from your team. Your final document should contain your Revised Backup Plan, your Original Backup Plan, and your team's comments. Send this document to your instructor as an e-mail attachment.

MULTIMEDIA PROJECT

Suppose you work for a software company and you are tasked with designing the user interface for a new handheld electronic toy for children ages 8-12. Write a paragraph describing how children will use the toy, then sketch out the main screen. Use callouts to describe how each of the screen elements is supposed to work.

 **RESUME BUILDER**

In today's job market, versatility is valuable. For this project, find a computer that runs an operating system different from the one you normally use. Spend at least 30 minutes working with this alternative operating system. Write a one-page description of your initial reaction, including aspects you liked and did not like.

 GLOBALIZATION

Computers are used worldwide, but all of the major operating systems originated in English-speaking countries. Take a look at the operating system that you use in the context of global users who might not speak English and who might not have grown up with Western customs. Describe at least five aspects of your operating system that would have to be modified to be acceptable to global users.

 ISSUE

The Issue section of this chapter focused on cybercrime. For this project, write a two- to five-page opinion paper about the "right to hack," based on information that you gather from the Internet. To begin this project, consult the Computer Crime InfoWeb (see page 233), and link to the recommended Web pages to get an in-depth overview of the issue. Armed with this background, select one of the following statements and argue for or against it:

• People have the "right" to hone their computing skills by breaking into computers.

• A person who creates a virus is perfectly justified in releasing it if the purpose is to make everyone aware of these security breaches.

• Computer crimes are no different from other crimes, and computer criminals should be held responsible for the damage they cause.

Whatever viewpoint you decide to present, make sure you back it up with facts and references to authoritative articles and Web pages. Follow your professor's instructions for submitting your paper by e-mail or as a printed document.

COMPUTERS IN CONTEXT

The Computers in Context section focused on computer use in law enforcement. For this project, use Web-based resources to search for cases in which computer forensic evidence was used in a criminal or civil investigation. Write a paragraph about the case's particulars, including a description of the alleged criminal activity. Next, create a list of elements, such as e-mail messages, attachments, files, and server logs, that were the focus of the forensic investigation. Follow up with a summary of the outcome. Was the suspect found guilty? Was a penalty imposed? Finally, state your opinion of how forensic evidence affected the case. Was it key evidence required to make the case, or did it simply support other physical evidence? Was the computer forensic evidence solid or open to interpretation and challenges from the defense? Make sure you include the URLs used for your research, and check with your professor for instructions on submitting this project on disk, by e-mail, or in print.

On the Web

STUDENT EDITION LABS

W **CLICK TO ACCESS THE NP11 WEB SITE**
or open your browser and connect to www.course.com/np/concepts11/ch04.
Lab results can be stored in the Universal Gradebook.

4

MAINTAINING A HARD DRIVE

In the Maintaining a Hard Drive Student Edition Lab, you will learn about the following topics:

- Defragmenting a hard disk
- Running ScanDisk
- Detecting system and program failure
- Freeing up disk space

MANAGING FILES AND FOLDERS

In the Managing Files and Folders Student Edition Lab, you will learn about the following topics:

- Using Windows Explorer to manage files and folders
- Deleting and restoring files
- Creating, naming, copying, and moving folders
- Changing folder options and properties

BACKING UP YOUR COMPUTER

In the Backing Up Your Computer Student Edition Lab, you will learn about the following topics:

- Creating a backup
- Creating an incremental backup
- Backing up the Windows Registry
- Scheduling backup jobs
- Restoring an entire backup

USING WINDOWS

In the Using Windows Student Edition Lab, you will learn about the following topics:

- Identifying common elements of Windows software
- Working with the taskbar and Start menu
- Using menus, toolbars, and dialog boxes

CHAPTER COURSECAST

Use your computer or iPod to hear a five-minute audio presentation of chapter highlights.

FLASHCARD COURSECAST

Interact with audio flashcards to review key terms from the chapter.

DETAILED OBJECTIVES

Make sure that you've achieved all the objectives for a chapter before it's time for your test!

TEST YOURSELF

Review chapter material by taking these ten-question tests, then send your results to the Universal Gradebook.

ONLINE GAMES

Have some fun while refreshing your memory about key concepts that might appear on the next test. You can even send your results to the Universal Gradebook!

AND MORE!

At the NP11 Web site you'll also find Extra Content and InfoWebLinks.

5

LANs and WLANs

LEARNING OBJECTIVES

- Describe the characteristics of PANs, NANs, LANS, MANs, and WANs
- Diagram the five most common network topologies
- Diagram Shannon's model of a communications network
- List the types of cables and other links typically used for data communications networks
- Make a list of network devices and explain the role of each one
- Describe the role of communications protocols
- Explain the difference between packet switching and circuit switching technology
- Describe how to set up wired and wireless networks
- List various ways to share files over a LAN
- List security measures for wired and wireless networks
- List and define types of encryption that help secure computer networks and data

PRE-ASSESSMENT QUIZ

Take the pre-assessment quiz to find out how much you know about the topics in this chapter. ▶

MULTIMEDIA and INTERACTIVE ELEMENTS
When using the BookOnCD, BookOnFlashDrive, or other NP11 BookOn product, the ▶ icons are clickable to access multimedia resources.

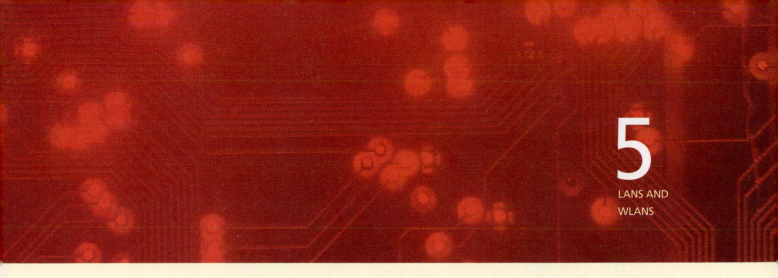

IS MY COMPUTER CONNECTED TO ANY NETWORKS?

Chapter 5 introduces computer networks and explains how handy they are for sharing files and accessing the Internet at home, at school, or in a business. Your computer might be connected to a home network or it might have access to a campus network or a local wireless hotspot. To discover the networks that your computer can access, do the following steps:

1. Click the Start button on the Windows taskbar, select Connect To. If you are using Windows XP, select Show all connections. If you're using Windows Vista, select Open Network and Sharing Center.

2. When the network dialog box appears, click the Maximize button so that the window fills the screen.

3. Study the information displayed in the window. How many networks are listed? _____

4. To view the status of a network in Windows XP, right-click it, then select Status from the pop-up menu. For Windows Vista, click the View status link.

5. Write down the status window information in any of the applicable red lines in the screen shot at right.

6. When you have recorded the information, close the Dialog boxes. You'll learn more about network status as you read this chapter.

Network Building Blocks

TODAY, NETWORKS ARE EVERYWHERE and network technology is evolving rapidly. Just when you think you have got a handle on your home wireless network, along come technologies like 802.11n, MIMO, and WPA2. Although network technology continues to evolve, it is based on a set of fairly stable concepts. If you understand the network building blocks introduced in Section A, working with new network technologies will be a piece of cake.

NETWORK CLASSIFICATIONS

What's the purpose of a network? In the early years of personal computers, networks were scarce. Most personal computers functioned as standalone units, and computing was essentially a solitary activity in which one person interacted with a limited set of software tools, such as a word processor, spreadsheet, database, and games.

Some computer engineers, however, had the foresight to anticipate that personal computers could be networked to provide advantages not available with standalone computers. One of the most significant network ideas was conceived by Bob Metcalfe in 1976. His plan for transporting data between computers, shown in Figure 5-1, has become a key element in just about every computer network.

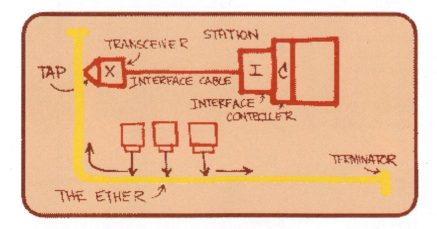

FIGURE 5-1

In 1976, Bob Metcalfe drew this diagram of a network technology, which he called Ethernet.

How are computer networks classified? Networks can be classified according to their size and geographic scope.

PAN (personal area network) is a term sometimes used to refer to the interconnection of personal digital devices within a range of about 30 feet (10 meters) and without the use of wires or cables. For example, a PAN could be used to wirelessly transmit data from a computer to a PDA, cell phone, or portable printer.

A **NAN** (neighborhood area network) provides connectivity within a limited geographical area, usually spread over several buildings. These networks are becoming popular as local coffee shops and computer hobbyists offer wireless Internet connections to the public.

A **LAN** (local area network) is a data communications network that connects personal computers within a very limited geographical area—usually a single building. LANs use a variety of wired and wireless technologies. School computer labs and home networks are examples of LANs.

A **MAN** (metropolitan area network) is a public high-speed network capable of voice and data transmission within a range of about 50 miles (80 km). Examples of MANs include local Internet service providers, cable television companies, and local telephone companies.

A **WAN** (wide area network) covers a large geographical area and usually consists of several smaller networks, which might use different computer platforms and network technologies. The Internet is the world's largest WAN. Networks for nationwide banks and multi-location superstores can also be classified as WANs.

Why is geographic scope important? Localized networks typically include a small number of computers, which can be connected using basic equipment. As the area of network coverage expands, the number of workstations grows, specialized devices are sometimes required to boost signals, and the diversity of devices requires sophisticated management tools and strategies.

FIGURE 5-2

The computer network in a dorm room is a LAN.

The focus of this chapter is on LANs because you are most likely to encounter this type of network in a school lab or small business. Also, if you intend to set up or upgrade a network in your home or dorm room, you will be working with LAN technologies (Figure 5-2).

LAN STANDARDS

Are there different kinds of LANs? In the past, a great diversity of LAN technologies existed as engineers pioneered various ideas to make data transport faster, more efficient, and more secure. Today, LANs are becoming more standardized, but several LAN standards remain necessary to accommodate networking environments that range from simple households to large businesses.

What are LAN standards? LAN technologies are standardized by the Institute of Electrical and Electronics Engineers (IEEE) *Project 802 - Local Network Standards*. IEEE standards are available for most types of commercial networks. An IEEE designation number, such as IEEE 802.3, is sometimes used to refer to a network standard in articles and advertisements. When you're shopping for equipment to connect your computer to a network, these designation numbers help you identify compatible network technologies.

What are the most popular LAN standards? Several LAN standards, including ARCnet, Token Ring, and FDDI, were popular in the past but are rarely used today. Today, most LANs are configured with Ethernet technology and use compatible Wi-Fi standards in applications that require wireless access. These standards are popular across the board for home and business installations. You'll learn more specifics about these popular networking technologies in sections B and C.

NETWORK DEVICES

What devices can be attached to a network? You can think of a network as a spider web with many interconnecting points. Each connection point on a network is referred to as a **node**. A network node typically contains computers, networked peripherals, or network devices.

How do computers connect to LANs? A personal computer connected to a network is sometimes called a workstation. Other classes of computers, such as mainframes, supercomputers, servers, and handhelds, can also connect to LANs.

To connect to a LAN, a computer requires network circuitry, sometimes referred to as a **network interface card** (NIC). Network circuitry is often built into personal computers. If not, a NIC can be added to a slot in the system board, a USB port, or a notebook's PC slot.

What is a networked peripheral? A **networked peripheral**, or network-enabled peripheral, is any device that contains network circuitry to directly connect to a network. Printers, scanners, and storage devices are examples of devices that can be equipped to directly connect to a network instead of connecting to a workstation. Network-enabled printers and scanners are sometimes described as having "built-in networking." Some devices offer networking as an optional add-on. A storage device that directly connects to a network is called **network attached storage** (NAS).

What are network devices? A **network device**, or network appliance, is any electronic device that broadcasts network data, boosts signals, or routes data to its destination. Network devices include hubs, switches, routers, gateways, bridges, and repeaters. You will learn more about these devices later in the chapter. In the meantime, study Figure 5-3 for an example of a LAN that connects a variety of computers, peripherals, and network devices.

FIGURE 5-3

A small LAN uses network devices to connect computers and peripherals.

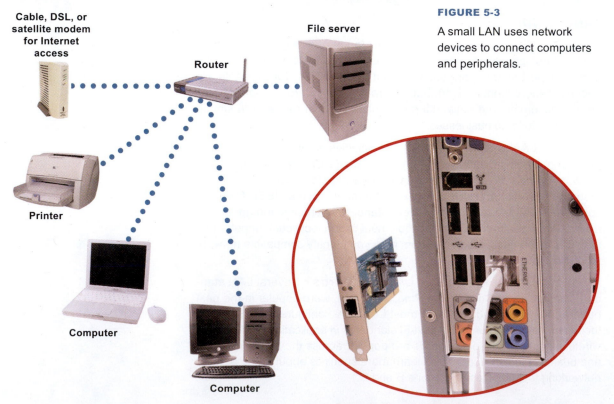

Cable, DSL, or satellite modem for Internet access

Router

File server

Printer

Computer

Computer

Every device on a network requires network circuitry, such as a network interface card.

CLIENTS, SERVERS, AND PEERS

What is the difference between a network client and a server?
Network devices can function as clients or as servers. A server is a computer that provides services to other computers called clients. For example, an **application server** runs application software for network workstations. A **file serve**r stores files and supplies them to workstations on request. A **print server** handles jobs sent to network printers.

Servers are often dedicated to the task they perform, which means they are not assigned to users as workstations. Computers can be configured to perform both functions at the same time, but will not perform optimally in either role.

Networks that include one or more servers can operate in **client/server mode**, which you can envision as a hierarchical structure with servers at the top of the hierarchy (Figure 5-4).

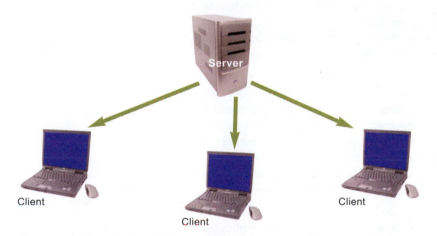

FIGURE 5-4

In client/server mode, a server is the most important resource. Client computers are usually personal computers that use locally installed client software, such as a browser or e-mail package, to access the server.

5

Can a network function without a server?
Networks do not require servers. Files and applications can be shared among workstations operating in **peer-to-peer mode**. In this mode, workstations can share responsibility for processing, storage, printing, and communications tasks (Figure 5-5). Popular file sharing networks such as Napster and BitTorrent operate in peer-to-peer mode.

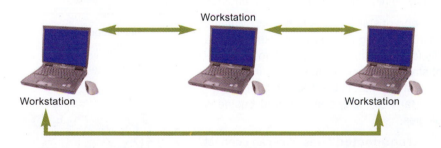

FIGURE 5-5

In peer-to-peer mode, workstations serve as both clients and servers.

Should I choose client/server or peer-to-peer?
You don't have to choose one or the other. A network can function in client/server mode when necessary and also exchange data in peer-to-peer fashion. You can, for example, share files in peer-to-peer mode with several other computers on the network during the day, then in the evening when your friends come over to play computer games, you can configure one of your computers as a server that oversees game play on the other computers in your network that operate as clients for the duration of the game.

PHYSICAL TOPOLOGY

How are the devices on a LAN physically arranged? The arrangement of devices in a network is referred to as its **physical topology**. Figure 5-6 illustrates star, ring, bus, mesh, and tree topologies; the pathways shown between nodes can be linked by physical cables or wireless signals.

What are the advantages of each topology? A network arranged as a **star topology** features a central connection point that links cables or handles wireless broadcasts to all workstations and peripherals. Many home networks are arranged in a star topology. The advantage of this topology is that any link can fail without affecting the rest of the network. Its primary disadvantage is that it requires quite a bit of cable to link all the devices—a disadvantage that disappears with wireless networks. Although the failure of a link does not affect the rest of the network, a device with a failed link would be cut off from the network and unable to receive data.

A **ring topology** connects all devices in a circle, with each device having exactly two neighbors. Data is transmitted from one device to another around the ring. This topology minimizes cabling, but failure of any one device can take down the entire network. Ring topologies, once championed by IBM, are infrequently used in today's networks.

A **bus topology** uses a common backbone to connect all network devices. The backbone functions as a shared communication link, which carries network data. The backbone stops at each end of the network with a special device called a terminator. Bus networks work best with a limited number of devices. Bus networks with more than a few dozen computers are likely to perform poorly, and if the backbone cable fails, the entire network becomes unusable.

A **mesh topology** connects each network device to many other network devices. Data traveling on a mesh network can take any of several possible paths from its source to its destination. These redundant data pathways make a mesh network very robust. Even if several links fail, data can follow alternative functioning links to reach its destination—an advantage over networks arranged in a star topology. The original plan for the Internet was based on mesh topology. Today, mesh topologies are used for some wireless networks. In a wireless mesh, data can be transported to nodes located far from a central access point, simply by hopping from one node to another.

A **tree topology** is essentially a blend of star and bus networks. Multiple star networks are connected into a bus configuration by a backbone. Tree topologies offer excellent flexibility for expansion—a single link to the backbone can add an entire group of star-configured devices. This link can be accomplished using the same type of hub that is used as the central connection point in a star network. Many of today's school and business networks are based on tree topologies.

Can various networks be interconnected? Yes. You can connect your home network to the Internet, for example. A LAN in your sorority or fraternity could be connected to your college campus network. A retail store might connect its cash register network to is financial network.

Two similar networks can be connected by a device called a **bridge**, which simply transfers data without regard to its format. Networks that use different topologies and technologies can be interconnected by using gateways.

FIGURE 5-6

Network Topologies

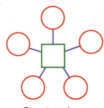

Star topology

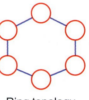

Ring topology

Bus topology

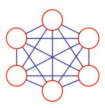

Mesh topology

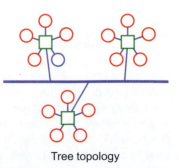

Tree topology

Gateway is a generic term for any device or software code used to join two networks, even if those networks use different protocols or address ranges. A gateway can be implemented completely in software, completely in hardware, or as a combination of the two. The device used to connect your home LAN to the Internet, for example, is a type of gateway.

NETWORK LINKS

What connects the nodes of a network? Data can travel from one network device to another over a cable or through the air. A **communications channel**, or link, is a physical path or a frequency for signal transmissions. For example, Channel 12 on your TV tuner is a specific frequency used to broadcast audiovisual data for a television station. This data might also be carried over another channel, such as coaxial cable, as part of a cable TV system.

Data in a network with wired links travels from one device to another over cables (Figure 5-7). You'll learn more about wired LANs, such as Ethernet, HomePNA, and HomePlug, in Section B. Networks without wires transport data through the air, eliminating the need for cables. Section C contains more information on popular wireless network technologies, such as Wi-Fi and Bluetooth.

FIGURE 5-7

Cables and wireless technologies transport data from one network device to another.

What's bandwidth? Network links must move data and move it quickly. **Bandwidth** is the transmission capacity of a communications channel. Just as a four-lane freeway can carry more traffic than a two-lane street, a high-bandwidth communications channel can carry more data than a low-bandwidth channel. For example, the coaxial cable that brings you more than 100 channels of cable TV has a higher bandwidth than your home telephone line. The bandwidth of a channel carrying digital data is usually measured in bits per second (bps). The bandwidth of a channel carrying analog data is typically measured in hertz (Hz).

To better grasp the significance of bandwidth in a communications network, imagine a dial-up connection's 56 Kbps bandwidth as a narrow bike path that allows a limited amount of slow traffic. A 6 Mbps (6,000 Kbps) connection through your cable TV company is equivalent to a two-lane highway. A typical LAN, such as a college computer lab, might provide 100 Mbps bandwidth—equivalent to a futuristic 260-lane expressway.

High-bandwidth communications systems, such as cable TV and DSL, are sometimes referred to as **broadband**, whereas systems with less capacity, such as dial-up Internet access, are referred to as **narrowband**.

TERMINOLOGY NOTE

Hz is an abbreviation for hertz, which refers to the number of times a wave oscillates, or peaks, per second. Telephone signals are transmitted in the 1,200 Hz range. Many wireless networks transmit a 2.4 GHz signal that peaks 2.4 billion times per second.

COMMUNICATIONS PROTOCOLS

What is a protocol? A protocol is a set of rules for interacting and negotiating. In some respects, it is like signals between the pitcher and catcher in a baseball game. Before the ball is thrown, the catcher and pitcher use hand signals to negotiate the speed and style of the pitch.

In the context of networks, a **communications protocol** refers to a set of rules for efficiently transmitting data from one network node to another. Just as a pitcher signals the catcher in baseball, two computers on a network might negotiate their communications protocols through a process called **handshaking**. The transmitting device sends a signal that means "I want to communicate." It then waits for an acknowledgement signal from the receiving device. The two devices negotiate a protocol that both can handle. The sounds you hear as two modems or fax machines connect are examples of handshaking.

The best-known communications protocol is probably TCP/IP. It is the protocol that regulates Internet data transport and has become a standard for LANs as well.

What can communications protocols do? Protocols set standards for encoding and decoding data, guiding data to its destination, and mitigating the effects of interference. Specifically, protocols are responsible for the following aspects of network communications:

- Dividing messages into packets
- Affixing addresses to packets
- Initiating transmission
- Regulating the flow of data
- Checking for transmission errors
- Acknowledging receipt of transmitted data

How does data travel over a network? In 1948, Claude Shannon, an engineer at the prestigious Bell Labs, published an article describing a communications system model applicable to networks of all types, including today's computer networks.

In Shannon's model, data from a source, such as a network workstation, is encoded and sent as signals over a communications channel to a destination, such as a network printer, storage device, server, or workstation. When data arrives at its destination, it is decoded. Transmission signals can be disrupted by interference called *noise*, which has the potential to corrupt data, making it erroneous or unintelligible (Figure 5-8).

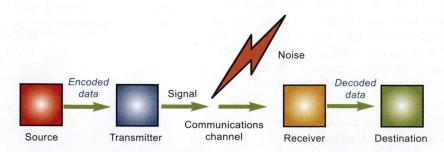

FIGURE 5-8

A communications system basically sends information from a source to a destination. Although the path between the source and destination might appear to be straight in the diagram, the data can pass through several devices, which convert it to electrical, sound, light, or radio signals; beam it up to satellites; route it along the least congested links; or clean up parts of the signal that have been distorted by noise.

What kind of signals travel over computer networks? When data is transmitted over a network link it usually takes the form of an electromagnetic signal. You can think of these signals as waves that ripple through cables or through the air. Digital signals are transmitted as bits using a limited set of frequencies. Analog signals can assume any value within a specified range of frequencies. Figure 5-9 helps you visualize the difference between digital and analog waves.

How can a network detect if a signal has been corrupted? Digital networks—those that transmit digital signals—can be easily monitored to determine if interference has corrupted any signals. At its most primitive level, digital equipment is sensitive to only two frequencies—one that represents 1s and one that represents 0s. Suppose that a 0 is sent as -5 volts and a 1 is sent as +5 volts. What if, during transmission, some interference changes the voltage of a "perfect" 1 to +3 volts? When the signal is received, the receiving device realizes that +3 volts is not one of the two valid voltages. It guesses that a 1 bit (+5 volts) was actually transmitted, and cleans the signal by reestablishing its voltage to +5. Correcting errors is one of the responsibilities of protocols.

What's a packet? When you send a file or an e-mail message, you might suppose that it is transmitted as an entire unit to its destination. This is not the case. Your file is actually chopped up into small pieces called packets. A **packet** is a parcel of data that is sent across a computer network. Each packet contains the address of its sender, the destination address, a sequence number, and some data. When packets reach their destination, they are reassembled into the original message according to the sequence numbers (Figure 5-10).

FIGURE 5-9

Digital and Analog Waves

The signals carried on a digital channel are depicted as a stepped wave.

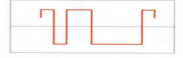

An analog signal is depicted as a smooth wave.

FIGURE 5-10

Before transmission, communications software divides messages into packets. Upon arriving at their destination, packets are reassembled into the original message.

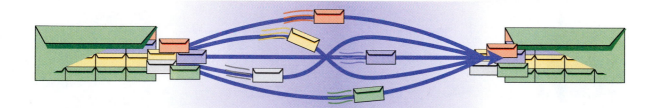

Why not just send an entire message? Some communications networks, such as the telephone system, use a technology called **circuit switching**, which essentially establishes a dedicated, private link between one telephone and another for the duration of a call. This type of switching provides callers with a direct pipeline over which streams of voice data can flow. Unfortunately, circuit switching is rather inefficient. For example, when someone is on hold, no communication is taking place—yet the circuit is reserved and cannot be used for other communications.

A more efficient alternative to circuit switching is **packet switching** technology, which divides a message into several packets that can be routed independently to their destination. Messages divided into equal-size packets are easier to handle than an assortment of small, medium, large, and huge files.

Packets from many different messages can share a single communications channel, or circuit. Packets are shipped over the circuit on a first-come, first-served basis. If some packets from a message are not available, the system does not need to wait for them. Instead, the system moves on to send packets from other messages. The end result is a steady stream of data (Figure 5-11).

FIGURE 5-11

Packet switching networks (top) provide a more efficient communications system than circuit switching networks (bottom).

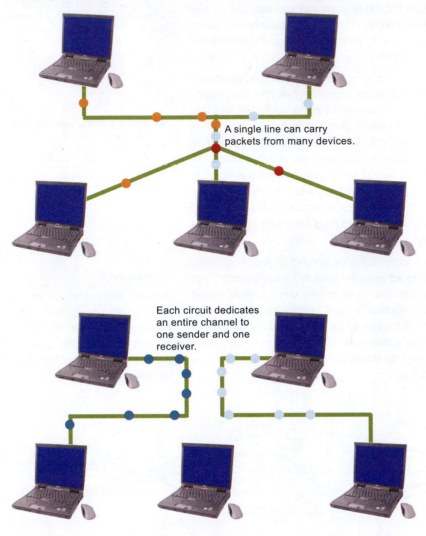

A single line can carry packets from many devices.

Each circuit dedicates an entire channel to one sender and one receiver.

How are packets routed to their destinations? Every packet that travels over a network includes the address of its destination device, similar to the way a letter contains the address of a house or mailbox. Communications protocols specify the proper format for addresses within a particular type of network. When a packet reaches a network node, a routing device examines the address and sends the packet along to its destination.

How do devices get an address? Network addresses are a potential source of confusion. Network devices can have a variety of addresses used for different purposes. Two commonly used addresses are MAC addresses and IP addresses.

What is a MAC address? In the context of networking, MAC stands for Media Access Control. A **MAC address** is a unique number assigned to a network interface card when it is manufactured. MAC addresses are used for some low-level network functions and can also be employed to establish network security.

What is an IP address?

An **IP address** is a series of numbers used to identify a network device. IP addresses were originally used on the Internet, but now are the standard used for assigning addresses to devices in virtually every type of computer network. IP addresses are assigned to network computers, servers, peripherals, and devices. When written, an IP address such as 204.127.129.1 is separated into four sections by periods for the convenience of human readers. Each section is called an **octet** because in binary it is represented by eight bits.

Where do IP addresses come from?

IP addresses can be assigned by ISPs or system managers. Assigned IP addresses are semi-permanent and stay the same every time you boot your computer. If you use an assigned IP address, you have to enter it when you configure your network access.

IP addresses can also be obtained through **DHCP** (Dynamic Host Configuration Protocol), a protocol designed to automatically distribute IP addresses. Most computers are preconfigured to get an IP address by sending a query to the network device acting as the DHCP server. The IP address assigned by DHCP is good for that session. The next time you boot up, you might be assigned a different address. The fact that your IP address changes each time you boot up isn't a problem. Your network keeps track of your IP address behind the scenes and unlike an e-mail address your IP address is not publicized as a permanent address that people use to send files and messages to you.

What happens when data reaches its destination?

Even on a small home network, packets might not travel from the source directly to their destination. Like travelers routed from one airline hub to another, network traffic often travels through intermediary routing devices. Some networks include protocols to keep track of each node that a packet traverses on its journey.

When data reaches its destination, it is checked for errors one last time and then the packets are reassembled into their original configuration. Tracking data is appended or stripped off, depending on the application, and then the newly delivered file is ready to be stored or viewed on the destination device.

QuickCheck

1. To connect to a LAN, a computer requires network circuitry, sometimes referred to as a network [_____] card.

2. A peer-to-peer network is simply a small version of a client/server network. True or false? [_____]

3. Communications [_____], such as TCP/IP, set standards for encoding and decoding data, guiding data to its destination, and mitigating the effects of noise.

4. A(n) [_____] switching network divides messages into small parcels and handles them on a first-come, first-served basis, whereas a(n) [_____] switching network establishes a dedicated connection between two devices.

5. A(n) [_____] address can be assigned to a network workstation by a DHCP server.

 CHECK ANSWERS

Wired Networks

WIRED NETWORKS offer clear advantages over their wireless counterparts for applications that require security and fast access. If you're planning to host a LAN party, for example; if you frequently transfer large video files from one computer to another; if you're nervous about the security of wireless networks, or if you're sending big graphics to a network printer, then a wired network connection should be your first choice. In Section B the focus is on wired technologies used for local area networks.

WIRED NETWORK BASICS

What is a wired network? A **wired network** is one that uses cables to connect network devices. Familiar technologies such as telephone and cable television make extensive use of wired networks. Much of the Internet infrastructure is also wired. Before wireless technologies became available, local area networks were exclusively wired. Today, wired networks are used less frequently for home, school, and business networks. They remain the network technology of choice, however, for LANs that require fast and secure connectivity.

What are the advantages of wired networks? Wired networks are fast, secure, and simple to configure. A wired network transfers data over cables, which typically have high bandwidth and are shielded against interference. Wired connections are characteristically fast and reliable. The speed of a wired network is useful when accessing large files from a local server; file transfers on wired networks are significantly faster than on wireless networks.

Wired networks also offer a faster infrastructure for playing multiplayer computer games within a LAN (Figure 5-12). For Internet based multiplayer games however, the speed of the Internet connection rather than the LAN is usually the limiting factor.

Wired networks are more secure than their wireless counterparts because a computer can only join a network if it is physically connected by a cable. When you set up a wired network you don't have to worry about LANjackers accessing your network from the sidewalk outside your house, or your neighbor stumbling across your files because your wireless signal reaches past your property line.

Today's wired LANs are easy to set up and configure. Most computers are preconfigured with the hardware and software needed to join a wired network. Whether you want to link up a desktop or notebook, PC or Mac, you can pretty much just plug in to connect.

What are the disadvantages of wired networks? The cables that offer speed and security for a wired network are also its main weakness. Devices tethered to cables have limited mobility. Desktop computers tend to be better candidates for wired networks, whereas notebook computers can retain their mobility when they are not tethered to a cable.

FIGURE 5-12

Discerning multiplayer game players prefer a fast wired connection when playing head to head on a LAN.

Cables are unsightly, tend to get tangled, and collect dust. Running cables through ceilings, walls, and floors can be tricky or banned by your landlord. Some building codes prohibit network cables from running through air conditioning and heating ducts. When drilling holes for network cables, installers should take care to avoid electrical wires and other hazards.

Are there various types of wired networks? In the past, many wired network technologies vied for popularity. Today, the most popular LAN technology is Ethernet. Alternatives such as HomePNA and HomePlug technologies are available but much less frequently used.

HOMEPNA AND POWERLINE NETWORKS

What's HomePNA? HomePNA (sometimes called HPNA) is a network technology that utilizes existing telephone wiring to connect network devices. Data transport follows the Ethernet model, but HPNA NICs and other network devices are specially designed to connect to standard telephone wall jacks and exchange data over premises telephone wiring (Figure 5-13).

TERMINOLOGY NOTE

In telecommunications and networking, premises wiring refers to cables and wires run within the structure of an office building, home, or other structure.

FIGURE 5-13

To form an HPNA network, workstations are equipped with HPNA NICs, which are connected to telephone wall jacks.

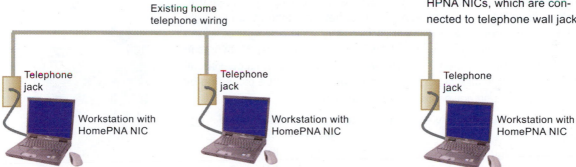

Who should use HomePNA network technology? If the structure of your building makes wiring difficult but you want the security of wired technology, then HomePNA might offer a solution. HomePNA works even when phone lines are not active, so as long as you have phone wires running throughout your building and telephone jacks are located where you want to put computers, you have a ready-made infrastructure for a HomePNA LAN. HomePNA also works in commercial settings. Several major hotels have found HomePNA to be a good solution to retrofit network access into guest rooms.

What is the speed and range of HomePNA? HomePNA operates at 10 Mbps, which is slower than Ethernet, and most wireless technologies. With a HomePNA network, data transport speeds are sufficient for average local file and printer sharing activities, as well as Web browsing. For exchanging lots of large files locally, Fast Ethernet or Gigabit Ethernet would be preferable technologies. HomePNA works with up to 32 devices and supports up to 1000 feet (304 meters) of wiring between devices.

INFOWEBLINKS

For the latest information on HomePNA and HomePlug networks, connect to the **Home Network InfoWeb**.

 **CLICK TO CONNECT**
www.course.com/np/concepts11/ch05

Can I talk on the phone while using the network? When your computer is connected to a HomePNA network, you can typically use the phone to make a call and send information over the network at the same time because the network frequency is different from the voice frequency. You cannot, however, make a voice call while a dial-up Internet connection is active.

What's a powerline network? A **powerline network** uses premises electrical wiring to form the infrastructure for a LAN. Data, transmitted as low-frequency radio waves, travels along the electrical wiring from one network device to another at speeds of about 10 Mbps. Powerline network equipment is sold under HomePLC, HPLC, or HomePlug network labels.

Why use powerline network technology? If you want a wired network, cannot run wires, and don't have telephone jacks where you want to locate computers, a powerline network might suit your needs. Network adapters can be attached to computers with Ethernet ports, then plugged into any electrical wall outlet (Figure 5-14).

What are the limitations of powerline networks? The ease with which you can link computers on a powerline network depends on the path of the wiring through your building's circuit box. The length of wiring between devices is limited to about 1000 feet (304 meters). Networks in apartment buildings are only secure if each apartment has its own circuit breaker box. Otherwise signals from your network could be picked up by neighbors also using powerline network equipment.

Another potential problem with powerline networks is that standard surge strips and UPSs suppress powerline network data signals as well as spikes and surges. Plugging your computer directly into a wall outlet risks damage by power fluctuations. To protect equipment on powerline networks, look for special power-line network rated surge strips from manufacturers such as Belkin or SurgeMaster.

ETHERNET

How does Ethernet work? **Ethernet**, defined by IEEE 802.3, simultaneously broadcasts data packets to all network devices. A packet is accepted only by the device to which it is addressed (Figure 5-15).

FIGURE 5-14

A powerline NIC is cabled to a computer's Ethernet port and plugs into a wall outlet.

FIGURE 5-15

On an Ethernet, a packet is broadcast to every device, but is accepted only by the device to which it is addressed.

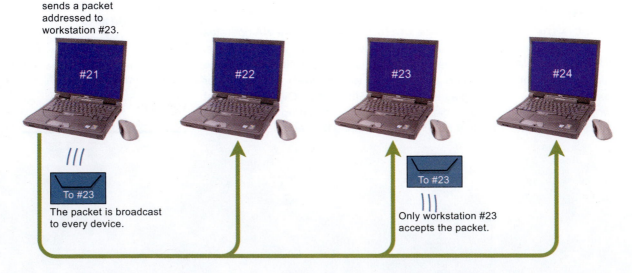

This workstation sends a packet addressed to workstation #23.

The packet is broadcast to every device.

Only workstation #23 accepts the packet.

An integral part of Ethernet technology relies on **CSMA/CD** protocol (Carrier Sense Multiple Access with Collision Detection). CSMA/CD takes care of situations in which two network devices attempt to transmit packets at the same time. A collision occurs and the signals do not reach their destination. CSMA/CD protocol detects the collision, deletes the colliding signals, resets the network, and prepares to retransmit the data. The two devices wait for random time periods before retransmitting to prevent a collision from reoccurring (Figure 5-16).

FIGURE 5-16

On an Ethernet, data travels on a first-come, first-served basis. If two workstations attempt to send data at the same time, a collision occurs. That data must be resent.

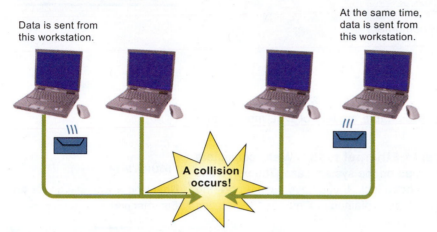

Data is sent from this workstation.

At the same time, data is sent from this workstation.

A collision occurs!

5

▶ CLICK TO START

How fast is an Ethernet network? The original Ethernet standard carried data over a coaxial cable bus topology at 10 Mbps. Today, Ethernet encompasses a family of LAN technologies that offer various data transmission rates over cables arranged in a bus or star topology. Of the Ethernet variations shown in Figure 5-17, **Fast Ethernet**, which operates at 100 Mbps, is currently the most popular for small to medium LANs, like those you might find in homes and small businesses. **Gigabit Ethernet**, with speeds of 1000 Mbps, is gaining popularity as equipment prices decrease.

Ethernet Standard	IEEE Designation	Speed
10BaseT Ethernet	IEEE 802.3	10 Mbps
Fast Ethernet	IEEE 802.3u	100 Mbps
Gigabit Ethernet	IEEE 802.3z	1000 Mbps
10 Gig Ethernet	IEEE 802.3ae	10 Gbps

FIGURE 5-17

Ethernet Standards

Why is Ethernet so popular? Despite challenges from other technologies, Ethernet has emerged as the leading LAN technology. It is currently used in a high percentage of LANs worldwide. Ethernet's success is attributable to several factors:

- Ethernet networks are easy to understand, implement, manage, and maintain.

- As a nonproprietary technology, Ethernet equipment is available from a variety of vendors, and market competition keeps prices low.

- Current Ethernet standards allow extensive flexibility in network topology to meet the needs of small and large installations.

- Ethernet is compatible with popular Wi-Fi wireless networks, so it is easy to mix wired and wireless devices on a single network.

INFOWEBLINKS

Ethernet is definitely cool. See what the "Ether" is all about at the **Ethernet InfoWeb**.

W CLICK TO CONNECT

www.course.com/np/concepts11/ch05

ETHERNET EQUIPMENT

What equipment do I need for an Ethernet network? Ethernet is the quintessential wired network technology. If you have a basic understanding of how it is installed, you can apply that knowledge to putting together just about any network.

Ethernet equipment is widely available and fairly inexpensive. For a typical home network that accesses the Internet, you need the following equipment:

- Two or more Ethernet-ready computers

- An Ethernet router

- Surge strip or UPS

- Cables for each computer

- Internet access device, such as cable modem or DSL modem and corresponding cables

How can I tell if a computer is Ethernet ready? Many computers have a built-in Ethernet port located on the system case. The port looks very similar to an oversized telephone jack. If you have such a port, the next step is to determine its speed, as explained in Figure 5-18.

INFOWEBLINKS

Your basic shopping list for a simple Ethernet LAN is at the **Building a LAN InfoWeb**.

 CLICK TO CONNECT
www.course.com/np/concepts11/ch05

FIGURE 5-18

Checking a workstation for an Ethernet port

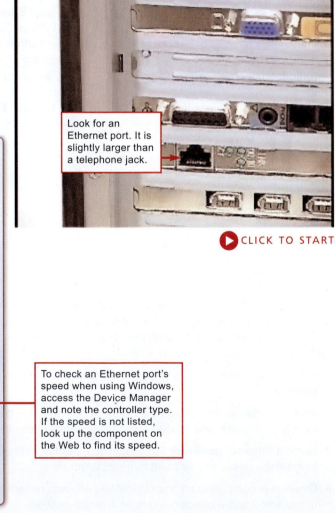

Look for an Ethernet port. It is slightly larger than a telephone jack.

CLICK TO START

To check an Ethernet port's speed when using Windows, access the Device Manager and note the controller type. If the speed is not listed, look up the component on the Web to find its speed.

What if a computer doesn't have an Ethernet port? If your computer has no Ethernet port, you can purchase and install an **Ethernet adapter** (also called an Ethernet card or NIC). USB and PC adapters simply plug into ports on the outside of your computer's system unit. Follow the manufacturer's installation instructions to install any necessary device drivers. Connecting an Ethernet adapter through the USB port is a good solution for notebook or desktop computers. If you're working with a desktop computer, you can install an Ethernet card in a PCI slot inside the computer case. For notebook computers, you can purchase and install an Ethernet adapter that slides into a PC card slot. Figure 5-19 illustrates some popular network adapters.

FIGURE 5-19

Ethernet adapters

Ethernet adapter for USB port   Ethernet adapter for PC slot   Ethernet adapter for PCI slot

Should I buy an Ethernet hub, switch, or router? A **network hub** is a device that links two or more nodes of a wired network. On a typical network, the hub accepts data from one of the computers and then broadcasts it to all of the other network nodes. Some devices receive data that is not meant for them, but their NICs filter out any data that is not intended for that destination.

A **network switch** is a more sophisticated connection device that sends data only to the devices specified as the destination. Using a switch instead of a hub can increase a network's performance and security because data isn't flowing indiscriminately to every device on the network.

A **network router** is a network device that can ship data from one network to another. Most routers are also switches that contain ports for connecting workstations. You might see a router/switch device advertised as "router with 4-port switch." A router/switch is particularly useful for connecting a home network to the Internet, so if you are planning to connect your network to the Internet, you should consider using one as the central point of your LAN (Figure 5-20).

FIGURE 5-20

An Ethernet router features a collection of ports for connecting servers, workstations, and peripheral devices.

How many ports do I need? Your hub, switch or router needs one port for each device you intend to wire to the network. A typical router, for example, has four or five ports for network devices. It also has a WAN port that is only used to connect the router to the Internet. If you want to attach more devices to a network, you can purchase an inexpensive hub that provides additional ports and connects to the router.

What do I need to know about speed? Ethernet routers are available at 10/100 Mbps or Gigabit speeds. If you have a Gigabit router and all the network computers have Gigabit Ethernet adapters, data will flow over all network connections at Gigabit speeds. If some computers have Gigabit adapters, whereas others have 10/100 Mbps adapters, a Gigabit router will ship data at a speed that corresponds to each adapter.

5

The only time you waste bandwidth is when you have a 10/100 Mbps router, but several of the network computers have Gigabit Ethernet adapters. In this case, the router cannot send data at Gigabit speeds, so the Gigabit adapters will receive data at the 100 Mbps rate.

Serious computer gamers who compete against each other over a LAN prefer Gigabit Ethernet equipment for adapters and routers. Some video-conferencing and streaming video applications might also benefit from high bandwidth equipment.

What kind of cable do I need? The devices in an Ethernet are connected with network cables terminated at each end with a plastic **RJ45 connector** (Figure 5-21).

Network cables contain four pairs of copper wires. Each pair of wires is independently insulated and then twisted together, which is why network cable is sometimes referred to as twisted-pair cable. Shielded twisted-pair cable (STP) contains shielding, which reduces signal noise that might interfere with data transmitted over unshielded cable (UTP). The shielded cable is not significantly more expensive.

When shopping for cables, look for Category 5 ("Cat5") or Category 6 ("Cat6") cables. You'll need one cable for each workstation. Network cables can be purchased in a variety of lengths. When you calculate the length of each cable, make sure you consider the path that the cable will follow as it snakes along walls from the router to the workstation.

ETHERNET SETUP

What's the general procedure for setting up Ethernet? Nowadays, it is easy to set up a wired network like the one in Figure 5-22.

To set up an Ethernet LAN:

- Run cables from the router to each workstation or server

- Run a cable between the router and the device used for your Internet connection

- Configure each workstation

- Configure the router

How do I run the wiring? Before you begin running wires, make sure the router, computers, and other devices are powered off. Connect cables between the router and the Ethernet ports on each workstation or server. Run a cable between your Internet device and the router's WAN port. Tuck the cables out of the way. You might want to use cable tacks to carefully secure each cable to the baseboards along your walls. Use the same precautions with your network cables as you would with power cords; do not run them across walkways or under carpets.

FIGURE 5-21

Network cables are terminated with plastic RJ45 connectors that are similar to, but larger than the connectors used for telephones.

FIGURE 5-22

A typical wired network uses a router as a central device for connecting workstations, a file server, and an Internet access device.

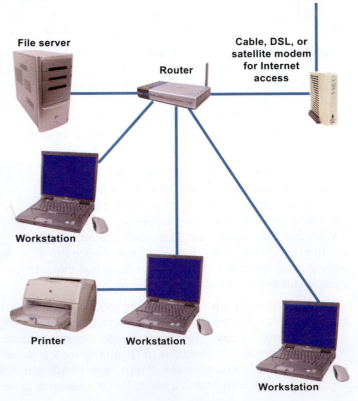

To an ISP and Internet

Cable, DSL, or satellite modem for Internet access

File server

Router

Workstation

Printer

Workstation

Workstation

When the cables are in place, plug in the router, preferably through a surge strip or UPS, and then turn it on. One by one, power up each network device. Figure 5-23 walks you through the basic setup.

FIGURE 5-23

Installing a LAN

1. Place the router in a central location and plug it into a surge-protected outlet.

2. Run cables from the router to the Ethernet adapter in each workstation.

3. Run a cable from your Internet device and your router's WAN port.

4. Turn on network devices one at a time. Your operating system should automatically detect the NICs and establish a connection to the network.

▶ CLICK TO START

5. Use your computer's operating system network utilities to verify each connection. When using Windows Vista, access the Network and Sharing Center where you can view the status of the Local Area Connection.

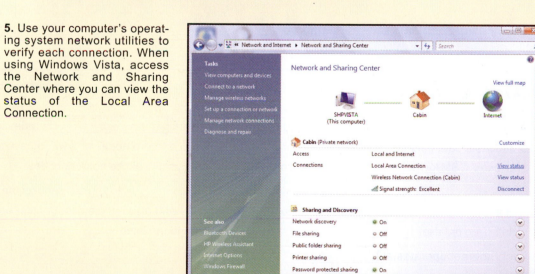

How do I configure each workstation? Turn on one of the workstations and wait for it to boot. Your computer's operating system should automatically sense the network connection. No additional configuration should be necessary.

How do I configure the router? The router's configuration data is stored in its EEPROM chip. To access the configuration data, open your browser and enter the router's address in the Address line as shown in Figure 5-24. Most routers use http://192.168.1.1 or http://192.168.1.100 as their configuration address. You can check your router's documentation to verify. It is essential that you change the router's password to prevent unauthorized changes to your network. If you are connecting your network to the Internet, additional configuration might be necessary, as explained in the Internet chapter.

How do I know when the network is ready? Your operating system usually displays a message or icon to let you know when you are connected to a network. For example, Windows displays the Local Area Connection icon on the taskbar to indicate the status of a wired network. If that icon indicates the network is connected, it is ready for use.

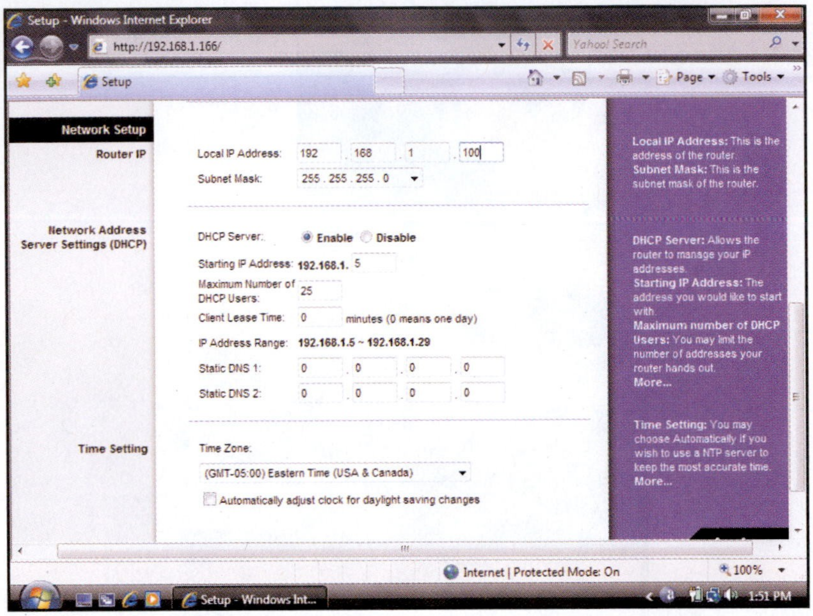

FIGURE 5-24

Most routers are configured using a browser. You should change the network administrator password, then verify that DHCP is enabled.

QuickCheck

SECTION B

1. A(n) _____ LAN simultaneously broadcasts data packets over all network links and uses CSMA/CD protocol to handle collisions.

2. A HomePNA network uses existing telephone wiring. True or false? _____

3. Fast Ethernet operates at _____ Mbps.

4. A network _____ is a device that links two or more nodes of a wired network and broadcasts it to all the network nodes.

5. A(n) _____ can connect the nodes of a LAN and also handle data transfer between a LAN and the Internet.

▶ CHECK ANSWERS

Wireless Networks

WHO WANTS LOTS OF unsightly wires and cables snaking through their living room or office space? Today's trend is to wireless LAN technology. Wireless LANs, dubbed WLANs, are easy to install, but it is important to secure them from intrusions. Section C supplies information on wireless LAN equipment and installation. You'll learn more about wireless security in Section E.

WIRELESS BASICS

What is a wireless network? A **wireless network** transports data from one device to another without the use of cables or wires. Networks of all sizes, from PANs to LANs and WANs, can use wireless technologies, such as radio signals, microwaves, and infrared light.

How do radio signals transport data? Wireless devices can transport data as radio, microwave, or infrared signals. Most wireless networks transport data as **RF signals** (radio frequency signals). RF signals—commonly called radio waves—are sent and received by a **transceiver** (a combination of a transmitter and a receiver) that is equipped with an antenna. Workstations, peripheral devices, and network devices can be equipped with transceivers to send and receive data on wireless networks (Figure 5-25).

How do microwaves transport data? **Microwaves** (the waves themselves, not your oven!) provide another option for transporting data over wireless networks. Like radio waves, microwaves are electromagnetic signals, but they behave differently. Microwaves can be aimed in a single direction and have more carrying capacity than radio waves. However, microwaves cannot penetrate metal objects and work best for line-of-sight transmission when a clear path exists between the transmitter and receiver. Microwave installations typically provide data transport for large corporate networks.

How does infrared transport data? Today most people are familiar with television remote controls that use **infrared light** beams. Infrared can also carry data signals, but only for short distances and with a clear line of sight. Its most practical use seems to be for transmitting data between devices connected to a PAN.

What are the advantages of wireless networks? The main advantage of wireless networks is mobility. Wireless devices are not tethered to network cables, so battery operated workstations can be easily moved from room to room, or even outdoors. With wireless networks, there are no unsightly cables, and power spikes are much less likely to run through cables to damage workstations.

Do wireless networks have disadvantages? In the past, wireless network equipment was quite a bit more expensive than equivalent wired equipment. With the current popularity of wireless technologies, however, prices have equalized. When compared to wired networks, the main disadvantages of wireless networks are speed, range, licensing, and security.

5

FIGURE 5-25

Wireless equipment often sports an antenna for transmitting and receiving data signals.

Why is wireless slower than wired? Wireless signals are susceptible to interference from devices such as microwave ovens, cordless telephones, and baby monitors. When interference affects a wireless signal, data must be re-transmitted.

Despite interference, wireless networks are fast enough for most applications. Even the slowest wireless LAN technologies are faster than most Internet services, so online access from a wireless LAN is no slower than from a wired LAN. Wireless LANs are slower for intra-LAN operations, such as exchanging files and sharing printers. When lots of computer game players compete against each other over a LAN, a fast, wired network is desirable.

What limits the range of a wireless network? The range of a wireless signal can be limited by the type of signal, the transmitter strength, and the physical environment. Just as radio stations fade as you move away from their broadcasting towers, data signals fade as the distance between network devices increases. Signal range can also be limited by thick walls, floors, or ceilings (Figure 5-26).

What's wrong with wireless security? Wireless signals float through the air and penetrate walls. The signals that carry your wireless data can be accessed from outside your premises. Someone outside of your house, for example, could surreptitiously join your network, access files, and piggyback on your Internet connection. To make wireless network data useless to intruders, it should be encrypted. Later in the chapter you'll learn how to use encryption to secure a wireless LAN.

How does licensing affect wireless networks? Signals that are sent through the air are regulated by government agencies such as the Federal Communications Commission (FCC). To broadcast at most frequencies, such as those used by radio or television, a license is required. Only certain frequencies are unlicensed and available for public use. Unlicensed frequencies include 2.4 GHz and 5.8 GHz used by cordless telephones and baby monitors, and the 460 MHz frequency used for two-way citizens band radios. Wireless networks use unlicensed frequencies so that they can be set up without applying to the FCC for permission. The few unlicensed frequencies are crowded, however, and neighboring home networks that are forced to use the same frequencies pose security risks.

What are the most popular technologies for wireless networks? By far the most popular wireless LAN technology is Wi-Fi. A second wireless technology called Bluetooth is useful for some applications. Other wireless technologies, such as WiMAX and Zigbee are MAN or WAN technologies, typically used for fixed Internet access. Let's take a brief look at Bluetooth technology and then examine Wi-Fi networks in more detail.

FIGURE 5-26

On a wireless network, signal strength varies depending on distance from a transmitter and obstacles that might interfere with the signal.

SSID: LAN Services
Speed: 54.0 Mbps
Signal: Excellent
Status: Connected
Address: 192.166.1.337
2:07 PM

BLUETOOTH

What is Bluetooth? **Bluetooth** is a short-range wireless network technology that's designed to make its own connections between electronic devices, without wires, cables or any direct action from a user. Bluetooth networks form automatically when two or more Bluetooth devices come within range of each other. A Bluetooth network is sometimes called a **piconet**.

To form a network, a Bluetooth device can search for other Bluetooth devices within range. When another Bluetooth device is detected, it typically broadcasts what it is, for example a printer, a PC, or a cell phone. Before data is exchanged, the owners of the two Bluetooth devices have to exchange passkeys, or PINs (Figure 5-27). Once passkeys have been exchanged, the two Bluetooth devices form a trusted pair. Future communication between these two devices does not require the passkey to be re-entered.

FIGURE 5-27

Owners of Bluetooth devices can beam data to other Bluetooth device owners.

5

Where is Bluetooth used? Bluetooth operates at the unlicensed 2.4 GHz frequency, so anyone can set up a Bluetooth network. Bluetooth is not typically used to connect a collection of workstations. Instead, Bluetooth connectivity replaces the short cables that would otherwise tether a mouse, keyboard, or printer to a computer.

Bluetooth can be used to link devices in a PAN, connect home entertainment system components, provide hands-free cell phone operation in an automobile, link a cell phone to a wireless headset (Figure 5-28), and synchronize PDAs with desktop base stations.

Bluetooth is built into some peripheral devices. If you want these devices to communicate with your computer you can use a variety of add-on cards.

FIGURE 5-28

Bluetooth technology is used for wireless keyboards and mice, but it is also the technology used for wireless headsets and devices like Motorola's Bluetooth headset that clips to a motorcycle helmet so you don't miss important cell calls.

What is the speed and range of Bluetooth? Bluetooth offers peak transmission rates of only 3 Mbps (version 2.0 +EDR) over a range of 3–300 feet (about 1–91 meters).

WI-FI

What is Wi-Fi? **Wi-Fi** refers to a set of wireless networking technologies defined by IEEE 802.11 standards that are compatible with Ethernet. A Wi-Fi network transmits data as radio waves over 2.4 GHz or 5.8 GHz frequencies. When people refer to wireless networks they are usually talking about Wi-Fi.

Wi-Fi encompasses several standards, designated by letters b, a, g, and n. Some of these standards are cross compatible, which means that you can use them on the same wireless network. Figure 5-29 summarizes the specifications for each Wi-Fi standard.

FIGURE 5-29

Wi-Fi Standards

IEEE Designation	Frequency	Speed	Range	Pros/Cons
IEEE 802.11b	2.4 GHz	11 Mbps	100–300 feet	Original standard
IEEE 802.11a	5 GHz	54 Mbps	25–75 feet	Not compatible with 802.11b, g, or n
IEEE 802.11g	2.4 GHz	54 Mbps	100–150 feet	Faster than, but compatible with, 802.11b
IEEE 802.11n	2.4/5 GHz	200 Mbps	100–150 feet	Faster but compatible with b and g

How do the speed and range of Wi-Fi compare to other network technologies? On a wired network, the rated speed and range are usually quite close to actual performance. Wireless network speed and range, however, are often theoretical maximums, because signals can easily deteriorate. Although Wi-Fi 802.11n is capable of 200 Mbps speeds, in actual performance it is unlikely to match Fast Ethernet and is far slower than Gigabit Ethernet.

FIGURE 5-30

MIMO-equipped devices usually have more than one antenna.

In a typical office environment, Wi-Fi's range varies from 25 to 150 feet (8–45 meters). Thick cement walls, steel beams, and other environmental obstacles can drastically reduce this range to the point that signals cannot be reliably transmitted. Wi-Fi signals can also be disrupted by interference from electronic devices operating at the same frequency, such as 2.4 GHz cordless telephones.

Wi-Fi speed and range can be improved with various technologies. For example, **MIMO** (multiple-input multiple-output) technology uses two or more antennas to essentially send multiple sets of signals between network devices (Figure 5-30).

WI-FI EQUIPMENT

What equipment is required for a Wi-Fi network? Wi-Fi equipment is widely available and fairly inexpensive. For a typical home network, you need the equipment listed in Figure 5-31.

FIGURE 5-31

Wireless Networking Equipment

Wireless-ready devices, such as computers and printers

Short piece of network cable to run between the router and one computer

Surge strip or UPS

Wireless router

How can I tell if a device is wireless-ready? Although cell phones and PDAs sometimes sport a small antenna that emphasizes their wireless communications capabilities, the antenna and transceiver for most notebook computers are hidden inside the case. You usually have to check your computer's documentation or on-screen utilities to discover if it has wireless capabilities (Figure 5-32).

FIGURE 5-32

Check the hardware listings to see if your computer has wireless capability. Use the System or Device Manager icon in the Windows Control Panel to look for a wireless or WLAN adapter.

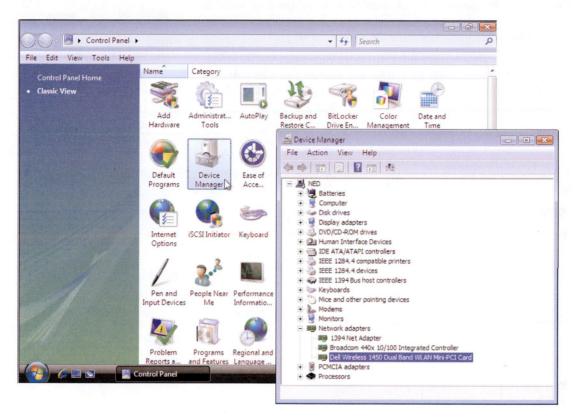

Can I add Wi-Fi? If your computer is not pre-equipped with wireless circuitry, you can purchase and install a Wi-Fi card. A **Wi-Fi card** (also called a Wi-Fi adapter) is a wireless NIC that includes a transmitter, receiver, and antenna to transmit signals. Wi-Fi cards for notebook or tablet computers can plug into a PC slot or USB port. Wi-Fi capability can be added to a desktop computer as a Wi-Fi card that fits into a system unit slot with the antenna protruding out of the back or as a small box that connects to a USB port. Yet another option is to use a wireless adapter to convert a standard Ethernet port into a wireless port. Figure 5-33 illustrates various Wi-Fi cards.

INFOWEBLINKS

For the latest information on Wi-Fi equipment and pricing, check out the **Wireless LAN InfoWeb**.

W CLICK TO CONNECT
www.course.com/np/concepts11/ch05

FIGURE 5-33

Wi-Fi Cards

Do I need a wireless router? You can set up a wireless network in two ways (Figure 5-34). First, you can set up a **wireless ad-hoc network** in which devices broadcast directly to each other. The advantage of this configuration is cost. If your devices include factory-installed wireless networking circuitry, you don't need additional equipment. The disadvantage of an ad-hoc network is Internet access. Although you can access the Internet from an ad-hoc network, you'll have to designate one of the network computers as the gateway device. It will require a cable connection to your Internet modem, and it will have to be left on during the time anyone on your network might want to access the Internet.

A second option called a **wireless infrastructure network** uses a centralized broadcasting device, such as a wireless access point or router. A **wireless access point** is a device that transmits and receives wireless signals. A **wireless router** is a wireless access point that also includes routing circuitry that can connect a Wi-Fi network to the Internet. Wireless routers offer the most flexibility for Internet access and the best security options, so most experts recommend using one as the central point in your wireless network. The remaining information in this section pertains to wireless infrastructure networks that use wireless routers.

WI-FI SETUP

What's the general procedure for setting up a Wi-Fi network?
Setting up a Wi-Fi network involves a few simple steps.

- Set up the router
- Connect to the router with a computer
- Configure the router
- Access the router setup utility
- Create a new router password
- Enter an SSID for the network
- Activate WEP, WPA, or WPA2 and create an encryption key
- Set up the wireless workstations
- Connect an Internet access device

Let's see how you can apply these steps to set up a basic wireless network similar to the one in Figure 5-35.

FIGURE 5-34

Wireless ad-hoc networks transmit from one workstation to another, whereas an infrastructure network uses a centralized access point or router to relay signals to workstations.

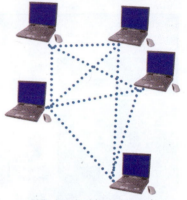

Wireless ad-hoc network

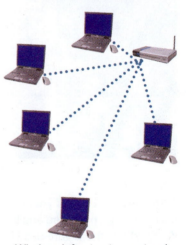

Wireless infrastructure network

FIGURE 5-35

A wireless network typically includes several workstations connected wirelessly to a router; an Internet device connected by a cable to the router's WAN port; and possibly a file server linked with a wired or wireless connection.

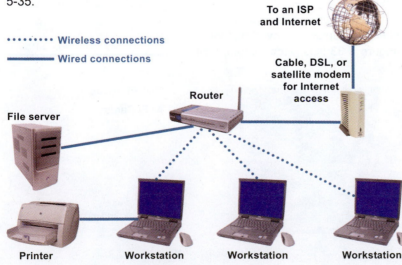

How do I set up a wireless router? Place the wireless router in a central location relative to the network devices. Thick concrete walls and floors can significantly lower signal strength, so if you encounter such obstacles, you might have to consider a signal booster.

Connect the wireless router to a power outlet through a surge strip or UPS. A UPS will keep your network operational during a power outage. Your ability to access the Internet during a power outage depends on the power situation at your ISP. However, a network that consists of battery operated notebook computers and a wireless router connected to a UPS should be able to run for several hours during a blackout.

If you want your wireless network to access the Internet, connect the router to an Internet access device, such as a cable or DSL modem. Internet modems are typically connected to the router's WAN port using an Ethernet cable.

How do I access the router's configuration utility? Before using your wireless network, you should adjust router configuration settings for the default password, SSID, and encryption, as described later in this section. The configuration settings are stored in the router's EEPROM memory. You'll need to log into the configuration software to adjust settings. A router has no screen or keyboard of its own, so to access the router's configuration software, you have to connect a computer to the router. The easiest way to make this connection is with a short Ethernet cable. Although it might seem nonintuitive to use a wire to create a wireless network, the use of a cabled connection is detected automatically by Windows and that provides a direct link to the router without any preliminary setup.

Documentation for the router supplies a LAN address for the router and might also supply a default password. A LAN address is typically something like 192.168.1.1 or 192.168.1.100. Open your browser and type http:// and the router's LAN address in the Address line. Enter the default password, if one is necessary (Figure 5-36).

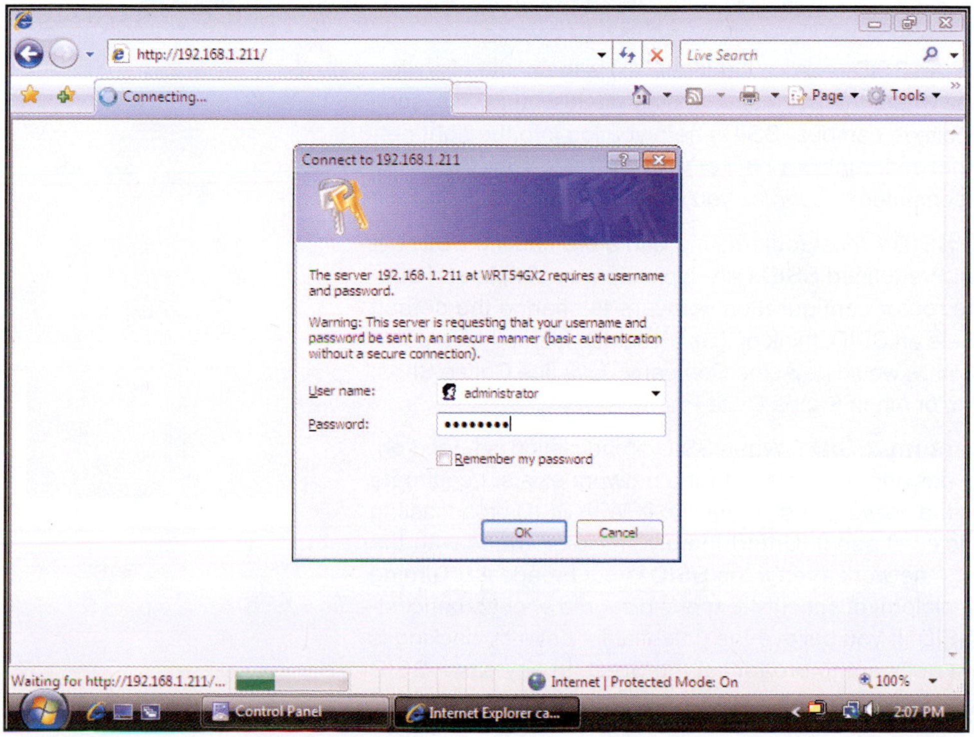

FIGURE 5-36

To access the router configuration utilities, use your browser.

How do I change the default password? Your wireless router configuration utility might look like the one in Figure 5-37. Your first step after logging on is to change the default password so that hackers can't gain access to your network and reconfigure it for their own malevolent schemes. Locate the setting for the administrator password and create a new one. Follow the recommendations in earlier chapters for creating a strong password. This password is only used to configure the router. It does not need to be conveyed to network users who simply want to set up their computers to send and receive data over the network.

FIGURE 5-37

Change the default password for your router when you install a wireless network.

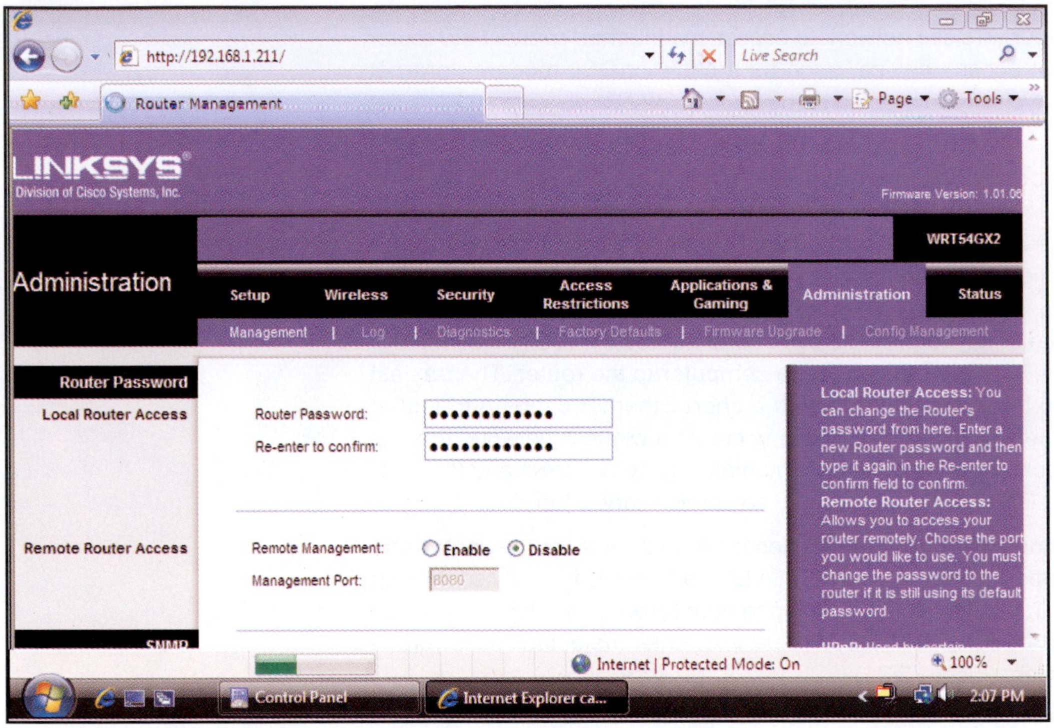

CLICK TO START

What is an SSID? An **SSID** (service set identifier) is the name of a wireless network. In areas where there are overlapping wireless networks, such as in a city or on a college campus, SSIDs help you log into the right network, rather than a network run by a hacker who will try to suck important information off your computer as soon as you connect.

How do I set the SSID? Most routers ship with a pre-defined SSID set by the manufacturer. Predefined SSIDs are typically very simple and publicly known. Use the router configuration software to change the default SSID. When you create an SSID, think of it as a user ID, rather than a password. Examples of SSIDs would be Acme Company, Java Joe Coffee Shop, Planters Inn of Miami, or Alpha Kappa Delta Phi.

Should I broadcast my SSID? When SSID broadcasting is turned on, any wireless device passing by can see that a network exists. Legitimate users can easily find the network and connect to it. With SSID broadcasting turned off, the public can't see it. Unfortunately, hackers armed with the right tools can see the network even if the SSID is not broadcast. Turning off SSID is a very weak form of security. Experts disagree about broadcasting your network's SSID. If you believe the potential for drive-by hacking is high, then you might not want to broadcast the SSID. In any case, SSID should be left on until you configure the rest of the devices that you plan to use on your network.

Do I need to take any special steps to secure my wireless network? Wireless networks are much more susceptible to unauthorized access and use than wired networks. Some measure of security can be gained by enabling encryption as explained in Section E.

When is the router configuration complete? Basic router configuration requires you to change the router password, enter an SSID, and activate encryption. Your wireless networking utility offers additional configuration options, but they are not needed for typical home and school networks. With your router configuration complete, you can close the router utility and set up the rest of the network.

How do I set up workstations and other network devices? To add computers and other devices to your wireless network, start by turning on another computer with wireless capability. Its wireless device driver should automatically find the network SSID and ask you to enter the wireless network key or passphrase.

Can I mix wireless and wired devices? Most wireless routers include ports for four Ethernet cables and a WAN port for a cable to an Internet device, such as a cable or DSL modem (Figure 5-38).

You can also wire some of your network workstations to the router. As a sample scenario, you might use a cable to connect the router and an old desktop computer that you plan to use as a game server or as a server for lots of video footage. You could also use a wired connection for the computer that you use to edit the video footage.

FIGURE 5-38

Most wireless routers (note the antenna) also include ports for wired Ethernet connections.

QuickCheck

1. Today's most popular wireless LAN technology is compatible with Ethernet and called [_____].

2. [_____] is a short-range wireless network technology used for PANs.

3. In a wireless [_____] network, devices broadcast directly to each other rather than through a central broadcasting device.

4. A wireless [_____] network uses a centralized broadcasting device, such as a wireless access point or router.

5. When setting up a wireless network it is important to change the username and password, create a unique [_____] and enable encryption. (Hint: Use the acronym.)

 CHECK ANSWERS

Using LANs

LANS HAVE BECOME an integral part of computing environments at home, at school, and at work. Many LANs are installed solely for distributing access to an Internet connection. That facet of LANs will be discussed in the next chapter. What else can you do with a LAN? Section D helps you explore the advantages and disadvantages of LANs, as well as providing practical tips on how to share files and printers.

LAN ADVANTAGES AND CHALLENGES

Why are LANs advantageous? Today, the pervasiveness of LANs and other types of networks has dramatically changed the face of computing by offering **shared resources**—hardware, software, and data made available for authorized network users to access. LANs offer the following advantages:

● **LANs enable people to work together.** Using groupware and other specialized network application software, several people can work together on a single document, communicate by e-mail and instant messaging, take part in multiplayer computer games, and participate in online conferences and Webcasts (Figure 5-39).

FIGURE 5-39

LANs can be used for intra-LAN collaboration, or they can be connected to other networks for broader participation.

● **Sharing networked software can reduce costs.** Although purchasing and installing a single software copy for an entire LAN might be technically possible, it is typically not allowed under the terms of a single-user license agreement. However, software site licenses for network use are usually less expensive than purchasing single-user versions of a product for each network user.

● **Sharing data on a LAN can increase productivity.** To transfer data between standalone computers, a file is usually copied to some type of removable storage media, and then carried or mailed to the other computer where it is copied onto the hard disk. LANs can provide authorized users with access to data stored on network servers or workstations.

- **Sharing networked hardware can reduce costs.** In an office environment, for example, a single expensive color printer can be purchased and attached to a LAN, instead of the costly alternative of purchasing color printers for each employee who wants to generate color printouts.

- **Sharing networked hardware can provide access to a wide range of services and specialized peripheral devices.** A LAN can allow multiple users to access Internet services, including voice over IP, through a single Internet connection. Networked peripheral devices, such as scanners, photo printers, plotters, and high-capacity storage devices can be accessed by any authorized LAN users. In a home environment, a LAN can offer access to surveillance and monitoring devices from inside or outside the home. LANs can control entertainment devices, and supply them with downloaded music and videos (Figure 5-40).

FIGURE 5-40

Music and video can stream over wireless LANs to projectors, speakers, and televisions when devices are equipped for 802.11 networking.

A wireless projector streams video signals from a remote PC.

A wireless receiver connects to an audio system, so you can listen to music from your PC in any room.

A wireless media player can stream video to your television, and play digital music on your stereo system.

Do LANs have disadvantages? One disadvantage of LANs is that when a network malfunctions, all the resources you're accustomed to accessing are unavailable until the network is repaired.

Another disadvantage of LANs is their vulnerability to unauthorized access. Whereas a standalone computer is vulnerable to on-premises theft or access, network computers are vulnerable to unauthorized access from many sources and locations.

Through unauthorized use of a LAN workstation, intruders can access data stored on the network server or other workstations. LANs connected to the Internet are vulnerable to intrusions from remote computers in distant states, provinces, or countries. Wireless LANs can be tapped from a specially equipped "snooping" computer in a car that's being driven by a hacker.

LANs are also more vulnerable than standalone computers to malicious code. Whereas the most prevalent threat to standalone computers is disk-borne viruses, networks are susceptible to an ever-increasing number of worms, Trojan horses, and blended threats. If a virus gets through LAN security, every computer on the network is at risk.

Most computer owners are enthusiastic about the benefits provided by LANs and believe that those benefits outweigh the risks of intrusions and viruses—especially if their computers can be protected by security tools, such as antivirus software and firewalls. You'll learn more about LAN security threats and countermeasures later in this chapter.

5

SHARING FILES

How do I access network resources? If you use Windows, it automatically detects available LANs any time you turn on a workstation. Depending on your network setup, you might be asked to log in by entering a user ID and password. Once access is established, you can use any shared resources for which you have been given authorization.

You can access shared data on other workstations in a variety of ways. For example, Windows Vista users can access the Start menu's Network option to access shared resources. These resources are listed as computers, folders, or drives; their names might indicate the computer on which they reside. Figure 5-41 shows a listing of available network resources.

FIGURE 5-41

The network on this Vista computer has access to five computers and one network printer.

A more general way to access network resources that works for most operating systems is to map a drive. **Drive mapping** assigns a drive letter to a storage device located on a network workstation (Figure 5-42).

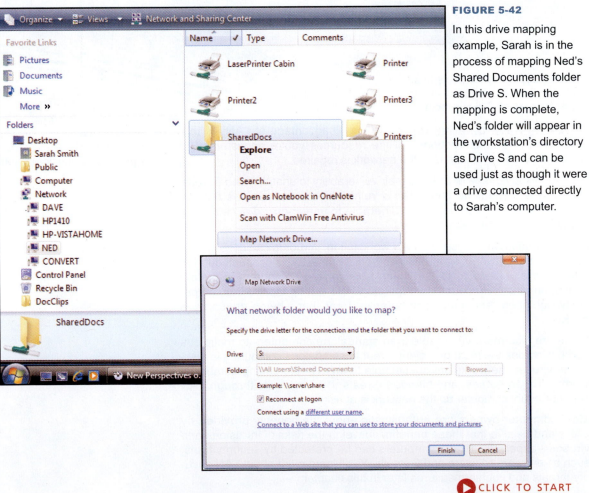

FIGURE 5-42

In this drive mapping example, Sarah is in the process of mapping Ned's Shared Documents folder as Drive S. When the mapping is complete, Ned's folder will appear in the workstation's directory as Drive S and can be used just as though it were a drive connected directly to Sarah's computer.

● CLICK TO START

How do I specify which resources can be shared by other workstations? If your computer is part of a network, you can typically specify which of your drives and folders can be accessed from other network workstations. For security reasons, however, it is not advisable to allow shared access to the root directory of drive C on your computer.

You can allow other network users to view and edit files in the folders you've designated as shared, or you can limit access only to viewing. Figure 5-43 explains how to use Windows Vista to designate a folder as shared.

FIGURE 5-43

To allow other network users to access files or folders on your Windows computer, you have to designate them as shared.

1. Right-click the file or folder you want to share, then select Share.

● CLICK TO START

2. Select who can access the shared files.

3. Decide if access is only for reading, or if access includes permission to modify and delete files.

What is a file server? A file server is a computer whose primary purpose is to be a repository for files that can be accessed by network workstations. A file server can reside on any personal computer. For example, you might designate one of your old desktop computers as a file server and use it to store lots of big video files that you don't want clogging up your local hard disk.

A file server connects to a LAN's router just like any other network device. You can also purchase a computing device advertised as a server. A server typically has no monitor or keyboard; its system unit contains a microprocessor, memory, high-capacity hard disk, and built-in network adapter. File servers are available as tower units or rack-mounted blade servers (Figure 5-44).

Are file servers a good idea for home networks? Whereas file servers are an essential component of most business networks, in many home networks, files are stored on workstations in shared folders rather than on a file server. A potential problem with this arrangement is that workstations must be turned on in order to access their files over a network. If you find yourself running all over the house turning on computers in order to find files, your network could be more effective with a file server. File servers are designed to run continuously day and night, so they are always on and their files are always accessible.

Another reason to consider a file server for a home network is backup. Rather than purchase external hard disk drives for each workstation's backup, one low-cost file server can supply enough space to back up files for several workstations.

Do file servers require any special setup? If you're using a file server without its own keyboard or monitor, its configuration software is accessible using a browser. To configure a file server, open a browser from any workstation, enter the file server's IP address, and provide the administrator ID and password.

SHARING PRINTERS

How can I set up a printer for network access? There are three ways to set up a printer so it can be accessed from any workstation. You can set up printer sharing using a workstation printer, set up printer sharing using a print server, or install a printer with built-in networking (Figure 5-45).

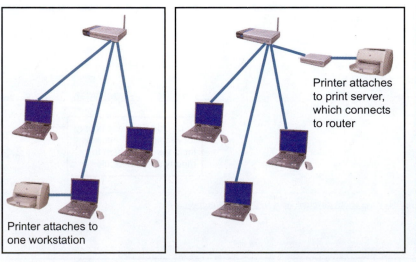

Printer attaches to print server, which connects to router

Printer attaches to one workstation

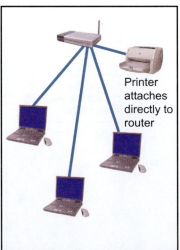

Printer attaches directly to router

How does printer sharing work? One way to share a printer over a network is to connect the printer to one of the workstations and then enable printer sharing. With printer sharing enabled, as long as the printer and workstation are turned on, any workstation on the network can send print jobs to the printer.

How do I enable printer sharing? If you're using Windows and you want to allow other users to share the printer that's attached to your workstation, access Printers from the Control Panel as shown in Figure 5-46.

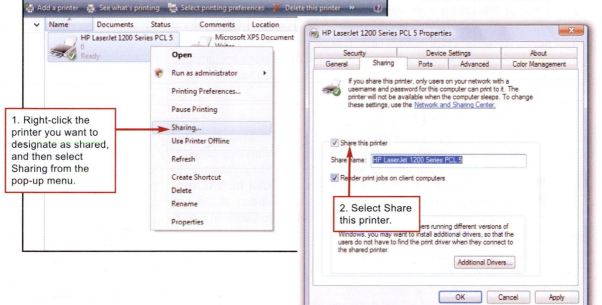

1. Right-click the printer you want to designate as shared, and then select Sharing from the pop-up menu.

2. Select Share this printer.

5

How do I send a print job to a shared printer? Before you can send a print job to a shared printer attached to someone else's workstation, you have to make sure that the printer driver is installed on your computer (Figure 5-47). Once you've added the printer to your list of printers and faxes, you can select the printer from your software's Print dialog box.

▶ CLICK TO START

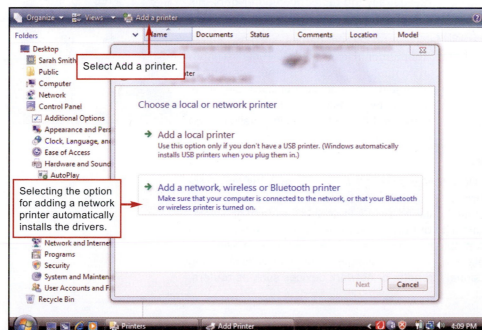

Select Add a printer.

Selecting the option for adding a network printer automatically installs the drivers.

Can I set up a shared printer without tying up a workstation?
You can use a network print server device to take the place of a workstation-controlled printer. By attaching a print server to a standard printer, you can access the printer from the network without going through a workstation. Print servers are available for wireless or wired networks. To set up a print server, connect it to the printer's USB port and access the configuration settings using your browser. Once the print server is configured, you can send print jobs to it using the same steps as for a shared printer.

What about attaching a printer directly to the network? A printer with built-in networking does not have to be attached to a workstation or a print server because it has its own NIC. This type of printer typically connects to the network hub or router using a cable or wireless transmitter. Once configured, print jobs are sent to it just as with shared printers.

LAN PARTIES

What is a LAN party? A **LAN party** is a gathering of people who connect their own computers to a LAN, usually to play multiplayer computer games. LAN parties can take place in private homes, community centers, or other venues. Most private LAN parties max out at 12 or so attendees. Commercialized LAN parties are sponsored by computer hardware or software companies and can sometimes involve hundreds of players (Figure 5-48). LANs can also be used for Xbox System Links, in which players link their Xboxes to a LAN for gaming.

FIGURE 5-48

LANs aren't just for business use!

Do LAN parties require special hardware? Small LAN parties can use just about any wired or wireless LAN. Attendees usually bring their own computer, keyboard, monitor, mouse, headphones, surge strip, and network cables. The host of a LAN party usually supplies the basic network infrastructure including hubs and routers. The host should also make a few calculations ahead of time to ensure that the party venue has adequate power to prevent circuits from popping. The LAN party host might also provide a computer that is used as a dedicated application server that coordinates game play. However, the game server can run on one of the player's computers—usually the fastest computer gets this honor.

What about software? Multiplayer computer games, such as Quake, Doom, Counter-Strike, Unreal Tournament, and Battlefield 1942 are popular at LAN parties. Players can compete against each other, team up to play against other teams, or play against the game's artificial intelligence. Each player should have the game software installed and a unique validation key to a legal copy of the software. LAN parties are not a valid reason to pirate software.

TROUBLESHOOTING

What if my network stops working? Network problems can stem from a variety of sources. Symptoms of network malfunctions are slow response time, intermittent outages, failure to access files from one workstation, and non-availability of network services to all workstations. To troubleshoot network problems, you have to consider the possibility of a problem with a workstation's hardware or settings; network links including cables and wireless signal strength; or network devices such as routers, servers, or NICs.

Cables. Make sure all network cables are firmly connected (Figure 5-49). If only one workstation is not accessing the network, you can try swapping cables with another workstation.

Signal strength. In a wireless network, check the signal strength. If the signal is weak, move the workstation closer to the access point, if possible.

Security. Make sure you are using the correct password and that your password has not expired.

Interference. If you have intermittent network outages, look for sources of interference, such as cordless phones, baby monitors, or construction equipment.

Network devices. Make sure your network hub, switch, router, or wireless access point is plugged in and functioning properly. Check the activity lights.

Settings. Make sure the network is enabled and then use Control Panel to check the drivers for your network equipment.

FIGURE 5-49

Windows can help you troubleshoot network problems.

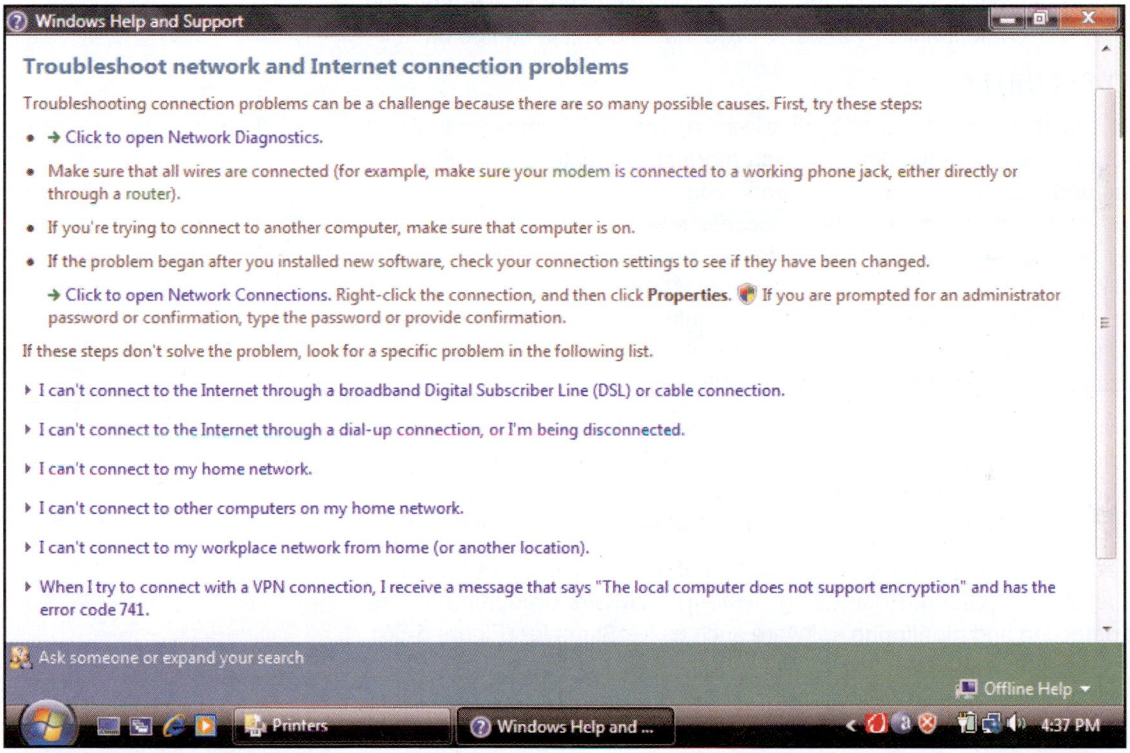

Troubleshoot network and Internet connection problems

Troubleshooting connection problems can be a challenge because there are so many possible causes. First, try these steps:

- → Click to open Network Diagnostics.
- Make sure that all wires are connected (for example, make sure your modem is connected to a working phone jack, either directly or through a router).
- If you're trying to connect to another computer, make sure that computer is on.
- If the problem began after you installed new software, check your connection settings to see if they have been changed.
  → Click to open Network Connections. Right-click the connection, and then click **Properties**. If you are prompted for an administrator password or confirmation, type the password or provide confirmation.

If these steps don't solve the problem, look for a specific problem in the following list.

▸ I can't connect to the Internet through a broadband Digital Subscriber Line (DSL) or cable connection.

▸ I can't connect to the Internet through a dial-up connection, or I'm being disconnected.

▸ I can't connect to my home network.

▸ I can't connect to other computers on my home network.

▸ I can't connect to my workplace network from home (or another location).

▸ When I try to connect with a VPN connection, I receive a message that says "The local computer does not support encryption" and has the error code 741.

QuickCheck

SECTION D

1. Networks offer shared [_____], such as printers, software applications, and storage space.

2. For security reasons it is not advisable to allow shared access to the [_____] directory of your C: drive.

3. Before you can send a print job to a shared printer attached to someone else's workstation,

you have to make sure that the printer [_____] is installed on your computer.

4. A(n) [_____] server is a computer whose primary purpose is to be a repository for files that can be accessed by network workstations.

5. A(n) [_____] server can be connected to a LAN to run software for workstations or coordinate game play for a LAN party.

● CHECK ANSWERS

Security Through Encryption

LOCAL AREA NETWORKS are susceptible to a variety of threats. Many threats can be handled using techniques for standalone computers. Network equipment should be connected to power strips to prevent damage from power spikes. Data should be backed up in case of a hard drive failure. Workstations should be protected by antivirus software, and passwords should be required for network access. Wireless networks also should be protected by the use of encryption. In Section E you'll learn how to enable encryption on a wireless network, you'll find out how encryption works, and become familiar with other ways that encryption can be useful.

WI-FI SECURITY

What are the threats to my wireless network? Compared to wired networks, wireless networks are much more susceptible to unauthorized access and use. To join a wired network, you have to gain physical access to the router and plug in a cable. To access many wireless networks, you simply boot up a wireless-enabled device such as a notebook computer within range of the wireless router. One threat to wireless network users is called an "evil twin." Users think they are logging onto a legitimate network, but its signals are being jammed by hackers who can extract passwords and credit card information from unsuspecting users.

With wireless network data floating freely through the air, hackers have an easy time intercepting signals by cruising through a business district or neighborhood with a Wi-Fi enabled notebook computer, a practice called **LAN jacking** or war driving ("war" stands for wireless access revolution).

LAN jackers can pinpoint the exact location of a wireless access point with the use of GPS (Global Positioning System) receivers or legitimate network-detecting and monitoring software such as NetStumbler (Figure 5-50).

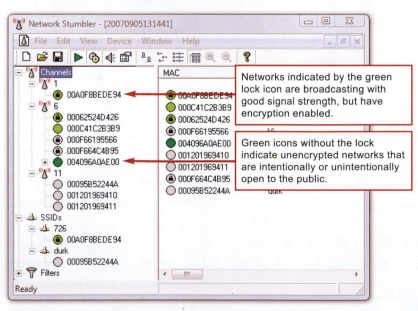

FIGURE 5-50

Software tools such as NetStumbler help locate and identify secured and unsecured networks. Once logged on to an unsecured wireless network, LAN jackers are free to do anything from stealing the network owner's credit card or bank information to attacking computers in other networks.

An offshoot of war driving is a gambit called **war chalking**. When wireless snoops find an unsecured network, they write specific symbols on walls, sidewalks, or lampposts to signal other wireless network seekers that they can tap into a wireless network in the area (Figure 5-51). War chalking is based on a convention established by hobos during the 1930's Great Depression. To help other vagabonds, hobos marked streets and homes with chalk symbols to indicate the best places for getting free handouts.

FIGURE 5-51

Warchalking identifies wireless networks. Open nodes are unsecured, closed nodes are well secured, WEP nodes are protected, but by easy-to-bypass security.

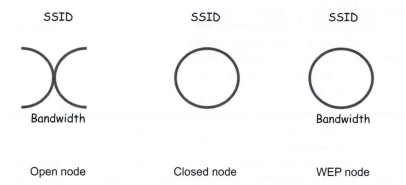

SSID	SSID	SSID
Bandwidth		Bandwidth
Open node	Closed node	WEP node

How can I secure my wireless network? Preventing Wi-Fi signal interception is difficult, but encrypting transmitted data makes it useless to intruders. **Wireless encryption** scrambles the data transmitted between wireless devices and then unscrambles the data only on devices that have a valid encryption key. Several types of encryption are available; some are more effective than others. You'll learn how encryption works later in the chapter.

What are the types of wireless encryption? The original wireless encryption was called **WEP** (Wired Equivalent Privacy) because it was designed to provide a level of confidentiality similar to that of a wired network. The original version of WEP is very easy to bypass. A second version of WEP uses stronger encryption but has several flaws that can easily be exploited by hackers.

WPA (Wi-Fi Protected Access) addresses some of WEP's weaknesses. It can encrypt data based on the user's password and implements message integrity checking, making sure that packets have not been intercepted or tampered with in any way. In contrast to WEP and WPA, much better security is offered by **WPA2**, which uses the same kind of strong encryption required by government agencies and businesses.

Which type of encryption should I use? All devices on a network must use the same type of encryption. If you have even one device on your network that only supports WEP, for example, you will have to use WEP for the entire network. Although WEP is fairly easy for hackers to neutralize, it is better than leaving a network totally unprotected. WEP can discourage casual hackers and keep your neighbors out of your files if the range of your networks overlap.

The best type of encryption is WPA2, so use it if all the devices on your network support it. Certified Wi-Fi devices manufactured after March 2006 must support WPA2. Devices manufactured before that date might support only WEP or WPA. The Wi-Fi Alliance Web site provides a list of WPA and WPA2 certified products. If you have older equipment in your network, you might want to phase out the older devices so that you can upgrade your encryption to WPA2.

5

How do I activate encryption? To activate encryption for your wireless network open the router's configuration software. Earlier in the chapter you learned that most wireless routers can be configured by opening a browser and entering the router's IP number. Use the router configuration utilities to select WEP, WPA, or WPA2. In addition, you must create a wireless network key.

A **wireless network key** (sometimes referred to as a network security key) is the basis for scrambling and unscrambling the data transmitted between wireless devices. The key is similar to a password, only it is often longer. Instructions for creating a valid key are usually given in the router's documentation or on-screen Help file. For example, you might be limited to using only numbers 0-9 and letters A-F. Alternatively, you might be allowed to use a passphrase, such as notrespassingthismeansu, as the key.

Don't use a key or passphrase that's easy for an intruder to guess. Remember the key or passphrase you use to configure the router. Later, when you set up computers and other network devices, you will enter the same key so that every device on your network can encrypt and decrypt the data flowing on the network. Figure 5-52 illustrates how to activate wireless encryption.

FIGURE 5-52

The configuration utility used to set up wireless security is supplied by the router manufacturer. In this example security is being configured for a Linksys router.

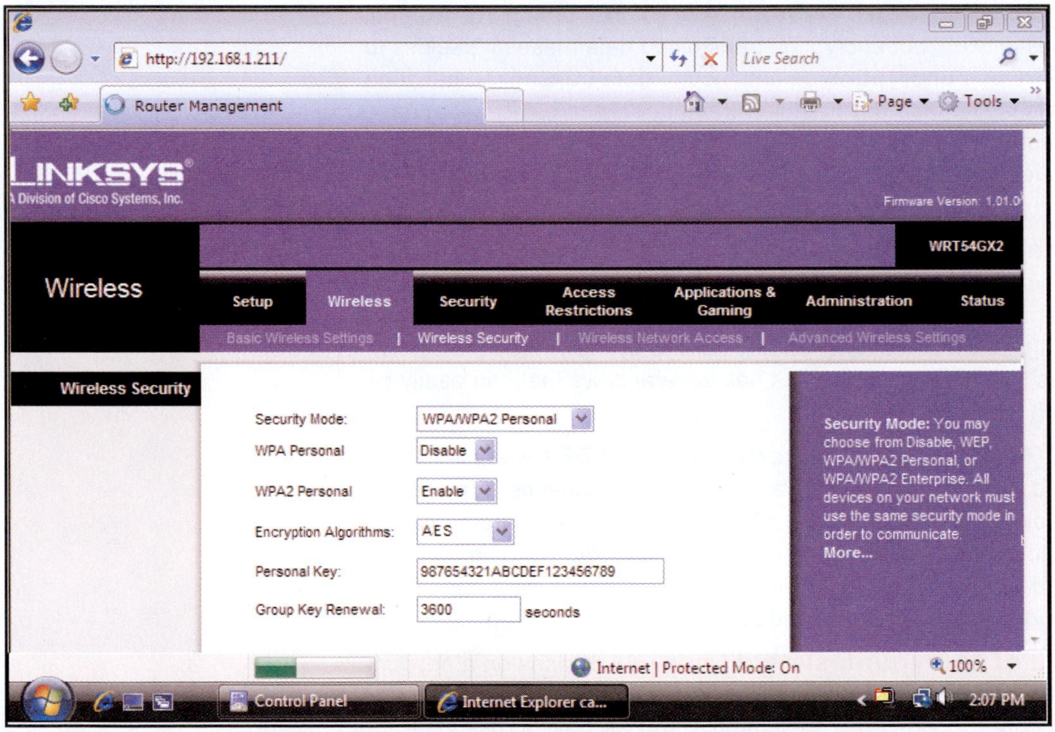

Do I need a wireless network key for other networks I use?

Many wireless networks are not encrypted and are open to the public. You'll find these networks in coffee shops, hotels, and airports. Other networks are available for public use, but are encrypted. To join your computer, PDA, or iPhone to an encrypted wireless hotspot on campus or at a friend's house, for example, you have to enter a wireless network key. When your computer is within range of an encrypted network, a network dialog box opens and prompts you to type the security key. Ask the person in charge of the network for the key or "network password." After you enter the key, your computer can transmit and receive data over the network. Your network software stores the key, too, so that in the future you can connect without re-entering it.

ENCRYPTION

Exactly what is encryption? **Encryption** transforms a message in such a way that its contents are hidden from unauthorized readers. Encryption is designed to keep messages secret. In the context of computing, encryption can be used in many ways, including the following.

- Scrambling data sent over wired or wireless networks to prevent intrusions

- Securing credit card numbers and other personal information transferred from shoppers' computers to e-commerce sites

- Encrypting computer archives so that data they contain is unusable if the the archive is lost or compromised

- Scrambling the contents of e-mail messages to maintain privacy

How does encryption work? An original message—one that has not yet been encrypted—is referred to as **plaintext** or cleartext. An encrypted message is referred to as **ciphertext**. The process of converting plaintext into ciphertext is called encryption. The reverse process—converting ciphertext into plaintext—is called **decryption**.

Messages are encrypted by using a cryptographic algorithm and key. A **cryptographic algorithm** is a procedure for encrypting or decrypting a message. A **cryptographic key** (usually just called a key) is a word, number, or phrase that must be known to encrypt or decrypt a message.

For example, Julius Caesar made extensive use of an encryption method called simple substitution, which could have been used to turn the plaintext message "Do not trust Brutus" into GRQRWWUXVWEUXWXV. The cryptographic algorithm was to offset the letters of the alphabet. The key was 3 (Figure 5-53).

FIGURE 5-53

The algorithm for Caesar's encryption technique was to offset the letters of the alphabet—in this case by three letters. A simple transformation table was used to encrypt or decrypt a message. For example, if a "G" appears in the encrypted message, it would be a "D" in the original unencrypted message.

5

Ciphertext letters:

D E F **G** H I J K L M N O P Q R S T U V W X Y Z A B C

Equivalent plaintext letters:

A B C **D** E F G H I J K L M N O P Q R S T U V W X Y Z

What's the difference between strong and weak encryption?

Caesar's simple substitution key is an example of **weak encryption** because it is easy to decrypt even without the algorithm and key. Unauthorized decryption is sometimes referred to as breaking or cracking a code. You could crack Caesar's code in several ways. For example, you could discover the key by making 25 different transformation tables, each with a different offset (assuming that the encryption method uses the letters of the alphabet in sequence and not at random). You could also analyze the frequency with which letters appear—in English documents, E, T, A, O, and N appear most frequently—and you can piece together the message by guessing the remaining letters.

Strong encryption is loosely defined as "very difficult to break." **AES** (Advanced Encryption Standard), the technology used for WPA2, is one of the strongest cryptographic algorithms. With continuous advances in technology, however, strong encryption is a moving target. Several encryption methods that were considered impossible to break 10 years ago have recently been cracked.

How long does it take to break strong encryption?
Encryption methods can be broken by the use of expensive, specialized, code-breaking computers. The cost of these machines is substantial, but not beyond the reach of government agencies, major corporations, and organized crime. Encryption methods can also be broken by standard computer hardware—supercomputers, mainframes, workstations, and even personal computers. These computers typically break codes using a brute force attack, which consists of trying all possible keys (Figure 5-54).

The length of a computer-readable encryption key is measured in bits. A 32-bit key, for example, could be one of 4.2 billion (2^{32}) numbers. Surprisingly, it would be possible to try all these numbers and discover the key in less than a day by using an average personal computer.

To discover a 40-bit key, you would have to try about 1 trillion possible combinations—a week's worth of processing time on a personal computer. 56-bit and 64-bit encryption—once thought to be unbreakable by any computer in the private sector—require a lot of computing power, but have been broken by combining the power of many personal computers connected over the Internet. 128-bit encryption and 256-bit encryption are probably secure for several years. Most encryption today uses a 128-bit key.

Another way to understand how the length of a key affects the strength of encryption is to consider this guideline: Beginning with a 40-bit key, each additional bit doubles the time it would take to discover the key. If a personal computer takes one week to crack a 40-bit key, it takes two weeks to crack a 41-bit key, four weeks to crack a 42-bit key, and eight weeks to crack a 43-bit key. A 128-bit key takes $2^{(128-40)}$ times longer to crack than a 40-bit key—that's 309,485,009,821,345,068,724,781,056 times longer!

What's public key encryption?
Caesar's encryption method is an example of **symmetric key encryption** in which the key used to encrypt a message is also used to decrypt the message. Symmetric key encryption is used to encrypt stationary data, such as corporate financial records. It is also used to encrypt the data that travels over wireless LANs.

Symmetric keys are not practical for e-mail and other situations in which the person receiving encrypted data does not have the key beforehand. E-mailing the key would be a major security problem because of the potential for a hacker to intercept it.

Public key encryption (PKE) eliminates the key-distribution problem, by using one key to encrypt a message, but another key to decrypt the message. Figure 5-55 illustrates how public key encryption works.

FIGURE 5-54

To discover a 4-digit PIN by brute force, a criminal must try, at most, 10,000 possibilities. Finding the key to computer data encrypted using a 32-bit key would involve about 4.2 billion possibilities.

FIGURE 5-55

Public key encryption uses two keys. A public key is used to encrypt a message. A private key is used to decrypt the message.

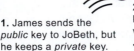

1. James sends the *public* key to JoBeth, but he keeps a *private* key.

2. JoBeth uses the public key to encrypt a message, which she sends back to James.

4. James can decrypt the message using his private key.

3. If the message and public key are intercepted by Draco, he cannot decrypt the message because he does not have the private key.

Public key encryption is a crucial technology for e-commerce and e-mail. When you use a secure connection to transmit a credit card number, the server sends a public key to your browser. Your browser uses this public key to encrypt the credit card number. After it is encrypted, no one—not even you—can use the public key to decrypt the message. The encrypted message is sent to a Web server, where the private key is used to decrypt it.

When personal computer users want to encrypt e-mail or other documents, they turn to public key encryption software called **PGP** (Pretty Good Privacy) software. When you first use PGP, the software generates a private key and a public key. You must keep your private key hidden. You e-mail the public key to the people you have authorized to send encrypted messages to you.

The people who receive your public key can store it in their PGP programs, which they then use to encrypt messages. When they send these messages to you, you can decrypt them using your private key. PGP software is available as a free download from several Web sites. Figure 5-56 contains an example of a public key generated by PGP.

INFOWEBLINKS

For additional resources on using ciphertext to protect data, including PGP software that you can use on your PC, connect to the **Encryption InfoWeb**.

 CLICK TO CONNECT
www.course.com/np/concepts11/ch05

```
-----BEGIN PGP PUBLIC KEY BLOCK-----

Version: 5.0

mQCNAi44C30AAAEEAL1r6BylvuSAvOKIk9ze9yCK+ZPPbRZrpXIRFBb
e+U8dGPMb9XdJS4L/cy1fXr9R9j4EfFsK/rgHV6i2rE83LjWrmsDPRPSaiz
z+EQTIZi4AN99jiBomfLLZyUzmHMoUoE4shrYgOnkc0u101ikhieAFje77j
/F3596pT6nCx/9/AAURtCRBbmRyZSBCYBNhcmQgPGFiYWNhcmRAd2
VsbC5zZi5jYS51cz6JAFUCBRAuOA6O7zYZz1mqos8BAXr9AgCxCu8C
wGZRdpfSs65r6mb4MccXvvfxO4TmPi1DKQj2FYHYjwYONk8vzA7XnE5
aJmk5J/dChdvfIU7NvVifV6of=GQv9

-----END PGP PUBLIC KEY BLOCK-----
```

FIGURE 5-56

PGP software generates a huge public key. Each person's public key is unique. You can e-mail this key to anyone who might want to send you an encrypted message.

QuickCheck

SECTION E

1. The original encryption method used for wireless networks was called [_____], but for the most secure wireless encryption you should use [_____].

2. [_____] key encryption uses the same key to encrypt a message as it does to decrypt the message.

3. [_____] key encryption uses one key to encrypt a message, but another key to decrypt the message.

4. [_____] is public key encryption software that is popular with personal computer owners who want to encrypt e-mail and data files. (Hint: Use the acronym.)

 CHECK ANSWERS

Who's Stealing My Signals?

A FLORIDA MAN WAS ARRESTED and charged with unauthorized access to a computer network, a crime that's a third-degree felony and carries punishment ranging from probation to five years in prison. The accused man was allegedly piggybacking on his neighbor's wireless network to access the Internet. It was one of the first cases of its kind in the United States.

Reporters and bloggers monitoring the case reported that the fault might actually rest with the network's owner who failed to implement wireless security. An especially aggressive posting on one blog also suggested that the network equipment manufacturer could be at fault for not enabling encryption as the default security setting.

With the proliferation of home, school, and corporate wireless networks, hackers are expected to increasingly capitalize on unprotected household wireless systems to download child pornography, send threatening e-mails, and steal financial information. But what about casual interlopers who just want to borrow a little bandwidth from time to time?

One tech-savvy reporter relates that "on a trip to Colorado a fellow skier told me that although the hotel we were both staying at did not have a wireless network, an apartment complex down the street did. So I sat on their doorstep in the freezing cold to check e-mail with my laptop." He then wonders wryly if he should have rung the bell and asked if he could "please use their Wi-Fi."

Free wireless access is not unusual. Free community wireless access is offered in cities as diverse as San Francisco, Miami, New York, Prague, and Amsterdam. You can find it in airports, hotels, and coffee shops. Free wireless access is also offered by rogue WLANs operated by public spirited individuals who are more than willing to share their bandwidth with passersby. Rogue WLAN operators typically subscribe to a high-speed Internet access service. They pay their monthly fees, but instead of limiting access to their own personal use, they distribute their connections over wireless LANs to friends, neighbors, and just about anyone who passes by with the right computer equipment.

Setting up a Wi-Fi antenna is simple and inexpensive. A basic Wi-Fi antenna can be created with a few wires and an empty Pringles container. Fancier antennas require a ravioli can—really!

The 802.11 standard uses an unlicensed telecommunications spectrum, so it is perfectly legal to set up an antenna to transmit and receive Wi-Fi signals without obtaining a broadcast license. FCC regulations even prohibit landlords from limiting tenant use of or access to wireless networks. For example, network administrators at the University of Texas at Dallas attempted to prohibit students from installing private wireless access points in their dorm rooms because the signals interfered with access to the campus-wide wireless network. The university reversed its policy after reviewing FCC regulations.

Some free WLAN advocates envision a nationwide web of interconnected Wi-Fi networks that will form "a seamless broadband network built by the people, for the people." In this vision of a world connected by free WLANs, libraries can offer Internet access to people in low-income neighborhoods. Local schools could get wired without exorbitant cabling expenses. Parents, kids, and grandparents, as well as corporate executives, could exchange e-mail and instant messages from locations that include the kitchen table, the corner coffee shop, and the Little League field.

But some broadband providers, such as AT&T and Comcast, fear that every user of a free wireless network is one less paying customer. According to one industry analyst, "The telecom industries are addicted to the one-wire, one-customer philosophy." Sharing an Internet connection that is intended for single-user access does not coexist with this philosophy. Most subscriber agreements contain wording that limits use of a broadband connection to one user and perhaps immediate family members. Although wording varies from one provider to another, most agreements expressly prohibit subscribers from using their connections for commercial purposes. Some free WLAN operators don't believe that sharing is commercial use. "I'm sharing it with people," says one free WLAN provider, "I'm not selling it. I'm not making a profit off it."

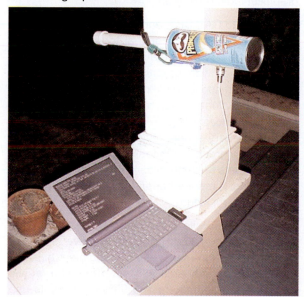

Whether or not free WLANs are legal, their benefits are tempered by several potentially negative repercussions. For example, tightening up subscriber agreements to eliminate the sharing loophole could affect many broadband subscribers who currently operate private wired or wireless networks that link several computers to a single Internet connection. Broadband providers could force private network

operators to purchase more expensive multiuser licenses—an option that might be too expensive for many home networks.

The wisdom of unregulated network availability is called into question by the proliferation of free WLANs. A publicly accessible LAN that requires no passwords or accounts can be used anonymously for a variety of illegal and dangerous activities. Like drug dealers who use public telephones to avoid taps and traces, terrorists and other criminals can simply walk into a free WLAN zone, tap into the Internet, and walk away without leaving a trace.

Widespread distribution of free WLANs can reduce the bandwidth available to paying customers. If your neighbor sets up a free WLAN that becomes popular with customers in a nearby coffee house, your previously sedate network neighborhood might suddenly become an overcrowded metropolis with major Internet access traffic jams.

Despite possible repercussions, the free WLAN movement appears to be growing and becoming more controversial. Some industry analysts expect a battle similar to the one that ensued when Napster's peer-to-peer music-sharing network was attacked by the music industry. The free WLAN controversy could pit a group of telecommunications giants against a rag-tag alliance of free WLAN advocates. The outcome has the potential to affect broadband subscribers everywhere.

5

INFOWEBLINKS

The **Free WLAN InfoWeb** provides more details about Wi-Fi technology and renegade LANs.

W CLICK TO CONNECT
www.course.com/np/concepts11/ch05

What Do You Think?

ISSUE

1. Have you ever accessed a free WLAN?

  ◯ Yes   ◯ No   ◯ Not sure

2. Do you believe that rogue WLANs can survive alongside for-profit broadband ISPs?

  ◯ Yes   ◯ No   ◯ Not sure

3. Are broadband providers justified in limiting the terms of their service agreements to "one subscription, one customer"?

  ◯ Yes   ◯ No   ◯ Not sure

▶ SAVE RESPONSES

COMPUTERS IN CONTEXT
Education

THE FIRST EDUCATIONAL application of computers emerged in the 1960s, when huge mainframes with clunky interfaces introduced students to computer-aided instruction (CAI). Based on operant conditioning research by B. F. Skinner and Ivan Pavlov—remember dogs salivating when a bell rings?—CAI uses basic drill and practice: The computer presents a problem, the student responds, and the computer evaluates the response. Studies in the 1970s indicated that CAI systems, such as PLATO (Programmed Logic for Automated Teaching Operations), improved student test scores, but students found the mainframe's monochrome display and the CAI's regimented drill format boring. Recent incarnations of CAI, such as an alien-invader style elementary math program, use snazzy graphics and arcade formats to grab learners' attention.

Educators looking for ways to harness computers' interactive and programmable nature arrived at the idea of computer-based training (CBT). CBT is formatted as a series of tutorials, beginning with a pretest to see whether students have the prerequisite skills and ending with a CAI-style drill and practice test to determine whether students can move on to the next tutorial segment. Today, CBT is a popular approach to learning how to use computer software.

Another educational approach, called computer-aided learning (CAL), uses the computer more as a source of information than an assessment mechanism. Students using CAL make decisions about their level of expertise, what material is relevant, and how to pace their own learning. Exploratory CAL environments include Seymour Papert's Logo programming language; students can investigate geometry concepts by using Logo to program a graphical turtle on-screen.

In addition to CAI, CBT, and CAL, simulations have become a popular educational tool. The computer mimics a real-world situation through a narrative description or with graphics. Students are given options and respond with a decision or an action. The computer evaluates each response and determines its consequences. Oregon Trail, a simulation popular with elementary school students, describes events that beset a group of pioneers traveling in a wagon train. Students respond to each event, while learning bits of history, money-handling skills, conservation, and decision making.

Most educators believe that computers can help create an individualized and interactive learning environment, which can make learning more effective and efficient. Although 99% of American public schools have computers and 93% of students use them in some way, these statistics can be deceiving. The reality falls far short of the ideal situation—every student having access to a computer throughout the school day.

The challenge is to figure out how to achieve the computers' potential in an educational setting when supplying computers for every student is often cost prohibitive. Compromise solutions have been tried with varying degrees of success. Some schools have installed learning labs where students go for scheduled lab time. In elementary schools, often a few computers are placed in special work areas of classrooms and used for small group projects or individual drill and practice. Some schools have relegated most computers to the library, where they are connected to the Internet and used for research. In some classrooms, a single computer can be used as an effective presentation device.

A few schools without the budget for enough desktop computers have opted for inexpensive PDAs instead. "Students need to use technology just as you and I do, not just one hour a day," says one teacher in support of PDAs. Students use standard PDA software for educational tasks: tracking nutritional intake for health class, collecting data from experiments in biology class, graphing functions in math class, translating phrases for French class, and maintaining to-do lists. The biggest drawback to more widespread educational use of PDAs, however, is a lack of software specifically designed for education.

As another option, some schools—primarily colleges—have confronted the problem of computer access by requiring all incoming first-year students to purchase notebook computers. Many colleges, for example, provide Internet connections in dorm rooms and library study carrels or offer campuswide Wi-Fi service. Students can tote their notebook computers to class and take notes. They can contact instructors via e-mail, use the Internet as a research resource, and run educational software.

Another educational use of computers can be seen in distance education (DE) courses (also called distance learning). Historically, distance education meant correspondence study or courses delivered by radio or television, but the meaning has been broadened to encompass any educational situation in which students and instructors aren't in the same place. Therefore, most DE courses today require students to have access to a computer and an Internet connection. DE courses are offered to K-12 students, college students, military personnel, business people, and the general public.

Most students who choose DE courses do so because they want to learn at their own pace, at a convenient time, and in a location close to home. Single parents who must deal with the realities of child care, working professionals who cannot relocate to a college town, and physically disabled students find distance education handy. Distance education has the potential of increasing the pool of students for a course by making it financially feasible; for example, an advanced Kanji course could be offered at a midwestern university with only 10 on-campus Japanese majors if enough distance education students can boost enrollment.

The Internet hosts a wide variety of DE courses, both credit-earning and noncredit courses. Several course management systems (CMSs), such as Blackboard and Moodle, help teachers prepare and manage DE courses. These systems are popular with degree-granting institutions that offer credit-earning DE courses in their course catalogs (subject to the usual course fees and requirements).

Course management software typically runs from a server maintained by a school system, college, or university. Using Web browsers, teachers access the CMS to post an online syllabus, develop Web pages with course content, create a database of questions for online assessment, manage e-mail, set up online discussion groups, and maintain a gradebook. Students using Internet-connected computers and standard Web browsers can access course materials, submit assignments, interact with other students, and take tests.

Computers and the Internet have opened opportunities for lifelong learning. Prospective students can use a search engine to easily find non-credit courses and tutorials for a wide range of topics, including pottery, dog grooming, radio astronomy, desktop publishing, and drumming. Some tutorials are free, and others charge a small fee. Several Web sites, such as Virtual University and OnlineLearning.com, offer a good choice of fee-based or free courses. In a society that promotes learning as a lifelong endeavor, the Internet has certainly made it possible for students of all ages to pursue knowledge and skills simply by using a computer and an Internet connection.

INFOWEBLINKS

You'll find lots more information related to this Computers in Context topic at the **Computers and Education InfoWeb**.

CLICK TO CONNECT
www.course.com/np/concepts11/ch05

New Perspectives Labs

On the BookOnCD

To access the New Perspectives labs for Chapter 5, start the BookOnCD, BookOnFlashDrive, or other NP11 BookOn product and then click the icon next to the lab title below.

▶ **LOCAL AREA NETWORKS**

IN THIS LAB YOU'LL LEARN:

- The basic technology specifications for Ethernet and Wi-Fi networks
- To identify the parts of a router
- How to open the router configuration utility
- How to change a router's default password
- How to create an SSID
- The advantages and disadvantages of WEP, WPA, and WPA2 encryption
- How to enable wireless encryption
- How to determine a computer's wired or wireless networking capability
- How to connect a LAN to the Internet
- How to make sure a router is configured for DHCP

LAB ASSIGNMENTS

1. Start the interactive part of the lab. Perform each lab step as directed, and answer all the lab QuickCheck questions.

2. Use your computer's networking utilities to find out if your computer is LAN and/or WLAN ready. Make a note of the type and specifications of any network adapters installed in your computer.

3. Using the information you gathered from assignment 2, draw a sketch showing how your computer could be linked into a LAN.

4. Examine the networking utilities installed on your computer. If you are using Windows, you might find utilities such as Network Connections, Wireless Network Setup Wizard, and others. Look at each utility and write a one-paragraph description for each utility.

Key Terms

Make sure you understand all the boldfaced key terms presented in this chapter. If you're using the NP11 BookOnCD, BookOnFlashDrive, or other NP11 BookOn product, you can use this list of terms as an interactive study activity. First, try to define a term in your own words, and then click the term to compare your definition with the definition presented in the chapter.

5

Interactive Summary

To review important concepts from this chapter, fill in the blanks to best complete each sentence. When using the NP11 BookOnCD or other BookOn product, click the Check Answers buttons to automatically score your answers.

SECTION A: Networks can be classified by geographical scope as PANs, [   ], MANs, NANs, and WANs. LAN technologies are standardized by the [   ] organization. Each connection point on a network is referred to as a [   ] and can contain computers, networked [   ], or network devices. Computers connected to a network require network circuitry, often housed on a network [   ] card (NIC). Networks that include one or more servers can operate in [   ] /server mode or peer-to-peer mode.

Networks without a server typically operate in peer-to-peer mode. Physical network topologies include star, bus, [   ], mesh, and tree. Network nodes are linked by communications channels. High bandwidth channels are referred to as [   ], whereas low bandwidth channels are referred to as [   ]. Communications [   ], such as TCP/IP, divide messages into [   ], handle addressing, and manage routing.

▶ CHECK ANSWERS

SECTION B: Wired networks are fast, secure, and simple to configure. HomePNA networks transport data over [   ] wiring and HomePlug networks transport data over [   ] wiring. Ethernet networks use CAT5 or CAT6 wiring with plastic [   ] connectors. Ethernet uses CSMA/CD protocol to detect [   ]. [   ] Ethernet operates at 100 Mbps, whereas Gigabit Ethernet operates at [   ] Mbps. Ethernet is usually wired in a [   ] topology to a central device. A network [   ] is a device that accepts data from one workstation and broadcasts it to all of the other network nodes. A network [   ] is a more sophisticated connection device that sends data only to the devices specified as the destination. A network [   ] is a network device that can ship data from one network to another. You typically use your [   ] software to access the router's configuration utilities.

▶ CHECK ANSWERS

SECTION C: Most wireless LANs transport data using [_____] frequency signals. The most popular WLAN technology is Wi-Fi, but [_____] is used for PANs and other short-range connections. Wi-Fi is defined by the IEEE [_____] standards, and there are versions denoted by the letters a, b, g, and n. Computers on a Wi-Fi network must have wireless circuitry, such as a Wi-Fi adapter. Wireless networks can be set up as a wireless [_____] network in which devices broadcast directly to each other, or as a wireless [_____] network that uses a centralized broadcasting device, such as a wireless [_____] point or a wireless router. When setting up a wireless network it is important to change the default router password, create an [_____] to uniquely identify the network, and enable wireless encryption for security.

▶ CHECK ANSWERS

SECTION D: LANs allow people to share network resources, such as files, printers, and Internet connections. Unfortunately, LANs are vulnerable to unauthorized access and malware. To view the files stored on other network workstations, you can use a technique called drive [_____] that assigns a drive letter and displays a remote drive's contents. Under Windows, you can designate folders and printers as [_____] if you want to allow other workstations to access them. If you have many files that need to be accessed from various workstations, you might want to add a [_____] server to the network. If you would like everyone on a network to have access to a printer, but you prefer not to send print jobs through any of the workstations, you can add a [_____] server or attach a network-ready printer directly to the router. When using a network for a LAN party, usually one of the computers will be used as an [_____] server to coordinate game play. Network problems can stem from a variety of sources. Symptoms of network malfunctions are slow response time, intermittent outages, failure to access files from one workstation, and non-availability of network services to all workstations. To troubleshoot network problems, you have to consider the possibility of a problem with a workstation's hardware or settings; network links including cables and wireless signal strength; or network devices such as routers, servers, or NICs.

▶ CHECK ANSWERS

SECTION E: Compared to wired networks, wireless networks are much more susceptible to unauthorized access and use. Hackers have an easy time intercepting signals by cruising through a business district or neighborhood with a Wi-Fi enabled notebook computer, a practice called LAN [_____]. Preventing Wi-Fi signal interception is difficult, but wireless [_____] scrambles transmitted data and makes it useless to intruders. Originally, wireless networks were secured with [_____], but it proved too easy to crack. Much better security is offered by WPA and WPA2. An original message—one that has not yet been encrypted—is referred to as [_____] or cleartext. An encrypted message is referred to as [_____]. Messages are encrypted by a cryptographic [_____], which is a specific procedure for encrypting or decrypting a message. A cryptographic [_____] is a word, number, or phrase that must be known to encrypt or decrypt a message. [_____] key encryption uses the same key to encrypt and decrypt a message. [_____] key encryption eliminates the key-distribution problem, by using one key to encrypt a message, but another key is used to decrypt the message. The software for a popular implementation of public key encryption called Pretty [_____] Privacy can be downloaded from several Web sites and used to encrypt e-mail or other documents.

▶ CHECK ANSWERS

Interactive Situation Questions

Apply what you've learned to some typical computing situations. When using the NP11 BookOnCD, BookOnFlashDrive, or any other NP11 BookOn product, you can type your answers, and then use the Check Answers button to automatically score your responses.

1. You're installing a LAN and you decide to go with Ethernet. You'll typically use Cat5 or Cat6 cables to connect each workstation to a(n) _____.

2. You're setting up an Ethernet wired network using a router. To access the router and its configuration software, you open your _____ and type the router's IP address.

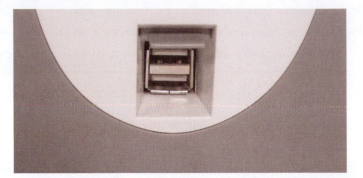

3. You're trying to figure out if your computer has a built-in Ethernet port. You see the port pictured to the right. Is that the port you should use for your RJ45 connector? _____

4. You install an 802.11b network, but it seems to stop working at various times. To begin troubleshooting, you look for any devices, such as cordless phones, that use the _____ GHz frequency.

5. Your PC is connected to a LAN, and you want to regularly access a file that's stored on one of the LAN workstations. You'd like to access that computer's hard disk as though it were connected to your own computer, so you decide to _____ the workstation's hard disk drive as drive F.

6. You arrive at work and one of your co-workers tells you that the router is down. Is it correct to surmise that your workstation will not be able to access other workstations, but will be able to access the Internet? Yes or no? _____

7. You're walking down the street in a large city and you spy a chalk circle on the sidewalk with "WEP" inside it. You realize that you're looking at an example of _____ chalking and there is probably a wireless LAN nearby.

8. You've set up a wireless network using some new equipment and a few old Wi-Fi cards given to you by your roommates. One of the cards is equipped only for WEP, whereas all the other cards support WPA2. Your roommate tells you that in order to use all the cards, you'll have to disable wireless encryption. Is your roommate right? _____

● CHECK ANSWERS

Interactive Practice Tests

Practice tests that consist of 10 multiple-choice, true/false, and fill-in-the-blank questions are available on both the NP11 BookOn products and the NP11 Web site. The questions are selected at random from a large test bank, so each time you take a test, you'll receive a different set of questions. Your tests are scored immediately, and you can print study guides that help you find the correct answers for any questions that you missed.

● CLICK TO START

Study Tips

Study Tips help you to organize and consolidate the information in a unit by making lists, outlines, charts, and sketches. You can use paper and pencil or word processing software to complete most of the Study Tip activities.

1. Make sure you can use your own words to correctly answer each of the red focus questions that appear throughout the chapter.

2. Make a list of the advantages and another list of the disadvantages of creating and using a computer network.

3. Describe the characteristics of PANs, NANs, LANS, MANs, and WANs, plus provide an example of each.

4. Create a list of network devices mentioned in this chapter. Write a brief description of each one, and indicate whether it would typically be part of the Internet, a LAN, or both.

5. Draw diagrams of star, ring, bus, mesh, and tree network topologies. Make sure that you can trace the route of data over an Ethernet. Discuss how collisions are detected and/or avoided.

6. Make a list of network cabling options and wireless options. Explain the advantages/disadvantages of each.

7. Explain the difference between an analog signal and a digital signal. Why do most modern communications systems use digital signals?

8. Draw a diagram of Shannon's communications model. Apply this model to a Wi-Fi LAN by indicating which real-world devices would exist at various points in the model to originate data, encode it, transmit signals, and so on.

9. Make a list of the LAN standards described in this chapter. For each one, indicate the type of technology it uses, its maximum speed, range, and the devices available to set up network communications.

10. Describe the differences between SSIDs, IP addresses, MAC addresses, and wireless network keys.

11. Make a list of security concerns that are related to local area networks.

12. Describe the steps that you would take to (a) secure a wired LAN and (b) secure a wireless LAN.

13. Describe the difference between symmetric encryption and public key encryption. List five uses for each one.

14. Fill in the blanks on the concept map shown below to show the hierarchy of LAN technology.

5

Concept Map

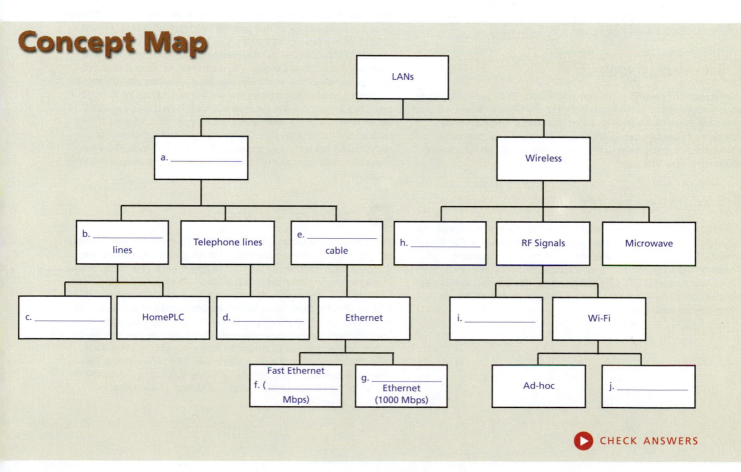

CHECK ANSWERS

Projects

 CRITICAL THINKING

Wireless technology has become quite pervasive. Not only are computing devices wireless, but most people have other devices, such as security systems, baby monitors, and entertainment systems, that could be wirelessly networked. Play the role of a futurist and think about the ultimate wired home. Sketch out floor plans and show how you would set up wireless devices, including wireless access points.

 **GROUP PROJECT**

Form a group with three or four other students. Suppose you are all living in adjacent dorm rooms and decide to create a LAN to connect your computers. For this project, first describe the number, type, and location of the computers that will form your network. Next, decide what type of network technology you want to use: Ethernet, HomePNA, Wi-Fi, HomePlug, or a mixture. Create a diagram showing the location of each computer, the wiring path (for Ethernet), the location of electrical outlets (for HomePlug), the location of telephone outlets (for HomePNA), or potential signal interference (for wireless). Create a shopping list of the network components you need to purchase, and then use the Web to locate prices for each item on your list. Make sure you supply your instructor with the URLs for sites where you found pricing information.

CYBERCLASSROOM

With a partner, research public key encryption (PKE) you could use to send encrypted e-mail back and forth. Do any utilities offered with your operating system offer PKE or would you have to use third-party software? If possible, set up encryption and send your partner an encrypted e-mail message or file. Describe the tools and procedure you used to your instructor.

MULTIMEDIA PROJECT

Wireless technology is increasingly being used for home entertainment systems, including stereos, television, and home theaters. For this project choose either television, stereo, or projection systems. Research the wireless options for the equipment of your choice. Write a two-page how-to article describing how to set up a cool wireless system. Be sure to describe the system's benefits as well as how to assemble the equipment.

 RESUME BUILDER

Bluetooth advocates champion the idea of using Bluetooth devices to exchange electronic business cards. Suppose you're working in the technology department of a corporation and your boss asks you to research the value of this concept for the company's sales representatives. After you complete your research, write a one-page memo describing your findings about cost and usefulness.

GLOBALIZATION

The model for telecommunications in most technologically advanced countries depends on large telecommunications corporations for telephone and Internet access. Can you envision ways in which people in technologically underdeveloped countries could benefit from inexpensive LAN and WLAN technologies? Jot down your initial thoughts, then search the Web for additional ideas. Write a one-page executive summary that describes your ideas.

ISSUE

The Issue section of this chapter focuses on the use of Wi-Fi technology to build wireless LANs that provide free Internet access. For this project, write a two- to five-page paper that examines one aspect of the free WLAN controversy. You might explore Wi-Fi technology to learn more about how it works. You might look for examples of free WLANs and try to find what motivates their operators. Or you might research how broadband providers are reacting to free WLANs. To begin this project, consult the Free WLAN InfoWeb (see page 289) to get an overview of the controversy. Using that information as background, choose the focus for your paper and continue your research. As you write your paper, make sure you can back up your statements with facts and references to authoritative articles and Web pages.

COMPUTERS IN CONTEXT

The Computers in Context section focuses on the many ways computers and Internet technology are used in education. For this project, identify a topic you'd like to learn more about, such as a hobby or your academic major. Under the heading "Topic Description," write a brief description of your topic, why it interests you, and what you would like to learn about it. Next, use a search engine, such as Google, to locate online tutorials about your topic. Under the heading "Available Tutorials," write a brief description of your search results. Indicate the number of tutorials you found on the topic, provide the URLs for at least three tutorials, and write a short description of each one. Take one of the free tutorials. Under the heading "Evaluation," describe the format for the tutorial, its ease of use, and what you learned.

On the Web

STUDENT EDITION LABS

W **CLICK TO ACCESS THE NP11 WEB SITE**

or open your browser and connect to www.course.com/np/concepts11/ch05. Lab results can be stored in the Universal Gradebook.

Work hands-on in structured simulations practicing important skills and concepts

NETWORKING BASICS

In the Networking Basics Student Edition Lab, you will learn about the following topics:

- Network architecture, hardware, and software
- Network protocols and utilities
- Networked resources
- Network security

WIRELESS NETWORKING

In the Wireless Networking Student Edition Lab, you will learn about the following topics:

- Implementing wireless networks
- Wireless security

CHAPTER COURSECAST

Use your computer or iPod to hear a five-minute audio presentation of chapter highlights.

FLASHCARD COURSECAST

Interact with audio flashcards to review key terms from the chapter.

DETAILED OBJECTIVES

Make sure that you've achieved all the objectives for a chapter before it's time for your test!

TEST YOURSELF

Review chapter material by taking these ten-question tests, then send your results to the Universal Gradebook.

ONLINE GAMES

Have some fun while refreshing your memory about key concepts that might appear on the next test. You can even send your results to the Universal Gradebook!

AND MORE!

At the NP11 Web site you'll also find Extra Content and InfoWebLinks.

5

6

The Internet

CHAPTER CONTENTS

LEARNING OBJECTIVES

- Briefly summarize the origins and development of the Internet
- Draw a conceptual diagram illustrating the Internet backbone, NAPs, NSPs, routers, and ISPs
- Draw a diagram to illustrate how computers on a LAN would access the Internet through a single DSL modem
- List at least five protocols used on the Internet and describe what they are used for
- Explain the differences between static IP addresses, dynamic IP addresses, private IP addresses, and domain names
- Explain when and why you might use Ping and Traceroute utilities
- Describe the advantages and disadvantages of dial-up, cable, DSL, ISDN, satellite, and fixed wireless Internet services
- Differentiate between portable Internet access and mobile Internet access
- Identify and describe the most prevalent types of portable Internet access
- Differentiate between WAP and wireless data services
- Describe the basic technology underlying chat and instant messaging services
- Explain how Voice over IP works
- Relate at least five examples of grid computing
- Describe how FTP differs from file sharing technologies such as BitTorrent
- Explain how hackers use the Internet to infiltrate computers
- List at least three steps you can take to secure your computer against Internet-based intrusions

☑ PRE-ASSESSMENT QUIZ

Take the pre-assessment quiz to find out how much you know about the topics in this chapter. ▶

MULTIMEDIA and INTERACTIVE ELEMENTS

When using the BookOnCD, BookOnFlashDrive, or other NP11 BookOn product, the ▶ icons are clickable to access multimedia resources.

BEFORE YOU READ ON, **TRY IT**

HOW FAST AND DEPENDABLE IS MY INTERNET CONNECTION?

You can access the Internet in various ways—using your phone line, your cable TV connection, or a personal satellite dish. Is your Internet connection fast enough for activities such as downloading DVDs and playing online multiplayer games? You can discover the speed of your Internet connection by doing the following steps.

1. Using Windows Vista, enter **command prompt** in the Search box. Using Windows XP, click the Start button, point to accessories, and then select Command Prompt from the list. This action opens what's called a "DOS Box."

2. Type **Ping www.google.com** and then press the Enter key.

3. Your computer makes four attempts to access the Google Web site and measures the time required for each attempt. Fill in the blanks below with the Ping statistics for your computer. When you read the chapter, you'll learn how those statistics stack up for videoconferencing, Voice over IP, and online multiplayer gaming.

4. Click the [X] button to close the DOS box.

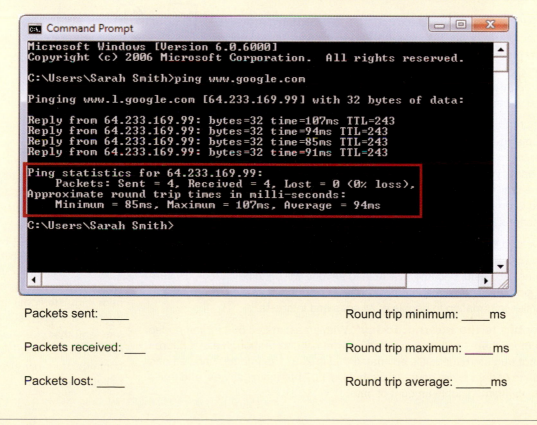

Packets sent: _____

Packets received: ___

Packets lost: _____

Round trip minimum: _____ms

Round trip maximum: _____ms

Round trip average: _____ms

WEB SITE

Visit the NP11 Web site to access additional resources Ⓦ that accompany this chapter.

Internet Technology

TO MOST PEOPLE, the Internet seems old hat. Even people who haven't used the Internet know a lot about it from watching the news, reading magazines, and watching movies. Using the Internet is actually pretty easy. Browsing Web sites, shopping at the Net mall, sending e-mail, and chatting online? No problem. But what makes the Internet "tick"? How can one network offer so much information to so many people? Section A pulls back the curtain and gives you a glimpse of what happens behind the scenes on the Net.

BACKGROUND

How did the Internet get started? The history of the Internet begins in 1957 when the Soviet Union launched Sputnik, the first man-made satellite. In response to this display of Soviet superiority, the U.S. government resolved to improve its scientific and technical infrastructure. One of the resulting initiatives was the Advanced Research Projects Agency (ARPA).

ARPA swung into action with a project designed to help scientists communicate and share valuable computer resources. The ARPANET, created in 1969, connected computers at UCLA, Stanford Research Institute, University of Utah, and University of California at Santa Barbara (Figure 6-1).

In 1985, the National Science Foundation (NSF) used ARPANET technology to create a similar, but larger, network, linking not just a few mainframe computers, but entire LANs at each site. Connecting two or more networks creates an internetwork, or internet. The NSF network was an internet (with a lowercase "i"). As this network grew throughout the world, it became known as the Internet (with an uppercase "I").

Early Internet pioneers—mostly educators and scientists—used primitive command-line user interfaces to send e-mail, transfer files, and run scientific calculations on Internet supercomputers. Finding information was not easy. Without search engines, Internet users relied on word of mouth and e-mail to keep informed about new data and its location. "The data you need is on the Stanford computer in a file called Chrome.txt" was typical of messages between colleagues.

How did the Internet become so popular? In the early 1990s, software developers created new user-friendly Internet access tools, and Internet accounts became available to anyone willing to pay a monthly subscription fee. Today, the Internet connects computers all over the globe and supplies information to people of all ages and interests.

How big is the Internet today? With an estimated 500 million nodes and more than 1 billion users, the Internet is huge. Although exact figures cannot be determined, it is estimated that in 2007 the Internet handled one exabyte of data every hour. An exabyte is 1.074 billion gigabytes, and that's a nearly unimaginable amount of data.

FIGURE 6-1

An original diagram of the ARPANET included four nodes, depicted as circles.

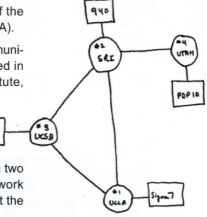

TERMINOLOGY NOTE

A few years ago, Wired News announced it would no longer capitalize the word *Internet*, a move supported by National Public Radio and several prominent linguists. Most style guides, however, still recommend that you capitalize references to the global communications network called the Internet.

INTERNET INFRASTRUCTURE

How is the Internet structured? Surprisingly, the Internet is not owned or operated by any single corporation or government. It is a data communications network that grew over time in a somewhat haphazard configuration as networks connected to other networks and to the Internet backbone.

What is the Internet backbone? The **Internet backbone** is a network of high-capacity communications links that provides the main routes for data traffic across the Internet. At one time, the topology of the Internet backbone and interconnected networks might have resembled a spine with ribs connected along its length. Today, however, it more resembles a map of interstate highways with many junctures and redundant routes.

How does the backbone tie the Internet together? The Internet backbone consists of high-speed fiber-optic links connecting high-capacity routers that direct network traffic. Backbone links and routers are maintained by **network service providers** (NSPs), such as AT&T, British Telecom, Deutsche Telekom, Sprint, and Verizon. NSP equipment and links are tied together by **network access points** (NAPs), so that, for example, data can begin its journey on a Verizon link and then cross over to a Sprint link, if necessary, to reach its destination.

NSPs supply Internet connections to large Internet service providers, such as AT&T WorldNet, AOL, and Comcast. An **Internet service provider** (ISP) is a company that offers Internet access to individuals, businesses, and smaller ISPs. Figure 6-2 shows a simplified conceptual diagram of the Internet backbone and its components.

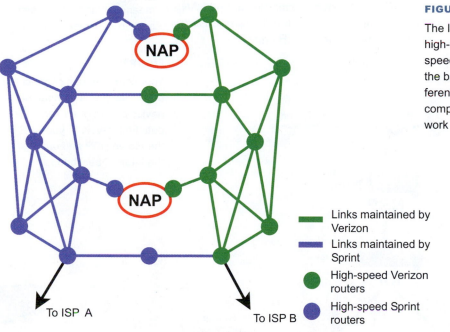

FIGURE 6-2

The Internet backbone includes high-speed routers and high-speed fiber-optic links. Parts of the backbone maintained by different communications companies are connected at network access points (NAPs).

Links maintained by Verizon

Links maintained by Sprint

High-speed Verizon routers

High-speed Sprint routers

To ISP A

To ISP B

What kinds of network devices are part of an ISP? An ISP operates routers, communication equipment, and other network devices that handle the physical aspects of transmitting and receiving data between their subscribers and the Internet. Many ISPs also operate e-mail servers to handle incoming and outgoing mail for their subscribers. Some ISPs have Web servers for subscriber Web sites. An ISP might operate a server that translates an address, such as *www.google.com*, into a valid IP address such as 208.50.141.12. ISPs can also maintain servers for chat groups, instant messaging, music file sharing, FTP, and other file transfer services (Figure 6-3).

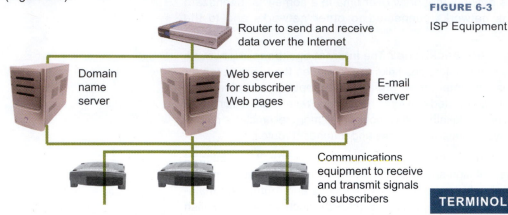

Router to send and receive data over the Internet

Domain name server

Web server for subscriber Web pages

E-mail server

Communications equipment to receive and transmit signals to subscribers

FIGURE 6-3

ISP Equipment

How does my computer fit into the structure of the Internet?

To communicate with an ISP, your computer uses some type of communications device, such as a modem. A **modem** contains circuitry that converts the data-carrying signals from your computer to signals that can travel over various communications channels. The kind of modem you use depends on whether your ISP supplies dial-up, cable, satellite, or DSL Internet service.

A standalone computer can communicate with an ISP directly through a modem, or through a combination of a router and modem. If your computer is part of a network, the network's router typically handles the Internet connection. Figure 6-4 illustrates the difference between standalone and LAN Internet access. You'll learn more about connecting to the Internet using telephone, cable, satellite, and cellular links in Sections B and C.

TERMINOLOGY NOTE

The word *modem* is derived from the words *modulate* and *demodulate*. In communications lingo, modulation means changing the characteristics of a signal, as when a dial-up modem changes a digital pulse into an analog audio signal that travels over telephone lines. Demodulation means changing a signal back to its original state.

FIGURE 6-4

Your computer can connect to the Internet as a standalone device or part of a LAN. Your data first travels to your ISP, then to an NSP and out over the Internet backbone.

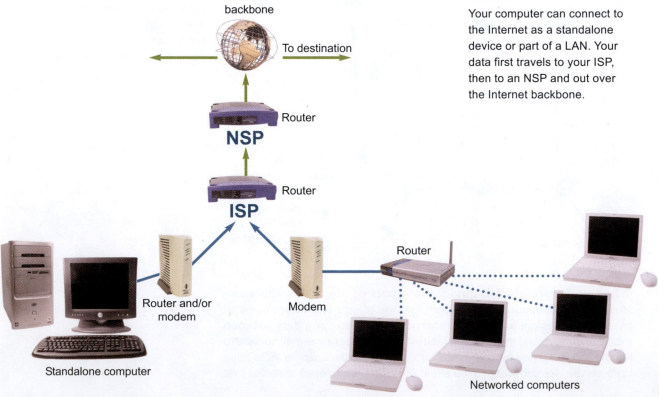

Internet backbone

To destination

Router

NSP

Router

ISP

Router and/or modem

Modem

Router

Standalone computer

Networked computers

INTERNET PROTOCOLS, ADDRESSES, AND DOMAINS

What protocols are used by the Internet? The Internet uses a variety of communications protocols to support basic data transport and services, such as e-mail, Web access, and downloading. Figure 6-5 briefly describes some of the main protocols used on the Internet.

FIGURE 6-5

Protocols Used on the Internet

Protocol	Name	Function
TCP	Transmission Control Protocol	Creates connections and exchanges packets of data
IP	Internet Protocol	Provides devices with unique addresses
UDP	User Datagram Protocol	An alternative data transport to TCP used for DNS, Voice over IP, and file sharing
HTTP	Hypertext Transfer Protocol	Exchanges information over the Web
FTP	File Transfer Protocol	Transfers files between local and remote host computers
POP	Post Office Protocol	Transfers mail from an e-mail server to a client Inbox
SMTP	Simple Mail Transfer Protocol	Transfers e-mail messages from client computers to an e-mail server
VoIP	Voice over Internet Protocol	Transmits voice conversations over the Internet
IRC	Internet Relay Chat	Transmits text messages in real time between online users
BitTorrent	BitTorrent	Distributes files using scattered clients rather than a server

6

How significant is TCP/IP? **TCP/IP** is the primary protocol suite responsible for message transmission on the Internet. A **protocol suite** is a combination of protocols that work together. **TCP** (Transmission Control Protocol) breaks a message or file into packets. **IP** (Internet Protocol) is responsible for addressing packets so that they can be routed to their destination. From a practical perspective, TCP/IP provides a protocol standard for the Internet that is easy to implement, public, free, and extensible.

Does the Internet use a special addressing scheme? In the previous chapter, you learned that IP addresses can be assigned to LAN workstations. IP addresses originated on the Internet as part of the TCP/IP protocol. IP addresses are used to uniquely identify computers on the Internet as well as on LANs. In the context of the Internet, these addresses are sometimes referred to as TCP/IP addresses or Internet addresses.

How do IP addresses work on the Internet? Every device on the Internet has an assigned IP address, such as 204.127.129.1, divided into four octets by periods. The numbers in each octet correspond to network classes. For example, an IP address that begins with a number between 128 and 191 corresponds to a Class B network, such as a large college campus. When delivering a packet of data, Internet routers use the first octet to get a general idea of where to send the packet. The rest of the IP address is used to drill down to the exact destination.

Do octets correspond to the parts of e-mail or Web site addresses? E-mail addresses, such as *imastudent@uga.edu* and Web site addresses such as *http://www.uga.edu* seem to be separated into parts with periods, similar to the octets in an IP address. The octets do not, however, map to the parts of a Web site address or e-mail address. So, even though *http://www.uga.edu* has an IP address of 128.192.1.9, the first octet, 128, does not correspond to *http://*. Nor does the second octet, 192, map to *www*.

Do I need a permanent IP address? A computer can have a permanently assigned **static IP address** or a temporarily assigned **dynamic IP address**. As a general rule, computers on the Internet that act as servers use static IP addresses. Typically, ISPs, Web sites, Web hosting services, and e-mail servers that always need to be found at the same address require static IP addresses. Most other Internet users have dynamic IP addresses. Figure 6-6 illustrates a tool you can use to find your IP address.

FIGURE 6-6

In Windows Vista you can use the Network and Sharing Center to find your computer's IP address. Other operating systems offer similar utilities.

Network Connection Details	
Network Connection Details:	
Property	Value
Connection-specific DN...	
Description	Broadcom 802.11b/g WLAN
Physical Address	00-1A-73-0E-77-75
DHCP Enabled	Yes
IPv4 IP Address	199.166.1.7
IPv4 Subnet Mask	255.255.255.0
Lease Obtained	November 09, 3:54:22 PM
Lease Expires	November 10, 3:54:23 PM
IPv4 Default Gateway	199.166.1.219
IPv4 DHCP Server	199.166.1.219
IPv4 DNS Server	137.118.1.32
IPv4 WINS Server	
NetBIOS over Tcpip En...	Yes
Link-local IPv6 Address	fe80:137b:6a1c:4413%10
IPv6 Default Gateway	
IPv6 DNS Server	

Close

 CLICK TO START

Why doesn't everyone have a static IP address? The use of 12-digit addresses such as 128.192.100.100 provides approximately 4.3 billion unique addresses, but many of these are reserved for special purposes and devices, leaving a meager number for the estimated 1.2 billion Internet users. To avoid running out of static IP addresses, dynamic addresses are used whenever possible. Dynamic IP addresses can be handed out as necessary and reused as needed.

How do I get a dynamic IP address? Every ISP controls a unique pool of IP addresses, which can be assigned to subscribers. If you have the type of Internet connection that requires a modem to make a telephone connection, for example, your ISP's DHCP server assigns a temporary IP address to your computer for use as long as it remains connected. When you end a session, that IP address goes back into a pool of addresses that can be distributed to other subscribers when they log in.

Your computer is rarely assigned the same dynamic IP address it had during a previous session. As an IP nomad with no permanent address, you can't feasibly run a Web site or perform other server-related activities on your computer. For example, if you try to run an online store, its address would change every time you connect to the Internet and customers would not be able to find it.

If you want to operate a server, your ISP should be able to supply you with a service plan that includes a static IP address and that will supply adequate bandwidth for server activity.

How does a dynamic IP address relate to an always-on connection? Most high-speed Internet connections use always-on technology. An **always-on connection** is linked to your ISP and is online whenever your computer and modem are on, even if you are not actively accessing the Internet. An always-on connection can have a static or dynamic IP address. With an always-on connection your dynamic IP address might seem like a static one because the address can remain the same unless you turn off your modem or your service provider has an outage.

Always-on connections are convenient. You don't have to wait for a connection to be established before using your browser or sending e-mail. If you have an always-on connection, however, you should be aware that it poses a security risk. With an always-on connection, your computer is connected to the Internet for long periods of time with the same IP address, making it particularly vulnerable to hackers. In Section E you'll learn how routers and firewalls can protect computers that have always-on Internet connections.

What's a domain name? Although IP addresses work for communication between computers, people find it difficult to remember long strings of numbers. Therefore, many Internet servers also have an easy-to-remember name, such as *nike.com*. The official term for this name is *fully qualified domain name (FQDN)*, but most people just refer to it as a **domain name**. By convention, you should type domain names using all lowercase letters.

A domain name is a key component of Web addresses, e-mail addresses, and addresses on the Web called URLs. It is the Web server name in a Web address and the e-mail server name in an e-mail address. For example, in the Web address *www.msu.edu/infotech*, the domain name is *msu.edu*. In the e-mail address *jbillings@msu.edu*, the domain name is also *msu.edu*.

A domain name ends with an extension that indicates its **top-level domain**. For example, in the domain name *msu.edu*, *edu* indicates that the computer is maintained by an educational institution. Some of the most commonly used top-level domains are listed in Figure 6-7.

FIGURE 6-7

Top-level Domains

Domain	Description
biz	Unrestricted use; usually for commercial businesses
com	Unrestricted use; usually for commercial businesses
edu	Restricted to North American educational institutions
gov	Restricted to U.S. government agencies
info	Unrestricted use
int	Restricted to organizations established by international treaties
mil	Restricted to U.S. military agencies
net	Unrestricted use; traditionally for Internet administrative organizations
org	Unrestricted use; traditionally for professional and nonprofit organizations

Country codes also serve as top-level domains. Canada's top-level domain is ca; the United Kingdom's is uk; Australia's is au. A domain with growing popularity is tv. Originally assigned to the small Polynesian island of Tuvalu, the tv domain is marketed by a professional management team and is available for a fee to media-related Web sites.

How are domain names related to IP addresses? Every domain name corresponds to a unique IP address that has been entered into a huge database called the **Domain Name System** (DNS). Any computer that hosts this database is referred to as a **domain name server**. A domain name, such as *travelocity.com*, must be converted into an IP address before packets can be routed to it. For example, when you type *www.travelocity.com* into your browser, the browser's first step is to contact a domain name server to get the IP address for the Travelocity Web server, as shown in Figure 6-8.

FIGURE 6-8

A domain name request is routed through your ISP to your designated domain name server, which searches through its database to find a corresponding IP address. The IP address can then be attached to packets, such as requests for Web pages.

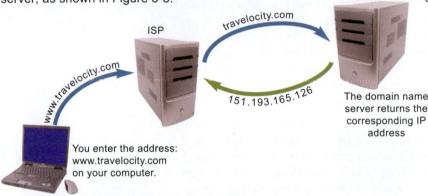

You enter the address:
www.travelocity.com
on your computer.

The domain name server returns the corresponding IP address

Is www part of domain names? No. Suppose that a corporation operates a server with an IP address of 192.150.18.61. The DNS links that address to the domain name *adobe.com*, not *www.adobe.com*. Prefixes such as *http://*, *www*, and *ftp* correspond to protocols, ports, and services offered by Internet computers.

A server can handle multiple tasks such as operating a corporate Web site, managing e-mail, and fulfilling FTP download requests. Each service uses a designated port. A **port** can be described as a virtual device because it is not a physical circuit or mechanism, but rather a conceptual or abstract concept that allows a computer to perform more than one type of service. Port 80, for example, typically corresponds to Web services, such as the corporate Web site. E-mail uses port 110. Ports 20 and 21 customarily host FTP downloads. A computer can have hundreds of ports.

When you enter *http://www.adobe.com* in a browser, the DNS gets your request as far as the *adobe.com* server. The server at *adobe.com* is listening to all the data packets that arrive. Packets sent to Web sites with URLs that begin *http://www* are handled by port 80, usually to display a Web page.

Do I need my own domain name? For client-style Internet activities, such as Web browsing, e-mail, and chat, you do not need your own domain name. You might, however, want a domain name if you plan to operate your own Web server or if you establish a Web site using servers provided by a Web site hosting service.

Suppose you decide to set up a Web site called Rocky Mountain Photos. For customers to access your site by typing *www.rockymtnphotos.com*, you must obtain the *rockymtnphotos.com* domain name. In contrast, if your Web site is set up on a Web server supplied by your ISP, your own domain name might not be necessary because you use the domain of the ISP's Web server. For example, if you set up your Rocky Mountain Photos site on AOL's Hometown Web server, its address might be *hometown.aol.com/rockymtnphotos*.

INFOWEBLINKS

Where can you register a domain name? What are the current fees? These questions are answered at the **Domain Name InfoWeb**.

CLICK TO CONNECT
www.course.com/np/concepts11/ch06

How do I get a domain name? An organization called **ICANN** (Internet Corporation for Assigned Names and Numbers) is recognized by the United States and other governments as the global organization that coordinates technical management of the Internet's Domain Name System. It supervises several for-profit Accredited Domain Registrars, which handle domain name requests.

The first step in registering a domain name is to find out whether the name is available. By connecting to an Accredited Domain Registrar Web site, you can enter a domain name, as shown in Figure 6-9.

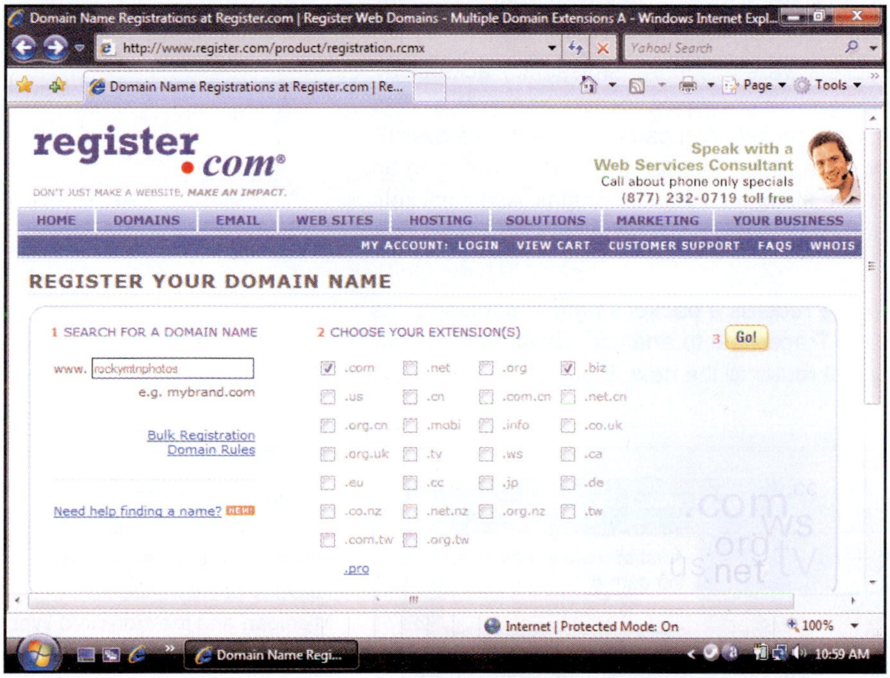

FIGURE 6-9

The first step in registering a domain name is to find out whether the name is currently in use or reserved for future use. If a domain name is not available, consider using a different top-level domain, such as biz instead of com. After you've found an available domain name, you can continue the registration process by filling out a simple online form.

▶ CLICK TO START

Is a fee required to obtain a domain name? You can register a domain name for a minimal annual fee—currently between US$10 and $50, depending on the registration service.

Some domain names are not currently in use, yet they are not available because they are reserved. Internet entrepreneurs have made a business of registering high-profile domain names with the intention of reselling them. Some domain names carry price tags of over $500,000. Most domain name shoppers, however, can come up with a perfectly suitable domain name that's not reserved or in use.

CONNECTION SPEED

How fast is the Internet? Data travels over the Internet at an incredible speed. On average, data within North America usually arrives at its destination in less than 1/10th of a second (100 ms) after it is sent. Data packets usually clip along the Internet backbone at blinding speeds. Data transport can slow down, however, when usage peaks during breaking news events, or when denial of service attacks break through security. Such slow-downs are temporary, however, and usually last only a few hours.

The elapsed time for data to make a round trip from point A to point B and back to point A is referred to as **latency**. Typically, latency averages 200 ms (milliseconds) or less in North America. Latency increases slightly for overseas transmissions. If you want to play online multiplayer games, it is best to have less than 100 ms latency. Good quality Voice over IP and videoconferencing require latency rates of 200 ms or less.

Can I measure speed and latency? You can run speed tests by linking to Internet-based utilities such as the Speakeasy Speed Test. You can also use a local Internet utility called **Ping** (Packet Internet Groper), which sends a signal to a specific Internet address and waits for a reply. If a reply arrives, Ping reports that the computer is online and displays the elapsed time for the round-trip message. You can use Ping before playing online games, using Voice over IP, or joining an online videoconference to make sure you have adequate speed for everything to run smoothly.

Ping also shows whether packets were lost in transmission. Packets can become lost when signal interference or network congestion overwhelms Internet servers and routers. Lost packets can cause jitter in Voice over IP communications and videoconferencing. Too many lost packets during an online gaming session can cause the game to stutter or stall. And if packets don't arrive in the correct order, your game character might seem to act randomly for a few seconds.

Another utility called **Traceroute** records a packet's path in addition to its round-trip speed. You can use Traceroute to analyze the latency of your data as it hops from one Internet router to the next. Figure 6-10 contains a Traceroute report.

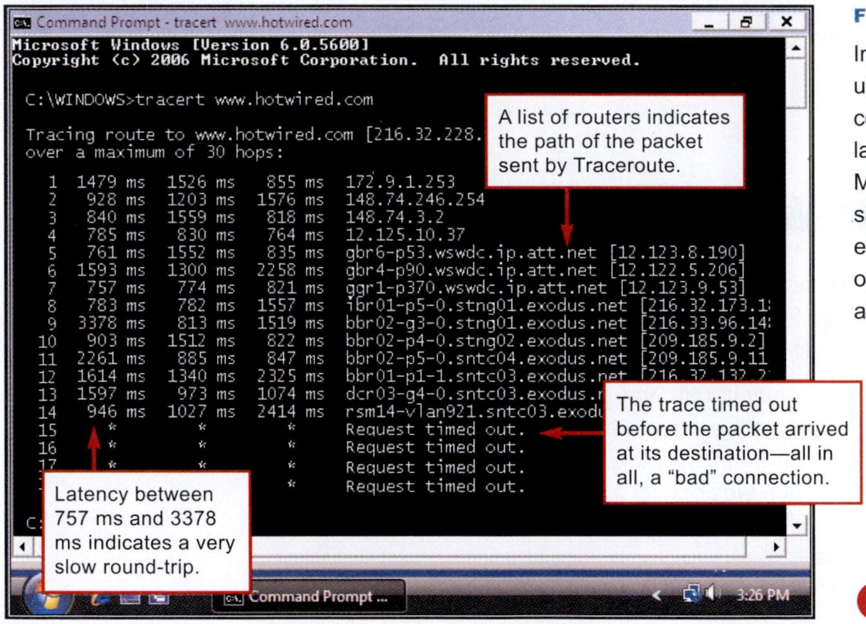

FIGURE 6-10

In this example, Traceroute is used to monitor an Internet connection between a small lakeside cabin in northern Michigan and the HotWired Web site. The satellite connection has extremely high latency and timed out before the Web site could be accessed.

▶ CLICK TO START

How fast is a typical Internet connection? The connection speeds you see advertised by ISPs refer to the amount of data that travels between a subscriber's computer and an ISP within a given time period. Connection speed is measured in Kbps (kilobits per second) or Mbps (megabits per second). The Internet connection speeds offered by various ISPs vary. Slow dial-up connections top out at 56 Kbps. High-speed (also called broadband) connections at 6000 Kbps (6 Mbps) are common. High-speed connections can display graphics quickly, show smoothly streaming video, handle net-based videoconferences, and deliver high-quality Voice over IP.

What factors affect connection speed? Your connection speed depends on whether you connect to your ISP using a telephone, cable television, satellite, or wireless link. Maximum speed can differ from actual speed because links are susceptible to interference that can hinder signals. Upstream speed can also differ from downstream speed.

What are upstream and downstream speeds? **Upstream speed** is the rate of data that is transmitted from your computer to the Internet. **Downstream speed** is the rate of data arriving at your computer. Many ISPs limit the speed of data flowing to and from their subscribers to make sure everyone gets an equal share of the bandwidth. In many cases, upstream speed is much slower than downstream speed.

When upstream speeds differ from downstream speeds, you have an **asymmetric Internet connection**. When upstream and downstream speeds are the same, you have a **symmetric Internet connection**. Asymmetric connections discourage subscribers from setting up Web and e-mail servers that would transmit lots of upstream data. For most users, however, an asymmetric connection is sufficient.

What are my connection options? Consumers have several options for connecting to the Internet. **Fixed Internet access** links your computer to an ISP from a stationary point, such as a wall socket or roof-mounted antenna. **Portable Internet access** allows you to easily move your access device, as in the case of vehicle-mounted satellite dishes that can be deployed when the vehicle is parked. **Mobile Internet access** allows you to use the Internet as you are on the go, such as using a cell phone to collect your e-mail while you are traveling by train.

You're not necessarily limited to a single Internet access option. Many consumers find it convenient to maintain fixed Internet access for home use, but use a portable or mobile method of Internet access while out and about. In Sections B and C you'll learn more about Internet access options.

> **TERMINOLOGY NOTE**
>
> In telecommunications, the term *asymmetric communications* refers to any system or device in which speed or quality differs between one direction and the other.

6

QuickCheck

1. The Internet _____ is a network of high-capacity communications links that provides the main routes for data traffic across the Internet.

2. An _____ is a company that offers Internet access to individuals, businesses, and smaller ISPs. (Hint: Use the acronym.)

3. On the Internet, _____ breaks a message into packets, and _____ is responsible for addressing packets so that they can be routed to their destination. (Hint: Use acronyms for these protocols.)

4. Computers on the Internet that act as servers use _____ IP addresses, whereas most other computers use _____ IP addresses.

5. An Internet address, such as *msu.edu*, is called a fully qualified _____ name.

6. The top-level domain for most schools and universities is _____ .

7. When upstream speeds differ from downstream speeds, you have an asymmetrical Internet connection. True or false? _____

 CHECK ANSWERS

Fixed Internet Access

ONE OF THE MOST challenging aspects of the Internet is selecting a service provider. In this section of the chapter, you'll learn about fixed Internet access, which is typically your main link to the Internet. You'll learn to evaluate the pros and cons of various fixed Internet options and discover why online interactive game players shun satellite Internet connections, but love cable Internet service. Plus, you'll find out which types of Internet access work best for Voice over IP.

DIAL-UP CONNECTIONS

What is a dial-up connection? A **dial-up connection** is a fixed Internet connection that uses a voiceband modem and telephone lines to transport data between your computer and your ISP. Many ISPs, including NetZero, AOL, and EarthLink offer dial-up Internet access. The service is typically less than $10 per month, but access speed is slow.

How does a dial-up connection work? When you use a dial-up connection, your computer's modem places a regular telephone call to your ISP. When the ISP's computer answers your call, a dedicated circuit is established between you and your ISP—just as though you had made a voice call and someone at the ISP had picked up the phone. The circuit remains connected for the duration of your call and provides a communications link that carries data between your computer and the ISP. As your data arrives at the ISP, a router sends it out over the Internet. Figure 6-11 illustrates the path of your data when you use a dial-up connection.

FIGURE 6-11

When you use an ISP to access the Internet, your data travels over local telephone lines to your ISP, which sends it onto the Internet.

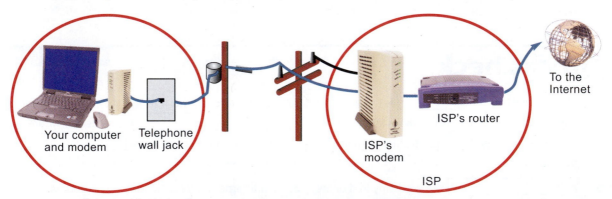

Your computer and modem · Telephone wall jack · ISP's modem · ISP's router · To the Internet · ISP

How does a voiceband modem work? The signals that represent data bits exist in your computer as digital signals. The telephone system, however, expects to work with human voices, so it carries analog audio signals. A **voiceband modem**—usually referred to simply as a modem—converts the signals from your computer into signals that can travel over telephone lines. A modem transmits a 1,070 Hz tone for a 0 data bit and a 1,270 Hz tone for a 1 data bit.

When your computer's modem initiates a connection, it sends a signal that is equivalent to picking up the receiver of a telephone to get a dial tone. It then dials the ISP by emitting a series of tones—the same tones you'd produce if you punched in the ISP's number using a phone keypad. The modem then waits for the ISP's modem to answer the call. After the ISP's modem answers, the two modems begin to negotiate communications protocols, such as transmission rate. The series of beeps, tones, and whooshing sounds you hear when you connect to your ISP is the sound of your modem "talking" to the ISP's modem. This process of negotiation is sometimes called handshaking. When the negotiation is complete, data transmission can begin (Figure 6-12).

FIGURE 6-12

When you transmit data, your voiceband modem modulates the signal that carries your data. A modem at the other end of the transmission demodulates the signal.

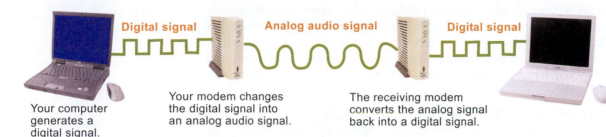

Digital signal   Analog audio signal   Digital signal

Your computer generates a digital signal.

Your modem changes the digital signal into an analog audio signal.

The receiving modem converts the analog signal back into a digital signal.

How fast is a voiceband modem? Modem speeds are measured in bits per second. (If you're a stickler for details, you'll realize that bps is actually a measure of capacity, but everyone calls it speed.) Since 1998, most modems use a standard called V.90 to provide a theoretical maximum speed of 56 Kbps. Actual data transfer speeds are affected by factors such as the quality of your phone line and connection. Even with an excellent connection, however, a 56 Kbps modem tops out at about 44 Kbps.

Dial-up connections are asymmetrical; 44 Kbps is a typical downstream speed for a 56 Kbps modem. Upstream, the data rate drops to about 33 Kbps or less.

Where can I get a voiceband modem? Most computers have built-in voiceband modem circuitry. You can check the ports of your computer for one that accepts a standard telephone RJ-11 connector (Figure 6-13). Voiceband modems are also available for internal slots or external USB ports. To get connected, plug one end of a telephone cable into your computer's RJ-11 port and the other end into a telephone wall jack. Your computer's operating system typically includes configuration software. Your ISP will supply information, such as the dial-in number, for completing the configuration.

FIGURE 6-13

An RJ-11 port on your computer can be connected by cable to a telephone wall jack.

RJ-11 port

Can I talk and send data at the same time? When your computer is connected to your ISP over a dial-up connection, data is transmitted over the same frequencies normally used for voice conversations. If you have only one telephone line, you cannot pick up your telephone receiver, dial your friend, and carry on a voice conversation while you are sending data. Some modems use technology similar to call waiting that allows you to remain connected to your ISP and temporarily suspend data transfers while answering a voice call.

Can I use an analog modem if my phone service is digital? In many areas of the world, the telephone system uses digital rather than analog signals to send voice conversations. You can still use an analog modem because the sounds it emits are transported just as if they were voices. Digital telephone systems open up the possibilities for digital data transport options such as ISDN, DSL, and dedicated lines.

DSL, ISDN, AND DEDICATED LINES

What are the options for transporting digital data over telephone lines? Although the standard equipment provided by telephone companies limits the amount of data you can transmit and receive over a voiceband modem, the telephone system's copper wire has a fair amount of capacity. Several services, such as ISDN, DSL, and dedicated lines take advantage of this capacity to offer high-speed digital communications links for voice and data.

What is a dedicated line? T1, T3, and T4 services are high-capacity dedicated lines that can be leased from the telephone company and are not shared by other customers. Speed ranges from 1.544 Mbps to 274 Mbps. These high-speed services are usually too expensive for individuals, but are leased by corporations and provide many of the links on the Internet backbone.

What is ISDN? ISDN (Integrated Services Digital Network) is a type of fixed Internet connection that moves data at speeds of 64 Kbps or 128 Kbps over ordinary telephone lines. Speed is symmetric, so you'll get the same data rates upstream as downstream. The service is usually obtained from a local telephone company or a dedicated ISDN service provider. ISDN availability and pricing vary from place to place.

Do I need a modem for ISDN? As with a dial-up connection, you use a telephone wall jack as your fixed point of connection, but instead of connecting your computer to a voiceband modem, you use a device called an **ISDN terminal adapter**, which sends digital signals. Although it is sometimes called an ISDN modem, a terminal adapter is not technically a modem because it doesn't modulate and demodulate the data signal. When installing ISDN, you typically receive an ISDN terminal adapter from your ISP (Figure 6-14).

Is an ISDN connection always on? Basic ISDN service is like dial-up in that it makes a connection when you open a browser, e-mail, or other Internet applications, and disconnects when you've closed those applications. Connections are almost instantaneous, however, so ISDN users don't have to wait for lengthy dialing and handshaking as with dial-up connections. Some ISDN providers offer a service called always-on dynamic ISDN (AO/DI), which remains connected to an ISP as long as the computer and terminal adapter are on. Although AO/DI offers a slight performance enhancement, an always-on connection increases your computer's vulnerability to hackers.

Why would I want ISDN? ISDN allows you to use your telephone line for voice calls and transmit data at the same time. ISDN service is faster than dial-up. It is sometimes classified as high-speed Internet service, but it is not in the league of truly high-speed Internet connections, such as DSL and cable. If you have no other high-speed options, if ISDN is available, and if the price isn't too exorbitant, you might consider replacing your dial-up connection with ISDN.

What is DSL? DSL (digital subscriber line) is a high-speed, digital, always-on, Internet access technology that runs over standard phone lines. It is one of the fastest Internet connections that's affordable to individual consumers. Several variations of this technology exist, including ADSL (asymmetric DSL, with downstream speed faster than upstream speed), SDSL (symmetric DSL, with the same upstream and downstream speed), HDSL (high-rate DSL), VDSL (very high speed DSL), and DSL lite.

FIGURE 6-14

ISDN requires a terminal adapter that can be added to an internal slot or USB port.

TERMINOLOGY NOTE

The acronym xDSL refers to the entire group of DSL technologies (including symmetric DSL, HDSL, and so on). xDSL is not a separate variation of DSL.

How does DSL work? Data is transmitted to and from your local telephone switching station in pure digital form, bypassing the bottleneck of analog-to-digital-to-analog conversion and escaping the requirement to use the narrow bandwidth allocated to voice transmissions. The result is fast data transmission over standard copper telephone cable.

DSL uses some fairly sophisticated technology to superimpose digital signals over the unused frequency spectrum of an ordinary telephone line. A DSL connection can simultaneously carry voice and data, if permitted by your DSL provider. Voice and data signals travel over telephone lines to your telephone company's local switching station. There, the voice signals are separated from the data signals. Voice signals are routed to the regular telephone system; data signals are routed to your ISP and then to the Internet (Figure 6-15).

INFOWEBLINKS

Nationwide, DSL vendors are grouping and regrouping. How might this affect your Internet access? You'll find up-to-date consumer information at the **DSL InfoWeb**.

 **CLICK TO CONNECT**
www.course.com/np/concepts11/ch06

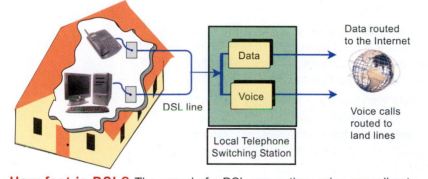

DSL line

Data

Voice

Local Telephone Switching Station

Data routed to the Internet

Voice calls routed to land lines

FIGURE 6-15

Voice and data signals travel over DSL to a special device at the local telephone switching station, where they are divided and routed to an ISP or to the regular telephone network.

How fast is DSL? The speed of a DSL connection varies according to the characteristics of your telephone line and your distance from the telephone company's switching station. Current DSL technology can transport data at speeds up to 6 Mbps downstream for a distance of about 1.25 miles (2 km). DSL signals deteriorate over distance, however. For DSL to work, your connection has to be within about 3 miles (5 km) of your telephone company's switching station. The distance requirement only pertains to the distance between you and the switching station. Once the signal arrives at the switch and is handed off to the ISP, it can travel the Internet backbone anywhere in the world.

How do I get DSL service? In many areas, DSL is a joint venture between the telephone company and an ISP. The telephone company is responsible for physical cabling and voice transmission. An ISP is responsible for data traffic. Some DSL installations require trained service technicians, whereas others can be handled by consumers. Prior to installation, you can contact your telephone company to find out if DSL is available in your area. Your DSL service provider will supply you with instructions for the installation.

Do I need special equipment for DSL? DSL installations typically require a modem and filters (Figure 6-16). DSL is digital, so data doesn't need to be changed into analog signals and then back to digital as it does when you use a dial-up connection. DSL signals have to be modulated, however, so they can travel on non-voice frequencies. A **DSL modem** is a device that connects a computer to a telephone line and converts computer data signs into signals compatible with DSL.

DSL filters prevent voiceband signals from interfering with DSL signals. Professionally installed business DSL systems typically use a single external filter. Self-installed DSL kits provide filters that you connect to every device in your home that uses the telephone line.

FIGURE 6-16

DSL Equipment

A DSL filter connects to lines used for handsets, answering machines and similar devices. For example to filter a telephone, unplug the phone, plug the filter into the wall jack, and plug the phone cable into the filter.

A DSL modem plugs into your computer's USB or Ethernet port.

6

CABLE INTERNET SERVICE

What is cable Internet service? **Cable Internet service** is a means of distributing always-on broadband Internet access over the same infrastructure that offers cable television service. Local and national cable companies, such as Comcast, Cox, and Charter, offer cable Internet service for a monthly subscription. Of all Internet services, cable Internet currently offers the fastest access speeds.

How does cable Internet service work? The cable television system was originally designed for remote areas where TV broadcast signals could not be received in an acceptable manner with an antenna. These systems were called community antenna television, or CATV. The CATV concept was to install one or more large, expensive satellite dishes in a community, catch TV signals with these dishes, and then send the signals over a system of cables to individual homes.

The topology of a CATV system looks a lot like the physical topology for a computer network. And that is just what is formed when your cable TV company becomes your Internet provider. Your computer becomes part of a neighborhood LAN joined by wiring for the cable TV infrastructure.

Are television and data signals carried over the same cable? CATV coaxial and fiber optic cables have plenty of bandwidth to carry television signals for hundreds of channels in addition to digital data. CATV cables provide bandwidth for television signals, incoming data signals, and outgoing data signals (Figure 6-17).

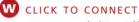

INFOWEBLINKS

For an in-depth look at cable modem technology, connections, bandwidth, and security, follow the links at the **Cable Internet Service InfoWeb**.

Ⓦ CLICK TO CONNECT
www.course.com/np/concepts11/ch06

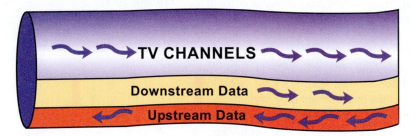

FIGURE 6-17

A CATV cable has enough bandwidth to support TV channels and data flowing downstream as well as data flowing upstream.

How fast is cable Internet service? Most cable Internet service is asymmetric, with upstream speeds considerably slower than downstream speeds to discourage subscribers from setting up public Web servers. A standard home service plan offers 6 Mbps (6000 Kbps) downstream and 384 Kbps upstream. Some premium plans offer speedier connections of 30 Mbps downstream and 2 Mbps upstream.

Cable signals are not particularly vulnerable to environmental interference, but data transport speeds are affected by subscriber use. The cable you share with your neighbors has a certain amount of bandwidth. As more and more neighbors use the service, it might seem to get slower and slower. As an analogy, consider the luggage conveyor belt in an airport, which moves at a constant speed. If you have three pieces of luggage and you are the only passenger on the plane, your bags arrive one right after another. However, if you just arrived on a full 747, your bags are intermixed with those of hundreds of other passengers, and it takes longer to collect them.

Your cable company's network carries packets at a constant speed. However, if many of your neighbors are sending and receiving packets at the same time, your packets seem to arrive more slowly. Cable Internet subscribers often find that their connection speed varies quite dramatically.

Do I need special equipment for cable Internet service? When you set up your computer for cable Internet service, you are essentially linking to the cable network's Ethernet-style LAN that connects a neighborhood of cable subscribers. The two requirements for this type of connection are circuitry to handle Ethernet protocols and a **cable modem**, which converts your computer's signal into one that can travel over the CATV network.

Most subscribers rent a cable modem from their cable company, and the rental fee is included in the monthly bill. Third-party cable modems manufactured by LinkSys, Motorola, DLink, and other companies can be purchased from electronic stores, but it is a good idea to check your cable company first to make sure the modem you select is compatible.

A cable modem can plug directly into a coaxial cable wall jack. If you need to connect your cable set-top box and cable modem to a single wall jack you can use a cable splitter as shown in Figure 6-18.

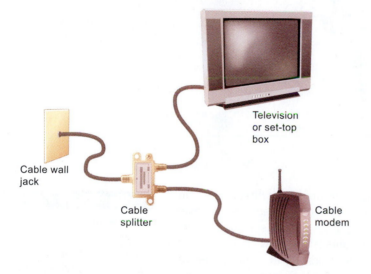

Television or set-top box

Cable wall jack

Cable splitter

Cable modem

FIGURE 6-18

If your home has only one CATV cable outlet, you need to use a splitter to link it to your cable modem and television. If you have multiple cable outlets, you can connect your cable modem directly to any one of them.

6

Most cable modems have USB and Ethernet ports, and you can use one or the other. Cable companies instruct subscribers to connect the modem directly to a computer. However, as you'll learn in the Internet Security section, the safest way to connect your computer to a cable modem is through a router.

How secure are cable Internet connections? In the early days of cable Internet service, some cable Internet subscribers were unpleasantly surprised when they happened to open Windows Network Neighborhood, only to be greeted with a list of their neighbors' computers! When you boot a PC, Windows automatically connects to available LANs and looks for shared files, folders, and printers on LAN workstations. Because cable Internet service uses LAN technology, computers in different households were treated as workstations on a shared LAN.

Today, most cable companies use DOCSIS-compliant cable modems that block crossover traffic between subscribers. **DOCSIS** (Data Over Cable Service Interface Specification) is a data transport technology that includes security filters. DOCSIS secures your computer from your neighbors, but it does not close up all the security holes that are opened when you use an always-on connection.

SATELLITE INTERNET SERVICE

What is satellite Internet service? Most people are familiar with services that provide access to television programming over a personal satellite dish. Many companies that provide satellite TV also offer Internet access. **Satellite Internet service** is a means of distributing always-on, high-speed asymmetric Internet access by broadcasting signals to and from a personal satellite dish. In many rural areas, satellite Internet service is the only alternative to a dial-up connection.

How does satellite Internet service work? Satellite Internet service uses a geostationary satellite to transmit computer data directly to and from a satellite dish owned by an individual (Figure 6-19).

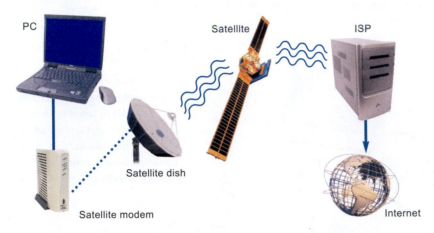

PC
Satellite
ISP
Satellite dish
Satellite modem
Internet

FIGURE 6-19

Satellite Internet services use geostationary satellites to transmit data between subscribers and ISPs.

Of all the Internet access services, satellite has the farthest range and ability to reach remote areas. Whereas ISDN and DSL services are limited to within several miles of a telephone company switching station, and cable Internet service is limited to areas where cable television is offered, satellite Internet service can be beamed to any customers whose property offers an unobstructed view of the orbiting satellite—in the U.S. that means an unobstructed view of the southern sky.

How fast is satellite Internet service? Satellite service typically averages 400–500 Kbps actual downstream speed but only 100–256 Kbps upstream. Satellite transmission and reception can be slowed or blocked by adverse weather conditions, such as rain and snow, which makes this type of data transport less reliable than wired Internet access services, such as cable and DSL.

Satellite data transport is subject to latency delays of one second or more, which occur as your data is routed between your computer and a satellite that orbits 22,200 miles above the Earth. Latency might not pose much of a problem for general Web surfing and downloading files, but it can become a showstopper for interactive gaming that requires quick reactions, and for Voice over IP.

As with cable Internet service, satellite data transport speeds might seem to decline when other users subscribe to the service because the satellite's bandwidth is shared among all users.

TERMINOLOGY NOTE

Communications satellites in geostationary orbits move in synchronization with the Earth's rotation and always appear to be in the same location of the sky.

INFOWEBLINKS

The **Satellite InfoWeb** dishes out lots of goodies about satellite Internet access—the technology, service providers, prices, and even reviews from disgruntled computer game players.

CLICK TO CONNECT
www.course.com/np/concepts11/ch06

Does satellite Internet service require special equipment? A satellite dish and modem are the two pieces of equipment required for satellite Internet access. If you are already receiving satellite television and your service provider offers Internet services, you can most likely use your current satellite dish. Most consumer satellite dishes used in the northern hemisphere are fixed in one position and 18–31 inches (46–79 cm) in diameter, as shown in Figure 6-20.

FIGURE 6-20

Today's satellite dishes are small and can be easily mounted on roofs or exterior walls.

A **satellite modem** (Figure 6-21) is a device that modulates the data signals from a computer into a frequency band that can be carried to the satellite dish where it is converted to another frequency, amplified, and transmitted. The modem usually connects to the satellite dish using two coaxial cables: one to transmit and one to receive. The modem then can be connected to the Ethernet port of a computer, or for better security to an Ethernet port of a router.

Equipment and installation costs for satellite Internet service are higher than other Internet services. Some companies charge US$500 or more for a satellite dish, though the cost is often spread over a 2–3 year service contract.

FIGURE 6-21

A satellite modem looks similar to cable and DSL modems, but is designed for entirely different technology.

FIXED WIRELESS SERVICE

What is fixed wireless Internet service? **Fixed wireless Internet service** (also called wireless broadband service) is designed to offer Internet access to homes and businesses by broadcasting data signals over areas large enough to cover most cities and outlying areas. Fixed wireless technologies are MAN (metropolitan area network) standards, in contrast to technologies such as Wi-Fi, which are LAN (local area network) standards. One of the most well-known fixed wireless standards is WiMAX, currently offered in the U.S. by companies such as Clearwire and in the UK by companies such as iAirWorks.

What is WiMAX? **WiMAX**, which stands for Worldwide Interoperability for Microwave Access, is an Ethernet-compatible network standard designated as IEEE 802.16. Its popularity is growing because it offers an alternative to wired technologies, such as DSL and cable Internet service, that require expensive infrastructures. WiMAX can be deployed in rural areas where cable service is not available and where customers are too far away from a telephone switching station for DSL service. In an urban environment, WiMAX can offer healthy competition to other Internet service providers.

How does WiMAX work? A WiMAX system transmits data to and from WiMAX antennas mounted on towers. A single tower can serve a large geographical area—up to 3,000 square miles (about 8,000 square KM). Towers can transmit data to subscribers, they can relay data to other towers using microwave links, and they can connect directly to the Internet backbone by cable. Within 3 miles/8 km of the tower, signals are strong enough to be picked up by subscribers on a non-line-of-sight device, similar to a Wi-Fi access point. Beyond that range, a line-of-sight antenna is required (Figure 6-22).

What is the speed of WiMAX? Under ideal conditions, WiMAX can transmit data at 70 Mbps. Actual speed, however, is affected by distance, weather, and usage. Current services claim speeds of 1.5–3 Mbps downstream. WiMAX can be distributed as symmetrical or asymmetrical service.

Fixed wireless technologies have less latency than satellite Internet service and can usually offer connection speeds suitable for online gaming, Voice over IP, and teleconferencing.

What equipment do I need for WiMAX access? Your wireless service provider typically supplies a wireless modem that you connect to your computer. The modem includes a transceiver to send and receive signals to a wireless point of access, usually located on a nearby communications tower. Subscribers on the outlying edges of the network's range might also require an antenna mounted on a window or roof, and line-of-sight range to the WiMAX tower.

INFOWEBLINKS

The **WiMAX InfoWeb** has the latest information on this up-and-coming Internet access technology.

 CLICK TO CONNECT
www.course.com/np/concepts11/ch06

FIGURE 6-22

A WiMAX tower broadcasts signals over a wide area. Subscribers close to the tower can use non-line-of-sight modems to pick up the signal.

FIXED INTERNET CONNECTION ROUNDUP

What's the best Internet connection for my PC? The best Internet connection depends on your budget, what's available in your area, and what you do while connected. For fixed Internet access, cable Internet service is usually the first choice, when available. If cable Internet service is not available, or proves slower or less dependable than expected, the next choice would be DSL or fixed wireless service, if available.

If several fixed Internet services are offered in your area, the table in Figure 6-23 can help you evaluate their requirements, costs, advantages, and disadvantages.

FIGURE 6-23

Fixed Internet Access Options

	Dial-up	ISDN	DSL	Cable	Satellite	WiMAX
Downstream speed (max)	56 Kbps	128 Kbps	384 Kbps–6 Mbps	1.5–6 Mbps	500 Kbps	70 Mbps
Upstream speed (max)	33 Kbps	128 Kbps	128 Kbps–6 Mbps	256–768 Kbps	40–60 Kbps	70 Mbps
Downstream speed (actual)	44 Kbps	128 Kbps	2 Mbps	3 Mbps	400 Kbps	1.5–3 Mbps
Latency	100–200 ms	10–30 ms	10–20 ms	10–20 ms	1–3 seconds	10–50 ms
Short video (72 MB) download	4 hours	78 minutes	5 minutes	3.2 minutes	24 minutes	6.4 minutes
Requirements	Telephone line, ISP, voiceband modem	Telephone line, ISDN service, ISDN terminal adapter	Computer located within 3 miles of local telephone switch; DSL modem	CATV service that provides Internet access; cable modem	Clear view of southern sky; satellite dish and modem	WiMAX modem, line-of-sight to WiMAX tower for distances > 3 miles
Monthly fee	$5–$25	$50–$150	$30–$200	$20–$50	$35–$80	$0–$60
Installation cost	$0	$0–$200	$0–$100	$0–$50	$200–$300	$50–$150
Always-on	N	N	Y	Y	Y	Y

QuickCheck

1. A _____ modem converts the signals from your computer into signals that can travel over telephone lines.

2. Always-on connections include dial-up, DSL, cable, and dedicated lines. True or false? _____

3. The two requirements for cable Internet service are circuitry to handle _____ protocols and a cable modem.

4. Satellite Internet service typically has a high _____ rate, which is unsuitable for some online gaming and Voice over IP.

5. _____, which adheres to IEEE 802.16 standards, is one of the most promising fixed wireless Internet technologies.

 CHECK ANSWERS

Portable and Mobile Internet Access

WHEN YOU'RE ON THE GO and away from your fixed Internet connection you are not necessarily cut off from your e-mail and other Internet activities. Portable and mobile Internet technologies can provide Internet access while you visit friends, commute to work or school, or take a vacation. In Section C, you'll find out what's available for portable and mobile access today and what's on the drawing board for the future.

INTERNET TO GO

What are the limitations of fixed Internet access? Fixed Internet access through dial-up, cable, ISDN, DSL, satellite, and 802.16 WiMAX tether your computer to a tangle of cables and equipment, such as modems, satellite dishes, and antennas. It can be a hassle even to relocate your Internet modem to another room.

In the days when bulky desktop computers were the norm, a fixed Internet connection seemed sensible. Today, however, with the proliferation of sleek notebook computers, PDAs, smartphones, and other portable computing appliances, Internet users are clamoring for the freedom to roam while accessing online information and services.

Suppose that you're on vacation and you want to download music for your iPod. What if you're visiting a friend across town and you want to get your e-mail? If you drop into your local video rental store with only your cell phone, can you access the Internet Movie Database to scan some reviews before you select a movie? If you're on a cross-country trip, would you be able to boot up your computer, access the MapQuest Web site, and give the driver directions to the nearest Cracker Barrel restaurant? (See Figure 6-24.)

FIGURE 6-24

Using mobile Internet access, you could find the location of the nearest roadside eatery.

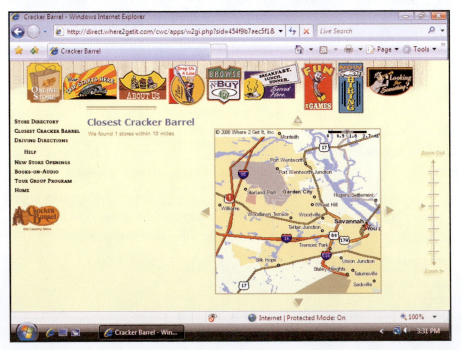

These scenarios are all possible, but not necessarily using a single Internet service provider, user account, or computer. Today's state-of-the-art is not an ideal "Internet anywhere" technology that allows you to use one Internet service and any digital device to tap into the global pool of Internet data from any location. Instead, Internet consumers have to contend with a hodgepodge of technologies, multiple accounts, and an unfortunate number of user fees for blanket Internet access.

Although the ideal Internet everywhere service has not yet arrived, looking at currently available portable and mobile Internet access options is worthwhile. Depending on your lifestyle, one or more of these options could be beneficial, productive, or just plain fun.

What is portable Internet access? Portable Internet access can be defined as the ability to easily move your Internet service from one location to another. It is portable in the sense that a hot plate is portable. It is light and compact enough to easily carry, even though you have to remain in one spot when it comes time to use it. Portable Internet access services include Wi-Fi, portable satellite, and portable wireless.

What is mobile Internet access? Mobile Internet access offers a continuous Internet connection as you are walking or riding in a bus, car, train, or plane. It is very similar in concept to cellular phone service that allows you to move freely within the coverage area as it seamlessly hands-off your signal from one tower to the next. Mobile Internet access includes Wi-Fi, mobile WiMAX, and cellular broadband service.

Let's take a look at some of the most popular and promising portable and mobile Internet access technologies.

WI-FI HOTSPOTS

How does Wi-Fi fit in with the Internet everywhere concept? As you learned in the previous chapter, Wi-Fi is a wireless LAN technology. In addition to being popular for home networks, Wi-Fi is also used for public networks, operated by merchants, hotels, schools, and municipalities. If your computer is equipped for Wi-Fi, as are most of today's notebooks, you have a portable means of accessing the Internet by carrying your computer to any Wi-Fi hotspot (Figure 6-25).

What is a Wi-Fi hotspot? A **Wi-Fi hotspot** is an area in which the public can access a Wi-Fi network that offers Internet service. You can find hotspots in coffee shops, RV parks, hotels, community centers, and airports. Wi-Fi hotspot availability is currently limited, but expanding even in small towns and rural areas. Web sites such as *www.jiwire.com* help you find Wi-Fi hotspots in a specific city.

How do Wi-Fi hotspots work? In a typical scenario, you might take your notebook computer—equipped with a Wi-Fi card—to your local Starbucks cafe. You buy a cup of cappuccino, sit down in a comfortable chair, and switch on your computer. Windows networking utilities automatically sense a Wi-Fi network and establish a connection. You can then surf the Web, just as though you were at home using a connection supplied by your desktop ISP.

Some Wi-Fi hotspots offer free service; others require a service plan or one-time use fee. Companies that offer hotspot service plans include T-Mobile, Verizon, Sprint, and AT&T Wireless. Hotspot service plans are not interchangeable. You cannot, for example, access a T-Mobile hotspot if you have a Verizon Wi-Fi Access service plan. Access plans can be expensive, too.

6

FIGURE 6-25

Starbucks Wi-Fi hotspots offer wireless Internet access to customers with T-Mobile accounts.

Daily plans for 24 hours of access run US$4–$10. Monthly unlimited access costs about the same as basic cell phone service.

Can I use hotspots for mobile Internet access? Although Wi-Fi is popular for portable Internet access, it does not typically provide acceptable mobile Internet access because you can only remain connected within range of the network's hotspot. The current model for using most Wi-Fi hotspots is that you enter the area of coverage, find a location with a strong signal, and remain there while accessing the Internet. Wi-Fi handoffs from one Wi-Fi network to another are clumsy and prone to packet loss, which is unacceptable for Voice over IP or streaming video applications. Although the IEEE has been working on standards for mobile Wi-Fi (sometimes called Mobile-Fi) protocols, new developments in WiMAX might make mobile enhancements to Wi-Fi unnecessary.

How fast is hotspot access? The speed of a hotspot is related to the speed of the wired line that connects it to the Internet. A hotspot that goes through a 1 Mbps DSL line will be slower than a hotspot that goes through a 6 Mbps cable Internet connection. Hotspot providers such as Verizon advertise peak speeds of 1.5 Mbps. Actual speed can vary depending on your distance from the access point, the number of people logged in, and interference from other networks.

Is hotspot access secure? Hotspots are as insecure as any wireless connection, so it is important for hotspot users to take steps to secure their computers with anti-virus software, firewalls, and encryption.

PORTABLE AND MOBILE WIMAX

What is portable WiMAX? WiMAX can be used as a portable technology because Internet access is available to subscribers anywhere within a tower's coverage area. WiMAX subscribers who use non-line-of-sight modems with an integrated antenna (Figure 6-26) can easily move their Internet service by relocating their modems anywhere within the service provider's coverage area. One WiMAX service provider encourages its customers to "Just plug in and jump online anywhere within the service area."

WiMAX-equipped computers make portable Internet access even easier. Just as many notebook computers are equipped with Wi-Fi circuitry, manufacturers can also add WiMAX circuitry and antennas, eliminating the need for an external modem.

What are the pros and cons of portable WiMAX? The big bonus of portable WiMAX is that you use the same Internet service provider whether you are at home or on the road. You do not need supplemental service contracts or day passes as you do for Wi-Fi hotspots. On the downside, WiMAX is not yet in widespread use and therefore coverage is limited.

What about mobile WiMAX? Mobile WiMAX is an up-and-coming standard destined to be deployed by ISPs and cell phone carriers because it is designed to offer Internet access with seamless handoff from the coverage area of one tower to the coverage area of another tower. Mobile WiMAX could make it possible for you to deal with a single service provider for all your cell phone and Internet access needs.

FIGURE 6-26

WiMAX modems are easy to transport and can be plugged in anywhere within the coverage area of a WiMAX tower.

PORTABLE SATELLITE SERVICE

What if I travel to remote areas? WiMAX and Wi-Fi hotspots provide coverage in cities and small towns, but do not typically extend far into sparsely populated areas. If you plan to remain in a single remote location, then fixed satellite Internet service is a good option. If, however, Internet access is required as you travel to various remote locations to hike, ski, or conduct research, then portable satellite technology is available (Figure 6-27).

How does portable satellite technology work? For portable satellite Internet service, a satellite dish is typically mounted on a vehicle. The disk is stowed while the vehicle is in motion, but can be quickly deployed when the vehicle stops.

Like a fixed satellite dish, a portable dish transmits signals to and receives signals from a geostationary satellite. If a fixed satellite dish moves out of alignment, signals can no longer be captured dependably. The challenge with mobile satellite service is to make sure the dish is correctly aimed from whatever location it is used.

Portable satellite systems have self-aiming hardware that automatically deploys the dish and rotates it until it locks onto the satellite signal (Figure 6-28).

FIGURE 6-27

Portable satellites are perfect for RVs and trucks, but remain a pricey technology.

▶ CLICK TO START

FIGURE 6-28

A vehicle-mounted satellite dish can be deployed from a control panel inside the vehicle.

6

How fast is portable satellite service? Portable satellite service providers advertise downstream speeds of 400–2000 Kbps and upstream speeds of 50–500 Kbps. Larger dishes offer faster speeds. Portable satellites work well for browsing the Web and working with e-mail. As with fixed satellite service, however, latency becomes a factor for real-time applications such as videoconferencing and online gaming.

What is the cost of portable satellite service? Portable satellite service doesn't work with tight budgets. Hardware, which includes the satellite dish, deployment mechanics, satellite modem, and interior control panel, can cost US$5,000–10,000. Hardware costs do not include installation, which has to be done by a professional according to FCC regulations. Monthly service fees range from US$100–300.

CELLULAR DATA SERVICE

How can I use my cell phone service to access the Internet?

In many countries, including the U.S., cell phone coverage is extensive and the technology is truly mobile; you can use cell phone service while walking or in a moving vehicle. The handoff as you travel from one cell area to another is seamless. Using cell phone technology to access the Internet offers mobility that is not yet possible with most of today's wired or wireless computer network technologies. And though in the past cellular-based Internet access was slower than dial-up, new technologies offer speeds that are more competitive with other broadband offerings.

How fast is cellular data transport?

Data transport rates depend on the technology of the cellular system. Cellular technology is classified by generation. First-generation (1G) technology is analog and offers few features beyond voice communications. Transmitting data requires a voiceband modem to convert data into analog tones. Transmission speed is glacial. Digital third-generation (3G) technologies offered by today's cellular service providers offer higher capacity for voice and data.

Within each generation are technology subcategories, such as CDMA, GSM, and GPRS. You can see from Figure 6-29 that 2.5G technology offers speeds equivalent to a 56 Kbps dial-up modem. 3G technologies have speeds similar to satellite Internet service, and can potentially match DSL speeds.

FIGURE 6-29

Cellular Network Technologies

Generation	Service	Speed *	Features
1G	AMPS	<10 Kbps	Analog voice service No standalone data service
2G	CDMA PDC GSM	14.4 Kbps 9.6 Kbps 9.6–14.4 Kbps	Digital voice service 9.6 Kbps–14.4 Kbps speed Enhanced calling features, such as caller ID No always-on data connection
2.5G	GPRS	56–114 Kbps	Adds always-on data transfers at 171.2 Kbps to CDMA and GSM networks
3G	UTMS EDGE EV-DO HSUPA	2 Mbps 384 Kbps 2.4 Mbps 5.76 Mbps	Superior digital voice service Broadband multimedia data services

* Maximum theoretical speed; actual speeds are slower

Can I get to the Internet from any cell phone? Most cellular service providers offer e-mail and Internet services. Basic phones can access a limited number of specially designed Web sites using WAP.

What is WAP? WAP (Wireless Access Protocol) is a communications protocol that provides Internet access from handheld devices, such as cell phones. WAP-enabled devices contain a microbrowser that displays simplified versions of popular Web sites, such as CNN, Google, Yahoo!, MSN, ESPN, UPS, FedEx, The Weather Channel, MapQuest, and Moviefone. WAP devices also include e-mail software formatted for small, low-resolution screens (Figure 6-30).

Can I use a cell phone to access regular Web sites and use other Internet services? Accessing the "real" Internet requires a different approach than offered by WAP. For the real Internet, cellular service providers offer data services, sometimes referred to as **mobile broadband**. Broadband access requires a fast connection, a data service subscription, and mobile broadband equipment.

What are the fastest cellular technologies? The fastest cellular technologies for Internet access are EDGE, EV-DO, and HSUPA.

EDGE (Enhanced Data rates for Global Evolution) is a 3G technology that works on GSM and GPRS cellular networks. EDGE can carry data at speeds up to 236 Kbps. AT&T, CellularOne, and T-Mobile are among the carriers in the U.S. that offer their subscribers EDGE technology for Internet access.

EV-DO (Evolution Data Optimized) is a 3G technology developed by Qualcomm and currently deployed by Alltel, Sprint, and Verizon in major U.S. markets. For mobile access, EV-DO offers average speeds of 400–700 Kbps, with peak speeds up to 2 Mbps.

HSUPA (High-speed Uplink Packet Access) is a 3.5G technology with theoretical maximum speeds in excess of 5 Mbps. AT&T is upgrading its EDGE technology to HSUPA in major markets.

Broadband speeds are not available in all of a cellular service provider's coverage area. Coverage maps can give you an idea of the service area, but actual coverage and speeds can vary. Where broadband coverage is not available, your device might operate at a much slower speed or might not have access to data services.

What is a data service plan? Most cellular service providers offer a data service plan for accessing the Internet. Prices for these plans fluctuate, but can range from $30 per month and up. Less expensive plans typically limit the amount of data you can send and receive, treating megabytes like minutes. Make sure you understand the terms of your service contract. Some service contracts prohibit users from streaming or downloading music, movies, or games; making Voice over IP phone calls; and using file-sharing networks.

What equipment do I need for mobile broadband Internet access? With a data service plan, there are four ways to take advantage of mobile broadband: using a handheld PDA or smartphone, using a mobile broadband card in a PC, using a mobile broadband-enabled computer, or using a cell phone as a modem for your desktop or notebook computer.

FIGURE 6-30

The advantage of WAP-enabled devices is their portability. The disadvantage is their small, low-res screens. Although various schemes for scrolling over a full-sized Web page have been tried, most WAP users stick to Web sites specially designed for small screen devices.

6

How do I access the Internet with a handheld device? You can use a smartphone or cellular-ready PDA to access the Internet by subscribing to a data service plan offered by a mobile phone provider such as AT&T or Sprint. Many handheld devices also have built-in Wi-Fi and can access the Internet when in range of a Wi-Fi LAN or hotspot. When the device senses the Wi-Fi network, it gives you the opportunity to connect and enter the wireless key if one is required. Once connected, your handheld device can access the Internet at Wi-Fi speeds.

PDAs such as Palm Tungstens, Blackberries, or HP iPAQs typically include browser and e-mail software (Figure 6-31). Like PDAs, smartphones are equipped with a browser and e-mail software. Some devices, such as the iPhone, include specialized software to access popular Web sites such as Google Maps and YouTube.

You can use a handheld device's QWERTY keyboard, stylus, or touch screen to manipulate icons for opening software, operating menus, and clicking links. Many of these devices use Windows Mobile OS, so the controls are similar to those on your desktop or notebook computer.

Although the screens on PDAs and smartphones have much higher resolution than the screens on basic WAP-enabled phones, they cannot display most Web pages at their normal size. To avoid excessive scrolling, you can use a service such as Skweezer (*www.skweezer.com*) to reformat Web pages to fit on a small screen (Figure 6-32).

FIGURE 6-31

Many PDAs offer a large color screen and can connect to Wi-Fi hotspots and cellular data services to access the Internet.

FIGURE 6-32

Skweezer and similar utilities shrink and reformat Web pages so that they fit on small screens.

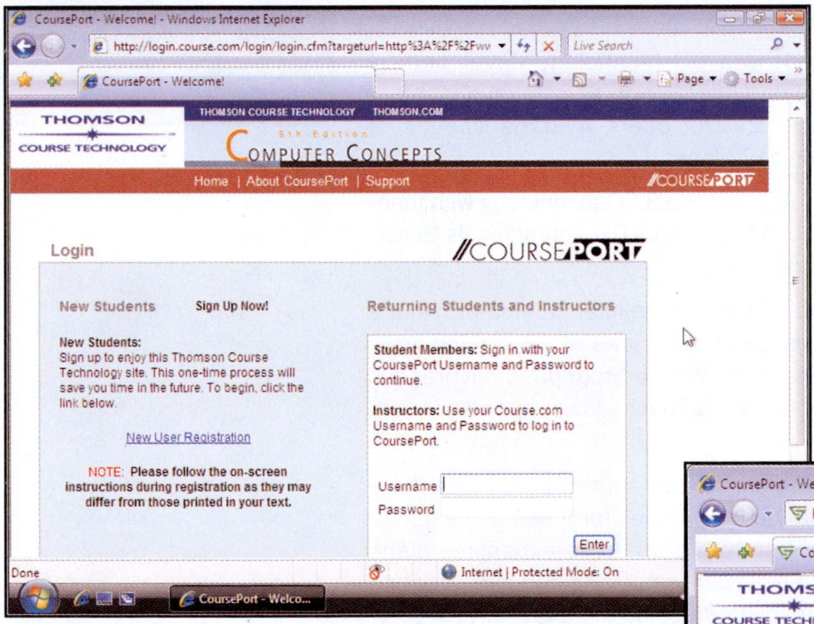

▶ CLICK TO START

Web page displayed on a computer screen

Web site displayed on a small screen using Skweezer

How do I access the Internet with a cellular wireless modem? Most cellular service providers offer wireless modems compatible with EDGE, EV-DO, or HSUPA technology (Figure 6-33). The modem slides into the PC card slot of your notebook computer and is installed following the manufacturer's instructions.

After the card has been installed, you can use it to connect to the Internet and use your usual set of tools, including your Web browser and e-mail software. With a full-size screen, you'll have the "real" Internet experience.

What is a mobile broadband-enabled computer? Just as many notebook computers come with Wi-Fi circuitry for accessing wireless LANs and hotspots, some manufacturers offer notebook computers with built-in EDGE, EV-DO, or HSUPA circuitry for mobile broadband access. Although these configurations reduce installation hassles, they are not in demand because they limit consumers to one mobile broadband technology and its corresponding cellular service provider.

How do I use a phone as a modem? Some cell phones connect to your computer and act as a wireless modem to transmit data over the Internet. Data speed depends on the phone's technology. A GSM/GPRS phone transmits data at a much slower speed than an EDGE, EV-DO, or HSUPA phone.

To make the connection, obtain a data cable that's compatible with your phone from your cellular service provider or an electronics outlet. Follow the manufacturer's instructions for installing the cable and setting up a modem connection. When you want to access the Internet, plug your cellular phone into your computer (Figure 6-34) and connect through your mobile data service. As with other connection options for desktop and notebook computers, you can use your usual suite of Internet software.

FIGURE 6-33

A cellular wireless modem slides into a notebook computer's PC slot.

FIGURE 6-34

Using a data cable such as CellularOne's QuickLink, your cellular phone can become a modem for your notebook computer.

6

QuickCheck

1. [   ] Internet access can be defined as the ability to easily move your Internet service from one location to another.

2. A Wi-Fi [   ] is an area in which the public can access a Wi-Fi network that offers Internet service.

3. Mobile [   ] is an up-and-coming standard destined to be deployed by ISPs and cell phone carriers because it is designed to

offer Internet access with seamless handoff from the coverage area of one tower to the coverage area of another tower.

4. [   ] is a protocol that provides Internet access from handheld devices with limited screen size and a cell phone-style keypad.

5. EV-DO, [   ], and HSUPA are examples of mobile broadband Internet services.

▶ CHECK ANSWERS

Internet Services

WHEN YOU HAVE an Internet connection, you have access to a global data communications system. You know that protocols such as TCP/IP and UDP handle basic data transport, but additional protocols, sometimes referred to as application protocols, make possible a variety of useful Internet applications, such as real-time messaging, Voice over IP, grid computing, FTP, and file sharing. Section D explains how these applications work.

REAL-TIME MESSAGING

What is real-time messaging? A networked-based **real-time messaging system** allows people to exchange short messages while they are online. One-on-one messaging is referred to as **instant messaging** (IM) and group communications are referred to as **chat**.

Everyday, millions of people use messaging systems, such as AOL Instant Messenger, Yahoo! Messenger, Google Talk, Apple iChat, and Windows Live Messenger, to communicate with friends, family, and coworkers. Some systems offer voice messaging options, so that participants can speak to each other using computer-based microphones. Video messaging is another option offered by some systems when both participants have computer-based cameras.

How does real-time messaging work? Most messaging is based on a client/server model that uses a server to handle communication packets between the participants (clients). When participants log on, they connect to the messaging server, which authenticates their user IDs and passwords. The server then sends back a list of participants or buddies. For a chat room, "participants" are those people who are currently logged into the discussion. For instant messaging, "buddies" are people in a participant's list of friends who are currently online.

Messages are typed into client software (Figure 6-35), which uses messaging protocols to break the message into packets and ship them to the server for distribution or directly to the recipient, depending on the system. Some protocols encrypt messages before they are transmitted. Messaging and chat protocols include IRC (Internet Relay Chat), MSNP (Mobile Status Notification Protocol), and Jabber.

FIGURE 6-35

IM client software displays a window for typing and viewing messages.

How do I set up a messaging system? Your first step is to select a service and get the client software. Messaging systems, such as Windows Live Messenger and Apple iChat, are packaged with computer operating systems and their client software might already be installed. Client software for other systems, such as AOL Instant Messenger, Yahoo! Messenger, and Google Talk, can be accessed by going to a Web site. When the client is installed, you can follow the configuration instructions to choose a nickname, "handle," or address, enter a buddy list, select chat rooms, and so on. Then you're ready to send messages and chat.

Is messaging safe? If you are using messaging services, you should take steps to protect your computer and your privacy. Instant messaging systems are vulnerable to instant message viruses and spyware hidden in files accessed by clicking a link in the message. To avoid these viruses, make sure your anti-virus software is active and up to date, use antispyware, and never open files or click links from someone you don't know (Figure 6-36). IM viruses take advantage of coding errors and vulnerabilities in instant messaging clients, so it is important to make sure you use the most recent version of the client and install updates as they become available.

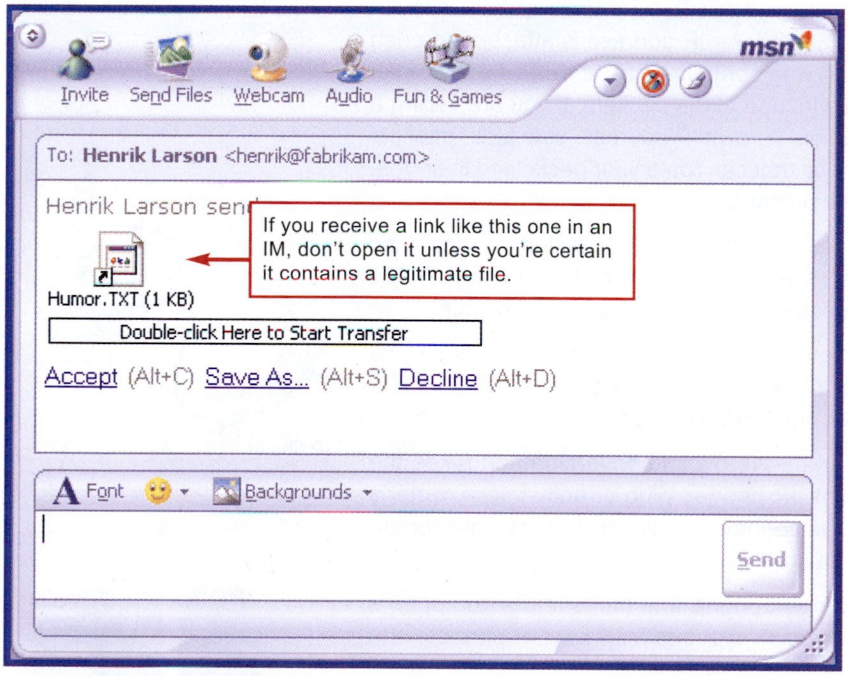

FIGURE 6-36

Clicking an IM link to a file could activate a virus, worm, or spyware.

6

To protect your privacy, be careful about revealing personal information in chat rooms. Many chat room participants are not who they appear to be. Some people are just having fun with fantasy identities, but others are trying to con people by telling hard luck stories and faking illnesses. In a chat room, never reveal personal information, such as your full name, address, or phone number. Resist the temptation to meet face to face with chat room participants. When using IM, be aware that messages can be recorded by your buddies and forwarded to others. Messages can also be intercepted, so before discussing sensitive health and financial matters, check to see if your IM system encrypts messages.

VOICE OVER IP

What is Voice over IP? As the Internet extended throughout the world, a cadre of IP telephony devotees began to spread the word about a technology called VoIP, which they claimed could make worldwide voice calling free, as in no monthly telephone or cellular phone bills. VoIP technology is finally here, but has not quite matched the hype.

VoIP (Voice over Internet Protocol) or Voice over IP, is a technology in which a broadband Internet connection is used to place telephone calls instead of the regular phone system. The earliest VoIP connections were computer-to-computer connections. Both the person initiating the call and the person receiving the call had to have computers with microphones and headsets or speakers. You could only call people who were using the same VoIP software and who happened to be online when you wanted to call them. These early VoIP systems worked more like instant messaging with voice than a traditional phone call.

You can still use VoIP to make calls from one computer to another, but today's VoIP systems allow you to use a standard telephone handset to make or receive calls. They also allow you to receive calls from regular telephones and to place calls to standard telephones.

How do today's VoIP systems work? Today's VoIP systems convert voice communications to data packets. An IP address is attached to each packet. If you are calling a friend with computer-based VoIP, for example, your friend's IP address will be attached to the packets. If you are calling a land line or other destination without its own IP address, your VoIP packets will carry an IP address of a service that can route your packets to their destination using land lines where necessary.

How do I set up VoIP? To set up a standard VoIP system, you can use an inexpensive ATA, IP phone, wireless IP phone, or USB phone. These devices can be obtained from an electronics store or a VoIP provider.

An **ATA** (Analog Telephone Adapter) is a device that converts analog voice signals into digital data packets. An ATA connects a standard telephone to an Ethernet port on a LAN router or broadband modem.

An IP phone contains built-in analog to digital conversion and takes the place of a conventional handset. IP phones plug directly into a router's Ethernet port. A wireless IP phone sends Wi-Fi signals to a wireless router, so the handset can be used like a cordless phone.

A USB phone is a VoIP-enabled telephone that plugs into a computer's USB port. Figure 6-37 illustrates configurations for ATAs, IP phones, and USB phones.

If you plan to call land lines (rather than limiting your calls to other computers), you must sign up for VoIP service, such as Vonage or Skype. VoIP services charge a fixed monthly fee to handle the handoff between your Internet-based call data and local telephone companies. When you sign up for VoIP service, you are assigned a standard telephone number. You might be surprised to learn that you can choose the area code for your VoIP number, and it doesn't have to be an area code from your physical location.

How do I use VoIP? When you pick up your VoIP handset, you hear a dial tone, just like with a regular phone. After you hear the dial tone, you can dial any phone, almost anywhere in the world just as you would from a regular phone.

FIGURE 6-37

Adding a VoIP handset to your computer system requires an ATA, an IP phone, or a USB phone.

Ethernet cable

Broadband modem or router

ATA

Standard telephone

Ethernet cable

Broadband modem or wired/wireless router

IP phone

Computer

USB cable

USB phone

What are the advantages of Voice over IP? VoIP service is still relatively new, but it already offers significant advantages over traditional phone service. For one monthly or annual fee, most VoIP services offer unlimited local and long distance calls in the U.S., Canada, and many other countries including most of Europe. That means no minute limitations, no roaming, no extra fees for long distance—not even for many international calls.

VoIP plans typically offer flexibility that regular phone service cannot match. Like a cell phone, your VoIP phone number moves with your IP phone or ATA. If you go away to school, you can continue to use your old number even though you may be in a different state or a different country. You can even carry your VoIP service on a portable USB flash drive for use in any public computer with an Internet connection (Figure 6-38).

Cell phones that offer Wi-Fi as well as cellular phone service can be used to make calls using your VoIP or cellular service. When you are within range of a Wi-Fi hotspot, the call is routed through the Internet as a VoIP call. If no hotspot is in range, the call is routed through the standard cellular service.

What are the disadvantages of VoIP? Like any technology, VoIP is not perfect. It does have disadvantages. The quality of VoIP calls can vary from good to very poor. If you have a fast Internet connection and if the packets flow freely over the Internet, the quality of the connection can be very good—basically as good as a telephone call using a land line. If your Internet connection is slow or if your packets encounter congestion, however, the quality of the connection can be very low, with clipped, almost unintelligible words.

VoIP service can let you down in an emergency. Like cordless phones, VoIP requires wall power. If the power goes out, you cannot use your VoIP phone. Since a VoIP number is not associated with a physical address, 911 systems cannot automatically direct emergency responders to your location in the event of an emergency. Most VoIP providers ask that you update your physical address when you move your VoIP phone so that 911 operators can find you in an emergency.

FIGURE 6-38

VoIP goes portable with a small set of earphones and software carried on a USB flash drive that can be plugged into any computer with Internet access.

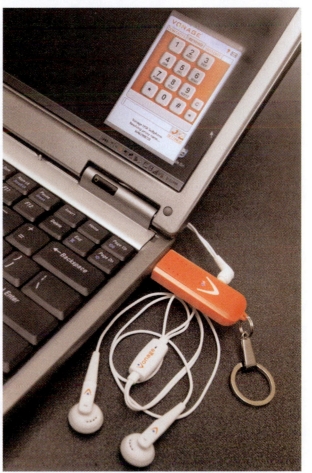

6

GRID COMPUTING

What is a grid computing system? In the days when the Internet was really taking off, computer scientists noticed that thousands of computers connected to the Internet sit idle for hours while the people who own them are in meetings, talking on the telephone, sleeping, or otherwise occupied. If these idle processing cycles could be harnessed, they could supply a tremendous amount of computing power—perhaps as much as a supercomputer.

A **grid computing system** is a network of diverse computers, such as PCs, Macs, workstations, and servers, in which each computer contributes processing resources to solving a single problem. Computer grids generate massive processing power by using many off-the-shelf personal computers, which work together to achieve processing speeds that rival some of the world's top supercomputers. Grid computing systems can be public or private. Some grid systems use computers connected to the Internet as resources; others operate on private networks.

How do grids work? Grid management software divides computational problems into pieces that are farmed out to individual computers on the grid for processing. Each computer on the grid runs grid client software that contains the program necessary to process a piece of the problem. In this manner, complex calculations or tasks can be performed in parallel by using as many computers as are available on the grid. Results are sent back to the grid management software for consolidation. Figure 6-39 illustrates the basic architecture of a grid computing system.

Where are grid systems used? Because of their scalability, low cost, and high performance, grid computing systems play a central role in scientific high-performance computing. One of the most famous examples of a grid system is the SETI@home project. People who wish to donate their computers' idle processing cycles to the SETI@home project can download and install grid client software (Figure 6-40).

FIGURE 6-39

A grid computing system uses a diverse variety of computers as generic and equal resources.

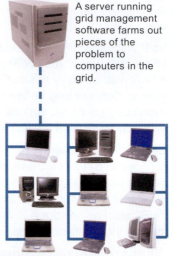

A server running grid management software farms out pieces of the problem to computers in the grid.

Computers in the grid run grid client software and send results back to the server.

INFOWEBLINKS

For more information about this fascinating use of grid computing, take a look at the **SETI@home InfoWeb**.

W CLICK TO CONNECT
www.course.com/np/concepts11/ch06

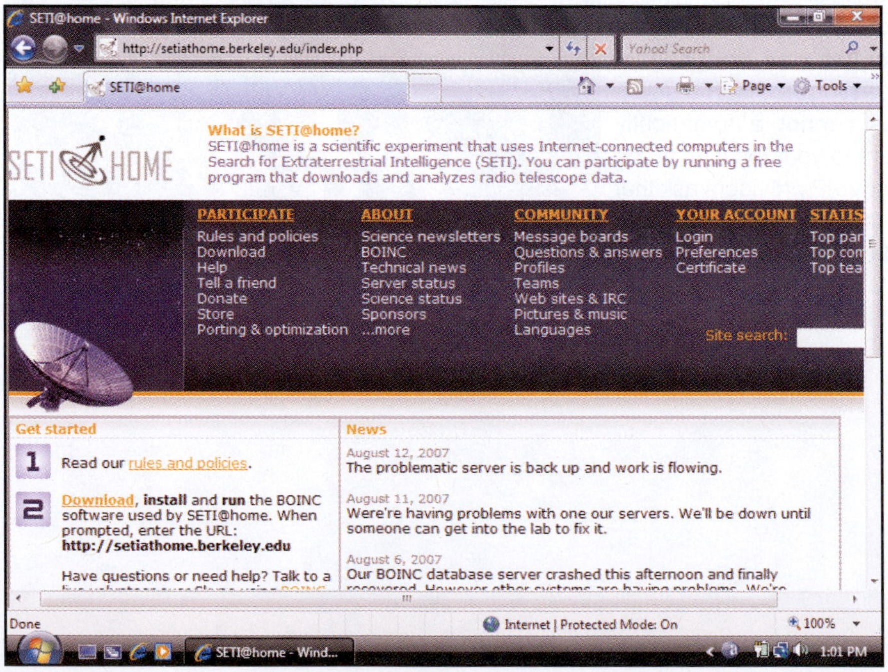

FIGURE 6-40

SETI@home consists of a grid management system and millions of privately owned personal computers whose owners donate idle processing time to the project. The SETI@home grid management system receives and stores raw data from the Arecibo radio telescope in Puerto Rico, divides this data into small segments for analysis, and farms out each segment to one of the privately owned computers.

What kinds of problems are best solved using grid systems?

Grid computing systems perform best on large, complex problems that can be divided into smaller problem segments, which can be processed in any sequence and at any time. One example of this type of problem is the process used to crack encryption algorithms, which are based on keys formed from very long numbers. The longer the number, the more keys are possible. For example, 56-bit encryption has many more possible keys than 12-bit encryption. Modern computerized encryption algorithms, which use 56-bit keys, were once thought to be unbreakable because the key can be any one of billions of numbers.

In 1997, a company called RSA Security Inc. set up a series of contests that awarded monetary prizes to the first person who could crack messages encrypted with a variety of common encryption algorithms. The contest caught the eye of a group of scientists who had an interest in encryption techniques and grid computing. The group, led by scientist Jeff Lawson, realized it would be possible to win the contest using simple brute force computing, which means trying every possible key. All that was needed was enough computer processing power to try all the different key combinations.

Lawson's group, Distributed.net, obtained the processing power by using a grid system. Group members created grid management software to divide keys into blocks and assign each block to one of the computers on the grid for processing. Each computer on the grid does the same thing—it starts with the first key in its block, checks it against the encrypted message to see if it's the correct key and, if unsuccessful, moves on to the next key. As more people donate their idle computer cycles to the project, the processing proceeds faster and faster. Using grid technology, Distributed.net cracked several encryption keys once thought to be unbreakable.

The first victory, RSA's RC5-56 challenge, was cracking a 56-bit code in 250 days. Over the course of the project, Distributed.net received donated cycles from more than 500,000 computers. The grid processed more than 34 quadrillion keys at a peak rate of 7 billion keys a second—the equivalent of 26,000 Pentium computers! In 2002, Distributed.net broke 64-bit encryption in 1,757 days with the help of 331,252 grid participants who tested 15,769,938,165,961,326,592 keys. Efforts to crack 72-bit encryption have been ongoing since 2002.

In addition to analyzing radio telescope signals and breaking codes, grid computing projects currently exist for applications such as studying global climate changes, predicting earthquakes, playing chess, and searching for new medicines (Figure 6-41). Sony is even considering a grid of Internet-connected PlayStation gaming consoles to enhance online game performance.

Not all computing tasks are suited to grid systems, however. Some problems cannot be divided into small processing segments for grid systems; other problems require extensive human interaction or highly specialized equipment.

FIGURE 6-41

Public Grid Computing Projects

First distributed computing network to play online chess.

Study climate change and improve the understanding of, and confidence in, climate change predictions for the 21st century.

Crack encryption algorithms.

Protein folding research related to neurological diseases such as Alzheimer's and Parkinson's, and many cancers and cancer-related syndromes.

Finding very large prime numbers.

fightAIDS@home

AIDS disease and drug modeling.

6

FTP

What is FTP? FTP (file transfer protocol) provides a way to transfer files from one computer to another over any TCP/IP network, such as a LAN or the Internet. The purpose of FTP is to make it easy to upload and download computer files without having to deal directly with the operating system or file management system of a remote computer. FTP also allows authorized remote users to change file names and delete files.

Do I need to use FTP? Many people use FTP without even knowing it. When you download an updated device driver from a technical support site, when you access a document in PDF format from a corporate Web site, or when you pull down an MP3 file from your favorite music site, FTP is in action although the mechanics of it are incorporated into other applications.

People who use FTP are often sharing large files stored on a file server in conjunction with a project. Files can be uploaded to the server by one participant and downloaded by others. An alternative to FTP, sending files as e-mail attachments, is not practical with very large files or for participants with slow Internet connections.

How does FTP work? An **FTP server** typically resides on a computer containing files that remote users might want to access. The server runs software that listens on ports 20 and 21 for requests coming in from other computers. When a request arrives, the server makes sure the user who made the request has rights to access the file. If the request is valid, the file is transferred over the Internet as a series of packets to the requesting computer, where it is saved in a designated location on a local storage device.

How can I access FTP servers? You can access FTP servers with FTP client software or with a browser. An **FTP client**, such as WSFTP, FTP Voyager, CuteFTP, or open-source FileZilla, offers an easy-to-use interface for accessing FTP servers. Convenient features allow you to save a list of server addresses and their corresponding user IDs and passwords, so you can connect to an FTP server with one click. FTP clients also allow you to download more than one file at a time and they can pick up where they left off if the transfer is interrupted by a glitch in your Internet connection (Figure 6-42).

FIGURE 6-42

FTP clients such as FileZilla make it easy to upload and download files from an FTP server.

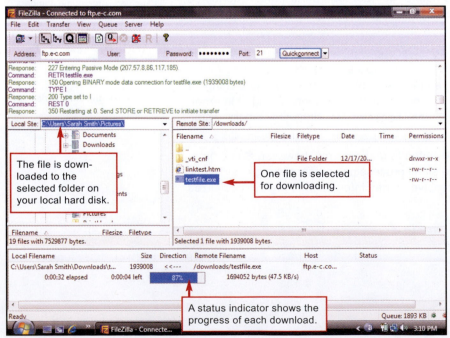

CLICK TO START

Web browsers also allow you to access FTP servers as shown in Figure 6-43. Not every FTP server is accessible from a browser, and those that are might work only for downloading files, not uploading them. If you plan to work with FTP a lot, you should get FTP client software.

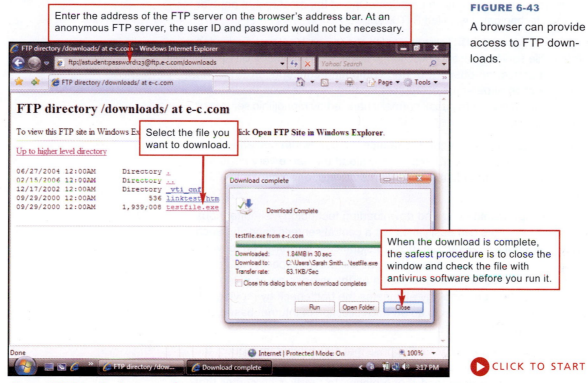

FIGURE 6-43

A browser can provide access to FTP downloads.

▶ CLICK TO START

6

Does FTP include security to prevent unauthorized access? Some FTP sites require remote users to log in before accessing files. A login ID and password can be obtained from the FTP site operator. Access rights can be configured in various ways to allow or prevent remote users from changing file names, deleting files, uploading files, or downloading files.

What is anonymous FTP? Anonymous FTP can be accessed by logging in without a password by using the user ID "anonymous." Some anonymous sites request users to enter their e-mail addresses as a password, but rarely is that piece of information used for verification or tracking.

FILE SHARING

What is file sharing? File sharing, sometimes called **P2P file sharing** uses peer-to-peer (P2P) protocols that allow users to obtain files from other users located anywhere on the Internet. In the late 1990s, file sharing burst onto the national scene when college students became aware of a technology called Napster that provided free access to hit songs.

File sharing originated on FTP-style servers, which held huge collections of popular music stored in digital MP3 files that could be easily downloaded and played on a computer or transferred to CD. Free distribution of music without the copyright holder's permission is illegal and file sharing server operators quickly encountered the legal ramifications of their computer's shady dealings.

To avoid legal hassles, file sharing technology evolved from thinly disguised client/server models to more distributed models that displaced legal responsibilities from a single operator of a central server to hundreds of users who each might store and share a dozen or fewer songs. Rather than store the actual files on a server, Napster stored only a list of song titles, with pointers to privately-owned computers from which the files could be downloaded. After a legal challenge shut down Napster, a more decentralized technology called Gnutella emerged. One of the most recent popular file sharing technologies is called BitTorrent.

What is BitTorrent? **BitTorrent** is a file sharing protocol that distributes the role of file server across a collection of dispersed computers. BitTorrent is, in some sense, an offshoot of grid computing concepts, in which an ad-hoc collection of personal computers located anywhere on the Internet can cooperate to complete a task normally handled by monolithic servers or supercomputers.

A BitTorrent network is designed to reduce the bandwidth bottleneck that occurs when many people attempt to download the same very large file, such as a feature-length film, application software, or an interactive 3-D computer game.

With conventional uploading and downloading technology, simultaneous requests for large files can easily max out a central server's capacity. Such a bottleneck could, for example, pose a significant barrier to nationwide movie distribution over the Internet. Imagine the server capacity needed to handle simultaneous download requests on the release dates of big box office hits. BitTorrent technology eliminates the bottleneck by moving the workload from a single server to an ad-hoc collection of Internet-based personal computers.

How does BitTorrent work? Suppose that 100 computers request the film *Hancock* at about the same time. A server breaks the movie file into pieces and begins to download those pieces to the first computer that requested the movie. As more computers request the file, they become part of a "swarm" that uses peer-to-peer technology to exchange file pieces with each other. After the server has downloaded all the file pieces to the swarm, its job is complete and it can service other requests. The swarm continues to exchange file pieces until every computer in the swarm has the entire file (Figure 6-44).

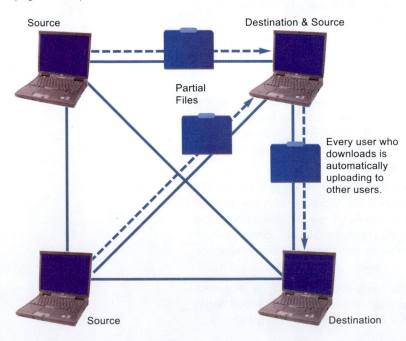

Source | Destination & Source

Partial Files

Every user who downloads is automatically uploading to other users.

Source | Destination

FIGURE 6-44

BitTorrent protocols dissect files into small chunks that might reside on different computers. Source computers have received parts of a file from a server. They then distribute these parts to other computers in the swarm.

How do I use BitTorrent? BitTorrent client software is currently available from several Web sites. After installing the client, you can use it to download from any BitTorrent-enabled site simply by clicking the file you want. The BitTorrent client handles the entire file-swapping procedure. After getting the entire file, good etiquette requires clients to remain connected to the swarm so that they can "seed" (see BitTorrent Lingo box, Figure 6-45) file pieces to others.

FIGURE 6-45

BitTorrent Lingo

Swarm: A group of computers temporarily networked to download a file.

Tracker: Server software that helps establish a swarm of end-user computers.

Seed or seeder: A computer that has downloaded an entire file and can upload pieces to other clients in a swarm.

Leech or leecher: A computer in the process of obtaining file pieces from a swarm.

Chokers: Clients that don't allow other clients to download file pieces.

Are BitTorrent and similar file swapping networks legal? File swapping networks are often used to illegally distribute copyrighted material. Napster, the original music file sharing network was closed down by court order in 2001 because most of the freely shared music was distributed without the permission of copyright holders. The Napster name and logo are now used by Roxio for an online music store similar to iTunes. Although BitTorrent technology differs from the Napster model, BitTorrent networks are not immune to the consequences of copyright infringement. Several U.S. and European BitTorrent sites have been raided for ignoring copyright laws.

Peer-to-peer file sharing networks and distributed technologies like BitTorrent have legitimate uses for distributing music, images, videos, and software with the approval of copyright holders. Peter Jackson's production diaries for King Kong have been posted for download using BitTorrent technology. Universal Studios and several independent film companies have released movie trailers with BitTorrent technology. The technology itself is not illegal; it is the use of the technology that is subject to legal scrutiny.

Is BitTorrent safe? Because BitTorrent files are assembled from little segments that come from a jumble of computers, they would seem on first thought to be bad candidates for distributing malware. Intelligent hackers would realize that their malicious code could easily be chopped up, too, and that pieces of it might not be delivered. And yet, BitTorrent files have become a source of adware and spyware. If you use BitTorrent make sure your computer is protected with a security software suite that offers good spyware protection.

QuickCheck

1. One-on-one messaging is referred to as instant messaging (IM) and group communications are referred to as _____ .

2. You can use VoIP to call other computers because it is an Internet service, but you cannot use it to call land lines. True or false? _____

3. SETI@home is an example of _____ computing, which generates massive processing power by using many off-the-shelf personal computers linked together by the Internet.

4. _____ makes it easy to upload and download computer files without having to deal directly with the operating system or file management system of a remote computer.

5. _____ is a peer-to-peer file sharing protocol that uses a "swarm" of computers to exchange chunks of data that can be eventually assembled into complete files.

▶ CHECK ANSWERS

Internet Security

WHEN COMPUTERS are connected to a network, the risk of intrusion has to be taken seriously. When the connection is Internet-based, billions of people are just an IP address away from your computer and its valuable, personal, and confidential data. Section E explains the mechanics of an intrusion attempt, and offers some practical advice for securing your computer against unauthorized access.

INTRUSION ATTEMPTS

Should I worry about intrusions? Suppose you live in a really dangerous neighborhood where gangs roam the streets, painting every available surface with graffiti and randomly attacking residents. A seemingly endless number of burglars creep from house to house looking for unlocked doors and windows, and occasionally trying to pick a lock or two. Punk kids rummage about looking for cars with keys in the ignition, unlocked doors, or loose hubcaps. Dark figures sift through your garbage cans searching for scraps of information that can be pieced together to steal your identity (Figure 6-46).

FIGURE 6-46

The Internet offers a wealth of useful tools and services, but it can be a dangerous neighborhood.

Unfortunately, this dangerous neighborhood has many similarities to the Internet where gangs of hackers deface Web sites, look for backdoors left open by network administrators, crack passwords to gain access to your data, and probe ports looking for ways to sneak bots into your computer. Your Internet connection puts you right in the middle of this dangerous neighborhood anytime you are connected—and with always-on connections like DSL and cable Internet service, that means any time your computer is turned on.

In the context of computers, an **intrusion** is any access to data or programs by hackers, criminals, or other unauthorized persons. As the result of an intrusion, data can be stolen or altered, system configurations can be changed to allow even more intrusions, and software can be surreptitiously installed and operated under the remote control of a hacker. Without any visible sign or warning, hackers can infiltrate your computer to obtain personal information or use your computer as a launching pad for attacks on other machines. Yes, you should worry about intrusions!

How do hackers use the Internet to infiltrate my computer?
One of the most common ways of gaining unauthorized access to a network-based computer is by looking for open ports. Earlier in this chapter you learned that network services, such as the Web, FTP, and e-mail operate on ports. As an example, you learned that Web requests use port 80.

If a port is open and listening for requests—on any computer, even your own—a hacker can exploit it like an unlocked door to gain access to your computer. Hackers are continuously canvassing the Internet and probing ports to find their next victims.

A **port probe** (or port scan) is the use of automated software to locate computers that have open ports and are vulnerable to unauthorized access. Software called a port scanner goes to a randomly selected IP address and systematically checks for a response from each port. Open ports can then be further tested to gauge their suitability for exploitation.

You might scoff at your computer's vulnerability to port probes. After all, there are millions and millions of computers on the Internet and a limited number of hackers. The chances of your computer becoming a target would seem to be slim, but the opposite is true. Port scanning software can examine more than 30,000 computers per minute. If you use security software to monitor port probes on an unprotected computer, you would see probes within seconds of going online. According to researchers, the average "survival time" for an unprotected computer to remain uncompromised is only 9 minutes.

How do I know if ports are open? You can check your computer for open ports using software tools such as Steve Gibson's Shields Up! at *www.grc.com*. You can initiate an "innocent" port probe to discover vulnerabilities. A security report like the one in Figure 6-47 is your goal.

FIGURE 6-47

Your computer's ports are most secure if they don't even appear to exist when probed using a port scanner.

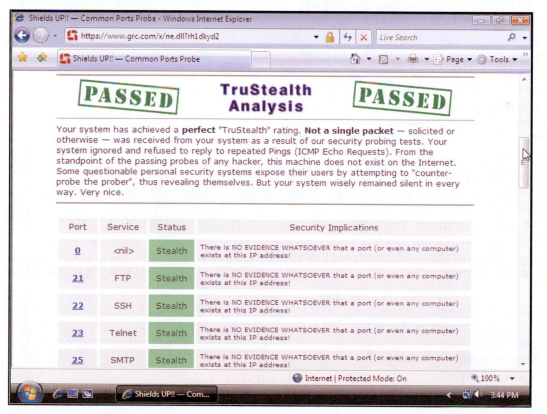

CLICK TO START

SECURING PORTS

How do I secure the ports on my computer? One of the easiest steps to enhance your computer's security is to turn it off when you aren't using it. When your computer is turned off, its ports are inactive and they are not vulnerable to intrusions. Putting your computer into sleep mode or activating a screen saver is not sufficient protection. Your computer must be shut down and turned off.

You should also keep your computer up-to-date with the latest operating system security patches and service packs. Operating systems are closely linked to port activity. Known vulnerabilities in Windows and Internet Explorer can be exploited to access ports or launch additional attacks once a port is breached. As Microsoft develops security patches, they are posted at Microsoft's Web site, *www.microsoft.com/security*. Check the site frequently to download the most recent patches. You can also configure Windows to automatically check for and install patches (Figure 6-48).

What about firewall protection? In the context of networking, a **firewall** is software or hardware designed to filter out suspicious packets attempting to enter or leave a computer. Firewall software helps keep your computer secure in several ways. It makes sure that incoming information was actually requested and is not an unauthorized intrusion. It blocks activity from suspicious IP addresses and—best of all—it reports intrusion attempts so that you can discover whether any hackers are trying to break into your computer.

You can use firewall software to open and close ports on your computer. Although it might seem safest to close all the ports, doing so would prevent you from accessing most Internet services, such as the Web, e-mail, instant messaging, and FTP. Most firewall software is preconfigured to block only unnecessarily open ports targeted by hackers.

Windows Vista includes firewall software that you can access and configure from the Security Center (Figure 6-49). Independently published firewall software includes Tiny Personal Firewall and BlackICE.

FIGURE 6-48

To configure a Windows Vista computer for Automatic Updates, type Security Center in the Start menu's Search box.

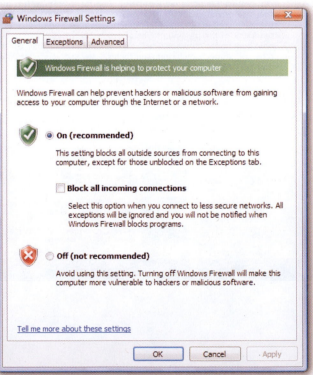

FIGURE 6-49

Windows includes a built-in firewall that can be activated to monitor intrusion attempts. Do not enable it, however, if your antivirus software firewall is activated.

What other Windows security options should I use? Sharing printers or files on a LAN or the Internet requires open ports so the data can be transferred to and from your computer. Those open ports can be a potential entryway for hackers. If no one else needs access to your printer, do not configure it for sharing. If you don't need to share files with other network users, you can turn off file sharing (Figure 6-50).

FIGURE 6-50

When you turn off file sharing, your files cannot be accessed by other network users.

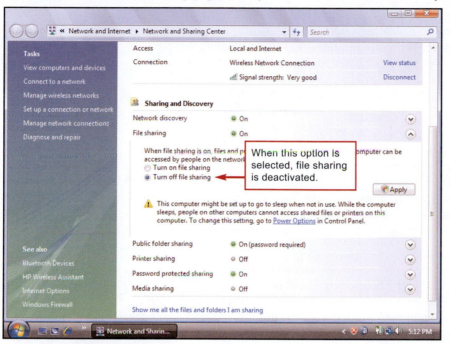

ROUTERS AND NAT

How does a router affect security? One of the most effective steps you can take to secure your computer from intrusions is to install a router. In the chapter on networking, you learned that a router can tie a LAN together and provide a portal to the Internet. Even if you have only one computer, however, a router can offer excellent security.

How does a router work? Routers are intended to work on LANs to monitor and direct packets being transported from one device to another. A router can also connect to the Internet through a DSL, cable, or satellite modem.

Routers are handy because they can screen IP addresses to keep locally addressed packets within the LAN so that they are delivered without traveling a circuitous route over the Internet and back (Figure 6-51).

FIGURE 6-51

A router monitors the IP addresses of packets on a LAN. Packets with local addresses (green) are kept within the LAN. Packets with external addresses are routed out to the Internet.

Packets with external addresses go to the Internet

Router

Packets with local addresses remain within the LAN

LAN workstations

▶ CLICK TO START

Your router has its own IP address, typically obtained from your Internet service provider's DHCP server. (Recall that a DHCP server assigns dynamic IP addresses to devices that request them.) It is also possible for your router to have a fixed IP address set up by you or an installer. The key point about your router's IP address is that it is routable. A **routable IP address** is one which can be accessed by packets on the Internet.

When you connect your computer to a router, and request an IP address, your *router* answers your request, not the ISP. Most routers are configured to assign private IP addresses. A **private IP address** is a non-routable IP address that can be used within a LAN, but not for Internet data transport. When the IP addressing scheme was devised, three ranges of addresses were reserved for internal or private use: 10.0.0.0–10.255.255.255, 172.16.0.0–172.31.255.255, and 192.168.0.0–192.168.255.255. If your computer has a private IP address it is essentially hidden from hackers.

But how do packets with private IP addresses get out to the Internet? Let's review the scenario. You have a router connected to an Internet device, such as a DSL or cable modem. The router has a routable IP address, visible to any device (and hackers) on the Internet. Your router isn't vulnerable to attacks because it doesn't contain any of your data. You've connected your computer to a router. Your computer has been assigned a private IP address.

Network address translation (NAT) is the process your router uses to keep track of packets and their corresponding private or public IP addresses. Jeff Tyson writing for *How Stuff Works* offers a useful analogy for how NAT works: "NAT is like the receptionist in a large office. Let's say you have left instructions with the receptionist not to forward any calls to you unless you request it. Later on, you call a potential client and leave a message for that client to call you back. You tell the receptionist that you are expecting a call from this client and to put her through. The client calls the main number to your office, which is the only number the client knows. When the client tells the receptionist that she is looking for you, the receptionist checks a lookup table that matches your name with your extension. The receptionist knows that you requested this call, and therefore forwards the caller to your extension."

A router and the receptionist perform essentially similar tasks. Your private IP address is like a private telephone extension in an office. Your router's public IP address is like the main switchboard number. Your router screens incoming packets and only lets one through to your private extension if you've requested it.

When you use the Internet, you initiate every valid transaction; you ask for a Web site, you ask to retrieve your mail, or you request a file from an FTP server. Only those requests that you initiate are valid. Suppose you want to download a file. You send a packet containing your request to the FTP server at 69.32.167.20. The packet goes to your router, which replaces your address with its own and makes an internal note that you initiated this FTP request. When the FTP server responds, it sends a packet addressed to the router. The router receives the packet, checks its internal note to see who made the original request, and then ships the FTP packet to your computer (Figure 6-52).

FIGURE 6-52

A router using NAT essentially cloaks your computer and makes it invisible from the Internet.

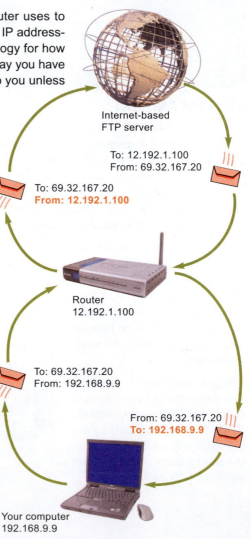

Internet-based
FTP server

To: 12.192.1.100
From: 69.32.167.20

To: 69.32.167.20
From: 12.192.1.100

Router
12.192.1.100

To: 69.32.167.20
From: 192.168.9.9

From: 69.32.167.20
To: 192.168.9.9

Your computer
192.168.9.9

VIRTUAL PRIVATE NETWORKS

Is it possible to secure connections for remote users? Sales representatives and telecommuters often have to access corporate networks by using a remote connection from home or a customer's office. It is possible to secure these remote connections by setting up **virtual private network** (VPN) access to a remote access server in the corporate office.

Who sets up VPNs? On the corporate end, setting up a secure VPN is not a trivial task and it is typically handled by specialists in the corporation's information technology department.

How do I access a VPN? Access to a VPN is usually by invitation only. Employees who need to access a VPN are given the necessary instructions, addresses, and passwords to make connections. In general, a person initiates a VPN connection by connecting to an ISP as usual. After the connection is established, a second connection to the remote access server creates an encrypted channel for data transmission. Figure 6-53 illustrates how a VPN operates.

How important is a VPN? A VPN is typically a corporate solution, whereas the other security suggestions in this section can be implemented by individuals. To recap the most important security precautions, you should turn your computer off when not in use, make sure all your computer's unnecessary ports are closed, activate firewall software, turn off file and printer sharing, and install a router. Taking these precautions might not make your computer invincible, but they offer very strong protection against intruders who might steal your identity or hijack your computer for various shady activities.

FIGURE 6-53

Virtual Private Network

6

QuickCheck

1. Hackers can use automated software to look for computers with open [_____] that are vulnerable to unauthorized access.

2. By downloading and applying operating system security [_____] and service packs, you can help to prevent unauthorized intrusions that exploit known operating system vulnerabilities.

3. [_____] software is designed to analyze incoming and outgoing packets to look for unusual activity that could be part of an intrusion.

4. One of the best defenses against intrusions is to use a(n) [_____] between your standalone or computer or LAN and your Internet connection device.

5. A(n) [_____] IP address is a non-routable IP address that can be used within a LAN, but not for Internet data transport.

▶ CHECK ANSWERS

What's Happening to Free Speech?

THE INTERNET offers instant access to information across national and cultural borders, but along with helpful information the Internet hosts a disturbing amount of unsavory material. Militias and hate groups use Web sites to spread their views. Hundreds of pornographic sites make a business of selling lewd images which can be accessed by anyone—even children. In chat rooms on innocent topics, the conversation can deteriorate into X-rated banter. Pedophile and bestiality sites that cater to warped sexual habits pop up in search engine lists. International terrorists use Web sites as recruiting tools and for boasting about suicide bombings. Criminals, terrorists, and hackers post guidebooks and tips on how to do all kinds of illegal activities, from making suitcase bombs to spreading computer viruses.

Some concerned netizens advocate cyber censorship to curtail irresponsible Web sites, blogs, discussion groups, and file sharing. Cyber censorship typically means blocking access to Web sites, but it can also mean closing sites and removing them from host servers. Censorship advocates are opposed by free speech supporters who believe that the right to free expression should be unshackled by laws or regulations.

The controversy over censorship is not new. Guidelines from the pre-Internet era also shape the cyber-censorship-vs-free-speech debate.

In most cases, words are acceptable, whereas actions can be punishable. Writing a mystery novel that describes how the main character cultivates botulism and then uses it to poison one of the other characters is acceptable. Actually carrying out such an act would be against the law. This concept was applied to cyberspace when the U.S. Supreme Court upheld a law that pornography featuring real children was illegal, but ruled that child pornography featuring computer-generated children is not illegal because children were not harmed when it was created.

Cyberlaw is not yet totally consistent on the words vs. deeds precedent, however. In some cases, words are punishable. For example, the Digital Millennium Copyright Act makes it illegal to even disseminate information on defeating software, CD, and DVD copy restrictions.

A second censorship guideline hinges on local standards of morality. Local communities can apply their own standards to determine whether material is obscene. Therefore, a raunchy magazine that you might find on a supermarket newsstand in New York City might be limited to adult bookstore shelves in a conservative Tennessee community.

Local standards, however, are difficult to sort out on the Internet where a Web surfer in Tennessee can easily access Web sites, bulletin boards, and chat groups that originate from anywhere in the world. Judges upheld the conviction of two sysops whose California-based porn site distributed obscene material to individuals in Tennessee. The sysops claimed that the Internet required a more flexible definition of "community" to account for the Internet's global accessibility; otherwise Web sites would be forced to eliminate all materials objected to by anyone. Judges denied that claim, saying that technology could be used to filter out objectionable material based on age and location information provided by member registration data.

Underlying a group of decisions on cyber censorship, the U.S. Supreme Court seems to support the concept of cyberzones that limit net access to certain materials in a way similar to how the adult sections of street-corner newsstands restrict children from browsing through certain magazines. As now-retired Justice O'Connor explained, "Cyberspace is malleable. Thus, it is possible to construct barriers in cyberspace and use them to screen for identity, making cyberspace more like the physical world and, consequently, more amenable to zoning laws." As an example, AOL is trying to develop a family-friendly Internet portal by enforcing policies against offensive speech, but has been criticized by free-speech advocates for its policies. AOL responds that it is a private company and members who disagree with AOL terms of use are free to terminate their subscriptions.

In some countries, however, cyber citizens have no choice but to use a government-controlled ISP. In many countries, free speech is not a basic right conferred to all citizens. Many dictatorial regimes want their citizens to receive news from the outside world only after it has been screened by a government censor. Officials in more than 20 countries use sophisticated tools to block Web sites, filter e-mail, and censor discussion groups.

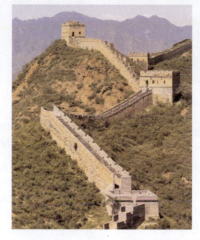

China has some of the most rigorous Internet censorship in the world. The "Great Firewall of China" as it is sometimes called, blocks Internet content by preventing IP addresses of objectionable sites from being routed through its gateways into China. The system also selectively engages in DNS poisoning, a technique that tricks a DNS server into believing it has received authentic information when, in reality, it has not. So Web surfers in China who attempt to access the Electronic Frontier Foundation's Web site that advocates free speech, might instead see a Chinese government site on social responsibility. In addition to blocking Web sites, the Chinese government filters e-mail, message boards, chat rooms, and blogs.

In Iran, government censors monitor political and news Web sites, and block access to many pornographic Web sites, anonymizer tools, sites with gay and lesbian content, politically sensitive sites, and women's rights sites. If you tried to access *Rolling*

Stone magazine's Web site from Saudi Arabia, you would find that access has been denied. The Saudi government claims it censors the Internet to preserve Islamic culture and heritage. That argument in many ways reflects the concept of cyberzones that conform to local standards of ethics and morality. Even free-speech activists at the OpenNet Initiative (ONI) seem to agree, "We do think that information should be free," states one ONI technician, "but we do need to find a balance for respect for sovereign states to preserve their own culture."

Despite such cultural sensitivity, technology giants, such as Microsoft, Yahoo!, and Cisco Systems have been criticized for providing foreign governments with tools for blocking culturally objectionable sites. Critics question whether companies in a free society should aid foreign governments' attempts to censor cyberspace.

For some people it is astonishing to realize that ideas such as liberty, equality, and women's rights would be subject to the same censorship attempts as pornography and hate speech. The solution to online censorship is still evolving as free speech comes into balance with cultural, ethical, and moral concerns in the global realm of cyberspace.

INFOWEBLINKS

You'll find more fascinating Internet myths and substantive articles about disinformation at the **Internet Censorship InfoWeb**.

W CLICK TO CONNECT

www.course.com/np/concepts11/ch06

6

What Do You Think?

ISSUE

1. Should governments be allowed to block access to Web sites based on local religions, politics, and customs?
   ○ Yes   ○ No   ○ Not sure

2. Do you believe that a privately-held Internet Service Provider like AOL has the right to censor the data posted on Web sites it hosts?
   ○ Yes   ○ No   ○ Not sure

3. Should companies like Microsoft, Yahoo!, and Cisco Systems provide blocking technology to foreign governments?
   ○ Yes   ○ No   ○ Not sure

4. Would you use filtering software that was preprogrammed to block pornographic and nuisance Web sites?
   ○ Yes   ○ No   ○ Not sure

▶ SAVE RESPONSES

Banking

FOR MOST OF HISTORY, banks used low-tech methods to track one of the world's most cherished commodities—wealth. Checking accounts were in widespread use as early as 1550, when wealthy Dutch traders began depositing money with cashiers for safekeeping. The use of printed checks became popular in England in the late 18th century—so popular that banks found it difficult to process a steadily increasing stream of checks, including those drawn on accounts from other banks.

An unverified story that has become part of bank lore describes the origin of a solution to the check processing problem. As the story goes, a London bank messenger stopped for coffee and got to talking with a messenger from another bank. Realizing that they were delivering checks drawn on each other's banks, the two messengers decided to exchange checks there in the coffee house. This event evolved into a system of check clearinghouses where representatives from various banks met periodically to exchange checks and reconcile totals in cash. By 1839, British clearinghouses were annually processing in excess of £954 million of checks—equivalent to U.S. $250 billion in today's money.

Bank clearinghouses were described in an essay, *The Economy of Machinery and Manufactures*, written by Charles Babbage in 1832. He also included a reference to the "possibility of performing arithmetical calculations by machinery" along with a description of the Difference Engine, then under construction in his workshop.

This dream of automated check clearing did not, however, become reality until more than a century later when S. Clark Beise, senior vice president at Bank of America, contracted with Stanford Research Institute (SRI) to develop a computer system to automate check processing. SRI completed a prototype in 1955 that used mechanical sorting equipment to queue up each check and MICR technology to read check numbers. In 1959, the first ERMA (Electronic Recording Machine-Accounting) system went into service. With ERMA handling calculations, 9 employees could handle the job that once required 50 people. By 1966, 32 regional ERMA systems operated by Bank of America were processing more than 750 million checks per year. ERMA and similar check processing technologies quickly integrated with bank transaction processing systems to become the bedrock of today's banking technology.

Output from check sorting machines can be submitted to the Automated Clearing House (ACH) network, which offers a secure, batch-oriented data exchange system that can be accessed by financial institutions. On a daily basis, banks submit check data and receive a report of balances due to other banks. These balances can be reconciled by electronic funds transfer over the Federal Reserve's FedWire telecommunications network.

An upswing in check fraud during the 1960s made it increasingly difficult to cash checks at local merchants. As an alternative to trying to cash checks at banks and local merchants, automatic teller machines (ATMs) were first installed in the 1970s. A typical ATM connects to a bank's front-end processor—a computer that maintains account balances for in-network customers and monitors suspicious activity. The front-end processor is separated from the bank's main computer system for security.

Some ATMs exchange data with the front-end processor by using dedicated dial-up telephone lines. Other ATMs use always-on leased lines. Legacy protocols such as SNA and 3270 bisync, are being replaced by the standard Internet Protocol (IP) that can be routed through more affordable connections, such as cable, ISDN, DSL, or Internet VPN.

ATMs are expensive—about $50,000 to purchase a machine, install it, and operate it for one year. Banks have offset this cost by charging transaction fees and reducing the number of bank tellers. Once a promising entry-level occupation, bank tellers today earn less than $20,000 per year. Although tellers continue to accept deposits, process withdrawals, and cash payroll checks, they are increasingly pressed into customer service roles—opening new accounts, issuing ATM cards, resolving disputed transactions, and assisting customers who have lost bank cards or checkbooks. Despite this shift in job description, the number of bank teller jobs is expected to fall at least 10% by 2010.

ATMs offer access to bank services from convenient locations where customers shop, eat, and hang out with friends. The Internet takes banking convenience one step further and provides round-the-clock account access from customers' homes, schools, or work PCs. Today, most banks and credit unions offer some type of online banking (also called home banking, Internet banking, or electronic banking).

Basic online banking services allow customers to access checking account and bankcard activity, transfer funds between checking and savings accounts, view electronic images of checks and deposit slips, download and print monthly statements, and reorder checks. Customers can also pay bills online by scheduling payment dates and amounts. Many credit card and utility companies offer e-billing services that automatically forward electronic bills to customers' online banking accounts. For monthly fixed-amount bills, such as car loans, online banking offers automatic payment options that deduct funds from specified checking or savings accounts.

For managing assets more effectively, online banking sites also offer sophisticated tools, including account aggregation, stock quotes, rate alerts, and portfolio management programs. Most online banking sites are also compatible with personal finance software, such as Managing Your Money, QuickBooks, AOL BankNOW, and Microsoft Money, so that transaction data can be shuttled between customer's local computers and their online banking services.

A cadre of customer support personnel staff online help desks for customers with questions about online banking. Webmasters, computer security specialists, and network technicians are also part of banking's new job corps.

Online banking services are typically housed on a well-secured Web server, and customers are not allowed direct access to the computer system that actually processes transactions. Customer privacy is maintained by the use of passwords and connections that encrypt data as it is sent to and from customers' computers.

Successful banks are built on good business decisions. Bank managers are increasingly working with business intelligence tools to look for trends in customer behavior, analyze competing financial institutions, and examine current business practices. Tools for these activities include data warehouses that collect and organize data, data mining software that organizes and analyzes data in a meaningful way, and statistical tools that formulate comparisons and trendlines.

Today, banking depends on multilayered technologies that incorporate check processing equipment, transaction processing systems, business intelligence software, ACH networks, FedWire, ATM networks, the Internet, and Web servers. Many banking practices originated from batch check processing, and only gradually have banks begun to move to more modern online transaction processing (OLTP) systems that store scanned images of checks and instantly update accounts when a purchase is made or a bill is paid.

6

New Perspectives Labs

On the BookOnCD

To access the New Perspectives labs for Chapter 6, start the BookOnCD, BookOnFlashDrive, or other NP11 BookOn product and then click the icon next to the lab title below.

▶ TRACKING PACKETS

IN THIS LAB YOU'LL LEARN:

- How Ping and Traceroute work
- How to use the Ping and Tracert utilities supplied by Windows
- How to interpret Ping and Tracert reports to determine the speed and reliability of your Internet connection
- How to access and use a graphical Traceroute utility
- How to find and use Web-based Ping and Traceroute utilities
- The advantages and disadvantages of Web-based Ping and Traceroute utilities
- How to access the Internet Traffic Report Web site and interpret its data and graphs
- How to use Internet traffic data, Ping, and Traceroute to pinpoint problems with your Internet connection

LAB ASSIGNMENTS

1. Start the interactive part of the lab. Make sure you've enabled Tracking if you want to save your QuickCheck results. Perform each lab step as directed, and answer all the lab QuickCheck questions. When you exit the lab, your answers are automatically graded and your results are displayed.

2. Use the Ping utility that's supplied by Windows to ping *www.abcnews.com*. Record the IP address for the ABC News site, plus the minimum, maximum, and average times. For each time, indicate whether it would be considered poor, average, or good.

3. Use the Tracert utility that's supplied by Windows to trace a packet between your computer and *www.excite.com*. Print the Traceroute report listing transmission times. Circle any pings on the report that indicate high latency.

4. Locate a Web-based Ping utility and use it to ping *www.gobledegok.com*. Indicate the address for the Web site where you found the Ping utility. Explain the ping results.

5. Connect to the Internet Traffic Report Web site, make a note of the date and time, and then answer the following questions:

   a. What is the traffic index for Asia?

   b. How does the index for Asia compare with the traffic index for North America?

   c. During the previous 24 hours in Europe, what was the period with the worst response time?

▶ SECURING YOUR CONNECTION

IN THIS LAB YOU'LL LEARN:

- How to use Windows utilities, online utilities, and firewall software to check the security of your Internet connection
- Why an unauthorized intruder might want to gain access to your computer
- The significance of communications ports as an intrusion risk factor
- How to use the Netstat utility to check your computer's open ports
- How to use an online utility to get a hacker's view of your computer
- Why Windows file and printer sharing can make your computer files vulnerable
- How to adjust settings for file and printer sharing
- How firewalls protect computers from intrusions
- How to adjust firewall settings

LAB ASSIGNMENTS

1. Start the interactive part of the lab. Make sure you've enabled Tracking if you want to save your QuickCheck results. Perform each lab step as directed, and answer all the lab QuickCheck questions. When you exit the lab, your answers are automatically graded and your results are displayed.

2. Use the Netstat utility to scan any computer that you typically use. Write out the Netstat report or print it. To print the report, copy it to Paint or Word, and then print. Explain what the Netstat report tells you about that computer's security.

3. Connect to *grc.com* and access the Shields Up! tests. Test the shields and probe the ports for the same computer you used for Assignment 2. Explain the similarities and differences between the Shields Up! report and the Netstat report for this computer. Which report indicates more security risks? Why?

4. In the lab, you learned how to adjust settings for Windows file and printer sharing. Without actually changing the settings, determine the status of file and printer sharing on your computer. Report your findings and indicate whether these settings are appropriate for network access and security.

5. Record the firewall settings on your computer. Indicate whether the settings are optimal for the way you use your computer on networks.

Key Terms

Make sure you understand all the boldfaced key terms presented in this chapter. If you're using the NP11 BookOnCD, BookOnFlashDrive, or other NP11 BookOn product, you can use this list of terms as an interactive study activity. First, try to define a term in your own words, and then click the term to compare your definition with the definition presented in the chapter.

Always-on connection, 307
Anonymous FTP, 337
Asymmetric Internet connection, 311
ATA, 332
BitTorrent, 338
Cable Internet service, 316
Cable modem, 317
Chat, 330
Dial-up connection, 312
DOCSIS, 317
Domain name, 307
Domain name server, 308
Domain Name System, 308
Downstream speed, 311
DSL, 314
DSL filter, 315
DSL modem, 315
Dynamic IP address, 306
EDGE, 327
EV-DO, 327
Firewall, 342
Fixed Internet access, 311
Fixed wireless Internet service, 320
FTP, 336
FTP client, 336

FTP server, 336
Grid computing system, 334
HSUPA, 327
ICANN, 309
Instant messaging, 330
Internet backbone, 303
Internet service provider, 303
Intrusion, 340
IP, 305
ISDN, 314
ISDN terminal adapter, 314
Latency, 309
Mobile broadband, 327
Mobile Internet access, 311
Modem, 304
Network access point, 303
Network address translation, 344
Network service provider, 303
P2P file sharing, 337
Ping, 310
Port, 308
Port probe, 341
Portable Internet access, 311
Private IP address, 344
Protocol suite, 305

Real-time messaging system, 330
Routable IP address, 344
Satellite Internet service, 318
Satellite modem, 319
Static IP address, 306
Symmetric Internet connection, 311
TCP, 305
TCP/IP, 305
Top-level domain, 307
Traceroute, 310
Upstream speed, 311
Virtual private network, 345
Voiceband modem, 312
VoIP, 332
WAP, 327
Wi-Fi hotspot, 323
WiMAX, 320

6

Interactive Summary

To review important concepts from this chapter, fill in the blanks to best complete each sentence. When using the NP11 BookOnCD or other BookOn product, click the Check Answers buttons to automatically score your answers.

SECTION A: The Internet infrastructure is based on high capacity communications links referred to as the Internet _____ , tied together at network _____ points where data can cross over from one NSP's equipment to another's. An Internet _____ provider offers Internet access to individuals, businesses, and smaller ISPs. The Internet uses several communications protocols, including _____ , which breaks a message or file into packets, and _____ , which is responsible for addressing packets. Every device on the Internet has an IP address, such as 204.127.128.1. _____ IP addresses are permanently assigned to computers, whereas _____ IP addresses are temporarily assigned by a DHCP server. Most high-speed Internet connections use _____ technology, and even dynamic IP addresses might seem permanent because they don't change unless you turn off your modem or your ISP has an outage. A _____ name server converts numeric IP addresses into familiar names, such as Travelocity.com. The speed of an Internet connection measured by utilities such as Ping and Traceroute refers to _____ , the elapsed time for data to make a round trip from point A to point B. The speed advertised by Internet service providers is a measure of the amount of data that travels between two points in a given amount of time. Many Internet connections are _____ , meaning the downstream speed is different than the upstream speed.

> ▶ CHECK ANSWERS

SECTION B: A _____ connection is a fixed Internet connection that uses a _____ modem and telephone lines to transport data between your computer and your ISP. Most modems use a standard called V.90 to provide a theoretical maximum speed of _____ Kbps. Dial-up connections are asymmetrical; 44 Kbps is a typical _____ speed for a 56 Kbps modem. _____ , the data rate drops to about 33 Kbps or less. _____ is a fixed, symmetric Internet connection that moves data at speeds of 64 Kbps or 128 Kbps over ordinary telephone lines through a device called a terminal adapter, which sends digital signals. _____ is a high-speed, digital, always-on, Internet access technology that runs over standard phone lines. _____ Internet service is a means of distributing always-on broadband Internet access over the same infrastructure that offers cable television service. Satellite Internet service is a means of distributing always-on, high-speed asymmetric Internet access by broadcasting signals to and from a personal satellite _____ . Fixed wireless Internet technologies are _____ area network standards, in contrast to technologies such as Wi-Fi, which are local area network standards. One of the most well-known fixed wireless standards is _____ , an Ethernet-compatible network standard designated as IEEE 802.16.

> ▶ CHECK ANSWERS

SECTION C: _____ Internet access can be defined as the ability to easily move your Internet service from one location to another. _____ Internet access offers a continuous Internet connection as you are walking or riding in a bus, car, train, or plane. Wi-Fi is an example of portable Internet access technology that allows public access to the Internet within the network's area of coverage, called a Wi-Fi _____ . Portable WiMAX and portable satellite offer additional Internet access options in the portable category. Cellular phone service providers offer two ways to access the Internet. _____ is a communications protocol that provides limited access to e-mail and Internet information from handheld devices with small screens and cell phone keypads. Mobile _____ services using EV-DO, EDGE, and HSUPA technologies offer faster access using conventional browsers and e-mail clients.

> ▶ CHECK ANSWERS

SECTION D: A networked-based real-time [_____] system allows people to exchange short messages while they are online. One-on-one messaging is usually referred to as [_____] messaging and group communications are referred to as [_____] . Most messaging is based on a client/server model that uses a server to handle communication packets between the participants. Instant messaging systems are vulnerable to instant message viruses and [_____] distributed by marketing companies. IM malware is often hidden in files accessed by clicking a link in the message. Many chat room participants are not who they appear to be. In a chat room, never reveal personal information, and resist the temptation to meet face to face with chat room participants. Voice over Internet [_____] is a technology in which a broadband Internet connection is used to place telephone calls instead of the regular phone system. An [_____] is a device that converts analog voice signals into digital data packets. It connects a standard telephone to an Ethernet port on a LAN router or Broadband modem. An [_____] phone plugs into an Ethernet port, contains built-in analog to digital conversion, and takes the place of a conventional handset. A USB phone is a VoIP-enabled telephone that plugs into a computer's [_____] port. A grid computing system is a network of diverse computers, such as PCs, Macs, workstations, and servers, in which each computer contributes processing resources to solving a single problem. One of the most famous examples of a grid system is the SETI@home project, but grid technology has been used to crack codes, analyze earthquake data, and crunch numbers for medical research. File transfer [_____] provides a way to transfer files from one computer to another over any TCP/IP network, such as a LAN or the Internet. The purpose of FTP is to make it easy to upload and download computer files without having to deal directly with the [_____] system or file management system of a remote computer. [_____] file sharing uses protocols that allow users to obtain files from other users located anywhere on the Internet. [_____] is an example of file sharing technology that links clients in a "swarm" for distributing files.

CHECK ANSWERS

SECTION E: In the context of computers, an [_____] is any access to data or programs by hackers, criminals, or other unauthorized persons. As the result of an intrusion, data can be stolen or altered, system configurations can be changed to allow even more intrusions, and software can be surreptitiously installed and operated under the remote control of a hacker. One of the most common ways of gaining unauthorized access to a network-based computer is by looking for open [_____] . A port [_____] is the use of automated software to locate computers that have open ports and are vulnerable to unauthorized access. One of the easiest steps to enhance your computer's security is to turn it off when you aren't using it. You should also keep your computer up-to-date with the latest operating system security [_____] and service packs. You can also install [_____] software designed to filter out suspicious packets attempting to enter or leave a computer. One of the most effective steps you can take to secure your computer from intrusions is to set up a [_____] , which assigns private IP addresses to the computers it controls. The process a router uses to keep track of packets and their corresponding private or public IP addresses is called [_____] address translation. Corporations try to limit intrusions by setting up virtual [_____] networks that offer encrypted connections for access to a remote server.

CHECK ANSWERS

Interactive Situation Questions

Apply what you've learned to some typical computing situations. When using the NP11 BookOnCD, BookOnFlashDrive, or any other NP11 BookOn product, you can type your answers, and then use the Check Answers button to automatically score your responses.

1. You've just got cable Internet service. Your computer is connected to a router, which you connect to the cable modem. The instructions provided by the cable company tell you to make sure [   ] is activated so that you can get a dynamic IP address.

2. You're finally ready to get a high-speed Internet connection. Because the cable modem provided by your CATV company contains Ethernet circuitry, you can simply connect the modem to your computer's [   ] port (shown in the photo at right).

3. Your Internet access seems very slow one day. You might be able to use a networking utility called [   ] to discover the source of the slowdown.

4. Suppose that you decide to open a little Web store to sell handcrafted pottery. Your Web site will need a(n) [   ] IP address, and you'll want to register a(n) [   ] name.

5. Imagine that your computer contains a 56 Kbps modem that uses the V.90 standard. You can expect about 44 Kbps [   ] speed and about 33 Kbps as the maximum [   ] speed.

6. Suppose you have installed a cable modem on a standalone PC. To secure your computer, you should first make sure that file [   ] is not activated. You should activate [   ] software to filter packets entering and leaving your computer.

7. Your friend, a film student, has created a 20 minute short film that she wants to distribute to friends. The file is much too large to be an e-mail attachment and she doesn't have access to a(n) [   ] server. You suggest that she try posting it at a [   ] P2P file sharing site where a swarm of computers can assist with the downloads.

8. You are going to be telecommuting two days a week, so your corporate information technology department has given you instructions to use the company [   ] private network.

 CHECK ANSWERS

Interactive Practice Tests

Practice tests that consist of 10 multiple-choice, true/false, and fill-in-the-blank questions are available on both the NP11 BookOn products and the NP11 Web site. The questions are selected at random from a large test bank, so each time you take a test, you'll receive a different set of questions. Your tests are scored immediately, and you can print study guides that help you find the correct answers for any questions that you missed.

 CLICK TO START

Study Tips

Study Tips help you to organize and consolidate the information in a unit by making lists, outlines, charts, and sketches. You can use paper and pencil or word processing software to complete most of the Study Tip activities.

1. Make sure you can use your own words to correctly answer each of the red focus questions that appear throughout the chapter.

2. Draw a conceptual diagram illustrating the Internet backbone, NAPs, NSPs, routers, and ISPs.

3. Draw a diagram to illustrate how computers on a LAN would access the Internet through a single DSL modem.

4. Explain the differences between static IP addresses, dynamic IP addresses, private IP addresses, and domain names.

5. Make sure that you can list the Internet access methods in which upstream transmission rates differ from downstream rates.

6. Study the Internet Access Options table in Figure 6-23. Add a statement for each column summarizing the strengths and weaknesses of each option.

7. List the options for mobile and portable Internet access and explain their strengths and weaknesses.

8. Explain the advantages of mobile broadband services compared to WAP service.

9. Create an outline to summarize the information in Section D about Internet services.

10. Make a list of security concerns that are related to Internet access.

11. Make a checklist of steps you can take to secure your computer from Internet-based intrusions.

12. Fill in the blanks on the concept map shown below to show the hierarchy of Internet access options.

6

Concept Map

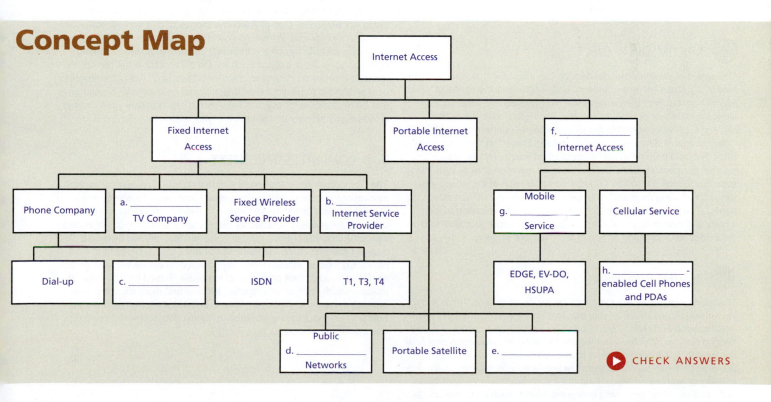

CHECK ANSWERS

Projects

CRITICAL THINKING

"The Internet treats censorship like damage and routes around it." Do you agree with this observation? Does it seem like the Internet—similar to banned books, music, videos, and satellite dishes—has a way of infiltrating even the most repressive societies? Does this tendency make censorship more tolerable in the short run?

GROUP PROJECT

Form a group with three or four other students and discuss the ways in which you secure your Internet connections. Compose a summary document that contains specific information about each group member's security and summarize the general level of security your group has in place.

CYBERCLASSROOM

Each member of your team should Ping Google and record results. Exchange your results with other students in your team to find out who has the fastest connection. How many members of the group have a connection fast enough to play online interactive multiplayer games? The member of your team with the fastest connection should summarize the team's data and submit it to your instructor.

MULTIMEDIA PROJECT

The speed of your Internet connection can affect the download time for media, such as photos and videos. Use Ping to find the speed of your Internet connection, then experiment with viewing five different short videos on news or entertainment Web sites. How does the performance of each video relate to the kind of Internet connection you have? Compile your findings into a well-organized PowerPoint presentation. Slide 1 should provide a brief description of your computer and Internet connection. Slide 2 should include a screen shot of your Ping statistics. Slides 3 through 7 should describe each of the videos you viewed, including their addresses and your evaluation of the video quality. The final slide should include your overall evaluation of the quality and convenience of Web-based video. Follow your instructor's guidelines for submitting and/or presenting your project.

RESUME BUILDER

The Internet provides resources for career development. Think about your ideal job and make a table that lists (in the first column) the top 10 qualifications and skills you'll need to be a successful applicant. In the second column, indicate whether you currently possess each qualification or skill. For those you need to develop in the future, indicate how you plan to obtain them, for example from a college course, on-the-job training, or self-paced study. Find out if you can develop any of these skills and qualifications using online resources, such as online courses. Provide addresses for any Internet resources that you find.

GLOBALIZATION

Worldwide, communications capabilities are growing at a rapid pace. Nonetheless, there exists among countries a great disparity in communications capabilities. For this project, use library and Internet resources to gather information about the communications options that are available throughout the world. You should consider which technologies are available and the number of people who use each technology. Your research can include any of the following: land-based phones, cellular phones, premium phone services such as ISDN and DSL, Internet access, broadcast television, and cable television. Once you have gathered these facts, consider how they might affect the lifestyles, politics, and economies of various regions. Suppose that you are organizing a high school debate about global communications technology. As the organizer, you must devise a controversial question on which the debate will be based. You should also write three "pro" and "con" paragraphs just to make sure that both sides of the issue will have substantial material to debate.

ISSUE

The Issue section of this chapter addressed the controversy over censorship on the Internet. Free speech is in constant struggle with individual rights and public safety. On the Web, some sites contain pornography, bigotry, and terrorist rhetoric that many people would rather not be public. One of the cornerstones of democracy, however, is freedom of speech. Where do you draw the line when it comes to censoring and filtering on the Internet? Explain your views, making sure you consider questions such as: Do parents have the right to monitor, screen, and filter their children's Web use? Are governments ever justified in regulating what their citizens can access? Should anyone be responsible for policing the Internet? Incorporate your ideas in a two-page summary and submit it to your instructor.

COMPUTERS IN CONTEXT

The Computers in Context section of this chapter focused on banking innovations and technology. The newest innovation to affect consumers is online banking. Although convenient, online banking has not been enthusiastically adopted by many consumers because of security concerns. For this project, research the services offered by online banking, then research the risks. Summarize your findings in a short paper. Connect to at least three banks that offer online banking services. Read through their promotional materials. Based on this material, indicate which bank seems to offer the best and most secure online banking services. Explain your choice in the last section of your paper. Follow your instructor's guidelines to submit your work as a printed document or by e-mail.

On the Web

STUDENT EDITION LABS

W CLICK TO ACCESS THE NP11 WEB SITE
or open your browser and connect to www.course.com/np/concepts11/ch06.
Lab results can be stored in the Universal Gradebook.

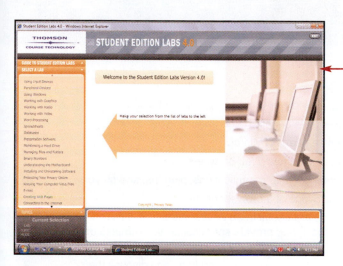

Work hands-on in structured simulations practicing important skills and concepts

PROTECTING YOUR PRIVACY ONLINE

In the Protecting Your Privacy Online Student Edition Lab, you will learn about the following topics:

- How cookies work
- Deleting cookies using a browser
- Adjusting your cookie settings in Internet Explorer

GETTING THE MOST OUT OF THE INTERNET

In the Getting the Most out of the Internet Student Edition Lab, you will learn about the following topics:

- Keeping track of your favorite Web sites
- Customizing your browser
- Searching the Web
- Online job hunting
- Online travel reservations
- Building communities

CONNECTING TO THE INTERNET

In the Connecting to the Internet Student Edition Lab, you will learn about the following topics:

- Establishing an Internet connection
- Connecting to the Internet using dial-up, DSL, cable, and wireless
- Installing ISP software
- Creating Internet connections manually

CHAPTER COURSECAST

Use your computer or iPod to hear a five-minute audio presentation of chapter highlights.

FLASHCARD COURSECAST

Interact with audio flashcards to review key terms from the chapter.

DETAILED OBJECTIVES

Make sure that you've achieved all the objectives for a chapter before it's time for your test!

TEST YOURSELF

Review chapter material by taking these ten-question tests, then send your results to the Universal Gradebook.

ONLINE GAMES

Have some fun while refreshing your memory about key concepts that might appear on the next test. You can even send your results to the Universal Gradebook!

AND MORE!

At the NP11 Web site you'll also find Extra Content and InfoWebLinks.

6

7

The Web and E-mail

LEARNING OBJECTIVES

- Describe the roles that HTML, XHTML, HTTP, URLs, browsers, and Web servers play in bringing Web pages to your desktop
- Illustrate an example of an HTML tag
- List the names of at least four Web browsers
- Describe the purpose of helper applications, plug-ins, and players
- Describe the significance of a browser cache
- Explain why cookies are useful in an environment that is based on a stateless protocol, and provide some concrete examples of their use
- Identify at least three Web page authoring tools and discuss their advantages and disadvantages
- Identify the elements that typically form a Web page
- Explain how to test and post Web pages
- List some advantages and disadvantages of HTML scripts
- List and describe the elements of a search engine
- Demonstrate that you can use a search engine to locate information on the Web
- Create advanced search queries and correctly format citations for Web-based materials
- Discuss why e-commerce has become so popular with consumers and merchants
- List some threats to the security of credit card numbers and other sensitive data during e-commerce transactions
- Describe how the following e-commerce technologies work: shopping carts, SSL, one-time-use credit cards, electronic wallets, and person-to-person payment systems
- List the features that you would expect to find in a typical e-mail software package
- Explain how an e-mail system works and describe the difference between POP and Web-based e-mail
- List security precautions you can take to avoid cookie exploits, spam, phishing, and pharming

☑ **PRE-ASSESSMENT QUIZ**
Take the pre-assessment quiz to find out how much you know about the topics in this chapter. ●

MULTIMEDIA and INTERACTIVE ELEMENTS
When using the BookOnCD, BookOnFlashDrive, or other NP11 BookOn product, the ● icons are clickable to access multimedia resources.

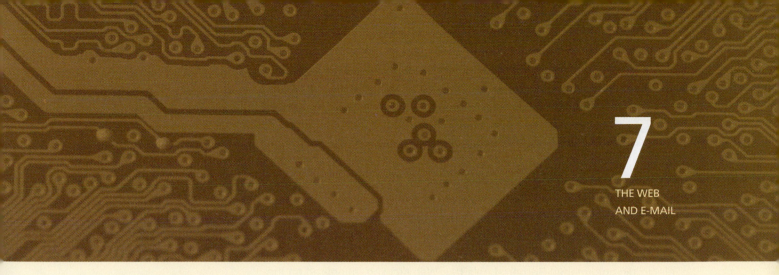

BEFORE YOU READ ON, **TRY IT**

WHAT'S MY BROWSER STATUS?

Chapter 7 focuses on the World Wide Web, or "Web" for short. The most important software tool for accessing the Web is called a browser. To learn about the browser on your computer, do the following steps:

1. Make sure your computer is on and displaying the Windows desktop.

2. Which browser do you typically use to access the Web? _____
If you don't know, look for browser icons on your desktop. Popular browsers include Internet Explorer, Safari, Firefox, and Opera.

3. What is the URL that your browser uses as your home page? _____
To find your browser's home page, start your browser. The home page is the first Web page displayed and the one displayed when you click the Home button.

4. What is the version number for the browser you are using? _____
To find your browser's version number, click Help and then click About. Your browser's version number should be displayed in a dialog box. After you write down the version number, close the dialog box.

5. Are you using the most recent version of your browser? _____

To find the most recent version for your browser, go to its Web site, for example *www.opera.com, www.mozilla.org/products/firefox, www.microsoft.com/windows/ie,* or *www.netscape.com.* You should be able to locate a download link that displays the latest version number. Unless you want to download the most recent version of your browser and have permission to do so, exit the download area and close your browser.

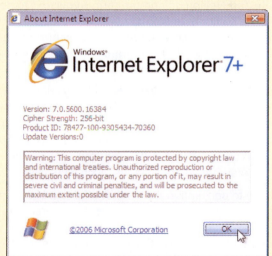

WEB SITE
Visit the NP11 Web site to access additional resources (w) that accompany this chapter.

SECTION A

Web Technology

IN 1990, a British scientist named Tim Berners-Lee developed specifications for URLs, HTML, and HTTP; a group of technologies designed to help researchers share information by creating access to a sort of "web" of electronic documents. Berners-Lee's free Web software appeared on the Internet in 1991, but the Web didn't take off until 1993 when Marc Andreessen and his colleagues at the University of Illinois created Mosaic, a graphical browser. Andreessen later formed his own company and produced a browser called Netscape, which put the Web into the hands of millions of Web surfers. In Section A, you'll peel back the layers of Web technologies to take a look at what happens behind your browser window.

WEB BASICS

What is the Web? One of the Internet's most captivating attractions, the **Web** (short for World Wide Web) is a collection of document, image, video, and sound files that can be linked and accessed over the Internet using a protocol called HTTP.

The concept of interlinking documents to access them pre-dates the Web by almost half a century. In 1945, an engineer named Vannevar Bush described a microfilm-based machine called the Memex that linked associated information or ideas through "trails."

The idea of linked documents resurfaced in the mid-1960s when Harvard graduate Ted Nelson coined the term **hypertext** to describe a computer system that could store literary documents, link them according to logical relationships, and allow readers to comment and annotate what they read. Nelson sketched the diagram in Figure 7-1 to explain his idea of a computer-based "web" of "links."

What is a Web site? A **Web site** typically contains a collection of related information organized and formatted so it can be accessed using software called a browser. You are probably familiar with informational Web sites such as HowStuffWorks, CNN, ESPN, and CNET. Websites can also offer Web-based applications, such as GoogleDocs.

In addition to conventional sites that offer text-based information and news, Web sites also host a diverse array of activities. Web sites that host amateur video, photos, and music get lots of traffic. Online shopping is a popular Web-based activity. From tiny niche boutiques to the Amazon.com superstore and countless eBay auctions, you can find just about any merchandise or service on the Web.

Many Web sites offer tools for creating your own blog and viewing blogs created by others. Blogs have become a frequently referenced source of commentary on news and politics. The Web also hosts a thriving selection of podcasts. A **podcast** (sometimes called a Webcast) is an audio file that is distributed through downloads or the use of a feed, such as **RSS** (Really Simple Syndication) or **Atom**. You can subscribe to a feed to make sure you automatically receive new podcasts as they are produced.

TERMINOLOGY NOTE

Although the terms *Internet* and *Web* are sometimes used interchangeably, they are not the same. The Web is an interlinked collection of information; the Internet is a communications system used to transport that information from computers that store it to clients who want to view it.

FIGURE 7-1

Ted Nelson's early sketch of project Xanadu—a distant relative of the Web—used the terms "links" and "web."

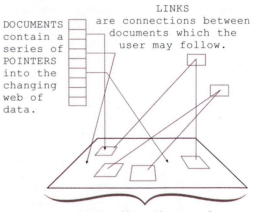

DOCUMENTS contain a series of POINTERS into the changing web of data.

LINKS are connections between documents which the user may follow.

Expanding Tissue of Text, Data, and Graphics

Podcasting was originally used to distribute radio show episodes, but is now widely used to distribute news, sports, music, educational tutorials, and blogs. **Videocasting** is similar to podcasting, but with video instead of audio files.

Social networking sites, such as Facebook, Classmates, MySpace, and Bebo link people together whether they are just down the street or on the other side of the globe. Members post their own profiles and invite friends to join. A **wiki**, such as Wikipedia, is a collaborative Web site which can be accessed and edited by anyone who wants to contribute.

Wikis, blogs, social networking sites, and Web-based applications are sometimes characterized as Web 2.0. Although the term **Web 2.0** sounds like a new version of the Web, it simply refers to new and innovative ways of using the Web. Web 2.0 uses the same Internet communications infrastructure as the "old" Web.

The activities that take place at Web sites are under the control of Web servers. A **Web server** is an Internet-based computer that accepts requests from browsers. Servers collect the requested information and transmit it back in a format that the browser can display, usually in the form of a Web page.

What is a Web page? A **Web page** is the product or output of one or more Web-based files displayed in a format similar to a page in a book. Unlike book pages, however, Web pages can dynamically incorporate videos, sounds, and interactive elements.

A Web page can be based on a document stored as a file or it can be assembled on the fly from information stored in a database. For example, a course syllabus that you view on the Web is probably written with a word processor and stored as a document on a Web server, whereas the Web page you view about a newly released CD on Amazon.com is assembled from a database that contains the CD name, artist name, song titles, price, album cover art, and other product information.

How do I access a Web page? Your main tool for accessing Web pages is browser software, such as Microsoft Internet Explorer, open-source Mozilla Firefox, or Apple's Safari. A **Web browser** (usually simply referred to as a browser) is client software that displays Web page elements and handles links between pages. When using a browser, you can access a Web page by clicking a **hypertext link** (usually referred to simply as a link) or by typing a URL (Figure 7-2).

What is a URL? Every Web page has a unique address called a **URL** (Uniform Resource Locator, pronounced "You Are ELL"). For example, the URL for the Cable News Network (CNN) Web site is *http://www.cnn.com*. Most URLs begin with http:// to indicate the Web's standard communications protocol. When typing a URL, the http:// can usually be omitted, so *www.cnn.com* works just as well as *http://www.cnn.com*.

FIGURE 7-2

Web page links can appear as underlined text, buttons, and graphics of varying size. When your pointer moves over a link, it changes from an arrow shape to a hand shape.

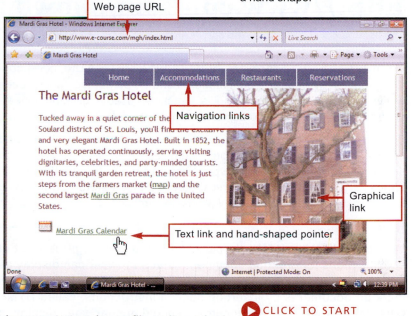

CLICK TO START

7

Most Web sites have a main page that acts as a doorway to the rest of the pages at the site. This main page is sometimes referred to as a home page, although this term can also refer to the page displayed by your browser each time it opens. The URL for a Web site's main page is usually short and to the point, like *www.cnn.com*.

The pages for a Web site are typically grouped into folders, which are reflected in the URL. For example, the CNN site might include weather information at *www.cnn.com/weather/* and entertainment information at *www.cnn.com/showbiz/*. The file name of a specific Web page always appears last in the URL. Web page file names usually have an .htm or .html extension, indicating that the page was created with Hypertext Markup Language. You'll learn more about HTML later in the chapter. Figure 7-3 identifies the parts of a URL.

FIGURE 7-3

The URL for a Web page indicates the computer on which it is stored, its location on the Web server, its file name, and its extension.

http://www.cnn.com/showbiz/movies.htm

| Web protocol standard | Web server name | Folder name | File name and file extension |

What are the rules for correctly typing a URL? A URL never contains spaces, even after a punctuation mark, so do not type any spaces within a URL. An underline symbol is sometimes used to give the appearance of a space between words, for example *www.detroit.com/top_10.html*.

Be sure to use the correct type of slash—always a forward slash (/)—and duplicate the URL's capitalization exactly. Some Web servers are case sensitive. On these servers, typing *www.cmu.edu/Info.html* (with an uppercase "I") will not locate the Web page that's stored on the Web server as *www.cmu.edu/info.html* (with a lowercase "i").

HTML

What is HTML? HTML (Hypertext Markup Language) is a set of specifications for creating documents that a browser can display as a Web page. HTML is called a **markup language** because authors mark up documents by inserting special instructions, called **HTML tags**, that specify how the document should appear when displayed on a computer screen or printed.

Tim Berners-Lee developed the original HTML specifications in 1990. These specifications were revised several times by the World Wide Web Consortium (W3C), but many of the early revisions did not gain widespread acceptance. HTML 3.2, introduced in 1997, was the first widely adopted revision of the original HTML specifications. HTML version 4.0 was introduced in late 1997, and HTML 4.01 in 1999.

XHTML is the follow-up version to HTML 4. Rather than calling it HTML 5, the W3C preferred to name it XHTML 1.0 to reflect its extensibility. XHTML includes all HTML 4 tags, but it can be extended by adding customized tags. Today's Web operates according to XHTML standards, even though people commonly refer to the technology simply as HTML. Variations of HTML, such as **DHTML** (dynamic HTML) and **Ajax** (Asynchronous JavaScript and XML) offer tools and techniques for extending basic HTML and making Web pages more interactive, visually appealing, and media-rich.

How do HTML tags work? HTML tags are incorporated into an **HTML document**, which is similar to a word processing file, but has an .htm or .html extension. HTML tags, such as <hr /> and <b>, are enclosed in angle brackets and embedded in the document. These tags are instruc-

INFOWEBLINKS

The W3C is a worldwide organization that formulates standards for the Web. Learn more by connecting to the **W3C InfoWeb**.

W CLICK TO CONNECT
www.course.com/np/concepts11/ch07

tions for the browser. When your browser displays a Web page on your computer screen, it does not show the tags or angle brackets. Instead, it attempts to follow the tags' instructions.

So HTML documents look a lot different from Web pages, right? Exactly. An HTML document is like a screenplay, and your browser is like a director who makes a screenplay come to life by assembling cast members and making sure they deliver their lines correctly.

As the HTML "screenplay" unfolds, your browser follows the instructions in an HTML document to display lines of text on your computer screen in the right color, size, and position. If the screenplay calls for a graphic, your browser collects it from the Web server and displays it. Although the HTML screenplay exists as a permanent file, the Web page you see on your computer screen exists only for the duration of the "performance."

Technically speaking, you can distinguish HTML documents (the screenplay) from Web pages (the performance). However, in everyday conversation, the term *Web page* is often used for the HTML document as well as the Web page displayed on screen.

An HTML document is sometimes referred to as a source document because it is the source of the HTML tags used to construct a Web page. You can view the HTML source documents for most Web pages if you are curious about how they were constructed. Figure 7-4 illustrates the difference between an HTML source document and the Web page it produces.

FIGURE 7-4

An HTML document (top) contains text and HTML tags. Formatting tags are used to change font size, separate paragraphs, and add rules. Other tags add graphics and links to a page. The HTML document produces a Web page (bottom).

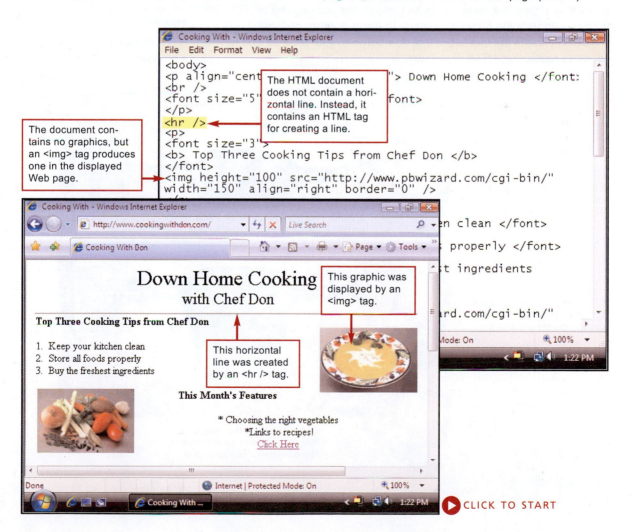

The document contains no graphics, but an <img> tag produces one in the displayed Web page.

The HTML document does not contain a horizontal line. Instead, it contains an HTML tag for creating a line.

This graphic was displayed by an <img> tag.

This horizontal line was created by an <hr /> tag.

CLICK TO START

HTTP

How does HTTP work? **HTTP** is a protocol that works with TCP/IP to get Web resources to your desktop. A Web resource can be defined as any chunk of data that has a URL, such as an HTML document, a graphic, or a sound file.

HTTP includes commands called *methods* that help your browser communicate with Web servers. GET is the most frequently used HTTP method. The GET method is typically used to retrieve the text and graphics files necessary for displaying a Web page. This method can also be used to pass a search query to a file server. HTTP transports your browser's request for a Web resource to a Web server. Next, it transports the Web server's response back to your browser.

An HTTP exchange takes place over a pair of sockets. A **socket** is an abstract concept that represents one end of a connection. Although a packet switching network doesn't actually make point-to-point connections between network nodes, many people find it handy to visualize network connections as a communication line with a doorway-like socket at each end. For HTTP, sockets usually are associated with port 80 on the client and server.

In an HTTP exchange, your browser opens a socket on your PC, connects to a similar open socket at the Web server, and issues a command, such as "send me an HTML document." The server receives the command, executes it, and sends a response back through the socket. The sockets are then closed until the browser is ready to issue another command. Figure 7-5 demonstrates the messages that flow between your browser and a Web server to retrieve an HTML document.

FIGURE 7-5

HTTP messages flow between a browser and a Web server.

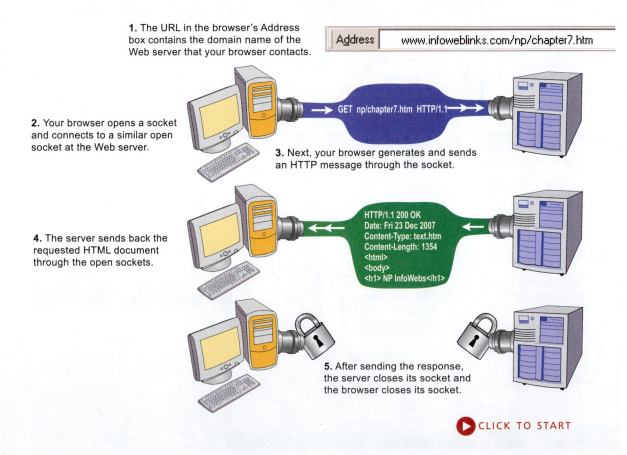

1. The URL in the browser's Address box contains the domain name of the Web server that your browser contacts.

Address   www.infoweblinks.com/np/chapter7.htm

2. Your browser opens a socket and connects to a similar open socket at the Web server.

GET np/chapter7.htm HTTP/1.1

3. Next, your browser generates and sends an HTTP message through the socket.

HTTP/1.1 200 OK
Date: Fri 23 Dec 2007
Content-Type: text.htm
Content-Length: 1354
<html>
<body>
<h1> NP InfoWebs</h1>

4. The server sends back the requested HTML document through the open sockets.

5. After sending the response, the server closes its socket and the browser closes its socket.

▶ CLICK TO START

Is each Web page element retrieved separately? Yes. HTTP is classified as a **stateless protocol**, which maintains no record of previous interactions and handles each request based entirely on information that comes with it.

HTTP generally allows only one request and response per session. As a result, your browser can request an HTML document during a session, but as soon as the document is sent, the session is closed, and the Web server forgets that your browser ever made a request. To make additional requests—for example, to request a graphic that's supposed to be displayed on a Web page—your browser must open another session. You can understand, then, that to assemble a complex Web page with several graphics, buttons, and sounds, your browser makes many HTTP requests to the Web server.

What if an element cannot be found? A Web server's response to a browser's request includes an **HTTP status code** that indicates whether the browser's request could be fulfilled. The status code 200 means that the request was fulfilled—the requested HTML document, graphic, or other resource was sent. Anyone who surfs the Web has encountered the "404 Not Found" message. Your browser displays this message when a Web server sends a 404 status code to indicate that the requested resource does not exist (Figure 7-6).

FIGURE 7-6

When a broken link points to a nonexistent HTML document, your browser typically produces a 404 Not Found error. When a broken link points to a nonexistent graphic or other non-HTML file, your browser usually displays one of the broken link icons, shown below.

WEB BROWSERS

What are some of today's most popular browsers? Today's most popular browsers include Microsoft Internet Explorer, Mozilla Firefox, Apple Safari, Netscape Navigator, and Opera. Figure 7-7 on this page and the next illustrates these popular programs.

Netscape Navigator was one of the first browsers with a graphical user interface. Published in December 1994, Netscape quickly became the most popular browser on Macintosh and PC platforms. Numerous revisions added pioneering features to enhance the overall browsing experience. Netscape is currently published by Netscape Communications and Weblogs, Inc., a subsidiary of AOL.

In 1998, Netscape source code became open source software, managed by an organization known as Mozilla. The organization's main product, a browser called Mozilla, was all but ignored by most computer owners. In 2004, however, a new version of Mozilla, dubbed Firefox, rapidly gained popularity because it offered effective security features.

Internet Explorer (IE) version 1.0 was published by Microsoft in August 1995. The program code for the original IE 1.0 browser was licensed from a Netscape spin-off called Spyglass, which provided IE with many of the same features as Netscape. Until IE 4.0 appeared in 1997, however, Microsoft's browser was unable to match Netscape's popularity. Today, IE has supplanted Netscape as the dominant browser for the PC platform. It is also available for Mac OS, Linux, and several versions of UNIX. AOL's browser is a slightly modified version of IE.

FIGURE 7-7

Shown on this page, Netscape Navigator and Firefox.

7

Before Firefox, Opera was one of the few alternatives to IE and Netscape. First published in December 1996, Opera began as a Norwegian phone company project to develop a small and fast browser for computers with meager memory and processing resources. Unlike IE and Netscape, which descended from Mosaic, Opera was written from scratch; as a result, it has features, such as page zoom and a multi-document display, that were later incorporated into IE and Firefox. Versions of Opera are available for Windows, Linux, UNIX, and Mac OS.

Macintosh computers were preloaded with Netscape Navigator until 1997, when Microsoft Internet Explorer for Mac replaced it. In 2003, however, Apple introduced a new browser called Safari, which is now included with Macintosh computers. Safari has the distinction of being the first browser to pass the Acid2 test, which means that it follows W3C standards and can correctly display all complying Web pages.

Should I upgrade my browser when new versions become available?
It is a good idea to upgrade when a new version of your browser becomes available. Because most browser updates are free, you can get up-to-date functionality simply by spending a few minutes downloading and installing an update.

The problem with using an old version of a browser is that some Web pages depend on new HTML features supported only by the latest browser versions. Without the latest upgrade, you might encounter errors when your browser tries to display a page, but cannot interpret some of the HTML. In other cases, your browser might display the Web page without errors, but you will not see all the intended effects.

Another important reason to upgrade is for increased security. As hackers discover and take advantage of security holes, browser publishers try to patch the holes. Upgrades usually contain patches for known security holes, although new features might sometimes open new holes.

Why do I have to download software to view some Web pages?
Browsers were originally limited to displaying documents in HTML format and graphics files in GIF and JPEG formats. Today, browsers work with additional file formats. Some browsers, however, do not have built-in support for proprietary file formats commonly used on the Web to display video, animation, and other media.

If you click a link that leads to a file stored in a format your browser does not handle, you can usually download software necessary to read the file format. For example, to read a PDF file, you might be directed to the Adobe Web site to download Acrobat Reader software that handles PDF files. To display an animation, you might need Adobe's Flash software. The software your browser calls upon to read non-native file formats can take the form of a helper application, plug-in, or player.

FIGURE 7-7 CONTINUED

Shown on this page, Internet Explorer, Opera, and Safari.

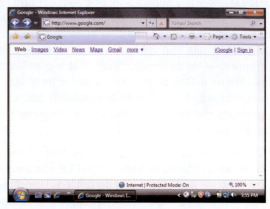

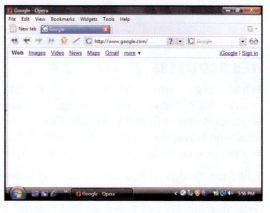

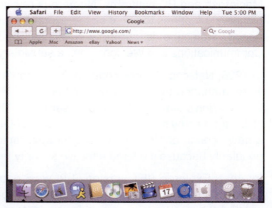

What is a helper application? A **helper application** (sometimes called a browser add-on) is a program that extends a browser's ability to work with file formats. Most helper applications can be downloaded from the Web. The process of installing a helper application creates an association between the browser and a file format, such as PDF, SWF, or MOV. Whenever your browser encounters one of these file formats, it automatically runs the corresponding helper application, which in turn opens the file.

Is a plug-in the same as a helper application? A **plug-in** is a type of helper application, pioneered by Netscape developers, that can be activated from an <embed> tag inserted in an HTML document. For example, <embed src = "sample.swf"> instructs a browser to activate the plug-in that works with the SWF file format, which can in turn open the sample.swf file.

Recent versions of Internet Explorer, however, do not respond to the <embed> tag and, therefore, are not able to use Netscape-style plug-ins. Instead, IE uses ActiveX components, which are activated by the <object> tag. Aside from this technical distinction, today's helper applications and plug-ins are very similar from the user's perspective.

The current trend is to use the terms player and add-on to refer to any helper application or plug-in that helps a browser display a particular file format. Figure 7-8 shows a list of players installed for use with Internet Explorer.

What is a Web cache? When your browser fetches pages and graphics to form a Web page, it stores that material on your computer in temporary files sometimes referred to as a **Web cache** or browser cache. These temporary files come in handy if you switch back and forth between pages or sites. Rather than fetch the entire page and all its graphics again, your browser can simply load them from the local cache. Files are deleted from the Web cache within days or weeks, depending on your browser's settings.

A potential problem with your Web cache is that it stores Web page elements from all the sites you've visited. If you use a public or lab computer, the Web page elements are stored there and can be viewed by others. To maintain your privacy, you might consider deleting these files periodically, adjusting browser settings to limit the time these files remain on your computer, or limiting the amount of space they can use on the hard disk.

FIGURE 7-8

You can usually find a list of players installed for use with your browser. If you use Internet Explorer, look for a Manage Add-ons option on the Tools menu. Your browser's list of players might include a PDF reader and spyware detectors used by your antivirus software.

Manage Add-ons

View and manage add-ons that are installed on your computer. Disabling or deleting add-ons might prevent some webpages from working correctly.

Show: Add-ons currently loaded in Internet Explorer

Name	Publisher	Status	Type
Enabled (6)			
Fill Forms		Enabled	Browser E>
Research		Enabled	Browser E>
RoboForm	Siber Systems	Enabled	Toolbar
RoboForm Toolbar		Enabled	Browser E>
RoboForm ver. 6-8-2 by Siber ...	Siber Systems	Enabled	Browser H
Save Forms		Enabled	Browser E>

Settings
Click an add-on name above and and then click Enable or Disable.
○ Enable
○ Disable

Delete ActiveX
Click the name of an ActiveX control above and then click Delete.
[Delete]

Download new add-ons for Internet Explorer
Learn more about add-ons

[OK]

▶ CLICK TO START

INFOWEBLINKS

For information about the most popular players, connect to the **Browser Players InfoWeb**.

CLICK TO CONNECT
www.course.com/np/concepts11/ch07

COOKIES

What is a cookie? A **cookie** (technically an HTTP cookie) is a small chunk of data generated by a Web server and stored in a text file on your computer's hard disk. Figure 7-9 contains an example.

ppkcookie1hellowww.quirksmode.org/1600182732736
02981171511470601282929810307*

Cookies allow a Web site to store information on a client computer for later retrieval. Web sites use cookies to:

- Monitor your path through a site to keep track of the pages you viewed or the items you purchased.

- Gather information that allows a Web server to present ad banners targeted to products you previously purchased at that Web site.

- Collect personal information you type into a Web page form and retain it for the next time you visit the Web site.

Why do Web sites need to use cookies? In many respects, cookies are a fix for problems caused by HTTP's stateless protocol. Cookies are frequently used to remind a Web server who you are each time your browser makes a request.

Suppose that you use your browser to visit a popular online music store. You search for your favorite bands, listen to some sample tracks, and select a few CDs you want to purchase. After browsing through 20 or 30 pages, you eventually go to the checkout counter where you see a list of the CDs you selected. You fill out a form that requests your name, shipping address, and payment information.

Although you might have been browsing at the music site for 30 minutes or more, from the perspective of the site's server, that activity could just as well have been carried out by several people, each one spending only a few seconds at the site. Because HTTP is a stateless protocol, each time you connect to a different page, the server regards it as a new visit.

Cookies allow the music site's server to identify you so that your requests won't get mixed up with those of other people visiting the site. Cookies also enable the server to keep track of your activity and compile a list of your purchases.

How do cookies work? When your browser connects to a site that uses cookies, it receives an HTTP "Set-cookie" message from the Web server. This cookie message contains some information that your browser stores on your computer's hard disk. The cookie information can include a customer number, a shopping cart number, a part number, or any other data. In addition, the cookie usually contains the date the cookie expires and the domain name of the host that created the cookie. A server that creates a cookie can request it the next time you connect to one of its Web pages.

How long do cookies stay on my computer? A Web developer can program a cookie to time out after a designated period of time. When a cookie reaches the end of its predefined lifetime, your Web browser simply erases it. Some cookies have no expiration date or a date far into the future, so cookies tend to accumulate on your computer's hard disk.

FIGURE 7-9

When you look at the cookies stored on your computer, most of the information is unintelligible. This cookie is called ppkcookie, its value is "hello," and it was created at *www.quirksmode.org*. The cookie contains an expiration date, but it is encoded so you can't decipher it.

INFOWEBLINKS

At the **Cookies InfoWeb**, you'll find links to a collection of articles that focus on cookie technology, including how they affect security and privacy.

 **CLICK TO CONNECT**
www.course.com/np/concepts11/ch07

Can I see the cookies stored on my computer? You can view a list of the cookies stored on your computer, but first you must discover where they are stored. Netscape stores cookies in one large file called *Cookies.txt* on a PC or in *Magiccookie* on a Macintosh. IE stores each cookie in a separate file. Refer to your browser documentation to discover which folder holds your cookies. Figure 7-10 shows a list of cookies stored for Internet Explorer.

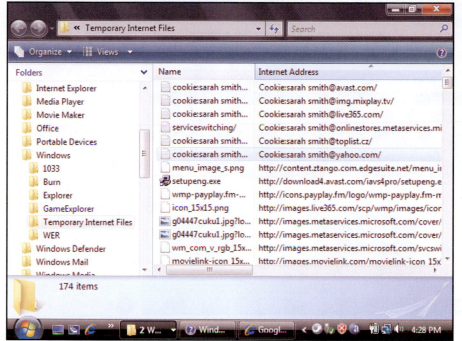

FIGURE 7-10

Internet Explorer typically stores cookies as individual files on your computer's hard disk. You can view a list of cookies stored on your computer. The information after the @ symbol usually indicates the domain name of the site that created the cookie.

WEB PAGE AUTHORING

What tools can I use to create Web pages? Your ISP or school might offer space for you to store your own Web pages, which you can keep private or open for public access. You have several choices when it comes to Web page authoring tools. You can use a text editor, HTML conversion utilities, online Web authoring tools, or Web authoring software.

The most difficult—and some would say old-fashioned—way to create Web pages is to use a text editor such as Notepad to type the HTML tags along with the text that you want the browser to display on a Web page.

An **HTML conversion utility** adds HTML tags to a document, spreadsheet, or other text-based file to create an HTML document that can be displayed by a browser. For example, you can work with Microsoft Word to create a standard DOC file and then use the File menu's Save As Web Page option to convert the document into HTML format. Converting a document into HTML format sometimes produces an unusual result, however, because some of the features and formatting in your original document might not be possible within the world of HTML.

A third option for creating Web pages is a special category of software called Web authoring software, which provides tools specifically designed to enter and format Web page text, graphics, and links. Popular Web authoring products include Microsoft FrontPage, Adobe Dreamweaver, and open source Nvu.

INFOWEBLINKS

Before you post Web pages, take a good look at them. For hints about creating effective Web pages and avoiding design disasters, check the links at the **Web Page Design Tips InfoWeb**.

 CLICK TO CONNECT
www.course.com/np/concepts11/ch07

INFOWEBLINKS

For help in selecting software to design your own Web pages, connect to the **Web Authoring Tools InfoWeb**.

CLICK TO CONNECT
www.course.com/np/concepts11/ch07

7

A fourth option for budding Web page authors is to use a set of online Web page authoring tools. These template-like tools are provided by some ISPs and other companies that host Web pages for individuals and businesses. Working with these tools is quite simple—you type, select, drag, and drop elements onto a Web page (Figure 7-11).

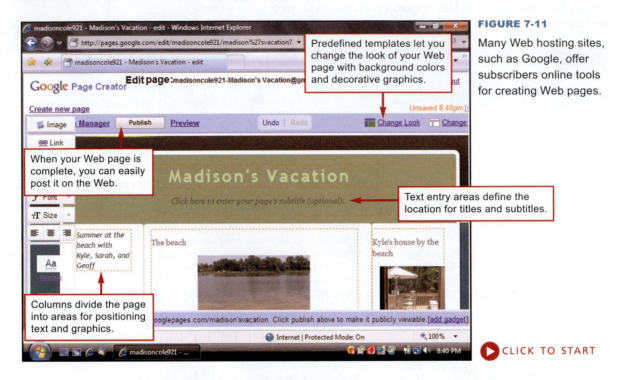

FIGURE 7-11

Many Web hosting sites, such as Google, offer subscribers online tools for creating Web pages.

How do I get my Web pages on the Internet? Creating a Web page is not the end of the publishing process. You also must test your pages, transfer them to a Web server, and test all your links, as explained by the steps in Figure 7-12.

FIGURE 7-12

Steps for Posting Web Pages

1. Test each page locally. When you complete the first draft of a Web page, you should test it to verify that every element is displayed correctly by any browsers that visitors to your Web page might use. You can accomplish this task without connecting to the Web. Simply open a browser, and then enter the local file name for the HTML document you created for your Web page. Repeat this process for any other browsers you expect visitors to use. One caution: Your hard disk drive is much faster than most Internet connections, so the text and graphics for your Web page are displayed faster during your local test than for someone viewing your page over the Internet.

2. Transfer pages to a Web server. Whether you're publishing a single page, a series of pages, or an entire Web site, you must put your pages on a Web server—a process called posting. To post Web page files manually you can use a file transfer utility, such as WSFTP. Web authoring software usually provides a menu option that automates the process of posting HTML documents and associated media files.

3. Test all pages and links. After you post your pages on a Web server, make sure you can access each page, and then test the links between your pages as well as any links to pages on other sites.

4. Update your site to keep it current. Periodically, you should review the information on your Web pages and verify that the links still connect to existing Web pages. You can easily change your pages and then test them offline before reposting them. You might encounter Under Construction signs at some Web sites, but they aren't usually necessary. You should handle your construction and revision work offline.

HTML SCRIPTS

Is it possible to add programs to a Web page?
Standard HTML provides a way to display text and graphics on a Web page and link to other Web pages, but because it isn't a programming language, HTML does not provide a way to perform complicated tasks or respond to user actions. A series of program instructions called an **HTML script** can be embedded directly into the text of an HTML document or in a file referenced from an HTML document. Scripts are not displayed by the browser; instead, they instruct the browser to perform specific actions or respond to specific user actions.

How would a Web page author use a script?
Scripts allow Web pages to become more interactive and incorporate activities that would otherwise require a computer program. Scripts enable e-commerce sites to verify credit card information. They also make it possible to create interactive Web pages, that include fill-in forms. Scripts work with cookies to deliver custom Web pages, such as those Amazon.com generates each time you return to the site. Scripts don't replace normal HTML—they extend and enhance it.

As an example of scripting, consider what happens when you use online forms. **HTML forms** are used to collect user input for e-commerce orders, site registrations, opinion polls, and so on. The information you enter into an HTML form is held in the memory of your computer, where your browser creates temporary storage bins that correspond to the input field names designated by the form's HTML tags.

Your address, in the form shown in Figure 7-13, might be temporarily held in a memory location that's called Customer Address. When you click a Submit button, your browser gathers the data from memory and sends it to a specially designated script on an HTTP server, where it can be processed and stored.

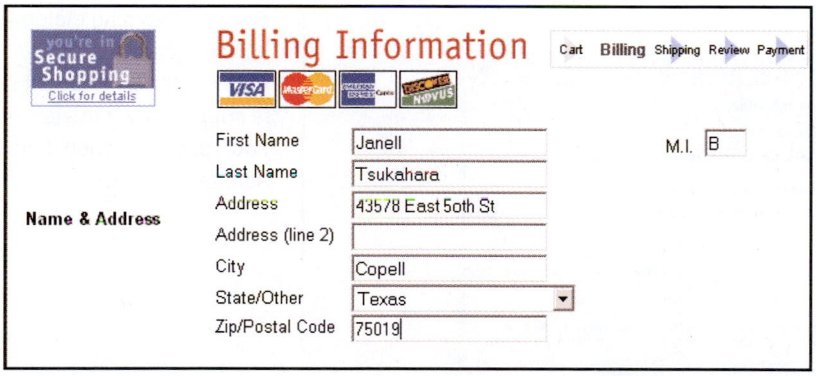

FIGURE 7-13

HTML forms are typically used to collect payment and shipping information at the checkout counter of e-commerce Web sites.

Do scripts run on my local computer or on a Web server?
Scripts can run on a client or a server. A **server-side script** consists of statements that run on a server. Server-side scripts accept data submitted by a form, process that data, and then generate a custom HTML document that is sent to the browser for display. These dynamically produced pages can often be identified because they contain question marks (?) in the URL displayed in the Address bar of your browser. Server-side scripts can be written using a variety of programming and scripting languages, such as Perl, C, C++, C#, and Java.

A **client-side script** consists of scripting statements that run on your local computer. The script is executed by the browser, which must have the capability to deal with the programming language used to write the script. Popular languages for client-side scripts include VBScript and JavaScript. Most of today's browsers can handle JavaScript, but only IE has the built-in capability to execute VBScript. Client-side scripts often take the form of Java applets or ActiveX controls.

What's a Java applet? A **Java applet** is an application written in the Java programming language. A programmer or Web page author places a reference to a Java applet in an HTML document using the <applet> HTML tag. When working with a Web page that contains an <applet> tag, your browser downloads the applet and executes its instructions. The applet is not installed on your computer, so it does not leave a permanent footprint.

You might wonder if a Java applet could contain a virus that would take up residence in your computer system or a worm that would spread over your network. Applets are fairly safe because they cannot open, modify, delete, or create files on your computer; they cannot make any network connections except to the originating site; and they cannot start other programs.

What is an ActiveX control? An **ActiveX control** is a compiled computer program that can be referenced from within an HTML document, downloaded, installed on your computer, and executed within the browser window. ActiveX controls can be used on the server side, too, but consumers typically encounter the client-side version when their browsers display a security warning and ask for permission to proceed with installation (Figure 7-14).

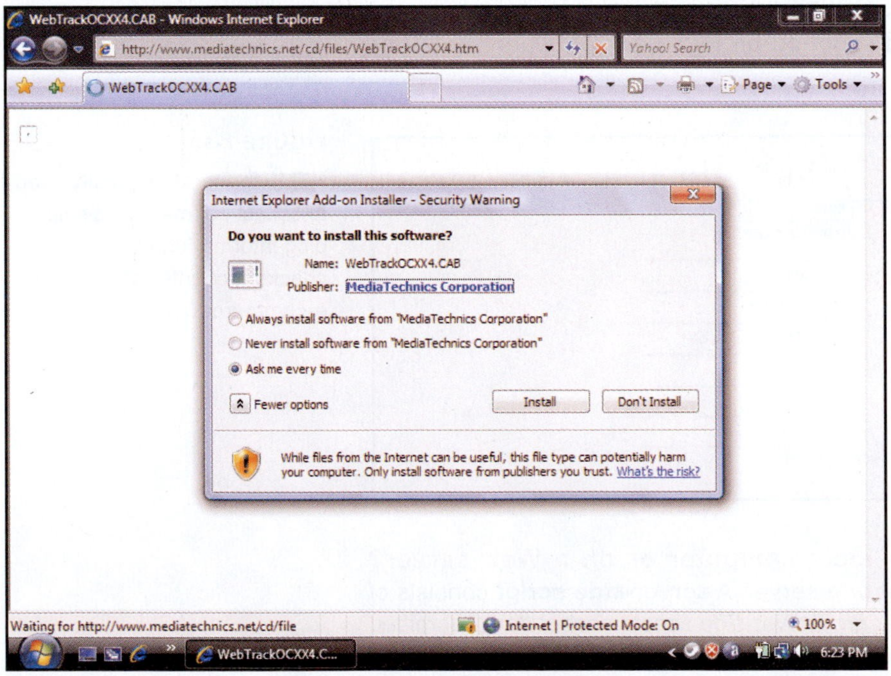

FIGURE 7-14

Web surfers who use Internet Explorer sometimes encounter the Security Warning dialog box for ActiveX components. If the component is supplied by a trusted source, then it should be safe to install it.

Programmers and Web page authors use programming languages such as C++ and Visual Basic to create ActiveX controls, which can be applied in a wide variety of ways to make Web pages interactive. ActiveX helps programmers provide the functionality many consumers expect after using full-featured applications, such as word processing, graphics, and entertainment software.

Most ActiveX controls are safe. However, an ActiveX control is a full-fledged program, which gives it the potential to include routines that alter or delete data on your computer's hard disk. ActiveX controls include digital certificates to increase their security. A **digital certificate** is an electronic attachment to a file that verifies the identity of its source (Figure 7-15).

Is it easy to create Java applets and ActiveX controls? Scripts are somewhat more difficult to write and test than HTML documents, so scripts are typically the domain of professional Web designers. A basic understanding of scripts, however, along with a grasp of HTML, HTTP, cookies, browsers, and hypertext, should give you a more complete understanding of how the Web works.

FIGURE 7-15

A digital certificate can be electronically attached to any ActiveX control. That control is then referred to as *signed*—it is as though the programmer signed his or her name to it. Theoretically, malicious programmers would not put their names on certificates that travel with an ActiveX control infected with a virus or worm.

QuickCheck

1. When using a browser, you can access a Web page by clicking a hypertext [ ] or by typing a URL.

2. When typing a URL, keep in mind that it can never contain a(n) [ ] , even after a punctuation mark.

3. [ ] software interprets and executes the special instructions embedded in HTML documents to display Web pages for you.

4. A(n) [ ] application is a program that extends a browser's ability to work with files in a variety of formats.

5. Cookies were developed because HTTP is a(n) [ ] protocol, so each time you connect to a different page, the Web server regards it as a new connection.

6. Some cookies can remain indefinitely on your computer's hard disk unless you manually delete them. True or false? [ ]

7. Because ActiveX controls are full-fledged programs that can alter, add, or delete data on your computer's hard disk, they include digital [ ] for security purposes.

 CHECK ANSWERS

Search Engines

THE WEB ENCOMPASSES hundreds of millions of pages stored on servers scattered all over the globe. To use this information, however, you have to find it. There is no rhyme or reason to the location of Web-based information; a particular fact you're trying to unearth could be located on an obscure server in Kazakhstan, or buried deep in the folder structure of a major e-commerce Web site. Modern Web surfers depend on search engines for help navigating the waves of information stored on the Web. In Section B you'll find out how Web search engines work, so that you can use them more efficiently.

SEARCH ENGINE BASICS

What is a Web search engine? A **Web search engine** (usually referred to simply as a search engine) is a program designed to help people locate information on the Web by formulating simple keyword queries. In response to a query, the search engine displays results or "hits" as a list of relevant Web sites, accompanied by links to source pages and short excerpts containing the keywords (Figure 7-16).

FIGURE 7-16

A query for "mountain bike" returns a list of links to relevant sites.

Popular search engines are located at Web sites such as *www.google.com*, *www.msn.com*, *www.ask.com*, and *www.yahoo.com*. You might say that the search engines at these sites build the equivalent of a book index. Whereas a book index helps readers turn to a page on which they can find a particular word or concept, a search engine helps Web surfers link to pages that contain the information they seek. Unlike a book, however, the information on the Web is too vast to catalog manually, so search engine software does it autonomously.

Although most search sites use automated search engines, a few sites specialize in human-powered searches, but within a limited range of topics. At search sites such as *www.mahalo.com* and *www.chacha.com* results are compiled and screened by human experts, usually called *guides*. You may find better quality results at these sites, but the range of topics is limited to those that have been compiled by the guides.

What is the difference between a search engine and a search engine site? It is easy to think of *www.google.com* as a search engine, but to be precise it is a Web site that offers access to a search engine. Search engine sites often contain a variety of tools and services in addition to search engine access. For example, Google's Web site offers maps, calendars, e-mail, photo sharing, Web-based apps, and blogs.

Google's search engine technology is used not only at the Google site, but also at search sites such as AOL and Netscape. Yahoo's search engine is used at search sites AltaVista and AlltheWeb. Ask.com uses Teoma search engine technology.

Many e-commerce, informational, and corporate sites offer query controls you can use to search the site or the entire Web. The sites that host these query controls typically link to major search engines or the sites that host them (Figure 7-17).

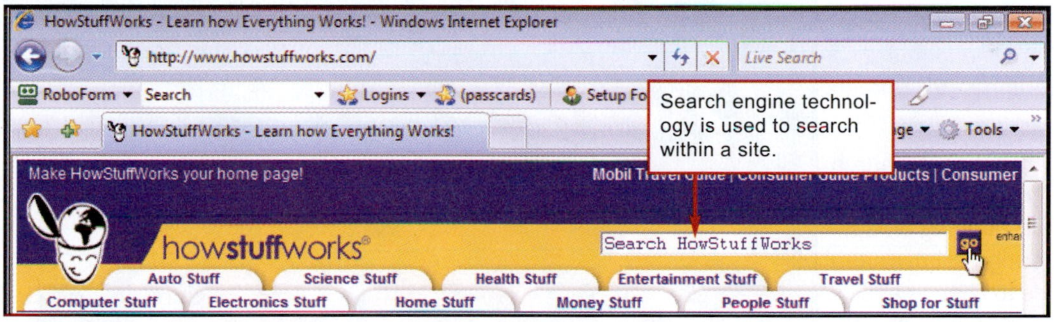

FIGURE 7-17

Many Web sites use search engine technology for searching within the site rather than searching the entire Web.

Search engine technology is used to search within a site.

How do search engines work? A search engine contains four components: a Web crawler, an indexing utility, a database, and a query processor. The Web crawler combs the Web to gather data that's representative of the contents of Web pages. The indexer processes the information gathered by the crawler into a list of key words and URLs stored in a database. The query processor allows you to access the database by entering key terms, and then produces a list of Web pages that contain content relevant to your query. Let's take a look at each of these components to find out how they affect your ability to mine information from the Web.

What is a Web crawler? A **Web crawler** (also referred to as a Web spider) is a computer program that is automated to methodically visit Web sites. Web crawlers can be programmed to perform various activities as they visit sites, but in the context of search engines, Web crawlers download Web pages and submit them to an indexing utility for processing.

How much of the Web does a Web crawler cover? A Web crawler begins with a list of URLs to visit. After copying the material at a specified URL, the Web crawler looks for hypertext links and adds them to the list of URLs to visit. To cover the Web as efficiently as possible, a Web crawler can run multiple processes in parallel. Sophisticated algorithms keep processes from overlapping, getting stuck in loops, or trying to capture Web pages dynamically produced by server-side scripts.

7

High performance Web crawlers can visit hundreds of millions of Web pages a day. Those pages, however, are only a fraction of the Web. Researchers estimate that the most extensive search engines cover less than 20% of the Web. Each search engine seems to focus on a slightly different collection of Web sites. The same search entered into different search engines can produce different results, so it is sometimes worthwhile to try alternative search engines.

Web crawlers typically do not gather material from the invisible Web, which encompasses pages that require password protected logins and pages that are dynamically generated with server-side scripts. The potential volume of dynamically generated pages, such as all the possible pages that Amazon.com could generate from its inventory database, is just too great to feasibly index. To access information related to e-commerce merchandise or library catalogs, you might have to go directly to the merchant's or library's Web site and use its search tools.

FIGURE 7-18

A search engine's indexer looks for keywords on each page the Web crawler retrieves.

How frequently do Web crawlers revisit sites?

When you query a search engine, you want the results to be up to date so that you don't waste time trying to link to pages that have changed or been deleted. Search engines use various algorithms to refresh their indexes.

The number of times a search engine's crawler visits a Web page varies, depending on several factors such as how often the page tends to change and its popularity. Obscure pages might be visited only once a month, whereas the pages at a news site would be visited daily.

How do search engine indexers work?

A **search engine indexer** is software that pulls keywords from a Web page and stores them in a database. The purpose of the indexer is to make pages easy to find based on their contents. For example, a Web page at a classic comic book site might contain information and covers from old comics (Figure 7-18). Key words that might help catalog this page for future access include classic, comic, comic book, artwork, cover, gallery, super-hero, crime, romance, Marvel, and Weird Science.

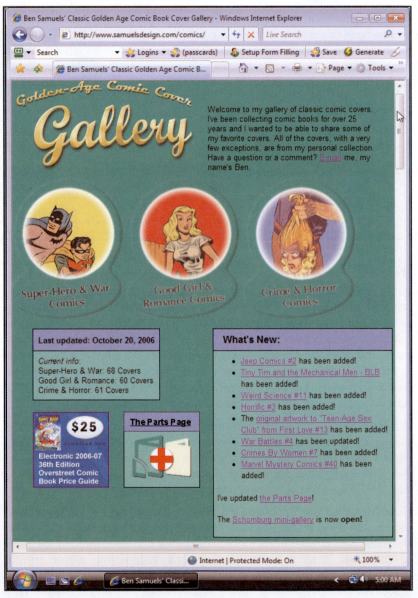

Which Web sites are shown at the top of the results list? A search engine's **query processor** looks for your search terms in the search engine's indexed database and returns a list of relevant Web sites. The order in which Web sites are listed in response to a search depends on relevancy criteria, such as key word matches and link popularity.

If a search is based on multiple keywords, pages that contain the most matching words are listed first. **Link popularity** is a measure of the quality and quantity of the links from one Web page to others. Pages with links to and from popular sites tend to get high relevancy ratings.

Can a search engine be manipulated into giving a high ranking to a page? Web sites can be added to a search engine index in several ways. Sites can automatically get discovered by a search engine's Web crawler, they can be submitted to a search engine by the Web masters who manage various Web sites, they can be submitted for a paid placement, or they can be submitted as banner or pop-up ads.

Most search engines make it easy to submit the URL for a Web site, so that Web masters don't have to wait for their sites to be discovered by a Web crawler. Manual submissions are added to the crawler's list of sites to visit and the site will eventually be indexed.

Some search engines accept paid placements, which are bumped to the top positions on the results list. Other search engines accept paid ads, but place them in a clearly marked area. For example, Google displays a column of ads related to the key words you enter for a search. Suppose you search for mountain bike trails. The main results list displays maps of mountain bike trails and reviews. An additional column of sponsored links are paid placements by merchants who have mountain-bike related products. Merchants are charged only if the ad is clicked (Figure 7-19).

FIGURE 7-19

Sponsored links on Google are paid placements that appear when users make queries using relevant keywords.

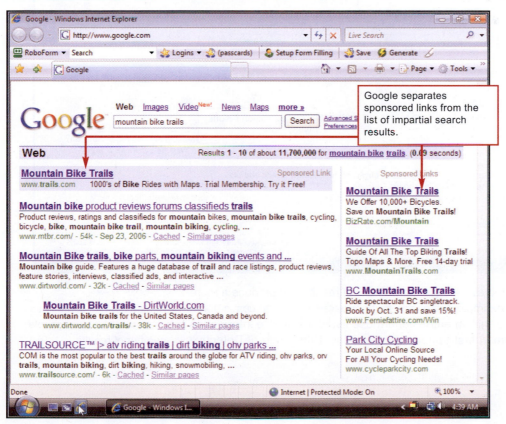

Disreputable Web site operators are constantly trying to devise schemes, such as manipulating meta keywords, to move their Web sites up to the top of search engine query results. A **meta keyword** is entered into a header section of a Web page when it is created and is supposed to describe the page contents.

Keyword stuffing is an unethical practice in which meta keywords are manipulated to gain high relevancy rankings. For example, a Web page author might include meta keywords such as "sex" (which happens to be the most frequently used search term) even though the term has little to do with the information on the page.

Socially responsible search engine sites take steps to foil practices that manipulate rankings and should make their policies on paid placements clear to users. When you use a search engine, read its About page to learn its placement policies and discover whether or not you can trust the search results to be unbiased.

FORMULATING SEARCHES

How do I formulate a basic search? Most search engines work with keyword queries in which you enter one or more words, called **search terms**, related to the information you want to find. For example, if you're interested in Batman comics, you can simply type the obvious: "Batman" (Figure 7-20).

Narrowing a search can reduce the number of results and produce a more targeted list. For example, the query "first appearance Batman comic book" produces under a million entries and those listed first link to information about when Batman first appeared in the May 1939 issue of Detective Comics.

FIGURE 7-20

Simple queries sometimes produce an unmanageable number of results.

 **CLICK TO START**

Searching is not a numbers game, however, because it is rare for a query to produce fewer than thousands of results. In fact, a game called Googlewhacking challenges you to type a two-word query that produces one and only one result. Try it! You need to choose two fairly unrelated words, but they cannot be totally unrelated or you'll get no results. You can view some googlewhacks at *www.googlewhack.com/tally.pl*.

When formulating queries, keep the simple guidelines from Figure 7-21 in mind.

FIGURE 7-21

Tips for Effective Queries

- Most search engines are not case sensitive, so you don't have to use the Shift key when entering proper names.
- Typically, search engines ignore common words, such as "and," "a," and "the," so don't bother to include them in your query.
- The top search engines use stemming technology that looks for plurals and other variations of the keywords you enter. For example, if you enter *diet*, the search engine also looks for pages with terms such as "diets," "dietary," and "dietician."
- To search for an exact phrase, enter it in quotes. For example, *"Dynamic Duo."*
- The asterisk (*) is sometimes referred to as a wildcard character. It allows a search engine to find pages with any derivation of a basic word. For example, the query *medic** would not only produce pages containing the word "medic," but also "medics," "medicine," "medical," "medication," and "medicinal."
- The NEAR operator tells a search engine that you want documents in which one of the keywords is located close to but not necessarily next to the other keyword. The query *library NEAR/15 congress* means that the words "library" and "congress" must appear within 15 words of each other. Successful searches could include documents containing phrases such as "Library of Congress" or "Congress funds special library research."
- When you enter multiple terms, the query processor assumes you want to see Web pages that include all your terms. Technically, the search engine inserts the Boolean operator "AND" between the keywords in your search. If you want to use other Boolean operators, however, you must enter them.

What are Boolean operators? A **Boolean operator** (sometimes called a search operator) is a word or symbol that describes a relationship between keywords and thereby helps you create a more focused query. They are called Boolean operators after George Boole, a 19th century English mathematician, who defined one of the first systems of logic. Figure 7-22 on the next page provides a quick overview of how to use Boolean operators when formulating searches.

FIGURE 7-22

Search Operators

AND	When two search terms are joined by AND, both terms must appear on a Web page before it can be included in the search results. The query *railroad AND cars* will locate pages that contain both the words "railroad" and "cars." Your search results might include pages containing information about old railroad cars, about railroad car construction, and even about railroads that haul automobiles ("cars"). Some search engines use the plus symbol (+) instead of the word AND.
OR	When two search terms are joined by OR, either one or both of the search words could appear on a page. Entering the query *railroad OR cars* produces information about railroad fares, railroad routes, railroad cars, automobile safety records, and even car ferries.
NOT	The keyword following NOT must not appear on any of the pages found by the search engine. Entering *railroad NOT cars* would tell the search engine to look for pages that include "railroad" but not the keyword "cars." In some search engines, the minus sign (-) can be used instead of the word NOT.

What is an advanced search? Many search engines provide ways to make your searches more precise and obtain more useful results. You might be able to use advanced search options to limit your search to material written in a specific language or stored in a specific file format. You might be able to specify a date, eliminate results from adult sites, and stipulate whether to look for your search terms in the title, URL, or body of the Web page (Figure 7-23).

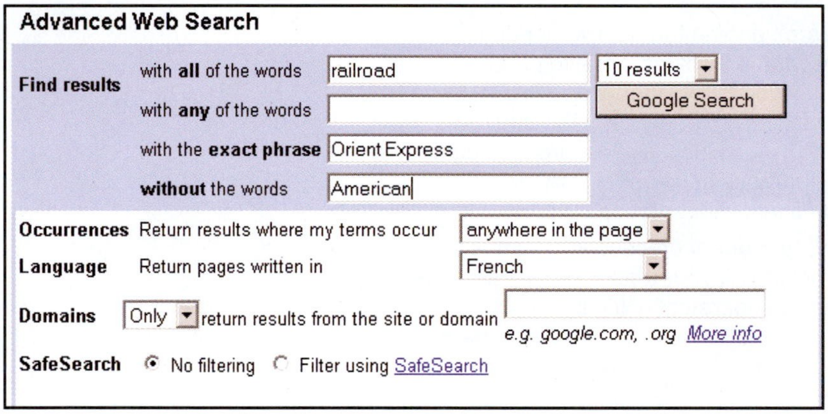

Advanced Web Search

Find results	with **all** of the words	railroad	10 results
	with **any** of the words		Google Search
	with the **exact phrase**	Orient Express	
	without the words	American	
Occurrences	Return results where my terms occur	anywhere in the page
Language	Return pages written in	French
Domains	Only	return results from the site or domain	*e.g. google.com, .org* *More info*
SafeSearch	⦿ No filtering ○ Filter using SafeSearch	

FIGURE 7-23

Many search engines provide forms designed to simplify the search process. These forms are usually accessible by clicking an Advanced Search link, which often is located on the main page of the search engine Web site.

Some search engine sites offer separate searches for academic works, images, videos, news, e-commerce merchandise, and blogs. Look for links to these specialized searches at your favorite search engine sites.

In addition to using search engines, you can also find Web-based information using a **metasearch engine** that searches a series of other search engines and compiles the search results. Popular metasearch sites include *www.mamma.com*, *www.dogpile.com*, and *www.metagopher.com*.

Do search engines keep records of my queries? Considering that a major search engine can receive upward of 100 million queries every day, the surprising answer to this question is "yes." Search engines at major sites such as Google, AOL, MSN, and Yahoo! save massive numbers of searches made by site visitors. Although most search sites do not specify how long this information is retained, industry analysts believe that some sites retain it for at least 30 days, and perhaps at least one search engine site has retained every search ever made at the site.

Privacy advocates question the wisdom of search engines retaining queries. They find difficulty in identifying any beneficial uses for such data and fear that it is of potential benefit only to marketing companies. Although the privacy policies of major search sites claim to protect personal information, in 2006, AOL released a database of 20 million queries collected by its search engine. The database was released publicly and online, ostensibly to help academic researchers. A few months earlier, the U.S. Department of Justice requested query databases from all major search engines in conjunction with a crackdown on Internet child pornography. Some search engine operators complied, whereas others did not. Anyone who uses search engines should be aware that the content of their searches could become public.

What kind of information does a search engine store? Although your queries do not contain your name, you are assigned a unique ID number that is stored in a cookie on your computer. In addition to storing an ID number, search engines store the IP address from which the query was initiated, the date and time of the query, the search terms, and the URL for the Web site linked to from the results list (Figure 7-24).

FIGURE 7-24

A database of 20 million AOL queries is still available to the public. You can use it to get a glimpse of the wide range of human interests and also understand how valuable such data can be to marketers. For example, you can see that in a three month period over 18,000 queries contained the words "mountain bike." If you click user 1404131, you can see that he or she was also interested in Sony PSP products.

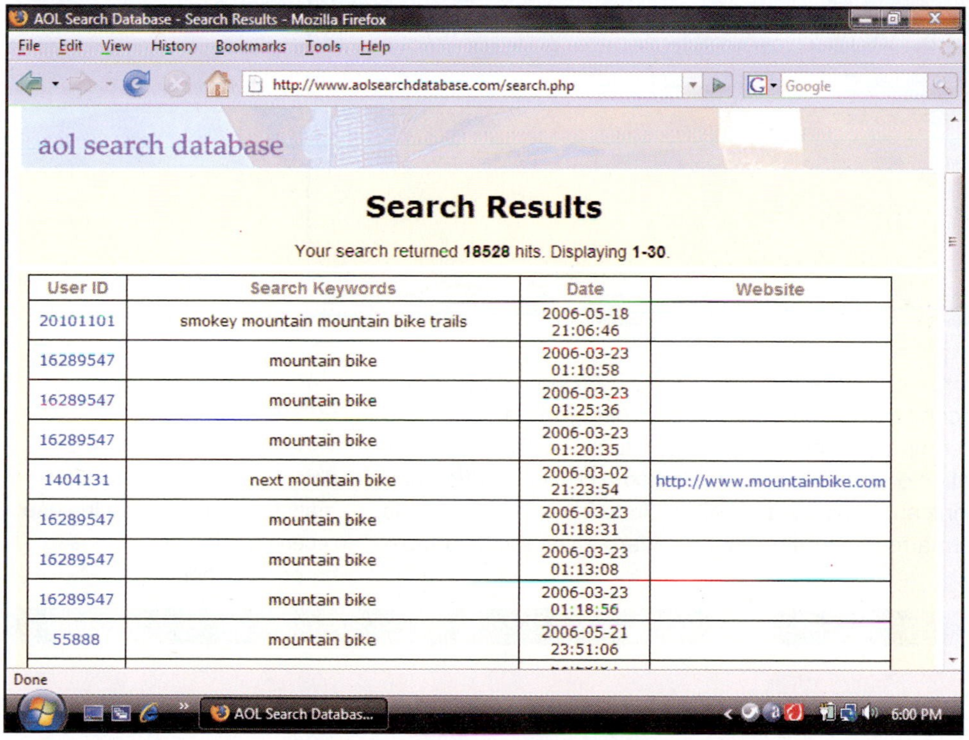

User ID	Search Keywords	Date	Website
20101101	smokey mountain mountain bike trails	2006-05-18 21:06:46	
16289547	mountain bike	2006-03-23 01:10:58	
16289547	mountain bike	2006-03-23 01:25:36	
16289547	mountain bike	2006-03-23 01:20:35	
1404131	next mountain bike	2006-03-02 21:23:54	http://www.mountainbike.com
16289547	mountain bike	2006-03-23 01:18:31	
16289547	mountain bike	2006-03-23 01:13:08	
16289547	mountain bike	2006-03-23 01:18:56	
55888	mountain bike	2006-05-21 23:51:06	

What can I do to keep my searches confidential? Your search-engine-assigned ID number is stored in a cookie and remains the same as long as the cookie remains on your computer. If you frequently delete your cookies as explained in Section E, a search engine's query database is unlikely to collect enough information to link back to you. You can block cookies from a specific search engine site, and that setting will force the search engine to assign a different ID number to you for each session. You can also download and use a cookie anonymizer that sets your Google ID number to 0. Scroogle, Tor, and other anonymizer sites act as relay stations to forward your searches to Google or other search engines without leaving a trail back to a cookie or IP address. These sites claim to delete all activity logs every day or two, but they are the subject of law enforcement scrutiny.

CITING WEB-BASED SOURCE MATERIAL

Can I copy text and graphics that I find on Web pages? Most browsers provide a Copy command that allows you to copy a section of text from a Web page, which you can then paste into one of your own documents. To keep track of the source for each text section, you can highlight the Web page's URL in the Address box, use the Copy command, and then paste the URL into your document (Figure 7-25).

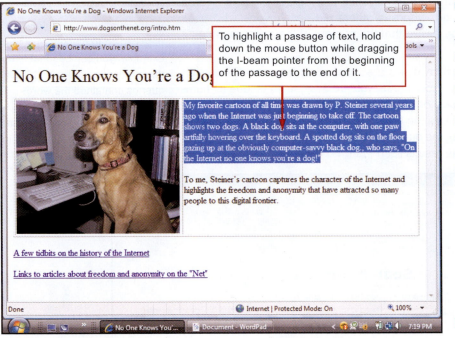

FIGURE 7-25

To copy a passage of text from a Web page, highlight the text, click the Edit menu, then select Copy. Next, switch to your own document and use the Paste option.
For a demonstration of this process, click the Start icon.

▶ CLICK TO START

How do I cite sources? Presenting someone else's work as your own is plagiarism. If you copy text, pictures, or other works from a Web page, make sure you give credit to the original author. Information that identifies the source of a quotation or excerpted work is called a citation. Written documents, such as reports and projects, typically include footnotes, endnotes, or in-line citations formatted according to a standard style, such as those listed in Figure 7-26.

FIGURE 7-26

Various style manuals suggest different punctuation and formats for citations. Use the one recommended by your instructor or publisher.

MLA Style

Du Bois, W.E.B. "Of the Dawn of Freedom." The Souls of Black Folk. 1903. Project Bartleby. 27 Nov. 2000 <http://www.bartleby.com/114/>.

APA Style

Du Bois, W.E.B. (1903). Of the dawn of freedom. In The Souls of Black Folk. Retrieved November 27, 2007, from Project Bartleby Web site: http://www.bartleby.com/114/.

Turabian Style

Du Bois, W.E.B. 1906. Of the dawn of freedom. In The Souls of Black Folk. On-line. Available from Internet, http://www.bartleby.com/114/, accessed November 27, 2007.

Chicago Style

Du Bois, W.E.B. 1906. Of the dawn of freedom. In The Souls of Black Folk. http://www.bartleby.com/114/ (accessed November 27, 2007).

When compiling the citation for online sources, make sure you provide sufficient information to allow readers to locate your source. Also, include the date when you accessed the source and the full URL. According to APA style, a citation to a Web-based source should provide a document title or description; author name if available; the date of publication, update, or retrieval; and a URL.

Do I need permission to use material? In the United States, a fair use doctrine allows you limited use of copyrighted material for scholarship and review without obtaining permission. For scholarly reports and projects, for example, you can use a sentence or paragraph of text without obtaining permission if you include a citation to the original source. Photos and excerpts from music and videos can be used within the context of critique, but their use purely as decorative elements for a document would, in most cases, not be considered fair use.

Some Web sites clearly state allowable uses for material on the site. Look for a link to Terms of Use on the site. For example, the YouTube Web site contains a collection of videos submitted by amateurs and semi-professionals, who retain the copyright to their materials. The Terms of Use section of the site allows the public to access, use, reproduce, distribute, create derivatives, display, and perform user-submitted works. Even with such broad terms of use, however, it is essential to cite the original source of the material if you incorporate it in your own work.

How do I get permission? To obtain permission to use text, photos, music, videos, and other elements you find on the Web, contact the copyright holder by e-mail, explain what you want to use and how you plan to use it. You can usually find contact information on the Web site, if not for the copyright holder, at least for a Web master who can direct you to the copyright holder.

7

QuickCheck

1. A Web _____ is a computer program designed to methodically visit Web sites, fetch Web pages and submit them to an indexing utility for processing.

2. Keyword _____ is an unethical practice in which meta keywords are manipulated to gain high relevancy rankings and move Web sites to the top of a search engine's results.

3. Most search engines are case sensitive, so you must make sure to capitalize the first letters of proper names and places. True or false? _____

4. "AND" is an example of a(n) _____ operator, also referred to as a search operator.

5. Because of the massive number of searches initiated by visitors of Google, AOL, MSN, and Yahoo!, these search engine sites are unable to maintain records of their visitors' queries. True or false? _____

6. Information that identifies the source of a quotation, photo, video, music, or excerpted work is called a(n) _____ .

 CHECK ANSWERS

E-commerce

ONE OF THE MOST POPULAR activities on the Web is shopping. Online shopping has the same allure as catalogs—you can shop at your leisure, anonymously, and in your pajamas. But the economics of the Web provide opportunities that go beyond retail catalogs. The Internet was opened to commercial use in 1991. Since then, thousands of businesses have set up shop at Web sites. This section of the chapter focuses on e-commerce and the technologies a typical shopper might encounter on the Web.

E-COMMERCE BASICS

What is e-commerce? Although the experts don't always agree on its definition, the term **e-commerce** typically refers to business transactions that are conducted electronically over a computer network. It encompasses all aspects of business and marketing processes enabled by Internet and Web technologies.

E-commerce wares include many kinds of physical products, digital products, and services. Physical products offered at e-commerce sites include such goods as clothing, shoes, skateboards, and cars. Most of these products can be shipped to buyers through the postal service or a parcel delivery service.

Increasingly, e-commerce goods include digital products, such as news, music, video, databases, software, and all types of knowledge-based items. The unique feature of these products is that they can be transformed into bits and delivered over the Web. Consumers can get them immediately upon completing their orders, and no one pays shipping costs.

E-commerce merchants also peddle services, such as online medical consultation, distance education, or custom sewing. Some of these services can be carried out by computers. Others require human agents. Services can be delivered electronically, as in the case of a distance education course, or they might produce some physical product, such as a custom-fit boat cover.

What are the most common e-commerce business models? Many e-commerce activities are classified as **B2C** (business-to-consumer) in which individual consumers purchase goods and services from online merchants. **C2C** (consumer-to-consumer) is another popular e-commerce model, in which consumers sell to each other at popular online auctions. **B2B** (business-to-business) e-commerce involves one enterprise buying goods or services from another enterprise. **B2G** (business-to-government) e-commerce aims to help businesses sell to governments. Figure 7-27 lists some popular B2C and C2C activities.

Is e-commerce more profitable than off-line business? E-commerce enhances traditional business models by offering efficiency and opportunities for automation, computerization, and digitization. As with a traditional brick and mortar business, profit in an e-commerce business is the difference between income and expenses.

FIGURE 7-27

B2C and C2C e-commerce offer consumers many types of goods and services.

Online storefronts sell a variety of goods, such as clothing, books, toys, music, food, sports gear, and electronics.

Online auctions provide consumers with a worldwide market for antiques, collectibles, and other new and used items.

Online schools offer credit and noncredit courses, tutorials, and even college degrees.

Online ticket and reservation systems provide concert and event tickets plus air, hotel, and car reservations.

Online information services sell subscriptions to news archives, databases, and online magazines.

One of the advantages of e-commerce is its ability to increase profit margins by cutting costs. For example, a typical catalog order placed over the phone costs the merchant US$2.50, whereas an online transaction costs about 35 cents. A hotel reservation made online costs the innkeeper 80% less than a booking by phone. A withdrawal or deposit costs a bank about a dollar when handled by a teller, about 25 cents on an ATM, and only a penny on the Web.

E-commerce merchants also gain income by hosting advertising space for marketers, who are creating increasingly hard-to-avoid styles of online advertisements, such as banner and pop-up ads. A **banner ad** is an advertisement, typically embedded at the top of a Web page. A **hover ad** overlays the content on a Web page, sometimes obscuring it until you click the ad or its timer expires and the ad disappears. A **pop-up ad**, such as the one in Figure 7-28, is an advertisement that appears in a separate window when you connect to a Web page. If you click a banner, hover, or pop-up ad, your browser connects directly to the advertiser's Web site, where you can find product information and make a purchase.

Banner, hover, and pop-up ads earn revenue for hosting merchants based on the **click-through rate**—the number of times that site visitors click the ad to connect to the advertiser's site. The hosting merchant is paid a small fee for each click through. Click-through rates have declined in recent years because most consumers simply ignore the ads or install **ad-blocking software** to prevent ads from appearing on their screens. Recent versions of Internet Explorer include a configurable feature to block pop-up ads.

Who benefits from e-commerce? Both merchants and consumers benefit from e-commerce because niche goods and small merchants can reach a global customer base. At online music shops and bookstores, for example, you can find obscure titles and alternative music that brick and mortar merchants haven't the space or inclination to stock.

Merchants are always looking for ways to attract customers. The Web and its search engines give small merchants without a budget for national advertising a way to be found by customers. When you're looking for handmade chainmail, for example, you're unlikely to find it at your local WalMart, but chances are good that you can find a chainmail merchant on the Web.

Is e-commerce popular worldwide? North America accounts for about half of all e-commerce activity, and Western Europe and Asian Pacific regions account for most of the rest. The low volume of e-commerce activity in Africa, Eastern Europe, and Russia can be attributed to several factors, including lack of Internet access, language barriers, depressed economies, shipping limitations, and merchant policies.

Today's e-commerce model is aimed at English speakers with Internet access and a credit card. Although an increasing number of e-commerce Web sites offer language alternatives, many e-commerce sites have not been internationalized. In regions where electricity and telephone service are not available, Internet access is simply not possible (Figure 7-29). Many e-commerce merchants do not accept checks or cash and might not accept credit cards issued by non-U.S. banks. Even if cash payment is accepted, the price of goods remains beyond the budget of many people in developing countries.

FIGURE 7-28

Pop-up ads appear as separate windows.

FIGURE 7-29

In some regions of the world, e-commerce obstacles include language barriers, economic factors, and even lack of electrical service.

ONLINE SHOPPING

What makes online shopping so special? E-commerce offers some unique advantages over brick-and-mortar stores and mail-order catalogs. Customers can easily search for specific merchandise. They can configure products online, see actual prices, and build an order over several days. Customers can easily compare prices between multiple vendors using Web sites such as BizRate, NexTag, and PriceGrabber. They can read professional and consumer reviews at sites like Epinions and ConsumerReports.org.

How does an e-commerce store work? E-commerce seems simple from the perspective of a shopper who connects to an online store, browses the electronic catalog, selects merchandise, and then pays for it. The screentour in Figure 7-30 walks you through a typical shopping session.

FIGURE 7-30

In a typical shopping session, you connect to an online storefront and use navigation controls to browse through the merchant's catalog. As you browse, you can drop items into your electronic shopping cart. At the checkout counter, you enter the information necessary to pay for the items you selected.

▶ CLICK TO START

Behind the scenes, an e-commerce site uses several technologies to display merchandise, keep track of shoppers' selections, collect payment data, attempt to protect customers' privacy, and prevent credit card numbers from falling into the wrong hands.

An e-commerce site's URL, such as *www.amazon.com*, acts as the entry to the online store. A Web page at this location—sometimes referred to as an electronic storefront—welcomes customers and provides links to various parts of the site. The goods and services for sale appear in a customer's browser window.

An e-commerce site usually includes some mechanism for customers to select merchandise and then pay for it. Customer orders might be processed manually in a small business. Most high-volume e-commerce businesses, however, use as much automation as possible; their order-processing systems automatically update inventories, and then print packing slips and mailing labels.

What's an online shopping cart? If you've done any shopping online, you've probably used an **online shopping cart**—a cyberspace version of the metal cart you wheel around a store and fill up with merchandise.

How do shopping carts work? As mentioned earlier, HTTP is a stateless protocol, which fulfills a single request for a Web resource and then immediately forgets about it. Under these circumstances, you might wonder how it is possible for an online retail store to remember the items you put in your shopping cart.

Most shopping carts work because they use cookies to store information about your activities on a Web site. Cookies work with shopping carts in one of two ways, depending on the e-commerce site. An e-commerce site might use cookies as a storage bin for all the items you load into your shopping cart, as shown in Figure 7-31.

FIGURE 7-31

Shopping cart items can be stored in a cookie.

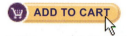

1. When you click the Add to Cart button, the merchant's server sends a message to your browser to add that item number to the cookie, which is stored on your computer.

ITEM #B7655

3. Your browser sends those cookies along with a request for an order summary.

VIEW CART

2. When you check out, the server asks your browser for all the cookie data that pertains to your shopping cart items.

Your order:

1 Blender $29.95

1 Wok $38.49

4. The Web server uses the cookies to produce a Web page listing the items you want to purchase.

FIGURE 7-32

Shopping cart items can be stored in a server-side database.

Some e-commerce sites use cookies simply as a way to uniquely identify each shopper. These sites generate a unique ID number that is stored along with your item selections in a server-side database (Figure 7-32).

1. When you connect to a merchant's site, the server assigns you a unique shopping cart ID number and sends it to your browser in a cookie.

DATABASE

WEB SERVER

CART # 2098-2

CART # 2098-2

ITEM # B7655

3. The Web server stores this number and your merchandise selection in the merchant's server-side database.

WEB SERVER

CART # 2098-2

BUY IT

2. When you select an item to purchase, your browser reads your shopping cart ID number from the cookie, and then sends this number to the merchant's Web server.

Order for CART #2098-2

1 Blender   B7655 $29.95

1 Wok   GJK4-31 $38.49

4. When you check out, your browser sends your shopping cart number to the server, which retrieves all your selections from the merchant's database.

7

ONLINE AUCTIONS

What is an online auction? If you're in a buying mood and looking for merchandise from tchotchkes to a new car, then you might turn first to an online auction, one of the hottest trends in online shopping. An **online auction** is the electronic equivalent to good old-fashioned yard sales, rummage sales, and auctions. Hosted by an Internet auction site, such as eBay, sellers post their merchandise or services and buyers bid for the posted items. The auction site does not own or hold the merchandise; rather, it merely facilitates the online bidding process and the transactions between buyers and sellers.

Online shoppers are attracted to online auctions for a number of reasons. Some merchandise can be obtained at bargain basement prices. Unique collectibles and memorabilia, which can be very difficult to find, are readily available for perusing and purchasing at auction. The greatest incentive, however, for participating in an online auction is perhaps the excitement of frenzied last-minute bidding to win an item you covet.

What can I buy at an online auction? You can expect to bid on new, used, closeout, overstock, or refurbished items at an online auction. Different types of services are also available. The merchandise covers a very broad spectrum of categories, such as antiques, collectibles, books and comics, coins, stamps, entertainment memorabilia, art, home and garden, cameras and camcorders, computers, cars and boats, sporting goods, apparel, jewelry, musical instruments, toys, and even theater tickets, special travel deals, and real estate (Figure 7-33).

The services up for auction are just as varied as the merchandise. For example, you can bid on tutoring lessons, printer repair, interior design, custom-made clothing, shopping assistance, printing and personalization, graphic design, and Web and computer services.

What are the largest auction sites? Originally founded in 1995 by Pierre Omidyar, eBay is by far the largest and most popular auction site. It is a virtual global marketplace that enables you to shop around the world. The number of confirmed registered users at eBay has risen year after year since it was founded, and had reached 222 million users at the beginning of 2007.

Amazon Auctions, uBid, eBid, Bidz, and Overstock.com also offer a wide range of products and bargains. Bid4Assets.com differs from other auction sites because it also provides seized, surplus, and tax-foreclosed properties from federal, state, and local government agencies. AuctionBytes is a Web site that provides up-to-date information on the numerous online auction sites.

How does an online auction work? At an online auction site specially designed computer software takes the place of an auctioneer. Server databases store information about auction items, and customer ratings of sellers. Server-side scripts accept bids and notify winners.

FIGURE 7-33

eBay and other auction sites offer a huge variety of goods and services.

Categories

Antiques
Art
Baby
Books
Business & Industrial
Cameras & Photo
Cars, Boats, Vehicles & Parts
Cell Phones
Clothing, Shoes & Accessories
Coins & Paper Money
Collectibles
Computers & Networking
Consumer Electronics
Crafts
Dolls & Bears
DVDs & Movies
Entertainment Memorabilia
Gift Certificates
Health & Beauty
Home & Garden
Jewelry & Watches
Music
Musical Instruments
Pottery & Glass
Real Estate
Specialty Services
Sporting Goods
Sports Mem, Cards & Fan Shop
Stamps
Tickets
Toys & Hobbies
Travel
Video Games
Everything Else
All Categories

ONLINE PAYMENT

How can I pay for merchandise from online shopping and auction sites? The most popular ways to make online payments include submitting your credit card number directly to a merchant and using a third-party payment service such as PayPal. Online wallets and one-time-use credit card numbers offer additional online payment options.

Is it safe to use my credit card online? Online shoppers are justifiably worried that personal information and credit card numbers supplied in the course of an e-commerce transaction might be hijacked and used inappropriately. Many shoppers worry that hackers might use packet sniffers to intercept credit card numbers traveling over the Internet.

To protect your credit card from packet sniffers, you should engage in electronic transactions only over a secure connection. A **secure connection** encrypts the data transmitted between your computer and a Web site. Even if a hacker can capture the packets containing payment data, your encrypted credit card number is virtually useless for illicit purposes. Technologies that create secure connections include SSL, TLS, and S-HTTP.

What are SSL and TLS? SSL (Secure Sockets Layer) and its successor **TLS** (Transport Layer Security) are protocols that encrypt data traveling between a client computer and an HTTP server. This encryption protocol creates a secure connection using a specially designated port—typically port 443 rather than port 80, which is used for unsecured HTTP communication. Web pages that provide a secure connection start with *https:* instead of *http:*.

What is S-HTTP? S-HTTP (secure HTTP) is an extension of HTTP that simply encrypts the text of an HTTP message before it is sent. Although SSL and S-HTTP both use encryption techniques to securely transmit data, they are technically different. Whereas SSL creates a secure connection between a client and a server over which any amount of data can be sent securely, S-HTTP is simply designed to encrypt and then transmit an individual message.

How do I know if a connection is secure? Your browser helps you identify when you are using a secure connection. Figure 7-34 explains.

INFOWEBLINKS

Connect to the **Safeguarding Your Credit Card InfoWeb** for tips on this important aspect of e-commerce.

W CLICK TO CONNECT
www.course.com/np/concepts11/ch07

TERMINOLOGY NOTE

Secure connections differ from secure Web sites. A secure connection encrypts the data transmitted between your computer and a Web site. A secure Web site, such as an online banking site, uses password security to prevent unauthorized access to pages on the site.

FIGURE 7-34

Secure connections are indicated by https in the URL and by the lock icon in Firefox (top) and Internet Explorer (bottom).

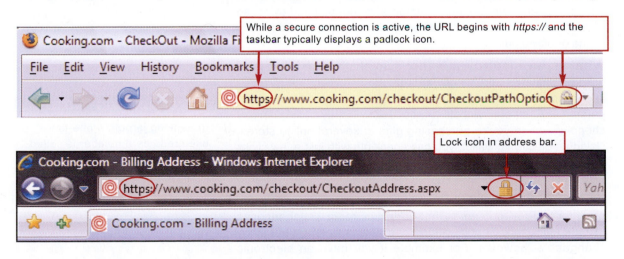

While a secure connection is active, the URL begins with *https://* and the taskbar typically displays a padlock icon.

Lock icon in address bar.

7

What is a person-to-person payment? A **person-to-person payment** (sometimes called a P2P payment, an online payment, or a third-party payment) offers an alternative to credit cards. It can be used to pay for online auction items and to wire money over the Internet. The online service called PayPal, now owned by eBay, pioneered person-to-person payments. PayPal's model has since been copied by several other service providers.

How does a person-to-person payment work? The process begins when you open an account at a person-to-person payment service. Some services require you to deposit money in your account—just as though you were opening a bank account. Other services allow you to supply your credit card number or bank account number, which is billed or debited only as you make purchases. You receive a user ID and password that enable you to access your account to make purchases and deposit additional funds. Money can be sent to anyone who has an e-mail account, as shown in Figure 7-35.

Is person-to-person payment safe? The major advantage of person-to-person payments is that the payment service is the only entity that sees your credit card number—merchants, auction dealers, and other payment recipients never receive your credit card number and, therefore, can't misuse it or store it on an unsecured computer. Currently, however, the person-to-person payment industry is relatively new, and companies are still scrambling to offer secure, reliable, long-term service to customers. Consumer advocates recommend using these services with caution and keeping your account balances low.

What is a one-time-use credit card? Several credit card companies offer one-time-use credit card numbers, which allow consumers to make purchases while keeping their actual card numbers hidden.

A one-time-use credit card number works for a single online purchase. Your credit card company tracks the purchases you incur with one-time-use numbers and adds the charges to your monthly credit card statement. One-time-use numbers cannot be used twice, so even if a hacker steals the number, it will not be accepted for any online or offline purchases.

What is an electronic wallet? An **electronic wallet** (also called a digital wallet) is software that stores billing and shipping information, which can be submitted when finalizing an e-commerce purchase. Electronic wallets are especially handy during holiday shopping, when you're purchasing gifts at several online stores. Using an electronic wallet, you can check out with just a few clicks instead of entering all the details of your billing address and credit card number.

You can create an electronic wallet by subscribing at a wallet provider's site. Companies that offer electronic wallet services include Microsoft, Google, and Yahoo! The wallets are not interchangeable, however. For example if you have an electronic

FIGURE 7-35

Using a person-to-person payment service.

1. To use a person-to-person payment service, simply log in to your account, enter the recipient's e-mail address, and indicate the payment amount.

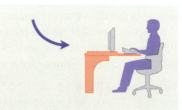

2. The recipient immediately receives an e-mail notification of your payment.

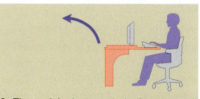

3. The recipient connects to the payment site to pick up the money by transferring the funds to his or her checking or payment account, requesting a check, or sending the funds to someone else.

TERMINOLOGY NOTE

In banking jargon, a one-time-use credit card number is called a controlled payment number. Banks and credit card companies offer this service under many different names, such as Citibank's Virtual Accounts and Discover Card's Deskshop.

wallet issued by Google, you can't use it at a Yahoo! merchant. To use an electronic wallet, look for a checkout button that corresponds to your digital wallet provider (Figure 7-36).

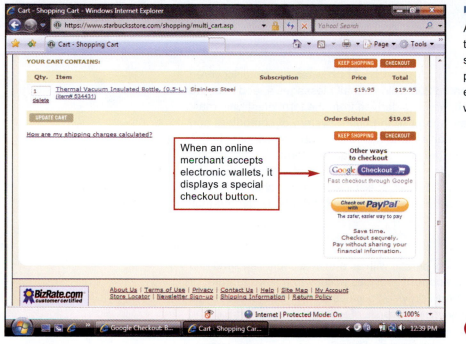

FIGURE 7-36

An electronic wallet can transfer your billing and shipping information to a participating site's e-commerce Web server when you check out.

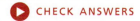 **CLICK TO START**

How safe is an electronic wallet? Electronic wallets are protected by passwords and encrypted to prevent unauthorized use. Hackers can potentially snag your data by using Trojan horse technology to collect your wallet password, however, so don't get fooled into entering your electronic wallet password by a bogus e-mail message instructing you to update your account. Consumers should carefully study current security bulletins before trusting their data to electronic wallets.

QuickCheck

1. An online auction is an example of C2C e-commerce. True or false? [ ]

2. A pop-up ad is an advertisement that appears in a separate window when you connect to a Web page. True or false? [ ]

3. One factor in the e-commerce economic model is ad revenue based on [ ] rates, the number of times that site visitors click an ad to connect to the advertiser's Web site.

4. Most online shopping carts work because they use [ ] to store information about your activities at a Web site.

5. Web sites that provide a secure connection display a padlock and start with sttp: instead of http:. True or false? [ ]

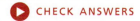 **CHECK ANSWERS**

E-mail

THE INTERNET REALLY TOOK OFF when people discovered electronic mail. An estimated 200 billion e-mail messages speed over the Internet each day. E-mail, which is derived from the term electronic mail, can refer to a single message or to the entire system of computers and software that transmits, receives, and stores electronic messages. In this section of the chapter, you get some background information about how e-mail works—in particular, the difference between Web-based e-mail and traditional client-based e-mail. E-mail labs at the end of the chapter provide hands-on overviews of how to read, compose, send, and reply to e-mail messages.

E-MAIL OVERVIEW

Who can use e-mail? Any person with an e-mail account can send and receive e-mail. An **e-mail account** provides access to a storage area, or mailbox, supplied by an e-mail provider, such as an ISP. Each mailbox has a unique address, which typically consists of a user ID, an @ symbol, and the name of the computer that maintains the mailbox. For example, suppose that a university student named Dee Greene has an electronic mailbox on a computer called rutgers.edu. If her user ID is dee_greene, her e-mail address would be *dee_greene@rutgers.edu*.

Exactly what is an e-mail message? An **e-mail message** is a document that is composed on a computer and remains in digital, or electronic, form so that it can be transmitted to another computer. A **message header** includes the recipient's e-mail address and message subject. It might also contain the address of anyone who is receiving a copy of the message, and the name of any file attachments that accompany the message. The body of the e-mail contains your message. The message header and body are usually displayed in a form, as shown in Figure 7-37.

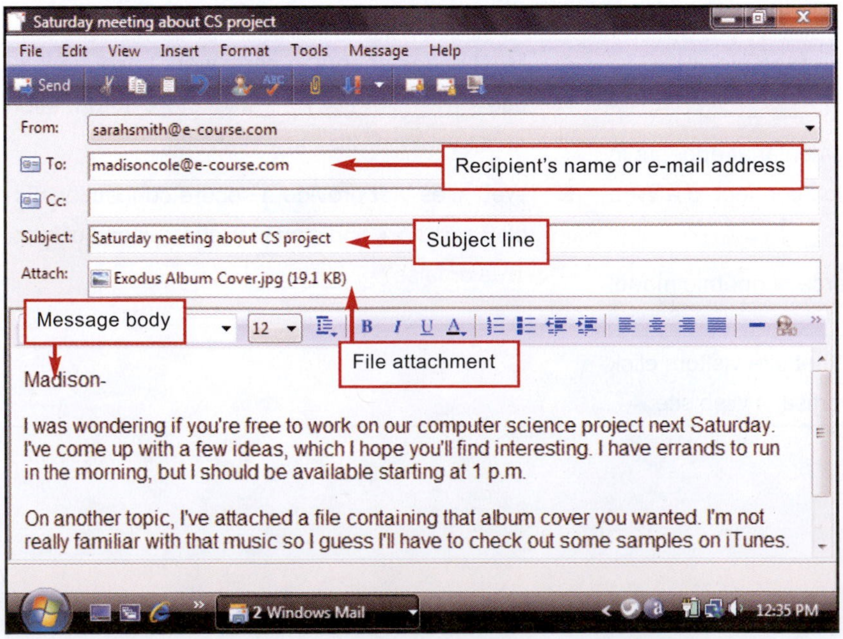

FIGURE 7-37

When you compose an e-mail message, you can begin by entering the address of one or more recipients and the subject of the message. You can also specify one or more files to attach to the message. The body of the e-mail message contains the message itself. When the message is sent, your e-mail software adds the date and your e-mail address to identify you as the sender.

CLICK TO START

What can I do with basic e-mail? Basic e-mail activities consist of writing, reading, replying to (Figure 7-38), and forwarding messages. Messages can be printed, kept for later reference, or deleted.

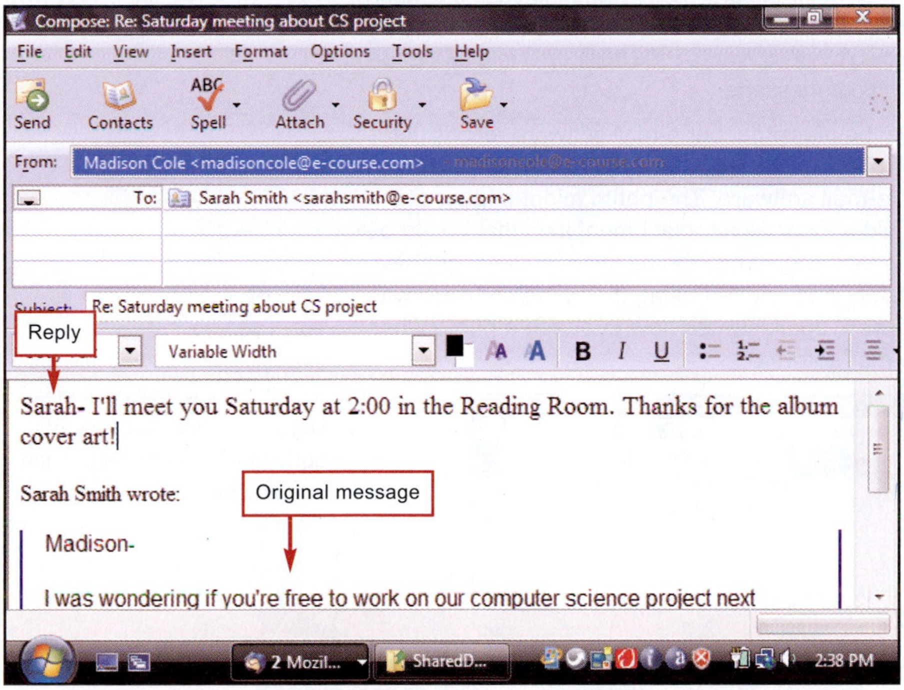

FIGURE 7-38

Your e-mail client's Reply button creates a new e-mail message and automatically addresses it to the person who sent the original message. Most e-mail systems also copy the text of the original message into the reply so that everyone has a complete transcript of the messages that were exchanged.

▶ **CLICK TO START**

How does forwarding work? After you receive an e-mail message, you can use the Forward feature to pass it on to other people. You might, for example, forward a message that was sent to you but that should be handled by someone else. When you initiate the forwarding process, the original e-mail message is copied into a new message window, complete with the address of the original sender. You can then enter the address of the person to whom you are forwarding the message. You can also add a note about why you are passing the message along.

Some e-mail systems allow you to alter the text of the original message before you forward it. If you do so, include a note explaining your changes, especially if they alter the intent of the original message. You should not forward messages that were intended to be confidential. If you think that such a message needs to be shared with other people, obtain permission from the author of the original message.

What's an e-mail attachment? Originally, e-mail messages were stored in a plain and simple format called ASCII text. No fancy formatting was allowed—no variation in font type or color, no underlining or boldface, and, of course, no pictures or sounds. Although you cannot insert a digital photo or sound file into a plain ASCII e-mail message, you can send these kinds of files as e-mail attachments.

Any file that travels with an e-mail message is called an **e-mail attachment**. A conversion process called **MIME** (Multi-Purpose Internet Mail Extensions) provides a clever way of disguising digital photos, sounds, and other media as plain ASCII code that can travel over the Internet as e-mail attachments. An electronic message incorporated in the e-mail header provides your e-mail software with information that allows it to reconstruct the attachment into its original form.

7

Suppose you want to e-mail a photo to a friend who is working on a brochure for the Humane Society. The photo is stored in a file called PICT0011.JPG. You can address an e-mail message to your friend, write a short note ("I've attached a photo that might work for the brochure."), and then use the Insert file or Attachment menu option provided by your e-mail software to specify PICT0011.JPG. Your e-mail software converts PICT0011.JPG into MIME format and sends it along with your message.

When your friend receives the message, her e-mail software reconstitutes the file into the original photo. The way the attachment is displayed depends on your friend's e-mail software. The photo might appear at the end of the e-mail, or it could appear as an attachment icon that has to be double-clicked. With some e-mail systems, the attachment file might have to be downloaded separately and opened using the same software with which it was created. Figure 7-39 illustrates how to attach a photo when using Microsoft Outlook e-mail software.

FIGURE 7-39

This sequence of screens demonstrates how to add an attachment to an e-mail message. Use the Click to Start button to find out how to open e-mail attachments and scan them for viruses.

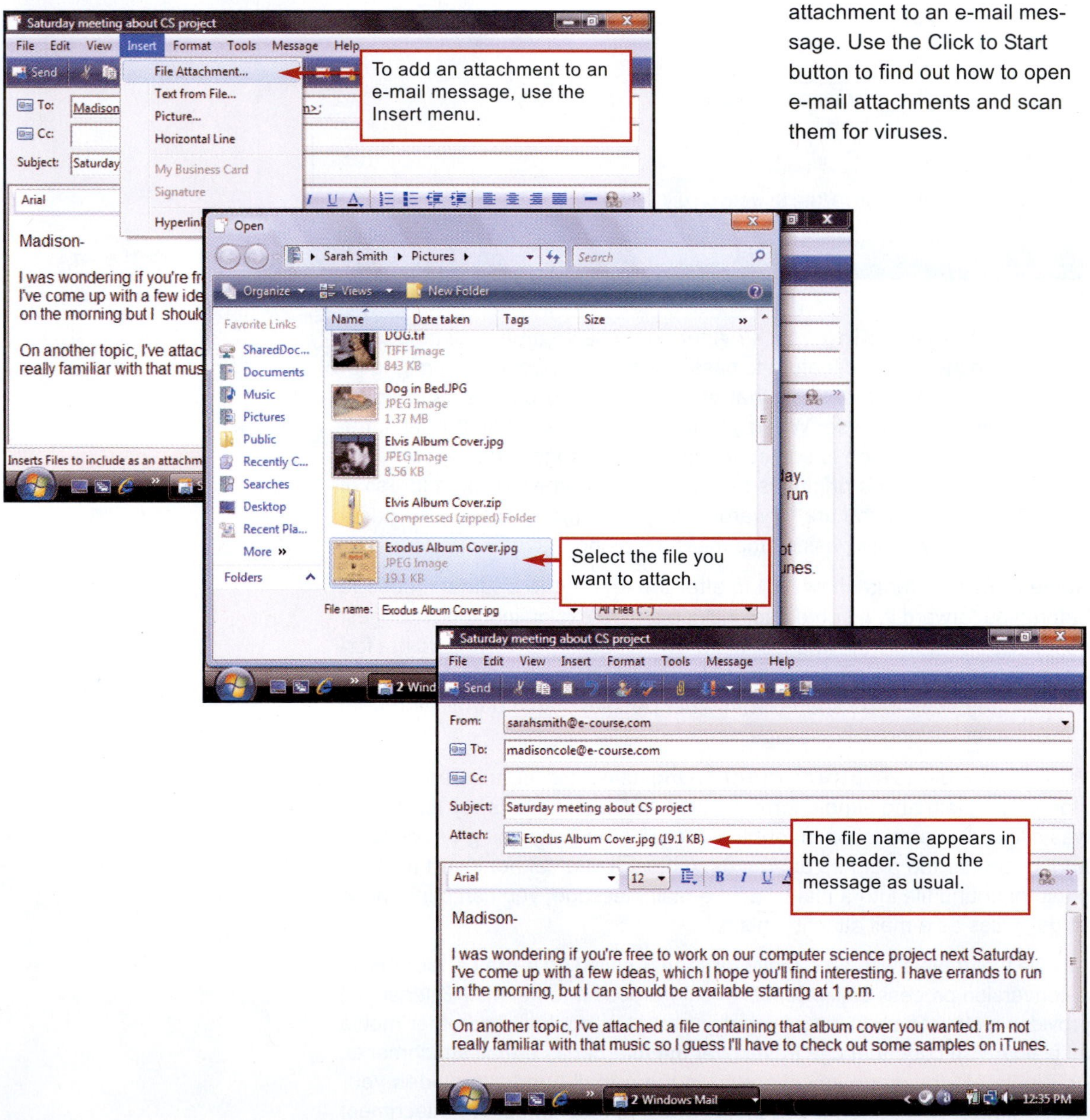

To add an attachment to an e-mail message, use the Insert menu.

Select the file you want to attach.

The file name appears in the header. Send the message as usual.

● CLICK TO START

How does HTML relate to e-mail? Most e-mail software offers an HTML formatting option to create e-mail messages that contain graphics and lots of elaborate formatting that's just not possible with plain ASCII text.

By selecting your e-mail software's HTML option, you enter a world of colorful, bold, italic, and underlined text; fancy fonts; embedded graphics; and various font sizes. Your e-mail recipients must have HTML-compliant e-mail software. Otherwise, your message will be delivered as plain, unformatted ASCII text. You should also be aware that HTML formatted e-mail messages can distribute viruses and open security holes that leave your computer vulnerable to hackers. Figure 7-40 illustrates an e-mail message in HTML format.

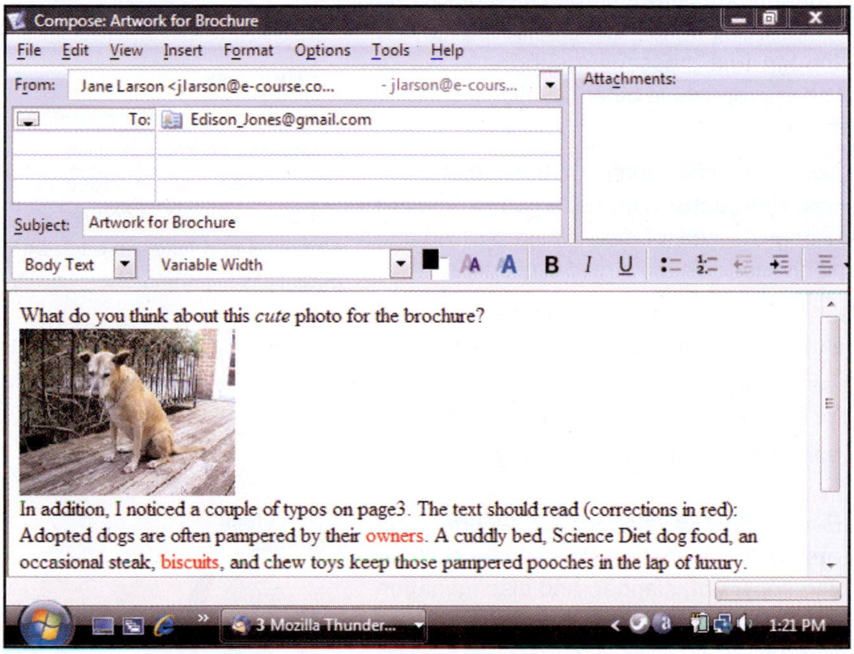

FIGURE 7-40

An e-mail message in HTML format can include graphics in addition to a variety of fonts and font colors.

What other e-mail features are available? In addition to attachments and HTML formatting, today's sophisticated e-mail systems typically offer features that help you perform the tasks listed in Figure 7-41.

FIGURE 7-41

E-mail features provide flexibility for sending and receiving messages.

- Maintain an address book and use it to select e-mail addresses instead of entering them every time you compose a message.
- Use the address book to send mail to a group that consists of several e-mail addresses.
- Send a carbon copy (Cc:) of a message to one or more recipients.
- Send a blind carbon copy (Bcc:), which hides the addresses in the Bcc: field from other recipients of the message.
- Assign a priority to a message—high priority is usually indicated by an exclamation point or red text.
- Find a particular message in your list of old mail.
- Enlarge text size for easier reading.
- Sort messages by date received, sender's name, subject, or priority.
- Refuse to accept messages that arrive from a particular e-mail address.
- Automate replies to messages that you receive while on vacation or when you will not be responding to e-mail messages for a few days.
- Automatically fetch mail at specified intervals.
- Check spelling before sending a message.

NETIQUETTE

Is e-mail different from other types of communication? In some respects, e-mail is similar to an old-fashioned letter because its message is conveyed without benefit of the facial expressions, voice inflections, and body gestures that accompany face-to-face conversations. When composing a message, it is important to carefully consider your audience and the message you want to convey.

For example, you might have gotten into the habit of using text messaging shorthand to write messages such as "thnq 4 spking w me 2day. c u 2moro at 10." (Translation: Thank you for speaking with me today. See you tomorrow at 10:00.) Text messaging shorthand recently emerged as a quick and convenient way to communicate when using e-mail, instant messaging, and cell phone text messaging. Although text messaging shorthand works among your friends, it would not be appropriate in other situations, such as confirming the time for a job interview.

By understanding netiquette, you can avoid some of the pitfalls and problems of e-mail communications. **Netiquette** is online jargon for Internet etiquette. It is a series of customs or guidelines for maintaining civilized and effective communications in online discussions and e-mail exchanges.

- **Put a meaningful title on the subject line.** The subject line of your message should clearly describe the content of your e-mail message.

- **Use uppercase and lowercase letters.** An e-mail message that's typed in all uppercase means that you're shouting.

- **Check spelling.** Most e-mail software offers a Check Spelling command. Use it.

- **Be careful what you send.** E-mail is not private, nor is it secure. Treat your messages as though they are postcards that can be read by anyone. Remember that all laws governing copyright, slander, and discrimination apply to e-mail.

- **Be polite.** Avoid wording that could sound inflammatory or argumentative. If you would not say it face-to-face, don't say it in e-mail.

- **Be cautious when using sarcasm and humor.** The words in your e-mail arrive without facial expressions or voice intonations, so a sarcastic comment can easily be misinterpreted.

- **Use smileys and text messaging shorthand cautiously.** **Smileys** are symbols that represent emotions (Figure 7-42). They can help convey the intent behind your words. Smileys and text messaging shorthand should be used only in correspondence with people who understand them.

- **Use the Bcc function for group mailings.** By placing e-mail addresses for secondary recipients in the Bcc box, the recipients of your message won't have to scroll through a long list of addresses before reaching the meat of your message.

- **Don't send replies to "all recipients."** Use the Reply All command only when there is a very specific need for everyone listed in the To, Cc, and Bcc boxes to receive the message.

- **Don't send huge attachments.** Try to limit the size of attachments to 50 KB or less for recipients who have dial-up connections. If necessary, use a compression program, such as WinZip, to shrink the attachment.

- **Explain all attachments.** Attachments can harbor computer viruses. To determine whether an attachment is legitimate, your correspondents will want to know the file name of the attachment, what the attachment contains, and the name of the software you used to create it.

INFOWEBLINKS

You can read more about netiquette, smileys, and text messaging shorthand at the **Netiquette InfoWeb**.

 **CLICK TO CONNECT**
www.course.com/np/concepts11/ch07

FIGURE 7-42

Smileys, which are sometimes called emoticons, are clever symbols that can be added to e-mail messages to convey emotions and take the edge off potentially inflammatory remarks.

:-)
"Don't take offense."

;-)
"Just kidding!"

:-(
"I'm not happy about that."

:-/
"I'm perplexed."

8-)
"I'm amazed."

- **Stay alert for viruses.** Because viruses can tag along with e-mail attachments, don't open an attachment unless it was sent from a reliable source, its purpose is clearly explained in the body of the e-mail, and it was scanned using antivirus software.

- **Notify recipients of viruses.** If you discover that your computer sent out infected attachments, use antivirus software to remove the virus, and then notify anyone to whom you recently sent mail.

E-MAIL TECHNOLOGY

What is an e-mail system? An **e-mail system** is the equipment and software that carries and manipulates e-mail messages. It includes computers and software called **e-mail servers** that sort, store, and route mail. An e-mail system also includes the personal computers that belong to individuals who send and receive mail. E-mail is based on **store-and-forward** technology—a communications method in which data that cannot be sent directly to its destination is temporarily stored until transmission is possible. This technology allows e-mail messages to be routed to a server and held until they are forwarded to the next server or to a personal mailbox.

Three types of e-mail systems are widely used today: POP, IMAP, and Web-based mail. **POP** (Post Office Protocol) temporarily stores new messages on an e-mail server. When you connect to your ISP and request your mail, it is downloaded from the e-mail server and stored on your computer. **IMAP** (Internet Messaging Access Protocol) is similar to POP, except that you have the option of downloading your mail or leaving it on the server. **Web-based e-mail** keeps your mail at a Web site, where it can be accessed using a standard Web browser (Figure 7-43).

FIGURE 7-43

You can use a browser to access your Web-based e-mail account.

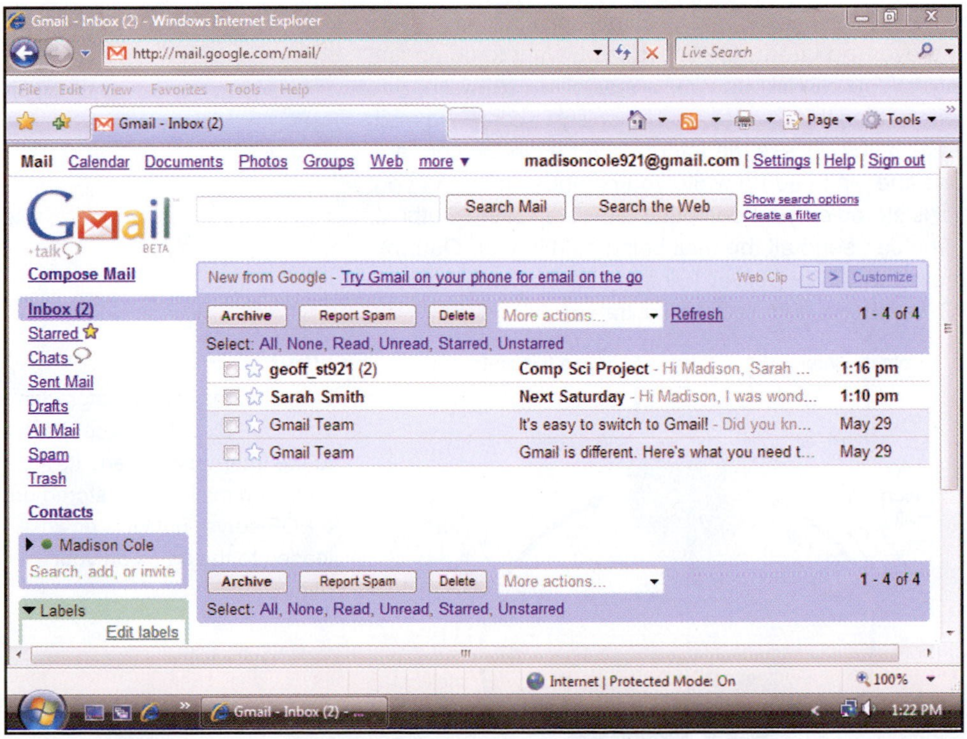

7

▶ CLICK TO START

How do I use Web-based e-mail? Before you can use Web-based e-mail, you need an e-mail account with a Web-based e-mail provider. Popular Web-based e-mail services include Google's Gmail, MSN's Hotmail, and Yahoo's Yahoo! Mail.

To obtain a Web-based e-mail account, connect to the provider's Web site and enter the information required to obtain an e-mail address, a user ID, and a password. Armed with these identifiers, you can use a browser to connect to the e-mail Web site from any computer that has access to the Internet. At the Web site, you can write, read, reply to, and delete e-mail messages. Some Web-based e-mail providers allocate a limited amount of space to each account, making it important to delete messages when you no longer need them. You don't want your electronic mailbox to overflow and cause some messages to be returned to the senders.

How do POP and IMAP work? Most people who use POP or IMAP e-mail have obtained an e-mail account from an ISP. POP mail accounts are more widely available. Such an account provides a mailbox on the ISP's **POP server**—a computer that stores your incoming messages until they can be transferred to your hard disk. Using POP requires **e-mail client software**, such as Microsoft Outlook, Mozilla Thunderbird (open source), or QUALCOMM Eudora. This client software, which is installed on your computer, provides an Inbox and an Outbox that allow you to work with your mail, even when your computer is not online.

An Inbox holds incoming messages. When you ask the e-mail server to deliver your mail, all your messages stored on the server are transferred to your computer, where they are stored on your computer's disk drive and listed as new mail in your Inbox. You can then disconnect from the Internet, if you like, to read and reply to the new mail at your leisure.

An Outbox temporarily holds messages you have composed and completed, but haven't transmitted over the Internet. Suppose you want to compose several e-mail messages. You can fire up your e-mail client software, but remain offline while you work on the messages. The ability to compose mail offline is especially useful if you access the Internet over a dial-up connection because the phone line isn't tied up while you compose mail. As you complete a message, it is stored on your computer and listed in the Outbox. When you go online, you can send all the mail being held in your Outbox. Outgoing mail is routed by an **SMTP server** (Simple Mail Transfer Protocol server) instead of a POP server, as Figure 7-44 illustrates.

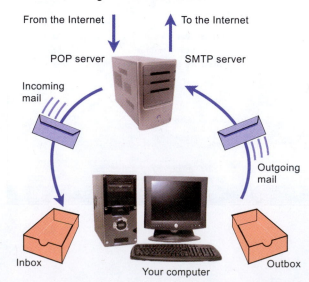

From the Internet   To the Internet

POP server   SMTP server

Incoming mail

Outgoing mail

Inbox   Your computer   Outbox

FIGURE 7-44

Outgoing mail can be stored in your Outbox until you connect to the Internet and send it. Incoming mail can be stored on a POP server until it is downloaded to the Inbox on your hard disk.

Does e-mail client software work only for offline e-mail tasks? No. Although you can use your e-mail client software to compose, read, and reply to messages while you're offline, you can also use it while you are online. In fact, this software often provides a setting that bypasses the Outbox and immediately sends messages out over the Internet.

How does POP mail compare to Web-based e-mail? Before answering this question, let's review the important distinctions between the two types of e-mail. First, POP mail requires you to install and use e-mail client software, whereas Web-based e-mail allows you to use a browser to work with your mail. Second, POP transfers messages to your computer's hard disk, whereas a Web-based e-mail system retains your messages on its server.

Both e-mail systems have similar features, allowing you to read, compose, reply to, delete, and forward e-mail messages; maintain an address book; and send attachments. Each system does, however, have unique advantages. In fact, many ISPs offer both POP and Web-based e-mail; POP for when customers are at their home computer, and Web mail for when they are traveling. You might consider using both.

● **Control.** POP mail gives you more control over your messages because they are transferred to your computer's hard disk, where you can control access to them. Web-based e-mail maintains your messages on its server, where you have less control over who can access them.

● **Security.** When messages are stored on your computer, a hard disk drive malfunction could wipe out all your correspondence (along with the rest of your files). A Web-based e-mail provider is rigorous about safeguarding its data, so your mail might be safer than if it was stored on your hard disk.

● **Travel.** The major advantage of Web-based e-mail is that you can access your messages from any computer connected to the Internet. Therefore, you can get your e-mail when you travel without taking your computer. In contrast, POP mail tools and data, such as your address book, e-mail software, and old mail are stored on your computer. To use your familiar POP mail tools on the road, you really have to carry your computer with you or store your e-mail files on a portable USB flash drive. Another solution is to temporarily forward your POP mail to a Web-based mail account that you can access from public computers.

QuickCheck

1. In an e-mail address, the [_____] symbol separates the user ID from the name of the e-mail server.

2. E-mail attachments are typically converted using [_____], which disguises media and other files as plain ASCII code. (Hint: Use the acronym.)

3. If you want an e-mail message to include various fonts, font colors, and graphics, you can use [_____] format for the message. (Hint: Use the acronym.)

4. Store-and-[_____] e-mail technology stores messages on an e-mail server until they are transmitted to an individual's computer.

5. For many client-based e-mail systems, a(n) [_____] server handles outgoing mail, and a(n) [_____] or IMAP server handles incoming mail. (Hint: Use acronyms.)

▶ CHECK ANSWERS

Web and E-mail Security

THE WEB AND E-MAIL abound with spam and scams engineered to monitor your online activities and collect confidential information, such as credit card numbers, passwords, and bank account numbers. You were introduced to spyware in an earlier chapter. Now you'll learn about specific spam and spyware exploits and find out how to minimize the risk they pose to computer security and your privacy.

COOKIE EXPLOITS

Can cookies be a security risk? Cookies have built-in safeguards designed to reduce their abuse, but marketers, hackers, and pranksters have discovered loopholes that twist cookies to serve the dark side. One of the most prevalent cookie exploits involves ad-serving cookies, and Flash cookies are a newly emerging problem.

What is an ad-serving cookie? When you connect to a Web site, you expect it to store an innocuous cookie on your computer's hard disk. Some Web sites, however, feature banner ads supplied by third-party marketing firms. If you click the ad, this third party can surreptitiously create an **ad-serving cookie** and use it to track your activities at any site containing banner ads from that third party. The marketing firms that distribute ad-serving cookies claim that the data in their cookies is used simply to select and display ads that might interest you, but privacy advocates worry that shopper profiles can be compiled, sold, and used for unauthorized purposes. Figure 7-45 illustrates how third parties use ad-serving cookies.

FIGURE 7-45

Third-party ad-serving cookies make it possible to track your Internet activities across sites.

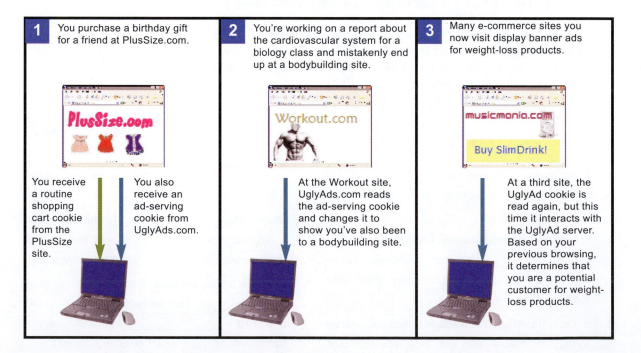

1	2	3
You purchase a birthday gift for a friend at PlusSize.com.	You're working on a report about the cardiovascular system for a biology class and mistakenly end up at a bodybuilding site.	Many e-commerce sites you now visit display banner ads for weight-loss products.

You receive a routine shopping cart cookie from the PlusSize site. | You also receive an ad-serving cookie from UglyAds.com.

At the Workout site, UglyAds.com reads the ad-serving cookie and changes it to show you've also been to a bodybuilding site.

At a third site, the UglyAd cookie is read again, but this time it interacts with the UglyAd server. Based on your previous browsing, it determines that you are a potential customer for weight-loss products.

Can I turn off cookies to foil ad-serving exploits? Most browsers include security settings that block cookies. Unfortunately, on many Web sites, cookies are the only mechanism available for tracking your activity or remembering your purchases. Cookies might also be required to join classes and chat groups.

If you disable cookies altogether, you might not be able to make online purchases, participate in online training classes, use Web-based mail, or register for premium services at search engine sites. In addition, you might have to manually enter your user ID and password every time you revisit a Web site. You won't be able to take advantage of targeted marketing, such as when a music Web site keeps track of your favorite band and notifies you when the band's new CDs are available.

Rather than block all cookies, you can block cookies from specific sites. For example, if you'd rather not have your favorite search engine compile and store your searches, you can block its cookies. Your browser might have a setting that blocks all third-party cookies to prevent ad-serving cookies from tracking your site visits (Figure 7-46).

FIGURE 7-46

Most browsers offer a way to turn off third-party cookies. When using Microsoft Internet Explorer, for example, you can adjust the setting using the Internet Options dialog box.

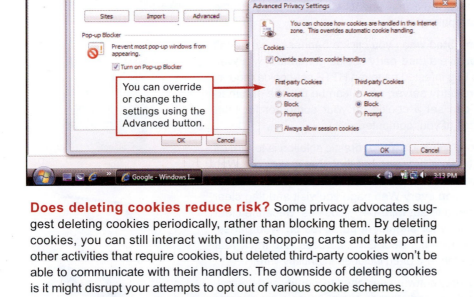

Does deleting cookies reduce risk? Some privacy advocates suggest deleting cookies periodically, rather than blocking them. By deleting cookies, you can still interact with online shopping carts and take part in other activities that require cookies, but deleted third-party cookies won't be able to communicate with their handlers. The downside of deleting cookies is it might disrupt your attempts to opt out of various cookie schemes.

An opt-out function allows you to refuse to participate in an activity or promotion. Similar to the National Do Not Call list, several third-party advertising companies, such as DoubleClick and ZEDO, now provide users with an opt-out mechanism to disallow ad-serving cookies. The Network Advertising Initiative (NAI) offers a tool to opt out of the targeted advertising by NAI's member firms. In most cases, however, opting out creates an opt-out cookie and if you delete all the cookies on your computer the opt-out cookie will also be deleted and third-party cookies will again start to accumulate.

What is a Flash cookie? A **Flash cookie**, also called a local shared object, is the Flash equivalent of a conventional Web cookie. Flash cookies are utilized and set by Adobe's Flash Player (previously distributed by Macromedia), which is installed on practically every computer to run movies, videos, and games. In the context of running Flash animations, Flash cookies can collect and store personal data, such as the user's name or the user's progress in a game.

Because so many computer users now delete or block conventional cookies, marketers are turning to Flash cookies for an alternative way to track and target consumers. United Virtualities (UV), an online marketing firm, developed the PIE (Persistent Identification Element) system, which essentially uses Flash cookies to track users even when they've deleted or aren't accepting conventional cookies.

Can I avoid Flash cookies? You can manually delete Flash cookies from your computer after locating the #Shared Objects file in which they are stored. You can also visit the Adobe Flash Player Web site to adjust your computer's settings for Flash cookies. You can choose your options from the Settings Manager, which consists of several panels. The Website Privacy Settings panel lists all the Web sites that currently store information about you and allows you to set your preferences on a per site basis. A tutorial for using the Settings Manager is also provided by the Web site.

What is a Web bug? A **Web bug** or clear GIF is typically a 1x1 pixel graphic embedded in a Web page or e-mail message. It is almost invisible due to its size, and is designed to track who's reading the Web page or e-mail message. Web bugs on a Web page can generate third-party ad-serving cookies. Junk e-mail messages use Web bugs for monitoring the number of people who view the e-mail and use that data to determine the direction of marketing campaigns.

Unlike cookies that are generated when you click a banner ad, you don't have to click anything to receive a third-party cookie generated by a Web bug. When you view a Web bug infested page, an HTTP set-cookie request automatically goes to a third-party server, which can be the site of a marketer or hacker. The site can set a cookie on your computer for later retrieval, or log the IP address of your computer.

Is there any way to avoid Web bugs? A drastic solution is to turn off all the graphics displayed by your browser, but that step makes the Web much less interesting. Bugnosis and similar Web bug detectors work with your browser to test graphics on every Web page you visit and flag clear GIF images that might be used to set third-party cookies. Because clear GIFs are also used legitimately for alignment purposes on Web pages, however, it is difficult to determine if a clear GIF's purpose is to track your surfing habits. Web bug detectors are often included in antispyware.

Antispyware is a type of security software designed to identify and neutralize Web bugs, ad-serving cookies, and other spyware. Antispyware such as Spy Sweeper, Ad-Aware, Spybot Search & Destroy, Pest Control, and Microsoft Antispyware can offer some degree of protection against browser parasites and other Web-based nuisances (Figure 7-47). Avoid responding to or downloading spyware from pop-up ads, however. Those ads often lead to infected software or other malware.

Can I surf the Internet anonymously? In addition to tracking cookies, Web sites can track IP addresses of computers that connect to their sites. IP addresses can sometimes be traced back to individuals, especially

FIGURE 7-47

Many computer owners use more than one antispyware utility if they suspect their computers are infested with spyware.

those who have fixed IP addresses or always-on connections that retain the same IP address for long periods of time. Individuals who prefer not to leave a trail of their Internet activities surf through an **anonymous proxy service**, which uses an intermediary, or proxy, server to relay Web page requests after masking the originating IP address (Figure 7-48).

Torpark and other anonymizer software allows you to browse through Web sites anonymously. It establishes an encrypted transport path from your computer to a Tor proxy server, which acts as a relay station to a destination site. Torpark can also be used as a portable application by storing it on a USB Flash drive that you plug into any Internet-enabled computer at work, school, or other public Internet facility.

A trade-off to the anonymity offered by anonymous proxies is that they tend not to operate at the same speed as your regular browser. In addition, some Web sites and discussion groups block access from proxy servers because they have been used to spam the site or flood it with traffic. Also, anonymous proxies can be compromised by malicious third parties or monitored under court order, so anonymity is never assured.

SPAM

What is spam? One of e-mail's main disadvantages is **spam**—unwanted electronic junk mail about medical products, low-cost loans, and fake software upgrades that arrives in your online mailbox. Today's proliferation of spam is generated by marketing firms that harvest e-mail addresses from mailing lists, membership applications, and Web sites.

Is spam dangerous? In the past, spam flooding your Inbox with unsolicited and often pornographic messages was merely an annoyance. These days, however, spam has turned into another major hacking tool for cyber criminals. Spam sometimes contains Web bugs, viruses, worms, or keyloggers that can wreak havoc on your computer or steal personal information such as passwords. Spam can also be used for phishing scams, which are described later in this section. In addition to being an annoyance, spam can pose a danger to you and your computer.

Can spam be blocked before it gets to my mailbox? With millions of copies of some spam floating around the Internet, it would seem possible to identify and delete it before individuals have to contend with it. ISPs have stepped up their role in the fight against spam. For example, Hotmail, MSN, and RoadRunner actively participate in Return Path's Bonded Sender Program, which requires e-mail senders to post a bond to guarantee that the messages they send are not spam. A charge is made against the bond if enough end-users complain that they received spam from the bonded e-mail sender. Bonded e-mail senders have to go through a strict accreditation procedure.

To combat spam sent by hijacked botnet computers, **e-mail authentication** techniques, such as Sender ID and DomainKeys, verify that e-mail messages originate from the Internet domain from which they claim to have been sent. For example, if Bank of America e-mail messages are supposed to originate from mail.bankofamerica.net, an ISP that uses e-mail authentication will filter out messages that originate from spoofed addresses such

FIGURE 7-48

An anonymous proxy server relays your Web page requests after stripping off your IP address.

3. The Web site you want to visit receives your request for a Web page.

4. The Web page is sent to the proxy server.

Unencrypted HTTP from 333.333.333.333

Web page to 333.333.333.333

2. A proxy server decrypts your HTTP request and resends it using a proxy IP address.

5. The proxy server receives the Web page, encrypts it, and sends it to you.

Encrypted HTTP from 111.111.111.111

Encrypted Web page to 111.111.111.111

1. Anonymizer software on your computer provides a specially equipped browser that encrypts its requests.

6. Your computer receives the encrypted Web page, the anonymizer software unencrypts it, and your browser displays it.

Your computer at IP address 111.111.111.111

▶ CLICK TO START

7

as *www.bankofamerica.ru*. Google, Yahoo!, and Earthlink use authentication techniques to filter out e-mail with a forged origination address.

Can I avoid spam? A **spam filter** is a type of utility software that captures unsolicited e-mail messages before they reach your inbox. It works by checking the text of e-mail headers and messages based on a series of rules. For example, a rule such as "Message header contains viagra, v1agra, or vi@gra" would help identify spam that's trying to hawk cheap pharmaceuticals.

Spam filters are available as standalone software, but often are included in e-mail clients and security suites. Most spam filters are shipped with a set of basic rules used to identify spam. The rules can be updated by downloads from the software publisher's Web site. Some spam filters also allow end-users to create their own rules to target spam that gets through the standard filters (Figure 7-49).

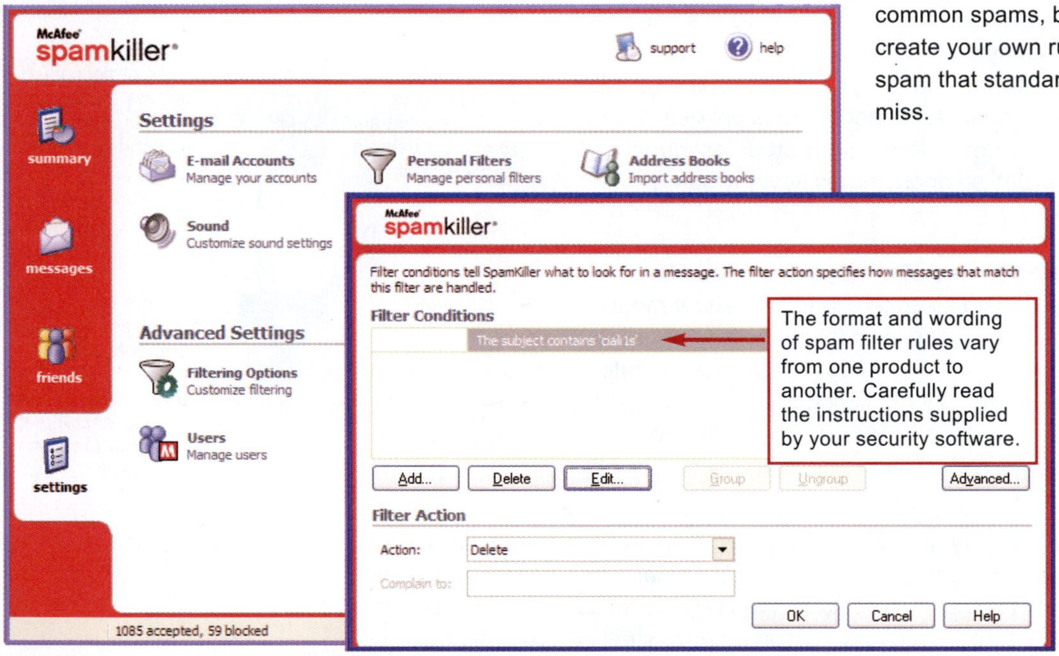

FIGURE 7-49

Spam filters usually include standard rules that block common spams, but you can create your own rules for spam that standard filters miss.

Spam filters tend to slow down the process of downloading mail and they sometimes trash legitimate mail. Periodically, you should look in the junk e-mail folder used by your spam filters to retrieve any mail that's not junk.

In addition to using spam filters, you can avoid being a spam victim by following the guidelines in Figure 7-50.

▶ **CLICK TO START**

FIGURE 7-50

Guidelines for Avoiding Spam

- Never reply to spam when you receive it.
- Don't click links in e-mail messages, even if it's an opt-out link.
- Give your e-mail address only to people from whom you want to receive e-mail. Be wary of providing your e-mail address at Web sites, entering it on application forms, or posting it in public places such as online discussion groups.
- Use a disposable e-mail address when you register for online sites. You can use this disposable address to get your confirmation number for online purchases you've made, but don't use it for regular e-mail correspondence.
- If your e-mail provider offers a way to report spam, use it.
- When spam gets out of hand, consider changing your e-mail account so that you have a different e-mail address.

PHISHING

What is phishing? **Phishing** is an e-mail based scam that's designed to persuade you to reveal confidential information such as your bank account number or Social Security number. Unlike pharming attacks, phishing scams require that you reply to the e-mail message or click an embedded Web site link for the scam to unfold.

If you've used e-mail for any length of time, you've probably encountered the granddaddy of all phishing scams, a letter from a Nigerian political refugee who wants to move a large sum of money to a bank in your country and needs a bank account (yours!) to stash it for a few days. Of course you'll get a percentage for your trouble. Don't even think about it. According to the FBI, several gullible individuals have been lured to foreign shores where they've been kidnapped and even killed.

More innocuous, but potentially damaging spam scams start with an e-mail message that appears to come from a legitimate organization such as a bank, an online payment service, an online store, or even your ISP. The message directs you to click a link to verify confidential data. The link connects you to a bogus site cleverly disguised to look very much like a legitimate Web site. There you are urged to enter your bank account number, PIN, password, credit card number, or other data.

How do I avoid phishing scams? If you don't want to become a phishing victim, be suspicious of e-mail messages that supposedly come from banks, ISPs, online payment services, operating system publishers, and online merchants. Even if the messages appear to be legitimate, do not click links in the messages, but instead go to the Web site using your browser and link to your account as you normally would. If your account needs updating, you should see instructions about how to proceed.

FAKE SITES

What is a fake site? A fake Web site looks legitimate, but has been created by a third party to be a very clever replica of a legitimate Web site, such as ebay.com or even the White House. Many fake Web sites are bogus storefronts designed exclusively for collecting credit card numbers from unwary shoppers. These sites might have the trappings of a real site. They might even offer a secure connection for transmitting your credit card number. When your data is received, however, it is stored in a database that belongs to a hacker, who can use the data for unauthorized transactions.

Some fake sites are not fake storefronts; rather, they are official-sounding sites, such as government agencies, that actually contain sexually explicit material. Other bogus sites simply present totally fabricated information or stories designed to fool the user. Fake sites are a key part of illegitimate pharming schemes.

What is pharming? **Pharming** is an exploit that redirects users to fake sites by "poisoning" a domain name server with a false IP address. Pharming and phishing are similar in many respects; both take advantage of fake sites. Phishing links, however, often lead to fake sites with URLs that are just slightly different from those of legitimate sites. Hackers depend on victims not paying close attention to the discrepancy when they click links.

Pharming is more sophisticated than phishing because the link appears to be for a legitimate URL. Even a close examination of the URL will not reveal anything suspicious because the URL's IP address has been changed at the domain name server.

7

TERMINOLOGY NOTE

Fake sites, URLs, and even e-mail addresses are often referred to as *spoofed* and the process of misdirection is called *spoofing*.

As you know from the Internet chapter, a domain name server is responsible for linking a domain name, such as YourBank.com, to its IP address, such as 64.191.203.33. Pharming attacks take advantage of a loophole in the domain name system that under certain circumstances permits third parties to change a record in a domain name server's database.

Hackers can attach the IP address of their own Web site to the URL of a legitimate site. For example, if a hacker manages to change the IP address for YourBank.com to the address of a fake site at 209.195.132.165, anyone who enters the legitimate URL of YourBank.com will be connected to the fake site.

How can I recognize a pharming attack? Pharming is more surreptitious and tougher to detect than most other hacker schemes. To detect a possible pharming attack, you have to be alert to the appearance of Web sites you frequently visit. Be cautious about revealing sensitive information if the site has changed since your last visit. You might want to call the business or organization that operates the Web site to learn whether the Web site has undergone a valid facelift or if the site is a slightly flawed replica of the legitimate one. You can also make sure that you see the lock or key icon at the bottom of the browser when a site claims to be a secure site.

A bank that offers online services recently implemented the use of personal digital images to counteract pharming. Each user chooses an image that is supposed to appear when he or she logs on. If the secret image does not appear, the site is not the legitimate one.

Anti-pharming tools are emerging in response to the growing security threat posed by fake sites. Mainstream browsers now include routines that compare IP addresses to a list of known fake sites and warn you of suspicious sites. Make sure your antipharming and antiphishing filters are activated (Figure 7-51).

FIGURE 7-51

Most browsers include antipharming and antiphishing routines. Make sure they are activated.

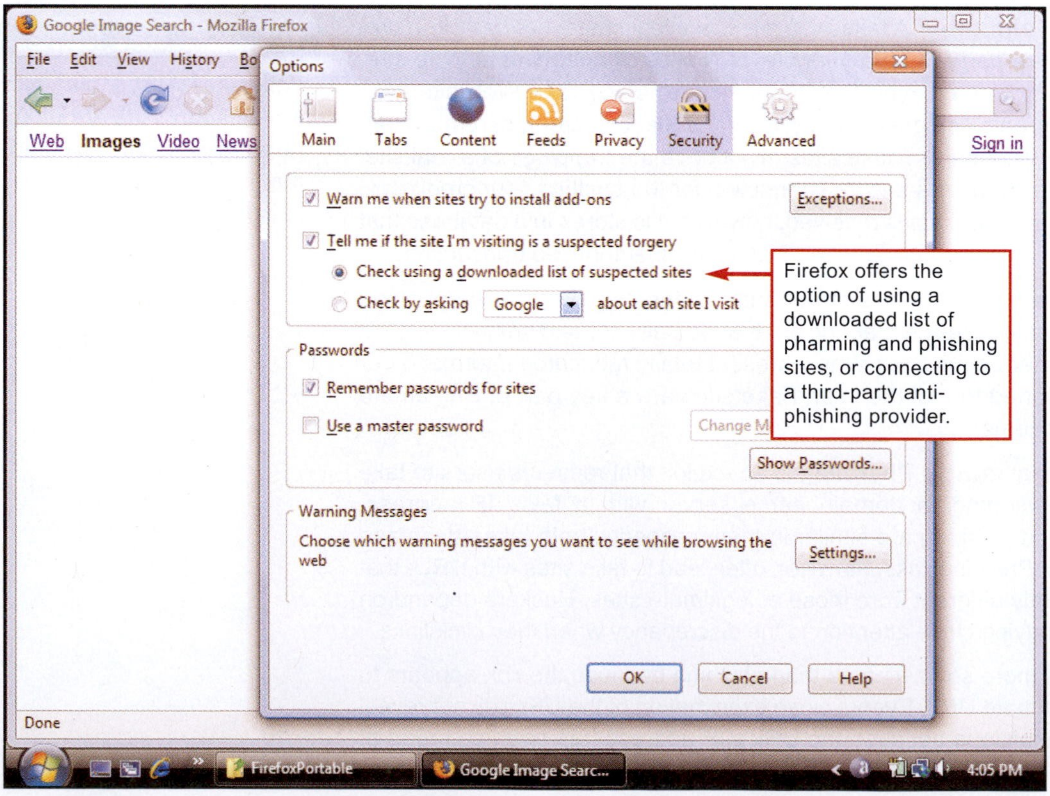

What's the best defense against all the bad stuff on the Web and in e-mail? First, understand that there is no perfect defense. Then understand that you should do all you can to safeguard your computer and your privacy. Use the list in Figure 7-52 as a starting point.

1. Use antispyware utilities to clean up any spyware that might be on your computer.

2. Run antispyware continuously just as you do antivirus software.

3. Set your browser to reject third-party cookies.

4. Register to reject Flash cookies.

5. Make sure your browser's antispoofing tools are activated; or install a third-party antispoofing tool to help you identify fake Web sites.

6. Set up a disposable e-mail address and use it as necessary.

7. Do not click links in untrusted e-mail or pop-up ads, and never respond to e-mail offers, especially those that seem too good to be true.

FIGURE 7-52

Guidelines for Secure and Private Web Surfing

QuickCheck

1. An anonymous [   ] service can prevent Web sites from tracking your activities on the Web.

2. Marketers are turning to [   ] cookies as a backup mechanism for conventional cookies.

3. A Web [   ] or clear GIF is typically a 1x1 pixel graphic embedded in a Web page or e-mail message.

4. [   ] is an exploit that redirects users to fake sites by "poisoning" a domain name server with false information.

5. A type of utility software that captures unsolicited e-mail before it reaches your Inbox is called a spam [   ].

6. For a pharming attack to take effect, you need to respond to an e-mail or click an embedded Web site link. True or false? [   ]

 CHECK ANSWERS

ISSUE

Who's Reading Your E-mail?

WHEN YOU DROP an envelope into the corner mailbox, you probably expect it to arrive at its destination unopened, with its contents kept safe from prying eyes. When you make a phone call, you might assume that your conversation will proceed unmonitored by wiretaps or other listening devices. Can you also expect an e-mail message to be read only by the person to whom it is addressed?

In the United States, the Electronic Communications Privacy Act of 2000 prohibits the use of intercepted e-mail as evidence unless a judge approves a search warrant. That doesn't mean the government isn't reading your mail. Heightened security concerns after the September 11, 2001 terrorist attacks resulted in the rapid passage of the Patriot Act, which became law on October 26, 2001. In an effort to assist law enforcement officials, among its other provisions the Patriot Act relaxes the rules for obtaining and implementing search warrants and lowers the Fourth Amendment standard for obtaining a court order to compel an ISP to produce e-mail logs and addresses.

To eavesdrop on e-mail from suspected terrorists and other criminals, the FBI uses commercially available sniffing software, which scans through messages entering and leaving an ISP's e-mail system to find e-mail associated with a person who is under investigation. Privacy advocates are concerned because the sniffing software scans all messages that pass through an ISP, not just those messages sent to or received by a particular individual.

Although law enforcement agencies are required to obtain a court order before intercepting e-mail, no

such restriction exists for employers who want to monitor employee e-mail. According to the American Management Association, 33% of U.S. businesses monitor employee e-mail. But this intentional eavesdropping is only one way in which the contents of your e-mail messages might become public. The recipient of your e-mail can forward it to one or more people—people you never intended for it to reach. Your e-mail messages could pop up on a technician's screen in the course of system maintenance, updates, or repairs.

Some Web-based e-mail providers—particularly those that make you look at ads in exchange for free accounts—collect information on how often you log in and might monitor your keystrokes to find out which ads and links you click. E-mail providers claim such information is used internally to deliver the best possible service, prevent fraud, and select the ads for products that you're most likely to buy. Also, keep in mind that e-mail messages—including those you delete from your own computer—can be stored on backups of your ISP's e-mail server.

You might wonder if such open access to your e-mail is legal. The answer in most cases is yes. Although the United States Omnibus Crime Control and Safe Streets Act of 1968 and the Electronic Communications Privacy Act of 1986 prohibit public and private employers from engaging in surreptitious surveillance of employee activity through the use of electronic devices, two exceptions to these privacy statutes exist. The first exception permits an employer to monitor e-mail if one party to the communication consents to the monitoring. An employer must inform employees of this policy before undertaking any monitoring. The second exception permits employers to monitor employees' e-mail if a legitimate business need exists, and the monitoring takes place within the business-owned e-mail system.

Employees generally have not been successful in defending their rights to e-mail privacy because courts have ruled that an employee's right to privacy does not outweigh a company's rights and interests. Courts seem to agree that because a company owns and maintains its e-mail system, it has the right to monitor the messages carried by the system.

Like employees of a business, students who use a school's e-mail system cannot be assured of e-mail privacy. When a CalTech student was accused of sexually harassing a female student by sending lewd e-mail to her and her boyfriend, investigators retrieved all the student's e-mail from the archives of the e-mail server. The student was expelled from the university even though he claimed that the e-mail had been spoofed to make it look as though he had sent it, when it had actually been sent by someone else.

Why would an employer want to know the contents of employee e-mail? Why would a school be concerned with the correspondence of its students? It is probably true that some organizations simply snoop on the off chance that important information might be discovered. Other organizations have more legitimate reasons for monitoring e-mail. An organization that owns an e-mail system can be held responsible for the consequences of actions related to the contents of e-mail messages on that system. For example, a school has a responsibility to protect students from harassment. If it fails to do so, it can be sued along with the author of the offending e-mail message. Organizations also recognize a need to protect themselves from false rumors and industrial espionage. For example, a business wants to know if an employee is supplying its competitor with information on product research and development.

Many schools and businesses have established e-mail privacy policies, which explain the conditions under which you can and cannot expect your e-mail to remain private. These policies are sometimes displayed when the computer boots or a new user logs in. Court decisions, however, seem to support the notion that because an organization owns and operates an e-mail system, the e-mail messages on that system are also the property of the organization. The individual who authors an e-mail message does not own all rights related to it. The company, school, or organization that supplies your e-mail account can, therefore, legally monitor your messages.

You should use your e-mail account with the expectation that some of your mail will be read from time to time. Think of your e-mail as a postcard, rather than a letter, and save your controversial comments for face-to-face conversations.

INFOWEBLINKS

You'll find lots more information about e-mail privacy (and lack of it) at the **E-mail Privacy InfoWeb**.

 CLICK TO CONNECT
www.course.com/np/concepts11/ch07

7

What Do You Think?

1. Do you think most people believe that their e-mail is private? ○ Yes ○ No ○ Not sure

2. Do you agree with CalTech's decision to expel the student who was accused of sending harassing e-mail to another student? ○ Yes ○ No ○ Not sure

3. Should the laws be changed to make it illegal for employers to monitor e-mail without court approval? ○ Yes ○ No ○ Not sure

4. Would you have different privacy expectations regarding an e-mail account at your place of work as opposed to an account you purchase from an e-mail service provider? ○ Yes ○ No ○ Not sure

▶ SAVE RESPONSES

COMPUTERS IN CONTEXT

Fashion Industry

FASHION IS BIG BUSINESS. Worldwide, clothing sales generate more than $200 billion in revenue. Shoes, accessories, and jewelry bump the industry's revenue even higher. Competition is tough as designers, manufacturers, and retailers compete for customer dollars. In the fashion industry, trends change quickly. As the saying goes, "Today's style is tomorrow's markdown." Fashion industry players look for every competitive advantage. It is no surprise that technology plays a major role in this glitzy industry.

Fashion begins with designers, such as Miuccia Prada, John Galliano, and Ralph Lauren. Their runway extravaganzas set off fashion trends that eventually work their way to retail stores. Fashion runways went high-tech in 1999 when lingerie manufacturer Victoria's Secret produced a Webcast watched by over 1 million viewers. Bravo television's Project Runway show has been one of the top iPod downloads. Fashion podcasts and blogs abound on the Web, as do fashion sites packed with news about the latest trends.

Although runway fashions are typically conceived with a sketch and stitched by hand, designs are adapted for the ready-to-wear market by using computer-assisted design (CAD) tools, such as pattern-making software. Garments are constructed by sewing together sections of fabric that form arms, fronts, backs, collars, and so forth. The set of templates used to cut fabric sections is called a pattern. Pattern-making is a tricky 3D challenge because flat pieces of fabric eventually become garments shaped to conform to curved body contours. Pattern making software helps designers visualize how flat pieces fit together and drape when sewn. Once a master pattern is complete, pattern-making software automatically generates a set of patterns for each garment size.

Fashion requires fabric, and computers play a major role in fabric design and manufacturing. Computer software, such as ArahWeave, lets fabric designers experiment with colors, yarns, and weaves while viewing detailed, realistic on-screen samples. Fabric

designs can be stored in a variety of formats for weaving machines. A few older mechanical weaving machines are controlled by punched cards. Digital fabric designs can be transferred to punched cards with a dedicated card punch machine. Most of today's weaving mills use computerized machinery that directly accepts digital input to control threads and patterns. Networks tie looms to CAD stations and to the Internet. Fabric designs can be stored in XML format, transmitted to a fabric manufacturer over the Internet, and used directly by computerized weaving machines.

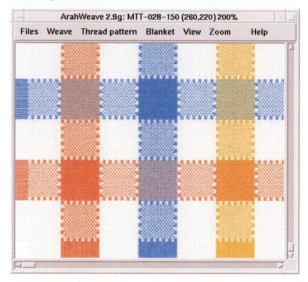

Clothing production, warehousing, and shipping are also highly automated. Benetton's high-tech facility at Castrette, Italy can produce over 110 million garments per year. Its automated distribution center uses a workforce of only 24 people to handle 40,000 boxes of merchandise daily. Radio frequency identification (RFID) tags—sometimes called smart labels—can be attached to individual garments or to packing boxes as an important tool for controlling inventory.

RFID technology uses an inexpensive, tiny computer chip with built-in antenna and the capacity to store between 64 and 128 bits of data about a garment— its SKU number, size, model, dye lot, manufacturing date, and so on. Tags can be attached to a garment or its label. An RFID reader that can retrieve data from tags is used to track merchandise from the manufacturing plant through the distribution chain to the retailer. RFID tags are becoming popular for all types of merchandise. Businesses that use them can save time and money. For example, RFID tags can reduce the time it takes to do a physical inventory by a factor of 10. Privacy advocates, however, are worried because these tags remain active even after you bring your merchandise home. Could a thief circle your house with an RFID scanner to find out what's inside? Could a stalker follow your movements by tracking the RFID tag embedded in your sweater? Next time you buy a garment, check to see if an RFID tag is attached. It would typically be sewn into a seam and may carry a warning "Remove before wearing."

In response to competition from offshore companies, U.S. clothing manufacturers pioneered Quick Response (QR)—a business model for compressing supply chains to quickly obtain raw materials, such as fabric, yarn, buttons, and zippers. Sophisticated software tools, such as the Sourcing Simulator, simplify QR planning.

Online shopping has become routine, but one drawback of catalog and online ordering is the cost associated with restocking returned merchandise. Can an online customer find out how a garment will fit and look before ordering it? In 1998, Lands' End introduced My Virtual Model technology that allows shoppers to create a custom model of themselves by choosing from a variety of hair colors and styles, face shapes, and body types. The model can "try on" clothes to show online customers how they would look when wearing the garments.

More recently, Lands' End toured the country with a body-scanning device to collect actual measurements from thousands of customers. Body-scanning devices use cameras and lasers to capture approximately 300,000 data points that can be pieced together into a 3D image.

Body scanners are also helping the fashion industry by collecting research data. Sizing standards fell by the wayside when vanity sizing added an inch or two to a garment so that consumers can feel good about themselves by fitting into smaller sizes. In the U.S. clothing industry, a comprehensive study of body shapes and sizes can help standardize sizing and eliminate much of the trial and error involved in finding apparel that fits. Collecting data from body scans is part of this ongoing research effort.

No discussion of fashion and computers would be complete without highlighting wearable technology. Clothing that contains digital devices has made its way out of the laboratory and onto store shelves. For example, Burton Snowboards, electronic fabric manufacturer SOFTswitch, and Apple teamed up to create the limited-edition Burton Amp, a jacket with integrated iPod controls designed for snowboarders to control music from the sleeves of their jackets without fumbling with zippers, gloves, and small control buttons.

Another wearable, originally popular with secret service agents, is the SCOTTeVEST, a jacket with pockets for cell phone, PDA, MP3 player, and built-in wiring to connect these devices into a personal area network (PAN). Available as a jacket or vest and in men's and women's sizes, the jacket can now be purchased by civilians.

With a growing emphasis on the use of technology in fashion design and manufacturing, fashion degree programs at colleges and technical schools have added courses such as computer-aided fashion design, computer-based pattern drafting, pattern grading and computer-aided drafting, and wearable computers.

INFOWEBLINKS

You'll find information related to this Computers in Context topic at the **Computers and Fashion InfoWeb**.

W **CLICK TO CONNECT**
www.course.com/np/concepts11/ch07

7

New Perspectives Labs

On the BookOnCD

To access the New Perspectives labs for Chapter 7, start the BookOnCD, BookOnFlashDrive, or other NP11 BookOn product and then click the icon next to the lab title below.

▶ BROWSER SECURITY SETTINGS

IN THIS LAB YOU'LL LEARN:

- How to adjust the security settings for Internet Explorer
- The significance of Internet, Local Intranet, Trusted, and Restricted security zones
- How to add sites to a security zone and adjust security zone settings
- Why ActiveX controls pose a potential security threat and how to adjust ActiveX control security settings
- Why downloads pose a potential security threat to your computer and how to activate the recommended download security settings
- Why Java applets pose a potential security threat to your computer
- The significance of Java permission levels
- How to activate the recommended Java security settings

LAB ASSIGNMENTS

1. Perform each lab step as directed, and answer all the lab QuickCheck questions.

2. Check the Internet zone security setting on the computer you typically use. Indicate whether the setting is High, Medium-high, Medium, Medium-low, Low, or Custom. Describe how this setting handles ActiveX controls, downloads, and Java applets.

3. On the computer you typically use, find out whether any Web sites are listed in the Trusted or Restricted zones. Would you make changes to the list of sites for these zones? Explain why or why not.

▶ WORKING WITH COOKIES

IN THIS LAB YOU'LL LEARN:

- How Web servers use cookies
- Why cookies might pose a threat to your privacy
- How to locate cookies stored on your computer
- How to view the contents of a cookie
- How to delete a single cookie created by Internet Explorer
- How to delete all the cookies stored on your computer
- How to limit the space allocated to cookies created by Internet Explorer
- How to block cookies
- What a session cookie is
- How to set cookie prompts and use the cookie prompt dialog box
- How to take advantage of P3P and Compact Privacy Policies
- The differences between first-party and third-party cookies

LAB ASSIGNMENTS

1. Perform each lab step as directed, and answer all the lab QuickCheck questions.

2. Use Windows Explorer to look at the cookies stored on your computer. Indicate how many cookies are currently stored. Examine the contents of one cookie, and indicate whether you think it poses a threat to your privacy.

3. Indicate the name and version of the browser you typically use. To find this information, open your browser, and then select the About option from the Help menu. Next, look at the cookie settings your browser provides. Describe how you would adjust these settings to produce a level of privacy protection that is right for your needs.

4. Adjust your browser settings so that you are prompted whenever a Web server attempts to send a cookie to your computer. Go to several of your favorite Web sites and watch for third-party cookies. When you receive a message from a third-party Web site, record the name of the third-party site and the contents of the cookie it is attempting to send. Finally, indicate whether you would accept such a cookie.

Key Terms

Make sure you understand all the boldfaced key terms presented in this chapter. If you're using the NP11 BookOnCD, BookOnFlashDrive, or other NP11 BookOn product, you can use this list of terms as an interactive study activity. First, try to define a term in your own words, and then click the term to compare your definition with the definition presented in the chapter.

ActiveX control, 372
Ad-blocking software, 385
Ad-serving cookie, 400
Ajax, 362
Anonymous proxy service, 403
Antispyware, 402
Atom, 360
B2B, 384
B2C, 384
B2G, 384
Banner ad, 385
Boolean operator, 379
C2C, 384
Click-through rate, 385
Client-side script, 372
Cookie, 368
DHTML, 362
Digital certificate, 373
E-commerce, 384
E-mail account, 392
E-mail attachment, 393
E-mail authentication, 403
E-mail client software, 398
E-mail message, 392
E-mail servers, 397
E-mail system, 397
Electronic wallet, 390
Flash cookie, 402
Helper application, 367
Hover ad, 385
HTML, 362
HTML conversion utility, 369

HTML document, 362
HTML forms, 371
HTML script, 371
HTML tags, 362
HTTP, 364
HTTP status code, 365
Hypertext, 360
Hypertext link, 361
IMAP, 397
Java applet, 372
Keyword stuffing, 378
Link popularity, 377
Markup language, 362
Message header, 392
Meta keyword, 378
Metasearch engine, 380
MIME, 393
Netiquette, 396
Online auction, 388
Online shopping cart, 386
Person-to-person payment, 390
Pharming, 405
Phishing, 405
Plug-in, 367
Podcast, 360
POP, 397
POP server, 398
Pop-up ad, 385
Query processor, 377
RSS, 360
Search engine indexer, 376
Search terms, 378

Secure connection, 389
Server-side script, 371
S-HTTP, 389
Smileys, 396
SMTP server, 398
Socket, 364
Spam, 403
Spam filter, 404
SSL, 389
Stateless protocol, 365
Store-and-forward, 397
TLS, 389
URL, 361
Videocasting, 361
Web, 360
Web 2.0, 361
Web browser, 361
Web bug, 402
Web cache, 367
Web crawler, 375
Web page, 361
Web search engine, 374
Web server, 361
Web site, 360
Web-based e-mail, 397
Wiki, 361
XHTML, 362

7

Interactive Summary

To review important concepts from this chapter, fill in the blanks to best complete each sentence. When using the NP11 BookOnCD or other BookOn product, click the Check Answers buttons to automatically score your answers.

SECTION A: The Web, one of the Internet's hottest attractions, is a collection of document, image, video, and sound files that can be linked and accessed over the Internet via the _____ protocol. The Web is an interlinked collection of information; whereas the _____ is the communications system used to transport Web information from computers that store it to client computers who request it. An Internet-based computer that stores and distributes Web files is called a Web _____. It can host one or more Web _____ such as *www.wikipedia.com* or *www.myspace.com* containing HTML _____ documents, which can be accessed and displayed using client software called a Web _____. Each Web page has a unique address called a _____. _____ markup language is a set of specifications for creating documents that a browser can display as a Web page. To create HTML documents, you can use a variety of Web authoring tools, such as a text _____, HTML conversion utility, online Web authoring tool, or Web authoring software. To enable your Web pages to perform tasks beyond what HTML can do, you can add programs by embedding a _____ in your HTML document, or by coding a Java _____ or _____ control, which you can refer to in your document.

> ▶ CHECK ANSWERS

SECTION B: To sift through massive amounts of information available on the Web and locate pertinent information about a topic, Web surfers utilize programs called search _____. These special programs have four major components. A Web _____, also called a Web spider, is automated to methodically visit Web sites and gather Web pages. A search engine _____ culls keywords from the gathered pages and stores them in a _____. The search engine's query _____ accepts one or more words called search _____, looks them up in the database, and produces a list of relevant Web sites. There are a number of ways to narrow searches and produce more targeted results, such as using _____ operators or putting exact phrases in _____. The order in which Web sites are returned in response to your query is dependent on relevancy criteria, such as keyword matches and _____ popularity.

> ▶ CHECK ANSWERS

SECTION C: Any business transaction that is conducted electronically over a computer network is typically referred to as a(n) _____ transaction. The most common business models are business-to-_____, consumer-to-consumer, business-to-business , and business-to-government. E-commerce merchants cut costs by taking advantage of efficiency and opportunities offered by _____, computerization, and digitization. They also increase their profits by providing space for third-party _____ ads and pop-up ads on their Web pages. Online stores use _____ to track customers' online shopping carts. At an online _____ site, sellers post their merchandise or services and consumers bid for the posted items. Online purchases can be paid for by submitting a credit card number directly to a merchant, using a person-to-_____ payment service, submitting payment data using an electronic wallet, or making use of a one-time-use credit card number.

> ▶ CHECK ANSWERS

SECTION D: E-mail, short for "electronic mail," can refer to a single electronic message or to the entire system of computers and software that transmits, receives, and stores digital e-mail messages. Any person with an e-mail [   ] can send and receive electronic mail. Basic e-mail activities include composing, reading, replying to, sending, forwarding, and deleting messages. More advanced activities include adding attachments and maintaining an address book. Most e-mail messages are created in a plain and simple format called [   ] text. It is also possible to create messages in [   ] format, which includes underlining, fancy fonts, colored text, and embedded graphics. An e-mail system consists of e-mail servers, which are accessible to e-mail account holders. Today, consumers can choose between three types of e-mail. [   ] mail holds your incoming mail on an e-mail server until you download it to your computer using e-mail [   ] software. [   ] mail gives you the option of downloading your mail or storing it on the e-mail server. [   ]-based mail allows you to use a browser as e-mail client software. E-mail has similarities with and differences from other forms of communications, but it is the differences that spawned a collection of online communications guidelines called [   ].

▶ CHECK ANSWERS

SECTION E: When you surf the Web or work with your e-mail, you need to be aware of potential spyware exploits, such as [   ] cookies from third-parties. While browsers and marketing firms are now providing opt-out mechanisms to block third-party cookies, it is not as easy to turn off all kinds of cookies. [   ] cookies, also called local shared objects, are used as an alternative to conventional cookies, and most users are not aware of their existence. Web [   ], or clear GIFs, are practically invisible 1x1-pixel graphics embedded in a Web page or e-mail message, that can be used to set cookies for third-party Web sites. [   ] redirects users to fake sites by tampering with the information in a [   ] name server. While these attacks don't need any action on your part to be effective, [   ] scams require you to respond to an e-mail message or click an embedded link in your e-mail. [   ] is unsolicited e-mail that you can avoid by practicing safe e-mail techniques such as using a spam [   ]. You can also use a [   ] e-mail address to receive confirmation for online purchases without getting added to a spam mailing list. A safe bet for combating most forms of spyware is by using a type of security software called [   ].

▶ CHECK ANSWERS

7

Interactive Situation Questions

Apply what you've learned to some typical computing situations. When using the NP11 BookOnCD, BookOnFlashDrive, or any other NP11 BookOn product, you can type your answers, and then use the Check Answers button to automatically score your responses.

1. Suppose that you are about to check out at an online store, but you don't see any indication that your transaction data will be protected by a secure connection. It would be best, under these circumstances, to use PGP software to encrypt your shipping and billing data. True or false? [_____]

2. Your friend, who is a little computer phobic, is going to be creating his first Web page and asks you to recommend some software for the task. Which one requires the least knowledge of HTML tags: Notepad or Microsoft Word? [_____]

3. Suppose you visit a Web site that has eye-catching pages. You want to know how these pages were formatted, so you use one of the options on your browser's menu to take a look at the HTML [_____] document.

4. Suppose you click a link at a Web site and get a message that the file cannot be displayed because it is in PDF format. To view the file, you need an updated version of your browser. True or false? [_____]

5. Suppose you're performing a local test of a Web page you created. All the page elements appear to be correctly positioned and formatted. You're also happy to discover that your large graphics files are displayed quite quickly by your browser. Can you expect similar performance after you post the page on a Web site? Yes or no? [_____]

6. You'd prefer not to have the search engine you use maintain accumulative records of your searches. You can block [_____] from a specific search engine site, and that setting will force the search engine to assign a different ID number to you for each session.

7. You're getting ready for a week-long trip. You'd rather not take your computer, but you'll have access to public computers. Rather than use Web-based e-mail while you're away from home, you decide to use your familiar POP e-mail [_____] software, by storing it and your e-mail files on a portable USB flash drive.

8. One of your relatives wants to try online shopping, but is suspicious that her credit card number might get stolen from a merchant's server by a hacker using a packet sniffer. Is it correct to tell her that she can best avoid these potential rip-offs by a secure connection, such as SSL? Yes or no? [_____]

9. Your inbox is getting more and more unsolicited messages with "fisd foos" in the header. You decide to generate a new rule for your security software's spam [_____] to block those irritating messages.

10. You're looking through a list of cookies stored on your computer, but don't remember visiting sites such as bannerbank, hotlog, and ad.bb. You can assume that these cookies were created by [_____], such as ad-serving cookies.

 CHECK ANSWERS

Interactive Practice Tests

Practice tests that consist of 10 multiple-choice, true/false, and fill-in-the-blank questions are available on both the NP11 BookOn products and the NP11 Web site. The questions are selected at random from a large test bank, so each time you take a test, you'll receive a different set of questions. Your tests are scored immediately, and you can print study guides that help you find the correct answers for any questions that you missed.

▶ CLICK TO START

Study Tips

Study Tips help you to organize and consolidate the information in a unit by making lists, outlines, charts, and sketches. You can use paper and pencil or word processing software to complete most of the Study Tip activities.

1. Make sure you can use your own words to correctly answer each of the red focus questions that appear throughout the chapter.

2. Draw a multi-panel cartoon that shows how a Web server and browser interact. Include the following terms: Web server, browser, HTTP, HTML, port, socket, HTML document, graphic file, and URL.

3. Make sure you can explain the relationship between an HTML source document and a Web page.

4. In your own words, explain what the term *stateless protocol* means, then describe how it relates to cookies.

5. Briefly sketch the evolution of Web browsers.

6. Describe the advantages and disadvantages of each type of Web page development tool discussed in this chapter.

7. Explain the purpose of HTML scripts and the differences between server-side scripts and client-side scripts.

8. Create a comic-strip like sequence of diagrams that illustrates how the following technologies interact: Web crawler, search engine database, indexer, query processor.

9. Use a search engine and Boolean operators to formulate a search for information about your favorite era in history. Can you make a more targeted search to find out what kind of slang was used during that time period?

10. List the four most commonly used styles of citation and make sure that you can correctly format a citation to a Web page using each style.

11. Explain two ways that shopping carts can work with cookies.

12. Outline what you've learned about online payment technologies.

13. List the advantages and disadvantages of HTML formatted mail.

14. Create a table that compares and contrasts POP mail with Web-based mail.

15. Make a list of security and privacy concerns discussed in this chapter. Describe each one and then describe procedures and technologies available to make your online experience more secure and private.

16. Fill in the blanks on the concept map below to show the hierarchy of Web technology concepts presented in this chapter.

7

Concept Map

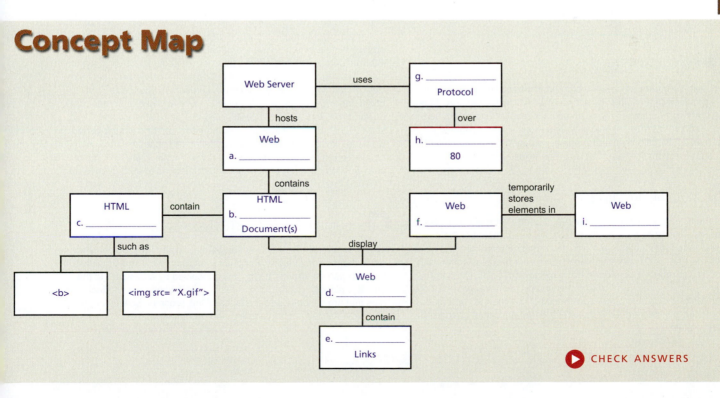

CHECK ANSWERS

Projects

CRITICAL THINKING

In this chapter you read about some of the pitfalls of shopping online. Reflect on what you read within the context of your own online usage habits. What aspects of your online activities could you change to become more secure, more private, or more efficient? What do you have to give up to get these benefits? Is it worth it to you? Incorporate your thoughts in a one-page summary. Follow your instructor's guidelines for submission.

GROUP PROJECT

Brainstorm with a group of three to five students to come up with an idea for an e-business. For this project assign tasks from the list below and create a schedule for completing them. Compile your work into a single document for submission.
Tasks:

• Decide on a name for the business after finding an available URL.

• Design a Web site for the business. Mock up the Web site home page using Web authoring software or simply a graphics program, such as Paint.

• Locate at least five partner sites that might provide synergistic cross-marketing.

• Make a list of 10 keywords that can be used in your Web page header so customers can easily find your site when using a search engine.

• Find a site to host your online business and work up a spreadsheet showing monthly and annual hosting costs.

CYBERCLASSROOM

Work with your team to create a blog on any topic. You can use the tools provided at any blogging site, such as *www.blogger.com*. Make sure that each person on the team posts at least one message to the blog. Send your instructor instructions for logging onto your blog. When all the blogs are up and running, your instructor might post the URLs so everyone in the class can judge whose blog is best.

MULTIMEDIA PROJECT

Surf the Web to select a home page that needs improvement. Use the Print Screen key on your keyboard to take a screenshot of the original page. Paste the page into graphics software such as Paint and store it as Home Page Original [Your Name]. Use your graphics software to create an improved home page by following some of the tips and recommendations offered in the chapter. Save your makeover as Home Page Makeover [Your Name]. Make a list of the changes you made. Submit the original page, the makeover page, and list of changes to your instructor.

RESUME BUILDER

Many companies have a Web site that provides information on their products and services. Use a search engine to locate a company in your career field. Suppose you are a recruiter for that company and you'll be attending a series of college career fairs. Create a one-page information flyer that you can hand out to prospective recruits. The flyer should include:

• The company name, URL, and physical location(s)

• A brief description of the company's mission, products, and services

• Instructions on how to submit a resume electronically

GLOBALIZATION

Examine trends in global e-commerce, and submit your answers to the following questions.

• Which countries are the top players in the e-commerce market?

• How big is your country's share of the e-commerce pie, and is it increasing or decreasing?

• How does e-commerce affect developing countries?

• What are the advantages and disadvantages of a global market?

ISSUE

The Issue section of this chapter focused on how much—or how little—privacy you can expect when using an e-mail account. For this project, write a two- to five-page paper about e-mail privacy based on information you gather from the Internet. To begin this project, consult the E-mail Privacy InfoWeb to get an in-depth overview of the issue. Next, determine the viewpoint you will present in your paper. You might, for example, decide to present the viewpoint of a student who believes that e-mail should be afforded the same privacy rights as a sealed letter. Or you might present the viewpoint of an employer who wants to explain why your company believes it is necessary to monitor employee e-mail. Whatever viewpoint you decide to present, make sure you can back it up with facts and references to authoritative articles and Web pages.

COMPUTERS IN CONTEXT

The Computers in Context section of this chapter focused on computers in the fashion industry. For this report, create a visual timeline that traces a garment from the time it is conceived by a designer to the time it is placed on a designer's rack or store shelf. Indicate technologies that are used at various stages of this process. Make sure that you provide citations for your text and graphical sources.

On the Web

STUDENT EDITION LABS

W CLICK TO ACCESS THE NP11 WEB SITE
or open your browser and connect to www.course.com/np/concepts11/ch07.
Lab results can be stored in the Universal Gradebook.

CREATING WEB PAGES

In the Creating Web Pages Student Edition Lab, you will learn about the following topics:

- Starting a Web page
- Formatting paragraphs and text on a Web page
- Using graphics and backgrounds on a Web page
- Linking to other Web pages
- Using tables on a Web page

E-MAIL

In the E-Mail Student Edition Lab, you will learn about the following topics:

- Composing, replying to, and printing e-mail messages
- E-mail organizational and management techniques such as moving messages to a folder and using an address book
- Signing up for and using Web-based e-mail to demonstrate your e-mail skills using your own e-mail account

E-COMMERCE

In the E-Commerce Student Edition Lab, you will learn about the following topics:

- Paying with electronic cash
- Ensuring security in an e-commerce transaction
- Technical components of an e-commerce Web site
- Developing an e-commerce Web site

WEB DESIGN PRINCIPLES

In the Web Design Principles Student Edition Lab, you will learn about the following topics:

- Designing the site structure
- Designing the site look and feel
- Designing for readability
- Using hypertext and images effectively

7

 CHAPTER COURSECAST

Use your computer or iPod to hear a five-minute audio presentation of chapter highlights.

 FLASHCARD COURSECAST

Interact with audio flashcards to review key terms from the chapter.

DETAILED OBJECTIVES

Make sure that you've achieved all the objectives for a chapter before it's time for your test!

 TEST YOURSELF

Review chapter material by taking these ten-question tests, then send your results to the Universal Gradebook.

 ONLINE GAMES

Have some fun while refreshing your memory about key concepts that might appear on the next test. You can even send your results to the Universal Gradebook!

 AND MORE!

At the NP11 Web site you'll also find Extra Content and InfoWebLinks.

8

Digital Media

LEARNING OBJECTIVES

- Describe the formats used for digital music

- Explain how to download music files and transfer them to portable audio players

- Describe the advantages, disadvantages, and uses for digital media, such as bitmap graphics, vector graphics, 3-D graphics, 3-D animations, desktop video, digital audio, and MIDI music

- List the equipment and software that can be used to work with various types of digital media

- Identify digital media files by their file extensions

- Understand the advantages and disadvantages of using each type of digital media on the Web

- Explain how resolution, image size, color depth, and color palettes can be manipulated to adjust the file size of a bitmap graphic

- Recap key points about image compression

- Describe procedures required to convert bitmap graphics into vector graphics and vector graphics into bitmaps

- Explain how wireframes, rendering, and ray tracing apply to 3-D graphics

- Define the differences between digital video and 3-D animation

- Describe how to shoot, capture, edit, and process digital video

- Explain how window size, frame rate, and compression affect file size for a desktop video

- Summarize the process for creating DVD-Video

- List and define digital rights management technologies used to protect content that is broadcast, downloaded, or delivered on CDs and DVDs

- Provide at least two examples of time shifting, place shifting, and format shifting

PRE-ASSESSMENT QUIZ

Take the pre-assessment quiz to find out how much you know about the topics in this chapter. ▶

MULTIMEDIA and INTERACTIVE ELEMENTS
When using the BookOnCD, BookOnFlashDrive, or other NP11 BookOn product, the ▶ icons are clickable to access multimedia resources.

BEFORE YOU READ ON, **TRY IT**

WHAT KINDS OF GRAPHICS, AUDIO, AND VIDEO FILES ARE ON MY COMPUTER?

You can use your computer to work with many types of media, such as photos, music, and videos. Your computer stores media that you've created and downloaded. It also stores images from Web sites you've recently visited. To discover what sort of media is stored on your computer, do the following steps:

1. Make sure your computer is turned on.

2. Click the Start button. If you're using Windows Vista, type **pictures** into the search box as shown below, and then press the Enter key.

If you are using Windows XP, click Search. The Search Results dialog box appears.

On the left side of the Search Results window, click the button for Pictures, Music, or Video.

Check the box for Pictures and Photos, then click the Search button. Your computer shows you a list of image files. If Windows displays a list of file names, but you'd rather see the images, click the View menu and select Thumbnails.

3. Repeat step 2 to search for **music** and then again to search for **video**.

4. When you're finished looking at your media files, click the ❌ button to close the Search Results dialog box.

Search for all files of a certain type, or search by type and name.

- ☑ **Pictures and Photos**
- ☐ Music
- ☐ Video

All or part of the file name:

You may also want to...

- ☑ Use advanced search options

[Back] [Search]

Digital Sound

COMPUTERS CAN RECORD, store, and play back sounds, such as narrations, sound effects, and music. Swapping music files over the Internet is currently the most popular use of digital audio, but this technology plays a key role in other very interesting applications. How would you like to quit messing with your computer keyboard and enter commands and documents simply by speaking into a microphone? Would you like to add music and sound effects to your Web pages? Maybe you'd like to pull tracks from your audio CDs and remaster them into your own collection of favorite songs. This section of the chapter covers a wide-ranging selection of digital audio concepts and technologies that you're likely to find handy for personal and professional use.

DIGITAL AUDIO BASICS

What is digital audio? **Digital audio** is music, speech, and other sounds represented in binary format for use in digital devices. Sound is produced by the vibration of matter such as a violin string or a drum head. This vibration causes pressure changes in the surrounding air creating waves.

The smooth, continuous curve of a sound wave can be directly recorded on analog devices, such as records. To digitally record sound, samples of the sound wave are collected at periodic intervals and stored as numeric data. Figure 8-1 shows how a computer digitally samples a sound wave.

FIGURE 8-1

Sampling a Sound Wave

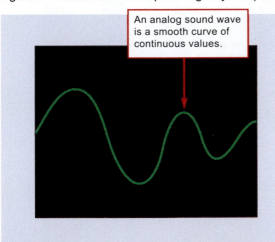

An analog sound wave is a smooth curve of continuous values.

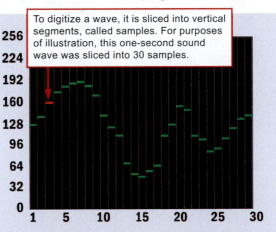

To digitize a wave, it is sliced into vertical segments, called samples. For purposes of illustration, this one-second sound wave was sliced into 30 samples.

Sample	Sample Height (Decimal)	Sample Height (Binary)
1	130	10000010
2	140	1000110
3	160	10100000
4	175	10101111
5	185	10111001

The height of each sample is converted into a binary number and stored. The height of sample 3 is 160 (decimal), so it is stored as its binary equivalent—10100000.

Does sampling rate affect sound quality? **Sampling rate** refers to the number of times per second that a sound is measured during the recording process. It is expressed in hertz (Hz). One thousand samples per second is expressed as 1,000 Hz or 1 KHz (kilohertz). Higher sampling rates increase the quality of the sound recording but require more storage space than lower sampling rates.

The height of each sound sample can be saved as an 8-bit number for radio-quality recordings or a 16-bit number for high-fidelity recordings. The audio CDs you buy at your favorite music store are recorded at a sampling rate of 44.1 KHz, which means a sample of the sound is taken 44,100 times per second. Sixteen bits are used for each sample. To achieve stereo effects, you must take two of these 16-bit samples. Therefore, each sample requires 32 bits of storage space. When you sample stereo CD-quality music at 44.1 KHz, one minute of music requires about 10 MB of storage space. Forty-five minutes of music—the length of a typical album—require about 450 MB.

To conserve space, applications that do not require such high-quality sound use much lower sampling rates. Voice-overs and narrations are often recorded with sampling rates of 11 KHz (11,000 samples per second). This rate results in lower quality sound, but the file is about one-fourth the size of a file for the same sound recorded at 44.1 KHz. Figure 8-2 illustrates how sampling rate affects sound quality.

FIGURE 8-2

A higher sampling rate produces more true-to-life sound quality. Use your BookOnCD to compare the quality of these audio clips, which were digitized at different sampling rates. You'll have to listen carefully to notice the differences.

Low sampling rate: File size = 66 KB

Medium sampling rate: File size = 124 KB

High sampling rate: File size = 235 KB

CLICK TO START

CLICK TO START

CLICK TO START

Regardless of sampling rate, digital audio file size can be reduced using audio compression techniques. **Audio compression** reduces the size of a sound file by removing bits that represent extraneous noise and sounds that are beyond the frequencies of normal hearing. In addition, general-purpose compression techniques explained later in the chapter can be applied to sound files. A compressed audio file requires less storage space than the uncompressed file and can be transmitted faster over a network. Popular portable music players typically work with compressed audio file formats.

How does a computer produce digital audio? Your computer's sound card is responsible for transforming the bits stored in an audio file into music, sound effects, and narrations. A **sound card** is a device that contains a variety of input and output jacks, plus audio-processing circuitry. A desktop computer's sound card is usually plugged into a PCI expansion slot inside the system unit. Alternatively, sound card circuitry might be built into the system board. Notebook computers rarely feature a separate sound card because manufacturers save space by incorporating sound circuitry into the system board.

8

A sound card is typically equipped to accept input from a microphone and send output to speakers or headphones. For processing digital audio files, a sound card contains a special type of circuitry called a **digital signal processor**, which performs three important tasks. It transforms digital bits into analog waves when you play back a digital audio file. It transforms analog waves into digital bits when you make a sound recording. It also handles compression and decompression, if necessary.

To play a digitally recorded sound, the bits from an audio file are transferred from disk to the microprocessor, which routes them to your computer's sound card. The digital signal processor handles any necessary decompression, and then transforms the data into analog wave signals. These signals are routed to the speakers and voilà! You have sound (Figure 8-3).

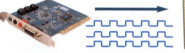 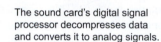 

FIGURE 8-3

Most sound cards use a digital signal processor to convert bits into an analog signal.

The sound card receives data from the microprocessor.

The sound card's digital signal processor decompresses data and converts it to analog signals.

The sound card sends analog signals to speakers.

How can I recognize a digital audio file? You can recognize a digital audio file by looking at its file extension. Digital audio can be stored in a variety of file formats. The table in Figure 8-4 provides an overview of the most popular digital audio formats, including **AAC**, **AIFF**, **MP3**, **RealAudio**, **Wave**, and **WMA**.

FIGURE 8-4

Popular Digital Audio File Formats

Audio Format	File Extension	Advantages	Disadvantages
AAC (Advanced Audio Compression)	.aac, .m4p, or .mp4	Very good sound quality; compressed format, used on iTunes music download site	Files are copy protected and use is limited to approved devices
AIFF (Audio Interchange Format)	.aif	Excellent sound quality; supported in browsers without a plug-in	Audio data is stored in raw, uncompressed format, so files are very large
MP3 (also called MPEG-1 Layer 3)	.mp3	Good sound quality even though the file is compressed; can be streamed over the Web	Requires a standalone player or browser plug-in
RealAudio	.ra, rx	High degree of compression produces small files; data can be streamed over the Web	Sound quality is not up to the standards of other formats; requires a player or plug-in
Wave	.wav	Good sound quality; supported in browsers without a plug-in	Audio data is stored in raw, uncompressed format, so files are very large
WMA (Windows Media Audio)	.wma	Compressed format, very good sound quality; used on several music download sites	Files can be copy protected; requires Windows Media Player 9 or above

What type of software is required to record and play digital audio files? To play an audio file on your computer, you must use audio or media player software. Player software tends to support several audio file formats. In the Windows environment, for example, you can use Windows Media Player to play Wave, WMA, AIF, and MP3 formats. Software that plays and records various audio file formats might be included with your computer's operating system, packaged with your sound card, or available on the Web. Open source offerings, such as QuickAudio and Audacity, are popular.

Audio player software typically also includes features that help you organize and modify your audio files. The ability to create playlists is a useful feature, as are links to an online music store and options for transferring music files to a portable music player.

Can I add digital audio files to my Web pages? Yes. Digital audio files can be embedded into a Web page using an HTML tag, such as <embed src="daisy.wav"> or <bgsound src="imagine.wav">. WAV files are supported by most Web browsers, so it is a popular audio file format. Other audio formats can be delivered over the Web, but might require plug-ins.

Web-based digital audio is often delivered in streaming format to avoid lengthy delays while the entire audio file is downloaded. **Streaming audio** plays as its file is downloaded and provides the technology for real-time Internet radio broadcasts, podcasts, RSS feeds, and voice chat sessions.

PORTABLE AUDIO PLAYERS

How can I listen to my digital music collection when I'm away from my computer? A **portable audio player** like the one in Figure 8-5 is a pocket-sized, battery-powered device that stores digital music. You can transfer a series of digital music tracks, called a playlist, from your computer's hard disk to your portable audio player and you'll have your personal collection of music wherever you go.

Where can I get digital music? Digital music is available from a wide variety of sources. At online music stores, such as iTunes Music Store, Rhapsody, Napster, MSN Music, Walmart Music Downloads, and the Zune Marketplace, individual songs can be downloaded for less than $1 each. The download price of an entire album is typically less than $10.

You can find free digital music, too. Famous performing artists and rock star wannabes post sample tracks from their CDs on Web sites. If fans like the music in these samples, they can purchase and download the entire song or CD. You can also digitize music from your CD collection by using CD ripper software that converts CD-audio music into computer-friendly digital audio format.

What are the most popular file formats for portable audio players? The first generation of online music was distributed in MP3 format. MP3 is a compressed digital audio format that stores digitized music, vocals, and narrations in such a way that the sound quality is very good, but the file size remains relatively small—small enough to download from the Web. A CD track that requires 32 MB of storage space shrinks to approximately 3 MB in MP3 format.

Although MP3 remains a popular audio file format, newer standards offer better sound quality and compression. Apple is promoting the AAC format at its iTunes Music Store. Microsoft is promoting its WMA format at the Zune online music store.

TERMINOLOGY NOTE

Portable audio players are also called MP3 players and digital music players.

FIGURE 8-5

Microsoft's Zune Portable Audio Player

8

Can I play any digital music format on my portable audio player? Some portable audio players support a variety of digital music formats, whereas others support only one or two formats. For example, Apple's iPod supports AAC, MP3, WAV, and AIFF formats, but it does not support the WMA format. When purchasing a portable audio player, you should consider which music formats you are likely to use. The specifications for a portable player include a list of compatible formats.

What are the most popular portable audio players? Consumers demand convenience and prefer not to purchase two devices when a single device meets their needs. Market demand and technological innovation produce convergence, such as when PDAs gain Wi-Fi compatibility or when cell phones feature digital cameras.

As an example of convergence, take a portable audio player, outfit it with a screen, add a high-capacity mini hard disk, include personal organizer software, throw in a few games, and provide connections for an external microphone and memory card reader. What you get is the Apple iPod (Figure 8-6). Not only can you use it to store a huge collection of digital music, you can use the hard disk drive as a portable mass storage device for document, photo, and video files. You can use it as a voice recorder and as a personal organizer for storing contacts and appointments. The iPod's versatility has made it one of the most popular portable audio players. Its popular cousin the iPhone takes convergence one step further by adding mobile phone and Wi-Fi Internet access.

With the popularity of portable audio players, new models appear frequently. Check your favorite music Web sites and blogs for reviews and opinions on the latest offerings.

MIDI MUSIC

What is MIDI music? Digital audio is a digital version of a real analog sound signal. In contrast, **synthesized sound** is an artificially created, or synthetic, sound. Synthesized sound can be classified as MIDI music or synthesized speech.

MIDI (Musical Instrument Digital Interface) specifies a standard way to store music data for synthesizers, electronic MIDI instruments, and computers. Unlike digital audio files, which contain digitized recordings of real sound passages, MIDI files contain instructions for creating the pitch, volume, and duration of notes that sound like various musical instruments.

MIDI is a music notation system that allows computers to communicate with music synthesizers. The computer encodes the music as a **MIDI sequence** and stores it as a file with a .mid, .cmf, or .rol file extension. A MIDI sequence is analogous to a player-piano roll that contains punched information indicating which musical notes to play. A MIDI sequence contains instructions specifying the pitch of a note, the point at which the note begins, the instrument that plays the note, the volume of the note, and the point at which the note ends.

Most computer sound cards are equipped to generate music from MIDI files, and many can capture music data from a MIDI instrument as well. A MIDI-capable sound card contains a **wavetable** (sometimes called a patch set), which is a set of prerecorded musical instrument sounds. The sound card accesses these sounds and plays them as instructed by the MIDI file. For example, if a sound card receives a MIDI instruction for a trumpet to play middle C, it accesses the trumpet's middle C patch and routes it to the speaker until it receives a MIDI instruction to stop the note.

FIGURE 8-6

Apple's iPod portable audio player is also a handy mass storage device.

What are the advantages and disadvantages of MIDI? MIDI files are much more compact than digital audio files. Depending on the exact piece of music, three minutes of MIDI music might require only 10 KB of storage space, whereas the same piece of music stored in a high-quality, uncompressed digital audio file might require 30 MB of storage space.

One of the big disadvantages of MIDI is that it does not produce high-quality vocals. Another disadvantage is that it does not have the full resonance of real sound. Most musicians can easily identify MIDI recordings because they simply lack the tonal qualities of symphony-quality sound. You can compare the differences by using the Click to Start buttons in Figure 8-7.

FIGURE 8-7

MIDI music tends not to have the full resonance of digital audio. Use your BookOnCD to listen to these two sound clips and see if you can hear a difference.

▶ CLICK TO START

▶ CLICK TO START

When would I use MIDI music? MIDI is a good choice for adding background music to multimedia projects and Web pages. Using a procedure similar to that for digital audio files, you can add a link to a MIDI file by inserting a tag such as `<embed src="sousa.mid">` within an HTML document. Most browsers include built-in support for MIDI music.

You can use music composition software, such as Finale, to create your own snappy tunes or get permission to use MIDI files you find on the Web. For composing your own MIDI music, you can input notes from a MIDI instrument directly to your computer. The input is typically handled by music composition software (Figure 8-8), which you can also use to edit notes and combine the parts for several instruments.

FIGURE 8-8

Music composition software provides tools for entering notes, specifying instruments, printing sheet music, and saving compositions in formats such as MIDI.

▶ CLICK TO START

8

SPEECH RECOGNITION AND SYNTHESIS

What's the difference between speech synthesis and speech recognition? **Speech synthesis** is the process by which machines, such as computers, produce sound that resembles spoken words. **Speech recognition** (or voice recognition) refers to the ability of a machine to understand spoken words.

If you've dialed Directory Assistance lately to obtain a telephone number, you've probably encountered speech recognition and speech synthesis. An automated operator asks you to speak the name of the person whose telephone number you seek. The name you speak is collected by a speech recognition unit, which attempts to spell out the name and then look for it in a database. If it locates the name and telephone number, a synthesized voice speaks the telephone number.

The use of digital spectrographic analysis to identify human speakers is an emerging part of law enforcement and homeland security. Not only can digitized samples of voices be analyzed to confirm identity, but real-time voice print identification can be used to match speakers with known recordings of their voices.

How does speech synthesis work? A basic sound unit, such as "reh" or "gay" is called a **phoneme**. Most speech synthesizers string together phonemes to form words. For example, the phonemes "reh" and "gay" produce the word "reggae." A basic speech synthesizer consists of **text-to-speech software**, which generates sounds that are played through your computer's standard sound card. As an alternative, some speech synthesizers are special-purpose hardware devices.

Speech synthesis is a key technology in mobile communication, such as accessing your e-mail using a cell phone—a speech synthesizer reads your e-mail messages to you. A speech synthesizer can also read a computer screen aloud, which unlocks access to computers and the Internet for individuals with visual disabilities.

How does speech recognition work? On a personal computer, a speech recognition system typically collects words spoken into a microphone that's attached to the sound card. The sound card's digital signal processor transforms the analog sound of your voice into digital data. This data is then processed by speech recognition software.

Speech recognition software analyzes the sounds of your voice and converts them to phonemes. Next, the software analyzes the content of your speech. It compares the groups of phonemes to the words in a digital dictionary that lists phoneme combinations along with their corresponding English (or French, Spanish, and so on) words. When a match is found, the software displays the correctly spelled word on the screen.

Speech recognition software can be integrated with word processing software so that you can enter text simply by speaking into a microphone. Going beyond word processing, speech recognition can be used to activate Windows controls instead of using a mouse. Most speech recognition software also works with your browser, allowing you to voice surf the Web.

Microsoft Office includes speech recognition software you can activate by using the Speech icon in the Windows Control Panel. The first step in using Microsoft speech recognition is training the computer to recognize your speaking style. Training consists of reading a series of short text passages into a microphone attached to your computer. Figure 8-9 lists tips for successful voice recognition training.

FIGURE 8-9

Tips for Voice Recognition Training

- Speak at a consistent volume.

- Speak at a steady pace, without speeding up and slowing down.

- Speak naturally, without exaggerated pauses between words or syllables.

- Work in a quiet environment so that the computer hears your voice instead of the sounds around you.

- Use a good quality microphone and keep it in the same position.

You can train your Windows computer by using the Voice Training Wizard, which displays paragraphs of text, waits for you to read them, and creates your personal speech profile (Figure 8-10).

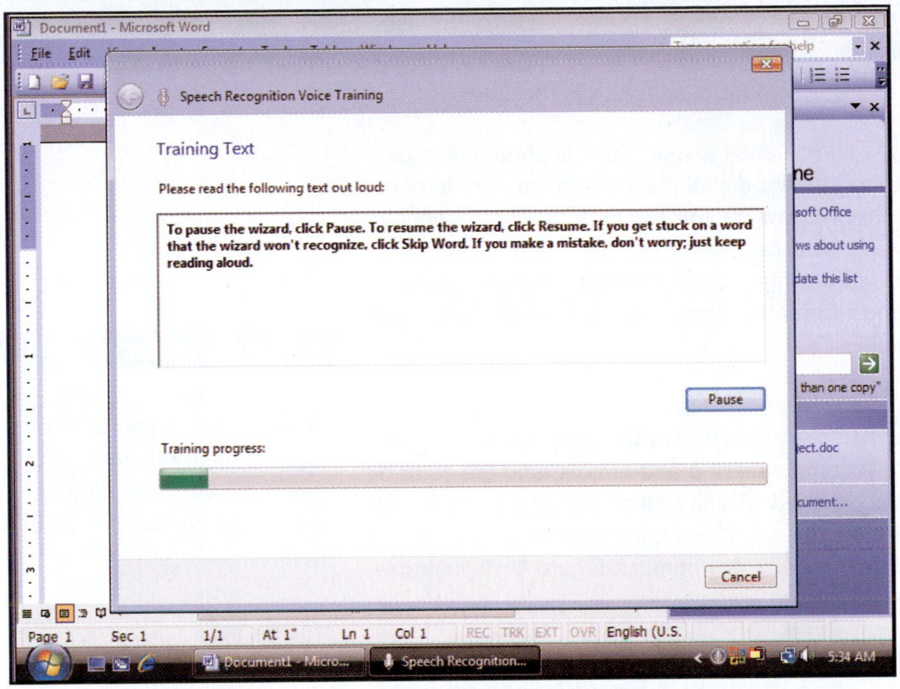

FIGURE 8-10

The Windows Voice Training Wizard displays short text passages. As you read each passage, the computer listens to the way you pronounce each word and stores it in your speech profile.

When training is complete, you can use Microsoft speech recognition to verbally issue commands in Windows and dictate text in Microsoft Word and Excel, plus any other Windows applications designed to support this feature.

QuickCheck

1. [_____] audio can deal with vocals, music, and narrations, whereas [_____] music is primarily designed for instrumental sounds. (Hint: Use the acronym.)

2. The number of times per second that the height of a sound wave is measured is referred to as the [_____] rate.

3. The .m4p music files on the iTunes site are stored in [_____] format. (Hint: Use the acronym.)

4. You can transfer digital music tracks, called a [_____], from your computer's hard disk to your portable audio player, and you'll have a great collection of music wherever you go.

5. Speech [_____] software translates spoken words into text that appears on a computer screen or is stored in a file.

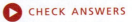 CHECK ANSWERS

Bitmap Graphics

A DIGITAL CAMERA seems easy to use. Point it, shoot the photo, and....what next? How do you transfer digital photos from camera to computer? How can you print them? How do you get them ready to become e-mail attachments? How do you prepare them for inclusion on Web pages? To understand the wide range of possibilities for digital photos, you'll need some background information about bitmap graphics—the topic for this section of the chapter.

BITMAP BASICS

What is a bitmap graphic? A **bitmap graphic**, also called a raster graphic or simply a bitmap, is composed of a grid of dots, and the color of each dot is stored as a binary number. Think of a grid superimposed on a picture. The grid divides the picture into cells, called pixels. Each pixel is assigned a color, which is stored as a binary number. Figure 8-11 illustrates these basic characteristics of a bitmap graphic.

> **TERMINOLOGY NOTE**
>
> The term *pixel* is derived from *picture element*. It is the smallest element that can be manipulated by a computer display device or printer.

FIGURE 8-11

A bitmap graphic is divided into a grid of individually colored pixels. The color number for each pixel is stored in binary format.

▶ CLICK TO START

Where would I encounter bitmap graphics? Bitmap graphics are typically used to create realistic images, such as photographs. You might also encounter bitmaps in the form of cartoons, images that appear in computer games, and rendered images produced by 3-D graphics software. When you use a digital camera or camera-enabled cell phone, your photos are stored as bitmaps. A scanner produces bitmaps. The photos you send or receive as e-mail attachments are bitmaps, as are most Web page graphics. Bitmap graphics formats include RAW, PNG, GIF, PCX, BMP, JPEG, and TIFF. Details about using these formats are presented later in this section.

How do I create bitmap images? You can create a bitmap graphic from scratch using the tools provided by graphics software—specifically a category of graphics software referred to as **paint software**. You might be familiar with paint software such as Adobe Photoshop, Corel Painter, and Microsoft Paint (included with Windows). These programs have tools for freehand sketching, filling in shapes, adding realistic shading, and creating effects that look like oil paints, charcoal, or watercolors. If your freehand sketching talent maxes out with stick figures, you can also create bitmap graphics by using a scanner or digital camera.

SCANNERS AND CAMERAS

How do I convert a printed image into a bitmap? When you have a printed image, such as a photograph, a page from a magazine, or a picture from a book, you can use a **scanner** to convert the printed image into a bitmap graphic. A scanner essentially divides an image into a fine grid of cells and assigns a digital value for the color of each cell. As the scan progresses, these values are transferred to your computer's hard disk and stored as a bitmap graphics file. Scanners, such as the one pictured in Figure 8-12, are inexpensive and easy to use.

When should I use a digital camera rather than a scanner? Whereas a scanner is designed to digitize printed images, a **digital camera** digitizes real objects. Instead of taking a photo with a conventional camera, developing the film, and then digitizing it with a scanner, a digital camera, such as the one in Figure 8-13, takes a photo in digital format, which you can then transfer directly to your computer or print directly to a photo printer.

Shutter release button

Viewfinder

Lens

FIGURE 8-12

To scan an image, turn on the scanner and start your scanner software. Place the image face down on the scanner glass, and then use the scanner software to initiate the scan. The scanned image is saved in RAM and can then be saved on your computer's hard disk.

▶ CLICK TO START

FIGURE 8-13

The controls for a digital camera are very similar to those for an analog, or film, camera. To take a photo, you simply point and shoot.

▶ CLICK TO START

8

How does a digital camera store images? Some digital cameras store photos on CDs, mini CDs, or microdrives, but the most popular digital camera storage is solid state memory cards. Like RAM, memory cards can be erased and reused. Unlike RAM, however, solid state storage holds data without consuming power, so it doesn't lose data when the camera is turned off. Figure 8-14 illustrates several digital camera storage options.

FIGURE 8-14

Storage options for digital cameras vary in capacity from 8 MB to 12 GB. The number of photos that can be stored depends on their resolution. High-resolution photos require more storage space than low-resolution photos. As few as five high-res photos might fit on a 64 MB card, whereas the same card might hold hundreds of low-res images.

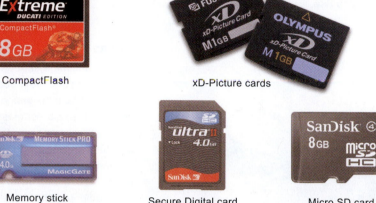

CompactFlash

xD-Picture cards

Memory stick

Secure Digital card

Micro SD card

Microdrive

How can I get images out of the camera? Digital cameras allow you to preview images while they are still in the camera and delete those you don't want. The photos you want to keep can be transferred directly to a properly equipped printer or transferred to your computer's hard disk. Depending on your camera, this transfer can be achieved in several ways:

● **Card readers.** A card reader is a small device designed to read data contained in a solid state memory card. Card readers can be connected to your computer's USB port, built into a computer system unit, or built into a photo-printer. To transfer photo data from a memory card, you remove it from the camera and insert it into the card reader, as shown in Figure 8-15.

● **Direct cable transfer.** If your computer and your camera have FireWire ports (also called IEEE-1394 ports), you can connect a cable between these two ports to transfer the photo data. You can use a similar transfer method if your computer and camera have USB ports or serial ports. A USB-2 or FireWire port provides good transfer speed. USB-1 ports are somewhat slower, and serial ports are quite slow.

● **Infrared port.** Some cameras can beam the data from your camera to your computer's infrared port. This method eliminates the need for a cable but is much slower than using a FireWire, USB, or serial port.

● **Media transfer.** If your camera stores data on CDs or similar optical media, you can simply remove the media from your camera and insert it into the appropriate drive of your computer.

● **Docking station.** Some camera manufacturers offer a camera docking station that connects to a computer by cable. A camera can be placed in the docking station to transfer photos to the computer's hard disk.

● **E-mail.** Cell phone photos can be transferred to a computer by e-mailing the photo to your e-mail account. The photo arrives as an attachment, which can be saved as a separate file.

FIGURE 8-15

A card reader transfers photo data from a memory card to your computer's hard disk.

Regardless of the technology you use, transferring photo data from your camera to your computer requires software, which might be supplied along with your camera, with your card reader, or by a standalone graphics software package, such as Adobe Photoshop. This software allows you to select a file format, specify a file name, and determine the location for each image file. You'll learn about your choices for file formats later in this section, but most cameras store photos in JPEG or TIFF formats.

After you store your digital photos on your computer's hard disk, you can modify them, send them as e-mail attachments, print them, post them on Web pages, or archive them onto a CD.

What characteristics of a bitmap can I modify? Because bitmap graphics are coded as a series of bits that represent pixels, you can use graphics software to modify or edit this type of graphic by changing individual pixels. You can retouch old photographs to eliminate creases, spots, and discoloration (Figure 8-16). You can modify photos to wipe out red eye or erase the "rabbit ears" that ruined an otherwise good family portrait. You can even design eye-catching new pictures with images you cut and paste from several photos or scanned images.

Whether you acquire an image from a digital camera or a scanner, bitmap graphics tend to require quite a bit of storage space. Although a large graphics file might provide the necessary data for a high-quality printout, these files take up space on your hard disk and can require lengthy transmission times that clog up mailboxes and make Web pages seem sluggish. The size of the file that holds a bitmap depends on its resolution and color depth. Read on to see how these factors affect file size and how you can alter them to create smaller graphics files, suitable for e-mail attachments and Web pages.

IMAGE RESOLUTION

How does resolution pertain to bitmap graphics? The dimensions of the grid that forms a bitmap graphic are referred to as its resolution. The resolution of a graphic is usually expressed as the number of horizontal and vertical pixels it contains. For example, a small graphic for a Web page might have a resolution of 150 x 100 pixels—150 pixels across and 100 pixels high.

How does resolution relate to image quality? High-resolution graphics contain more data than low-resolution graphics. With more data, it is possible to display and print high-quality images that are sharper and clearer than images produced using less data. For example, a photograph of a cat taken with an inexpensive digital camera might produce a graphic with a resolution of 1600 x 1200, but a more expensive camera with 3888 x 2592 resolution contains more pixels and produces a higher-quality image.

Camera manufacturers sometimes express the resolution of digital cameras as megapixels. A **megapixel** is 1 million pixels. A camera with resolution of 1600 x 1200 has the capability of producing photos containing 1.9 megapixels (1600 multiplied by 1200). A camera with 3888 x 2592 resolution is technically 10.1 megapixels, but might be rounded off and called a 10 megapixel camera by its manufacturer.

How does resolution relate to the file size of a graphic? Each pixel in a bitmap graphic is stored as one or more bits. The more pixels in a bitmap, the more bits needed to store the file.

FIGURE 8-16

Bitmap graphics can be easily modified. Many graphics software products include wizards that help you retouch photographs.

Before

After

8

How does resolution relate to the physical size of an image?

A bitmap graphic is simply a collection of data. Unlike a printed photograph, a bitmap has no fixed physical size. The size at which a bitmap is displayed or printed depends on the density as well as the resolution (dimensions) of the image grid.

Imagine that each bitmap image and its grid come on a surface that you can stretch or shrink. As you stretch the surface, the grid maintains the same number of horizontal and vertical cells, but each cell becomes larger and the grid becomes less dense. As you shrink the surface, the grid becomes smaller and more dense. The graphic retains the same resolution no matter how much you stretch or shrink the graphic's physical size, as shown in Figure 8-17.

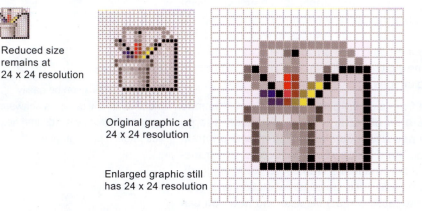

Reduced size
remains at
24 x 24 resolution

Original graphic at
24 x 24 resolution

Enlarged graphic still
has 24 x 24 resolution

FIGURE 8-17

When a bitmap graphic is enlarged or reduced in size, it still retains its original resolution—24 x 24.

This concept of stretching and shrinking without changing resolution is important for understanding what happens when bitmaps are displayed and printed. The denser the grid, the smaller the image will appear. The density of an image grid can be expressed as dots per inch (dpi) for a printer or scanner or as pixels per inch (ppi) on a monitor.

How do I specify the size of a printed image?

Most graphics software allows you to specify the size at which an image is printed without changing the resolution of the bitmap graphic. You'll get the highest print quality if the resolution of the graphic meets or exceeds the printer's dpi. An ink jet printer with a resolution of 1440 x 720 dpi produces a very dense image grid. If each pixel of a 1600 x 1200 graphic was printed as a single dot on this printer, the resulting image would be very high quality but just a bit wider than 1 inch. You can specify a larger size for the printout, in which case the printer must create additional data to fill the print grid. This process can produce a fuzzy and blocky image if the printed image gets very large.

As a general rule, when you incorporate an image in a desktop-published document, or when you print photographs, you should work with high-resolution bitmaps so that you can produce high-quality output. To capture high-resolution bitmaps, use the highest resolution provided by your digital camera. When scanning an image, choose a dpi setting on your scanner that is at least as high as the dpi for the printout.

How does a bitmap's resolution relate to what I see on the screen?

In Chapter 2, you learned that you can set your computer monitor to a particular resolution, such as 1024 x 768. When you display a bitmap graphic on the screen, each pixel of the graphic typically corresponds to one pixel on the screen. If the resolution of your graphic is

1024 x 768 and your monitor is set at 1024 x 768 resolution, the image appears to fill the screen. If you view a 4.0 megapixel image on the same monitor, the image is larger than the screen, and you have to scroll or change the zoom level to view it (Figure 8-18).

Can I change a graphic's file size? The resolution and corresponding file size of a graphic might not be right for your needs. For example, if you take a photo with a 4.0 megapixel camera, it is unsuitable for a Web page. Not only would it take a long time to download, but it would be larger than most screens. A 4.0 megapixel graphic is also not suitable for an e-mail attachment. Uploading and downloading such a large file—especially over a dial-up connection—would take much too long. Reducing the resolution of a bitmap can reduce its file size and on-screen display size. Most experts recommend that Web graphics not exceed 100 KB and that e-mail attachments not exceed 500 KB.

You can reduce the size of a bitmap by cropping it. **Cropping** refers to the process of selecting part of an image—just like cutting out a section of a photograph. Cropping decreases resolution and file size by reducing the number of pixels in a graphic. You can also reduce file size by removing pixels from the entire graphic; however, this process changes the image quality.

Bitmap graphics are **resolution dependent**, which means that the quality of the image depends on its resolution. If you reduce the resolution, the computer eliminates pixels from the image, reducing the size of the image grid. For example, if you reduce the resolution from 2160 x 1440 (3.1 megapixels) to 1080 x 720 (.8 megapixels), the image grid becomes a quarter of its original size. The file size is reduced by a similar amount. However, the computer threw away data with the pixels, which can reduce image quality.

If you attempt to enlarge a bitmap by increasing its resolution, your computer must somehow add pixels because no additional picture data exists. But what colors should these additional pixels become? Most graphics software uses a process called **pixel interpolation** to create new pixels by averaging the colors of nearby pixels. For some graphics, pixel interpolation results in an image that appears very similar to the original. Other images—particularly those with strong curved or diagonal lines—develop an undesirable **pixelated**, or "bitmappy," jagged appearance (Figure 8-19).

FIGURE 8-18

When viewing an image larger than the screen, you must scroll to see all parts of the image or set the zoom level of your graphics software to less than 100%. You should understand, however, that changing the zoom level stretches or shrinks only the size of the image grid. It has no effect on the printed size of a graphic or the graphic's file size.

8

FIGURE 8-19

When you increase the resolution of an existing graphic, the file size increases, but the quality might deteriorate.

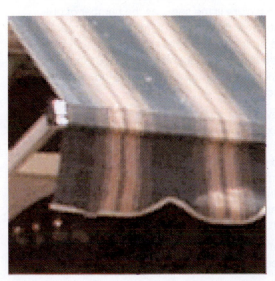

The figure above has a resolution of 130 x 130. The figure at right was enlarged to a resolution of 260 x 260, but it has a rough, pixelated appearance.

COLOR DEPTH AND PALETTES

What is color depth? As you learned in Chapter 2, color depth is the number of colors available for use in an image. As the number of colors increases, image quality improves, but file size also increases. You can limit color depth to decrease the file size required for a graphic. To find out how this works, take a look at the storage requirements for various color depths. Then you can turn to the procedures for reducing color depth.

How does color depth relate to file size? To answer this question, go back to the old days of computing when monitors were simple monochrome devices. Each screen pixel could be either "on" or "off." A **monochrome bitmap** is displayed by manipulating the pattern of "off" and "on" pixels displayed on-screen. To store the data for a monochrome bitmap, an "on" pixel is represented by a 1 bit. An "off" pixel is represented by a 0 bit. Each row of the bitmap grid is stored as a series of 0s and 1s, as shown in Figure 8-20.

FIGURE 8-20

Each pixel in a monochrome bitmap graphic is stored as a bit.

1. This image originated as a black-and-white silhouette.

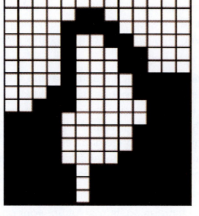

2. The computer divides the picture into a matrix.

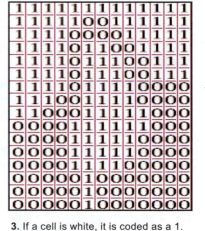

3. If a cell is white, it is coded as a 1. If the cell is black, it is coded as a 0.

Monochrome bitmaps require very little storage space. Suppose you create a full-screen monochrome bitmap with your monitor's resolution set to 640 x 480. Your screen displays 307,200 pixels (that's 640 multiplied by 480). Each pixel is set to display a black dot or a white dot. When you store the graphic, each dot requires only one bit. Therefore, the number of bits required to represent a full-screen picture is the same as the number of pixels on the screen. At a resolution of 640 x 480, a full-screen graphic requires 307,200 bits of storage space. The number of bytes required to store the image is 307,200 divided by 8 (remember that there are eight bits in a byte). Your full-screen monochrome bitmap would, therefore, require only 38,400 bytes of storage space.

But what about color? Today's color monitors require a more complex storage scheme. Each screen pixel displays a color based on the intensity of red, green, and blue signals it receives. A pixel appears white if the red, green, and blue signals are set to maximum intensity. If red, green, and blue signals are equal but at a lower intensity, the pixel displays a shade of gray. If the red signal is set to maximum intensity, but the blue and green signals are off, the pixel appears in brilliant red. A pixel appears purple if it receives red and blue signals, and so forth.

Each red, green, and blue signal is assigned a value ranging from zero to 255. Zero represents the absence of color, and 255 represents the highest intensity level for that color. These values produce a maximum of 16.7 million colors. A graphic that uses this full range of colors is referred to as a **True Color bitmap** or a **24-bit bitmap**. You might be able to guess where the *24-bit* term comes from. The data for each pixel requires three bytes of storage space—eight bits for blue, eight bits for green, and eight bits for red—for a total of 24 bits. Although True Color bitmaps produce photographic-quality images, they also produce very large files. Because each pixel requires three bytes, a 3.1 megapixel True Color bitmap would require a 9.3 MB file!

You might occasionally encounter a **32-bit bitmap**. Just like a 24-bit bitmap, it displays 16.7 million colors. The extra bits are used to define special effects, such as the amount of transparency, for a pixel. These files are even larger than those containing 24-bit bitmaps. A 3.1 megapixel 32-bit bitmap would be about 10 MB.

Files containing full-screen 24-bit and 32-bit bitmaps are typically too large for Web pages because they require excessively long upload and download times. Earlier in the chapter, you learned that you can reduce a bitmap's file size by removing pixels. Another way to shrink a bitmap file is to reduce its color depth.

How can I reduce color depth? To reduce the color depth of a bitmap, you can use your graphics software to work with color palettes. A **color palette** (also called a color lookup table or color map) is the digital version of a kidney-shaped artist's palette that holds the selection of colors an artist uses for a particular painting. A digital color palette allows you to select a group of colors to use for a bitmap graphic.

The advantage of a palette is that if it contains only 256 colors, you can store the data for each pixel in 8 bits instead of 24 bits, which reduces the file to a third of the size required for a True Color bitmap.

How does a color palette work? A color palette is stored as a table within the header of a graphics file. Each palette contains a list of 256 color numbers. Each of these numbers is mapped to a 24-bit number that corresponds to the actual levels of red, green, and blue required to display the color. Figure 8-21 explains how this table works.

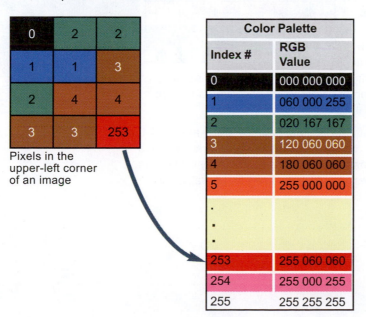

Pixels in the
upper-left corner
of an image

FIGURE 8-21

A color palette is a subset of all possible colors. Each color in the palette is numbered, and its number points to the full 24-bit RGB (red, green, blue) value stored in the graphics file header.

How do I select a color palette? Most graphics software offers a selection of ready-made palettes that you can choose by using the color palette or color picker tool. Ready-made palettes usually include a grayscale palette, a system palette, and a Web palette.

A **grayscale palette** uses shades of gray, or "gray scales," to display images that look similar to black-and-white photographs. Most grayscale palettes consist of 256 shades of gray. Figure 8-22 illustrates a grayscale palette and a grayscale bitmap graphic.

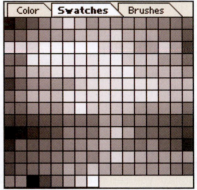

A **system palette** is the collection of colors the operating system uses for graphics that represent desktop icons and controls. Windows, for example, uses a system palette containing 20 permanent colors and 236 colors that can be changed, depending on the application.

A **Web palette** (also called a Web-safe palette or a browser palette) contains a standard set of colors used by Internet Web browsers. Because most browsers support this palette, it is typically regarded as a safe choice when preparing graphics for Internet distribution. Figure 8-23 shows the collection of colors used by system and Web palettes.

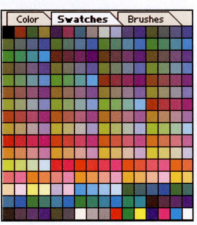

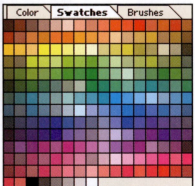

Your graphics software might offer additional palettes. They are likely to include a "woodsy" palette that works well for outdoor photographs, a pastel palette that works well with images filled with predominantly light colors, and a flesh-tone palette that's designed to work nicely for portraits.

IMAGE COMPRESSION

What is image compression? **Image compression** refers to any technique that recodes the data in an image file so that it contains fewer bits. Smaller files produced as a result of image compression require less storage space and can be transmitted more rapidly than the larger, original files. Images can be compressed using lossless or lossy compression.

What is the difference between lossless and lossy compression? **Lossless compression** provides the means to compress a file and then reconstitute all the data into its original state. TIFF, PCX, and GIF graphics formats offer lossless compression. In contrast, **lossy compression** throws away some of the original data during the compression process. In theory, the human eye won't miss the lost information. JPEG files are compressed using lossy compression. Most lossy compression techniques have adjustable compression levels so that you can decide how much data you can afford to lose.

How does lossless compression shrink a file without throwing away data? Various techniques exist for lossless image compression. As a simple example, consider a type of lossless compression called run-length encoding. **Run-length encoding** (RLE) replaces a series of similarly colored pixels with a code that indicates the number of pixels and their colors. Suppose that a section of a picture has 167 consecutive white pixels, and each pixel is described by one byte of data, as in a 256-color bitmap image. RLE compresses this series of 167 bytes into as few as two bytes, as shown in Figure 8-24.

FIGURE 8-24

In an uncompressed file, each pixel of a 256-color bitmap requires one byte to indicate its color. For example, a white pixel might be coded 11111111. Run-length encoding compresses graphical data by recoding like-colored pixels when they appear in a series.

1. The data for the first 167 white pixels can be compressed as 10100111 11111111. The first byte is the binary representation of 167. The second byte is the code for white.

2. The next five pixels are coded 00000101 00000000. The first byte is the binary representation of the number 5. The second byte is the code for black.

3. With compression, the first nine rows of the graphic require only 30 bytes—the binary numbers in columns 2 and 4 of this table. The uncompressed graphic requires 288 bytes.

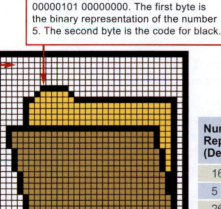

Number of Repetitions (Decimal)	Number of Repetitions (Binary)	Pixel Color	Pixel Color (Binary)
167	10100111	White	11111111
5	00000101	Black	00000000
26	00011010	White	11111111
1	00000001	Black	00000000
5	00000101	Yellow	10100000
1	00000001	Black	00000000
23	00010111	White	11111111
2	00000010	Black	00000000
7	00000111	Yellow	10100000
18	00010010	Black	00000000
5	00000101	White	11111111
1	00000001	Black	00000000
25	00011001	Yellow	10100000
1	00000001	White	11111111
1	00000001	Black	00000000

8

What happens during lossy compression? Lossy compression techniques discard some data from an image to shrink its file size. JPEG is a lossy version of run-length encoding that can be applied to images, such as photographs, that don't have large areas of solid color. A True Color photograph might not have any adjoining pixels of the same color. Applying RLE to such a photo would not result in any compression whatsoever. JPEG preprocesses an image by tweaking the colors in adjoining pixels so that they are the same color whenever possible. After this preprocessing is complete, run-length encoding can be applied with more success.

For many images, lossy compression results in only a minor reduction in the sharpness of the image. The reduction in quality can be unnoticeable in many circumstances. Figure 8-25 illustrates a section of a noncompressed image and a section of that same image after JPEG compression has been applied. Can you see the difference?

FIGURE 8-25

JPEG compression can slightly adjust the colors of adjacent pixels to make them the same. These like-colored pixels can then be compressed with RLE.

Non-compressed JPEG image

JPEG image with 35% compression

How do I compress image files? Some graphics file formats automatically compress file data. You can also compress files using a general-purpose file compression utility.

PCX, GIF, JPEG, PNG, and TIFF file formats support compression. Software that works with these file formats might allow you to select compression levels before saving a graphics file. For example, when saving an image in JPEG format, you might be given the option of selecting compression settings from 1 (worst quality) to 99 (best quality).

Some bitmap formats, such as BMP and RAW, do not support compression. If you want to compress these files before sending them as e-mail attachments, for example, you can do so manually using a file compression utility. A **file compression utility** uses lossless compression to shrink one or more files into a single new file. PKZIP and WinZip are popular shareware programs that compress and decompress files. 7-Zip is a popular open source compression utility. You can compress any kind of file, including programs and data files, graphics and document files. BMP file sizes might shrink by as much as 70% when compressed. Files stored in formats such as PNG, GIF, and JPEG hardly shrink at all when you use compression utilities because they are already stored in compressed format.

Compressing files is sometimes called zipping, and decompressing files is sometimes called unzipping. Most file compression utilities not only zip single files, but can also zip several files into a single compressed file that can later be unzipped into the original separate files.

For example, suppose you want to send three files to your boss. The original files are called Technology.xls, Award.doc, and Insurance.bmp. You can zip all three files into a single compressed file called Management 212.zip (Figure 8-26). Simply attach this one file to an e-mail and send it to your boss. When Management 212.zip is unzipped, it produces the three original files.

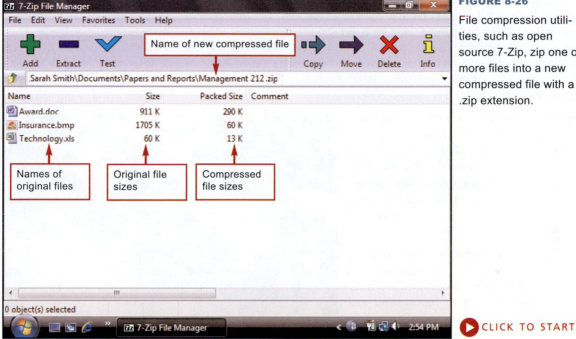

FIGURE 8-26

File compression utilities, such as open source 7-Zip, zip one or more files into a new compressed file with a .zip extension.

► CLICK TO START

If you have not installed compression software such as PKZIP, you can use a feature of Windows to create compressed folders (Figure 8-27). Any files that you drag into a compressed folder are automatically compressed. You don't have to do anything special to open a file from a compressed folder. Simply double-click the file as usual, and Windows automatically decompresses the file before displaying its contents.

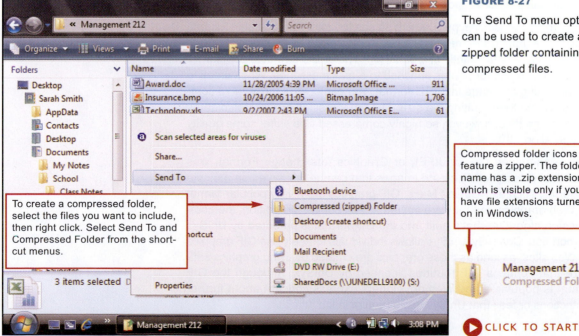

FIGURE 8-27

The Send To menu option can be used to create a zipped folder containing compressed files.

Compressed folder icons feature a zipper. The folder name has a .zip extension, which is visible only if you have file extensions turned on in Windows.

► CLICK TO START

8

BITMAP GRAPHICS FORMATS

Are there different kinds of bitmap graphics? Many graphics file formats exist, and most graphics software offers a choice of popular formats, such as BMP, RAW, PCX, TIFF, JPEG, GIF, and PNG.

BMP, pronounced "bee-em-pee" or "bump," is the native bitmap graphics file format of the Microsoft Windows environment. Microsoft Paint, included as part of Microsoft Windows, creates BMP graphics files. The BMP format supports True Color and can be used for a wide variety of graphics applications, such as photographs, illustrations, and graphs. BMP files are not compressed in any way, so this format typically creates very large files that are not suitable for e-mail attachments. BMP graphics are not supported by most browsers, so they are not used on the Web.

FIGURE 8-28

Digital cameras use a sensor array to capture an image. The sensor is packed with millions of light sensitive cells that record color and brightness for millions of points in the image grid.

RAW image formats contain the unprocessed pixel data generated directly by a digital camera's sensor (Figure 8-28). Up to 12 bits of data can be stored for each of the red, blue, and green values for a pixel, so RAW files are very large. Cameras that offer a RAW format also supply proprietary software to convert RAW data to JPEG or TIFF.

PCX is one of the original personal computer bitmap graphics file formats. PCX graphics are usually 8-bit (256 colors) and are automatically compressed to reduce file size without any loss of image quality. Because it's not supported by browsers, PCX is not used on the Web.

TIFF (Tag Image File Format), or TIF, is a flexible and platform-independent graphics file format supported by most photo-editing software packages. Scanners and digital cameras commonly store bitmaps in TIFF format because it supports True Color and can be easily converted into other graphics file formats. TIFF is an excellent choice for desktop publishing projects, but it is not supported by most browsers.

JPEG (pronounced JAY peg), which stands for Joint Photographic Experts Group, is a graphics format with built-in compression that stores True Color bitmap data very efficiently in a small file. The JPEG format is popular for Web graphics and for photos attached to e-mail messages. When creating or converting an image in JPEG format, you can control the level of compression and the resulting file size. The compression process eliminates some image data, however, so highly compressed files suffer some quality deterioration.

GIF (pronounced GIF or JIFF), or Graphics Interchange Format, was specifically designed to create images that can be displayed on multiple platforms, such as PCs and Macs. GIF graphics are a very popular format for Web graphics, but they are limited to 256 colors. In addition, the compression algorithm that's built into the GIF format is patented by UniSys Corporation. Currently, UniSys allows individuals to freely use GIF graphics on Web sites, as long as those graphics are created by using graphics software that contains GIF routines licensed by UniSys. Although the GIF format is popular, some Web developers express concern about further restrictions or fees that UniSys might require in the future.

PNG (Portable Network Graphic), pronounced "ping," is a graphics format designed to improve on the GIF format. A PNG graphic can display up to 48-bit True Color (trillions of colors). Unlike JPEG, PNG compresses bitmap data without losing any data, so compressed images retain the same high quality as the originals. Unlike GIF, PNG is a public domain format without any restrictions on its use.

How do I determine which graphics format to use? Selecting the best graphics file format to use depends on what you intend to do with the image. Figure 8-29 summarizes popular uses for each format.

Format	Use
BMP	Graphical elements, such as buttons and other controls used in computer programs
RAW	Used by professional and semi-professional photographers to manually adjust images before they are stored in other formats
PCX	Older graphics format not used much today
TIFF	High-resolution scanned images and digital photos used in desktop publishing; high-quality digital photos reproduced on special photo printers
JPEG	Photographic or scanned images that might be used in a variety of applications, such as DTP or Web pages, where flexibility in file size is important
GIF	Popular format for Web graphics
PNG	An alternative to GIF for Web graphics

FIGURE 8-29

Choosing a bitmap graphics format depends on how the image is used.

QuickCheck   SECTION B

1. Images from a digital camera can be transferred to a computer by using a USB cable, serial cable, or ☐ cable.

2. A 10 megapixel digital camera captures images with a 3888 x 2592 ☐.

3. Bitmap graphics are resolution ☐, so that reducing the resolution also reduces the image quality.

4. A(n) ☐ palette produces images that resemble black and white photographs.

5. The ☐ format is a good choice for desktop publishing, but not for Web graphics. (Hint: Use the acronym.)

6. The most popular 256-color formats for Web graphics include ☐ and PNG. (Hint: Use the acronym.)

7. Unlike ☐ compression, ☐ compression shrinks a file without throwing away any data.

 CHECK ANSWERS

Vector and 3-D Graphics

IF YOU'VE PLAYED any computer games recently or watched an animated movie, you've seen the product of computer-generated 3-D animated graphics. To the uninformed, these photorealistic action characters might seem little more than fancy cartoons. After you understand the way they are created, however, you'll appreciate the incredible amount of computing power they require. This section begins with two-dimensional vector graphics. You'll find out how they differ from bitmaps and why you might want to use them. After covering the basics for two-dimensional graphics, the section progresses to static 3-D graphics and then to animated 3-D graphics.

VECTOR GRAPHICS BASICS

What is a vector graphic? Unlike a bitmap graphic created by dividing an image into a grid of pixels, a **vector graphic** consists of a set of instructions for re-creating a picture. Instead of storing the color value for each pixel, a vector graphic file contains the instructions the computer needs to create the shape, size, position, and color for each object in an image. These instructions are similar to those a drafting teacher might give students: "Draw a 2-inch (or 112-pixel) circle. Locate this circle 1" down and 2" in from the right edge of the work area. Fill the circle with yellow." The Stonehenge image shown in Figure 8-30 was created as a vector graphic.

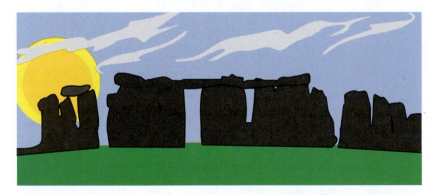

FIGURE 8-30

The parts of a vector graphic are created as separate objects. This image was created with a series of roughly rectangular objects for the stones and a circular object for the sun. The objects are layered and can be manipulated individually. This characteristic of vector graphics gives artists flexibility in arranging and editing image elements.

How can I identify vector graphics? It can be difficult to accurately identify a vector graphic just by looking at an on-screen image. One clue that an image might be a vector graphic is a flat, cartoon-like quality. Think of clip art images—they are typically stored as vector graphics. For a more definitive identification, however, you should check the file extension. Vector graphics files have file extensions such as .wmf, .ai, .dxf, .eps, .swf, and .svg.

How do vector graphics compare with bitmap graphics? Vector graphics are suitable for most line art, logos, simple illustrations, and diagrams that might be displayed and printed at various sizes. When compared to bitmaps, vector graphics have several advantages and a few disadvantages. You should take the following distinctions into account when deciding which type of graphic to use for a specific project.

- **Vector graphics resize better than bitmaps.** When you change the size of a vector graphic, the objects change proportionally and maintain their smooth edges. Whereas shapes in a bitmap graphic might appear to have jagged edges after they are enlarged, shapes in a vector graphic appear smooth at any size, as shown in Figure 8-31.

FIGURE 8-31

Unlike bitmaps, vector graphics can be resized without becoming pixelated and blurry.

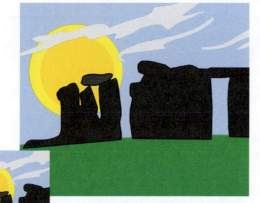

Vector graphic at 200% (above) and 50% (left)

Bitmap graphic at 200% (above) and 50% (right)

- **Vector graphics usually require less storage space than bitmaps.** The storage space required for a vector graphic reflects the complexity of the image. Each instruction requires storage space, so the more lines, shapes, and fill patterns in the graphic, the more storage space it requires. The Stonehenge vector graphic used as an example in this chapter requires less than 4 KB of storage space. A True Color photograph of the same image requires 1,109 KB.

- **Vector graphics are not usually as realistic as bitmap images.** Most vector images tend to have a cartoon-like appearance instead of the realistic appearance you expect from a photograph. This cartoon-like characteristic of vector images results from the use of objects filled with blocks of color. Your options for shading and texturing objects are limited, which tends to give vector graphics a flat appearance.

- **It is easier to edit an object in a vector graphic than an object in a bitmap graphic.** In some ways, a vector graphic is like a collage of objects. Each object can be layered over other objects, but moved and edited independently. You can individually stretch, shrink, distort, color, move, or delete any object in a vector graphic. For example, if you delete some of the stones from the Stonehenge vector image, the background layers remain. In contrast, most bitmap graphics are constructed as a single layer of pixels. If you erase the pixels for some of the stones in the Stonehenge photograph, you'll create a hole of white pixels (Figure 8-32).

FIGURE 8-32

Vector graphic objects are layered, so it is easy to move and delete objects without disrupting the rest of the image. In contrast, deleting a shape from a bitmap image leaves a hole because the image is only one layer of pixels.

8

What tools do I need to create vector graphics? Neither scanners nor digital cameras produce vector graphics. Architects and engineers sometimes use a digitizing tablet to turn a paper-based line drawing into a vector graphic. A **digitizing tablet** (sometimes called a 2-D digitizer) is a device that provides a flat surface for a paper-based drawing and a pen or mouse-like puck that you can use to click the endpoints of each line on the drawing. The endpoints are converted into vectors and stored.

Usually, vector graphics are created from scratch with vector graphics software, referred to as **drawing software**. Popular drawing software includes Adobe Illustrator, Corel Designer, OpenOffice Draw, and open source Inkscape. Drawing software is sometimes packaged separately from the paint software used to produce bitmap graphics. In other cases, it is included with bitmap software as a graphics software suite.

Vector graphics software provides an array of drawing tools that you can use to create objects, position them, and fill them with colors or patterns. For example, you can use the filled circle tool to draw a circle filled with a solid color. You can create an irregular shape by connecting points to outline the shape. Figure 8-33 illustrates how to use drawing tools to create a vector graphic.

INFOWEBLINKS

To learn more about popular vector graphics software, you can connect to the **Vector Graphics Software InfoWeb**.

W CLICK TO CONNECT

www.course.com/np/concepts11/ch08

FIGURE 8-33

To draw a circle, select the filled circle tool, and then drag the mouse pointer to indicate the circle's location and size. A color palette allows you to select the circle color. After you create the circle object, you can move it and change its size or color. You can also create irregular shapes for objects, such as clouds, by connecting short line segments.

▶ CLICK TO START

The clouds are created as a series of short line segments and filled with color.

The stones are created as a series of short line segments and filled with black.

The sun is two circles, each filled with a slightly different shade of yellow.

Vector graphics software helps you easily edit individual objects within a graphic by changing their sizes, shapes, positions, or colors. For example, the data for creating a circle for the sun is recorded as an instruction, such as CIRCLE 40 Y 200 150, which means create a circle with a 40-pixel radius, color it yellow, and place the center of the circle 200 pixels from the left of the screen and 150 pixels from the top of the screen. If you move the circle to the right side of the image, the instruction that the computer stores for the circle changes to something like CIRCLE 40 Y 500 150—500 pixels from the left instead of 200.

When filling a shape with color, your graphics software might provide tools for creating gradients. A **gradient** is a smooth blending of shades from one color to another or from light to dark. Gradients, as shown in Figure 8-34, can be used to create shading and three-dimensional effects.

Some vector graphics software provides tools that apply bitmapped textures to vector graphic objects, giving them a more realistic appearance. For example, you can create a vector drawing of a house, and then apply a brick-like texture derived from a bitmap photograph of real bricks. A graphic that contains both bitmap and vector data is called a **metafile**.

VECTOR-TO-BITMAP CONVERSION

Is it possible to convert a vector graphic into a bitmap? A vector graphic can be converted quite easily into a bitmap graphic through a process called rasterizing. **Rasterization** works by superimposing a grid over a vector image and determining the color for each pixel. This process is typically carried out by graphics software, which allows you to specify the output size for the final bitmap image. On a PC, you can also rasterize a vector graphic by using the Print Screen key to take a screenshot of a vector image. It is important to rasterize images at the size you ultimately need. If you rasterize a vector image at a small size and then try to enlarge the resulting bitmap image, you will likely get a poor-quality pixelated image, such as the one in Figure 8-35.

After a vector graphic is converted to a bitmap, the resulting graphic no longer has the qualities of a vector graphic. For example, if you convert the Stonehenge vector graphic into a bitmap, the sun is no longer an object that you can easily move or assign a different color.

How about converting a bitmap graphic into a vector graphic? Converting a bitmap graphic into a vector graphic is more difficult than converting from a vector to a bitmap. To change a bitmap graphic into a vector graphic, you must use tracing software. **Tracing software** locates the edges of objects in a bitmap image and converts the resulting shapes into vector graphic objects.

Tracing software products, such as ImpressionX, work best on simple images and line drawings. They do not usually produce acceptable results when used on complex, detailed photos. Tracing capabilities are included in some general-purpose graphics software, but standalone tracing software offers more flexibility and usually produces better results.

FIGURE 8-34

Gradients can create the illusion of three dimensions, such as making this shape appear to be a tube.

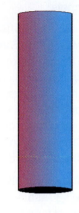

FIGURE 8-35

When vector images are rasterized, they become bitmaps and can't be enlarged without becoming pixelated.

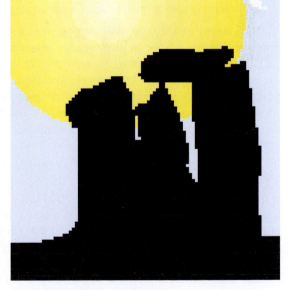

8

VECTOR GRAPHICS ON THE WEB

Do vector graphics work on the Web? Web browsers were originally designed to support a limited number of graphics formats—GIF and JPEG—and these formats were exclusively bitmaps. Plug-ins and players are currently available for several of the most popular Web-based vector graphics formats.

Which vector graphics formats can be used on the Web? A graphics format called **SVG** (Scalable Vector Graphics) is designed specifically for the Web (Figure 8-36). Graphics in SVG format are automatically resized when displayed on different screens or when printed. SVG supports gradients, drop shadows, multiple levels of transparency, and other effects, along with portability to other platforms, such as handheld computers and cellular phones. SVG graphic objects can include regular and irregular shapes, images, and text, and they can be animated. You can add SVG files to HTML and XML documents by using the <embed> tag.

Flash is another popular vector graphics format frequently used on the Web. Adobe's Flash software creates vector graphics that are stored in files with .swf extensions. Flash graphics can be static or animated. Flash players are shipped with most browsers, and player updates can be downloaded from the Adobe site.

Flash animations have advantages over other formats, such as animated GIFs. An **animated GIF** is essentially a series of slightly different bitmap images displayed in sequence to achieve animation effects. As a bitmap-based format, GIF files are fairly large. Most Flash animations fit in compact files and, therefore, can be transferred from a Web server to a browser more rapidly than animated GIFs.

What are the advantages of using vector graphics on the Web? Vector graphics have several advantages:

● **Consistent quality.** On Web pages, vector graphics appear with the same consistent quality on all computer screens. This capability makes it possible for browsers to adjust the size of an image on the fly to fit correctly on a screen, regardless of its size or resolution. These adjustments don't carry any penalty in terms of image quality—a large version of a vector graphic displayed on a monitor set at 1024 x 768 resolution has the same sharp detail and smooth curves as the original image sized to fit a smaller screen set at 640 x 480 resolution. This flexibility is important for Web pages that might be viewed at different resolutions on PCs, Macs, or other platforms.

● **Searchable.** Another advantage is that any text contained in a vector image is stored as actual text, not just a series of colored dots. This text can be indexed by search engines so that it can be included in keyword searches. For example, suppose a vector drawing was used to produce a diagram describing the service box where your telephone line enters your house. One of the components in this diagram is labeled "telephone test jack." If you enter *telephone test jack* into a search engine, the service box diagram will likely turn up in the list of search results.

● **Compact file size.** A third advantage of vector graphics on the Web is their compact file sizes. A fairly complex graphic can be stored in a file that is under 30 KB—that's kilobytes, not megabytes. These files require little storage space and can be transmitted swiftly from a Web server to your browser.

FIGURE 8-36

SVG graphics are typically used on the Web for maps, ads, organizational charts, and flow-charts.

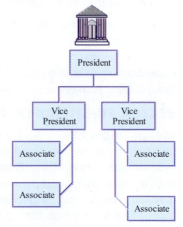

3-D GRAPHICS

How do vector graphics relate to 3-D graphics? Like vector graphics, **3-D graphics** are stored as a set of instructions. For a 3-D graphic, however, the instructions contain the locations and lengths of lines that form a wireframe for a three-dimensional object. The **wireframe** acts in much the same way as the framework of a pop-up tent. Just as you would construct the framework for the tent, and then cover it with a nylon tent cover, a 3-D wireframe can be covered with surface texture and color to create a graphic of a 3-D object. The process of covering a wireframe with surface color and texture is called **rendering**. The rendering process, shown in Figure 8-37, outputs a bitmap image.

FIGURE 8-37

3-D graphics are based on a wireframe, which can be rendered into a bitmap image that looks three-dimensional.

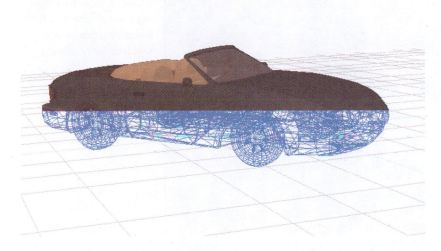

For added realism, the rendering process can take into account the way that light shines on surfaces and creates shadows. The technique for adding light and shadows to a 3-D image is called **ray tracing**. Before an image is rendered, the artist selects a location for one or more light sources. The computer applies a complex mathematical algorithm to determine how the light source affects the color of each pixel in the final rendered image. This process can take time—hours for a complex image, even using today's most powerful personal computers. Figure 8-38 shows the image from the previous figure rendered with an additional light source and ray tracing.

FIGURE 8-38

Ray tracing adds realism to 3-D graphics by adding highlights and shadows that are produced by a light source.

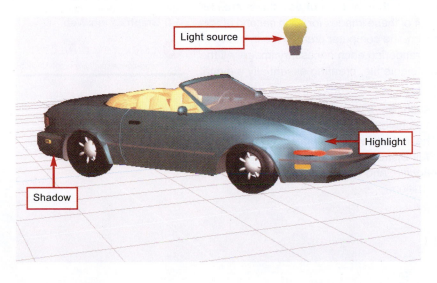

8

What tools do I need to create 3-D graphics? 3-D graphics software runs on most personal computers, although some architects and engineers prefer to use high-end workstations. A fast processor, lots of RAM, and a fast graphics card with its own video RAM all speed up the rendering process. To create 3-D graphics, you need 3-D graphics software, such as AutoCad or Caligari trueSpace. This software has tools for drawing a wireframe and viewing it from any angle. It provides rendering and ray tracing tools, along with an assortment of surface textures that you can apply to individual objects. Figure 8-39 takes you on a tour of a popular 3-D graphics software package.

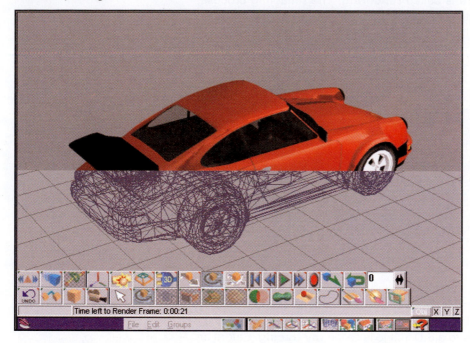

FIGURE 8-39

3-D graphics software provides tools for drawing a wireframe and then specifying colors and textures for rendering.

▶ CLICK TO START

Is it possible to animate 3-D graphics? 3-D graphics can be animated to produce special effects for movies or to create interactive, animated characters and environments for 3-D computer games. Animated special effects, such as massive battle scenes, are created by rendering a sequence of bitmaps, in which one or more objects are moved or otherwise changed between each rendering. In traditional hand-drawn animation, a chief artist draws the keyframes, and then a team of assistants creates each of the in-between images—24 of these images for each second of animation. For 3-D computer animation, the computer creates the in-between images by moving the object and rendering each necessary image. All the images are then combined into a single file, creating essentially a digital movie.

Graphics design companies such as Pixar Animation Studios and DreamWorks use 3-D animation techniques to produce animated feature films as well as special effects. The first full-length animated 3-D movie was *Toy Story*, released in 1995 by Walt Disney Studios and Pixar. Digitally animated films, such as *Cars*, *Ratatouille*, and *Shrek the Third*, illustrate the growing sophistication of 3-D animation.

INFOWEBLINKS

For additional resources about 3-D software (and shareware), rendering, ray tracing, and 3-D animated graphics, check out the **3-D Graphics InfoWeb**.

Ⓦ CLICK TO CONNECT
www.course.com/np/concepts11/ch08

Do game and movie animation require similar tools and techniques? An important characteristic of special effects and animated films is that rendering can be accomplished during the production phase of the movie and incorporated into the final footage. In contrast, 3-D computer game animation happens in real time. Each frame that makes the image seem to move must be rendered while you are playing the game—a process that requires an incredible amount of computer power. To give you a handle on the immensity of the task, consider a game like Doom displayed on a computer monitor that's set at 1024 x 768 resolution (Figure 8-40). At this resolution, the screen contains 786,432 pixels (1024 multiplied by 768). If the game is presented in 32-bit color, each frame of the animation requires 25,165,824 bits (multiply 786,432 times 32).

Computer game designers believe that on-screen animation looks smoothest at 60 frames per second, which means your computer must handle 1,509,949,440—that's more than 1 billion—bits of information every second just to put the 3-D image onto the screen. In addition, the computer must process even more data to keep track of the movements of each player. To handle all this data, your computer's main processor gets help from a graphics processor located on your computer's graphics card. These graphics processors vary in their capabilities. For the fastest graphics capability, look for graphics cards billed as 3-D accelerators.

Can I create my own animated 3-D graphics? You can create 3-D animations on a standard PC or Mac with commercially available software, but professional 3-D software, such as Maya and Autodesk 3ds Max, is expensive and has a steep learning curve. If you want to dabble with 3-D animations before making an expensive software investment, you might try Curious Labs Poser, DAZ Bryce, or one of the shareware programs listed in the 3-D Graphics InfoWeb. Whether you use a commercial or shareware package, be prepared to spend lots of time with the manual before you are able to produce any original animations.

FIGURE 8-40

Classic computer games, such as Doom, established building blocks for animation technologies used to create today's fast-action, visually detailed computer games.

QuickCheck

1. Unlike bitmaps, vector graphics can be enlarged without becoming pixelated. True or false? [＿＿＿＿＿]

2. Whereas the software used to work with bitmap graphics is often referred to as paint software, vector graphics software is usually referred to as [＿＿＿＿＿] software.

3. 3-D graphics are constructed based on a(n) [＿＿＿＿＿] that can be covered with surface texture and color.

4. The technique of adding light and shadows to a 3-D image is called ray [＿＿＿＿＿].

5. A vector graphic can be easily converted into a bitmap through a process called [＿＿＿＿＿].

6. Today, SVG and [＿＿＿＿＿] are the most popular vector graphics formats for the Web.

▶ CHECK ANSWERS

Digital Video

IN THE PREVIOUS SECTION, you learned about GIF and Flash animations—popular options for adding motion to Web pages. You also learned about using animated 3-D graphics for movie special effects and computer games. Digital animation is typically created from scratch by an artist with the help of a computer. In contrast, digital video is based on footage of real objects filmed and then stored as bits. Digital video encompasses several technologies, including those that produce theater-quality DVD movies, desktop videos, Web-based videos, and PDA videos. In this section, you'll take a look at what you can do with affordable, easy-to-use desktop video tools. You'll also explore how to transfer digital videos onto DVD and then add interactive menus to access selected scenes and special features.

DIGITAL VIDEO BASICS

What is digital video? A video is a series of still frames, like those in Figure 8-41, projected at a rate fast enough to fool the human eye into perceiving continuous motion. **Digital video** uses bits to store color and brightness data for each video frame. The process is similar to storing the data for a series of bitmap images in which the color for each pixel is represented by a binary number.

Unlike analog video, digital video retains image quality no matter how many times it is copied. Videos in digital format can be easily manipulated on a personal computer, putting the world of movie-making at your fingertips.

Footage for digital videos can be supplied by a video camera, videotape, television, DVD, or even a digital video recording device such as TiVo. You can shoot footage with a consumer-quality camcorder and use your personal computer to edit this footage into videos suitable for a variety of personal and professional uses, such as video wedding albums, product sales videos, training videos, video holiday greeting cards, documentaries for nonprofit organizations, and video scrapbooks. These videos can be stored on a hard disk or distributed on CDs, DVDs, videotapes, memory cards, or the Web.

Digital video is stored in a variety of file formats including ASF, AVI, QuickTime Movie, Windows Media, Flash Video, MPEG-4, Ogg, and RealMedia. Later in the chapter, you'll learn about video file formats in more detail.

Are there different kinds of digital videos? Digital video is sometimes classified by its platform. The term **desktop video** refers to videos that are constructed and displayed using a personal computer. **Web-based video** is incorporated in Web pages and accessed with a browser. **DVD-Video** refers to a DVD format used for commercial DVDs that contain feature-length films. **PDA video** refers to small-format video designed to be viewed on a PDA or cell phone screen.

FIGURE 8-41

A video is composed of a series of bitmap graphics, each one called a frame.

How do I create digital video? To understand how you can create your own digital videos, you'll need information about four procedures summarized in Figure 8-42 and explained in the rest of this section.

FIGURE 8-42

Desktop video requires a few fairly simple steps.

1. **Produce video footage.** Select equipment for filming videos and use effective filming techniques.

2. **Transfer video footage to a computer.** Use a cable or a video capture card to move video footage from cameras, videotapes, television, and DVDs to your computer's hard disk.

3. **Edit video footage.** Use software to select video segments, arrange them into a video, and add a soundtrack.

4. **Store and play.** Select digital video file formats for playback on desktop, Web, PDA, and DVD platforms.

PRODUCING VIDEO FOOTAGE

Is it necessary to use a digital video camera for filming digital video? You can use a digital or an analog video camera to shoot video footage. As you might expect, a digital video camera stores footage as a series of bits. The video data can be stored on a tape in much the same way that computer data is stored on a backup tape. Video data can also be stored on 3" miniDVDs. Digital videotape formats include miniDV, DVCPro, and DVCam. MiniDV is the most popular and generally the format used by consumer digital video cameras.

You can also use an analog video camera to shoot footage that eventually becomes digital video. As with digital video cameras, the footage is stored on tape, but instead of storing bits, an analog video camera stores video signals as a continuous track of magnetic patterns. The three most popular analog video formats are Hi8, S-VHS, and VHS.

Another option for shooting video footage is a small, inexpensive **videoconferencing camera** (often called a Web cam or Web camera) that attaches directly to a computer (see Figure 8-43). These cameras capture a series of still photos, which are stored in digital format directly on your computer's hard disk. Web cameras typically produce rather low-quality video. These cameras are not usually battery powered and must remain tethered to your computer, which tends to limit your videos to "talking heads."

What are the advantages of a digital video camera? A digital video camera captures video data in digital format, which can then be transferred directly to a computer for editing. In addition, digital cameras generally produce higher quality video than analog or videoconferencing cameras. Images tend to be sharper and more colorful. A common

FIGURE 8-43

A Web camera sits on top of a computer monitor. It is designed mainly for "talking head" applications, such as online video chats and video conferences.

8

misconception is that because desktop, Web-based, and PDA videos are shown on a small computer screen at a fairly low resolution, a cheap camera won't make a difference. Just the opposite is true. The higher the quality of the original video, the better the final video will look.

Does desktop video require special filming techniques? When videos are processed and stored on a personal computer, some of the image data is eliminated to reduce the video file to a manageable size. Simpler videos tend to maintain better quality as they are edited, processed, and stored. Camera movements, fast actions, patterned clothing, and moving backgrounds all contribute to the complexity of a video and should be minimized. The techniques listed in Figure 8-44 can help you produce video footage that maintains good quality as it is edited and processed.

- Use a tripod to maintain a steady image.
- Move the camera slowly if it is necessary to pan from side to side.
- Zoom in and out slowly.
- Direct your subjects to move slowly, when possible.
- Position your shot to eliminate as much background detail and movement as possible.
- Ask the subjects of your video to wear solid-colored clothing, if possible.

FIGURE 8-44

Video Filming Tips

VIDEO TRANSFER

How do I transfer video footage to my computer? Video footage can originate from a variety of sources, including video cameras, videotape, DVRs (digital video recorders), and even your TV. To digitally edit and process digital video, you must transfer the video footage from its source to your computer. After the footage is transferred and stored on a random-access device, such as your computer's hard disk, you can easily cut out unwanted footage, rearrange clips, and add a soundtrack.

The basic method for transferring video footage to your computer is to send the data over a cable that connects your video source to your computer (Figure 8-45). Analog video footage from TV, videotape, and analog video cameras must be converted into digital format before it is stored on your computer's hard disk. Video that originates as a digital signal usually can be transferred directly to your computer without conversion.

How do I convert video from analog devices? The process of converting analog video signals into digital format is referred to as **video capture** and requires a video capture device. Your computer's graphics card might include video capture capabilities. If not, you can purchase a separate video capture device that connects to your computer's USB port or a video capture card that plugs into one of your computer's PCI slots.

FIGURE 8-45

You can transfer video footage to a hard disk by connecting a cable between a video camera and a computer. When the transfer is complete, the cable can be disconnected.

Most video capture devices support a variety of analog video sources, such as cameras and VCRs. The trick is to find a cable with a connector at one end that plugs into the video output port of your analog video source and a plug at the other end that's compatible with your video capture device. Figure 8-46 illustrates the equipment necessary for capturing video from an analog camera.

How do I transfer data from a digital camera to my computer?

The data from a digital camera typically requires no conversion, so it can be transferred directly to your computer's hard disk. Most digital cameras provide a USB or FireWire port for this purpose. Your computer needs a corresponding port to accept the cable from the camera.

Can I capture video from a digital video recorder?

A **digital video recorder** (DVR), like those used with TiVo service, is a device that records television signals received by an antenna, through a cable, or from a satellite. Signals that originate from antenna or cable are converted from analog into digital format and stored on a built-in hard disk. Satellite signals, already in digital format, are converted or unscrambled as necessary before being stored. DVRs are controlled by customized operating systems, usually based on Linux.

It seems like it would be easy to transfer video files from this computer-like device to your personal computer for editing, but some DVRs store data in proprietary formats designed to discourage copying and distribution. These proprietary formats can make it difficult to convert DVR videos into formats that can be manipulated on a computer. Consumers, however, are demanding more compatibility between DVRs and computers. Until DVR manufacturers provide standard video formats, you can capture analog video direct from the TV using a video capture device.

How do I control the transfer process?

Whether you transfer footage from an analog camera or a digital camera, you must use video capture software to control the transfer process. Video capture software allows you to start and stop the transfer, select a file format for storing your video footage, and specify the file name for each video clip. Video capture software is supplied with video editing software and with video capture devices.

Videos are easier to edit if you divide them into several files, each containing a one- or two-minute video clip. Some video capture software automatically creates clips by detecting frame changes, such as when you turn your camera off, pause, or switch to a new scene (Figure 8-47).

FIGURE 8-46

After it has been installed in your computer, a video capture card can be connected to an analog camera's video-out and audio-out ports.

FIGURE 8-47

Most video editing software offers an option for transferring video footage from a camera.

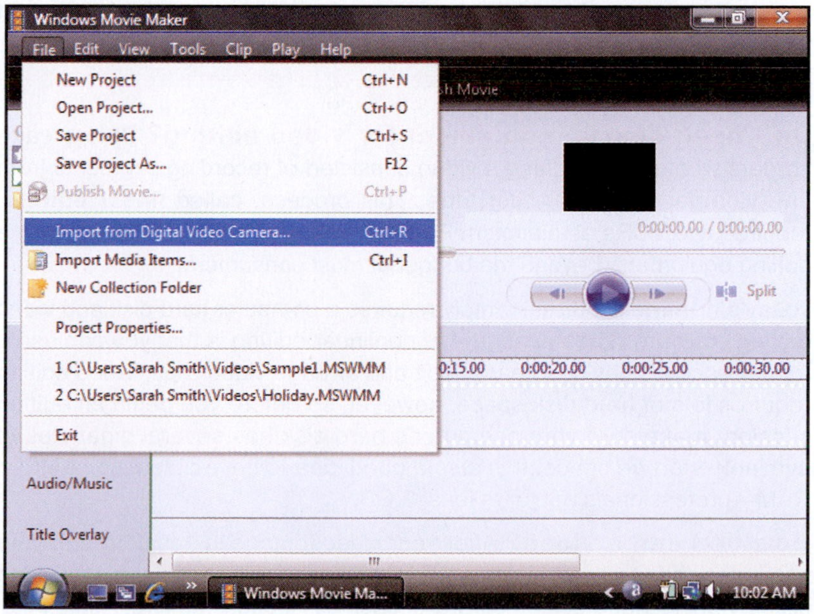

8

What format should I use for video files? For the best quality final product, experts recommend that you store video in a raw, non-compressed format for editing. After you trim out unwanted footage, arrange your clips, and add a soundtrack, you might want to convert your completed video into other formats for distribution. You'll learn more about distribution formats later in this section.

Most digital video cameras store data in DV format. Despite the use of real-time compression to filter out unnecessary data as you record with your camera, DV format contains lots of data. When transferred to your computer, a DV clip requires roughly 1 GB of storage per 5 minutes of video. If you have the disk capacity, you'll get the best quality video if you transfer all this data. If disk space is tight, however, you can whittle digital video down to a more manageable size by using your video capture software to decrease the video display size, reduce the frame rate, and compress file data.

● **Decrease video display size.** A smaller video window contains fewer pixels than a full-screen window and requires fewer bits to represent the data. Whereas a 720 x 480 video window contains 345,600 pixels, a 320 x 240 window contains only 76,800 pixels and fits in a file one-fourth the size. That's a big advantage. If you're creating Web-based videos designed to be displayed in a small window, or if you're designing video for handheld devices, consider decreasing the resolution at this stage of the process.

● **Reduce the frame rate.** **Frame rate** refers to the number of frames shown per second. Digital video cameras record 30 frames per second (fps). Feature films are typically projected at a rate of 24 frames per second. If you intend to output your digital videos to DVDs, you should maintain a high frame rate. Most desktop video, however, has a frame rate of only 15 fps. Reducing the frame rate tends to increase the blurriness of a video, especially for fast-action sequences. If your videos are destined for desktop, Web, or PDA playback, you can reduce the frame rate at this stage of the process because the finished video will be displayed at a lower frame rate.

● **Compress data.** Most video capture software offers a variety of compression options to reduce the size of video files. If storage space is a concern or if your videos are destined for the Web or a PDA, you might want to compress your video clips before you edit them.

VIDEO EDITING

Do I need special equipment for video editing? Before camcorders went digital, editing a video consisted of recording segments from one videotape onto another tape. This process, called **linear editing**, required two VCRs at minimum. Professional video editors used expensive editing equipment, beyond the budget of most consumers.

Today's **nonlinear editing** simply requires a computer hard disk and video editing software. The advantage of nonlinear editing is that you can use a random-access device to easily edit and arrange video clips. Video editing requires lots of hard disk space, however, so before you begin an editing session, make sure your computer's hard disk has several gigabytes of available storage space. It is also a good idea to have at least 512 MB of RAM—professionals opt for at least 2 GB.

How do I edit a video? After your video footage is transferred to your computer and stored on the hard disk, you can begin to arrange your video clips by using video editing software, such as Adobe Premiere, Apple Final Cut Pro, Windows Movie Maker, or Ulead VideoStudio. Your completed

video consists of video tracks containing video segments and transitions, plus audio tracks containing voices and music. Most video editing software allows you to overlay a video track with several audio tracks. Figure 8-48 illustrates how to lay out video and audio tracks.

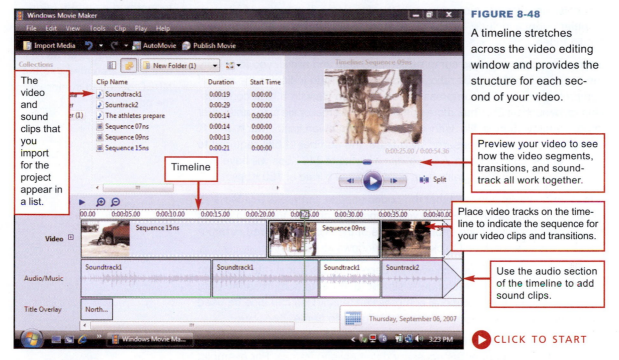

FIGURE 8-48

A timeline stretches across the video editing window and provides the structure for each second of your video.

Preview your video to see how the video segments, transitions, and soundtrack all work together.

Place video tracks on the timeline to indicate the sequence for your video clips and transitions.

Use the audio section of the timeline to add sound clips.

▶ CLICK TO START

VIDEO OUTPUT

How does video footage become a digital video? After you edit your video clips, arrange them on a timeline, and specify a soundtrack, your video editing software combines the data from all the video and audio files you selected into a single file, which is stored on your computer's hard disk as a digital video. You can think of the files that store your digital videos as containers because they can hold video and audio streams. Digital video file formats are sometimes referred to as **container formats** because they are essentially a receptacle for the elements of a video. Figure 8-49 describes some popular video container formats—**AVI**, **QuickTime Movie**, **MPEG**, **RealMedia**, **ASF**, **Flash Video**, and **VOB**.

FIGURE 8-49

Popular Digital Video Formats

Format	Extension	Platform	Description and Use
AVI (Audio Video Interleave)	.avi	PC	Often the format for storing digital clips from video cameras; used for desktop video on the PC platform
QuickTime Movie	.mov	PC, Mac, UNIX, Linux	One of the most popular formats for desktop and streaming Web videos
MPEG (Moving Pictures Experts Group)	.mpg or .mpeg	PC, Mac, UNIX, Linux	Versions include MPEG1, MPEG2, and MPEG4; used for desktop video, PDA video, and streaming Web video
RealMedia	.rm	PC, Mac, UNIX, Linux	Produced by RealNetworks, a popular format for streaming Web videos
ASF (Advanced Systems Format)	.asf or .wmv	PC	Container format for Microsoft's Windows Media Video (WMV) desktop, PDA, and streaming video
Flash Video	.flv	PC, Mac	Popular for Web-based video; requires Adobe Flash Player
VOB (Video Object)	.vob	Standalone DVD players, PCs, Macs, Linux	Industry-standard format for standalone DVD players

8

Which compression techniques should I use? Suppose you decide to store your video in an AVI container file for desktop viewing. You can compress the video stream using various codecs. A **codec** (compressor/ decompressor) is the software that compresses a video stream when a video is stored and decompresses the file when the video is played. Popular codecs include MPEG, Sorenson, Cinepak, DivX, and Windows Media Video.

Each codec uses a unique compression algorithm and allows you to specify the compression ratio or bit ratio. A **compression ratio** indicates the ratio of compressed data to uncompressed data. A video file with a high compression ratio, such as 35:1 has more compression, a smaller file size, and lower image quality than a file with a lower compression ratio, such a 5:1. Compression can be measured by **bitrate**, the number of bits required to display one second of video. A video with a bitrate of 340 Kbps will have less compression and better quality than a video with a bitrate of 150 Kbps.

It is important to understand that the codec used to compress a video also must be used to decompress the video when it is played. Videos intended for a widespread audience should use one of the codecs included in popular video players, such as QuickTime or Windows Media Player.

Video compression can be achieved by decreasing the frame rate, reducing the frame size, or using techniques similar to JPEG to compress the data stored for each frame. Temporal compression techniques can also be used to eliminate data that doesn't change from frame to frame.

Temporal compression is a technique that can be applied to video footage to eliminate redundant or unnecessary data between frames. For example, if you are working with a video of a "talking head," the background image is likely to contain lots of redundant information that doesn't change from one frame to the next.

As the temporal compression algorithm begins to analyze frames, the first frame becomes a **key frame** that contains all the data. Key frames are stored at preset intervals or whenever a cut, wipe, or transition changes the scene. As the compression algorithm analyzes subsequent frames in the video, it stores only the data that is different from data in the key frame.

The videos in Figure 8-50 illustrate the differences in image quality and file size that result from using various compression ratios and frame rates.

Uncompressed video

TERMINOLOGY NOTE

MPEG is potentially confusing because it is a file format and a codec. Files in MPEG format use the MPEG codec. Files in other formats, such as AVI and MOV, can also use the MPEG codec to compress file contents.

FIGURE 8-50

Different bitrates and frame rates can have a remarkable effect on video quality and file size.

Bitrate: 90 Kbps
Frame rate: 10
File size: 359 KB

▶ CLICK TO START

Bitrate: 448 Kbps
Frame rate: 15
File size: 1177 KB

▶ CLICK TO START

Bitrate: 928 Kbps
Frame rate: 30
File size: 2448 KB

▶ CLICK TO START

DESKTOP, PDA, AND WEB VIDEO

How are desktop videos used? Desktop videos are usually displayed on a computer screen with popular video player software, such as the RealMedia player, Windows Media Player, or Apple's QuickTime player. Desktop videos are typically stored on hard disk or CD, and they are sometimes sent as e-mail attachments.

Can I view movies on my PDA? Some PDAs and smartphones can be configured to play digital videos (Figure 8-51), including movie trailers, TV shows, and even feature-length movies. The device requires video or multimedia player software, such as Pocket TV or Windows Media Player, and storage capacity for the video file—usually on a solid-state memory card. Videos specially optimized for handheld devices can be downloaded from Web sites to your computer, then transferred to handheld storage and played. Popular formats for handheld video include MPEG and WMV.

FIGURE 8-51

You can watch digital videos on some PDAs and cell phones.

How do Web-based videos work? A video for a Web page is stored on a Web server in a file. Usually, a link for the video file appears on the Web page. When you click the link, the Web server transmits a copy of the video file to your computer. If you have the correct video player installed on your computer, the video appears on your computer screen.

The transfer of a digital video file from the Web to your computer can happen in one of two ways, depending on the video format. In one case, your computer waits until it receives the entire video file before starting to play it. For large video files, you might wait several minutes or more before the video starts. An alternative method, called **streaming video**, sends a small segment of the video to your computer and begins to play it. While this first segment plays, the Web server sends the next part of the file to your computer, and so on, until the video ends. With streaming video technology, your computer essentially plays the video while it continues to receive it.

How do I post a video to YouTube or a similar file-sharing site? YouTube is a video-sharing Web site which encourages members to upload, view, and rate video clips. YouTube and similar sites typically accept most popular video file formats directly from digital cameras, camcorders, and cell phones. Usually, however, you would edit the video first and save it in a standard video container format such as AVI, QuickTime Movie, or MPEG. YouTube automatically converts all submitted files into Flash Video format. Most sites have a length and file limitation, so you should check those before you finalize your video.

How do I add a video to my own Web pages? You can add two styles of video to your Web pages. The first style, called external video, simply displays a link to a video file. An HTML tag, such as <a href="ducks.avi"> 1.5 MB AVI Video </a>, indicates the file that contains the video (ducks.avi) and the text for the link (1.5 MB AVI Video). When the link is clicked, the video file is downloaded, and the video player is opened and displayed as a separate window in which the video appears.

A second style of Web video uses the <embed> tag to create an internal video, also referred to as an in-place video. Instead of opening a separate window for the video player, an internal video plays within the Web page. Figure 8-52 on the next page illustrates external and internal Web page videos.

8

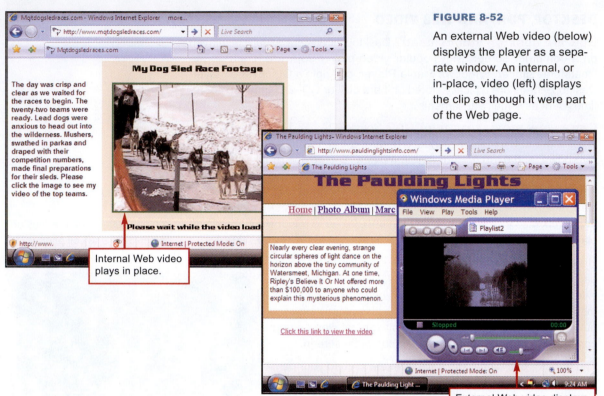

FIGURE 8-52

An external Web video (below) displays the player as a separate window. An internal, or in-place, video (left) displays the clip as though it were part of the Web page.

How does Internet connection speed affect Web videos? Although it is possible to play streaming videos over a dial-up connection, it is truly an unsatisfying experience. New compression techniques are able to jam more video data into a smaller package, but with a dial-up connection images tend to be fuzzy and motion is often jerky.

High-speed Internet connections provide much more bandwidth for streaming video. Videos designed to be transmitted over high-speed connections can play in a larger video window, use less compression, and display better image quality. Until everyone has a high-speed connection, however, many Web sites provide one video file that's optimized for dial-up connections and a better quality video file that's optimized for high-speed connections.

What are the best formats for Web videos? Today's most popular Web video formats include Flash Video, MPEG4, QuickTime Movie, Windows Movie, and RealMedia. All these formats offer streaming video and allow developers to adjust compression levels to produce file sizes optimized for dial-up or broadband connections.

DVD-VIDEO

Can I incorporate my digital videos onto DVDs with interactive menus like commercial movies? Suppose you've used video editing software to create a short documentary on sled dogs. You can package the completed video footage into a professional-style DVD that can be played on computer DVD drives (if your computer is equipped with DVD player software) or standalone DVD players. It can include interactive menus with options, such as Play Video, Select a Scene, and Special Features, that viewers can select using their DVD remote controls.

What equipment do I need? To create video DVDs, you need a writable DVD drive (sometimes called a DVD burner) plus software that includes tools for DVD menu creation and writing data onto a DVD-Video—a process sometimes called burning. These tools are offered by DVD authoring software, such as Adobe Encore, Sonic MyDVD, Nero, and Ulead DVD MovieFactory. Many video editing software packages and suites also include tools for creating DVD menus and burning projects onto DVDs.

What's the process for making a video DVD? To create a video DVD, you usually begin by selecting one or more completed videos that include soundtracks, transitions, titles, special effects, and so on. You then use DVD authoring software to design menus and buttons that viewers can use to navigate to specific parts of your video. To complete the project, you can test your project and then burn it to DVD.

What are my options for creating interactive DVD menus? A DVD menu is a screen that provides viewers with navigation tools to start a video, skip to specific scenes, play special features, and link to other menus. A typical DVD menu consists of a decorative background and option buttons that viewers can select using their DVD players' remote control. Static backgrounds are simply bitmap images, such as a frame from the video or an abstract design. Motion backgrounds display animations or video segments.

Option buttons can be a variety of shapes and sizes. They typically change appearance when selected. For example, when a viewer selects the Play button, it might light up or an icon might appear next to it.

Some DVD authoring software offers a selection of predesigned menu and button templates that you can easily incorporate with your videos. Your software might also provide the option to create your own backgrounds and buttons using graphics software, such as Adobe Photoshop or Microsoft Paint. Figure 8-53 illustrates a DVD menu being created using a simple DVD authoring software package.

FIGURE 8-53

DVD authoring software offers a selection of backgrounds and button styles for creating DVD menus.

CLICK TO START

Are menus easy to create? Yes, they just require a little advance planning. As you design the menu flow, remember that you want to provide viewers with a way to return to the main menu from each submenu. You might also want viewers to return to the main menu after viewing individual clips. If a submenu offers options for outtakes or other special features, you should provide a way for viewers to return to the submenu when the special feature ends. To help visualize the way your menus will work you can draw a diagram similar to the one in Figure 8-54.

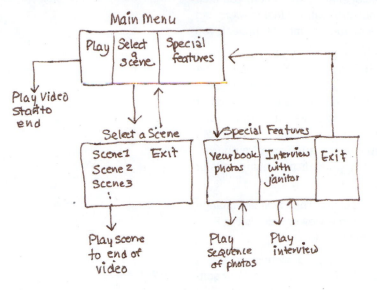

FIGURE 8-54

Sketching a diagram of the menus for your DVD can help you envision how viewers will navigate to selected scenes and special features.

How do I output my video to DVD? To create a DVD that can be viewed on a standalone DVD player, you have to output your video in DVD-Video format, which requires video encoded with MPEG2 and stored in VOB (video object) files. Your DVD authoring software can generate MPEG2-encoded video clips and menus, store them in VOB files, and lay them out on a DVD according to industry standards.

Most DVD authoring software can accomplish the MPEG encoding on the fly as it burns the DVD. This process takes time, however, so if you are burning more than one copy, or if you want to test your menu structure before burning the video onto a DVD, you might want to consider creating a DVD image.

What's a DVD image? A **DVD image** (sometimes called a DVD volume) is essentially a prototype of your DVD, but it is stored on your computer's hard disk. If you have space to store a DVD image, it is a good idea to make one before burning a DVD. You can use a DVD image for testing. You can also use the image to burn multiple DVDs without waiting for your software to prepare the files for each burn.

Can I simply copy a desktop video to a DVD using the Copy command? Desktop videos are typically stored in AVI or MOV format and most standalone DVD players are not equipped to handle those formats. So, although you can use the Copy command to copy MOV and AVI files to a DVD and distribute them, these files can be viewed on most computers, but not on all DVD players.

Even copying files stored in MPEG format might not produce a DVD that works in a standalone player. The DVD-Video format specification requires a specific layout for data on the DVD surface. The method you use to copy computer data files does not produce the required layout, so most DVD players will not be able to play the video.

How do I test my DVD image? Your DVD is ready for production and distribution if the video quality looks good and the menus work correctly. Use the tips listed below to test your DVD on your computer before you burn a DVD.

- Test each button to make sure it links to the correct clip.

- Play each clip to the end and make sure it returns to the correct menu when completed.

- Watch the video carefully and look for any poor quality segments with distracting artifacts, such as blurs or halos. Artifacts can sometimes be removed by revisiting your MPEG coding options.

- Listen to the soundtrack to make sure the audio is clear, smooth, and synchronized with the video.

Does it make a difference if I use recordable or rewritable DVDs? Commercial DVD movies are stamped onto DVD-ROM disks during the manufacturing process—something you can't do with your computer's DVD drive. Your computer can burn data on DVD-R, DVD+R, or DVD-RW disks. Because the DVD industry has not achieved a single media standard, some standalone DVD players—particularly those manufactured before 2004—are not able to read one or more of these disk types. DVD+R and DVD-R seem to be compatible with the widest variety of DVD players, whereas DVD-RWs seem to be the least compatible. Before you distribute your DVDs make sure you test them in a standalone DVD player.

> **TERMINOLOGY NOTE**
>
> In the world of video production, an artifact is any visible degradation in the image quality, such as shimmering where contrasting colors meet or backgrounds that become wavy during fast pans or zooms.

QuickCheck

8

1. _____ video refers to digital videos constructed and displayed using a personal computer.

2. The process of converting analog video signals into digital format is referred to as video _____.

3. The size of a video file can be reduced by three techniques: shrinking the size of the video window, reducing the _____ rate, and compressing the video data.

4. Compressing a video at a ratio of 35:1 produces higher quality than compressing it at a 5:1 ratio. True or false? _____

5. PDA videos are stored in MP3 files, similar to those used on portable audio players. True or false? _____

6. Some Web pages feature _____ video, which sends a small segment of the video to your computer and begins to play it. While this first segment plays, the Web server sends the next part of the file to your computer, and so on, until the video ends.

7. DVD-Video requires files in _____ format.

 CHECK ANSWERS

Digital Rights Management

THE SECURITY SECTIONS of earlier chapters looked at security from the user perspective. In contrast, the security section for this chapter examines the techniques used by content providers to protect digital media from unlicensed duplication and use. Pirating music and movies is a multi-billion dollar worldwide activity that is increasingly controlled by organized crime. Legitimate content providers are taking steps to reduce piracy by prosecuting digital pirates and using digital rights management technologies to deter duplication. Unfortunately, technical measures taken to reduce illicit duplication can be inconvenient for legitimate users. In this section, you'll learn about DRM technologies you may have already encountered and some that are likely to affect your ability to use digital media in the future.

DRM BASICS

What is DRM? **Digital rights management** (DRM) is a collection of techniques used by copyright holders to limit access and use of digital content. Because DRM is primarily used to protect products of the entertainment industry, in the context of DRM, **digital content** (or simply content) usually refers to movies, music, e-books, and computer games.

Digital content is accessed by means of a player. Keep in mind that the term *player* can refer to a hardware device or software. Software players include familiar media players, such as iTunes, Windows Media Player, and QuickTime. Hardware players include standalone devices such as CD players, VCRs, DVD players, and portable music players. Computer devices, such as CD, DVD, and Blu-ray drives, are also considered players, though they require software to play back content.

Every hardware device and software program that interacts with digital content poses a potential vulnerability that can be exploited by pirates. Software that encrypts content can be cracked, signals that travel from one device to another can be intercepted, and when all else fails, the **analog hole** allows pirates to capture content by using a microphone to record songs as they are output to speakers or using a camcorder to film movies as they are projected in a movie theater.

In response to the creativity and sheer stubbornness of digital pirates, modern DRM systems include layers of protection, with the goal of controlling content from its distribution point through to its playback (Figure 8-55).

How does DRM affect my use of digital media? The average consumer uses a variety of electronic devices to play digital content. Many of these devices offer convenient time and place shifting, but DRM technologies can curtail their use.

FIGURE 8-55

The threat of legal penalties has not been enough to discourage digital piracy, so copyright holders are working on increasingly sophisticated ways to prevent illegal copying.

The unauthorized reproduction or distribution of this copyrighted work is illegal. Criminal copyright infringement, including infringement without monetary gain, is investigated by the FBI and is punishable by up to 5 years in federal prison and a fine of $250,000.

Time shifting is the process of recording a broadcast, such as a television show, so that it can be played back at a more convenient time. **Place shifting** allows media that originates in one place to be accessed from another place without changing the device on which it is stored (Figure 8-56). Place shifting is often achieved using computer networks, as when you view a cable television broadcast sent from your Wi-Fi equipped set-top box to your Wi-Fi equipped notebook.

Format shifting is the process of converting media files from a format suitable to one device to a format suitable for a different kind of device. A common use of format shifting is ripping audio tracks from a CD and converting them into MP3 format for playback on a portable audio device, such as an iPod.

Is DRM effective? DRM has not lived up to the expectation of copyright holders and it has disappointed consumers by curtailing their options for using content they have legitimately purchased. Digital piracy continues to run rampant and hackers stubbornly continue to devise work-arounds to defeat DRM. There is evidence that the incidence of casual copying has decreased, but some of this casual copying might actually be legitimate, fair use. The Issue section of this chapter looks at the relationship between DRM technologies and the concept of fair use.

To judge whether DRM technologies are effective and to gauge their effect on consumers, it is helpful to take a more detailed look at the evolution of DRM technologies from their first applications for scrambling cable television signals to more recent applications designed to protect online delivery of digital content.

SIGNAL SCRAMBLING AND DIGITAL WATERMARKS

What is signal scrambling? **Signal scrambling** is a term commonly used for obscuring cable or satellite television images until they are unscrambled by a set-top box or other authorized mechanism. The first scrambling systems were based on various proprietary algorithms that transmitted unsynchronized video signals designed to be resynchronized by a set-top box. With the advent of digital content, scrambling was implemented by encrypting the digital bits of the signal.

It is technically possible to build a device to descramble signals, but it is illegal to use one. For the most part, consumers accept signal scrambling technology with the understanding that once signals are received and unscrambled, they can be recorded for later viewing. DRM technologies such as digital watermarks, however, can limit the use of unscrambled content.

What is a digital watermark? A **digital watermark** is a pattern of bits inserted at various places in an image or a content stream that can be used to track, identify, verify, and control content use. Watermarks, such as broadcast flags, are usually imperceptible to viewers or listeners, but can be picked up by compliant devices.

A **broadcast flag** is a set of bits inserted into the data stream of digital television or radio programs that specifies how the stream can and cannot be used. Broadcast flags can prohibit a program from being unencrypted or

8

copied. They can limit copies to low resolution, such as by reducing high-definition video to the resolution of a standard television. In addition, broadcast flags can prevent fast forwarding past commercials.

Broadcast flags are intended to combat indiscriminate use of digital video recorders, such as TiVos. In the United States, many HDTVs are equipped to recognize broadcast flags, but the number of consumers who own HDTVs is not high, making it unlikely for broadcast flags to be widely used in the near future. Nevertheless, consumers should be aware that future implementations of broadcast flags are possible and can affect use of digital media.

CD COPY PROTECTION

How does digital rights management affect music and other media distributed on CDs?
Compact disc (CD) technology was introduced in 1982. It was originally developed for storing digital audio and is still a primary distribution method for recorded music. CDs adhere to a standardized format commonly called the Red Book, which implements DRM with a data bit that can be set to "no-copy." The Red Book no-copy bit is easy to defeat, so the recording industry has attempted to use more robust DRM technologies, such as copy protection.

What is copy protection?
Copy protection refers to technologies designed to prohibit consumers from copying content. CDs with copy protection cannot be duplicated and music that is ripped to another format does not play back correctly. Copy protection technologies include Copy Control, CDS (Cactus Data Shield), and XCP (Extended Copy Protection).

How does CD copy protection work?
Most CD copy protection technologies rely on two techniques: multiple sessions and corrupted data. A copy protected CD with multiple sessions is essentially divided into two parts called sessions. The first session contains an audio stream of recorded music that has been intentionally corrupted. The second session contains a computer program that can essentially reverse the corruption.

The audio stream is corrupted by replacing certain frames (about 1/75th of a second of music) with data, rather than sound. Dedicated CD players simply skip the data, but computer CD drives tend to play the data frames, resulting in loud pops and other audio glitches. On some drives, the CD seems to pause every few seconds while the drive attempts to make sense of the data. Ripping and pirating the corrupted audio tracks is pointless because they don't play back correctly. To filter out the corrupted data, your computer requires specialized software. This software is stored as the CD's data session and is installed the first time that you use the CD (Figure 8-57).

FIGURE 8-57

Copy protected CDs contain a software program that strips out intentionally corrupted data.

Copy protected CD contains music and computer software

The corrupted audio stream makes popping sounds

Software is installed on hard drive the first time CD is accessed

Software filters out intentionally corrupted data

How do I know if a CD is copy protected? Some distributors, such as Amazon.com, do their best to identify copy protected CDs in product descriptions. The existence of a data session and intentionally corrupted audio on copy protected CDs does not adhere to the Red Book standard for audio CDs, so the official CDDA logo is missing on the CD packaging. Most copy protected CDs also carry warnings that they might not function on some equipment, such as car CD players.

How prevalent is CD copy protection? Copy protected CDs have become much less common since the 2005 Sony BMG rootkit incident. Several Sony BMG CDs were copy protected by software that limited duplication to three copies. The copy protection software was surreptitiously installed and once installed used a rootkit to conceal itself. Not only was the software installed without user consent, once installed, the software made consumers' computers more open to Internet viruses. The copy protection software had no uninstall routine and if users deleted the files, their CD drives no longer worked. After a high-profile rash of negative publicity, the CDs were recalled and music publishers quietly began to abandon copy protection.

DVD DRM

Do DVDs and CDs use similar DRM? The first DVD players were introduced in 1996 primarily as a distribution medium for mainstream movies. Based on prior experience with CD and VHS piracy, technologies to discourage piracy were built into the DVD standard from its inception.

Unlike CD DRM, protection for DVD content did not have to be tacked onto the distribution media as corrupted data and rootkits. DRM designed for DVDs could take advantage of more sophisticated technologies both on disks and on players. The major DRM technologies for DVDs include copy generation management, analog output protection, and CSS. These technologies can be implemented individually or together to provide layers of protection.

What is copy generation management? **Copy generation management** is a digital watermark that specifies the number of times a content stream can be duplicated. Compliant players recognize the watermark and abide by it. With the watermark set to no copy, for example, a video stream cannot be copied to other compliant devices. If a content stream carries a one-copy-only watermark, compliant devices can make a copy, but will change the watermark to no-copies-allowed. As a result, second generation copies cannot be used to make additional copies (Figure 8-58).

FIGURE 8-58

Watermarks are read by devices that comply with the limitations embedded in the content stream.

Original DVD with   Compliant DVD burner   DVD copy now contains   Compliant DVD burner
one-copy-only   do-not-copy watermark   will not copy the DVD
watermark

What is an analog protection system? An **analog protection system** is any DRM technology that interjects signals into the video stream to prevent analog output from being copied. As used in the context of protecting DVDs, an analog protection system places signals within the content stream that disrupt playback on VCRs by making the image appear dim or scrambled. The intended use of this technology is to prevent DVD video streams from being output to videotape, then being converted back into digital format.

What is CSS? **CSS** (Content Scramble System) is a digital rights management technology designed to encrypt and control the use of content stored on DVDs. It is intended to render DVD copies nonfunctional and enforces additional restrictions, such as region coding. CSS is the most well-known DRM technology for DVDs.

How does CSS work? CSS technology is a type of authentication-and-encryption DRM technology built into standalone DVD players and computer DVD players/burners. A key aspect of CSS is the use of authentication keys that allow a DVD disk and player to prove to each other that they are legitimately licensed to use CSS. Only after authentication can the encrypted video stream be decoded.

DVD players are manufactured with a built-in set of CSS keys. When a DVD is inserted, the player runs through every key until one unlocks the disc. Once this disc key is known, the player uses it to retrieve a title key from the disc. The title key allows the player to unscramble the DVD video stream (Figure 8-59).

Title key

1. DVD Player decrypts title key using one of 400 pre-programmed keys

Key to decrypt content stream

DVD protected by CSS

2. The title key contains a unique key to decrypt the data stream

DVD Player

FIGURE 8-59

In addition to limiting playback to compliant devices, CSS prevents DVDs from being successfully duplicated by end-users using standard copy utilities. Decryption keys are stored on a hidden area of the DVD which is not copied to the new DVD during duplication.

What is a region code? The CSS authentication process includes checking region codes. A DVD **region code** specifies a geographical area of legitimate use for DVD disks and players. For example, the United States, Canada, Bermuda, and U.S. territories make up region 1. DVD players are sold according to region, so in Canada consumers purchase region 1 DVD players, while consumers in India purchase players for region 5. A DVD player will play only DVDs encoded for its region. Region codes allow the film industry to charge higher prices in some countries than others without worrying about cheaper versions affecting sales in more expensive regions.

Has CSS been cracked? Soon after CSS appeared, hackers were able to crack it. **DeCSS** is the most well-known software for decrypting DVD content that is protected by CSS. New DRM technologies, such as RipGuard, have emerged as replacements for CSS, but most of these have also been cracked. Although DeCSS and other tools for bypassing DVD protection are widely available on the Internet, their distribution and use is illegal in the United States or other countries with similar copyright laws or treaties.

What about copy protection for Blu-ray and HD-DVDs? Like earlier DVD standards, Blu-ray and HD-DVD incorporate layers of DRM technologies, but they use AACS instead of CSS for authorization and encryption. **AACS** (Advanced Access Content System) is a DRM technology designed to encrypt and protect content on optical disks. Additional DRM layers include BD+ and BD ROM Mark.

How does AACS work? Like CSS, AACS works with an encrypted content stream. AACS, however, uses a much stronger encryption key, which makes it quite difficult for hackers to break the encryption using brute force methods. Another difference between the two methods is that CSS uses a shared set of encryption keys, and all devices of a specific model use the same key. In contrast, AACS compliant devices each contain their own unique set of keys and these keys can be revoked if a player is found to be compromised. The concept of **authorization and revocation** can be applied to hardware devices and software players to give licensing bodies the means to keep non-complying players off the market and deny further access to complying devices that have become compromised (Figure 8-60).

FIGURE 8-60

AACS depends on authentication and revocation built into devices and content.

In addition to encryption, AACS protects content with two types of digital watermarks, a theatrical mark and a consumer mark. The theatrical mark is inserted into the soundtrack of films actually shown in theaters. If a home player detects this watermark, playback stops because the disk is suspected to be one created using an illicitly borrowed professional reel of the film. The second AACS watermark is inserted into legitimate DVDs sold to consumers. If the mark is not detected on a DVD that is supposed to have it, playback will terminate.

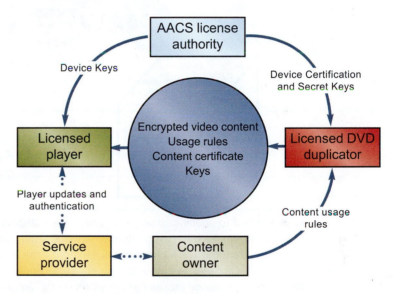

Do video disc DRM technologies make my computer less secure? DVD publishers can use DRM to prevent consumers from making a copy of a DVD in case the original is damaged, force viewers to watch the ubiquitous FBI warning, and prohibit viewers from fast-forwarding through commercials. Using DRM in such a manner annoys consumers, but does not threaten the security of their computers. So far, the technologies used to protect video disc content have not opened security holes that are widely exploited by hackers.

DRM FOR DIGITAL DOWNLOADS

Can DRM protect downloaded files? As you have learned so far, DRM technologies can be applied to broadcasts and to content distributed on physical storage media, such as CDs and DVDs. DRM also plays a role in controlling the use of downloaded audio, video, and e-book files.

Free file-sharing sites popular in the 1990s had a devastating effect on the recording industry. Free sites still exist, but the recording industry is waging war against site operators and users. In addition to legal recourse, the recording industry reportedly pays private firms to seed file-sharing

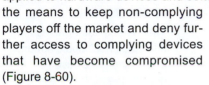

networks with fake versions of popular copyrighted songs, so that it is difficult to find genuine versions. After litigation shut down many free sites, a new crop of legitimate sites offered to pay royalties by charging customers for downloads.

Many consumers seem content to pay a dollar or less to download a song from a legitimate online music store, so iTunes, Zune, and others do a booming business. Part of the agreement between the recording industry and online music stores is that music downloads have to be distributed in a way that prevents unauthorized copying and sharing. Apple uses a DRM technology called **FairPlay** to control music stored in protected AAC format and downloaded from the iTunes store. Microsoft supplies DRM technologies for several online music stores, including Zune.

How does FairPlay work? FairPlay packages iTunes in a standard M4P container format as described in Figure 8-61.

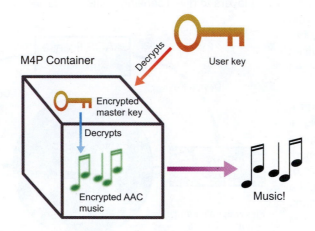

FairPlay user keys are tied to specific computers, which are authorized to play the track. You can authorize other computers to play the songs you've purchased and you can deauthorize a computer, for example, before you send it for repair or sell it. Changes in authorization require a connection to the iTunes store where a database stores customer accounts, authorized machine identifiers, a list of purchased tracks, and user keys.

User accounts add a dimension to DRM technology that is not possible with standalone CD and DVD players. Your keys open only your copy of downloaded content and may allow illicit copies of songs or players to be traced back to their source. This concept, sometimes referred to as **DRM individualization**, has become a key component of digital rights management for downloaded content.

iTunes software is stored on subscriber computers and can be updated by Apple as necessary to plug vulnerabilities in its DRM. Subscribers are forced to install new versions of the iTunes software before they can continue to purchase content from the iTunes store. The iTunes EULA prohibits subscribers from attempting to "circumvent or modify any security technology or software" and Apple's policy is to aggressively prosecute anyone who develops or distributes software to bypass its DRM.

How does Windows Media DRM work? **Windows Media DRM** was developed by Microsoft to provide secure digital content delivery over networks and from Web sites such as the Zune Marketplace. Its purpose is similar to FairPlay—to make sure that digital music and movies can be used only by consumers who purchase them legitimately—but the two

FIGURE 8-61

The M4P container holds an encrypted AAC audio stream and a master key used to decrypt the audio. The master key is also encrypted, so before you can play iTunes music, you need a so-called user key that decrypts the master key. Each time you purchase an iTunes track, a unique user key is generated for your computer. The user key is stored on your computer so that you can decrypt the master key, which is then used to decrypt the track before you can play it.

▶ CLICK TO START

DRM technologies differ slightly. Like FairPlay, Windows Media DRM encrypts the content stream. The key is stored in an encrypted license, which unlike FairPlay is distributed separately. The digital media file contains an encrypted link to the license.

Files protected by Windows Media DRM can be distributed from a Web site, on a CD, or as an e-mail attachment. If you receive one of these files from a friend and try to access it, you will be prompted to get a license. This process of sharing files but forcing users to pay for licenses before accessing content is sometimes referred to as **super distribution**.

Files protected by Windows Media DRM can be accessed only when using a compliant hardware or software player. Before producing a compliant player, companies must be authorized by Microsoft. Authorization can be revoked from players that become compromised. Windows Media DRM is designed to be updatable. It has been cracked several times, but in every case quick updates from Microsoft have patched the vulnerabilities.

What about movie download sites? Movie download technology at legitimate online stores such as CinemaNow, Vongo, and MovieLink has lagged behind music downloads. Movie files are huge and take time to download—about 30 minutes for a low resolution version or more than an hour for DVD quality. Lengthy downloads are not only inconvenient for users, but also create a burden on servers that subsequently limits availability. In addition, movie download sites tend to have a somewhat skimpy selection, a factor that can be attributed in part to the reluctance of copyright holders to release content on a platform that seems so inherently easy for pirating.

DRM technologies such as watermarks and copy generation management are used in various ways to limit how you can use movies you've downloaded. At some movie download stores, content viewing is limited to your computer screen. At other sites, you are allowed to burn a limited number of DVDs. DRM can also limit the length of time you are allowed to view a movie. Often the limit is 24 hours, but some sites offer a 30-day or unlimited viewing window. Most movie download sites require a monthly subscription fee, so before you subscribe, carefully examine the Terms of Use and FAQs to become familiar with download and copy policies.

8

QuickCheck

SECTION E

1. _____ shifting is the process of recording a broadcast, such as a television show, so that it can be played back at a more convenient time.

2. A digital _____ inserted into an audio or video stream is imperceptible to users, but can be read by complying devices.

3. When first accessing a copy _____ audio CD, software is installed on your computer that essentially reverses the intentionally corrupted data inserted into the audio track.

4. _____ is the primary technology used to protect DVDs, but it was cracked soon after it was introduced. (Hint: Use the acronym.)

5. A key aspect of protecting content downloaded from online music and video stores is the concept of DRM _____ that ties decryption keys to a user account.

6. Microsoft DRM allows _____ distribution, a process whereby consumers can share protected files with friends, who are required to obtain their own license for accessing the content.

 CHECK ANSWERS

ISSUE

What Happened to Fair Use?

SUPPOSE YOU PURCHASE a music CD of your favorite recording group. Now you want to transfer the file to your computer, rip the best tracks, and transfer them to your portable audio player. But wait! That CD is copy protected and your computer CD drive won't read it. You purchased the disk. Can't you listen to the music on any device you choose? The answer depends on a concept called fair use.

Fair use is the right to use portions of copyrighted material without the permission of the copyright holder for purposes such as review, criticism, or parody. Under certain circumstances, fair use is also a successful defense for practices, such as time shifting, in which whole works are copied for limited personal use.

Exactly what does or does not constitute fair use, however, is only sketched out in copyright law. The precise nature of fair use is shaped by a somewhat amorphous cloud of court decisions covering situations and devices as disparate as player piano rolls, printer toner cartridges, video tape recorders, and file-sharing networks.

As one of the original time-shifting technologies, VCRs made it possible to set a recording time to capture movies and shows broadcast on television or cable channels. Digital video recorders, such as TiVo, make time shifting possible by saving content to a digital storage device, such as a hard disk.

The legal precedent for time shifting is the landmark 1984 Betamax case in which Universal Studios attempted to hold Sony Corp. of America liable for copyright infringement by people who used video recorders to tape movies from their televisions. The U.S. Supreme court sided with Sony and concluded that some instances of time shifting were legal.

The court's decision, however, was based on a definition of time-shifting as "the practice of recording a program to view it once at a later time." Note the word "once." The Betamax case did not offer legal precedent for copying and saving content for viewing multiple times. The Supreme Court was also influenced by testimony from copyright holders, such as the host of the well-known children's show *Mister Rogers' Neighborhood*, who welcomed the practice of time shifting. At the time, some TV guides even listed shows that networks permitted viewers to copy.

The proliferation of computer networks and streaming media has made place shifting a reality. You can, for example, view a cable television broadcast sent from your Wi-Fi equipped set-top box in your living room to your Wi-Fi equipped notebook out on the deck. The network, however, is transmitting a copy of the broadcast, a use of copyrighted work that is not explicitly allowed by copyright law in most countries. Therefore, unless a user agreement extends the basic rights granted by copyright law, place shifting would be considered to be a questionable practice.

So how about format shifting? Surely, it must be legal to rip tracks from a CD that you own, save them as an MP3 file, and play them on your iPod.

Many consumers believe that format shifting is a legal type of adaptation. That is true for computer software. According to section 117 of the United States Code "it is not an infringement for the owner of a copy of a computer program to make or authorize the making of another copy or adaptation."

It might seem that digital content is similar to computer programs because both are in digital formats that can be manipulated by computers. The courts, however, do not agree that the two are the same, so consumers do not have a right to format-shift movies and music. Copyright holders can, however, allow format shifting for specific works if they choose to do so.

It is interesting to consider the basis for the widely held belief that once a song or video has been purchased, consumers have a right to use it in any manner they please short of redistributing it for profit. Precedents for this belief exist in the music and publishing industries.

Although it is not well known, until 1971 no U.S. law protected recorded music. Sheet music and the underlying composition could be copyrighted, but a particular artist's performance was not. So-called "record pirates" could freely copy, say, an Elvis Presley recording without violating U.S. Federal law until an amendment to the copyright law was passed in 1971.

A statement accompanying the 1971 amendment seemed to approve of copying music for personal use: "Specifically, it is not the intention of Congress to restrain the home recording, from broadcasts or from tapes or records, of recorded performances, where the home recording is for private use and with no purpose of reproducing or otherwise capitalizing commercially on it."

Consumers are also familiar with copyright restrictions on printed books and have an expectation that digital media can be legally used in parallel ways. Readers expect to be able to carry a book with them to any location, read it at any time they like, use any type of reading light or reading glasses, loan the book to friends, and sell the book when they have finished using it. No wonder consumers are peeved when e-book vendors and other digital content providers use DRM technology to limit how much of an e-book can be viewed, whether the text can be printed or shared, and how long it can be viewed.

Although it is convenient to focus on the "once I buy it I can use it as I like" rationale, we tend to ignore situations in which our expectations about content use are more limited. For example, we do not expect that after attending a Widespread Panic concert, we are entitled to a free DVD or video of the performance. If we pay to see a movie at a theater, we don't then expect not to pay for the DVD or soundtrack CD when they are released.

From rock concerts to theaters, consumers are familiar with the idea that different venues and formats might require separate payments. Digital rights management technologies simply enforce this idea in practice.

Advocates of DRM even contend that it broadens the scope of what consumers can do with digital content because EULAs often provide consumers with more flexibility than today's copyright laws.

Circumventing DRM is possible and it would seem okay to do so for legitimate reasons, such as making backup or archival copies. However, the Digital Millennium Copyright Act makes it illegal to circumvent any technological measure that controls access to a work.

The current status of DRM seems to conflict with consumer fair-use expectations for manipulating and copying music, video, and other digital content. DRM technologies are still evolving, however, as are copyright laws. The Digital Millennium Copyright Act undergoes a formal review every three years, and a bill is circulating in Congress to revise the DMCA ban on circumventing DRM protection for noninfringing activities. Let's see whether the future produces a shift in the balance between fair use, digital rights management, and copyright law.

INFOWEBLINKS

You'll find information related to this controversy at the **Digital Rights Management InfoWeb**.

W **CLICK TO CONNECT**
www.course.com/np/concepts11/ch08

8

What Do You Think?

ISSUE

1. Have you had trouble using software, music CDs, or movie DVDs because of copy protection?

   ○ Yes   ○ No   ○ Not sure

2. In your opinion, do sites like the iTunes Music Store provide consumers with enough flexibility for copying files and creating playlists?

   ○ Yes   ○ No   ○ Not sure

3. Do you think digital rights management technologies are justified because of the high rate of piracy?

   ○ Yes   ○ No   ○ Not sure

   ▶ SAVE RESPONSES

COMPUTERS IN CONTEXT

Film

IN 1895, eager Parisians crowded into a busy café to watch the first public presentation of an exciting new invention—the Cinematograph. The 10-minute film, mostly scenes of everyday life, was a smashing success and ushered in the motion picture era. Early films were short, grainy, grayscale, and silent, but technology quickly improved. In the New York debut of *The Jazz Singer* (1927), Al Jolson spoke the first words in a feature film, "Wait a minute, wait a minute. You ain't heard nothin' yet!" The audience rose to its feet, applauding wildly. In 1935, RKO studios released *Becky Sharp*, the first feature-length movie filmed from beginning to end in Technicolor—a real milestone for the film industry.

Even before "talkies" and Technicolor, filmmakers sought ways to escape the bounds of reality through special effects. As early as 1925, directors such as Willis O'Brien used stop-motion photography to animate dinosaurs, giant gorillas, and sword-wielding skeletons. Special-effects technologies—miniatures, blue screens, puppets, claymation, and composite shots—were used with varying degrees of skill over the next 50 years. Films such as Stanley Kubrick's masterpiece, *2001: A Space Odyssey* (1968), and George Lucas's original *Star Wars* (1977) stretched these technologies to their limits, but audiences demanded even more spectacular, yet "realistic," effects.

In 1982, Disney released *TRON*, a movie about a computer programmer who becomes trapped in the depths of a computer where programs are human-like creatures that serve every whim of an evil Master Control Program. The movie included the first primi-tive attempts at computer-generated footage—30 minutes of computer-generated imagery (CGI) created by two Cray XMP supercomputers.

CGI uses rendering techniques to create a 3-D scene from a 2-D image, a camera angle, and a light source. Sophisticated algorithms determine how textures, colors, and shadows appear in the rendered scene. Camera angles can be changed at will, and fantastic effects can be created by bending or stretching the image, manipulating light, creating textures, and adding movement to the scene.

Rendered scenes can be set in motion with computer animation techniques. Manual animation requires a painstaking process called in-betweening, in which an artist draws a series of incrementally different images to produce the illusion of movement. Computers can easily generate in-between images and free up human animators for more challenging work.

A captivating animation special effect called morphing was first seen on the big screen in James Cameron's *Abyss* (1989) and later used in *Terminator 2* (1991) and other movies. Like in-betweening, morphing starts out with animators defining the morph's start and end points—for example, in *Terminator 2*, the liquid metal face of the T-1000 robot and actor Robert Patrick's face. The start and end points are rendered into digital images, and then the computer generates all the in-between images. Human animators tweak the images by inserting small discrepancies for a touch of less-than-perfect realism in the final footage.

Although the process might sound simple, morphing complex objects realistically and believably takes a tremendous amount of time and computer power. The five-minute morphing sequence in *Terminator 2* took special-effects company Industrial Light and Magic a year to create.

Memorable computer-generated scenes from 2002 blockbusters include the breathtaking aerial scenes in *Spiderman*, a furry blue monster called Sully careening downhill in *Monsters, Inc.*, and the endless army of Uruk-hai marching down the valley toward Helm's Deep in *The Two Towers*. Spiderman's acrobatic swing through Manhattan was generated with three professional rendering products: Maya, Houdini, and RenderMan. The Uruk-hai were created with MASSIVE, a custom program that gave each computer-generated warrior a unique sequence of actions. To individually animate each of Sully's 2,320,413 blue hairs, animators developed software called Fizt, a dynamic simulator.

Rendering, morphing, and other special-effects processing require sophisticated computer systems. Pixar Inc., the company that provided the technology behind *Toy Story*, *Shrek*, *Ratatouille*, and many other feature-length animated films, uses a cluster of computers dubbed the "RenderFarm." A movie such as *Toy Story* took more than 800,000 computer hours to produce using the RenderFarm. That might seem like a long time, but if Pixar animators had attempted to use a single-processor computer, it would have taken 43 years to finish the job!

Other CGI variations are being used for increasingly sophisticated effects. Special-effects guru John Gaeta developed bullet time and image-based rendering for *The Matrix* (1999). They have been used for stunning visual effects in movies such as *The Matrix: Reloaded* (2003), *The Matrix: Revolutions* (2003), and *Hero* (2002/2004). Bullet time produces reality-defying action sequences that slow time to a tantalizing crawl and then crank it back up to normal speed as the camera pivots rapidly around the scene. The effect requires a computer to meticulously trigger a circular array of more than 100 still cameras in sequence.

Image-based rendering generates a digital image based on photos of objects, scenes, or people. The 2-D photos can be digitally manipulated to create 3-D objects, eliminating the need for conventional CGI's computationally intensive 3-D wireframes and ray tracing.

Films, such as *Sky Captain And The World Of Tomorrow* (2004) and *Sin City* (2005), took green screen special effects to a new level. Filmed entirely

indoors on a sound stage, these movies used a technique called compositing that layers two or more video clips over each other and merges them into one image. Actors were filmed against a green background screen. During post-production, video editing software removed the background and layered in scenery created with CGI or from real footage on location.

Sin City is also notable as one of the first fully digital live action motion pictures. It was filmed in full color with high-definition digital cameras. The footage was converted to black and white and then color was reintroduced digitally with the use of a DLP Cinema projector.

Sophisticated animation and rendering techniques now come close to producing realistic human figures. Animations were once clearly two-dimensional and far from lifelike, but CGI renderings are becoming more difficult to distinguish from real actors. What might happen in the future is the subject of *Simone* (2002), starring Al Pacino as a washed-up director who is given a hard disk containing code for a computer-generated movie star. Pacino uses her as the leading lady in a string of hits, all the while keeping her identity secret. According to reviewer Leigh Johnson, it becomes clear that Simone, a computer-generated image, is more authentic than the people watching her. It is one of the film's main themes, expressed by Pacino's character: "Our ability to manufacture fraud now exceeds our ability to detect it."

The implications of computer-generated actors are just emerging. Not only do they blur the line between reality and fiction, but they also raise puzzling questions for actors and their agents, directors, and programmers. Is it possible to create CGI doubles for long-dead actors, such as Marilyn Monroe and James Dean? If so, who controls their use and profits from their work? Can aging actors sign contracts for use of their "young" CGI counterparts? Would it be legal and ethical for programmers to create and market virtual characters based on real actors or a compilation of the best traits of popular stars? As is often the case, new technologies present issues along with their benefits—issues you might want to consider the next time you watch a movie.

8

INFOWEBLINKS

To find more information on this topic, visit the **Computers and Film InfoWeb**.

W CLICK TO CONNECT

www.course.com/np/concepts11/ch08

New Perspectives Labs

On the BookOnCD

To access the New Perspectives labs for Chapter 8, start the BookOnCD, BookOnFlashDrive, or other NP11 BookOn product and then click the icon next to the lab title below.

▶ WORKING WITH BITMAP GRAPHICS

IN THIS LAB YOU'LL LEARN:

- How to identify common bitmap graphics file extensions
- How to capture an image from the Web
- How to find the properties of a graphic
- How to eliminate red eye and manipulate brightness, contrast, and sharpness of photos
- How to make a photo look "old"
- How to select a palette and apply a dithering technique
- How to prepare graphics for the Web and e-mail attachments
- The effects of lossy compression

LAB ASSIGNMENTS

1. Start the interactive part of the lab. Make sure you've enabled Tracking if you want to save your QuickCheck results. Perform each lab step as directed, and answer all the lab QuickCheck questions. When you exit the lab, your answers are automatically graded and your results are displayed.

2. Use the Start button to access the All Programs menu for the computer you typically use. Make a list of the available bitmap graphics software.

3. Capture a photographic image from a digital camera, scanner, or Web page. Save it as "MyGraphic." Open the image using any available graphics software. Use this software to discover the properties of the graphic. Indicate the source of the graphic, and then describe its file format, file size, resolution, and color depth.

4. Prepare this graphics file to send to a friend as an e-mail attachment that is smaller than 200 KB. Describe the steps that were required.

5. Suppose you want to post the image from #4 on a Web page. Make the necessary adjustments to file size and color depth. Describe the resulting graphic in terms of its resolution, color depth, palette, and dithering.

Key Terms

Make sure you understand all the boldfaced key terms presented in this chapter. If you're using the NP11 BookOnCD, BookOnFlashDrive, or other NP11 BookOn product, you can use this list of terms as an interactive study activity. First, try to define a term in your own words, and then click the term to compare your definition with the definition presented in the chapter.

24-bit bitmap, 437
32-bit bitmap, 437
3-D graphics, 449
AAC, 424
AACS, 469
AIFF, 424
Analog hole, 464
Analog protection system, 468
Animated GIF, 448
ASF, 457
Audio compression, 423
Authorization and revocation, 469
AVI, 457
Bitmap graphic, 430
bitrate, 458
BMP, 442
Broadcast flag, 465
Codec, 458
Color palette, 437
compression ratio, 458
Container formats, 457
Copy generation management, 467
Copy protection, 466
Cropping, 435
CSS, 468
DeCSS, 468
Desktop video, 452
Digital audio, 422
Digital camera, 431
Digital content, 464
Digital rights management, 464
Digital signal processor, 424
Digital video, 452
Digital video recorder, 455
Digital watermark, 465
Digitizing tablet, 446
Drawing software, 446

DRM individualization, 470
DVD image, 462
DVD-Video, 452
FairPlay, 470
File compression utility, 440
Flash, 448
Flash Video, 457
Format shifting, 465
Frame rate, 456
GIF, 442
Gradient, 447
Grayscale palette, 438
Image compression, 439
JPEG, 442
Key frame, 458
Linear editing, 456
Lossless compression, 439
Lossy compression, 439
Megapixel, 433
Metafile, 447
MIDI, 426
MIDI sequence, 426
Monochrome bitmap, 436
MP3, 424
MPEG, 457
Nonlinear editing, 456
Paint software, 430
PCX, 442
PDA video, 452
Phoneme, 428
Pixel interpolation, 435
Pixelated, 435
Place shifting, 465
PNG, 443
Portable audio player, 425
QuickTime Movie, 457
Rasterization, 447

RAW, 442
Ray tracing, 449
RealAudio, 424
RealMedia, 457
Region code, 468
Rendering, 449
Resolution dependent, 435
Run-length encoding, 439
Sampling rate, 423
Scanner, 431
Signal scrambling, 465
Sound card, 423
Speech recognition, 428
Speech synthesis, 428
Streaming audio, 425
Streaming video, 459
Super distribution, 471
SVG, 448
Synthesized sound, 426
System palette, 438
Temporal compression, 458
Text-to-speech software, 428
TIFF, 442
Time shifting, 465
Tracing software, 447
True Color bitmap, 437
Vector graphic, 444
Video capture, 454
Videoconferencing camera, 453
VOB, 457
Wave, 424
Wavetable, 426
Web palette, 438
Web-based video, 452
Windows Media DRM, 470
Wireframe, 449
WMA, 424

8

Interactive Summary

To review important concepts from this chapter, fill in the blanks to best complete each sentence. When using the NP11 BookOnCD or other BookOn product, click the Check Answers buttons to automatically score your answers.

SECTION A: Music, voice, and sound effects can all be recorded and digitally stored as [_____] audio. To digitally record sound, [_____] of the sound are collected at periodic intervals and stored as numeric data. High-quality sound is usually sampled at 44.1 [_____], and each stereo sample requires 32 bits of storage space. To conserve space, radio-quality recordings of speaking voices are often recorded at lower sampling rates. A computer's [_____] card is responsible for transforming the bits stored in an audio file into music, sound effects, and narrations. It contains digital [_____] processing circuitry that transforms bits into analog sound, records analog sounds as digital bits, and handles audio compression. Digital audio file formats include Wave, Audio Interchange Format, RealAudio, AAC, WMA, and MP3. Most portable audio players work with MP3 format or with the [_____] format, used for the .m4p files at the iTunes Music Store.

MIDI music is [_____] sound that is artificially created. Unlike digital audio sound files, which contain digitized recordings of real sound passages, MIDI files contain [_____] for creating the pitch, volume, and duration of notes made by musical instruments. MIDI files are typically much smaller than digital audio files for similar musical passages, so they are ideal for Web pages. However, MIDI music tends to lack the full resonance of symphony-quality sound that can be achieved with digital audio. Speech [_____] is the process by which machines, such as computers, produce sound that resembles spoken words. Speech [_____] refers to the ability of machines to "understand" spoken words.

 CHECK ANSWERS

SECTION B: A [_____] graphic is composed of a grid of dots, and the color of each dot is stored as a binary number. Both scanners and cameras produce images in bitmap format. The dimensions of the grid that forms a bitmap graphic is referred to as its [_____]. High-resolution graphics typically produce better image quality than low-resolution graphics, but require more storage space. It is possible to change the resolution and/or the file size of a bitmap graphic, but because bitmaps are resolution [_____], these changes can reduce image quality. For example, enlarging a bitmap requires your computer to fill in missing pixels, which often results in a jagged or [_____] image. As a general rule, images that you intend to print should remain at full size and resolution. When sending bitmap files as e-mail attachments, they can be [_____] in size or resolution to produce a file that is less than 500 KB.

Color [_____] refers to the number of colors available for use in an image. For example, a bitmap graphic composed of 256 colors requires only [_____] bits to store the data for each pixel, whereas 24 bits are required for each pixel in a [_____] Color graphic. Grayscale, system, and Web palettes use eight bits to represent each pixel. Image [_____] shrinks the size of a graphics file. [_____] compression permanently removes data, but [_____] compression shrinks files without removing any data. Popular bitmap graphics formats include BMP, PCX, TIFF, GIF, JPEG, RAW, and PNG. Of these formats, GIF, JPEG, and PNG are supported by most Web browsers.

 CHECK ANSWERS

SECTION C: Unlike a bitmap graphic, created by superimposing a grid of pixels over an image, a [_____] graphic consists of a set of instructions for creating a picture. These graphics are created by using a type of graphics software called [_____] software. They are stored as a collection of [_____] and their corresponding sizes, colors, and positions. You can identify these graphics by their flat cartoon-like appearance and their file extensions: .wmf, .ai, .dxf, .eps, .svf, and .svg. A vector graphic can be converted into a bitmap by a process called [_____]. Once converted, however, the resulting graphic loses the object-editing qualities it had in its vector state. Two vector graphics formats, [_____] and Flash, are popular for Web-based graphics. 3-D graphics are stored as a set of instructions that contain the locations and lengths of lines that form a [_____] for a 3-D object. These lines form a framework that can be covered by colored, patterned, and textured surfaces. This process, called [_____], produces a bitmap image of the 3-D object. [_____] tracing adds highlights and shadows to the image. 3-D graphics can be animated to produce special effects for movies and animated characters for 3-D computer games.

► CHECK ANSWERS

SECTION D: Videos that are constructed and played on a personal computer are called [_____] videos. Video footage can be stored on a computer's [_____] disk for editing, and then it can be transferred to CDs, DVDs, or videotape. A video is composed of a series of bitmap graphics. Each one is called a [_____]. Popular desktop video file [_____] include AVI, QuickTime Movie, MPEG-4, RealMedia, Windows Media, ASF, Flash Video, Ogg, and VOB. When video footage is filmed using an analog camera, it can be converted into digital format by a video [_____] device. Footage from a digital video camera requires no conversion and can be streamed directly from camera to computer through a serial, [_____], or USB port. Raw video footage contains a huge amount of data. The size of a video file can be reduced by three techniques, including shrinking the size of the video window, reducing the [_____] rate, and [_____] the video data. A [_____] is the software or hardware that compresses and decompresses files, such as graphics and videos. Videos can be added to Web pages by using techniques such as [_____] video, which transmits the first segment of a video, begins to play it, and then continues to transfer additional segments. Digital videos can be transferred to DVDs, which use files in the [_____] format.

► CHECK ANSWERS

SECTION E: Digital [_____] management is a collection of techniques used by copyright holders to limit access to and use of digital content. DRM technologies can limit or prevent convenient [_____], place, and format shifting. A digital [_____] is a DRM technology that is inserted into the content stream in such a way that it is imperceptible to users, but can be recognized by complying devices. Copy [_____] DRM for CDs depends on intentionally [_____] data and CD-based software. The major DRM technology to protect DVD content called [_____] was cracked shortly after it was introduced. A somewhat more sophisticated DRM technology called [_____] is used on Blu-ray and HD-DVD. The concept of authorization and [_____] can be applied to hardware devices and software players to give licensing bodies the means to keep non-complying players off the market and deny further access to complying devices that have become compromised. Content downloaded from online music and video stores is heavily protected by DRM technologies, such as Apple's [_____] and Microsoft's Windows Media DRM.

► CHECK ANSWERS

8

Interactive Situation Questions

Apply what you've learned to some typical computing situations. When using the NP11 BookOnCD, BookOnFlashDrive, or any other NP11 BookOn product, you can type your answers, and then use the Check Answers button to automatically score your responses.

1. Suppose you are creating an English-as-a-Second-Language Web page and you want to add links to sound files that pronounce English phrases. Would it be better to store the files in Wave or MIDI format? ⬚

2. Imagine that you're a musician and you are asked to synthesize some music for the opening screen of a Web site. For this project, you would most likely work with ⬚ music.

3. Suppose you visit a Web site that allows you to enter sentences, and then it reads the sentences back to you. The site even gives you a choice of a female or male voice. You assume that this site uses speech ⬚ technology.

4. You have an old photograph that you want to incorporate in a brochure for your antiques business. To convert the photo into digital format, you use a(n) ⬚ .

5. Imagine that you are preparing a series of bitmap graphics for a Web site. To decrease the download time for each graphic, you can remove pixels or reduce the color ⬚ .

6. You've taken a photo with a high resolution digital camera and you want to send it as an e-mail attachment. You decide to use PKZIP to ⬚ the image into a more manageable size.

7. Suppose you are designing a logo for a client. You know the design will undergo several revisions, and you understand

that the logo will be used at various sizes. You decide it would be best to use drawing software to create the logo as a(n) ⬚ graphic.

8. After you finish arranging video clips and adding a soundtrack, you can select a video file format and a compression technique. For example, you might store the video in AVI container format and use the Cinepak ⬚ to compress the file.

9. After purchasing a CD of your favorite rock group you try to rip one of the tracks to your computer and convert it to MP3 format. When you play the file on your computer, you notice loud pops in the audio that indicate that the CD was probably copy ⬚ .

10. Your friend sends you an e-mail attachment containing a music video from the Zune site. Your ability to access the file after paying for your own license is an example of ⬚ distribution.

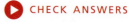 ▶ CHECK ANSWERS

Interactive Practice Tests

Practice tests that consist of 10 multiple-choice, true/false, and fill-in-the-blank questions are available on both the NP11 BookOn products and the NP11 Web site. The questions are selected at random from a large test bank, so each time you take a test, you'll receive a different set of questions. Your tests are scored immediately, and you can print study guides that help you find the correct answers for any questions that you missed.

 ▶ CLICK TO START

Study Tips

Study Tips help you to organize and consolidate the information in a unit by making lists, outlines, charts, and sketches. You can use paper and pencil or word processing software to complete most of the Study Tip activities.

1. Make sure you can use your own words to correctly answer each of the red focus questions that appear throughout the chapter.

2. Make a list of 10 digital audio applications and indicate whether each one would use Wave or MIDI.

3. Make a list of the file extensions that were mentioned in this chapter and group them according to digital media type: bitmap graphic, vector graphic, digital video, digital audio, and MIDI. Circle any formats that are used on the Web.

4. Make a list of the software mentioned in this chapter, indicating the type of task that it helps you accomplish.

5. Describe the devices that transfer photos from a digital camera to a computer.

6. Describe how resolution and color depth contribute to the size of a graphics file.

7. Summarize how you would prepare bitmap graphics for the following uses: e-mail attachment, Web page, desktop publishing, and printed photo.

8. Explain how a computer monitor displays color, and how that relates to the way it stores a color palette.

9. Explain how the concept of layering relates to your ability to modify a vector graphic.

10. Make a list of the advantages and disadvantages of bitmaps and vector graphics.

11. Make a series of quick sketches that illustrates the evolution of a 3-D graphic from wireframe to rendered image, and to ray-traced image.

12. Explain the different procedures required to transfer analog or digital video from camera to computer.

13. Define the differences between linear and non-linear editing.

14. List three ways in which you can reduce the file size of a desktop video.

15. Explain how streaming audio and video work, and contrast them to non-streaming technology.

16. Use your own words to make a list of the steps required to burn video onto a DVD that can be viewed on standalone DVD players.

17. In your own words describe each type of compression mentioned in the chapter.

18. Explain how specific DRM technologies are used to prevent consumers from a) recording television broadcasts, b) making a copy of a music CD, c) ripping tracks from a music CD, d) copying a DVD movie, and e) watching a movie captured on TiVo and streamed over a network to a PC.

19. Fill in the blanks on the concept map shown below to show the hierarchy of digital media described in this chapter.

Concept Map

8

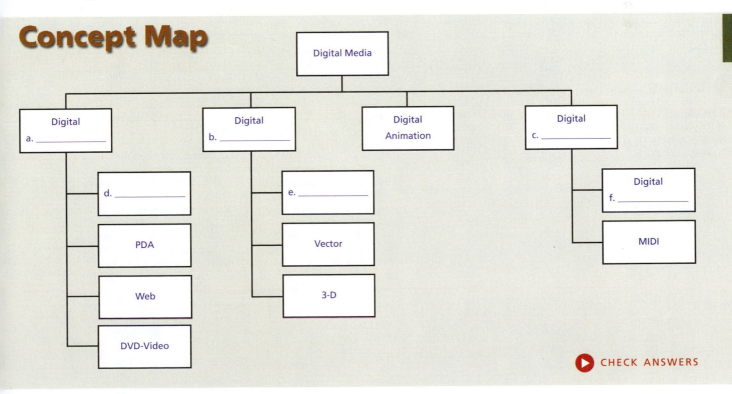

CHECK ANSWERS

Projects

CRITICAL THINKING

Copyright laws are changing as digital sound, image, and video technologies evolve and become easier to use. Although the courts seem to clearly hold that it is illegal to copy media for profit, they are not as clear about the acceptability of modifications. For example, video editing software makes it relatively simple for people to clip out parts of movies they find to be objectionable for themselves or their children. Should it be legal to do so for personal use? What if an organization wanted to rent out such edited copies? What if DVD players and movies were set up so that the devices would edit and display the revised version on the fly? After you consider your own opinion, you might check the Web to see the latest information about this issue.

GROUP PROJECT

Work with a group of four students to research Web-based music download sites. Create one PowerPoint slide for each site. The slide should give a basic overview of the site, including its name, URL, price, pros, and cons. For the final slide in the presentation, create a table comparing the features and prices of each site.

CYBERCLASSROOM

Each person on your team should e-mail a photo in JPEG format to the other members of the group. The photo can be one you've taken or one you find on the Web. If you get your photo from the Web, make sure there are no prohibitions for using it for a personal project and keep track of the Web site so you have a record of your source. When you receive the photos from your teammates, be creative and use Photoshop or similar photo editing software to create a composite image that contains elements from all the photos. Submit your original photo and your composite photo to your instructor.

MULTIMEDIA PROJECT

Use Windows Sound Recorder or similar software to record your own 15-second radio ad for your favorite music or video download service. Submit the text of your script along with the .wav file containing your ad.

RESUME BUILDER

Artists routinely create a portfolio containing examples of their best work. How can you apply the portfolio concept to your job search? Suppose you've decided to create a multimedia portfolio that showcases your talents. Describe what you'd like your portfolio to contain, indicating which of the items you currently have and which you'd like to create and add in the future. Also, describe the format for each item: photo, document, scan, audio, or video. Finally, describe whether you envision delivering your portfolio on CD or the Web, and then discuss the advantages and limitations of your choice.

GLOBALIZATION

The United States has been accused of exporting its culture and values through films and television. Sometimes referred to as Coca Colonization, the mass exportation of American culture is expected to increase as more and more people have access to the Internet. But is digital distribution a two-way street? What can you find out about the *importation* of cultures to the United States (or your country)? Incorporate your findings into a two-page paper. Make sure you cite specific examples and offer your ideas on how technology aids or discourages cross cultural interchanges. Include a list of references on a third page.

ISSUE

The Issue section of this chapter focused on digital rights controversies, such as your rights to share music files, copy DVD movies, or use software to break copy protection. To begin the project, consult the Digital Rights Management InfoWeb and link to the recommended Web sites to get an in-depth overview of the issues. With this background, work with a partner and select a digital rights controversy that seems interesting. Use the Web to research the controversy. Collaborate with your partner to write a dialog between two people who are arguing both sides of the issue.

COMPUTERS IN CONTEXT

The Computers in Context section of this chapter focused on digital special effects technology used in recent films. For this project, conduct your own exploration of the special effects that have appeared in your favorite movies. To begin the project, browse through the material presented in the Computers and Film InfoWeb on page 475. Look for information about specific movies using Web sites such as the Internet movie database (*www.imdb.com*). Many movies also have dedicated Web sites that you can find using a search engine. To complete the project, select one of your favorite movies and write a two- to four-page movie review that focuses on how its special effects contribute to the movie's overall quality.

On the Web

STUDENT EDITION LABS

W **CLICK TO ACCESS THE NP11 WEB SITE**
or open your browser and connect to www.course.com/np/concepts11/ch08.
Lab results can be stored in the Universal Gradebook.

Work hands-on in structured simulations practicing important skills and concepts

WORKING WITH GRAPHICS

In the Working with Graphics Student Edition Lab, you will learn about the following topics:

- Downloading images from the Web
- Enhancing an image with filters and manipulating brightness, contrast, and sharpness
- Incorporating type in an image and working with layers
- Cropping vs. resizing and reducing file size
- Creating Web graphics

WORKING WITH VIDEO

In the Working with Video Student Edition Lab, you will learn about the following topics:

- Viewing digital video
- Importing and working with clips
- Using the storyboard
- Adding transitions and including audio
- Saving the video

WORKING WITH AUDIO

In the Working with Audio Student Edition Lab, you will learn about the following topics:

- Audio file formats and extensions
- Importing and downloading audio files
- Burning audio CDs
- Including audio files on a Web site

 CHAPTER COURSECAST

Use your computer or iPod to hear a five-minute audio presentation of chapter highlights.

FLASHCARD COURSECAST

Interact with audio flashcards to review key terms from the chapter.

DETAILED OBJECTIVES

Make sure that you've achieved all the objectives for a chapter before it's time for your test!

 TEST YOURSELF

Review chapter material by taking these ten-question tests, then send your results to the Universal Gradebook.

 ONLINE GAMES

Have some fun while refreshing your memory about key concepts that might appear on the next test. You can even send your results to the Universal Gradebook!

 AND MORE!

At the NP11 Web site you'll also find Extra Content and InfoWebLinks.

8

9

The Computer Industry: History, Careers, and Ethics

LEARNING OBJECTIVES

- Outline the development of calculating and computer devices, beginning with simple counting aids and continuing through developments that led to today's computer technology

- Describe the hardware, software, and operating system characteristics for computer prototypes and the four generations of computers

- List the factors that changed personal computers from hobbyists' kits to widely used productivity and communications tools

- Describe the role of the computer and IT industries in today's global economy

- Explain the life cycle of typical hardware and software products

- Discuss the advantages and disadvantages of various marketing channels for consumers who want to purchase computers and related products

- Summarize the job outlook and working conditions for computer professionals

- Differentiate between computer engineering, computer science, information systems, information technology, and software engineering degree programs

- Demonstrate how to create a resume that works in today's technology-driven job market

- Describe the professional resources available to computer professionals who are faced with ethical decisions

- List health risks that are suspected of being linked to the use of computers and other digital devices

- Describe ergonomic principles of setting up computer work areas

PRE-ASSESSMENT QUIZ

Take the pre-assessment quiz to find out how much you know about the topics in this chapter. ▶

MULTIMEDIA and INTERACTIVE ELEMENTS
When using the BookOnCD, BookOnFlashDrive, or other NP11 BookOn product, the ▶ icons are clickable to access multimedia resources.

BEFORE YOU READ ON, **TRY IT**

DO I HAVE A SAFE AND HEALTHY COMPUTING ENVIRONMENT?

If you spend hours at your computer each day working, studying, chatting online, or playing games, you might begin to feel stresses and strains in your back, neck, wrist, fingers, or eyes. OSHA (Occupational Safety and Health Administration) experts on work area health and safety have identified sources for many work-related physical maladies. Often the culprit is a work area that does not fit your body. To find out how your computer work area stacks up to OSHA standards, complete the following steps. You'll learn more about setting up an ergonomic workstation in Section E.

1. If possible, ask a friend to snap a digital photo of you sitting in a position similar to the person in the illustration. Otherwise, sit at your computer while a friend compares your desk, chair, and posture to those in the illustration.

2. On the illustration, circle any of the equipment, angles, or positions that are not optimal in your work area.

3. Consider how you could change your work area to achieve OSHA standards and help prevent muscle soreness, joint pain, eye strain, and headaches.

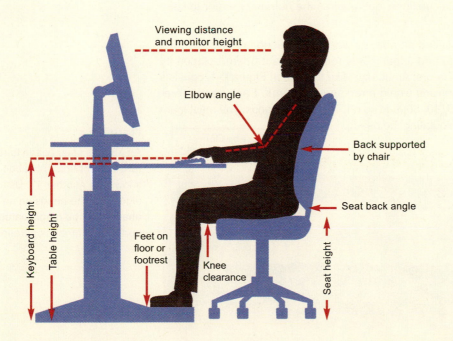

WEB SITE
Visit the NP11 Web site to access additional resources **w** that accompany this chapter.

Computer History

LIKE MOST INVENTIONS throughout history, computer technology evolved as inventors tinkered with various devices. With so many pioneering efforts, historians cannot pinpoint one development and say that it represents the first calculator or the first computer. Keeping that uncertainty in mind, it is, nonetheless, interesting to trace the development of computers. Knowing the history of computers helps you understand the design and capabilities of today's ever-expanding assortment of digital devices. It also helps you understand how the computer industry of today came into being.

MANUAL CALCULATORS

What came before computers? Even before recorded history, humans used counting aids, such as pebbles and notched sticks, to keep track of quantities—the number of sheep in a flock, for example, or the number of oil jars purchased from a merchant. Many transactions, however, required calculations.

A calculation is based on an algorithm—the step-by-step process by which numbers are manipulated. Even simple paper-and-pencil addition requires an algorithm. The steps include adding the rightmost digits first, carrying a 1 if necessary, and then moving left to any remaining digits, where the process is repeated. A **manual calculator** is a device that assists in the process of numeric calculations, but requires the human operator to keep track of the algorithm.

A manual calculator called an **abacus** was initially used in ancient Rome, Greece, India, China, and Japan. Only recently has it been replaced by handheld digital calculators. An abacus, like the one in Figure 9-1, consists of beads mounted on rods within a rectangular frame. Each bead represents a quantity—1, 5, 10, 50, and so on. To use an abacus, you must learn the algorithm for manipulating the beads.

Each of these beads represents the quantity "5."

Each of these beads represents the quantity "10."

Each of these beads represents the quantity "1."

FIGURE 9-1

An abacus uses beads to represent numbers. This abacus shows the number 17. Using an algorithm, the beads on an abacus can be manipulated to perform arithmetic operations.

▶ CLICK TO START

Other manual calculators include the oddly named Napier's Bones and the slide rule. John Napier, the Scottish Laird of Merchiston, made two contributions to the field of mathematics. He invented logarithms and a device for multiplication and division. The device consisted of several rods, divided into 10 squares, each labeled with 2 numbers. The rods were positioned according to the numbers in a calculation, and the result was determined by adding values shown in a specific location on the rods. These rods were often constructed out of bones, so they came to be called **Napier's Bones** (Figure 9-2).

In 1621, an English mathematician named William Oughtred used Napier's logarithms to construct the first **slide rule**. Slide rules, like the one pictured in Figure 9-2, remained in use as an essential tool for students, engineers, and scientists through the 1960s.

FIGURE 9-2

Napier's Bones (left) evolved into the slide rule (right).

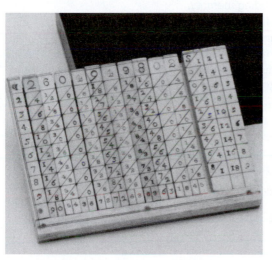
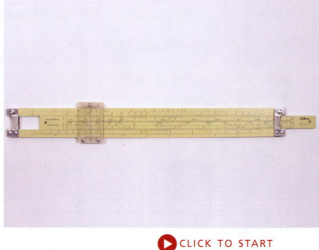

▶ CLICK TO START

MECHANICAL CALCULATORS

When did machines begin to perform calculations? Manual calculators, such as the abacus and slide rule, require the operator to apply algorithms to perform calculations. In contrast, a **mechanical calculator** implements algorithms autonomously. To work a mechanical calculator, the operator simply enters the numbers for a calculation, and then pulls a lever or turns a wheel to carry out the calculation. No thinking—or at least very little—is required.

Mechanical calculators were developed as early as 1623, when a German professor named Wilhelm Schickard created a mechanical calculator (called **Schickard's Calculator**) with a series of interlocking gears. Each of the 10 spokes on a gear represented a digit. Every time a gear completed a full circle, it moved the next gear one notch to the left to "carry the 1." A similar mechanism is used to advance the mileage on a car's odometer.

In 1642, a Frenchman named Blaise Pascal developed the **Pascaline**, a mechanical device that could be used to perform addition, subtraction, multiplication, and division. Yet another mechanical calculator—now called the **Leibniz Calculator**—was created by a German baron named Gottfried Wilhelm von Leibniz in 1673. It was not until 1820, however, that Thomas **deColmar's Arithmometer** became the first mass-produced calculator. These devices, unlike today's battery-powered calculators, operated under manual power by turning a crank or pulling a lever.

9

When did calculating devices begin to operate without human power? In 1822, an English mathematician named Charles Babbage proposed a device called the **Difference Engine** that would operate using steam power—cutting-edge technology during Babbage's lifetime. The Difference Engine was intended to quickly and accurately calculate large tables of numbers used for astronomical and engineering applications. The blueprints for the Difference Engine called for more than 4,000 precision-engineered levers, gears, and wheels. Babbage worked on the Difference Engine until 1833, but he was unable to fabricate gears with the necessary precision to create a working version of this complex mechanical device.

In 1834, Babbage began designing a new general-purpose calculating device, called the **Analytical Engine**. Although the Analytical Engine was never completed, computer historians believe that its design embodies many of the concepts that define the modern computer, including memory, a programmable processor, an output device, and user-definable input of programs and data. Babbage proposed storing programs and data for calculations on punched cards, an idea that probably came from using punched cards to control the color and patterns of yarns used in the Jacquard loom. Punched cards were later used in the first generation of electronic computing devices (Figure 9-3).

INFOWEBLINKS

At the **Charles Babbage InfoWeb**, you'll find sketches, photos, and original documents describing the Analytical and Difference Engines, including programming notes by mathematician Ada Byron.

W CLICK TO CONNECT
www.course.com/np/concepts11/ch09

FIGURE 9-3

Charles Babbage conceived of a device called the Analytical Engine, which embodied many of the characteristics that define modern computers. For example, he proposed storing programs and data for calculations on punched cards, much like those used in 1970s mainframes.

The U.S. Census provided incentive for the next generation of calculating machines. Compiling data from the 1880 census dragged on until 1887—just three years before the next census was to begin. With a surge in population, Census Bureau administrators feared that the 1890 census could not be completed before the 1900 census would begin. Clearly a faster way of tabulating census results was required.

The U.S. Census Bureau held a competition to find a way to tabulate the 1890 census. Herman Hollerith won the competition with a design for an electronic punched card tabulating device. Each card contained areas to represent fields, such as "nationality." Once punched, the cards were fed into a card reader that used an array of metal rods to electronically read data from the cards and tabulate the results. The **Hollerith Tabulating Machine** was effective. The 1890 census was tallied in six months, and only two additional years were required to complete all statistical calculations.

Hollerith incorporated The Tabulating Machine Company in 1896. In 1924, the name of the company was changed to International Business Machines, better known today as IBM. Since it was founded, IBM has become a major player in the computer industry.

The first half of the 20th century ushered in an era of growth in the business machine industry, which at that time produced typewriters and mechanical calculating devices. IBM faced tough competition from companies such as Burroughs, National Cash Register, Olivetti, and Remington. Some of these companies would later venture into the computer industry.

COMPUTER PROTOTYPES

Who invented the computer? The question "Who invented the computer?" doesn't have a simple answer because the modern digital computer evolved from a series of prototypes developed by various groups of people. A **prototype** is an experimental device that typically must be further developed and perfected before going into production and becoming widely available.

Between 1937 and 1942, an Iowa State University professor, John V. Atanasoff, and a graduate student, Clifford E. Berry, worked on a prototype for an electronic computer. The **Atanasoff-Berry Computer** (ABC) was the first to use vacuum tubes instead of mechanical switches for processing circuitry. Its design also incorporated the idea of basing calculations on the binary number system. The ABC, shown in Figure 9-4, is often considered the first electronic digital computer. According to one historian, "The ABC first demonstrated in 1939 may not have been much of a computer, just as the Wrights' model was not much of an airplane, but it opened the way."

FIGURE 9-4

The Atanasoff-Berry Computer (ABC) gained national attention when it was pulled from obscurity in a 1972 patent dispute. The Sperry Rand company claimed to have a patent on digital computer architecture, but the court declared the patent claim invalid because it was based on the work of Atanasoff and Berry.

9

While Atanasoff worked on the ABC, a German engineer named Konrad Zuse developed a computer called the **Z3**, which, like the ABC, was designed to work with binary numbers. Built in Nazi Germany during World War II, the Z3 was cloaked in secrecy, even though Hitler believed that computers had no strategic use in the war effort. Information on Zuse's invention did not surface until long after the war ended. So although Zuse was on the trail of modern computer architecture, his work had little effect on the development of computers.

Even with the work of Atanasoff and Zuse, it was not clear that computers were destined to be binary electronic devices. IBM had an entirely different computer architecture in mind. In 1939, IBM sponsored an engineer named Howard Aiken, who embarked on an audacious plan to integrate 73 IBM Automatic Accounting Machines into a single unified computing unit. What emerged was a mechanical computer officially named the IBM Automatic Sequence Controlled Calculator (ASCC), but now usually referred to as the **Harvard Mark I** (Figure 9-5) because it was moved to Harvard University shortly after completion.

FIGURE 9-5

Constructed of relay switches, rotating shafts, and clutches, the Harvard Mark I was described as sounding like a "roomful of ladies knitting." The device was 51 feet long and 8 feet tall and weighed about 5 tons.

Although the Harvard Mark I was one of the first working computers, as a prototype, it strayed considerably from the path of development leading to modern computers. The Harvard Mark I was digital but used decimal rather than binary representation, which is used by today's computers. In contrast, the ABC, with its electronic vacuum tubes and binary representation, was a much closer prototype of the generations of computers to come.

Aiken was a fine engineer but did not quite grasp the far-reaching potential of computers. In 1947, he predicted that only six electronic digital computers would be required to satisfy the computing needs of the entire United States—a sentiment that echoed an earlier statement made by Thomas J. Watson, then chairman of IBM.

Were prototypes able to perform any real computing? Some computer prototypes were pressed into service barely before they were completed. In 1943, a team of British developers created **COLOSSUS**, an electronic device designed to decode messages encrypted by the German Enigma machine. COLOSSUS contained 1,800 vacuum tubes, used binary arithmetic, and was capable of reading input at the rate of 5,000 characters per second. COLOSSUS successfully broke the Enigma codes and gave the Allies a major advantage during World War II.

In 1943, a team headed by John W. Mauchly and J. Presper Eckert started work on ENIAC, a gigantic, general-purpose electronic computer. **ENIAC** (Electronic Numerical Integrator and Computer) was designed to calculate trajectory tables for the U.S. Army, but wasn't finished until November 1945, three months after the end of World War II. ENIAC was over 100 feet long and 10 feet high and weighed 30 tons. This gigantic machine contained over 18,000 vacuum tubes and consumed 174,000 watts of power. It could perform 5,000 additions per second and was programmed by manually connecting cables and setting 6,000 switches—a process that generally took two days to complete.

ENIAC was formally dedicated at the Moore School of Electrical Engineering of the University of Pennsylvania on February 15, 1946, and immediately pressed into service making atomic energy calculations and computing trajectories for new missile technologies. ENIAC received several upgrades and remained in service until 1955.

INFOWEBLINKS

Read more about the ABC, Z3, COLOSSUS, ENIAC, and other early computers at the **Computer Prototype InfoWeb**.

W CLICK TO CONNECT
www.course.com/np/concepts11/ch09

GENERATIONS OF COMPUTERS

What was the first commercially successful computer? A computer called the **UNIVAC** is considered by most historians to be the first commercially successful digital computer. The first UNIVAC computer was constructed under the auspices of the Eckert-Mauchly Computer Corp. By the time the first UNIVAC was completed in 1951, the Eckert-Mauchly Computer Corp. had fallen into financial distress and been acquired by Remington Rand, one of IBM's chief rivals in the business machine arena. Forty-six UNIVAC computers were delivered to Remington Rand's customers between 1951 and 1958.

At 14.5 feet long, 7.5 feet high, and 9 feet wide, UNIVAC was physically smaller than ENIAC, but more powerful. UNIVAC could read data at the rate of 7,200 characters per second, and complete 2.25 million instruction cycles per second. It had RAM capacity of 12,000 characters (12 KB), and used magnetic tape for data storage and retrieval. The cost of a UNIVAC averaged about $930,000—almost $7 million in today's currency.

How did computers progress from room-sized behemoths to modern personal computers? Early computers, such as the Harvard Mark I, ENIAC, and UNIVAC, used technology that required lots of space and electrical power. As technology evolved, relay switches and vacuum tubes were replaced with smaller, less power-hungry components. Most computer historians agree that computers have evolved through four distinct generations, and in each generation, computers became smaller, faster, more dependable, and less expensive to operate.

What characterized the first generation of computers? **First-generation computers** can be characterized by their use of vacuum tubes, such as those in Figure 9-6, to store individual bits of data. A **vacuum tube** is an electronic device that controls the flow of electrons in a vacuum. Each tube can be set to one of two states. One state is assigned a value of 0 and the other a value of 1. Vacuum tubes respond more quickly than mechanical relays, resulting in faster computations, but they also have several disadvantages. They consume a lot of power, much of which is wasted as heat. They also tend to burn out quickly. ENIAC, the prototype for first-generation computers, contained about 18,000 tubes, and every tube was replaced at least once in the first year of operation.

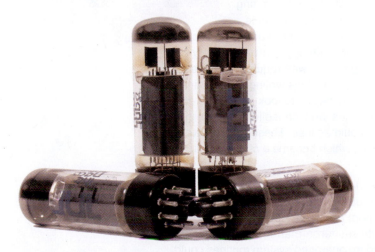

INFOWEBLINKS

Historians are not in total agreement about the number of computer generations. You can find more information about historians' views regarding this topic by connecting to the **Computer Generations InfoWeb**.

Ⓦ CLICK TO CONNECT
www.course.com/np/concepts11/ch09

9

FIGURE 9-6

Vacuum tubes resemble light bulbs and were used as the main processing and memory technology for first-generation computers. Although no longer used in computers, vacuum tubes can still be found in some televisions, computer monitors, high-end stereo systems, and guitar amplifiers.

In addition to vacuum tube technology, first-generation computers were characterized by custom application programs, made to order for the specific task the computer was to perform. Programming first-generation computers was difficult. As the computer era dawned, programmers were forced to think in 1s and 0s to write instructions in machine language. Before the first generation ended, programmers had devised rudimentary compilers that allowed them to write instructions using assembly language op codes, such as LDA and JNZ. Assembly language was a small step forward, but like machine language, it was machine specific and required programmers to learn a different set of instructions for each computer.

Although many companies recognized the potential of machines to perform fast calculations, first-generation computers did not seem ready for prime time. That said, many business machine companies, such as IBM, Burroughs, and National Cash Register (NCR), began research and development efforts into fledgling computer technologies. Companies in the electronics industry, such as General Electric, RCA, Control Data, and Honeywell, also showed interest in the new field of computing.

How did second-generation computers differ from first-generation computers?
Second-generation computers used transistors instead of vacuum tubes. First demonstrated in 1947 by AT&T's Bell Laboratories, **transistors** regulate current or voltage flow and act as a switch for electronic signals. Transistors performed functions similar to vacuum tubes, but they were much smaller, cheaper, less power hungry, and more reliable. By the late 1950s, transistors, such as those in Figure 9-7, had replaced vacuum tubes as the processing and memory technology for most computers.

Several successful transistorized computers were manufactured by companies such as IBM, Burroughs, Control Data, Honeywell, and Sperry Rand (which was the new name given to Remington Rand after its merger with Sperry Corp). In addition to the important hardware breakthrough provided by transistors, an equally important development in software differentiated second-generation computers from their first-generation ancestors.

First-generation computers didn't have operating systems as we know them today. Instead, each software application included the instructions necessary for every aspect of the computing job, including input, output, and processing activities. Programmers were quick to realize that this style of programming was terribly inefficient. For example, although virtually every program sent results to a printer, every program was required to have its own print routine. As programmers found themselves writing print routines over and over again for every program, they began to look for a more efficient method to standardize such routines and consolidate them into programs that any application software could access. These routines were gathered together into operating systems, which became a characteristic of second-generation computers.

Computer manufacturers such as IBM developed operating systems that provided standardized routines for input, output, memory management, storage, and other resource management activities. Application programmers were no longer required to write resource management routines. Instead, simple commands to call standard operating system routines could be easily incorporated into program code for application software.

FIGURE 9-7

Transistors first sparked a revolution in the entertainment industry by providing a small, power-efficient technology for portable radios. Later, transistors were incorporated in computers to replace large, hot, power-hungry vacuum tubes.

Early proprietary operating systems developed by IBM and other computer manufacturers were designed to work only on a particular computer model. Each of these operating systems had a unique set of commands to call its routines. Early operating systems were a step in the right direction, but unfortunately, learning to use each one was like learning a new and unique programming language. It was not until the third generation of computers that portable operating systems, such as CP/M and UNIX, provided programmers with similar operating system commands across hardware platforms.

In addition to operating systems, second-generation computers also ran programming language compilers that allowed programmers to write instructions using English-like commands rather than machine language 1s and 0s or cryptic assembly language commands. High-level languages, such as COBOL (Common Business-Oriented Language) and FORTRAN (Formula Translator), were available for use on second-generation computers and remain in use today. The availability of high-level computer programming languages made it possible for third parties to develop software, and that capability was instrumental in the birth of the software industry.

What are the characteristics of third-generation computers?

Third-generation computers became possible in 1958, when Jack Kilby at Texas Instruments and Robert Noyce at Fairchild Semiconductor independently developed integrated circuits (Figure 9-8). Integrated circuit technology made it possible to pack the equivalent of thousands of vacuum tubes or transistors onto a single miniature chip, vastly reducing the physical size, weight, and power requirements for devices such as computers.

FIGURE 9-8

Jack Kilby's original integrated circuit was a key development for creating today's small, fast, and efficient computers.

Two of the first computers to incorporate integrated circuits were the **RCA Spectra 70** and the wildly successful **IBM 360**. The first orders for IBM 360s computers were filled in 1965—a date regarded by many historians as the advent of third-generation computers.

In 1965, Digital Equipment Corp. (DEC) introduced the **DEC PDP-8**, the first commercially successful minicomputer. Minicomputers were designed to be smaller and less powerful than mainframe computers, while maintaining the capability to simultaneously run multiple programs for multiple users. Thousands of manufacturing plants, small businesses, and scientific laboratories were attracted to the speed, small size, and reasonable cost of the PDP-8.

DEC introduced a succession of minicomputers that stole a share of the mainframe market. Eventually, IBM and other mainframe makers introduced their own minicomputers, but the star for minicomputers faded as microcomputers gained processing power and networking became easier. DEC was purchased by Compaq in 1998. Compaq was later purchased by Hewlett-Packard.

By 2000, the **IBM AS/400** (renamed the iSeries 400) was one of the few remaining devices that could be classified as a minicomputer. Today, demand for minicomputers is satisfied by high-end personal computers and servers, and the term *minicomputer* has generally fallen into disuse.

9

How did microprocessor technology affect the computer industry? The technology for **fourth-generation computers** appeared in 1971, when Ted Hoff developed the first general-purpose microprocessor. Called the Intel 4004, this microprocessor dramatically changed the computer industry, resulting in fourth-generation microprocessor-based computer systems that were faster, smaller, and even less expensive than third-generation computers.

Microprocessor manufacturers soon flourished. Early industry leaders included Intel, Zilog, Motorola, and Texas Instruments. Intel's 4004 microprocessor (Figure 9-9) was smaller than a corn flake but matched the computing power of ENIAC. The 4004 packed the equivalent of 2,300 transistors or vacuum tubes on a single chip and was able to perform 60,000 instructions per second. The 4004 was followed by the 8008, the first commercial 8-bit microprocessor, and then the 8080.

In 1974, Motorola released the 6800 8-bit microprocessor. A few months later, ex-Motorola engineers working at MOS Technologies created the 6502, an 8-bit microprocessor that was used in the Apple II and Commodore personal computer systems.

In 1976, Zilog introduced the Z80 microprocessor, an enhanced 8080 microprocessor that was used in many early computer systems. In the same year, Intel released the 8085, a further enhancement of the 8080.

Both Intel and Motorola continued development of advanced microprocessors. The Intel line, used in most Windows-compatible and Intel Mac computers, included the 8086, 8088, 80286, 80386, 80486, Pentium, Itanium, and multi-core microprocessors. The Motorola line of microprocessors grew to include the 68000 series processors used in Apple Macintosh computers, plus the PowerPC processors developed in the early 1990s and used in Macintosh computer systems.

Today, microprocessors are a key component of all types of computers—ranging from PDAs to supercomputers. Intel reigns as the world's leading microprocessor manufacturer, although microprocessors are also produced by companies such as Hitachi, Texas Instruments, Toshiba, Sun Microsystems, AMD, and Motorola.

PERSONAL COMPUTERS

Who invented the personal computer? In the early 1970s, many hobbyists built their own computer systems based on integrated circuit and microprocessor technologies. One such system was the **Mark-8** developed by Jonathan A. Titus, who was featured in the July 1974 issue of *Radio-Electronics*. These early personal computers were not commercially produced or widely available, but they are often considered forerunners of today's personal computer.

In 1975, Ed Roberts and the MITS (Micro Instrument and Telemetry Systems) company announced the **MITS Altair**, which many historians believe to be the first commercial microcomputer (Figure 9-10). The Altair was based on the Intel 8080 processor and sold as a kit for $395 or fully assembled for $650—about one-fourth the price of a 1975 Volkswagen Beetle. The Altair was a computer for the hobbyist. The kit came unassembled in a box containing a processor and 256 bytes of memory—not 256 KB, just 256 bytes. It had no keyboard, no monitor, and no permanent storage device.

FIGURE 9-9

The Intel 4004 microprocessor was small. Its chip (lower right) was only 1/8" by 1/16". Even in the chip carrier (top left) the microprocessor was less than 1" in length.

FIGURE 9-10

The Altair computer made the cover of *Popular Electronics* in January 1975.

Programming the Altair computer meant flipping individual switches on the front of the system unit. Output consisted of flashing lights, and the only programming language available was 8080 machine language. Although it was typically sold as a kit, required assembly, and was too limited to perform significant computational tasks, the Altair was snapped up by hobbyists interested in learning how computers worked.

In 1976, Steve Jobs and Steve Wozniak founded Apple Computer Corporation and released the **Apple I**, a kit containing a system board with 4 KB of RAM that sold for $666.66. Other companies, such as Commodore, Atari, and Radio Shack, pursued the hobbyist market, but with preassembled computers.

How did personal computers become so successful? In 1978,
Apple introduced a preassembled computer called the **Apple II**, which featured color graphics, expansion slots, a disk drive, a 1.07 MHz 6502 processor, and 16 KB of RAM for $1,195. The Apple II, shown in Figure 9-11, was a very successful product. One of the main reasons behind its success was a commercial software program called **VisiCalc**—the first electronic spreadsheet. This program landed computers on the radar screen of business users and clearly marked a turning point where personal computers appealed to an audience beyond hobbyists.

In 1981, IBM began marketing what it called a *personal computer* or *PC*, based on the 8088 processor. When the PC version of VisiCalc became available, the IBM PC quickly became the top-selling personal computer, far surpassing IBM's expectations.

The $3,000 **IBM PC**, shown in Figure 9-12, shipped with a 4.77 MHz Intel 8088 processor, 16 KB of RAM, and single-sided 160 KB floppy disk drives. The IBM PC was soon followed by the **IBM PC XT**, which featured RAM upgradable to 640 KB, and a 10 MB hard disk drive.

IBM PCs were constructed with off-the-shelf parts that could be easily obtained from many electronics wholesalers. Within months, dozens of companies used these parts to produce clones of IBM-compatible computers that could run the same software and use the same expansion cards as the IBM PC and XT. These companies were also able to obtain essentially the same operating system used by IBM.

The IBM PC used an operating system called PC-DOS that was marketed by a young entrepreneur named Bill Gates, founder of a fledgling software company called Microsoft. Microsoft marketed a similar operating system, called MS-DOS, to PC clone makers. Many of the companies that produced IBM clones failed, but some, such as Dell and Hewlett-Packard, became major forces in the personal computer industry.

Although hobbyists and the business community had embraced computers, these machines were still considered difficult for the average person to use. That perception began to change in 1983, when Apple introduced a product called the **Apple Lisa**. A key feature of the Lisa was its graphical user interface—an idea borrowed from the **Xerox Alto** computer. At $10,000, the Lisa proved too expensive for most consumers. Apple

FIGURE 9-11

The Apple II was the most popular computer of its time.

FIGURE 9-12

The IBM PC, launched in 1981, evolved into today's popular Windows-based PCs.

9

remained committed to graphical user interfaces, however, and in 1984, released the first **Apple Macintosh** (Figure 9-13). The $2,495 Macintosh featured a graphical user interface that made programs easier to use than those on the command-line-based IBM PC. The Macintosh became the computer of choice for graphical applications such as desktop publishing.

By the late 1980s, the computer industry had begun to consolidate around two primary platforms—the MS-DOS-based IBM-compatible platform and the Apple Macintosh. Although dozens of companies produced IBM-compatible systems that ran the same software and used the same hardware as the IBM PC, Apple attempted to keep its system proprietary. As more IBM-compatible computers were sold, the market for IBM-compatible hardware and software continued to grow. By the mid-1990s, IBM-compatible computer systems accounted for more than 90% of all personal computer sales. The Apple Macintosh accounted for most of the remainder, with other proprietary platforms accounting for a very small percentage of new computer sales.

Even as computer sales soared, and graphical user interfaces, such as Windows 3.1, made computers easier to use, many people simply could not think of any reason to own one. They preferred to write short notes on paper rather than learn how to use a word processor. It seemed easier to punch numbers into a handheld calculator than tackle the complexities of electronic spreadsheets. Why buy a computer if it didn't offer some really enticing perks? That attitude began to change in the late 1980s when the Internet opened to public use. In a flurry of activity, graphical browsers appeared, ISPs provided inexpensive connections, e-mail began to fly, and e-commerce sites opened their doors. By the mid 1990s, personal computers had finally achieved mass popularity.

INFOWEBLINKS

At the **Computer Museum InfoWeb** you'll find links to detailed timelines of computer history, photos of old computers, plus additional accounts of the computer industry's early days.

W CLICK TO CONNECT
www.course.com/np/concepts11/ch09

QuickCheck

SECTION A

1. The abacus and slide rule are examples of _____ calculators, which require the operator to apply an algorithm to perform calculations.

2. Charles _____ designed a general-purpose calculating device, called the Analytical Engine, that embodied many of the concepts that define the modern computer.

3. Computers designed by Atanasoff, Zuse, and Aiken are usually considered to be computer _____ because they were experimental models.

4. The first generation of computers can be characterized by its use of _____ tubes to store individual bits of data, whereas second-generation computers used _____ .

5. Third-generation computers were based on _____ circuit technology, and fourth-generation computers are characterized by _____ technology.

▶ CHECK ANSWERS

SECTION B

The Computer and IT Industries

THE INDUSTRIES that supply computer goods and services are in a continual state of change as new products appear and old products are discontinued; as corporations form, merge, and die; as corporate leadership shifts; as consumers' buying habits evolve; and as prices steadily decrease. Before you venture out to buy computers, peripheral devices, or software; before you commit yourself to a computer career; or before you buy stock in computer companies, you should arm yourself with some basic knowledge about the computer and information technology industries. In this section of the chapter, you'll learn about the scope and economics of these dynamic industries.

INDUSTRY OVERVIEW

Is there a difference between the computer industry and the information technology industry? The term *computer industry* is used in a variety of ways. Narrowly defined, the **computer industry** encompasses those companies that manufacture computers (Figure 9-14) and computer components, such as microprocessors. The term *computer industry* is also used more broadly to include software publishers and peripheral device manufacturers.

An even broader term, **information technology industry** (or IT industry), is typically used to refer to the companies that develop, produce, sell, or support computers, software, and computer-related products. It includes companies in the computer industry; software publishers; communications service vendors, such as AT&T; information services, such as the Lexis/Nexis online law library; and service companies, such as EDS (Electronic Data Systems).

The terms *computer industry* and *IT industry* are sometimes used interchangeably in news reports and publications, leaving the reader to discern whether the subject is limited to computer manufacturers and distributors. In this textbook, the term *computer industry* is used in its more limited sense, and *IT industry* refers to the broader group of companies that provide computer, telecommunications, and software equipment and services.

FIGURE 9-14

Manufacturers such as Apple, Dell, Hewlett-Packard, IBM, and Intel, are representative of companies in the computer industry.

9

Is every company that uses computers part of the IT industry? No. A bank uses computers to track money flowing in and out of accounts, but it is classified as part of the banking industry. A clothing store might use computers to monitor inventory, but it is classified as part of the apparel industry. Such businesses make use of information technology, but they are definitely not part of the computer industry and are not considered part of the IT industry either.

What kinds of companies are included in the IT industry?

Companies in the IT industry can be separated into several broad categories, sometimes referred to as *sectors* or *segments*, including equipment manufacturers, chipmakers, software publishers, service companies, and retailers.

Equipment manufacturers design and manufacture computer hardware and communications products, such as personal computers, mainframe computers, PDAs, mice, monitors, storage devices, routers, scanners, and printers. Examples of these companies include computer manufacturers IBM and Hewlett-Packard. Network hardware companies, such as Cisco and its subsidiary Linksys, are also examples of equipment manufacturers.

Chipmakers design and manufacture computer chips and circuit boards, including microprocessors, RAM, system boards, sound cards, and graphics cards. Intel, Transmeta, Texas Instruments, and AMD, are examples of chipmakers.

Software publishers create computer software, including applications, operating systems, and programming languages. Examples of software companies include Microsoft, Adobe Systems, Electronic Arts (EA), and Computer Associates (CA).

Service companies provide computer-related services, including business consulting, Web site design, Web hosting, Internet connections, computer equipment repair, network security, and product support. Classic examples of service companies include AOL and the computer consulting giant, EDS (Electronic Data Systems).

Computer retailers (sometimes called *resellers*) include companies that sell computer products through retail stores, direct sales representatives, mail-order catalogs, and Web sites. Well-known computer resellers include CompUSA, which operates retail stores, and mail-order retailers PC Connection and CDW.

Although some companies fit neatly into one of the above categories, other companies operate in two or more areas. For example, Dell manufactures hardware but also resells that hardware directly to individuals and businesses. Sun Microsystems is known for its Sun servers and workstations but also develops and sells software, such as operating systems and the Java programming language. IBM designs and manufactures computer chips and circuit boards as well as producing workstations, servers, and mainframes.

The IT industry also encompasses large conglomerates with one or more divisions devoted to computer hardware, software, or services. As an example, Japanese-owned Hitachi produces a wide variety of electronic devices, but it is also one of the world's largest chipmakers.

What about dot coms? The 1990s spawned a group of Internet-based companies that came to be called *dot coms*. The dot com moniker came from the companies' domain names, which inevitably ended with .com; many of the companies even incorporated .com into their official company names.

Amazon.com was one of the first Internet-based companies. Founded in 1995, the company's mission is to "use the Internet to transform book buying into the fastest, easiest, and most enjoyable shopping experience possible." To transform book buying, Amazon.com set up a Web site where customers can buy books online, without walking into a physical brick-and-mortar store.

Unless a dot com sells computers, peripherals, or software online, it is probably not considered part of the computer industry, but experts disagree on whether dot coms rightfully belong to the IT industry. Some experts group dot coms under the IT umbrella because they make extensive use of computer equipment and have developed key e-commerce technologies. Other analysts classify dot coms by their core businesses. For example, dot coms that sell clothing would be in the apparel industry, music vendors would be in the entertainment industry, and an online stock broker would be in the financial industry.

What is the significance of Silicon Valley?

The area of California called Silicon Valley that stretches south and east from San Francisco's Golden Gate bridge was the birthplace of integrated circuits, microprocessors, and personal computers. Early IT industry pioneers attracted the attention of many other technology companies who wanted to be in the middle of the action. Today, well-known companies, such as Cisco Systems, Sun Microsystems, Oracle, Hewlett-Packard, AMD, and Silicon Graphics, all have headquarters in or near California's Silicon Valley (Figure 9-15).

Although Silicon Valley has a reputation as the home of the IT industry, many top IT players are located elsewhere. Microsoft is located near Seattle. EDS is headquartered in Plano, Texas and Dell is just outside Austin. North Carolina's Research Triangle (Raleigh-Durham-Chapel Hill) is home base for IBM's largest hardware lab and several small research startups. Colorado's Front Range (the Boulder-Denver-Longmont area) hosts desktop publishing software vendor Quark, Inc. Software publisher Computer Associates is based in New York. Unisys, a high-end server manufacturer, has its headquarters near Philadelphia. Outsourcing and offshoring spread the computer industry to additional locations both in the United States and abroad.

What are outsourcing and offshoring?

Like companies in many industries, computer companies make significant use of outsourcing to reduce the price of materials and labor. **Outsourcing** is defined as the use of components or labor from outside suppliers. Most computer companies do not manufacture all the components used to assemble their computers. Instead they depend on components from other companies, such as microprocessors from Intel, hard drives from Seagate, and LCD panels from Samsung. Software publishers also make use of outsourcing

FIGURE 9-15

Silicon Valley is home to many companies in the IT industry.

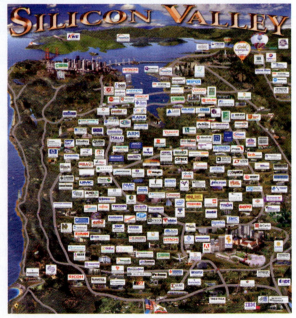

9

by hiring outside firms to develop products and manufacture packaging. Outsourcing offers economies of scale and expertise to companies in the highly competitive computer industry.

Computer companies also make use of offshoring to help keep product prices competitive. **Offshoring** is defined as relocating business processes, such as development and production, to lower-cost locations in other countries.

U.S. computer companies have established manufacturing and development facilities in countries such as China, India, Malaysia, Thailand, and Mexico, where labor is inexpensive but reliable. Computer manufacturer Dell Inc. maintains a cadre of offshore technicians to staff customer call centers. The next time you dial technical support, you might be connected to a technician in India. Companies such as Microsoft and Oracle make extensive use of programmers based in India, who telecommute, when necessary, using the Internet (Figure 9-16). The use of offshore resources has become increasingly controversial. You can read about the pros and cons in the Offshoring Issue at the end of this chapter.

FIGURE 9-16

The IT industry reaches globally for programmers and manufacturing facilities.

Where can I find information about the IT industry? Whether you are planning to purchase a computer, embark on a computing career, or invest in a computer company, you can dig up lots of information on IT and computer companies from a wide variety of computer and business publications. The IT Sources InfoWeb provides an up-to-date guide to publications and other IT industry resources.

ECONOMIC FACTORS

How has the IT industry affected the economy? The IT industry has been described as the most dynamic, most prosperous, most economically beneficial industry the world has ever known. That statement might be a bit of an exaggeration, but the IT industry unquestionably has fueled the economies of many countries. Worldwide consumers spend more than U.S. $1 trillion on information technology each year.

By dollar value, the biggest computer hardware producing countries are the United States, Japan, Taiwan, Singapore, and China. Despite the increasing globalization of the IT industry, however, it remains dominated by the United States. The majority of IT workers are in the United States, even though about two-thirds of industry revenues are from non-U.S. companies.

INFOWEBLINKS

The **IT Sources InfoWeb** contains a comprehensive list of links to IT industry information resources.

Ⓦ CLICK TO CONNECT
www.course.com/np/concepts11/ch09

INFOWEBLINKS

The computer industry makes a tremendous contribution to global financial resources. For links to information on company stock values, venture over to the **NASDAQ InfoWeb**.

Ⓦ CLICK TO CONNECT
www.course.com/np/concepts11/ch09

What about the dot com bubble? A stock market *bubble* refers to a sharp rise in stock values of a particular industry, which is later followed by a sudden decline. During the later part of the 1990s, the information technology sector experienced a stock market bubble, which burst in 2001 (Figure 9-17). The bubble was fueled by a dot com frenzy. Entrepreneurs seemed to believe that any Internet-based business was destined for success. Investors believed that dot coms were the key to quick profits. Stock sold like hotcakes on the technology-specialized NASDAQ stock exchange.

Dot com stock values soared as investors poured money into online businesses. These businesses needed equipment and employees, which had a positive effect on other sectors of the IT industry by boosting computer sales, networking equipment sales, and IT employment. Unfortunately, many dot coms lacked experienced management teams and realistic business plans, burned through startup capital without making a profit, and then went bankrupt.

A high rate of dot com business failures during 2001 and 2002 meant a decline in equipment orders, Web site hosting contracts, and IT sector job openings. Nonetheless, strength in worldwide markets for IT equipment and services continues to buoy up the industry, and most analysts believe that tech stocks have now normalized. Analysts believe that well-conceived and professionally managed online businesses can be a profitable part of the IT industry.

Although another dot com boom is doubtful, tech stocks still offer some surprises. An initial public offering of VMWare stock in 2007 raked in nearly $20 billion in the largest IPO since Google went public in 2004.

What accounts for the success of the IT industry? As with many situations involving the economy, the factors that account for the success of the IT industry cannot be pinpointed with certainty. It is likely, however, that population growth and business globalization are two important factors that contribute to huge investments in information technology.

The worldwide population more than doubled over the past 50 years, and a recent study predicts that the population will peak at 9 billion by 2070. Keeping track of the information relating to all these people—births, deaths, marriages, property ownership, taxes, purchases, banking records, and licenses—certainly seems impossible without the use of computers. Governments and private businesses have discovered that they can become much more efficient with a liberal application of computers and other information technologies.

As a business globalizes, it encounters new competitors with technological advantages. Intense global competitive pressure keeps companies looking for ways to cut costs and raise productivity. Staying ahead of the competition becomes a priority for survival. If your business competitor offers automated online order tracking, for example, you might lose customers unless you can offer the same service. Bottom line: If your business competitors turn to technology, so must you. In our highly populated global economy, information technology products are an effective alternative to manual record-keeping systems (Figure 9-18).

FIGURE 9-17

Dot Com Bubble Timeline

May 1997 Amazon.com stock initial public offering (IPO) kicks off the dot com frenzy.

November 1998 theglobe.com earns $100 million during its IPO, making it the most successful stock offering in history.

March 2000 NASDAQ reaches its all-time high of 5048; stocks are trading for an average of $55.92 per share.

December 2000 By year's end, venture capitalists have invested an estimated $20 billion in 12,450 dot com startups.

January 2001 17 dot coms each spend over $2 million for a 30-second ad during the Super Bowl.

June 2001 By mid-year, 345 dot coms have closed their doors or filed for bankruptcy protection.

August 2001 theglobe.com goes out of business.

September 2002 NASDAQ bottoms out at 1,184, much lower than its 5,048 peak. Average price per share is $14.07.

August 2004 Google has a successful IPO—a sign that consumers are regaining confidence in dot com stocks.

FIGURE 9-18

Manual record-keeping systems of the past have gradually been replaced by computerized archives.

9

PRODUCT DEVELOPMENT

Why do so many new computer products appear each year?

Automobile manufacturers introduce new models every year, which incorporate new features and give customers an incentive to buy. IT manufacturers and publishers introduce new products for the same reasons as their counterparts in the automotive industry. New products, such as a computer with a faster microprocessor, a Blu-ray DVD player, or a new version of Windows, are designed to attract customers and generate sales.

In contrast to the automotive industry, however, the IT industry is not on an annual cycle. As a result, the computer marketplace seems rather chaotic because new product announcements, availability dates, and ship dates occur sporadically.

The equipment manufacturing segment of the IT industry is relatively young, and technology, rather than marketing, is the major force that drives product development. New technologies spur a flurry of development activity and generate new products designed to increase sales. For example, the debut of Wi-Fi technology stimulated development of Wi-Fi hubs and cards, Wi-Fi enabled notebook computers, Internet access points in coffee shops and airports, and Wi-Fi access plans from companies such as T-Mobile.

Technological breakthroughs do not necessarily adhere to a schedule, however. Companies cannot always predict when a new technology will appear or how it might be incorporated into new products. As a result, the life cycle of computer hardware and some computer products is short, whereas other products have a long life cycle.

What are the stages in the life cycle of a typical hardware product?

In the computer industry, the life cycle of a new computer model usually includes five stages: product development, product announcement, introduction, maintenance, and retirement, as shown in Figure 9-19.

Product Development
Create product specifications and prototypes.

FIGURE 9-19

Five-stage life cycle of a computer product.

Product Announcement
Publicize information about new product features, advantages, and projected price.

Introduction Roll out the product at a trade show or press conference, formalize the product's list price, and begin to ship it to vendors and customers.

Maintenance
Adjust manufacturing capacity to meet product demand.

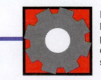

Retirement
Discontinue manufacturing product and eventually discontinue product support.

● **Product development.** Product development often takes place under wraps. Developers use fanciful code names, such as Sawtooth and Longhorn, to refer to their products. Inevitably, news of these products leaks out and causes much speculation among industry analysts.

● **Product announcement.** Some time during the development process, a company makes a product announcement to declare its intention to introduce a new product. Products are often announced at trade shows and press conferences. As a consumer, you should be wary of making purchase or investment decisions based on product announcements. A product announcement can precede the actual launch by months or even years. Some products, referred to as **vaporware**, are announced but never produced.

● **Introduction.** When a new product becomes available, it is usually added to the vendor's product line and featured prominently in advertisements. Initial supplies of the product generally remain low while manufacturing capacity increases to meet demand. Consumers who want a scarce product must pay a relatively high list price—sometimes called **MSRP** (manufacturer's suggested retail price)—set by the manufacturer.

● **Maintenance.** As supply and demand for a product reach an equilibrium, the price of the product decreases slightly. Usually the price decrease is caused by retail discounting rather than a change to the MSRP. This discounted price is sometimes referred to as the **street price**. Over time, the manufacturer might also reduce the MSRPs of products with older technology to keep them attractive to buyers.

● **Retirement.** Gradually, a company's oldest products are discontinued as demand for them declines. As you can see from the ad in Figure 9-20, the least expensive products tend to have slower processors, less RAM, and lower-capacity hard disk drives. If your budget is not severely limited, a computer in the middle of a vendor's product line usually gives you the most computing power per dollar.

FIGURE 9-20

A typical manufacturer's product line.

9

Edge 2500 Notebook

- AMD Turion Dual-Core 1.6 GHz
- 17" WXGA TFT Display
- 1 GB DDR2 SDRAM
- 80 GB SATA HD
- 24X CD-RW Drive
- Shared Video RAM
- Dial-up, Ethernet, Wi-Fi

$549

Edge 4200 Notebook

- AMD Athlon Dual-Core 1.7 GHz
- 17" WXGA+ TFT Display
- 1 GB DDR2 SDRAM
- 200 GB SATA HD
- 5-in-1 Media Card Reader
- 12X CD-RW/8X DL DVD Drive
- 256 MB Video RAM
- Dial-up, Ethernet, Wi-Fi

$859

Edge 8200 Notebook

- Intel Core 2 Duo T7600G 2.33 GHz
- 17" WXGA+ TFT Display
- 4 GB DDR2 RAM
- 400 GB Ultra ATA HD
- 5-in-1 Media Card Reader
- 12X CD/DVD +RW +R Dual layer Drive
- 512 MB NVIDIA GeForce Video RAM
- Dial-up, Ethernet, Wi-Fi

$2,099

Is the life cycle of a software product similar to that of a hardware product? Software, like hardware, begins with an idea that is shaped by a design team and marketing experts. A team of programmers then works to produce executable programs and support modules for the new software product.

Most software products undergo extensive testing before they are released. The first phase of testing, called an **alpha test**, is carried out by the software publisher's in-house testing team. Errors, or bugs, found during the alpha test phase are fixed, and then the software enters a second testing phase called a **beta test**. Typically, a beta test is conducted by a team of off-site testers, such as a professional testing company. Sometimes a software publisher releases a beta version of the software to select individuals and companies in the general public to expose the software to the widest possible variety of computers and operating environments. Although it can be exciting to test a yet-to-be-released software package, beta versions are typically "buggy" and can cause unexpected glitches in your computer. Beta testing requires a high tolerance for frustration.

A newly published software package can be an entirely new product, a new version (also called a release) with significant enhancements, or a revision designed to add minor enhancements and eliminate bugs found in the current version. When a new software product first becomes available, the publisher often offers a special introductory price that's designed to entice customers. Even after the introductory price expires, most vendors offer sizable discounts. Expect software with a list price of $495 to be offered for a street price of about $299.

Unlike computer hardware products, older versions of software typically do not remain in the vendor's product line. When a publisher offers a new version of the software that you are using, it is a good idea to upgrade, but you can wait to upgrade, however, for several months until the initial rush for technical support on the new product subsides. Upgrading your existing software is typically less expensive than replacing it with a brand-new program. If you don't upgrade, you might find that the software publisher offers minimal technical support for older versions of the program. Also, if you let several versions go by without upgrading, you might lose your eligibility for special upgrade pricing.

MARKET SHARE

How do computer companies stack up against each other?
Industry analysts often use market share as a gauge of a company's success. **Market share** refers to a company's share, or percentage, of the total market. For example, Microsoft's share of the total personal computer operating system market is about 90%. The remaining 10% share is distributed among Apple and several Linux vendors.

In worldwide hardware sales, Hewlett-Packard leads the pack with more than 18% market share, followed closely by Dell. The pie chart in Figure 9-21 illustrates market share for PC vendors. Lenovo is the China-based company that purchased IBM's PC division in 2005.

FIGURE 9-21

Worldwide market share for personal computer vendors in the second quarter of 2007.

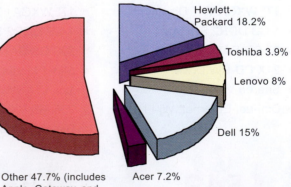

Hewlett-Packard 18.2%

Toshiba 3.9%

Lenovo 8%

Dell 15%

Acer 7.2%

Other 47.7% (includes Apple, Gateway, and other vendors)

Source: Gartner, Inc.

Market share graphs for personal computer manufacturers, software publishers, operating system developers, Internet service providers, and handheld computer manufacturers provide a roadmap to the changing fortunes of companies in the computer industry. Competition is fierce in all segments of the industry, and market share is one indicator of a company's ability to steal sales from its rivals. The top companies are constantly challenged, not only by their peers, but by startup companies in lower tiers of the industry.

What's the relevance of market tiers? Since 1981, hundreds of companies have produced personal computers. Industry analysts have classified these companies into **market tiers**, or categories. Although analysts do not agree on which companies belong in each tier, the concept of tiers helps explain price differences and changing market shares.

The top (first) tier in any segment of the computer industry consists of large companies that have been in the computer business for many years, and have an identifiable share—usually more than 2%—of total computer sales. IBM, Hewlett-Packard, and Dell are three venerable members of the top tier of the computer industry. The second tier includes newer companies with sales volume just below the cutoff level for identifiable market share and somewhat fewer financial resources than companies in the first tier. Most analysts place companies such as Gateway in this tier. The third tier consists of smaller startup companies that sell primarily through mail order (Figure 9-22).

FIGURE 9-22

Computer Industry Market Tiers

First Tier

Prices Computer prices from first-tier vendors are generally higher than computers offered by second-tier or third-tier vendors. Pricing reflects overhead costs that include facilities, professional management teams, a large workforce, and cutting-edge research.

Quality Many consumers believe that computers sold by first-tier companies offer better quality and are a safer purchasing decision than computers from other tiers.

Resources Substantial financial resources help these companies contribute many of the innovations that make computers faster, more powerful, and more convenient.

Service A stable first-tier company is likely to provide continuing support, honor warranties, and maintain an inventory of replacement parts.

Second Tier

Prices Computers from second-tier companies are typically less expensive than those from first-tier firms.

Quality Most PCs are constructed from off-the-shelf circuit boards, cases, and chips. Components in the computers sold by second-tier companies are often the same as those in computers sold by first-tier firms.

Resources Second-tier companies typically maintain low prices by minimizing operating costs. These companies have limited research and development budgets.

Service Some second-tier companies maintain a relatively small workforce by contracting with other companies to provide repair and warranty work.

Third Tier

Prices Computers from third-tier companies often appear to be much less expensive than those in other tiers.

Quality A consumer who is knowledgeable about the market and has technical expertise can often get a bargain on a good-quality computer from a third-tier company. Low pricing might reflect low overhead costs of a small company, but it could reflect poor-quality components.

Resources Third-tier companies usually do not have substantial financial resources and are more likely to go out of business than companies in the other tiers.

Service If a company goes out of business, its customers may be left without technical support.

9

MARKETING CHANNELS

Why are computer equipment and software sold through so many outlets?

Hardware manufacturers and software publishers try to reach consumers by making their products available through a variety of sources. Computer hardware and software are sold through marketing outlets called **marketing channels**. These channels, shown in Figure 9-23, include computer retail stores, mail-order/Internet outlets, value-added resellers, and manufacturer direct.

FIGURE 9-23

Computer hardware and software are sold through several marketing channels.

Distribution centers stock products from many different manufacturers and then sell the products to retailers.

Computer retailers stock products from several manufacturers and sell these products to customers.

Manufacturers produce products and ship them to resellers, distribution centers, computer retailers, and mail-order suppliers.

Some manufacturers ship products directly to customers.

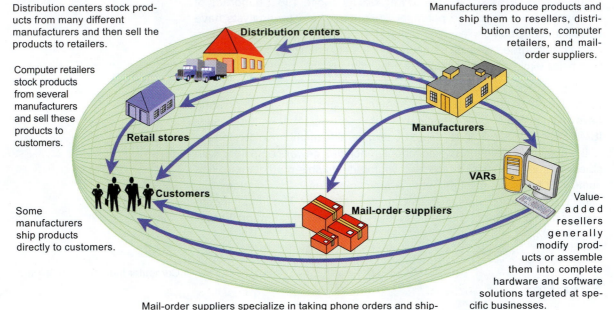

Value-added resellers generally modify products or assemble them into complete hardware and software solutions targeted at specific businesses.

Mail-order suppliers specialize in taking phone orders and shipping products to customers using U.S. mail or courier services.

Isn't a computer retail store the best channel for hardware and software products?

A **computer retail store** purchases computer products from a variety of manufacturers, and then sells those products to consumers. Computer retail stores are either small local shops or nationwide chains, such as CompUSA, that specialize in the sale of microcomputer software and hardware. Computer retail store employees are often knowledgeable about a variety of computer products and can help you select a hardware or software product to fit your needs. Many computer retail stores also offer classes and training sessions, answer questions, provide technical support, and repair hardware products.

A computer retail store is often the best shopping option for buyers who are likely to need assistance after their purchases, such as beginning computer users or those with plans for complex computer networks. Retail stores can be a fairly expensive channel for hardware and software, however. Their prices reflect the cost of purchasing merchandise from a distributor, maintaining a retail storefront, and hiring a technically qualified staff.

What about office and electronics stores?

Today, computers, peripherals, and software are sold from a variety of retail outlets, including electronics stores, such as Best Buy, Circuit City, and Radio Shack. Office superstores, such as Staples, Office Depot, and OfficeMax, also sell computer wares.

Prices at these outlets vary. Service tends to be less professional than from a dedicated computer retail store, so it is important for consumers to ask about service facilities and policies.

How does the mail-order channel compare to retail? **Mail order** is a special type of retailing in which a vendor takes orders by telephone or from an Internet site, and then ships the product directly to consumers. Mail-order suppliers, such as TigerDirect and CDW, generally offer low prices but might provide only limited service and support. A mail-order supplier is often the best source of products for buyers who are unlikely to need support or who can troubleshoot problems by calling a help desk.

Experienced computer users who can install components, set up software, and do their own troubleshooting are often happy with mail-order suppliers. Inexperienced computer users might not be satisfied with the assistance they receive.

Do some manufacturers and publishers sell direct? **Manufacturer direct** refers to hardware manufacturers that sell their products directly to consumers without a middleman, such as a retail store. IBM has a long tradition of direct sales, and that model has been emulated by several hardware manufacturers and some software publishers. A company's sales force usually targets large corporate or educational customers, where large-volume sales can cover the sales representative's costs and commissions.

For personal computer hardware, Dell Computers pioneered Web-based direct sales to individual customers. Its innovative Web site allows customers to select from a variety of standard models or configure their own custom builds (Figure 9-24). A just-in-time inventory model allows Dell to build each customer's computer as it is ordered, which eliminates costly inventories of computers that quickly become outdated. The obvious advantage of direct sales is that by cutting out the retailer, a manufacturer can make more profit on each unit sold. The disadvantage is that the manufacturer must provide customers with technical support—a potentially costly service that requires large teams of technical support personnel.

FIGURE 9-24

At Dell's Web site, customers can order a custom-built computer by simply clicking to add various hardware options.

9

▶ CLICK TO START

What's a VAR? VAR stands for value-added reseller. A value-added reseller combines commercially available products with specialty hardware or software to create a computer system designed to meet the needs of a specific industry. Although VARs charge for their expertise, they are often the only source for specialized computer systems. For example, if you own a video rental store and want to automate the rental process, the best type of vendor might be a VAR that offers a complete hardware and software package tailored to the video rental business. Otherwise, you must piece together the computer, scanner, printer, and software components yourself. VARs are often the most expensive channel for hardware and software, but their expertise can be crucial to ensure that the hardware and software work correctly in a specific environment.

Do so many channels confuse consumers? Consumers can benefit from a variety of channels. Because the price of computer equipment and software tends to vary by channel, consumers can shop for the best price and the most appropriate level of support.

Although consumers benefit from a variety of channels, vendors within the channels often find that other channel vendors pirate their sales—a process referred to as **channel conflict**. In the early days of the IT industry, hardware manufacturers and software publishers awarded exclusive territories to their retail vendors. An Apple computer dealer in Spokane, for example, was assured of sales to any customers in the local area who wanted a Macintosh. Mail-order vendors, however, were also able to attract the business of Spokane customers, creating a channel conflict. To avoid such conflicts, Apple did not allow its computers to be sold through mail-order channels.

INDUSTRY REGULATION

Is the IT industry regulated in any way? Some aspects of the IT industry are regulated by government agencies, but many aspects are self-regulated. Unlike the airline industry, which is regulated by agencies such as the Federal Aviation Authority (FAA), most countries do not have a single government agency dedicated to regulating the IT industry. The IT industry encompasses many activities, however, and consequently it is subject to regulation from a variety of broad-based government agencies, such as the FCC and FTC (Figure 9-25).

Many governments are enacting laws that restrict access to particular Internet activities and content. For example, several Caribbean countries recently enacted laws that regulate online casino operators. In 1996, the U.S. Congress enacted the Communications Decency Act, which made it illegal to put indecent material online where children might see it. Parts of this legislation were contested and ultimately nullified by the U.S. Supreme Court, but the desire for decency without censorship has not died among lawmakers. In an effort to avoid further government regulations, many Internet service companies are establishing their own policies for policing and monitoring their customers' online activity.

In many countries, export restrictions affect the type of technology that can be sold to foreign governments and individuals. For example, before being exported from the United States, software and hardware products that contain certain encryption algorithms must be registered with the U.S. government. Additional government regulations that pertain to law enforcement, national security, e-commerce, and taxation can also affect the way the IT industry conducts its business and how it engineers products.

FIGURE 9-25

IT Industry Regulation

Internet activity is affected by policies of the U.S. Federal Communications Commission (FCC), which regulates interstate and international communications by television, wire, radio, satellite, and cable.

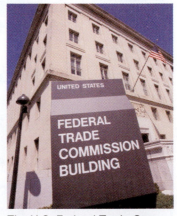

The U.S. Federal Trade Commission (FTC) and Department of Justice police the business practices of the IT industry, just as they police other industries.

How does the IT industry perceive government regulation?

Most IT industry leaders oppose further regulation of their industry. They remain skeptical of government regulations that might limit their ability to explore new technologies and offer them to the public. To avoid further government intervention, the IT industry has taken steps toward self-regulation.

Several organizations provide a forum for the IT industry to examine issues, express views, work out self-governing policies, and set standards. The Information Technology Industry Council has become one of the major trade associations for computer manufacturers, telecommunications suppliers, business equipment dealers, software publishers, and IT service providers. As part of its mission, this organization provides a powerful lobbying group, which works with lawmakers to minimize legislation that might curtail technology innovation and use.

The Software & Information Industry Association, formerly known as the Software Publishers Association, has 600 member companies and organizations. This organization focuses on protecting the intellectual property of members and lobbying for a legal and regulatory environment that benefits the entire IT industry. Its anti-piracy program is instrumental in identifying and prosecuting software and Internet piracy cases.

Organizations such as the IEEE Standards Association help the IT industry standardize technology, such as microprocessor architecture and network protocols, as well as programming languages and multimedia components.

QuickCheck

1. The computer industry can be divided into broad categories called [_____] or segments.

2. [_____] Valley is regarded as the birthplace of integrated circuits, microprocessors, and personal computers.

3. To stay competitive, many companies turn to [_____], which locates development and production to lower-cost locations in other countries.

4. Internet-based companies called [_____] coms fueled a stock market boom that turned into a bust.

5. The life cycle of a new computer model typically evolves through five stages: product development, product announcement, introduction, maintenance, and [_____].

6. Some products, which are referred to as [_____], are announced but never produced.

7. Computer companies use a variety of marketing [_____], such as retail stores and VARs, to reach consumers.

 CHECK ANSWERS

Careers for Computer Professionals

TODAY, IT SEEMS that just about everyone uses computers at work. In fact, it is difficult to find a job nowadays that does not make use of computers in some capacity. But who writes the software that's used by all these workers? Who designs their hardware, configures their networks, and troubleshoots their technical glitches? In this part of the chapter, you'll learn about a special cadre of workers within the IT industry called computer professionals. You'll find out who they are, what they do, who employs them, and how much they're paid. Maybe you'll even get a glimpse of your own future, if you're considering a career in IT.

JOBS AND SALARIES

What is a computer professional? In 1999, the U.S. Congress crafted an amendment to the Fair Labor Standards Act that essentially defines a **computer professional** as any person whose primary occupation involves the design, configuration, analysis, development, modification, testing, or security of computer hardware or software.

What kinds of jobs are typically available to computer professionals? Many computer professionals work in an **Information Systems department**—the wing of a business or organization responsible for computer, data, software, and support services. An IS department is also responsible for prioritizing an organization's information needs, modifying old systems as necessary, and creating new systems.

Historically, IS departments were part of an organization's Finance department because computers were initially deployed for accounting and inventory management functions. As computers began to assist with a wider variety of business tasks, some organizations changed their organizational charts to make the IS department a separate entity reporting directly to the chief executive officer or president. This reorganization provided IS departments with more autonomy to make budget decisions and prioritize projects. In addition, it provided more interaction with employees and managers from other departments.

Most IS departments are headed by a **chief information officer** (CIO), or director. The CIO heads a hierarchy of computer professionals, who might be organized as in Figure 9-26. The following descriptions highlight typical responsibilities and skills for various IS department jobs:

A **systems analyst** investigates the requirements of a business or organization, its employees, and its customers in order to plan and implement new or improved computer services. This job requires the ability to identify problems and research technical solutions. Good communications skills are essential for interacting with managers and other employees.

FIGURE 9-26

The organizational structure of information systems departments vary. This organizational structure might typically be found in a mid-size business.

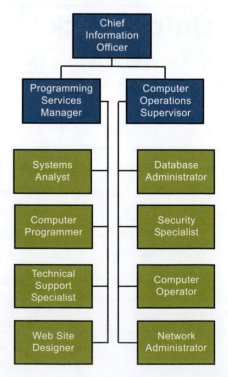

A **computer programmer** (sometimes described as a programmer/analyst) designs, codes, and tests computer programs. In addition, programmers modify existing programs to meet new requirements or eliminate bugs. Computer programming requires concentration and a good memory for the countless details that pertain to a programming project. Programming projects range from entertainment and games to business and productivity applications. Programmers get satisfaction from devising efficient ways to make a computer perform specific jobs, tasks, and routines.

A **security specialist** analyzes a computer system's vulnerability to threats from viruses, worms, unauthorized access, and physical damage. Security specialists install and configure firewalls and antivirus software. They also work with management and employees to develop policies and procedures to protect computer equipment and data. Computer security is punctuated by crises when a virus hits or a security breach is discovered. A security specialist must have wide-ranging knowledge of computers as well as communications protocols that can be applied for a quick resolution to any crisis that occurs.

A **database administrator** analyzes a company's data to determine the most effective way to collect and store it. Database administrators create databases, data entry forms, and reports. They also define backup procedures, provide access to authorized users, and supervise the day-to-day use of databases.

A **network specialist/administrator** plans, installs, and maintains one or more local area networks. These specialists also provide network accounts and access rights to approved users. They troubleshoot connectivity problems and respond to requests from the network's users for new software. Network specialists/administrators might be responsible for maintaining the security of a network, plus they often pick up Webmaster duties to maintain an organization's Web site.

A **computer operator** typically works with network servers, mainframes, and supercomputers. Computer operators monitor computer performance, install software patches and upgrades, perform backups, and restore data as necessary.

A **technical support specialist** troubleshoots hardware and software problems. Good interpersonal skills and patience are required for this job (Figure 9-27).

A **Web site designer** creates, tests, posts, and modifies Web pages. A good sense of design and artistic talent are required for this job, along with an understanding of how people use graphical user interfaces. Familiarity with Web tools, such as HTML, XML, JavaScript, and ActiveX, is becoming more important for this job, as is a knowledge of computer programming and database management.

Do computer professionals work outside of IS departments?

In addition to jobs in IS departments, computer professionals also find work in companies that produce computer hardware and software. Some of these jobs are listed on the next page.

INFOWEBLINKS

Before making a career decision, it is important for you to research current industry trends and the general economic outlook. The **Career Outlook InfoWeb** will help you access Web resources on this topic.

CLICK TO CONNECT
www.course.com/np/concepts11/ch09

FIGURE 9-27

Some technical support specialists work inhouse with company employees, whereas others provide remote phone support for customers.

9

A **technical writer** creates documentation for large programming projects and writes the online or printed user manuals that accompany computers, peripheral devices, and software. Some technical writers work for computer magazines, writing columns about the latest hardware products, software, and automated business solutions. Good writing and communications skills are valuable for this job, as is an ability to quickly learn how to use new computers and software.

A **computer salesperson**, or sales rep, sells computers. Sales reps might pay personal visits to potential corporate customers or staff the order desk of a mail-order computer company. Sales reps' starting salaries tend to be low but are usually supplemented by commissions. Effective sales reps have good interpersonal skills, an ability to remember technical specifications, and an understanding of business problems and solutions.

A **quality assurance specialist** participates in alpha and beta test cycles of software, looking for bugs or other usability problems. This job title sometimes refers to assembly-line workers who examine and test chips, circuit boards, computers, and peripheral devices. An effective QA specialist has a good eye for detail and a passion for perfection.

A **computer engineer** designs and tests new hardware products, such as computer chips, circuit boards, computers, and peripheral devices.

A **manufacturing technician** participates in the fabrication of computer chips, circuit boards, system units, or peripheral devices. Some of these jobs require basic screwdriver skills, whereas others require special training in microlithography.

These job descriptions are but a sample of those in IS departments and the IT industry. Additional job titles are listed in Figure 9-28.

What's the outlook for computer careers? According to an Information Technology Association of America study, the U.S.-based IT workforce totaled about 10.4 million in 2000, but lost 500,000 jobs in 2001 as the dot com bubble burst. A small but steady upswing from 2002 through 2006 brought the IT workforce close to its year 2000 peak. In coming years, the highest demand may be for technical support specialists, network system designers and administrators, and security specialists.

As in the past, economic trends could cause significant changes in the job market. In preparing for an IT career, flexibility is the key. You should be willing to train and then retrain as new skills are needed to work with emerging technologies.

What can I expect as a salary for an IT industry job? Web sites such as *www.bls.gov* provide salary data for various IT industry jobs. In addition to data from the Bureau of Labor Statistics, you can find comparative IT industry salary averages using a standard Web search engine.

As with almost every industry, the compensation rates for jobs in the IT industry vary. Jobs that require college degrees and certification typically pay more than jobs that require a high school diploma and some on-the-job training. IT industry salaries also vary by geographic location. In the United States, the highest salaries tend to be offered in the Northeast and on the West Coast—two regions where the cost of living is relatively high.

FIGURE 9-28

The Information Technology Association of America (ITAA) categorizes IT jobs into eight clusters, shown in bold. Sample job titles are listed here and in the continuation of this figure on the next page.

Database Administration and Development
Database Administrator
Database Analyst
Database Developer
Database Manager
Database Security Expert
DSS (Decision Support Services)
Knowledge Architect

Digital Media
2-D/3-D Artist
Animator
Audio/Video Engineer
Designer
Media Specialist
Media/Instructional Designer
Multimedia Author
Multimedia Authoring Specialist
Multimedia Developer
Multimedia Specialist
Producer
Streaming Media Specialist
Virtual Reality Specialist

Enterprise Systems Analysis and Integration
Application Integrator
Business Continuity Analyst
Cross-Enterprise Integrator
Data Systems Designer
Data Systems Manager
E-business Specialist
Information Systems Architect
Information Systems Planner
Systems Analyst
Systems Architect
Systems Integrator

Network Design and Administration
Communications Analyst
Network Administrator
Network Analyst
Network Architect
Network Engineer
Network Manager
Network Operations Analyst
Network Security Analyst
Network Specialist
Network Technician

What are the advantages of working in the computer industry? Many technology companies offer employee-friendly working conditions that include child care, flexible hours, and the opportunity to work from home. As in any industry, the exact nature of a job depends on the company and the particular projects that are in the works. Some jobs and projects are more interesting than others.

What about part-time or contract work? The average IT industry employee works a 40-hour week, and often longer hours are required. Part-time workers are defined as those who are required to be on the job for fewer than 40 hours a week. The number of part-time workers in the computer industry is similar to other industries.

The IT industry has an unusually large number of contract and temporary workers. A **contract worker** is typically hired as a consultant. Contract workers are not official employees of a company. They might be paid by the job, rather than by the hour; they are not eligible for a company's health insurance benefits or retirement plan, and they must pay self-employment taxes.

IT businesses benefit from the ability to hire contract workers. The pool of IT contract workers offers a selection of people with specialized skills. Contract workers can be added to a company's staff when needed, instead of hiring full-time workers who might later be laid off if the company is forced to downsize. A few businesses, however, have been accused of misusing contract workers by hiring them for years at a time without paying benefits. Potential contract workers are advised to carefully read their contracts and understand the terms of employment.

Can I work at an IT job from home? Workers in many industries are interested in **telecommuting**—using available technology to work from home or an off-site location. In recent years, businesses have begun to allow telecommuting because it makes financial sense. Telecommuters tend to be more productive and work longer hours because they have no commute time, and they are not interrupted by routine office chatter.

Telecommuting also has disadvantages. Some workers need supervision or they procrastinate. The home environment can be distracting, which reduces productivity. Security is also a concern—especially the security of data transmitted from home workers to corporate networks.

The Internet and telecommunications technologies have made an impact on the availability of telecommuting opportunities for workers. It has become common for employees to collaborate through e-mail, fax, groupware, and videoconferencing. Although the majority of IT workers still commute to work, industry observers expect the number of telecommuting IT workers to increase. Programming and customer support are likely to be the first jobs with a significant number of telecommuting workers.

FIGURE 9-28 (CONTINUED)

Programming/Software Engineering
Applications Analyst
Applications Engineer
Business Analyst
Computer Engineer
OS Designer/Engineer
OS Programmer/Analyst
Program Manager
Programmer
Programmer/Analyst
Software Applications Specialist
Software Architect
Software Design Engineer
Software Engineer
Software QA Specialist
Software Tester

Technical Support
Call Center Support Rep
Customer Liaison
Customer Service Rep
Customer Support Professional
Help Desk Specialist
Help Desk Technician
PC Support Specialist
PC Systems Coordinator
Product Support Engineer
Sales Support Technician
Technical Account Manager
Technical Support Engineer
Technical Support
    Representative

Technical Writing
Desktop Publisher
Document Specialist
Documentation Specialist
Editor
Electronic Publications
    Specialist
Electronic Publisher
Instructional Designer
Online Publisher
Technical Communicator
Technical Editor
Technical Publications Manager
Technical Writer

Web Development and Administration
Web Administrator
Web Architect
Web Designer
Web Page Developer
Web Site Developer
Web Specialist
Webmaster

9

EDUCATION AND CERTIFICATION

What are the basic qualifications for IT industry jobs?

Qualifications for most IT industry jobs include some type of higher education, certification, or computer experience. A bachelor's degree in a computer-related discipline is the most prevalent requirement, but some employers accept a two-year associate's degree. The table in Figure 9-29 shows the education and experience employers seek in IT job applicants.

Do I need a computer science degree to work in the computer industry?

Computer science is only one of many computer-related degrees that colleges and universities offer. According to the Association for Computing Machinery (ACM), there are five major computing disciplines, as described here.

Computer engineering focuses on the design of computer hardware and peripheral devices, often at the chip level. The curriculum includes basic studies in calculus, chemistry, engineering, physics, computer organization, logic design, computer architecture, microprocessor design, and signal processing. Students learn how to design new computer circuits, microchips, and other electronic components, plus they learn how to design new computer instruction sets and combine electronic or optical components to provide powerful, cost-effective computing. A degree in computer engineering provides excellent qualifications for working at a chip manufacturer, such as Intel, Motorola, IBM, or Texas Instruments.

Computer science focuses on computer architecture and how to program computers to make them work effectively and efficiently. The curriculum includes courses in programming, algorithms, software development, computer architecture, data representation, logic design, calculus, discrete math, and physics. Students investigate the fundamental theories of how computers solve problems, and they learn how to write application programs, system software, computer languages, and device drivers. Computer science graduates generally find jobs as programmers, with good possibilities for advancement to software engineers, object-oriented/GUI developers, and project managers in technical applications development. Computer scientists work as theorists, inventors, and researchers in fields as diverse as artificial intelligence, virtual reality, and computer games.

Information systems degree programs, typically offered by a university's College of Business, focus on applying computers to business problems. The curriculum includes course work in business, accounting, computer programming, communications, systems analysis, and human psychology. For students who want to become computer professionals but lack strong math aptitude, most academic advisors recommend the information systems degree. An information systems degree usually leads to a programming or technical support job, with good possibilities for advancement to systems analyst, project manager, database administrator, network manager, or other management positions.

Information technology degree programs focus on the computer equipment and software used by businesses and organizations—how they work, how they are secured, upgraded, maintained, and replaced. Students in an IT program typically work hands-on with hardware, networks, Web pages, multimedia, e-mail systems, and security. Graduates work as network specialists and administrators, systems analysts, and help desk technicians.

FIGURE 9-29

Across all IT job categories, the highest percentage of employers are looking for applicants with previous work experience in a similar job and relevant four-year degrees.

Credentials Wanted by Employers	
Previous experience in a similar job	46%
Four-year college degree in a related field	41%
Two-year degree	16%
Vendor certification	14%
Four-year degree in non-related field	3%
Advanced degree	3%

INFOWEBLINKS

If you're still not sure about the right career path, connect to the **Career Assessment InfoWeb**, where you'll find links to interactive materials that help you evaluate your aptitude for various jobs.

W **CLICK TO CONNECT**
www.course.com/np/concepts11/ch09

Software engineering takes a disciplined approach to developing software that is reliable, efficient, affordable, user-friendly, and scalable. Often this degree program includes courses from Information Systems and Computer Science curricula. Graduates with software engineering degrees often work on large-scale, safety-critical applications.

What kinds of computer jobs require only an associate's degree? Colleges, community colleges, and technical schools offer several computer-related associate's degrees, ranging from computer programming to graphic design, networking, and telecommunications. The curriculum for these programs varies from one degree program to another, but all tend to require intensive course work. Graduates of two-year programs typically find employment as entry-level technicians, programmers, and support personnel. Advancement opportunities might be limited, however, without additional education or certification.

Do I need a graduate degree? Master's degrees in software engineering have been difficult to find, except at large research universities with well-established computer science programs. A master's degree in computer science is available at most four-year colleges and universities that offer graduate degrees. Another option at the graduate level is to pursue a master's degree in information systems or a master's degree in business administration (MBA). Any of these graduate degrees would help you get a management position in the computer industry.

Doctoral degrees are available in software engineering, applications software engineering, systems software development, and management information systems. A doctoral degree in any of these areas would qualify you for advanced technical research or for a position as a college professor.

Where can I find information on computer-related degree programs? Peterson's is a comprehensive resource for educational services. Its Web site at *www.petersons.com* has become a primary resource for locating educational programs as well as providing testing services for admissions and certification. Peterson's maintains a searchable database of two-year and four-year programs that prepare you for a variety of IT jobs. You can find additional information at the Web sites of various technical schools, community colleges, and universities.

What type of certification is available? Certification falls into two broad categories: certificates of completion and certification exams (Figure 9-30). **Certificates of completion** are offered to students who successfully complete one or more courses on a specific topic. Community colleges and technical schools often offer certificates of completion in a variety of computer-related areas, such as Information Technology Specialist, LAN Administrator, User Support Specialist, PC/Hardware Support Specialist, and IT Operations Specialist.

How important is certification? Certification alone is rarely sufficient to qualify you for a job in the IT industry. Paired with a college degree or extensive experience, however, several studies suggest that certification can improve your chances for employment, increase your credibility in the workplace, and lead to higher salaries. Many employers view certification with some degree of skepticism, so the value of a certificate depends on where, when, and how it is obtained. Critics of certification exams, for example, maintain that a multiple-choice test cannot accurately measure a person's ability to deal with real-world equipment and software. Bottom line: Certification is only part of your total package of qualifications.

FIGURE 9-30

Certification exams are offered in a variety of formats. Some are offered online, but most take place in authorized testing venues, such as schools.

9

A **certification exam** is an objective test that verifies your level of knowledge about a particular technology or subject. Approximately 300 computer-related certification exams are offered in areas of specialty that range from desktop publishing to network installation. Most of these exams use multiple-choice format, last several hours, and require substantial testing fees.

You can prepare for a certification exam with independent study materials (Figure 9-31), online tutorials, or an exam preparation class. Certification exams can be divided into several categories:

● **General computer knowledge.** IC3 certification, offered by Certiport, covers basic computing knowledge and skills. General certification is also offered by the International Computer Driving License (ICDL).

The Institute for Certification of Computing Professionals (ICCP) offers several generalized certification exams, such as the Information Systems CORE, leading to CCP (Certified Computing Professional) certification. According to the ICCP Web site, "Professionals certified with ICCP serve as consultants, working with local, state, and federal government; in accounting and banking; in high schools, technical schools, and universities; in the manufacturing industry; in insurance and numerous other fields."

● **Software applications.** Many certification exams allow you to demonstrate your prowess with a specific software application. The Microsoft Office Specialist certification is perhaps the most popular, but of limited value to most computer professionals who are expected to be able to quickly learn such applications on their own. Certification in productivity applications is most valuable for entry-level secretarial and clerical positions as well as help desk personnel.

Autodesk offers the AutoCAD Certified User exam on the use of its 3-D design software. Certification is also available for popular Adobe software applications, such as Illustrator, InDesign, PhotoShop, and Premiere. Adobe offers certification for Dreamweaver, Flash, and ColdFusion software products previously marketed by Macromedia.

● **Database administration.** Databases require a high level of expertise, not only in the use of database software, but in the conception and design of database structures. Many computer professionals have sought certification in database systems, such as Oracle, Access, Sybase, and DB2. The most popular database certification exams include the Microsoft Certified Database Administrator (MCDBA) and Oracle Certified Professional.

● **Networking.** Among computer professionals, network certification might be the most useful. One of the earliest network certification exams was offered by Novell, publisher of the NetWare network operating system. Microsoft offers a corresponding MCSE certification (Microsoft Certified Systems Engineer). Network hardware certification includes the Cisco Certified Network Professional (CCNP), offered by network equipment supplier Cisco Systems. Wireless network certification, such as Planet3 Wireless CWNP certification, is available too.

● **Computer hardware.** One of the most popular computer hardware certification exams is the A+ Certification, sponsored by the Computing Technology Industry Association (CompTIA). This exam is designed to certify the competency of entry-level computer service technicians for installing, configuring, upgrading, troubleshooting, and repairing personal computer systems. A+ Certification provides good credentials for employment in a computer store or computer repair shop.

FIGURE 9-31

Your local bookstore and the Internet provide sources for independent study materials that can help you prepare for an IT certification exam.

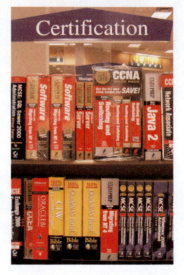

INFOWEBLINKS

For a comprehensive list of certification exams and tips on how to prepare for them, connect to the **Certification InfoWeb**.

W CLICK TO CONNECT
www.course.com/np/concepts11/ch09

- **Computer security.** With the proliferation of computer viruses and worms, analysts predict that computer security will become a hot niche for IT workers. CompTIA offers the Security+ certification exam, which covers topics such as cryptography, access control, authentication, external attack, and operational security. The International Information Systems Security Consortium offers a Certified Information System Security Professional (CISSP) exam.

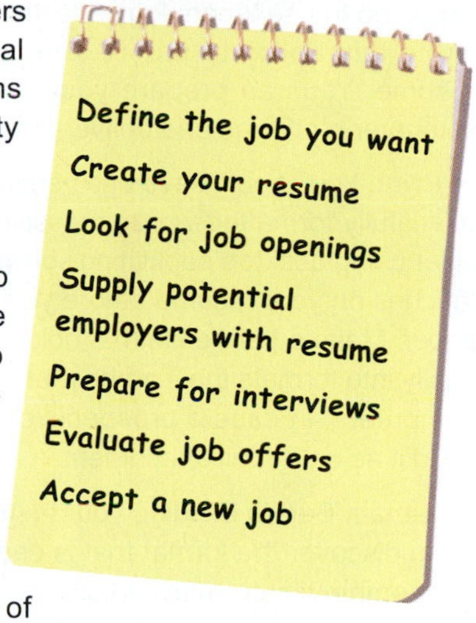

JOB HUNTING BASICS

How do I find a job in the IT industry? In many ways, finding a job in the IT industry is just like finding a job in any other industry. Effective job seekers begin by taking stock of their qualifications, identifying job titles relevant to their skills, identifying potential employers, and considering the geographic area in which they want to work. They then create a carefully worded resume, look for job openings, contact potential employers, and work with employment agencies and recruiting firms. Figure 9-32 summarizes the steps in a job hunt.

Conventional wisdom about job hunting applies to a broad spectrum of industries, such as financial, automotive, hospitality, and even entertainment. But one job-hunting strategy is not necessarily effective for every job in every industry. Take a closer look at the job hunting process, and examine how hunting for an IT job might differ from a job search in other industries.

How can I use the Internet to find a job? The Internet has become an important tool for job hunters. In 1994, about 10,000 resumes were posted on the Web. Today, the Web plays host to millions of resumes.

The Internet can figure into your job hunt in several ways, including researching potential jobs and employers, posting your resume, locating job leads, and corresponding with potential employers. Career counselors warn of placing too much emphasis on the online aspects of your job search. "Don't put all your eggs in the online basket" is often-repeated advice. Job-hunting experts advise IT job seekers to spend no more than 50% of their total job-hunting efforts online; the other 50% should be spent making contacts with recruiters, placement agencies, career counselors, and mentors. Rather than accept that advice outright, consider it with regard to your employment needs, geographical location, and current employment situation.

Where do I start? You should begin by defining the jobs for which you are qualified. In the IT industry, job titles are not standardized. For example, the job title for a person who provides employee or customer support over the phone might be Help Desk Operator, Customer Support Technician, Support Specialist, Personal Computer Specialist, Technology Support Specialist, or Inbound Telephone Service Consultant.

Nonstandardized job titles can pose a problem for job hunters, especially those who use search engines to locate job openings. Failure to enter one of the many titles for a job might mean that a job hunter misses a good opportunity. Although many job search sites maintain their own lists of equivalent job titles, job hunters in the IT industry should take some time to compile their own lists of equivalent job titles and relevant search terms. You can compile such a list by entering the key phrases *job titles* and *computer industry* into a general search engine such as Google. Connect to the sites the search produces, and take note of any job titles that seem applicable.

FIGURE 9-32

Job Hunting Steps

Define the job you want
Create your resume
Look for job openings
Supply potential employers with resume
Prepare for interviews
Evaluate job offers
Accept a new job

INFOWEBLINKS

At the **Online Job Hunting InfoWeb**, you'll find lots of tips for using technology to find a job.

W CLICK TO CONNECT
www.course.com/np/concepts11/ch09

9

RESUMES AND WEB PORTFOLIOS

Do I need an online resume? As a computer professional, you are expected to use technology effectively for everyday tasks. You can demonstrate this ability to prospective employers by the way you treat your resume. You can prepare your resume in formats suitable for different computer platforms and delivery methods, as shown in Figure 9-33.

- **Print.** You should save one version of your resume as a beautifully formatted word processing file. You might consider using desktop publishing software to put the finishing touches on your resume before you print it on high-quality paper. Make sure the file that holds your resume converts easily into formats that can be read by Mac, PC, and Linux computers, in case a prospective employer asks you to send it as an e-mail attachment.

- **E-mail.** Before sending your resume as an attachment, try to discover the format that is easiest for your prospective employer to use. Microsoft's Rich Text Format produces files with .rtf extensions, which can be read by a variety of word processing software. Microsoft's DOC format is widely used, but its DOCX format is less popular.

Some career counselors advise against the use of e-mail attachments, suggesting that many employers never open attachments for fear of e-mail viruses. Instead of attaching your resume, you can simply paste it into the body of an e-mail message. To make sure it is formatted for maximum readability, you might want to create a plain ASCII version of your resume, without fancy fonts, bullets, or symbols. This ASCII version might also be useful for online job posting sites that store your resume information in a searchable database.

- **HTML and XML.** You might also want to create HTML and XML versions of your resume. You can paste the HTML version into an HTML-formatted e-mail message or post it on a Web site provided by your school or ISP. You might also consider developing an XML resume based on standard XML stylesheets. For more information, refer to *xmlresume.sourceforge.net*.

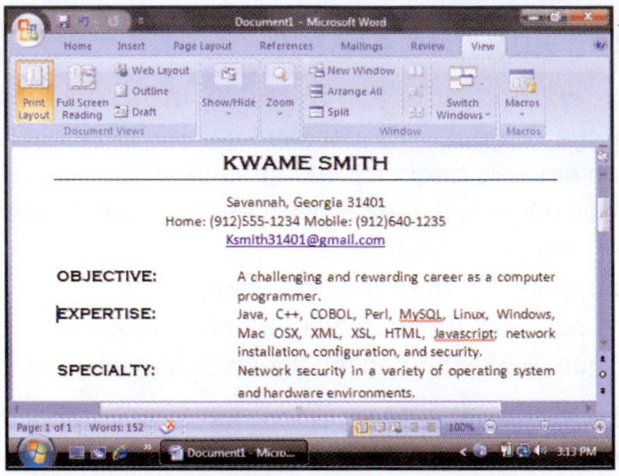

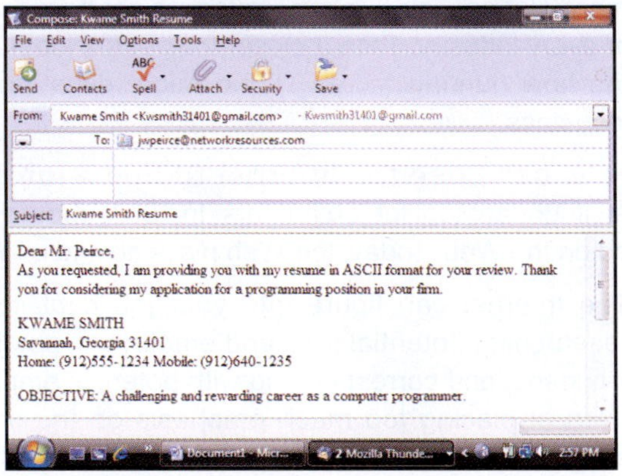

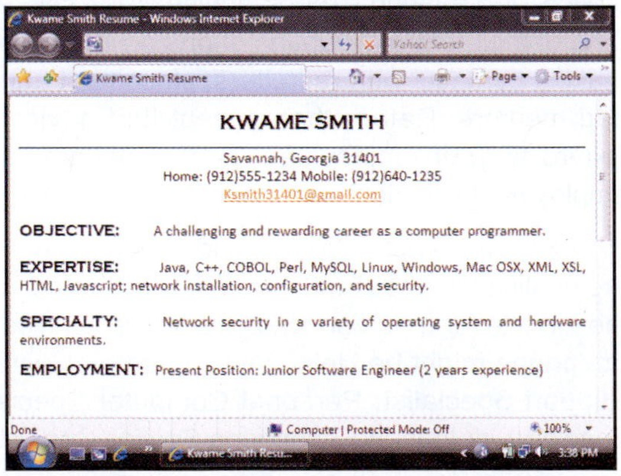

Should an IT industry resume contain any special elements? Regardless of the industry in which you seek employment, an effective resume is clear, correct, and easy to read. When developing your resume, you can ask friends, coworkers, and career counselors to review your drafts and provide suggestions for improvement. Figure 9-34 on the next page shows a short checklist of resume writing guidelines.

FIGURE 9-33

Job seekers can format their resumes for printed output, e-mail delivery, or Web posting.

In the past, tips on how to create the perfect resume applied to a conventional process in which a recruiter sifted through a pile of resumes that arrived by surface mail. Job seekers spent hours agonizing over the weight, texture, and color of the paper on which they printed their resumes.

Conventional tips about paper color, fonts, and wording remain valid for hard-copy resumes. Today, however, resumes are often stored in online databases, which are initially scanned not by human eyes, but by a computer.

How can my resume get maximum exposure in an online job database? For resumes that become part of a computer-searchable database, experts recommend that you focus on nouns, not verbs. At one time, the trend was to pepper your resume with action phrases and power verbs, such as "implemented successful solutions" and "created innovative algorithms." When employers use a job site's search engine to locate potential employees, however, they typically search for particular skills by entering nouns associated with programming language names, software, computer equipment, analysis methodologies, and business sectors. They might also enter buzzwords and acronyms, such as XML, B2B, client/server, API, and P2P, which relate to specific IT tools and methods. Job seekers should try to envision the search terms that employers might enter, and then include applicable terms in their resumes.

In addition to computer-related search terms, employers sometimes search for terms that indicate a job applicant's personality, communication skills, and work ethic. When appropriate, adjectives such as "enthusiastic," "team player," "industrious," "honest," "capable," and "experienced" can be effective in helping an online recruiter pull your resume from those submitted by thousands of other applicants.

What other factors are important for online resumes? Today's trend to search resumes online has implications for all job seekers, not just those in the IT industry. For example, you should avoid formatting your resume into side-by-side columns because the columns could get scrambled when transferred to an online job database.

Experience is important, but the old style of dating your tenure at a job supplies little information for online searches. Information such as "Intern IBM from 2003-2005" does not produce a hit for a recruiter searching online for "IBM >2 years." By modifying your online resume to "Intern IBM, 2 years: 2003-2005," you provide better information for electronic searches.

What is a Web portfolio? A **Web portfolio** is a hypertext version of your resume, which might contain links to relevant Web sites, such as past employers, your alma mater, and samples of your work. For example, a programmer might include a link to one of her particularly well-documented and elegant programs, or a Web designer might provide links to sites that he designed.

Should I jazz up my Web portfolio with multimedia? Current technology gives you the ability to personalize your Web portfolio with photos, your favorite music, or even video portraits that demonstrate your speaking and communications abilities. Forget the music—it is more likely to irritate prospective employers than impress them. Photos and videos that indicate an applicant's age, gender, ethnicity, or physical characteristics also

FIGURE 9-34

Resume Writing Guidelines

Tips for an Effective Resume

Be clear and concise

- Eliminate unnecessary words, phrases, and sentences.
- Be economical with words when describing tasks, duties, titles, and accomplishments.
- Be brief and to the point without selling yourself short.

Place the most important point first

- List your qualifications by importance and relevance to the job you seek.
- Summarize skills at the top of the resume.
- Use a bold font to emphasize skills and accomplishments that are required for the position you seek.
- Include pertinent information about training, certification, and professional affiliations, but avoid personal information, such as church affiliation and hobbies, that is not directly related to the job.

Use language effectively

- Target terms and wording to prospective employers.
- Use industry jargon wherever appropriate.
- Use action verbs to maintain the reader's interest.
- Use past and present tenses consistently. Double-check grammar and spelling.
- When posting information in a database, use nouns that describe your skills.

INFOWEBLINKS

Because of their extensive knowledge about computers, job seekers in the IT industry may be able to understand the implications of online resume searches better than their counterparts in other industries. It doesn't hurt to get some tips from the experts at the **Resume Guide InfoWeb**.

CLICK TO CONNECT

www.course.com/np/concepts11/ch09

9

have potential drawbacks. Decisions based on such characteristics could be viewed as discriminatory. You might want to keep such multimedia presentations on hand but supply them only when requested.

Where do I post my Web portfolio? You can post your Web portfolio on your personal Web site. If you don't already have such a site, your school or ISP might offer tools to build one. Just remember that your personal Web site is an open book to prospective employers. If you don't want them to know the details about last summer's vacation, you should remove such extraneous material from your Web site. Even if you don't supply the URL for your Web site to prospective employers, remember that your Web site can be easily found simply by entering your name in a search engine, such as Yahoo!

JOB LISTINGS

Where can I find a list of job openings? To find job openings, you can begin with the usual sources of job listings: the newspaper's Help Wanted section, your school's career placement office, and your local state employment agency. Typically, you'll move quickly to online resources, such as online newspapers, company Web sites, and job banks.

On the Web you can access the Help Wanted sections from major metropolitan newspapers. Many companies maintain Web sites that include links to information about their job openings. If you have a short list of companies that you'd like to work for, check out their Web sites.

How do online job banks work? An **online job bank** maintains a database that contains thousands of job openings posted by employers. The largest job banks span just about every industry. Others are devoted to specific industries. Several online job banks specialize in the IT industry.

Job banks typically offer free access to job seekers, although you might be required to register before searching. You can search most online job databases by job title, geographic location, or company (Figure 9-35).

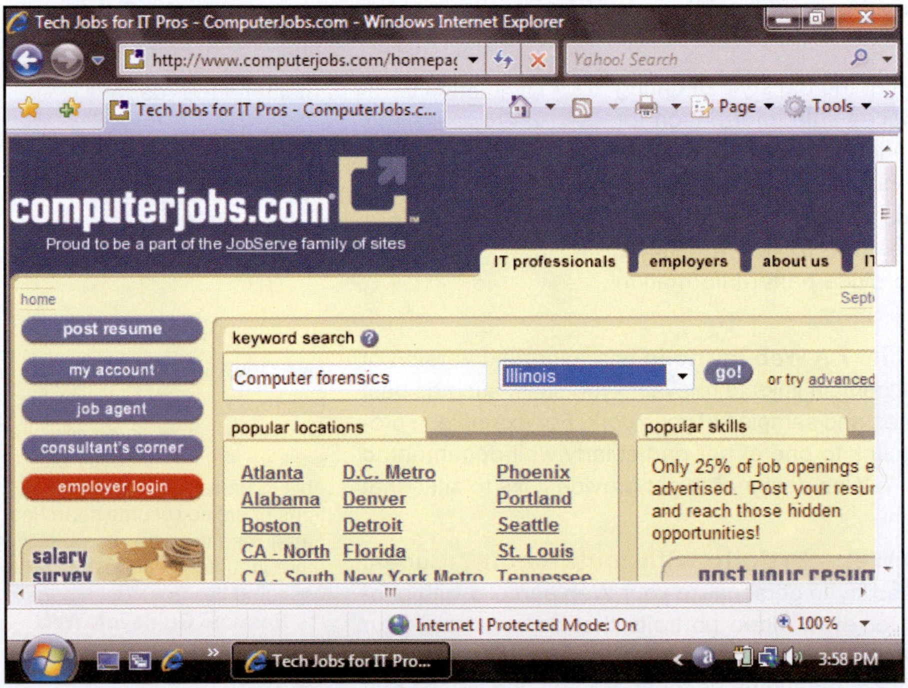

FIGURE 9-35

If your search turns up a job that looks promising, most job banks provide a way to apply online by sending your resume information to the employer through the job bank's Web site. To use the *apply online* feature, you're typically required to register with the job bank.

▶ CLICK TO START

Do I have to manually search every online job bank? The Internet offers thousands of job banks, each with unique job announcements. Searching all these sites manually would be a full-time job in itself! Search agents and metasearch tools allow you to automate the search process across many sites.

A **job search agent** is an automated program that searches one or more databases and notifies you when it finds any leads that match your specified criteria. To use a job search agent, you configure it with keywords that describe the type of job you want, your geographical limitations, and salary requirements. You then launch the agent and it searches for matching job announcements. When a match is found, the search agent generates an e-mail message with the information you need to view the job posting. Most job banks provide access to free job search agents.

Some search agents work within one specific site—typically an online job bank. Other search agents visit multiple Web sites. The key advantage of a job search agent, such as the one shown in Figure 9-36, is that you don't have to be online while it works.

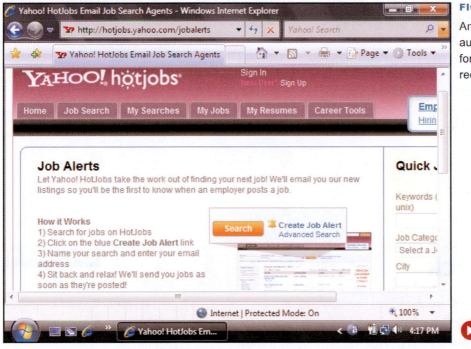

FIGURE 9-36

An online search agent autonomously searches for jobs that match your requirements.

▶ CLICK TO START

9

A **metasearch tool** is a software program that performs broad-based Web searches, such as searching more than one job database at a time. In some respects, a metasearch tool is similar to a multi-site job search agent, except that when you use a metasearch tool, you must remain online. Instead of notifying you by e-mail, a metasearch tool supplies a list of links to applicable job postings, similar to the links provided by a standard search engine, such as Google.

How well do job banks protect my privacy? Job seekers who post their resumes at online job banks should be aware of potential threats to their privacy. Without privacy safeguards, the information in your online resume could be used to compile a profile of you, which could be misused by advertisers or individuals interested in stealing identities. Some job banks might distribute your resume or personal information without your authorization. Sometimes job banks sell resumes to employers and pass personal information to advertisers. Before posting your resume, always check the job bank's privacy policy.

If a job bank requires you to register, follow common sense to protect your privacy. Do not, for example, provide your Social Security number. Although it is required for jobs in the United States, your Social Security number should be given only to your employer after you receive a job offer.

If your job bank allows you to set an expiration date for your resume, do so just in case you forget to manually remove it when your job search is complete.

To protect your privacy, you might also consider removing most of the contact information, such as your address and phone number, from your online resume. You should provide an e-mail address, but not the address of the business e-mail account supplied by your employer. Also, make sure your e-mail address is not linked to a personal profile, as it is on America Online (AOL) and some other Internet provider sites. You can open a Web-based e-mail account specifically devoted to job hunting. By the way, consider your e-mail user ID carefully. Employers might respond better to an e-mail address such as excellentprogrammer@hotmail.com than an address such as bigbertha@hotmail.com.

Many job seekers are hesitant to post their resumes for fear that their current employers will learn they are preparing to jump ship. Some job banks allow you to block access to your resume by specific employers. You can learn about the features of each job bank by connecting to its links for Help, Privacy, and Terms of Use.

INFOWEBLINKS

Connect to the **Online Job Banks InfoWeb** for links to the most popular Web-based job databases.

 CLICK TO CONNECT
www.course.com/np/concepts11/ch09

QuickCheck

1. The term *computer professional* is loosely defined as programmers and systems analysts who work in the IT industry. True or false? [   ]

2. A(n) [   ] specialist analyzes a computer system's vulnerability to viruses, worms, unauthorized access, and physical damage.

3. The advantage of [   ] is reduced commute time, but disadvantages include distractions and security risks.

4. [   ] systems degree programs focus on applying computers to business problems.

5. IC3, ICDL, and MCSE are examples of computer [   ] exams.

6. A Web [   ] is a hypertext version of your resume, which might include links to Web sites and samples of your work.

7. A(n) [   ] tool performs broad-based Web searches similar to the way a search engine works.

 CHECK ANSWERS

Professional Ethics

WHEN DISCUSSING ETHICAL ISSUES, we often do so from the perspective of the victim. We imagine how it might feel if someone else—an employer, the government, cyberpunks, and so on—pilfered our original artwork from a Web site, read our e-mail, or stole our credit card number from an e-commerce site. It is quite possible, however, that at some time in your career, you could become the perpetrator—the copyright violator, the snoop, or the thief—without intending to cause harm. Section D presents information about professional ethics as they relate to computing and digital technologies.

ETHICS BASICS

What are professional ethics? The term **professional ethics** refers to on-the-job choices and actions that reflect a person's values. Ethics define standards of conduct that specify how workers should behave, particularly in situations where doing the right thing might not seem to have short-term benefits, or when doing something of questionable legality seems to offer attractive benefits. Situations, like the one in Figure 9-37, in which you ask yourself, "What's the right thing to do?" often require you to make ethical decisions.

Professional ethics are derived from principles of right and wrong. In most modern societies, the foundation for ethical decisions and actions is based on values such as impartiality, fairness, objectivity, honesty, regard for privacy, commitment to quality, and respect for others.

How are ethics related to laws? Laws are legislated documentation of permissible behavior based on a community's ethics. As computers and digital technologies play a more central role in every aspect of daily life, laws have been created to deal with computer uses and abuses. It is important to consider applicable laws as you make ethical decisions. Keep in mind, too, that laws relating to computers vary from country to country. Figure 9-38 on the next page provides a brief overview of the most significant computer laws and court decisions in the United States.

Although most laws try to promote ethical behavior, laws and ethics are not necessarily the same. Some behaviors are legal, but not necessarily ethical. Some laws are not ethical or their ethics are controversial. An act isn't ethical simply because it is permissible or you can get away with it. An ethical person often chooses to do more than the law requires and less than the law allows.

Are ethics different for various career fields? Ethical values such as honesty, fairness, respect, responsibility, and caring are reasonably universal and apply to any career field. The situations that require ethical decisions can vary from one career field to another, however. For example, medical ethics typically involve doctors and nurses in situations that are different from computer ethics situations that are encountered by programmers, network administrators, and other IT professionals.

FIGURE 9-37

If your boss asks you to divulge information about your work on a competing project with a previous employer, you'll score some points with your new employer if you give over the information, but doing so might not be fair or right.

INFOWEBLINKS

You'll find additional information about professional ethics at the **Ethics in Computing InfoWeb**.

Ⓦ **CLICK TO CONNECT**
www.course.com/np/concepts11/ch09

9

FIGURE 9-38

Significant U.S. Computer Laws
and Court Decisions

United States Copyright Act (1976) extends copyright protection beyond print media to "original works of authorship fixed in any tangible medium of expression, now known or later developed, from which they can be perceived, reproduced, or otherwise communicated, either directly or with the aid of a machine or device."

The **Fair Use Doctrine**, a part of the U.S. Copyright Act, generally allows copying if it is for educational or personal use, if only a portion of the original work is copied, and if it does not have substantial effect on the market for the original work.

Sony Corp. v. Universal Studios (1984) sets a precedent that companies are not liable for user infringements, such as using VCRs to make unauthorized copies of videotapes, so long as the technology has valid, non-infringing uses, such as copying personal home videos. In recent cases, the defense for peer-to-peer file sharing networks was based on this decision.

Computer Fraud and Abuse Act (1986 amended in 1994, 1996, 2001, and Patriot Act) makes it a criminal offense to knowingly access a computer without authorization, transmit a program, information, code, or command that causes damage, or distribute passwords that would enable unauthorized access.

Electronic Communications Privacy Act (1986) extends telephone wiretap laws by restricting government agents and unauthorized third parties from tapping into data transmissions without a search warrant. The law does not apply to data, such as e-mail, transmitted on employer-owned equipment.

Health Insurance Portability and Accountability Act (1996) requires healthcare providers to take reasonable procedural and technical safeguards to insure the confidentiality of individually identifiable health information.

Digital Millennium Copyright Act (1998) makes it illegal to circumvent copy-protection technologies, such as those used to prevent unauthorized copying of software CDs, music CDs, and movie DVDs. In addition, it is illegal to distribute any type of cracking software technology that would be used by others to circumvent copy protection. Protects ISPs against copyright infringement by subscribers if the ISP takes prompt action to block the infringement as soon as it discovers illegal activity.

Communications Decency Act (1996) protects ISPs from liability for defamatory statements made by customers. Prohibits material deemed offensive by local community standards from being transmitted to minors. The latter section was overturned in 2002.

Child Online Privacy Protection Act (1998) attempted to protect children from Internet pornography. Overturned in 1999.

Gramm-Leach-Bliley Act (1999) requires financial institutions to protect the confidentiality and security of customers' personal information.

Children's Internet Protection Act (2000) requires schools and libraries that receive federal funds to implement filtering software that protects adults and minors from obscenity and pornography.

USA Patriot Act (2001) enhances the authority of law enforcement agents to preempt potential terrorist acts by various means, such as monitoring electronic communications without first obtaining a search warrant in situations where there is imminent danger. Offers safe harbor to ISPs who voluntarily disclose potentially threatening activities of users. Increases maximum penalties for hackers.

Homeland Security Act (2002) establishes a Department of Homeland Security with an agency to monitor threats to the communications infrastructure, including the Internet, and exempts from the Privacy Act any information about infrastructure vulnerabilities to terrorism submitted by individuals or non-federal agencies.

Sarbanes-Oxley Act (2002) establishes financial reporting regulations to prevent corporate fraud. Requires full disclosure in accounting systems and protects corporate whistleblowers.

CAN-SPAM Act (2003) establishes national standards for sending commercial e-mail by requiring senders to use a valid subject line, include the sender's legitimate physical address, and provide an opt-out mechanism.

Greene v. America Online (2003) interprets sections of the Communications Decency Act to mean that ISPs are not responsible for malicious software transmitted over their services by hackers.

MGM v. Grokster (2005) refines the precedent set in the 1984 Sony Corp. v. Universal Studios case. Companies that actively encourage infringement, as seemed to be true of peer-to-peer file-sharing networks such as Grokster, can be held accountable for user infringement.

IT ETHICS

Why are professional ethics important for IT workers? Most computer professionals are hard-working and honest. They take pride in their work and strive to offer excellent products and services that benefit consumers. They want to do what's right. Sometimes, however, computer professionals have to cope with ethical dilemmas in which the right course of action is not entirely clear, or in which the right course of action is clear, but the consequences—such as getting fired—are not easy to face.

Ethical dilemmas in the workplace are more common than you might imagine. It is likely that you'll find yourself in an ethical quandary about some aspect of your job even before you've completed your first year. Some situations that call for an ethical decision offer you the luxury of time—you don't have to respond or act right away—so you can think about what you'll do. Other situations require an immediate response. If an immediate response is required, you'll be less likely to take action that you'll later regret if you have considered potentially compromising situations ahead of time and have prepared some general guidelines you can use if necessary.

What kinds of situations in an IT career might require ethical decisions? Situations that require computer professionals to make ethical decisions often involve software copyrights, privacy, conflict of interest, use of work computers, software quality, hacking, and social responsibility. Sometimes, computer professionals are pressured to participate in activities that border on being illegal and are clearly unethical. These marginal activities are sometimes justified with statements such as "Everyone does it" or "No one will know." Employees might be assured, "You won't be responsible" or "It's for the good of the company." Such justifications are not, however, always true or appropriate.

Outside of corporate IT departments, individual entrepreneurs sometimes get caught up in unethical activities because they make bad judgments or have not done their homework regarding applicable laws and regulations.

How would software copyrights become an ethical issue? Most computer professionals are familiar with the general principles of copyright law and the provisions of the Digital Millennium Copyright Act. They understand it is illegal to make unauthorized copies of software and other copyrighted media, such as commercial music and movies. Programmers, Web designers, and other creative professionals tend to respect intellectual property and try to adhere to copyright laws and license agreements. It is not unusual, however, to find yourself in a software copyright dilemma like the one described in Figure 9-39.

Business managers are not always familiar with current copyright restrictions or choose to ignore them. Computer professionals should stay up-to-date on current copyright law that applies to software and other digital media. Asking for a copy of the software license agreement is considered standard practice and can help resolve questions about the legality of copying software for use in multiple-user installations.

FIGURE 9-39

Copyrights can trigger ethical dilemmas.

On your first day of work, your employer hands you CDs containing the latest upgrade for Microsoft Office and asks you to install it on every computer in the organization. When you ask if the company owns a site license, your boss responds, "No, do you have a problem with that?" What would you reply? Would you risk your job by insisting that the company order enough copies for all the computers before you install it? Or would you go ahead and install the software, assuming that your boss would take responsibility for this violation of the software license agreement?

9

What kinds of ethical issues revolve around privacy?
You know it is ethical to respect the privacy of others, but business practices can clash with privacy rights. Network technicians sometimes see the content of e-mail messages or files in the course of system maintenance or troubleshooting. Typically, professionals simply try to forget what they see. However, computer professionals sometimes come across a file or an e-mail message that's troubling. It might be a message from an employee who is corresponding with a competing company about a job offer. More seriously, a message might divulge proprietary information to the competitor, harass another employee, or outline other illegal activities. If your employer has no guidelines for reporting suspicious activities, you'll have to make your own decision about what kinds of information are serious threats.

Computers are increasingly used to monitor employee activities. RFID chips embedded in ID badges can be used to keep track of employee locations in an office or manufacturing facility. Keystroke monitors, random samples of active programs, Web browsing history, network logs, and e-mail volume offer additional ways to monitor employee activities to make sure they are working productively. Some surveillance is done with employee knowledge and consent, such as when it is clearly explained in an employment contract or company policy. Other surveillance is surreptitious.

Either way, surveillance is set up by someone, often a programmer or network administrator. How would you respond if asked to set up a surveillance system like the one in Figure 9-40?

Employees—particularly computer professionals—should be familiar with laws and company policy applicable to privacy. Privacy laws differ from one country to the next, and most companies have unique privacy policies, so rather than assume you know the rules, make an effort to check applicable documents before you take action.

How might confidentiality lead to ethical dilemmas?
Confidentiality is the obligation not to disclose willingly any information obtained in confidence. Confidentiality rights apply to individuals and organizations. With respect to individuals, confidentiality means not disclosing names and associated data from databases and other information repositories. Laws in most countries restrict the disclosure of an individual's medical or financial information. Marketers, however, currently take advantage of gray areas in these laws to distribute names, addresses, and phone numbers collected with consent on forms, applications, and Web sites. The ethics of such practices is doubtful.

With respect to organizations, confidentiality means protecting **proprietary information** about company finances, procedures, products, and research that competitors would find valuable. Computer professionals can find themselves in compromising situations where they are asked to disclose confidential information gathered while employed in previous jobs.

FIGURE 9-40

Privacy rights sometimes clash with safety issues or business goals.

Imagine that you're a programmer for a local public school system. One day, the superintendent of schools calls you into her office and asks if you can write software that supplies the administration with a log of Web sites visited by students and teachers. From your understanding of the school's network and Web access, you realize that it would be easy to write such monitoring software. You also realize, however, that the superintendent could use the software to track individual teachers and students as they visit Web sites. You ask the superintendent if faculty and students would be aware of the monitoring software, and she replies, "What they don't know won't hurt them." Should you write the program? Should you write the program, but start a rumor that monitoring software is being used to track faculty and student Web access? Should you pretend that it would be technically impossible to write such software? Should you tell the superintendent that federal law does not permit interception of electronic communications without consent?

Job mobility is one of the perks of a hot career field. Most employers agree that employees have a right to switch jobs to seek higher pay, more responsibility, better working conditions, a better location, or more challenging projects. The skills you pick up on one job can increase your qualifications for other jobs. For example, you might learn about multimedia production while working for an educational software company, and those skills might provide you with qualifications to switch to a higher-paying and more challenging job working for an online game company. Using your skills as a springboard to a new job in a case like this one is perfectly acceptable, but disclosing confidential information is not ethical in most cases, including the one in Figure 9-41.

Many employment contracts contain a non-compete clause designed to prevent employees from divulging proprietary information to competitors or opening competing businesses. Non-compete clauses can extend beyond the period of employment and can remain in effect for a specified time after you leave a job. Most non-compete clauses, however, fail to delineate exactly what information cannot be divulged, and so ex-employees are forced to make ethical decisions about competitive information. To avoid compromising situations, check the business plans of prospective employers so that you won't be working on projects that compete directly with those at your previous place of employment. You can also have a frank discussion with your new boss to outline the boundaries of the knowledge you are able to share from your old job.

Can I get into trouble using my work computer for personal activities?
When surveyed, a majority of computer professionals admit that they see no problem using their work computers for personal activities as long as it has no adverse affect on the employer. It seems innocent enough to send and receive personal e-mail over your account at work or place bids on an online auction, especially if you do so during your lunch hour. Maybe it also seems okay to use your corporate e-mail server to send bulk mail to raise money for a private, non-profit relief organization. Your employer might not agree, however.

There is a temptation to use computers, copiers, and network connections at work for personal activities; the equipment is convenient and usually cutting edge. Most companies have explicit policies about what is and what is not acceptable use. Some policies are strict, but designed to prevent conflicts like the one in Figure 9-42.

It is never a good practice to use facilities at work for personal activities, unless you have a specific agreement with your employer and your activities do not breach your employment contract. Some employment contracts have restrictions pertaining to intellectual

FIGURE 9-41

Disclosures about your previous employer might violate the confidentiality clause of your employment contract.

Suppose you take a new job and then discover that your new employer—at an online game company—wants to produce online educational games that will directly compete with your previous employer's products. Your new boss wants you to lead the team that creates its first educational product, which sounds suspiciously like a rip off of your old employer's best selling software. What should you do?

FIGURE 9-42

Use of your employer's equipment and computer facilities could lead to a conflict of interest.

You might believe it is perfectly fine to spend your lunch hour writing a Linux media player—not because your company can use it, but because one of your friends wants to listen to iTunes music on a Linux computer. You finish the program and realize there's a market for it. You begin selling it as shareware. The response is overwhelming. You quit your job and go into business marketing your product. Unfortunately, your old employer claims to own your software because you used company computers to develop it. How would you respond?

9

property. In the most restrictive contracts, anything employees develop at work or at home using on-the-job equipment or knowledge during their tenure of employment belongs to the company. If your contract does not limit outside development, you might still have to make an ethical decision about what rightfully belongs to your company and what you created outside of your company's sphere of influence.

Why would I get involved in hacking?

Computer professionals have to keep up with the latest threats from viruses and intrusion attempts, but "knowing your enemy" can be a two-edged sword. Most computing students learning about virus and intrusion countermeasures become more than a little curious about these technologies. "Is it really so easy to design and launch viruses?" they wonder. "Are passwords easy to crack? Do I have the skill to do it?" Pursuing these questions can get students and computer professionals into sticky ethical situations like the one in Figure 9-43.

Many computer scientists have toyed with the idea of creating virus-killing programs that autonomously prowl the Internet to eradicate viruses before they cause widespread damage. Is anything wrong with that? The answer—or part of it—relates to problems with antispyware technologies. Antispyware technology watches network packets heading into a computer, and filters out those suspected to be parts of Trojan horses or bots.

Unfortunately, not everything caught in the antispyware net is malware. Some legitimate programs—at least their authors claim they are legitimate—are also filtered out. When antispyware applications reside on a computer's hard disk, it is a relatively easy task to update the antispyware definitions to exclude erroneously filtered, but legitimate, programs. An autonomous virus killer set loose on the Internet would not be so easy to modify, however, unless it contains some kind of recall mechanism or expiration date. The problem is not insurmountable, but as of yet no one has wanted to take the responsibility for such a program and its potential repercussions. The legality of "good" viruses is questionable, so the decision whether to create and distribute such programs becomes an ethical one.

Am I responsible for software quality?

Most computer professionals believe that software should be thoroughly tested to produce the most reliable and accurate product possible, but what if you encounter a situation like the one in Figure 9-44?

Software development is an incredibly complex undertaking. Bugs are virtually impossible to completely eradicate, so most companies have policies that guide

FIGURE 9-43

Even an academic interest in hacking can raise sticky ethical issues.

In the course of your computing career, you might be tempted to try some passwords at a protected site. What if you get in? Should you poke around? Should you notify the system administrator that the network password is not secure? If you do so, you'll have to admit that you were doing a bit of illegal hacking, so your decision about a course of action might not be an easy one.

FIGURE 9-44

A decision to short-cut software testing should not be taken lightly.

Suppose your project team has spent the better part of a year developing a new software product. The project is scheduled for release in four weeks, but to meet the deadline, you'll have to cut testing time in half. The team leader tells you to pare down the testing plan to a bare minimum. What should you do? Does the type of software you're developing make a difference in your response? What if you're working on an arcade-style game? What if it is a government project to help the IRS audit tax returns? What if it is an ambulance dispatch system or an air traffic control system?

developers on the number, severity, and type of bugs that are and are not acceptable when the software ships to customers. Although developers, managers, and marketers are supposed to be governed by these policies, software testing cycles are sometimes cut short when deadlines loom. Computer professionals working on such projects should think carefully about the repercussions of shortened test cycles and speak out when serious risks to users might result.

Am I responsible for how my software is used? Technology may be neutral in and of itself, but technology can be put to use in both positive and negative ways.

Some IT projects are clearly not socially responsible. Society would be better off without spam and viruses. Filtering software and monitoring software can be misused. If you are assigned to a project of questionable social value like the one in Figure 9-45, you might have to make an ethical decision about whether to participate or look for another job.

FIGURE 9-45

Sorting out issues of social responsibility can be tough.

Decisions pertaining to social responsibility are not always easy. Members of a project team might not be supplied with enough information to make value judgments about the projects to which they are assigned.

Laws and court decisions sometimes conflict with regard to whether programmers and members of software development teams are responsible for the way their software is used. In the landmark case Sony Corp. vs. Universal City Studios, the U.S. Supreme Court set a precedent that Sony was not responsible when individuals used Sony betamax recording technology to make and distribute illegal copies of movies. When applied to the IT industry, the Sony case seemed to absolve software developers from any illegal actions taken by users.

After graduating, your first big software development project was creating adaptive software to help people with physical handicaps use computers in productive careers. That product had clear social benefits. You've now been assigned to a project team working on automated garment production software. You have an uneasy feeling about its benefits. Will it displace hundreds of garment workers? What if those workers are domestic? Does it make a difference if those workers are offshore?

However, the Digital Millennium Copyright Act explicitly states that it is illegal to produce any product that allows individuals to circumvent copyright law or copy protection methods. Therefore, a programmer who produces software to crack DVD copy protection can be held responsible when individuals use it to make illegal copies of DVDs. Peer-to-peer file sharing networks such as Napster and Grokster can be held accountable for users who illegally share copyrighted music and movies—especially if such illegal sharing is encouraged and the networks are not also used for legal file sharing. As with laws governing non-technical aspects of society, like parking and speeding, ignorance of the law is not an excuse for breaking it.

ETHICAL DECISION MAKING

How do I make ethical decisions? Ethical decisions that you make on the job can have long-term consequences for your career and lifestyle, so it is important to approach these decisions seriously. First, take time to think about your situation before responding or taking action. Before you begin to examine the immediate situation, make sure you have a good handle on your long-term and short-term career goals. Gather the information needed for a decision, and make sure the facts are credible. Use Web resources and legal services, if necessary, to check applicable laws. With the facts in hand, list your options and consider the advantages and disadvantages of each one. For help in defining and evaluating your options, you can use strategies, such as those listed below.

- **Talk to people whose judgment you respect.** Mentors and responsible friends might be willing to help you evaluate your options. Your workplace might provide access to an arbitrator, ombudsman, or counselor. Remember, however, that after you've gathered opinions and advice, you are ultimately responsible for the outcome of your decision.

- **Consider what the most ethical person you know would decide to do.** Think of a real-life person or fictional character who has strong values and impeccable ethical judgment. Use that person as your decision-making role model and ask yourself what he or she would do in your situation.

- **Think about what you would do if your actions were made public.** Ask yourself how you would feel if you made a particular decision and everyone found out about it. Would you be proud or uncomfortable? Decisions that look good only if no one knows are usually wrong. When you've made a good decision, you should feel comfortable talking about it as long as it doesn't abuse confidentiality.

- **Look at the problem from the opposite perspective.** Put yourself in the place of other stakeholders, such as your boss, your clients, or consumers. How would you want to be treated if you were them?

- **Consult a code of professional ethics.** The guidelines contained in a code of professional ethics might offer a path of action suitable for your situation.

What is a code of ethics? A **code of ethics** is a set of guidelines designed to help professionals thread their way through a sometimes tangled web of ethical on-the-job decisions. Some codes of ethics are short and pithy, whereas others are long and detailed. Even with a detailed code of ethics, however, don't expect a cookbook that tells you exactly what to do in a particular situation. Expect instead to be offered some general guidelines that you will have to apply to a specific situation. Most codes of ethics are created for a specific career field, such as medicine, accounting, or IT. Figure 9-46 contains a code of ethics from the Computer Ethics Institute.

FIGURE 9-46

Many IT professional organizations offer codes of ethics.

How effective are codes of ethics? Professional codes of ethics are not without controversy. For example, the code published by the Computer Ethics Institute has drawn fire from critics, such as Dr. N. Ben Fairweather, the Centre for Computing and Social Responsibility's resident philosopher and research fellow, who states, "It is easy to find exceptions to the short dos and don'ts of the 'ten commandments'... indeed, every time such a short code of ethics falls into unwarranted disrepute, the whole idea of acting morally is brought into disrepute too." Dr. Fairweather seems to suggest that hard and fast rules might not apply to all situations.

"Ten Commandments" from the Computer Ethics Institute Professional Code

- Thou shalt not use a computer to harm other people.
- Thou shalt not interfere with other people's computer work.
- Thou shalt not snoop around in other people's files.
- Thou shalt not use a computer to steal.
- Thou shalt not use a computer to bear false witness.
- Thou shalt not use or copy software for which you have not paid.
- Thou shalt not use other people's computer resources without authorization.
- Thou shalt not appropriate other people's intellectual output.
- Thou shalt think about the social consequences of the program you write.
- Thou shalt use a computer in ways that show consideration and respect.

For the situations in which these guidelines clearly apply, however, they are a valuable resource. In some cases a code might include guidelines whose intent is not accurately reflected in their wording. For example, the Computer Ethics Institute guideline "Thou shalt not use or copy software for which you have not paid" obviously does not include public domain and open source software, or software for which your employer has paid.

Similarly, the idea that you should "think about the social consequences of the program you write" is valid, but what should you think about? This guideline does not offer helpful criteria for distinguishing between socially useful programs and those that might be damaging. Furthermore, what is socially acceptable for one programmer may be unacceptable for another. When a code of ethics does not offer a complete solution, professionals might have to refer to other resources before making a decision and taking action.

Some codes of ethics attempt to offer more complete guidelines. A comprehensive approach can be useful, but it can sometimes become so complex that it seems to contradict itself. For example, the ACM's Code of Ethics and Professional Conduct contains a guideline that begins, "ACM members must obey existing local, state, province, national, and international laws unless there is a compelling ethical basis not to do so." It goes on, however, to offer a series of caveats that add complexity to the decision-making process, "...sometimes existing laws and rules may be immoral or inappropriate and, therefore, must be challenged. Violation of a law or regulation may be ethical when that law or rule has inadequate moral basis or when it conflicts with another law judged to be more important. If one decides to violate a law or rule because it is viewed as unethical, or for any other reason, one must fully accept responsibility for one's actions and for the consequences."

Where can I find codes of ethics for IT? IT professionals have access to codes of ethics published by many professional organizations, such as the Association for Computing Machinery (Figure 9-47), the British Computer Society, the Australian Computer Society, and the Computer Ethics Institute. Each code varies in detail but supplies a similar set of overall guiding principles for professional conduct. Codes of ethics are published at organization Web sites and are available to the public as well as to members of the professional organization.

FIGURE 9-47

The ACM (Association for Computing Machinery) posts a code of ethics at its Web site.

9

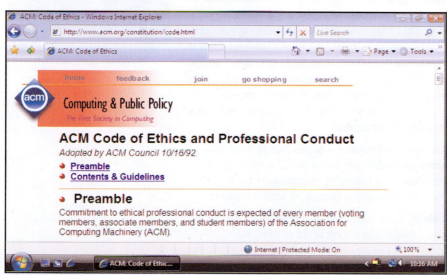

How should I apply codes of ethics to my situation? A code of ethics can provide guidelines, but it might not offer ready answers to every dilemma that arises in the course of your career. When confronted with a difficult ethical decision, you should consider ethical guidelines, but also consider the policies of your workplace and relevant laws. You might also seek legal advice, consult the human resources advocate at your job, or ask advice from your union representative. Sometimes even talking to a trusted friend helps you recognize the correct course of action.

Ethical decisions can be difficult and sometimes the results of your decision—good or bad—are not apparent right away. A decision with immediate negative repercussions might have beneficial long-term advantages that you cannot foresee. Ultimately, a decision about the right course of action is yours, and you must be willing to take responsibility for the consequences of your decision.

WHISTLEBLOWING

Should I blow the whistle on unethical practices? A widely accepted definition of **whistleblowing** is the "disclosure by an employee (or professional) of confidential information which relates to some danger, fraud, or other illegal or unethical conduct connected with the workplace, be it of the employer or of fellow employees." A whistleblower is someone in an organization who decides to speak out against on-the-job activities that are contrary to the mission of the organization or threaten the public interest.

Is whistleblowing effective? Whistleblowers have focused public attention on corporate abuses at Enron and WorldCom, revealed major problems in the way the FBI investigated potential terrorists prior to 9-11, and uncovered defects in the body armor supplied to the U.S. president and combat troops (Figure 9-48).

Although whistleblowing might seem effective, the consequences of whistleblowing can often be extreme. Even with strong legal protection under the Sarbanes-Oxley Act, whistleblowers are often fired or forced out of their jobs. If they keep their jobs, they might be excluded from promotions and shunned by coworkers. They are sometimes branded as tattletales and have difficulty finding other jobs in their career field.

Is there any way to safely blow the whistle on unethical business practices? Whistleblowing is risky under any circumstances. For example, a computer system administrator working for a state agency noticed his boss spent the majority of his time playing solitaire on his computer. After several e-mail messages up the chain of command were ignored, the system administrator installed Win-Spy software, which grabbed incriminating screenshots of his boss's computer several times per day over a period of several months. When the system administrator showed this evidence to his superiors, he was fired for violating his boss's privacy. His boss received only a light reprimand.

As a whistleblower, the system administrator did some things right, but he missed some important measures that might have led to a more positive outcome. Employee advocates have the following suggestions for reducing the risk of career repercussions so often experienced by whistleblowers.

● **Examine your motives.** Make sure your cause is significant. Don't act out of frustration or because you feel underappreciated or mistreated.

FIGURE 9-48

The head of research for a company that manufactures body armor blew the whistle on his company for not notifying consumers that fibers in the company's bullet proof vests break down over time, significantly reducing their protection against gunfire.

- **Try the normal chain of command.** Before you blow the whistle, try to correct the problem by reporting up the normal chain of command. Consider every possible way to work within the system before you take your concerns public.

- **Collect evidence to back up your accusations.** Gather documentary evidence that proves your case and keep it in a safe place. Do not break any laws while collecting evidence. Try to collect evidence before you draw attention to your concerns.

- **Record events as they unfold.** Keep detailed, dated notes about events before and after you blow the whistle. Keep in mind that your notes might become public if they are used as evidence in a trial.

- **Act ethically.** Do not embellish your case and do not violate any confidentiality agreements you may have. Engage in whistleblowing activities on your own time, not your employer's.

- **Be ready to accept repercussions.** Think through the effect your actions might have on your family. Be prepared for unemployment and the possibility of being blacklisted in your profession.

- **Establish a support network.** Seek out potential allies, such as elected officials, journalists, and activists that can support your cause.

- **Consult a lawyer.** Make sure you understand your rights as an employee.

- **Consider your strategy.** You might reduce the risk of repercussions if you lodge your complaint anonymously or as part of a group.

As with other ethical decisions, your resolution to become a whistleblower can have a long-term affect on your career, family, and lifestyle. Think about your situation carefully and make use of whatever resources are available to you.

QuickCheck

1. The term professional [_____] refers to on-the-job choices and actions that reflect a person's values.

2. [_____] are legislated documentation of permissible behavior based on a community's ethics.

3. The [_____] Millennium Copyright Act makes it illegal to circumvent copy-protection technology.

4. [_____] is the obligation not to disclose willingly any information obtained in confidence.

5. Computer professionals sometimes have difficulty evaluating whether a project is socially [_____] because project team members might not be given detailed information about a product's application.

6. A(n) [_____] is someone in an organization who decides to speak out against on-the-job activities that are contrary to the mission of the organization or threaten the public interest.

 CHECK ANSWERS

9

SECTION E

Work Area Safety and Ergonomics

MORE AND MORE WORKERS spend an entire eight-hour day or longer in front of a computer screen. Road warriors are lugging notebook computers through airports and trying to get work done in the cramped confines of economy seats. As computers and other digital devices continue to infiltrate the workplace, worker advocates are concerned about health risks associated with computer use. Questions about the safety of digital devices affect ordinary consumers, too. Consumers own more digital gadgets than ever before and spend more time using them. Studies have shown that the average American spends about two hours a day using a computer. The popularity of LAN parties has spawned intensive day-long competitions, and many serious gamers are still hunched over their keyboards in the wee hours of the morning. It is rare to go anywhere and not see someone talking on a cell phone or plugged into a portable music player. Section E focuses on how this digital lifestyle affects health.

RADIATION RISKS

What is radiation? Although we tend to associate radiation with the fallout from nuclear blasts and debilitating cancer treatments, the term refers simply to any energy that is emitted in the form of waves or particles. Radiation streams out of the sun in the form of heat and out of your stereo system as sound waves. Even more radiation pulses out from electrical appliances, wireless networks, cell phone towers, and electrical power lines. Most of the radiation in your everyday world is considered safe, especially in moderation (Figure 9-49).

A few types of radiation can be harmful. Gamma rays and X-rays, for example, contain enough electromagnetic energy to alter chemical reactions in the body and disrupt molecules in human tissue. Shielding against these types of radiation is an important safety factor.

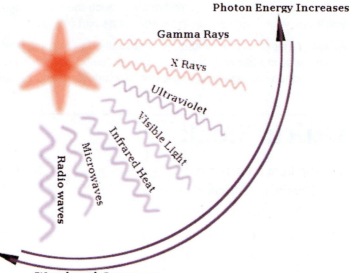

FIGURE 9-49

Some types of radiation, such as light, heat, microwaves, and radio waves, are generally considered safer than Gamma rays, X-rays, and ultraviolet light.

What kinds of radiation are emitted by digital devices? Every electronic device emits some type of radiation, otherwise they would be useless. The light emitted by computer, PDA, cell phone, and portable music player screens is essential for their use. Cell phones emit sound waves so we can listen to the person at the other end of the connection. Wireless routers emit radio waves to carry data from one workstation to another.

Although the radiation from most digital gadgets is considered harmless, researchers have raised concerns about radiation from cell phones and computer CRT display devices.

What's the problem with CRTs? Bulky cathode ray tubes (CRTs) used in older computer monitors and televisions are electronic vacuum tubes containing a mechanism that essentially shoots a stream of high-speed electrons at the front of the screen as shown in Figure 9-50.

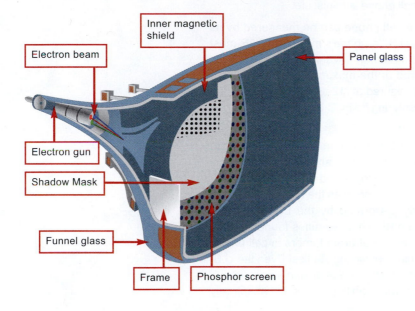

Electron beam

Inner magnetic shield

Panel glass

Electron gun

Shadow Mask

Funnel glass

Frame

Phosphor screen

FIGURE 9-50

The electron gun in a CRT sprays a beam of electrons at the screen.

The electron beam in a CRT generates X-rays, very low frequency (VLF) radiation, and extremely low frequency (ELF) radiation. Consumers became concerned that these emissions might be a health risk. In some studies, emissions from CRTs have been associated with increased risk of cancer, birth defects, and miscarriages, but a large collection of research carried out over the last 30 years has been unable to find a definitive link.

How much harmful radiation does a CRT emit? Most harmful X-rays from a CRT are blocked by leaded glass that forms the tube. Radiation that escapes through the tube is primarily ELF and VLF, which deteriorates over a fairly short distance. For example, the level of emissions 20 inches (50 cm) from the screen is considerably less than emissions 10 inches away. Emission levels differ for different CRTs. Some manufacturers use extra shielding to produce low-emission devices. In Europe display devices are manufactured to meet strict TCO and MPR standards. Emissions are typically low, but some consumer advocates argue they are not low enough.

Do LCD screens emit radiation? LCD displays generate an image by illuminating a matrix of tiny lights. Unlike a CRT, an LCD has no tube, no electron spray, and generates no X-rays. LCD devices do, however, emit low levels of radiation. Emission levels vary depending on manufacturer, brand, and model.

Can I take steps to block emissions from my computer display device? Monitors that meet TCO or MPR standards have emission levels believed to be safe. An LCD monitor would typically have lower emission levels than a CRT, so use an LCD if possible. Various devices supposed to block radiation are on the market, but their effectiveness is questionable. Whatever type of display device you use, sit at least an arm's length away from it to reduce your exposure.

9

How much radiation does a typical cell phone emit? A cell phone is a radio transmitter and receiver so it emits RF (radiofrequency) energy. High levels of RF energy can heat human tissue much like the way a microwave oven heats food. Compared to a microwave oven, however, the amount of radiation emitted by a cell phone is miniscule.

The amount of radiation emitted by a cell phone can be measured by its specific absorption rate (SAR). In the U.S., a phone's maximum SAR must be less than 1.6W/kg; in Europe the maximum level is 2.0W/kg. Phones with the highest SAR levels registered at the maximum allowable level. Phones with the lowest levels were measured at .12-.33W/kg. You can find the SAR level for your cell phone by entering its FCC ID number (look for it in the user manual) at *www.fcc.gov/oet/*.

Are the current limits safe? The scientific community continues to study and debate the amount of RF radiation that should be considered safe for long-term use. A recent Swedish study found evidence that long-term, extensive cell phone use significantly increases the risk of developing a brain tumor. A contradictory study performed by the London-based Institute of Cancer Research and three British universities found that cell phone risk does not increase the incidence of brain tumors in cell phone users. Research literature is full of similar conflicting studies. Even the U.S. Food and Drug Administration (FDA) admits, "the available scientific evidence does not allow us to conclude that mobile phones are absolutely safe, or that they are unsafe."

What can I do to avoid excess cell phone radiation? The easiest way to reduce your exposure to cell phone radiation is to use a hands-free headset. Headsets, which many states require for use while driving, offer the additional benefit of reducing your chance of becoming involved in a traffic accident.

REPETITIVE STRESS INJURIES

What is a repetitive stress injury? Most of the health risks associated with computer use are not caused by the equipment itself, but how it is set up and used. Improper positioning of your keyboard and mouse can cause repetitive stress injuries to wrists, arms, neck, back, and shoulders. A **repetitive stress injury** (RSI) is not a specific disease but a group of similar overuse disorders that affect tendons, muscles, and nerves. Symptoms include stiffness and minor pain in your hands, wrists, arms, or shoulders. Your symptoms might appear while you're working, or they might appear several hours or days later. With rest, these injuries tend to heal, although some problems, such as carpal tunnel syndrome might require medical intervention.

What is carpal tunnel syndrome? Your wrist contains eight carpal bones surrounding a large nerve that controls your thumb, index, and middle fingers. Anything that compresses this nerve, such as arthritis or thickened tendons, can cause numbness, pain, or tingling in your fingers, a condition called carpal tunnel syndrome (Figure 9-51). At one time it was generally accepted that keyboarding was a major cause of carpal tunnel syndrome. A recent Mayo Clinic study, however, concluded that keyboarding does not cause carpal tunnel syndrome, though it can make the condition worse. Most computer-related hand and arm injuries are repetitive stress injuries, which can be avoided by following ergonomic guidelines.

FIGURE 9-51

Carpal tunnel syndrome is a condition affecting the nerve that runs to your thumb, index and middle fingers.

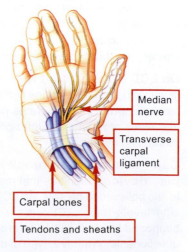

Median nerve

Transverse carpal ligament

Carpal bones

Tendons and sheaths

What is ergonomics? **Ergonomics** is the study of safe and efficient environments, particularly working environments. Ergonomics provides guidelines for making work environments safer and healthier.

In the U.S., the Occupational Safety and Health Administration (OSHA) sets and enforces standards for the safety and health of American workers. Although a federal law to enforce ergonomic standards in the workplace was repealed in 2001, many states have regulations designed to protect workers from repetitive stress injuries.

How should I set up my work area? At the beginning of the chapter, you had an opportunity to evaluate the ergonomics of your current work area. To avoid future computer-related stress injuries, keep ergonomic principles in mind wherever you work. The key to avoiding uncomfortable stress injuries is in the placement and use of your keyboard, mouse, monitor, desk, and chair. Figure 9-52 provides an overview of ergonomic workstation guidelines and offers some specific tips for setting up your keyboard and mouse.

FIGURE 9-52

Set up and use your computer equipment according to ergonomic guidelines to avoid repetitive stress injuries.

- Position the keyboard so that it is just above your lap and your elbows are able to extend past the 90 degree angle when you type. When shopping for a computer desk, make sure it has a keyboard tray, adjustable if possible, and look for one with a small lip that reduces the distance between the tray and your thighs.

- Angle the keyboard so that your wrists are straight when typing.

- If you have a wrist-rest, use it only when you are not typing; resting your palm on a wrist-rest while typing usually creates an angle in your wrist that is not efficient.

- Use a keyboard that fits the size of your hands and fingers. When you rest your fingers on the home keys (asdf and jkl;), there should be 1/8 to 1/4 inch of space between them so you are not trying to type with your fingers cramped together or overextending.

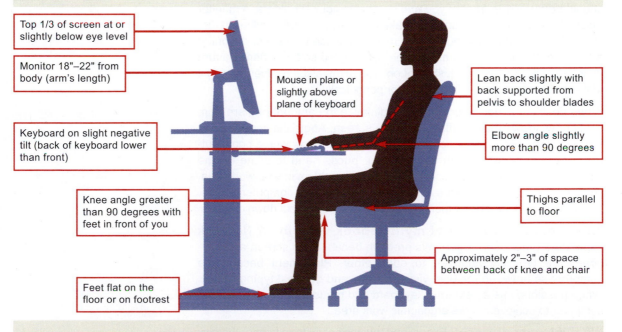

Top 1/3 of screen at or slightly below eye level

Monitor 18"–22" from body (arm's length)

Mouse in plane or slightly above plane of keyboard

Lean back slightly with back supported from pelvis to shoulder blades

Keyboard on slight negative tilt (back of keyboard lower than front)

Elbow angle slightly more than 90 degrees

Knee angle greater than 90 degrees with feet in front of you

Thighs parallel to floor

Approximately 2"–3" of space between back of knee and chair

Feet flat on the floor or on footrest

- Make sure your mouse is positioned close by so that you don't have to reach for it.

- Keep the mouse at the same height as your keyboard to minimize arm movements.

- Use your mouse with a relaxed arm and wrist.

- When working at mouse-intensive activities, change mouse hands occasionally or change to an air mouse or trackball, which require a different set of muscles.

EYE STRAIN

What about computer-related eye problems? Studies have found links between computer use and eye problems. The most common symptoms are sore, tired, burning, or itching eyes, watery eyes, dry eyes, blurred or double vision, headaches, difficulty shifting focus between the screen display and printed documents, and increased sensitivity to light. For many computer users, eye problems can be avoided by proper monitor placement and adjustment.

What is the optimal placement for my monitor? To correctly position your monitor, sit back slightly in your chair and stretch your right arm out straight ahead of you. Your middle finger should almost touch the center of your screen as shown in Figure 9-53.

FIGURE 9-53

You can position your monitor by stretching out your arm parallel to the ground. Your finger tips should just touch the center of the screen.

Once the screen is set at the proper height, tilt it backwards just a bit. You should feel like you are looking down slightly at the screen. Your screen should be directly in front of you and parallel to your shoulders. A monitor that's tilted to one side or another makes your eyes focus at different distances, which is tiring. If you use two monitors, place your second monitor as close to the first monitor as possible, but angled so that when you turn your head slightly you face it straight on. You might also consider moving it to the other side of your primary monitor periodically.

When positioning your monitor, try to minimize the amount of glare from lights or windows that is reflected on the screen. Angle the screen away from windows, but it is best not to end up facing a window where bright outdoor light can interfere with the way your pupils need to dilate for the brightness of your computer screen. If glare is a problem in your work area, you can purchase an antiglare screen that fits over your computer screen. Keeping the surface of your monitor free of dust can also cut down on glare.

What about placement of my notebook computer? Notebook computers present an ergonomic problem because the screen and keyboard are typically attached to each other. Placement becomes a compromise between the best viewing angle and the best typing height. When possible, use an external keyboard and mouse with your notebook computer to achieve a more ergonomic work area.

What if I wear glasses? Bifocal and trifocal lenses tend to offer the correct focus for computer work through the bottom of the lens. Wearers raise their chins to view the screen, which puts stress on neck muscles and causes headaches. To avoid this situation, bifocal and trifocal wearers might have to lower their screens or ask their optometrist for eyewear dedicated to viewing the computer screen.

How about adjusting the resolution? One of the most effective steps you can take to avoid eye strain is to adjust the resolution of your monitor so that you can easily read the text displayed on your screen. Remember that you can make two types of adjustments. You can adjust the resolution of your monitor through the operating system, which globally affects window, icon, and text size. LCD screens have a **native resolution** which displays one pixel for each tiny light in the display matrix. Selecting a resolution lower than a screen's native resolution forces the display device to interpolate pixels and results in a slightly fuzzy display. Figure 9-54 explains how to find your monitor's native resolution.

FIGURE 9-54

To find your screen's native resolution when using Windows, check the display settings. Typically, the highest resolution available is your screen's native resolution.

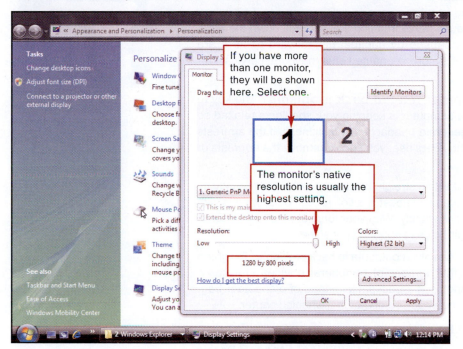

Once your monitor is set to its native resolution, you might find that the text on Web pages and in documents is too small to view comfortably. In that situation, you can adjust the zoom level within various applications. For example, you might set your browser to display larger text and set your word processor to display text at 125% or 150% (Figure 9-55).

FIGURE 9-55

If the text is too small at your monitor's native resolution, try increasing the zoom level within applications.

9

BACK PAIN

How can computer use affect my back and spine? Back pain can be caused by many factors, including poor posture and careless lifting of heavy objects.

What about posture? Doctors and physical therapists commonly use the term *flex-forward posture* to describe the sitting posture shared by many computer users. The layman's term *computer slump* refers to the same thing: sitting hunched over a computer keyboard with your neck craned forward (Figure 9-56).

Habitual slouching can lead to stiffness and muscle tenderness. Left uncorrected, the problem can cause nerve irritation that spreads down the arms and back. Back problems caused by habitual flex-forward posture are sometimes referred to as T4 syndrome, named after the fourth cervical vertebra that is most affected.

How can I avoid computer related back problems? The key to comfort while working on a computer is keeping your shoulders relaxed so that tense muscles don't generate headaches and stiffness. If the armrests on your chair make your shoulders rise, you should remove the armrests or get another chair.

Conventional wisdom about sitting straight has been challenged recently by a body of evidence that indicates the best position for computer work is with your upper torso leaning back slightly. With your torso at a 100-110 degree angle, the back of your chair helps to support your spine.

Carrying a heavy computer can also contribute to back problems. To lighten your load, try to reduce the number of peripheral devices you carry. Consider toting your computer in a backpack instead of a shoulder bag. When traveling, place your notebook computer in a wheeled carrier.

SEDENTARY LIFESTYLE

Does computer use affect my overall physical fitness? People who live and work in digital cultures tend to spend many hours each day in sedentary pursuits, such as watching television and using computers. Many researchers believe that there is a link between our increasingly sedentary lifestyle and a steady climb in obesity and cardiovascular disease. To counteract the effects of a sedentary lifestyle, it is important to exercise and eat right. A good balance of stretching and cardiovascular exercise can help you keep physically fit and has the additional benefit of helping to prevent repetitive stress injuries and back pain.

What about circulatory problems? Sitting still for long periods of time, especially in positions that limit blood circulation can be a health risk, similar to the risk of long haul air travel. A condition called deep vein thrombosis is the formation of blood clots that commonly affect veins in the legs. Symptoms include pain, swelling, and redness in the affected area. Deep vein thrombosis requires treatment to prevent life threatening complications if the clot moves to the heart. Although the condition is not common in young people, good work habits can help you maintain healthy circulation.

FIGURE 9-56

Bad posture can lead to back pain.

What factors help maintain good circulation? Your chair should not prevent good circulation to your legs. Make sure there is at least 2 inches (5 cm) of clearance between your calf and the front of your chair. Your thighs should be parallel to the ground to allow for good blood flow; if necessary use a foot rest to raise your feet and reduce the pressure on the backs of your thighs.

What else can I do? To combat potential health hazards associated with computer use you should try to take breaks periodically, say, every 20 minutes or at least once every hour. At minimum try the 20/20/20 break: Every 20 minutes, take 20 seconds and look 20 feet away. Longer breaks of two to five minutes are more effective. During a longer break, stand up to change your circulation. Rest your eyes by focusing on distant objects. Gently rotate and stretch your wrists, shoulders, and neck. **Break reminder software** such as RSIGuard, Stress buster, Easy Rest Break, and open source Workrave, can help you remember when it's time to take a break from your work (Figure 9-57).

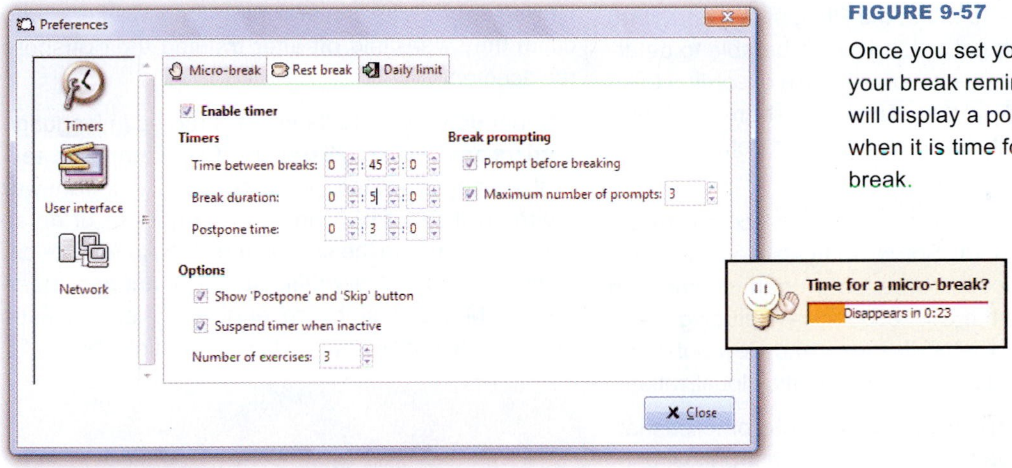

FIGURE 9-57

Once you set your preferences, your break reminder software will display a pop-up window when it is time for you to take a break.

QuickCheck

1. Monitors that comply with TCO and MPR standards are considered to emit safe levels of _____ such as ELF and VLF.

2. If you are curious about the amount of radio frequency emitted by your cell phone, you can check its _____ level on the FCC Web site. (Hint: Use the acronym.)

3. A(n) _____ stress injury is not a specific disease but a group of similar disorders that can affect the tendons, muscles, and nerves when a keyboard or mouse are overused.

4. According to ergonomic guidelines, you should use the arms of your chair to keep your shoulders elevated. True or false? _____

5. LCD screens have a(n) _____ resolution which displays one pixel for each tiny light in the display matrix.

6. Break _____ software such as RSIGuard, Stress buster, Easy Rest Break, and Workrave can help you remember when it's time to take a break from your work.

CHECK ANSWERS

ISSUE

ISSUE
Are Tech Jobs Heading Offshore?

HAVE YOU EVER called a customer service number and encountered a friendly voice with a foreign accent on the other end of the line? Has it ever occurred to you that this support technician might be sitting at a desk on the other side of the world—in India, Singapore, or the Philippines, for example?

Computer and telecommunications technologies have made it possible for companies such as American Express, America Online, and Dell to move their call centers to India, the Philippines, and other countries. You might not, however, be able to determine a call center's location because according to an article in the *New York Times*, offshore customer service representatives are instructed not to disclose their locations to customers.

Outsourcing and offshoring have come under increasing criticism. Some analysts believe these business practices are causing unemployment in many sectors of the U.S. economy—including the IT industry. Other experts disagree, and view outsourcing and offshoring as part of economic globalization.

Outsourcing is an established business practice that can reduce product costs, cut consumer prices, and help businesses remain competitive. The range of outsourced jobs includes manufacturing; electrical engineering; back-office functions like accounting, human resources, call centers, and data analysis; and IT-related work, such as software development, maintenance, support, and quality assurance.

Electronic Data Systems (EDS), founded in 1962 by former presidential candidate Ross Perot, gets credit for turning IT outsourcing into a major business. In 1969, when Blue Shield of Pennsylvania could no longer handle the state's Medicare processing workload, EDS took over responsibility for managing the system and hiring employees.

Outsourcing seemed a good business practice and did not generate much controversy when jobs remained within national boundaries. As jobs were outsourced to other countries with significantly cheaper labor, the term *offshoring* was born and analysts became increasingly concerned about its effect on unemployment at home.

India, the first country to host offshore contact centers for U.S. businesses, is currently on the leading edge of IT offshoring. China, the Philippines, Mexico, Canada, and Russia are also considered strong contenders.

The major lure of offshoring is reduced cost of labor in developing nations. Whereas the salary for a U.S.-based programmer with three to four year's experience would be US$60,000 to $75,000 a year, programmers in India can easily charge a fraction of the cost—around US$15,000 to $30,000 a year. News reports cite several high-tech workers who claim they were laid off after training their offshore replacements.

Another downside of offshoring is rooted in language barriers and cultural differences. For example, in several Asian countries, it is customary to answer indirectly instead of giving an outright yes or no as would normally be the case in the U.S. An Asian technician who says "very difficult" might actually mean "no." A Mexican software engineer's enthusiastic "Yes!" might really mean, "I'll have to think about it."

Miscommunication can be costly. Dell Computers was forced to discontinue its offshore business-customers call center because of mounting complaints about bad service. New York financial services firm Lehman Brothers stopped offshoring its computer help desk to Wipro in India because of unsatisfactory service.

On both the national and state levels, politicians are faced with a dilemma: Should they focus on protecting their constituents' jobs or saving taxpayer money? Voters are clearly voicing their anxiety over job security. Because it became a major election issue, the State of Indiana prematurely ended a $15.2 million offshoring contract to upgrade the state's unemployment claims computer system, even though the contract would have saved taxpayers $8.1 million.

Consumers, however, vote with their wallets, and few are willing to pay more for U.S.-produced goods and services. Businesses that maintain a high-cost U.S. workforce could find themselves unable to compete in a global marketplace. If the business goes bankrupt, all its employees join the unemployment ranks.

It is difficult to precisely assess the pros and cons of offshoring. A survey conducted by *CFO* magazine reported that some companies had no cost savings whatsoever, or only nominal savings of less than 15%. Less than half of the companies in the study reported savings of more than 20%. In contrast to this data, Forrester Research, an independent technology research company, claims that its offshoring clients typically reap benefits ranging from 25% to 45%. How many domestic jobs have moved offshore? Estimates vary between 300,000 and 1 million—less than 2 tenths of a percent of all U.S. workers. Forrester Research projects a loss of 3.4 million U.S. jobs to offshoring by 2015.

As the offshoring debate continues, IEEE-USA, an organizational unit of the world's largest technical professional society, recommends the following:

- The Federal Government must collect and publish reliable statistics on the kinds and numbers of manufacturing and service jobs that are being moved offshore.

- Government procurement rules should favor work done in the United States and should restrict the offshoring of work in any instance where there is not a clear long-term economic benefit to the nation or where the work supports technologies that are critical to our national economic or military security.

- New U.S. workforce assistance programs should be created to help displaced high-tech workers regain productive employment and ensure that employed workers can acquire the knowledge and skills they need to remain competitive.

- A coordinated national strategy must be developed to sustain U.S. technological leadership and promote jobs creation in response to the concerted strategies other countries are using to capture U.S. industries, jobs, and markets.

Not since the industrial revolution has technology provided tools for such a significant change as economic globalization. Our response as individuals and as a nation is likely to have a far-reaching effect on future lifestyles, so keeping tabs on this issue is important.

INFOWEBLINKS

You'll find additional information about this issue at the **Offshoring InfoWeb**.

W **CLICK TO CONNECT**
www.course.com/np/concepts11/ch09

9

ISSUE

What Do You Think?

1. Have you ever contacted a call center that you suspected was located outside the United States?   ○ Yes ○ No ○ Not sure

2. Are you surprised that high-tech jobs, such as software engineering, requiring advanced skills can be handled by offshore firms?   ○ Yes ○ No ○ Not sure

3. Are you against offshoring?   ○ Yes ○ No ○ Not sure

▶ **SAVE RESPONSES**

COMPUTERS IN CONTEXT

Travel

RAMON STOPPELENBURG LEFT his home in the Netherlands with a backpack, a digital camera, a laptop computer, and a cell phone. He left behind the one thing most travelers would never be caught without—money! Instead, he set up a Web site called Let Me Stay For a Day. Every few days, Ramon updated his Web site with a journal entry, a picture or two, and his travel itinerary. After viewing the Web site, more than 3,600 people from 72 different countries have offered money, meals, and lodging.

Using the Web as his travel agent, Ramon has traveled through 17 countries, written more than 500 journal entries, taken more than 7,000 photographs, and spent US$0.00 of his own money. Ramon Stoppelenburg's adventure might be unconventional, but it demonstrates the growing role that computers play in the travel industry.

Since the 1960s, computer-based GDSs (global distribution systems) have managed and distributed travel related information, such as flight schedules, ticket prices, and passenger itineraries. GDSs were originally proprietary systems installed in airport terminals and used only by authorized airline employees. Today, GDSs are used by travel agents, hotel employees, and airline ticketing clerks. They also provide the power behind some travel-related Web sites.

The SABRE system, one of the oldest and largest GDSs, caters primarily to travel industry professionals. In 1953, American Airlines president C. R. Smith happened to be seated next to IBM sales representative R. Blair Smith on a flight from Los Angeles to New York. Their chance meeting led to the development of the Semi-Automatic Business Research Environment—commonly known as SABRE. When SABRE went online in 1964, it became the first e-commerce system in the world, allowing American Airlines agents in airport terminals to automate up to 26,000 passenger reservation transactions per day. Other airlines quickly followed suit, and competing GDSs were launched by United Airlines, TWA, and Amadeus, a partnership of European Airlines.

Before SABRE, flight reservations required cumbersome manual transactions. Travel agents used teletypes to communicate with airlines to reserve seats and generate tickets. Processing a round-trip reservation could take up to 3 hours and involved as many as 12 people. Today, SABRE and other GDSs manage information from hundreds of airlines, thousands of hotels, and a multitude of other travel-related organizations, such as car rental companies, cruise lines, and tour operators. Travel agents can use these systems to compare fare information, generate itineraries, and print tickets instantly. Schedule and rate changes are available immediately—no waiting for new rates to be printed and distributed.

Although GDSs are still in demand, some experts believe that their early popularity is now contributing to their demise. Most GDSs were built before the Internet and the Web were invented, and the hardware and software they rely on is now considered outdated. Compared to modern information systems, GDSs are difficult and expensive to maintain, and their use often requires special training. The information stored on a GDS was historically available only to professional travel agents.

The use of GDSs has been affected by a fundamental change in the travel industry characterized by a shift away from marketing through tour guides and travel agents. Many travel-related companies now prefer to market directly to consumers through Web sites and telephone sales. Some GDSs have been modified for consumer-level Web accessibility. These GDSs now provide the power behind popular travel Web sites such as Expedia.com and Travelocity.com.

GDS-powered Web sites offer consumers the same information that was previously available only to travel professionals who subscribed to a GDS service. Consumers can search for flights, compare fares, research travel destinations, and find hotel and car rental fees from one easy-to-use Web site. The GDS components of these systems continue to use old hardware and software, however, and the ongoing cost of maintenance is high.

In 2001, five airlines—American, Continental, Delta, Northwest, and United—launched a new travel-related Web site called Orbitz.com. Unlike other travel Web sites, this new site was not powered by a traditional GDS. Instead, Orbitz.com was built from the ground up, using modern hardware and software. Like GDS-based sites, Orbitz.com maintains information about flights, fares, hotels, rental cars, and cruises. Consumers can search for travel deals and discounts or research specific destinations.

Even before Orbitz.com went live, it was the subject of criticism and lawsuits. For example, the American Association of Travel Agents (AATA) claimed that Orbitz.com could publish special pricing not available through the standard fare schedules. If travel agents were unable to access the special online pricing, the AATA predicted that consumers would eventually stop using the services of travel agencies to book flights, rental cars, and other travel services. In July 2003, the Department of Transportation Inspector General closed the federal review after finding no evidence of any anti-competitive behavior by Orbitz, and in fact determined that Orbitz provides a valuable service to consumers and promotes competition in the travel marketplace. Despite a federal probe, Orbitz.com opened to much fanfare in June 2001 and quickly became one of the most popular travel-related Web sites.

Web-based travel services represented one of the few bright spots on the e-commerce landscape after the dot com bubble burst. Online travel sites appear to be flourishing.

Going a step beyond Orbitz, travel consolidators such as Kayak.com use metasearch technology to search hundreds of airline, hotel, and cruise sites to help customers find the best deals. Revenues garnered from ad clickthroughs keep these sites in business and travel planners benefit from the convenience of using a single site to search for travel deals.

Hotel and transportation reservations are one aspect of the travel-related services found on the Internet. The Web provides an abundance of trip planning information. Google Maps and MapQuest provide road maps and driving destinations between cities all over the globe. Web sites maintained by popular travel guides, such as Frommers.com and Fodors.com, provide information that helps travelers plan where to eat, where to stay, and what to see. The Web also offers travelogues, reviews, blogs, and message boards with postings from individual travelers. Web sites and blogs, such as TravelAdvisor.com and Epinions.com, encourage tourists and business travelers to post reviews about favorite restaurants, hotels, and tourist attractions.

Computers aren't used only for planning travel. Many travelers opt to take PDAs or laptops on the road, or stop at local Internet cafes and spend some time browsing the Web or sending e-mail messages. Web-based e-mail services such as Hotmail, Gmail, and Yahoo! Mail make it simple and inexpensive to keep in touch with friends, family, clients, and colleagues while on the road. Travelers with digital cameras can even send vacation photos to friends and relatives by e-mail or post the photos on a personal Web site. Travelers can download street maps and tourist information to their PDAs or iPhones, calculate exchange rates, and even translate simple phrases from one language to another.

INFOWEBLINKS

You'll find lots more information and links related to this Computers in Context topic at the **Computers and Travel InfoWeb**.

W CLICK TO CONNECT
www.course.com/np/concepts11/ch09

9

New Perspectives Labs

On the BookOnCD

To access the New Perspectives labs for Chapter 9, start the BookOnCD, BookOnFlashDrive, or other NP11 BookOn product and then click the icon next to the lab title below.

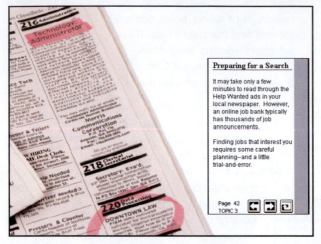

ONLINE JOB HUNTING

IN THIS LAB YOU'LL LEARN:

- How to register with an online job bank

- How to submit your resume online

- Why the file that you use for your printed resume might not be appropriate for posting online

- The characteristics of an ASCII document

- How to convert a formatted resume to an ASCII resume

- How to fix an ASCII resume so that it presents information in an easy-to-read format

- How to post an ASCII resume at a job bank

- How to enter a job search by keyword or category

- Creative ways to use keywords in a search specification

- How to configure a search agent

- How to find information on salaries, employers, and places to live

LAB ASSIGNMENTS

1. Start the interactive part of the lab. Make sure you've enabled Tracking if you want to save your QuickCheck results. Perform each lab step as directed, and answer all the lab QuickCheck questions. When you exit the lab, your answers are automatically graded and your results are displayed.

2. Write a paragraph that describes your ideal job. Next, create a list of search specifications that you could enter at an online job bank to find job openings for your ideal job. Connect to an online job bank and enter your search specifications. Describe the results. If your results were not satisfactory, try modifying your search specifications. Record what seems to be the most effective search, and, if possible, print the job listings that resulted from your search.

3. Using word processing or desktop publishing software, create a one-page resume that highlights your current skills and experience. Print this resume. Convert the resume into an ASCII document, tidy up the format, and then print it.

4. Use the Web to find information about the corporate culture at Microsoft. Summarize your findings, and list each Web site you visited to find information.

5. Use the Web to compare Macon, GA to San Diego, CA in terms of salaries, cost of living, job opportunities, and other factors. Write a one-page summary of the strengths and weaknesses of each city, and then explain which city you would prefer to live in. List the URLs for any Web sites you used for this assignment.

Key Terms

Make sure you understand all the boldfaced key terms presented in this chapter. If you're using the NP11 BookOnCD, BookOnFlashDrive, or other NP11 BookOn product, you can use this list of terms as an interactive study activity. First, try to define a term in your own words, and then click the term to compare your definition with the definition presented in the chapter.

Abacus, 486
Alpha test, 504
Analytical Engine, 488
Apple I, 495
Apple II, 495
Apple Lisa, 495
Apple Macintosh, 496
Atanasoff-Berry Computer, 489
Beta test, 504
Break reminder software, 541
Certificates of completion, 515
Certification exam, 516
Channel conflict, 508
Chief information officer, 510
Chipmakers, 498
Code of ethics, 530
COLOSSUS, 490
Computer engineer, 512
Computer engineering, 514
Computer industry, 497
Computer operator, 511
Computer professional, 510
Computer programmer, 511
Computer retail store, 506
Computer retailers, 498
Computer salesperson, 512
Computer science, 514
Confidentiality, 526
Contract worker, 513
Database administrator, 511
DEC PDP-8, 493
deColmar's Arithmometer, 487
Difference Engine, 488
ENIAC, 490

Equipment manufacturers, 498
Ergonomics, 537
First-generation computers, 491
Fourth-generation computers, 494
Harvard Mark I, 490
Hollerith Tabulating Machine, 488
IBM 360, 493
IBM AS/400, 493
IBM PC, 495
IBM PC XT, 495
Information systems, 514
Information Systems department, 510
Information technology, 514
Information technology industry, 497
Job search agent, 521
Leibniz Calculator, 487
Mail order, 507
Manual calculator, 486
Manufacturer direct, 507
Manufacturing technician, 512
Mark-8, 494
Market share, 504
Market tiers, 505
Marketing channels, 506
Mechanical calculator, 487
Metasearch tool, 521
MITS Altair, 494
MSRP, 503
Napier's Bones, 487
Native resolution, 539
Network specialist/administrator, 511
Offshoring, 500
Online job bank, 520
Outsourcing, 499

Pascaline, 487
Professional ethics, 523
Proprietary information, 526
Prototype, 489
Quality assurance specialist, 512
RCA Spectra 70, 493
Repetitive stress injury, 536
Schickard's Calculator, 487
Second-generation computers, 492
Security specialist, 511
Service companies, 498
Slide rule, 487
Software engineering, 515
Software publishers, 498
Street price, 503
Systems analyst, 510
Technical support specialist, 511
Technical writer, 512
Telecommuting, 513
Third-generation computers, 493
Transistors, 492
UNIVAC, 491
Vacuum tube, 491
Vaporware, 503
VAR, 508
VisiCalc, 495
Web portfolio, 519
Web site designer, 511
Whistleblowing, 532
Xerox Alto, 495
Z3, 489

9

Interactive Summary

To review important concepts from this chapter, fill in the blanks to best complete each sentence. When using the NP11 BookOnCD or other BookOn product, click the Check Answers buttons to automatically score your answers.

SECTION A: Even before recorded history, humans used various [_____] aids, such as pebbles and notched sticks, to keep track of quantities. By 1200, a [_____] calculator, called the abacus, had appeared in China. In Europe, a popular calculating device called Napier's Bones was transformed into the slide rule in 1621, and became the calculating tool of choice in Europe and later the Americas. Manual calculators require the operator to apply an [_____] to perform calculations. In contrast, [_____] calculators, such as the Pascaline and deColmar's Arithmometer, are designed to carry out calculations autonomously. In 1822, an English mathematician named Charles [_____] proposed to build a device, called the Difference Engine, that would operate using

steam power. He also designed a second device, called the [_____] Engine, which embodied many of the concepts that define the modern computer. In the 1930s and 1940s, several [_____] computers were developed, including the Atanasoff-Berry Computer, Z3, Harvard Mark I, COLOSSUS, and ENIAC. Most of these early computers used [_____] tubes, which paved the way for the architecture of first-generation computers, such as UNIVAC. Second-generation computers were smaller and less power hungry because they used [_____]. Third-generation computers were even smaller because they used [_____] circuits. The key technology for fourth-generation computers, including personal computers, is the [_____].

▶ CHECK ANSWERS

SECTION B: The [_____] industry encompasses those companies that manufacture computers. A broader term, IT industry, is typically used to refer to the companies that develop, produce, sell, or support computers, software, and computer-related products. The IT industry has fueled the economies of many countries, but despite a trend toward [_____], the IT industry remains dominated by the United States. A high rate of dot com business failures during 2001 and 2002 meant a decline in equipment orders, Web site hosting contracts, and IT sector job openings. During that time, strength in worldwide markets for IT equipment and services continued to buoy up the industry. The life cycle of a typical hardware product includes product development, product announcement, introduction, [_____], and retirement. The life cycle of a software product is similar, except that old versions of a

software product do not typically remain in the publisher's product line. Soon after a new version of a software product is released, the publisher discontinues sales of the old version. Hardware and software products are sold through marketing [_____], such as retail stores, mail-order/Internet outlets, value-added resellers, and manufacturer direct. Retail stores and VARs tend to have the highest prices. In most countries, including the United States, the IT industry is not regulated by a dedicated government agency. Instead, the IT industry is subject to broad-based [_____] that pertains to anti-monopoly laws, communications rules, and gambling restrictions. To avoid government regulations that target technology companies, the IT industry has attempted to regulate itself by creating organizations to set standards and disseminate information to technology companies, government, and the general public.

▶ CHECK ANSWERS

SECTION C: A computer [ ] is defined as any person whose primary occupation involves the design, configuration, analysis, development, modification, testing, or security of computer hardware or software. The IT industry encompasses a wide variety of jobs for computer professionals, and the career outlook appears to be relatively positive. Salaries and working conditions are quite favorable. The typical IT worker puts in a 40+ hour week, although part-time work is also available. Many computer professionals are [ ] workers, who arrange to work for a company on a temporary basis, usually as consultants for particular projects. Although these workers are usually highly paid, they are not official employees of a company and are not eligible for company health care or retirement benefits. Education is an important key to most high tech jobs. Computer [ ] degree programs focus on the design of computer hardware and peripheral devices. Computer [ ] degree programs focus on digital computer architecture and how to program computers to make them work effectively and efficiently. Information [ ] degree programs focus on applying computers to business problems. In addition to a college degree, [ ] provides job applicants with marketable credentials, through certificates of completion or certification exams. Finding a job in the IT industry is similar to finding any job. Preparing a resume is essential, and it can be supplemented by a Web [ ] with links to relevant Web sites, such as past employers, your alma mater, and samples of your work. Job seekers can make use of online search [ ] and [ ] tools that can be automated to search one or more job databases. Before posting a resume at an online job bank, you should always check the job bank's [ ] policy. ▶ CHECK ANSWERS

SECTION D: Computer professionals sometimes encounter situations in which the right course of action requires a decision based on evaluating what's right and wrong. Professional [ ] refers to on-the-job choices and actions that reflect a person's values. Ethical decisions should take into account applicable [ ], such as the Digital Millennium Copyright Act. Laws and ethics are not the same thing, however, and sometimes following the letter of the law does not result in ethical behavior. Situations that require computer professionals to make ethical decisions often involve software copyrights, privacy, conflict of interest, use of work computers, software quality, hacking, and social [ ]. Ethical decisions made on the job can have long-term career effects. Many IT organizations have [ ] of ethics designed to help computer professionals make tough decisions. Additional help in making ethical decisions can also be obtained from knowledgeable friends, mentors, lawyers, and workplace counselors. Computer professionals who are compelled to become [ ] and speak out against on-the-job activities that threaten the public interest should understand the potential legal and career risks before they proceed. ▶ CHECK ANSWERS

SECTION E: As computers and other digital devices became a fixture in modern workplaces and everyday life, questions were raised about health risks associated with computer use. All electronic devices emit various types of [ ] in the form of light, heat, and radio waves. Some consumer watchdogs have suggested that cathode ray [ ] monitors pose a potential health risk because they generate X-rays. Researchers have explored the link between cell phones and brain cancer with inconclusive results, however, government standards limit emissions to 1.6W/kg, measured by [ ]. To avoid [ ] stress injuries, equipment and furniture in a computer work area should be arranged according to [ ] guidelines. Taking frequent rest breaks while using a computer can also help to avoid eyestrain and stress injuries. [ ] reminder software can help workers remember when to take a break. Television and digital gadgets seem to contribute to a sedentary lifestyle. To counteract health problems associated with sitting for long periods of time, regular exercise and good nutrition are essential. ▶ CHECK ANSWERS

9

Interactive Situation Questions

Apply what you've learned to some typical computing situations. When using the NP11 BookOnCD, BookOnFlashDrive, or any other NP11 BookOn product, you can type your answers, and then use the Check Answers button to automatically score your responses.

1. Suppose that you were an accountant in 1979, and you wanted to use a state-of-the-art personal computer and software for your work. You would probably have selected an Apple II computer and [_____] software.

2. You work as a manufacturing technician in a chip fabrication plant. Your aunt asks if you're in the IT industry. Your response: [_____]

3. Suppose that you visit a software publisher's Web site and gather information about a software package that has an MSRP of $495. Instead of purchasing the software from the publisher's site, you check a few other sites because you expect the [_____] price to be less.

4. You receive an e-mail from a software publisher that offers to supply you with a free copy of a new operating system if you become part of a beta test program. You are hesitant about participating because beta software versions often contain [_____] that can cause unexpected glitches in your computer.

5. After studying and gaining practical experience on how to analyze a computer system's vulnerability to threats from viruses, worms, unauthorized access, and physical damage, you are ready for a job as a(n) [_____] specialist.

6. You accepted a position with an IT company as a(n) [_____] worker, fully realizing that you will not be considered an official employee of the company, nor will you be eligible for the company's health care or retirement benefits.

7. Your friend is not strong in math, but really wants to work with computers. You suggest that your friend consider a(n) [_____] systems degree.

8. To supplement your computer science degree, you decide to take a(n) [_____] exam to become a Microsoft Certified Systems Engineer.

9. As part of your job hunting activities, you plan to create your resume in several different [_____], for use in the body of an e-mail message, as a Web page, and as a printed document.

10. You're working with a friend on an assignment and she proudly shows you a program she's developing to shut down hate sites on the Web. Her plan gives you an uneasy feeling. You'll have to make an [_____] decision about what to do.

11. You've discovered your company's accounting system was intentionally modified to disguise certain expenses. You're contemplating what might happen if you become a [_____], and expose this unethical practice.

12. You want to make sure your computer is set up so that you can avoid disabling musculoskeletal injuries, like carpal tunnel syndrome. You can look for [_____] guidelines on the Web, which offer advice on how to position your computer monitor and where to place lighting.

 CHECK ANSWERS

Interactive Practice Tests

Practice tests that consist of 10 multiple-choice, true/false, and fill-in-the-blank questions are available on both the NP11 BookOn products and the NP11 Web site. The questions are selected at random from a large test bank, so each time you take a test, you'll receive a different set of questions. Your tests are scored immediately, and you can print study guides that help you find the correct answers for any questions that you missed.

CLICK TO START

Study Tips

Study Tips help you to organize and consolidate the information in a unit by making lists, outlines, charts, and sketches. You can use paper and pencil or word processing software to complete most of the Study Tip activities.

1. Make sure you can use your own words to correctly answer each of the red focus questions that appear throughout the chapter.

2. Create a timeline of the computer history events described in Section A.

3. Supply examples and explain the differences that characterize counting aids, manual calculators, and mechanical calculators.

4. Define how the term prototype applies to the history of computing, and list at least five computer prototypes that were developed between 1937 and 1951.

5. Make a list of the computer companies mentioned in the chapter. What was the contribution of each company to the evolution of computers, from the prototypes of the 1940s to the personal computers that we use today?

6. Discuss the key developments that changed the personal computer's target market from a small group of hobbyists to a diverse population.

7. Define the terms outsourcing and offshoring then explain how they relate to the computer industry.

8. List five stages in the life cycle of a typical computer hardware product, then explain the similarities and differences that exist in the life cycle of a software product.

9. List the various marketing channels that exist in the computer industry, and explain the advantages and disadvantages of each channel for consumers.

10. Define the term computer professional, and list at least eight job titles that it encompasses.

11. Explain in your own words the focuses of computer engineering, computer science, information technology, software engineering, and information systems degree programs.

12. List four ways in which the Internet can figure into your job search.

13. Suppose you have a version of your resume in DOC, RTF, ASCII, and HTML formats. Explain the circumstances under which you would use each of these versions.

14. Make a list of the situations described in this chapter that required a computer professional to make an ethical decision.

15. Make a list of the resources mentioned in this chapter that can help computer professionals resolve ethical issues.

16. List and briefly describe the major health risks that have been associated with computer use.

17. Draw a diagram showing ergonomic placement for equipment and furniture in a computer work area.

18. Fill in the blanks on the concept map below to show the hierarchy of computer generations described in this chapter.

Concept Map

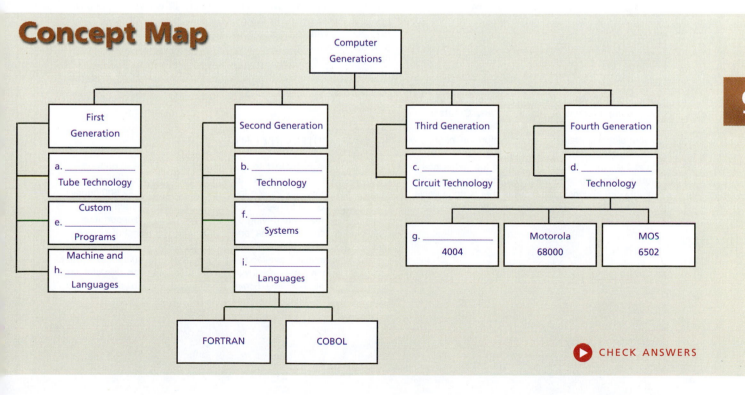

9

CHECK ANSWERS

Projects

 CRITICAL THINKING

Before you find yourself in a compromising situation involving computer use, it might be useful to consider your own ethical principles. Organize your thoughts into a set of ethical guidelines in a paper that's one or two pages in length.

GROUP PROJECT

Form a team of six people. Select two members of the team to be "head hunters," who work together to post a job description. The other four team members write fictional cover letters and resumes to apply for the job, and then send them to the head hunters. The head hunters should rank the resumes and then compare results. Were the rankings the same? Why or why not? Remember that real-life head hunters are suspicious of resumes that seem too good to be true, so try to be realistic. Your group should submit the job description, cover letters, resumes, and rankings to your instructor.

CYBERCLASSROOM

Provide your team members with access to your resume. If it is posted on a Web site, provide the URL. If it is stored as an electronic document format that all your team members can read, you can e-mail it to them as an attachment. As a last resort, you can copy and paste it into the body of an e-mail message. Solicit comments from your team to help improve your resume. Use cut and paste to combine the comments from your team members into a document. Submit your original resume, your team members' comments, and your revised resume to your instructor.

MULTIMEDIA PROJECT

Locate information about an interesting technology company on the Web. Now suppose you are a recruiter for that company. Create a 10–15 slide PowerPoint presentation to show to college students at a job fair. Make sure your slides contain substantive information, presented in a quick-to-understand format for students who are moving from booth to booth at a job fair. Use photos to make the slides interesting and, since you are trying to capture student interest in a busy atmosphere, you might want to consider music or other sound effects, too. Follow your instructor's guidelines for submitting your PowerPoint presentation.

 **RESUME BUILDER**

What does it take today to create an effective online resume? Use the Web to locate information and tips about creating effective online resumes. Using the guidelines you find, create a resume using word processing software or Web page authoring software. Show your initial draft to two other students in your class. Collect their feedback and make any necessary revisions. Submit your completed resume in the format specified by your instructor, accompanied by a description of the features you included to make your resume easy to find and understand.

 GLOBALIZATION

With growing trends to outsourcing, some economists are pointing to the emergence of "globalized professionals," who are developing qualifications necessary to succeed in the global job market. For this project use Web resources to research about globalized professionals. Pay particular attention to the way this concept relates to your chosen career field. Using the information you've found, write a one-page paper outlining your thoughts. If the idea of becoming a globalized professional appeals to you, describe how you might enhance your qualifications. If the idea does not appeal to you, explain why.

ISSUE

The Issue section of this chapter focused on outsourcing and offshoring. Both are controversial business practices that many people believe affect the economy, wages, and employment. For this project, research the Web for information on offshoring. Make a list of as many pros as you can find. Make another list of as many cons as you can find. To conclude the project, suppose that you were asked to participate in a panel discussion about offshoring. The panel will begin with a 30-second position statement from each of the participants. Write out your statement and submit it.

 **COMPUTERS IN CONTEXT**

The Computers in Context section of this chapter focused on travel-related uses of computers. For this project, suppose that you are planning a one-week vacation for two, and you have a $2,500 budget. Use the Web to find transportation. Include your flight, train, or boat schedule or a map with driving directions. Calculate transportation costs. Find accommodations, and calculate the total cost of lodging for the week-long trip. Next, find restaurants for two special dinners during your trip. If menus are available, indicate what you would order. Finally, make a list of the sights you'll visit. Include a brief description of each and indicate entrance fees. Provide your instructor with your trip itinerary and costs, along with the URLs of all Web sites you used to gather information.

On the Web

STUDENT EDITION LABS

W **CLICK TO ACCESS THE NP11 WEB SITE**
or open your browser and connect to www.course.com/np/concepts11/ch09.
Lab results can be stored in the Universal Gradebook.

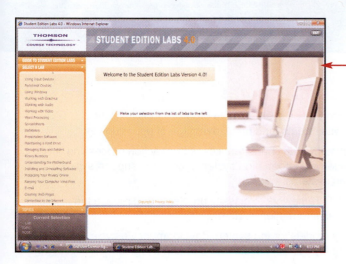

Work hands-on in structured simulations practicing important skills and concepts

COMPUTER ETHICS

In the Computer Ethics Student Edition Lab, you will learn about the following topics:

- Intellectual property rights and copyrights for images, video, and text
- Using company resources
- Fair use and public domain issues
- File sharing issues

CAREERS AND TECHNOLOGY: GETTING AHEAD

In the Careers and Technology Student Edition Lab, you will learn about the following topics:

- The use of technology in IT and non-IT jobs
- Education and certification IT jobs
- Creating resumes
- The hiring manager's perspective

CHAPTER COURSECAST

Use your computer or iPod to hear a five-minute audio presentation of chapter highlights.

FLASHCARD COURSECAST

Interact with audio flashcards to review key terms from the chapter.

DETAILED OBJECTIVES

Make sure that you've achieved all the objectives for a chapter before it's time for your test!

TEST YOURSELF

Review chapter material by taking these ten-question tests, then send your results to the Universal Gradebook.

ONLINE GAMES

Have some fun while refreshing your memory about key concepts that might appear on the next test. You can even send your results to the Universal Gradebook!

AND MORE!

At the NP11 Web site you'll also find Extra Content and InfoWebLinks.

9

10

Information Systems Analysis and Design

LEARNING OBJECTIVES

- Describe how information systems help organizations fulfill their missions, deal with threats, and take advantage of opportunities

- Contrast and compare the characteristics of transaction processing systems, management information systems, decision support systems, and expert systems

- Apply the PIECES framework to classify problems that reduce the effectiveness of an information system

- Describe various models for the system development life cycle (SDLC), and identify system development methodologies

- List the activities that take place in each phase of the system development life cycle

- Describe alternative hardware and software solutions that a project team might consider

- Explain the differences between unit testing, integration testing, system testing, and acceptance testing

- Describe the advantages and disadvantages of direct, parallel, phased, and pilot conversion techniques

- List the major threats to data stored on corporate information systems

- List five guidelines for mitigating the effects of corporate identity theft

PRE-ASSESSMENT QUIZ

Take the pre-assessment quiz to find out how much you know about the topics in this chapter. ▶

MULTIMEDIA and INTERACTIVE ELEMENTS

When using the BookOnCD, BookOnFlashDrive, or other NP11 BookOn product, the ▶ icons are clickable to access multimedia resources.

BEFORE YOU READ ON, **TRY IT**

HOW EFFECTIVE IS MY INFORMATION SYSTEM?

One of the first steps in the systems analysis process is to uncover problems and opportunities with computer systems currently in use. Although systems analysts typically work on large organizational projects, you can use some of their techniques to analyze your personal computer. Apply the PIECES framework to your computer system to complete the table below. You'll learn more about PIECES when you read the chapter.

P	Performance	List any tasks your computer performs slowly or software that doesn't respond as quickly as you would like.	
I	Information	List any examples of applications that don't provide you with the right information at the right time or in the most useable format.	
E	Economics	List any computing tasks that seem to cost too much.	
C	Control	List any computing tasks that make it difficult to control unauthorized access to your data.	
E	Efficiency	List any tasks that seem to take longer than necessary.	
S	Service	List any computing tasks which seem too complex or inconvenient.	

WEB SITE

Visit the NP11 Web site to access additional resources  that accompany this chapter.

Information Systems

YOU ARE PROBABLY a member of an organization, such as a student club, fraternity or sorority, sports team, or political party. You also deal with all kinds of organizations every day: your school, stores, banks, and government agencies. Most organizations use information systems to operate more effectively, gather information, and accomplish tasks. In this section, you'll review some basic concepts about organizations and find out how information systems enhance organizational activities.

INFORMATION SYSTEMS IN ORGANIZATIONS

What is an information system? An **information system** collects, stores, and processes data to provide useful, accurate, and timely information, typically within the context of an organization. Information systems encompass data, the people and machines that collect, process, output, and store data, the networks that transmit and receive data, and the procedures that govern the way data is handled.

Although an information system does not necessarily have to be computerized, today most information systems rely on computers and communications networks to store, process, and transmit information with far more efficiency than would be possible with manual systems. In this textbook, the term *information system* refers to a system that uses computers and usually includes communications networks.

What's the official definition of organization? An **organization** is a group of people working together to accomplish a goal. According to Peter Drucker, who was an influential writer about business and management, "the purpose of an organization is to enable ordinary people to do extraordinary things." Organizations have accomplished amazing feats, such as sending astronauts into space, providing live television coverage of global events, and inventing freeze-dried ice cream. They also accomplish all kinds of day-to-day, routine tasks, such as offering banking services, selling merchandise, and policing neighborhoods.

Any organization that seeks profit by providing goods and services is called a **business**. Some organizations are formed to accomplish political, social, or charitable goals that do not include amassing profit. Such an organization is known as a **nonprofit organization**.

Every organization has a goal or plan that's referred to as its **mission**. All activities that take place in an organization, including those that involve computers, should contribute to this mission. The written expression of an organization's mission is called a mission statement. A **mission statement** describes not only an organization's goals, but also the way in which those goals will be accomplished. Companies publish their mission statements in corporate reports and on the Web (Figure 10-1).

FIGURE 10-1

Many organizations, such as Expedition 360, publish their mission statements on the Web.

to circle the world by means of human power alone

to use the adventure as a classroom learning tool

to encourage world citizenship between cultures

to promote environmental responsibility

to live fully and enjoy the experience

Who uses information systems? An information system is used by the people in an organization and its customers. You've undoubtedly used many information systems—for example, when registering for classes, getting cash from an ATM, and purchasing merchandise on the Web. You might even work for a business or nonprofit organization where you access an information system as part of your job.

Not everyone in an organization uses an information system in the same way. An information system must support the needs of people who engage in many different organizational activities.

To coordinate the activities of employees, most organizations use a hierarchical structure. An **organizational chart**, such as the one in Figure 10-2, depicts the hierarchy of employees in an organization.

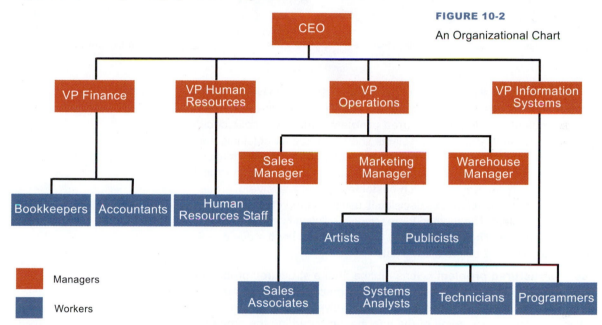

FIGURE 10-2

An Organizational Chart

In many organizations, and most businesses, employees can be classified as workers or managers. **Workers** are the people who directly carry out the organization's mission. For example, they assemble cars, write newspaper articles, sell merchandise, answer telephones, lay bricks, cut trees, fix engines, or perform other types of labor. Workers typically collect data for information systems. For example, as a checkout clerk rings up sales, her cash register records each item in a database.

Managers determine organizational goals and plan how to achieve those goals. They approve new products, authorize new construction, and supervise workers. Executive managers plan an organization's long-range goals for profitability, market share, membership levels, and so on. This emphasis on long-range and future goals is referred to as **strategic planning**.

Mid-level managers are responsible for figuring out how to achieve those long-range goals through sales, marketing, or new product development. They set incremental goals that can be achieved in a year or less—a process referred to as **tactical planning**. Low-level managers are responsible for scheduling employees, ordering supplies, and other activities that make day-to-day operations run smoothly—a process referred to as **operational planning**. Information systems can provide some or all of the data needed for strategic, tactical, and operational planning.

10

How do information systems help the people in an organization?

An information system can help the people in an organization perform their jobs more quickly and effectively by automating routine tasks, such as reordering inventory, taking customer orders, or sending out renewal notices. Information systems can also help people solve problems.

One of the major functions of an information system is to help people make decisions in response to problems. According to Herbert Simon, who was well known for his insights into organizational behavior, the decision-making process has three phases, shown in Figure 10-3.

Phase 1: Recognize a problem or a need to make a decision.

Phase 2: Devise and analyze possible solutions or actions to solve the problem.

Phase 3: Select an action or a solution.

FIGURE 10-3

The three decision-making phases are usually clear cut, leading to decisions that are objective, standardized, and based on factual data.

All problems are not alike, but they can be classified into three types: structured, semi-structured, and unstructured. An everyday, run-of-the-mill, routine problem is called a **structured problem**. When you make decisions in response to structured problems, the procedure for obtaining the best solution is known, the objective is clearly defined, and the information necessary to make the decision is easy to identify. An example of a structured problem is figuring out which customers should receive overdue notices. The information for this decision is usually stored in a file cabinet or computer system. The method for reaching a solution is to look for customers with outstanding balances, and then check whether the due dates for their payments fall before today's date.

A **semi-structured problem** is less routine than a structured problem. When solving a semi-structured problem, the procedure for arriving at a solution is usually known; however, it might involve some degree of subjective judgment. Also, some of the information regarding the problem might not be available, might lack precision, or might be uncertain. An example of a semi-structured problem for a retail business is deciding how much inventory to stock for the holidays. The decision can be based on the previous year's sales, with some adjustment for the current year's consumer confidence index. The consumer confidence index, however, might or might not accurately predict consumer spending over the holidays. Because of this uncertainty, determining the appropriate amount of holiday inventory would be classified as a semi-structured problem.

An **unstructured problem** requires human intuition as the basis for finding a solution. Information relevant to the problem might be missing, and few, if any, parts of the solution can be tackled using concrete models. If experts are presented with the same problem data, but they disagree on a solution, it is likely an unstructured problem. An example of an unstructured problem might be whether Saks Fifth Avenue should stock Japanese-inspired evening gowns. The purchasing agent for women's clothing makes this decision based on her intuition of customer taste and fashion trends.

Can an information system solve all three types of problems?

Traditionally, information systems have contributed most to solving structured problems, but tools have emerged to help people tackle semi-structured and unstructured problems as well. Despite these tools and the data they provide, many semi-structured and unstructured problems continue to be solved based on "guesstimates."

An information system's ability to assist with problem solving and decision making depends on the data it collects and makes available. Some information systems collect and store **internal information** generated by the organization itself. Other information systems store or provide access to **external information** generated by sources outside the organization. Later in this section, you'll learn how different types of information systems deal with internal and external information.

Do organizations require different kinds of information systems? Because organizations have different missions and face different problems, they require different kinds of information systems. A small business might require a basic information system for accounting, inventory, and payroll. A large business might require several information systems integrated into an **enterprise computer system** that supports a variety of business activities such as inventory management, point-of-sale cash registers, e-commerce, payroll, and managerial planning.

An information system or its components can be classified as transaction processing systems, management information systems, decision support systems, or expert systems.

TRANSACTION PROCESSING SYSTEMS

What's a transaction? In an information system context, a **transaction** is an exchange between two parties that is recorded and stored in a computer system. When you order a product at a Web site, buy merchandise in a store, or withdraw cash from an ATM, you are involved in a transaction.

What is a transaction processing system? Many organizational activities involve transactions. A **transaction processing system** (TPS) provides a way to collect, process, store, display, modify, or cancel transactions. Most transaction processing systems allow many transactions to be entered simultaneously. The data collected by a TPS is typically stored in databases, and can be used to produce a regularly scheduled set of reports, such as monthly bills, weekly paychecks, annual inventory summaries, daily manufacturing schedules, or periodic check registers. Figure 10-4 lists some examples of business transaction processing systems.

FIGURE 10-4

Business Transaction Processing Systems

10

Payroll

Accounting

Inventory

Point of sale

Early transaction processing systems, such as banking and payroll applications of the 1970s, used **batch processing** to collect and hold a group of transactions until the end of a day or pay period, when the entire batch is processed. Batch processing proceeds without human intervention, until all transactions are completed or until an error occurs.

In contrast to batch processing, most modern transaction processing systems use **online processing**—a real-time method in which each transaction is processed as it is entered. Such a system is often referred to as an **OLTP system** (online transaction processing system). OLTP uses a *commit or rollback* strategy to ensure that each transaction is processed correctly. This strategy is crucial because most transactions require a sequence of steps, and every step must succeed for the transaction to be completed.

How does commit or rollback work? If you withdraw cash from an ATM, the bank's computer must make sure your account contains sufficient funds before it deducts the withdrawal from your account and allows the ATM to deliver cash. If the ATM is out of cash, however, the transaction fails, and the withdrawal should not be deducted from your account. A TPS can **commit** to a transaction and permanently update database records only if every step of the transaction can be successfully processed. If even one step fails, however, the entire transaction fails and a **rollback** returns the records to their original state. Figure 10-5 diagrams the processes that take place in a typical TPS, and the video that accompanies the figure provides additional information about commit and rollback.

FIGURE 10-5

A transaction processing system (TPS) is characterized by its ability to:
■ Collect, display, and modify transactions
■ Store transactions
■ List transactions

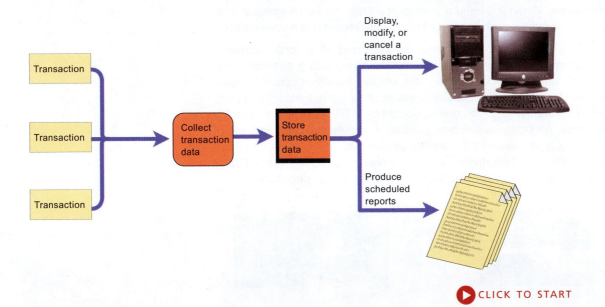

CLICK TO START

What are the limitations of transaction processing systems?
Although a TPS excels at maintaining transaction data entered by clerical personnel and online customers, its reporting capabilities are limited. A typical TPS generates **detail reports**, which provide a basic record of completed transactions. However, managers need more sophisticated reports to help them understand and analyze data. These reports are usually created by a management information system.

MANAGEMENT INFORMATION SYSTEMS

What is a management information system? The term *management information system* is used in two contexts. It can be a synonym for the term *information system*, or it can refer to a specific category or type of information system. We'll use the term **management information system** (MIS, pronounced em-eye-ess) in this second context, to refer to a type of information system that uses the data collected by a transaction processing system, and manipulates the data to create reports that managers can use to make routine business decisions in response to structured problems. As Figure 10-6 shows, an MIS is characterized by the production of periodic reports that managers use for structured and routine tasks.

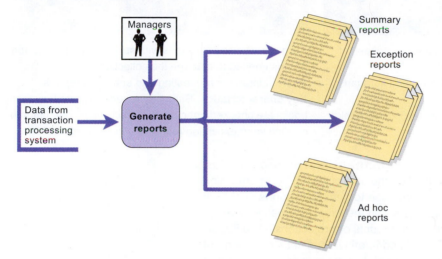

FIGURE 10-6

A management information system is characterized by its ability to:

- Produce routine and on-demand reports
- Provide useful information for managerial activities
- Increase managerial efficiency
- Provide information used for structured, routine decisions

▶ **CLICK TO START**

One of the major goals of an MIS is to increase the efficiency of managerial activity. Different levels of management have different information needs. In response to these different needs, an MIS can produce scheduled reports or ad hoc reports. **Scheduled reports**, such as monthly summaries, follow a fixed format and are produced according to a preset timetable. An **ad hoc report** (sometimes called a demand report) is a customized report, generated to supply specific information not available in scheduled reports.

The scheduled reports produced by an MIS include summary and exception reports. A **summary report** combines, groups, or totals data. For example, a summary report might show total annual sales for the past five years. Summary reports are useful in tactical and strategic planning. An **exception report**, such as the one shown in Figure 10-7, contains information that is outside normal or acceptable ranges.

FIGURE 10-7

Exception reports help managers take action, such as reordering inventory. Managers also use exception reports to analyze potential problems, such as continued inventory shortages or an excessive number of customers making late payments.

Low Inventory-May 30

Item#	Description	Minimum Quantity	Current Quantity	Vendor
J506	Qualo-bag	12	10	REI
05D-8	Sm. Backpack	48	22	REI
B99A	Med. Backpack	48	40	REI
L2020	Canteen	24	3	ZB Ind.
D2990	Flashlight	36	8	ZB Ind.
6-334	Tent stakes	112	24	Granot

10

How does an MIS differ from a TPS? Whereas a TPS simply records data, an MIS can consolidate data by grouping and summarizing it. For example, modern library systems typically contain both a TPS and an MIS, which serve different functions, as Figure 10-8 explains.

FIGURE 10-8

A library's TPS performs different functions than its MIS.

TPS

Purpose: Track books by maintaining a database of titles, checkout dates, and so forth
Users: Library patrons locating books and librarians checking books in and out
Key characteristic: Managing transactions as books are checked in and out

MIS

Purpose: Provide librarians with summary and exception reports needed to manage the collection
Users: Librarians requesting and analyzing reports
Key characteristics: Summary reports indicate how many books are checked out each day, each week, each month, or each year; exception reports list long-overdue books

What are the limitations of a management information system? A traditional MIS is based on the data collected by a transaction processing system. The MIS software used to generate reports might not be flexible enough to provide managers with the exact information needed. Further, an MIS usually cannot create models or projections—two important strategic planning tools. Today's competitive business environment calls for more sophisticated data manipulation tools, such as those that decision support systems provide.

DECISION SUPPORT SYSTEMS

What's a decision support system? A **decision support system** (DSS) helps people make decisions by directly manipulating data, analyzing data from external sources, generating statistical projections, and creating data models of various scenarios. A DSS provides tools for routine decisions, non-routine decisions, structured problems, and even semi-structured problems in which a decision might be based on imprecise data or require "guesstimates."

A special type of decision support system, called an **executive information system** (EIS), is designed to provide senior managers with information relevant to strategic management activities—such as setting policies, planning, and preparing budgets—based on information from internal and external databases.

A decision support system derives its name from the fact that it *supports* the decision maker; that is, it provides the tools a decision maker needs to analyze data. A DSS does not make decisions, however. That task remains the responsibility of the human decision maker.

Decision makers use DSSs to design decision models and make queries. A **decision model** is a numerical representation of a realistic situation, such as a cash-flow model of a business that shows how income adds to cash accounts and expenses deplete those accounts. A **decision query** is a question or set of instructions describing data that must be gathered to make a decision.

A DSS typically includes modeling tools, such as spreadsheets, so that managers can create a numerical representation of a situation and explore *what-if* alternatives. DSS statistical tools help managers study trends before making decisions. In addition, a DSS usually includes data from an organization's transaction processing system, and it might include or access external data, such as stock market reports, as shown in Figure 10-9.

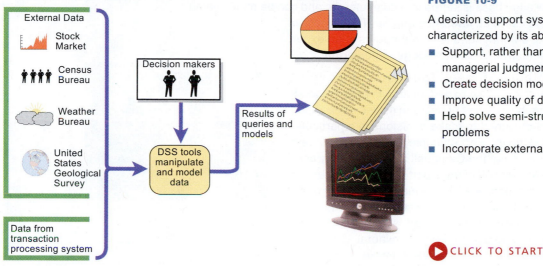

FIGURE 10-9

A decision support system is characterized by its ability to:

- Support, rather than replace, managerial judgment
- Create decision models
- Improve quality of decisions
- Help solve semi-structured problems
- Incorporate external data

▶ CLICK TO START

What kinds of decisions can a DSS handle?

A DSS can be used to tackle diverse problems because it contains a good selection of decision support tools. A manager of a camping supply business might use a DSS to project demand for camping equipment before deciding how much new inventory to order. The DSS can access data on past sales from the company's transaction processing system. It can also access external data from government reports and commercial information services. This data can be manipulated to examine what-if scenarios, such as "What if higher national park fees decrease the number of campers, and demand for camping equipment declines by 2%?"

What are the limitations of a DSS?

A DSS helps people manipulate the data needed to make a decision but does not actually make a decision. Instead, a person must analyze the data and reach a decision. A DSS is not a substitute for human judgment. Therefore, a DSS is appropriate in situations where it is used by trained professionals.

Many organizations, however, would like an alternative in which not every decision needs to be made by a highly paid expert. The major limitation of most decision support systems is they require users to have in-depth knowledge of the business problem that underlies the decision, plus a good background on what-if models and statistics. When organizations want an information system to make decisions without direct guidance from an experienced decision maker, they turn to expert systems.

INFOWEBLINKS

The Web contains lots of information about DSSs. At the **DSS InfoWeb**, you can explore their history and learn about state-of-the-art DSS software.

Ⓦ CLICK TO CONNECT
www.course.com/np/concepts11/ch10

10

EXPERT SYSTEMS AND NEURAL NETWORKS

What is an expert system? An **expert system**, sometimes referred to as a *knowledge-based system*, is a computer system designed to analyze data and produce a recommendation, diagnosis, or decision based on a set of facts and rules, as shown in Figure 10-10.

The facts and rules for an expert system are usually derived by interviewing one or more experts, and then incorporated into a **knowledge base**. The knowledge base is stored in a computer file and can be manipulated by software called an **inference engine**. The process of designing, entering, and testing the rules in an expert system is referred to as **knowledge engineering**.

What kinds of decisions can an expert system make? An expert system is not a general-purpose problem solver or decision maker. Each expert system is designed to make decisions in a particular area or *domain*. For example, an expert system created for use at the Campbell Soup Company captured the knowledge of an expert cooking-vat operator to help less experienced employees troubleshoot problems that might arise during the cooking and canning process. Other expert systems have been developed to locate mineral deposits, diagnose blood diseases, evaluate corporate financial statements, underwrite complex insurance policies, order a customized personal computer, and recommend stock purchases.

How are expert systems built?
Expert systems can be created with a computer programming language, but an expert system shell offers a set of tools designed to simplify the development process. An **expert system shell** is a software tool containing an inference engine and a user interface that developers use to enter facts and rules for a knowledge base. An expert system shell also has tools for testing a knowledge base to make certain it produces accurate decisions.

Can an expert system deal with uncertainty? Expert systems are often designed to deal with data that is imprecise, or with problems that have more than one solution. Using a technique called **fuzzy logic**, an expert system can deal with imprecise data by asking for a level of confidence. For example, suppose an expert system is helping you identify a whale you spotted off the California coast. The expert system asks, "Did you see a dorsal fin?" You're not sure. You think you saw one, but it could have been a shadow. If the expert system is using fuzzy logic, it will let you respond with something like "I'm 85% certain I saw a dorsal fin." Based on the confidence level of your answers to this and other questions, the expert system might be able to tell you that it is "pretty sure," maybe 98% confident, that you saw a gray whale.

How does an expert system work? When it is time to make a decision, the inference engine begins analyzing the available data by following the rules in the knowledge base. If the expert system needs additional data, it checks external databases, looks for the data in a transaction processing system, or asks the user to answer questions. Figure 10-11 on the next page outlines the flow of information in an expert system and summarizes its capabilities.

FIGURE 10-10

A simple expert system, such as this automechanic expert, collects information about car trouble by asking questions. Answers are analyzed according to a set of facts and rules to produce a repair recommendation.

```
What happens when you
turn the key to start
your car?
a. no response
b. the engine sputters
c. the engine sounds
   normal
d. none of the above

Your response:_
```

RULE 1:
IF you turn the key and there is no response,
THEN the battery is dead and you should recharge the battery.

RULE 2:
IF you turn the key and the engine sputters,
THEN you might be out of gas and you should check the fuel gauge.

RULE 3:
IF you turn the key and the engine sounds normal,
THEN the transmission might be malfunctioning. Check the position of the shift lever.

RULE 4:
IF none of the above choices applies to the problem,
THEN the expert system will ask additional questions.

INFOWEBLINKS

At the **Expert System and Neural Network InfoWeb**, you'll find information about the history and current availability of these fascinating technologies.

W **CLICK TO CONNECT**
www.course.com/np/concepts11/ch10

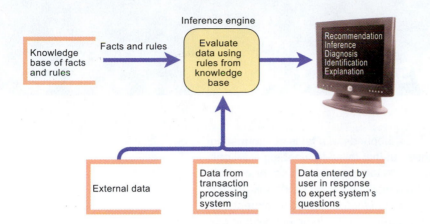

FIGURE 10-11

An expert system is characterized by its ability to:

- Replicate the reasoning of a human expert
- Work with internal or external data
- Produce a recommendation or decision

▶ CLICK TO START

Is it possible to build an expert system without an expert? An expert system begins with a set of facts and rules. But if the rules are not known, a computer can "learn" how to make decisions based on hundreds or thousands of lightning-fast trial-and-error attempts. A **neural network** uses computer circuitry to simulate the way a brain might process information, learn, and remember. For example, a neural network could be connected to a digital projector that displays photos of people's faces. Which faces are males and which are females? The neural network begins with a list of criteria with no values attached. "Hair length" might be one criteria, but the neural network is not programmed to expect that females usually have longer hair than men. Based on the evidence, a neural network begins to establish its own criteria—its own rules—about the data.

Neural networks have been successfully implemented in many business and financial applications where identification and trend analysis are important. A useful application of neural networks takes place in video surveillance systems, such as one that analyzes video footage of busy central London streets, watching for faces that match those of known terrorists (Figure 10-12).

FIGURE 10-12

Neural networks have been developed for a variety of applications, including surveillance.

QuickCheck

1. Effective information systems are designed to support goals that help an organization carry out its _____ statement.

2. Mid-level managers are typically responsible for _____ planning, whereas executive managers engage in _____ planning.

3. Information systems are effective for solving everyday, run-of-the-mill _____ problems.

4. _____ processing holds a group of transactions for later processing, whereas _____ processing handles each transaction as it is entered.

5. A(n) _____ makes it possible to produce scheduled, ad hoc, and exception reports. (Hint: Use the acronym.)

6. A(n) _____ model is a numerical representation of a realistic situation that can be incorporated in a DSS.

7. A(n) _____ system uses an inference engine.

10

▶ CHECK ANSWERS

Systems Analysis

THE COMPUTER INDUSTRY abounds with tales of information systems developed at great expense but that failed to meet expectations because they didn't work correctly, were too complex to use, or weren't flexible enough to meet changing business needs. As Frederick Brooks observes in his book *The Mythical Man-Month*, "One can expect the human race to continue attempting systems just within or just beyond our reach, and software systems are perhaps the most intricate and complex of all man's handiwork." Whether you are part of a team that is developing a complex corporate information system, or you are developing a small information system for your own use, you will be more likely to succeed if you analyze the purpose of the information system, carefully design the system, test it thoroughly, and document its features. In this section of the chapter, you'll learn about the planning and analysis that's required for an information system.

SYSTEM DEVELOPMENT LIFE CYCLE

What is a system development life cycle? An information system progresses through several phases as it is developed, used, and finally retired. These phases are referred to as a **system development life cycle**—usually referred to as the **SDLC**. Figure 10-13 illustrates a typical sequence of SDLC phases.

FIGURE 10-13

System Development Life Cycle

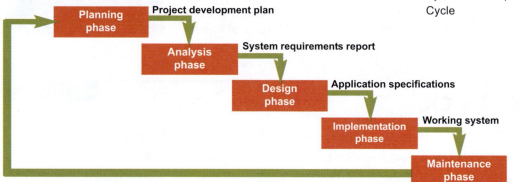

The original **waterfall SDLC**, shown above, approaches each phase in the life cycle as a discrete step. In real systems, however, the phases are not so neatly compartmentalized. The analysis, design, and implementation phases often overlap. For example, as programmers begin producing code in the implementation phase, user feedback might require changes to the design from a previous phase.

Variations of the waterfall SDLC take into account overlapping phases and the necessity of backtracking during system development. A **modified waterfall SDLC** accounts for overlap between SDLC phases. An **iterative SDLC** depicts phases as repeating as necessary.

How does the SDLC apply to systems analysis and design? The SDLC provides a general outline of how an information system evolves. **Systems analysis and design** is a discipline that focuses on developing information systems according to the phases of an SDLC.

The scope of systems analysis and design encompasses the people, procedures, computers, communications networks, and software involved with handling information in an organization. Its scope is much broader than software engineering, which focuses on developing computer programs during the design and implementation phases of the SDLC. Systems analysts deal with information systems within the broad context of an organization and have to be aware of the way new systems and procedures affect an organization's employees and customers.

PLANNING PHASE

How does an information system project begin? Creating an information system can be compared to building a house. You don't just grab a hammer and start nailing pieces of wood together. It is important to have a plan. Initial plans for an information system are developed during the planning phase.

What does the planning phase entail? The **planning phase** for an information system project includes the activities listed in Figure 10-14. The goal of these activities is to create a **Project Development Plan**. Before the project proceeds beyond the planning phase, the Project Development Plan must typically be reviewed and approved by management. This planning document includes:

- A short description of the project, including its scope
- A justification for the project, which includes an estimate of the project costs and potential financial benefits
- A list of project team participants
- A schedule for the project, including an outline of its phases

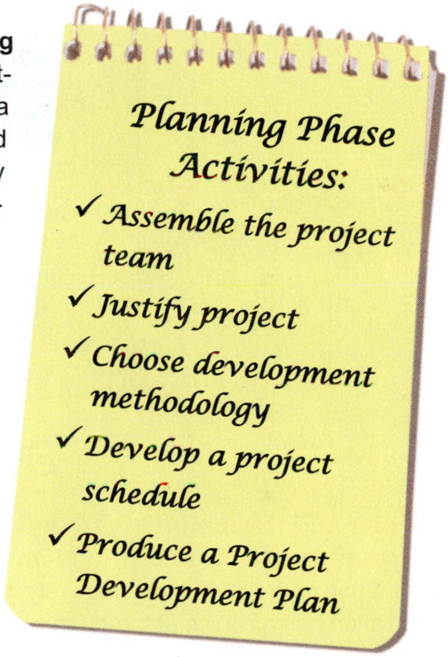

Who supervises the development project? Depending on the scope of the problem and the expertise of the professional staff, an information systems project can be managed by an in-house Information Systems department or outsourced to a development firm.

A system development project team, or project team for short, is assigned to analyze and develop an information system. The project team has a leader, sometimes referred to as the project manager, who supervises the project team's work flow and output.

Who participates in the process of building an information system? The composition of a project team depends on the scope of the project. Large and complex projects tend to have sizable project teams, and a majority of team members are systems analysts or other computer professionals. Smaller projects tend to have fewer members on the project team, and a higher percentage of team members are likely to be users rather than computer professionals.

In addition to the project team, other members of an organization might be asked to participate in various phases of the project. A widely accepted technique called **joint application design** (JAD) is based on the idea that the best information systems are designed when end users and systems analysts work together on a project as equal partners. JAD provides a structured methodology for planning and holding a series of meetings, called JAD sessions, in which users and analysts jointly identify problems and look for solutions.

FIGURE 10-14

Planning Phase Activities:
✓ Assemble the project team
✓ Justify project
✓ Choose development methodology
✓ Develop a project schedule
✓ Produce a Project Development Plan

10

TERMINOLOGY NOTE

As described in Chapter 9, systems analysts are responsible for analyzing information requirements, designing new information systems, and supervising their implementation. Systems analysts also create specifications for application software, and then give those specifications to computer programmers, who, in turn, create software to meet those specifications.

Why are new information systems developed? The justification for a new information system usually emerges from a serious problem with the current system, a threat to the organization's success, or an opportunity to improve an organization's products or services through technology. If the current information system is manual, for example, it might not be cost effective, efficient, or competitive. Computerized information systems can become obsolete when hardware becomes outdated, or when the software no longer meets the needs of the business mission.

What kinds of threats and opportunities can affect an organization? Most organizations exist in a rapidly changing and competitive environment, where many opportunities and threats can be effectively handled only by using computers. A well-known business analyst, Michael Porter, created the Five Forces model, shown in Figure 10-15, to illustrate how opportunities and threats can affect an organization.

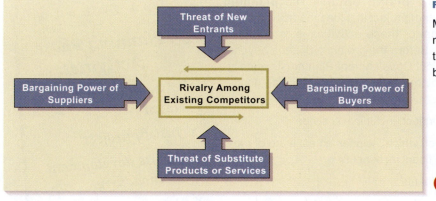

FIGURE 10-15

Michael Porter's Five Forces model illustrates the factors that affect competition among business rivals.

▶ CLICK TO START

How can an information system help an organization respond to threats and opportunities? To be successful in its mission, an organization must respond effectively to opportunities and threats. An organization has a choice of three fundamental responses:

● **Make improvements.** An organization can become better at what it does by cutting costs, lowering prices, improving its products, offering better customer service, and so on. Computers often provide ways to make businesses run more efficiently, and they can supply timely information that helps improve customer service. For example, to keep up with other automakers, DaimlerChrysler developed a new information system that uses the Internet to track vehicle design, manufacturing, and supply.

● **Change the industry.** An organization can change the nature of an industry. Computers and related technologies, such as the Internet, often make such changes possible. For example, Amazon.com pioneered the idea of selling books on the Web, which was a major change to an industry in which success depended on the number of store franchises that could be placed in shopping malls.

● **Create new products.** An organization can create a new product, such as flavored potato chips, or a new service, such as overnight package delivery. Although creativity and invention usually spring from the minds of people, computers can contribute to research and development efforts by collecting and analyzing data, helping inventors create models and explore simulations, and so on.

A new information system might be only one aspect of a larger plan to evolve an organization into a stronger, more competitive entity. The business community has embraced several business practices, summarized in Figure 10-16, that use information systems as a key component for transforming organizations.

FIGURE 10-16

Business Practices Glossary

BI (Business Intelligence): An integrated set of technologies and procedures used to collect and analyze data pertaining to sales, production, and other internal operations of a business in order to make better business decisions.

BPR (Business Process Reengineering): An ongoing iterative process that helps businesses rethink and radically redesign practices to improve performance, as measured by cost, quality, service, and speed.

CRM (Customer Relationship Management): A technique for increasing profitability by improving the relationship between a company and its customers. It helps a business increase sales by identifying, acquiring, and retaining customers. It can also cut costs by automating sales, marketing, and customer service. Information systems make it possible to collect and process the large volumes of customer data required for CRM and to efficiently transform this data into useful information.

EAI (Enterprise Application Integration): The use of networked, compatible software modules and databases to provide unrestricted sharing of data and business processes throughout an organization, for example between CRM and BI systems.

EDI (Electronic Data Interchange): The ability to transfer data between different companies using networks, such as the Internet, which enables companies to buy, sell, and trade information.

ERP (Enterprise Resource Planning): A system of business management that integrates all facets, or resources, of a business, including planning, manufacturing, sales, and marketing. An information system running special ERP software is a key technology that allows a business to track the information necessary to monitor its resource use.

JIT (Just In Time): A manufacturing system in which the parts needed to construct a finished product are produced or arrive at the assembly site just when they are needed. JIT typically reduces costs by eliminating substantial warehousing costs and obsolete parts.

MRP (Manufacturing Resource Planning): Calculates and maintains an optimum manufacturing plan based on master production schedules, sales forecasts, inventory status, open orders, and bills of material. If properly implemented, it improves cash flow and increases profitability. MRP provides businesses with the ability to be proactive rather than reactive in the management of their inventory levels and material flow.

TQM (Total Quality Management): A technique initiated by top management that involves all employees and all departments and focuses on quality assurance in every product and service offered to customers.

How does the project team identify problems and opportunities?

Justifying a project often involves identifying problems and opportunities within an organization's current information system. By eliminating problems and taking advantage of opportunities, an organization can become more competitive.

Project team members can identify problems and opportunities using a variety of techniques, such as interviews and data analysis. For example, James Wetherbe's **PIECES framework** helps classify problems in an information system. Each letter of PIECES stands for a potential problem, as shown in Figure 10-17.

INFOWEBLINKS

You'll find more information about terms such as BPR, TQM, JIT, and CRM at the **Business Practices InfoWeb**.

CLICK TO CONNECT
www.course.com/np/concepts11/ch10

FIGURE 10-17

Wetherbe's PIECES

10

P I E C E S

Performance
A performance problem means that an information system does not respond quickly enough to users or takes too long to complete processing tasks.

Information
An information problem means that users don't receive the right information at the right time in a usable format.

Economics
An economics problem means that the system costs too much to operate or use.

Control
A control problem means that information is available to unauthorized users or that authorized users are not given the authority to make decisions based on the information they receive.

Efficiency
An efficiency problem means that too many resources are used to collect, process, store, and distribute information.

Service
A service problem means that the system is too difficult or inconvenient to use.

What is a system development methodology? As part of the planning phase, the project team typically selects one or more methodologies that provide structure for the development effort. Earlier in the chapter you learned that the SDLC delineates the phases of system development. A system development methodology specifies what takes place in each phase; it encompasses the activities, procedures, methods, best practices, deliverables, and automated tools that systems developers follow to complete the SDLC. In short, a system development methodology guides developers through the phases of system development.

There are many standard system development methodologies. **Structured methodology** focuses on the processes that take place within an information system. **Information engineering methodology** focuses on the data an information system collects before working out ways to process that data. **Object-oriented methodology** treats an information system as a collection of objects that interact with each other to accomplish tasks.

How is the project schedule developed? Project planning begins in the planning phase, but stretches throughout the entire project. Project managers organize the work into tasks and milestones, which can be scheduled and assigned. As tasks are completed, the schedule is updated and adjusted. Industry standard tools for scheduling and project management include PERT, WBS, and Gantt charts.

PERT (Program Evaluation and Review Technique) is a method for analyzing the time needed to complete each project task and identifying the minimum time needed to complete the total project. A PERT diagram shows tasks as arrows and events as the completion of tasks (Figure 10-18).

FIGURE 10-18

PERT chart elements are arranged to show which tasks must be completed before subsequent dependent tasks can begin. By tracing paths through the diagram, project managers can determine the best-case and worst-case scheduling scenarios. The longest path through the tasks, shown in red, is called the critical path.

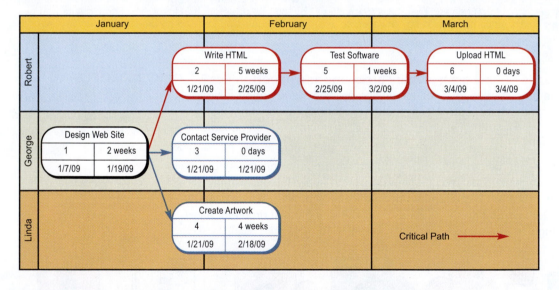

A **WBS** (work breakdown structure) breaks a complex task into a series of subtasks. The hierarchy of tasks is typically shown as a hierarchical diagram, but it can also be formatted as a simple outline. A WBS can be activity-oriented to list tasks, or deliverable-oriented to list project milestones (Figure 10-19).

A **Gantt chart** uses bars to show the timing of development tasks as they occur over time. Each bar on the chart represents a task; the length of a bar indicates the task's expected duration (Figure 10-20).

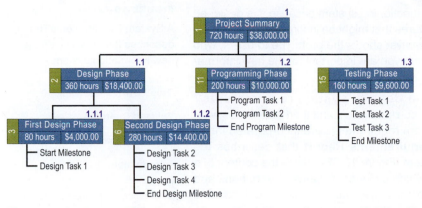

FIGURE 10-19

The top element on a WBS chart represents the entire project. At the next level, the project is broken down into subtasks, and those tasks are in turn broken down into even smaller tasks.

Do computers offer tools for planning phase activities?

Project management software is an effective tool for planning and scheduling. It helps managers track and visualize the complex interactions between tasks using tools such as Gantt charts, PERT, and WBS. Popular project management offerings include open source software, such as Open WorkBench, and commercial software, such as Microsoft Project.

ANALYSIS PHASE

What happens in the analysis phase? The analysis phase begins after the project team selects a development methodology, draws up the Project Development Plan, and receives permission to proceed from management. The goal of the **analysis phase** is to produce a list of requirements for a new or revised information system. Tasks for the analysis phase are listed in Figure 10-21.

Why study the current system? Typically, a new information system is designed to replace a system or process that is already in place. It is important to study the current system to understand its strengths and weaknesses before designing a new system.

How does the project team discover what happens in the current system? Some members of the project team might have first-hand experience with the current system. They can often provide an overview of the system and identify key features, strengths, and weaknesses. To obtain additional information about the current system, project team members can observe the system in action and interview people who use the system.

How does the project team determine what the new system should do? **System requirements** are the criteria for successfully solving problems identified in an information system. These requirements guide the design and implementation for a new or updated information system. They also serve as an evaluation checklist at the end of the development project, so they are sometimes called **success factors**. A new or updated information system should meet requirements defined by the project team.

The project team determines requirements by interviewing users and studying successful information systems that solve problems similar to those in the current system. Another way to determine requirements is to construct a prototype as an experimental or trial version of an information system.

FIGURE 10-20

Gantt charts indicate the duration of each task. They can also show milestones and compare planned completion dates with actual completion dates.

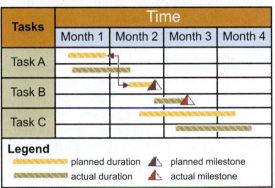

FIGURE 10-21

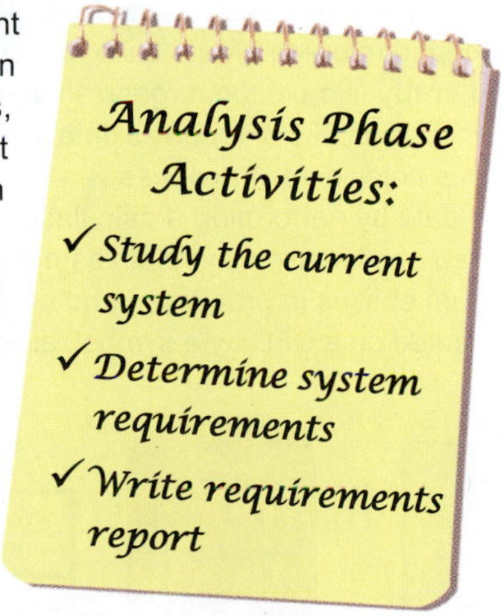

Analysis Phase Activities:

✓ *Study the current system*

✓ *Determine system requirements*

✓ *Write requirements report*

10

Often the prototype is not a fully functioning system because it is designed to demonstrate only selected features that might be incorporated into a new information system. A systems analyst shows the prototype to users, who evaluate which features of the prototype are important for the new information system.

What does the project team do with system requirements?

After the project team studies the current system and then determines what the new system should do, system requirements are incorporated into a document called a **System Requirements Report** that describes the objectives for an information system. Figure 10-22 outlines the content of a System Requirements Report, which includes narrative descriptions and diagrams showing the new system's users, data, processes, objects, and reports. When management approves the report, the project can move on to the design phase.

DOCUMENTATION TOOLS

How does the project team document system requirements?

The project team can use a variety of tools to diagram the current system and produce documentation that is also useful in later phases of the SDLC. Documentation tools vary according to development methodology. For example, a project team following a structured methodology will use different documentation tools than a project group using object-oriented methodology. To understand some of the most popular documentation tools, consider a project to develop an information system for a for-profit organization that offers business seminars and workshops throughout the world. The new information system must keep track of workshop schedules and student enrollments. Students have to be able to select workshops, and instructors must be supplied with a roster of students.

What are structured documentation tools?

The core documentation tool for project teams using structured methodology is the **data flow diagram** (DFD), which graphically illustrates how data moves through an information system.

You can think of a DFD as a map that traces the possible paths for data traveling from entities (such as students) to processes (such as enrolling in a workshop) or storage areas (such as databases). In DFD terminology, an **external entity** is a person, organization, or device outside the information system that originates or receives data. A **data store** is a filing cabinet, disk, or tape that holds data. A **process** is a manual or computerized routine that changes data by performing a calculation, updating information, sorting a list, and so on. An arrow symbolizes a **data flow** and indicates how data travels from entities to processes and data stores. Each of these elements is represented on a DFD by a symbol, as shown in Figure 10-23.

FIGURE 10-23

Data Flow Diagram Symbols

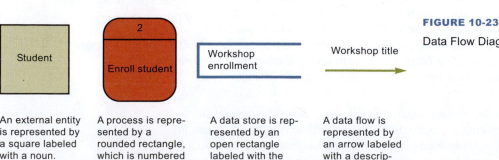

An external entity is represented by a square labeled with a noun.

A process is represented by a rounded rectangle, which is numbered and labeled with a verb phrase.

A data store is represented by an open rectangle labeled with the name of a data file.

A data flow is represented by an arrow labeled with a description of the data.

What does a DFD look like? In a completed DFD, data flow arrows show the path of data to and from external entities, data stores, and processes. Figure 10-24 explains how to read a DFD.

FIGURE 10-24

To read a DFD, begin at any one of the square entities and follow the arrows to trace the flow of data. The label on each data flow arrow identifies the data that moves through the system. Arrows moving into a process indicate input data. Arrows that emerge from a process show output. Rectangular data stores represent data stored on computer disks and in databases.

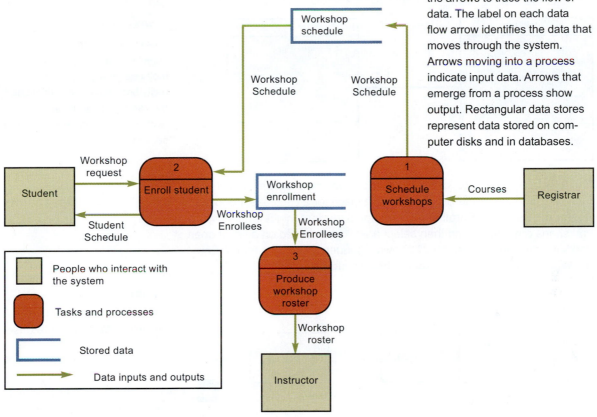

How do documentation tools differ for object-oriented analysis and design? Structured documentation tools such as DFDs help analysts decide how to design databases and write applications that allow people to interact with those databases. In contrast, object-oriented design tools provide blueprints for creating data objects and the routines that allow people to interact with those objects. The current standard for object-oriented documentation is called **UML** (Unified Modeling Language). Three of the most frequently used UML tools include use case diagrams, sequence diagrams, and class diagrams.

What is a use case diagram? A **use case diagram** documents the users of an information system and the functions they perform. In object-oriented jargon, the people who use the system are called **actors**. Any task an actor performs is called a **use case**. Figure 10-25 shows a simple use case diagram for a workshop registration system.

What is the composition of an object? A key element of object-oriented development is defining objects. In the use case diagram, a student interacted with two objects: a Workshop object and a Section object. A **class diagram** provides the name of each object, a list of each object's attributes, a list of methods, and an indication of the cardinality between objects. An attribute is simply any data element that is stored as part of an object. A method is any behavior that an object is capable of performing.

FIGURE 10-25

A use case diagram for a workshop registration system depicts two use cases—one in which a student enrolls in a workshop and one in which the student drops the workshop.

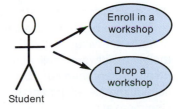

Cardinality refers to the number of associations that can exist between objects. You'll find detailed definitions of object-oriented terms, such as classes, attributes, and methods, in Chapter 12. Figure 10-26 illustrates a class diagram for the workshop registration system.

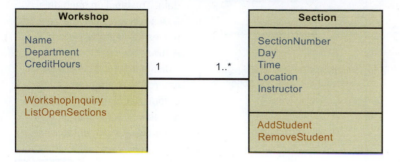

FIGURE 10-26

This class diagram shows each object's attributes (in blue) and methods (in brown). The cardinality between objects (indicated by 1 and 1..*) means that each workshop may have one or more sections.

What is a sequence diagram? A **sequence diagram** depicts the detailed sequence of interactions that take place for a use case. For example, for the use case Enroll in a Workshop a student might inquire which workshops are offered and then select a workshop based on a list of open workshop sections. Figure 10-27 shows a sequence diagram for the Enroll in a Workshop use case and explains how to interpret it.

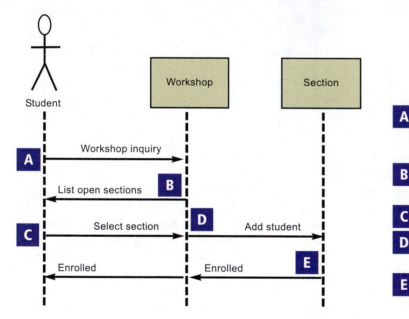

FIGURE 10-27

Sequence Diagram for the Enroll in a Workshop Use Case

A A student enters the title or number of a workshop that he or she wants to take.

B The Workshop object displays a list of sections that are open.

C The student selects a section.

D The student is added to the workshop roster for the section.

E The student receives confirmation of the enrollment.

Are diagramming tools computerized? Maintaining documentation can become a complex task as the project progresses and system requirements are revised. A **CASE tool** (computer-aided software engineering tool) is a software application designed for documenting system requirements, diagramming current and proposed information systems, scheduling development tasks, and developing computer programs. Commercial CASE tools such as Visible Analyst, and open source tools such as ArgoUML automate many of the routine housekeeping tasks required for systems analysis and design, such as changing the name of a data element on one diagram and making sure the change is reflected in other diagrams and program code. Figure 10-28 on the next page explains some of the features of CASE tools.

INFOWEBLINKS

You'll find more information about CASE software, including links to downloads, at the **CASE Tools InfoWeb**.

W **CLICK TO CONNECT**
www.course.com/np/concepts11/ch10

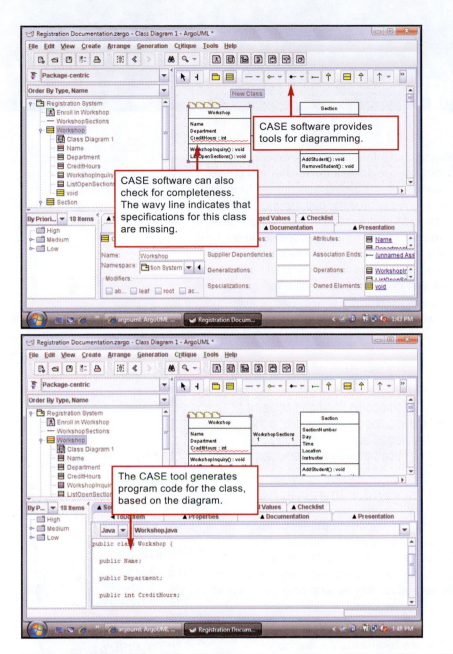

FIGURE 10-28

CASE tools help project team members manage all the details of system documentation. In this example, the project team is developing a course registration system. The top screen shows how the CASE tool helps developers create diagrams and how it points out missing elements in the design. The second screen shows how the CASE tool generates program code.

 CLICK TO START

QuickCheck

SECTION B

10

1. Project [_____] software helps project leaders schedule and track a project's milestones and tasks.

2. In the planning phase, one of the main goals is to produce a Project [_____] Plan.

3. When justifying a new information system, the project team should consider threats and [_____] that affect the organization.

4. In the [_____] SDLC, one phase of the process must be completed before the next phase can begin.

5. To fulfill the main goal of the analysis phase, the project team produces a System [_____] Report for a new or revised information system.

6. DFDs are used with structured methodology, whereas object-oriented methodology uses [_____] case, class, and sequence diagrams.

CHECK ANSWERS

System Design

MANY ASPECTS of designing an information system resemble an architectural construction project. Suppose that during the analysis phase, an architect determines the elements a new building will contain. A single-family home, for example, might require bedrooms, bathrooms, closets, a kitchen, living room, dining room, and laundry room. In the design phase, the architect must figure how to arrange these elements. Should all the rooms be on the same floor? How many bedrooms? Where will the closets be located? Where will the doors be placed to create the best traffic pattern? As the architect answers these questions, the design for the house begins to emerge. In Section C, you'll learn how a project team applies the same approach to design a new information system.

DESIGN PHASE

What happens in the design phase? In the analysis phase, the project team determines *what* the new information system must do. In the **design phase** of the SDLC, the project team must figure out *how* the new system will fulfill the requirements specified in the System Requirements Report. The activities that typically take place during the design phase for an information system are listed in Figure 10-29.

FIGURE 10-29

Design Phase Activities:

✓ Identify potential solutions

✓ Evaluate solutions and select the best

✓ Select hardware and software

✓ Develop application specifications

✓ Obtain approval to implement the new system

How does the project team come up with solutions? There might be more than one way to solve the problems and meet the requirements identified in the analysis phase of the SDLC. Some potential solutions might be better than others. They might be more effective, less costly, or less complex. Therefore, it is not a good idea to proceed with the first solution that comes to mind. The project team should instead identify several potential hardware and software solutions by brainstorming and researching case studies at Web sites and in computer publications.

What hardware alternatives are available? A myriad of hardware options are available for information systems. Mainframes, servers, and personal computers are the most commonly used components, but in some information systems, handhelds or even supercomputers play a role. When evaluating hardware solutions for a new information system, a project team considers the overall architecture of the information system based on level of automation, processing methodology, and network technology.

● **Level of automation and computerization.** Some information systems provide a higher level of automation than others. For instance, a point-of-sale system with a low level of automation might require the checkout clerk to enter credit card numbers from a keypad. At a higher level of automation, a magnetic strip reader automates the process of entering a credit card number. A further level of automation is achieved by using a pressure-sensitive digitizing pad and stylus to collect customer signatures (Figure 10-30). With signatures in digital format, the entire transaction record becomes electronic, and the business does not need to deal with paper credit card receipts.

FIGURE 10-30
Automation options, such as this device that digitizes signatures, might be considered by the project team as it brainstorms solutions.

Automation alternatives can affect many aspects of an information system. In the point-of-sale example, a credit card number can be stored using a few bytes. Storing a digitized signature, however, might require far more disk space, a special type of database software, and specialized input devices. The project team should consider the pros and cons of different levels of computerization and automation because they affect all aspects of the planned information system.

● **Processing methodology.** An information system can be designed for **centralized processing**, in which data is processed on a centrally located computer. An alternative design option is **distributed processing**, in which processing tasks are distributed to servers and workstations. Typically, centralized processing requires a more powerful computer—usually a mainframe—to achieve the same response speed as distributed processing. Distributed processing in a client/server or peer-to-peer environment is very popular because it provides high levels of processing power at a low cost. However, these distributed architectures present more security problems than a single, centralized computer—a factor that the project team must consider within the context of selecting a solution.

● **Network technology.** An information system, by its very nature, is designed to serve an entire organization. That organization includes many people who work in different rooms, different buildings, and perhaps even different countries. Virtually every information system requires a network, so the project team must examine network alternatives, such as LANs, extranets, intranets, and the Internet. Many information systems require a complex mixture of networks, such as a LAN in each branch office connected to a company intranet, with customers accessing selected data using the Internet.

10

What software alternatives are available? The project team might consider software alternatives, such as whether to construct the system from scratch in a programming language, use an application development tool, purchase commercial software, or select a turnkey system (Figure 10-31).

Creating an information system from scratch using a programming language can take many months or years. It is usually costly, but offers the most flexibility for meeting the system requirements. As an analogy, baking a cake from scratch allows you some flexibility in the ingredients you choose—margarine instead of shortening, for example. However, baking from scratch requires a lot of time and work to sift the flour with the salt; mix the sugar, eggs, shortening, and milk; combine the dry and wet ingredients; and so forth.

During the design phase, the project team can analyze the costs and benefits of developing an information system from scratch. If it appears to be a feasible solution, the team can also select the programming language to use.

An **application development tool** is essentially a type of software construction kit containing building blocks that can be assembled into a software product. Application development tools include expert system shells and database management systems.

An application development tool is the programmer's "cake mix," which contains many of the ingredients necessary for quickly and easily developing the modules for an information system. Although application development tools usually speed up the development process, they might not offer the same level of flexibility as a programming language.

Commercial software for an information system is usually a series of preprogrammed software modules, supplied by a software developer or value added reseller (VAR). Commercial software eliminates much of the design work required with programming languages or application development tools. However, commercial software requires extensive evaluation to determine how well it meets the system requirements. Following through with the cake analogy, commercial software is equivalent to buying a premade cake that you simply slice and serve.

Commercial software is available for standard business functions, such as human resource management, accounting, and payroll. It is also available for many vertical market businesses and organizations, such as law offices, video stores, medical offices, libraries, churches, e-commerce, and charities. Although most commercial software has some customization options, in many cases, it cannot be modified to exactly meet every system requirement, which necessitates adjustments in an organization's procedures. The project team must decide if the benefits of commercial software can offset the cost and inconvenience of procedural changes.

A **turnkey system** is essentially an "information system in a box," which consists of hardware and commercial software designed to offer a complete information system solution. In terms of the cake analogy, a turnkey system is like going out to dinner and simply ordering your choice of cake for dessert. A turnkey system might seem like a quick and easy solution, and it looks attractive to many project teams. Like commercial software, however, a turnkey system must be extensively evaluated to determine whether it can satisfy system requirements.

FIGURE 10-31

Software Alternatives

Programming Language
Pros: Can be exactly tailored to system requirements
Cons: Requires development time and expertise

Application Development Tool
Pros: Requires less time than programming languages
Cons: Might limit developers on the way they implement some system features

Commercial Software
Pros: Little or no programming required, so requires minimal development time
Cons: Software features might not exactly match business needs; might require extensive customization

Turnkey System
Pros: Minimal effort required to select and set up equipment and software
Cons: Requires time and expertise to evaluate

EVALUATION AND SELECTION

How does the team choose the best solution? To determine the best solution, the project team devises a list of criteria for comparing each potential solution. This list includes general criteria related to costs, benefits, and development time. The list also includes technical criteria, such as the flexibility of the solution and its adaptability for future modifications and growth. Finally, the list includes functional criteria that indicate how well the solution satisfies the specified requirements.

Each criterion is assigned a weight to indicate its importance. The project team then evaluates the criteria for each solution and assigns raw scores. A raw score of 10, for example might indicate a highly valued feature. The raw score for each criterion is multiplied by the weight, and these weights are added to produce a total score for each solution. Sound complicated? It isn't, especially if the project team uses a **decision support worksheet**. Take a few moments to study Figure 10-32, and you'll quickly see how it works.

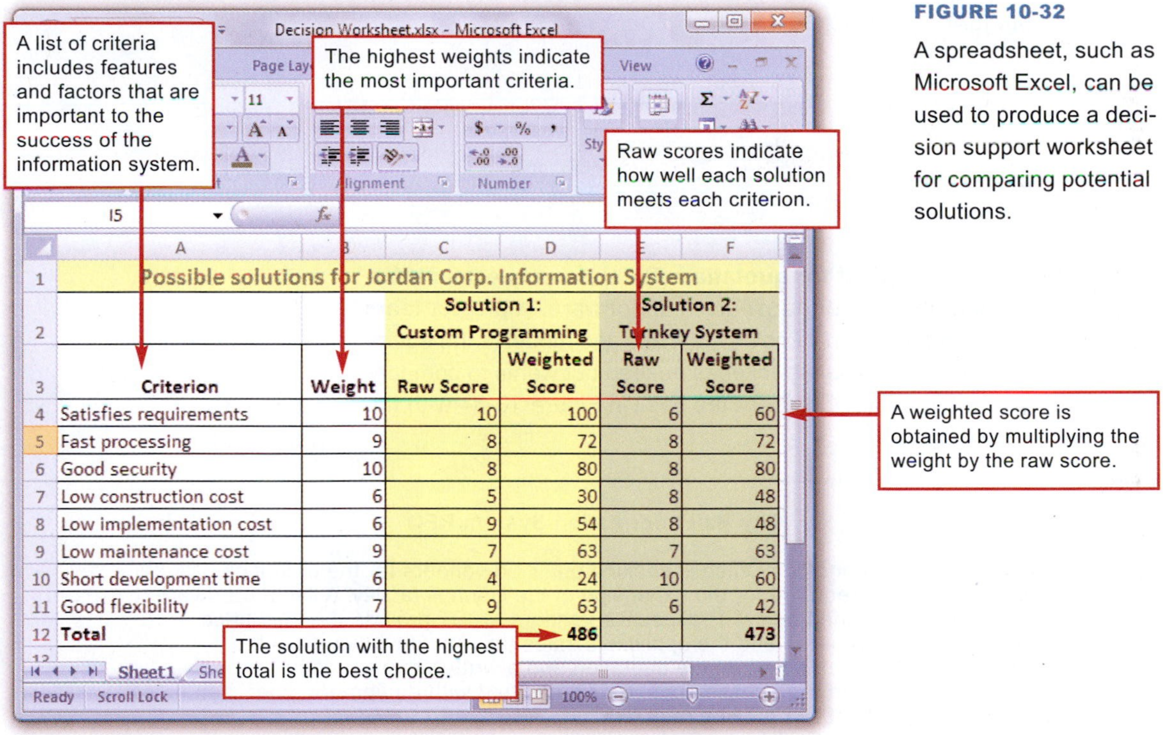

FIGURE 10-32

A spreadsheet, such as Microsoft Excel, can be used to produce a decision support worksheet for comparing potential solutions.

A list of criteria includes features and factors that are important to the success of the information system.

The highest weights indicate the most important criteria.

Raw scores indicate how well each solution meets each criterion.

A weighted score is obtained by multiplying the weight by the raw score.

The solution with the highest total is the best choice.

Possible solutions for Jordan Corp. Information System

Criterion	Weight	Solution 1: Custom Programming Raw Score	Solution 1: Custom Programming Weighted Score	Solution 2: Turnkey System Raw Score	Solution 2: Turnkey System Weighted Score
Satisfies requirements	10	10	100	6	60
Fast processing	9	8	72	8	72
Good security	10	8	80	8	80
Low construction cost	6	5	30	8	48
Low implementation cost	6	9	54	8	48
Low maintenance cost	9	7	63	7	63
Short development time	6	4	24	10	60
Good flexibility	7	9	63	6	42
Total			**486**		**473**

How does the project team find the right hardware and software for the new information system? After the project team selects a solution, the next task is to select the hardware and software needed to implement the solution. Sometimes more than one vendor sells the hardware and software necessary for the new system, so an organization might have a choice of vendors.

The method for selecting the hardware, software, and vendor depends on the project team's understanding of what is required for the solution. Sometimes the team knows exactly what brand, model, or version of hardware and software are required. At other times, the team has a general understanding, but needs vendor help selecting specific products. RFPs and RFQs (described on the next page) help the team collect information for these important decisions.

10

What's an RFP? A **request for proposal** (RFP) is a document that describes the information system problem and the requirements for the solution. An RFP essentially asks a vendor to recommend hardware and software for the solution and to describe the vendor's qualifications for implementing the solution. A project team usually issues an RFP when its members believe that a vendor has more knowledge and experience in the solution area. Look at the sample RFP in Figure 10-33.

FIGURE 10-33

RFP Excerpt

> ### RFP for The University Library Information System
>
> The purpose of this request for proposal (RFP) and subsequent vendor presentations is to identify a vendor with whom The University will negotiate a contract to supply, install, and support an integrated library system. This system must be capable of supporting an online public access catalog, cataloging and authority control, acquisitions and serials control, circulation, and reserve. It should be capable of supporting media booking, interlibrary loan and document delivery, and preservation control. Proposals are due 10 August 3:00pm, Purchasing Dept.
>
> A letter of intent to propose should be received by the University by 5:00pm CDT, July 13, 2009. Letters should be sent to the following address:

What's an RFQ? A **request for quotation** (RFQ) is a request for a formal price quotation on a list of hardware and software. A project team issues an RFQ to vendors when it knows the make and model of the equipment and the titles of the software packages needed but wants to compare prices from different vendors. Compare the RFQ in Figure 10-34 with the RFP in the previous figure.

FIGURE 10-34

RFQ Excerpt

> ### City Hall Information System RFQ
>
> The Information Technology Office is seeking qualified vendors for the quotation of network equipment required for the expansion of the city hall facility. A list of hardware and software is provided below. Prospective vendors MUST provide the total price including shipping charges and the applicable sales tax. Any deviation from the specifications MUST be noted on the quotation and a written explanation is strongly encouraged to support the substitutions. Bids submitted with equipment other than those stated in the specifications may be rejected.
>
> | Part Description | Part Number | Quantity | Price |
> |---|---|---|---|
> | 1. Cisco Catalyst 3750 24 10/100/1000T + 4 SFP Enhanced Multilayer Switch | WS-C3750G-24TS-E | 1 | |
> | 2. Cisco Catalyst 3750 24 10/100/1000T + 4 SFP Standard Multilayer Switch | WS-C3750G-24TS-S | 2 | |

How does the project team evaluate an RFP or RFQ? The project team can evaluate RFPs or RFQs by constructing a decision table similar to the one used for evaluating solutions. The basis for choosing hardware and software typically includes general criteria, such as cost and delivery time. In addition, it is important for the project team to consider the vendor's reliability, expertise, and financial stability. Technical criteria for hardware might include processing speed, reliability, upgradability, maintenance costs, and warranty. Technical criteria for software might include reliability, compatibility, and the availability of patches to fix program errors.

APPLICATION SPECIFICATIONS

What happens after the project team selects a solution? Exactly what happens next in the system design phase depends on the type of solution selected. If a turnkey solution is selected, the next step might be to get approval to move into the implementation phase of the SDLC. In contrast, if the project team selects a solution that requires custom programming, the team's systems analysts will create a set of **application specifications** that describe the way the information system's software should interact with users, store data, process data, and format reports.

This part of the SDLC is sometimes referred to as the detailed design phase because its goal is to create very detailed specifications for the completed information system, such as a detailed description of the process for discontinuing an inventory item in Figure 10-35.

```
BEGIN

FIND item in INVENTORY with matching inventory-ID

IF record cannot be found

        DISPLAY "No inventory item matches the Inventory ID."

ELSE

        READ item record

        SET discontinued-item to YES

        WRITE item record

        DISPLAY "Item [inventory-ID] is now marked as
        discontinued."

ENDIF

END
```

FIGURE 10-35

This excerpt from a project team's application specifications describes in detail the process for discontinuing an inventory item.

Detailed application specifications can be developed only after selecting the hardware and software for an information system. For example, the specifications for a program that runs on a Windows-based LAN might require quite a different user interface and processing model than a program that runs on a centralized mainframe computer and is accessed via the Internet.

What is the importance of application specifications? Application specifications are a key element in developing an effective information system. Not only do these specifications serve as a blueprint for the new system, but they play a critical role in ensuring that the development process proceeds efficiently.

10

Many projects fail because of constant, unmanaged demand for changes, even before the system is implemented. This failure to constrain change is often referred to as **feature creep** because new features tend to creep into the development process with a snowballing effect on other features, costs, and schedules. It might be important to change some specifications during the development process because of changes in business needs, laws, or regulations. Proposed changes should be managed within a formal process that includes written **change requests**, which detail the scope of a proposed change and can be evaluated by project team members.

What happens to the completed specifications? Application specifications are similar to the pages of an architectural blueprint that show the detailed plan for electrical wiring or plumbing. In a large information systems project, the specifications are given to a programming team or application developer who creates the software. In a small information systems project, you as the user might develop your own specifications. Then you might give the specifications to a programmer or, if you have the expertise, you might create the software yourself.

When can the project team actually begin to build the new information system? In the design phase of the SDLC, the project team chooses a solution, selects hardware and software, and designs detailed application specifications. Before the solution is implemented, the project team typically must seek approval from management. The approval process might be fairly informal, simply involving a discussion with the CIO. In contrast, some organizations require a much more formal process for obtaining approval, in which the project team submits a written proposal that's supplemented by presentations to management and user groups. After the project team's proposal is approved, the project can move to the next phase of development.

QuickCheck

1. In the design phase of the SDLC, a project team identifies several potential [   ] and then selects the one that offers the most benefits at the lowest cost.

2. Project team members should consider various [   ] processing methodologies, such as a client/server and peer-to-peer.

3. A(n) [   ] development tool is essentially a software construction kit containing building blocks that can be assembled into the software for an information system.

4. The project team can develop and send out a(n) [   ] to ask vendors to recommend solutions. (Hint: Use the acronym.)

5. Application [   ] describe the way an application should interact with users, store data, process data, and format reports.

 CHECK ANSWERS

Implementation and Maintenance

AFTER THE PLAN for an information system is approved, it's time to start building it. During the implementation phase of the SDLC, an organization puts together the components for the new information system. After an information system is installed and tested, it enters the final phase of the SDLC—the maintenance phase. Most people have experience with information systems in the maintenance phase because that is when a system provides its services. At the end of this section, you'll learn what happens during the maintenance phase and the important role played by people who use the system.

IMPLEMENTATION PHASE

FIGURE 10-36

What happens during the implementation phase? During the **implementation phase** of the SDLC, the project team supervises the tasks necessary to construct the new information system. The tasks that take place during the implementation phase can include any of those listed in Figure 10-36.

Does a new information system typically require new hardware? As the implementation phase begins, programming languages, development tools, and application software needed for the new information system are purchased, installed, and tested to ensure that they work correctly.

Software testing can reveal problems that result from incompatibilities with the existing hardware or an incorrect installation of the software. These problems must be corrected before continuing with system development. Some problems might result from bugs (errors) in the software, which must be corrected by the software publisher.

In addition to new software, the specifications for most new information systems require new hardware, which can either replace old equipment or supplement existing equipment. During the implementation phase, new hardware is purchased, installed, and tested to ensure that it operates correctly.

Implementation Phase Activities:

✓ *Purchase and install hardware and/or software*
✓ *Create applications*
✓ *Test applications*
✓ *Finalize documentation*
✓ *Train users*
✓ *Convert data*
✓ *Convert to new system*

DEVELOPMENT AND TESTING

What's the next step in the implementation phase? The next step in the implementation phase depends on the software tools selected for the project.

When the software for an information system is created by using a programming language or application development tool, programmers must create and test all the new software modules. Chapter 12 provides more information about the programming process.

When an information system is constructed using commercial software, that software has been written and tested by the software publisher. Nevertheless, the software sometimes must be customized. **Software customization** is the process of modifying a commercial application to reflect an organization's needs. Customization might include modifying the

10

user interface, enabling or disabling the mouse, selecting the menus that appear on-screen, and designing forms or reports. The extent to which commercial software can be customized depends on the options available in the application. For example, some commercial software offers options for customizing report formats, while other software does not.

How can the team ensure that a new information system works? A rigorous testing process is the only way to make sure a new information system works. Different types of testing during the implementation phase help identify and fix problems before the information system is incorporated into day-to-day business activities.

What is application testing? **Application testing** is the process of trying out various sequences of input values and checking the results to verify that the application works correctly. Application testing is performed in three ways: unit testing, integration testing, and system testing.

As each application module is completed, it undergoes **unit testing** to ensure that it operates reliably and correctly. When all modules have been completed and tested, **integration testing** is performed to ensure that the modules operate together correctly. Unit testing and integration testing are usually performed in a test area. A **test area** is a place where software testing can occur without disrupting the organization's regular information system. A test area might be located in an isolated section of storage on the computer system that runs the organization's regular information system, or it might be located on an entirely separate computer system.

When a problem is discovered during unit testing or integration testing, the team must track down the source of the problem and correct it. Unit testing and integration testing are then repeated to make sure the problem is corrected, and no new problems were introduced when the original problem was fixed.

After unit and integration testing are completed, **system testing** ensures that all hardware and software components work together correctly. If an existing information system is modified, system testing is performed when the new or modified units are combined with the rest of the existing system. In a completely new information system, system testing is performed to simulate daily work loads and make sure processing speed and accuracy meet the specifications. Figure 10-37 summarizes the three stages of application testing.

FIGURE 10-37

Unit, integration, and system testing ensure that applications work.

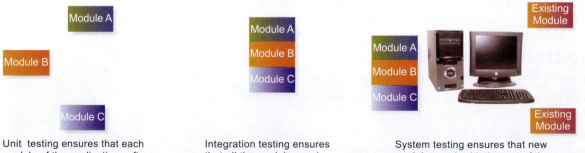

Unit testing ensures that each module of the application software works correctly.

Integration testing ensures that all the modules work together correctly.

System testing ensures that new modules work with the rest of the system hardware and software.

DOCUMENTATION AND TRAINING

What kinds of documentation does the project team create during the implementation phase? One of the most important tasks during the implementation phase is to make sure the information system is completely documented so that it can be used effectively and modified easily. The documentation for an information system can be broadly categorized as system or user documentation.

System documentation describes a system's features, hardware architecture, and programming. The target audience for system documentation is programmers, designers, and analysts who might maintain the system on a day-to-day basis and implement modifications. Much of the information required for system documentation is generated in the analysis and design phases of the SDLC. During the implementation phase, these documents should be reviewed for accuracy because features sometimes change as a result of problems or opportunities encountered during implementation.

For system documentation, many project teams turn to automated applications that produce documentation from completed source code. These tools help the team retrofit the documentation to the actual system, which might differ somewhat from the original system specifications.

User documentation describes how to interact with the system to accomplish specific tasks. It typically includes a list of features and instructions on how to use them.

Both system and user documentation can be supplied in printed format, but the current trend is to supply documentation in digital format as electronic documents, online help, or hyperlinked HTML documents. Electronic documents are often stored in a standard format, such as PDF, which can be accessed using Adobe Acrobat. Online help systems, such as the familiar Windows Help files, can be customized to provide help for information system modules. HTML documents can be posted for Web access over the Internet or a corporate intranet.

How do employees learn how to use the new information system? In preparation for using a new information system, users need extensive training, which might include software orientation, hardware operation, data entry, and backup procedures (Figure 10-38).

During training sessions, users learn how to interact with the interface, use the new system to perform day-to-day tasks, and find additional information in user manuals or procedure handbooks. A **procedure handbook** is a type of user documentation that contains step-by-step instructions for performing specific tasks. It often takes the place of a lengthy user manual because in a large organization, an employee in a particular department usually performs specific tasks and does not need to know how all features of the system work.

CONVERSION AND CUTOVER

What happens to data from the old system? The data for a new information system might exist in card files, file folders, or an old information system. This data must be loaded into the new system—a process called data conversion. For example, suppose that a local building inspector's office has a manual system for issuing and renewing construction permits. It has more than 8,000 permits on record. If this office computerizes its operations, it must convert these 8,000 records into an electronic

FIGURE 10-38

Training sessions for a new information system can be conducted by members of the project team or outsourced to professional trainers.

10

format that the new computerized system can access. When converting data from a manual system to a computer system, the data can be typed or scanned electronically into the appropriate storage media (Figure 10-39).

When converting data from an existing computer system to a new system, a programmer typically writes conversion software to read the old data and convert it into a format that is usable by the new system. Without such software, users would be forced to manually reenter data from the old system into the new system.

How does a business switch from the old information system to the new system? **System conversion** refers to the process of deactivating an old information system and activating a new one. It is also referred to as *cutover* or *go live*. There are several strategies for converting to a new system.

Direct conversion means that the old system is completely deactivated and the new system is immediately activated. Direct conversion usually takes place during non-peak hours to minimize disruption to normal business routines. Direct conversion is risky, however, because if the new system does not work correctly, it might need to be deactivated and undergo further testing. In the meantime, the old system must be reactivated, and transactions that were entered into the new system must be reentered into the old system so that business can continue.

Parallel conversion avoids some of the risk of direct conversion because the old system remains in service while some or all of the new system is activated. Both the old and new systems operate in parallel until the project team can determine whether the new system is performing correctly. Parallel conversion often requires that all entries be made in both the new and old systems, which is costly in terms of time, computer resources, and personnel. If financial and personnel resources are available, however, parallel conversion offers a good safety net in case a new information system fails to operate reliably or accurately.

Phased conversion works well with large, modularized information systems because the new system is activated one module at a time. After the project team determines that one module is working correctly, the next module is activated, and so on, until the entire new system is operational. In a phased conversion, however, each module of the new system must work with both the old and new systems, which greatly increases the complexity and cost of application development.

Pilot conversion works well in organizations with several branches that have independent information processing systems because the new information system is activated at one branch at a time. If the new system works correctly at one branch, it is activated at the next branch. To prepare for a pilot conversion, system developers must devise methods to integrate information from branches using the new system with information from branches still using the old system.

When is the new information system formally "live"? A new or upgraded information system undergoes a final test called acceptance testing. **Acceptance testing** is designed to verify that the new information system works as required. Procedures for acceptance testing are typically designed by users and systems analysts, and often include the use of real data to demonstrate that the system operates correctly under normal and peak data loads. Acceptance testing usually marks the completion of the implementation phase.

FIGURE 10-39

Some organizations have a lot of data that must be converted from paper-based documents into digital format. Even using scanners, this process can take a long time, require extra personnel, and be quite costly.

MAINTENANCE PHASE

What happens during the maintenance phase? The **maintenance phase** of the SDLC involves day-to-day operation of the system, making modifications to improve performance, and correcting problems. After an information system is implemented, it remains in operation for a period of time. During this time, maintenance activities ensure that the system functions as well as possible. Figure 10-40 lists the major maintenance activities for a typical information system.

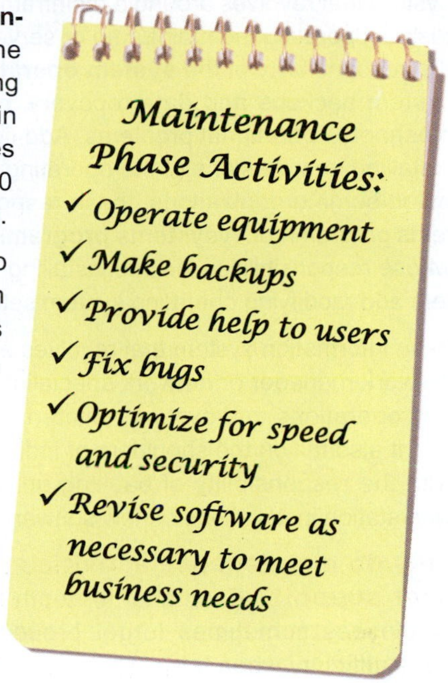

The term *maintenance phase* is a bit misleading because it seems to imply that the information system is maintained in a static state. On the contrary, during the maintenance phase, an information system is likely to undergo many changes to meet an organization's needs. Changes during the maintenance phase can include the following:

- Upgrades to operating system and commercial software
- User interface revisions to make the system easier to use
- Application software revisions to fix bugs and add features
- Hardware replacements to retire defective equipment or enhance performance
- Security upgrades (You'll find more on this topic in the next section of the chapter.)
- Hardware, software, or network adjustments to maintain and enhance quality of service

FIGURE 10-40

Maintenance Phase Activities:
✓ Operate equipment
✓ Make backups
✓ Provide help to users
✓ Fix bugs
✓ Optimize for speed and security
✓ Revise software as necessary to meet business needs

What is quality of service? The term **quality of service** (QoS) refers to the level of performance a computer system provides. When quality of service is good, data flows swiftly through the system, software is easy and intuitive to use, and work is completed quickly and without error. When quality of service is poor, users experience long waits, software is clumsy to use, and information is difficult to find.

Three key concepts ensure good quality of service: reliability, availability, and serviceability. Computer systems are reliable when they can be counted on to function correctly. Availability refers to the ability of the system to be continuously accessible to all the people who use it. Systems exhibit serviceability when they are easily upgraded or repaired.

What are quality-of-service metrics? A **quality-of-service metric** is a technique for measuring a specific QoS characteristic. Data for these metrics can be gathered by monitoring system performance and analyzing responses to user satisfaction surveys. Businesses typically use several QoS metrics, such as those described in Figure 10-41.

FIGURE 10-41

QoS Metrics

10

QoS Metric	Description
Throughput	Amount of data processed in a particular time interval
Accuracy	Number of errors occurring in a particular time interval for a particular function
Downtime	Amount of time a system is not available for processing
Capacity	Available storage space, number of users, number of connections, or number of packets
User levels	Number of users at peak, average, and low times
Response time	Time period between when a user initiates a request for information and when the request is fulfilled

Who is responsible for system maintenance?

In an information system that revolves around a mainframe computer or network servers, the task of operating the mainframe or servers on a day-to-day basis is usually the responsibility of the **system operator**. The system operator performs system backups and data recovery, monitors system traffic, and troubleshoots operational problems. Additional responsibilities might include installing new versions of the operating system and software applications, but in some organizations, these responsibilities are delegated to a systems programmer. A **systems programmer** is the operating system "guru," whose responsibilities include installing new versions of the operating system and modifying operating system settings to maximize performance.

In an information system that revolves around a microcomputer network, a network manager or network specialist is typically responsible for day-to-day operations and system maintenance. Some maintenance activities might also fall on the shoulders of individual users, who are often charged with the responsibility of backing up their workstations and performing workstation installations of new software.

Why do maintenance activities include user support?

Even after in-depth training, employees sometimes forget procedures or have difficulty when they encounter a new set of circumstances. These employees turn to the IS department for help. Many organizations establish a help desk to handle end-user problems. The **help desk** is staffed by technical support specialists who are familiar with the information system's software. Support specialists keep records of problems and solutions.

When you use an information system, you are likely to have questions. Your first source of information is your procedure handbook or user manual. It might be similar to the one in Figure 10-42 or it could be accessible online.

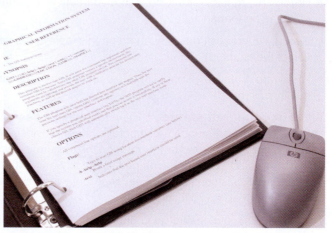

FIGURE 10-42

When you have questions about how to use an information system, first check the documentation. If you can't find an answer there, call the help desk.

Help desk personnel have little tolerance for people who ask questions that are clearly answered in the documentation. You should not hesitate, however, to ask about procedures or problems that are not covered in the documentation. Your questions can often promote much-needed modifications in the information system. For example, suppose you encounter a problem with an update procedure and call the help desk. The help desk technician begins to troubleshoot the problem and soon realizes that it is caused by a programming error not caught during system testing. This bug is recorded in a bug report that is routed to the programming group, which can determine its severity and take steps to fix it.

How long does the maintenance phase last?

The maintenance phase is the longest SDLC phase and lasts until the system is retired. Although the analysis, design, and implementation phases of the SDLC are costly, for many organizations, the maintenance phase is the most expensive because it is the longest.

The maintenance phase often accounts for 70% of the total cost of an information system. As shown in Figure 10-43 on the next page, maintenance costs follow a U-shaped curve—an information system requires the most maintenance at the beginning and end of its life cycle.

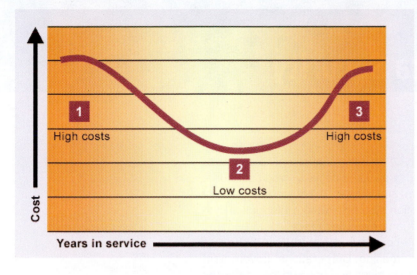

FIGURE 10-43

Maintenance Phase Costs

FIGURE 10-43

Maintenance Phase Costs

1. When a new information system first goes "live," maintenance costs are high while programmers work out the bugs and users clamor for support.

2. After most of the bugs are fixed and users become familiar with the information system, maintenance costs decrease.

3. As an information system nears the end of its useful life span, repair costs rise, and changing business practices begin to require modifications that are time consuming and expensive to implement.

When does the maintenance phase end? The maintenance phase continues until an information system is no longer cost effective or until changes in the organization make the information system obsolete. It is not unusual for an information system to remain in operation for 20 years or more. Eventually an information system's useful or cost-effective life nears a close. It is then time to begin the system development life cycle again.

QuickCheck

1. The _____ phase follows the design phase.

2. When the project team selects commercial software, it usually has to be _____ to reflect the organization's needs.

3. _____ testing ensures that a software module operates reliably and correctly, whereas _____ testing checks to make sure all the modules work with each other.

4. The target audience for _____ documentation is programmers, designers, and analysts.

5. A(n) _____ handbook can take the place of a lengthy user manual.

6. A(n) _____ conversion is more risky than other types of conversion because all parts of the new system go live at once.

7. The final phase of testing, in which users verify that the entire system works as specified, is called _____ testing.

8. During the maintenance phase, three key concepts ensure good quality of service: _____ , availability, and serviceability.

10

 CHECK ANSWERS

Corporate Data Security

BANKING, MEDICAL CARE, air traffic control, online access to public records, e-commerce, next-day package delivery, credit card use, e-mail, telecommunications, discount superstores...all of these aspects of modern life are powered by information systems. Without information systems and the data they contain, many everyday tasks would become impossibly cumbersome and time-consuming. Unfortunately, threats against information systems are increasing. Corporations, government agencies, and other organizations are constantly shoring up their defenses to protect data and the people to whom it refers. In this security section, you'll learn about threats to corporate data and methods for protecting that data. You can then draw some informed conclusions about the risks you might face when data about you is stored in information systems and when you depend on information systems for key aspects of your lifestyle.

INFORMATION SYSTEM DATA VULNERABILITIES

What are the most common threats to the data stored on corporate information systems? As with personal computers, common threats to corporate information systems include natural disasters, power outages, software failures, hardware breakdowns, human error, security breaches, acts of war, and viruses. When disaster strikes the PC on your desktop, it is a major inconvenience, but just for one person. In contrast, threats to a corporate information system can affect thousands of people.

● **Natural disasters** include fires, floods, hurricanes, and other such unforeseeable events. A natural disaster can completely shut down a computer system, cut off service to customers, and potentially destroy the system completely. For example, when Hurricane Katrina tore through Louisiana, it left a swath of destruction in its wake. In many businesses, computer systems were drenched with rain and flood waters. During the storm, power outages knocked down several major Internet hosting services. Power remained out for weeks in some places, and businesses without generators scrambled to continue operating.

● **Power outages** can be caused by natural disasters, overloaded power grids, planned brownouts, and rolling blackouts. For example, the IS Departments of many California businesses had to contend with rolling blackouts in the early 2000s when power grids in the area could not keep up with rising power demands.

● **Hardware breakdowns** can occur in any hardware component of a computer system. The risk of breakdown increases as a hardware component ages, but breakdowns can occur in brand-new hardware. Many devices are rated with a mean time between failures (MTBF) statistic. For example, an MTBF rating of 125,000 hours means that, on average, a device could function for 125,000 hours before failing. MTBF ratings are averages, however, so a server with a 125,000 MTBF rating might operate for only 10 hours before it fails, for example.

- **Human errors** refer to mistakes made by computer operators. Common errors within an information system include entering inaccurate data and failing to follow required procedures. Poorly trained computer operators were blamed for the biggest North American blackout in history, which left more than 50 million people without power in the summer of 2003 (Figure 10-44).

- **Software failures** can be caused by bugs or flawed software design. A tiny memory leak might be undetectable in a small computing system, but it can be disastrous on a system consisting of hundreds or thousands of computers. Other bugs may cause security leaks. Hackers continue to discover bugs in Microsoft Windows and other software products that allow unauthorized access to servers.

- **Security breaches** include stolen data, physical intrusions, and deliberate sabotage. In one of the most publicized security cases, Omega Engineering Corporation, an instrumentation manufacturer for customers such as NASA and the U.S. Navy, fired a network administrator for performance problems. Before leaving work, the disgruntled employee wrote a six-line computer program that ultimately cost his former employer $10 million dollars in financial losses. The six line program was a "time bomb" that erased information on the company's file server and destroyed data on all the backup tapes. The employee was eventually tried and convicted of computer sabotage, but Omega Engineering never regained its foothold in the market.

- **Acts of war** once affected only computer systems located on battle fronts. With a recent increase in terrorist incidents, however, civilian areas have become targets. Acts of war, such as bombing, can cause physical damage to computer systems. Cyberterrorism can also cause damage, using viruses and worms to destroy data and otherwise disrupt computer-based operations, which now include critical national infrastructures such as power grids and telecommunications systems.

- **Viruses** can damage just about any computer system. You might have experienced the nuisance of rooting out a virus from your personal computer. That inconvenience pales when compared to the potential effect of a virus on a corporate information system. The MyDoom worm, spread through e-mail, infected Web sites, and caused an estimated $250 million in damage when it infected millions of computers worldwide.

10

INFORMATION SYSTEM DATA SECURITY

How is the data on corporate information systems protected from threats? No computer system can be completely risk-free, but several proactive measures can protect information systems from threats. These countermeasures can be grouped into four categories: deterrents, preventive countermeasures, corrective procedures, and detection activities.

- **Deterrents** reduce the likelihood of deliberate attack. Common deterrents include security features such as multilevel authentication and password protection. Physical deterrents, such as limiting access to critical servers, also fall under this category (Figure 10-45).

- **Preventive countermeasures** shield vulnerabilities to render an attack unsuccessful or reduce its impact. Firewalls that prevent unauthorized access to a system are one example of a preventive countermeasure.

- **Corrective procedures** reduce the effect of an attack. Data backups, disaster recovery plans, and the availability of redundant hardware devices all are examples of corrective procedures.

- **Detection activities** recognize attacks and trigger preventive countermeasures or corrective procedures. For example, antivirus software detects viruses entering a system and can be configured to automatically clean the system or quarantine infected files. Theft or vandalism can be detected by periodic hardware inventories. The use of monitoring software to track users, file updates, and changes to critical systems can also help detect anomalies that indicate an intrusion or threat.

Does a data center help minimize risks? The hardware and software for most corporate information systems are housed in a data center. A **data center** is a specialized facility designed to hold and protect computer systems and data. A data center typically includes special security features, such as fireproof construction, earthquakeproof foundations, sprinkler systems, power generators, secure doors and windows, and antistatic floor coverings.

Data centers are designed to proactively reduce the risk of data loss that might occur as a result of a disaster. The best way to protect against risk is to avoid it altogether, and data centers can reduce or negate the effects of specific types of disasters. For example, NTT/Verio, an ISP that supplies Web hosting services in more than 200 countries, currently operates from more than 20 data centers located in the United States, Europe, Australia, and Asia. The company stores data for thousands of organizations, and loss of information in even one data center would be a disaster. NTT/Verio managers designed a series of data centers with risk prevention in mind. Each data center incorporates special risk management features for dealing with fires, power outages, security, and environmental concerns.

Data centers can be located in the basement of a building or even underground. For example, a commercial data center based in a former NATO command bunker dug into the Lincolnshire Wolds advertises that it is the "most secure non-government site in the U.K." Underground data centers provide protection against many natural disasters, such as storms and forest fires, and are not susceptible to extreme changes in surface

FIGURE 10-45

Physical deterrents, such as fingerprint and retinal scans, provide one line of defense against disasters.

temperature. In general, data centers are not located in earthquake, flood, or tornado prone areas.

Data centers typically include equipment to keep computers functioning during power outages. Most areas experience occasional power failures or blackouts, which can be costly to organizations whose goal is to offer 24/7 coverage. To avoid downtime, one of the most basic requirements for a data center is a supply of uninterrupted power from high-capacity, battery-operated UPSs (uninterruptible power supplies) and backup power generators. A data center must also protect and maintain its own power grid. For example, fuel tanks must be protected against explosions or fire, and batteries must be kept at room temperature for proper functioning.

Physical security is critical to data centers. Most data centers limit physical access using fingerprint identification systems, badges, or security guards. Steel doors divide the centers into secure areas. Motion detectors and automated alarm systems prevent unauthorized movement through the building. In addition, many data centers are located close to police and fire departments.

Conditions in a data center must be monitored at all times. Computerized detection systems monitor sensing devices that track temperature, humidity, water, smoke, fire, air flow, power levels, security systems, and many other metrics. Cameras can be placed in air ducts, under raised floors, and in computer chassis to detect intruders, pests such as mice or rats, or chemical leaks.

What if disaster strikes? A particularly heavy rainfall in the United States Virgin Islands a few years ago caused massive water damage to the local driver's license offices. The computer system containing license data was soaked and the hard drive damaged beyond repair. There were no backups. Residents were asked to appear in person at the license bureau so that government employees could re-enter license data. Episodes such as this one can be avoided when organizations create and implement a disaster recovery plan.

A **disaster recovery plan** is a step-by-step plan that describes the methods used to secure data against disaster and explains how an organization will recover lost data if and when a disaster occurs. One of the most destructive corporate disasters in recent history was the September 11, 2001 terrorist attack that caused the World Trade Center collapse. Surprisingly, very few companies affected by the disaster experienced critical data loss. Most companies were able to reconstitute their computer systems because a bomb eight years earlier at the World Trade Center prompted many companies in the towers to design disaster recovery plans.

For example, Kemper Insurance, located on the 35th and 36th floors of the World Trade Center north tower, designed a disaster recovery plan after the 1993 bombing. Kemper's plan not only detailed what to do in case of disaster, but it also required a mock disaster recovery exercise at least once a year. In these yearly exercises, IT employees went through the process of reconstructing the company's computer system from scratch at an off-site location. They configured new hardware, installed the required software, and restored data from backup tapes. In response to the 9/11 catastrophe, Kemper Insurance IT employees followed the disaster recovery plan and re-created the computer system at another Kemper Insurance site. Kemper Insurance was up and running by 4:00 a.m. on September 12—less than 24 hours after its main office was destroyed.

10

Disaster recovery plans must deal not only with calamities such as the World Trade Center collapse; they also must take into account day-to-day events that could potentially cause data loss. Backup tapes can become corrupted, an employee might spill coffee onto the most critical storage device in the building, or a virus can slow down the network to the point that it's unusable. A well-formulated disaster recovery plan should account for all kinds of trouble, from the most minor glitch to the most destructive disaster. Specifically, an enterprise-wide disaster recovery plan should:

- Ensure the safety of people on the premises at the time of a disaster

- Continue critical business operations

- Minimize the duration of a serious disruption to operations

- Minimize immediate damage and prevent additional losses

- Establish management succession and emergency powers

- Facilitate effective coordination of recovery tasks

A disaster recovery plan can mean the difference between an organization rebounding after a disaster or simply ceasing to exist. The Kemper Insurance example illustrates how quickly and easily information can be recovered, even after severe disasters. Disaster recovery plans are as critical to data security as data backups, firewalls, and password protection. As a key component of computer system management, disaster recovery is the focus of numerous publications and conferences (Figure 10-46).

FIGURE 10-46

Publications such as the *Disaster Recovery Journal* help risk management professionals design and update disaster recovery plans.

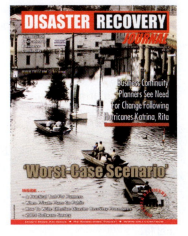

CORPORATE IDENTITY THEFT

What is corporate identity theft? In the corporate world, a brand symbolizes a company and its products or services. A brand typically includes a name, logo, trademark, and other visual elements. Brands are used on catalogs, store fronts, merchandise, letterheads, and Web sites, to help build customer trust and confidence. When a company's brand is used without authorization, the company has become a victim of identity theft. Corporate identity attacks can undermine customer confidence, overwhelm customer service, generate bad publicity, and result in lost revenues. With the escalation of online crime, corporate identity theft has become a major security threat.

How are corporate identities stolen? The Internet makes it easy to steal corporate identities and use them for phishing scams and fake Web sites. The key to a phishing scam is an e-mail that looks like it originated from a legitimate company, such as Bank of America, the IRS, PayPal, or Microsoft. It is not difficult for hackers to copy logos and other graphic elements from Web pages of legitimate sites and compile them into an official-looking e-mail message. Creating a fake Web site is also easy. Hackers can obtain a URL that's similar to one used by a legitimate company, perhaps by using a different country code or using .biz instead of .com. By copying and pasting a few graphics, the site looks legitimate, too.

Why does corporate identity theft matter to consumers? Savvy consumers are on the lookout for phishing attacks and avoid clicking links embedded in e-mail messages. Unfortunately, other consumers unknowingly click fake links and divulge personal information. These unfortunate consumers in turn can become the victims of fraud and identity theft.

What can companies do about fake sites and phishing scams?

Preventing corporate identity theft is not really feasible. With current HTTP and HTML technologies, corporations have no way to lock down their branding elements, so hackers can easily misappropriate them. Secure Web site identification has been in the works for many years, but a worldwide standard that is recognized and understood by consumers does not yet exist. Consumers will remain at risk until there is universal implementation of technology that verifies a Web site's legitimacy.

Companies can take steps to protect their customers, and deal quickly with identity theft incidents. The American Management Association and other business advocates offer guidelines, such as those listed in Figure 10-47, to help corporations minimize the effects of identity theft.

FIGURE 10-47

Guidelines help corporations deal with identity theft

- **Help customers report scams** Provide a simple way for employees and customers to report phishing attacks that appear to originate from the company and fake versions of the corporate Web site.

- **Educate customers** Let customers know what kinds of legitimate communications they can expect from the company. Avoid acclimatizing customers to e-mail notifications that can make them vulnerable to future attacks. Never send customers mass-mailings that contain links to the company's site or ask them to send personal data as an e-mail reply. Instead, ask customers to connect to the company's site using their browsers and provide instructions for accessing a data collection form.

- **Manage URLs** Make sure the company Web site is easy to find online. Keep the company URL simple so that users can access it directly, rather than through search engines or partner sites. Consider typical typographic errors that customers might make when typing the company URL. Try to reserve those URLs so that hackers can't take advantage of them. To minimize typographic errors, encourage customers to bookmark the company site by adding it to their Favorites lists.

- **Monitor domain name registration** Keep up-to-date on the corporation's domain registration and periodically check for new registrations that might make unauthorized use of the company name or trademarks.

- **Be prepared** Prepare for an attack before it happens by establishing relationships with law enforcement, ISPs, and others who can help locate and take down fraudulent sites.

QuickCheck

SECTION E

1. A(n) [_____] rating of 125,000 hours means that, on average, a device could function for 125,000 hours before failing. (Hint: Use the acronym.)

2. A disaster recovery plan focuses on how to back up data. True or false? [_____]

3. Preventive [_____], such as firewalls, can help to shield a system's vulnerabilities.

4. A data center is a storage facility specifically designed to withstand attacks from internal auditors. True or false? [_____]

5. Corporate [_____] theft has become a major security concern because of increasing numbers of [_____] scams and fake Web sites.

10

► CHECK ANSWERS

ISSUE

What's Wrong with Online Voting?

A COMPLEX INFORMATION SYSTEM now on the drawing board would make it possible for Americans to vote online. The idea of online voting surfaced years ago as the Internet gained popularity. Early enthusiasts envisioned it as a technology solution to the problems of representative democracy. They expected the rapid emergence of a new e-democracy in which citizens had a direct vote in every issue with the ease of dashing off an e-mail or logging on to a Web site.

The term online voting usually refers to a remote voting system that allows voters to cast their ballots from any computer connected to the Internet—typically from personal computers, but possibly from other devices as well, such as interactive television, cell phones, handheld computers, or game machines.

In the early days of the Internet, online voting looked easy, but the feasibility of an easy solution died with the advent of viruses, worms, bots, Denial of Service attacks, unauthorized intrusion attempts, and the growing threat of international terrorists. Computer scientists, systems analysts, security experts, and election officials now have a pretty good idea of the problems associated with online voting, but they disagree about the best solutions.

Whether manual or electronic, there are six basic requirements for a voting system (see box).

BASIC REQUIREMENTS FOR DEMOCRATIC VOTING SYSTEMS

- Encourage and allow voters to register
- Provide voters with an easy-to-decipher ballot
- Allow voters to make their selections, review them, and revise them before casting their ballots
- Collect ballots and filter out those that are invalid or fraudulent
- Accurately tabulate votes from every valid ballot
- Allow officials to recount ballots if an election is challenged

---

Online voting meets some of these basic requirements better than current voting methods, but faces challenges in adequately fulfilling other requirements.

Online voting has several advantages. It is convenient. Voters can cast ballots from home or work, or even while on vacation. It is quick. Casting an online ballot doesn't require driving to a polling station and waiting in line.

Because of its advantages, online voting has the potential to attract net-savvy young voters who historically have voted in lower numbers than other segments of the population. It also simplifies the voting process for elderly and homebound voters. The convenience of online voting might also increase participation in local elections.

Online voting has the potential to decrease the number of ballots that are invalidated because of procedural problems, such as failing to completely punch out the "chad" on a ballot card, or checking more than one candidate on a paper ballot. Voting software can prevent voters from erroneously selecting more than one candidate and make sure that voters can revise their selections without invalidating their ballots.

Online voting trial runs have a good track record. In 2000, Arizona Democrats had the opportunity to vote online in the Democratic primaries. Michigan Democrats were given the opportunity to vote online in the 2004 primaries. The success of these online experiments is viewed by online voting supporters as evidence that Internet voting can be effective and secure. Several states, including Michigan and West Virginia, plan to offer access to online voting for primaries running up to the 2008 U.S. presidential election.

Although previous experiments with online voting in Michigan and Arizona appeared to go without a hitch, a more comprehensive online voting project called Secure Electronic Registration and Voting Experiment (SERVE) was scrapped shortly before the 2004 presidential election. SERVE was initiated by the U.S. Department of Defense with a goal of offering online voting to overseas military personnel. The project expanded to include 50 counties in seven states and 100,000 American military personnel and civilians living abroad. The decision to scrap the project came shortly after a panel of security experts, the Security Peer Review Group (SPRG), analyzed SERVE and criticized its vulnerabilities.

SPRG reported that Internet voting was susceptible to a variety of well-known cyber attacks that could prevent votes from reaching a tabulating center, alter votes, or stuff electronic ballot boxes with thousands of fraudulent votes. The report went on to say that "Such attacks could occur on a large scale, and could be launched by anyone, including disaffected lone individuals to well-financed enemy agents outside the reach of U.S. law. These attacks could result in large-scale, selective voter disenfranchisement, privacy violations, vote buying and selling, and vote switching even to the extent of reversing the outcome of many elections at once, including the presidential election."

The SPRG report also noted that successful attacks might go completely undetected, but even if attacks were detected and neutralized, they could have a devastating effect on public confidence in elections. Members of SPRG concluded that the vulnerabilities were not specific to the SERVE system, but rather were inherent in the Internet itself and the relatively unsecured personal computers used to access it.

In addition to technical issues with Internet security, online voting opponents have concerns about voter fraud and privacy.

Voter fraud includes voting multiple times, stuffing the ballot box with ballots from nonexistent voters, and buying votes. To reduce voter fraud, voters must be identified to make sure they are eligible to vote and vote only once. When a person logs on to vote remotely, it is difficult to verify his or her identity. Passwords are not effective in controlling fraud because they can be shared and distributed. Biometric devices that offer more positive identification are not typically part of personal computer systems.

A partial solution might be for online voters to submit their names and Social Security numbers along with their votes. Computers at vote-tabulation centers could screen out duplicate voters. However, secret ballots are a cornerstone of democracy. In a physical polling place, voters provide identification at the door and are checked against voter registration records. Registered voters are allowed to proceed to voting booths where their votes are cast in secret. Nothing allows that vote to be traced back to the individual who voted.

Politically, skeptics of online voting are uncomfortable with its affect on voting demographics. Some Republican strategists are concerned about a sudden upswing in young voters—not a block of traditionally Republican supporters—who might take advantage of online polling. Democrats, on the other hand, have intimated that online voting would disproportionately increase the number of high-income voters because many economically deprived voters do not have access to a computer and an Internet connection.

For a democracy to function properly, its citizens should be confident that the electoral system is honest and works. Online voting presents some sticky technological and social challenges. Although these challenges exist, secure technologies for online banking and e-commerce are working, so shouldn't it be possible to design an online voting system that's secure enough to conduct our elections?

INFOWEBLINKS

You'll find additional information about online voting at the **Online Voting InfoWeb**.

Ⓦ CLICK TO CONNECT
www.course.com/np/concepts11/ch10

10

What Do You Think?

ISSUE

1. Would you prefer online voting to voting at a polling place? ⭕Yes ⭕ No ⭕ Not sure

2. Do you think online voters would disproportionally vote for Republicans? ⭕Yes ⭕ No ⭕ Not sure

3. Should online voting be available only to specific groups, such as elderly voters and military personnel stationed abroad, who currently have trouble reaching polling places? ⭕Yes ⭕ No ⭕ Not sure

▶ SAVE RESPONSES

COMPUTERS IN CONTEXT
Architecture and Construction

A CLUSTER OF HARDHATS study a dog-eared blueprint. Sun-bronzed laborers perch on a makeshift bench, munching sandwiches and waving to a group of carpenters hauling 2x4s onto a foundation. The sounds of hammers, shovels, and power tools fill the air from early morning through late afternoon. It is a typical construction site: an ant hill of activity where a structure of some sort is eventually assembled—a house, a shopping mall, or a skyscraper.

Behind the scenes of this busy ant hill, computer technology has added a high-tech flavor to construction projects with real-time interactive computer graphics, broadband wireless communications, distributed database management systems, wearable and vehicle-mounted computers, global positioning satellites, and laser-guided surveying systems. Architects use computers to create blueprints. Contractors use computers for cost estimates and scheduling. Computers are even starting to appear on the job site, carried as handheld devices and embedded in construction equipment.

In the past, architects typically drew construction plans by hand on semitransparent film called vellum. To create a blueprint, they overlaid the vellum on special blue paper and then ran it through a machine that exposed it to intensified light and ammonia. Minor changes to a design were possible, but for major changes, architects often needed to create a new set of vellum drawings.

With the advent of computers and computer-aided design (CAD) software, architects realized they could be more productive—and make design changes more easily—by replacing their drafting tables with computers running CAD software, much as writers replaced their typewriters with computers running word processing software. Using plotters with wide print beds, architects were able to produce computer-generated blueprints similar to those they created at a drafting table.

Initially, architects used CAD software to create 2-D floor plans and elevations. Today architects use 3-D CAD software that offers a greatly expanded toolset. Architects can begin with a simple 2-D floor plan, and then use CAD tools to draw interior and exterior walls, ceilings, and roofs. Standard building materials, such as doors and windows, can be selected from a list of clip-art objects and dragged into position with a mouse. Electrical, plumbing, and framing schematics can also be added. Any elements of the drawing can be displayed or hidden—for example, when discussing the design with an electrical contractor, an architect can hide the plumbing details. These 3-D wireframe drawings with building, electrical, and plumbing elements included can be rotated and viewed from any angle.

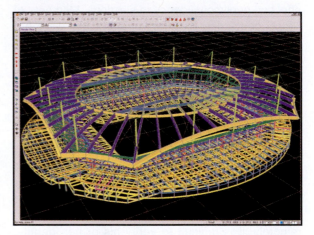

Inexpensive inkjet printers have replaced expensive first-generation plotters and give architects the option of printing in realistic color. Using 3-D CAD software, they can also apply textures and colors to convert wireframes into 3-D models that can be viewed from the inside or outside. Architects sometimes use an animated version of a 3-D model for virtual reality walkthroughs.

After an architect has completed the building plans, a contractor estimates the project's price tag by calculating the cost of materials and labor. Computerized spreadsheets, such as Excel, are a popular tool for cost estimates. Large contracting firms often use commercial software specifically designed for construction estimates.

Contractors are also responsible for scheduling the tasks in a construction project, such as excavating the building site, erecting the foundation and frame, assembling the roof, adding wiring and plumbing, and doing interior finish work. Large construction projects, such as malls and government buildings, can involve thousands of tasks and many subcontractors. Computerized scheduling tools, such as Gantt charts, PERT (program evaluation and review technique) diagrams, and WBS software, make it possible to plan and track each construction phase and break a project down into a series of tasks. For each task, planners enter its estimated duration and how it relates to other tasks. For example, drywall work that requires eight days depends on interior framing, electrical work, and plumbing being finished first. Given information about all the tasks in a project, planning software can create a master schedule showing both best- and worst-case completion dates, and contractors can easily update the schedule based on actual construction progress.

At a high-tech construction site, computers can play several roles. A site supervisor can use a wireless handheld computer to view and update the construction schedule stored on a desktop computer at the contractor's main office. Rather than refer to a set of printed—and possibly outdated—plans, the supervisor can refer to up-to-date plans transmitted from the home office. A supervisor might even wear a hardhat-mounted computer that collects multimedia data, such as video and sound, to document site inspections. A voice-activated microphone records the supervisor's comments and adds them to the digital video, which can be uploaded to a database in the contractor's main office.

Computers also play a role in guiding bulldozers during site preparation by using construction software developed at Ohio State University that works with the global positioning system (GPS). A GPS receiver is mounted on a vehicle that traverses the site. GPS signals are collected and entered in the software program, which creates a map and a plan for site preparation. A wireless computer monitor mounted in each bulldozer's cab receives data from the software and displays it to the operator. The system allows construction crews to stake and grade a site with to-the-centimeter accuracy.

Computers embedded in robots are used extensively on large construction projects in Japan. These single task robots perform specific jobs. For example, a concrete-task robot might lay forms, bend rebar, pour concrete, and screed the surface to a smooth finish. Other robots weld steel components, apply paint, or install tile. Single-task robots have been successful because they shield human workers from dangerous and difficult jobs and typically work faster and more consistently than humans. However, trained technicians are required to set up and monitor robot work.

Although construction robots are widely used in Japan, they aren't popular with contractors in many other parts of the world. Industry observers speculate that Japan's shortage of unskilled laborers differentiates it from countries where labor is readily available and relatively inexpensive. In the United States, for example, college students working in construction is a long-standing summer tradition—but one that might be changing. In a recent survey, students viewed construction work as dirty and undesirable and, out of 252 career choices, ranked it as 251.

Construction robots might help fill the labor gap in countries such as the United States, but potential barriers, such as union regulations, could discourage their use. Some observers question how building trade union agreements might affect construction site robots. According to one supervisor's worst-case scenario, "Millwrights will want to set up the device, electricians will want to fix the electronic controls, equipment operators will want to run it, cement finishers will want to adjust it, and laborers will be expected to clean it." The future of computer-powered robots at construction sites is still unclear and illustrates the controversies that sometimes surround technology as it filters into society and the workplace.

10

INFOWEBLINKS

You'll find lots more information related to this topic by connecting to the **Computers and Construction InfoWeb**.

W **CLICK TO CONNECT**
www.course.com/np/concepts11/ch10

New Perspectives Labs

On the BookOnCD

To access the New Perspectives labs for Chapter 10, start the BookOnCD, BookOnFlashDrive, or other NP11 BookOn product and then click the icon next to the lab title below.

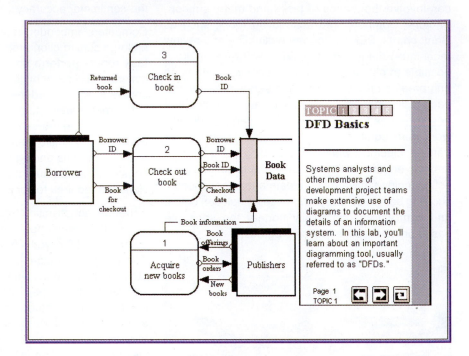

▶ **WORKING WITH DFDS**

IN THIS LAB YOU'LL LEARN:

- The purpose of data flow diagrams (DFDs) in the system development life cycle

- How to read a leveled set of DFDs

- The meaning of each DFD symbol

- The differences between Gane/Sarson DFD notation and Yourdon/Coad DFD notation

- How to label data flows, entities, data stores, and processes

- How to create a context DFD

- How to "explode" a DFD to show additional levels of detail

- Why "black holes" and "miracles" indicate DFD errors

LAB ASSIGNMENTS

1. Start the interactive part of the lab. Make sure you've enabled Tracking if you want to save your QuickCheck results. Perform each lab step as directed, and answer all the lab QuickCheck questions. When you exit the lab, your answers are automatically graded and your results are displayed.

2. Use paper and pencil, graphics software, or a CASE tool to create a context DFD for a video rental store. Use Gane/Sarson notation. Remember that the store purchases as well as rents videos and DVDs.

3. Explode the DFD you created in Assignment 2 so that it represents the main processes and data stores for the video rental store. Make sure you label data flows, processes, entities, and data stores. Before you finalize your DFD, make sure it contains no black holes or miracles.

4. Convert the DFD you drew in Assignment 3 to Yourdon/Coad notation.

Key Terms

Make sure you understand all the boldfaced key terms presented in this chapter. If you're using the NP11 BookOnCD, BookOnFlashDrive, or other NP11 BookOn product, you can use this list of terms as an interactive study activity. First, try to define a term in your own words, and then click the term to compare your definition with the definition presented in the chapter.

Acceptance testing, 586
Actors, 573
Ad hoc report, 561
Analysis phase, 571
Application development tool, 578
Application specifications, 581
Application testing, 584
Batch processing, 560
BI, 569
BPR, 569
Business, 556
CASE tool, 574
Centralized processing, 577
Change requests, 582
Class diagram, 573
Commit, 560
CRM, 569
Data center, 592
Data flow, 572
Data flow diagram, 572
Data store, 572
Decision model, 562
Decision query, 562
Decision support system, 562
Decision support worksheet, 579
Design phase, 576
Detail reports, 560
Direct conversion, 586
Disaster recovery plan, 593
Distributed processing, 577
EAI, 569
EDI, 569
Enterprise computer system, 559
ERP, 569
Exception report, 561
Executive information system, 562
Expert system, 564
Expert system shell, 564
External entity, 572
External information, 559
Feature creep, 582
Fuzzy logic, 564

Gantt chart, 570
Help desk, 588
Implementation phase, 583
Inference engine, 564
Info. engineering methodology, 570
Information system, 556
Integration testing, 584
Internal information, 559
Iterative SDLC, 566
JIT, 569
Joint application design, 567
Knowledge base, 564
Knowledge engineering, 564
Maintenance phase, 587
Management information system, 561
Managers, 557
Mission, 556
Mission statement, 556
Modified waterfall SDLC, 566
MRP, 569
Neural network, 565
Nonprofit organization, 556
Object-oriented methodology, 570
OLTP system, 560
Online processing, 560
Operational planning, 557
Organization, 556
Organizational chart, 557
Parallel conversion, 586
PERT, 570
Phased conversion, 586
PIECES framework, 569
Pilot conversion, 586
Planning phase, 567
Procedure handbook, 585
Process, 572
Project Development Plan, 567
Project management software, 571
Quality of service, 587
Quality-of-service metric, 587
Request for proposal, 580
Request for quotation, 580

Rollback, 560
Scheduled reports, 561
SDLC, 566
Semi-structured problem, 558
Sequence diagram, 574
Software customization, 583
Strategic planning, 557
Structured methodology, 570
Structured problem, 558
Success factors, 571
Summary report, 561
System conversion, 586
System development life cycle, 566
System documentation, 585
System operator, 588
System requirements, 571
System Requirements Report, 572
System testing, 584
Systems analysis and design, 566
Systems programmer, 588
Tactical planning, 557
Test area, 584
TQM, 569
Transaction, 559
Transaction processing system, 559
Turnkey system, 578
UML, 573
Unit testing, 584
Unstructured problem, 558
Use case, 573
Use case diagram, 573
User documentation, 585
Waterfall SDLC, 566
WBS, 570
Workers, 557

10

Interactive Summary

To review important concepts from this chapter, fill in the blanks to best complete each sentence. When using the NP11 BookOnCD or other BookOn product, click the Check Answers buttons to automatically score your answers.

SECTION A: [   ] systems play a key role in helping organizations achieve goals, which are set forth in a [   ] statement. Computers can be used by people at all levels of an organization. Workers use information systems to produce and manipulate information. Managers depend on information systems to supply data that is essential for long-term [   ] planning and short-term tactical planning.

Transaction [   ] systems provide an organization with a way to collect, display, modify, or cancel transactions. These systems encompass activities such as general accounting, inventory tracking, and e-commerce. [   ] information systems typically build on the data collected by a TPS to produce reports that managers use to make the business decisions needed to solve routine, structured problems.

A decision [   ] system helps workers and managers make non-routine decisions by constructing decision models that include data collected from internal and external sources.

An [   ] system is designed to analyze data and produce a recommendation or decision based on a set of facts and rules called a [   ] base. These facts and rules can be written using an expert system shell or a programming language. An [   ] engine evaluates the facts and rules to produce answers to questions posed to the system. Using a technique called [   ] logic, these systems can deal with imprecise data and problems that have more than one solution. If the rules for an expert system are not known, a neural [   ] might be used to enable a computer to "learn" how to make a decision. ▶ CHECK ANSWERS

SECTION B: The process of planning and building an information system is referred to as systems [   ] and design. The development process is supervised by an organization's Information Systems (IS) department, but the [   ] team usually includes members from other departments as well. System development follows some type of system development [   ] cycle (SDLC), which consists of several phases. In the [   ] SDLC, one phase of the SDLC must be completed before the next phase can begin. In practice, however, most project teams use a modification of this model in which phases can overlap or repeat.

A project team can use one of several approaches to the system development process. For example, the [   ] methodology focuses on the processes that take place in an information system. The information [   ] methodology focuses on the data that an information system collects. The object-[   ] methodology treats an information system as a collection of interacting objects.

A project begins with a [   ] phase in which a member of the IS department creates a Project Development Plan. The project team then proceeds to the [   ] phase, with the goal of producing a list of requirements for a new or revised information system.

▶ CHECK ANSWERS

SECTION C: In the [＿＿＿＿＿＿＿] phase of the SDLC, the project team identifies potential solutions, evaluates those solutions, and then selects the best one. The team members might consider various levels of [＿＿＿＿＿＿＿] , such as scanning magnetic credit card strips instead of entering credit card numbers from a keyboard. The project team might also consider whether a [＿＿＿＿＿＿＿] processing model would be better than a distributed processing model. Several alternative [＿＿＿＿＿＿＿] technologies might provide connectivity solutions. Alternative software solutions for a project include the use of programming languages, application development tools, or commercial software. A [＿＿＿＿＿＿＿] system might offer a complete hardware and software solution.

After the project team selects a solution, team members can then select specific hardware and software products to build the new information system. The project team might send out a request for [＿＿＿＿＿＿＿] , asking vendors to recommend a solution. As an alternative the project team can send out a request for [＿＿＿＿＿＿＿] , which simply asks for vendor prices. After selecting hardware and software, the project team can develop [＿＿＿＿＿＿＿] specifications that describe the way the new information system should interact with the user, store data, process data, and format reports.

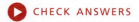 CHECK ANSWERS

SECTION D: During the [＿＿＿＿＿＿＿] phase of the SDLC, the project team supervises the technicians who set up new hardware, install programming languages and other application [＿＿＿＿＿＿＿] tools, create and test applications, and customize software. The team also finalizes the system documentation and trains users. In this phase, three types of testing ensure that new software works correctly. [＿＿＿＿＿＿＿] testing is performed on each module, and then [＿＿＿＿＿＿＿] testing is performed to make sure that all the modules work together correctly. [＿＿＿＿＿＿＿] testing ensures that the software components work correctly on the hardware and with other, perhaps older, elements of the information system.

When application testing is complete, data is converted from the old system to the new one, users are trained, and the new system goes live. Four types of information system "go live" conversions are possible: direct, parallel, phased, or pilot. At the end of the conversion process, the information system undergoes a final test called [＿＿＿＿＿＿＿] testing, designed to assure the system's owner that the new system works as specified.

After testing and installation, an information system enters the [＿＿＿＿＿＿＿] phase of its life cycle. During this phase, a [＿＿＿＿＿＿＿] operator typically performs backups, monitors system utilization, and troubleshoots operational problems. As users discover bugs, programmers must fix them. Ongoing user support from a help [＿＿＿＿＿＿＿] might also be required.

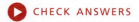 CHECK ANSWERS

SECTION E: The most common threats to corporate information systems include natural disasters, power outages, hardware breakdowns, human errors, [＿＿＿＿＿＿＿] breaches, acts of war, and viruses. These threats can be handled in several ways. [＿＿＿＿＿＿＿] reduce the likelihood of deliberate attack. [＿＿＿＿＿＿＿] countermeasures shield vulnerabilities to render an attack unsuccessful. [＿＿＿＿＿＿＿] procedures reduce the effect of an attack. [＿＿＿＿＿＿＿] activities recognize attacks and trigger a corrective response. To protect hardware, software, and data, corporate systems are often housed in a protective facility called a [＿＿＿＿＿＿＿] center. Most companies have a disaster [＿＿＿＿＿＿＿] plan that describes how to secure data against disaster, recover lost data, and restore normal operations after a disaster. Companies also have established policies that guard against corporate identity [＿＿＿＿＿＿＿] and protect personal data of employees and clients.

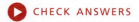 CHECK ANSWERS

10

Interactive Situation Questions

Apply what you've learned to some typical computing situations. When using the NP11 BookOnCD, BookOnFlashDrive, or any other NP11 BookOn product, you can type your answers, and then use the Check Answers button to automatically score your responses.

1. Suppose that you own a small bookstore located in a mall. Business seems to be declining, and you suspect that many of your former customers are now shopping at online bookstores. What can you do about declining sales? You realize that this problem falls into the category of a(n) [   ] problem, and you might not be able to solve it using the data supplied by your MIS.

2. Your friend just graduated and started work in a local pharmacy. She tells you about the pharmacy's computer system that warns of dangerous drug interactions by examining the patient's prescription record and sometimes asking the pharmacist to enter age and allergy information. The system that she has been describing sounds like a(n) [   ] system.

3. An article in your local newspaper describes a new airport security system as "a sophisticated facial-recognition system powered by advanced computer technology that learns on its own." This technology sounds like a(n) [   ] network.

4. As a member of the IS staff at a large corporation, you often hear about problems with the current information system. One recently discovered problem is that when an employee quits (or gets fired), sometimes the network manager is not notified, and the former employee continues to have access to company data over the Internet. Using the PIECES framework, you would classify this as a(n) [   ] problem.

5. Your county provides online access to property records. You simply enter the address of the property or the owner's name. However, each search seems to take longer than one minute. According to the PIECES framework, this delay would be classified as a(n) [   ] problem.

6. Your roommate works in the Data Entry department for a large corporation and has been asked to participate in a JAD session. When asked about it, you explain to your roommate that JAD stands for [   ] application design, and this probably means the corporation is working on a new information system.

7. You just started working in the IS department for a very small company that's developing a new information system. Your coworkers are trying to track down a discrepancy that resulted from a change in the name of a data field. Although you don't say it, you realize that such a problem would not have occurred if the project team used [   ] tools. (Hint: Use the acronym.)

8. On your last job, you worked as an admitting clerk in a hospital. One day you were told to begin using the hospital's new information system. The next day, you were told to go back to using the old system until further notice. You suspect that these events occurred as a result of a failed attempt at a(n) [   ] conversion.

 CHECK ANSWERS

Interactive Practice Tests

Practice tests that consist of 10 multiple-choice, true/false, and fill-in-the-blank questions are available on both the NP11 BookOn products and the NP11 Web site. The questions are selected at random from a large test bank, so each time you take a test, you'll receive a different set of questions. Your tests are scored immediately, and you can print study guides that help you find the correct answers for any questions that you missed.

 CLICK TO START

Study Tips

Study Tips help you to organize and consolidate the information in a unit by making lists, outlines, charts, and sketches. You can use paper and pencil or word processing software to complete most of the Study Tip activities.

1. Make sure you can use your own words to correctly answer each of the red focus questions that appear throughout the chapter.

2. Explain the differences between strategic, tactical, and operational planning. Provide an example of each.

3. Explain the differences between structured, semi-structured, and unstructured problems. Provide an example of each type, and describe how an information system might contribute to solving the problems.

4. Using your own examples, discuss the ways in which an organization can respond to opportunities and threats.

5. Using the figure on page 560, explain how a TPS might handle a specific type of transaction, such as signing up for a college course, or making a deposit to your checking account.

6. Revise the labels on the diagram in the figure on page 563 so that it explains how a DSS might help the Krispy Kreme Doughnut franchisers decide whether to construct a new doughnut shop in your town.

7. Suppose that a mail-order merchant runs out of an item featured in its recent catalog. Revise the labels on the diagram on page 565 so that it specifically illustrates how an expert system might produce a recommendation to place the out-of-stock item on backorder, or simply cancel the order.

8. Create a table that summarizes the characteristics of TPSs, MISs, DSSs, expert systems, and neural networks.

9. For each letter of the PIECES framework, create your own example of a problem that a systems analyst might discover in an obsolete information system.

10. Make sure that you can list the phases of the SDLC and the tasks that occur in each phase.

11. Make sure that you can describe how PERT, WBS, and Gantt techniques help systems analysts.

12. List some of the hardware and software alternatives that the project team must consider in the design phase.

13. Describe the five types of testing used during the implementation phase.

14. Use your own words to describe the advantages and disadvantages of direct, parallel, phased, and pilot conversions.

15. Draw a DFD showing the flow of data (ingredients) when you make a grilled cheese sandwich.

16. Fill in the blanks on the concept map below to show the hierarchy of SDLC phases and outputs described in this chapter.

Concept Map

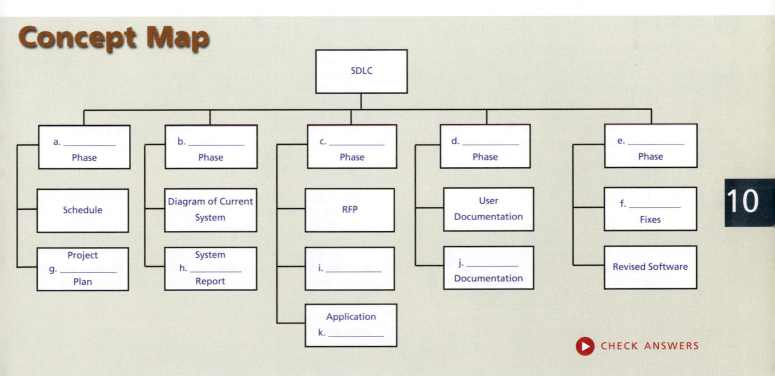

10

CHECK ANSWERS

Projects

CRITICAL THINKING

An important part of any new computer or software installation is training. Suppose you are a cashier at a large discount store that is getting new checkout software and terminals. List the number of ways you could envision your company conducting training sessions. Which type of training would you prefer? Why? Consolidate and list your ideas, and then submit them to your instructor using e-mail.

GROUP PROJECT

Form a group of two to five students as the project team for a systems development project. Elect one person as the team leader, who will assign tasks to each group member. Your team's mission is to complete the planning phase for a systems development project and produce a Project Development Plan. The first task is to identify and briefly describe an information system at school, work, or a local business that needs improvement. The second task is to make a list of problems and opportunities that exist in that system by applying Porter's Five Forces Model and Wetherbe's PIECES framework. The third task is to select a project development methodology, such as structured analysis, object-oriented analysis, or RAD, and make a list of tasks your team would perform to design, construct, and implement a new information system using the methodology you've selected. Finally, incorporate all your findings into a document that would serve as the Project Development Plan. Submit this plan to your instructor, who might provide additional directions for your group work and report format.

CYBERCLASSROOM

Describe a problem that you've encountered with an online information system such as student registration, driver's license renewal, or e-commerce site. Distribute the description to the members of your team. Each person who receives your description should e-mail back and tell you which one of the PIECES problems best describes it. Respond to each of your team members to indicate whether they were correct and explain why or why not. Use cut and paste to consolidate all the responses into a single document. Indicate which of the responses are correct and then send the final document to your instructor.

MULTIMEDIA PROJECT

Suppose you're an instructor preparing a lecture about how information systems help organizations respond to threats and opportunities. You need to create a PowerPoint presentation about an organization's three fundamental responses. The presentation should consist of about 10 slides. To make it interesting you decide to illustrate your slides with photos you take or find on the Web. Try to use examples different from those in the textbook. You might try businesses in industries such as athletic footwear, frozen treats, or sports equipment. Submit your PowerPoint presentation on disk, by e-mail, or on paper following guidelines provided by your instructor.

RESUME BUILDER

Create 10 rules for an expert system that pertains to your career field. To complete the assignment, think of a set of simple decisions that someone on the job might be required to perform. For example, a loan officer might be required to make a quick evaluation of a borrower, an auto mechanic might be required to figure out what various tapping noises mean, or a fitness instructor might be required to recommend the best type of fitness class for clients. Make a list of 10 rules that would help make the decision. The rules should be in the format IF... THEN... Submit your rules to your instructor.

GLOBALIZATION

Suppose that you are a systems analyst for a major city. You're in the process of purchasing new desktop computers for city hall. Your city has an active and vocal interest group that wants you to purchase equipment made within your state or country. Select a computer vendor and try to determine the country of origin for as many of its parts as you can. Alternatively, if you have access to a computer and permission to take it apart, you can examine the "Made in" labels on its component parts. Write up your findings in a one-page summary and conclude with your thoughts about the feasibility of sourcing locally.

ISSUE

The Issue section of this chapter focused on online voting. For this project, you will write a two- to five-page paper about online voting based on information you gather from the Internet. To begin this project, consult the Online Voting InfoWeb and link to the recommended Web pages to get an in-depth overview of the issue. Next, determine which aspect of the online voting controversy you want to discuss in your paper. You might, for example, decide to focus on potential political ramifications of online voting, you might want to delve into the potential for online fraud, or you might want to emphasize the impact of viruses and other security problems. Present your discussion as a debate between two people who take different sides on the issue. Follow your instructor's guidelines for submitting your paper.

COMPUTERS IN CONTEXT

The Computers in Context section focused on architects' and contractors' use of computers. Today, many architects use CAD software to create floor plans, elevations, and 3D walkthroughs. Similar software is available to consumers. For this project, complete one of the following assignments:

• Use the Computers and Construction InfoWebLinks to take a tutorial on floor plan software. When you have finished the tutorial, select two of your favorite features of the software, and briefly explain how to use them.

• Use the Computers and Construction InfoWebLinks to download basic floor plan software, and use it to draw and print a floor plan of your dorm room, apartment, or house. If you are using lab computers, make sure you have permission to download and install software. Instead of downloading floor plan software, your professor might instruct you to use CAD software already installed on your school's lab computers.

On the Web

STUDENT EDITION LABS

W **CLICK TO ACCESS THE NP11 WEB SITE**
or open your browser and connect to www.course.com/np/concepts11/ch10.
Lab results can be stored in the Universal Gradebook.

Work hands-on in structured simulations practicing important skills and concepts

PROJECT MANAGEMENT

In the Project Management Student Edition Lab, you will learn about the following topics:

- Introduction to project management software
- Entering project tasks to determine scope
- Developing the project schedule
- Entering cost and human resource information
- Communicating project information

ADVANCED SPREADSHEETS

In the Advanced Spreadsheets Student Edition Lab, you will learn about the following topics:

- Sorting and filtering lists and creating subtotals
- Using conditional formatting, data validation, Goal Seek and macros
- Creating PivotTables
- Protecting and documenting a worksheet

CHAPTER COURSECAST

Use your computer or iPod to hear a five-minute audio presentation of chapter highlights.

FLASHCARD COURSECAST

Interact with audio flashcards to review key terms from the chapter.

DETAILED OBJECTIVES

Make sure that you've achieved all the objectives for a chapter before it's time for your test!

TEST YOURSELF

Review chapter material by taking these ten-question tests, then send your results to the Universal Gradebook.

ONLINE GAMES

Have some fun while refreshing your memory about key concepts that might appear on the next test. You can even send your results to the Universal Gradebook!

AND MORE!

At the NP11 Web site you'll also find Extra Content and InfoWebLinks.

10

11 Databases

CHAPTER CONTENTS

LEARNING OBJECTIVES

- Define basic database terminology, such as fields, records, record types, and cardinality
- Describe six database models and their applications
- Explain the capabilities of various data management tools, such as commercial applications, word processing software, spreadsheet software, file management software, and database management software
- Describe various ways to provide access to databases over the Web
- Explain how to design an effective relational database
- List the principles for creating effective report templates
- Describe how to add records, delete records, search for information, update fields, and simultaneously access data from multiple tables using SQL queries
- Explain how database vulnerabilities affect individuals and organizations
- Describe the legal, regulatory, and procedural methods that pertain to database security
- List the steps you can take when working with databases to protect your privacy and identity

☑ **PRE-ASSESSMENT QUIZ**

Take the pre-assessment quiz to find out how much you know about the topics in this chapter. ▶

MULTIMEDIA and INTERACTIVE ELEMENTS
When using the BookOnCD, BookOnFlashDrive, or other NP11 BookOn product, the ▶ icons are clickable to access multimedia resources.

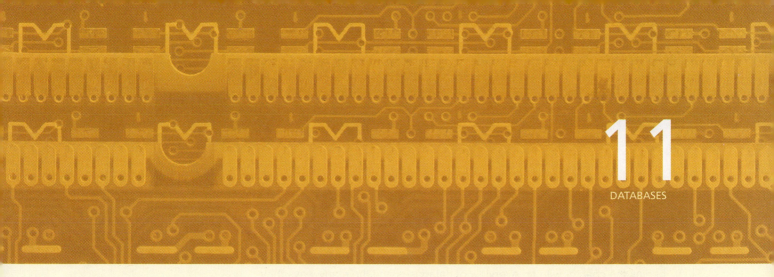

BEFORE YOU READ ON, **TRY IT**

HOW DOES "BAD" DATA GET INTO DATABASES?

Databases are everywhere and information about you is in many of them. You might wonder if that information is accurate. Data entry mistakes are easy to make, but a well designed database can prevent some common data entry errors. To start exploring databases, you can check the design of a database that's on most computers—the e-mail address book.

1. Start your e-mail program and access its address book function.

2. Use the menu bar or toolbar option to add an address or contact.

3. A typical address book stores data for each person in a record. The record is divided into fields, such as name and e-mail address. Many address books also store additional data such as phone numbers and physical addresses. How many fields does your address book provide?

4. Begin to fill in fields with data for one of your friends. Are the field names clearly labeled so you know what you're supposed to enter into them?

5. Does your address book divide the first name and last name into two fields or does it combine that data into one field?

6. Try entering the data for the Name field in all uppercase. When you move to the next field, does the database maintain the uppercase format? Go back and modify the field using an initial capital letter.

7. Try entering an e-mail address that does not contain an @ sign. Does the database accept e-mail addresses that are not valid?

8. Try entering invalid data in other fields. What happens if you enter an invalid state abbreviation, like XX?

9. It is not necessary to save the address you've entered. Close the address book. As you read Chapter 11, you'll discover the significance of field normalization, case sensitivity, and validity checks.

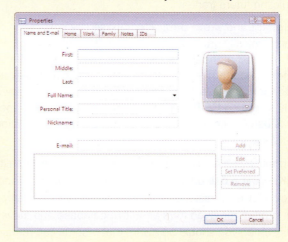

WEB SITE

Visit the NP11 Web site to access additional resources **w** that accompany this chapter.

File and Database Concepts

DATABASES ARE AN ESSENTIAL aspect of modern life. Most businesses could not function without them and they are the backbone of popular Internet services such as iTunes, MySpace, and eBay. Section A begins the chapter with an overview of databases and the many ways they are used today. Throughout the chapter, many of the examples focus on Vintage Music Shop, a fictitious Web-based music store that specializes in LP vinyl record albums. Vintage Music Shop's information system stores data about album prices, monitors inventory levels, maintains customer data, and reports which albums are top sellers. It also keeps track of customer orders, prints shipping labels, and produces quarterly sales reports. The characteristics of Vintage Music Shop's database are typical of many databases you encounter on and off the Web.

DATABASE BASICS

What is a database? In the broadest definition, a **database** is a collection of information. Today, databases are typically stored as computer files. A database can be a simple personal list, such as your address book, or it can be a massive list, such as New York City telephone numbers.

Databases can even incorporate several lists. For example, the database for an e-commerce site, such as Amazon.com, includes inventory lists and customer lists.

How is database information used? The tasks associated with creating, maintaining, and accessing the information in databases are referred to as data management, file management, or database management. Databases can be used in a variety of ways, from a simple tool for collecting and tracking data, to a comprehensive source for making decisions and predicting future trends.

● **Collect and store data.** A database is a collection of data, but that collection typically grows as additional data is obtained. Data can be collected and entered manually or electronically. For example, you manually add names to your address book. The Red Cross manually adds new names to its donor list as donations arrive. WalMart updates its inventory by electronically scanning RFID tags affixed to palettes of new merchandise. FedEx clerks use bar code readers to enter package information into the shipping database.

Information can also be removed from a database when it is no longer needed. Keeping a database lean can speed up searches and conserve storage space. However, historical data can be valuable, so rather than delete it, old data is often removed from an active database and moved to an archive. As a consumer, you should be aware that records can remain in databases and archives years after transactions have been completed, your name has been "removed," or your records are designated as "inactive." (See Figure 11-1.)

● **Update data.** One of the primary database management activities is keeping data up to date. As with collecting data, updates can be made manually or electronically. For example, your friend moves to a different

FIGURE 11-1

Database data that is no longer current is typically moved to an archive, which can be stored on a hard drive, secondary server, or tape. High-volume archives can be stored in a tape silo containing thousands of data tapes and a tape robot that pulls tapes off the shelves and loads them into a tape drive.

apartment, so you have to change her address in your address book. If an employee claims an additional deduction for a new baby, her employer has to update the payroll database. When a BestBuy customer purchases a digital camera, the store's point-of-sale system automatically decreases the quantity of that item in the inventory database.

Database updates are sometimes problematic. Data entry errors can result in database inaccuracies. When meter readers issue tickets for improperly parked vehicles, they write the tickets by hand. License plate numbers of ticketed vehicles are later entered into a database. If the data entry operator misreads or miskeys a license plate number, the database will contain inaccurate data and the wrong person could receive a "Failure to Pay" notice.

Data entry errors are not always easy to correct (Figure 11-2). Horror stories about data entry errors abound, including individuals—very much alive—whose records were mistakenly marked "deceased" and victims of identity theft who had trouble restoring their credit ratings. Organizations that maintain databases should be held accountable for data accuracy, especially when the data relates to individuals. Most countries, however, have only rudimentary regulations that offer consumers minimal recourse for mopping up after database snafus.

FIGURE 11-2

Data entry errors that pertain to confidential information are sometimes difficult to rectify until the correct data is validated and approved.

● **Organize and output data.** The data in a typical database is stored in no particular order. New data is appended to the end of the file because it is too cumbersome to insert it in, say, alphabetical order, then rearrange all the records that come after it. Reports created with this jumble of raw data would not be particularly useful. To make data into a more suitable report, it can be organized in a variety of ways. It can be alphabetized, placed in numeric order, grouped, and subtotaled.

Database output is easy to organize and reorganize without actually rearranging the physical data on the disk. A librarian can extract from a database the list of patrons with overdue books organized by date while at the same time a student can look for a list of books written by Elizabeth Peters. Businesses can save money on bulk mailings if envelopes are organized by zip code. It is most efficient to sort the database by zip code before printing the envelopes, rather than printing them in alphabetic order by customer and then later sorting by hand.

● **Distribute data.** Databases, combined with mailmerge and other computerized technologies, offer efficient ways to distribute information to customers, employees, the press, government agencies, and other companies. Your monthly electric bill is generated from the power company's database. That recall notice you received about the braking system in your 6-month old car, your monthly bank statement, your class schedule for next semester—all are generated from databases.

Unfortunately, databases also generate mountains of Publisher's Clearinghouse mailings and an irritating amount of v1agr*a spam that lands in your e-mail inbox. Today's digital databases are much more portable than old-fashioned paper-based databases, but the convenience of digital formats makes computer databases easier to misuse. Spammers, junk mailers, and telemarketers pay only a fraction of a penny for each name on a mailing list or call list. Millions of records can be easily copied, sent over the Internet, and stored on a single data DVD. The legal system has yet to iron out details regarding database ownership and under what conditions it is allowable to share database data.

● **Find data.** Databases make it easy to locate information. You can use an online library card catalog to find books. A pharmacist can check a pharmaceutical database for drug interactions before filling a prescription. A computer tech can check a manufacturer's database to find the part number for replacing your computer's fried hard drive.

In the Software chapter, you learned about several ways to locate data in a database. A query language, such as SQL, offers a set of commands to help you formulate searches such as *Select from MusicCollection where Artist = 'Elvis'* that finds all the songs performed by Elvis Presley in your mp3 music collection. Natural query languages allow you to search by asking questions such as "Show me a list of Elvis songs." You can also query by example using a fill-in form, like the one in Figure 11-3.

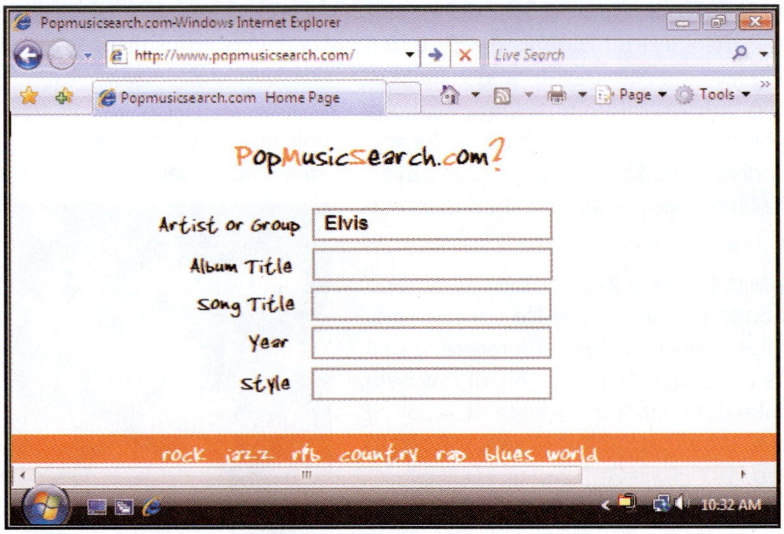

FIGURE 11-3

A query-by-example interface displays a form and formulates a query based on what the user enters.

- **Analyze data.** A database includes certain facts as raw data, such as names, addresses, bank balances, prices, and merchandise counts. Analyzing this data using statistics and other interpretive tools can produce information that is not readily apparent from simply looking at raw data. For example, a nationwide chain of bookstores issues discount cards and tracks the books purchased using each card. An analysis of sales data shows that customers who purchase self-help books typically purchase other similar books within six months. Nowhere in the database does it explicitly state "self-help book purchasers tend to buy additional self-help books." This conclusion is "new" information that can be gleaned from the raw data. Techniques for data analysis include data mining and OLAP.

What is data mining? **Data mining** refers to the process of analyzing existing information in databases to discover previously unknown, and potentially useful information, including relationships and patterns. The data accessed by data mining and other analysis techniques is often stored in a **data warehouse**, which is a repository for data from more than one database. Data from operational databases—those used for daily transactions—is transferred to a data warehouse where it can be combined with data from other databases to enhance the data set.

Data mining can reveal relationships. For example, an analysis of over 10 million policies and accident claims in the Farmers Insurance Group database revealed a relationship between age, marital status, second car ownership, sportscar ownership, and accident claims. Married baby boomers who owned a full size car or minivan in addition to a sportscar tended to make far fewer claims than younger, single sportscar owners. As a result of the data analysis, lower insurance rates were offered to sportscar owners who fit the low-risk profile.

A more complex type of data analysis can reveal sequences of events that predict future trends and patterns. **Predictive analytics** refers to a branch of data mining that focuses on predicting future probabilities and trends. It makes use of statistical algorithms, neural networks, and optimization research to discover patterns in data that predict the dynamics of customer behavior, market trends, and other critical business transactions.

Data mining and predictive analytics are sometimes criticized for finding relationships, patterns, and trends when none actually exist. You could, for example use data mining to look for trends in lottery numbers and locations. Data mining reveals that October's winning numbers always include more even numbers than odd ones, and were purchased at convenience stores. Unhappily, probability theory would tell you that the pattern is an anomaly and won't help you predict next week's winning numbers. The misuse of data mining is sometimes called data dredging or data fishing.

What is OLAP? One of today's most advanced data analysis methods, **OLAP** (online analytical processing), allows decision makers to look for relationships between multiple data dimensions. It is a technology used in the context of business intelligence and decision support systems which help decision makers by providing timely, accurate, and relevant information for business decisions.

To understand how OLAP works, imagine a sales history database for a nationwide chain of bookstores. A manager might use OLAP to look for trends in fiction, nonfiction, and reference book sales across three states and over a three-month time span. The analysis includes three dimensions—book type, store location, and month. OLAP might show that trends seem to originate in State A and spread to State C, then to State B. Based on this analysis, a decision maker could assume that book-buying trends in State A can be used to stock bookstores in the other states.

To analyze and mine complex data sets, decision makers sometimes use **executive dashboard software**, which provides tools for formulating OLAP queries and displaying results visually (Figure 11-4).

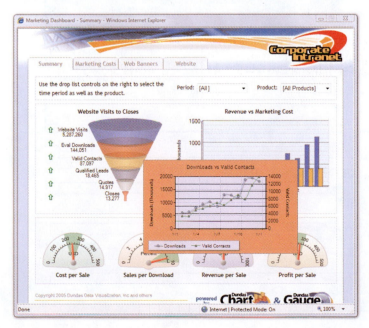

FIGURE 11-4

Executive dashboard software helps decision makers visualize data from complex data sets.

11

DATABASE MODELS

What is the underlying structure of a database? Computer databases evolved from manual filing systems. A filing cabinet full of folders and papers would be classified as an **unstructured file** or database because every document has a unique structure and contains different kinds of data. For example, some documents might be old receipts, others could be photos or product brochures, whereas other documents might be handwritten letters. The electronic equivalent to this jumble of information might be the collection of documents and graphics stored at a Web site. In contrast, library card catalogs and Rolodexes would be classified as structured files.

A **structured file** uses a uniform format to store data for each person or thing in the file. The focus of this chapter is on databases that are constructed with structured files because they comprise the majority of databases used in business, e-commerce, and government activities. Structured files can be used in different ways to build databases. The underlying structure of a database is referred to as a **database model**. Figure 11-5 lists basic database models.

Some of these models are becoming obsolete, whereas other models are just beginning to develop a track record. Understanding the characteristics of each model will help you determine which type of database is right for your needs, and understand why certain types of databases are popularly deployed for various business and organizational applications.

What's the simplest way to store data? The simplest model for storing data is a **flat file** that consists of a single, two-dimensional table of data elements. Each row in the table is a record, and each column of the table is a field. Computer databases typically display records as rows in a table or as forms as shown in Figure 11-6.

FIGURE 11-5

Database Models

- Flat file
- Hierarchical database
- Networked database
- Relational database
- Dimensional database
- Object database
- Object-relational database

FIGURE 11-6

Records can be displayed as rows in a table or as forms.

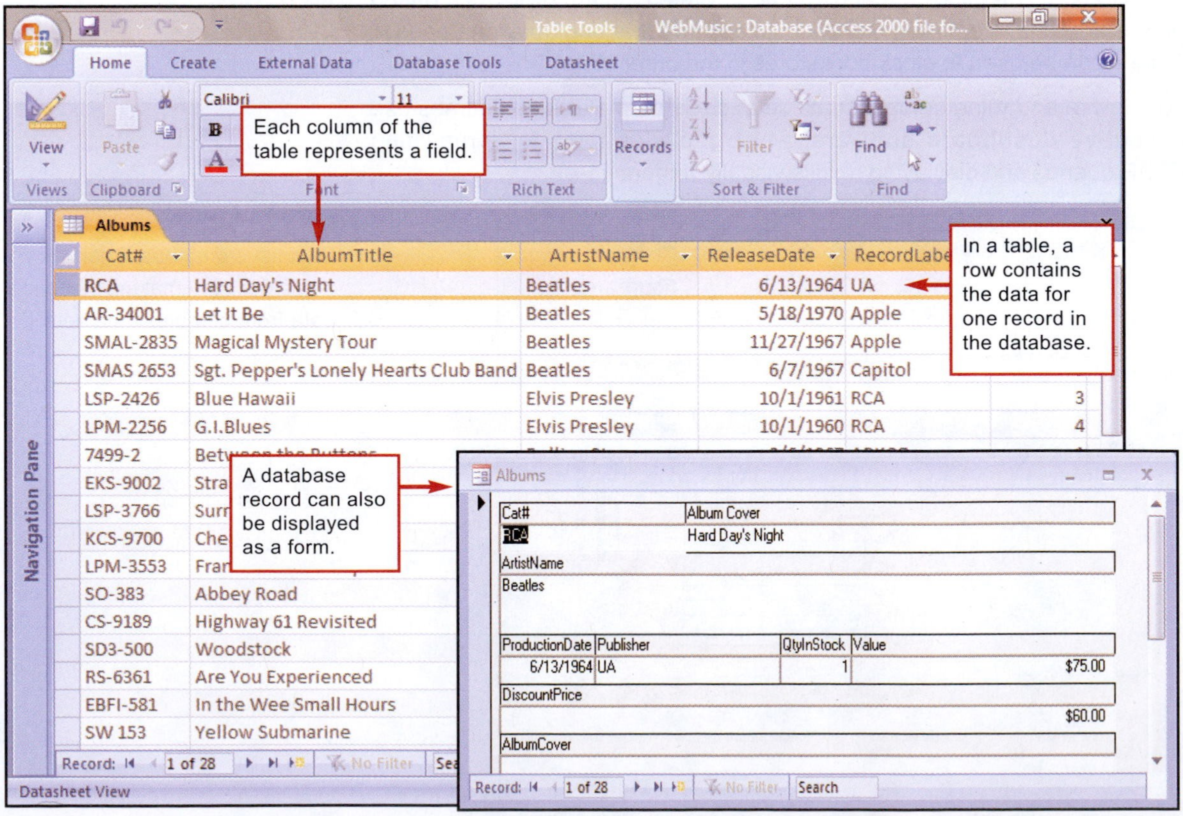

CLICK TO START

A **field** contains the smallest unit of meaningful information, so you might call it the basic building block for a structured file or database. Each field has a unique **field name** that describes its contents. For example, in an iTunes playlist, the field called Name would hold the name of a song, the Time field holds the song length, the Artist field holds the name of the performer, the Album field holds the name of the album that the song came from, and the Genre field holds the type of song.

A field can be variable length or fixed length. A **variable-length field** is like an accordion—it expands to fit the data you enter, up to some maximum number of characters. A **fixed-length field** contains a predetermined number of characters (bytes). The data you enter in a fixed-length field cannot exceed the allocated field length. Moreover, if the data you enter is shorter than the allocated length, blank spaces are automatically added to fill the field. The fields in Figure 11-7 are fixed length. The underscores indicate the number of characters allocated for each field.

Name:	**Can't Buy Me Love**_ _ _ _ _ _ _ _ _ _ _ _ _ _
Time:	**2:11** _
Artist:	**The Beatles** _
Album:	**A Hard Day's Night** _ _ _ _ _ _ _ _ _ _ _ _ _ _
Genre:	**Rock** _ _ _ _ _ _ _ _ _ _ _ _ _ _ _ _ _ _

Field name Field data

Dashes indicate length of fixed-length fields

FIGURE 11-7

When setting up a database, the length of text fields should be adequate to store the longest names or titles. The Time field can be shorter because the longest tracks are 60 minutes or less, which can be expressed in the format MM:SS, where MM is minutes and SS is seconds.

In the world of databases, a **record** refers to a collection of data fields. You're already familiar with several types of records, such as student records, medical records, and dental records. Each record stores data about one entity—a person, place, thing, or event. For example, a record in an iTunes playlist stores fields of data about a digital music track.

The template for a record is referred to as a **record type**. It contains field names, but no data. Creating record types is part of the design process that lets database designers specify the information needed to complete each record. A record type, similar to a blank form, is usually shown without any data in the fields. A record that contains data is referred to as a **record occurrence**, or simply a record (Figure 11-8).

FIGURE 11-8

A record type (left) is simply a list of fields, whereas a record occurrence (right) contains data for a particular entity. In this case, the entity is a track called "Can't Buy Me Love" on The Beatles' album *A Hard Day's Night*.

Record Type
Name
Time
Artist
Album
Genre

Record Occurrence	
Name	Can't Buy Me Love
Time	2:11
Artist	The Beatles
Album	A Hard Day's Night
Genre	Rock

11

The flat file model is the foundation for simple databases, such as an e-mail address book, an iTunes playlist, or the addresses for a mail merge. It is also the model used for spreadsheets. With a flat file, you can search for, update, group, and organize records. Each record in a flat file, however, is an independent entity and no relationships can be established between records. For example, you can't set up links between all The Beatles' songs in your iTunes playlist. If you are listening to A Hard Day's Night, you can't automatically link to The Beatles' next most popular top ten song.

Why would a database need to keep track of relationships? In database jargon, a **relationship** is an association between data that's stored in different record types. Relationships are important because there are important associations among the real-life things that database data represents. There are, for example, relationships between customers and the goods they purchase and between an album and the song tracks it contains. Although you can work with an iTunes playlist without establishing relationships, other databases, such as the one used at the Vintage Music Shop, are more efficient if relationships can be defined.

An important aspect of the relationship between record types is cardinality. **Cardinality** refers to the number of associations that can exist between two record types. For example, a Vintage Music Shop customer can place more than one order. The reverse is not true, however. A particular order cannot be placed jointly by two customers. When one record is related to many records, the relationship is referred to as a **one-to-many relationship**.

In contrast, a **many-to-many relationship** means that one record in a particular record type can be related to many records in another record type, and vice versa. For example, an album contains many songs. At the same time, a song could be included on several different albums. George Harrison's song "Something" was included in The Beatles' *Abbey Road* album and the best hits release, *The Beatles 1*.

A **one-to-one relationship** means that a record in one record type is related to only one record in another record type. This kind of relationship is rare in the world of databases. It is sometimes used to conserve disk space when an item of information will not be stored for every record in the database.

For example, the marketing director at Vintage Music Shop sometimes wants to include a description of an album in the database, but only for historically notable albums. If a Description field is included in the Albums record type, it will be empty for most records. Empty fields take up space on the disk, so it's not desirable to have fields that will most likely be blank. Creating another record type, called Album Description, allows this data to be stored efficiently. Only historically significant albums would have a corresponding Album Description record. The Album record and its corresponding description would have a one-to-one relationship.

The relationship between record types can be depicted graphically with an **entity-relationship diagram** (sometimes called an ER diagram or ERD). Figure 11-9 shows ERDs for one-to-many, many-to-many, and one-to-one relationships.

FIGURE 11-9

An entity-relationship diagram depicts each record type as a rectangle. Relationships and cardinality are shown by connecting lines.

One-to-many relationship
One customer can order many albums.

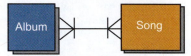

Many-to-many relationship
One album contains many songs, and a song can be included on several different albums.

One-to-one relationship
An album has only one description.

KEY TO ERD SYMBOLS

The crossbar indicates exactly one occurrence.

The crossbar and crow's foot indicate one or more occurrences.

What kind of databases track relationships? Except for flat files, other database models allow you to track relationships. The way database models work with relationships is a key to their differences. A **hierarchical database** allows one-to-one and one-to-many relationships, linked in a hierarchical structure. A **network database** uses a mesh-like structure to offer the additional capacity to define many-to-many relationships. Compare the structures of these two database models in Figures 11-10 and 11-11.

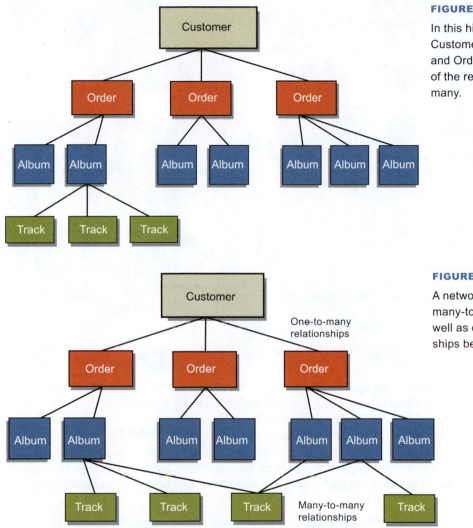

FIGURE 11-10

In this hierarchical database, Customers, Albums, Tracks, and Orders are record types. All of the relationships are one-to-many.

FIGURE 11-11

A network database allows many-to-many relationships as well as one-to-many relationships between record types.

Although hierarchical and network databases offer lightning quick searches and utilize a minimum amount of disk space for storage, they are rarely used today for business, consumer, and other mainstream database applications. Instead, they remain in use only for specialized applications. For example, Windows uses a hierarchical database to store Registry data that keeps track of the software and hardware configuration of your PC. The DNS system that keeps track of Internet addresses uses a network database structure. Outside of such specialized applications, databases built on hierarchical and network models have been replaced by relational or object databases.

11

What's a relational database? A **relational database** stores data in a collection of related tables. Each **table** is a sequence of records, similar to a flat file. All the records in a table are of the same record type. Each row of a table is equivalent to a record. Each column of the table is equivalent to a field. A relational database typically contains several tables. For example, the Vintage Music Shop's database uses six tables to store data, as shown in Figure 11-12.

FIGURE 11-12

Vintage Music Shop stores data in six tables.

ALBUM DESCRIPTION

Cat#	Description

TRACKS

Cat#	TrackTitle	Track Length	TrackSample

ORDER DETAILS

OrderNumber:	Cat#	QTY	DiscountPrice

ORDERS

OrderNumber:	CustomerNumber:	TotalPrice:	OrderDate:

CUSTOMERS

CustomerNumber	FirstName:	LastName:	Street:	City:

ALBUMS

Cat#	AlbumTitle	ArtistName	Release Date	In Stock	Value
LPM-2256	G.I. Blues	Elvis Presley	10/1/1960	4	20.00
7499-2	Between the Buttons	Rolling Stones	2/6/1967	1	13.99
LSP-246	Blue Hawaii	Elvis Presley	10/1/1961	5	50.00
N16014	Surfin Safari	Beach Boys	10/29/1963	8	18.95

In a relational database, relationships are specified by joining common data stored in the fields of records in different tables. For example, most albums contain many tracks, an example of a one-to-many relationship. The Vintage Music database stores general information about an album in one table and information about individual tracks in another table. Both tables have a Cat# field containing album numbers and that field can be used to establish a relationship between the two tables, as shown in Figure 11-13.

FIGURE 11-13

In a relational database, two tables can be joined by similar fields—in this example, by Cat#.

ALBUMS

Cat#	AlbumTitle	ArtistName	Release Date	In Stock	Value
LPM-2256	G.I. Blues	Elvis Presley	10/1/1960	4	20.00
7499-2	Between the Buttons	Rolling Stones	2/6/1967	1	13.99
LSP-246	Blue Hawaii				
N16014	Surfin Safari				

The Cat# LPM-2256 links records in both tables that refer to Elvis Presley's album *G.I. Blues*.

TRACKS

Cat#	TrackTitle	Track Length	TrackSample
LPM-2256	Blue Suede Shoes	104	BlueSuede.mp3
LPM-2256	Frankfort Special	132	FrankSpec.mp3
LPM-2256	Wooden Heart	163	WoodenHE.mp3
7499-2	Ruby Tuesday	197	RubyT.mp3

The way a relational database establishes relationships allows the tables to be essentially independent, but the tables can be joined for a particular task as required. Relationships can be added, changed, or deleted on demand, making this database model very flexible. The relational database model's flexibility is a major factor in its use for the majority of databases that handle the everyday query and reporting needs of businesses, government agencies, and organizations. It is also the database model supported by many consumer-level database products, such as Microsoft Access.

What's a dimensional database? A **dimensional database**, sometimes referred to as a multidimensional database, organizes relationships over three or more dimensions. Each field is contained within a cell that can be accessed directly from a query or from following a relationship. Dimensional databases are an extension of the relational database model in which tables are stacked in addition to being linked side by side. One way to visualize the dimensional database model is as a three-dimensional cube (Figure 11-14).

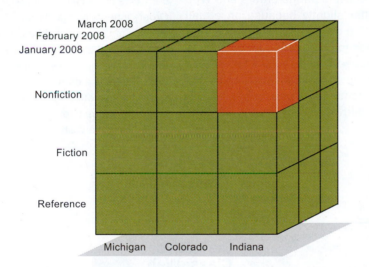

Compared to a relational database with complex queries based on relationships and joins, a dimensional database offers a simpler way to visualize data and formulate queries. Dimensional databases are easy to maintain and efficient to use because data is stored in the same way as it is viewed. However, formulating and populating a dimensional database requires more expertise than a relational database. Consequently, dimensional databases are most often deployed for data analysis and decision support systems in which data from operational databases is moved into a dimensional data warehouse before being queried by managers.

11

What's an object database? An **object database**, also referred to as an object-oriented database, stores data as objects, which can be grouped into classes and defined by attributes and methods. The Programming chapter covers object-oriented terminology in detail, but in the context of object databases, a class defines a group of objects by specifying the attributes and methods these objects share.

The attributes for an object are equivalent to fields in a relational database. A method is any behavior that an object is capable of performing. For example, the Vintage Music Shop has to keep track of objects that represent customer orders. To set up an object database for this task, the first step would be to define a class called Orders that can hold data such as the order number, order date, customer number, and the albums ordered. A method called Check Inventory can be defined for this class. Its job is to make sure the album is in stock.

Object databases excel in representing objects that have slightly different attributes, which is the case in many real-world business applications. Suppose that the Vintage Music Shop accepts phone orders and Web orders. These two types of orders differ slightly because an e-mail address is used to communicate with Web customers, whereas a telephone number and order clerk name need to be recorded for customers who order by phone. A relational database would require two record types, but an object database can be set up so that the Orders class has two derivative classes, one for Web customers and one for phone customers. Figure 11-15 illustrates classes, derivative classes, and methods in an object database.

FIGURE 11-15

An object database can easily store data about different types of orders. A class called Orders holds data and methods common to all types of orders. A derivative class called Phone Orders inherits all the characteristics of Orders, but it has attributes and methods unique to orders placed by telephone. Web Orders is a derivative class that has attributes and methods unique to orders placed over the Web.

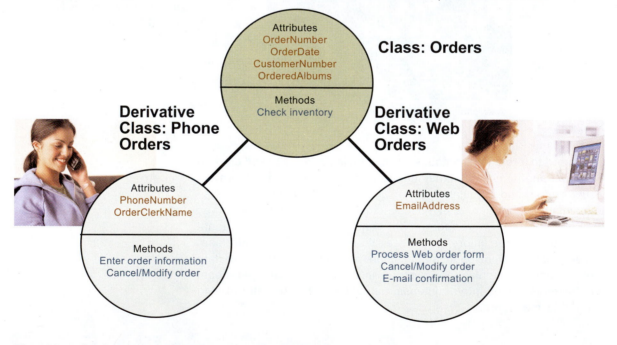

The object database model is newer than the relational model and has not yet gained a substantial foothold in mainstream database applications. Its advocates, however, cite advantages over rival database models, including the idea that object databases best reflect real-world entities and relationships.

What's an object-relational database? The term **object-relational database** is used to describe a variety of technologies that combine object-oriented and relational concepts. The object-relational database model has been described as an attempt to "add OO-ness to tables." Basically, an object-relational database is organized as one or more tables, just as in a traditional relational database. Object-relational databases, however, have the flexibility to store unique types of data and program code necessary to access that data.

To understand the distinction between relational databases and object-relational databases, suppose you restructure your iTunes playlist as a table in a relational database containing fields for the song title, artist, time, and so on. The database does not actually contain the .m4p data for the song, but it probably contains the name of the computer file that holds the song. When you select a song to play, the database doesn't play it. Instead, the file name is passed to your iTunes jukebox, which plays the song.

In contrast, you could use an object-relational database to store the actual digital data for songs in a field called SongFile. Your database could also hold a routine called PlaySong. If you select the database record for Blue Suede Shoes, for example, the database uses its PlaySong routine to play the data stored in the SongFile field, so there is no need to use external music player software (Figure 11-16).

Most of today's relational database tools offer object-oriented features. For example the popular database query language SQL, which you'll learn about later in the chapter, can be used to define custom functions to process the data in a database. However, object-relational hybrids do not typically support a full set of object-oriented characteristics. The distinction is somewhat technical. Suffice it to say that database models are still evolving as the best elements are blended and optimized to meet the needs of today's complex database applications.

FIGURE 11-16

A relational database sends a file name to an external player (top), but an object-relational database can store the song data and the routine to play it.

Relational Database

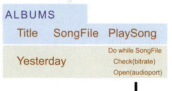

Object-relational Database

QuickCheck

1. Data _____ refers to the process of analyzing existing information in databases to discover previously unknown, and potentially useful information.

2. Online _____ processing allows decision makers to look for relationships between multiple data dimensions.

3. A database consists of one or more record _____ that contain data.

4. A(n) _____ file is a structured file containing only one record type.

5. In an ERD, relationships and _____ are shown by connecting lines.

6. A(n) _____ database is one that can link record types through shared fields on demand.

7. The _____ database model uses classes, derivative classes, and methods to reflect real-world relationships.

● CHECK ANSWERS

11

Data Management Tools

ONE OF THE FIRST decisions to make when creating a database is what type of data management tools to use. Different tools are designed for different uses. Simple tools that easily store address book information might not be suited for managing a worldwide airline reservation system. On the other hand, database software designed for huge corporations might be overkill for keeping track of your social calendar or storing customer data for a small business. Some tools provide ways to display information on the Web from a database, and some are designed only to print basic reports. How do you know which data management tools to use for a project? Section B describes the different types of tools available and explains how to decide which one best suits your needs.

DATA MANAGEMENT SOFTWARE

Are simple data management tools available? Yes. The simplest tools for managing data are software packages dedicated to a specific data management task, such as keeping track of appointments or managing your checking account. You can purchase these tools or download them from various Web sites. Some are available as shareware or open source software. Although these tools are easy to use, they don't generally allow you to create new record types because the record types are predefined. To use one of these tools, you simply enter your data. The software includes menus that allow you to manipulate your data after entering it.

How about a simple, generic tool that allows me to define a file structure? Most spreadsheet and word processing software packages feature simple tools that allow you to specify fields, enter data, and manipulate it. For example, your word processing software probably allows you to maintain data as a set of records, as shown in Figure 11-17.

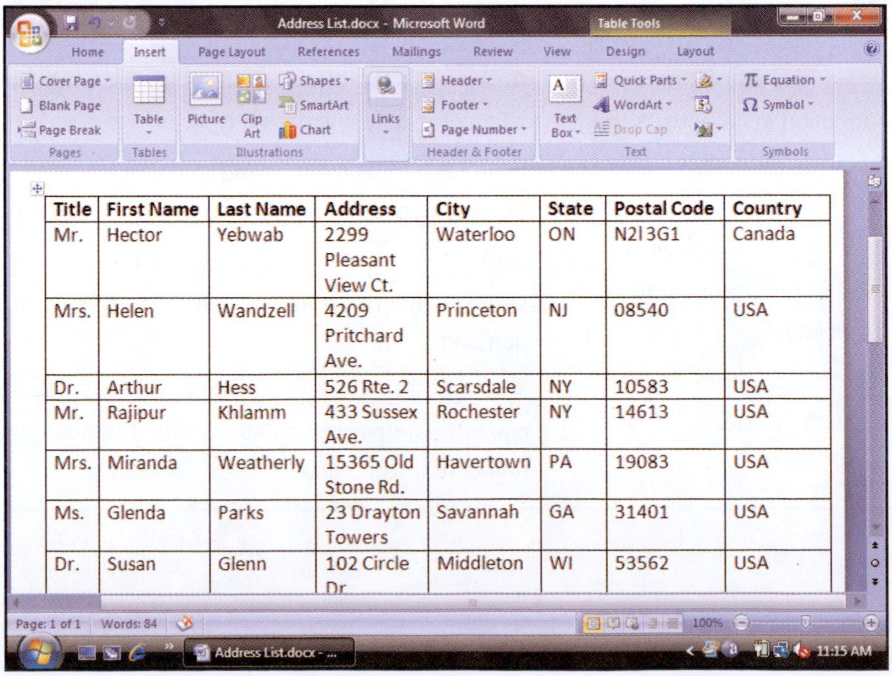

FIGURE 11-17

Microsoft Word allows you to create a table of information, such as a mailing list, which you can edit, sort, search, and print. In addition, you can merge data from the table with a template letter to create form letters, mailing labels, and envelopes.

► CLICK TO START

Some spreadsheet software also includes basic data management features. It's quite easy to create simple flat files using a spreadsheet. Depending on the spreadsheet software, it may be possible to sort records, validate data, search for records, perform simple statistical functions, and generate graphs based on the data. Figure 11-18 illustrates Microsoft Excel data management functions applied to a list of merchandise.

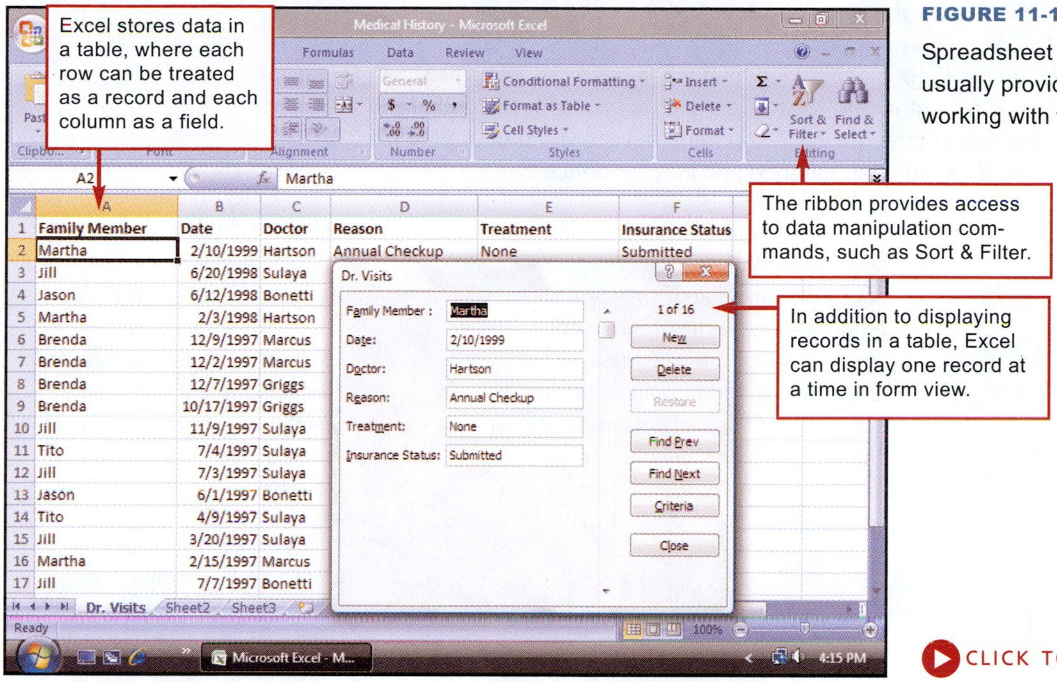

Excel stores data in a table, where each row can be treated as a record and each column as a field.

The ribbon provides access to data manipulation commands, such as Sort & Filter.

In addition to displaying records in a table, Excel can display one record at a time in form view.

FIGURE 11-18

Spreadsheet software usually provides tools for working with flat files.

▶ CLICK TO START

The simple file management tools provided by word processing and spreadsheet software are popular for individuals who want to maintain flat files that contain hundreds, not thousands, of records. These tools work well for a simple address book, an inventory of household goods, a record of health insurance costs, and a variety of other simple lists. They do not, however, offer database capabilities for establishing relationships between different record types, and they are not powerful enough to maintain the large volume of records required for business information systems.

Can I create my own data management software? It is possible to simply enter data as an ASCII text file, and then use a programming language to write routines to access that data. Custom software can be created to accommodate flat files and other database models.

Custom data management software has the advantage of being tailored to the exact needs of a business or an individual. This advantage is offset, however, by several disadvantages. Custom software requires skilled programmers. The development time for each module can be lengthy and costly. In addition, programmer efforts are sometimes redundant because similar modules are often required for different data files. For example, programmers who write a report routine for one data file might have to repeat their efforts a few weeks later for a different data file.

11

Poorly designed custom software can result in **data dependence**—a term that refers to data and program modules being so tightly interrelated that they become difficult to modify. Imagine a database in which programs and data all exist in one large file! It would be impossible to access the data while editing any of the programs. Furthermore, changing the file structure in any way might make the programs unusable.

Modern database software supports **data independence**, which means separating data from the programs that manipulate data. As a result, a single data management tool can be used to maintain many different files and databases. In addition, standard search, sort, and print routines continue to function, regardless of changes to field names or record structure. Figure 11-19 further explains data dependence and independence.

FIGURE 11-19

Data dependence is typically found in poorly written custom software when programmers tie the program code too tightly to specific field names, record structures, report formats, and calculations. If these aspects of the database change, programs cannot adapt and must be rewritten.

Data independence is a design concept based on the idea that databases are most flexible when programs that manipulate a database are not too tightly tied to the structure of fields, records, calculations, and reports.

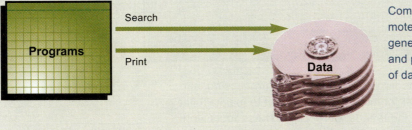

Commercial database software promotes data independence because a generic set of programs for searching and printing can be used on any set of data.

What's the best data management tool? The best tool depends on several factors. When selecting a data management tool, consider its cost, versatility, and ease of use (Figure 11-20).

FIGURE 11-20

Data Management Tools

Tool	Cost	Versatility	Ease of Use
Dedicated software, such as an address book	Inexpensive shareware available for simple applications; dedicated software for business applications can be costly	Typically dedicated to a single type of database	Easy; minimal setup required because fields are predefined
Word processing software	Most computers include word processing software	Best for simple flat files, such as mailing lists	Easy; uses an interface familiar to most users
Spreadsheet software	Most computers include spreadsheet software	Best for simple flat files that involve calculations	Easy; uses an interface familiar to most users
Custom software	Expensive development and programming time	Very versatile because programs can be tailored to any data	The programming can be difficult, but the final result may be easy to use
Database software	Basic shareware database software is inexpensive; high-end database software can be expensive	High-end packages provide excellent versatility	High-end database software often has a steep learning curve

DATABASE MANAGEMENT SYSTEMS

What kinds of tools are specifically designed for creating and manipulating databases? The term **DBMS** (database management system) refers to software that is designed to manage data stored in a database. Each DBMS typically specializes in one database model, but some DBMS software offers versatility by dealing with a variety of models and data.

An **XML DBMS**, for example, is optimized for handling data that exists in XML format. (You'll learn more about XML later in the chapter.) An **ODBMS** (object database management system) is optimized for the object database model, allowing you to store and manipulate data classes, attributes, and methods. An **RDBMS** (relational database management system) allows you to create, update, and administer a relational database. Most of today's popular RDBMS software also provides the capability to handle object classes and XML data, making it unnecessary to purchase a separate ODBMS or XML DBMS.

Which DBMS should I use for my projects? Today most database projects are implemented with a relational database management system. The particular RDBMS package you choose, however, depends on the scope of your project, the number of people who will simultaneously access the database, and the expected volume of records, queries, and updates.

Entry-level RDBMS software, such as Microsoft Access, is a good fit for small businesses and individuals whose data can't be efficiently handled as a flat file spreadsheet. An entry-level DBMS typically includes all the tools you need to manipulate data in a database, specify relationships, create data entry forms, query the database, and generate reports, as shown in Figure 11-21.

TERMINOLOGY NOTE

An ODBMS is also referred to as an OODBMS (object-oriented database management system).

INFOWEBLINKS

Get the latest scoop on relational, object, and XML database software at the **DBMS InfoWeb**.

 CLICK TO CONNECT
www.course.com/np/concepts11/ch11

FIGURE 11-21

An entry-level DBMS usually includes all the tools you need to manipulate data in a database.

Microsoft Access provides tools for working with tables and for creating queries, forms, reports, and Web pages.

Database table

Concert	Performer	Gross Sales	Promoter	Tickets Sold
1	Stone Temple Pilots	$246,375	1	10,950
2	Reba McEntire	$263,410	2	10,800
3	Van Halen	$243,865	4	10,975
4	Tori Amos	$196,580	3	10,473
5	BlackHawk/Teri Clark	$206,550	2	9,897
6	Blues Traveler	$199,475	3	9,759
7	Brooks & Dunn	$255,940	3	11,128
8	Sheryl Crow	$212,575	4	10,634
9	Smashing Pumpkins	$256,805	2	11,348
10	Alan Jackson	$231,800	3	10,536
11	Melissa Etheridge	$217,420	2	10,042
12	Nine Inch Nails	$213,590	1	10,621
13	Alanis Morisette	$219,350	4	10,973
14	John Mellencamp	$226,990	2	9,947
15	Tracy Chapman	$193,000	4	9,852
16	Vince Gill	$241,100	3	10,668

Record: 1 of 65   No Filter   Search

11

If an entry-level DBMS is located on a network, it is possible for multiple users to access the database at the same time. As shown in Figure 11-22, each workstation typically uses database client software to communicate with the DBMS. **Database client software** allows any remote computer or network workstation to access data in a database.

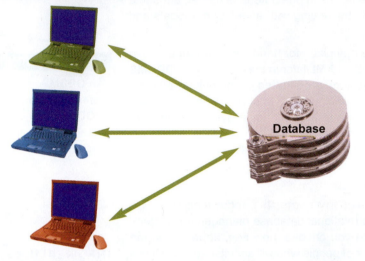

FIGURE 11-22

Multiple users can access a database using client software.

An entry-level DBMS that resides on a network server might be able to handle many simultaneous searches. However, these DBMSs are limited in their ability to deal with problems that arise when multiple users attempt to update the same record at the same time. This limited multiuser capability might be able to handle, for example, a civic center ticketing system operated by a box office clerk. It would not be sufficient, however, to handle the volume of simultaneous transactions for Ticketmaster's 6,500 retail ticket center outlets, 20 telephone call centers worldwide, and online Web site.

In situations with many users who make simultaneous updates, it is usually necessary to move to database server software, such as Oracle Database, IBM DB2 Universal Database, Microsoft SQL Server, or the open source favorite SQLite. **Database server software** is designed to manage billions of records and several hundred transactions every second. It provides optimum performance in client/server environments, such as LANs and the Internet. It can also handle a **distributed database**, in which a database is stored on several computers, on multiple networks, or in different geographical locations. As shown in Figure 11-23, database server software passes query requests from client software to the database and sends query results back to the client.

FIGURE 11-23

Database server software is optimized to provide fast access to multiple simultaneous users.

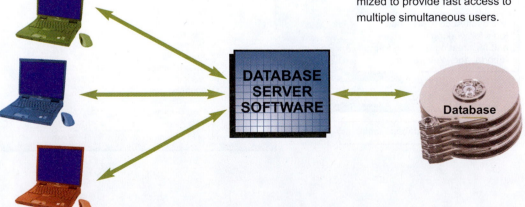

DATABASES AND THE WEB

Is it possible to access a database over the Web?
The Web allows access to many databases. When you shop at an online store, for example, the photos, descriptions, and prices you see are pulled from the merchant's database and displayed as Web pages. More direct database access is offered by online card catalogs, such as the U.S. Library of Congress. A database also provides the foundation for online access to course registration systems, yellow pages, real estate listings, movie reviews, flight schedules, and a host of other information.

The Web provides both opportunities and challenges for accessing the information in a database. Obviously, with its global reach, the Web provides an opportunity for many people to gain access to data from multiple locations. Web access is constrained, however, by the stateless nature of HTTP and the necessity to provide access by using a browser as client software. Providing access to databases over the Web requires some tricks. It does not, however, require special databases or special DBMSs.

What's the simplest way to provide Web access to a database?
A technique called **static Web publishing** is a simple way to display the data in a database by converting a database report into an HTML document, which can be displayed as a Web page by a browser. Static publishing provides extremely limited access to a database because it creates a Web page that essentially displays a snapshot of your data at the time the report was generated. Data on the Web page cannot be manipulated, except to be searched in a rudimentary way by the Find feature of your Web browser.

The advantages of static publishing include security and simplicity. Your data remains secure because you have not provided direct access to your database, so unauthorized users cannot change your data. Static publishing is simple because most entry-level DBMS software includes a menu option that allows you to easily produce an HTML page from a database report, as shown in Figure 11-24.

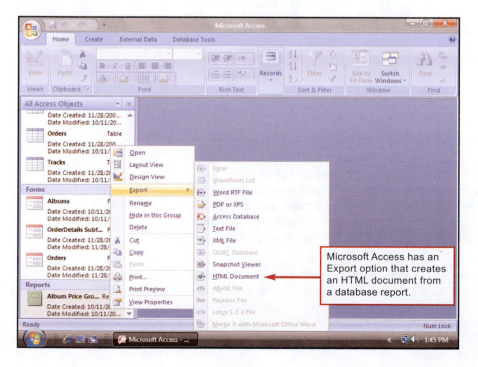

Microsoft Access has an Export option that creates an HTML document from a database report.

FIGURE 11-24

Many entry-level DBMSs include an easy way to turn a report into an HTML document that you can post as a Web page.

 CLICK TO START

What if I want to provide access to current data? Each time regular customers at Vintage Music Shop connect to the site, they see Web pages tailored to their music preferences. Country music fans, for example, see descriptions of Nashville classics and a list of discount albums by their favorite artists. Obviously, these pages cannot be the result of static publishing. They are created by a **dynamic Web publishing** process that generates customized Web pages as needed, or "on the fly."

Dynamic Web publishing relies on a program or script, referred to as a **server-side program**, that resides on a Web server and acts as an intermediary between your browser and a DBMS. In the Vintage Music Shop example, a server-side program reads a cookie from the customer's computer to find the unique number assigned to the customer. The server-side program then uses the customer number to generate a query, which is sent to the database server software. This software accesses the database to locate the customer's music preferences and favorite artists. The server-side program then asks the database server software to locate all the specials that apply to this customer's preferences. A list of applicable albums, descriptions, and prices is sent back to the Web server, where it is formulated as an HTML document and sent to the browser. The architecture for dynamic publishing requires a Web server in addition to database server software, a database, and a browser, as shown in Figure 11-25.

FIGURE 11-25

Dynamic Web publishing requires several components, including a browser, Web server, database server software, and database.

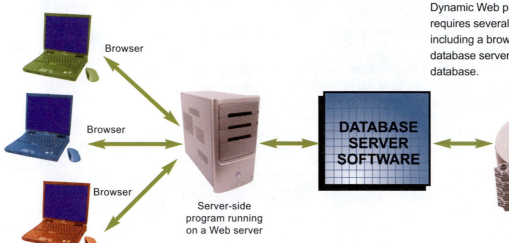

Browser

Browser

Browser

Server-side
program running
on a Web server

DATABASE
SERVER
SOFTWARE

Database

Is it possible to add and update database records over the Web? In several situations, such as e-commerce, it is important for people to use a browser to add or update records in a database. For example, the process of ordering merchandise at Vintage Music Shop creates a new order record, changes the InStock field in the Albums table, and creates a customer record for first-time customers. These dynamic database updates require an architecture similar to that used for dynamic Web publishing, plus the use of forms.

A form can collect data, such as customer name and address, or it can collect the specifications for a query, such as a search for Frank Sinatra albums. A completed form is sent from your browser to the Web server, which strips the data or query out of the document and sends it to the DBMS. Results are sent to the Web server, formatted into an HTML document, and sent back to your browser.

A form usually exists on a Web server, which sends the form to your browser. Most forms are created using the HTML <form> tag and <input> tag. Figure 11-26 illustrates an HTML document with <input> tags and shows the Web page form it produces.

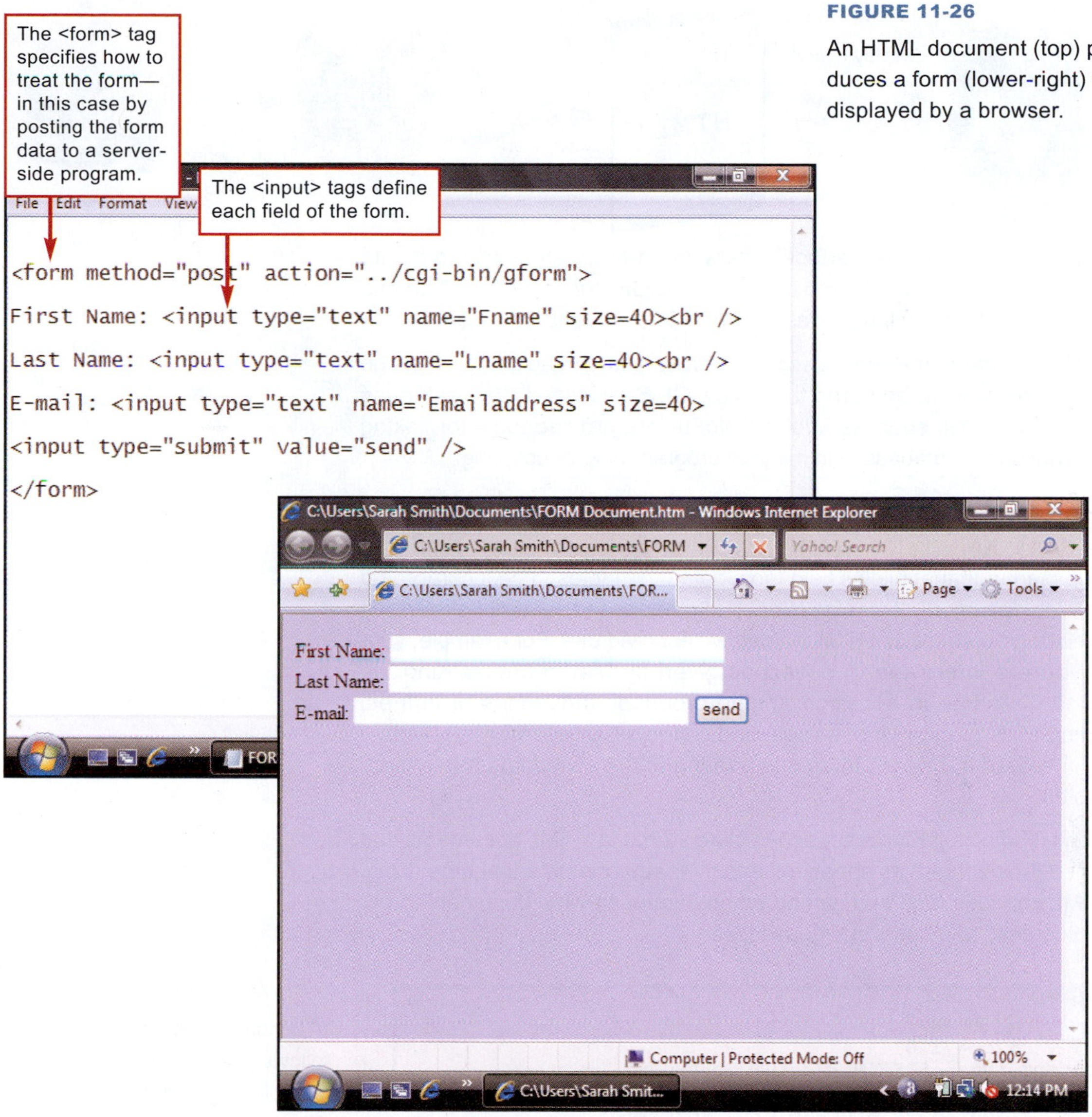

FIGURE 11-26

An HTML document (top) produces a form (lower-right) when displayed by a browser.

The <form> tag specifies how to treat the form—in this case by posting the form data to a server-side program.

The <input> tags define each field of the form.

```
<form method="post" action="../cgi-bin/gform">

First Name: <input type="text" name="Fname" size=40><br />

Last Name: <input type="text" name="Lname" size=40><br />

E-mail: <input type="text" name="Emailaddress" size=40>

<input type="submit" value="send" />

</form>
```

A technology called **XForms** provides an alternative to HTML forms. XForms offer more flexibility than HTML forms, and they interface with XML documents. XForms are designed as the successor to HTML forms for interactive exchange of data over the Web, such as e-commerce payment information. Use of XForms requires an XForms-enabled browser or a plug-in that adds XForms capability.

How do I create server-side programs? Several tools, including ASP, CGI, and PHP, help you create server-side programs. ASP (Active Server Pages) technology can be used to generate an HTML document that contains scripts, which are run before the document is displayed as a Web page. These scripts are small embedded programs that can be designed to get user input, run queries, and display query results.

11

ASP technology, developed by Microsoft, originally worked only on Windows-based Web servers. A plug-in is now available for UNIX servers. Figure 11-27 illustrates how an ASP script displays database information that has been requested by a remote user.

FIGURE 11-27

An ASP script can collect user input, run queries, and display query results.

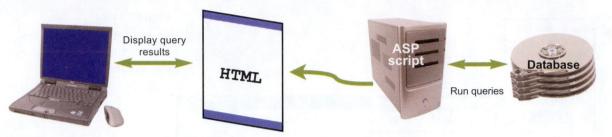

Display query results

HTML

ASP script

Database

Run queries

CGI (Common Gateway Interface) offers a non-proprietary way to create HTML pages based on data in a database. A CGI script can be written in a variety of programming languages, such as C, C++, Java, and Perl.

PHP (PHP: Hypertext Preprocessor) is a cross-platform scripting language that can accomplish the same tasks as CGI. Specialized Web database development tools, such as Adobe ColdFusion, provide tools for linking HTML pages to a database with minimal programming or scripting.

XML

How does XML relate to the Web and databases? XML is a markup language that allows field tags, data, and tables to be incorporated into a Web document. It was developed in response to several deficiencies that became apparent as HTML gained widespread use. For example, suppose you are interested in speeches given by Martin Luther King, Jr. Entering his name in a search engine produces thousands of entries, including MLK biographies, streets and schools named after the famous civil rights leader, historic locations relating to the civil rights movement, and so on.

Wouldn't it be nice if King's speeches were stored in HTML documents that identified their content as speeches and their author as Martin Luther King, Jr.? XML provides tags that can be embedded in an XML document to put data in context, as shown in Figure 11-28.

FIGURE 11-28

A document with XML tags allows you to make a targeted search for author = Martin Luther King, Jr. and document_type = SPEECH.

```
mlk2.htm - Notepad
File  Edit  Format  View  Help
<?xml version="1.0"?>
<document_type> SPEECH </document_type>

<speechtitle>I Have a Dream </speechtitle>

<author>Martin Luther King, Jr.</author>

<place>Delivered on the steps at the Lincoln Memorial
in Washington D.C. </place>
<date> August 28, 1963 </date>

<speechtext>Five score years ago, a great American, in
whose symbolic shadow we stand signed the Emancipation
Proclamation. This momentous decree came as a great
beacon light of hope to millions of Negro slaves who
had been seared in the flames of withering injustice.
It came as a joyous daybreak to end the long night of
captivity.

But one hundred years later, we must face the tragic
```

mlk2.htm - Notepad   6:34 AM

How is XML typically used today? One of XML's most positive contributions to data management is the potential to add context to the information contained in a widely diverse pool of documents on the Web. Although it is easy to see how XML tags might make the free-form documents currently on the Web much easier to manage, today XML is more often used for structured data.

XML can be used to specify a standard structure of fields and records, such as SportsML and Chemical Markup Language, for storing data that can be accessed from a browser. Using this standard structure, data entered into an XML document can be identified by field names. Figure 11-29 provides an example of an XML document that contains data similar to that in Vintage Music Shop's Albums table.

FIGURE 11-29

This XML document contains data that looks similar to the fields and records from a table of a relational database.

Can I search the data in an XML document? Yes. Access to XML data is provided by XML query engines, such as XPath and XQuery. Direct access to structured data like that shown in Figure 11-29 above, however, requires knowledge of its location, access rights, and a list of field names. Therefore, like many relational databases, access to structured data in XML documents is typically provided by some type of client software designed specifically to accept queries, access the data, and return results. XML clients can be offered as browser plug-ins.

What are the pros and cons of XML for storing data? Storing data in an XML document offers several advantages. It exists as a document in human-readable format. It is also portable so that it can be easily accessed from virtually any computer platform—PCs, Macs, Linux computers, mainframes, and even handhelds. All that's required on the platform is an XML-enabled browser, such as Internet Explorer or Firefox.

XML documents are not, however, optimized for many operations you would customarily associate with databases, such as fast sorts, searches, and updates.

11

To get the best out of XML and relational databases, some experts recommend storing data in a relational database, managing it with RDBMS software, and using server-side software to generate XML documents for exchanging data over the Web. Some RDBMSs include features that allow a database server to receive queries in the form of XML commands. After receiving a query, the database compiles the results and uses XML to format the data into a Web page, as shown in Figure 11-30.

FIGURE 11-30

Manipulating XML data with an RDBMS.

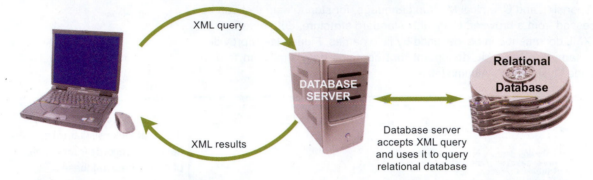

XML query

DATABASE SERVER

Relational Database

XML results

Database server accepts XML query and uses it to query relational database

As you can see, many techniques exist for storing, accessing, and displaying the data from databases. Individuals can use simple tools to create personal databases, such as address books. Corporate database managers, however, need to be familiar with more complex tools used to distribute data over networks and the Web. Sometimes more than one tool has the potential to work for a specific application. Now that you've had an introduction to the options, you should be able to evaluate when and how to use them.

QuickCheck

1. A custom database can be stored as a simple _____ file and can be accessed by routines written in a standard programming language. (Hint: Use the acronym.)

2. Spreadsheet software typically includes some data management features suitable for working with relational databases. True or false? _____

3. Modern database software supports data _____, which means keeping data separated from the program modules that manipulate the data.

4. _____ Web publishing uses the data in a database to generate customized Web pages as needed.

5. ASP, CGI, and PHP are used to create XML documents that are processed on a server before being sent to your browser. True or false? _____

 CHECK ANSWERS

Database Design

THE KEY to an effective database is its initial design. In a well-designed database, data can be flexibly manipulated to produce timely, meaningful, and accurate information for decision making. Bad database design can lead to messy databases, lost records, and inaccurate data. The goal of good database design is to store information so that it is easy to access and maintain, but concise enough to take up as little disk space as possible. Section C looks at databases from the perspective of the database designer and describes how to create an efficient structure for a relational database. You can apply many of these design principles when you create your own databases.

DEFINING FIELDS

How does a database designer know what data to store? The term **database structure** refers to the arrangement of fields, tables, and relationships in a database. The first step in structuring a relational database is to determine what data must be collected and stored. To do so, a database designer might begin by consulting users and studying the current filing system to compile a list of available data as well as any additional data necessary to produce on-screen output or printed reports.

If you are designing the database structure for Vintage Music Shop, for example, you would probably recognize that data such as the album title, artist name, release date, catalog number, record label, quantity in stock, value, discount price, and album cover photo should be collected and stored.

After the database designer determines what data to store, the next step is to organize that data into fields. It is usually easy to break data into fields just by using common sense and considering how people might want to access the data. Any data that people would want to search for, sort on, or use in a calculation should be in its own field.

Why are last names stored in a different field than first names? The treatment of first and last names illustrates the concept of breaking data into fields. A database designer could define a field called Name to hold an entire customer's name, such as Gilbert B. Grape. With the entire name in one field, however, the database would not be able to easily access individual parts of the name, making it difficult to alphabetize customers by last name or to produce a report in which names appear in a format such as Grape, Gilbert B. (Figure 11-31).

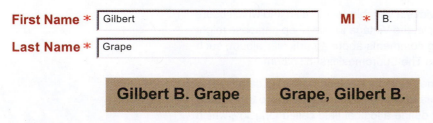

FIGURE 11-31

When a field contains an entire name, it is difficult to individually manipulate the first name, last name, and middle initial. A more flexible design provides separate fields for each part of the name.

What makes each record unique? Although two people might have the same name or two paychecks might contain the same amount, a computer must have some way to differentiate between records. A **primary key** is a field that contains data unique to a record. Designers commonly designate fields such as SocialSecurityNumber and PartNumber as primary keys.

How does a database designer know what data types to use? The data that can be entered into a field depends on the field's data type. From a technical perspective, a **data type** specifies the way data is represented on the disk and in RAM. From a user perspective, the data type determines the way data can be manipulated. When designing a database, each field is assigned a data type.

Data can be broadly classified as numeric or character. As you learned in earlier chapters, character data contains letters, numerals, and symbols not used for calculations. Numeric data contains numbers that can be manipulated mathematically by adding, averaging, multiplying, and so forth. As an example, the Price field in Figure 11-32 contains numeric data, which can be added to the prices for other albums to calculate a total price when a customer buys more than one album.

FIGURE 11-32

Numeric data can be used for calculations.

Price | $70.00 |

```
INVOICE
Qty  Album Title      Price

1    That's All       $70.00
1    Surfin Safari    $10.00
1    Blue Hawaii      $18.00

     Total            $98.00
```

There are several numeric data types, including real, integer, and date. Database designers assign the **real data type** to fields that contain numbers with decimal places—prices, percentages, and so on. The **integer data type** is used for fields that contain whole numbers—quantities, repetitions, rankings, and so on. Database designers typically use the integer data type unless the data requires decimal places because real numbers require more storage space. As you might expect, the **date data type** is used to store dates in a format that allows them to be manipulated, such as when you want to calculate the number of days between two dates.

The **text data type** is typically assigned to fixed-length fields that hold character data—people's names, album titles, and so on. Text fields sometimes hold data that looks like numbers, but doesn't need to be mathematically manipulated. Telephone numbers and ZIP codes are examples of data that looks numeric, but is stored in text fields because database users would never want to add two telephone numbers together or find the average of a group of ZIP codes. As a general rule, information such as telephone numbers, ZIP codes, Social Security numbers, and item numbers should be stored in text fields.

A **memo data type** usually provides a variable-length field into which users can enter comments. For example, the Vintage Music Shop database might contain a memo field for storing comments about a particular album, such as "Where Did Our Love Go was The Supremes' first hit album."

The **logical data type** (sometimes called a Boolean or yes/no data type) is used for true/false or yes/no data using minimal storage space. For example, a database designer might define a logical field called OrigCov, which would contain a Y if an album includes the original dust cover.

Some file and database management systems also include additional data types, such as BLOBs and hyperlinks. A **BLOB** (binary large object) is a collection of binary data stored in a single field of a database. BLOBs can be just about any kind of data you would typically store as a file, such as an MP3 music track. For example, the Vintage Music Shop database stores a short sample of each song on an album in a BLOB field called TrackSample.

The **hyperlink data type** stores URLs used to link directly from a database to a Web page. For example, data stored in a hyperlink field of the Vintage Music Shop database could provide a link to a musician's Web site. Figure 11-33 summarizes the most commonly used data types in today's databases.

INFOWEBLINKS

BLOBs are a relatively new data type. Learn more about them at the **BLOB InfoWeb**.

Ⓦ CLICK TO CONNECT
www.course.com/np/concepts11/ch11

FIGURE 11-33

Commonly Used Data Types

Data Type	Description	Sample Field	Sample Data
Real	Numbers that include decimal places	DiscountPrice	9.99
Integer	Whole numbers	QTY	5
Date	Month, day, and year	OrderDate	9/30/2005
Text	Letters or numerals not used for calculations	Name ZipCode	Gilbert 49866
Logical	Data that can have one of two values	InStock	Y
Memo	Variable length comment field	Condition	Some wear on album cover
BLOB	Binary data	SampleTrack	[An MP3 file]
Hyperlink	URLs	MusicianWebSite	www.bobdylan.com

How does a database handle computations? When a customer looks for an album at Vintage Music Shop's Web site, three pieces of pricing information are provided. The first is the value. The second is the discounted price that Vintage Music Shop offers. The third is the amount of money a customer will save by purchasing the album through Vintage Music Shop. The Albums record type, however, contains only two pieces of pricing information—Value and DiscountPrice. The third piece of information—the amount of money a customer saves by purchasing through Vintage Music Shop—is a computed field.

A **computed field** is a calculation that a DBMS performs during processing, and then temporarily stores in a memory location. An efficiently designed database uses computed fields whenever possible because they do not require disk storage space. Figure 11-34 illustrates how a computed field produces the amount saved with purchases at Vintage Music Shop's discount price.

TERMINOLOGY NOTE

A computed field works somewhat like a function in a spreadsheet; you set up a formula for the calculation, which is applied to compute the data.

FIGURE 11-34

Creating a Computed Field

Value	$47.00
DiscountPrice	$45.00

The database includes a field containing the value and another field containing the discount price.

RAM

Amount Saved

$2.00

The amount in one field can be subtracted from the amount in the other field. The result is temporarily stored in a "field" in RAM and can appear on a screen or report.

Can a database designer prevent people from entering inaccurate data? There's an old saying in the computer industry: "garbage in, garbage out." This adage is especially true when dealing with databases. The information produced by reports and processing routines is only as accurate as the information in the database. Unfortunately, data entry errors can compromise the accuracy and validity of a database. When designing a database, it is important to think ahead and envision potential data entry errors. Most DBMSs provide tools that database designers can use to prevent some, but not all, data entry errors.

People who enter data into a database sometimes have difficulty deciding whether to use uppercase or lowercase characters. In a **case sensitive database**, uppercase letters are not equivalent to their lowercase counterparts. For example, in a case sensitive database, the artist name *Elvis* is not equivalent to *elvis*. Inconsistent use of case can lead to several problems. A search for *elvis* will not produce records for *Elvis* or *ELVIS*. Furthermore, in a sorted or indexed list, *elvis* and *ELVIS* might not be grouped together.

Most, but not all, DBMSs give database designers an option to turn case sensitivity on or off. They might also have the option to force data to all uppercase or all lowercase as it is entered. Neither technique is an infallible solution to case sensitivity, but as you gain experience designing databases, you'll become familiar with the advantages and disadvantages of each technique.

People who enter data might not be consistent about the way they enter numbers. For example, a data entry operator might enter a telephone number as 555-555-7777, (555) 555-7777, or 1-555-555-7777. If multiple data entry operators enter telephone numbers in different formats, it becomes difficult to produce nicely formatted reports or locate a particular telephone number. To prevent this sort of inconsistent formatting, a database designer can specify a field format. A **field format** is a picture of what the data is supposed to look like when it's entered. If someone attempts to enter data in the wrong format, the database rejects that entry. A telephone number field might use a field format such as the one shown in Figure 11-35.

FIGURE 11-35

A field format helps maintain consistent data by providing a structure for entering data into a field.

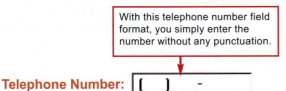

With this telephone number field format, you simply enter the number without any punctuation.

Telephone Number: [ ] -

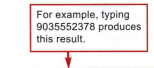

For example, typing 9035552378 produces this result.

Telephone Number: (903) 555-2378

Sometimes people who enter data simply make a mistake and press the wrong keys. Preventing every typographical error is not possible. However, it is possible to catch some of these errors by using field validation rules, list boxes, or lookups.

A **field validation rule** is a specification that the database designer sets up to filter data entered into a particular field. For example, the price of albums in the Vintage Music Shop database ranges from $0 (for promotions) to $800. No albums have a value greater than $1000. When intending to enter $19.98 in the value field, however, the omission of a decimal point could set the price of an album to $1998.00! When designing the Vintage Music Shop database, a database designer can use a field validation rule to limit entries in the Value field to less than $1000. If the DBMS receives a number such as 1998 in the value field, it displays a message requesting the correct price.

Another technique that prevents typographical and case-sensitivity errors is to limit data entry to the items on a specified list. For example, the state abbreviation for Michigan might be entered as MI, Mi, Mich, or NI if your fingers slipped. However, most databases allow the database designer to specify a list of acceptable entries for each field. Most people are familiar with clickable lists of states, such as the one in Figure 11-36.

Database designers can also prevent entry errors by using lookup routines. A **lookup routine** validates an entry by searching for the same data in a file or database table. For example, suppose that a Vintage Music Shop employee is entering new albums. It is important that each album has a unique catalog number. When data is entered in the Cat# field, the database can use a lookup routine to search every existing record to make sure the new catalog number does not duplicate an existing catalog number.

NORMALIZATION

How does a database designer group fields into tables? A process called **normalization** helps database designers create a database structure that can save storage space and increase processing efficiency. The goal of normalization is to minimize **data redundancy**—the amount of data that is repeated or duplicated in a database. To normalize a database, one of the designer's main tasks is to decide how best to group fields into tables.

The first step to grouping fields is to get an idea of the big picture of the data. Often, groupings correspond to the physical items, or entities, that are tracked in the database. For example, Vintage Music Shop data is grouped into several tables: Albums, Tracks, Customers, Orders, and Order Details. Some of these groupings seem obvious, but other groupings might seem a bit puzzling. You might wonder why it is necessary to use three tables—Customers, Orders, and Order Details—to store data about an order. Why won't one table suffice? To answer this question, first take a look at the data relevant to each order in Figure 11-37.

FIGURE 11-36

Clickable lists are an easy way for users to enter data in a standard format.

FIGURE 11-37

A typical Vintage Music Shop order contains customer data and data about the merchandise being ordered.

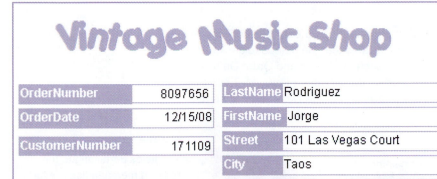

11

If customer information and order information are grouped in the same table, each time Jorge Rodriguez places an order, his name, shipping address, billing address, telephone number, and e-mail address must be entered and stored. This data redundancy not only requires extra storage space, but also could lead to storing inconsistent or inaccurate data. The solution is to create separate tables for Orders and Customers, which can be related by including a CustomerNumber field in both tables, as shown in Figure 11-38.

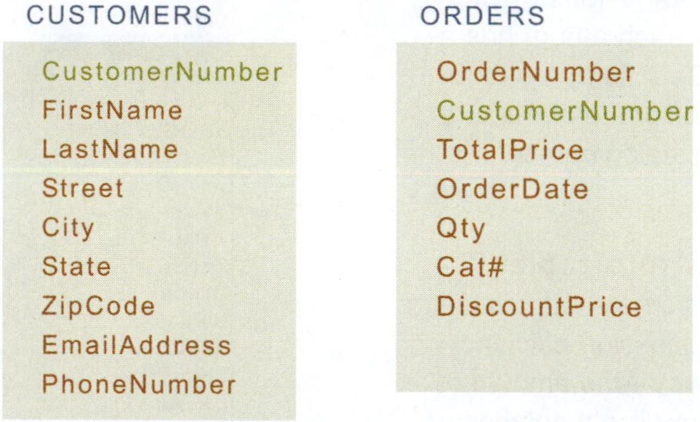

CUSTOMERS

CustomerNumber
FirstName
LastName
Street
City
State
ZipCode
EmailAddress
PhoneNumber

ORDERS

OrderNumber
CustomerNumber
TotalPrice
OrderDate
Qty
Cat#
DiscountPrice

FIGURE 11-38

Fields for each order are separated into two tables—one for customer information and one for order information.

Even after separating customer data from order data, the structure of the Vintage Music Shop database can be further improved. The Orders table in the previous figure allows customers to order only one album per order because the fields Cat# and DiscountPrice occur only once. Obviously, the Vintage Music Shop database is required to handle orders for more than one album.

It might seem reasonable to provide several fields for the albums on an order. Perhaps they could be named AlbumNumber1, AlbumNumber2, AlbumNumber3, and so on. But how many fields should the database designer provide? If the designer provides fields for ordering 10 albums, the database still cannot handle large orders for more than 10 albums. Furthermore, if a customer orders fewer than 10 albums, space is wasted by having empty fields in each record.

You might recognize that a one-to-many relationship exists between an order and the ordered items. That clue indicates that the database designer should separate the data into two tables, such as Orders and Order Details. These two tables are related by the OrderNumber field. Figure 11-39 illustrates how the Orders table is further normalized into two tables to store data more efficiently.

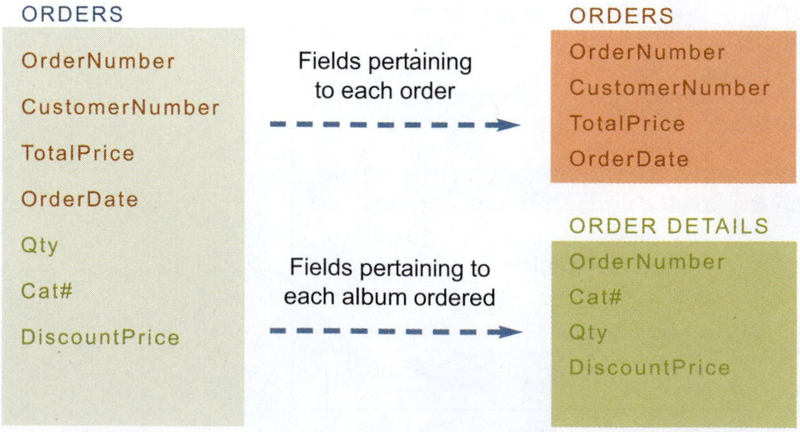

ORDERS

OrderNumber

CustomerNumber

TotalPrice

OrderDate

Qty

Cat#

DiscountPrice

Fields pertaining to each order
- - - - - - - ->

Fields pertaining to each album ordered
- - - - - - - ->

ORDERS

OrderNumber
CustomerNumber
TotalPrice
OrderDate

ORDER DETAILS

OrderNumber
Cat#
Qty
DiscountPrice

FIGURE 11-39

The fields pertaining to the ordered merchandise are further divided into two record types and related by the OrderNumber field.

ORGANIZING RECORDS

How are database records organized? Records can be organized in different ways depending on how people want to use them. For example, a customer visiting Vintage Music Shop's Web site will most often view the information in the Albums table by AlbumTitle or ArtistName. The inventory manager usually wants the data sorted by quantity in stock so that it is easy to see which albums are overstocked. In contrast, the marketing manager is more interested in the Value field, so that rare and expensive albums can be aggressively marketed. No single way of organizing the data accommodates everyone's needs, but tables can be sorted or indexed in multiple ways.

What happens when the data in a table is sorted? A table's **sort order** is the order in which records are stored on disk. Sorted tables typically produce faster queries and updates because they take advantage of clever algorithms that quickly pinpoint records. In a sorted table, new records are inserted to maintain the order. If no sort order is specified, new records are appended to the end of the file, resulting in a file that is not in any particular order. Queries and updates within an unsorted database are slow because the only algorithm for searching an unsorted table requires a sequential look at each record.

Most DBMSs use a sort key to determine the order in which records are stored. A table's **sort key** is one or more fields used to specify where new records are inserted in a table. A table can have only one sort key at a time, but the sort key can be changed. Changing a sort key can take a long time, however, because the process physically rearranges records on the disk. The database designer usually specifies the sort key for a database table at the time the database structure is created.

How is indexing different from sorting? A database index can be used to organize data in alphabetical or numeric order. It is very similar to an index in a book that contains a list of keywords and pointers to the pages where they can be found. A **database index** contains a list of keys, and each key provides a pointer to the record that contains the rest of the fields related to that key. Figure 11-40 illustrates how an index works.

FIGURE 11-40

When arranged by date, Blue Hawaii is the second record in the index. The index file contains a list of keys and the record number (R#) that contains more information about the album released on that date.

INDEX

Key	R#
10/1/1960	1
10/1/1961	3
10/29/1961	4
2/6/1967	2

ALBUMS

R#	Cat#	AlbumTitle	ArtistName	Release Date	In Stock	Value
1	LPM-2256	G.I. Blues	Elvis Presley	10/1/1960	4	20.00
2	7499-2	Between the Buttons	Rolling Stones	2/6/1967	1	13.99
3	LSP-246	Blue Hawaii	Elvis Presley	10/1/1961	5	50.00
4	N16014	Surfin Safari	Beach Boys	10/29/1961	8	18.95

11

CLICK TO START

Unlike a sort order, an index has no bearing on the physical sequence of records on disk. An index simply points to the record where the data can be found. The advantage of an index over a sort is that a table can have multiple indexes, but only one sort order. For example, the Albums table could be indexed by AlbumTitle to facilitate searches for specific albums. The same table could also be indexed by ArtistName to facilitate searches using artist names.

Database tables should be indexed by any field or fields that are commonly used as search fields. The database designer typically creates indexes at the time the database structure is designed. Indexes can also be created at a later date, as needed.

DESIGNING THE INTERFACE

Does a database designer have control over the user interface? The way that database records, queries, and reports appear on the screen depends on the user interface. An operating system typically provides some conventions for the user interface, such as dialog and button styles, but additional design decisions must be made for the database user interface.

Designing the database user interface can be a challenging task. If a company's database includes multiple tables used by many different people, a professional user interface designer usually creates and maintains the user interface. Large databases might even require a group of user interface designers.

The interface for smaller databases, such as those used by small businesses or individuals, is most likely created by the database designer. Some DBMSs include tools to create database interfaces. Others require separate tools for this task.

What makes a good database interface? A well-defined user interface for a database should be clear, intuitive, and efficient. Take a moment to look at the data entry screen in Figure 11-41, and imagine that you are using the screen to finalize the purchase of several albums.

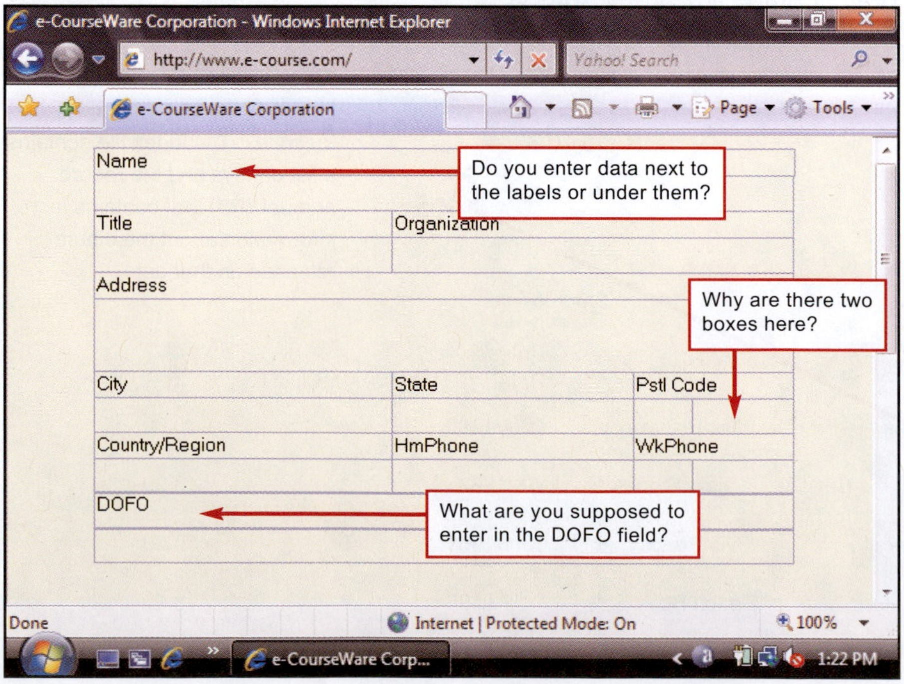

FIGURE 11-41

Imagine entering your own name and address using this on-screen form. Does it seem easy to use?

Using the data entry screen pictured on the previous page might be awkward because it does not follow good user interface design principles. The data entry fields seem out of order, and users might have difficulty discerning which entry box corresponds to each label. In addition, several fields have cryptic labels that don't provide good clues about the data you're supposed to enter.

To improve this database interface, a designer might consider the following principles:

- Arrange fields in a logical order beginning at the top-left of the screen. The first fields should be those used most often or those that come first in the data entry sequence.

- Provide visual clues to the entry areas. An edit box, line, or shaded area can delineate data entry areas.

- Entry areas should appear in a consistent position relative to their labels. By convention, labels are placed left of the entry areas or above them.

- Provide a quick way to move through the fields in order. By convention, the tab key performs this function.

- If all fields do not fit on a single screen, use scrolling or create a second screen.

- Provide buttons or other easy-to-use controls for moving from one record to another.

- Supply on-screen instructions to help ensure that data is entered correctly. Web databases can benefit from links to help pages.

Figure 11-42 contains an improved interface for the database in the previous figure.

INFOWEBLINKS

Compare the good, the bad, and the ugly at the **Database Interface InfoWeb**.

Ⓦ CLICK TO CONNECT
www.course.com/np/concepts11/ch11

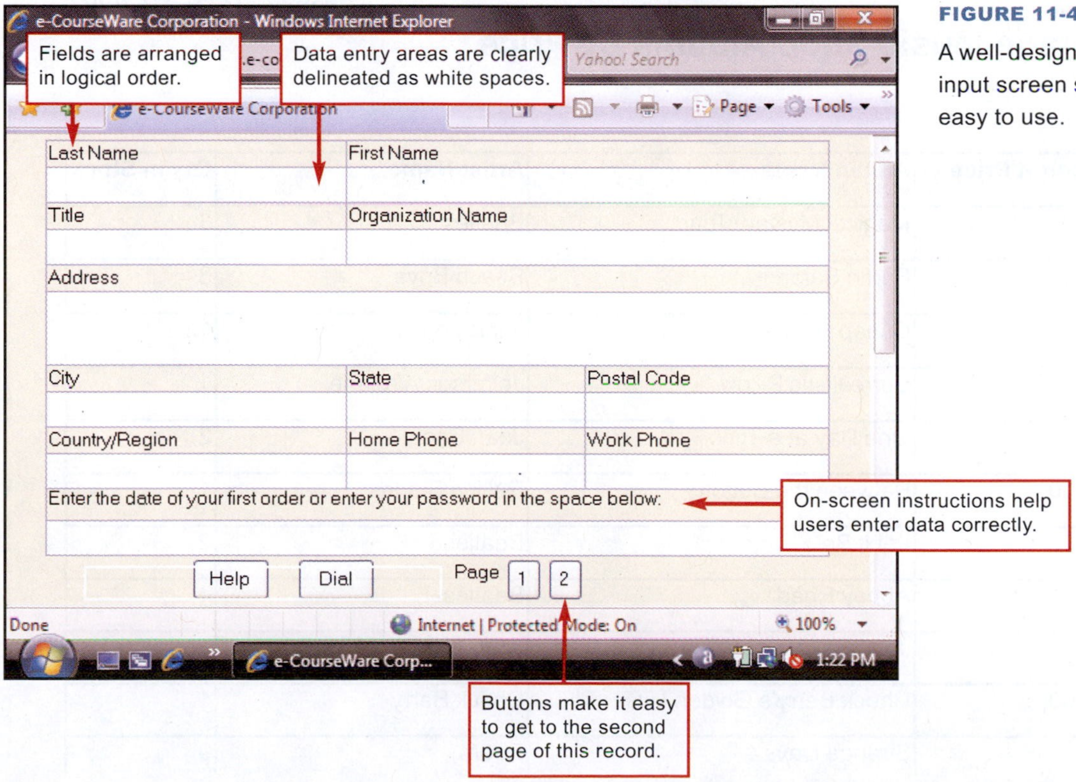

FIGURE 11-42

A well-designed data input screen should be easy to use.

DESIGNING REPORT TEMPLATES

How can I display or print data as a formatted report? A report is a printed or on-screen list of some or all of the data in a database. To create reports, most DBMSs include a **report generator**, which is a software tool for specifying the content and format for a database report. End users might use report generators, but more typically they are used by database designers.

A **report template** contains the outline or general specifications for a report, including such elements as the report title, fields to include, fields to subtotal or total, and report format specifications. The template does not, however, contain data from the database. Data is merged into the template when you actually run a report.

As an example, suppose that a manager at the Vintage Music Shop wants to create a report that lists albums arranged by price. The manager can create a report template called AlbumPriceGroup, which specifies the following:

- The title of the report is Vintage Music Shop Albums by Price.

- The report contains data from the Albums table, arranged in four columns, with data from the DiscountPrice, AlbumTitle, ArtistName, and InStock fields.

- The headings for the columns are Discount Price, Album Name, Artist Name, and Qty In Stock.

- The report is grouped by price.

These specifications would be used to produce a report similar to the one shown in Figure 11-43.

FIGURE 11-43

A report template contains the specifications to produce this report.

Report Date: 8/21/08

Vintage Music Shop Albums by Price

Discount Price	Album Name	Artist Name	Qty in Stock
$9.00	Magical Mystery Tour	Beatles	3
$10.00	Surfin Safari	Beach Boys	3
	Cheap Thrills	Janis Joplin	12
	Surrealistic Pillow	Jefferson Airplane	1
	One Day at a Time	Joan Baez	2
$14.00	Between the Buttons	Rolling Stones	1
$15.00	Let it Be	Beatles	2
	Abbey Road	Beatles	4
	Joan Baez	Joan Baez	1
$18.00	Chuck Berry's Golden Hits	Chuck Berry	1
	Strange Days	Doors	9

When a report is actually produced, it is based on the data currently contained in the database table. For example, the report on the previous page was produced on August 21st and includes albums that were stored in the database as of that date. Now suppose that at the beginning of October, Vintage Music Shop receives a new shipment of vintage albums. The AlbumPriceGroup report template is used again to print a report on October 12th. This report, shown in Figure 11-44, follows the same format as the previous report, but includes the new albums.

FIGURE 11-44

Using the same report specifications as the 08/21/08 report, but different data.

Report Date: 10/12/08

Vintage Music Shop Albums by Price

Discount Price	Album Name	Artist Name	Qty in Stock
$9.00	Magical Mystery Tour	Beatles	3
	In Person	Kingsmen	1
$10.00	Cheap Thrills	Janis Joplin	8
	About this Thing Called Love	Fabian	2
	One Day at a Time	Joan Baez	2
$14.00	Between the Buttons	Rolling Stones	1

How does the database designer create effective report templates? The reports created by a report generator can be displayed, printed, saved as files, or output as Web pages. Some data management software also provides tools to output data as graphs, sounds, or graphics. The database designer can create templates for reports that effectively present information by observing the following guidelines:

- Supply only the information required. Too much information can make it difficult to identify what is essential.

- Present information in a usable format. For example, if subtotals are necessary for making a decision, include them. The people who use reports should not have to make additional manual calculations.

- Information should be timely. Reports must arrive in time to be used for effective decision making. Some decisions require periodic information—for example, monthly sales reports. Other decisions require ongoing information, such as current stock prices, that will be best satisfied by a continuous display.

- Information should be presented in a clear, unambiguous format and include necessary titles, page numbers, dates, labels, and column headings.

- Present information in the format most appropriate for the audience. In many cases, a traditional report organized in rows and columns is most appropriate. In other cases, graphs might be more effective.

11

LOADING DATA

How is data loaded into database tables? After the design for the database structure is complete, it is time to load the database with an initial set of data. For example, before the Vintage Music Shop database went online, it was populated with data for all the albums in the inventory.

Data can be loaded into a database manually by using generic data entry tools supplied with the DBMS or by using a customized data entry module created by the database designer. Entering data manually can take a long time, however, and mistakes such as misspellings are common.

If the data exists electronically in another type of database or in flat files, it is usually possible to transfer the data using a custom-written conversion routine or import and export routines. A conversion routine converts the data from its current format into a format that can be automatically incorporated into the new database. It takes some time and requires knowledge about database formats to write conversion routines, but for large databases, it's much quicker to convert data than to re-enter it manually. Converting data also results in fewer errors.

Some DBMSs provide built-in import and export routines that automatically convert data from one file format to another. An import routine brings data into a database. For example, if data was previously stored as a spreadsheet file, an import routine in Microsoft Access can be used to transfer data from the spreadsheet to an Access database. In contrast, an export routine copies data out of a software package, such as spreadsheet software, and into the database. Typically, you would use either an import routine or an export routine to move data from one location to another, but not both.

QuickCheck

1. A primary [_____] contains data unique to a record, such as a Social Security number or ISBN.

2. Real, integer, text, logical, BLOB, and date are examples of data [_____].

3. A computed field is calculated during processing and stored temporarily in memory. True or false? [_____]

4. In a case [_____] database, a data entry such as MI is not the same as Mi.

5. To filter data entered into a field, the database designer can set up a field [_____] rule.

6. One of the goals of the normalization process is to minimize data [_____].

7. A report [_____] contains the outline or general specifications for a report, but does not contain data from the database.

 CHECK ANSWERS

SQL

ADDING RECORDS, finding information, and making updates are all important aspects of database use. Most people who access a database on a casual basis—to shop online or withdraw cash from an ATM, for example—interact with very simple user interfaces. These user interfaces shield users from the intricacies of sophisticated query languages. Nevertheless, a little background in query languages can help you understand the power and capabilities of databases. In Section D, you'll explore the SQL database query language by working with examples that illustrate major database functions, such as deleting records, adding records, searching for information, updating records, and joining tables.

SQL BASICS

How does a query language like SQL work? Query languages like **SQL** (Structured Query Language) typically work behind the scenes as an intermediary between the database client software provided to users and the database itself. Database client software provides an easy-to-use interface for entering search specifications, new records, data updates, and so on. The client software collects your input, and then converts it into an **SQL query**, which can operate directly on the database to carry out your instructions, as shown in Figure 11-45.

SQL commands interact directly with the database to locate data, update records, and perform other functions the user requests

Database

Client software converts the entries in a form into SQL commands

**SELECT AlbumTitle FROM Albums
WHERE ArtistName = 'Beatles'
and Format = 'LP'**

Search

Artist: | Beatles
Title: |
Label: |
Format: ⊙ LP ○ Cassette ○ Single

[Search Now] [Clear the Form]

Form-based user interface

TERMINOLOGY NOTE

The American National Standards Institute's official pronunciation of SQL is "ESS que el," but you also hear it called "SEE quell."

FIGURE 11-45

Database client software provides database users with simple forms that can be used to enter search specifications or update data. Here a customer uses an online form to search for Beatles albums in LP (long-playing 33 rpm) format.

11

What does a simple SQL query look like? An SQL query is a sequence of words, much like a sentence. For example, an SQL query that searches for a song called "Ruby Tuesday" in Vintage Music Shop's database might look like this:

SELECT TrackTitle FROM Tracks WHERE TrackTitle = 'Ruby Tuesday'

The SQL query language provides a collection of special command words called **SQL keywords**, such as SELECT, FROM, INSERT, and WHERE, which issue instructions to the database. Although the SQL examples in this section of the chapter use uppercase letters for keywords, most implementations of SQL accept either uppercase or lowercase keywords.

Most SQL queries can be divided into three simple elements that specify an action, the name of a database table, and a set of parameters. Let's look at each of these elements.

How does SQL specify the action that I want carried out in the database? An SQL query typically begins with an action keyword, or command, which specifies the operation you want carried out. For example, the command word **DELETE** removes a record from a table. Figure 11-46 lists some of the most commonly used SQL command words.

FIGURE 11-46

SQL Command Words

Command	Description	Example
CREATE	Create a database or table	CREATE TABLE Album
DELETE	Remove a record from a table	DELETE FROM Tracks WHERE TrackTitle = 'Blue Suede Shoes'
INSERT	Add a record	INSERT INTO AlbumDescription (Cat#, Condition) VALUES ('LPM-2256', 'Mint condition; no visible scratches; original album cover')
JOIN	Use the data from two tables	SELECT FROM Albums JOIN Tracks ON Albums.Cat# = Tracks.Cat#
SELECT	Search for records	SELECT FROM Albums WHERE ArtistName = 'Beatles'
UPDATE	Change data in a field	UPDATE Albums SET DiscountPrice = 15.95 WHERE Cat# = 'LPM-2256'

How does SQL specify which table to use? SQL keywords such as USE, FROM, or INTO can be used to construct a clause specifying the table you want to access. The clause consists of a keyword followed by the name of the table. For example, the clause **FROM Tracks** indicates that you want to use the Tracks table from Vintage Music Shop's database.

An SQL query that begins with **DELETE FROM Tracks** means that you want to delete something from the Tracks table. To complete the query, you provide parameters that specify which record you want to delete.

How does SQL specify parameters? **Parameters** are detailed specifications for a command. Keywords such as WHERE usually begin an SQL clause containing the parameters for a command. Suppose that Vintage Music Shop's inventory manager wants to delete all the albums in the Vintage Music Shop database recorded by Bobby Darin. The SQL looks like this:

DELETE **FROM Albums**	**WHERE ArtistName = 'Bobby Darin'**
SQL command word / FROM clause specifies the table to use	WHERE clause specifies the field name and its contents

Now that you've learned the basic structure of an SQL query, take a closer look at the SQL for specific database tasks, such as adding records, searching for information, updating fields, organizing records, and joining tables.

ADDING RECORDS

How are records added to a database? Suppose you want to purchase an album from the Vintage Music Shop's Web site. As a first-time customer, you fill out a form with your name, address, and so on. The client software that you use collects the data you enter in the form and generates an SQL statement using the **INSERT** command, which adds your data to the Customers table of the Vintage Music Shop database. Figure 11-47 shows the Customer form, the SQL statement that adds the customer data to the database, and the data that is added to the Customers table.

FIGURE 11-47

Data from the Customer form is added to the database.

Customer form

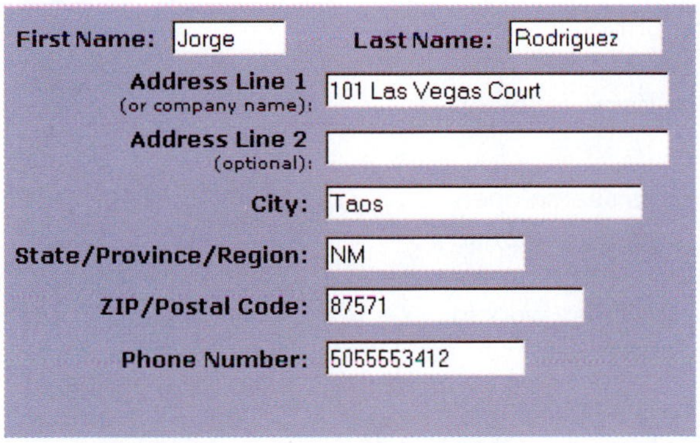

| First Name: | Jorge | Last Name: | Rodriguez |

Address Line 1 (or company name): 101 Las Vegas Court

Address Line 2 (optional):

City: Taos

State/Province/Region: NM

ZIP/Postal Code: 87571

Phone Number: 5055553412

SQL statement

INSERT INTO Customers (LastName, FirstName, Street, City, State, ZipCode, PhoneNumber) VALUES ('Rodriguez', 'Jorge', '101 Las Vegas Court', 'Taos', 'NM', '87571', '5055553412')

Customers table

LastName	FirstName	Street	City	State	ZipCode	PhoneNumber
Rodriguez	Jorge	101 Las Vegas Court	Taos	NM	87571	505-555-3412
Bleuman	Jonathan	5022 Lake St.	Negaunee	MI	49866	906-555-2131
Wincheta	Daisy	499 Table Mesa	Boulder	CO	80301	303-555-6902
Venkata	Patel	872 Old York Way	Durango	CO	81301	970-555-4438
Wong	Joy	822 Park Place	New York	NY	10023	212-555-9903
Helwig	Nathaniel	5 Winsome Drive	Cheyenne	WY	82003	303-555-3223
Chen	Lu-Chi	2235 Overview Trail	San Francisco	CA	94118	415--555-9001
Walton	William	500 Vista Mesa Bl		NM	87504	505-555-1111
Bolduc	Luc	41 Rue S				487
	Kallie					

11

SEARCHING FOR INFORMATION

How do SQL queries carry out searches? One of the most common database operations is to query for a particular record or group of records by using the **SELECT** command. Suppose you're looking for Jefferson Airplane albums. You fill in the Search box at the Vintage Music Shop site, as shown in Figure 11-48.

Search
Artist: Jefferson Airplane
Title:
Label:
Format: ● LP ○ Cassette ○ Single

[Search Now] [Clear the Form]

The database client software uses your search specification to create the SQL query:

> **SELECT AlbumTitle, AlbumCover FROM Albums**
>
> **WHERE ArtistName = 'Jefferson Airplane'**

As a result of this query, the Vintage Music Shop Web page displays a list beginning with *Jefferson Airplane Takes Off*—the band's first album—and a photo of the album cover. Take a closer look at the parts of this query.

The phrase **SELECT AlbumTitle, AlbumCover** specifies that the database should show you only the album title and cover. Until you confirm that this is the album you're interested in, it will not show you additional information, such as the price or list of tracks. **FROM Albums** tells the DBMS to search for the album in the Albums table. **WHERE ArtistName = 'Jefferson Airplane'** specifies that the record you want contains the data "Jefferson Airplane" in the ArtistName field.

Can SQL perform complex searches? Yes. SQL uses search operators such as AND, OR, and NOT to form complex queries. Because search operators were originally the idea of mathematician George Boole, they are also referred to as Boolean operators. Let's see how they work in the context of SQL queries.

How does AND work in an SQL query? AND (sometimes indicated by a + sign) is used when you want to retrieve records that meet more than one criteria. For example, suppose a customer wants to find all the albums by Jefferson Airplane, but wants to display only albums that are on sale for less than $10.00. You might enter something like **Jefferson Airplane <$10.00** in the Vintage Music Shop search box. The database client creates an SQL query:

> **SELECT AlbumTitle FROM Albums**
> **WHERE ArtistName = 'Jefferson Airplane' AND**
> **DiscountPrice < 10.00**

In this example, a record is selected only if the ArtistName field contains Jefferson Airplane and the value in the DiscountPrice field is less than $10.00. If the discount price is $10.00 or more, the record is not selected. The AND operator specifies that both of the search criteria must be true for the record to be selected.

FIGURE 11-48

Search form used by customers to query the database. Here the search is for Jefferson Airplane albums.

INFOWEBLINKS

At the **Boolean InfoWeb**, you can learn how a guy born in 1815 had such an immense effect on a modern technology like the Web.

 **CLICK TO CONNECT**
www.course.com/np/concepts11/ch11

How does OR differ from AND? Two variations of the OR operator exist. One variation, the inclusive OR, designates records that meet one of the criteria or both. The other variation, called the exclusive OR, designates records that meet one criterion or the other, but not both.

SQL uses the inclusive OR. A query such as:

```
SELECT AlbumTitle FROM Albums
WHERE ArtistName = 'Jefferson Airplane' OR
DiscountPrice < 10.00
```

produces all the Jefferson Airplane albums, regardless of price. It also produces any albums that are less than $10.00, regardless of the artist.

You can combine AND and OR clauses to formulate complex queries. For example, Jefferson Airplane became Jefferson Starship in 1974. If you'd like a list of Jefferson Airplane or Starship albums for less than $10.00, you can use a query like the following:

```
SELECT AlbumTitle FROM Albums
WHERE (ArtistName = 'Jefferson Airplane' OR ArtistName =
'Jefferson Starship') AND DiscountPrice < 10.00
```

Note the use of parentheses around the OR clause. Parentheses tell the DBMS to process this part of the query first. The placement of parentheses can change the results of a query, sometimes drastically. Compare the previous query to the following query:

```
SELECT AlbumTitle FROM Albums
WHERE ArtistName = 'Jefferson Airplane' OR (ArtistName =
'Jefferson Starship' AND DiscountPrice < 10.00)
```

The first query (in blue) returns albums by Jefferson Airplane or Starship that are less than $10.00. The second query (in green) returns all albums by Jefferson Airplane, regardless of price, and any albums by Jefferson Starship that cost less than $10.00.

How does NOT work in an SQL query? The NOT operator can be used to omit records from a search by specifying a not-equal relationship. For example, the following query returns all records in the Albums table where the ArtistName is not equal to Jefferson Airplane:

```
Select AlbumTitle from Albums
WHERE NOT(ArtistName = 'Jefferson Airplane')
```

Sometimes NOT relationships are specified with a not-equal operator, such as <> or !=, depending on the specifications of the query language. For example, the following query returns the same records as one that uses the NOT operator:

```
Select AlbumTitle from Albums
WHERE ArtistName <> 'Jefferson Airplane'
```

11

UPDATING FIELDS

Can I change the contents of a record? You can change records in a database only if you have authorization to do so. At Vintage Music Shop's site, for example, customers do not have authorization to change album prices or alter the name of the songs on an album. The process of purchasing an album, however, does cause an update in the Vintage Music Shop database. Suppose you purchase Elvis Presley's *G.I. Blues* album. Your purchase reduces the number of *G.I. Blues* albums in Vintage Music Shop's inventory. To accomplish this update, one of the software modules in Vintage Music Shop's inventory system issues an SQL **UPDATE** command to reduce the number in the InStock field of the *G.I. Blues* record:

```
UPDATE Albums
SET InStock = InStock - 1
WHERE AlbumTitle = 'G.I. Blues'
```

Is it possible to update a group of records? In addition to changing the data in a single record, SQL can perform a **global update** that changes the data in more than one record at a time. Suppose you're Vintage Music Shop's marketing manager, and you want to put all The Rolling Stones albums on sale by reducing the DiscountPrice to $9.95. You could do it the hard way by searching for an ArtistName field that contains "Rolling Stones," adjusting the DiscountPrice field for that record, and then looking for the next Rolling Stones album. However, it would be easier to change all the records with a single command. The following SQL statement accomplishes this global update:

```
UPDATE Albums
SET DiscountPrice = 9.95
WHERE ArtistName = 'Rolling Stones'
```

Let's see how this command performs a global update. The UPDATE command means you want to change the data in some or all of the records. Albums is the name of the record type containing the data you want to change. **SET DiscountPrice = 9.95** tells the DBMS to change the data in the DiscountPrice field to $9.95. **WHERE ArtistName = 'Rolling Stones'** tells the DBMS to change only those records where the artist name is Rolling Stones.

What are the limitations of the global UPDATE command? Although the global update function is powerful, it works only for records that have similar characteristics—for example, all albums by the Rolling Stones or all albums produced in 1955. Custom programming is required to perform global operations on information that does not have any similar characteristics. Figure 11-49 provides an example.

Vintage Music Shop's marketing manager picks 10 albums each week to place on a special promotional sale. These albums have no common data that can be used to formulate a global UPDATE command.

FIGURE 11-49

Database designers can write modules that provide custom update capabilities.

> Hard Day's Night
> Blue Hawaii
> Strange Days
> Cheap Thrills
> Yellow Submarine
> Surfin Safari
> Blonde on Blonde
> Dragon Fly
> Rubber Soul
> Anthem of the Sun

Custom programming would allow the marketing manager to simply submit a list of 10 albums as a document. The module would "read" the document and issue an UPDATE command for each of the chosen albums.

JOINING TABLES

How is data retrieved from more than one table at a time?

Recall that the process of normalization creates tables that can be related by fields that exist in both tables. In SQL terminology, creating a relationship between tables is referred to as **joining tables**.

Suppose you want some information on Elvis Presley's *G.I. Blues* album. It would be nice to see not only the album name and cover, but also a list of the songs included on the album. The songs, however, are not stored in the same table as the rest of the album data. The Albums table holds the album name, the artist's name, the release date, and other data about the album. The Tracks table holds the name of each song track, the track length, and an MP3 sample of the track. Both tables also contain a Cat# field.

Earlier in the chapter you learned that a relationship can exist between Vintage Music Shop's Albums table and Tracks table, based on the data in the Cat# field, as shown in Figure 11-50.

FIGURE 11-50

Records in the Albums table and Tracks table both include a Cat# field. When the data in these fields is the same, the records refer to the same entity—in this case, an Elvis Presley album called *G.I. Blues*.

ALBUMS

R#	Cat#	AlbumTitle	ArtistName	Release Date	In Stock	Value
1	LPM-2256	G.I. Blues	Elvis Presley	10/1/1960	4	20.00
2	7499-2	Between the Buttons	Rolling Stones	2/6/1967	1	13.99
3	LSP-246	Blue H				
4	N16014	Surfin				

TRACKS

Cat#	TrackTitle	Track Length	TrackSample
LPM-2256	Blue Suede Shoes	104	BlueSuede.mp3
LPM-2256	Frankfort Special	132	FrankSpec.mp3
LPM-2256	Wooden Heart	163	WoodenHE.mp3
7499-2	Ruby Tuesday	197	RubyT.mp3

To take advantage of the relationship between these two tables, you first have to join the tables. Why? Remember that in a relational database, the tables are essentially independent unless you join them together. The SQL **JOIN** command allows you to temporarily join and simultaneously access the data in more than one table.

How does the JOIN command work?

A single SQL query can retrieve data from the Albums table and the Tracks table for Elvis Presley albums. To do so, however requires some way to distinguish the data contained in each table. In the example, both tables contain a field called Cat#. How can you differentiate the Cat# field that belongs to the Albums table from the Cat# field in the Tracks table?

SQL uses dot notation to make this distinction. Albums.Cat# is the full specification for the Cat# field in the Albums table. Tracks.Cat# specifies its counterpart in the Tracks table.

11

When joining two tables, the convention is to use the full specification for table and field name. Figure 11-51 dissects an SQL query that joins two Vintage Music Shop tables.

FIGURE 11-51

The JOIN command links the Albums and Tracks tables to produce the album name, cover, price, and tracks for item number LPM-2256.

SELECT Albums.AlbumTitle, ◄—————

Albums.AlbumCover,

Albums.DiscountPrice,

Tracks.TrackTitle

FROM Albums JOIN Tracks on ◄—————

Albums.Cat# = Tracks.Cat# ◄—————

WHERE Album.Cat# = 'LPM-2256' ◄—————

The SELECT clause specifies the fields that should appear. Albums.AlbumTitle refers to the AlbumTitle field of the Albums table.

The JOIN command links the Albums and Tracks tables.

The tables are joined when the same data appears in the Cat# fields of records from the two tables.

The WHERE clause specifies that you want to see the album with item number LPM-2256.

How extensive is SQL? In this section, you were introduced to some of the most commonly used SQL commands, and you explored how they might be used in the context of an e-commerce music business. SQL is a very extensive and powerful language that can be used not only to manipulate data, but also to create databases, tables, and reports. Because SQL is one of the most popular database tools, many computer professionals consider SQL fluency an essential career skill.

QuickCheck

SECTION D

1. SQL [_____] include SELECT, FROM, and INSERT.

2. The term *parameter* refers to detailed specifications for a command. True or false? [_____]

3. In search specifications, AND, OR, and NOT are examples of [_____] operators and are used to specify relationships between search criteria.

4. In SQL, the DATA command adds fields to a database. True or false? [_____]

5. To search for data in a specific field, you can use the SQL command [_____].

6. The SQL [_____] command can change the data in a specified field in one or more records.

7. In SQL, the JOIN command allows you to add fields to a database. True or false? [_____]

 CHECK ANSWERS

SECTION E

Database Security

IN THE PAST FEW YEARS, data for millions of people has been stolen, hacked, or simply gone missing. No one is quite sure what happened to a Bank of America backup tape containing personal information for 1.2 million federal employees, senators, and representatives. A U.S. Air Force spokesperson confirmed that personal data for 33,000 soldiers was hacked from an online system. A hacker gained access to a research database of 600,000 people registered with the California Department of Social Services. ChoicePoint, a consumer data firm, was duped into distributing personal information for more than 145,000 people. Computer hackers obtained access to personal information for 32,000 Lexis-Nexis subscribers. Consumers are alarmed that databases are so vulnerable. In Section E you'll learn why.

DATABASE VULNERABILITIES

How vulnerable are databases? Databases are vulnerable to theft, hacking, and unauthorized access. A disk or tape containing a backup or archive could be stolen. A notebook computer containing a database used by a field representative or teleworker can go missing. Hackers can gain unauthorized access to a database over the Internet or an unsecured wireless connection. Legitimate database entry personnel might make unauthorized copies, changes, and deletions.

The qualities that make databases efficient also make them vulnerable. Data stored in digital format is easy to copy, back up, store, and transmit. Although it would be impractical to steal millions of paper records from filing cabinets, to steal a digital database a criminal simply has to pocket a small backup tape or make a copy of the original database (Figure 11-52).

Electronic databases can typically be accessed over local area networks and the Internet, offering convenience to customers, clients, and employees. Security holes can allow intruders to infiltrate computer systems housing databases, copy data, delete it, or change it.

When a database is illicitly copied, it is stolen but not missing, as it would be if a crook made off with the folders in a filing cabinet. The theft might not be discovered for days or weeks, if ever, preventing organizations and individuals from taking steps to prevent pilfered data from being misused.

Easy access to information is an essential characteristic of a database. Many databases, however, contain confidential information, such as medical records, corporate memos, military plans, or financial data. Confidentiality breaches can occur when intruders gain access to a database, as well as when curious insiders make unauthorized queries.

How do database security breaches affect individuals? There is hardly a person in America who is not in at least one computer database. Every time you fill out a survey, register to use a Web site, visit your doctor, use your credit card, or make a phone call, that information is stored somewhere in a database. According to the Electronic Frontier Foundation, the average American is in at least 50 databases. With personal data stored in so many databases and those databases at risk for being stolen or misused, citizens have valid concerns about their privacy, the validity of recorded data, and the security of their identities.

FIGURE 11-52

Database theft is all too common.

11

Privacy is typically viewed as an inherent right. You expect personal information to remain confidential. When your data is in a computer database, there is risk that it can be viewed by unauthorized individuals or distributed without your permission. Many people are concerned about misuse of medical records. Pregnant women are not always happy to get stacks of unsolicited mail with baby food, crib, and car seat ads. More insidious is the use of medical information by prospective employers, who might not hire at-risk employees who would become a burden on the corporate health insurance plan. But what about seemingly innocuous databases? Your local Blockbuster probably has a list of the movies you've rented. A preferred customer card at your favorite supermarket could be used to collect data about the groceries you purchase.

Accepting the fact that personal data is stored in countless databases, it would be comforting to know that the data is accurate. However, data entry errors, update errors, and hacking all add to doubt about the veracity of database data. A mistake in your credit rating could prevent you from purchasing a car or home. A mixup in your student records could keep you out of graduate school.

Criminals have become sophisticated in the use of cybertools, using bots, keyloggers, and redirection to access data stored on personal computers and corporate databases. The data stored in a single database is often enough to provide a criminal with enough information to access your bank account or use your credit card. New trends in data aggregation and analysis make it possible to assemble a fairly detailed picture of an individual's life with enough critical ID numbers and PINs to steal an entire identity and then run up debt, acquire a criminal record, evade taxes, and put a real person's life in shambles.

How do database security breaches affect organizations?

When a database security breach occurs in a legitimate organization, its customers lose confidence and might take their business elsewhere. Conscientious businesses will try to assist victims of a data break-in by notifying them and offering guidance for changing PINs and watching for unauthorized account activity. The customer notification process is usually costly and can affect profitability. It also reduces productivity while the business devotes time and computer system resources to the notification effort. Most legitimate businesses are serious about database security and take steps—sometimes costly steps—to protect personal and corporate data.

DATABASE SECURITY MEASURES

Can databases be secured?
Today's computers are under assault from hackers and natural disasters. Although no computer system can be 100% secure, system administrators can take steps to secure computer systems and the databases they contain. Security measures include encryption, access controls, data security policies, and intrusion monitoring.

How does encryption secure a database?
Although encryption cannot prevent a database from being lost or stolen, it can make the data it contains unintelligible to a hacker. It might seem that a prudent approach to database security would be encrypting the entire database and leaving it that way, but encrypted databases are not always practical.

The act of processing queries for a database can sometimes reveal information to savvy hackers. Consequently, the encryption might not offer full protection. Also, it is difficult to query an encrypted database. Typically all or part of the database has to be decrypted for the query to locate information.

The process of decrypting database information in response to a query typically decreases efficient query processing. A computer hosting a database that is constantly queried by hundreds of users would spend most of its processing resources in an endless cycle of encryption and decryption.

Most active, operational databases are not encrypted while being used, but the data they contain can be encrypted before it is archived. Thieves who gain access to a database archive cannot make sense of the data if it is encrypted. Also, database data that's transmitted over the Web can be encrypted using encryption technologies such as SSL or SHTTP. Encryption is a useful tool in the security arsenal, but database administrators must take additional steps to secure database data.

What are access controls? An **access control** limits access to systems, such as computer databases. Access controls can block unauthorized users and limit activities of authorized users. IT professionals sometimes classify access controls as identification and authentication, authorization, and accountability. Identification and authentication determine who can log on to a system, authorization defines what an authenticated user can do, and accountability tracks what a user did. A simpler way to understand access controls is that they restrict the who and how of data access. Access controls do the following:

● **Control who accesses the database** by restricting network and physical access to the computer that hosts the database. Physical access can be limited to authorized personnel by housing the computer in a locked data center. Online access can be limited by firewalls and passwords. System administrators should be sure to change all default administrator passwords before opening the database to internal and external users. Most DBMSs ship with a standard administrator password. Hackers know it. Surveys show that as many as 25% of businesses never remember to change it, leaving their systems wide open to unauthorized access. Security experts also recommend separating the server that hosts the database from the server that hosts publicly accessible services, such as Web pages. Database servers that supply information to Web servers should be configured to allow connections only from that Web server to prevent port-jumping exploits from unauthorized intruders.

● **Control how users interact with the database** by defining user privileges and views. Customers, clients, and even most employees who use a database have no need to change its structure by adding fields, changing field names, and setting keys. **User privileges** (also referred to as user rights or permissions) delineate what activities a user can perform within a database. The lowest level privilege is read access, which allows a user to see the data, but not change it. Adding the write privilege allows a user to also change data in the database. Privileges can also be granted for deleting, adding, indexing, printing, and copying (Figure 11-53). A **data view** establishes which fields and records a particular user is allowed to access. In a medical insurance database, for example, a customer service representative might be allowed to view an insured person's account, including the customer name and address; however the treatment summary might display only dates and charges, not the nature of the treatment.

FIGURE 11-53

A database administrator can limit the way individuals or groups access data. In this example, library patrons are given permission to read data, but not update, insert, or delete it.

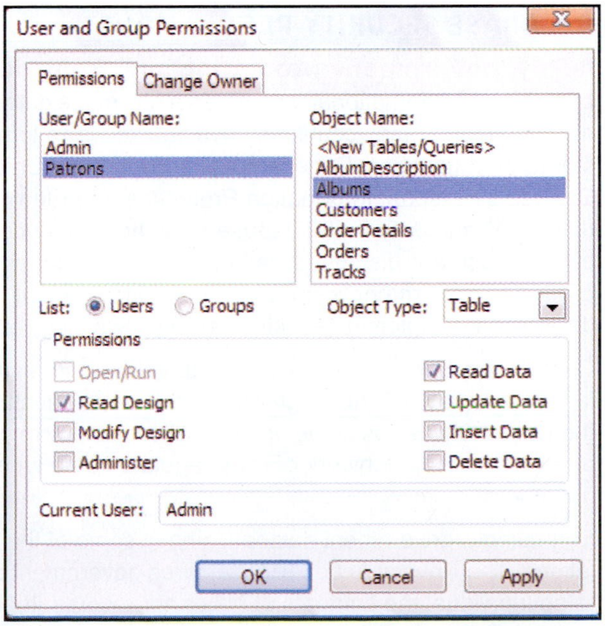

11

How can policies help to secure databases? A notebook computer is an easy target. Most thieves are after the hardware, but they might hit the jackpot if a computer contains a company database that a careless worker wants to work with while on a business trip. To minimize vulnerabilities caused by employee inattention, organizations can formulate database use policies, such as requiring employees to log off the system before going to lunch and prohibiting employees from removing sensitive data from the workplace. A good set of policies decreases the risk of unauthorized access within the workplace, minimizes the chance of confidential data escaping from the workplace, and helps improve data entry accuracy.

What can monitoring accomplish? A **database audit** is a procedure that monitors and records user activity within a database. In some instances, auditing can identify potential intruders before they can compromise a system. If an intruder breaches database security, an audit can help to identify the damage and correct it. Database auditing tools can be configured to keep a record of who is accountable for changes to the database, gather general usage statistics, or investigate suspicious activity.

Tracking who makes changes in a database helps an organization maintain accountability, trace the source of errors, and make comprehensive corrections. If a database had been compromised by a hacker, for example, an audit report can be used to check recent changes to the database to make sure they are legitimate.

General usage statistics help database administrators maintain optimal performance, so that query response is quick even at peak usage times. General statistics can also reveal abnormal usage patterns and alert system administrators to possible intrusion attempts (Figure 11-54).

If abnormal usage patterns become evident, database auditing tools can be configured to check specific types of database activity. For example, if a system administrator suspects that data is being surreptitiously deleted or changed, an audit can be set up to record any successful or unsuccessful deletions from tables in the database.

FIGURE 11-54

Database monitoring software such as Cisco Management Center can be used to track intrusion attempts.

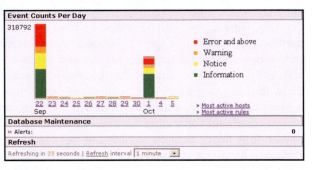

DATABASE SECURITY REGULATIONS

Is my government protecting me from database security breaches? International e-commerce has made database security a global concern and many countries have enacted laws to protect personal data stored on databases. For example, the European Union's Privacy Act and Canada's Personal Information Protection and Electronics Document Act (PIPEDA) mandate that database breaches from accidental loss or electronic attack are disclosed, rather than swept under the carpet. Despite progress, governments around the world still have much work to do in designing and enforcing effective privacy laws.

Canada, the European Union, and Japan have more stringent privacy regulations than the U.S. Although it leads the world in technology development, the United States has some of the weakest privacy regulations in the developed world. Its patchwork of laws regulate some types of databases, but not others.

Surprisingly, government databases have some of the most stringent regulations. The Privacy Act of 1974 requires government agencies to disclose to an individual the contents of his or her records. It places restrictions on how agencies can share an individual's data with other people and agencies. The Act also requires agencies to follow "fair information practices" when gathering and handling personal data, and allows individuals to sue the government for violating its provisions. There are exceptions to the restrictions, such as when information is needed in the course of a criminal investigation. In addition, subsequent legislation, such as the Patriot Act, further delineates the rules governing the collection and use of data about U.S. citizens and visitors.

Regulations in the private sector are, in many cases, less stringent than those imposed on the government. Most consumers probably have more to fear from private sector criminals than from government misuse of databases. One particularly worrisome development has been criminal database aggregation. Here's how it works. A hacker obtains a database containing moderately sensitive data, such as e-mail addresses and frequent flier account numbers. The list is sold for a modest sum to the highest bidder who devises a data-rich phishing attack, like the one in Figure 11-55, to gain even more data.

The hacker's database now includes additional legitimate information. This enriched list, now containing e-mail addresses, frequent flyer numbers and PINs, can be sold at a profit to another hacker who can devise other phishing schemes to gather even more data. Eventually, the database will contain a fairly complete dossier on its subjects, and it will be worth big bucks when sold to identity theft criminals.

FIGURE 11-55

A bland but irritating spam that appears to originate from a legitimate air carrier might contain an opt-out clause that contains accurate data, such as your frequent flyer number. An average person reads this message and reasons, "If they have my frequent flyer number, it must be a legitimate site," and proceeds to enter his or her PIN, which gets sent directly to a hacker.

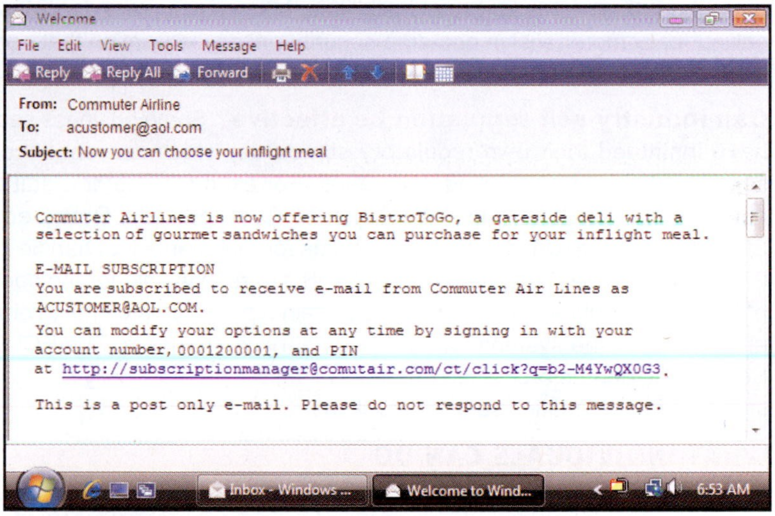

Laws governing private sector databases offer only spot coverage of specific types of data, such as telephone records. Laws dating back to the 1950s cover disclosure of telephone and cable records. A U.S. law also prohibits video rental stores from disclosing the titles of videos rented by customers. The Video Privacy Protection Act, passed in 1988, requires video stores to provide consumers with the opportunity to opt out from mailing lists that might be sold to other businesses.

The Health Insurance Portability and Accountability Act (HIPAA) of 1996 addresses the security and privacy of medical records. Its privacy provisions protect all individually identifiable health information. Medical records that include an individual's name, Social Security number, or other personal identification cannot be disclosed without consent. HIPAA's security provisions prescribe a number of required policies, procedures, and reporting mechanisms that must be in place for all information systems that process medical records.

The Gramm-Leach-Bliley Act of 1999 requires financial institutions to establish security standards that protect customer data from internal and external threats, including unauthorized access that occurs through networks and online systems. The law also contains an opt-out clause designed to protect consumer data from being sold or disclosed to third parties. Laws are complex, however, and the Gramm-Leach-Bliley Act includes a number of cases in which data can be shared.

11

Seemingly reasonable steps to protect U.S. consumers have not yet been incorporated into comprehensive national database legislation. For example, in 2003 California passed CA SB1386, usually referred to as California's Database Breach Act, which requires businesses to make timely disclosure of database security breaches to any California residents whose personal information might have been compromised. Unfortunately, an attempt to pass a similar law on the national level failed.

The patchwork of U.S. law that applies to database security offers no guidelines that apply to all databases, leaving irritating loopholes that allow some types of personal data to be gathered, aggregated, and shared with third parties. Rules for financial databases are slightly different than for medical, telephone, cable, or video rental databases. Even if businesses adhere to the applicable database laws, consumers cannot be expected to understand the nuances for different types of databases and are therefore in the dark about their rights and responsibilities. Many consumer advocates are calling for comprehensive one-stop security-privacy legislation that applies to all databases.

Can industry self-regulation be effective? Some business sectors have instituted their own regulatory standards, which can enhance the security blanket surrounding databases. For example, major credit card companies formulated the PCI (Payment Card Industry) Data Security Standards that specifies security standards for merchants that handle credit card information. Participating merchants are responsible for the security of cardholder data and must not store certain types of data on their computer systems or the systems of third party service providers. The PCI Data Security Standards are based on ISO 17799, an internationally recognized standard for information security practices.

WHAT INDIVIDUALS CAN DO

What can I do to minimize my vulnerability to database security breaches? You can't protect your personal data once you've released it, so the key to minimizing your risk is to be vigilant about the information you divulge.

Be aware of any activities that can possibly collect information about you for a database, such as registering to use a Web site, participating in a survey, submitting your resume to an online data bank, sending for a product rebate, participating in online discussion groups, clicking pop-up ads, and so on. Sometimes the gains aren't worth the risk or the potential nuisance of dealing with a deluge of junk mail.

When asked for information, supply only what's required. Never divulge your Social Security number and be cautious about other personal information, such as your telephone number or address. When in doubt, you might consider using phony data.

Make sure you look for the opt-out button if you don't want your data distributed to third parties. Some Web sites have the opt-in button selected as the default and if you don't want your data distributed, you will need to change to the opt-out status.

Consider using a portable password manager that stores strongly encrypted passwords, enters them when you want to access a password protected database or site, but can be removed from your computer when it is not in use to foil intrusion attempts (Figure 11-56).

FIGURE 11-56

Portable password managers that you can use from a Flash drive include:

- Siber Systems RoboForm2go
- Key Chain Technologies Portable Password Manager
- Dobysoft KeyPass
- Bruce Schneier's Password Safe
- Dominik Reichl's KeePass

Be wary of offers for free services in exchange for personal information or permission to track your online footprints.

Make sure your antivirus software is running and up-to-date. Use a personal firewall and pop-up blocker to protect your computer from unauthorized intrusions.

Never send personal information in response to an e-mail request that could be a phishing attack from an illegitimate source.

When a privacy policy exists, check it out—especially the part that explains whether your data might be shared with a third party (Figure 11-57). Even if the policy indicates that data will not be shared, don't assume the data will never be released. You'll have to weigh the sensitivity of the data and the dependability of the source to decide whether to supply the requested data.

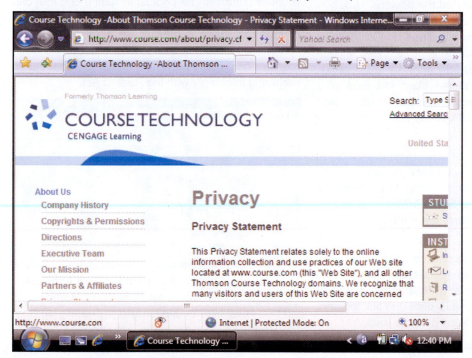

FIGURE 11-57

Investigate a site's privacy policy before you provide personal information.

▶ CLICK TO START

QuickCheck

1. _____ cannot prevent a database from being lost or stolen, but it can make the data it contains unusable.

2. The lowest level privilege allows users _____ access to a database.

3. A database _____ is a procedure that monitors and records user activity within a database.

4. The Gramm-Leach-Bliley Act of 1999 requires _____ institutions in the U.S. to establish security standards that protect customer data from internal and external threats.

5. A(n) _____ password manager stores strongly encrypted passwords, enters them when you want to access a password protected database or site, but can be removed from your computer when it is not in use to foil intrusion attempts.

 CHECK ANSWERS

ISSUE

Do You Want a National ID Card?

THE 9/11 TERRORIST ATTACKS were a wake-up call for America to shore up its defenses. Terrorists who boarded planes that September morning were ready to show legitimate driver licenses if questioned about their identity. The ensuing national security investigation reported the obvious: U.S. borders were porous and there was really no way to tell who was in the country legally. The 9/11 Commission recommended ID cards as an important step in combating terrorist threats. Shortly after the 9/11 attacks, 70% of Americans surveyed liked the idea of a national ID card. That sentiment had not decreased much by 2005 when a USA Today poll showed 66% approval.

National ID cards are used all over the world to enhance national security, unmask potential terrorists, and guard against illegal immigrants. More than 100 European, Asian, and South American countries require their citizens to carry government-issued ID cards at all times.

In 2005, the U.S. Congress passed the Real ID Act, a cleverly crafted piece of legislation that doesn't directly establish a national ID, but forces individual states to issue an approved ID card and link together the databases that contain card holder data.

Starting in 2010, people who live or work in the United States will be able to obtain a federally approved ID card. Without an approved ID card, it will be much more difficult to open a bank account, travel on an airplane, collect Social Security payments, or obtain other government services.

The ID cards can be issued by states, but the card format must be approved by the federal Department of Homeland Security. The cards must include anti-counterfeiting technology and contain a version of the data in a standardized machine-readable format, such as on a magnetic strip or an embedded RFID chip. Civil liberties watchdogs are suspicious of RFID chips, which can be read from a distance without notifying the card holder. Unauthorized access and abuse of data contained on the card could lead to security breaches. Magnetic strip technology, however, is less threatening because it is used for credit cards that many people currently carry.

Most states are expected to offer federally approved ID cards through their departments of motor vehicles and the cards will most likely take the place of today's driver licenses. Florida began issuing new driver licenses two years ago with 17 layers of security. The licenses contain three photos, including one that can be seen only under ultraviolet light. The card's security features make it difficult for a terrorist, illegal immigrant, or identity thief to alter or forge the data. Florida's card could become a model for other states preparing to comply with the Real ID Act.

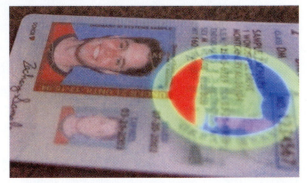

So now that a national ID card is about to become reality, why are states such as New Hampshire, with its "live free or die" motto, rebelling against the Real ID Act? Why is the Act opposed by more than 600 organizations, including the American Library Association, the American Association of Motor Vehicle Administrators, the National Association of Evangelicals, the Association for Computing Machinery, the American Immigration Lawyers Association, the National Council of State Legislatures, and the National Governors Association?

The card in and of itself is harmless. People carry all kinds of identification cards. The controversy stems from a clause in the Real ID Act that requires states to link their ID databases in order to discover duplicate applications, monitor potential terrorists, and uncover illegal immigrants. Opponents to the Real ID Act fear that a massive centralized ID database could be abused by government agencies, businesses, and criminals. Although 66% of Americans say they support a national ID card, only 26% of Americans support a national ID database.

The Real ID Act contains provisions that require states to store and share ID data, including name, birth date, gender, ID number, address, digitized photo, and biometric data such as a digitized fingerprint or retinal scan. Barry Steinhardt, director of the American Civil Liberties Union's technology and liberty program, explains, "It's going to result in everyone, from the 7-Eleven store to the bank and airlines, demanding to see the ID card. They're going to scan it in. They're going to have all the data on it from the front of the card...It's going to be not just a national ID card but a national database."

Presumably, the database and electronic scanning technology will work together so that the card can be swiped, data transmitted to the central database, and verified. That scheme has privacy advocates worried. Will a simple ID card scan to verify your identity at your neighborhood supermarket add data about the transaction to the national database? How much other data might be collected? Will the government ID database eventually contain detailed dossiers on every citizen?

Privacy watchdogs continue to monitor a National Security Agency data mining project designed to preemptively identify terrorists by looking for suspicious patterns in library book borrowing, car rental, e-mail, banking, and other transactions. A similar system applied to a dossier-like national ID database has ramifications even for law abiding citizens. As an editorial in Scientific American points out, "Suppose that there are 1,000 terrorists in the U.S. and that the data-mining process has an amazing 99 percent success rate. Then 10 of the terrorists will probably still slip through—and 2.8 million innocent people will also be fingered."

The government is only one potential source of abuse for a national ID database; businesses are another. If a business can scan an ID card to validate it, the reader might also be able to copy the data into the business's own database to use for mass mailings and other marketing activities. Some stores would want to collect and store ID data "just until the check clears," but who is to say that the data would not be stored longer and sold to a credit union, for example, or mailing list broker?

A national ID database would also draw the attention of every hacker in the world. The database would be, as one analyst colorfully put it, the "big red target, the bullseye, the holy grail of black hats." Optimists hope that encryption will protect the data. However, the encryption technology used for a prototype RFID passport planned for use by the Netherlands was hacked in just two hours by a security firm partnering with a local television show.

Laws to limit additional data collection and restrict access could help prevent abuse of a national ID database, just as the Fourth Amendment protects citizens against illegal searches and seizures. However, many citizens in this country founded on liberty do not find that idea reassuring.

INFOWEBLINKS

You'll find lots more information about this issue at the **Database Privacy InfoWeb**.

W **CLICK TO CONNECT**
www.course.com/np/concepts11/ch11

What Do You Think?

ISSUE

1. Do you support the idea that a national ID card can help combat terrorism and help secure U.S. borders?   ○ Yes ○ No ○ Not sure

2. Are you comfortable about the tradeoff between privacy and security that accompanies a national ID database?   ○ Yes ○ No ○ Not sure

3. Do you think most citizens are well informed about the privacy risks associated with a national ID database?   ○ Yes ○ No ○ Not sure

4. Will you get a national ID card?   ○ Yes ○ No ○ Not sure

▶ SAVE RESPONSES

11

COMPUTERS IN CONTEXT

Medicine

THE HEALTH CARE INDUSTRY was an early adopter of computer technology for traditional data processing applications, such as client billing and employee payroll. A computer's ability to process and store thousands of records helps reduce hospital administrative costs. Linking hospital billing to health insurance companies streamlines cumbersome manual procedures for submitting insurance claims. These "behind-the-scenes" applications do not, however, directly affect the quality of health care, where computer technology has recently made a significant contribution.

Until recent years, paper charts dangled from the foot of every hospital bed and additional information was stored in thick file folders in nursing stations or the hospital's medical records department. Patient records include doctors' diagnoses, laboratory test results, medication schedules, and charts depicting a patient's vital signs. The process of maintaining these paper-based records is time consuming and quite open to errors. Effective treatments might be dangerously delayed while a slip of paper that holds laboratory results wends its way through the hospital corridors. In a hospital where a patient's condition can change suddenly and unexpectedly, health care providers need instant and ubiquitous access to the information contained in the patient's record.

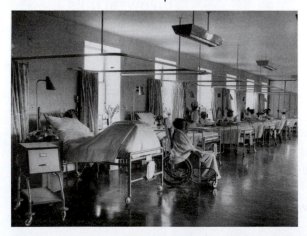

Today, technology allows hospitals to store patient records in computer databases that are instantly accessible to doctors, nurses, and other health care workers. A nurse can access a patient's record from a computer in the nursing station to check care

instructions and enter vital statistics. Doctors can access a patient's record from an office or home computer to check progress, order tests, and make decisions when minutes count. Lab technicians can enter test results immediately into a patient's record. Patient records tie into a comprehensive hospital information system (HIS) that integrates just about every aspect of hospital management. Even the hospital dietitian can access relevant parts of a patient's record to work out menus that fit a patient's dietary needs, while avoiding allergies.

According to technology pioneer Ray Kurzweil, "medicine is among the most knowledge-intensive professions." Most doctors agree that medicine has grown too complex to have all the answers "in their heads." Today, in just about every aspect of their practices, doctors use computer applications and Internet technologies.

At one time, doctors dictated the results of an examination or surgical procedure. The dictated notes were later transcribed into computer records by staff members. Today's technology allows doctors to enter this information directly into computerized patient records by typing or by dictating into a speech recognition system that digitally converts the spoken word into computer text.

The Internet supplies physicians with many informational and diagnostic resources. Health libraries provide online access to reference databases, such as MEDLINE, and medical reference books, such as *Stat Ref*. Doctors use drug databases to choose appropriate medications, avoid dangerous drug interactions, determine correct dosages, and print out prescriptions. One pediatrician says, "I use the computer to make sure the medicine will work with any other medicines the patient takes, the patient won't be allergic, and to check for warnings about certain foods or alcohol."

Hospitals are ideal candidates for wireless technologies because just about everything and everyone is on the move, including doctors, nurses, patients, and equipment. Overlake Hospital in Bellevue, Washington is a model of future wired, paperless hospitals. Nurses tote portable computer stations, physicians use voice recognition software to enter prescriptions, and bar coded patient wrist bands help caregivers administer and track medications.

The Internet's ability to rapidly disseminate information worldwide makes it a crucial tool for tracking global health threats. During the SARS outbreak in 2003, Web sites maintained by the World Health Organization (WHO) and Centers for Disease Control (CDC) provided statistics on the spread of infection. They also kept doctors, researchers, and reporters up to date on efforts to identify the virus, develop a vaccine, and devise treatment options.

Many doctors use Internet technology to communicate with their colleagues by e-mail and send imaging data, such as X-rays, to specialists. Telemedicine uses communications links to supply medical services at a distance. It can be used to provide specialty medical services to rural patients, and allow medical personnel from several locations to collaborate on patient diagnosis and treatment.

Once limited to telephone consultations and fax transmission of paper-based patient records, today telemedicine takes full advantage of the Internet to transfer electronic patient records, still images, and even full motion video sequences. Images from diverse sources, such as X-rays, MRIs, and CT scans, stored in the standard DICOM (Digital Imaging and Communications in Medicine) format, can be easily transferred over the Internet and displayed using a single software package.

Computers have become an integral part of modern medical equipment. The use of X-rays was a huge medical breakthrough in the early 1900s, but X-rays capture only a two-dimensional image. A technology called CT (computerized tomography) essentially assembles a series of X-ray images taken from slightly different angles. A computer works with the data to generate a three-dimensional image that can be rotated and viewed from any angle.

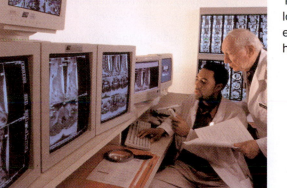

Computers, data, and telecommunications technology team up in a number of mobile medical devices that have revolutionized emergency medical services. An EMS worker describes a device used to monitor suspected heart attack patients: "We can do a comprehensive 12-lead EKG at the scene and the computer inside the LifePak 12 tells us what kind of arrhythmia we may be dealing with and even gives us suggestions for treatments."

Today, most patients want to be informed participants in their health care team. Patients use the Web to find information on diseases, drugs, and treatment options. Doctors frequently recommend health-related Web sites and support groups to patients. Patients can gather information from these sites at their own pace and refer back to it as necessary. The availability of information on the Web reduces the need for doctors to make lengthy explanations that patients often cannot absorb or remember during an office visit.

The computer's use in medicine is not without potential pitfalls. Online patient records raise issues of confidentiality. Many patients are concerned about unauthorized access to their records by employers, Human Resources staff, and hackers.

The Health Insurance Portability and Accountability Act (HIPAA) requires insurance companies to protect the privacy of its policy holders from inappropriate use or disclosure. Insurance company employees are allowed to look at clients' personal health information only in the course of administering claims. Insurance companies are not allowed to disclose personal health information to any other company or to a client's employer without permission. Insurance companies are, however, allowed to divulge information to government agencies if a serious threat to public health and safely exists. HIPAA also gives patients the right to amend incorrect or missing information in their records, and it allows clients to request a list of the disclosures.

The next time you're in a hospital or doctor's office, look around for computers. You're sure to find these essential tools used to improve the effectiveness of health care.

INFOWEBLINKS

You can find more information for this Computers in Context topic at the **Computers and Medicine InfoWeb**.

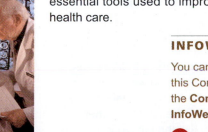

W **CLICK TO CONNECT**
www.course.com/np/concepts11/ch11

11

New Perspectives Labs

On the BookOnCD

To access the New Perspectives labs for Chapter 11, start the BookOnCD, BookOnFlashDrive, or other NP11 BookOn product and then click the icon next to the lab title below.

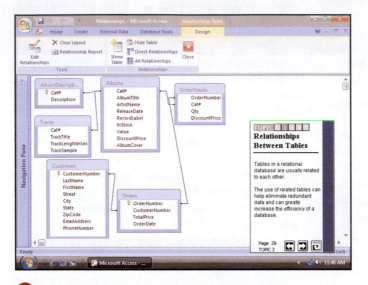

▶ **WORKING WITH DATABASE SOFTWARE**

IN THIS LAB YOU'LL LEARN:

- How relational database software depicts data as tables, records, and fields
- How to use tables and forms to view data
- How to create a table
- How to use primary keys
- How to enter and edit data
- Why relationships between tables are so important
- How to sort data and create an index
- How to search for data
- How to set filters
- How to create queries
- How to view the SQL code for a query
- How to create a report
- How to modify a report in Design view

LAB ASSIGNMENTS

1. Start the interactive part of the lab. Make sure you've enabled Tracking if you want to save your QuickCheck results. Perform each lab step as directed, and answer all the lab QuickCheck questions. When you exit the lab, your answers are automatically graded and your results are displayed.

2. A friend wants to create a table to store information about a collection of old books. List the fields you might include in the table to store information about the books. For each field, specify the field name, data type (text, numeric, date, etc.), and field length. Indicate the primary key(s), and describe how you would sort and/or index the data.

3. Use Microsoft Access or any available file or database management software to create the structure for the table you specified in Assignment 2. Enter at least 10 records. Print a list of all your data.

4. Make a list of five queries that might be useful if your database had hundreds of records. Try these queries on your table. For each query, list the records that were selected.

5. Sketch a report on paper that uses some of the fields in your table. Make sure your report contains a title and headings for each field. Specify whether you would like to align your data at the right, center, or left of each column. Use your software to generate and print the report.

Key Terms

Make sure you understand all the boldfaced key terms presented in this chapter. If you're using the NP11 BookOnCD, BookOnFlashDrive, or other NP11 BookOn product, you can use this list of terms as an interactive study activity. First, try to define a term in your own words, and then click the term to compare your definition with the definition presented in the chapter.

11

Interactive Summary

To review important concepts from this chapter, fill in the blanks to best complete each sentence. When using the NP11 BookOnCD or other BookOn product, click the Check Answers buttons to automatically score your answers.

SECTION A: A [_____] is a collection of information, typically stored as computer files. The information it contains can be stored, updated, organized, output, distributed, searched, and analyzed. A filing cabinet full of folders and papers would be classified as an [_____] file. A [_____] file uses a uniform format to store data for each person or thing in the file. The simplest model for storing data is a [_____] file that consists of a single, two-dimensional table of data elements. Each row in the table is a [_____], and each column of the table is a [_____]. Each kind of record is referred to as a record [_____]. A record that contains data is sometimes referred to as a record [_____]. In databases, records can be related by one-to- [_____] relationships, one-to-many relationships, or many-to-many relationships. The number of associations that can exist between two record types is referred to as [_____]. Relationships can be depicted graphically by using [_____]-relationship diagrams. [_____] databases allow only one-to-many relationships. [_____] databases allow one-to-many and many-to-many relationships. [_____] databases exist as a series of tables that can be related by common fields. A [_____] database, organizes relationships over three or more dimensions. An [_____] database stores data in objects that can be grouped into classes and defined by attributes and methods.

▶ CHECK ANSWERS

SECTION B: Flat files can be created and manipulated by using a variety of tools, including word processing and spreadsheet software. For databases composed of more than one record type, however, it is best to use a database management system, which is abbreviated as [_____].

An [_____]-level database management system typically handles many simultaneous searches, but has limited capability to deal with multiple simultaneous updates. Handling billions of records and performing hundreds of transactions every second requires database [_____] software.

The data in a database can be accessed over the Web. A simple process called [_____] Web publishing converts a database report into an HTML document, which can be displayed by a browser. More sophisticated [_____] Web publishing produces data from a database on demand. HTML forms and XForms not only provide search capabilities, but can also be used to add or modify data in a database with a Web browser. [_____] documents provide a Web-based data management tool that uses special tags as field names within a document.

▶ CHECK ANSWERS

SECTION C:

The first step in designing a relational database is to define its fields by specifying a field name and data type. Integer, date, and [＿＿＿＿＿＿＿] data types are used for fields containing data that might be mathematically manipulated. The [＿＿＿＿＿＿＿] data type is used for fixed-length fields containing text that is not intended to be mathematically manipulated. The [＿＿＿＿＿＿＿] data type is a variable-length field for entering text. The [＿＿＿＿＿＿＿] data type is used to store true/false or yes/no data. The [＿＿＿＿＿＿＿] data type can be used to store URLs. The [＿＿＿＿＿＿＿] data type is used to store binary data, such as MP3 files or graphics. When designing fields, a database designer can also include field formats, field [＿＿＿＿＿＿＿] rules, and lookup routines to reduce data entry errors.

The number of tables in a database can be determined by a process called [＿＿＿＿＿＿＿], which helps a database designer group fields into record types and avoid data redundancy. A database designer must also consider how to sort or index records. The [＿＿＿＿＿＿＿] key for a table specifies the order in which records are stored and indicates where new records are inserted in a table. A database [＿＿＿＿＿＿＿] provides an alternative way to organize records, using a series of keys and pointers to temporarily arrange data without affecting the physical sequence of records specified by the sort order.

▶ CHECK ANSWERS

SECTION D:

SQL is a database query language that typically works behind the scenes as an intermediary between the database [＿＿＿＿＿＿＿] software provided to users and the database itself. Although the specifications for searches and other database tasks are collected by easy-to-use graphical user interfaces, those specifications are converted into SQL [＿＿＿＿＿＿＿], which can communicate directly with the database.

An SQL query contains SQL [＿＿＿＿＿＿＿], such as SELECT, FROM, INSERT, JOIN, and WHERE, plus [＿＿＿＿＿＿＿] that specify the details of the command. Records can be removed from a database using the SQL [＿＿＿＿＿＿＿] command. Records can be added to a table using the SQL [＿＿＿＿＿＿＿] command. To search for data, you can use the SQL [＿＿＿＿＿＿＿] command. To change or replace the data in a field requires the SQL [＿＿＿＿＿＿＿] command. SQL also provides a [＿＿＿＿＿＿＿] command that can be used to temporarily consolidate two tables so that data can be accessed simultaneously from both of them.

▶ CHECK ANSWERS

SECTION E:

Databases are vulnerable to theft, hacking, and unauthorized access. Although [＿＿＿＿＿＿＿] cannot prevent a database from being lost or stolen, it can make the data it contains unusable. This security technique, however, is typically used for archived databases, rather than operational databases. Access controls can be used to restrict physical access to a database, limit user privileges, and regulate data [＿＿＿＿＿＿＿] that establish which fields a particular user is allowed to access. Tracking database use is also an important security tool. If an intruder breaches database security, an [＿＿＿＿＿＿＿] can help to identify the damage and correct it. A patchwork of database security laws in the U.S. leaves loopholes that allow some types of personal data to be gathered, aggregated, and shared with third parties. Individuals can take steps to protect their personal data by vigilantly monitoring what information is released, using strong passwords, running security software, and becoming familiar with the [＿＿＿＿＿＿＿] policy for sites that store personal data.

▶ CHECK ANSWERS

Interactive Situation Questions

Apply what you've learned to some typical computing situations. When using the NP11 BookOnCD, BookOnFlashDrive, or any other NP11 BookOn product, you can type your answers, and then use the Check Answers button to automatically score your responses.

1. You're working for a company that's just getting started with a database project. Your supervisor wants "the most standard kind of database," so you recommend using _____ database management software.

2. You are analyzing a company's customer and order information. Because each customer can place multiple orders, you know this is a(n) _____ -to-many relationship.

3. You are designing a record type that holds customer information. You should use a(n) _____ data type for the fields that hold information such as telephone numbers and Social Security numbers because although this data looks like numbers, you'll never need to use it to perform mathematical calculations.

4. You are creating a movie review database, and one field stores the "star rating" that a popular reviewer gave each movie. Movies are rated from one to four stars, so the "Stars" field is valid only if the number is between 1 and 4. To ensure that nobody enters a value below 1 or above 4, you can use a field _____ rule to filter the data as it's entered into the table.

5. You want to print a professionally designed list of all the records in your database. To organize and format the list, you use a report generator to create a reusable report _____ .

6. You own a fly-fishing shop and maintain an inventory database that, along with inventory data, stores the names

of the wholesalers from which you buy each item. Hot Rod Wholesalers just changed its name to Northern Rod and Reel, so you need to update your database. The best way to accomplish this task would be to perform a(n) _____ update that changes every instance of "Hot Rod Wholesalers" to "Northern Rod and Reel."

7. You are designing the structure for a mail-order catalog company. You recognize that a many-to-many relationship exists between an order and the items listed on the order. That clue indicates that you should separate the data into two _____ , one called Orders and the other called Order Details.

8. Your friend is working on some Web pages, and you notice that they contain tags such as <editor>Ella Ellison</editor>

    <born>1960/05/26</born>

    You surmise that your friend is using _____ instead of HTML.

CHECK ANSWERS

Interactive Practice Tests

Practice tests that consist of 10 multiple-choice, true/false, and fill-in-the-blank questions are available on both the NP11 BookOn products and the NP11 Web site. The questions are selected at random from a large test bank, so each time you take a test, you'll receive a different set of questions. Your tests are scored immediately, and you can print study guides that help you find the correct answers for any questions that you missed.

CLICK TO START

Study Tips

Study Tips help you to organize and consolidate the information in a unit by making lists, outlines, charts, and sketches. You can use paper and pencil or word processing software to complete most of the Study Tip activities.

1. Make sure you can use your own words to correctly answer each of the red focus questions that appear throughout the chapter.

2. Create a descriptive example that would help explain the concepts of data mining, data warehouses, predictive analytics, and OLAP to an average non-technical adult.

3. Make a list of the three different types of cardinality, and write down an example of each.

4. For each of the following pairs of record types, draw an ERD showing whether the relationship is one-to-one, one-to-many, or many-to-many.

   Author—Book   Person—Social Security number

   House—Mailbox   Musician—CD

5. Take a "real-world" entity, like a comic book collection or a recipe file that you might want to store information about in a database, and divide the information into fields and record types.

6. Explain the differences between a record occurrence and a record type.

7. Provide five examples of data you would store in real, integer, text, logical, date, memo, and BLOB data fields.

8. Describe the differences between hierarchical, network, relational, dimensional, object, and object-relational databases.

9. Explain the advantages of using computed fields in a database application.

10. List the techniques that a database designer can use to reduce data entry errors.

11. Use your own words and examples to explain how normalization relates to the way you divide fields into records when designing a database.

12. Explain the differences between sorting and indexing.

13. Use diagrams to explain different ways of providing Web access to the data in a database.

14. Imagine that you must access a library card catalog using SQL. Write an SQL query that you would use to search for any books by J. K. Rowling in a table called Books, where authors' names are stored in a field called AuthorName and book titles are stored in a field called Title.

15. Fill in the blanks on the concept map shown below to show the hierarchy of relationships among the database terms used in this chapter.

Concept Map

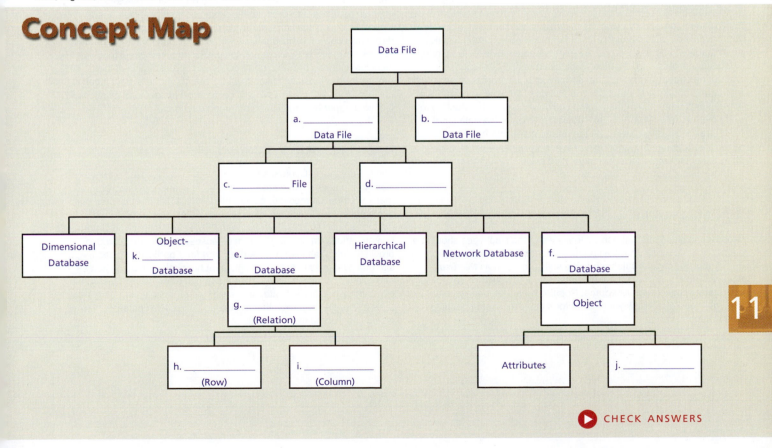

CHECK ANSWERS

11

Projects

CRITICAL THINKING

Type your name into the Google search engine. How much information can you currently find about yourself? How much privacy are you willing to release? Create a table with rows for the following: Name, address, e-mail address, SS#, credit card #, phone number, height, weight, gender, hobbies, medical history, employer, spouse name, children's names. Put the following columns across the top: Applying for a job, visiting the doctor, subscribing to a Web site, making an online purchase, opening a bank account, responding to an e-mail message, registering for classes. Add two more situations to the list. Use a check mark or "OK" to indicate if you would be willing to provide each type of information. Put an "R" in a column if you believe the information is legitimately required. Use a question mark when you're not sure if the information is required.

GROUP PROJECT

Form a group of four to five students. Suppose you must design the record structure for a new information system that holds drivers' license data. Using your own driver licenses, design an effective record structure, indicating record types, field names, field lengths, and data types. Where appropriate, indicate ways that you could minimize data entry errors. Submit your record structure to your instructor.

CYBERCLASSROOM

Look at the Internet Movie Database (*www.imdb.com*) and search for your favorite movie. Examine the field names and content (i.e., title, genre, tagline) imdb uses to organize data about movies. How would you distribute these fields among tables in a relational database? Create the structure for a database that you think duplicates the fields for the Internet Movie Database. You can use Microsoft Access or similar relational database management software. Send your structure to one other member of your team who will try to enter the data for at least three movies (you can limit the number of actors to five per movie). Your team partner should also send you comments for changes or improvements. When you are satisfied with the structure of your database, send it to your instructor.

MULTIMEDIA PROJECT

Create a multimedia database. At least two of the field types should be defined to hold media, such as photos, sounds, narration, or video. Set up a prototype of your database using software, such as Microsoft Access. You can create the media or download it from the Web, giving appropriate citations for its source. Populate your database with at least five records. Follow your instructor's guidelines for submitting your database.

RESUME BUILDER

When you look for a job, you might send query letters and resumes out to several employers. To track the status of each, you can use a database. Use database or spreadsheet software to create a job-hunting database that includes company contact information plus fields to indicate the status of your inquiry. Load the database with at least five sample contacts. Make sure you can use the database to generate mailing labels. You should also be able to make queries to determine which job prospects are still "active" possibilities. Follow your instructor's guidelines for submitting your database and mailing labels.

GLOBALIZATION

Computer databases often store personal information about the citizens of more than one country, yet privacy expectations and laws differ. For this project, explore the differences in privacy laws around the globe. Which countries have the strongest privacy laws and which have the weakest? Which laws would govern the data stored by multinational companies? As a global consumer, which databases would concern you most for potential privacy violations? Consolidate your thoughts into a one- to two-page paper and submit it to your instructor.

ISSUE

The Issue section of this chapter focused on the controversy surrounding national ID cards. To begin this project, consult the Database Privacy InfoWeb and link to the recommended Web pages to get an in-depth overview of the issue. Next, script the dialog for a town meeting between a group of typical small-town citizens and a panel that includes the head of Homeland security, a representative of the American Civil Liberties Union (ACLU), and the head of your local driver's license office. Follow your professor's instructions for submitting your paper by e-mail or as a printed document.

COMPUTERS IN CONTEXT

The Computers in Context section of this chapter focused on several ways computers are used to enhance health care. It pointed out that many Web-based medical resources are available. For this project, explore the Web to find five sites: 1) a site that attempts to make a diagnosis based on a set of symptoms, 2) a site that provides information on various drugs used to treat diseases, 3) a site dedicated to providing information and patient support for a particular disease, 4) a site that evaluates medical care given at hospitals or nursing homes, and 5) a government site dedicated to health or medicine. Record the URL and name for each site, along with the organization that maintains it. Write a paragraph that describes each site's content and who would find the site most useful.

On the Web

STUDENT EDITION LABS

W **CLICK TO ACCESS THE NP11 WEB SITE**
or open your browser and connect to www.course.com/np/concepts11/ch11.
Lab results can be stored in the Universal Gradebook.

Work hands-on in structured simulations practicing important skills and concepts

ADVANCED DATABASES

In the Advanced Databases Student Edition Lab, you will learn about the following topics:

- Using primary and foreign keys
- Identifying relationships between tables
- Identifying determinants, partial dependencies, and transitive dependencies
- Using normalization to design a collection of tables without redundancy

 CHAPTER COURSECAST

Use your computer or iPod to hear a five-minute audio presentation of chapter highlights.

 FLASHCARD COURSECAST

Interact with audio flashcards to review key terms from the chapter.

 DETAILED OBJECTIVES

Make sure that you've achieved all the objectives for a chapter before it's time for your test!

 TEST YOURSELF

Review chapter material by taking these ten-question tests, then send your results to the Universal Gradebook.

ONLINE GAMES

Have some fun while refreshing your memory about key concepts that might appear on the next test. You can even send your results to the Universal Gradebook!

 AND MORE!

At the NP11 Web site you'll also find Extra Content and InfoWebLinks.

11

12 Computer Programming

CHAPTER CONTENTS

LEARNING OBJECTIVES

- Describe the roles of computer programmers and software engineers
- Categorize today's popular computer programming languages by generation and paradigm
- Explain the process of planning, coding, and testing a computer program
- Describe the advantages and disadvantages of generic text editors, program editors, and VDEs for coding computer programs
- Define the term *algorithm* and describe how it relates to procedural programming
- Identify various tools that programmers use to plan programs, such as flowcharts, structured English, pseudocode, UML diagrams, and decision tables
- Follow the control structures for a procedural program
- Describe the major concepts of object-oriented programming, such as objects, classes, inheritance, messages, methods, polymorphism, and encapsulation
- Create some basic facts and rules using Prolog syntax
- Describe how a declarative language, such as Prolog, satisfies goals by instantiation
- Describe vulnerabilities in software program code and explain the steps programmers can take to write more secure code
- List steps that consumers can take to avoid vulnerabilities that exist in software with code defects

☑ PRE-ASSESSMENT QUIZ

Take the pre-assessment quiz to find out how much you know about the topics in this chapter. ▶

MULTIMEDIA and INTERACTIVE ELEMENTS
When using the BookOnCD, BookOnFlashDrive, or other NP11 BookOn product, the ▶ icons are clickable to access multimedia resources.

BEFORE YOU READ ON, **TRY IT**

CAN I WRITE A SIMPLE COMPUTER PROGRAM?

Think about your favorite computer game. Chances are the program that makes it tick is huge and complex. Yet, all computer programs are based on simple ideas that are easy to grasp. Do the following steps to try your hand at writing a program that changes the display color based on the current time. If it is before noon, the color will change to yellow, which is designated by the letter E. If it is afternoon, the color will change to blue, which is designated by the number 9.

1. Start your computer and use the Start button to access the All Programs menu. Select Accessories, then click Notepad.

2. When the Notepad window opens, type the following program:

```
REM Program to change display colors

@echo off

set time = %time%

echo %time%

if %time% lss 12 color E

if %time% gtr 12 color 9

pause

color
```

3. Save the program in your main user folder (not in your Documents folder) with the name C:Change.bat. Make sure you use bat as the file extension! Write down the full path (such as C:\Users\Your Name).

4. Click the Start button, point to All Programs, point to Accessories, and then select Command Prompt.

5. When the black Command Prompt window opens, make sure the command prompt lists your main user folder, i.e., C:\Users\Your Name. If you need to change it, type CD\ followed by the full path that you wrote down in step 3.

6. Type **change** and press the Enter key. Your program should start, display the time, turn the type either yellow or blue, and then display the message "press any key to continue." After you do so, the display will return to its original color.

7. Close the Command Prompt window. You'll discover more about the program you wrote as you read Chapter 12.

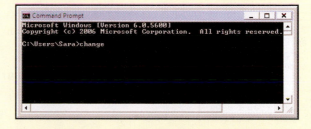

WEB SITE

Visit the NP11 Web site to access additional resources (w) that accompany this chapter.

Programming Basics

EVEN IF you are not planning to become a computer programmer or software engineer, you are likely to use many computer programs during your career. When you realize that your word processing software contains in excess of 750,000 lines of code, you can understand how a few bugs might exist. You can also understand why you would not want to undertake the task of writing word processing software on your own—that project is best left to professional programming teams. Although you would not typically write the productivity software you use, you might have the opportunity to participate in the development of software applications that are specific to your needs. Understanding the basics of computer programming can help you constructively plan and productively participate in the development process.

COMPUTER PROGRAMMING AND SOFTWARE ENGINEERING

What is program code? As you learned in earlier chapters, a computer program is a set of step-by-step instructions that tell a computer how to solve a problem or carry out a task. The instructions that make up a computer program are sometimes referred to as **code**, probably because program instructions for first-generation computers were entered as binary codes. Coding refers to entering a list of commands that become a computer program. Today, program code contains familiar English-like words. Figure 12-1 illustrates the code for a short program that converts feet and inches into centimeters.

FIGURE 12-1

A typical computer program consists of lines of code that tell a computer how to solve a problem or carry out a task. This program is written in a computer programming language called Pascal.

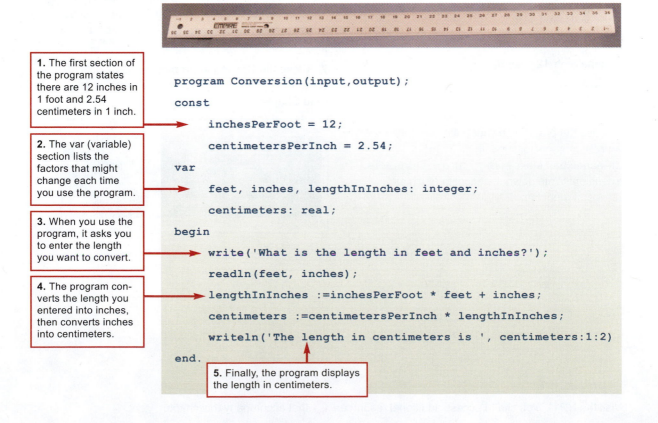

1. The first section of the program states there are 12 inches in 1 foot and 2.54 centimeters in 1 inch.

2. The var (variable) section lists the factors that might change each time you use the program.

3. When you use the program, it asks you to enter the length you want to convert.

4. The program converts the length you entered into inches, then converts inches into centimeters.

5. Finally, the program displays the length in centimeters.

```pascal
program Conversion(input,output);
const
    inchesPerFoot = 12;
    centimetersPerInch = 2.54;
var
    feet, inches, lengthInInches: integer;
    centimeters: real;
begin
    write('What is the length in feet and inches?');
    readln(feet, inches);
    lengthInInches :=inchesPerFoot * feet + inches;
    centimeters :=centimetersPerInch * lengthInInches;
    writeln('The length in centimeters is ', centimeters:1:2)
end.
```

A computer program is typically stored as a file and transferred into RAM when needed, but a computer program can also be embedded in computer hardware—in a ROM chip, for example. A computer program can exist as a single module that provides all the instructions necessary for a software application, device driver, or operating system. Alternatively, a computer program might consist of several modules that form a software application or operating system.

How big is a typical computer program? Compared to commercial application software, the programs that you'll work with in this chapter are relatively tiny. Windows Vista contains about 50 million lines of code. Even a typical cell phone contains over a million lines of code. Research has shown that, on average, one person can write, test, and document only 20 lines of code per day. It is not surprising, then, that most commercial programs are written by programming teams and take many months or years to complete.

Who creates computer programs? Computer programs are developed by computer programmers (programmers for short) or software engineers. Computer programmers typically focus on coding computer programs, whereas software engineers tend to focus on designing and testing activities (Figure 12-2).

FIGURE 12-2

Like a computer programmer, a software engineer designs, codes, tests, and documents software, but tends to focus on designing and testing activities. Software engineers approach these activities using formalized techniques based on mathematical proofs, computer science research, and engineering theory. For example, a computer programmer might code a search routine by simply instructing the computer to step through a list looking for a match. In contrast, a software engineer might consider several sophisticated methods for implementing the search, and select the one that provides the greatest efficiency based on the computer architecture and the data being processed.

What's the difference between computer programming and software engineering? **Computer programming** encompasses a broad set of activities that include planning, coding, testing, and documenting. Most computer programmers participate to some extent in all of these phases of program development, but focus on the coding process.

Software engineering is a development process that uses mathematical, engineering, and management techniques to reduce the cost and complexity of a computer program while increasing its reliability and modifiability. It can be characterized as more formalized and rigorous than computer programming. It is used on large software projects where cost overruns and software errors might have disastrous consequences.

Some software engineering activities overlap with the systems analysis and design activities presented in Chapter 10. To distinguish between the two, remember that systems analysis and design encompass all aspects of an information system, including hardware, software, people, and procedures. In contrast, software engineering tends to focus on software development.

12

PROGRAMMING LANGUAGES AND PARADIGMS

What is a programming language? A **programming language**, or computer language, is a set of keywords and grammar rules designed for creating instructions that a computer can ultimately process or carry out. Most people are familiar with names of popular programming languages, such as BASIC, C, Pascal, FORTRAN, Java, and COBOL. But many other programming languages, such as 8088 assembly, FORTH, LISP, and APL, remain relatively unknown to the general public.

The program you wrote at the beginning of the chapter to change the text color displayed on your computer screen was written in DOS scripting language, which is supported in most versions of Windows.

Just as an English sentence is constructed from various words and punctuation marks that follow a set of grammar rules, each instruction for a computer program consists of keywords and parameters that are held together by a set of rules. A **keyword**, or command, is a word with a predefined meaning for the compiler or interpreter that translates each line of program code into machine language. Keywords for the Pascal computer language include WRITE, READ, IF...THEN, and GOSUB. The Change.bat program you wrote used keywords such as ECHO, SET, IF, PAUSE, and COLOR.

Keywords can be combined with specific **parameters**, which provide more detailed instructions for the computer to carry out. Keywords and parameters are combined with punctuation according to a series of rules called **syntax**, as shown in Figure 12-3.

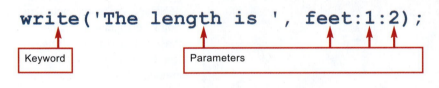

FIGURE 12-3

An instruction for a computer program consists of keywords and parameters, formed into sentence-like statements according to a set of syntax rules.

How are programming languages categorized? Programming languages are categorized in several ways. They can be divided into two major categories: low-level languages and high-level languages. They are also categorized by generation and by paradigm.

What is a low-level language? A **low-level language** typically includes commands specific to a particular CPU or microprocessor family. Low-level languages require a programmer to write instructions for the lowest level of the computer's hardware—that is, for specific hardware elements, such as the processor, registers, and RAM locations. Low-level languages include machine languages and assembly languages.

What is a high-level language? A **high-level language** uses command words and grammar based on human languages to provide what computer scientists call a *level of abstraction* that hides the underlying low-level assembly or machine language. High-level languages, such as COBOL, BASIC, Java, and C, make the programming process easier by replacing unintelligible strings of 1s and 0s or cryptic assembly commands with understandable commands, such as PRINT and WRITE. High-level language commands eliminate many lines of code by substituting a single high-level command for multiple low-level commands (Figure 12-4).

FIGURE 12-4

A single high-level command does the work of multiple low-level commands.

High-level Pascal command

```
Total:=5+4
```

Low-level assembly commands

```
LDA 5
STA Num1
LDA 4
ADD Num1
STA Total
END
```

How did programming evolve from low-level to high-level languages? The first computers were programmed without programming languages. Technicians rewired a computer's circuitry to prepare it for various processing tasks (Figure 12-5). The idea of storing programs in computer memory paved the way for computer programming languages, which allowed a programmer to write commands and load them into the computer for execution. Programming languages were very primitive at first, but they evolved through many generations into the computer languages of today.

What was the first generation of programming languages? Machine languages were the first languages available for programming computers and, therefore, they are sometimes referred to as **first-generation languages**. In Chapter 1, you learned that a machine language consists of a set of commands, represented as a series of 1s and 0s, corresponding to the instruction set that is hardwired into the circuitry of a microprocessor.

A machine language is specific to a particular CPU or microprocessor family. For example, the machine language that is hardwired into a Pentium 4 processor includes many unique commands that are not wired into older PCs with Intel 8088 microprocessors or Macintosh-based PowerPC microprocessors. Although machine languages still work on today's computers, programmers rarely use machine languages to write programs.

What is a second-generation language? An **assembly language** allows programmers to use abbreviated command words, called op codes, such as LDA for load, rather than the 1s and 0s used in machine languages. At the time assembly languages were first introduced, they were hailed as a significant improvement over machine languages, and came to be known as **second-generation languages**.

Like a machine language, an assembly language is classified as a low-level language because it is machine specific—each assembly language command corresponds on a one-to-one basis to a machine language instruction. As you might expect, the assembly language instructions for an Intel Core 2 microprocessor differ from those for an 8088 or a PowerPC microprocessor. An assembly language is useful when a programmer wants to directly manipulate what happens at the hardware level. Today, programmers typically use assembly languages to write system software, such as compilers, operating systems, and device drivers.

What is a third-generation language? When high-level languages were originally conceived in the 1950s, they were dubbed **third-generation languages** because they seemed a major improvement over machine and assembly languages. Third-generation languages used easy-to-remember command words, such as PRINT and INPUT, to take the place of several lines of assembly language op codes or lengthy strings of machine language 0s and 1s. Third-generation languages, such as COBOL and FORTRAN, were used extensively for business and scientific applications. Pascal and BASIC were popular teaching languages. C and its derivative languages remain popular today for system and application software development, for example to develop Microsoft Windows and Linux.

Many computer scientists believed that third-generation languages would eliminate programming errors. Errors certainly became less frequent, and program development time decreased significantly. Programmers using third-generation languages still made a variety of errors, however, so computer language development continued to progress.

FIGURE 12-5

Technicians programmed the first computers by changing the circuitry.

12

What is a fourth-generation language? In 1969, computer scientists began to develop high-level languages, called **fourth-generation languages**, which more closely resemble human languages, or natural languages, than do third-generation languages. Fourth-generation languages, such as SQL and RPG-I, eliminate many of the strict punctuation and grammar rules that complicate third-generation languages. Today, fourth-generation languages are typically used for database applications. A single SQL command, such as SORT TABLE Kids on Lastname, can replace many lines of third-generation code, as shown in Figure 12-6.

FIGURE 12-6

A single command written in a fourth-generation language can replace many lines of third-generation code.

```
SORT TABLE Kids on Lastname
```

```
PUBLIC SUB Sort(Kids As Variant, inLow As Long, inHi As Long)
    DIM pivot   As Variant
    DIM tmpSwap As Variant
    DIM tmpLow  As Long
    DIM tmpHi   As Long
    tmpLow = inLow
    tmpHi = inHi
     pivot = Kids((inLow + inHi) \ 2)
    WHILE (tmpLow <= tmpHi)
       WHILE (Kids(tmpLow) < pivot And tmpLow < inHi)
          tmpLow = tmpLow + 1
       WEND
       WHILE (pivot < Kids(tmpHi) And tmpHi > inLow)
          tmpHi = tmpHi - 1
       WEND
     IF (tmpLow <= tmpHi) THEN
          tmpSwap = Kids(tmpLow)
          Kids(tmpLow) = Kids(tmpHi)
          Kids(tmpHi) = tmpSwap
          tmpLow = tmpLow + 1
          tmpHi = tmpHi - 1
       END IF
    WEND
    IF (inLow < tmpHi) THEN Sort Kids, inLow, tmpHi
    IF (tmpLow < inHi) THEN Sort Kids, tmpLow, inHi
END SUB
```

What about fifth-generation languages? In 1982, a group of Japanese researchers began work on a fifth-generation computer project that used Prolog—a computer programming language based on a declarative programming paradigm, which is described in detail later in the chapter. Prolog and other declarative languages became closely identified with the fifth-generation project and were classified by some experts as **fifth-generation languages**. Other experts disagree with this classification and instead define fifth-generation languages as those that allow programmers to use graphical or visual tools to construct programs, instead of typing lines of code. You'll learn more about visual programming later in the chapter.

What is the best programming language? Hundreds of programming languages exist, and each has unique strengths and weaknesses. Although it might be possible to select the best language for a particular project, most computer scientists would find it difficult to agree on one all-around best language. The table in Figure 12-7 on the next page briefly describes some of the programming languages discussed in this chapter.

INFOWEBLINKS

Programmers can choose from a wide array of programming languages. You can learn more about the most popular languages by visiting the **Programming Languages InfoWeb**.

W CLICK TO CONNECT
www.course.com/np/concepts11/ch12

FIGURE 12-7 Selected Programming Languages

Ada: A high-level programming language developed under the direction of the Department of Defense and originally intended for military applications.

APL (A Programming Language): A scientific language used to manipulate tables of numbers.

BASIC (Beginner's All-purpose Symbolic Instruction Code): Developed by John Kemeny and Thomas Kurtz in the mid-1960s, BASIC is a simple, interactive programming language.

C: Developed in the early 1970s by Dennis Ritchie at Bell Laboratories, C is used today for a wide range of commercial software.

C++ and **C#**: Languages derived from C that provide object-oriented (OO) capabilities.

COBOL (COmmon Business Oriented Language): A procedural language developed in the early 1960s and used extensively for mainframe business applications.

CPL (Combined Programming Language): A language developed in the 1960s for scientific and commercial programming.

Eiffel: An advanced OO language developed in 1988 with syntax similar to C.

FORTRAN (FORmula TRANslator): One of the original third-generation languages; developed in the 1950s and is still used today for scientific applications.

Haskell: A functional programming language named for the mathematician Haskell Brooks Curry.

Java: A C++ derivative developed by Sun Microsystems used extensively for Web-based programming.

LISP (LISt Processing): Developed in 1959 by famed artificial intelligence researcher John McCarthy, LISP is used for artificial intelligence applications.

Pascal: Named in honor of Blaise Pascal, who invented one of the first mechanical adding machines, Pascal is a third-generation language developed to teach students programming concepts.

PL/1 (Programming Language 1): A complex business and scientific language developed in 1964 by IBM that combines FORTRAN, COBOL, and ALGOL.

Prolog (PROgramming in LOGic): A declarative language developed in 1972 and used for artificial intelligence applications.

REALbasic (RB): A modern OO version of BASIC that works cross platform on Windows, Macs, and Linux.

RPG (Report Program Generator) and **RPG-II**: An IBM programming platform introduced in 1964 for easily generating business reports.

Scheme: A dialect of LISP, used for computer research and teaching.

SIMULA (SIMUlation LAnguage): Believed to be the first object-oriented programming language.

Smalltalk: A classic object-oriented programming language developed by Xerox researchers in 1980.

Visual Basic: Windows-based software development kit created by Microsoft in the early 1990s designed for developing Windows-based applications.

What is a programming paradigm? In addition to being classified by level and by generation, programming languages can also be classified by paradigm. Programmers approach problems in different ways. Whereas one programmer might focus on the steps required to complete a specific computation, another programmer might focus on the data that forms the basis for the computation. The phrase **programming paradigm** refers to a way of conceptualizing and structuring the tasks a computer performs. Quite a number of programming paradigms exist, and they are not mutually exclusive. A programmer might use techniques from multiple paradigms while planning and coding a program.

Some programming languages support a single paradigm. Other programming languages—referred to as **multiparadigm languages**—support more than one paradigm. Figure 12-8 provides a brief description of today's most popular programming paradigms. Sections B, C, and D of this chapter give you a detailed look at three classic paradigms—procedural, object-oriented, and declarative.

FIGURE 12-8

Programming Paradigms

Paradigm	Languages	Description
Procedural	BASIC, Pascal, COBOL, FORTRAN, Ada	Emphasizes linear steps that provide the computer with instructions on how to solve a problem or carry out a task
Object-oriented	Smalltalk, C++, Java	Formulates programs as a series of objects and methods that interact to perform a specific task
Declarative	Prolog	Focuses on the use of facts and rules to describe a problem
Functional	LISP, Scheme, Haskell	Emphasizes the evaluation of expressions, called functions
Event-driven	Visual Basic, C#	Focuses on selecting user interface elements and defining event-handling routines that are triggered by various mouse or keyboard activities

12

PROGRAM PLANNING

How does a programmer plan a computer program? Suppose a group of market analysts—or even a group of hungry students—wants to determine which pizza shop offers customers the best deal. Problems you might try to solve using a computer often begin as questions—for example, "Which pizza place has the best deal?" But such questions might not be stated in a way that helps you devise a method for a computer to arrive at an answer.

A question like "Which pizza place has the best deal?" is vague. It does not specify what information is available or how to determine the best deal. Do you know the price of several pizzas at different pizza places? Do you know the sizes of the pizzas? Do you know how many toppings are included in each price? What does "best deal" mean? Is it merely the cheapest pizza? Is it the pizza that gives you the most toppings for the dollar? Is it the biggest pizza you can get for the $24.63 that you and your friends managed to scrape together? The programming process begins with a problem statement that helps you clearly define the purpose of a computer program.

What is a problem statement? In the context of programming, a **problem statement** defines certain elements that must be manipulated to achieve a result or goal. A good problem statement for a computer program has three characteristics:

- It specifies any assumptions that define the scope of the problem.
- It clearly specifies the known information.
- It specifies when the problem has been solved.

Study Figure 12-9 and see if you can formulate a problem statement that is better than the initial vague question, "Which pizza place has the best deal?"

What is an assumption? In a problem statement, an **assumption** is something you accept as true in order to proceed with program planning. For example, with the pizza problem, you can make the assumption that you want to compare two pizzas. Furthermore, you can assume that some pizzas are round and others are square. To simplify the problem, you might also assume that none of the pizzas are rectangular—that is, none will have one side longer than the other. This assumption simplifies the problem because you need to deal only with the size of a pizza, rather than the length and width of a pizza. A fourth assumption for the pizza problem is that the pizzas you compare have the same toppings. Finally, you can assume that the pizza with the lowest cost per square inch is the best buy.

How does known information apply to a problem statement? The **known information** in a problem statement is the information that you supply to the computer to help it solve a problem. For the pizza problem, the known information includes the prices, shapes, and sizes of pizzas from two pizzerias. The known information is often included in the problem statement as *givens*. For example, a problem statement might include the phrase, "given the prices, shapes, and sizes of two pizzas... ."

Factors, such as price, shape, and size, are often treated as variables in computer programs. A **variable** represents a value that can change. For example, the price of a pizza can vary or change, depending on the pizza shop from which it is purchased, so PizzaPrice could become a variable in the pizza program. In contrast, a **constant** is a factor that remains the same throughout a program. For example, the mathematical constant pi always

FIGURE 12-9

Two pizza shops advertise special prices. Which one offers the best deal? Can you formulate a problem statement that describes the pizza problem?

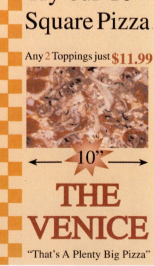

has a value of 3.142. Computer programmers think of variables and constants as named memory locations, equivalent to empty boxes where data can be temporarily stored while being manipulated by a computer program. In your Change.bat program %time% was a variable. The command `set time = %time%` put the value for the actual time into the %time% variable.

How can a problem statement specify when a problem is solved? After identifying the known information, a programmer must specify how to determine when the problem has been solved. Usually this step means specifying the output you expect. Of course, you cannot specify the answer in the problem statement. You won't know, for example, whether VanGo's Pizzeria or The Venice has the best deal before you run the program, but you can specify that the computer should output which pizza is the best deal.

Suppose we assume that the best deal is the pizza with the lowest price per square inch. For example, a pizza that costs 5¢ per square inch is a better deal than a pizza that costs 7¢ per square inch. The problem is solved, therefore, when the computer has calculated the price per square inch for both pizzas, compared the prices, and printed a message indicating which one has the lower price per square inch. You could write this part of the problem statement as, "The computer will calculate the price per square inch of each pizza, compare the prices, then print a message indicating which pizza has the lower price per square inch."

What's the problem statement for the pizza program? You can incorporate your assumptions, known information, and expected output into a problem statement, such as the one in Figure 12-10.

Does the problem statement provide sufficient planning to begin coding? Formulating a problem statement provides a minimal amount of planning, which is sufficient for only the simplest programs. A typical commercial application requires far more extensive planning, which includes detailed program outlines, job assignments, and schedules. Several software development methodologies exist to help program designers and coders plan, execute, and test software. Methodologies can be classified as predictive or agile.

A **predictive methodology** requires extensive planning and documentation up front. It allows little room for adaptation and change once specifications for the software have been completed in the design phase. Predictive methodologies are typically preferred for large software development projects involving more than 10 developers, geographically dispersed development teams, and life-critical applications.

In contrast to predictive methodologies, an **agile methodology** focuses on flexible development and specifications that evolve as a project progresses. In an agile-driven project, for example, programmers might produce a subset of the entire project, show it to users and then plan the next phase of development based on the feedback received. Agile methods seem best for projects with a small core of developers working at a single location.

To some extent, program planning depends on the language and paradigm used to code a computer program. Program planning tools, such as flowcharts, structured English, pseudocode, UML diagrams, and decision tables, are discussed in Sections B, C, and D of this chapter.

Regardless of the tools used, when planning is complete, programmers can begin coding, testing, and documenting.

FIGURE 12-10

Pizza Problem Statement

Assuming that there are two pizzas to compare, that both pizzas contain the same toppings, and that the pizzas could be round or square, and given the prices, shapes, and sizes of the two pizzas, the computer will print a message indicating which pizza has the lower price per square inch.

12

PROGRAM CODING

How do I code a computer program? The process of coding a computer program depends on the programming language you use, the programming tools you select, and the programming paradigm that best fits the problem you're trying to solve. Programmers typically use a text editor, program editor, or VDE to code computer programs.

What is a text editor? A text editor (sometimes referred to as a *generic text editor*) is any word processor that can be used for basic text editing tasks, such as writing e-mail, creating documents, or coding computer programs. Notepad, the accessory program supplied with Microsoft Windows that you used to write Change.bat, is one of the most popular text editors used for programming PCs. When using a text editor to code a computer program, you simply type in each instruction. The lines of code are stored in a file, which can be opened and modified using the usual editing keys.

What is a program editor? A **program editor** is a type of text editor specially designed for entering code for computer programs. These editors are available from several commercial, shareware, and freeware sources. Features vary, but can include helpful programming aids, such as keyword colorizing, word completion, keyboard macros, and search/replace. Figure 12-11 illustrates the difference between a text editor and a program editor.

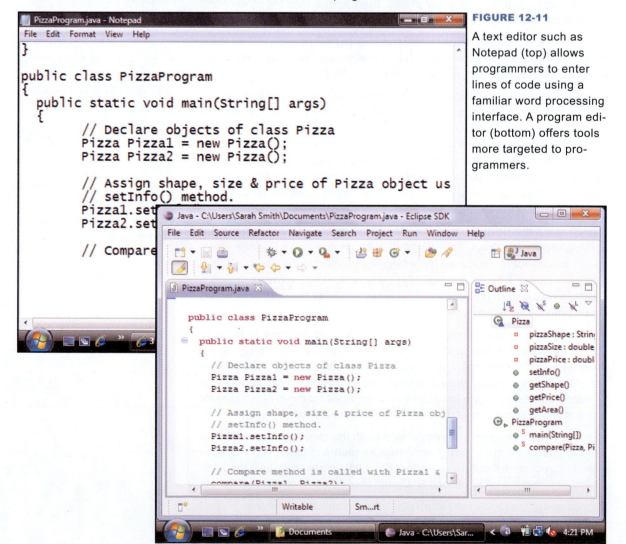

FIGURE 12-11

A text editor such as Notepad (top) allows programmers to enter lines of code using a familiar word processing interface. A program editor (bottom) offers tools more targeted to programmers.

What is a VDE? A **VDE** (visual development environment) provides programmers with tools to build substantial sections of a program by pointing and clicking rather than typing lines of code. A typical VDE is based on a **form design grid** that a programmer manipulates to design the user interface for a program.

By using various tools provided by the VDE, a programmer can add objects, such as controls and graphics, to the form design grid. In the context of a VDE, a **control** is a screen-based object whose behavior can be defined by a programmer. Frequently used controls include menus, toolbars, list boxes, text boxes, option buttons, check boxes, and graphical boxes. Figure 12-12 shows a form design grid and illustrates a variety of controls that can be added.

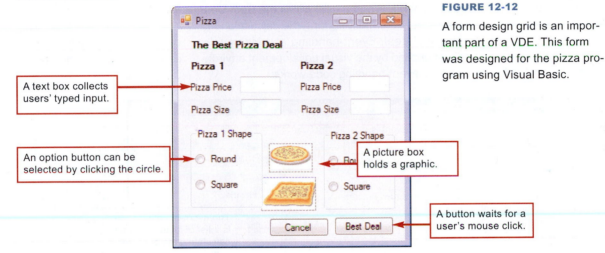

FIGURE 12-12

A form design grid is an important part of a VDE. This form was designed for the pizza program using Visual Basic.

A control can be customized by specifying values for a set of built-in **properties**. For example, a button control can be customized for the pizza program by selecting values for properties such as shape, color, font, and label (Figure 12-13).

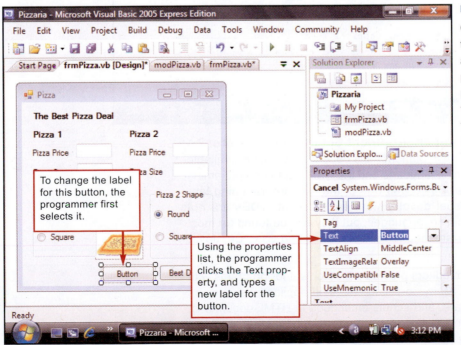

FIGURE 12-13

Controls, such as buttons, can be selected by a programmer from a properties list. Here a programmer is changing the text property of a button so that its label will be "Cancel".

CLICK TO START

12

In a visual development environment, each control comes with a predefined set of events. Within the context of programming, an **event** is defined as an action, such as a click, drag, or key press, associated with a form or control. A programmer can select the events that apply to each control. For example, a programmer might decide that pizza program users will be allowed to left-click either the Round Pizza or Square Pizza button in each Pizza Shape box. Users will not be allowed to right-click, double-click, or drag these buttons, however.

An event usually requires the computer to make some response. Programmers write **event-handling code** for the procedures that specify how the computer responds to each event. For example, if a user clicks an icon depicting a round pizza, an event-handling procedure might set a variable called pizzashape equal to *round*. When a user clicks the Best Deal button, another event-handling procedure must perform the calculations to determine which pizza is the best deal. Event-handling code is usually entered using a program editor supplied by the visual development environment. Figure 12-14 illustrates how event-handling code works.

FIGURE 12-14

The "Best Deal" event-handling code tells the computer what to do when users click the Best Deal button.

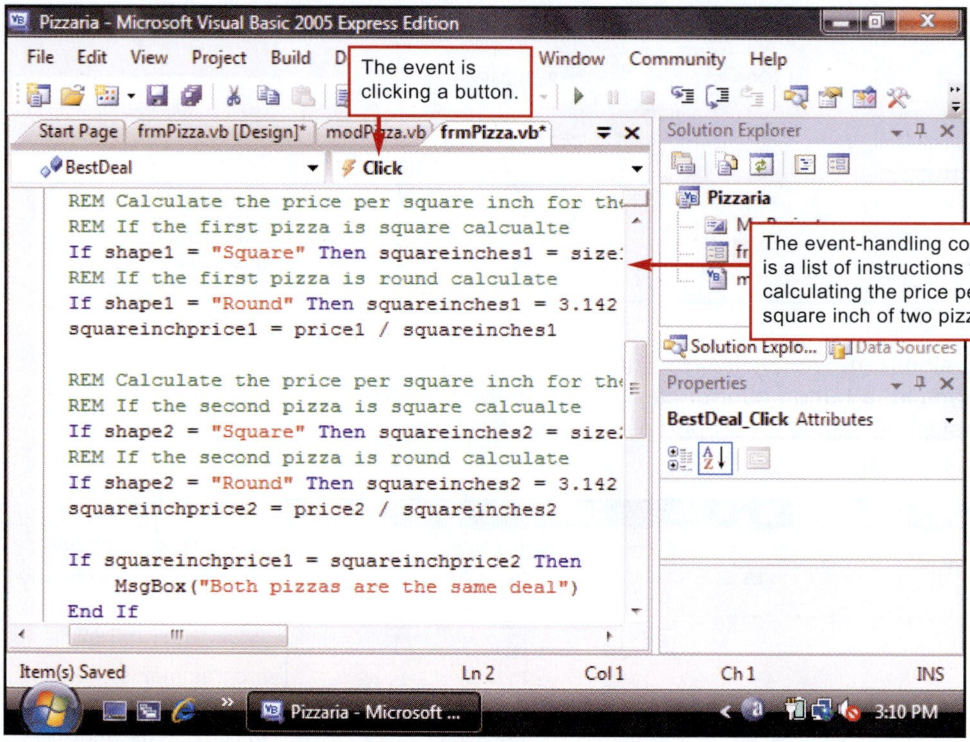

The event is clicking a button.

The event-handling code is a list of instructions for calculating the price per square inch of two pizzas.

Is a visual development environment better than an editor? A

programmer's choice of development tools depends on what is available for a particular programming language and the nature of the programming project. Microsoft Visual Basic was one of the first programming languages to feature a visual development environment. VDEs are not available for all programming languages, but they can be found for most of today's popular programming languages, including C++, C#, Java, REALbasic, and Prolog.

Text editors and program editors provide a fine toolset for programs with minimal user interfaces. Many so-called back-end applications, such as device drivers, middleware, and scripts embedded in HTML documents, require little or no user interaction and, therefore, can be created just as easily with an editor as with a visual development environment.

A visual development environment is a powerful tool for programming software applications for GUI environments, such as Windows, Linux desktops, and Mac OS. Most GUI applications are event-driven, which means that when launched, the program's interface appears on the screen and waits for the user to initiate an event by clicking a menu, dragging an object, double-clicking an icon, typing text, or clicking a button. The fact that the sequence of user actions cannot be predicted introduces a level of complexity that doesn't fit well with traditional programming languages, which tend to approach programs as a fixed sequence of procedures.

Visual development environments have spawned an approach to programming that is sometimes referred to as the **event-driven paradigm**, in which a programmer develops a program by selecting user interface elements and specifying event-handling routines. The programmer is never required to deal with the overall program sequence because the VDE automatically combines user interface elements and event-handling routines into a file that becomes the final computer program. This event-driven paradigm can significantly reduce development time and simplify the entire programming process.

PROGRAM TESTING AND DOCUMENTATION

How does a programmer know if a program works? A computer program must be tested to ensure that it works correctly. Testing often consists of running the program and entering test data to see whether the program produces correct results. If testing does not produce the expected results, the program contains an error, sometimes called a *bug*. This error must be corrected, and then the program must be tested again and again until it runs error-free.

What can cause program errors? When a program doesn't work correctly, it is usually the result of an error made by the programmer. A **syntax error** occurs when an instruction does not follow the syntax rules, or grammar, of the programming language. For example, the BASIC command `If AGE = 16 Then "You can drive."` produces a syntax error because the command word PRINT is missing. The correct version of the command is `If AGE = 16 Then Print "You can drive."` Syntax errors are easy to make, but they are usually also easy to detect and correct. Figure 12-15 lists some common syntax errors.

Another type of program bug is a **runtime error**, which, as its name indicates, shows up when you run a program. Some runtime errors result from instructions that the computer can't execute. The BASIC instruction `DiscountPrice = RegularPrice/0` produces a runtime error because dividing by 0 is a mathematically impossible operation that the computer cannot perform.

Some runtime errors are classified as logic errors. A **logic error** is an error in the logic or design of a program, such as using the wrong formula to calculate the area of a round pizza. Logic errors can be caused by an inadequate definition of the problem or an incorrect formula for a calculation, and are usually more difficult to identify than syntax errors.

How do programmers find errors? Programmers can locate errors in a program by reading through lines of code, much like a proofreader. They can also use a tool called a **debugger** to step through a program and monitor the status of variables, input, and output. A debugger is sometimes packaged with a programming language or can be obtained as an add-on.

FIGURE 12-15

Common Syntax Errors

- Omitting a keyword, such as THEN

- Misspelling a keyword, such as PIRNT

- Omitting required punctuation, such as a period

- Using incorrect punctuation, such as a colon where a semicolon is required

- Forgetting to close parentheses

12

Do computer programs contain any special documentation?
Anyone who uses computers is familiar with program documentation in the
form of user manuals and help files. Programmers also insert documentation called **remarks** into the program code. Remarks are identified by
language-specific symbols, such as // in Java, or keywords, such as Rem in
BASIC.

Remarks are useful for programmers who want to understand how a program works before modifying it. For example, suppose you are assigned to
make some modifications to a 50,000-line program that calculates income
tax. Your task would be simplified if the original programmer included
remarks that identify the purpose of each section of the program and
explain the basis for any formulas used to perform tax calculations.

A well-documented program contains initial remarks that explain its purpose
and additional remarks in any sections of a program where the purpose of
the code is not immediately clear. For example, in the pizza program, the
purpose of the expression `3.142 * (size1 / 2) ^2` might not be immediately obvious. Therefore, it would be helpful to have a remark preceding
the expression, as shown in Figure 12-16.

FIGURE 12-16

A series of remarks in a BASIC
program can explain to programmers the method used to
calculate the square inches in a
round pizza.

```
Rem The program calculates the number of square inches

Rem in a round pizza using the formula pi r squared

Rem pi = 3.142, size/2 = radius,

Rem and (size/2)^2 = radius squared

Rem SquareInches = 3.142*(size/2)^2
```

PROGRAMMING TOOLS

Where can I get programming tools? Some programmers like to
obtain programming tools a la carte by picking up a compiler from one Web
site, selecting an interactive debugger from another Web site, and using
any handy editor, such as Notepad. More typically, programmers download
or purchase an SDK or IDE that contains a collection of programming tools.

An **SDK** (software development kit) is a collection of language-specific programming tools that enables a programmer to develop applications for a
specific computer platform, such as Windows PCs. A basic SDK includes a
compiler, documentation about the language and syntax, and installation
instructions. More sophisticated SDKs might also include an editor, a
debugger, a visual user interface design module, and APIs. The components of an SDK are sometimes a hodgepodge of tools without consistent
user interfaces for the programmer. For a more polished development environment, programmers turn to IDEs.

An **IDE** (integrated development environment) is a type of SDK that packages a set of development tools into a sleek programming application. The
modules in the application—editor, compiler, debugger, and user interface
development tool—have a uniform set of menus and controls, which
simplifies the programming process.

SDKs and IDEs are available on the Web as shareware or commercial products. Some of these development tools—especially IDEs—are so large that they are not practical to download without a high-speed Internet connection. For programmers limited to dial-up speeds, SDKs and IDEs can be ordered on the Web and shipped on CDs.

Do I need components for my programming projects? Every feature of a lengthy computer program is not necessarily created from scratch. Components can be incorporated into a program, saving days, weeks, or months of programming time. A **component** is a prewritten module, typically designed to accomplish a specific task. For example, one component might provide spreadsheet capabilities, while another component might provide encryption capabilities.

What's an API? In the context of computer programming, **API** is an abbreviation for application program interface or application programming interface. An API is a set of application program or operating system functions that programmers can access from within the programs they create. For example, the Windows API includes code for an assortment of dialog box controls familiar to anyone who uses a PC. The ability to browse through file folders is one element of the Windows API that might be useful in any application program that allows users to open or save files. APIs are usually supplied as part of an SDK.

Do programmers use standard programming tools to develop computer games? Creating a computer game is a multifaceted project that includes creating a multiple-level virtual world, populating it with autonomous and user-controlled characters, providing characters with weapons and food, determining how characters interact with objects, adding sound effects, and keeping score (Figure 12-17).

At the core of every computer game is a program that ties together the virtual game world, characters, weapons, and other objects. Most of these programs are written using standard SDK and IDE programming tools.

What's the most popular programming language for game development? C and C++ are the most popular programming languages for commercial games. Serious game programmers universally learn those languages and Microsoft's Visual C++ is their IDE of choice. MinGW Studio and DevC++ offer lower-cost alternatives with almost as much power.

Although many independent game developers use C and C++, some indies prefer languages such as BASIC and Java. Popular IDEs and SDKs for these languages include DarkBasic, Purebasic, REALBasic, Visual Basic, JCreator, Sun Java Studio Creator, and Eclipse.

What other tools are handy for game programmers? Computer games take place in virtual 3-D worlds populated by animated characters and objects that characters can pick up, move, open, and shoot. On commercial game projects, artists usually create, render, and animate game objects using bitmap, vector, 3-D, and animation graphics software. For indies without artistic talent, 3-D animated characters can be obtained from freelance artists who peddle their creations on the Web at sites such as *www.3dcafe.com/*.

A type of special effects software called a **particle renderer** helps developers create explosions, flares, fog, and fairy dust. **Pathfinder algorithms** distributed as APIs map character routes, limiting them to valid paths and preventing them from walking through walls (unless they are magic users).

FIGURE 12-17

Game development is a hot career field. Independent, or indie, game developers work on a freelance basis for game publishers or create their own games and market them as shareware. Commercial game developers collaborate with artists, animators, musicians, and even Hollywood stars to create arcade-style and adventure games for companies such as Electronic Arts, LucasArts, Nintendo, and Sony.

12

Developers also use a variety of audio and sound software to record, edit, and mix sound effects for gun shots, explosions, footsteps, and so on. Even non-musicians can generate upbeat background music by using MIDI or tracker software. The tracker file format, popular for PC-based computer games, combines MIDI music and instrument sound patches in one file.

Commercially available artificial intelligence APIs and components can plug into programs to control the actions of autonomous, non-player controlled monsters and foes. Physics APIs can tie into objects to make them respond with life-like realism to gravity, momentum, and collisions. Digital Rights Management (DRM) software is also available to help game developers protect their creations from piracy and illegal copying.

Developers on the Windows platform use Microsoft's DirectX SDK, a library of APIs designed specifically for game programming to quickly and efficiently communicate with video hardware, sound hardware, networks, and input devices.

Figure 12-18 lists graphics, audio, API, and DRM tools that are popular with game developers. You'll find more information about game programming tools at the Programming Tools InfoWeb.

How can I learn computer programming? You can learn the fundamentals of programming by taking a class or working with an online tutorial. When you've gained fluency in a programming language, you can hone your skills by participating in an open source software development project. When you join, you'll be given a programming task by an online project manager. Your work will be reviewed by experienced members of the team who will help you meet the exacting standards of professional developers.

FIGURE 12-18

Game Programming Tools

3-D Object Modeling
Maya
OpenGL
3D Studio

Special Effects
LHFire
ParticleIllusion

Audio Recording and Mixing
Ardour
Audition
Audacity

MIDI Music Generators
Acid Music
Psycle

DRM
Armadillo
Themidia

General Purpose API Libraries
DirectX
Allegro

Artificial Intelligence
AI.implant
DirectAI
OpenAI

Pathfinding
MicroPather
PATHEngine

Physics
Havok
Tokamak
True Axis

QuickCheck

1. The instructions that make up a computer program are sometimes referred to as code. True or false? [   ]

2. Software [   ] plan and develop computer software using formalized techniques based on mathematical proofs, computer science research, and engineering theory.

3. A programming language typically supports one or more programming [   ], such as procedural, object-oriented, or declarative.

4. [   ] -generation programming languages, such as COBOL and FORTRAN, use easy-to-remember command words.

5. A(n) [   ] development environment provides programmers with tools to build substantial sections of a program by pointing and clicking.

6. Programmers can use a software tool called a(n) [   ] to step through a program and find errors.

7. A(n) [   ] is a set of application program or operating system functions that programmers can access from within the programs they create. (Hint: Use the acronym.)

 ► CHECK ANSWERS

Procedural Programming

EARLY APPROACHES to computer programming were based on writing step-by-step instructions for the computer to follow. This technique is still in widespread use today and provides an easy starting point for learning what programming is all about. In this section, the examples are written in BASIC because it is one of the easiest programming languages to grasp.

ALGORITHMS

What is procedural programming? The traditional approach to programming uses a **procedural paradigm** (sometimes called an imperative paradigm) to conceptualize the solution to a problem as a sequence of steps. A program written in a procedural language typically consists of self-contained instructions in a sequence that indicates how a task is to be performed or a problem is to be solved.

A programming language that supports the procedural paradigm is called a **procedural language**. Machine languages, assembly languages, COBOL, FORTRAN, C, and many other third-generation languages are classified as procedural languages. Procedural languages are well suited for problems that can be easily solved with a linear, or step-by-step, algorithm. Programs created with procedural languages have a starting point and an ending point. The flow of execution from the beginning to the end of a program is essentially linear—that is, the computer begins at the first instruction and carries out the prescribed series of instructions until it reaches the end of the program.

What is an algorithm? An **algorithm** is a set of steps for carrying out a task that can be written down and implemented. For example, the algorithm for making a batch of macaroni and cheese is a set of steps that includes boiling water, cooking the macaroni in the water, and making a cheese sauce (Figure 12-19). The algorithm is written down, or expressed, as instructions in a recipe. You can implement the algorithm by following the recipe instructions.

An important characteristic of a correctly formulated algorithm is that carefully following the steps guarantees that you can accomplish the task for which the algorithm was designed. If the recipe on a macaroni package is a correctly formulated algorithm, by following the recipe, you should be guaranteed a successful batch of macaroni and cheese.

How do I write an algorithm? An algorithm for a computer program is a set of steps that explains how to begin with known information specified in a problem statement and how to manipulate that information to arrive at a solution. Algorithms are usually written in a format that is not specific to a particular programming language. This approach allows you to focus on formulating a correct algorithm, without becoming distracted by the detailed syntax of a computer

> **TIP**
> This chapter presents some fairly technical material. You might want to consider taking a break between sections.

FIGURE 12-19

The algorithm for making macaroni and cheese is expressed as a recipe.

12

programming language. In a later phase of the software development process, the algorithm is coded into instructions written in a programming language so that a computer can implement it.

How do I figure out an algorithm? To design an algorithm, you might begin by recording the steps you take to solve the problem manually. If you take this route with the pizza problem, you must obtain initial information about the cost, size, and shape of each pizza. The computer also needs this initial information, so part of your algorithm must specify how the computer gets it. When the pizza program runs, it should ask the user to enter the initial information needed to solve the problem. Your algorithm might begin like this:

> **Ask the user for the shape of the first pizza and hold it in RAM as Shape1.**
>
> **Ask the user for the price of the first pizza and hold it in RAM as Price1.**
>
> **Ask the user for the size of the first pizza and hold it in RAM as Size1.**

Next, your algorithm should specify how to manipulate this information. You want the computer to calculate the price per square inch, but a statement like "Calculate the price per square inch" neither specifies how to do the calculation, nor deals with the fact that you must perform different calculations for square and round pizzas. A more appropriate set of statements for the algorithm is shown in Figure 12-20.

INFOWEBLINKS

Donald Knuth's multivolume collection of programming algorithms, called *The Art of Computer Programming*, is considered one of the best scientific monographs of the twentieth century. You'll find information about this book and more at the **Algorithms InfoWeb**.

 **CLICK TO CONNECT**
www.course.com/np/concepts11/ch12

FIGURE 12-20

The algorithm for calculating the price per square inch must work for square pizzas as well as round ones.

1. To calculate the area of a square pizza, multiply the length of one side by the length of the other side. The sides are the same size in a square, so you can use the formula Size1 * Size1.

2. To calculate the area of a round pizza, use the formula for the area of a circle: πr^2. π is approximately 3.142. r^2 is the square of the radius of the circle. The size of a pizza is its diameter, so you need to divide the diameter by 2 to get the radius, using Size1 / 2. Then you need to square the radius. ^2 is the notation that you use on a computer to indicate the exponent 2.

10" length

8" diameter

4" radius

3. After calculating the area of a pizza, the computer can calculate the price per square inch.

```
If Shape1 is square then
    calculate square inches using the formula:
    SquareInches1 = Size1 * Size1
If Shape1 is round then
    calculate square inches using the formula:
    SquareInches1 = 3.142 * (Size1 / 2) ^2
SquareInchPrice1 = Price1 / SquareInches1
```

So far, the algorithm describes how to calculate the price per square inch of one pizza. It should specify a similar process for calculating the price per square inch of the second pizza.

Finally, the algorithm should specify how the computer decides what to display as the solution. You want the computer to display a message indicating which pizza has the lowest square-inch cost, so your algorithm should include steps like the following:

If SquareInchPrice1 is less than SquareInchPrice2 then display the message "Pizza 1 is the best deal."

If SquareInchPrice2 is less than SquareInchPrice1 then display the message "Pizza 2 is the best deal."

But don't forget to indicate what you want the computer to do if the price per square inch is the same for both pizzas:

If SquareInchPrice1 equals SquareInchPrice2 then display the message "Both pizzas are the same deal."

The complete algorithm for the pizza problem is shown in Figure 12-21.

FIGURE 12-21

The algorithm for the pizza problem, written in structured English, has five main sections.

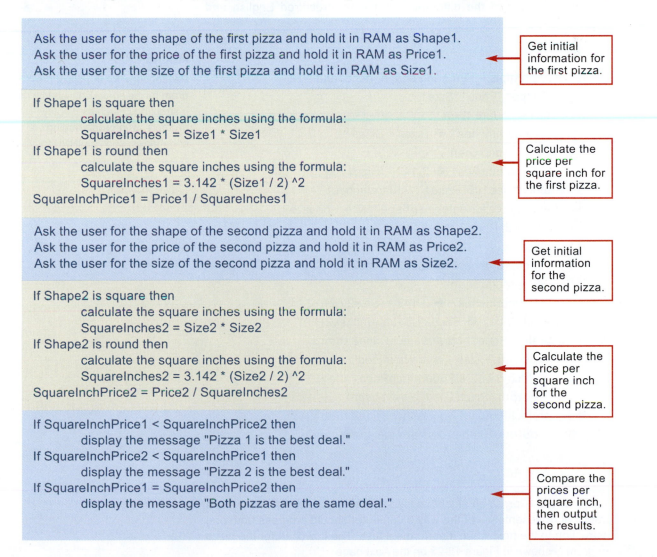

Ask the user for the shape of the first pizza and hold it in RAM as Shape1.
Ask the user for the price of the first pizza and hold it in RAM as Price1.
Ask the user for the size of the first pizza and hold it in RAM as Size1.

Get initial information for the first pizza.

If Shape1 is square then
     calculate the square inches using the formula:
     SquareInches1 = Size1 * Size1
If Shape1 is round then
     calculate the square inches using the formula:
     SquareInches1 = 3.142 * (Size1 / 2) ^2
SquareInchPrice1 = Price1 / SquareInches1

Calculate the price per square inch for the first pizza.

Ask the user for the shape of the second pizza and hold it in RAM as Shape2.
Ask the user for the price of the second pizza and hold it in RAM as Price2.
Ask the user for the size of the second pizza and hold it in RAM as Size2.

Get initial information for the second pizza.

If Shape2 is square then
     calculate the square inches using the formula:
     SquareInches2 = Size2 * Size2
If Shape2 is round then
     calculate the square inches using the formula:
     SquareInches2 = 3.142 * (Size2 / 2) ^2
SquareInchPrice2 = Price2 / SquareInches2

Calculate the price per square inch for the second pizza.

If SquareInchPrice1 < SquareInchPrice2 then
     display the message "Pizza 1 is the best deal."
If SquareInchPrice2 < SquareInchPrice1 then
     display the message "Pizza 2 is the best deal."
If SquareInchPrice1 = SquareInchPrice2 then
     display the message "Both pizzas are the same deal."

Compare the prices per square inch, then output the results.

12

EXPRESSING AN ALGORITHM

What's the best way to express an algorithm? You can express an algorithm in several different ways, including structured English, pseudocode, and flowcharts. These tools are not programming languages, and they cannot be processed by a computer. Their purpose is to give you a way to document your ideas for program design.

Structured English is a subset of the English language with a limited selection of sentence structures that reflect processing activities. Refer to Figure 12-21 on the previous page to see how structured English can be used to express the algorithm for the pizza problem.

Another way to express an algorithm is with pseudocode. **Pseudocode** is a notational system for algorithms that has been described as a mixture of English and your favorite programming language. Pseudocode is less formalized than structured English, so the structure and wording are left up to you. Also, when you write pseudocode, you are allowed to incorporate command words and syntax from the computer language you intend to use for the actual program. Compare Figure 12-22 with Figure 12-21 and see if you can identify some of the differences between structured English and pseudocode.

FIGURE 12-22

Pseudocode for the pizza program mixes some English-like instructions, such as display prompts, with programming commands, such as INPUT.

```
display prompts for entering shape, price, and size
input Shape1, Price1, Size1
if Shape1 = square then
        SquareInches1 ← Size1 * Size1
if Shape1 = round then
        SquareInches1 ← 3.142 * (Size1 / 2) ^2
SquareInchPrice1 ← Price1 / SquareInches1
display prompts for entering shape, price, and size
input Shape2, Price2, Size2
if Shape2 = square then
        SquareInches2 ← Size2 * Size2
if Shape2 = round then
        SquareInches2 ← 3.142 * (Size2 / 2) ^2
SquareInchPrice2 ← Price2 / SquareInches2
if SquareInchPrice1 < SquareInchPrice2 then
        output "Pizza 1 is the best deal."
if SquareInchPrice2 < SquareInchPrice1 then
        output "Pizza 2 is the best deal."
if SquareInchPrice1 = SquareInchPrice2 then
        output "Both pizzas are the same deal."
```

A third way to express an algorithm is to use a **flowchart**. A flowchart is a graphical representation of the way a computer should progress from one instruction to the next when it performs a task. The flowchart for the pizza program is shown in Figure 12-23 on the next page.

CLICK TO START

FIGURE 12-23

The pizza program flowchart illustrates how the computer should proceed through the instructions in the final program.

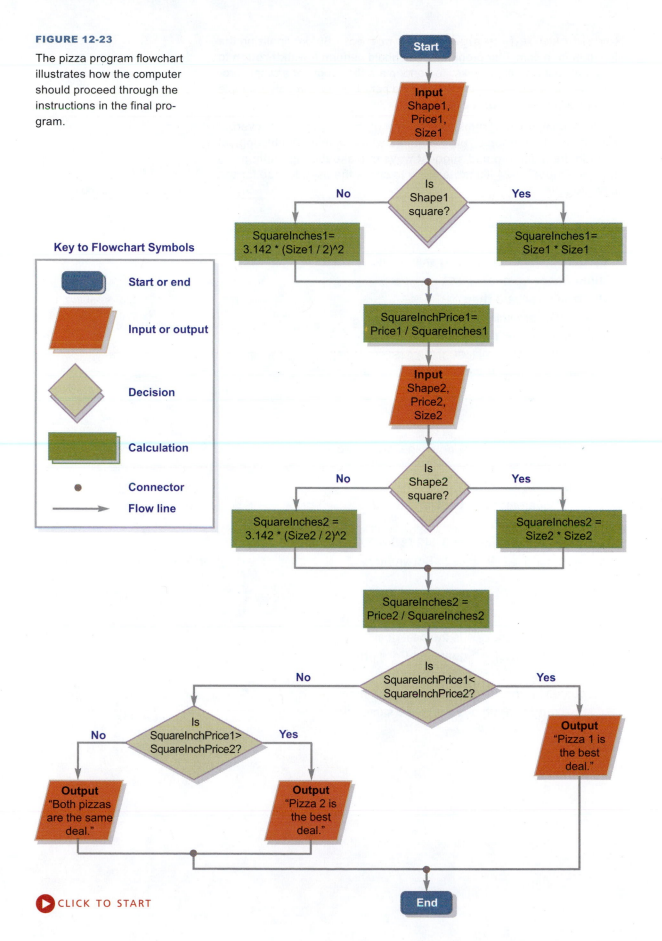

Key to Flowchart Symbols

- Start or end
- Input or output
- Decision
- Calculation
- Connector
- Flow line

12

How do I know if my algorithm is correct? Before finalizing the algorithm for a computer program, you should perform a **walkthrough** to verify that your algorithm works. To perform a walkthrough for a simple program, you can use a calculator, paper, and pencil to step through a sample problem using realistic test data.

For more complex programs, a walkthrough might consist of a verbal presentation to a group of programmers who can help identify logical errors in the algorithm and suggest ways to make the algorithm more efficient. Figure 12-24 illustrates how to check the pseudocode for the pizza program.

FIGURE 12-24

Pseudocode Walkthrough

display prompts for entering shape, price, and size	User asked to enter the first pizza's shape, price, and size
input Shape1, Price1, Size1	User enters square, $10.00, 12

if Shape1 = square **then**
        SquareInches1 ← Size1 * Size1
if Shape1 = round **then**
        SquareInches1 ← 3.142 * (Size1 / 2) ^2
	The first pizza is square, so the computer calculates:
	12 * 12 = 144 for SquareInches1

SquareInchPrice1 ← Price1 / SquareInches1	The computer also calculates: $10.00/144 = .069 for SquareInchPrice1
display prompts for entering shape, price, and size	User asked to enter the second pizza's shape, price, and size:
input Shape2, Price2, Size2	User enters round, $10.00, 12

if Shape2 = square **then**
        SquareInches2 ← Size2 * Size2
if Shape2 = round **then**
        SquareInches2 ← 3.142 * (Size2 / 2) ^2
	The second pizza is round, so the computer calculates:
	$3.142*(12/2)^2 = 113.112$ for SquareInches2

SquareInchPrice2 ← Price2 / SquareInches2	The computer also calculates $10.00/113.112 = .088 for SquareInchPrice2

if SquareInchPrice1 < SquareInchPrice2 **then**
        output "Pizza 1 is the best deal."
if SquareInchPrice2 < SquareInchPrice1 **then**
        output "Pizza 2 is the best deal."
if SquareInchPrice1 = SquareInchPrice2 **then**
        output "Both pizzas are the same deal."
	.069 < .088 so pizza 1 is the best deal

SEQUENCE, SELECTION, AND REPETITION CONTROLS

How do I specify the order in which program instructions are performed by the computer? Unless you specify otherwise, sequential execution is the normal pattern of program execution. During **sequential execution**, the first instruction in the program is executed first, then the second instruction, and so on, to the last instruction in the program. Here is a simple program written in the BASIC programming language that outputs `This is the first line.`, and then outputs `This is the next line`.

```
Print "This is the first line."
Print "This is the next line."
```

Is there an alternative to sequential execution? Some algorithms specify that a program must execute instructions in an order different from the sequence in which they are listed, skip some instructions under certain circumstances, or repeat instructions. **Control structures** are instructions that specify the sequence in which a program is executed. Most programming languages have three types of control structures: sequence controls, selection controls, and repetition controls.

A **sequence control structure** changes the order in which instructions are carried out by directing the computer to execute an instruction elsewhere in the program. In the following simple BASIC program, a GOTO command tells the computer to jump directly to the instruction labeled "Widget." By performing the GOTO statement, the program never carries out the command `Print "This is the next line."`

```
Print "This is the first line."
Goto Widget
Print "This is the next line."
Widget: Print "All done!"
End
```

The flowchart in Figure 12-25 shows how the computer follows a series of sequential commands, and then jumps past other commands as the result of a GOTO command.

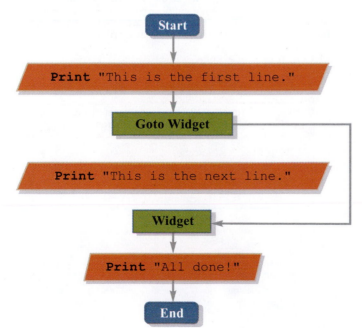

FIGURE 12-25

Executing a GOTO command directs the computer to a different part of the program.

12

▶ CLICK TO START

Although it is the simplest control structure, the GOTO command is rarely used by skilled programmers because it can lead to programs that are difficult to understand and maintain. In 1968, the journal *Communications of the ACM* published a now-famous letter from Edsger Dijkstra, called "Go To Statement Considered Harmful." In his letter, Dijkstra explained that injudicious use of the GOTO statement in programs makes it difficult for other programmers to understand the underlying algorithm, which in turn means that such programs are difficult to correct, improve, or revise.

Experienced programmers prefer to use sequence controls other than GOTO to transfer program execution to a subroutine, procedure, or function. A **subroutine**, **procedure**, or **function** is a section of code that is part of a program, but is not included in the main sequential execution path. A sequence control structure directs the computer to the statements they contain, but when these statements have been executed, the computer neatly returns to the main program. Figure 12-26 shows the execution path of a program that uses the GOSUB command to transfer execution to a subroutine.

INFOWEBLINKS

Read Dijkstra's letter and find out why the GOTO command is considered bad programming at the **GOTO InfoWeb**.

 **CLICK TO CONNECT**
www.course.com/np/concepts11/ch12

FIGURE 12-26

Executing a GOSUB command directs the computer to a different section of the program.

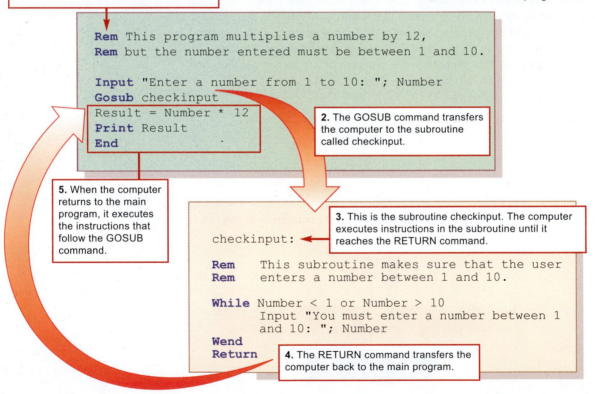

1. This is the main program. The computer executes the main program instructions until it reaches the GOSUB command.

```
Rem This program multiplies a number by 12,
Rem but the number entered must be between 1 and 10.

Input "Enter a number from 1 to 10: "; Number
Gosub checkinput
Result = Number * 12
Print Result
End
```

2. The GOSUB command transfers the computer to the subroutine called checkinput.

5. When the computer returns to the main program, it executes the instructions that follow the GOSUB command.

3. This is the subroutine checkinput. The computer executes instructions in the subroutine until it reaches the RETURN command.

```
checkinput:

Rem   This subroutine makes sure that the user
Rem   enters a number between 1 and 10.

While Number < 1 or Number > 10
      Input "You must enter a number between 1
      and 10: "; Number
Wend
Return
```

4. The RETURN command transfers the computer back to the main program.

Can the computer make decisions while it executes a program? A **selection control structure** tells a computer what to do, based on whether a condition is true or false. A simple example of a selection control structure is the IF...THEN...ELSE command.

The following program uses this command to decide whether a number entered is greater than 10. If the number is greater than 10, the computer prints `That number is greater than 10`. If the number is not greater than 10, the program performs the ELSE instruction and prints `That number is 10 or less`.

```
Input "Enter a number from 1 to 10: "; Number

If Number > 10 Then Print "That number is greater than 10."

Else Print "That number is 10 or less."

End
```

Figure 12-27 uses a flowchart to illustrate how a computer follows commands in a decision structure.

TERMINOLOGY NOTE

Selection control structures are also referred to as decision structures or branches.

FIGURE 12-27

The computer executes a decision indicated on the flowchart by the question in the diamond shape.

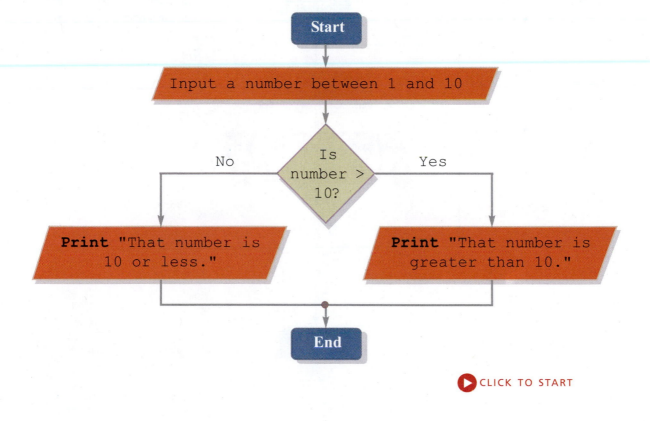

CLICK TO START

Can a computer automatically repeat a series of instructions? A **repetition control structure** directs the computer to repeat one or more instructions until a certain condition is met. The section of code that repeats is usually referred to as a **loop** or **iteration**. Some of the most frequently used repetition commands are FOR...NEXT, DO...WHILE, DO...UNTIL, and WHILE...WEND.

The keyword FOR, DO, or WHILE marks the beginning of a loop. The keyword NEXT, UNTIL, or WEND (which means *while ends*) marks the end of a loop. The following simple BASIC program uses a FOR...NEXT command to print a message three times:

```
For N = 1 to 3

   Print "There's no place like home."

Next N

End
```

Follow the path of program execution in Figure 12-28 to see how a computer executes a series of commands in a repetition structure.

FIGURE 12-28

To execute a loop, the computer repeats one or more commands until some condition indicates that the looping should stop.

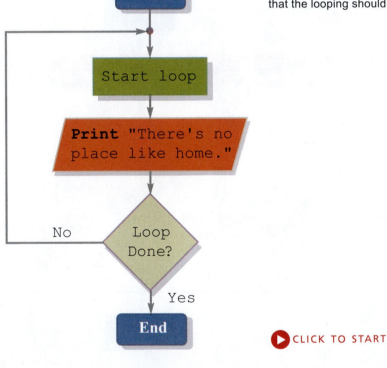

▶ CLICK TO START

To get a better idea of how a FOR...NEXT loop works, pretend that you're the computer executing the FOR...NEXT instructions below. You can use the box labeled N in the margin as a RAM location. As the computer, you would also have a screen on which to display output—use the Screen Output box. Now, walk through the loop.

```
For N = 1 to 3

   Print "There's no place like home."

Next N

End
```

1. As the computer, the first time you see the instruction `For N = 1 to 3`, you set N equal to 1. To do so, write the number 1 in the N box in the margin.

2. You would then execute the next instruction, `Print "There's no place like home."` To do so, write the phrase "There's no place like home." in the Screen Output box.

N

3. The instruction `Next` sends you back to the command `For N = 1 to 3`. Because this occasion is the second time you have executed this statement, put a 2 in the N box in the margin (you can erase the 1 that was there previously).

4. You must check whether the value in box N is greater than 3. Why? Because the command `For N = 1 to 3` means you can continue to loop only if N is 3 or less. N is only 2, so you can proceed.

5. Go to the next instruction, which is `Print "There's no place like home."` Write this sentence again in the Screen Output box.

Screen Output

6. Moving on, you reach the `Next` statement again, which sends you back to the For statement.

7. Continue by changing the value in the N box to 3. Check the N box to make sure it does not contain a value greater than 3. It doesn't, so continue.

8. The next line instructs you to `Print "There's no place like home."` Write this sentence again in the Screen Output box. The `Next` statement sends you back to the For statement. Increase the value in the N box to 4.

9. This time when you check whether the value in N is greater than 3, it is. That means the loop is complete, and you should jump to the statement past the end of the loop.

10. The next statement is `End`, so you've completed the program.

11. When your program is complete, the variable N should contain the number 4, and the screen output box should contain three lines of "There's no place like home."

12

How do I use control structures to write a program? To write the code for the pizza program, you use the control structures, keywords, and syntax provided by your programming language. The completed pizza program, written in BASIC, is provided in Figure 12-29.

FIGURE 12-29

Each line of code for the pizza program consists of keywords (shown in blue) and parameters.

```
Rem The Pizza Program
Rem This program tells you which of two pizzas is the best deal
Rem    by calculating the price per square inch of each pizza.
Rem Collect initial information for first pizza.
Input "Enter the shape of pizza 1:"; Shape1$
Input "Enter the price of pizza 1:"; Price1
Input "Enter the size of pizza 1:"; Size1

Rem Calculate price per square inch for first pizza.
Rem If the first pizza is square, calculate square inches by multiplying one side
Rem    by the other.
If Shape1$ = "square" Then SquareInches1 = Size1 * Size1
Rem If the first pizza is round, calculate the number of square inches where
Rem    pi = 3.142, size / 2 = radius, and (size / 2) ^2 = radius squared.
If Shape1$ = "round" Then SquareInches1 = 3.142 * (Size1 / 2)^2
SquareInchPrice1 = Price1 / SquareInches1

Rem Collect initial information for second pizza.
Input "Enter the shape of pizza 2:"; Shape2$
Input "Enter the price of pizza 2:"; Price2
Input "Enter the size of pizza 2:"; Size2

Rem Calculate price per square inch for second pizza.
If Shape2$ = "square" Then SquareInches2 = Size2 * Size2
If Shape2$ = "round" Then SquareInches2 = 3.142 * (Size2 / 2)^2
SquareInchPrice2 = Price2 / SquareInches2

Rem Decide which pizza is the best deal and display results.
If SquareInchPrice1 < SquareInchPrice2 Then Message$ = "Pizza 1 is the best deal."
If SquareInchPrice2 < SquareInchPrice1 Then Message$ = "Pizza 2 is the best deal."
If SquareInchPrice1 = SquareInchPrice2 Then Message$ = "Both pizzas are the same deal."
Print Message$
End
```

Lines that begin with Rem contain remarks that explain each section of the program. The computer does not execute the remarks.

Data is stored in variables, or memory locations, in RAM. The variable Shape2$ stores text, such as the word *round*. The $ indicates a text variable. Other variables, such as Price1 and Size1, store numbers; they do not include $ as part of the variable name.

PROCEDURAL LANGUAGES AND APPLICATIONS

What are the most popular procedural languages? All the first programming languages were procedural. FORTRAN, developed in the United States in 1954, was the first widely used, standardized computer language. Its implementation of the procedural paradigm set the pattern for other popular procedural languages, such as COBOL, FORTH, APL, ALGOL, PL/1, Pascal, C, Ada, and BASIC.

In 1958, a group of European researchers created a new programming language, dubbed ALGOL, an acronym for ALGOrithmic Language. ALGOL was used for research applications and is the ancestor of several languages in widespread use today. CPL, created by Ken Thompson of AT&T Bell Laboratories, descended from ALGOL and evolved into the C language. Pascal, the popular teaching language created by Niklaus Wirth, was an important step in the development of Ada.

What kinds of problems are best suited to the procedural approach? The procedural approach is best used for problems that can be solved by following a step-by-step algorithm. One of the original problems tackled by computers was computing missile trajectories. Missiles follow an arcing path called a trajectory. Aim too high or too low, and the missile misses its target.

The factors that affect a missile's trajectory include the angle of the gun, weight of the missile, wind direction, wind speed, temperature, and distance to target. However, after these factors are known for a particular target, the calculation follows a simple mathematical algorithm. Therefore, the steps for calculating trajectories remain the same, regardless of the data. That concept is the key to understanding the kinds of problems that are best suited for the procedural approach.

The procedural approach has been widely used for transaction processing, which is characterized by the use of a single algorithm applied to many different sets of data. For example, in the banking industry, the algorithm for calculating checking account balances is the same, regardless of the amounts deposited and withdrawn. Many problems in math and science also lend themselves to the procedural approach.

What are the advantages and disadvantages of the procedural paradigm? The procedural approach and procedural languages tend to produce programs that run quickly and use system resources efficiently. It is a classic approach understood by many programmers, software engineers, and system analysts. The procedural paradigm is quite flexible and powerful, which allows programmers to apply it to many types of problems. For example, although the programming example in this section worked only for round and square pizzas, it could be modified to handle rectangular pizzas, too.

The downside of the procedural paradigm is that it does not fit gracefully with certain types of problems—those that are unstructured or those with very complex algorithms. The procedural paradigm has also been criticized because it forces programmers to view problems as a series of steps, whereas some problems might better be visualized as interacting objects or as interrelated words, concepts, and ideas.

QuickCheck

1. BASIC is an easy to understand programming paradigm because it requires no algorithms. True or false? _____

2. COBOL, FORTRAN, and C are examples of _____ languages.

3. Structured English, _____ , and pseudocode are used by programmers to express algorithms.

4. A decision control tells a computer what to do, based on whether a condition is true or false, whereas a(n) _____ control can change the order in which program instructions are executed.

5. A subroutine is a section of code that is part of a program, but is not included in the main execution path. True or false? _____

6. The section of a program that contains a repetition control is sometimes referred to as an iteration or a(n) _____ .

12

▶ CHECK ANSWERS

Object-Oriented Programming

THE PROCEDURAL PARADIGM forced programmers to view every problem in terms of a step-by-step algorithm. It soon became clear, however, that not every problem fit into the procedural pigeonhole. Alternative programming paradigms and languages were quick to appear, but none achieved the widespread popularity of the procedural paradigm until the emergence of OO. The abbreviation OO, which stands for object oriented, is used to describe a programming paradigm as well as a variety of computer programming languages. In this section, you'll find out what OOP (object-oriented programming) is all about. Java is used for the examples in this section of the chapter because it is today's most popular language for implementing object-oriented programs.

OBJECTS AND CLASSES

What is the basic focus of the object-oriented paradigm? The **object-oriented paradigm** is based on the idea that the solution for a problem can be visualized in terms of objects that interact with each other. In the context of this paradigm, an **object** is a unit of data that represents an abstract or a real-world entity, such as a person, place, or thing. For example, an object can represent a $10.99 small round pepperoni pizza. Another object can represent a pizza delivery guy named Jack Flash. Yet another object can represent a customer who lives at 22 W. Pointe Rd.

What's the difference between an object and a class? The real world contains lots of pizzas, customers, and delivery guys. These objects can be defined in a general way by using classes. Whereas an object is a single instance of an entity, a **class** is a template for a group of objects with similar characteristics. For example, a Pizza class defines a group of gooey Italian snacks that are made in a variety of sizes, crafted into rectangular or round shapes, and sold for various prices. A class can produce any number of unique objects, as shown in Figure 12-30.

CLASS: Pizza

Pizza objects

FIGURE 12-30

A class, such as the Pizza class, is a general template for a group of objects with similar characteristics.

How do I define the classes I need to solve a problem? When taking the object-oriented approach to a problem, one of the first steps is to identify the objects that pertain to a solution. As you might expect, the solution to the pizza problem requires some pizza objects.

Certain characteristics of pizzas provide information necessary to solve the problem. This information—the price, size, and shape of a pizza—provides the structure for the Pizza class. A class is defined by attributes and methods. A **class attribute** defines the characteristics of a set of objects. You will learn about methods, which define actions, later in this section.

Each class attribute typically has a name, scope, and data type. One class attribute of the Pizza class might be named pizzaPrice. Its scope can be defined as public or private. A **public attribute** is available for use by any routine in the program. A **private attribute** can be accessed only from the routine in which it is defined. The pizzaPrice attribute's data type can be defined as double, which means that it can be any decimal number, such as 12.99. Figure 12-31 describes the data types most often used to describe class attributes.

TERMINOLOGY NOTE

The data types used to define class attributes are similar to the data types for defining database fields, but the terminology is slightly different.

FIGURE 12-31

Class Attribute Data Types

Data Type	Description	Example
Int	Integer whole numbers	10
Double	Numbers with decimal places	12.99
String	Multiple characters, symbols, and numerals	Square
Boolean	Limited to two values	T or F

OO programmers often use UML (Unified Modeling Language) diagrams to plan the classes for a program. The UML diagram in Figure 12-32 shows one possible way to envision the Pizza class.

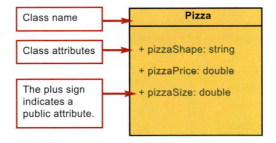

FIGURE 12-32

The core of a UML diagram is a rectangular shape that contains information about a class.

12

How do I code a class when writing a program? Although a programmer typically completes the overall program plan before coding, jump ahead to take a quick look at the Java code for the attributes in the Pizza class. The first line of code defines the name of the class. Each subsequent line defines the scope, data type, and name of an attribute. The curly brackets simply define the start and end of the class.

```
class Pizza
{
  public string pizzaShape;
  public double pizzaPrice;
  public double pizzaSize;
}
```

INHERITANCE

How flexible are classes for defining different types of objects?
The object-oriented paradigm endows classes with quite a bit of flexibility. For the pizza program, objects and classes make it easy to compare round pizzas to rectangular pizzas rather than just to square pizzas.

Suppose you want to compare a 10-inch round pizza to a rectangular pizza that has a length of 11 inches and a width of 8 inches. The Pizza class in Figure 12-32 on the previous page holds only one measurement for each pizza—pizzaSize. This single attribute won't work for rectangular pizzas, which might have a different length and width. Should you modify the class definition to add attributes for pizzaLength and pizzaWidth? No, because these attributes are necessary only for rectangular pizzas, not for round pizzas. An OO feature called inheritance provides flexibility to deal with objects' unique characteristics.

What is inheritance?
In object-oriented jargon, **inheritance** refers to passing certain characteristics from one class to other classes. For example, to solve the pizza problem, a programmer might decide to add a RoundPizza class and a RectanglePizza class. These two new classes can inherit attributes from the Pizza class, such as pizzaShape and pizzaPrice. You can then add specialized characteristics to the new classes. The RectanglePizza class can have attributes for length and width, and the RoundPizza class can have an attribute for diameter.

The process of producing new classes with inherited attributes creates a superclass and subclasses. A **superclass**, such as Pizza, is any class from which attributes can be inherited. A **subclass** (or derived class), such as RoundPizza or RectanglePizza, is any class that inherits attributes from a superclass. The set of superclasses and subclasses that are related to each other is referred to as a **class hierarchy**. The UML diagram in Figure 12-33 shows the Pizza class and its subclasses.

FIGURE 12-33

The subclass attributes shown in blue (pizzaShape and pizzaPrice) are inherited from the Pizza superclass. The attributes in red are unique to the subclasses. The plus sign indicates that these attributes are public.

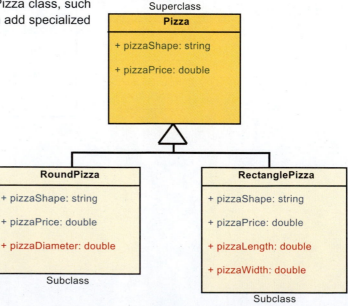

How do I code a subclass? Java uses the extends command to link a subclass to a superclass. The statement `class RectanglePizza extends Pizza` means "create a class called RectanglePizza that's derived from the superclass called Pizza." Figure 12-34 contains the Java code that creates attributes for the RectanglePizza class.

```
class RectanglePizza extends Pizza
{
        double pizzaLength;
        double pizzaWidth;
}
```

FIGURE 12-34

Using the extends command, the RectanglePizza class inherits the pizzaShape and pizzaPrice attributes from the Pizza superclass. The pizzaLength and pizzaWidth attributes are unique to the RectanglePizza class.

METHODS AND MESSAGES

How does an OO program use objects? An OO program can use objects in a variety of ways. A basic way to use objects is to manipulate them with methods. A **method** is a segment of code that defines an action. The names of methods usually end in a set of parentheses, such as compare() or getArea().

What can a method do? A method can perform a variety of tasks, such as collecting input, performing calculations, making comparisons, executing decisions, and producing output. For example, the pizza program can use a method named compare() to compare the square-inch prices of two pizzas and display a message indicating which pizza is the best deal.

What does a method look like when it has been coded in Java? A method begins with a line that names the method and can include a description of its scope and data type. The scope—public or private—specifies which parts of the program can access the method. The data type specifies the kind of data, if any, that the method produces. The initial line of code is followed by one or more lines that specify the calculation, comparison, or routine that the method performs. Figure 12-35 illustrates the code for the compare() method.

FIGURE 12-35

Java code for the compare() method.

```
public compare( Pizza Pizza1, Pizza Pizza2 )
{
        if (Pizza1.SquareInchPrice < Pizza2.SquareInchPrice )
            System.out.println("Pizza 1 is the best deal!");

        if (Pizza1.SquareInchPrice > Pizza2.SquareInchPrice )
            System.out.println("Pizza 2 is the best deal!");

        if (Pizza1.SquareInchPrice == Pizza2.SquareInchPrice
            System.out.println("The pizzas are the same deal!");
}
```

The method manipulates pizza objects.

The method title includes its scope and name.

The body of the method contains logic statements that determine which pizza is the best deal and print the result.

12

What activates a method? A method is activated by a **message**, which is included as a line of program code that is sometimes referred to as a *call*. For example, in a Java program, a line of code such as `compare(Pizza1, Pizza2)` produces a message used to activate or call the compare() method.

In the object-oriented world, objects often interact to solve a problem by sending and receiving messages. For example, a pizza object might receive a message asking for the pizza's area or price per square inch.

How do methods relate to classes? Methods can be defined along with the class they affect. The getSquareInchPrice() method pertains to pizzas of any shape, so it can be defined as part of the Pizza class. To calculate the square-inch price, however, it is necessary to know the area of a pizza. That calculation can be achieved by defining a getArea() method.

The area calculation for round pizzas is different from the calculation for rectangular pizzas, so the getArea() method should become part of the RoundPizza and RectanglePizza subclasses, as indicated by the UML diagram in Figure 12-36.

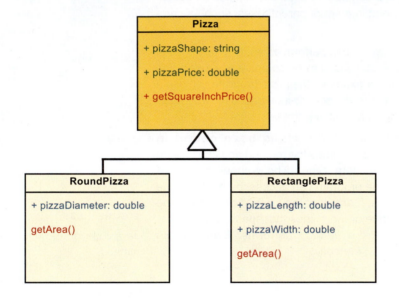

FIGURE 12-36

The getSquareInchPrice() method is defined as part of the Pizza class, whereas the getArea() method is defined within the RoundPizza and RectanglePizza classes.

How does the getArea() method work? If you have been thinking ahead a bit, you might wonder how a programmer can define the getArea() method to perform two different calculations—one that calculates the area of a rectangle by multiplying its length times its width, and another that calculates the area of a circle using the formula πr^2. An object-oriented concept called polymorphism makes it possible to assign more than one formula to the getArea() method.

What is polymorphism? **Polymorphism**, sometimes called overloading, is the ability to redefine a method in a subclass. It allows programmers to create a single, generic name for a procedure that behaves in unique ways for different classes.

In the pizza program, for example, both the RectanglePizza and RoundPizza classes can have a getArea() method. The calculation that getArea() performs is defined one way for the RectanglePizza class and another way for the RoundPizza class. Figure 12-37 illustrates how polymorphism allows subclasses to tailor methods to fit their unique requirements.

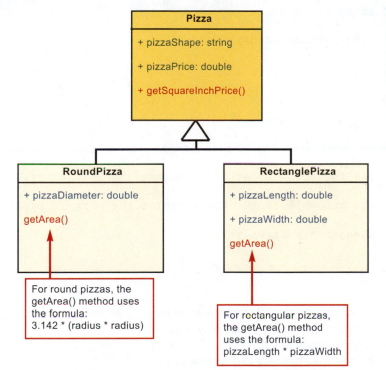

FIGURE 12-37

Polymorphism allows a programmer to define different getArea() methods for each subclass. When the completed program runs, pizza shapes are collected from the user and the corresponding getArea() method can be applied to calculate the area of a pizza.

12

How does the code for the round getArea() method differ from the code for the rectangle getArea() method? The code for the getArea() method defined in the RoundPizza class asks users to key in, or enter, the pizza's diameter. The method then divides the diameter by 2 to arrive at the radius. The value for the radius is used in the πr^2 calculation—3.142 * (radius * radius)—for the area of a circle.

The getArea() method defined in the RectanglePizza class asks users to key in the length of the pizza and then its width. This data is used in the calculation that multiplies length times width to produce the area of a rectangular pizza. Figure 12-38 illustrates the Java code for the getArea() methods. The lines that begin with // are remarks.

FIGURE 12-38

The getArea() methods for round and rectangular pizzas.

```
getArea()

//Method to calculate the area of a round pizza
{
        pizzaDiameter = Keyin.inDouble("Enter the diameter of the pizza: ");

        radius = pizzaDiameter/2;

        pizzaArea = 3.142 * (radius*radius);

}
```

```
getArea()

//Method to calculate the area of a rectangular pizza
{
        pizzaLength = Keyin.inDouble("Enter the length of the pizza: ");

        pizzaWidth  = Keyin.inDouble("Enter the width of the pizza: ");

        pizzaArea = pizzaLength * pizzaWidth;

}
```

What are the advantages of polymorphism? Polymorphism provides OO programs with easy extensibility and can help simplify program code. For example, it would be easy to extend the pizza program to work with triangular pizzas, if one of the pizzerias decides to get creative with pizza shapes. To extend the program, you would simply define a TrianglePizza class that includes attributes for pizzaWidth and pizzaHeight and tailor its getArea() method for calculating the area of a triangle.

The ability to tailor the getArea() method for round and square pizzas allows programmers to avoid complex logic and to simplify program code. As you can imagine, creating separate methods with unique names, such as getAreaRoundPizza(), getAreaRectanglePizza(), and getAreaTrianglePizza(), would add to the program's complexity and make it more difficult to extend the program for other pizza shapes.

OBJECT-ORIENTED PROGRAM STRUCTURE

What does the completed pizza program look like in Java? So far in this section of the chapter, you have learned how objects and methods interact to solve the pizza problem. You know that the pizza program uses a Pizza class and two subclasses: RectanglePizza and RoundPizza. You also know that these classes include getSquareInchPrice() and getArea() methods to perform calculations that supply data for solving the problem. You should also remember that the compare() method is used to manipulate pizza objects to determine which is the best deal.

The classes and methods defined for the pizza program must be placed within the structure of a Java program, which contains class definitions, defines methods, initiates the comparison, and outputs results. Figure 12-39 provides an overview of the program structure.

FIGURE 12-39

Program Structure for the Pizza Program

Pizza Class Definition

Define Pizza as a class with attributes for shape and price. Define the getSquareInchPrice() method that collects input for the pizza price, then calculates a pizza's square-inch price.

RectanglePizza Class Definition

Define RectanglePizza as a subclass of Pizza with attributes for length and width. Define the getArea() method that collects input for the pizza length and width to calculate area.

RoundPizza Class Definition

Define RoundPizza as a subclass of Pizza with an attribute for diameter. Define a getArea() method that collects input for the pizza diameter, then calculates area.

Compare() Method

Compare the square-inch price of two pizzas and output results.

Main Module

Set up variables, create objects for Pizza1 and Pizza2, and activate the getArea(), getSquareInchPrice(), and compare() methods.

12

How does a Java program work? The computer begins executing a Java program by locating a standard method called main(), which contains code to send messages to objects by calling methods. For the pizza program, the main() method includes code that defines a few variables and then asks the user to enter the shape of the first pizza. If the shape entered is Round the program creates an object called Pizza1 that is a member of the RoundPizza class. If the shape entered is Rectangle the program creates an object called Pizza1 that is a member of the RectanglePizza class.

After the pizza object is created, the program uses the getArea() method to calculate its area. The program then uses the getSquareInchPrice() method to calculate the pizza's square-inch price. When the calculations are complete for the first pizza, the program performs the same process for the second pizza. Finally, the program uses the compare() method to compare the square-inch prices of the two pizzas and output a statement about which one is the best deal.

Because it is not the goal of this section to teach you the particulars of Java programming, don't worry about the detailed syntax of the Java code. Instead, refer to Figure 12-40 to get an overview of the activity that takes place in the main() method for the pizza program.

FIGURE 12-40

Java code for the main module of the Pizza Program.

```java
public static void main(String[] args)    ◄─ 1. Main() method title
   {

      Pizza Pizza1;    ◄─ 2. Define variables used
      Pizza Pizza2;          in the main() method.
      String pizzaShape;


      pizzaShape = Keyin.inString("Enter the shape of the first pizza: ");
      if (pizzaShape.equals("Round"))    ◄─ 3. Collect input for the shape of the
        {                                     first pizza, then create an object
         Pizza1 = new RoundPizza();           called Pizza1 that belongs to the
        }                                     RoundPizza or RectanglePizza class.
      else
         Pizza1 = new RectanglePizza();

                                          4. Use the getArea() and
                                          getSquareInchPrice() methods to calculate
      Pizza1.getArea();    ◄─             area and square-inch price for the first pizza.
      Pizza1.getSquareInchPrice();

      pizzaShape = Keyin.inString("Enter the shape of the second pizza: ");
      if (pizzaShape.equals("Round"))    ◄─ 5. Collect input for the shape of the second pizza,
         Pizza2 = new RoundPizza();          then create an object called Pizza2 that belongs
      else                                   to the RoundPizza or RectanglePizza class.
         Pizza2 = new RectanglePizza();

                                          6. Use the getArea() and getSquareInchPrice() methods to
      Pizza2.getArea();    ◄─             calculate area and square-inch price for the second pizza.
      Pizza2.getSquareInchPrice();

      compare(Pizza1, Pizza2);    ◄─ 7. Use the compare() method
   }                                  to determine which pizza is the
                                      best deal, then print results.
```

What happens when the completed pizza program runs? When you run the pizza program, it looks for the main() method. This method displays an onscreen prompt that asks for the pizza's shape. The getArea() method displays a prompt for the pizza's diameter (for a round pizza) or the pizza's length and width (for a rectangular pizza). A similar series of prompts appears for the second pizza. The program concludes when the compare() method displays a statement about which pizza is the best deal. The software tour for Figure 12-41 lets you see what happens when the OO pizza program runs.

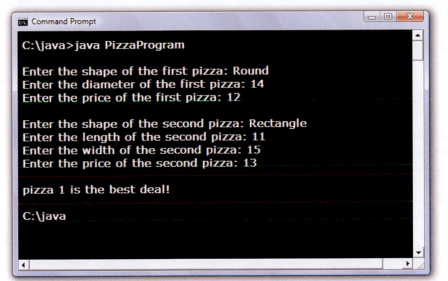

FIGURE 12-41

When the pizza program runs, on-screen prompts ask for the shape, size, and price of each pizza; then the program displays a message that indicates which pizza is the best deal.

▶ CLICK TO START

OBJECT-ORIENTED LANGUAGES AND APPLICATIONS

How did object-oriented languages originate? Computer historians believe that SIMULA (SIMUlation LAnguage) was the first computer language to work with objects, classes, inheritance, and methods. SIMULA was developed in 1962 by two Norwegian computer scientists for the purpose of programming simulations and models. SIMULA laid the foundation for the object-oriented paradigm, which was later incorporated into other programming languages, such as Eiffel, Smalltalk, C++, and Java.

The second major development in object-oriented languages came in 1972 when Alan Kaye began work on the Dynabook project at the Xerox Palo Alto Research Center (PARC). Dynabook was a prototype for a notebook-sized personal computer, intended to handle all the information needs of adults and children. Kaye developed a programming language called Smalltalk for the Dynabook that could be easily used to create programs based on real-world objects. Dynabook never became a commercial product, but Smalltalk survived and is still in use today. Smalltalk is regarded as a classic object-oriented language, which encourages programmers to take a pure OO approach to the programming process.

Which object-oriented languages are popular today? As the object-oriented paradigm gained popularity, several existing programming languages were modified to allow programmers to work with objects, classes, inheritance, and polymorphism. The concept for the Ada programming language originated in 1978 at the U.S. Department of Defense. The first versions of Ada were procedural, but in 1995, the language was modified to incorporate object-oriented features. A similar transformation took place with the C language in 1983, except that the

12

object-oriented version earned a new name—C++. Hybrid languages, such as Ada95, C++, Visual Basic, and C#, give programmers the option of using procedural and object-oriented techniques.

Java is one of the newest additions to the collection of object-oriented languages. Originally planned as a programming language for consumer electronics, such as interactive cable television boxes, Java evolved into an object-oriented programming platform for developing Web applications. Java was officially launched by Sun Microsystems in 1995 and has many of the characteristics of C++, from which it derives much of its syntax. Like C++, Java can also be used for procedural programming, so it is sometimes classified as a hybrid language.

What kinds of applications are suitable for object-oriented languages? The object-oriented paradigm can be applied to a wide range of programming problems. Basically, if you can envision a problem as a set of objects that pass messages back and forth, the problem is suitable for the OO approach.

What are the advantages and disadvantages of the OO paradigm? The object-oriented paradigm is cognitively similar to the way human beings perceive the real world. Using the object-oriented approach, programmers might be able to visualize the solutions to problems more easily. Facets of the object-oriented paradigm can also increase a programmer's efficiency because encapsulation allows objects to be adapted and reused in a variety of different programs. **Encapsulation** refers to the process of hiding the internal details of objects and their methods. After an object is coded, it becomes a black box, which essentially hides its details from other objects and allows the data to be accessed using methods. Encapsulated objects can be easily reused, modified, and repurposed.

A potential disadvantage of object-oriented programs is runtime efficiency. Object-oriented programs tend to require more memory and processing resources than procedural programs. Programmers, software engineers, and system analysts can work together to weigh the tradeoffs between the OO approach and runtime efficiency.

QuickCheck

1. The [_____] paradigm is based on the idea that computer programs can be visualized in terms of objects that interact with each other.

2. A class is a template for a group of objects with similar characteristics. True or false? [_____]

3. OO programmers often use [_____] diagrams to plan the classes for a program. (Hint: Use the abbreviation.)

4. The process of passing certain characteristics from a superclass to a subclass is referred to as [_____].

5. In an OO program, objects send and receive [_____] to initiate actions, which a programmer defines by creating a(n) [_____].

CHECK ANSWERS

Declarative Programming

AS THE 1950S drew to a close, computers were primarily used for number-crunching tasks, such as calculating missile trajectories, tabulating census data, and processing payrolls. A few visionary computer scientists saw beyond these limited number-crunching applications and began to explore ways in which computers could make decisions and solve problems by manipulating non-numeric data, including words and concepts. Procedural programming languages, such as FORTRAN and COBOL, did not have the flexibility to deal efficiently with non-numeric data, so non-procedural languages were developed. This section explains a type of non-procedural programming that follows the declarative paradigm and gives you a little taste of the Prolog language.

THE DECLARATIVE PARADIGM

What is the declarative paradigm? Non-procedural languages, such as LISP, Scheme, Haskell, and Prolog, can be grouped into one of two paradigms, functional or declarative. The **functional paradigm** emphasizes the evaluation of expressions, called functions, rather than the execution of commands. The **declarative paradigm** attempts to describe a problem without specifying exactly how to arrive at a solution.

What is unique about the declarative paradigm? In earlier sections of this chapter, you learned that procedural programming focuses on a step-by-step algorithm that instructs the computer how to arrive at a solution. You also learned that the object-oriented approach emphasizes classes and methods that form objects. In contrast, the declarative paradigm describes aspects of a problem that lead to a solution. Although the declarative paradigm might sound similar to the procedural paradigm, the procedural paradigm focuses on an algorithm that describes the solution, whereas the declarative paradigm focuses on describing the problem. Figure 12-42 summarizes these differences.

What are the building blocks for the declarative paradigm? Many declarative programming languages, such as Prolog, use a collection of facts and rules to describe a problem. In the context of a Prolog program, a **fact** is a statement that provides the computer with basic information for solving a problem. In the pizza problem, for example, these facts might include:

> **A pizza has a price of $10.99, a size of 12 inches, and a round shape.**

> **Another pizza has a price of $12.00, a size of 11 inches, and a square shape.**

In the context of a Prolog program, a **rule** is a general statement about the relationship between facts. For example, the following rule is useful for solving the problem of which pizza is a better deal:

> **A pizza is a better deal if its square-inch price is less than the square-inch price of another pizza.**

FIGURE 12-42

Paradigm Comparison

Procedural paradigm:
- Programs detail how to solve a problem

- Very efficient for number-crunching tasks

Object-oriented paradigm:
- Programs define objects, classes, and methods

- Efficient for problems that involve real-world objects

Declarative paradigm:
- Programs describe the problem

- Efficient for processing words and language

12

To apply the betterdeal rule, additional rules are necessary to calculate the square-inch price of each pizza. You'll look at these rules in more detail later in this section.

How does a programmer plan a declarative program? The core of most declarative programs is a set of facts and rules that describe a problem. The logic for the pizza program is very simple because the solution depends on a single factor: the lowest square-inch price. Declarative programs with such simple logic don't require much planning. In contrast, programs that deal with multiple factors have more complex logic and often require planning tools, such as decision tables.

A **decision table** is a tabular method for visualizing and specifying rules based on multiple factors. As an example, suppose your decision to buy a pizza depends not just on its price, but on whether you can get it delivered and how soon it is ready. These three factors produce eight possible situations. In which of those eight situations would you purchase a pizza? What if the best-priced pizza is ready in less than 30 minutes, but it can't be delivered? What if the best-priced pizza won't be ready for an hour? Figure 12-43 illustrates how a programmer might construct a decision table that describes all the rules pertaining to pizza prices, delivery, and time.

FIGURE 12-43

Decision Table

Lowest price	Y	N	Y	N	Y	N	Y	N
Delivery available	Y	Y	N	N	Y	Y	N	N
Ready in less than 30 minutes	Y	Y	Y	Y	N	N	N	N
Buy it?	Y	Y	N	N	Y	N	N	N

PROLOG FACTS

How does a programmer code facts? Return to the simple problem of deciding which of two round or square pizzas is the best deal based on price per square inch. The first step in coding the program is to enter facts that describe the prices, shapes, and sizes of two pizzas. The fact "The shape of a pizza is round." can be coded in Prolog like this:

```
shapeof(pizza,round).
```

The words in parentheses are called arguments. An **argument** represents one of the main subjects that a fact describes. The word outside the parentheses, called the **predicate**, describes the relationship between the arguments. In other words, the predicate shapeof describes the relationship between pizza and round. Figure 12-44 points out some important syntax details pertaining to capitalization and punctuation for Prolog facts.

FIGURE 12-44

A Prolog fact follows specific syntax rules.

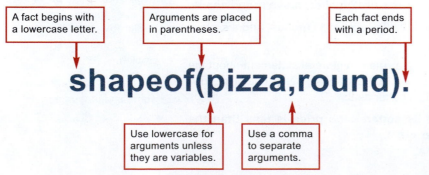

A fact begins with a lowercase letter.

Arguments are placed in parentheses.

Each fact ends with a period.

shapeof(pizza,round).

Use lowercase for arguments unless they are variables.

Use a comma to separate arguments.

Although it might seem obvious that round describes the shape of a pizza, the predicate cannot be omitted. In many cases, the predicate can drastically change the meaning of a fact. For example, the facts in Figure 12-45 have the same arguments, (joe,fish), but the predicates give the facts very different meanings.

FIGURE 12-45

The predicate can drastically change the meaning of a fact.

`hates(joe,fish).`
Joe hates fish.

`name(joe,fish).`
Joe is the name of a fish.

`playscardgame(joe,fish).`
Joe plays a card game called fish.

For the pizza program, a series of facts can be used to describe a pizza:

```
priceof(pizza1,10).

sizeof(pizza1,12).

shapeof(pizza1,square).
```

Another set of similar facts can be used to describe a second pizza:

```
priceof(pizza2,12).

sizeof(pizza2,14).

shapeof(pizza2,round).
```

Facts can have more than two arguments. For example, a single fact can be used to fully describe a pizza:

```
pricesizeshape(pizza1,10,12,square).
```

Using a series of facts to describe a pizza has some advantages and some disadvantages over using a single fact. A single fact tends to make a program more compact, whereas multiple facts might provide more flexibility. The structure of a fact also affects the syntax for goals that produce information.

What is a goal? The facts in a Prolog program are useful even without any rules. Prolog can manipulate facts in several ways without explicit programming. Each fact in a Prolog program is similar to a record in a database. You can query a program's database by asking a question, called a **goal** in Prolog jargon. Suppose you have entered the following facts:

```
priceof(pizza1,10).

sizeof(pizza1,12).

shapeof(pizza1,square).

priceof(pizza2,12).

sizeof(pizza2,14).

shapeof(pizza2,round).
```

12

You can ask questions by entering goals from the ?- prompt. For example, the goal `?- shapeof(pizza1,square)` means "Is the shape of pizza1 square?" Prolog searches through the facts to see if it can satisfy the goal by finding a match. If a match is found, Prolog responds with yes; otherwise, it responds with no. This exercise might seem trivial because you are working with a small set of facts, which are all visible on the screen. Many programs, however, contain hundreds of facts, which cannot be displayed on a single screen or easily remembered by a programmer.

Prolog allows you to ask open-ended questions by replacing constants with variables. A constant, such as pizza1, square, or 10, represents an unchanging value or attribute. A Prolog variable is like a placeholder or an empty box, into which Prolog can put information gleaned from a fact. A Prolog variable begins with an uppercase letter to distinguish it from a constant. The argument Pizza is a variable, whereas pizza1 is a constant. The argument Inches is a variable, whereas 14 is a constant.

Prolog variables are handy tools for formulating open-ended goals. As an example, suppose you want to find the size of pizza2. You can obtain this information by using the variable Inches in the goal:

```
?- sizeof(pizza2,Inches).
```

Prolog looks for any facts that have sizeof as a predicate and pizza2 as the first argument. It responds with the actual value of the second argument:

```
Inches = 14
```

Much of the power and flexibility of the Prolog language stem from its ability to sift through facts trying to match predicates, compare constants, and instantiate variables. The screentour for Figure 12-46 demonstrates various Prolog goals.

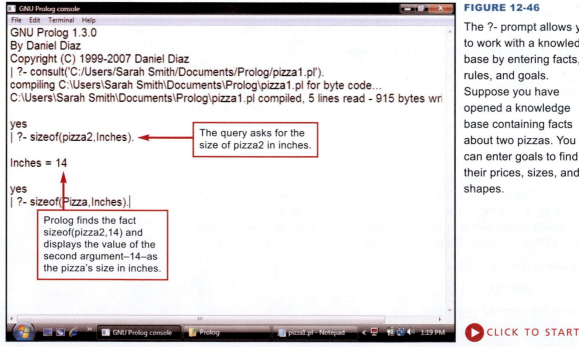

FIGURE 12-46

The ?- prompt allows you to work with a knowledge base by entering facts, rules, and goals. Suppose you have opened a knowledge base containing facts about two pizzas. You can enter goals to find their prices, sizes, and shapes.

CLICK TO START

What is instantiation? Finding a value for a variable is referred to as **instantiation**. To solve the goal `?- sizeof(pizza2,Inches)`, Prolog instantiates the value 14 to the variable Inches. Instantiation means "to make a temporary assignment." When a Prolog program discovers that the size of pizza2 is 14 inches, it instantiates, or assigns, the value 14 to the variable Inches.

Prolog can perform multiple instantiations. You can ask for the sizes of both pizzas by using the query `?- sizeof(Pizza,Inches)`. Capitalizing the words Pizza and Inches signifies that both are variables. Prolog can instantiate Pizza to pizza1 and then instantiate it to pizza2:

```
Pizza = pizza1
Inches = 12
Pizza = pizza2
Inches = 14
```

You can also formulate queries in which you tell Prolog not to instantiate a variable. For example, suppose you want to know the prices of the pizzas, but you don't need to know which price corresponds to a particular pizza. You can enter the query `?- priceof(_,Price)`, which means, "What are the prices?" Prolog would reply with:

```
Price = 10
Price = 12
```

Instantiation can be used to produce information that is not implicitly stored in the database. Suppose you want to know the size of the round pizza. The knowledge base does not contain a fact like `sizeof(roundpizza,14)`; however, you can use a conjunction of two goals, as shown in Figure 12-47, to obtain the size of the round pizza.

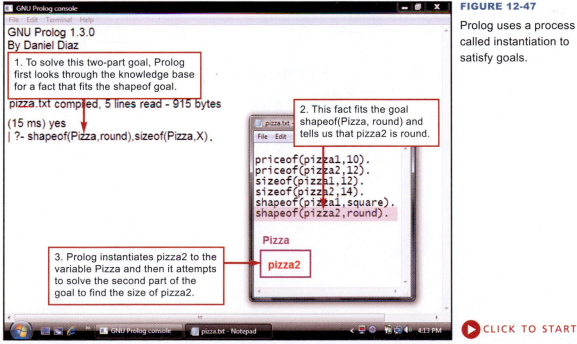

FIGURE 12-47

Prolog uses a process called instantiation to satisfy goals.

1. To solve this two-part goal, Prolog first looks through the knowledge base for a fact that fits the shapeof goal.

2. This fact fits the goal shapeof(Pizza, round) and tells us that pizza2 is round.

3. Prolog instantiates pizza2 to the variable Pizza and then it attempts to solve the second part of the goal to find the size of pizza2.

```
GNU Prolog 1.3.0
By Daniel Diaz

pizza.txt compiled, 5 lines read - 915 bytes

(15 ms) yes
| ?- shapeof(Pizza,round),sizeof(Pizza,X).
```

```
priceof(pizza1,10).
priceof(pizza2,12).
sizeof(pizza1,12).
sizeof(pizza2,14).
shapeof(pizza1,square).
shapeof(pizza2,round).
```

Pizza

pizza2

CLICK TO START

12

Instantiation is one of the keys to understanding how Prolog works. Unlike a procedural programming language, which is designed to step through a series of statements in a path prescribed by the programmer, Prolog can autonomously run through every possible instantiation, backtracking if necessary to deal with multiple variables.

PROLOG RULES

How does a programmer code Prolog rules? The pizza program requires a rule that states, "A pizza is a better deal if its price per square inch is less than the price per square inch of the other pizza." Translated into Prolog code, this rule becomes:

```
betterdeal(PizzaX,PizzaY) :-
    squareinchprice(PizzaX,AmountX),
    squareinchprice(PizzaY,AmountY),
    AmountX < AmountY.
```

Take a look at the logic behind this rule. A Prolog rule consists of a head, body, and connecting symbol, as described in Figure 12-48.

FIGURE 12-48

A Prolog rule consists of a head and one or more clauses that form the body of the rule.

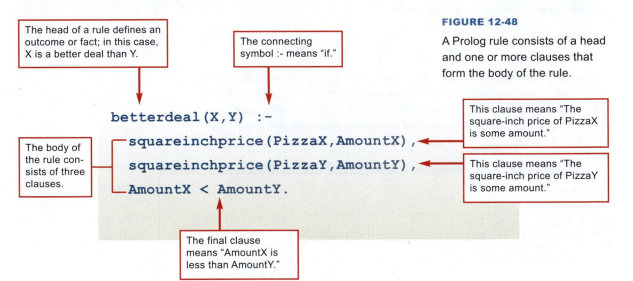

The head of a rule defines an outcome or fact; in this case, X is a better deal than Y.

The connecting symbol :- means "if."

The body of the rule consists of three clauses.

```
betterdeal(X,Y) :-
    squareinchprice(PizzaX,AmountX),
    squareinchprice(PizzaY,AmountY),
    AmountX < AmountY.
```

This clause means "The square-inch price of PizzaX is some amount."

This clause means "The square-inch price of PizzaY is some amount."

The final clause means "AmountX is less than AmountY."

How do Prolog rules work? To understand how the betterdeal rule works, you'll need to perform a bit of magic to determine the price per square inch of each pizza. In the completed pizza program, the computer can calculate the square-inch price using a rule the programmer provides. Because you don't yet have such a rule, temporarily assume that the square-inch price of the first pizza is .0694 (6.94 cents) and the square-inch price of the second pizza is .0779 (7.79 cents). These facts would be stated as:

`squareinchprice(pizza1,.0694).` and
`squareinchprice(pizza2,.0779).`

Now, suppose you enter the query `?- betterdeal(pizza1,pizza2).`, which translates to "Is pizza1 a better deal than pizza2?" Figure 12-49 illustrates how Prolog uses the betterdeal rule to answer your query.

FIGURE 12-49

Prolog executes the betterdeal rule.

Facts for the pizza program

```
priceof(pizza1,10).

sizeof(pizza1,12).

shapeof(pizza1,square).

priceof(pizza2,12).

sizeof(pizza2,14).

shapeof(pizza2,round).

squareinchprice(pizza1,.069).

squareinchprice(pizza2,.0779).
```

The betterdeal rule

```
betterdeal(PizzaX,PizzaY) :-

    squareinchprice(PizzaX,AmountX),

    squareinchprice(PizzaY,AmountY),

    AmountX < AmountY.
```

The query

```
?- betterdeal(Pizza1,Pizza2)
```

1. Prolog instantiates pizza1 to PizzaX and pizza2 to PizzaY.

```
betterdeal(pizza1,pizza2) :-

    squareinchprice(pizza1,AmountX),

    squareinchprice(pizza2,AmountY),

    AmountX < AmountY.
```

2. Prolog looks through the facts to find the squareinchprice for pizza1 and pizza2. These prices are instantiated to AmountX and AmountY.

```
betterdeal(pizza1,pizza2) :-

    squareinchprice(pizza1,.0694),

    squareinchprice(pizza2,.0779),

    .0694 < .0779.
```

3. The last line now contains a statement that is true—.0694<.0779—which validates the rule and produces "yes" as a response to your query, "Is pizza1 a better deal than pizza2?"

12

Does the order of rules affect the way a Prolog program runs?
When coding programs in a procedural language, such as C, Pascal, or
BASIC, the order of program instructions is critically important. For example, if you place input statements for pizza size and price after the code that
calculates the price per square inch, the program produces an error. In contrast, the order or sequence of rules in a Prolog program is usually not
critical.

What does the complete pizza program look like in Prolog?
The complete pizza program includes the facts that describe two pizzas
and rules that describe betterdeal, square-inch price, and area. Figure 12-
50 contains the Prolog code for the entire pizza program.

FIGURE 12-50

The complete Prolog program.

```
priceof(pizza1,10).
sizeof(pizza1,12).
shapeof(pizza1,square).
priceof(pizza2,12).
sizeof(pizza2,14).
shapeof(pizza2,round).
betterdeal(PizzaX,PizzaY) :-
    squareinchprice(PizzaX,Amount1),
    squareinchprice(PizzaY,Amount2),
    Amount1 < Amount2.
area(Pizza,Squareinches) :-
    sizeof(Pizza,Side),
    shapeof(Pizza,square),
    Squareinches is Side * Side.
area(Pizza,Squareinches) :-
    sizeof(Pizza,Diameter),
    shapeof(Pizza,round),
    Radius is Diameter/2,
    Squareinches is 3.142 * (Radius * Radius).
squareinchprice(Pizza,Amount) :-
    area(Pizza,Squareinches),
    priceof(Pizza,Dollars),
    Amount is Dollars / Squareinches.
```

INPUT CAPABILITIES

Can I generalize the program for any pizzas? A version of the
pizza program that contains facts, such as `priceof(pizza1,10)` and
`priceof(pizza2,12)` is limited to specific pizzas that cost $10.00 and
$12.00. The program can be generalized by collecting input from the
user and storing it in variables or by asserting new facts at runtime.

How do I collect input from the user? If you think back to the procedural programming section of this chapter, you might recall that the BASIC program collected the size, shape, and price of each pizza by using Input statements such as:

```
Input "Enter the size of pizza1: ", Size1
```

That Input statement displayed the prompt "Enter the size of pizza1:" and then stored the number entered in a variable called Size1. Prolog has similar capabilities. Examine the following program code to see how a Prolog program collects user input, then take the screentour in Figure 12-51 to see how the program interacts with users when it is run.

Prolog uses the write predicate to display a prompt for input.

The read predicate gathers input entered by the user, then the assertz predicate creates a fact, such as priceof(pizza1,12).

```
write(user,'enter price of pizza1: '),
read(user,Price1), assertz(priceof(pizza1,Price1)),
write(user,'enter size of pizza1: '),
read(user,Size1), assertz(sizeof(pizza1,Size1)),
write(user,'enter shape of pizza1: '),
read(user,Shape1), assertz(shapeof(pizza1,Shape1)),
write(user,'enter price of pizza2: '),
read(user,Price2), assertz(priceof(pizza2,Price2)),
write(user,'enter size of pizza2: '),
read(user,Size2), assertz(sizeof(pizza2,Size2)),
write(user,'enter shape of pizza2: '),
read(user,Shape2), assertz(shapeof(pizza2,Shape2)),
```

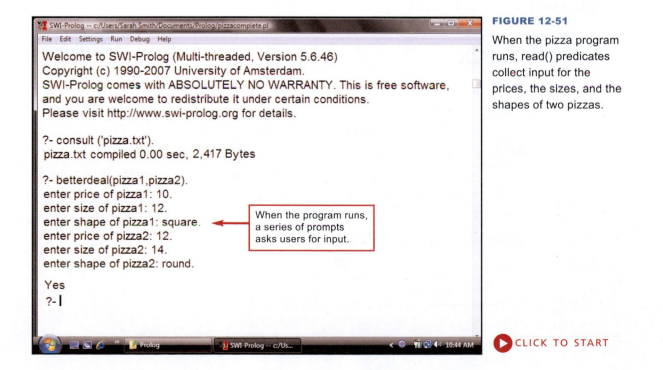

FIGURE 12-51

When the pizza program runs, read() predicates collect input for the prices, the sizes, and the shapes of two pizzas.

```
Welcome to SWI-Prolog (Multi-threaded, Version 5.6.46)
Copyright (c) 1990-2007 University of Amsterdam.
SWI-Prolog comes with ABSOLUTELY NO WARRANTY. This is free software,
and you are welcome to redistribute it under certain conditions.
Please visit http://www.swi-prolog.org for details.

?- consult ('pizza.txt').
pizza.txt compiled 0.00 sec, 2,417 Bytes

?- betterdeal(pizza1,pizza2).
enter price of pizza1: 10.
enter size of pizza1: 12.
enter shape of pizza1: square.
enter price of pizza2: 12.
enter size of pizza2: 14.
enter shape of pizza2: round.

Yes
?-
```

When the program runs, a series of prompts asks users for input.

12

CLICK TO START

DECLARATIVE LANGUAGES AND APPLICATIONS

What kinds of problems are suitable for the declarative approach? As you have seen from the pizza example, it is possible to use a declarative language to solve a problem that involves calculations. However, problems that require intensive computation are not usually best suited for the declarative paradigm. As a general rule, declarative programming languages are most suitable for problems that pertain to words and concepts rather than to numbers. These languages are a good choice for applications such as those listed in Figure 12-52.

What are the advantages and disadvantages of declarative languages? Declarative languages offer a highly effective programming environment for problems that involve words, concepts, and complex logic. As you learned in this chapter, declarative languages offer a great deal of flexibility for querying a set of facts and rules. These languages also allow you to describe problems using words rather than the abstract structures procedural and object-oriented languages require.

Currently, declarative languages are not commonly used for production applications. To some extent, today's emphasis on the object-oriented paradigm has pushed declarative languages out of the mainstream, both in education and in the job market. Many aspiring programmers are never introduced to declarative languages, so they are not included in the languages evaluated for a specific project.

Declarative languages have a reputation for providing minimal input and output capabilities. Although many of today's Prolog compilers provide access to Windows and Mac user interface components, programmers are often unaware of this capability.

A final disadvantage of declarative languages is their relatively poor performance on today's personal computer architecture, which is optimized for sequential processing. Declarative languages run much more efficiently on parallel architectures, which have only recently emerged in the personal computer market.

FIGURE 12-52

Examples of applications that are suitable for declarative languages.

- Databases that contain complex relationships—for example, a genealogy database used to trace ancestral lineage or a street and highway database used for mapping routes

- Decision support systems that handle semi-structured problems—for example, a decision support system that helps determine tactics for military campaigns or a system that helps planners efficiently allocate energy resources

- Expert systems that require analysis of multiple, interrelated factors—for example, an expert system that helps troubleshoot appliance repairs or a program that translates documents from one language to another

---

QuickCheck

1. The declarative programming paradigm focuses on describing a(n) [＿＿＿＿], whereas the procedural paradigm focuses on algorithms that describe a(n) [＿＿＿＿].

2. A(n) [＿＿＿＿] table is a tabular method for visualizing and specifying rules based on multiple factors.

3. In the Prolog fact partnumber(desk,12367), desk and 12367 are referred to as [＿＿＿＿], whereas partnumber is referred to as the [＿＿＿＿].

4. A Prolog attribute can either be a(n) [＿＿＿＿], such as pizza (with a lowercase p), or it can be a(n) [＿＿＿＿], such as Pizza (with an uppercase P).

5. Finding the value for a variable while solving a Prolog goal is called [＿＿＿＿].

6. In a Prolog rule, the :- connecting symbol means [＿＿＿＿].

 CHECK ANSWERS

SECTION E

Secure Programming

HACKERS, CRACKERS, CYBERCRIMINALS, and black hats—no matter what you call them, their goal is to gain unauthorized access to information. The first line of defense in cyber security is the programmers who create applications, operating systems, and utilities that you use every day. Section E looks at program-level security vulnerabilities and what programmers can do to shore up security defenses.

BLACK HAT EXPLOITS

What makes my computer vulnerable to attack? Viruses, worms, bots, malicious Web scripts, and other exploits plague computer users. Many of these black-hat exploits creep into computer systems through security holes. Computer users have a vague notion that such holes exist and that antivirus software and firewalls are necessary to plug those holes, prevent intrusions, foil identity thieves, evade botnets, and avoid all the headaches associated with cleaning up after successful attacks.

Consumers are led to believe that their computers are vulnerable because they don't take rigorous steps to secure their computer by installing the latest antivirus software or firewall, keeping it up to date, and renewing their costly security software subscriptions. Those steps are essential in today's computing environment, but consumers should also be asking significant questions, such as: What makes my computer vulnerable to these attacks in the first place? Exactly what are these security holes? Who is responsible for allowing security holes to exist? The answer to these questions turns the focus to program code because that is the source of the porous net which allows malware to wiggle into your computer.

Today's operating systems, utilities, and application software are full of defects that create security holes, which are exploited by black hats. Software security defects include buffer overflows and verbose error messages.

What is a buffer overflow? According to most experts the most prevalent cause of security holes is program code that allows buffer overflows. A **buffer overflow** (also called a buffer overrun) is a condition in which data in memory exceeds its expected boundaries and flows into memory areas intended for use by other data. Figure 12-53 offers a simplified example of the problem.

FIGURE 12-53

A buffer overflow allows attackers to surreptitiously change the way a program works.

1. The programmer expects to collect a 2-byte state abbreviation as input for variable A. Variable B holds the address of the next instruction.

Variable A		Variable B		
		0	1	9

2. An attacker enters MI999. The 5-byte string overflows the buffer for variable A and spills over into variable B. Now variable B holds 999, which is not the correct address for the next instruction.

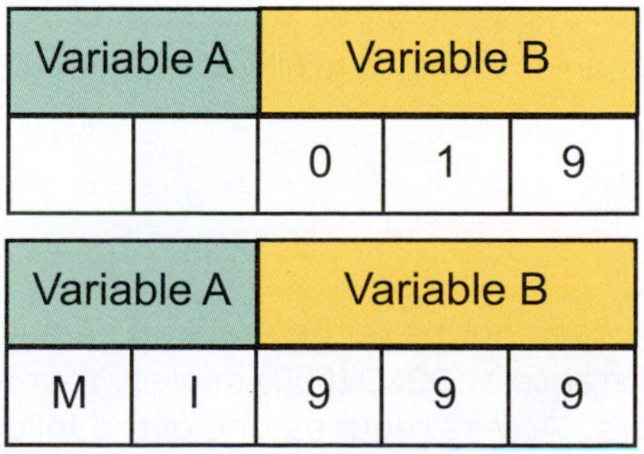

Variable A		Variable B		
M	I	9	9	9

3. When the program checks variable B to locate the next instruction, it goes to 999, where an attacker might have stored code for a virus, worm, or bot.

12

Buffer overflows can be triggered by input specifically designed to execute malicious code. One of the first exploits to take advantage of buffer overflows was the Morris worm, which attacked the Internet in 1988. Since that time, Microsoft alone has disclosed hundreds of buffer overflow vulnerabilities in commonly used Windows components, such as Internet Explorer, Outlook, Outlook Express, Troubleshooter, Plug and Play, the file decompression routine, and the routine that renders Windows Metafiles.

Sloppy C and C++ programming sets the stage for buffer overflows. C and C++, the two languages most commonly used for professional software development, offer little protection against buffer overflows. Commonly used routines, such as get() and strcpy(), from the standard C libraries perform no bounds checking and therefore allow buffer overflows.

Buffer overflows can be prevented. The techniques have been known for over a decade. Programmers can prevent buffer overflows by controlling pointers (or simply not using them), scrupulously checking input for suspicious characters, and placing strict boundaries on the values that can be stored in variables. Programming languages such as D, Cyclone, Java, and C# have some similarities to C and C++, but offer a more structured programming environment with fewer treacherous commands.

What is a verbose error message? Applications fail for many reasons including hardware malfunctions, program bugs, and incompatibility with other software. Good programmers try to anticipate how a program might fail and include code to handle the failure as gracefully as possible. Typically, the result is an error message displayed to the user. When software is in developmental and testing phases, error messages can help programmers locate the source of errors if they contain information pertinent to the location of defective code and the state of variables. If those information-rich and verbose error messages remain when the software ships, hackers can use them to identify security vulnerabilities.

Verbose error messages can also present attackers with information about the directory location of programs or files, the structure of a database, or the layout of the program in memory. The solution to verbose error messages is simple: Identify verbose error messages and sanitize them before shipping software.

Some of the most common examples of verbose error messages appear during unsuccessful attempts to log in or access files. Those error messages, like the one in Figure 12-54, often give attackers information that makes break-ins easier.

FIGURE 12-54

This verbose error message provides attackers with information about restricted-access folder names and locations, as well as account names (Manager, Member, and Owner) that can gain access to these folders.

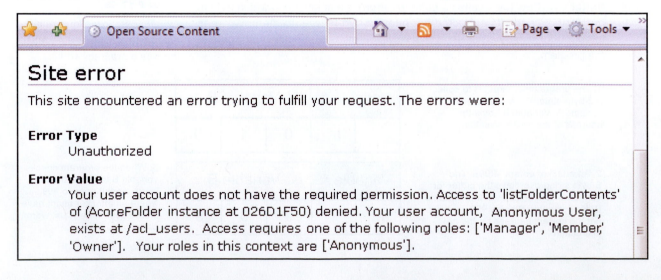

Site error

This site encountered an error trying to fulfill your request. The errors were:

Error Type
Unauthorized

Error Value
Your user account does not have the required permission. Access to 'listFolderContents' of (AcoreFolder instance at 026D1F50) denied. Your user account, Anonymous User, exists at /acl_users. Access requires one of the following roles: ['Manager', 'Member,' 'Owner']. Your roles in this context are ['Anonymous'].

SECURE SOFTWARE DEVELOPMENT

Is it possible to develop secure software? According to security experts, most software security problems can be traced back to defects that programmers unintentionally introduce in software during design and development. The general nature of the defects that open security holes is widely known and most can be eliminated.

Software security begins when the program specifications are formulated. Techniques such as formal methods, threat modeling, attack trees, and defensive programming help programmers remain aware of security throughout the software development life cycle.

What are formal methods? **Formal methods** help programmers apply rigorous logical and mathematical models to software design, coding, testing, and verification. Some software development methodologies incorporate formal methods and organizations that use them tend to produce more secure software. Formal methods, however, add to the cost and time of software development, so they tend to be used only for life-critical systems, such as air traffic control and nuclear reactor control systems, where security and safety are crucial.

What is threat modeling? **Threat modeling** (also called risk analysis) is a technique that can be used to identify potential vulnerabilities by listing the key assets of an application, categorizing the threats to each asset, ranking the threats, and developing threat mitigation strategies that can be implemented during coding. Threats can be categorized using a model like STRIDE as described in Figure 12-55.

Spoofing: Pretending to be someone else

Tampering: Changing, adding, or deleting data

Repudiation: Covering tracks to make attacks difficult to trace

Information disclosure: Gaining unauthorized access to information

Denial of service: Making a system unavailable to legitimate users

Elevation of privilege: Modifying user rights to gain access to data

FIGURE 12-55

STRIDE categories help software developers anticipate threats from attackers.

Threats are ranked using DREAD categories based on how much Damage they could cause, how easy they are to Reproduce, how much effort and skill is needed to Exploit a vulnerability, how many users would be Affected, and how likely it is that the vulnerability will be Discovered by hackers. After potential threats have been identified and ranked, software designers can work with programmers to devise appropriate security strategies.

12

What is an attack tree? Attack trees offer another way to get a handle on potential threats. An **attack tree** is a hierarchical diagram of potential attacks against a system. The root of the upside-down tree-shaped diagram represents an attacker's ultimate objective, such as stealing passwords. The branches of the tree represent actions that attackers might take to achieve the objective. By tracing paths through the diagram, developers can discover which kinds of attacks are easiest, which are most difficult to detect, and which have the potential to cause the most damage. Figure 12-56 shows an attack tree for opening a safe.

FIGURE 12-56

Attack trees are used by security analysts in many fields. This diagram illustrates an attack tree that might be devised by a bank security officer examining the vulnerability of the bank vault.

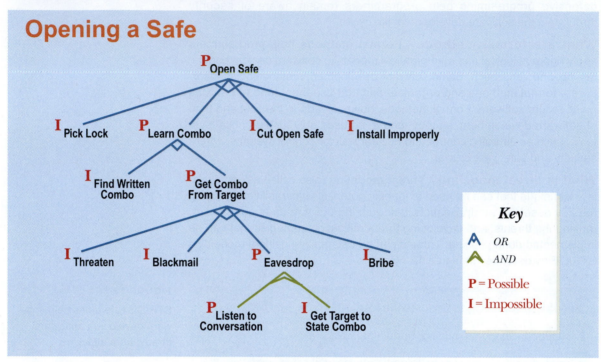

What is defensive programming? **Defensive programming** (also referred to as secure programming) is an approach to software development in which programmers anticipate what might go wrong as their programs run, and take steps to smoothly handle those situations. It is analogous to defensive driving that requires drivers to anticipate dangerous situations arising from adverse conditions or the mistakes of other drivers. Defensive programmers have to anticipate ways in which their programs could be compromised by legitimate users, intruders, other applications, the operating system, or third party security software. Avoiding code that could lead to buffer overflows is an example of defensive programming. Trapping program failures with error messages is another example.

Techniques associated with defensive programming include:

● **Source code walkthroughs.** Open source software goes through extensive public scrutiny that can identify security holes, but proprietary software can also benefit from a walkthrough with other in house programmers.

● **Simplification.** Complex code is more difficult to debug than simpler code. Sometimes sections of code should be rewritten to reduce their complexity.

● **Filtering input.** It is dangerous to assume that users will enter valid input. Attackers have become experts at concocting input that causes buffer overflows and runs rogue HTML scripts. Programmers should use a tight set of filters on all input fields.

How does signed code help? **Signed code** is a software program that identifies its source and carries a digital certificate attesting to its authenticity. Its main advantage is to help users avoid downloading and running virus-infected or intrusive software. Signed code is wrapped in a sort of security blanket that contains the name of the software developer and ensures that the software will not run if even one bit of the source code is changed by a virus or any other factor.

Programmers who want to deliver signed code have to provide proof of their identity to a trusted third-party certification authority, such as Verisign. Upon verification, the programmer is issued a code-signing utility and a certificate that can be used to sign any number of software products. To sign a product, the programmer uses the code-signing utility to encrypt the digital signature and program length. That encrypted information is incorporated in the product's executable file.

When a signed product is downloaded and launched, the encrypted signature is opened first, the browser uses a client-side certificate validation routine to make sure the signature is valid, and the program is the expected length before the actual product is opened and installed.

Signed certificates have been deployed for downloaded software, using a browser on the client end to verify the digital signature. Microsoft's Authenticode technology, for example, uses Internet Explorer as the verification client.

Signed certificates are not bullet proof. Fake certificates can be fashioned to look like the real ones and are likely to fool consumers who don't click the link to the certificate authority. Also, a signed certificate does not assure users that the original code was free of viruses or bugs. There is no third-party verification of the program's content, but programmers are unlikely to knowingly distribute infected code that could be traced back to its source through a signed certificate like the one in Figure 12-57.

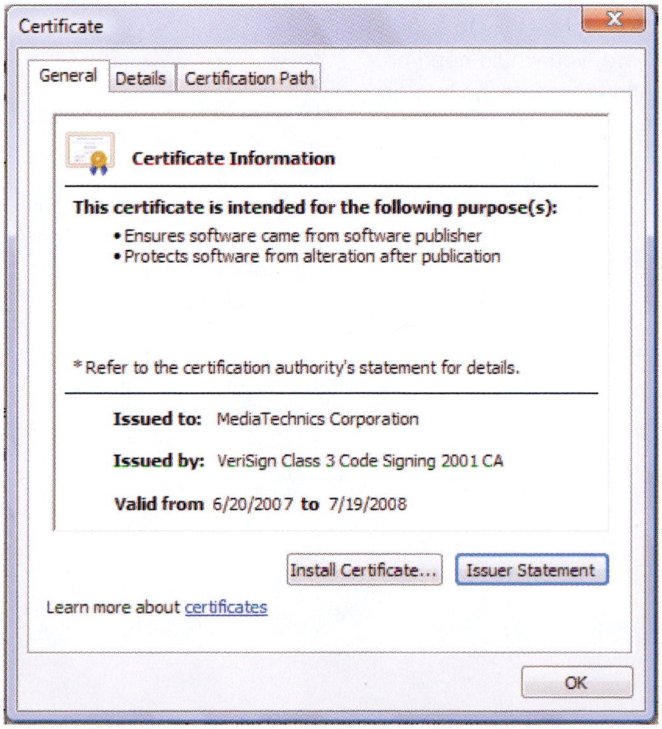

FIGURE 12-57

A signed digital certificate identifies the source of a software program.

12

MITIGATION

What happens when vulnerabilities are discovered in products that have already shipped? Despite defensive programming and other tactics to produce secure software, some defects inevitably remain undiscovered in products that end up in the hands of consumers. Some of those defects could be discovered and exploited by attackers. To be fair, some exploits are caused by factors that didn't exist when a software product was in development. For example, features of a new operating system might interact with a product in such a way that previously secure code suddenly becomes vulnerable. When bugs are discovered—especially if the bugs are being exploited by attackers—the programmer's remaining line of defense is to produce a bug fix, or patch.

What's up with all these patches? In today's computing environment, patches seem to pop up like mushrooms after a spring rain. Computer users are encouraged to apply all available patches, and some software publishers such as Microsoft, virtually force users to apply patches through an auto-update service.

To create a software patch, programmers first locate the source of the defect and make a judgment about its scope. Some patches require reworking an entire module, whereas small patches might affect just a few lines of code. Before being posted for users, patches should be thoroughly tested.

Patches can be supplied as complete files that simply overwrite an entire bad file with a more secure version. Patches can also be supplied as an in-line code segment, which overwrites only a targeted section of code.

Are there steps consumers can take to mitigate security vulnerabilities that exist because of programming flaws? You might remember seeing an error message like the one in Figure 12-58. The question, "Do you want to debug?" could lead you to believe that you can simply correct program errors on your own. That is rarely the case. To debug software, you need access to source code or scripts. Even if those are available, as in the case of open source software, you would need programming expertise and knowledge of the application to locate the bug and fix it.

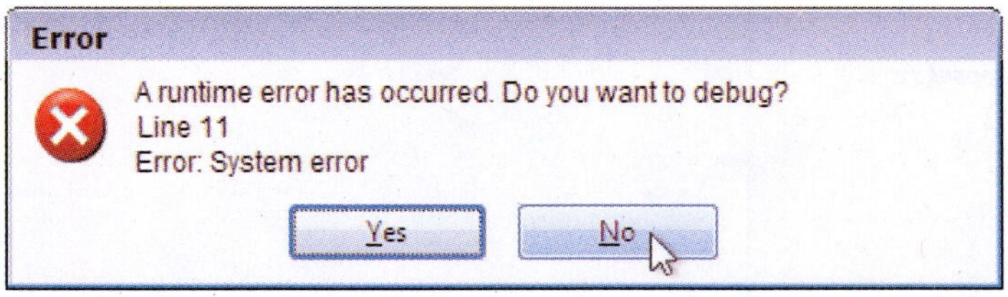

FIGURE 12-58

An error message that seems to offer an opportunity to fix a bug really isn't much use to most consumers.

Realistically, computer users have no control over software at the code level, but there are a few steps they can take to avoid security problems that stem from software defects.

- Select applications from software publishers with a good security track record.

- Watch for patches and apply them.

- Consider using open source software, which has been extensively reviewed by the programming community.

- And yes, keep your firewall and antivirus software deployed and up to date.

Security experts anticipate that buffer overflow and scripting attacks may decline because social engineering exploits like phishing scams require much less technical expertise. Social engineering exploits pit attackers directly against consumers and the techniques for fending off such attacks are typically out of the hands of programmers. Until that time, however, consumers should remain aware of the vulnerabilities related to software defects and factor that into software purchase decisions.

QuickCheck

1. A buffer [_____] is a condition in which data in memory exceeds its expected boundaries and flows into memory areas intended for use by other data.

2. [_____] error messages can present attackers with information about the directory location of programs or files, the structure of a database, or the layout of the program in memory.

3. The basic objective of [_____] programming methods is to generate proofs that the program code meets requirements.

4. [_____] programmers have to anticipate ways in which their programs could be compromised by legitimate users, intruders, other applications, the operating system, or third party security software.

5. Programmers can offer a(n) [_____] to fix a defect in a software product that is in the hands of consumers.

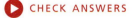 CHECK ANSWERS

12

Who's Minding the Asylum?

A STUDENT IN SINGAPORE found her 15 minutes of fame when she thumbed 26 words into her cell phone in less than 44 seconds, beating the previous 67-second record. Although some people can use a cell phone keypad to rapidly enter text messages, for most people, a numeric keypad is a frustrating tool for entering text. In addition to the exasperation of dealing with controls for gadgets such as cell phones and remote controls, you probably have pet peeves about the software interfaces for Web sites, productivity software, and computer games.

Today's programming languages provide programmers with sophisticated tools for coding and testing software. Why then, are computers and computer software so often characterized as being difficult to use? How is it that one of the new words in the computer lexicon is *techno-rage*? What prompts comments such as "My machine sometimes makes me feel like an idiot!"

Programmer and user interface designer Alan Cooper offers an explanation and solution in his book *The Inmates Are Running the Asylum*. The book's title is a metaphor for what Cooper perceives as the current state of computer programming. The *inmates* are computer programmers and the *asylum* is the frustrating, seemingly demented world of computer technology, with its cryptic error messages, puzzling user manuals, and inscrutable modes of operation.

According to Cooper, programmers don't intentionally create bad technology products. "Programmers aren't evil. They work hard to make their software easy to use. Unfortunately, their frame of reference is themselves, so they only make it easy to use for other software engineers, not for normal human beings." Cooper suggests that it is possible to create intuitive, easy-to-use technology products by devoting more time to developing detailed product specifications with the assistance of an interactive designer who is familiar with the psychology and habits of a typical computer user.

Paul Somerson, writing in *PC Computing* magazine, asserts, "You shouldn't have to plod through manuals, or spend hours waiting on support lines just to get your work done. This stuff is way, way too hard and overcomplicated." Somerson proposes a 10-point User's Bill of Rights that begins "All computers should be forced to work the way people do, rather than the other way around."

The first point of Somerson's Bill of Rights echoes the last point of another User's Bill of Rights, developed by Clare-Marie Karat, a psychologist and IBM researcher.

The Computer User's Bill of Rights

1. The user is always right. If there is a problem with the use of the system, the system is the problem, not the user.
2. The user has the right to easily install software and hardware systems.
3. The user has the right to a system that performs exactly as promised.
4. The user has the right to easy-to-use instructions for understanding and utilizing a system to achieve desired goals.
5. The user has the right to be in control of the system and to be able to get the system to respond to a request for attention.
6. The user has the right to a system that provides clear, understandable, and accurate information regarding the task it is performing and the progress toward completion.
7. The user has the right to be clearly informed about all system requirements for successfully using software or hardware.
8. The user has the right to know the limits of the system's capabilities.
9. The user has the right to communicate with the technology provider and receive a thoughtful and helpful response when raising concerns.
10. The user should be the master of software and hardware technology, not vice-versa. Products should be natural and intuitive to use.

Source: Clare-Marie Karat, IBM Thomas J. Watson Research Center

Karat agrees with Cooper's comments about programmers being unable to understand the people who use their software. She says, "The profile of the people who use systems has changed, while the system, and the culture in which they have developed, have not adjusted…The engineers and computer scientists who design hardware and software know little about the needs and frustrations of consumers."

BusinessWeek columnist Stephen H. Wildstrom published Karat's Bill of Rights and asked for reader feedback. The response was overwhelming and led Wildstrom to comment in a follow-up article, "The computer industry has a lot of baffled, frustrated, and unhappy customers." Surprisingly, many readers disagreed with the tenets of the Bill of Rights. For example, Jef Raskin, a member of the Macintosh computer design team, pointed out that "the mouse was not intuitive. A person seeing one for the first time had no idea how to use it."

Until we are able to implant some kind of instant-computer-genius chip at birth, it might be that people will just have to invest some time learning how to use a computer. "It shouldn't take a Ph.D. to understand that a few hours invested in learning about the computer and its software will make subsequent products intuitively usable," wrote one concerned *BusinessWeek* reader. Other readers questioned how much simplicity one could really expect from a computer. A computer that is as simple to use as a toaster would seem unlikely. As readers pointed out, a toaster is designed to do only one thing, whereas a computer can perform many different tasks, depending on the software it uses.

Some efforts to simplify operating system software have created another band of disgruntled users who complain that important features are now hidden because of feedback from novice testers who considered such features too advanced or confusing. Some

controls, such as those for setting up networks, are not easy to understand, but could be crucial for a successful installation. Hiding those controls because they might confuse beginners has only caused advanced users to become frustrated.

Who is right? Can technology be simplified, yet remain powerful enough to accomplish complex tasks? A branch of ergonomics called Human Factors, or Human-Computer Interaction (HCI), focuses on factors that make computers easy or difficult to use. The Human Factors InfoWeb provides more information about HCI and offers some additional food for thought on the usability controversy.

INFOWEBLINKS

You can read more about user-oriented software design at the **Human Factors InfoWeb**.

W **CLICK TO CONNECT**
www.course.com/np/concepts11/ch12

What Do You Think?

ISSUE

1. Can you think of a specific instance when you have become frustrated with a software user interface? ○ Yes ○ No ○ Not sure

2. Is it possible to make computer software significantly easier to use? ○ Yes ○ No ○ Not sure

3. Would you agree that programmers do not understand the viewpoint of a typical computer user and consequently produce bad software? ○ Yes ○ No ○ Not sure

▶ SAVE RESPONSES

12

COMPUTERS IN CONTEXT

Agriculture

AGRICULTURE MIGHT SEEM like a low-tech enterprise, but many farmers are turning to technology for help managing their finances, crops, and livestock. Even home gardeners who need little more than a few seed packets and a hoe are digging into computer and Internet resources for tips on combating garden pests, growing spectacular roses, and producing a bumper crop of veggies. Need to identify the pesky insect that's eating your tomatoes? Worried about the black spots appearing on your apple trees? Trying to figure out if that sprout is a flower or a weed? Many of your gardening questions are answered at sites sponsored by state and province extension services, the National Gardening Association, Organic Gardening.com, and many more.

Computers first sprouted up on farms to take care of financial matters. Farming, like any business, is all about the bottom line—the profit that's left after paying for seed, feed, fertilizer, machinery, taxes, utilities, and labor. Tracking income and expenses provides essential information for analyzing ways to improve operations and generate more profit. To keep track of finances, farmers typically use generic small-business accounting software, such as Quicken, or vertical market software designed especially for farming.

Farmers also use computers to maintain and analyze production records for crops and livestock. The Manitoba Milk Revenue Analyzer is an Excel spreadsheet template designed to help farmers pick the best dairy management scenario by analyzing factors such as feed costs and milk production levels. Cow Sense decision support software can help farmers improve cow herds and explore production, marketing, and financial alternatives.

How does a farmer decide whether to plant fields with soybeans or wheat? The Internet offers resources such as The Alberta Agriculture, Food, and Rural Development Web site where farmers can use an interactive crop cost calculator to compare profit potential for up to four crops. The calculator uses average market value for each crop and expected yield per acre based on the farm's growing zone. It produces a table that shows costs and estimated profit for each crop.

Suppose that a farmer decides to plant durum wheat. How much seed is needed? Too much seed is wasted money. Not enough seed produces scanty crops. A Web-based seed calculator helps farmers decide how much seed is necessary to produce the desired plant population. It also provides instructions for calibrating the seeder so that it sows the correct amount of seed. And what if chickweeds are choking out the sunflower crop? Alberta's Agriculture Web site offers an expert system to determine the most effective herbicide.

Farmers use the Internet to gather information about weather, market reports, farm equipment, loans, crops, and livestock. Lively discussions take place in "ag" chat groups, such as Farm Business, Crop Talk, Cattle Chat, Hog Talk, and Bug Talk. Farmers subscribe to e-mail newsletters, such as Amber Waves, and tap government resources, such as the USDA (United States Department of Agriculture) Hogs and Pigs Quarterly report.

The cutting edge of agricultural technology revolves around remote sensing, satellite imaging, geographical information systems, and global positioning systems. Remote sensing involves gathering information about an object without being in physical contact with it. For agriculture, two of the most often used remote sensing tools are satellite imaging and aerial photography. Weather satellite images are readily available and help farmers decide the best days to plant and harvest crops. Topographical satellite images can help farmers analyze drainage patterns to prevent crops from being flooded. Other satellite images can be used for crop surveillance—looking for areas of low yield, drought, disease, and infestation.

A geographical information system (GIS) is a computer-based tool for storing data and creating layered maps of the earth's surface. A GIS can store data about many factors important to farmers, such as soil moisture, salinity, nitrogen levels, and acidity. To collect data for a GIS, farmers use a global positioning system (GPS) and a variety of monitoring devices. Throughout the growing season, farmers use GPSs to find specific locations in their fields where they record data from soil sampling and observations of weed growth, unusual plant stress, and growth conditions. They can enter this data into a GIS program, along with data from satellite images, to create maps that help them gauge where to plant, what to plant, and how to care for plants.

The experience of a North Dakota farmer illustrates how data from satellite images and GPS observations can be combined in a GIS to create valuable agricultural maps. The farmer was producing a bountiful harvest of sugar beets, but the crop's sugar content was low. The farmer enlisted the help of agriculture experts at a nearby university who obtained a satellite image of the fields that showed areas of high and low production. The next step was to take soil samples—one every half acre. A handheld GPS was used to make sure samples were taken in an exact half-acre grid pattern. The satellite and soil sample data were then entered into a GIS, which produced a map overlaid with a multicolored grid. Grid colors corresponded to the amount of nitrogen that should be applied for best production. But how to apply these varying levels of nitrogen in each small area? The farmer used GPS-equipped machinery to spread the correct amount of nitrogen in each area of the field. This selective fertilization, along with crop rotation to further even out nitrogen levels, increased the beets' sugar content and the farmer's income.

Applying detailed agricultural data collected with a GPS is called *precision farming*. Several specialized tools, such as GPS-equipped yield monitors, help farmers collect data on bushels per acre, wet and dry bushels, total pounds, acres per hour, acres worked, and grain moisture content. Yield monitors are usually installed on the combines that harvest crops. The data is recorded on a memory card for later analysis and mapping.

Although a variety of agricultural technologies are available, not all farmers embrace them with equal enthusiasm. Barriers to using technology such as computers, GISs, GPSs, and satellite imaging include cost, training, and concerns about reliability, privacy, and security. The cost of obtaining satellite images, for example, has been the biggest deterrent to regular use of this data; the main barrier to the use of computers is simply a lack of expertise. Busy farmers might not have time to learn how to use even basic computer programs, and a fairly complex GIS database application can seem particularly daunting. University and government agencies are targeting farmers with special extension courses on agriculture-specific software for accounting, livestock decision support, and crop management. The goal is to make these technology tools part of the legacy that's handed down to the next generation of farmers.

INFOWEBLINKS

You'll find lots more information at the **Computers and Agriculture InfoWeb**.

Ⓦ CLICK TO CONNECT
www.course.com/np/concepts11/ch12

12

New Perspectives Labs

On the BookOnCD

To access the New Perspectives labs for Chapter 12, start the BookOnCD, BookOnFlashDrive, or other NP11 BookOn product and then click the icon next to the lab title below.

 USING A VISUAL DEVELOPMENT ENVIRONMENT

IN THIS LAB YOU'LL LEARN:

- To use the basic tools provided by the Visual Basic VDE

- How to work with a form design grid

- How to select controls, such as buttons, menus, and dialog boxes, for the graphical user interface of a computer program

- The way that a visual development environment displays properties for a control

- How to set properties that modify the appearance and operation of a control

- About the variety of events that can affect a control

- How to add code that specifies how a control responds to events

- How to add a component to the Visual Basic toolbox, and then incorporate it into a program

- How to save and test a program

- How to compile a program and run the executable version

LAB ASSIGNMENTS

1. Start the interactive part of the lab. Make sure you've enabled Tracking if you want to save your QuickCheck results. Perform each lab step as directed, and answer all the lab QuickCheck questions. When you exit the lab, your answers are automatically graded and your results are displayed.

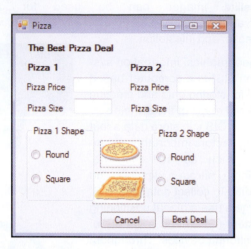

2. Draw a sketch of the main screen of your favorite word processing program. Identify five controls (such as menus, toolbars, lists, buttons, and scroll bars) provided by the programmer. Describe the external events (such as clicks, double-clicks, right-clicks, and mouseovers) to which each control responds.

3. Suppose you are preparing to write a program that calculates the number of calories you burn while exercising. The program requires users to enter their weight, the distance travelled, and the elapsed time in minutes from the beginning of the exercise to the end. Users should also be able to select from the following types of exercises: jogging, walking, swimming, and bicycling. After these calculations are entered, users should click a Calculate button to display the results of the calorie calculation. A Clear button should allow users to enter a new set of weight, distance, and time data. Sketch a form design grid like the one you used in the lab, and indicate where you would place each control necessary for this program's user interface.

Key Terms

Make sure you understand all the boldfaced key terms presented in this chapter. If you're using the NP11 BookOnCD, BookOnFlashDrive, or other NP11 BookOn product, you can use this list of terms as an interactive study activity. First, try to define a term in your own words, and then click the term to compare your definition with the definition presented in the chapter.

Ada, 679
Agile methodology, 681
Algorithm, 689
API, 687
APL, 679
Argument, 714
Assembly language, 677
Assumption, 680
Attack tree, 726
BASIC, 679
Buffer overflow, 723
C, 679
C#, 679
C++, 679
Class, 702
Class attribute, 703
Class hierarchy, 704
COBOL, 679
Code, 674
Component, 687
Computer programming, 675
Constant, 680
Control, 683
Control structures, 695
CPL, 679
Debugger, 685
Decision table, 714
Declarative paradigm, 713
Defensive programming, 726
Eiffel, 679
Encapsulation, 712
Event, 684
Event-driven paradigm, 685
Event-handling code, 684
Fact, 713
Fifth-generation languages, 678
First-generation languages, 677
Flowchart, 692

Formal methods, 725
Form design grid, 683
FORTRAN, 679
Fourth-generation languages, 678
Function, 696
Functional paradigm, 713
Goal, 715
Haskell, 679
High-level language, 676
IDE, 686
Inheritance, 704
Instantiation, 717
Iteration, 698
Java, 679
Keyword, 676
Known information, 680
LISP, 679
Logic error, 685
Loop, 698
Low-level language, 676
Message, 706
Method, 705
Multiparadigm languages, 679
Object, 702
Object-oriented paradigm, 702
Parameters, 676
Particle renderer, 687
Pascal, 679
Pathfinder algorithms, 687
PL/1, 679
Polymorphism, 707
Predicate, 714
Predictive methodology, 681
Private attribute, 703
Problem statement, 680
Procedural language, 689
Procedural paradigm, 689
Procedure, 696

Program editor, 682
Programming language, 676
Programming paradigm, 679
Prolog, 679
Properties, 683
Pseudocode, 692
Public attribute, 703
REALbasic, 679
Remarks, 686
Repetition control structure, 698
RPG, 679
Rule, 713
Runtime error, 685
Scheme, 679
SDK, 686
Second-generation languages, 677
Selection control structure, 697
Sequence control structure, 695
Sequential execution, 695
Signed code, 727
SIMULA, 679
Smalltalk, 679
Structured English, 692
Subclass, 704
Subroutine, 696
Superclass, 704
Syntax, 676
Syntax error, 685
Third-generation languages, 677
Threat modeling, 725
Variable, 680
VDE, 683
Visual Basic, 679
Walkthrough, 694

12

Interactive Summary

To review important concepts from this chapter, fill in the blanks to best complete each sentence. When using the NP11 BookOnCD or other BookOn product, click the Check Answers buttons to automatically score your answers.

SECTION A: Each line of instructions for a computer program is referred to as [_____] . Computer programmers focus on [_____] computer programs, but also plan, test, and document computer programs. In contrast, software [_____] tend to focus on designing and [_____] activities.

A computer programming language is a set of grammar rules and [_____] for creating instructions that can ultimately be processed by a computer. The first programming languages were low-level [_____] languages. Second-generation languages, called [_____] languages, allowed programmers to write programs consisting of abbreviated op codes instead of 1s and 0s. Third-generation languages provided programmers with easy-to-remember command words, such as PRINT and INPUT. Fourth-generation languages were designed to eliminate many of the strict punctuation and [_____] rules that complicated third-generation languages.

Some experts believe that [_____] languages, such as Prolog, constitute a fifth generation of computer languages. Other experts define fifth-generation languages as those that allow programmers to use graphical or visual tools to construct programs.

Before program code can be written, a programmer needs a clear problem [_____] , which includes a list of assumptions, a description of known information, and a specification for what constitutes a solution. With a clear plan, a programmer can begin coding using a text editor, program editor, or [_____] development environment. A program is not complete until it has been tested to ensure that it contains no [_____] errors or runtime errors. All computer programs should include internal documentation in the form of [_____] , which are explanatory comments inserted into a computer program along with lines of code.

▶ CHECK ANSWERS

SECTION B: A programming [_____] is an approach that affects the way programmers conceptualize and approach a computer program. Every programming language supports one or more programming approaches. Languages such as COBOL and FORTRAN support a traditional approach to programming called the [_____] paradigm, which is based on a step-by-step [_____] . Various planning tools, such as structured English, [_____] , and flowcharts, help programmers plan the steps for a procedural program.

Procedural languages provide programmers with a variety of [_____] structures for specifying the order of program execution. A [_____] control structure directs the computer to execute one or more instructions, not coded as a simple succession of steps. A [_____] control provides a choice of paths, based on whether a condition is true or false. A [_____] control, or loop, repeats one or more instructions until a certain condition is met. The procedural paradigm provides a solid approach to problems that can be solved by following a set of steps. Procedural languages tend to produce programs that run quickly and use [_____] resources efficiently.

▶ CHECK ANSWERS

SECTION C: The object-oriented paradigm is based on the idea that the solution to a problem can be visualized in terms of objects that [_____] with each other. An object is a single instance of an entity. Programmers can use a [_____] as a template for a group of objects with similar characteristics. Classes can be derived from other classes through a process called [_____]. The set of superclasses and subclasses that are related to each other is referred to as a class [_____]. OO programmers often use [_____] Modeling Language diagrams to plan the classes for a program.

Objects interact to solve problems by exchanging [_____], which initiate an action, process, or procedure. OO programmers can create [_____] to define what happens once an action is initiated. Methods provide excellent flexibility because a concept called [_____], or overloading, allows programmers to create a single, generic name for a procedure that behaves in unique ways for different classes. The OO paradigm allows programmers to hide the internal details of objects and their methods. This process, called [_____], allows objects to be easily reused, modified, and repurposed.

► CHECK ANSWERS

SECTION D: Programming languages such as Prolog support the [_____] programming paradigm because they encourage programmers to describe a [_____] rather than its solution.

Prolog programs are typically built from a collection of facts and rules. A Prolog fact begins with a [_____], such as shapeof, followed by a series of [_____] within parentheses, such as (pizza,round). Each Prolog rule has a [_____], which defines an outcome or fact, followed by the notation :-, which means "if." The body of the rule consists of one or more clauses that define conditions that must

be satisfied to validate the head of the rule. Prolog uses a process called [_____] to evaluate facts and rules to determine whether they are true. In Prolog jargon, a question or query to a program's database is called a [_____].

Declarative languages, such as Prolog, can be used for problems that require calculations, but those problems are typically better suited to [_____] languages. As a general rule, declarative languages are best suited for problems that pertain to words and concepts rather than numbers.

► CHECK ANSWERS

SECTION E: According to most experts the primary cause of security holes is a [_____] overflow, a condition in which data in memory exceeds its expected boundaries and flows into memory areas intended for use by other data. Hackers also use verbose [_____] messages to uncover security vulnerabilities. Developing secure software depends on rigorous software development techniques, such as [_____] methods, which generate proof that the program code meets listed requirements, and [_____] modeling that can be used to identify potential vulnerabilities to

security breaches. A technique called [_____] programming focuses on source code walkthroughs, simplification, and filtering input. [_____] code is a software program that identifies its source and carries a digital certificate attesting to its authenticity. Despite the best development efforts, code defects are sometimes found after products ship and must be remedied with [_____]. Consumers should remain aware of the vulnerabilities related to software defects and factor that into software purchase decisions.

► CHECK ANSWERS

12

Interactive Situation Questions

Apply what you've learned to some typical computing situations. When using the NP11 BookOnCD, BookOnFlashDrive, or any other NP11 BookOn product, you can type your answers, and then use the Check Answers button to automatically score your responses.

1. A friend asks you for help writing a computer program to calculate the square yards of carpet needed for a dorm room. The statement "the living room floor is rectangular" is an example of a(n) [_____] . The length and width of the room are examples of [_____] information, which you can obtain as [_____] from the user.

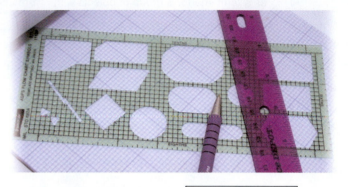

2. Continuing with the carpet example, you devise a set of steps, or a(n) [_____] , to solve the problem. You then use a programming language to write the [_____] shown below, which expresses the algorithm.

```
Input "Enter the width of the room in
    feet: "; width
Input "Enter the length of the room in
    feet: "; length
Print "Carpet needed:"
Print length*width & " square feet"
Print (length*width)/9 & "square yards"
```

3. Examine the code shown below. This program prints [_____] lines of text.

```
For n = 1 To 5
    Print "Loop number " & n
Next n
```

4. You've just joined a programming team that is developing a Java program for an earth-moving equipment vendor. The lead programmer shows you a UML with labels such as Cranes, Trucks, and Front-end Loaders. With your background in object-oriented programming, you can tell immediately that these are [_____] , which will be coded as a series of attributes, such as `private string manufacturer.`

5. While browsing through several programs posted online, you come across the following code and realize it is written using the [_____] programming language.

```
male(frodo).
male(mungo).
male(largo).
male(balbo).
female(berylla).
female(belladonna).
female(primula).
female(sella).
parents(mungo,berylla,balbo).
parents(frodo,primula,drogo).
parents(largo,berylla,balbo).
parents(sella,berylla,balbo).
brother_of(X,Y):-
    male(Y),
    parents(X,Mother,Father),
    parents(Y,Mother,Father).
```

▶ CHECK ANSWERS

Interactive Practice Tests

Practice tests that consist of 10 multiple-choice, true/false, and fill-in-the-blank questions are available on both the NP11 BookOn products and the NP11 Web site. The questions are selected at random from a large test bank, so each time you take a test, you'll receive a different set of questions. Your tests are scored immediately, and you can print study guides that help you find the correct answers for any questions that you missed.

▶ CLICK TO START

Study Tips

Study Tips help you to organize and consolidate the information in a unit by making lists, outlines, charts, and sketches. You can use paper and pencil or word processing software to complete most of the Study Tip activities.

1. Make sure you can use your own words to correctly answer each of the red focus questions that appear throughout the chapter.

2. Describe how the job of a systems analyst differs from the job of a software engineer.

3. Create a diagram that shows how low-level and high-level languages relate to the five generations of computer languages.

4. Describe the three elements of a problem statement, and provide examples within the context of the pizza problem.

5. Explain the differences between an algorithm and a computer program.

6. Describe three ways to express an algorithm, and try to create your own short examples to illustrate your descriptions.

7. Give an example of a sequence control structure, a selection control structure, and a repetition control structure.

8. Using the pizza program as the basis for an example, describe how to test a program to make sure that it works correctly.

9. Explain the differences between a syntax error and a logic error.

10. Make sure you can define each of these terms associated with object-oriented programming: object, class, superclass, subclass, attribute, message, method, inheritance, polymorphism, and encapsulation.

11. Describe the differences between event-driven, procedural, object-oriented, and declarative paradigms, and provide at least one example of a language that supports each paradigm.

12. Make sure you can use your own words to define the following terms associated with the declarative paradigm: fact, rule, predicate, arguments, goal, instantiation, and backtracking.

13. Write a few Prolog facts that describe your relationships to members of your family.

14. Describe two ways in which a Prolog program can be set up to accept user input.

15. Create a sentence outline for Section E that focuses on techniques for secure programming.

16. Fill in the blanks on the concept map shown below to show the hierarchy of programming paradigms described in this chapter.

Concept Map

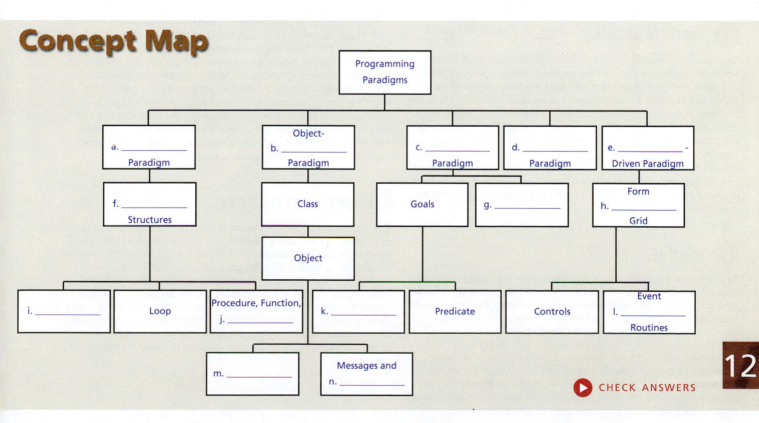

CHECK ANSWERS

12

Projects

CRITICAL THINKING

Think like a programmer and write a detailed description of making a peanut butter sandwich. Next, look at your detailed instructions and circle any looping or branching activities. If you don't have any, your description wasn't detailed enough and you should rework it. When you've completed the description, submit it to your instructor, who might compare the most and least detailed descriptions submitted by all students in your class.

GROUP PROJECT

In a group of three students, create the specifications for a program to operate a gas pump. Make sure you create a problem statement, complete with assumptions and known information. Design the algorithm, making sure it dispenses the customer's choice of Regular, Mid-grade, or Premium gas. Assume that all customers will pay cash (credit cards are not accepted). Create mockups of the input/output displays shown to the customer. Create a test plan with a comprehensive set of inputs and outputs that could be used to check the accuracy of your finished program. You can collaborate on each aspect of the specifications, or assign one student to each. Consolidate your completed specifications into a single document to submit to your instructor.

 CYBERCLASSROOM

Computer programmers often develop user interfaces for programs. For this project, your team will use an online program and evaluate its interface. Your team leader should initiate the project by finding a free online tutorial about 1 hour in length that will be of interest to the rest of the team. A good place to find tutorials is *www.e-learningcentre.co.uk /eclipse/showcase/academic.htm.* All team members should complete the tutorial and then send the team leader answers to the following questions: 1) From a learner's perspective, did the tutorial hold your interest and help you learn? 2) If you were redesigning the user interface for this program, what improvements would you make? The team leader should compile everyone's comments and forward them to the instructor.

 MULTIMEDIA PROJECT

To appreciate the complexity of game programming, play a computer game. Make a list of the objects you encounter during the first five minutes of the game. You might have to stop and restart the game several times to complete your list. Don't forget to include the title screen, introductory music, video, and so on. Expand your list of objects by adding descriptions of what happens to the objects. For example, the background scenery object might move when the game character reaches a certain point on the screen, or a sound might be emitted by a character that gets struck by a weapon. Take a screenshot of the game during your observation period. Submit your list and screenshot. Indicate the name of the game you observed on the screenshot.

RESUME BUILDER

The computer game industry is hot and employs professionals from a wide variety of career fields. How would a professional in your career field fit into a computer game development team? What aspect of the game would they work on? Jot down your thoughts, and then go online and search for information about computer game development. What can you learn about jobs in the computer game industry for people with skills in your career field? Submit your findings in a format of your choice. You can write a one-page summary or get creative and work up a brochure or 30-second radio spot.

GLOBALIZATION

There is a growing trend to develop software that can be used globally. Suppose you are supervising a programming team and you have directed them to internationalize a software application and make sure it can be easily converted into a variety of languages. After researching on the Web, create a list of best practices for software globalization that you will distribute to your programming team.

ISSUE

The Issue section of this chapter focused on why computers seem difficult to use. Some critics accuse software engineers of designing software for their fellow engineers rather than non-technical computer users. On the other side of the argument are people who believe that computers perform complex tasks, which can never be simplified enough to become totally intuitive. Which side do you support? To begin this project, access the Human Factors InfoWeb to get an in-depth overview of the issue. Next, determine the viewpoint that you want to present and write a 2-3 page article suitable for a computer magazine. Follow your professor's instructions for submitting your paper by e-mail or as a printed document.

COMPUTERS IN CONTEXT

The Computers in Context section focused on technologies used in agriculture, farming, and gardening. For this project, research one of these technologies. Find out how it works, how much it costs, and how it is applied to farming. Now imagine you are a county agriculture agent whose job is to inform farmers of new and useful agricultural technologies. You have a booth at the county fair. Design an eye-catching poster that fair-goers could understand in about two minutes. You can design your poster on poster board, or you can use an electronic medium, such as a word processor. When you submit your poster, provide a list of the sources you used to gather information and graphics.

On the Web

STUDENT EDITION LABS

W CLICK TO ACCESS THE NP11 WEB SITE
or open your browser and connect to www.course.com/np/concepts11/ch12.
Lab results can be stored in the Universal Gradebook.

Work hands-on in structured simulations practicing important skills and concepts

VISUAL PROGRAMMING

In the Visual Programming Student Edition Lab, you will learn about the following topics:

- Introduction to the basics of visual programming
- Understanding structured vs. object-oriented programming
- Using Visual Basic
- Designing a user interface
- Writing and running a program

CHAPTER COURSECAST

Use your computer or iPod to hear a five-minute audio presentation of chapter highlights.

FLASHCARD COURSECAST

Interact with audio flashcards to review key terms from the chapter.

DETAILED OBJECTIVES

Make sure that you've achieved all the objectives for a chapter before it's time for your test!

TEST YOURSELF

Review chapter material by taking these ten-question tests, then send your results to the Universal Gradebook.

ONLINE GAMES

Have some fun while refreshing your memory about key concepts that might appear on the next test. You can even send your results to the Universal Gradebook!

AND MORE!

At the NP11 Web site you'll also find Extra Content and InfoWebLinks.

12

QUICK CHECK ANSWERS

ORIENTATION

QuickCheck A
1. unit
2. Start
3. False
4. Backspace
5. menu

QuickCheck B
1. save
2. browser
3. search
4. @
5. account

QuickCheck C
1. False
2. security
3. Spyware
4. spam

QuickCheck D
1. Annotation
2. False
3. Labs
4. Tracking

QuickCheck E
1. True
2. Home
3. Overview
4. Labs

CHAPTER 1

QuickCheck A
1. Internet
2. networks
3. Cyberspace
4. Digitization
5. Convergence

QuickCheck B
1. output
2. False
3. stored
4. supercomputer
5. microcontroller

QuickCheck C
1. digital
2. binary
3a. ASCII
3b. binary
4. gigabyte
5. integrated

QuickCheck D
1. source
2. object
3. operands
4. arithmetic
5. control

QuickCheck E
1. authentication
2. Biometrics
3. keylogger
4. True
5. password

CHAPTER 2

QuickCheck A
1. peripheral
2. desktop
3. tablet computers
4. Media
5. compatible

QuickCheck B
1. clock
2. processor
3. bus
4. core
5. volatile
6. virtual
7. EEPROM

QuickCheck C
1. Access
2a. random, direct
2b. sequential
3. density
4. head
5. crashes
6. lands
7. True
8. state

QuickCheck D
1. pointing
2. refresh
3. resolution
4. duplex
5. slots
6. USB

QuickCheck E
1. Slot
2. surge
3. battery
4. death
5. Safe

CHAPTER 3

QuickCheck A
1. system
2. Productivity
3. groupware
4. utility
5. driver

QuickCheck B
1. document
2. False
3. Spreadsheet
4. Database
5. ripper
6. DVD

QuickCheck C
1. suite
2. requirements
3. False
4. Public
5. concurrent
6. Open

QuickCheck D
1. executable
2. local
3. True
4. Portable
5. patch

QuickCheck E
1. blended
2. viruses
3. worm
4. rootkit
5. quarantines

CHAPTER 4

QuickCheck A
1. resources
2. memory, RAM
3. kernel
4. bootstrap
5. interface

QuickCheck B
1. False
2. backward
3. dual
4. virtual
5. fork
6. Linux
7. True

QuickCheck C
1. conventions
2. True
3. C:
4. subdirectories
5. folders
6. size
7. header
8. native

QuickCheck D
1. Save
2. metaphor, model
3. Explorer
4a. tracks
4b. sectors
5. shredder

QuickCheck E
1. Registry
2. folder
3. external
4. incremental
5. recovery

CHAPTER 5

QuickCheck A
1. interface
2. False
3. protocols
4a. packet
4b. circuit
5. IP

QuickCheck B
1. Ethernet
2. True
3. 100
4. hub
5. router

QuickCheck C
1. Wi-Fi
2. Bluetooth
3. ad-hoc
4. infrastructure
5. SSID

QuickCheck D
1. resources
2. root
3. driver
4. file
5. application

QuickCheck E
1a. WEP
1b. WPA2
2. Symmetric
3. Public
4. PGP

CHAPTER 6

QuickCheck A
1. backbone
2. ISP
3a. TCP
3b. IP
4a. static
4b. dynamic
5. domain
6. .edu
7. True

QuickCheck B
1. voiceband
2. False
3. Ethernet
4. latency
5. WiMAX

QuickCheck C
1. Portable
2. hotspot
3. WiMAX
4. WAP
5. EDGE

QuickCheck D
1. chat
2. False
3. grid
4. FTP
5. BitTorrent

QuickCheck E
1. ports
2. patches
3. Firewall
4. router
5. private

CHAPTER 7

QuickCheck A
1. link
2. space
3. Browser
4. helper
5. stateless
6. True
7. certificates

QuickCheck B
1. crawler, spider
2. stuffing
3. False
4. Boolean
5. False
6. citation

QuickCheck C
1. True
2. True
3. clickthrough
4. cookies
5. False

QuickCheck D
1. @
2. MIME
3. HTML
4. forward
5a. SMTP
5b. POP

QuickCheck E
1. proxy
2. Flash
3. bug
4. Pharming
5. filter
6. False

CHAPTER 8

QuickCheck A
1a. digital
1b. MIDI
2. sampling
3. AAC
4. playlist
5. recognition

QuickCheck B
1. FireWire, IEEE 1394
2. resolution
3. dependent
4. grayscale
5. TIFF, TIF
6. GIF
7a. Lossy
7b. lossless

QuickCheck C
1. True
2. drawing
3. wireframe
4. tracing
5. rasterization
6. SWF, Flash

QuickCheck D
1. Desktop
2. capture
3. frame
4. False
5. False
6. streaming
7. VOB, Video Object

QuickCheck E
1. Time
2. watermark
3. protected
4. CSS
5. individualization
6. super

CHAPTER 9

QuickCheck A
1. manual, hand
2. Babbage
3. prototypes
4a. vacuum
4b. transistors
5a. integrated
5b. microprocessor

QuickCheck B
1. sectors
2. Silicon
3. offshoring
4. dot
5. retirement
6. vaporware
7. channels

QuickCheck C
1. False
2. security
3. telecommuting
4. Information
5. certification
6. portfolio
7. metasearch

QuickCheck D
1. ethics
2. Laws
3. Digital
4. Confidentiality
5. responsible
6. whistleblower

QuickCheck E
1. radiation
2. SAR
3. repetitive
4. False
5. native
6. reminder

CHAPTER 10

QuickCheck A
1. mission
2a. tactical
2b. strategic
3. structured
4a. Batch
4b. online
5. MIS
6. decision
7. expert

QuickCheck B
1. management
2. Development
3. opportunities
4. waterfall
5. Requirements
6. use

QuickCheck C
1. solutions
2. distributed
3. application
4. RFP
5. specifications

QuickCheck D
1. implementation
2. customized
3a. unit
3b. integration
4. system
5. procedure
6. direct
7. acceptance
8. reliability

QuickCheck E
1. MTBF
2. False
3. countermeasures
4. False
5a. identity
5b. phishing

CHAPTER 11

QuickCheck A
1. mining
2. analytical
3. occurrences
4. flat
5. cardinalities
6. relational
7. object

QuickCheck B
1. ASCII
2. False
3. independence
4. Dynamic
5. False

QuickCheck C
1. key
2. types
3. True
4. sensitive
5. validation
6. redundancy
7. template

QuickCheck D
1. keywords
2. True
3. Boolean
4. False
5. SELECT
6. UPDATE
7. False

QuickCheck E
1. Encryption
2. read
3. audit
4. financial
5. portable

CHAPTER 12

QuickCheck A
1. True
2. engineers
3. paradigms
4. Third
5. visual
6. debugger
7. API

QuickCheck B
1. False
2. procedural
3. flowcharts
4. sequence
5. True
6. loop

QuickCheck C
1. object-oriented
2. True
3. UML
4. inheritance
5a. messages
5b. method

QuickCheck D
1a. problem
1b. solution
2. decision
3a. arguments
3b. predicate
4a. constant
4b. variable
5. instantiation
6. if

QuickCheck E
1. overflow
2. Verbose
3. formal
4. Defensive
5. patch

CREDITS

Page v, Shutterstock photo by Graham Tomlin
Page xiv, Shutterstock illustration by Marko Nesic
Page xi, Shutterstock photo by Mark Aplet
Page xvi, Shutterstock photo by Daniel Sroga
Page xix, Shutterstock photo by Jaimie Duplass
Orientation 2, Courtesy of Sony Electronics
Orientation 5, Courtesy of Kensington Technology Group
Orientation 6, Photodisc/Getty Images
Orientation 14, Courtesy of Stephen G. Eick, SSS Research Inc.
Figure 1-02, © Time & Life Pictures/Getty Images
Figure 1-06, © Walt Disney Pictures/courtesy Everett Collection
Figure 1-07, Courtesy of iLounge.com : All Things iPod
Figure 1-08, Courtesy Everett Collection
Figure 1-09, © Motion Picture Association of America, Inc.
Figure 1-10, © Joel W. Rogers/CORBIS
Figure 1-11, AP Photo/Pavel Rahman
Figure 1-14, Courtesy of IBM Corporation
Figure 1-14, Courtesy of AlienWare
Figure 1-14, Courtesy of Apple
Figure 1-14, Courtesy of Acer Inc. and Microsoft Corporation
Figure 1-15, Courtesy of Sun Microsystems
Figure 1-16, Courtesy of Nintendo Corporation
Figure 1-17, Courtesy of IBM Corporation
Figure 1-18, Courtesy of IBM Corporation
Figure 1-19a, BlackBerry Curve image courtesy of Research In Motion
Figure 1-19b, iStockphoto
Figure 1-20, Courtesy of Intel Corporation
Figure 1-21, © Getty Images
Figure 1-41, © Brand X Pictures/Alamy
Figure 1-44, Courtesy of www.rantsandraves.co.uk
Figure 1-48, Courtesy of SanDisk Corporation
Issue 1a, © Warner Brothers/courtesy Everett Collection
CinC-1a, Image courtesy of The Advertising Archives
CinC-1b, Napster advertisement reprinted with permission of Napster, LLC
Figure 2-02b, Courtesy of MonarchComputer.com
Figure 2-02c, Courtesy of Apple
Figure 2-03b, Courtesy of Fujitsu Ltd. and Microsoft Corporation
Figure 2-03c, Courtesy of OQO
Figure 2-04, AP Photo/Damian Dovarganes
Figure 2-05, Courtesy of NVIDIA
Figure 2-06, Courtesy of Hewlett-Packard Company
Figure 2-07, Courtesy of Hewlett-Packard Company
Figure 2-10, Courtesy of Jonathan Atwell
Figure 2-11, Courtesy of Intel Corporation
Figure 2-14a, Courtesy of Intel Corporation
Figure 2-14b, AMD, the AMD Arrow logo, and combinations, thereof are trademarks of Advanced Micro Devices, Inc.
Figure 2-26, Courtesy of IBM Research
Figure 2-30, Courtesy of Hewlett-Packard Company
Figure 2-31, Courtesy of Sony Electronics, Inc.
Figure 2-36a, Courtesy of IBM Corporation
Figure 2-36c, Courtesy of Kensington Technology Group
Figure 2-36d, Courtesy of Saitek USA
Figure 2-37, Courtesy of Microsoft Corporation
Figure 2-38a, Courtesy of Sony Electronics, Inc.
Figure 2-38b, Courtesy of Sony Electronics, Inc.
Figure 2-38c, Courtesy of ViewSonic Corporation
Figure 2-41, Courtesy of ATI Technologies Inc.
Figure 2-42, Courtesy of Epson America Inc.
Figure 2-52, Courtesy of Kensington Technology Group
Figure 2-53, Courtesy of AnchorPad
Figure 2-54, Courtesy of Kensington Technology Group
Figure 2-55, Courtesy of American Power Conversion
Issue-2b, © Gabe Palmer/CORBIS
CinC-2a, © Bettmann/CORBIS
CinC-2b, Courtesy of Business Wire and Lages & Associates
Figure 3-04, Courtesy of Microsoft Corporation
Figure 3-05, Courtesy of Microsoft Corporation

Figure 3-07a, Courtesy of Microsoft Corporation
Figure 3-07b, Reprinted with permission of Quark, Inc. and its affiliates.
Figure 3-07c, Courtesy of Adobe Systems Incorporated
Figure 3-16a, Courtesy of Wolfram Research
Figure 3-16b, Photo: Julie Cooke, www.lightdrawing.com
Figure 3-28, Courtesy of Microsoft Corporation
Figure 3-28, Courtesy of Norton by Symantec
Figure 3-28, Courtesy of Adobe Systems Incorporated
Figure 3-28, Courtesy of InterVideo, Inc.
Figure 3-33, Copyright © 2006 by the Open Source Initiative
Figure 3-44, David Woolley/Getty Images
Figure 3-49, Courtesy of ClamWin Free Antivirus
Issue-3a, Courtesy of Software & Information Industry Association
CinC-3a, © Eli Reed/Magnum
CinC-3b, © Ashley Gilbertson/Aurora
Figure 4-08, Courtesy of Microsoft Corporation
Figure 4-15, Courtesy of Microsoft Corporation
Figure 4-18, Courtesy of Apple
Figure 4-23, Courtesy of Microsoft Corporation
Figure 4-23, Courtesy of Palm, Inc.
Figure 4-23, Courtesy of Symbian
Figure 4-47, Courtesy of Seagate Technology
Issue-4 © Dennis O'Clair/Getty Images
CinC-4a, Courtesy of the Fond du Lac Police Department
CinC-4b, Courtesy of the Fond du Lac Police Department
Figure 5-01, Courtesy of Bob Metcalfe
Figure 5-02, © Gail Mooney/Masterfile
Figure 5-12, AP Photo/Eckehard Schulz
Figure 5-14, Courtesy of Iogear
Figure 5-19a, Courtesy of NETGEAR, Inc.
Figure 5-19b, Courtesy of D-Link Systems
Figure 5-19c, Courtesy of D-Link Systems
Figure 5-20, Courtesy of Linksys
Figure 5-25, Courtesy of Dell Inc.
Figure 5-27, Courtesy of Bluetooth SIG
Figure 5-27b, Courtesy of Nokia
Figure 5-28, Courtesy of Motorola
Figure 5-30, Courtesy of D-Link Systems
Figure 5-33a, Courtesy of Nokia
Figure 5-33c, Courtesy of NETGEAR, Inc.
Figure 5-39, © Steve Chenn/CORBIS
Figure 5-40a, Courtesy of Sonos, Inc.
Figure 5-40b, Courtesy of D-Link Systems
Figure 5-40c, Courtesy of Toshiba America Information Systems
Figure 5-44b, Courtesy of Intel Corporation
Figure 5-48, AP Photo/Matthias Rietschel
Figure 5-54, © A. Ramey/Photo Edit—all rights reserved.
Issue-5a, Courtesy of Ken Pau and Stone Creek Coffee Company
Issue-5b, Courtesy of Rob Flickenger
   (http://www.oreillynet.com/pub/wlg/448)
CinC-5a, Photography courtesy of the University of Illinois at Urbana-Champaign Archives
CinC-5b, © Tom Stewart/CORBIS
Figure 6-01, Computer History Museum
Figure 6-06, Courtesy of DNSstuff.com
Figure 6-14, Courtesy of Zyxel
Figure 6-16a, Courtesy of 2Wire.com
Figure 6-16b, Courtesy of Zoom Technologies
Figure 6-20, © Siri Stafford/Getty Images
Figure 6-20, © Bryce Kroll/iStockphoto.com
Figure 6-20, © Jonathan Ling/iStockphoto.com
Figure 6-21, Courtesy of Hughes Network Systems, LLC
Figure 6-22, Courtesy of Intel Corporation
Figure 6-24, Cracker Barrel Old Country Store, Inc.
Figure 6-25, Royalty-Free/CORBIS
Figure 6-26, Siemens Press Photo
Figure 6-27, Courtesy of Ground Control
Figure 6-28, Courtesy of Ground Control
Figure 6-31, Opera Software ASA

GLOSSARY

24-bit bitmap A True Color graphic, which requires 24 bits for each pixel, used for photographic-quality images that can include any of 16.7 million colors. 437

3-D graphics A type of digital graphics format that displays a three-dimensional image on a two-dimensional space. 449

3-D graphics software The software used to create three-dimensional wireframe objects, then render them into images. 137

32-bit bitmap A graphical image which requires 32 bits for each pixel. 437

AAC (Advanced Audio Compression) A file format that provides highly compressed audio files with very little loss of sound quality and is promoted by Apple on its iTunes Web site. 424

AACS (Advanced Access Content System) A digital rights management system that uses encryption to restrict access and copying content from optical media. 469

Abacus A manual calculator that consists of beads mounted on sticks inside a frame with each bead representing a specific quantity. 486

Absolute reference In a worksheet formula, cell references (usually preceded by a $ symbol) that cannot change as a result of a move or copy operation. 132

Acceptance testing The final phase of testing for a new information system, in which the system's new owner determines whether the system performs as required. 586

Access control Security measures that limit access to systems, such as databases. 655

Access time The estimated time for a storage device to locate data on a disk, usually measured in milliseconds. 77

Accounting software A category of software that includes accounting, money management, and tax preparation software. 142

ActiveX control A set of commands and components that can be used by programmers to add interactive features to Web pages. 372

Actors Object-oriented jargon for people who use an information system. 573

Ad hoc report A customized report (also called a demand report) generated according to supplied specific information not available in scheduled reports. 561

Ad-blocking software A type of software that prevents ads from appearing on your computer screen. 385

Ad-serving cookie A cookie installed by a marketing firm to track user activities on Web sites containing their ads. 400

Ada A high-level programming language developed by the Department of Defense and originally intended for military applications. 679

AES (Advanced Encryption Standard) An encryption standard that uses three separate key sizes and is based on the Rijndael encryption algorithm. 285

Agile methodology An approach to software development that produces programs in an incremental way allowing specification to evolve at each iteration. 681

AGP (Accelerated Graphics Port) A type of interface, or slot, that provides a high-speed pathway for advanced graphics. 96

AIFF (Audio Interchange File Format) An audio file format developed by Apple that is popular for cross-platform use. 424

Ajax An approach to developing interactive Web sites that uses tools such as JavaScript and XML. 362

Algorithm An abstract or general procedure for solving a problem, typically expressed as pseudocode, structured English, or a flowchart. 689

Alpha test One of the first phases of software testing, usually conducted by the software publisher's in-house testing team. 504

ALU (Arithmetic Logic Unit) The part of the CPU that performs arithmetic and logical operations on the numbers stored in its registers. 31

Always-on connection In the context of Internet access, a permanent connection, as opposed to a connection that is established and dropped as needed. 307

Analog data Data that is measured or represented on a continuously varying scale, such as a dimmer switch or a watch with a sweep second hand. 22

Analog hole Any device or technique that allows digital content to be copied legally or illegally from an analog device. 464

Analog protection system (APS) A DVD copy prevention technology developed by Macromedia that scrambles data copied to video tape. 468

Analysis phase Tasks performed by the project team whose goal is to produce a list of requirements for a new or revised information system. 571

Analytical Engine A mechanical calculator designed by Charles Babbage that included memory and a programmable processor and is widely regarded as the most important ancestor to modern computer design. 488

Animated GIF A type of GIF image that displays a sequence of frames to create the appearance of continuous motion. 448

Anonymizer tools Software and/or hardware that cloaks the origination of an e-mail or Web page request. 10

Anonymous FTP A type of FTP access that requires no account on a server, but rather can be accessed using "anonymous" as the user ID. 337

Anonymous proxy service A server on the Internet that can be used to forward Web requests after cloaking the originating address for users who want to surf anonymously. 403

Antispyware Software that blocks spyware from entering a computer. 402

Antivirus software A computer program used to scan a computer's memory and disks to identify, isolate, and eliminate viruses. 167

API (Application Program(ming) Interface) A set of application programs or operating system functions that can be utilized by a program. 687

APL The acronym for A Programming Language, a high-level scientific programming language used to manipulate tables of numbers. 679

Apple I An unassembled computer kit released in 1977 by Apple Computer Corp. for computer hobbyists. 495

Apple II A complete microcomputer system developed by Apple Computer Corp. introduced in 1978 that helped broaden the personal computer market beyond hobbyists. 495

Apple Lisa A personal computer system developed and manufactured by Apple Computer Corp. that featured one of the first graphical user interfaces. 495

Apple Macintosh First released in 1984, it was one of the first commercially successful personal computers sold with graphical user interface software. 496

Application development tool Software, such as 4GLs, expert system shells, and component objects that can be assembled into the applications software for an information system. 578

Application server A computer on a network that is dedicated to running applications and delivering applications to client computers. 249

Application software Computer programs that help you perform a specific task such as word processing. Also called application programs, applications, or programs. 16

Application specifications A detailed description of the way that the software for an information system should interface with the user, store data, process data, and format reports. 581

Application testing The process of testing newly developed application software by running unit tests, integration tests, and system tests. 584

Argument In the context of Prolog programming, an argument describes a predicate and is enclosed in parentheses in a Prolog fact. 714

ASCII (American Standard Code for Information Interchange) A code that represents characters as a series of 1s and 0s. Most computers use ASCII code to represent text, making it possible to transfer data between computers. 24

ASF (Advanced System Format) Microsoft's proprietary container format for streaming digital multimedia; typically holds WMV and WMA files. 457

Assembly language A low-level computer programming language that uses simple commands and is translated into machine language by an assembler. 677

Assumption In the context of programming, a condition that you accept to be true, which often places limits on the scope of the programming problem. 680

Asymmetric Internet connection Any connection to the Internet in which the upstream speed differs from the downstream speed. 311

ATA (Analog Telephone Adapter) A device used with VoIP systems to convert analog voice signals from a standard telephone into digital data. 332

Atanasoff-Berry Computer (ABC) An early electronic computer prototype that incorporated the use of vacuum tubes for data processing instead of mechanical switches. 489

Atom A syndicated data feed technology for the Web similar to RSS. 360

Attack tree A hierarchical diagram of potential threats to a system used as one tool in creating more secure software. 726

Audio compression Techniques used to reduce the size of files that contain audio data. 423

Audio editing software A program that enables users to create and edit digital voice and music recordings. 139

Audio encoding software A computer program designed to convert sound files into a digital sound format, such as MP3 or AAC. 139

Authentication protocol Passwords, user IDS, and biometric measures used to verify a person's identity. 34

Authorization and revocation A component of digital rights management that can be used to disable compromised players. 469

Automatic recalculation A feature found in spreadsheet software that automatically recalculates every formula after a user makes a change to any cell. 132

AVI (Audio Video Interleave) A video file format, developed by Microsoft, that was once the most common format for desktop video on the PC. 457

B2B (Business-to-Business) An e-commerce exchange of products, services, or information between businesses. 384

B2C (Business-to-Consumer) An e-commerce exchange of products, services, or information between businesses and consumers. 384

B2G (Business-to-Government) An e-commerce exchange of products, services, or information between businesses and governments. 384

Backup A duplicate copy of a file, disk, or tape. Also refers to a Windows utility that allows you to create and restore backups. 222

Backup software A set of utility programs that performs a variety of backup related tasks, such as helping users select files for backup. 226

Backward compatibility The ability to work with products designed for prior generations of the product. 198

Bandwidth The data transmission capacity of a communications channel. Digital signals are measured in bits per second, analog signals in Hertz. 251

Banner ad A type of advertisement typically embedded at the top of a Web page. 385

BASIC (Beginners All-purpose Symbolic Instruction Code) A simple high-level programming language that was popularized by Microsoft in the 1970s. 679

Batch processing A processing system that involves holding a group of transactions for processing until the end of a specified period of time. 560

Benchmarks A set of tests used to measure computer hardware or software performance. 69

Beta test A testing phase near the end of the software development process in which a software product is tested in real-world computer environments, often by end-users. 504

BI (Business Intelligence) An integrated set of technologies and procedures used to collect and analyze data pertaining to sales, production, and other internal operations of a business in order to make better business decisions. 569

Binary number system A method for representing numbers using only two digits, 0 and 1. Contrast to the decimal number system, which uses ten digits: 0, 1, 2, 3, 4, 5, 6, 7, 8, and 9. 23

Biometrics The use of physical attributes such as a fingerprint to verify a person's identity. 34

Bit The smallest unit of information handled by a computer. A bit is one of two values, either a 0 or a 1. Eight bits comprise a byte, which can represent a letter or number. 23

Bitmap graphic An image, such as a digital photo, that is stored as a grid work of colored dots. 430

Bitrate A ratio such as 5:1 that indicates the ratio of compression that has been applied to a file. High compression ratios, such as 35:1 indicate more compression so data can be contained in smaller files. 458

BitTorrent A peer-to-peer technology in which pieces of files are distributed to and from a collection of networked computers; used for distributing music and movies over the Internet. 338

Blended threat A combination of more than one type of malicious program. 162

BLOB (Binary Large OBject) A collection of binary data, such as a graphic or audio clip, that is stored in a single field of a database. 635

Blogs (WeB LOG) A publicly-accessible personal journal posted on the Web. Blogs often reflect the personality of the author and are typically updated daily. 6

Blu-ray DVD A high-capacity DVD that holds up to 25 GB per layer; also called Blu-ray Discs or BDs. 81

Blue screen of death An error condition in which a PC "freezes" and displays a blue screen; usually turning the computer off and turning it on again clears the error. 103

Bluetooth A wireless technology used in conjunction with standard Ethernet networks that allows data transfer rates between 200 and 700 Kbps up to a maximum range of 35 feet. 267

BMP The native bitmap graphic file format of the Microsoft Windows OS. 442

Boolean operator A logical search operator such as AND, OR, and NOT that helps form complex queries. 379

Boot disk A floppy disk or CD that contains the files needed for the boot process. 229

Boot process The sequence of events that occurs within a computer system between the time the user starts the computer and the time it is ready to process commands. 192

Bootstrap program A program stored in ROM that loads and initializes the operating system on a computer. 192

Bot An intelligent agent that autonomously executes commands behind the scenes. Sometimes used to refer to a remote access Trojan horse that infects computers. 164

Botnet A group of bots under the remote control of a botmaster, used to distribute spam and Denial of Service attacks. 164

BPR (Business Process Redesign) A technique for improving a business by making radical changes to existing business procedures or organizational structure. 569

Break reminder software Software designed to signal users when it is time to take a break in order to avoid various repetitive-use and stress injuries. 541

Bridge A device that connects two similar networks by simply transferring data without regard to the network format. 250

Broadband A term used to refer to communications channels that have high bandwidth. 251

Broadcast flag A status flag inserted into the data stream of digital television to indicate whether it can be copied. 465

Brute force attack A method of breaking encryption code by trying all possible encryption keys. 37

BSD license (Berkeley Software Distribution) An open source software license patterned on a license originally used by the University of California. 150

Buffer overflow A condition that can be exploited by hackers in which data overflows its intended memory space to affect other variables. 723

Bulletin boards One of the original communications and social network technologies used on the Internet. 6

Bus topology A network arranged on a common backbone that connects all the network devices. If the backbone fails the network becomes unusable. 250

Business An organization that seeks profit by providing goods and services. 556

Button An onscreen graphical control that can be clicked to initiate an action or command. 190

Byte An 8-bit unit of data that represents a single character. 26

C A compiled procedural language that provides both high-level commands and low-level access to hardware. 679

C# A derivative of C++ programming language developed by Microsoft. 679

C++ An object-oriented version of the C programming language. 679

C2C (Consumer-to-Consumer) An e-commerce exchange of products, services, or information between consumers; for example online auctions. 384

Cable Internet service A type of Internet connection offered to subscribers by cable television companies. 316

Cable modem A communications device that can be used to connect a computer to the Internet via the cable TV infrastructure. 317

Cache Special high-speed memory that gives the CPU rapid access to data that would otherwise be accessed from disk. Also called RAM cache or cache memory. 68

CAD software (Computer-Aided Design software) A program designed to draw 3-D graphics for architecture and engineering tasks. 138

Capacitors Electronic circuit components that store an electrical charge; in RAM, a charged capacitor represents an "on" bit, and a discharged one represents an "off" bit. 72

Card reader A device that can be used to read and record data on solid stage storage devices, such as flash memory cards. 84

Cardinality A description of the numeric relationship (one-to-one, one-to-many, or many-to-many) that exists between two record types. 616

Case sensitive A condition in which uppercase letters are not equivalent to their lowercase counterparts. 35

Case sensitive database A database in which uppercase letters are not equivalent to their lowercase counterparts. 636

CASE tool (Computer-Aided Software Engineering) Software that is used to summarize system requirements, diagram current and proposed information systems, schedule development tasks, prepare documentation, and develop computer programs. 574

CD (Compact Disc) An optical storage medium used to store digital information. CD-ROMs are read only. CD-R and CD-RWs can be used to record data. 81

CD drive An optical drive that can work with one or more CD formats, such as CD-ROM, CD-R, or CD-RW. 81

CD ripper software Software that converts the music on an audio CD to a WAV file. 139

CD-DA (Compact Disc Digital Audio) The format for commercial music CDs, typically recorded by the manufacturer. 82

CD-R (Compact Disc Recordable) CD-R is a type of optical disk technology that allows the user to record data once on a disc. 83

CD-ROM (Compact Disc Read-Only Memory) The read-only data format that is stamped onto a CD, usually by the manufacturer. 83

CD-RW (Compact Disc ReWritable) CD-RW is a type of optical disk technology that allows the user to write data onto a CD, then change that data much like on a floppy or hard disk. 83

Cell In spreadsheet terminology, the intersection of a column and a row. In cellular communications, a limited geographical area surrounding a cellular phone tower. 130

Cell references The column letter and row number that designate the location of a worksheet cell. For example, the cell reference C5 refers to a cell in column C, row 5. 131

Central processing unit (CPU) The main processing unit in a computer, consisting of circuitry that executes instructions to process data. 15

Centralized processing An information system design in which data is processed on a centrally located computer, usually a mainframe. 577

Certificates of completion A certification offered to students who successfully complete one or more courses on a specific topic. 515

Certification exam An objective test that verifies your level of knowledge about a particular technology or subject. 516

Change requests A formal, written request to add, delete, or change the features of an information system. 582

Channel conflict A situation in which computer vendors from retail, wholesale, or mail-order channels compete for customers. 508

Character data Letters, symbols, or numerals that will not be used in arithmetic operations (name, social security number, etc.). 24

Chat Interactive real-time person-to-person communication over a network. 330

Chat groups A discussion in which a group of people communicates online simultaneously. 6

Chief information officer (CIO) The highest-ranking executive responsible for information systems. 510

Chipmakers Companies that design and manufacture computer chips used in a wide variety of computer related applications. 498

Ciphertext An encrypted message. 285

Circuit switching The method used by the telephone network to temporarily connect one telephone with another for the duration of a call. 253

CISC (Complex Instruction Set Computer) A general-purpose microprocessor chip designed to handle a wider array of instructions than a RISC chip. 69

Class In object-oriented terminology, a group with specific characteristics to which an object belongs. 702

Class attribute In the context of object-oriented programming, a class attribute defines a characteristic for the members of a class. Similar to a field in a database. 703

Class diagram A diagram that provides the name of each object, a list of the object's attributes, a list of methods, and an indication of the cardinality between objects. 573

Class hierarchy Like a hierarchical diagram, a class hierarchy is a set of related superclasses and subclasses defined within the object-oriented paradigm. 704

Click-through rate The number of times Web site visitors click an ad to connect to an advertiser's site. 385

Client A computer or software that requests information from another computer or server. 18

Client-side script Scripting statements embedded in an HTML document that are executed by a client's browser. 372

Client/server mode A network where processing is split between workstations (clients) and the server. 249

Clip art Graphics designed to be inserted into documents, Web pages, and worksheets, usually available in CD-ROM or Web-based collections. 129

Cluster (1) A group of sectors on a storage medium that, when accessed as a group, speeds up data access. (2) A group of two or more devices connected together to share processing, storage, input, or output tasks. 219

COBOL (COmmon Business-Oriented Language) A high-level programming language used for transaction processing on mainframe computers. 679

Code In the context of computer programming, code can be used as a noun to refer to the set of instructions that form a program, or as a verb that refers to the process of writing a program. 674

Code of ethics A set of guidelines designed to help professionals make on-the-job ethical decisions. 530

Codec Short for COmpressor/DECompressor, a hardware or software routine that compresses and decompresses digital graphics, sound, and video files. 458

Color depth The number of bits that determines the range of possible colors that can be assigned to each pixel. For example, an 8-bit color depth can create 256 colors. 91

Color palette The selection of colors used in a graphic. 437

COLOSSUS An early electronic computer prototype that used binary data representation and was used during WWII to decode messages encrypted by ENIGMA. 490

Command-line interface A style of user interface which requires users to type commands, rather than use a mouse to manipulate on-screen controls. 189

Commercial software Copyrighted computer applications sold to consumers for profit. 149

Commit The act of permanently updating database records only if every step of the transaction can be successfully processed. 560

Communications channel Any pathway between the sender and receiver; channel may refer to a physical medium or a frequency. 251

Communications protocol A set of rules that ensures the orderly and accurate transmission and reception of data. 252

Compiler Software that translates a program written in a high-level language into low-level instructions before the program is executed. 30

Component Prewritten objects or modules that programmers can customize and add to their own programs. 687

Compression ratio A ratio such as 5:1 that indicates the ratio of compression that has been applied to a file. High compression ratios, such as 35:1 indicate more compression so data can be contained in smaller files. 458

Compute-intensive Refers to any task, problem, or product that is able to handle massive amounts of data and complex mathematical calculations. 19

Computed field A calculation that a DBMS performs during processing and then temporarily stores in a memory location. 635

Computer A device that accepts input, processes data, stores data, and produces output according to a stored program. 14

Computer engineer A computer professional who focuses on the design and development of computer hardware and peripheral devices. 512

Computer engineering A career that focuses on the design and development of computer hardware and peripheral devices. 514

Computer industry The corporations and individuals that supply computer-related goods and services to individuals and organizations. 497

Computer network A collection of computers and related devices, connected in a way that allows them to share data, hardware, and software. 7

Computer operator A computer professional who works directly with and maintains mainframe computers. 511

Computer professional Any person whose primary occupation involves one or more aspects of computer technology. 510

Computer program A detailed set of instructions that tells a computer how to solve a problem or carry out a task. 15

Computer programmer A person who designs, codes, and tests computer programs. 511

Computer programming The process of designing, coding, and testing computer programs. 675

Computer retail store A store that typically sells several brands of computers from a store-front location, such as a mall or shopping center. 506

Computer retailers Also called resellers, companies that sell computer-related products. 498

Computer salesperson A computer professional who sells computers and computer-related products. Also called a sales rep. 512

Computer science A career field that focuses on developing fast and efficient computers from their construction to their programming and operating systems. 514

Computer virus A program designed to attach itself to a file, reproduce, and spread from one file to another, destroying data, displaying an irritating message, or otherwise disrupting computer operations. 163

Computer worm A software program designed to enter a computer system, usually a network, through security "holes" and then replicate itself. 163

Computer-aided music software Software used to generate unique musical compositions with a simplified set of tools, such as tempo, key, and style. 139

Concurrent-use license Legal permission for an organization to use a certain number of copies of a software program at the same time. 147

Confidentiality The obligation not to disclose willingly any information obtained in confidence. 526

Constant In the context of programming, a constant represents an unchanging value. In contrast, the data held in a variable can change. 680

Container formats File formats, typically for storing sound and video, that contain one or more types of data that is compressed using standard codecs. 457

Contract worker A computer professional who does not work directly for one company and often is paid by the job instead of a salary. 513

Control In the context of graphical user interfaces, a control is a screen-based object whose behavior can be specified by a programmer. 683

Control structures Instructions that specify the sequence in which a program is to be executed: sequence, selection, and repetition controls. 695

Control unit The part of the microprocessor that directs and coordinates processing. 31

Convergence In the context of technology, the melding of digital devices into a single platform that handles a diverse array of digital content, such as cell phones also playing digital music and displaying digital video. 8

Cookie A message sent from a Web server to a browser and stored on a user's hard disk, usually containing information about the user. 368

Copy generation management A digital rights management technology that controls the number of times that a CD, DVD, or tape can be recopied. 467

Copy protection Any digital rights management technology designed to prevent duplication of digital content; also referred to as copy prevention or copy restriction. 466

Copyright A form of legal protection that grants certain exclusive rights to the author of a program or the owner of the copyright. 146

Copyright notice A line such as "Copyright 2007 by ACME CO" that identifies a copyright holder. 147

CPL (Combined Programming Language) A programming language developed in the 1960s for scientific and commercial applications. 679

CPU (Central Processing Unit) The main processing circuitry within a computer or chip that contains the ALU, control unit, and registers. 15

CRM (Customer Relationship Management) A technique for increasing profitability by improving the relationship between a company and its customers. 569

Cropping The process of selecting and removing part of an image. 435

CRT (Cathode Ray Tube) A display technology that uses a large vacuum tube, similar to that used in television sets. 90

Cryptographic algorithm A specific procedure for encrypting and decrypting data. 285

Cryptographic key A specific word, number, or phrase that must be used to encrypt or decrypt data. 285

CSMA/CD (Carrier Sense Multiple Access with Collision Detection) A method of responding to an attempt by two devices to use a data channel simultaneously. Used by Ethernet networks. 259

CSS (1) (Content Scramble System) A DRM technology designed to prevent unauthorized duplication of DVDs. (2) (Cascading Style Sheets) A Web technology for specifying Web page styles. 468

Custom Recovery CD A CD that can be used to reboot a computer after a hard disk failure and can be used to begin restoring programs to it. 231

Cyberspace A term coined by William Gibson and now used to refer to information and other resources offered in virtual "worlds" based on computer networks and the Internet. 7

Data In the context of computing and data management, data refers to the symbols that a computer uses to represent facts and ideas. 15

Data bus An electronic pathway or circuit that connects the electronic components (such as the processor and RAM) on a computer's motherboard. 95

Data center A specialized facility designed to house and protect computer systems and data. 592

Data dependence The undesirable situation in which data and program modules become so interrelated that modifications become difficult. 624

Data flow On a DFD, a line with an arrow on the end, which indicates the direction in which data flows. 572

Data flow diagram (DFD) A diagram that illustrates how data moves through an information system. 572

Data fork An element of the Macintosh file system that comprises the part of the file that contains the text, audio, or video data; contrast with resource fork. 200

Data independence The separation of data from the programs that manipulate the data. 624

Data mining Analyzing data to discover patterns and relationships that are important to decision making. 612

Data redundancy Repetition of data within a database. 637

Data representation The use of electronic signals, marks, or binary digits to represent character, numeric, visual, or audio data. 22

Data store A filing cabinet, disk, or tape that holds data. On a DFD, usually represented by an open-ended rectangle. 572

Data transfer rate The amount of data that a storage device can move from a storage medium to computer memory in one time unit, such as one second. 77

Data type The characteristics of data that can be entered into a field in a data file; data types include character, numeric, date, logical, and memo. 634

Data view A mechanism typically applied to databases in which different forms or reports are displayed depending on a query, and can be customized for different categories of users. 655

Data warehouse A collection of information organized for analysis. 612

Database A collection of information that might be stored in more than one file or in more than one record type. 134, 610

Database administrator A person who supervises database design, development, testing, and maintenance. 511

Database audit A procedure that monitors or records user activity within a database, often for security purposes. 656

Database client software Software that allows any remote computer or network workstation to access data in a database. 626

Database index A file of keys and pointers used to display a list of database records organized according to the data in one or more fields. 639

Database model The underlying structure or category of a database, such as relational, hierarchical, network, or object. 614

Database server software Software that is designed to manage a large number of records and perform many simultaneous transactions. 626

Database software Software designed for entering, finding, organizing, updating, and reporting information stored in a database. 134

Database structure The arrangement of the fields, tables, and relationships in a database. 633

Date data type A data type that indicates that the data in a field represents a date. 634

DBMS (DataBase Management System) Application software that assists the user in manipulating, storing, and maintaining database files. 625

Debugger A programming utility that helps programmers test and correct a computer program. 685

DEC PDP-8 Built by Digital Equipment Corp. and introduced in 1965, the PDP-8 is the first commercially successful minicomputer. 493

Decision model A numerical representation of a realistic situation, such as a cash flow model of a business. 562

Decision query A question or set of instructions that describes the data that needs to be gathered to make a decision. 562

Decision support system (DSS) A computer system that allows decision makers to manipulate data directly, to incorporate data from external sources, and to create data models or "what-if" scenarios. 562

Decision support worksheet A comparison table used by a project team to evaluate solutions by assigning a score and a weight to each criterion. 579

Decision table A tabular method for listing rules and specifying the outcomes for various combinations of rules. 714

Declarative paradigm An approach to the programming process in which a programmer writes a program by specifying a set of statements and rules that define the conditions for solving a problem. 713

deColmar's Arithmometer The first commercially successful, mass-produced mechanical calculator. 487

Decryption The process of converting ciphertext into plaintext. 285

DeCSS A program that defeats the CSS copy protection and allows users to copy DVDs. 468

Defensive programming An approach to programming that attempts to identify possible threats and proactively create code to avoid them. 726

Defragmentation utility A software tool used to rearrange the files on a disk so that they are stored in contiguous clusters. 221

DELETE An SQL keyword that removes a record from a table. 646

Demoware Commercial software that is distributed free, but expires after a certain time limit and then requires users to pay to continue using it. 149

Design phase The process a project team uses for figuring out how to implement a new system. This phase is undertaken after the analysis phase is complete. 576

Desktop A term used to refer to the main screen of a graphical user interface that can hold objects such as folders and widgets. 189

Desktop computer A computer that is small enough to fit on a desk and built around a single microprocessor chip. 58

Desktop operating system An operating system specifically designed for use on personal computers, such as Windows Me or Mac OSX. 188

Desktop publishing software (DTP) Software used to create high-quality output suitable for commercial printing. DTP software provides precise control over layout. 125

Desktop video Videos stored in digital format on a PC's hard disk or CD. 452

Desktop widget An interactive program that is represented on the desktop by an information-rich graphic, such as a clock or graph. 123

Detail reports Organized lists generated by a management information system (for example, an inventory list). 560

Device driver A type of system software that provides the computer with the means to control a peripheral device. 124

DHCP (Dynamic Host Configuration Protocol) A set of rules that allow network client computers to find and use the Internet address that corresponds to a domain name. 255

DHTML (Dynamic HTML) A collection of technologies such as HTML and JavaScript used to create animated and interactive Web pages. 362

Dial-up connection A connection that uses a phone line to establish a temporary Internet connection. 312

Dialog box An element of graphical user interfaces that appears in a window and requests information, such as command parameters, from a user. 191

Dictionary attack A method of discovering a password by trying every word in an electronic dictionary. 36

Difference Engine A mechanical calculator design created by Charles Babbage that was to use steam power for fully automatic operation. It was never built. 488

Differential backup A copy of all the files that changed since the last full backup of a disk. 227

Digital audio Music or voice that has been digitized into files using sampling techniques; sometimes referred to as waveform audio. 422

Digital camera A camera that takes and stores a digital image instead of recording onto film. 431

Digital certificate A security method that identifies the author of an ActiveX control. A computer programmer can "sign" a digital certificate after being approved. 373

Digital content A term popularized in the content of multimedia that refers to digital music, video, text, and images. 464

Digital data Text, numbers, graphics, or sound represented by discrete digits, such as 1s and 0s. 22

Digital divide A gap between those who have access to digital technologies and those who do not. 12

Digital revolution A set of significant changes brought about by computers and other digital devices during the second half of the 20th Century. 4

Digital rights management (DRM) A set of techniques and technologies designed to discourage and prevent unauthorized duplication of digital content. 464

Digital signal processor Circuitry that is used to process, record, and playback audio files. 424

Digital video A series of still frames stored sequentially in digital format by assigning values to each pixel in a frame. 452

Digital video recorder (DVR) A time-shifting device, such as a TiVo, that captures television and cable TV programs then stores them on a built-in hard disk for later viewing. 455

Digital watermark A digital rights management technology that inserts a hidden signal into multimedia content as an identifying marker that can be tracked or verified. 465

Digitization To convert non-digital information or media to a digital format through the use of a scanner, sampler, or other input device. 7

Digitizing tablet A device that provides a flat surface for a paper-based drawing and a "pen" used to create hand-drawn vector drawings. 446

Dimensional database A database often created for data analysis that has a more complex structure than a simple 2-dimensional table. 619

Direct conversion The simultaneous deactivation of an old computer system and activation of a new one. 586

Directory In the context of computer file management, a list of files contained on a computer storage device. 206

Disaster recovery plan A step-by-step plan that describes the methods used to secure equipment and data against disasters, and how to recover from disasters. 593

Disk mastering The process of creating a CD or DVD by selecting all the files to be copied and then writing them in a single session. Contrast with packet writing. 219

Disk partition An area of a hard disk created by dividing a large hard disk into several smaller virtual ones, such as when using two operating systems on a single computer. 205

Distributed database A database that is stored on different computers, on different networks, or in different locations. 626

Distributed processing An information system design in which data is processed on multiple workstations or servers. 577

Distribution media One or more floppy disks, CDs, or DVDs that contain programs and data, which can be installed on a hard disk. 146

DOCSIS (Data Over Cable Services Interface Specification) A security technology used for filtering packets and maintaining customer privacy on cable Internet services. 317

Document production software Computer programs that assist the user in composing, editing, designing, and printing documents. 125

Domain name Short for "fully qualified domain name"; an identifying name by which host computers on the Internet are familiarly known (for example, "cocacola.com"). 307

Domain name server A computer that hosts the domain name system database. 308

Domain Name System (DNS) A large database of unique IP addresses that correspond with domain names. 308

DOS (Disk Operating System) The operating system software shipped with the first IBM PCs, then used on millions of computers until the introduction of Microsoft Windows. 202

Dot matrix printer A printer that creates characters and graphics by striking an inked ribbon with small wires called "pins," generating a fine pattern of dots. 92

Dot pitch The diagonal distance between colored dots on a display screen. Measured in millimeters, dot pitch helps to determine the quality of an image displayed on a monitor. 90

Double layer DVD A DVD that essentially stacks data in two different layers on the disk surface to store 8.5 GB, twice the capacity of a standard DVD. 81

Download The process of transferring a copy of a file from a remote computer to a local computer's storage device. 8

Downstream speed The rate at which transmitted data flows from a host or server to a local computer (contrast with upstream speed). 311

Drawing software Programs that are used to create vector graphics with lines, shapes, and colors, such as logos or diagrams. 137, 446

Drive bays Areas within a computer system unit that can accommodate additional storage devices. 86

Drive mapping A process of assigning a drive letter to a storage device located on a different network workstation. 276

DRM individualization A digital rights management concept that ties access to digital content to individual subscribers, whose access can be tracked, if necessary. 470

DSL (Digital Subscriber Line) A high-speed Internet connection that uses existing telephone lines, requiring close proximity to a switching station. 314

DSL filters Devices that are commonly used to prevent interference from analog devices, such as telephones, that use the same line as DSL devices. 315

DSL modem A device that sends and receives digital data to and from computers over telephone lines. 315

Dual boot A computer that contains more than one operating system and can boot into either one. 199

Duplex printer A printer that prints on both sides of the paper in a single pass. 93

Duty cycle A measurement of how many pages a printer is able to produce per day or month. 93

DVD (Digital Video Disc or Digital Versatile Disk) An optical storage medium similar in appearance and technology to a CD but with higher storage capacity. 81

DVD authoring software Computer programs that offer tools for creating DVD menus and transferring digital video onto DVDs that can be played in a computer or standalone DVD player. 140

DVD drive An optical storage device that reads data from CDs and DVDs. 81

DVD image A series of files containing the data needed for a video DVD. The image is typically stored on a hard disk for testing before the image is transferred or "burned" to the DVD. 462

DVD+R (Digital Versatile Disk Recordable) A DVD data format that, similar to CD-R, allows recording data but not changing data on a DVD. 83

DVD+RW (Digital Versatile Disk ReWritable) A DVD technology that allows recording and changing data on DVDs. 83

DVD-R (Digital Versatile Disk Recordable) A DVD data format that, similar to CD-R, allows writing data but not changing data on a DVD. 83

DVD-ROM A DVD disk that contains data that has been permanently stamped on the disk surface. 83

DVD-RW A DVD technology similar to DVD+RW that allows recording and changing data on DVDs. 83

DVD-video A DVD format used for commercial movies shipped on DVDs. 82, 452

Dynamic IP address A temporarily assigned IP address usually provided by an ISP. 306

Dynamic Web publishing A way of displaying data from a database as customized Web pages, which are generated as the page is sent to the browser. 628

E-commerce Short for electronic commerce, it is the business of buying and selling products online. 384

E-mail Messages that are transmitted between computers over a communications network. Short for electronic mail. 6

E-mail account A service that provides users with an e-mail address and a mailbox. 392

E-mail attachment A separate file that is transmitted along with an e-mail message. 393

E-mail authentication A technology designed to defeat spam by checking to make sure that messages originate from valid addresses. 403

E-mail client software Software that is installed on a client computer and has access to e-mail servers on a network. This software is used to compose, send, and read e-mail messages. 398

E-mail message A computer file containing a letter or memo that is transmitted electronically via a communications network. 392

E-mail servers A computer that uses special software to store and send e-mail messages over the Internet. 397

E-mail system The collection of computers and software that works together to provide e-mail services. 397

EAI (Enterprise Application Integration) The use of networked software and databases for providing unrestricted sharing of data in an organization. 569

Ear training software Software used by musicians to develop tuning skills, recognize keys, and develop musical skills. 139

EBCDIC (Extended Binary-Coded Decimal Interchange Code) A method by which digital computers, usually mainframes, represent character data. 25

EDGE (Enhanced Data Rates for GSM Evolution) A cell phone technology that offers faster data transport than basic GSM service. 327

EDI (Electronic Data Interchange) The ability to transfer data between different companies using networks which enable companies to buy, sell, and trade information. 569

Educational software Software used to develop and practice skills. 140

EEPROM (Electrically Erasable Programmable Read-Only Memory) A type of non-volatile storage typically used in personal computers to store boot and BIOS data. 74

Eiffel An object-oriented programming language with syntax similar to C. 679

Electronic wallet Software that stores personal information used during e-commerce transactions. 390

Encapsulation An object-oriented technique in which the internal details of an object are "hidden" in order to simplify their use and reuse. 712

Encryption The process of scrambling or hiding information so that it cannot be understood without the key necessary to change it back into its original form. 285

ENIAC (Electronic Numerical Integrator and Computer) An early electronic computer prototype that was designed for the U.S. Army for calculating trajectories and was completed in 1945. 490

Enterprise computer system The use of one or more information systems that share data and typically provide information to hundreds or thousands of users who may be located in diverse locations. 559

Entity-relationship diagram (ERD) A diagram that graphically depicts relationships between record types. 616

Equipment manufacturers Companies that design and manufacture computer hardware and communication products. 498

Ergonomics The science of designing safe, comfortable, efficient machines and tools for human use. 537

ERP (Enterprise Resource Planning) A system of business management that integrates all resources of a business, including planning, manufacturing, sales, and marketing. 569

Ethernet A type of network in which network nodes are connected by coaxial cable or twisted-pair wire; the most popular network architecture, it typically transmits data at 10 or 100 megabits per second. 258

Ethernet adapter A type of network interface card designed to support Ethernet protocols. 261

EULA (End User License Agreement) A type of software license that appears on the computer screen when software is being installed and prompts the user to accept or decline. 148

EV-DO (Evolution-Data Optimized) A technology used by cell phone companies to offer faster data transport than basic CDMA service. 327

Event In the context of programming, an action or change in state, such as a mouse click, that requires a response from the computer. 684

Event-driven paradigm An approach to programming in which a programmer creates programs that continually check for, and respond to, program events, such as mouse clicks. 685

Event-handling code The program segment that instructs the computer how to react to events, such as mouse clicks. 684

Exception report A report generated by a management information system, listing information that is outside normal or acceptable ranges, such as a reorder report showing low-stock inventory items. 561

Executable file A file, usually with an .exe extension, containing instructions that tell a computer how to perform a specific task. 152

Executive dashboard software Software designed for managers that typically uses widgets to graphically display statistics relevant to business decisions. 613

Executive information system (EIS) A special type of a decision support system that is designed to provide senior managers with information relevant to strategic management activities. 562

Expansion bus The segment of the data bus that transports data between RAM and peripheral devices. 95

Expansion card A circuit board that is plugged into a slot on a computer motherboard to add extra functions, devices, or ports. 95

Expansion port A socket into which the user plugs a cable from a peripheral device, allowing data to pass between the computer and the peripheral device. 96

Expansion slot A socket or "slot" on a PC motherboard designed to hold a circuit board called an expansion card. 95

Expert system A computer system incorporating knowledge from human experts, and designed to analyze data and produce a recommendation or decision (also called knowledge-based system). 564

Expert system shell A software tool used for developing expert system applications. 564

Extended ASCII Similar to ASCII but with 8-bit character representation instead of 7-bit, allowing for an additional 128 characters. 24

External entity A person, organization, or device that exists outside an information system, but provides it with input or receives output. On a DFD, usually represented by a square. 572

External information Information obtained by organizations from outside sources. 559

Fact In the context of Prolog programming, a fact is a statement incorporated into a program that provides basic information for solving a problem. 713

FairPlay A digital rights management technology used to protect content distributed at the iPod store. 470

Fast Ethernet A type of Ethernet that operates at 100 Mbps. 259

FAT32 A file system used by Microsoft Windows 95, 98, and Me operating systems to keep track of the name and location of files on a hard disk. 219

Feature creep An undesirable occurrence during information system development when users, customers, or designers attempt to add features after the final specifications have been approved. 582

Field The smallest meaningful unit of information contained in a data file. 134, 615

Field format A specification for the way that data is displayed on the screen and printouts, usually using a series of Xs to indicate characters and 9s to indicate numbers. 636

Field name A name that identifies the contents of a field. 615

Field validation rule A specification that a database designer sets up to filter the data entered into a particular field. 636

Fifth-generation languages Either declarative languages, such as Prolog, or programming languages that allow programmers to use graphical or visual tools to construct programs. 678

File A named collection of data (such as a computer program, document, or graphic) that exists on a storage medium, such as a hard disk or CD. 15

File Allocation Table (FAT) A special file that is used by some operating systems to store the physical location of all the files on a storage medium, such as a hard disk or floppy disk. 219

File compression utility A type of data compression software that shrinks one or more files into a single occupying less storage space than the files did separately. 440

File date The date that a file was created or last modified. 206

File extension A set of letters and/or numbers added to the end of a file name that helps to identify the file contents or file type. 204

File format The method of organization used to encode and store data in a computer. Text formats include DOC and TXT. Graphics formats include BMP, TIFF, GIF, and PCX. 207

File header Hidden information inserted at the beginning of a file to identify its properties, such as the software that can open it. 207

File management utilities Software, such as Windows Explorer, that helps users locate, rename, move, copy, and delete files. 214

File server A network computer that is dedicated to storing and distributing files to network clients. 249

File shredder software Software designed to overwrite sectors of a disk with a random series of 1's and 0's to ensure deletion of data. 220

File size The physical size of a file on a storage medium, usually measured in kilobytes (KB). 206

File specification A combination of the drive letter, subdirectory, file name, and extension that identifies a file (such as, A:.doc). Also called a "path." 206

File system A method that is used by an operating system to keep files organized. 219

File tag In the context of Windows, a piece of information that describes a file. Tags, such as Owner, Rating, and Date Taken, can be added by users. 212

File-naming conventions A set of rules, established by the operating system, that must be followed to create a valid file name. 204

Firewall Software or hardware designed to analyze and control incoming and outgoing packets on a network, used to enhance security by filtering out potential intrusion attempts. 342

First-generation computers Computers that use vacuum tubes to process and store data such as UNIVAC. 491

First-generation languages Machine languages that were available for programming the earliest computers. 677

Fixed Internet access Any Internet access service designed to be used from a fixed, non-portable location, i.e., dial-up, ISDN, DSL, and cable Internet service. 311

Fixed wireless Internet service High-speed, wide area Internet service alternative to cable and DSL that transmits data wirelessly using RF signals. 320

Fixed-length field A field in a data file that has a predetermined number of characters. 615

Flash A file format developed by Macromedia and marketed by Adobe that has become popular for animations on Web pages. 448

Flash cookie A cookie-like object that is created and used by the Adobe Flash player; also referred to as a local shared object. 402

Flash Video A popular video file format developed by Adobe systems and used for Web-based video at sites such as YouTube. 457

Flat file A single file that is the electronic version of a box of index cards, in which all records use the same record format. 614

Floppy disk A removable magnetic storage medium, typically 3.5" in size, with a capacity of 1.44 MB. 80

Flowchart In software engineering, a graphical representation of the way a computer should progress from one instruction to the next when it performs a task. 692

Folder The subdirectories, or subdivisions of a directory, that can contain files or other folders. 206

Font A typeface or style of lettering, such as Arial, Times New Roman, and Gothic. 127

Footer Text that appears in the bottom margin of each page of a document. 128

Form design grid A visual programming tool that allows programmers to drag and drop controls to form the user interface for a program. 683

Form factor The configuration of a computer's system unit; examples include, tower, mini-tower, pizza box, and cube. 58

Formal methods Mathematically-based techniques for specifying and developing reliable and robust software or hardware. 725

Format (1) Specified properties for setting a document's appearance. (2) File type, i.e. BMP format. 127

Format shifting The process of converting media into a different file format to use it on a device other than the original one. 465

Formatting The process of dividing a disk into sectors so that it can be used to store information. 218

Formula In spreadsheet terminology, a combination of numbers and symbols that tells the computer how to use the contents of cells in calculations. 131

FORTRAN (FORmula TRANslator) The oldest high-level computer programming language still in use for scientific, mathematical, and engineering programs. 679

Fourth-generation computers Computers, such as today's personal computer, servers, and mainframes, that use a general purpose microprocessor for data processing. 494

Fourth-generation languages Programming and query languages, such as SQL and RPG, that more closely resemble human languages than did third-generation languages. 678

Fragmented files Files stored in scattered, noncontiguous clusters on a disk. 221

Frame rate Refers to the number of frames displayed per second in a video or film. 456

Frames An outline or boundary, frequently defining a box. For document production software, a pre-defined area into which text or graphics may be placed. 129

Freeware Copyrighted software that is given away by the author or copyright owner. 150

Front side bus (FSB) The data bus that carries signals between the CPU and RAM, disks, or expansion slots. 68

FTP (File Transfer Protocol) A set of rules for uploading and downloading files between a client computer and a remote server. 336

FTP client The computer or software that is used to access an FTP server and transfer files to it or from it. 336

FTP server A computer that stores and distributes files to remote client computers. 336

Full backup A copy of all the files for a specified backup job. 226

Fully justified The horizontal alignment of text where the text terminates exactly at both margins of the document. 128

Function In spreadsheet software, a built-in formula for making a calculation. In programming, a section of code that manipulates data, but is not included in the main sequential execution path of a program. 131, 696

Functional paradigm An approach to programming that emphasizes the use of expressions called "functions". 713

Fuzzy logic A technique used by an expert system to deal with imprecise data by incorporating the probability that the input information is correct. 564

Gantt chart A chart that depicts a project schedule by showing each task as a bar on the chart. 570

Gateway A network device that connects two dissimilar networks even if the networks use different protocols. 251

GIF (Graphics Interchange Format) A bitmap graphics file format, popularized by CompuServe, for use on the Web. 442

Gigabit (Gb or Gbit) Approximately one billion bits, exactly 1,024 megabits. 26

Gigabit Ethernet An Ethernet standard that carries data at speeds up to 1 Gbps. 259

Gigabyte (GB) Approximately one billion bytes; exactly 1,024 megabytes (1,073,741,824 bytes). 26

Gigahertz (GHz) A measure of frequency equivalent to one billion cycles per second. 67

Global update In the context of databases, changing data in more than one record at a time, i.e., changing the due date in all the records. 650

Globalization A group of social, economic, political, and technological interdependencies linking people and institutions from all areas of the world. 12

Goal In the context of Prolog programming, a goal is a query that searches for an answer based on a set of Prolog facts and rules. 715

GPL (General Public License) A software license often used for freeware that insures it will be distributed freely whether in its original form or as a derivative work. 151

Gradient A smooth blending of shades of different colors, from light to dark. 447

Grammar checker A feature of word processing software that coaches the user on correct sentence structure and word usage. 127

Graphical user interface (GUI) A type of user interface that features on-screen objects, such as menus and icons, manipulated by a mouse. 189

Graphics Any picture, photograph, or image that can be manipulated or viewed on a computer. 137

Graphics card A circuit board inserted into a computer to handle the display of text, graphics, animation, and videos. Also called a "video card." 91

Graphics processing unit (GPU) A microprocessor dedicated to rendering and displaying graphics on personal computers, workstations, and videogame consoles. 91

Graphics software Computer programs for creating, editing, and manipulating images; types include paint software and drawing software. 137

Grayscale palette Digital images that are displayed in shades of gray, black, and white. 438

Grid computing system A network of diverse computers in which each computer is treated as a generic and equal processing resource. 334

Groupware Software that enables multiple users to collaborate on a project, usually through a pool of data that can be shared by members of the workgroup. 121

Handheld computer A small, pocket-sized computer that is designed to run on its own power supply and provide users with basic applications. 19

Handshaking A process where a protocol helps two network devices communicate. 252

Hard disk controller A circuit board in a hard drive that positions the disk and read-write heads to locate data. 79

Hard disk drive A computer storage device that contains a large-capacity rigid storage surface sealed inside a drive case. Typically used as the primary storage device in personal computers. 78

Hard disk platter The component of a hard disk drive on which data is stored. It is a flat, rigid disk made of aluminum or glass and coated with a magnetic oxide. 78

Harvard Mark I An early computer prototype also known as the ASCC (Automatic Sequence Controlled Calculator), developed by IBM that used decimal data representation rather than binary. 490

Hash value A number produced by a hash function to create a unique digital "fingerprint" that can be used to allow or deny access to a software application. 157

Haskell A functional programming language. (See functional paradigm.) 679

HD-DVD A high-density DVD that stores up to 15 GB in a single layer or 30 GB in dual layers. 81

Head crash A collision between the read-write head and the surface of the hard disk platter, resulting in damage to some of the data on the disk. 80

Header Text that is placed in the top margin of each page of a document. 128

Help desk Part of the Information Systems department designated to assist users experiencing problems with their computers or applications. 588

Helper application An external program that is used to display content retrieved using a Web browser. 367

Hierarchical database A database model in which record types are arranged as a hierarchy, or tree, of child nodes that can have only one parent node. 617

High-level language A programming language that allows a programmer to write instructions using human-like language. 676

Hollerith Tabulating Machine A mechanical calculator first used in 1890 by the U.S. Census Bureau that used punch cards to store data and led to the creation of IBM. 488

Home computer system A personal computer designed for use with mainstream computer applications such as Web browsing, e-mail, music downloads, and productivity software. 60

HomePNA A network technology that uses a building's existing phone lines to connect nodes. 257

Horizontal market software Any computer program that can be used by many different kinds of businesses (for example, an accounting program). 142

Hover ad An advertisement, created using interactive Web tools such as DHTML, that appears on top of Web pages sometimes obscuring parts of them. 385

HSUPA (High Speed Uplink Packet Access) A data transmission standard used by cell phone companies for high-speed data transport. 327

HTML (Hypertext Markup Language) A standardized format used to specify the layout for Web pages. 362

HTML conversion utility Utility software that converts documents, spreadsheets, and databases into HTML files that can be posted on the Web. 369

HTML document A plain text or ASCII document with embedded HTML tags that dictate formatting and are interpreted by a browser. 362

HTML forms An HTML document containing blank boxes that prompt users to enter information that can be sent to a Web server. Commonly used for e-commerce transactions. 371

HTML script A series of instructions embedded directly into the text of an HTML document or a file referenced from an HTML document. 371

HTML tags A set of instructions, such as <B>, inserted into an HTML document to provide formatting and display information to a Web browser. 362

HTTP (Hypertext Transfer Protocol) The communications protocol used to transmit Web pages. HTTP:// is an identifier that appears at the beginning of Web URLs (for example, http://www.fooyong.com). 364

HTTP status code A code used by Web servers to report the status of a browser's request. The HTTP status code 404 means document not found. 365

Hyper-Threading technology A feature of microprocessors that allows a single processor to simulate the operation of two processors. 69

Hyperlink data type A data type assigned to fields that store URLs used to link directly to a Web page. 635

Hypertext A way of organizing a collection of documents by assigning an address to each and providing a way to link from one address to another. 360

Hypertext link Also referred to simply as a "link", an underlined word or phrase on a Web page that when clicked, takes you to a designated URL. 361

HyperTransport A computer bus technology that increases the speed at which data is transported to a microprocessor. 68

IBM 360 An early third generation computer that is widely regarded as the first general purpose mainframe. 493

IBM AS/400 IBM's most successful legacy minicomputer. 493

IBM PC An early, commercially successful personal computer system that featured a 4.77 MHz Intel 8088 processor, 64 KB RAM, and a floppy disk drive. Ancestor to today's PCs. 495

IBM PC XT An early, commercially successful personal computer system that included a hard disk drive. 495

ICANN (Internet Corporation for Assigned Names and Numbers) A global organization that coordinates the management of the Internet's domain name system, IP addresses, and protocol parameters. 309

Icon A graphical object, such as those that represent programs or folders on a computer desktop. 189

IDE (Integrated Development Environment) A set of programming tools, typically including editor, compiler, and debugger, packaged into an application for creating programs. 686

Identity theft An illegal practice in which a criminal obtains enough information to masquerade as someone. 36

Image compression Any technique that is used to reduce the size of a file that holds a graphic. 439

IMAP (Internet Messaging Access Protocol) A protocol similar to POP that is used to retrieve e-mail messages from an e-mail server, but offers additional features, such as choosing which e-mails to download from the server. 397

Implementation phase A set of tasks performed with the supervision of a system development project team in which a new information system is constructed. 583

Incremental backup A backup that contains files that changed since the last backup. 227

Inference engine Software that can analyze and manipulate a knowledge base or expert system. 564

Information engineering methodology A method of developing an information system that focuses on data the information system collects before finding ways to process that data. 570

Information system A computer system that collects, stores, and processes information, usually within the context of an organization. 556

Information systems (IS or CIS) The career field or academic major that focuses on developing computer systems and networks for businesses. 514

Information Systems department The part of a business or organization responsible for developing and maintaining the computers, data, and programs for an information system. 510

Information technology (1) A degree program that focuses on the computer equipment and software used by businesses and organizations. (2) The use of computers and software to manipulate data. 514

Information technology industry (IT industry) Companies involved in the development, production, sales, and support of computers and software. 497

Infrared light A transmission technology that uses a frequency range just below the visible light spectrum to transport data. 265

Inheritance In object-oriented terminology, a method for defining new classes of objects based on the characteristics of existing classes. 704

Ink jet printer A non-impact printer that creates characters or graphics by spraying liquid ink onto paper or other media. 92

Input As a noun, "input" means the information that is conveyed to a computer. As a verb, "input" means to enter data into a computer. 15

INSERT An SQL keyword that adds a record to a table. 647

Instant messaging A private chat in which users can communicate with each other in real time using electronically transmitted text messages. 330

Instantiation A programming term that refers to the process of assigning a value to a variable. 717

Instruction cycle The steps followed by a computer to process a single instruction; fetch, interpret, execute, then increment the instruction pointer. 32

Instruction set The collection of instructions that a CPU is designed to process. 30

Integer data type A numeric data type used for fields that contain whole numbers. 634

Integrated circuit (IC) A thin slice of silicon crystal containing microscopic circuit elements such as transistors, wires, capacitors, and resistors; also called chips and microchips. 27

Integration testing The testing of completed modules of an application to ensure that they operate together correctly. 584

Intellectual property A legal concept that refers to ownership of intangible information, such as ideas. 11

Internal information Information obtained by an organization from its own resources, such as from accounting or personnel systems. 559

Internet The worldwide communication infrastructure that links computer networks using TCP/IP protocol. 6

Internet backbone The major communications links that form the core of the Internet. 303

Internet service provider (ISP) A company that provides Internet access to businesses, organizations, and individuals. 303

Interpreter A program that converts high-level instructions in a computer program into machine language instructions, one instruction at a time. 30

Intrusion In the context of computer security, the unauthorized access to a computer system. 340

IP (Internet Protocol) One of the main protocols of TCP/IP; responsible for addressing packets so that they can be routed to their destinations. 305

IP address Unique identifying numbers assigned to each computer connected to the Internet. 255

iPhone OSX A streamlined version of Mac OS X operating system, designed for the iPhone. 203

ISA (Industry Standard Architecture) A standard for moving data on the expansion bus. Can refer to a type of slot, a bus, or a peripheral device. An older technology, it is rapidly being replaced by PCI architecture. 96

ISDN (Integrated Services Digital Network) A telephone company service that transports data digitally over dial-up or dedicated lines. 314

ISDN terminal adapter A device that connects a computer to a telephone jack and translates the data into a signal that can travel over an ISDN connection. 314

Iteration In the context of computer programming, a section of code that is repeated; also called a loop. 698

Iterative SDLC A series of phases that outlines the development process of an information system where each phase is allowed to repeat as needed in the development process. 566

Java A platform-independent, object-oriented, high-level programming language based on C++, typically used to produce interactive Web applications. 679

Java applet Small programs that add processing and interactive capabilities to Web pages. 372

JIT (Just In Time) A manufacturing system in which the parts needed to construct a product are received at the assembly site only as needed. 569

Job search agent An automated program that searches one or more databases and notifies you when it finds a lead on a specific job type. 521

JOIN An SQL command that temporarily joins data from more than one table in order to allow simultaneous access to both tables. 651

Joining tables In SQL terminology, the act of creating a relationship between tables. 651

Joint application design (JAD) A widely accepted design technique that is based on the idea that the best information systems are designed when end-users and systems analysts work together on a project as equal partners. 567

Joystick An input device that looks like a small version of a car's stick shift. Popular with gamers, moving the stick moves objects on the screen. 89

JPEG (Joint Photographic Experts Group) A format that uses lossy compression to store bitmap images. JPEG (pronounced JAY-peg) files have a .jpg extension. 442

Kernel The core module of an operating system that typically manages memory, processes, tasks, and storage devices. 192

Key frame Frames at intervals in a digital video clip that contain all data for that frame. The rest of the frames in the video contain only the information that is different from the preceding key frame. 458

Keylogger A program, sometimes part of a Trojan Horse, that records a person's keystrokes, saves them, and then sends them to a system administrator or remote hacker. 163

Keyword 1) A word or term used as the basis for a Web page search. 2) A command word provided by a programming language. 676

Keyword stuffing An unpopular practice of including a huge variety of keywords in the header of an HTML document in the hopes that a search engine will display it even when the content of the page is not relevant to the search. 378

Kilobit (Kbit or Kb) 1024 bits. 26

Kilobyte (KB) Approximately 1,000 bytes; exactly 1,024 bytes. 26

Knowledge base The collection of facts and rules obtained from experts that are incorporated into an expert system. 564

Knowledge engineering The process of designing, entering rules into, and testing rules in an expert system. 564

Known information In a problem statement, information supplied to the computer to help it solve a problem. 680

Label In the context of spreadsheets, any text used to describe data. 130

LAN (Local Area Network) An interconnected group of computers and peripherals located within a relatively limited area, such as a building or campus. 247

LAN jacking Unauthorized access to a wireless network; also called war driving. 282

LAN party An assembly of computer users and their computers for the purpose of creating a temporary local area network for gaming. 280

Lands Non-pitted surface areas on a CD that represent digital data. (See also Pits.) 81

Laser printer A printer that uses laser-based technology, similar to that used by photocopiers, to produce text and graphics. 92

Latency The elapsed time it takes for a packet of data to arrive at its destination. 309

LCD (Liquid Crystal Display) Technology used for flat panel computer screens typically found on notebook computers. 90

Leading Also called line spacing, the vertical spacing between lines of text. 128

Leibniz Calculator A mechanical calculator capable of performing the four arithmetic functions that helped develop the technology for the first commercially successful calculator. 487

Level 1 cache (L1 cache) Cache memory built into a microprocessor chip. L1 cache typically can be read in one clock cycle. 68

Level 2 cache (L2 cache) Cache memory that is located in a chip separate from the microprocessor chip. 68

Line spacing Also called leading, the vertical spacing between lines of text. (See leading.) 128

Linear editing A video editing technique involving recording segments of video from one tape to another. 456

Link popularity A metric used by some search engines to rank the sites that are relevant to a query. 377

Linux An operating system that is a derivative of UNIX, available as freeware, and widely used for servers though it is also used on personal computers and workstations. 201

Linux distribution Usually a download that includes the Linux operating system, a Linux desktop, and other Linux utilities. 201

Linux platform A computer that is running the Linux operating system. 64

LISP (LISt Processor) A declarative programming language that excels at handling complex data structures, artificial intelligence projects, and very complex programs. 679

Local application Software designed to be installed on and run from a hard disk. 154

Logic error A run-time error in the logic or design of a computer program. 685

Logical data type A data type specifying that a field in a data file is used to store true/false or yes/no data. 634

Logical storage models Any visual or conceptual aid that helps a computer user visualize a file storage system. Also called a storage metaphor. 215

Lookup routine A validation process used by database designers to prevent data entry errors by searching for an entry such as a state abbreviation in a file or database table. 637

Loop The section of program code that is repeated because of a repetition control structure. 698

Lossless compression A compression technique that is able to reconstitute all of the data in the original file, hence "lossless" means that this compression technique does not lose data. 439

Lossy compression Any data compression technique in which some of the data is sacrificed to obtain more compression. 439

Low-level language A programming language that requires a programmer to write instructions for specific hardware elements such as the computer processor, registers, and RAM locations. 676

MAC address (Media Access Control) A unique identifier similar to a serial number assigned to networking equipment at time of manufacture. 254

Mac OS The operating system software designed for use on Apple Macintosh computers. 197

Mac platform A family or category of Macintosh-compatible personal computers designed and manufactured by Apple Computers. 64

Machine code Program instructions written in binary code that the computer can execute directly. 30

Machine language A low-level language written in binary code that the computer can execute directly. 30

Magnetic storage A technology for recording data onto disks or tape by magnetizing particles of an oxide-based surface coating. 78

Mail merge A feature of document production software that automates the process of producing customized documents, such as letters and advertising flyers. 129

Mail order A type of retailing in which a merchant takes orders by telephone or from an Internet site, then ships orders by mail or other courier service. 507

Mainframe computer A large, fast, and expensive computer generally used by businesses or government agencies to provide centralized storage, processing, and management for large amounts of data. 18

Maintenance phase The day-to-day operation of an information system, including making modifications and correcting problems to insure correct operation. 587

Malicious software Any program or set of program instructions, such as a virus, worm, or Trojan horse, designed to surreptitiously enter a computer and disrupt its normal operations. 162

Malware (Malicious software) Programs such as viruses, worms, and bots designed to disrupt computer operations. 162

MAN (Metropolitan Area Network) A public, high-speed network that can transmit voice and data within a range of 50 miles. 247

Management information system (MIS) A type of information system that manipulates the data collected by a transaction processing system to generate reports that managers can use to make business decisions. 561

Managers People who make decisions about how an organization carries out its activities. 557

Manual calculator A device that helps solve mathematical calculations, but does not contain sophisticated built-in algorithms. 486

Manufacturer direct The selling of products by hardware manufacturers directly to consumers by means of a sales force or mail order. 507

Manufacturing technician A computer professional who participates in the fabrication of computer chips, systems, and devices. 512

Many-to-many relationship A relationship in which one record in a particular record type can be related to more than one record in another record type, and vice versa. 616

Mark-8 A microprocessor based computer system developed by Jonathan A. Titus in 1974 that helped lead to the development of personal computers. 494

Market share A company's share, or percentage, of the total market. 504

Market tiers Categories of computer companies based on size, longevity, and market share. 505

Marketing channels Marketing outlets such as retail stores or mail order for computer-related products. 506

Markup language A language that provides text and graphics formatting through the use of tags. Examples of markup languages include HTML, XML, SGML. 362

Mass-mailing worm A worm that sends itself to every e-mail address in the address book of an infected computer. 163

Master File Table An index file used in NTFS storage systems to maintain a list of clusters and keep track of their contents. 219

Mathematical modeling software Software for visualizing and solving a wide range of math, science, and engineering problems. 133

Mathematical operators Symbols such as + - / * that represent specific mathematical functions in a formula. 131

Mechanical calculator A machine capable of implementing algorithms used to solve mathematical calculations. 487

Media Center PC A personal computer system designed to be a home entertainment hub; a computer system that includes Microsoft Windows Media Center operating system. 60

Megabit (Mb or Mbit) 1,048,576 bits. 26

Megabyte (MB) Approximately one million bytes; exactly 1,048,576 bytes. 26

Megahertz (MHz) A measure of frequency equivalent to 1 million cycles per second. 67

Megapixel One million pixels; expresses the resolution and quality of an image; usually used in reference to digital cameras. 433

Memo data type A data type that specifies that a field in a data file can contain variable-length text comments (also called memo field). 634

Memory The computer circuitry that holds data waiting to be processed. 15

Memory leak An undesirable state in which an operating system does not correctly allocate memory for programs causing parts of one program to overwrite parts of others and malfunction. 187

Menu In the context of user interfaces, a list of commands or options often displayed as a list. 190

Menu bar A standard component of most graphical user interfaces that is displayed as a strip of clickable options, that in turn display a list of commands. 190

Mesh topology A network arranged in such a way that each device is connected to many other devices. Data traveling on a mesh network can take any of several possible paths. 250

Message In the context of object-oriented programming, input that is collected and sent to an object. 706

Message header The section of an e-mail file that contains address, subject, and file attachment information. 392

Meta keyword A word that is included in the header of an HTML document in order to describe the document's contents. 378

Metafile In the context of graphics, a file that contains both vector and bitmap data. 447

Metasearch engine A search engine that searches other search engines. 380

Metasearch tool A program that performs broad-based Web searches, such as searching more than one job database at a time. 521

Method In the context of object-oriented programming, any action that an object can perform. 705

Microcontroller A special purpose microprocessor that is built into the device it controls. 20

Microprocessor An integrated circuit that contains the circuitry for processing data. It is a single-chip version of the central processing unit (CPU) found in all computers. 15

Microprocessor clock A timing signal that sets the pace for executing instructions in a microprocessor. 67

Microsoft Windows An operating system, developed by Microsoft Corporation, that provides a graphical interface. Versions include Windows 3.1, Windows 95, 98, Me, NT, 2000, XP, and Vista. 194

Microwaves Electromagnetic waves with a frequency of at least 1 gigahertz; one type of channel for transmitting data over communications networks. 265

MIDI (Musical Instrument Digital Interface) A standardized way in which sound and music are encoded and transmitted between digital devices that play music. 426

MIDI sequence Digitally encoded MIDI music stored on a digital device, such as a computer or MIDI instrument. 426

MIDI sequencing software Software that uses a standardized way of transmitting encoded music or sounds for controlling musical devices, such as a keyboard or sound card. 139

MIME (Multi-purpose Internet Mail Extensions) A standard for formatting non-ASCII messages so that they can be sent over the Internet, typically as e-mail messages. 393

MIMO (Multiple Input Multiple Output) A wireless communications device that uses an array of antennas to transmit data over more than one channel. 268

Mission An organization's goal or plan, which is reflected by the organization's activities. 556

Mission statement The written expression of an organization's goals and how those goals will be accomplished. 556

MITS Altair The first commercial microcomputer. It was based on the Intel 8080 processor and sold primarily to computer hobbyists. 494

Mobile broadband High bandwidth wireless technology that was developed for sending digital data over cell phone systems. 327

Mobile Internet access Any service that allows subscribers to access the Internet while on the go. 311

Mod In the context of personal computers, a customized or "modified" system unit typically jazzed up with lights, chrome, and decals. 65

Modem A device that modulates and demodulates a signal, typically used to send data from a computer to the Internet over telephone, cable television, or satellite networks. 304

Modified waterfall SDLC A series of phases that outlines the development process of an information system where each phase can overlap and be repeated as necessary in the development process. 566

Money management software Software used to track monetary transactions and investments. 133

Monochrome bitmap A bitmap image that contains only the colors black and white. 436

Mouse An input device that allows the user to manipulate objects on the screen by clicking, dragging, and dropping. 88

MP3 A file format that provides highly compressed audio files with very little loss of sound quality. 424

MPEG (Moving Pictures Experts Group) A family of highly compressed container file formats and codecs for digital multimedia; MPEG-1, MPEG-2, and MPEG-4. 457

MRP (Manufacturing Resource Planning) A business management technique in which an optimum manufacturing plan is generated based on a wide variety of data. 569

MSRP (Manufacturer's suggested retail price) The suggested price of a product that is set by the manufacturers, usually higher than the street price. 503

Multi-core processor A microprocessor that contains circuitry for more than one processing unit. 69

Multiparadigm languages A programming language that supports more than one paradigm, such as object-oriented and procedural paradigms. 679

Multiple-user license Legal permission for more than one person to use a particular software package. 147

Multiprocessing The ability of a computer or operating system to support dual core processors or multiple processors. 186

Multitasking The ability of a computer, processor, or operating system to run more than one program, job, or task at the same time. 186

Multithreading A technology that allows multiple parts or threads from a program to run simultaneously. 186

Multiuser operating system An operating system that allows a single computer to deal with simultaneous processing requests from multiple users. 187

NAN (Neighborhood Area Network) A network with a range of a few blocks, such as a Wi-Fi hotspot offered by a coffee shop or neighborhood free Wi-Fi organization. 246

Nanosecond A unit of time representing 1 billionth of a second. 73

Napier's Bones A manual calculator created by John Napier that could be used to perform mathematical calculations by manipulating numbered rods. 487

Narrowband A term that refers to communications channels that have low bandwidth. 251

Native file format A file format that is unique to a program or group of programs and has a unique file extension. 209

Native resolution The dimensions of the grid that holds LEDs in a flat screen, LCD display device; the resolution at which an LCD offers the clearest display. 539

Natural language query A query formulated in human language, as opposed to an artificially constructed language such as machine language. 136

Netiquette (Internet etiquette) A set of guidelines for posting messages and e-mails in a civil, concise way. 396

Network access points (NAP) An Internet node that links together different network service providers so that data can be transferred from one service provider to the other. 303

Network address translation (NAT) A security technique that allows a LAN to use one type of IP address for intra-network data and another type of address for data traveling to and from the Internet. 344

Network attached storage (NAS) Storage devices that are designed to be attached directly to a network, rather than to a workstation or server. 248

Network database A collection of physically linked records in a one-to-many relationship in which a member (child) can have more than one owner (parent). 617

Network device Any device, such as a gateway, hub, or router, that is used to broadcast network data, boost signals, or route data to its destination. 248

Network hub A network device that connects several nodes of a local area network. 261

Network interface card Circuitry, often on an expansion card mounted inside a computer, that transmits and receives data on a local area network. Also called a NIC, network card, or network adapter. 248

Network router A device found at each intersection on the Internet backbone that examines the IP address of incoming data, and forwards the data towards its destination. 261

Network service providers (NSP) A company that maintains a series of nationwide Internet links. 303

Network specialist/administrator A computer professional who plans, installs, and maintains one or more local area networks. 511

Network switch A network device that sends data to a specific address instead of broadcasting it over an entire network. 261

Networked peripheral A peripheral device that contains circuitry that allows it to be directly connected to a network, rather than connecting to a computer that transfers data to a network. 248

Neural network A type of expert system that uses computer circuitry to simulate the way in which the brain processes information, learns, and remembers. 565

Node In a network, a connection point; in a hierarchical database, a segment or record type. 248

Non-executing zip file A type of compressed file that has to be unzipped manually to extract the file or files contained within it. 157

Non-volatile Any electronic component that does not require a constant supply of power to hold data. 84

Nonlinear editing A digital video editing technique that requires a personal computer and video editing software. 456

Nonprofit organization Organizations with political, social, or charitable goals that are not intended to generate a profit. 556

Normalization The process of analyzing data to create the most efficient database structure. 637

Notation software Software used to help musicians compose, edit, and print their compositions. 139

Notebook computer A small, lightweight, portable computer that usually runs on batteries. Sometimes called a laptop. 59

NTFS (New Technology File System) A file system used by Microsoft Windows NT, 2000, and XP operating systems to keep track of the name and location of files on a hard disk. 219

Numeric data Numbers that represent quantities and can be used in arithmetic operations. 23

Object In an object database or OO programming language, a discrete piece of code describing a person, place, thing, event, or type of information. 702

Object code The low-level instructions that result from compiling source code. 30

Object database A database model that organizes data into classes of objects that can be manipulated by programmer-defined methods; also referred to as object-oriented database. 620

Object-oriented methodology An approach to system development that regards the elements of a system as a collection of objects that interact with each other to accomplish tasks. 570

Object-oriented paradigm An approach to programming that focuses on the manipulation of objects rather than on the generation of procedure-based code. 702

Object-relational database A database that uses object-oriented and relational concepts. 621

Octet One of four sections of an IP address. 255

ODBMS (Object database management system) Database management software used to construct an object-oriented database. 625

Offshoring The corporate practice of relocating production, manufacturing, or customer service to lower-cost overseas locations. 500

OLAP (Online Analytical Processing) A system that consists of computer hardware, database software, and analytical tools that are optimized for analyzing and manipulating data. 613

OLTP system (Online Transaction Processing Systems) Interactive online transaction processing methods that use a "commit or rollback" strategy to ensure accurate transaction processing. 560

One-to-many relationship A relationship in which one record in a particular type may be related to more than one record of another record type. 616

One-to-one relationship An association between database entities in which one record type is related to one record of another type. 616

Online auction A consumer-to-consumer form of e-commerce in which merchandise and services are sold to the highest bidder. eBay is a popular example. 388

Online job bank An online database of job opening announcements that spans many industries or just one specific industry. 520

Online processing An interactive method of processing transactions in which each transaction is processed as it is entered. 560

Online shopping cart A feature of e-commerce sites that stores information about items selected for purchase often by creating a cookie on a shopper's computer. 386

Online social networks Web sites that provide ways for people to communicate and socialize. MySpace is a popular example. 6

Op code Short for operation code, an op code is an assembly language command word that designates an operation, such as add (ADD), compare (CMP), or jump (JMP). 31

Open source An approach to developing and licensing software in which source code remains public so it can be improved and freely distributed. 12

Open source software Software that includes its source code, allowing programmers to modify and improve it. 150

Operand The part of an instruction that specifies the data, or the address of the data, on which the operation is to be performed. 31

Operating system The software that controls the computer's use of its hardware resources, such as memory and disk storage space. Also called OS. 16, 184

Operational planning The scheduling and monitoring of workers and processes. 557

Optical storage A technology that records data as light and dark spots on a CD, DVD, or other optical media. 81

Organization A group of people working together to accomplish a goal. 556

Organizational chart A diagram showing the hierarchy of workers in an organization. 557

Output The results produced by a computer (for example, reports, graphs, and music). 15

Outsourcing The corporate practice of using third-party contractors to supply raw goods, manufacturing, or services. 499

Overclocking Forcing a computer component, such as a microprocessor, to run at a higher speed than intended by the manufacturer. 70

P2P file sharing A practice in which individuals can obtain music, video, and other types of files from other users on a network; sometimes the files are shared without authorization from the copyright holder. 337

Packet A small unit of data transmitted over a network. 253

Packet switching A technology used by data communications networks, such as the Internet, where a message is divided into smaller units called "packets" for transmission. 253

Packet writing The process of recording data to a CD or DVD in multiple sessions. Contrast with disk mastering. 219

Page layout The physical positions of elements on a document page such as headers, footers, page numbering, and graphics. 128

Paint software Software that creates and manipulates bitmap graphics. 137, 430

Palm OS A popular type of operating system produced by PalmSource specifically for handheld computers. 202

PAN (Personal Area Network) An interconnected group of personal digital devices located within a range of about 30 feet. 246

Paragraph alignment The horizontal position (left, right, justified, centered, for example) of the text in a document. 128

Paragraph style A specification for the format of a paragraph, which includes the alignment of text within the margins and line spacing. 128

Parallel conversion A type of system conversion in which the old computer system remains in service while some or all of the new system is activated. 586

Parallel processing The simultaneous use of more than one processor to execute a program. 69

Parameters A delimiting variable used to modify a command, e.g., /ON modifies the DIR command so it displays files in order by name. 647, 676

Particle renderer Graphics software that generates special effects for explosions, flares, fog, and smoke. 687

Pascal A high-level, procedural programming language developed to help computer programming students learn the structured approach to programming. 679

Pascaline An early mechanical calculator capable of performing addition, subtraction, division, and multiplication. 487

Password A special set of symbols used to restrict access to a user's computer or network. 35

Password manager Software that keeps track of sites at which a user has registered and the password that corresponds to each site. 40

Path A file's location specified by the drive on which it is stored and the hierarchy of folders in which it is stored. (See File specification.) 206

Pathfinder algorithms Program code used to control the routes characters take as they move through the virtual world of a computer game. 687

Payroll software A type of horizontal market software used to maintain payroll records. 142

PC card (Personal Computer Memory Card International Association or PCMCIA card) A credit card-sized circuit board used to connect a modem, memory, network card, or storage device to a notebook computer. 96

PC platform A family of personal computers that use Windows software and contain Intel-compatible microprocessors. 64

PC slot (Personal Computer Memory Card International Association or PCMCIA slot) An external expansion slot typically found on notebook computers. 96

PCI (Peripheral Component Interconnect) A method for transporting data on the expansion bus. Can refer to type of data bus, expansion slot, or transport method used by a peripheral device. 96

PCX The PC Paintbrush file format that incorporates a compression algorithm. 442

PDA (Personal Digital Assistant) A computer that is smaller and more portable than a notebook computer (also called a palm-top or handheld computer). 19

PDA video Digital video formatted for viewing on a PDA or other hand-held device. 452

Peer-to-peer mode A method of using a network in which workstations act as both file servers and clients. 249

Peripheral device A component or equipment, such as a printer, that expands a computer's input, output, or storage capabilities. 56

Person-to-person payment A method of e-commerce payment that uses an intermediary or third party such as PayPal to handle payment between a buyer and seller. 390

Personal computer A microcomputer designed for use by an individual user for applications such as Web browsing and word processing. 17

Personal finance software Software geared toward individual finances that helps track bank account balances, credit card payments, investments, and bills. 133

PERT (Program Evaluation and Review Technique) A technique for project management by displaying interconnected events and task milestones on a timeline. 570

PGP (Pretty Good Privacy) A popular program used to encrypt and decrypt files and e-mail messages. 287

Pharming An exploit that redirects users to fake Web sites. 405

Phased conversion A type of information system conversion in which one module of a new information system is activated at a time. 586

Phishing An e-mail based scam that's designed to fool users into revealing confidential information. 405

Phoneme A unit of sound that is a basic component of words and is produced by speech synthesizers. 428

Photo editing software The software used to edit, enhance, retouch, and manipulate digital photographs. 137

Physical storage model A representation of data as it is physically stored. 218

Physical topology The actual layout of network devices, wires, and cables. 250

Piconet A network formed by Bluetooth devices. 267

PIECES framework A concept developed by James Wetherbe, to help identify problems in an information system. Each letter of PIECES stands for a potential problem (Performance, Information, Economics, Control, Efficiency, and Service). 569

Pilot conversion A type of system conversion in which a new information system is first activated at one branch of a multi-branch company. 586

Ping (Packet INternet Grouper) A command on a TCP/IP network that sends a test packet to a specified IP address and waits for a reply. 310

Pipelining A technology that allows a processor to begin executing an instruction before completing the previous instruction. 69

Pits Spots on a CD that are "burned" onto an optical storage medium to represent digital data. 81

Pixel interpolation A process that is used by graphics software to average the color of adjacent pixels in an image, usually when the image is enlarged. 435

Pixelated Describes the effect of increasing the size and thus decreasing the quality of an image. 435

Pixels Short for picture element, a pixel is the smallest unit in a graphic image. Computer display devices use a matrix of pixels to display text and graphics. 90

PL/1 (Programming Language 1) A business and scientific programming language developed by IBM in 1964. 679

Place shifting The practice of accessing media from a remote location, such as over a network. 465

Plaintext An original, un-encrypted message. 285

Planning phase The first phase of an information system development project with the goal of creating a Project Development Plan. 567

Plasma screen A compact, lightweight, flat panel computer display that uses a technology similar to that of neon lights. 90

Plug and Play The ability of a computer to automatically recognize and adjust the system configuration for a newly added device. 97

Plug-in A software module that adds a specific feature to a system. In the context of browsers, a plug-in adds the ability to play files referenced from the EMBED tag. 367

PNG (Portable Network Graphics) A type of graphics file format similar to but newer than GIF or JPEG. 443

Podcast An audio file that is distributed over the Internet through downloads or the use of an RSS feed or Atom. 360

Point size A unit of measure (1/72 of an inch) used to specify the height of characters in a font. 127

Pointing device An input device such as a mouse, trackball, pointing stick, or trackpad, that allows users to manipulate an on-screen pointer and other screen-based graphical controls. 88

Pointing stick A mouse-substitute input device that looks like the tip of an eraser embedded in the keyboard of a notebook computer. 89

Polymorphism In the context of object-oriented programming, the ability to redefine a method for a subclass. Also called overloading. 707

POP (Post Office Protocol) A standard for retrieving e-mail messages from an e-mail server. 397

POP server A computer that receives and stores e-mail data until retrieved by the e-mail account holder. 398

Pop-up ad A type of advertisement that usually appears in a separate window when you enter a Web site. 385

Port In the context of computer networks, a virtual device that sets up one or more connections over which data can flow. 308

Port probe An exploit used by hackers to locate computer ports that can be used for surreptitious access. 341

Portable audio player A digital device designed to store and play digital music; also called MP3 player. 425

Portable computer Any type of computer, such as a notebook computer, that runs on batteries and is designed to be carried from one location to another. 59

Portable Internet access Any type of Internet service, such as portable satellite, that can be moved from one place to another. 311

Portable media player A small, lightweight, battery-powered device designed to store and play audio, video, or image files stored in such formats as MP3 and AAC. 20

Portable software Software designed to be stored on a flash drive or CD, and that does not require installation before it is used. 158

PostScript A printer language, developed by Adobe Systems, which uses a special set of commands to control page layout, fonts, and graphics. 94

Power surge A spike in electrical voltage that has the potential to damage electronic equipment such as computers. 99

Powerline network A network that uses a building's existing power line cables to connect nodes; also called HomePlug, HPLC, or HomePLC. 258

Predicate In a Prolog fact, such as likes(John, Mary), the predicate "likes" describes the relationship between the arguments in parentheses, such as (John, Mary). 714

Predictive analytics A branch of data mining that focuses on predicting future probabilities and trends using statistical algorithms, neural networks, and optimization research. 613

Predictive methodology The traditional approach to software development in which detailed specifications are created before coding begins. 681

Presentation software Software that provides tools to combine text, graphics, graphs, animation, and sound into a series of electronic "slides" that can be output on a projector, or as overhead transparencies, paper copies, or 35-millimeter slides. 138

Primary key A field in a database that contains data, such as a social security number, that is unique to a record. 634

Print server A device that controls a cluster of printers by distributing jobs that arrive in its print queue—a list of documents that require printing. 249

Printer Control Language (PCL) A standard for formatting codes embedded within a document that specify how a printer should format each page. 94

Private attribute An attribute for an object, class, or record that can be accessed only from the program routine in which it is defined. 703

Private IP address An IP address that cannot be routed over the Internet. 344

Problem statement In software engineering a concise summary of elements that must be manipulated in order to achieve a result or goal. 680

Procedural language Any programming language used to create programs composed of a series of statements that tell the computer how to perform a specific task. 689

Procedural paradigm An approach to programming in which a programmer defines the steps for solving a problem. 689

Procedure In the context of computer programming, a section of code that performs activities but is not included in the main sequential execution path of a program. 696

Procedure handbook Step-by-step instructions for performing a specific job or task. 585

Process A systematic series of actions that a computer performs to manipulate data; typically represented on a DFD by a rounded rectangle. 572

Processing The manipulation of data by a computer's microprocessor or central processing unit. 15

Product activation The process of becoming a registered user of a software product; the process might include entering a validation code to unlock the software. 157

Productivity software Software that helps people work more efficiently; traditionally word processing, spreadsheet, presentation, e-mail, and database software. 121

Professional ethics On-the-job actions and choices that reflect a person's values. 523

Program editor A programming tool, similar to a word processor, but that provides specialized editing and formatting features to streamline the programming process. 682

Programming language A set of keywords and grammar (syntax) that allows a programmer to write instructions that a computer can execute. 29, 676

Programming paradigm A programming methodology or approach, as in the object-oriented paradigm. 679

Project Development Plan A planning document that is the final result of a planning phase and is reviewed and approved by management. 567

Project management software Software specifically designed as a tool for planning, scheduling, and tracking projects and their costs. 142, 571

Prolog A declarative programming language used to develop expert systems modeled after human thinking. 679

Properties The characteristics of an object in a program. 683

Proprietary information Financial and product data, procedures, or concepts created by an individual or organization that are not made public because they would aid the competition. 526

Proprietary software Software that carries restrictions on its use that are delineated by copyright, patents, or license agreements. 149

Protocol suite A group of protocols, such as TCP and IP, that work together. 305

Prototype An experimental or trial version of a device or system. 489

Pseudocode A notational system for algorithms that combines English and a programming language. 692

Public attribute An attribute for an object, class, or record that can be accessed from any routine in a program. 703

Public domain software Software that is available for public use without restriction except that it cannot be copyrighted. 149

Public key encryption (PKE) An encryption method that uses a pair of keys, a public key (known to everyone) that encrypts the message, and a private key (known only to the recipient) that decrypts it. 286

Quality assurance specialist A computer professional who participates in alpha and beta test cycles of software. Also refers to a person who examines and tests computer chips and devices. 512

Quality of service (QoS) The level of performance that is provided by a computer system and measured by factors such as response time, downtime, and capacity. 587

Quality-of-service metric A technique for measuring a particular quality-of-service characteristic, such as response time. 587

Quarantined file A file suspected to be infected with a virus that antivirus software moves to a special folder to prevent accidental access to it. 169

Query A search specification that prompts the computer to look for particular records in a file. 136

Query by example (QBE) A type of database interface in which the user fills in a field with an example of the type of information that she is seeking. 136

Query language A set of command words that can be used to direct the computer to create databases, locate information, sort records, and change the data in those records. 136

Query processor The component of a search engine that examines keywords entered by users and fetches results that match the query. 377

QuickTime Movie A video and animation file format developed by Apple Computer that can also be run on PCs. QuickTime files have a .mov extension. 457

RAM (Random Access Memory) Computer memory circuitry that holds data, program instructions, and the operating system while the computer is on. 71

Random access The ability of a storage device (such as a disk drive) to go directly to a specific storage location without having to search sequentially from a beginning location. 77

Rasterization The process of superimposing a grid over a vector image and determining the color depth for each pixel. 447

RAW In the context of digital graphics, a file that contains unprocessed image data directly from a digital camera's sensors. 442

Ray tracing A technique by which light and shadows are added to a 3-D image. 449

RCA Spectra 70 An early third generation computer that was among the first to use integrated circuits for data processing. 493

RDBMS (Relational Database Management System) Database management software used to create, update, and administer a relational database. 625

Read-only technology Storage media that can only be read from, but not recorded on. 82

Read-write head The mechanism in a disk drive that magnetizes particles on the storage disk surface to write data, or senses the bits that are present to read data. 78

Readability formula A feature found in some word processing software that can estimate the reading level of a written document. 127

Real data type A numeric data type used for fields that contain numbers with decimal places. 634

Real-time messaging system Technologies, such as instant messaging and chat that allow people to exchange messages when they are online. 330

RealAudio An audio file format developed by Real Networks especially for streaming audio data over the Web. 424

REALbasic A modern OO version of the BASIC programming language that works cross platform on Windows, Macs, and Linux. 679

RealMedia A video file format developed by Real Networks that is popular for streaming Web videos. 457

Record In the context of database management, a record is the fields of data that pertain to a single entity in a database. 134, 615

Record occurrence A record that has been filled with data for a particular entity. 615

Record type The structure of a record, including the names, length, and data types for each field. 615

Recordable technology The devices and standards that allow computers to write data permanently on CDs and DVDs, but does not allow that data to be changed once it has been recorded. 82

Recovery disk A CD that contains all the operating system files and application software files necessary to restore a computer to its original state. 229

Reference software Software that contains a large database of information with tools for sorting, viewing, and accessing specific topics. 141

Refresh rate The speed at which a computer monitor is rewritten, measured in Hertz. Faster refresh rates reduce flickering. 90

Region code A signal added to commercial DVDs that limits playback to devices that have a corresponding region code. 468

Registers A sort of "scratch pad" area of the microprocessor into which data or instructions are moved so that they can be processed. 31

Relational database A database structure that incorporates the use of tables that can establish relationships with other, similar tables. 618

Relationship In the context of databases, an association between entities that can be used to link records in more than one file. 616

Relative reference In a worksheet, a cell reference that can change if cells change position as a result of a move or copy operation. 132

Remarks Explanatory comments inserted into lines of code in a computer program. 686

Remote Access Trojan (RAT) A type of Trojan horse malware that allows remote hackers to transmit files to victims' computers. 163

Rendering In graphics software, the process of creating a 3-D solid image by covering a wireframe drawing and applying computer-generated highlights and shadows. 449

Repetition control structure A component of a computer program that repeats one or more instructions until a certain condition is met (also called loop or iteration). 698

Repetitive stress injury An injury that occurs from overuse over a period of time. 536

Report generator The component of a data management environment that provides a user with the ability to design reports. 642

Report template A predesigned pattern that provides the outline or general specifications for a report. 642

Request for proposal (RFP) A document sent by an organization to vendors to solicit proposals; it specifies the problem that needs to be solved and the requirements that must be met. 580

Request for quotation (RFQ) A document sent by an organization to vendors requesting a formal price quotation on a list of hardware and/or software. 580

Reserved words Special words used as commands in some operating systems that may not be used in file names. 205

Resolution The density of the grid used to display or print text and graphics; the greater the horizontal and vertical density, the higher the resolution. 91

Resolution dependent Graphics, such as bitmaps, in which the quality of the image is dependent on the number of pixels comprising the image. 435

Resource A component, either hardware or software, that is available for use by a computer's processor. 185

Resource fork A storage characteristic of Mac OS that creates a file containing a description of the data stored in an accompanying raw data file. 200

Restore point Data stored about the state of files and the operating system at a given point in time, then used to roll back the computer system to that state. 228

Rewritable technology The devices and standards that allow users to write data on a storage medium and then change that data. 82

RF signals (Radio Frequency Signals) Data that is broadcast and received via radio waves with a transceiver. 265

Ribbon An element of the user interface popularized by Microsoft Office 2007 that presents users with multiple tabs instead of menus at the top of the application window. 190

Ring topology A network in which all devices are connected in a circle with each device having exactly two neighbors. 250

RISC (Reduced Instruction Set Computer) A microprocessor designed for rapid and efficient processing of a small set of simple instructions. 69

RJ45 connector A square plastic cable connector that resembles an oversized telephone connector, and is used to connect Ethernet devices. 262

Rollback The act of returning database records back to their original states if one or more steps of the transaction cannot be successfully processed. 560

ROM (Read-Only Memory) Refers to one or more integrated circuits that contain permanent instructions that the computer uses during the boot process. 73

ROM BIOS A small set of basic input/output system instructions stored in ROM. 74

Root directory The main directory of a disk. 206

Rootkit Software that conceals running processes; used by hackers to disguise security breaches and breakins. 165

Routable IP address A network address that can be routed over the Internet; contrast to private IP address. 344

RPG (Report Program Generator) A programming language used to generate business reports. 679

RSS (Really Simple Syndication) Delivers files called "feeds" from Websites to subscribers. 360

Rule In the context of Prolog programming, a rule is a general statement about the relationship between facts. 713

Run-length encoding A graphics file compression technique that looks for patterns of bytes and replaces them with messages that describe the patterns. 439

Runtime error An error that occurs when a computer program is run. 685

S-HTTP (Secure HTTP) A method of encrypting data transmitted between a computer and a Web server by encrypting individual packets of data as they are transmitted. 389

Safe Mode A menu option that appears when Windows is unable to complete the boot sequence. By entering Safe Mode, a user can gracefully shut down the computer, then try to reboot it. 105

Sampling rate The number of times per second a sound is measured during the recording process. 423

Satellite Internet service A high-speed Internet service that uses a geosynchronous or low-earth orbit satellite to send data directly to satellite dishes owned by individuals. 318

Satellite modem A device that connects a computer to a satellite for purposes of accessing the Internet. 319

Scanner A device that converts a printed image into a bitmap graphic. 431

Scheduled reports Reports such as monthly sales summaries that follow a fixed format and are produced according to a preset time table. 561

Scheme A dialect of LISP, used for computer research and teaching. 679

Schickard's Calculator An early mechanical calculator consisting of a series of gears and spokes representing numerical values. 487

SDK (Software Development Kit) A collection of language-specific programming tools. 686

SDLC (System Development Life Cycle) The series of phases that outlines the development process of an information system. 566

Search and Replace A feature of document production software that allows the user to automatically locate all instances of a particular word or phrase and substitute another word or phrase. 127

Search engine indexer The component of a search engine that reviews the Web pages brought back by a crawler and creates pointers to them so that they can be quickly accessed. 376

Search terms The words entered into a search engine or database to form a query. 378

Second-generation computers Computers that use transistors for data processing and storage instead of vacuum tubes. 492

Second-generation languages Assembly languages that followed machine languages. 677

Sectors Subdivisions of the tracks on a storage medium that provide storage areas for data. 218

Secure connection An internet connection that encrypts data transmitted between your computer and a Web site. 389

Security software Any software package that is designed to protect computers from destructive software and unauthorized intrusions. 162

Security specialist A computer professional who analyzes security threats, implements solutions, and develops policies and procedures to protect computer equipment and data. 511

Security suite A software suite containing modules to protect computers against viruses, worms, intrusions, spyware, and other threats. 166

SELECT An SQL keyword that queries for a particular record or group of records from a table. 648

Selection control structure A component of a computer program that tells a computer what to do, depending on whether a condition is true or false (also called decision structure or branch). 697

Self-executing zip file A type of compressed file that can be run to unzip the file or files contained within it. 157

Self-installing executable file A program that automatically unzips and then initiates its setup program. 157

Semi-structured problem A problem for which a general procedure has been established, but which requires some degree of discretionary judgment to arrive at a solution. 558

Semiconducting materials (Semiconductors) Substances, such as silicon or germanium, that can act either as a conductor or insulator. Used in the manufacture of computer chips. 27

Sequence control structure A programming construct which alters the order in which instructions are executed. 695

Sequence diagram A tool used by a project team that depicts the detailed interactions that take place within an information system. 574

Sequential access A characteristic of data storage, usually on computer tape, that requires a device to read or write data one record after another, starting at the beginning of the medium. 77

Sequential execution The computer execution of program instructions performed in the sequence established by a programmer. 695

Serial processing Processing of data one instruction at a time, completing one instruction before beginning another. 69

Server A computer or software on a network that supplies the network with data and storage. 18

Server operating system A type of operating system, sometimes called a network operating system, that provides management tools for distributed networks, e-mail servers, and Web hosting sites. 187

Server-side program A program or scripting statement that resides on a Web server and acts as an intermediary between a user's browser and a DBMS. 628

Server-side script Scripting statements that are executed by a Web server in response to client data. 371

Service companies Companies that provide computer-related services such as consulting or support. 498

Service pack A collection of patches designed to correct bugs and/or add features to an existing software program. 159

Setup program A program module supplied with a software package for the purpose of installing the software. 154

Shared resources On a network, resources such as hardware, software, and data, made available for authorized users to share. 274

Shareware Copyrighted software marketed under a license that allows users to use the software for a trial period and then send in a registration fee if they wish to continue to use it. 149

Shrink-wrap license A legal agreement printed on computer software packaging, which becomes binding when the package is opened. 147

Signal scrambling A technique that encrypts or otherwise disrupts broadcast signals so that they have to be unscrambled before they are sensible. 465

Signed code Program code that has an associated digital certificate identifying the programmer; used to reduce susceptibility to malware. 727

SIMULA (SIMUlation LAnguage) Believed to be the first object-oriented programming language. 679

Single-user license Legal permission for one person to use a particular software package. 147

Single-user operating system A type of operating system that is designed for one user at a time using one set of input devices. 187

Site license Legal permission for software to be used on any and all computers at a specific location (for example, within a corporate building or on a university campus). 147

Slide rule A manual calculator invented by William Oughtred that uses John Napier's logarithms to solve complex engineering and scientific calculations. 487

Smalltalk A classic object-oriented programming language. 679

Smart phone A handheld device that integrates the functions of a mobile phone, PDA, portable music player, or other digital device. 20

Smileys Text-based symbols used to express emotion. 396

SMTP server (Simple Mail Transfer Protocol Server) A computer used to send e-mail across a network or the Internet. 398

Sniffing In the context of computer hacking, a technique that uses packet sniffer software to capture packets as they are sent over a network. 37

Socket A communication path between two remote programs. 364

Software The instructions that direct a computer to perform a task, interact with a user, or process data. 15

Software customization The process of modifying a commercially available software application to meet the needs of a specific user or organization. 583

Software engineering The process of developing software using systematic mathematical, engineering, and management techniques. 515

Software installation The process by which programs and data are copied to the hard disk of a computer system and otherwise prepared for access and use. 153

Software license A legal contract that defines the ways in which a user may use a computer program. 147

Software patch A section of software code designed to modify an existing program to fix a specific error or add a feature. 159

Software publishers Companies that produce computer software. 498

Software suite A collection of individual applications sold as one package. 144

Solid state storage A technology that records data and stores it in a microscopic grid of cells on a non-volatile, erasable, low-power chip. 84

Sort key A field used to arrange records in order. 639

Sort order In a database table, the order in which records are stored on disk. 639

Sound card A circuit board that gives the computer the ability to accept audio input from a microphone, play sound files stored on disks and CD-ROMs, and produce audio output through speakers or headphones. 423

Source code Computer instructions written in a high-level language. 29

Spam Unsolicited e-mail typically sent as a bulk or mass-mailing and often used for fraudulent or deceptive marketing. 403

Spam filter Software that identifies unsolicited and unwanted e-mail messages and blocks them from the recipient's inbox. 404

Speech recognition The process by which computers recognize voice patterns and words, then convert them to digital data. 428

Speech synthesis The process by which computers produce sound that resembles spoken words. 428

Spelling checker A feature of document production software that checks each word in a document against an electronic dictionary of correctly spelled words, then presents a list of alternatives for possible misspellings. 126

Spelling dictionary A data module that is used by a spelling checker as a list of correctly spelled words. 126

Spreadsheet A numerical model or representation of a real situation, presented in the form of a table. 130

Spreadsheet software Software for creating electronic worksheets that hold data in cells and perform calculations based on that data. 130

Spyware Any software that covertly gathers user information without the user's knowledge, usually for advertising purposes. 164

SQL A popular query language used by mainframes and microcomputers. 645

SQL keywords A collection of command words that issue instructions to an SQL database. 646

SQL query A command created using SQL database client software that operates directly on the record in a database. 645

SSID (Service Set IDentifier) A code that identifies a wireless network and is attached to every packet that travels on that network. 272

SSL (Secure Sockets Layer) A security protocol that uses encryption to establish a secure connection between a computer and a Web server. 389

Star topology A network configured with a central connection point or hub for all workstations and peripherals. 250

Stateless protocol A protocol, such as HTTP, that allows one request and response per session. 365

Static IP address A permanently assigned and unique IP address, used by hosts or servers. 306

Static Web publishing A simple way to display the data in a database by converting a database report into an HTML document. 627

Statistical software Software for analyzing large sets of data to discover patterns and relationships within them. 133

Storage The area in a computer where data is retained on a permanent basis. 15

Storage density The closeness of the particles on a disk surface. As density increases, the particles are packed more tightly together and are usually smaller. 77

Storage device A mechanical apparatus that records data to and retrieves data from a storage medium. 76

Storage medium The physical material used to store computer data, such as a floppy disk, a hard disk, or a CD-ROM. 76

Store-and-forward A technology used by communications networks in which an e-mail message is temporarily held in storage on a server until it is requested by a client computer. 397

Stored program A set of instructions that resides on a storage device, such as a hard drive, and can be loaded into computer memory and executed. 16

Strategic planning The process of developing long-range goals and plans for an organization. 557

Streaming audio An audio file format that allows the audio clip to begin before the file is entirely downloaded. 425

Streaming video An Internet video technology that sends a small segment of a video file to a user's computer and begins to play it while the next segment is being sent. 459

Street price The average discounted price of a product. 503

Strong encryption Encryption that is difficult to decrypt or "break" without the encryption key. 285

Structured English Vocabulary and syntax used by systems analysts to concisely and unambiguously explain the logic of a process. It is limited to words defined in a data dictionary and to specific logical terms such as "if...then,". 692

Structured file A file that consists of a collection of data organized as a set of similarly structured records. 614

Structured methodology A method of developing an information system that focuses on the processes that take place within the information system. 570

Structured problem A problem for which there exists a well-established procedure for obtaining the best solution. 558

Style A feature in many desktop publishing and word processing programs that allows the user to apply numerous format settings with a single command. 128

Subclass In object-oriented programming, a subclass is derived from a superclass and inherits its attributes and methods. 704

Subdirectory A directory found under the root directory. 206

Submenu A user interface element that emerges after a menu is selected to offer additional options. 191

Subroutine A section of code that performs activities or manipulates data but is not included in the main sequential execution path of a program. 696

Success factors System requirements that also serve as an evaluation checklist at the end of a development project. 571

Summary report A report generated by a management information system that combines or groups data and usually provides totals, such as a report of total annual sales for the past five years. 561

Super distribution A concept incorporated into Microsoft DRM that allows users to share protected media with others who can access it after they obtain their own license for it. 471

Superclass In object-oriented programming, a superclass can provide attributes and methods for subclasses. 704

Supercomputer The fastest and most expensive type of computer, capable of processing trillions of instructions per second. 18

Surge strip A device that filters out electrical spikes that could damage computer equipment. 100

SVG (Scalable Vector Graphics) A graphics format designed specifically for Web display that automatically resizes when displayed on different screens. 448

SVGA (Super Video Graphics Array) SVGA typically refers to 800 x 600 resolution. 91

SXGA (Super eXtended Graphics Array) A screen resolution of 1280 x 1024. 91

Symbian OS An operating system typically used on mobile phones and open to programming by third-party developers. 203

Symmetric Internet connection Any connection to the Internet in which the upstream speed is the same as the downstream speed. 311

Symmetric key encryption An encryption key that is used for both encryption and decryption of messages. 286

Syntax In the context of programming languages, syntax refers to the grammar rules that create valid program statements. 676

Syntax error An error that results when an instruction does not follow the syntax rules, or grammar, of the programming language. 685

Synthesized sound Artificially created sound, usually found in MIDI music or synthesized speech. 426

System board The main circuit board in a computer which houses chips and other electronic components. 28

System conversion The process of deactivating an old information system and activating a new one. 586

System development life cycle (SDLC) The series of phases that outlines the development process of an information system. 566

System documentation Descriptions of the features, hardware architecture, and programming of an information system written for programmers, designers, and analysts who maintain the system. 585

System operator The person responsible for the day-to-day operation of a computer—usually a mainframe or supercomputer. 588

System palette A selection of colors that are used by an operating system to display graphic elements. 438

System requirements The criteria for developing a successful information system; compiled into a System Requirement Report at the conclusion of the analysis phase. 145, 571

System Requirements Report A report generated at the conclusion of the analysis phase by a project team that has studied a system and determined the system requirements. 572

System software Computer programs, such as an operating system or utility software, that help the computer carry out essential operating tasks. 16

System testing The process of testing an information system to ensure that all the hardware and software components work together. 584

System unit The case or box that contains the computer's power supply, storage devices, main circuit board, processor, and memory. 57

Systems analysis and design The process of planning and building an information system. 566

Systems analyst A computer professional responsible for analyzing requirements, designing information systems, and supervising the implementation of new information systems. 510

Systems programmer The person responsible for installing, modifying, and troubleshooting the operating system of a mainframe or supercomputer. 588

Table (1) An arrangement of data in a grid of rows and columns. (2) In a relational database, a collection of record types with their data. 129, 618

Tablet computer A small, portable computer with a touch-sensitive screen that can be used as a writing or drawing pad. 59

Tactical planning Short- or near-term decisions and goals that deploy the human, financial, and natural resources necessary to meet strategic goals. 557

Tape drive A device that stores data on magnetic tape. 80

Taskbar A graphical user interface element usually displayed near the bottom of the screen to help users launch and monitor applications. 190

Tax preparation software Personal finance software that is specifically designed to assist with tax preparation. 133

TCP (Transmission Control Protocol) The protocol within TCP/IP that is responsible for establishing a data connection between two hosts and breaking data into packets. 305

TCP/IP (Transmission Control Protocol/Internet Protocol) The primary protocol suite for transmitting messages over the Internet. 305

Technical support specialist A computer professional who provides phone or online help to customers of computer companies and software publishers. 511

Technical writer A person who specializes in writing explanations of technical concepts and procedures. 512

Telecommuting The act of using available technologies, such as computers, telephones, and the Internet, to work from home or another off-site location. 513

Temporal compression A data compression scheme that, when applied to video or audio data, eliminates unnecessary data between video frames or audio samples. 458

Test area A portion of a computer system where software testing can occur without disrupting an organization's regular information system. 584

Text data type A data type used for fixed-length fields that hold character data such as people's names or CD titles. 634

Text-to-speech software Software that generates speech based on written text that is played back through a computer's sound card. 428

Thesaurus A feature of documentation software that provides synonyms. 127

Third-generation computers Computers characterized by using integrated circuits instead of transistors or vacuum tubes for data processing. 493

Third-generation languages Programming languages, such as FORTRAN, BASIC, and COBOL, that followed assembly languages and provided English-like keywords. 677

Threat modeling A component of defensive programming that helps programmers identify ways in which their programs might be compromised. 725

TIFF (Tag Image File Format) A bitmap image file format with .tif extension that automatically compresses the file data. 442

Time shifting The practice of recording digital content for later playback. 465

TLS (Transport Layer Security) An update of the Secure Sockets Layer (SSL) protocol for encrypting data before it is transmitted over a network. 389

Toolbar A component of graphical user interfaces that displays icons representing tools, commands, and other options. 190

Top-level domain A major domain category into which groups of computers on the Internet are divided, such as com, edu, gov, int, mil, net, and org. 307

Touch screen A display device that accepts input from being touched with a stylus or fingertip. 89

TQM (Total Quality Management) The process by which an organization analyzes and implements ways to improve the quality of its products and/or services. 569

Traceroute A network utility that records a packet's path, number of hops, and the time it takes for the packet to make each hop. 310

Tracing software Software that locates the edges of objects in a bitmap graphic and converts the resulting shape into a vector graphic. 447

Trackball An input device that looks like an upside down mouse. The user rolls the ball to move the on-screen pointer. 89

Trackpad A touch-sensitive surface on which you slide your fingers to move the on-screen pointer. 89

Tracks A series of concentric or spiral storage areas created on a storage medium during the formatting process. 218

Transaction An exchange between two parties that can be recorded and stored in a computer system. 559

Transaction processing system (TPS) A system that keeps track of transactions for an organization by providing ways to collect, display, modify, and cancel transactions. 559

Transceiver A combination of a transmitter and a receiver used to send and receive data in the form of radio frequencies. 265

Transistors A computer processing technology created by Bell Laboratories in 1947, characterizing second generation computers, which replaced vacuum tubes for data processing. 492

Tree topology Multiple star networks connected into a bus configuration by a backbone. 250

Trojan horse A computer program that appears to perform one function while actually doing something else, such as inserting a virus into a computer system or stealing a password. 163

True Color bitmap A color image with a color depth of 24 bits or 32 bits. Each pixel in a true color image can be displayed using any of 16.7 million different colors. 437

Turnkey system A complete information system that consists of both hardware and commercial software. 578

U3 drive A specially formatted USB flash drive that autoplays when inserted and requires special U3 versions of application software. 85

Ultra-mobile PC (UMPC) A small form-factor PC with a touch-sensitive screen. 59

UML (Unified Modeling Language) A tool for diagramming a set of object classes. 573

Unicode A 16-bit character-representation code that can represent more than 65,000 characters. 25

Uninstall routine A program that removes software files, references, and registry entries from a computer's hard disk. 160

Unit testing The process of testing a completed application module to make sure that it operates reliably and correctly. 584

UNIVAC The first commercially successful digital computer. 491

UNIX A multi-user, multitasking server operating system developed by AT&T Bell Laboratories in 1969. 201

Unstructured file A file that contains data, but that is not in a structured format of fields and records. 614

Unstructured problem A problem for which there is no established procedure for arriving at a solution. 558

Unzipped Refers to files that have been uncompressed. 156

UPDATE An SQL keyword used to alter the values in a database record. 650

UPS (Uninterruptible Power Supply) A battery-backed device designed to provide power to a computer during blackouts, brownouts, or other electrical disruptions. 100

Upstream speed The rate at which data is transmitted from your home computer to the Internet. 311

URL (Uniform Resource Locator) The address of a Web page. 361

USB (Universal Serial Bus) A high-speed bus commonly used for connecting peripheral devices to computers. 94

USB flash drive A portable solid state storage device nicknamed "pen drive" or "keychain drive" that plugs directly into a computer's USB port. 85

Use case Tasks performed by an actor in an information system. 573

Use case diagram Documentation of the users of an information system and their functions. 573

User documentation Descriptions of how to interact with an information system or program, including instructions on use, features, and troubleshooting. 585

User ID A combination of letters and numbers that serves as a user's "call sign" or identification. Also referred to as a user name. 34

User interface The software and hardware that enable people to interact with computers. 189

User privileges A set of assigned rights that specify what data is accessible to a particular user on a network or on a database. 655

Utility software A type of system software provided by the operating system or third-party vendors that specializes in tasks such as system maintenance, security, or file management. 122

UXGA (Ultra eXtended Graphics Array) A screen resolution of 1600 x 1200. 91

Vacuum tube An electronic device that controls the flow of electrons in a vacuum and represents binary data; used in the construction of first generation computers. 491

Value A number used in a calculation. 130

Vaporware Software or other products that are announced, but never produced. 503

VAR (Value-Added Reseller) A company that combines one product with additional hardware, software, and/or services to create a system designed to meet the needs of specific customers or industries. 508

Variable A named storage location that is capable of holding data, which can be modified during program execution. 680

Variable-length field A field in a data file that can expand to accept any number of characters up to a maximum limit. 615

VDE (Visual Development Environment) Programming tools that allow programmers to build substantial parts of computer programs by pointing and clicking, rather than entering code. 683

Vector graphic An image generated from descriptions that specify the position, length, and direction in which lines and shapes are drawn. 444

Vertical market software Computer programs designed to meet the needs of a specific market segment or industry, such as medical record-keeping software for use in hospitals. 142

VGA (Video Graphics Array) A screen resolution of 640 x 480. 91

Video capture The process of converting analog video signals into digital data stored on a hard drive. 454

Video editing software Software that provides tools for capturing and editing video from a camcorder. 140

Videocasting Online delivery of a video clip as an Atom or RSS feed; also referred to as a video podcasting or vodcasting. 361

Videoconferencing camera (Also called a Web camera.) An inexpensive digital camera that attaches directly to a computer and creates a video by capturing a series of still images. 453

Videogame console A computer specifically designed for playing games using a television screen and game controllers. 17

Viewable image size (vis) A measurement of the maximum image size that can be displayed on a monitor screen. 90

Viewing angle width The angle at which you can clearly see the screen image from the side. 90

Virtual machine Software that creates an operating environment that emulates another computer platform; as an example, Parallels Desktop creates a virtual PC on an Intel Macintosh computer. 199

Virtual memory A computer's use of hard disk storage to simulate RAM. 72

Virtual private network (VPN) A network connection that typically carries encrypted data over the Internet to and from a remote access server. 345

Virus definitions A group of virus signatures used by antivirus software to identify and block viruses and other malware. 168

Virus hoax A message, usually e-mail, that makes claims about a virus problem that doesn't actually exist. 166

Virus signature The unique computer code contained in a virus that security software uses to identify it. 167

VisiCalc First released on the Apple II, VisiCalc was the first electronic spreadsheet. 495

Visual Basic An event-driven programming environment where the programmer designs forms graphically and codes procedures in BASIC which responds to all form options. 679

VOB (Video OBject) An industry-standard video format for standalone DVD players. 457

Voiceband modem The type of modem typically used to connect a computer to a telephone line. 312

VoIP (Voice over Internet Protocol) Hardware, software, and protocols used to make telephone-style calls over the Internet. Also referred to as Internet telephony. 332

Volatile A term that describes data (usually in RAM), which can exist only with a constant supply of power. 72

Walkthrough In the context of programming, a method of verifying that an algorithm functions properly when using realistic test data. 694

WAN (Wide Area Network) An interconnected group of computers and peripherals that covers a large geographical area, such as multiple branches of a corporation. 247

WAP (Wireless Access Protocol) A communications protocol that provides Internet access for handheld devices. 327

War chalking The practice of locating Wi-Fi networks and identifying them for public access, often by writing the SSID with chalk on a nearby sidewalk. 283

Waterfall SDLC A series of phases that outlines the development process of an information system where each phase is a discrete step in the development process. 566

Wave An audio format with .wav extension that was Windows original "native" sound format. 424

Wavetable A set of pre-recorded musical instrument sounds in MIDI format. 426

WBS (Work Breakdown Structure) A project management tool based on a hierarchical structure of tasks and deliverables. 570

Weak encryption Encryption that is relatively easy or simple to decrypt without the encryption key. 285

Web Short for World Wide Web. An Internet service that links documents and information from computers located worldwide, using the HTTP protocol. 7, 360

Web 2.0 A group of new and innovative ways to use the Web, such as for social networking, blogging, and wikis. 361

Web application Applications software that is accessed and used from within a browser. 158

Web authoring software Computer programs for designing and developing customized Web pages that can be published electronically on the Internet. 125

Web browser A program that communicates with a Web server and displays Web pages. 361

Web bug A small graphic on a Web page that installs cookies designed to track your online activities. Also known as a Clear GIF. 402

Web cache A collection of Web pages and associated graphics that have been accessed and are temporarily stored locally to speed up subsequent access to them. 367

Web crawler The component of a search engine that autonomously visits Web sites collecting Web page data that will be indexed and available for searching. 375

Web page Information displayed by a Web browser that's produced from an HTML document or generated on the fly from data in a database. 361

Web palette A standard selection of colors that all Internet browsers can display. 438

Web portfolio A hypertext version of a resume containing links to Web sites of former employers or schools. 519

Web search engine A program that uses keywords to find information on the Internet and returns a list of links to relevant documents. 374

Web server A computer that listens for queries from Web browsers and transmits HTML documents over the Internet. 361

Web site A Web address that holds a collection of information identified by a common domain name, such as www.cnn.com. 360

Web site designer A computer professional who creates, tests, posts, and modifies HTML documents and other data for a Web site. 511

Web-based e-mail An e-mail system that allows users to access e-mail messages using a browser. 397

Web-based video Digital video designed to be accessed using a browser and played on a computer. 452

WEP (Wired Equivalent Privacy) An encryption algorithm used to protect data on Wi-Fi networks. 283

What-if analysis The process of setting up a model in a spreadsheet and experimenting to see what happens when different values are entered. 130

Whistleblowing The disclosure by an employee of confidential information that relates to some danger, fraud, or other illegal or unethical conduct connected with the workplace. 532

Wi-Fi An Ethernet-compatible wireless network that uses 802.11 a, b, g, and n standards. 268

Wi-Fi card A type of network interface card that includes a transmitter and a receiver using Wi-Fi protocols. 269

Wi-Fi hotspot The geographical area in which you can connect to a Wi-Fi signal, such as a Wi-Fi equipped campus or coffeehouse. 323

Wiki Software that allows users to collaborate to create, change, and link Web pages. Used for applications such as Wikipedia and open source project management. 361

WiMAX Fixed wireless Internet service based on Ethernet protocols with range of 30 miles and transmission speed of 70 Mbps. 320

Window An element of graphical user interfaces that is rectangular in shape and displays the controls for a program or a dialog box. 189

Windows Explorer A file management utility included with most Windows operating systems that helps users manage their files. 216

Windows Media DRM Microsoft's digital rights management technology. 470

Windows Mobile OS An operating system designed by Microsoft for hand-held computers. 203

Windows Registry A crucial set of data files maintained by the operating system that contains the settings needed by a computer to correctly use any hardware and software that has been installed. 154

Wired network A network that uses cables or wires to transmit data from one network device to another. 256

Wireframe A representation of a 3-D object using separate lines, which resemble wire, to create a model. 449

Wireless access point A network device that connects several devices of a local area network by broadcasting signals to any device with compatible Wi-Fi cards. 270

Wireless ad-hoc network A wireless network in which devices broadcast directly to each other instead of to a central access point. 270

Wireless encryption A security measure for wireless networks that scrambles data transmitted between network devices. 283

Wireless infrastructure network A wireless network in which devices communicate through a central access point. 270

Wireless network Networks that use radio or infrared signals (instead of cables) to transmit data from one network device to another. 265

Wireless network key The encryption key used to encrypt and decrypt data that travels over a wireless network protected by WEP, WPA, or WPA2. 284

Wireless router A network device that contains circuitry for a wireless access point and routing data to the Internet. 270

WMA (Windows Media Audio) A file format with .wma extension that is promoted by Microsoft and provides highly compressed audio files with very little loss of sound quality. 424

Word processing software Computer programs that assist the user in producing documents, such as reports, letters, papers, and manuscripts. 125

Word size The number of bits that a CPU can manipulate at one time, which is dependent on the size of the registers in the CPU, and the number of data lines in the bus. 68

Workers People who perform the tasks necessary to carry out an organization's mission. 557

Worksheet A computerized, or electronic, spreadsheet. 130

Workstation (1) A computer connected to a local area network. (2) A powerful desktop computer designed for specific tasks. 17

WPA (Wi-Fi Protected Access) A method for encrypting data transmitted over wireless networks. 283

WPA2 (Wi-Fi Protected Access 2) The second generation of WPA encryption for data transmitted over wireless networks. 283

WUXGA (Widescreen Ultra eXtended Graphics Array) A display resolution of 1920 X 1200 pixels. 91

Xerox Alto An early personal computer prototype developed by Xerox Corp. that featured, among other things, a graphical user interface that became influential in the development of the Apple Macintosh. 495

XForms A database technology that provides an alternative to HTML forms by providing more flexibility and an interface to XML documents. 629

XGA Extended Graphics Array or XGA usually refers to 1024 x 768 resolution. 91

XHTML The follow-up version to HTML 4. 362

XML (eXtensible Markup Language) A document format similar to HTML, but that allows the Web page developer to define customized tags, generally for the purpose of creating more interactivity. 630

XML DBMS An XML DBMS is a database management system that provides authoring and query tools for designing and managing collections of XML documents. 625

Z3 An early electronic computer prototype designed by Konrad Zuse that was the first to incorporate the use of binary numbers for data representation. 489

Zipped Refers to one or more files that have been compressed. 156

Zombie A computer that has been compromised by malware that allows it to be controlled by a remote user. 164

INDEX